HOUSING STATISTICS OF THE UNITED STATES

FIFTH EDITION

2012

HOUSING STATISTICS OF THE UNITED STATES

FIFTH EDITION

2012

Bernan Press
Lanham, MD

Published in the United States of America
by Bernan Press, a wholly owned subsidiary of
The Rowman & Littlefield Publishing Group, Inc.
4501 Forbes Boulevard, Suite 200
Lanham, Maryland 20706

Bernan Press
800-865-3457
www.bernan.com

ISBN-13: 978-1-59888-575-0

ISSN: 1521-5601

∞™ The paper used in this publication meets the minimum requirements of American National Standard for Information Sciences—Permanence of Paper for Printed Library Materials, ANSI/NISO Z39.48-1992.
Manufactured in the United States of America.

CONTENTS

New Residential Construction

Primary Mortgage Market Survey

Monthly Interest Rate Survey

Census Bureau/Department of Housing and Urban Development Joint Initiative

Manufacturer's Reports to the Institute for Building Technology and Safety (IBTS)

PREFACE

Today's housing market bears little resemblance to the housing market of 2000. The years since the turn of the 21st century have seen steep drops in housing prices and value and sharp increases in foreclosures, short sales, and homeowners who are "underwater" on their investments.

This book provides detailed data about the current state of the market, covering such broad topics as mortgage status, demographics, physical characteristics, and income. However, in order to understand the present, it is also critical to examine the past. Many of the tables provided give historical scope to housing trends.

HISTORY OF THE HOUSING BUBBLE

Perhaps the first inklings of the crisis to come occurred with the advent of Section 121 in 1978. In this law, allowance was made for one-time capital gains exclusions for real estate sales. This was repealed in the 1990s, although the $250,000 single/$500,000 married exclusions remained in force under the Taxpayer Relief Act of 1997.[1,2]

Another factor that contributed to the bubble was the deregulation of the financial industry. In addition to the legislation that loosened the requirements for financial institutions to merge, adjustable-rate mortgages (ARMs) became possible in this environment. According to the Garn-St. Germain Depository Institutions Act of 1982, which was passed by Congress, these provisions were made "to revitalize the housing industry by strengthening the financial stability of home mortgage lending institutions and ensuring the availability of home mortgage loans."[3]

This new freedom, coupled with the booming economy of the 1990s and early 2000s, created an environment in which consumers were able to take out loans for housing that depended on the economy's continuing to function at a high level. This type of lending occurred despite risk that the lendee would not be able to repay the loan, giving rise to the "subprime lending" crisis, which encompassed not only mortgage loans, but also loans for refinancing in other areas.[4]

In the end, the financial crisis ended certain features of lending and ushered in a new era: the time of the housing crisis. Although it seemed to hit with a sudden blow, the foundations had been laid years before.

THE UNITED STATES: STATE OF THE COUNTRY'S DEMOGRAPHICS[5]

The Census Bureau's 3-year estimates from the American Community Survey state that in the 2008–2010 time period, there were 114.6 million households in the United States, with an average of 2.6 people per household. Approximately two-thirds of all households consisted of families, with married-couple families representing 49 percent and other families representing 17 percent of the total. Nonfamily households mainly comprised people living alone, although there were some households in which no one was related to the householder. Approximately 34 percent of households included members under 18 years old, while 24 percent of households had members over 65 years old. Approximately 52 percent of males and 48 percent of females over 15 years old were married. Grandchildren lived with their grandparents in approximately 6.7 million households, with 40 percent of these grandparents responsible financially for the grandchildren.

Almost 60 percent of these residents of the United States were living in the same state in which they were born. Native-born residents made up 87 percent of the population. Almost a third of the foreign-born population entered the country in or after the year 2000. A fifth of all people over 5 years old spoke a language other than English at home, with over 60 percent of these people speaking Spanish and over 30 percent reporting not speaking English "very well."

Approximately 59 percent of the ACS-surveyed population over 16 years old was employed, while 35 percent was not in the labor force. Almost 80 percent of workers were private wage and salary workers. Almost 23 percent of workers were employed in the educational services and health care and social assistance sector, while only 1.9 percent worked in agriculture, forestry, fishing and hunting and mining. In regard to occupations, 35.6 percent worked in management, business, science, and arts occupations, while 9.5 percent were employed in natural resources, construction, and maintenance occupations.

The American Community Survey's 2006–2010 (5-year) observations of the United States list the national median income for this timeframe as $51,914. Incomes by state (excluding Puerto Rico) ranged from $70,647 in Maryland to $37,881 in Mississippi. The Northeast and West Census regions also outearned the South and the Midwest. According to the 3-year estimates (2008–2010), 13 percent of households had incomes below $15,000 per year, while 9 percent of households had incomes of greater than $150,000 per year. Households who received earnings comprised 79 percent of all households.

People living in poverty totaled 14 percent of the population in the ACS 3-year estimates, with 10.5 percent of all families, 29.2 percent of female householder families, 9.4 percent of people over 65 years old, and 19.7 percent of related children under 18 years old also falling below the poverty threshold. Approximately 15 percent of people did not have health insurance coverage.

HOUSING IN THE 2000s

The ACS also shows some related information about housing; specifically, that housing has become a burden to homeowners, especially renters. The 2008–2010 (i.e., 3-year estimate) population profile shows that while less than a

Figure A. Median Household Income (in 2010 Inflation-Adjusted Dollars), United States and Five Highest-Earning and Five Lowest-Earning States (ACS 5-Year Estimates)

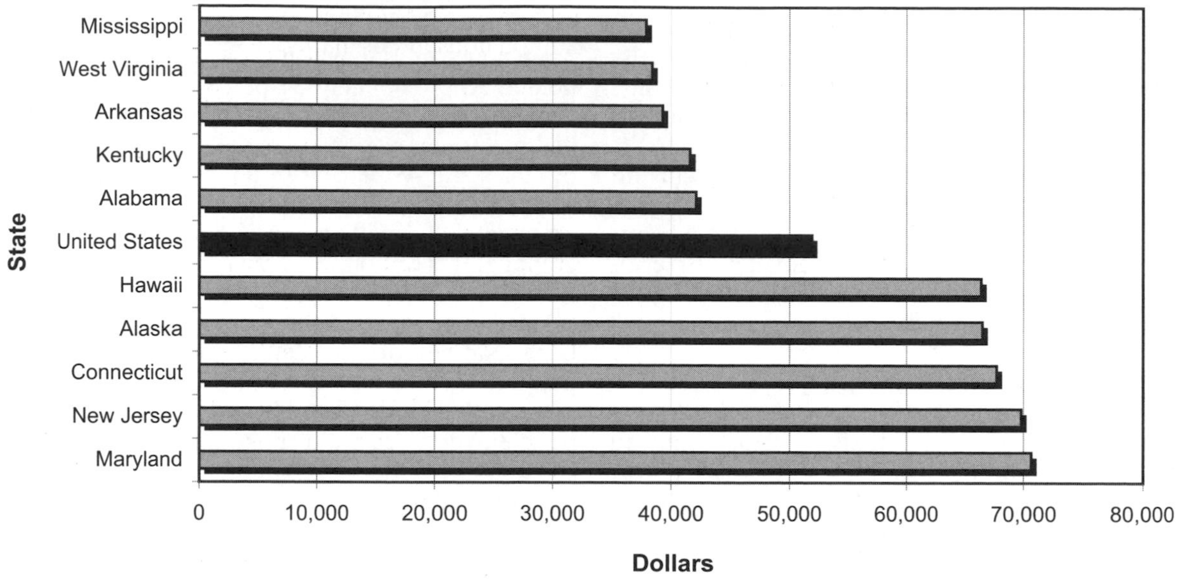

Figure B. Occupants with a Housing Burden in the United States in 2008–2010, 2010 American Community Survey, 3-Year Estimates

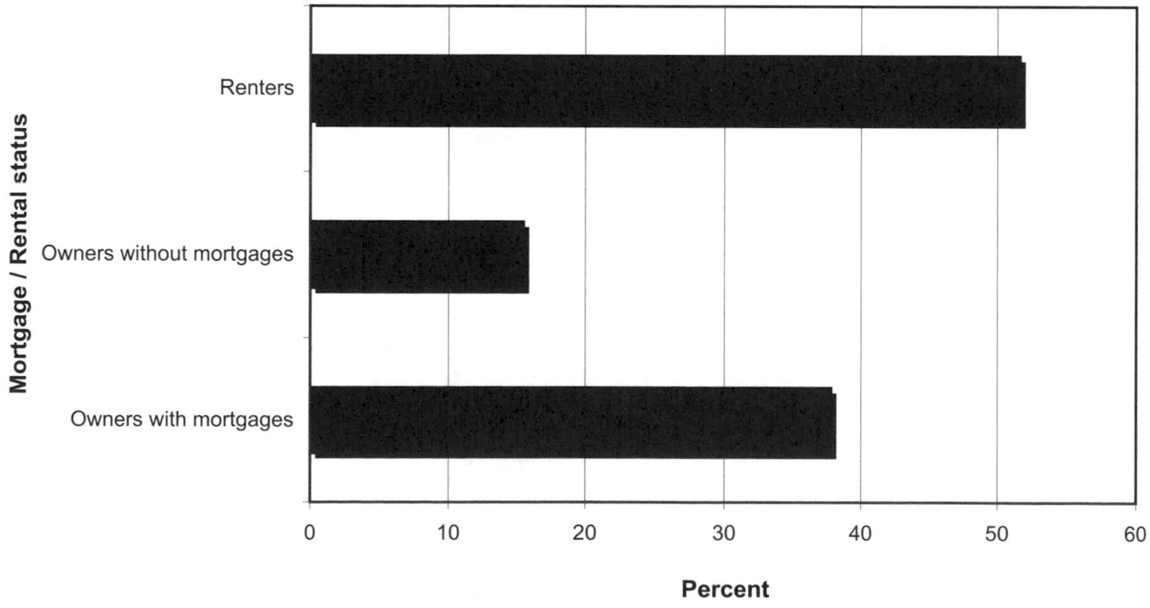

fifth of homeowners without a mortgage spent more than 30 percent of their income on housing, more than triple that percentage of renters were forced to do so.

According to the ACS, median monthly housing costs for mortgaged owners was $1,521, while nonmortgaged owners spent a median of $431 and renters spent a median of $850.

Housing characteristics provide a picture of how a "median" family lives in the United States. The median number of rooms per dwelling is 6, and 60 percent of units have 3 or more bedrooms. Of the 114.6 million occupied housing units reported in ACS's 3-year estimates, 66 percent are occupied by owners and 34 percent are occupied by renters. Mortgages were held by 68 percent of units for which this criterion applies. Approximately 61 percent of households of occupied units had moved in since 2000. About 2 percent of households lacked telephone service, while 9 percent had no vehicles available; in contrast, a fifth of all households had three or more vehicles available.

Gas—including bottled, natural, LP, utility, and tank—was the most popular method of heating housing units.

The 2008–2010 ACS estimates delineate the types of housing that make up the householder units. Approximately two-thirds of all households live in single-family units.

A majority of occupied housing units (approximately 85 percent, although only 70 percent of rental units) had the additional benefit of a porch, deck, balcony, or patio, and a garage or carport, according to the 2009 American Housing Survey. (A fraction of a percent of households did not report.) As seen in Figure 1-3, also derived from AHS data, selected amenities, such as having 2 or more recreation/living rooms, usable fireplaces, and a garage or carport, were much more present in owner-occupied units than in renter-occupied units.

Major deficiencies noted in this same survey included signs of rats and mice (approximately 6.7 million households) and open holes or cracks inside the dwelling (approximately 5.5 million households). The AHS counts 111.8 million households in this survey. However, when asked for their opinions of their homes, on a scale of 1 (worst) to 10 (best), approximately 80 percent of householders rated their units as 8s, 9s, or 10s. Just over 1 percent of householders gave their dwellings 1s, 2s, or 3s.(Approximately 3.8 percent did not report.) A majority of AHS-surveyed units also had two or more bathrooms.

HOUSING FINANCIALS IN THE 2000s

As mentioned, the housing market of today is vastly different than that of a decade ago. Periodic jumps in prices of such items as gasoline and food have not helped to lessen the impact of subprime lending, adjustable-rate mortgages, and the number of householders struggling with outsize debt. Measures have been taken by two presidents to ease the plight of this debt. President Bush signed the Economic Stimulus Act of 2008 into law in order to ease the recession through the issuance of tax rebates.[6] In 2009, President Obama initiated the Homeowner Affordability and Stability Plan, which works to modify loans and is allocated $75 billion dollars to assist homeowners at risk of foreclosure. Fannie Mae and Freddie Mac are also part of this program, working to help homeowners refinance at the lower contemporary interest rates.[7] The government is continuing to work toward long-ranging reform in order to insulate the market from ever again experiencing such a crash.

Figure C. Types of Housing Structures in 2008–2010, 2010 American Community Survey, 3-Year Estimates

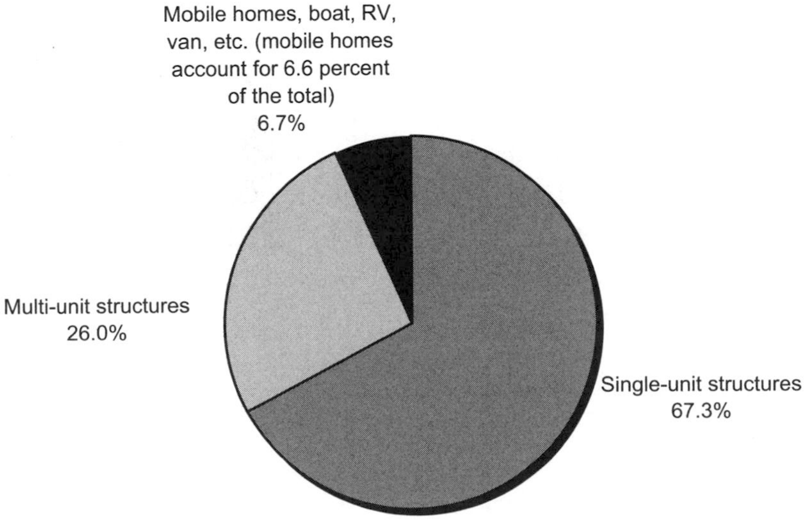

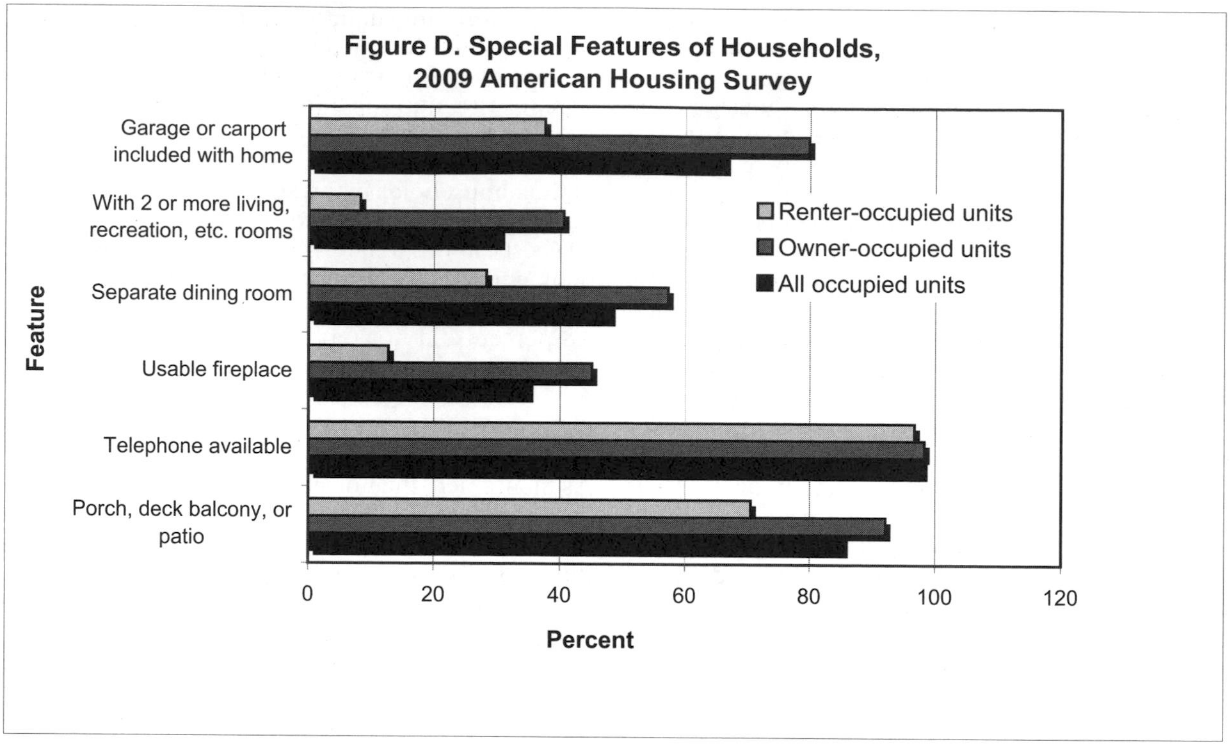
Figure D. Special Features of Households, 2009 American Housing Survey
Garage or carport included with home
With 2 or more living, recreation, etc. rooms
Separate dining room
Usable fireplace
Telephone available
Porch, deck balcony, or patio
Feature
Renter-occupied units
Owner-occupied units
All occupied units
0
20
40
60
80
100
120
Percent

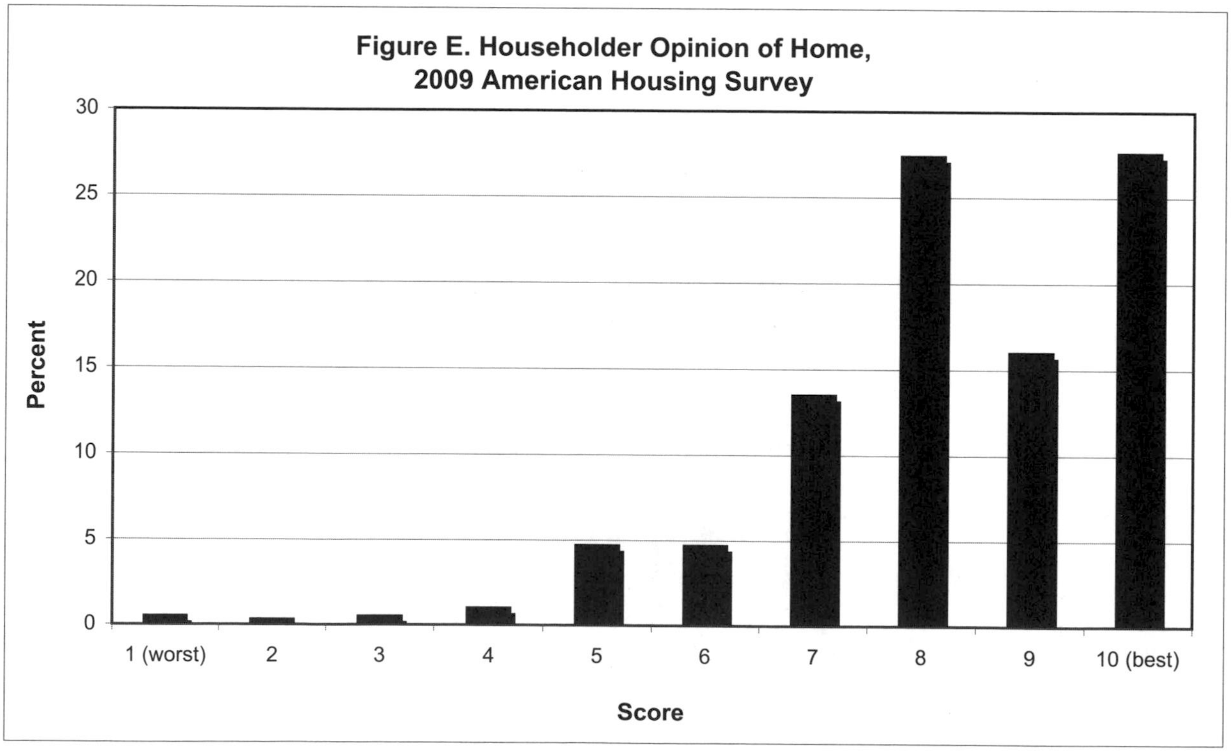
Figure E. Householder Opinion of Home, 2009 American Housing Survey
30
25
20
15
10
5
0
Percent
1 (worst)
2
3
4
5
6
7
8
9
10 (best)
Score

HOW TO USE THIS BOOK

This volume is a compilation of many sources of statistics about housing. One of its most important features is the tables within. Tables are organized into relevant sections for demographic, financial, and physical characteristics of housing and are derived from a number of different sources. The origination and the methodology of the source material can be found in Appendix A, with definitions following in Appendix B.

It is important to note that in all sections, data may not sum to perfect totals due to rounding.

ABOUT THE EDITOR

Shana Hertz Hattis is an editor with over a decade of experience in statistical and government research publications. Past titles include *The United States Government Internet Directory*, *Crime in the United States*, and *Employment, Hours, and Earnings*. She earned her bachelor of science in journalism and master of science in education degrees from Northwestern University.

NOTES

1. § 1978. Repealed. 1997, No. 121 (Adj. Sess.), {39(6). <http://law.justia.com/citations.html - 24%20VT%20Stats%20%C2%A7%201978.%20%282011%20through%20Adj%20Sess%29>

2. "Taxpayer Relief Act of 1997." <www.gpo.gov/fdsys/pkg/PLAW.../PLAW-105publ34.pdf>

3. FDIC. "Garn-St. Germain Depository Institutions Act of 1992." <http://www.fdic.gov/regulations/laws/rules/8000-4100.html>

4. Lee, Mara. "Subprime Mortgages: A Primer." March 23, 2007. <http://www.npr.org/templates/story/story.php?storyId=9085408>

5. Formal data and analysis are derived and taken from the American Community Survey and the American Housing Survey, both conducted by the U.S. Census Bureau. Differentiation and attribution are contained within the text that follows.

6. CNN.com. "Bush signs stimulus bill; rebate checks expected in May." February 13, 2008. <http://articles.cnn.com/2008-02-13/politics/bush.stimulus_1_rebate-checks-economic-stimulus-act-stimulus-bill?_s=PM:POLITICS>

7. FDIC. "Homeowner Affordability and Stability Plan." <http://www.fdic.gov/consumers/loans/hasp/>

PART I
DEMOGRAPHIC CHARACTERISTICS

PART I: DEMOGRAPHIC CHARACTERISTICS

Figure 1-1. Units Occupied by Owners, by Special Demographic Group, American Housing Survey, 2009

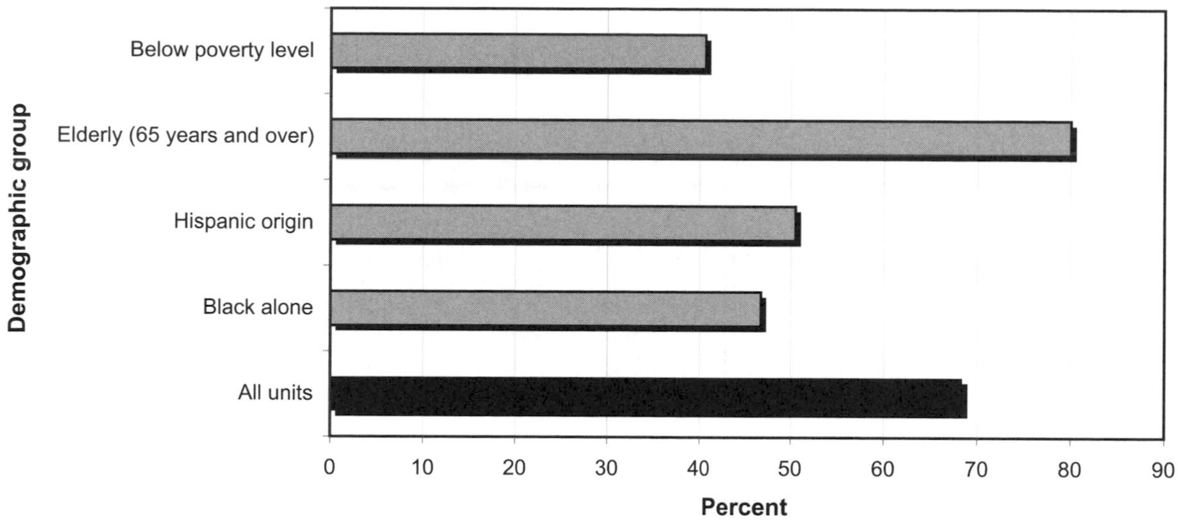

- In 2009, owners occupied 68.4 percent of all occupied units. However, AHS householder respondents designated as Black alone owned only 46.8 percent of all relevant occupied units, while Hispanic householders owned 50.5 percent of the units they occupied. (Table 1-1) According to the American Community Survey's 3-year estimates, the poverty rate for the United States was 10.5 for all families and 14 percent for all people for 2008–2010.

- The median household income ranged from $42,000 in the South to $53,300 in the West in 2009. The median income of households with a householder age 65 years or over was $27,000. (Table 1-16)

- The 2009 AHS reported that most respondents chose to move due to added convenience, either to a job or to friends and relatives. The look/appeal of a neighborhood and the assessment of the house itself were also popular considerations. (Table 1-13)

Table 1-1. Introductory Characteristics, Occupied Units, 2009

[Numbers in thousands.]

Characteristics	Total occupied units	Tenure		Housing unit characteristics		Household characteristics				Regions			
		Owner	Renter	New construction 4 years	Manufactured/ mobile homes	Black alone	Hispanic	Elderly (65 years or over)	Below poverty level	Northeast	Midwest	South	West
Sample size	45,057	30,228	14,829	1,692	2,048	5,555	5,276	10,152	6,377	10,279	11,575	14,543	8,660
Total	111,806	76,428	35,378	4,771	6,839	13,993	12,739	23,095	15,739	20,451	25,368	41,586	24,401
Tenure													
Owner occupied	76,428	76,428	X	3,830	5,418	6,547	6,439	18,472	6,405	13,378	18,249	29,193	15,607
Percent of all occupied	68.4	100.0	X	80.3	79.2	46.8	50.5	80.0	40.7	65.4	71.9	70.2	64.0
Renter occupied	35,378	X	35,378	941	1,421	7,446	6,300	4,623	9,334	7,073	7,119	12,392	8,794
Race and Hispanic origin													
White alone	91,137	65,935	25,202	3,838	5,953	X	11,804	19,943	10,840	16,971	21,801	32,251	20,115
Non-Hispanic	79,333	59,905	19,427	3,432	5,272	X	X	18,564	8,328	15,336	20,858	27,689	15,449
Hispanic	11,804	6,030	5,775	406	681	X	11,804	1,379	2,512	1,634	943	4,562	4,666
Black alone	13,993	6,547	7,446	562	643	13,993	384	2,246	3,864	2,428	2,533	7,720	1,312
Non-Hispanic	13,609	6,415	7,195	548	633	13,609	X	2,201	3,761	2,261	2,503	7,590	1,256
Hispanic	384	132	252	14	10	384	384	44	103	168	31	130	56
American Indian or Alaska Native alone	968	503	466	33	101	X	238	119	212	75	213	221	459
Asian alone	4,003	2,516	1,487	263	28	X	64	482	505	776	490	827	1,910
Pacific Islander alone[1]	281	141	140	26	–	X	40	47	49	14	24	55	189
Two or more races	1,423	786	637	50	114	X	210	258	268	187	308	512	416
Hispanic or Latino (any race)[2]	12,739	6,439	6,300	438	722	384	12,739	1,482	2,717	1,879	1,057	4,851	4,952
Units in structure													
1, detached	73,079	63,324	9,755	3,311	X	6,850	6,807	15,913	6,949	11,431	17,944	28,063	15,642
1, attached	5,973	3,952	2,021	417	X	1,095	597	1,190	841	1,810	1,055	1,935	1,172
2 to 4	8,350	1,353	6,998	157	X	1,699	1,456	1,177	2,154	2,571	1,792	2,096	1,892
5 to 9	5,269	632	4,637	116	X	1,184	1,061	672	1,382	944	1,043	1,818	1,465
10 to 19	4,661	483	4,178	144	X	1,004	815	474	1,022	741	962	1,819	1,139
20 to 49	3,630	499	3,131	136	X	719	724	628	859	914	673	1,049	994
50 or more	4,004	768	3,237	191	X	801	557	1,504	1,039	1,501	756	887	860
Manufactured/mobile home or trailer	6,839	5,418	1,421	301	6,839	643	722	1,537	1,492	540	1,145	3,918	1,236
Cooperatives and condominiums													
Cooperatives	651	429	222	3	23	101	66	216	71	440	79	67	65
Condominiums	6,580	4,399	2,181	406	15	593	810	1,577	728	1,312	1,291	2,075	1,902
Year structure built[3]													
2005 to 2009	5,884	4,601	1,283	4,771	378	687	557	496	429	533	957	2,921	1,473
2000 to 2004	8,102	6,371	1,731	X	768	783	841	1,105	782	719	1,671	3,764	1,947
1995 to 1999	7,825	6,221	1,603	X	1,459	757	669	1,386	797	690	1,603	3,774	1,756
1990 to 1994	5,995	4,715	1,280	X	811	592	546	1,047	571	607	1,337	2,556	1,495
1985 to 1989	7,648	5,159	2,489	X	669	836	753	1,427	856	1,132	1,358	3,184	1,974
1980 to 1984	6,380	4,201	2,179	X	697	734	787	1,229	1,016	627	1,023	3,254	1,477
1975 to 1979	11,835	7,471	4,364	X	701	1,458	1,484	2,450	2,006	1,476	2,692	4,823	2,843
1970 to 1974	9,413	5,696	3,718	X	795	1,385	1,190	2,303	1,578	1,389	1,989	3,938	2,097
1960 to 1969	13,326	8,917	4,409	X	401	1,865	1,530	3,692	2,052	2,451	2,957	4,832	3,086
1950 to 1959	11,771	8,528	3,243	X	56	1,579	1,530	3,112	1,609	2,609	3,002	3,591	2,569
1940 to 1949	6,745	4,423	2,322	X	54	1,121	1,087	1,570	1,235	1,645	1,503	2,110	1,488
1930 to 1939	4,828	2,904	1,924	X	49	737	608	949	894	1,411	1,292	1,192	933
1920 to 1929	4,331	2,520	1,811	X	X	633	500	804	677	1,603	1,379	721	627
1919 or earlier	7,724	4,703	3,021	X	X	827	658	1,524	1,235	3,560	2,604	924	635
Median	1974	1975	1971	2007	1990	1971	1972	1970	1971	1958	1970	1979	1976
Metropolitan/ nonmetropolitan areas													
Inside metropolitan statistical areas	89,949	60,102	29,846	3,965	3,807	12,529	11,644	17,483	12,232	18,029	18,611	32,121	21,188
In central cities	32,645	17,809	14,837	1,372	566	6,687	5,432	6,048	6,088	6,062	6,868	11,138	8,577
Suburbs	57,303	42,294	15,009	2,593	3,241	5,842	6,212	11,435	6,144	11,967	11,743	20,982	12,612
Outside metropolitan statistical areas	21,857	16,326	5,532	806	3,032	1,465	1,095	5,612	3,507	2,422	6,758	9,465	3,212
Regions													
Northeast	20,451	13,378	7,073	412	540	2,428	1,879	4,638	2,632	20,451	X	X	X
Midwest	25,368	18,249	7,119	763	1,145	2,533	1,057	5,364	3,385	X	25,368	X	X
South	41,586	29,193	12,392	2,414	3,918	7,720	4,851	8,505	6,695	X	X	41,586	X
West	24,401	15,607	8,794	1,181	1,236	1,312	4,952	4,587	3,027	X	X	X	24,401

Table 1-1. Introductory Characteristics, Occupied Units, 2009—*Continued*

[Numbers in thousands.]

Characteristics	Total occupied units	Tenure		Housing unit characteristics		Household characteristics				Regions			
		Owner	Renter	New construction 4 years	Manufactured/ mobile homes	Black alone	Hispanic	Elderly (65 years or over)	Below poverty level	Northeast	Midwest	South	West
Place size													
Less than 2,500 persons....	5,254	3,982	1,271	192	471	290	280	1,281	603	698	2,102	1,799	655
2,500 to 9,999 persons.....	13,093	9,298	3,795	498	680	1,174	1,322	2,866	1,781	2,284	3,156	4,932	2,720
10,000 to 19,999 persons..............................	9,487	6,314	3,173	265	245	1,047	868	1,925	1,290	1,776	2,581	3,707	1,422
20,000 to 49,999 persons..............................	14,846	9,643	5,204	408	278	2,013	1,947	3,111	2,161	2,334	3,745	4,882	3,885
50,000 to 99,999 persons..............................	10,783	6,549	4,235	362	204	1,328	1,819	1,932	1,518	1,710	2,703	2,727	3,643
100,000 to 249,999 persons..............................	8,793	5,108	3,685	242	99	1,569	1,285	1,626	1,361	1,021	1,567	2,961	3,244
250,000 to 499,999 persons..............................	6,110	3,329	2,781	284	70	1,310	955	936	1,140	338	1,112	2,353	2,307
500,000 to 999,999 persons..............................	3,716	2,073	1,644	144	44	920	749	737	671	225	837	1,523	1,130
1,000,000 persons or more................................	6,906	2,928	3,978	118	12	1,892	1,661	1,335	1,585	3,364	1,111	940	1,492

– = Zero or rounds to zero.
X = Not applicable.
[1] = Native Hawaiian and Other Pacific Islander.
[2] = Because Hispanics may be any race, data can overlap slightly with other groups. Most Hispanics report themselves as White, but some report themselves as Black or in other categories.
[3] = For manufactured/mobile homes, oldest category is 1939 or earlier.

Source: U.S. Census Bureau, American Housing Survey

Table 1-2. Introductory Characteristics, Owner-Occupied Units, 2009

[Numbers in thousands.]

Characteristics	Total occupied units	Housing unit characteristics		Household characteristics				Regions			
		New construction 4 years	Manufactured/ mobile homes	Black alone	Hispanic	Elderly (65 years and over)	Below poverty level	Northeast	Midwest	South	West
Total	76,428	3,830	5,418	6,547	6,439	18,472	6,405	13,378	18,249	29,193	15,607
Race and Hispanic origin											
White alone	65,935	3,171	4,745	X	6,030	16,387	5,026	11,904	16,589	24,114	13,327
Non-Hispanic	59,905	2,856	4,285	X	X	15,460	4,265	11,450	16,062	21,481	10,912
Hispanic	6,030	315	460	X	6,030	927	761	454	528	2,633	2,416
Black alone	6,547	364	503	6,547	132	1,460	1,024	903	1,120	4,014	510
Non-Hispanic	6,415	356	498	6,415	X	1,436	1,012	863	1,101	3,955	496
Hispanic	132	8	5	132	132	24	12	40	19	59	14
American Indian or Alaska Native alone	503	26	62	X	108	98	69	32	82	138	250
Asian alone	2,516	217	14	X	32	306	165	444	309	558	1,206
Pacific Islander alone[1]	141	18	–	X	14	32	25	7	9	24	101
Two or more races	786	34	94	X	123	189	96	89	140	344	213
Hispanic or Latino (any race)[2]	6,439	339	490	132	6,439	995	810	522	589	2,788	2,540
Units in Structure											
1, detached	63,324	3,067	X	5,100	5,249	14,990	4,732	10,439	15,964	23,924	12,998
1, attached	3,952	324	X	594	298	961	343	1,294	682	1,265	711
2 to 4	1,353	41	X	165	185	396	97	607	251	221	274
5 to 9	632	38	X	43	69	150	64	114	102	186	230
10 to 19	483	26	X	42	41	121	53	75	102	166	140
20 to 49	499	17	X	44	45	169	36	133	64	177	124
50 or more	768	46	X	57	62	306	71	281	142	181	164
Manufactured/mobile home or trailer	5,418	272	5,418	503	490	1,379	1,009	436	943	3,072	966
Cooperatives and condominiums											
Cooperatives	429	1	23	60	28	165	29	305	51	49	24
Condominiums	4,399	301	15	237	397	1,253	355	844	935	1,297	1,323
Year structure built[3]											
2005 to 2009	4,601	3,830	301	419	413	390	204	387	797	2,342	1,075
2000 to 2004	6,371	X	650	503	613	852	417	555	1,348	3,021	1,447
1995 to 1999	6,221	X	1,272	484	463	1,128	430	607	1,269	3,022	1,324
1990 to 1994	4,715	X	607	322	387	846	298	494	1,066	2,017	1,137
1985 to 1989	5,159	X	511	337	356	1,058	368	884	970	2,202	1,102
1980 to 1984	4,201	X	545	297	367	904	410	448	727	2,067	960
1975 to 1979	7,471	X	532	527	592	1,827	664	906	1,708	3,135	1,722
1970 to 1974	5,696	X	595	529	513	1,736	542	791	1,260	2,439	1,205
1960 to 1969	8,917	X	263	860	713	3,109	828	1,664	2,132	3,277	1,844
1950 to 1959	8,528	X	48	757	878	2,750	772	1,969	2,306	2,559	1,693
1940 to 1949	4,423	X	48	588	508	1,295	516	1,063	1,123	1,370	867
1930 to 1939	2,904	X	46	355	229	740	342	787	860	733	524
1920 to 1929	2,520	X	X	261	213	609	218	854	909	414	342
1919 or earlier	4,703	X	X	308	195	1,228	395	1,970	1,774	593	366
Median	1975	2007	1991	1971	1975	1968	1971	1960	1970	1980	1978
Metropolitan/ nonmetropolitan areas											
Inside metropolitan statistical areas	60,102	3,150	2,961	5,691	5,791	13,676	4,708	11,575	13,063	22,085	13,380
In central cities	17,809	930	434	2,617	2,328	4,219	1,706	2,549	3,999	6,425	4,836
Suburbs	42,294	2,220	2,527	3,074	3,462	9,457	3,001	9,026	9,064	15,660	8,544
Outside metropolitan statistical areas	16,326	680	2,457	857	649	4,796	1,697	1,803	5,187	7,108	2,227
Regions											
Northeast	13,378	317	436	903	522	3,368	875	13,378	X	X	X
Midwest	18,249	642	943	1,120	589	4,277	1,310	X	18,249	X	X
South	29,193	1,972	3,072	4,014	2,788	7,239	3,090	X	X	29,193	X
West	15,607	899	966	510	2,540	3,588	1,130	X	X	X	15,607
Place size											
Less than 2,500 persons	3,982	156	391	187	207	1,093	267	553	1,598	1,341	490
2,500 to 9,999 persons	9,298	412	501	582	763	2,345	799	1,667	2,319	3,362	1,950
10,000 to 19,999 persons	6,314	197	143	448	472	1,459	421	1,178	1,861	2,426	849
20,000 to 49,999 persons	9,643	295	210	891	954	2,406	777	1,514	2,587	3,104	2,437
50,000 to 99,999 persons	6,549	271	140	535	832	1,446	473	957	1,792	1,567	2,232
100,000 to 249,999 persons	5,108	136	78	629	570	1,185	445	451	979	1,686	1,992
250,000 to 499,999 persons	3,329	203	67	426	489	620	262	140	616	1,288	1,285
500,000 to 999,999 persons	2,073	92	37	432	436	548	214	77	406	909	681
1,000,000 persons or more	2,928	58	9	707	450	766	364	1,274	546	467	641

– = Zero or rounds to zero.
X = Not applicable.
[1] = Native Hawaiian and Other Pacific Islander.
[2] = Because Hispanics may be any race, data can overlap slightly with other groups. Most Hispanics report themselves as White, but some report themselves as Black or in other categories.
[3] = For manufactured/mobile homes, oldest category is 1939 or earlier.

Source: U.S. Census Bureau, American Housing Survey

Table 1-3. Introductory Characteristics, Renter-Occupied Units, 2009

[Numbers in thousands.]

Characteristics	Total occupied units	Housing unit characteristics		Household characteristics				Regions			
		New construction 4 years	Manufactured/ mobile homes	Black alone	Hispanic	Elderly (65 years and over)	Below poverty level	Northeast	Midwest	South	West
Total	35,378	941	1,421	7,446	6,300	4,623	9,334	7,073	7,119	12,392	8,794
Race and Hispanic origin											
White alone	25,202	667	1,207	X	5,775	3,555	5,814	5,067	5,212	8,137	6,787
Non-Hispanic	19,427	576	987	X	X	3,104	4,062	3,886	4,797	6,208	4,537
Hispanic	5,775	91	221	X	5,775	451	1,751	1,181	415	1,929	2,250
Black alone	7,446	198	140	7,446	252	786	2,841	1,525	1,413	3,706	802
Non-Hispanic	7,195	192	135	7,195	X	765	2,749	1,398	1,402	3,635	760
Hispanic	252	6	5	252	252	20	91	127	11	71	42
American Indian or Alaska Native alone	466	7	39	X	130	21	143	43	131	82	209
Asian alone	1,487	46	14	X	31	176	340	333	181	269	704
Pacific Islander alone[1]	140	8	–	X	26	15	24	7	15	31	87
Two or more races	637	16	20	X	87	70	172	98	168	168	203
Hispanic or Latino (any race)[2]	6,300	98	232	252	6,300	487	1,906	1,358	468	2,062	2,412
Units in structure											
1, detached	9,755	244	X	1,750	1,558	923	2,217	992	1,980	4,140	2,644
1, attached	2,021	93	X	501	299	228	498	516	374	670	461
2 to 4	6,998	116	X	1,533	1,271	782	2,057	1,964	1,541	1,874	1,619
5 to 9	4,637	78	X	1,141	993	522	1,318	830	940	1,632	1,235
10 to 19	4,178	118	X	962	774	352	969	666	860	1,653	999
20 to 49	3,131	119	X	674	679	460	823	781	609	872	870
50 or more	3,237	145	X	745	495	1,198	968	1,220	614	707	696
Manufactured/mobile home or trailer	1,421	28	1,421	140	232	158	483	104	201	845	270
Cooperatives and condominiums											
Cooperatives	222	3	–	42	38	51	43	135	28	18	41
Condominiums	2,181	105	–	356	413	324	374	468	355	778	579
Year structure built[3]											
2005 to 2009	1,283	941	77	268	144	106	224	146	160	579	397
2000 to 2004	1,731	X	118	279	227	254	365	165	324	743	500
1995 to 1999	1,603	X	187	273	206	259	367	84	335	753	433
1990 to 1994	1,280	X	204	270	159	201	273	113	271	539	358
1985 to 1989	2,489	X	158	499	398	369	488	248	388	982	872
1980 to 1984	2,179	X	153	437	421	325	606	179	296	1,187	517
1975 to 1979	4,364	X	169	931	892	623	1,342	570	984	1,688	1,121
1970 to 1974	3,718	X	200	857	677	567	1,037	597	729	1,499	893
1960 to 1969	4,409	X	138	1,005	817	583	1,225	787	824	1,555	1,242
1950 to 1959	3,243	X	7	822	652	362	837	641	696	1,031	876
1940 to 1949	2,322	X	6	533	579	275	719	581	380	740	621
1930 to 1939	1,924	X	3	383	378	208	552	624	433	459	409
1920 to 1929	1,811	X	X	372	287	195	459	749	470	307	285
1919 or earlier	3,021	X	X	519	463	297	839	1,590	830	331	270
Median	1971	2007	1986	1971	1970	1973	1970	1950	1969	1976	1974
Metropolitan / nonmetropolitan areas											
Inside metropolitan statistical areas	29,846	815	846	6,838	5,854	3,807	7,524	6,454	5,548	10,036	7,808
In central cities	14,837	442	132	4,070	3,104	1,829	4,381	3,513	2,869	4,714	3,740
Suburbs	15,009	373	714	2,768	2,750	1,978	3,143	2,941	2,679	5,322	4,068
Outside metropolitan statistical areas	5,532	126	575	608	446	816	1,809	619	1,571	2,357	985
Regions											
Northeast	7,073	95	104	1,525	1,358	1,270	1,757	7,073	X	X	X
Midwest	7,119	121	201	1,413	468	1,088	2,075	X	7,119	X	X
South	12,392	442	845	3,706	2,062	1,267	3,605	X	X	12,392	X
West	8,794	282	270	802	2,412	999	1,896	X	X	X	8,794
Place size											
Less than 2,500 persons	1,271	35	79	104	73	188	336	145	504	457	165
2,500 to 9,999 persons	3,795	86	179	592	559	520	982	618	838	1,570	770
10,000 to 19,999 persons	3,173	68	102	599	396	465	869	598	721	1,281	574
20,000 to 49,999 persons	5,204	114	68	1,122	993	705	1,384	820	1,157	1,779	1,448
50,000 to 99,999 persons	4,235	91	64	793	987	486	1,045	753	911	1,160	1,411
100,000 to 249,999 persons	3,685	106	21	940	715	441	917	570	588	1,276	1,252
250,000 to 499,999 persons	2,781	81	2	884	466	316	878	198	496	1,065	1,023
500,000 to 999,999 persons	1,644	52	7	487	313	189	457	148	432	615	449
1,000,000 persons or more	3,978	60	3	1,185	1,211	570	1,220	2,090	565	473	851

– = Zero or rounds to zero.
X = Not applicable.
[1] = Native Hawaiian and Other Pacific Islander.
[2] = Because Hispanics may be any race, data may overlap slightly with other groups. Most Hispanics report themselves as White, but some report themselves as Black or in other categories.
[3] = For manufactured/mobile homes, oldest category is 1939 or earlier.

Source: U.S. Census Bureau, American Housing Survey

Table 1-4. Neighborhood, Occupied Units, 2009

[Numbers in thousands.]

Characteristics	Total occupied units	Tenure		Housing unit characteristics		Household characteristics				Regions			
		Owner	Renter	New construction 4 years	Manufactured/ mobile homes	Black alone	Hispanic	Elderly (65 years or over)	Below poverty level	Northeast	Midwest	South	West
Total	111,806	76,428	35,378	4,771	6,839	13,993	12,739	23,095	15,739	20,451	25,368	41,586	24,401
Overall opinion of neighborhood													
1 (worst)	837	338	499	24	72	291	148	116	354	164	201	323	149
2	637	289	348	29	59	170	94	65	166	105	156	268	108
3	1,002	459	543	15	100	195	111	99	263	184	229	372	217
4	1,633	766	867	58	132	291	190	178	429	217	419	536	462
5	6,332	3,356	2,976	176	474	1,250	964	1,003	1,526	980	1,323	2,554	1,476
6	5,919	3,454	2,465	210	380	959	735	823	972	1,080	1,285	2,120	1,434
7	14,767	9,603	5,164	489	808	2,028	1,633	2,194	1,828	2,628	3,324	5,344	3,472
8	29,794	20,808	8,986	1,156	1,646	3,379	3,373	5,394	3,467	5,506	6,751	10,793	6,745
9	18,017	13,454	4,563	776	874	1,725	1,902	3,821	1,804	3,243	4,220	6,472	4,082
10 (best)	28,465	20,891	7,575	1,663	2,073	3,019	3,198	8,502	4,053	5,437	6,704	10,873	5,452
No neighborhood	60	31	29	–	4	8	3	12	16	13	10	26	11
Not reported	4,341	2,979	1,362	175	220	677	388	888	860	895	746	1,905	794
Street noise or traffic													
Bothersome street noise or heavy traffic present	111,806	76,428	35,378	4,771	6,839	13,993	12,739	23,095	15,739	20,451	25,368	41,586	24,401
Yes	25,381	15,223	10,158	716	1,335	4,099	3,143	4,574	4,659	5,203	6,006	8,466	5,706
No	85,122	60,264	24,858	4,009	5,442	9,731	9,517	18,242	10,812	15,052	19,132	32,519	18,418
Not reported	1,303	941	362	46	62	163	79	279	268	196	230	600	276
Neighborhood crime													
Serious crime in past 12 months	111,806	76,428	35,378	4,771	6,839	13,993	12,739	23,095	15,739	20,451	25,368	41,586	24,401
Yes	19,299	11,649	7,650	778	944	3,473	2,626	2,763	3,205	2,912	4,318	7,482	4,586
No	90,116	63,230	26,886	3,905	5,796	10,104	9,943	19,836	12,008	17,159	20,615	33,055	19,287
Not reported	2,391	1,549	842	88	99	416	170	496	526	379	435	1,049	528
Odors													
Bothersome smoke, gas, or bad smells	111,806	76,428	35,378	4,771	6,839	13,993	12,739	23,095	15,739	20,451	25,368	41,586	24,401
Yes	5,434	3,278	2,156	159	386	944	725	827	1,115	1,053	1,379	1,732	1,271
No	105,015	72,168	32,847	4,563	6,385	12,890	11,931	21,974	14,347	19,194	23,756	39,229	22,836
Not reported	1,356	982	375	49	68	159	83	293	276	205	233	625	293
Other bothersome neighborhood conditions													
No other problems	93,262	63,858	29,404	3,884	5,591	11,180	10,674	20,098	12,825	17,280	21,418	34,624	19,941
With other problems[1]	16,876	11,359	5,517	838	1,163	2,595	1,961	2,650	2,566	2,926	3,663	6,150	4,137
Noise	2,950	1,733	1,217	80	157	473	381	477	496	646	598	965	741
Litter or housing deterioration	1,691	1,101	590	26	97	399	212	309	333	300	376	659	356
Poor city or county services	694	440	254	11	74	181	86	91	161	110	170	292	123
Undesirable commercial, institutional, or industrial	415	247	168	27	17	62	52	60	73	104	91	133	87
People	4,521	2,706	1,815	178	393	758	566	624	879	679	1,108	1,678	1,056
Other	9,539	6,748	2,791	583	618	1,415	1,082	1,489	1,235	1,611	1,902	3,565	2,461
No problem	151	90	61	7	8	24	22	27	32	42	28	41	39
Type of problem not reported	5	–	5	–	–	5	–	3	2	3	2	–	–
Other problems not reported	1,667	1,210	457	49	84	219	104	347	348	245	288	811	323
Public elementary school[1]													
Households with children aged 5 through 15	26,636	18,509	8,127	1,429	1,576	3,973	4,760	527	4,309	4,576	5,869	9,994	6,196
Attend public school (K-12)	22,140	14,932	7,208	1,168	1,422	3,497	4,251	421	3,840	3,675	4,878	8,384	5,203
Attend private school (K-12)	2,583	2,203	380	142	42	277	228	41	163	511	626	905	541
Attend ungraded school, preschool, etc.	438	327	111	30	7	46	52	22	78	105	83	136	114
Home schooled	382	294	88	28	32	11	25	8	37	51	86	172	73
Not in school	497	317	180	35	29	65	91	6	80	103	106	172	115
Not reported	1,208	922	286	70	54	157	184	33	166	239	237	457	275
Households with children aged 0 through 13	30,976	20,490	10,486	1,823	1,782	4,467	5,550	493	5,217	5,251	6,931	11,733	7,061
Satisfactory public elementary school	25,297	16,966	8,331	1,471	1,538	3,583	4,615	433	4,186	4,304	5,762	9,560	5,671
Unsatisfactory public elementary school	2,146	1,422	724	145	119	431	296	23	428	331	422	862	532
Not reported or don't know	3,532	2,102	1,431	207	125	453	638	36	603	616	747	1,311	859
Public elementary school less than 1 mile	18,667	11,571	7,096	832	533	3,068	4,252	260	3,382	3,261	4,128	6,059	5,220
Public elementary school 1 mile or more	10,526	7,785	2,741	882	1,160	1,179	954	195	1,494	1,673	2,416	5,019	1,417
Not reported	1,783	1,134	649	109	89	220	344	38	342	317	386	655	425
Academic comparison to other area elementary schools													
Households with children aged 0 through 13 dissatisfied with local elementary school	2,146	1,422	724	145	119	431	296	23	428	331	422	862	532
Better	216	154	63	16	12	53	40	3	56	30	34	103	50
About the same	714	490	224	59	48	115	86	12	119	124	149	287	154
Worse	1,082	696	386	53	60	237	151	2	230	155	202	428	297
Not reported	133	83	51	16	–	26	19	6	22	21	37	44	31
Building neighbor noise[2]													
Neighbor noise present	18,015	3,360	14,655	604	X	3,832	2,789	2,280	4,216	4,659	3,837	5,115	4,404
Loudness bothersome	5,189	717	4,472	152	X	1,258	974	422	1,467	1,172	1,104	1,527	1,385
Loudness not bothersome	12,820	2,641	10,180	453	X	2,572	1,815	1,857	2,749	3,485	2,733	3,588	3,015
Loudness bothersome not reported	6	3	3	–	X	3	–	1	1	2	–	–	3
Time of noise bothersome	5,219	736	4,483	150	X	1,311	974	434	1,498	1,179	1,114	1,584	1,342
Time of noise not bothersome	12,777	2,618	10,159	454	X	2,512	1,814	1,843	2,714	3,479	2,722	3,519	3,056
Time bothersome not reported	19	6	14	–	X	8	–	3	4	1	–	12	7
Neighbor noise not present	12,399	4,065	8,334	500	X	2,353	2,195	3,053	2,646	3,437	2,198	3,941	2,824
Not reported	1,474	261	1,213	56	X	317	227	312	435	384	246	549	295

Table 1-4. Neighborhood, Occupied Units, 2009—*Continued*

[Numbers in thousands.]

Characteristics	Total occupied units	Tenure: Owner	Tenure: Renter	Housing unit characteristics: New construction 4 years	Housing unit characteristics: Manufactured/ mobile homes	Household characteristics: Black alone	Household characteristics: Hispanic	Household characteristics: Elderly (65 years or over)	Household characteristics: Below poverty level	Regions: Northeast	Regions: Midwest	Regions: South	Regions: West
Public transportation													
With public transportation	60,257	35,616	24,641	1,501	1,468	9,575	8,993	11,528	9,376	13,375	12,758	16,507	17,617
Travel time to nearest bus stop, train station, or subway stop													
Less than 5 minutes	21,258	10,929	10,328	469	479	3,688	3,153	3,527	3,656	4,795	5,287	5,228	5,947
5-9 minutes	21,699	12,830	8,869	495	486	3,554	3,499	4,156	3,311	4,691	4,230	5,972	6,807
10-14 minutes	8,606	5,853	2,753	270	175	1,308	1,295	1,731	1,133	2,075	1,460	2,582	2,489
15-29 minutes	4,224	3,125	1,099	105	160	542	591	966	509	1,007	647	1,317	1,252
30 minutes or longer	618	449	169	18	53	88	42	141	131	107	119	269	123
Not reported	3,852	2,430	1,422	144	115	395	414	1,007	636	700	1,014	1,139	999
Household uses public transportation regularly for commuting to school or work	10,212	3,817	6,395	200	157	2,679	2,252	1,146	2,397	3,639	1,738	1,948	2,887
Household does not use public transportation regularly for commuting to school or work	49,681	31,606	18,075	1,279	1,309	6,801	6,696	10,350	6,900	9,570	10,982	14,470	14,659
Not reported	364	194	170	23	2	95	45	32	79	166	38	89	71
No public transportation	48,532	38,848	9,684	3,085	5,191	4,128	3,526	10,964	5,859	6,630	11,939	23,794	6,168
Not reported	3,017	1,964	1,053	185	180	291	220	603	503	447	671	1,285	615
Neighborhood shopping													
Grocery stores or drug stores within 15 minutes of the home	106,737	72,548	34,189	4,433	6,142	13,275	12,346	21,692	14,669	19,618	24,433	39,153	23,532
Satisfactory	103,482	70,400	33,082	4,267	5,876	12,658	11,983	20,982	14,003	19,007	23,830	37,985	22,660
Not satisfactory	2,769	1,805	964	152	238	535	330	596	587	517	528	932	792
Not reported	486	343	143	15	29	81	32	113	79	94	75	237	80
No grocery stores or drug stores within 15 minutes of the home	3,596	2,819	777	201	549	519	276	1,116	734	609	700	1,728	560
Not reported or don't know	1,473	1,061	412	136	148	199	118	287	335	224	235	705	309
Police protection													
Satisfactory police protection	101,373	69,633	31,740	4,245	5,992	12,163	11,365	21,223	13,526	18,594	23,406	37,316	22,056
Unsatisfactory police protection	7,356	4,800	2,556	352	678	1,351	1,111	1,244	1,598	1,304	1,444	3,004	1,604
Not reported	3,078	1,995	1,082	174	168	480	263	628	615	553	519	1,266	740
Secured communities													
Community access secured with walls or fences	10,759	5,337	5,422	736	566	1,738	1,992	2,339	1,832	1,355	883	4,346	4,175
Special entry system present	6,091	2,682	3,410	529	133	940	1,061	1,405	923	613	320	2,651	2,507
Special entry system not present	4,653	2,648	2,005	207	433	791	931	934	910	742	559	1,688	1,664
Special entry system not reported	14	7	7	–	–	8	–	–	–	–	3	8	3
Community access not secured	100,124	70,410	29,714	3,993	6,222	12,152	10,665	20,542	13,696	18,964	24,337	36,821	20,002
Community access not reported	923	682	242	42	51	104	82	214	211	132	149	418	224
Secured multiunits													
Multiunit access secured	7,211	1,357	5,854	328	X	1,406	1,133	1,880	1,621	2,043	1,637	1,688	1,843
Multiunit access not secured	16,741	2,151	14,590	373	X	3,622	2,985	2,175	4,292	4,187	3,291	5,314	3,949
Multiunit access not reported	1,963	226	1,737	42	X	378	495	401	544	440	297	667	558
Senior citizen communities													
Households with person 55 and over	45,684	36,591	9,093	1,208	2,989	4,975	3,706	23,095	6,408	8,991	10,259	16,945	9,489
Community age restricted	3,080	1,457	1,624	145	401	389	241	2,453	782	601	553	1,105	821
No age restriction or restriction not reported	42,603	35,134	7,469	1,063	2,588	4,585	3,465	20,642	5,626	8,390	9,706	15,840	8,667
Community age specific	10,302	8,867	1,435	139	700	1,058	688	5,831	1,298	1,744	2,550	4,206	1,802
Community not age specific	29,683	24,100	5,583	854	1,706	3,174	2,572	13,624	3,873	6,085	6,706	10,591	6,302
Community age specific not reported	2,618	2,167	451	69	183	352	205	1,187	455	561	449	1,043	564
Community quality													
Some or all community activities present[1]	49,962	33,117	16,845	2,052	2,272	5,962	5,194	11,087	6,666	9,066	13,917	15,732	11,247
Community center or clubhouse	24,410	14,707	9,703	1,298	1,370	3,260	2,474	6,193	3,523	3,967	6,260	8,613	5,569
Golf in community	16,709	12,762	3,947	384	528	1,082	1,192	4,015	1,712	3,058	6,507	3,890	3,254
Trails in community	21,609	15,300	6,309	1,014	565	2,000	1,975	4,336	2,350	3,815	6,791	6,213	4,791
Shuttle bus	9,933	5,718	4,215	185	288	1,124	1,249	3,291	1,643	2,308	2,998	2,275	2,352
Daycare center	15,883	10,633	5,249	322	441	2,454	1,728	2,938	2,390	3,734	5,844	3,646	2,658
Private or restricted beach, park, or shoreline	21,432	15,124	6,308	733	761	1,979	2,303	4,058	2,431	4,427	7,197	5,092	4,716
Description of area within 300 feet[1]													
Single-family detached houses	95,916	68,909	27,007	3,899	5,080	11,377	10,548	19,890	12,500	17,146	22,159	35,417	21,194
Single-family attached	21,832	10,973	10,860	810	323	3,870	2,982	3,857	3,498	5,223	4,052	6,962	5,595
Multiunit residential buildings[3]	33,635	11,514	22,121	930	578	6,524	5,709	5,779	7,283	7,455	7,311	10,123	8,747
1- to 3-story multiunit is tallest	25,143	9,014	16,130	664	525	4,638	4,160	3,951	5,409	3,838	5,936	8,134	7,235
4- to 6-story multiunit is tallest	4,937	1,464	3,473	138	34	1,056	914	964	1,023	1,997	739	1,202	1,000
7-or-more-story multiunit is tallest	3,172	929	2,243	128	10	746	548	740	739	1,486	543	705	437
Manufactured/mobile homes	13,388	10,276	3,112	590	5,413	1,272	1,361	3,087	2,472	1,205	2,022	7,346	2,815
Commercial or institutional	35,649	16,992	18,657	840	1,336	6,563	5,566	6,183	7,048	8,083	7,766	11,498	8,302
Industrial or factories	5,376	2,520	2,856	110	342	1,147	954	810	1,289	1,450	1,365	1,627	934
Open space, park, woods, farm, or ranch	45,816	33,110	12,706	2,610	4,132	4,658	3,664	9,155	5,705	8,549	11,430	16,958	8,878
4-or-more-lane highway, railroad, or airport	19,612	10,380	9,232	566	1,155	3,450	2,748	3,633	3,539	2,994	4,483	7,846	4,289
Not reported	2,624	1,836	788	111	133	407	233	466	500	460	447	1,150	567

Table 1-4. Neighborhood, Occupied Units, 2009—*Continued*

[Numbers in thousands.]

Characteristics	Total occupied units	Tenure		Housing unit characteristics		Household characteristics				Regions			
		Owner	Renter	New construction 4 years	Manufactured/ mobile homes	Black alone	Hispanic	Elderly (65 years or over)	Below poverty level	Northeast	Midwest	South	West
Bodies of water within 300 feet													
Water in area	18,656	13,824	4,832	1,050	1,541	1,548	1,332	3,818	1,980	3,548	4,498	8,188	2,422
With waterfront property	3,331	2,653	678	166	197	152	187	991	294	555	800	1,595	382
Waterfront property not reported	360	266	94	15	24	26	36	83	52	59	81	182	38
With flood plain	2,622	1,929	692	114	268	232	241	614	300	487	318	1,477	340
Flood plain not reported	116	41	74	21	10	17	20	12	17	18	17	66	15
Water not reported	676	521	156	58	35	107	40	88	141	162	121	209	185
No water in area	92,474	62,083	30,390	3,663	5,263	12,339	11,368	19,189	13,618	16,742	20,750	33,189	21,793
Age of other residential buildings within 300 feet													
Older	12,638	7,710	4,928	81	1,138	1,516	1,387	2,918	2,424	2,641	2,791	4,639	2,568
About the same	75,613	52,299	23,313	2,557	2,892	9,928	8,987	14,750	9,632	13,485	17,353	27,703	17,071
Newer	9,774	7,126	2,648	1,716	1,382	988	876	1,974	1,307	1,886	2,151	3,893	1,844
Very mixed	6,701	4,582	2,120	81	867	697	722	1,800	1,072	1,225	1,386	2,576	1,515
No other residential buildings	3,316	2,425	891	217	390	262	289	901	520	459	1,005	1,264	589
Not reported	3,764	2,286	1,478	119	170	603	478	753	783	756	682	1,511	814
Other buildings vandalized or with interior exposed within 300 feet													
None	98,452	67,919	30,533	4,242	5,762	11,263	11,151	20,573	12,918	18,277	22,080	36,453	21,643
1 building	3,246	2,034	1,211	90	265	660	457	575	650	550	727	1,258	711
More than 1 building	3,856	2,031	1,825	105	275	1,366	576	529	1,084	637	1,029	1,393	796
No buildings	2,871	2,245	626	195	385	155	217	774	382	345	926	1,104	497
Not reported	3,381	2,198	1,182	140	153	550	337	644	704	642	607	1,378	754
Bars on windows of buildings within 300 feet													
No bars on windows	93,406	66,383	27,024	4,267	6,045	9,933	9,012	19,383	11,822	16,564	22,498	35,261	19,083
1 building with bars	2,108	1,256	851	33	105	377	366	424	422	253	342	824	689
2 or more buildings with bars	9,101	3,927	5,174	126	135	2,721	2,654	1,618	2,209	2,481	841	2,730	3,049
No buildings	2,871	2,245	626	195	385	155	217	774	382	345	926	1,104	497
Not reported	4,320	2,617	1,703	151	169	807	490	896	903	808	762	1,667	1,083
Condition of streets within 300 feet													
No repairs needed	63,186	44,404	18,782	3,237	2,987	6,701	7,287	13,742	7,666	10,223	13,227	24,274	15,462
Minor repairs needed	36,976	24,133	12,843	952	2,646	5,391	4,153	6,935	5,750	8,050	9,438	12,555	6,932
Major repairs needed	6,604	4,375	2,228	336	864	1,221	818	1,389	1,385	1,239	1,762	2,673	930
No streets	1,678	1,259	419	99	166	182	170	363	255	279	358	636	405
Not reported	3,362	2,257	1,106	147	174	499	312	665	683	660	583	1,446	672
Trash, litter, or junk on streets or any properties within 300 feet													
None	99,010	69,415	29,595	4,344	5,953	11,403	10,964	21,173	12,771	17,954	22,740	36,992	21,324
Minor accumulation	7,250	3,491	3,759	210	474	1,569	1,081	956	1,762	1,494	1,548	2,386	1,822
Major accumulation	2,519	1,426	1,093	81	261	552	428	390	624	438	540	917	623
Not reported	3,027	2,096	931	136	151	469	267	576	582	565	540	1,290	631
Parking lots													
With parking lots	33,562	14,581	18,981	948	1,272	5,571	4,455	5,907	6,445	6,377	8,678	11,083	7,424
No parking lots within 300 feet	75,433	59,870	15,563	3,708	5,433	7,989	8,038	16,660	8,770	13,554	16,201	29,298	16,380
Parking lots not reported	2,811	1,977	833	116	133	434	246	528	523	520	489	1,205	597
Manufactured/mobile homes in groups													
Manufactured/mobile homes	6,839	5,418	1,421	301	6,839	643	722	1,537	1,492	540	1,145	3,918	1,236
1 to 6	4,918	3,952	966	251	4,918	546	399	1,010	1,093	312	707	3,135	764
7 to 20	370	217	153	19	370	46	64	61	86	46	49	228	48
21 or more	1,550	1,249	301	30	1,550	50	260	465	313	182	389	555	424

– = Zero or rounds to zero.
X = Not applicable.
[1] = Figures may not add to total because more than one category may apply to a unit.
[2] = Limited to single attached and multiunits.
[3]= Figures do not add up because of nonrespondents.

Source: U.S. Census Bureau, American Housing Survey

Table 1-5. Neighborhood, Owner-Occupied Units, 2009

[Numbers in thousands.]

Characteristics	Total occupied units	Housing unit characteristics		Household characteristics				Regions			
		New construction 4 years	Manufactured/ mobile homes	Black alone	Hispanic	Elderly (65 years and over)	Below poverty level	Northeast	Midwest	South	West
Total	76,428	3,830	5,418	6,547	6,439	18,472	6,405	13,378	18,249	29,193	15,607
Overall opinion of neighborhood											
1 (worst)	338	10	41	51	31	91	78	41	77	160	61
2	289	24	51	34	28	48	24	40	77	120	52
3	459	12	67	71	37	72	48	62	132	192	73
4	766	35	99	77	70	138	112	84	220	246	216
5	3,356	144	368	438	346	713	437	477	768	1,399	713
6	3,454	151	272	388	321	618	292	590	791	1,322	751
7	9,603	371	627	931	848	1,716	702	1,643	2,250	3,571	2,138
8	20,808	891	1,305	1,709	1,746	4,346	1,477	3,678	4,966	7,778	4,386
9	13,454	628	744	953	1,084	3,136	831	2,287	3,308	4,945	2,915
10 (best)	20,891	1,419	1,678	1,605	1,723	6,860	1,962	3,934	5,118	8,120	3,718
No neighborhood	31	–	4	4	1	8	1	4	1	20	6
Not reported	2,979	145	164	284	203	725	440	541	542	1,320	577
Street noise or traffic											
Bothersome street noise or heavy traffic present	76,428	3,830	5,418	6,547	6,439	18,472	6,405	13,378	18,249	29,193	15,607
Yes	15,223	482	1,008	1,639	1,419	3,497	1,549	2,926	3,793	5,343	3,161
No	60,264	3,313	4,361	4,836	4,972	14,744	4,692	10,316	14,269	23,435	12,245
Not reported	941	35	49	72	48	231	164	136	188	415	202
Neighborhood crime											
Serious crime in past 12 months	76,428	3,830	5,418	6,547	6,439	18,472	6,405	13,378	18,249	29,193	15,607
Yes	11,649	598	739	1,428	1,223	2,105	951	1,567	2,679	4,779	2,624
No	63,230	3,165	4,605	4,958	5,129	15,983	5,194	11,581	15,283	23,703	12,663
Not reported	1,549	67	74	161	87	383	259	230	288	711	320
Odors											
Bothersome smoke, gas, or bad smells	76,428	3,830	5,418	6,547	6,439	18,472	6,405	13,378	18,249	29,193	15,607
Yes	3,278	125	311	330	367	663	389	563	895	1,071	749
No	72,168	3,669	5,054	6,142	6,024	17,567	5,843	12,673	17,156	27,686	14,653
Not reported	982	35	52	76	48	243	174	142	198	437	205
Other bothersome neighborhood conditions											
No other problems	63,858	3,125	4,411	5,217	5,316	15,939	5,319	11,378	15,425	24,369	12,687
With other problems[1]	11,359	666	944	1,235	1,058	2,239	872	1,843	2,578	4,254	2,684
Noise	1,733	58	114	176	165	382	156	344	402	541	446
Litter or housing deterioration	1,101	18	78	196	85	266	121	160	268	444	229
Poor city or county services	440	11	67	80	49	70	72	59	106	199	77
Undesirable commercial, institutional, or industrial	247	20	14	25	15	52	20	65	56	77	49
People	2,706	129	303	298	269	510	249	372	704	1,042	587
Other	6,748	475	537	705	638	1,272	452	1,091	1,403	2,564	1,691
No problem	90	7	6	12	11	19	8	23	15	24	27
Type of problem not reported	–	–	–	–	–	–	–	–	–	–	–
Other problems not reported	1,210	39	63	95	64	294	213	157	247	570	236
Public elementary school[1]											
Households with children aged 5 through 15	18,509	1,180	1,168	1,759	2,442	452	1,503	3,163	4,432	6,928	3,986
Attend public school (K-12)	14,932	948	1,054	1,486	2,148	352	1,309	2,488	3,599	5,638	3,206
Attend private school (K-12)	2,203	125	32	180	149	37	75	415	568	774	446
Attend ungraded school, preschool, etc.	327	25	6	20	26	22	23	80	63	104	80
Home schooled	294	25	23	5	20	8	19	45	62	130	57
Not in school	317	28	15	21	41	6	22	55	75	115	71
Not reported	922	65	45	80	107	31	82	163	190	346	223
Households with children aged 0 through 13	20,490	1,520	1,235	1,786	2,651	420	1,549	3,485	4,995	7,654	4,355
Satisfactory public elementary school	16,966	1,223	1,078	1,462	2,203	370	1,323	2,924	4,246	6,302	3,494
Unsatisfactory public elementary school	1,422	119	88	172	164	19	106	218	265	587	353
Not reported or don't know	2,102	178	69	153	284	31	120	343	484	766	508
Public elementary school less than 1 mile	11,571	662	346	1,110	1,985	210	845	1,969	2,820	3,656	3,125
Public elementary school 1 mile or more	7,785	756	846	589	500	177	598	1,318	1,921	3,592	955
Not reported	1,134	102	43	87	165	32	106	198	255	406	276
Academic comparison to other area elementary schools											
Households with children aged 0 through 13 dissatisfied with local elementary school	1,422	119	88	172	164	19	106	218	265	587	353
Better	154	16	12	15	24	–	17	19	25	76	34
About the same	490	55	35	53	47	12	26	88	102	201	99
Worse	696	41	41	91	80	1	56	95	110	287	204
Not reported	83	7	–	13	13	6	7	15	27	23	17

Table 1-5. Neighborhood, Owner-Occupied Units, 2009—*Continued*

[Numbers in thousands.]

Characteristics	Total occupied units	Housing unit characteristics		Household characteristics				Regions			
		New construction 4 years	Manufactured/ mobile homes	Black alone	Hispanic	Elderly (65 years and over)	Below poverty level	Northeast	Midwest	South	West
Building neighbor noise[2]											
Neighbor noise present	3,360	207	X	422	295	696	277	1,096	618	832	814
Loudness bothersome	717	50	X	94	85	117	71	236	121	163	197
Loudness not bothersome	2,641	157	X	325	210	579	207	860	497	669	615
Loudness bothersome not reported	3	–	X	3	–	–	–	–	–	–	3
Time of noise bothersome	736	54	X	98	95	114	82	243	115	169	210
Time of noise not bothersome	2,618	152	X	322	200	582	195	853	503	660	602
Time bothersome not reported	6	–	X	3	–	–	–	–	–	3	3
Neighbor noise not present	4,065	273	X	488	386	1,322	332	1,333	697	1,246	789
Not reported	261	11	X	34	19	85	55	74	27	119	40
Public transportation											
With public transportation	35,616	994	1,183	3,719	3,998	8,283	2,815	7,543	8,055	9,598	10,421
Travel time to nearest bus stop, train station, or subway stop											
Less than 5 minutes	10,929	278	385	1,221	1,174	2,309	873	2,392	2,947	2,606	2,983
5-9 minutes	12,830	346	378	1,438	1,574	2,994	1,015	2,619	2,744	3,392	4,075
10-14 minutes	5,853	175	144	570	721	1,351	429	1,303	1,079	1,757	1,715
15-29 minutes	3,125	76	139	305	316	794	220	740	524	968	892
30 minutes or longer	449	13	37	42	25	121	44	70	83	203	94
Not reported	2,430	105	99	144	188	714	233	419	679	671	661
Household uses public transportation regularly for commuting to school or work	3,817	100	117	720	569	582	308	1,260	726	726	1,104
Household does not use public transportation regularly for commuting to school or work	31,606	887	1,063	2,963	3,411	7,679	2,473	6,204	7,311	8,826	9,265
Not reported	194	8	2	37	17	21	33	78	18	45	52
No public transportation	38,848	2,686	4,110	2,689	2,309	9,728	3,337	5,570	9,757	18,754	4,767
Not reported	1,964	150	126	138	132	461	254	266	437	842	419
Neighborhood shopping											
Grocery stores or drug stores within 15 minutes of the home	72,548	3,537	4,860	6,155	6,240	17,257	5,781	12,732	17,526	27,288	15,002
Satisfactory	70,400	3,386	4,632	5,922	6,042	16,688	5,523	12,374	17,153	26,473	14,401
Not satisfactory	1,805	135	207	202	177	493	216	300	318	643	543
Not reported	343	15	21	31	22	77	42	58	56	172	58
No grocery stores or drug stores within 15 minutes of the home	2,819	182	451	293	130	968	415	499	537	1,398	385
Not reported or don't know	1,061	111	107	100	69	246	209	148	186	508	219
Police protection											
Satisfactory police protection	69,633	3,399	4,753	5,837	5,742	16,929	5,501	12,283	16,927	26,267	14,156
Unsatisfactory police protection	4,800	294	544	516	568	1,051	608	786	943	2,072	999
Not reported	1,995	138	121	194	129	492	296	309	380	854	453
Secured communities											
Community access secured with walls or fences	5,337	459	487	367	656	1,512	440	606	480	2,281	1,969
Special entry system present	2,682	284	121	150	273	829	184	239	113	1,281	1,048
Special entry system not present	2,648	175	366	213	383	683	257	367	364	996	921
Special entry system not reported	7	–	–	4	–	–	–	–	3	4	–
Community access not secured	70,410	3,336	4,893	6,124	5,736	16,783	5,831	12,680	17,644	26,614	13,472
Community access not reported	682	35	39	56	47	177	134	92	126	297	166
Secured multiunits											
Multiunit access secured	1,357	79	X	106	135	454	118	366	281	334	375
Multiunit access not secured	2,151	82	X	216	237	608	163	774	348	524	506
Multiunit access not reported	226	6	X	29	30	81	40	70	32	74	51
Senior citizen communities											
Households with person 55 and over	36,591	1,021	2,669	3,132	2,451	18,472	3,763	6,629	8,363	14,189	7,409
Community age restricted	1,457	94	366	89	71	1,079	194	223	113	683	437
No age restriction or restriction not reported	35,134	927	2,303	3,043	2,379	17,393	3,569	6,406	8,250	13,506	6,972
Community age specific	8,867	125	637	793	551	5,031	884	1,393	2,164	3,726	1,584
Community not age specific	24,100	735	1,513	2,006	1,667	11,359	2,364	4,588	5,700	8,881	4,931
Community age specific not reported	2,167	67	154	244	161	1,003	321	424	386	899	457
Community quality											
Some or all community activities present[1]	33,117	1,460	1,854	2,570	2,547	8,356	2,468	5,860	9,765	10,437	7,054
Community center or clubhouse	14,707	818	1,178	1,181	1,127	4,306	1,177	2,307	4,016	5,260	3,125
Golf in community	12,762	329	447	611	694	3,410	832	2,307	5,041	3,064	2,350
Trails in community	15,300	839	451	983	1,099	3,509	981	2,619	4,925	4,416	3,339
Shuttle bus	5,718	106	216	422	536	2,033	482	1,303	1,923	1,196	1,297
Daycare center	10,633	251	339	1,157	795	2,392	822	2,318	4,242	2,441	1,632
Private or restricted beach, park, or shoreline	15,124	584	592	925	1,158	3,327	964	2,982	5,282	3,693	3,167
Description of area within 300 feet[1]											
Single-family detached houses	68,909	3,347	4,020	5,906	5,760	16,439	5,400	12,034	16,618	26,160	14,097
Single-family attached	10,973	521	242	1,330	1,021	2,522	889	2,583	2,075	3,662	2,653
Multiunit residential buildings[3]	11,514	364	438	1,457	1,383	2,805	1,228	2,507	2,801	3,346	2,860
1- to 3-story multiunit is tallest	9,014	259	398	1,046	1,100	2,098	981	1,567	2,352	2,682	2,413
4- to 6-story multiunit is tallest	1,464	65	28	263	170	412	141	562	245	385	271
7-or-more-story multiunit is tallest	929	40	6	130	96	264	95	348	174	242	165

Table 1-5. Neighborhood, Owner-Occupied Units, 2009—*Continued*

[Numbers in thousands.]

Characteristics	Total occupied units	Housing unit characteristics		Household characteristics				Regions			
		New construction 4 years	Manufactured/ mobile homes	Black alone	Hispanic	Elderly (65 years and over)	Below poverty level	Northeast	Midwest	South	West
Manufactured/mobile homes	10,276	512	4,318	824	877	2,758	1,464	969	1,630	5,713	1,964
Commercial or institutional	16,992	492	1,023	2,240	1,841	3,820	1,703	3,641	4,158	5,590	3,603
Industrial or factories	2,520	81	269	401	311	515	317	585	743	830	363
Open space, park, woods, farm, or ranch	33,110	2,169	3,281	2,289	1,894	7,548	2,540	6,027	8,566	12,502	6,015
4-or-more-lane highway, railroad, or airport	10,380	324	882	1,215	1,112	2,513	1,015	1,569	2,529	4,218	2,065
Not reported	1,836	96	91	184	132	408	285	315	320	793	408
Bodies of water within 300 feet											
Water in area	13,824	859	1,294	714	727	3,192	990	2,575	3,454	6,126	1,668
With waterfront property	2,653	139	163	59	132	846	178	423	623	1,322	286
Waterfront property not reported	266	12	16	10	22	62	29	39	62	136	30
With flood plain	1,929	77	215	115	144	539	169	360	236	1,108	225
Flood plain not reported	41	11	10	6	2	2	2	7	6	21	7
Water not reported	521	51	30	64	29	83	101	120	96	169	135
No water in area	62,083	2,920	4,094	5,769	5,683	15,197	5,314	10,683	14,699	22,090	13,003
Age of other residential buildings within 300 feet											
Older	7,710	67	892	527	556	2,351	1,003	1,601	1,823	2,991	1,295
About the same	52,299	2,097	2,198	4,836	4,704	12,054	3,806	8,975	12,558	19,445	11,322
Newer	7,126	1,311	1,216	487	518	1,452	526	1,263	1,602	3,042	1,218
Very mixed	4,582	59	690	331	349	1,377	461	815	1,025	1,833	909
No other residential buildings	2,425	192	305	131	133	707	253	288	822	918	398
Not reported	2,286	103	118	235	180	530	355	436	420	964	466
Other buildings vandalized or with interior exposed within 300 feet											
None	67,919	3,400	4,572	5,398	5,666	16,456	5,352	12,186	15,974	25,871	13,888
1 building	2,034	70	215	294	226	464	228	326	490	805	414
More than 1 building	2,031	68	225	528	267	391	282	245	589	741	457
No buildings	2,245	177	300	91	113	646	220	240	786	856	363
Not reported	2,198	116	106	236	167	515	324	381	411	921	486
Bars on windows of buildings within 300 feet											
No bars on windows	66,383	3,427	4,831	4,888	4,840	15,868	5,118	11,849	16,458	25,220	12,856
1 building with bars	1,256	21	63	181	187	326	155	119	184	495	459
2 or more buildings with bars	3,927	81	106	1,058	1,092	987	533	708	356	1,568	1,295
No buildings	2,245	177	300	91	113	646	220	240	786	856	363
Not reported	2,617	124	118	330	206	645	379	461	466	1,055	635
Condition of streets within 300 feet											
No repairs needed	44,404	2,581	2,355	3,294	3,795	11,022	3,190	7,018	9,874	17,383	10,129
Minor repairs needed	24,133	757	2,059	2,406	1,984	5,515	2,182	5,019	6,490	8,448	4,175
Major repairs needed	4,375	279	749	545	423	1,132	577	752	1,187	1,851	586
No streets	1,259	81	134	104	77	287	129	190	300	501	269
Not reported	2,257	132	121	198	160	517	327	400	398	1,010	447
Trash, litter, or junk on streets or any properties within 300 feet											
None	69,415	3,481	4,748	5,639	5,752	17,001	5,507	12,189	16,765	26,480	13,981
Minor accumulation	3,491	167	367	505	342	673	396	611	779	1,274	828
Major accumulation	1,426	62	197	201	193	318	187	208	316	544	357
Not reported	2,096	120	106	202	151	479	315	370	389	895	441
Parking lots											
With parking lots	14,581	456	964	1,435	1,296	3,223	1,246	2,799	4,145	4,595	3,041
No parking lots within 300 feet	59,870	3,274	4,363	4,914	5,000	14,799	4,868	10,228	13,747	23,757	12,138
Parking lots not reported	1,977	100	91	198	143	450	292	351	357	841	428
Manufactured/mobile homes in groups											
Manufactured/mobile homes	5,418	272	5,418	503	490	1,379	1,009	436	943	3,072	966
1 to 6	3,952	234	3,952	440	269	903	756	256	572	2,557	567
7 to 20	217	19	217	35	38	47	28	29	35	119	34
21 or more	1,249	19	1,249	28	183	429	225	152	337	396	365

– = Zero or rounds to zero.
X = Not applicable.
[1] = Figures may not add to total because more than one category may apply to a unit.
[2] = Limited to single attached and multiunits.
[3] = Figures do not add up because of nonrespondents.

Source: U.S. Census Bureau, American Housing Survey

Table 1-6. Neighborhood, Renter-Occupied Units, 2009

[Numbers in thousands.]

Characteristics	Total occupied units	Housing unit characteristics: New construction 4 years	Housing unit characteristics: Manufactured/ mobile homes	Household characteristics: Black alone	Household characteristics: Hispanic	Household characteristics: Elderly (65 years and over)	Household characteristics: Below poverty level	Regions: Northeast	Regions: Midwest	Regions: South	Regions: West
Total	35,378	941	1,421	7,446	6,300	4,623	9,334	7,073	7,119	12,392	8,794
Overall opinion of neighborhood											
1 (worst)	499	13	31	240	118	24	276	124	124	163	88
2	348	5	8	136	66	16	142	65	78	148	56
3	543	3	33	124	74	27	215	123	98	179	144
4	867	23	32	214	121	41	317	133	199	289	246
5	2,976	32	106	812	618	290	1,089	503	555	1,155	763
6	2,465	60	108	571	413	205	680	490	494	798	683
7	5,164	118	180	1,097	784	478	1,126	984	1,073	1,773	1,334
8	8,986	265	341	1,670	1,627	1,048	1,989	1,828	1,785	3,015	2,359
9	4,563	149	130	772	818	684	973	957	912	1,527	1,167
10 (best)	7,575	244	395	1,414	1,475	1,642	2,090	1,503	1,586	2,752	1,733
No neighborhood	29	–	–	3	2	4	15	9	10	6	5
Not reported	1,362	30	56	393	184	164	420	355	205	586	217
Street noise or traffic											
Bothersome street noise or heavy traffic present	35,378	941	1,421	7,446	6,300	4,623	9,334	7,073	7,119	12,392	8,794
Yes	10,158	234	326	2,460	1,725	1,077	3,110	2,277	2,213	3,123	2,546
No	24,858	696	1,081	4,895	4,545	3,498	6,119	4,736	4,863	9,084	6,174
Not reported	362	11	14	91	30	48	104	60	42	185	74
Neighborhood crime											
Serious crime in past 12 months	35,378	941	1,421	7,446	6,300	4,623	9,334	7,073	7,119	12,392	8,794
Yes	7,650	179	205	2,045	1,403	658	2,254	1,345	1,639	2,702	1,963
No	26,886	740	1,190	5,146	4,814	3,853	6,813	5,578	5,333	9,351	6,623
Not reported	842	21	25	255	83	112	267	149	147	338	208
Odors											
Bothersome smoke, gas, or bad smells	35,378	941	1,421	7,446	6,300	4,623	9,334	7,073	7,119	12,392	8,794
Yes	2,156	34	74	614	359	164	727	490	484	661	522
No	32,847	894	1,331	6,749	5,907	4,408	8,505	6,521	6,600	11,543	8,184
Not reported	375	13	16	83	35	51	102	63	35	189	88
Other bothersome neighborhood conditions											
No other problems	29,404	759	1,181	5,963	5,357	4,159	7,505	5,903	5,993	10,255	7,253
With other problems[1]	5,517	172	219	1,360	903	411	1,694	1,083	1,085	1,896	1,453
Noise	1,217	22	43	296	217	95	340	302	195	424	296
Litter or housing deterioration	590	8	19	203	127	43	213	140	109	215	127
Poor city or county services	254	–	7	101	37	21	89	52	64	93	46
Undesirable commercial, institutional, or industrial	168	6	3	37	36	8	53	39	35	56	38
People	1,815	49	90	460	297	115	630	307	403	636	468
Other	2,791	108	81	710	444	217	782	521	499	1,001	770
No problem	61	–	3	12	11	8	24	19	13	17	12
Type of problem not reported	5	–	–	5	–	3	2	3	2	–	–
Other problems not reported	457	11	21	124	40	53	135	88	41	241	87
Public elementary school[1]											
Households with children aged 5 through 15	8,127	249	408	2,214	2,319	74	2,807	1,413	1,438	3,066	2,210
Attend public school (K-12)	7,208	220	368	2,011	2,103	69	2,531	1,187	1,279	2,746	1,996
Attend private school (K-12)	380	16	10	96	79	3	88	96	58	131	95
Attend ungraded school, preschool, etc.	111	5	1	27	26	–	55	25	20	32	34
Home schooled	88	2	9	5	4	–	17	6	24	41	16
Not in school	180	7	14	43	50	–	58	49	31	56	44
Not reported	286	4	9	77	78	2	84	76	47	110	53
Households with children aged 0 through 13	10,486	303	547	2,681	2,899	73	3,668	1,766	1,935	4,079	2,706
Satisfactory public elementary school	8,331	248	460	2,121	2,413	64	2,863	1,380	1,516	3,258	2,177
Unsatisfactory public elementary school	724	26	31	259	132	4	322	113	157	275	179
Not reported or don't know	1,431	29	55	300	354	5	483	273	262	546	350
Public elementary school less than 1 mile	7,096	170	187	1,957	2,267	50	2,536	1,292	1,308	2,402	2,094
Public elementary school 1 mile or more	2,741	127	314	590	454	17	896	355	496	1,428	463
Not reported	649	7	46	134	178	5	236	119	131	249	149
Academic comparison to other area elementary schools											
Households with children aged 0 through 13 dissatisfied with local elementary school	724	26	31	259	132	4	322	113	157	275	179
Better	63	–	–	38	16	3	40	11	9	27	16
About the same	224	4	13	62	39	–	93	36	47	86	55
Worse	386	13	18	146	71	1	175	60	92	141	93
Not reported	51	9	–	13	6	–	15	6	9	21	15

Table 1-6. Neighborhood, Renter-Occupied Units, 2009—*Continued*

[Numbers in thousands.]

Characteristics	Total occupied units	Housing unit characteristics: New construction 4 years	Housing unit characteristics: Manufactured/ mobile homes	Household characteristics: Black alone	Household characteristics: Hispanic	Household characteristics: Elderly (65 years and over)	Household characteristics: Below poverty level	Regions: Northeast	Regions: Midwest	Regions: South	Regions: West
Building neighbor noise[2]											
Neighbor noise present	14,655	398	X	3,410	2,494	1,584	3,939	3,563	3,219	4,283	3,590
Loudness bothersome	4,472	102	X	1,163	889	305	1,396	936	983	1,364	1,189
Loudness not bothersome	10,180	296	X	2,246	1,604	1,278	2,542	2,625	2,236	2,919	2,400
Loudness bothersome not reported	3	–	X	–	–	1	1	2	–	–	1
Time of noise bothersome	4,483	96	X	1,214	880	320	1,416	936	1,000	1,415	1,132
Time of noise not bothersome	10,159	302	X	2,190	1,614	1,261	2,519	2,626	2,219	2,859	2,454
Time bothersome not reported	14	–	X	5	–	3	4	1	–	9	4
Neighbor noise not present	8,334	227	X	1,865	1,809	1,731	2,314	2,104	1,501	2,695	2,035
Not reported	1,213	45	X	282	208	227	381	310	218	430	255
Public transportation											
With public transportation	24,641	507	285	5,856	4,996	3,245	6,562	5,832	4,703	6,909	7,196
Travel time to nearest bus stop, train station, or subway stop											
Less than 5 minutes	10,328	191	93	2,468	1,978	1,218	2,783	2,403	2,340	2,622	2,964
5-9 minutes	8,869	149	108	2,116	1,925	1,162	2,296	2,072	1,486	2,580	2,732
10-14 minutes	2,753	95	30	738	574	380	704	772	382	825	774
15-29 minutes	1,099	29	22	237	275	172	288	267	123	348	360
30 minutes or longer	169	5	16	46	17	20	87	37	37	66	29
Not reported	1,422	38	16	251	227	293	404	281	336	468	337
Household uses public transportation regularly for commuting to school or work	6,395	100	39	1,959	1,682	564	2,089	2,378	1,012	1,221	1,783
Household does not use public transportation regularly for commuting to school or work	18,075	392	246	3,838	3,285	2,670	4,427	3,366	3,672	5,644	5,394
Not reported	170	15	–	59	28	11	46	88	19	44	19
No public transportation	9,684	399	1,081	1,438	1,217	1,236	2,522	1,060	2,182	5,040	1,401
Not reported	1,053	35	54	152	88	142	250	181	234	443	196
Neighborhood shopping											
Grocery stores or drug stores within 15 minutes of the home	34,189	896	1,282	7,120	6,106	4,434	8,888	6,887	6,907	11,866	8,530
Satisfactory	33,082	880	1,244	6,736	5,941	4,294	8,481	6,634	6,677	11,511	8,259
Not satisfactory	964	16	31	334	153	104	371	216	210	289	249
Not reported	143	–	8	50	11	36	37	36	20	65	22
No grocery stores or drug stores within 15 minutes of the home	777	20	98	226	146	148	319	110	162	330	174
Not reported or don't know	412	25	41	100	49	41	126	76	50	197	90
Police protection											
Satisfactory police protection	31,740	846	1,240	6,325	5,623	4,294	8,025	6,311	6,479	11,049	7,900
Unsatisfactory police protection	2,556	58	134	835	543	193	990	518	501	931	606
Not reported	1,082	36	47	286	135	135	319	244	139	412	287
Secured communities											
Community access secured with walls or fences	5,422	277	79	1,371	1,336	827	1,392	749	403	2,065	2,205
Special entry system present	3,410	245	13	790	788	576	739	374	207	1,370	1,459
Special entry system not present	2,005	32	67	577	547	251	653	375	195	692	743
Special entry system not reported	7	–	–	4	–	–	–	–	–	4	3
Community access not secured	29,714	657	1,329	6,028	4,930	3,758	7,865	6,284	6,693	10,207	6,530
Community access not reported	242	7	12	48	35	38	76	40	23	121	58
Secured multiunits											
Multiunit access secured	5,854	249	X	1,301	998	1,426	1,503	1,677	1,356	1,354	1,467
Multiunit access not secured	14,590	290	X	3,406	2,749	1,567	4,129	3,414	2,943	4,790	3,444
Multiunit access not reported	1,737	37	X	349	465	321	504	370	266	593	508
Senior citizen communities											
Households with person 55 and over	9,093	186	320	1,842	1,255	4,623	2,645	2,362	1,895	2,757	2,080
Community age restricted	1,624	51	35	300	169	1,374	588	377	440	422	384
No age restriction or restriction not reported	7,469	135	285	1,542	1,086	3,249	2,057	1,984	1,455	2,334	1,695
Community age specific	1,435	14	63	265	137	800	414	351	386	480	218
Community not age specific	5,583	119	193	1,168	906	2,265	1,509	1,497	1,006	1,710	1,371
Community age specific not reported	451	3	29	109	43	184	134	137	63	144	106
Community quality											
Some or all community activities present[1]	16,845	592	418	3,392	2,647	2,731	4,197	3,206	4,151	5,294	4,193
Community center or clubhouse	9,703	479	192	2,078	1,347	1,888	2,346	1,660	2,245	3,354	2,445
Golf in community	3,947	55	82	471	499	604	880	751	1,466	826	904
Trails in community	6,309	175	113	1,017	876	826	1,369	1,196	1,865	1,797	1,451
Shuttle bus	4,215	79	72	702	713	1,258	1,161	1,005	1,075	1,080	1,055
Daycare center	5,249	70	102	1,297	934	546	1,568	1,416	1,602	1,205	1,026
Private or restricted beach, park, or shoreline	6,308	149	168	1,053	1,145	731	1,466	1,445	1,916	1,399	1,548

Table 1-6. Neighborhood, Renter-Occupied Units, 2009—*Continued*

[Numbers in thousands.]

Characteristics	Total occupied units	Housing unit characteristics		Household characteristics				Regions			
		New construction 4 years	Manufactured/ mobile homes	Black alone	Hispanic	Elderly (65 years and over)	Below poverty level	Northeast	Midwest	South	West
Description of area within 300 feet[1]											
Single-family detached houses	27,007	552	1,060	5,471	4,789	3,451	7,099	5,112	5,540	9,258	7,097
Single-family attached	10,860	289	81	2,541	1,961	1,336	2,609	2,640	1,977	3,300	2,942
Multiunit residential buildings[3]	22,121	566	140	5,067	4,326	2,974	6,055	4,948	4,510	6,777	5,887
1- to 3-story multiunit is tallest	16,130	405	127	3,592	3,060	1,853	4,428	2,271	3,583	5,452	4,823
4- to 6-story multiunit is tallest	3,473	73	6	793	744	552	883	1,435	493	816	728
7-or-more-story multiunit is tallest	2,243	88	4	615	452	476	644	1,138	369	463	272
Manufactured/mobile homes	3,112	78	1,096	448	484	329	1,007	236	392	1,633	851
Commercial or institutional	18,657	348	313	4,324	3,726	2,363	5,345	4,442	3,608	5,909	4,699
Industrial or factories	2,856	29	72	746	642	295	972	865	622	798	571
Open space, park, woods, farm, or ranch	12,706	441	851	2,369	1,770	1,606	3,165	2,522	2,864	4,456	2,863
4-or-more-lane highway, railroad, or airport	9,232	242	273	2,236	1,636	1,121	2,524	1,425	1,955	3,628	2,224
Not reported	788	15	42	222	101	59	215	145	126	357	159
Bodies of water within 300 feet											
Water in area	4,832	191	247	834	605	626	990	973	1,044	2,062	754
With waterfront property	678	28	34	93	55	145	116	131	177	273	96
Waterfront property not reported	94	3	8	16	15	21	23	20	19	47	8
With flood plain	692	36	53	117	96	74	132	128	82	369	114
Flood plain not reported	74	10	–	11	18	10	15	11	11	45	7
Water not reported	156	7	5	42	11	5	40	42	24	40	49
No water in area	30,390	743	1,169	6,570	5,684	3,992	8,304	6,059	6,051	10,290	7,990
Age of other residential buildings within 300 feet											
Older	4,928	14	245	989	831	566	1,421	1,040	968	1,648	1,273
About the same	23,313	459	694	5,092	4,283	2,696	5,826	4,510	4,795	8,259	5,750
Newer	2,648	405	166	501	358	521	781	623	549	851	625
Very mixed	2,120	22	177	365	374	423	611	410	361	742	606
No other residential buildings	891	26	85	131	156	194	266	171	184	346	191
Not reported	1,478	15	52	368	299	223	428	320	262	547	348
Other buildings vandalized or with interior exposed within 300 feet											
None	30,533	842	1,190	5,864	5,485	4,117	7,566	6,091	6,105	10,582	7,755
1 building	1,211	20	50	365	231	112	422	224	237	453	297
More than 1 building	1,825	37	50	838	310	138	802	392	441	652	339
No buildings	626	18	84	65	104	128	163	105	139	248	134
Not reported	1,182	24	47	314	170	129	380	261	196	457	268
Bars on windows of buildings within 300 feet											
No bars on windows	27,024	840	1,215	5,046	4,172	3,515	6,703	4,715	6,041	10,041	6,227
1 building with bars	851	12	42	196	178	98	267	133	158	330	230
2 or more buildings with bars	5,174	44	29	1,663	1,562	631	1,676	1,773	485	1,162	1,754
No buildings	626	18	84	65	104	128	163	105	139	248	134
Not reported	1,703	27	50	477	284	251	524	347	296	612	448
Condition of streets within 300 feet											
No repairs needed	18,782	656	633	3,406	3,492	2,721	4,476	3,205	3,353	6,892	5,333
Minor repairs needed	12,843	194	588	2,985	2,169	1,421	3,568	3,032	2,948	4,107	2,757
Major repairs needed	2,228	57	115	676	394	257	807	487	575	823	344
No streets	419	18	33	78	93	76	126	89	58	135	136
Not reported	1,106	15	53	300	153	148	357	260	185	436	225
Trash, litter, or junk on streets or any properties within 300 feet											
None	29,595	864	1,205	5,764	5,211	4,172	7,264	5,765	5,975	10,512	7,344
Minor accumulation	3,759	43	107	1,064	738	283	1,366	883	769	1,112	994
Major accumulation	1,093	19	64	351	235	72	437	230	224	373	266
Not reported	931	15	45	268	116	96	267	195	151	395	190
Parking lots											
With parking lots	18,981	492	308	4,136	3,160	2,684	5,199	3,578	4,533	6,488	4,382
No parking lots within 300 feet	15,563	433	1,071	3,075	3,038	1,861	3,903	3,326	2,454	5,541	4,242
Parking lots not reported	833	15	42	236	103	78	232	169	132	363	169
Manufactured/mobile homes in groups											
Manufactured/mobile homes	1,421	28	1,421	140	232	158	483	104	201	845	270
1 to 6	966	17	966	107	130	107	337	57	135	577	197
7 to 20	153	–	153	11	25	15	58	17	14	109	14
21 or more	301	11	301	22	77	36	88	30	53	159	59

– = Zero or rounds to zero.
X = Not applicable.
[1] = Figures may not add to total because more than one category may apply to a unit.
[2] = Limited to single attached and multiunits.
[3] = Figures do not add up because of nonrespondents.

Source: U.S. Census Bureau, American Housing Survey

Table 1-7. Household Composition, Occupied Units, 2009

[Numbers in thousands, except as noted.]

Characteristics	Total occupied units	Tenure		Housing unit characteristics		Household characteristics				Regions			
		Owner	Renter	New construction 4 years	Manufactured/ mobile homes	Black alone	Hispanic	Elderly (65 years or over)	Below poverty level	Northeast	Midwest	South	West
Population in housing units	283,089	200,336	82,753	13,203	17,068	35,069	41,231	39,508	38,094	50,935	62,940	104,344	64,870
Total	111,806	76,428	35,378	4,771	6,839	13,993	12,739	23,095	15,739	20,451	25,368	41,586	24,401
Persons													
1 person	30,108	16,777	13,331	977	1,940	4,499	2,171	10,312	6,823	5,829	7,015	11,082	6,182
2 persons	37,086	27,633	9,453	1,557	2,343	3,767	3,019	10,462	3,211	6,550	8,723	13,976	7,837
3 persons	17,568	12,223	5,345	770	960	2,409	2,330	1,576	1,892	3,234	3,644	6,933	3,757
4 persons	15,807	11,791	4,016	881	845	1,855	2,355	417	1,684	2,957	3,626	5,719	3,505
5 persons	7,117	5,207	1,910	348	454	848	1,580	192	1,147	1,226	1,574	2,484	1,833
6 persons	2,577	1,797	780	159	203	353	718	90	532	407	494	880	797
7 persons or more	1,543	1,000	543	80	93	262	567	45	450	248	293	512	490
Number of single children under 18 years													
None	73,604	50,579	23,026	2,669	4,619	8,399	6,305	22,323	9,426	13,917	16,843	27,138	15,706
1	16,145	10,796	5,349	781	925	2,477	2,248	503	2,335	2,738	3,467	6,457	3,484
2	13,934	9,828	4,106	805	724	1,822	2,310	176	1,904	2,502	3,263	5,050	3,119
3	5,689	3,760	1,928	352	383	866	1,205	69	1,267	990	1,244	2,026	1,429
4	1,672	1,040	632	119	143	259	439	16	489	204	389	628	451
5	503	281	222	32	26	115	165	6	196	71	97	187	148
6 or more	258	143	115	14	19	56	69	2	123	29	65	100	64
Persons 65 years and over													
None	85,652	55,429	30,223	4,254	5,078	11,379	10,807	X	11,552	15,188	19,500	31,926	19,038
1 person	17,640	13,187	4,453	314	1,293	2,097	1,408	14,794	3,561	3,680	3,893	6,461	3,606
2 persons or more	8,513	7,812	701	203	468	518	524	8,301	625	1,584	1,976	3,198	1,756
Age of householder													
Under 25 years	6,083	1,284	4,799	310	395	949	955	X	2,104	807	1,490	2,399	1,386
25 to 29	8,614	3,541	5,072	634	410	1,245	1,418	X	1,325	1,293	2,053	3,343	1,924
30 to 34	10,093	5,532	4,561	726	624	1,287	1,712	X	1,313	1,653	2,161	3,812	2,467
35 to 44	21,908	14,932	6,976	1,247	1,259	3,005	3,128	X	2,444	4,129	4,798	8,034	4,947
45 to 54	23,505	17,743	5,762	808	1,427	3,049	2,441	X	2,493	4,404	5,387	8,537	5,177
55 to 64	18,509	14,924	3,585	635	1,186	2,214	1,604	X	2,150	3,525	4,115	6,955	3,913
65 to 74	11,938	9,818	2,120	295	909	1,374	877	11,938	1,669	2,301	2,729	4,573	2,335
75 years and over	11,157	8,653	2,503	115	628	872	604	11,157	2,240	2,337	2,635	3,933	2,252
Median (years)	48	52	39	39	50	46	42	74	47	50	48	48	47
Household composition by age of householder													
2-or-more-person households	81,698	59,651	22,047	3,795	4,899	9,494	10,568	12,783	8,915	14,622	18,354	30,503	18,219
Married-couple families, no nonrelatives	55,817	47,008	8,808	2,912	3,157	4,051	6,323	9,967	3,315	9,923	12,815	20,834	12,245
Under 25 years	1,203	495	707	64	118	65	268	X	248	141	237	524	301
25 to 29 years	3,320	2,007	1,313	358	167	221	647	X	298	441	789	1,312	778
30 to 34 years	5,143	3,646	1,497	473	358	335	889	X	335	755	1,158	1,960	1,269
35 to 44 years	12,504	10,336	2,168	867	619	992	1,799	X	719	2,366	2,781	4,546	2,812
45 to 64 years	23,681	21,352	2,329	930	1,278	1,865	2,092	X	1,050	4,428	5,516	8,655	5,082
65 years and over	9,967	9,174	793	220	616	572	628	9,967	665	1,793	2,334	3,837	2,003
Other male householder	9,385	4,712	4,673	327	658	1,237	1,710	813	1,210	1,614	2,054	3,364	2,353
Under 45 years	5,800	2,170	3,629	258	364	697	1,220	X	763	882	1,312	2,091	1,515
45 to 64 years	2,773	1,878	895	56	226	389	403	X	336	580	575	974	644
65 years and over	813	663	150	14	68	150	87	813	111	152	167	299	194
Other female householder	16,496	7,931	8,565	555	1,084	4,207	2,536	2,004	4,391	3,085	3,485	6,306	3,620
Under 45 years	9,066	2,948	6,119	384	538	2,450	1,488	X	2,952	1,590	2,082	3,430	1,964
45 to 64 years	5,426	3,397	2,030	150	403	1,371	824	X	1,071	1,109	1,025	2,073	1,219
65 years and over	2,004	1,587	417	22	144	385	224	2,004	368	386	377	802	438
1-person households	30,108	16,777	13,331	977	1,940	4,499	2,171	10,312	6,823	5,829	7,015	11,082	6,182
Male householder	13,357	6,770	6,588	438	860	1,940	1,154	2,754	2,577	2,470	3,095	4,816	2,976
Under 45 years	5,682	2,142	3,540	253	310	912	570	X	969	979	1,332	2,075	1,296
45 to 64 years	4,922	2,810	2,112	136	347	711	391	X	1,014	863	1,163	1,796	1,099
65 years and over	2,754	1,818	936	48	203	317	193	2,754	594	629	600	945	581
Female householder	16,750	10,007	6,743	539	1,080	2,560	1,017	7,558	4,246	3,358	3,920	6,266	3,206
Under 45 years	3,980	1,547	2,434	261	215	812	332	X	902	730	811	1,651	788
45 to 64 years	5,212	3,231	1,981	172	359	927	335	X	1,173	950	1,222	1,994	1,046
65 years and over	7,558	5,230	2,328	106	506	821	350	7,558	2,172	1,678	1,886	2,622	1,371
Adults and single children under 18 years													
Total households with children	38,201	25,849	12,352	2,102	2,220	5,594	6,434	772	6,313	6,534	8,525	14,447	8,695
Married couples	25,451	20,367	5,084	1,599	1,293	2,042	4,116	349	2,028	4,433	5,667	9,313	6,039
One child under 6 years only	3,570	2,644	926	301	165	225	537	47	176	629	708	1,419	813
One under 6 years, one or more 6 to 17 years	4,291	3,254	1,037	301	266	376	1,024	42	501	727	904	1,524	1,136
Two or more under 6 years only	2,623	1,946	677	220	92	155	379	4	248	479	664	906	575
Two or more under 6 years, one or more 6 to 17 years	1,299	898	401	128	124	102	360	8	265	193	275	478	353
One or more 6 to 17 years only	13,669	11,626	2,043	649	646	1,184	1,817	247	839	2,406	3,116	4,985	3,161

Table 1-7. Household Composition, Occupied Units, 2009—*Continued*

[Numbers in thousands, except as noted.]

Characteristics	Total occupied units	Tenure		Housing unit characteristics		Household characteristics				Regions			
		Owner	Renter	New construction 4 years	Manufactured/ mobile homes	Black alone	Hispanic	Elderly (65 years or over)	Below poverty level	Northeast	Midwest	South	West
Other households with two or more adults	5,905	2,822	3,083	185	439	1,490	1,373	311	1,529	967	1,306	2,272	1,360
One child under 6 years only	1,174	488	686	36	89	217	257	37	256	170	306	478	220
One under 6 years, one or more 6 to 17 years	849	367	483	26	56	234	256	17	267	139	193	319	199
Two or more under 6 years only	460	134	326	13	26	131	112	12	197	89	99	183	89
Two or more under 6 years, one or more 6 to 17 years	312	122	190	14	46	98	127	20	142	40	74	133	65
One or more 6 to 17 years only	3,109	1,711	1,398	96	221	810	621	224	666	529	634	1,158	788
Households with one adult or none	6,845	2,660	4,185	318	487	2,062	945	112	2,756	1,134	1,553	2,863	1,296
One child under 6 years only	830	143	687	15	48	280	102	3	393	107	239	358	126
One under 6 years, one or more 6 to 17 years	903	294	609	34	81	341	144	6	440	173	212	364	154
Two or more under 6 years only	367	65	302	12	17	135	71	–	259	55	89	150	73
Two or more under 6 years, one or more 6 to 17 years	276	54	221	18	20	129	64	3	207	30	47	154	45
One or more 6 to 17 years only	4,469	2,104	2,365	238	321	1,177	564	101	1,457	768	965	1,837	898
Total households with no children	73,604	50,579	23,026	2,669	4,619	8,399	6,305	22,323	9,426	13,917	16,843	27,138	15,706
Married couples	31,036	27,102	3,934	1,336	1,896	2,031	2,402	9,689	1,367	5,594	7,291	11,744	6,408
Other households with two or more adults	12,874	6,890	5,984	424	848	1,955	1,743	2,322	1,487	2,550	2,599	4,545	3,180
Households with one adult	29,694	16,587	13,108	909	1,874	4,412	2,160	10,312	6,572	5,773	6,953	10,850	6,117
Own never-married children under 18 years													
No own children under 18 years	77,557	53,128	24,429	2,836	4,932	9,327	6,975	22,981	10,477	14,517	17,629	28,884	16,527
With own children under 18 years	34,249	23,300	10,949	1,935	1,906	4,666	5,764	114	5,262	5,934	7,739	12,701	7,874
Under 6 years only	8,154	4,779	3,375	585	382	962	1,310	13	1,341	1,393	1,908	3,091	1,762
1 child	4,959	2,784	2,174	346	245	598	798	13	707	816	1,096	1,975	1,072
2 children	2,720	1,747	974	190	110	294	442	–	477	506	679	933	602
3 or more children	475	248	227	49	27	69	70	–	157	71	133	182	89
6 to 17 years only	19,322	14,229	5,093	857	1,043	2,718	2,838	94	2,422	3,411	4,358	7,101	4,451
1 child	9,460	6,848	2,613	335	525	1,478	1,281	73	1,144	1,700	2,020	3,632	2,109
2 children	7,070	5,367	1,703	375	358	821	1,092	15	733	1,250	1,670	2,479	1,670
3 or more children	2,792	2,014	778	147	160	420	465	6	544	460	668	991	672
Both age groups	6,773	4,292	2,480	493	481	987	1,617	7	1,499	1,129	1,473	2,509	1,661
2 children	3,048	2,006	1,043	209	189	442	639	5	475	532	679	1,173	664
3 or more children	3,724	2,287	1,438	284	292	545	977	2	1,024	598	793	1,336	996
Persons other than spouse or children[1]													
With other relatives	23,656	17,454	6,202	676	1,475	3,997	4,316	3,644	3,024	4,721	4,594	8,806	5,535
Single adult offspring 18 to 29 years	13,511	10,481	3,030	408	827	2,088	2,215	366	1,478	2,866	2,796	4,861	2,989
Single adult offspring 30 years of age or over	3,862	3,148	714	58	235	723	608	2,275	489	768	698	1,542	854
Households with three generations	3,301	2,342	958	90	197	749	762	569	675	572	586	1,292	850
Households with 1 subfamily	2,622	1,837	784	76	173	551	730	466	570	397	452	1,000	772
Subfamily householder age under 30 years	1,318	858	459	26	89	343	362	52	340	172	264	557	325
30 to 64 years	1,219	906	314	44	82	198	335	413	224	212	171	421	415
65 years and over	85	73	11	6	2	9	33	1	6	14	16	22	32
Households with 2 or more subfamilies	111	74	37	–	4	27	55	10	18	20	22	30	39
Households with other types of relatives	7,165	4,543	2,622	223	488	1,481	1,689	1,172	1,213	1,332	1,213	2,756	1,865
With nonrelatives	10,717	4,816	5,901	439	825	1,153	1,705	607	1,521	1,819	2,406	3,702	2,790
Co-owners or co-renters	3,428	1,000	2,427	165	192	281	440	137	477	505	852	1,079	992
Lodgers	1,207	533	674	39	76	86	339	64	144	185	190	436	397
Unrelated children, under 18 years old	1,133	647	486	36	75	140	166	57	214	180	293	409	250
Other nonrelatives	6,049	3,160	2,889	229	594	763	996	383	874	1,125	1,326	2,158	1,440
One or more secondary families	621	352	269	21	52	85	119	20	87	92	184	211	133
2-person households, none related to each other	5,403	2,440	2,963	253	339	482	539	401	492	985	1,184	1,806	1,428
3-to-8-person households, none related to each other	862	190	672	22	50	64	132	11	184	144	167	292	260
Educational attainment of the householder													
Less than 9th grade	5,257	3,025	2,232	85	691	520	2,516	2,339	1,798	694	762	2,450	1,350
9th to 12th grade, no diploma	9,972	5,517	4,455	228	1,222	1,985	2,089	3,047	3,124	1,763	2,021	4,425	1,763
High school graduate (includes equivalency)	34,389	22,665	11,724	1,131	2,957	4,916	3,775	8,155	5,576	6,605	8,819	12,757	6,208
Additional vocational training	3,697	2,553	1,144	151	277	465	332	729	455	602	1,054	1,304	736
Some college, no degree	19,583	12,659	6,924	868	998	2,877	1,790	3,480	2,693	2,797	4,575	7,220	4,991
Associate's degree	9,244	6,722	2,522	517	519	1,106	736	1,064	826	1,762	2,162	3,208	2,111
Bachelor's degree	21,077	15,894	5,183	1,229	360	1,752	1,251	2,761	1,204	4,071	4,563	7,440	5,002
Graduate or professional degree	12,285	9,947	2,338	712	92	838	582	2,250	518	2,759	2,465	4,086	2,975
Percent high school graduate or higher	86.4	88.8	81.1	93.4	72.0	82.1	63.9	76.7	68.7	88.0	89.0	83.5	87.2
Percent bachelor's degree or higher	29.8	33.8	21.3	40.7	6.6	18.5	14.4	21.7	10.9	33.4	27.7	27.7	32.7

Table 1-7. Household Composition, Occupied Units, 2009—*Continued*

[Numbers in thousands, except as noted.]

Characteristics	Total occupied units	Tenure		Housing unit characteristics		Household characteristics				Regions			
		Owner	Renter	New construction 4 years	Manufactured/ mobile homes	Black alone	Hispanic	Elderly (65 years or over)	Below poverty level	Northeast	Midwest	South	West
Citizenship of householder													
Citizen of the United States	104,356	73,334	31,022	4,481	6,482	13,330	8,527	22,643	14,092	19,064	24,563	38,943	21,786
Naturalized citizen of the United States	6,861	4,732	2,129	267	167	669	2,150	1,551	1,062	1,671	795	1,917	2,478
Year householder immigrated to the United States													
2005 to 2009	1,129	156	973	42	64	138	444	20	312	252	179	414	284
2000 to 2004	2,060	659	1,402	105	91	174	1,016	55	421	434	262	783	580
1995 to 1999	2,056	998	1,058	122	106	232	1,022	58	429	408	268	755	625
1990 to 1994	1,926	1,037	889	76	70	184	934	95	427	361	231	589	745
1980 to 1989	3,342	2,175	1,167	112	107	358	1,487	284	522	675	270	1,003	1,393
1979 or before	3,797	2,801	996	100	86	248	1,460	1,492	599	928	390	1,014	1,465
Year householder moved into unit													
2005 to 2009	46,108	20,126	25,982	4,712	2,609	7,023	6,664	3,507	8,148	7,185	9,917	18,062	10,944
2000 to 2004	22,490	17,520	4,970	31	1,775	2,528	2,733	3,314	2,672	3,912	5,124	8,156	5,298
1995 to 1999	13,131	11,217	1,914	13	1,262	1,391	1,251	2,697	1,352	2,509	3,002	4,793	2,827
1990 to 1994	8,763	7,706	1,057	6	565	926	728	2,047	978	1,720	2,100	3,200	1,742
1985 to 1989	5,844	5,362	482	6	290	515	447	1,734	590	1,210	1,430	2,057	1,146
1980 to 1984	3,436	3,124	312	3	156	360	262	1,274	433	908	794	1,178	556
1975 to 1979	3,978	3,734	244	–	99	411	256	1,969	430	905	1,039	1,383	651
1970 to 1974	2,698	2,548	151	–	64	312	163	1,835	354	614	641	1,042	401
1960 to 1969	3,300	3,142	158	–	17	363	142	2,859	431	896	819	1,098	487
1950 to 1959	1,592	1,522	70	–	–	135	74	1,441	267	439	391	471	291
1940 to 1949	357	334	23	–	2	21	19	308	61	116	85	114	42
1939 or earlier	110	93	17	–	–	8	–	110	24	36	27	32	15
Median	2003	1999	2007	2007	2002	2005	2005	1990	2005	2001	2002	2003	2004
Household moves and formation in last year													
Total with a move in last year	22,726	8,394	14,332	1,809	1,366	3,586	3,703	1,301	4,658	3,186	4,954	8,822	5,764
Household all moved here from one unit	14,975	3,961	11,014	1,412	812	2,645	2,365	836	3,500	2,026	3,219	5,963	3,767
Householder of previous unit did not move here	2,808	460	2,349	148	172	601	507	71	932	380	644	1,149	636
Householder of previous unit moved here	10,898	3,165	7,733	1,165	569	1,875	1,652	709	2,215	1,453	2,325	4,311	2,808
Householder of previous unit not reported	1,269	337	932	100	71	169	207	56	354	193	250	503	323
Household moved here from two or more units	1,691	304	1,387	82	95	204	307	24	237	167	445	561	517
No previous householder moved here	324	42	282	17	21	44	56	–	48	31	90	100	102
1 previous householder moved here	438	79	359	27	26	43	82	6	57	37	135	170	96
2 or more previous householders moved here	679	156	523	32	39	82	118	11	84	70	158	223	227
Previous householder(s) not reported	251	28	223	7	8	34	51	8	48	29	62	68	92
Some already here, rest moved in	6,057	4,129	1,928	315	459	737	1,031	442	921	993	1,289	2,294	1,480
No previous householder moved here	3,336	2,331	1,006	190	268	406	560	137	541	546	759	1,219	812
1 or more previous householders moved here	2,200	1,497	703	108	147	255	362	266	284	321	423	910	546
Previous householder(s) not reported	521	301	220	18	44	76	109	39	96	126	107	166	122
Number of previous units not reported	4	–	4	–	–	–	–	–	–	–	–	4	–
Households with disabled persons													
Households without a disabled person	91,621	62,765	28,856	4,198	5,052	11,375	10,902	14,149	11,139	16,725	20,647	33,901	20,347
Households with a disabled person[1, 2]	19,182	12,948	6,234	540	1,754	2,477	1,785	8,738	4,381	3,478	4,541	7,232	3,931
Hearing disability	6,077	4,498	1,578	185	561	412	494	3,581	1,073	1,077	1,472	2,159	1,370
Vision disability	2,993	1,940	1,053	61	306	413	372	1,383	792	509	612	1,212	661
Mental disability	5,817	3,498	2,320	208	600	825	561	1,842	1,626	1,022	1,400	2,184	1,211
Physical disability	11,651	7,880	3,771	319	1,115	1,704	1,039	5,938	2,804	2,118	2,739	4,603	2,192
Self-care disability	2,969	2,038	931	78	238	462	315	1,439	771	502	641	1,187	638
Go-outside-home disability	6,206	4,140	2,065	174	550	935	594	3,121	1,614	1,100	1,499	2,340	1,267
Disability not reported	1,003	715	288	33	33	141	52	209	218	247	181	453	122

– = Zero or rounds to zero.
X = Not applicable.
[1] = Figures may not add to total because more than one category may apply to a unit.
[2] = Mental, physical, and self-care disabilities are limited to household members at least 5 years of age. Go-outside-home disabilities are limited to household members at least 15 years of age.

Source: U.S. Census Bureau, American Housing Survey

Table 1-8. Household Composition, Owner-Occupied Units, 2009

[Numbers in thousands, except as noted.]

Characteristics	Total occupied units	Housing unit characteristics		Household characteristics				Regions			
		New construction 4 years	Manufactured/ mobile homes	Black alone	Hispanic	Elderly (65 years and over)	Below poverty level	Northeast	Midwest	South	West
Population in housing units	200,336	10,956	13,179	17,149	21,623	33,085	14,795	35,269	47,621	74,798	42,647
Total	76,428	3,830	5,418	6,547	6,439	18,472	6,405	13,378	18,249	29,193	15,607
Persons											
1 person	16,777	653	1,555	1,725	890	7,048	2,915	2,944	3,986	6,619	3,227
2 persons	27,633	1,286	1,978	1,962	1,593	9,381	1,541	4,615	6,785	10,717	5,516
3 persons	12,223	626	738	1,148	1,160	1,380	563	2,233	2,657	4,871	2,461
4 persons	11,791	760	585	987	1,195	368	554	2,206	2,937	4,300	2,348
5 persons	5,207	297	349	445	886	170	445	943	1,283	1,760	1,222
6 persons	1,797	145	154	170	396	84	206	281	392	587	537
7 persons or more	1,000	63	59	111	319	41	181	156	209	339	296
Number of single children under 18 years											
None	50,579	2,089	3,821	4,167	3,286	17,825	4,396	8,980	11,986	19,482	10,130
1	10,796	645	689	1,132	1,085	421	776	1,785	2,460	4,347	2,204
2	9,828	670	499	830	1,116	143	596	1,746	2,481	3,579	2,022
3	3,760	292	264	294	624	63	367	697	946	1,253	864
4	1,040	103	114	73	220	16	166	112	273	374	281
5	281	27	15	37	80	3	57	44	60	108	70
6 or more	143	3	16	14	29	–	47	14	43	51	35
Persons 65 years and over											
None	55,429	3,412	3,833	4,846	5,122	X	3,791	9,515	13,542	20,989	11,383
1 person	13,187	241	1,145	1,255	893	10,842	2,085	2,478	2,862	5,209	2,638
2 persons or more	7,812	177	440	446	424	7,630	529	1,385	1,846	2,995	1,586
Age of householder											
Under 25 years	1,284	139	179	74	136	X	344	180	347	516	241
25 to 29	3,541	480	240	240	426	X	219	466	986	1,384	705
30 to 34	5,532	590	436	352	668	X	297	782	1,365	2,159	1,227
35 to 44	14,932	1,060	937	1,399	1,682	X	846	2,709	3,597	5,551	3,075
45 to 54	17,743	684	1,169	1,669	1,487	X	1,103	3,224	4,248	6,563	3,708
55 to 64	14,924	554	1,079	1,352	1,046	X	1,149	2,650	3,430	5,781	3,063
65 to 74	9,818	242	814	887	606	9,818	1,007	1,733	2,294	3,932	1,860
75 years and over	8,653	81	565	573	389	8,653	1,441	1,636	1,983	3,307	1,728
Median (years)	52	40	52	52	47	74	58	52	51	52	51
Household composition by age of householder											
2-or-more-person households	59,651	3,177	3,863	4,822	5,549	11,424	3,490	10,434	14,263	22,575	12,380
Married-couple families, no nonrelatives	47,008	2,627	2,673	2,936	4,054	9,174	1,946	8,207	11,418	17,724	9,658
Under 25 years	495	38	60	13	63	X	88	77	127	219	73
25 to 29 years	2,007	305	114	80	261	X	55	243	564	795	405
30 to 34 years	3,646	431	272	147	455	X	118	516	930	1,396	804
35 to 44 years	10,336	792	488	701	1,166	X	385	1,930	2,482	3,793	2,131
45 to 64 years	21,352	867	1,160	1,503	1,596	X	733	3,883	5,133	7,904	4,432
65 years and over	9,174	195	579	492	514	9,174	566	1,559	2,184	3,617	1,814
Other male householder	4,712	219	448	480	579	663	424	811	1,124	1,722	1,054
Under 45 years	2,170	160	214	195	327	X	193	314	568	790	498
45 to 64 years	1,878	48	172	179	186	X	152	384	419	676	399
65 years and over	663	11	62	106	65	663	80	113	136	256	158
Other female householder	7,931	330	743	1,405	916	1,587	1,120	1,415	1,721	3,128	1,667
Under 45 years	2,948	205	282	486	399	X	431	484	705	1,148	611
45 to 64 years	3,397	108	329	646	389	X	448	657	710	1,323	706
65 years and over	1,587	17	131	273	128	1,587	240	274	306	656	351
1-person households	16,777	653	1,555	1,725	890	7,048	2,915	2,944	3,986	6,619	3,227
Male householder	6,770	272	662	660	439	1,818	936	1,140	1,637	2,582	1,410
Under 45 years	2,142	151	209	214	144	X	183	326	576	778	462
45 to 64 years	2,810	99	291	305	193	X	444	436	673	1,100	601
65 years and over	1,818	22	163	142	102	1,818	309	378	389	704	347
Female householder	10,007	381	893	1,065	452	5,230	1,979	1,805	2,349	4,037	1,817
Under 45 years	1,547	187	153	229	98	X	252	247	343	691	266
45 to 64 years	3,231	117	296	389	168	X	474	514	744	1,339	633
65 years and over	5,230	77	444	446	185	5,230	1,253	1,044	1,262	2,006	918

Table 1-8. Household Composition, Owner-Occupied Units, 2009—*Continued*

[Numbers in thousands, except as noted.]

Characteristics	Total occupied units	Housing unit characteristics		Household characteristics				Regions			
		New construction 4 years	Manufactured/ mobile homes	Black alone	Hispanic	Elderly (65 years and over)	Below poverty level	Northeast	Midwest	South	West
Adults and single children under 18 years											
Total households with children	25,849	1,741	1,597	2,380	3,154	647	2,009	4,398	6,263	9,711	5,477
Married couples	20,367	1,433	1,002	1,398	2,439	315	971	3,580	4,933	7,465	4,389
One child under 6 years only	2,644	271	125	127	278	43	61	456	601	1,021	566
One under 6 years, one or more 6 to 17 years	3,254	278	196	253	582	37	217	552	773	1,170	759
Two or more under 6 years only	1,946	194	51	68	168	4	61	366	560	641	379
Two or more under 6 years, one or more 6 to 17 years	898	113	96	45	201	8	121	138	215	329	216
One or more 6 to 17 years only	11,626	578	536	904	1,209	223	512	2,069	2,784	4,305	2,467
Other households with two or more adults	2,822	134	307	535	459	259	420	424	729	1,086	583
One child under 6 years only	488	26	37	72	69	28	51	62	155	187	84
One under 6 years, one or more 6 to 17 years	367	13	46	90	75	15	68	52	92	157	66
Two or more under 6 years only	134	10	6	16	24	12	35	29	42	46	17
Two or more under 6 years, one or more 6 to 17 years	122	12	39	19	47	18	36	13	38	51	20
One or more 6 to 17 years only	1,711	74	180	337	243	186	231	268	402	645	396
Households with one adult or none	2,660	174	288	447	256	73	617	393	602	1,160	506
One child under 6 years only	143	7	17	27	9	3	33	20	42	62	19
One under 6 years, one or more 6 to 17 years	294	17	40	65	26	6	73	32	59	149	54
Two or more under 6 years only	65	3	6	13	4	–	12	15	13	20	17
Two or more under 6 years, one or more 6 to 17 years	54	3	4	12	19	3	30	2	17	21	14
One or more 6 to 17 years only	2,104	144	222	330	197	62	469	324	471	907	402
Total households with no children	50,579	2,089	3,821	4,167	3,286	17,825	4,396	8,980	11,986	19,482	10,130
Married couples	27,102	1,215	1,692	1,551	1,701	8,925	1,016	4,700	6,589	10,415	5,399
Other households with two or more adults	6,890	277	625	896	695	1,852	570	1,347	1,444	2,572	1,526
Households with one adult	16,587	597	1,504	1,720	890	7,048	2,811	2,934	3,953	6,495	3,205
Own never-married children under 18 years											
No own children under 18 years	77,557	53,128	24,429	2,836	4,932	9,327	6,975	22,981	10,477	14,517	17,629
With own children under 18 years	34,249	23,300	10,949	1,935	1,906	4,666	5,764	114	5,262	5,934	7,739
Under 6 years only	8,154	4,779	3,375	585	382	962	1,310	13	1,341	1,393	1,908
1 child	4,959	2,784	2,174	346	245	598	798	13	707	816	1,096
2 children	2,720	1,747	974	190	110	294	442	–	477	506	679
3 or more children	475	248	227	49	27	69	70	–	157	71	133
6 to 17 years only	19,322	14,229	5,093	857	1,043	2,718	2,838	94	2,422	3,411	4,358
1 child	9,460	6,848	2,613	335	525	1,478	1,281	73	1,144	1,700	2,020
2 children	7,070	5,367	1,703	375	358	821	1,092	15	733	1,250	1,670
3 or more children	2,792	2,014	778	147	160	420	465	6	544	460	668
Both age groups	6,773	4,292	2,480	493	481	987	1,617	7	1,499	1,129	1,473
2 children	3,048	2,006	1,043	209	189	442	639	5	475	532	679
3 or more children	3,724	2,287	1,438	284	292	545	977	2	1,024	598	793
Persons other than spouse or children[1]											
With other relatives	17,454	568	1,152	2,288	2,479	3,094	1,405	3,368	3,632	6,638	3,817
Single adult offspring 18 to 29 years	10,481	343	669	1,203	1,423	301	631	2,149	2,346	3,836	2,150
Single adult offspring 30 years of age or over	3,148	48	216	518	399	1,965	342	599	592	1,290	666
Households with three generations	2,342	75	156	413	449	506	304	383	453	887	619
Households with 1 subfamily	1,837	63	137	287	408	429	259	260	340	690	547
Subfamily householder age under 30 years	858	21	63	168	198	49	129	104	190	353	211
30 to 64 years	906	36	72	113	183	380	127	145	134	317	310
65 years and over	73	6	2	6	27	1	3	11	16	20	26
Households with 2 or more subfamilies	74	–	4	14	37	6	5	6	14	24	29
Households with other types of relatives	4,543	189	327	774	824	958	528	800	812	1,795	1,137
With nonrelatives	4,816	290	577	348	491	486	390	794	1,184	1,686	1,152
Co-owners or co-renters	1,000	81	118	45	110	96	44	196	227	349	228
Lodgers	533	22	50	18	112	51	37	68	98	194	173
Unrelated children, under 18 years old	647	25	54	62	55	48	82	107	185	200	155
Other nonrelatives	3,160	182	421	266	288	313	277	523	826	1,093	718
One or more secondary families	352	15	42	36	32	17	31	60	124	109	59
2-person households, none related to each other	2,440	160	261	135	153	311	145	415	566	845	614
3-to-8-person households, none related to each other	190	2	14	11	19	4	29	42	27	59	61

Table 1-8. Household Composition, Owner-Occupied Units, 2009—*Continued*

[Numbers in thousands, except as noted.]

Characteristics	Total occupied units	Housing unit characteristics		Household characteristics				Regions			
		New construction 4 years	Manufactured/ mobile homes	Black alone	Hispanic	Elderly (65 years and over)	Below poverty level	Northeast	Midwest	South	West
Educational attainment of the householder											
Less than 9th grade	3,025	64	527	240	1,222	1,597	748	243	485	1,655	641
9th to 12th grade, no diploma	5,517	148	937	737	794	2,205	1,143	817	1,204	2,681	816
High school graduate (includes equivalency)	22,665	840	2,311	2,116	1,746	6,627	2,241	4,290	6,244	8,501	3,630
Additional vocational training	2,553	127	211	192	190	585	171	408	795	905	446
Some college, no degree	12,659	654	790	1,253	983	2,873	994	1,727	3,000	4,802	3,129
Associate's degree	6,722	448	458	566	449	919	383	1,246	1,638	2,393	1,444
Bachelor's degree	15,894	1,040	311	1,025	818	2,334	605	2,862	3,605	5,806	3,620
Graduate or professional degree	9,947	635	85	610	427	1,917	291	2,192	2,073	3,354	2,327
Percent high school graduate or higher	88.8	94.5	73.0	85.1	68.7	79.4	70.5	92.1	90.7	85.1	90.7
Percent bachelor's degree or higher	33.8	43.7	7.3	25.0	19.3	23.0	14.0	37.8	31.1	31.4	38.1
Citizenship of householder											
Citizen of the United States	73,334	3,596	5,215	6,352	4,839	18,226	6,007	12,968	17,904	27,981	14,481
Naturalized citizen of the United States	4,732	229	125	360	1,355	1,090	446	1,023	597	1,383	1,728
Year householder immigrated to the United States											
2005 to 2009	156	29	12	14	57	–	19	31	27	72	27
2000 to 2004	659	93	45	24	250	13	82	79	104	302	174
1995 to 1999	998	98	69	99	392	12	117	165	156	361	315
1990 to 1994	1,037	59	46	73	405	37	119	164	148	332	392
1980 to 1989	2,175	92	74	200	892	151	191	372	184	723	896
1979 or before	2,801	92	81	146	959	1,123	317	622	324	804	1,051
Year householder moved into unit											
2005 to 2009	20,126	3,787	1,546	1,622	2,015	1,678	1,417	2,898	4,558	8,170	4,500
2000 to 2004	17,520	17	1,544	1,452	1,837	2,261	1,325	2,697	4,120	6,760	3,944
1995 to 1999	11,217	13	1,206	1,009	927	2,091	840	1,965	2,660	4,282	2,310
1990 to 1994	7,706	3	527	654	550	1,691	671	1,353	1,914	2,946	1,494
1985 to 1989	5,362	6	276	417	357	1,530	430	1,042	1,345	1,926	1,048
1980 to 1984	3,124	3	140	272	193	1,108	340	763	737	1,121	503
1975 to 1979	3,734	–	96	346	202	1,861	363	766	1,009	1,330	629
1970 to 1974	2,548	–	64	287	142	1,746	315	550	622	1,000	376
1960 to 1969	3,142	–	17	336	135	2,735	379	802	805	1,063	472
1950 to 1959	1,522	–	–	130	63	1,386	248	408	380	454	280
1940 to 1949	334	–	2	15	19	291	53	110	78	109	37
1939 or earlier	93	–	–	8	–	93	24	24	22	32	15
Median	1999	2007	2000	1999	2002	1985	1997	1997	1999	2000	2001
Household moves and formation in last year											
Total with a move in last year	8,394	1,211	713	681	949	675	737	1,173	1,916	3,239	2,067
Household all moved here from one unit	3,961	912	342	303	365	281	348	533	887	1,544	997
Householder of previous unit did not move here	460	75	74	39	60	20	71	53	123	193	91
Householder of previous unit moved here	3,165	775	222	245	266	235	227	450	700	1,210	805
Householder of previous unit not reported	337	63	46	19	39	26	50	30	64	141	101
Household moved here from two or more units	304	31	31	19	35	5	12	31	77	87	108
No previous householder moved here	42	6	10	–	–	–	3	4	15	12	11
1 previous householder moved here	79	12	14	2	5	–	2	10	27	21	21
2 or more previous householders moved here	156	13	4	11	24	5	3	13	29	46	67
Previous householder(s) not reported	28	–	3	6	6	–	3	4	7	8	9
Some already here, rest moved in	4,129	267	340	359	549	390	377	608	952	1,608	961
No previous householder moved here	2,331	171	187	185	306	111	221	334	588	877	532
1 or more previous householders moved here	1,497	81	125	132	205	242	120	218	301	634	344
Previous householder(s) not reported	301	15	28	42	38	36	36	56	63	97	85
Number of previous units not reported	–	–	–	–	–	–	–	–	–	–	–
Households with disabled persons											
Households without a disabled person	62,765	3,388	3,946	5,295	5,433	11,681	4,446	11,076	14,990	23,717	12,981
Households with a disabled person[1, 2]	12,948	424	1,453	1,213	973	6,614	1,845	2,161	3,113	5,154	2,520
Hearing disability	4,498	151	480	216	272	2,827	535	749	1,162	1,595	992
Vision disability	1,940	38	257	166	193	995	327	293	398	835	415
Mental disability	3,498	148	446	346	294	1,377	553	549	852	1,411	686
Physical disability	7,880	243	945	900	587	4,357	1,244	1,296	1,835	3,357	1,392
Self-care disability	2,038	68	210	255	165	1,066	338	314	426	893	405
Go-outside-home disability	4,140	129	450	504	335	2,251	689	648	1,015	1,680	797
Disability not reported	715	18	19	39	34	177	114	141	146	321	107

– = Zero or rounds to zero.
X = Not applicable.
[1] = Figures may not add to total because more than one category may apply to a unit.
[2] = Mental, physical, and self-care disabilities are limited to household members at least 5 years of age. Go-outside-home disabilities are limited to household members at least 15 years of age.

Source: U.S. Census Bureau, American Housing Survey

Table 1-9. Household Composition, Renter-Occupied Units, 2009

[Numbers in thousands, except as noted.]

Characteristics	Total occupied units	Housing unit characteristics		Household characteristics				Regions			
		New construction 4 years	Manufactured/ mobile homes	Black alone	Hispanic	Elderly (65 years and over)	Below poverty level	Northeast	Midwest	South	West
Population in housing units	82,753	2,247	3,889	17,919	19,608	6,424	23,299	15,666	15,319	29,546	22,223
Total	35,378	941	1,421	7,446	6,300	4,623	9,334	7,073	7,119	12,392	8,794
Persons											
1 person	13,331	323	385	2,774	1,280	3,264	3,908	2,884	3,029	4,463	2,954
2 persons	9,453	271	365	1,805	1,426	1,082	1,669	1,935	1,938	3,259	2,321
3 persons	5,345	145	222	1,261	1,170	195	1,329	1,001	986	2,062	1,296
4 persons	4,016	121	260	868	1,160	49	1,130	751	689	1,418	1,157
5 persons	1,910	50	105	403	694	22	702	284	291	725	611
6 persons	780	13	50	183	322	6	326	125	102	292	261
7 persons or more	543	17	33	151	248	5	269	92	84	173	194
Number of single children under 18 years											
None	23,026	580	798	4,232	3,020	4,498	5,029	4,937	4,857	7,656	5,575
1	5,349	136	236	1,345	1,163	81	1,558	953	1,007	2,109	1,280
2	4,106	135	225	992	1,194	32	1,308	756	782	1,471	1,097
3	1,928	60	120	571	581	7	900	293	298	773	565
4	632	15	29	186	219	–	323	91	116	255	170
5	222	5	11	78	85	2	139	28	37	79	77
6 or more	115	10	3	42	40	2	77	15	22	49	29
Persons 65 years and over											
None	30,223	842	1,244	6,533	5,685	X	7,761	5,673	5,958	10,937	7,655
1 person	4,453	73	148	842	516	3,952	1,476	1,202	1,031	1,252	968
2 persons or more	701	26	28	71	100	671	97	199	130	203	170
Age of householder											
Under 25 years	4,799	171	216	874	819	X	1,760	628	1,143	1,883	1,145
25 to 29	5,072	154	170	1,005	993	X	1,106	827	1,068	1,959	1,219
30 to 34	4,561	137	188	934	1,044	X	1,016	871	796	1,653	1,240
35 to 44	6,976	187	323	1,606	1,446	X	1,598	1,420	1,202	2,482	1,872
45 to 54	5,762	124	258	1,379	954	X	1,390	1,181	1,139	1,974	1,469
55 to 64	3,585	81	107	861	558	X	1,001	875	685	1,175	850
65 to 74	2,120	53	95	487	271	2,120	662	569	435	641	475
75 years and over	2,503	35	63	298	216	2,503	799	701	652	626	524
Median (years)	39	35	38	40	36	75	39	43	39	37	38
Household composition by age of householder											
2-or-more-person households	22,047	618	1,036	4,672	5,020	1,359	5,426	4,189	4,090	7,929	5,839
Married-couple families, no nonrelatives	8,808	285	484	1,115	2,269	793	1,369	1,716	1,397	3,109	2,587
Under 25 years	707	26	58	52	205	X	160	64	110	305	228
25 to 29 years	1,313	52	53	141	386	X	243	198	225	517	373
30 to 34 years	1,497	43	87	188	433	X	217	239	229	564	465
35 to 44 years	2,168	75	130	291	634	X	334	436	299	753	681
45 to 64 years	2,329	63	119	362	496	X	316	546	383	750	650
65 years and over	793	25	38	80	114	793	99	234	150	220	189
Other male householder	4,673	108	210	756	1,131	150	786	803	930	1,642	1,299
Under 45 years	3,629	97	150	502	893	X	570	568	743	1,301	1,018
45 to 64 years	895	8	54	210	217	X	185	196	156	298	246
65 years and over	150	2	6	44	22	150	31	39	31	44	36
Other female householder	8,565	225	341	2,801	1,620	417	3,271	1,670	1,764	3,178	1,953
Under 45 years	6,119	178	255	1,964	1,089	X	2,520	1,106	1,378	2,282	1,353
45 to 64 years	2,030	42	73	725	435	X	623	452	315	750	513
65 years and over	417	5	13	112	95	417	128	113	71	146	87
1-person households	13,331	323	385	2,774	1,280	3,264	3,908	2,884	3,029	4,463	2,954
Male householder	6,588	165	198	1,280	715	936	1,641	1,330	1,457	2,234	1,566
Under 45 years	3,540	102	101	698	427	X	787	653	756	1,297	835
45 to 64 years	2,112	37	57	406	198	X	570	427	491	696	498
65 years and over	936	26	40	175	91	936	285	251	211	241	234
Female householder	6,743	158	187	1,495	565	2,328	2,267	1,554	1,571	2,230	1,388
Under 45 years	2,434	75	62	583	234	X	650	484	468	959	523
45 to 64 years	1,981	55	63	537	166	X	698	436	479	654	412
65 years and over	2,328	29	62	375	165	2,328	919	634	624	616	453
Adults and single children under 18 years											
Total households with children	12,352	361	623	3,214	3,281	125	4,304	2,136	2,262	4,736	3,218
Married couples	5,084	166	291	644	1,677	34	1,057	853	734	1,847	1,650
One child under 6 years only	926	30	40	97	259	5	115	173	107	399	247
One under 6 years, one or more 6 to 17 years	1,037	22	70	123	441	5	284	175	131	354	376
Two or more under 6 years only	677	27	41	87	211	–	187	113	104	265	196
Two or more under 6 years, one or more 6 to 17 years	401	15	29	57	159	–	144	55	59	150	137
One or more 6 to 17 years only	2,043	71	110	280	607	24	327	338	332	680	694

Table 1-9. Household Composition, Renter-Occupied Units, 2009—*Continued*

[Numbers in thousands, except as noted.]

Characteristics	Total occupied units	Housing unit characteristics		Household characteristics				Regions			
		New construction 4 years	Manufactured/ mobile homes	Black alone	Hispanic	Elderly (65 years and over)	Below poverty level	Northeast	Midwest	South	West
Other households with two or more adults	3,083	51	132	955	914	52	1,109	543	577	1,186	778
One child under 6 years only	686	10	53	144	188	9	206	108	151	291	137
One under 6 years, one or more 6 to 17 years	483	13	10	144	180	2	199	87	101	162	133
Two or more under 6 years only	326	3	20	115	88	–	162	60	57	138	71
Two or more under 6 years, one or more 6 to 17 years	190	2	8	80	80	2	106	27	36	82	45
One or more 6 to 17 years only	1,398	23	41	473	378	38	435	261	232	513	392
Households with one adult or none	4,185	144	200	1,615	689	39	2,139	740	951	1,703	790
One child under 6 years only	687	8	31	253	93	–	360	87	197	296	107
One under 6 years, one or more 6 to 17 years	609	18	42	276	117	–	366	141	153	215	100
Two or more under 6 years only	302	9	12	122	67	–	247	40	77	129	57
Two or more under 6 years, one or more 6 to 17 years	221	14	16	116	45	–	177	27	31	133	31
One or more 6 to 17 years only	2,365	95	98	847	367	39	988	445	495	931	496
Total households with no children	23,026	580	798	4,232	3,020	4,498	5,029	4,937	4,857	7,656	5,575
Married couples	3,934	121	204	480	702	764	350	894	702	1,329	1,009
Other households with two or more adults	5,984	146	224	1,060	1,048	470	918	1,204	1,154	1,972	1,654
Households with one adult	13,108	313	371	2,692	1,270	3,264	3,761	2,840	3,001	4,355	2,912
Own never-married children under 18 years											
No own children under 18 years	24,429	615	854	4,707	3,347	4,596	5,598	5,211	5,097	8,248	5,874
With own children under 18 years	10,949	326	567	2,739	2,953	27	3,735	1,862	2,022	4,145	2,920
Under 6 years only	3,375	87	190	748	847	3	1,174	540	667	1,383	786
1 child	2,174	52	117	469	508	3	626	351	435	908	480
2 children	974	27	54	212	285	–	407	165	185	369	255
3 or more children	227	8	19	67	54	–	141	24	47	106	51
6 to 17 years only	5,093	159	237	1,355	1,254	22	1,489	885	936	1,858	1,414
1 child	2,613	71	107	673	584	13	690	482	472	960	699
2 children	1,703	57	85	428	468	8	455	297	323	581	503
3 or more children	778	32	46	253	202	–	344	107	141	318	212
Both age groups	2,480	79	139	637	852	2	1,072	437	419	904	720
2 children	1,043	38	60	243	346	–	333	213	201	376	253
3 or more children	1,438	42	80	393	506	2	739	224	219	527	467
Persons other than spouse or children[1]											
With other relatives	6,202	108	323	1,709	1,837	550	1,619	1,353	962	2,168	1,718
Single adult offspring 18 to 29 years	3,030	65	158	886	792	64	847	717	450	1,025	839
Single adult offspring 30 years of age or over	714	10	19	205	208	310	147	169	106	251	188
Households with three generations	958	14	41	337	313	63	371	189	133	405	231
Households with 1 subfamily	784	13	36	263	322	37	311	137	111	310	225
Subfamily householder age under 30 years	459	5	25	175	165	3	211	68	74	204	114
30 to 64 years	314	7	11	86	152	33	97	67	37	104	106
65 years and over	11	–	–	3	5	–	3	3	–	3	6
Households with 2 or more subfamilies	37	–	–	13	18	4	13	14	8	6	10
Households with other types of relatives	2,622	34	161	708	865	214	685	532	402	961	728
With nonrelatives	5,901	149	247	805	1,214	122	1,131	1,025	1,222	2,016	1,638
Co-owners or co-renters	2,427	84	74	236	330	41	433	309	624	730	764
Lodgers	674	17	26	67	227	13	107	117	91	242	224
Unrelated children, under 18 years old	486	11	21	78	110	9	132	73	108	210	94
Other nonrelatives	2,889	46	173	497	707	70	597	602	500	1,065	722
One or more secondary families	269	6	10	49	87	3	56	32	60	102	74
2-person households, none related to each other	2,963	93	78	347	386	90	347	569	618	961	814
3-to-8-person households, none related to each other	672	20	36	54	113	7	155	102	139	233	198
Educational attainment of the householder											
Less than 9th grade	2,232	21	164	279	1,294	742	1,050	451	277	795	709
9th to 12th grade, no diploma	4,455	80	285	1,247	1,294	842	1,981	946	817	1,744	947
High school graduate (includes equivalency)	11,724	291	647	2,801	2,029	1,527	3,335	2,315	2,576	4,255	2,578
Additional vocational training	1,144	24	66	273	142	144	284	195	260	399	290
Some college, no degree	6,924	214	208	1,624	807	607	1,699	1,069	1,575	2,418	1,862
Associate's degree	2,522	69	61	539	286	145	444	516	524	815	667
Bachelor's degree	5,183	189	49	728	433	427	599	1,209	959	1,634	1,382
Graduate or professional degree	2,338	77	7	228	155	333	226	567	391	732	648
Percent high school graduate or higher	81.1	89.3	68.4	79.5	58.9	65.7	67.5	80.2	84.6	79.5	81.2
Percent bachelor's degree or higher	21.3	28.3	4.0	12.8	9.3	16.4	8.8	25.1	19.0	19.1	23.1
Citizenship of householder											
Citizen of the United States	31,022	885	1,267	6,978	3,688	4,417	8,085	6,096	6,659	10,962	7,305
Naturalized citizen of the United States	2,129	38	43	308	795	461	616	648	198	534	749

Table 1-9. Household Composition, Renter-Occupied Units, 2009—*Continued*

[Numbers in thousands, except as noted.]

Characteristics	Total occupied units	Housing unit characteristics		Household characteristics				Regions			
		New construction 4 years	Manufactured/ mobile homes	Black alone	Hispanic	Elderly (65 years and over)	Below poverty level	Northeast	Midwest	South	West
Year householder immigrated to the United States											
2005 to 2009	973	12	52	124	387	20	293	221	152	342	257
2000 to 2004	1,402	13	46	150	766	42	339	355	159	481	407
1995 to 1999	1,058	23	37	133	630	46	312	243	112	393	309
1990 to 1994	889	17	24	110	529	58	308	197	83	257	353
1980 to 1989	1,167	20	33	158	595	133	331	303	86	280	497
1979 or before	996	8	5	102	501	369	282	305	66	210	414
Year householder moved into unit											
2005 to 2009	25,982	924	1,063	5,401	4,649	1,829	6,731	4,286	5,359	9,892	6,444
2000 to 2004	4,970	13	231	1,076	896	1,052	1,347	1,216	1,004	1,396	1,354
1995 to 1999	1,914	–	56	382	324	606	512	544	342	511	517
1990 to 1994	1,057	3	38	272	178	356	307	367	186	254	249
1985 to 1989	482	–	14	98	91	204	160	168	84	131	98
1980 to 1984	312	–	16	87	69	166	93	145	56	58	53
1975 to 1979	244	–	3	66	54	108	67	139	30	53	22
1970 to 1974	151	–	–	24	22	88	39	64	19	42	25
1960 to 1969	158	–	–	28	7	124	52	94	15	34	15
1950 to 1959	70	–	–	6	11	55	19	31	11	16	11
1940 to 1949	23	–	–	5	1	18	7	6	7	4	6
1939 or earlier	17	–	–	–	–	17	–	12	5	–	–
Median	2007	2008	2007	2007	2007	2003	2007	2006	2007	2007	2007
Household moves and formation in last year											
Total with a move in last year	14,332	598	653	2,905	2,754	626	3,920	2,013	3,038	5,584	3,698
Household all moved here from one unit	11,014	500	470	2,343	2,000	555	3,152	1,493	2,332	4,419	2,770
Householder of previous unit did not move here	2,349	73	97	562	447	51	860	327	522	956	544
Householder of previous unit moved here	7,733	390	347	1,630	1,385	474	1,987	1,003	1,625	3,102	2,003
Householder of previous unit not reported	932	37	25	150	168	30	304	163	186	361	222
Household moved here from two or more units	1,387	51	64	185	272	19	225	135	368	474	409
No previous householder moved here	282	11	11	44	56	–	45	27	76	89	90
1 previous householder moved here	359	15	12	41	77	6	55	27	108	148	75
2 or more previous householders moved here	523	19	35	71	94	6	81	57	129	177	160
Previous householder(s) not reported	223	7	6	29	45	8	45	25	55	60	83
Some already here, rest moved in	1,928	48	120	378	482	52	543	385	337	686	519
No previous householder moved here	1,006	19	81	221	254	25	320	212	171	342	280
1 or more previous householders moved here	703	26	23	123	157	24	164	103	122	276	202
Previous householder(s) not reported	220	2	15	34	72	2	60	70	44	69	37
Number of previous units not reported	4	–	–	–	–	–	–	–	–	4	–
Households with disabled persons											
Households without a disabled person	28,856	810	1,106	6,080	5,469	2,467	6,693	5,649	5,657	10,184	7,367
Households with a disabled person[1, 2]	6,234	117	302	1,264	813	2,124	2,537	1,317	1,427	2,078	1,411
Hearing disability	1,578	34	81	195	222	755	537	327	310	563	378
Vision disability	1,053	23	49	247	179	387	465	216	214	377	246
Mental disability	2,320	60	154	478	267	465	1,073	473	549	773	525
Physical disability	3,771	76	170	804	452	1,581	1,560	822	904	1,246	800
Self-care disability	931	10	28	207	150	373	433	189	215	295	232
Go-outside-home disability	2,065	44	100	431	259	870	925	452	484	660	470
Disability not reported	288	15	13	102	19	32	104	107	35	131	16

– = Zero or rounds to zero.
X = Not applicable.
[1] = Figures may not add to total because more than one category may apply to a unit.
[2] = Mental, physical, and self-care disabilities are limited to household members at least 5 years of age. Go-outside-home disabilities are limited to household members at least 15 years of age.

Source: U.S. Census Bureau, American Housing Survey

Table 1-10. Previous Unit of Recent Movers, Occupied Units, 2009

[Numbers in thousands.]

Characteristics	Total occupied units	Tenure		Housing unit characteristics		Household characteristics				Regions			
		Owner	Renter	New construction 4 years	Manufactured/ mobile homes	Black alone	Hispanic	Elderly (65 years or over)	Below poverty level	Northeast	Midwest	South	West
Householder moved during the past year from within the United States													
Total	16,763	4,341	12,422	1,511	926	2,901	2,685	868	3,700	2,190	3,686	6,585	4,303
Structure type of previous residence													
Moved from within the United States	16,763	4,341	12,422	1,511	926	2,901	2,685	868	3,700	2,190	3,686	6,585	4,303
House	8,531	2,595	5,936	897	438	1,245	1,212	486	1,708	991	1,956	3,391	2,193
Apartment	6,437	1,208	5,228	442	157	1,381	1,253	261	1,490	1,058	1,363	2,373	1,643
Manufactured/mobile home	783	238	545	79	283	79	99	59	238	30	160	433	159
Other	499	119	380	52	16	71	57	37	131	56	124	150	169
Not reported	513	182	331	41	32	125	65	26	133	55	83	237	138
Tenure of previous residence													
House, apartment, manufactured/mobile home in the United States	15,751	4,041	11,710	1,418	878	2,705	2,563	805	3,435	2,079	3,479	6,198	3,996
Owner occupied	5,023	2,032	2,991	701	322	552	569	431	831	628	1,166	2,026	1,203
Renter occupied	10,728	2,009	8,719	717	556	2,153	1,994	375	2,605	1,450	2,313	4,172	2,793
Persons – previous residence													
House, apartment, manufactured/mobile home in the United States	15,751	4,041	11,710	1,418	878	2,705	2,563	805	3,435	2,079	3,479	6,198	3,996
1 person	2,414	579	1,835	234	72	438	232	369	520	336	570	943	565
2 persons	4,390	1,420	2,970	449	247	595	463	336	591	629	903	1,769	1,089
3 persons	3,257	778	2,480	262	190	567	536	54	734	428	788	1,232	809
4 persons	2,733	654	2,080	264	168	494	530	14	638	337	618	1,095	683
5 persons	1,408	353	1,055	121	98	278	320	6	416	178	296	538	396
6 persons	712	122	589	53	50	137	218	12	271	69	139	285	220
7 persons or more	567	98	469	15	39	132	209	4	220	54	126	218	168
Not reported	270	38	232	20	13	65	55	9	46	48	38	119	66
Previous home owned or rented by someone who moved here													
House, apartment, manufactured/mobile home in the United States	15,751	4,041	11,710	1,418	878	2,705	2,563	805	3,435	2,079	3,479	6,198	3,996
Owned or rented by a mover	11,933	3,420	8,513	1,211	626	1,969	1,879	716	2,340	1,572	2,575	4,689	3,098
Owned or rented by other	3,463	540	2,923	192	211	684	628	71	1,033	441	851	1,333	838
By a relative	2,076	303	1,773	85	124	448	348	35	633	238	512	808	518
By a nonrelative	1,387	238	1,149	107	86	235	280	36	400	202	340	525	320
Not reported	1	–	1	–	–	1	–	–	–	1	–	–	–
Not reported	354	80	274	15	41	52	56	18	62	66	53	176	59
Change in housing costs													
House, apartment, manufactured/mobile home in the United States	15,751	4,041	11,710	1,418	878	2,705	2,563	805	3,435	2,079	3,479	6,198	3,996
Increased with move	7,590	2,455	5,135	913	269	1,266	1,141	292	1,413	1,060	1,725	2,840	1,965
Decreased	4,520	801	3,719	219	335	773	817	234	1,087	550	969	1,807	1,194
Stayed about the same	3,107	663	2,444	245	227	577	533	223	807	360	694	1,311	743
Don't know	310	60	250	23	28	42	57	30	80	68	57	115	69
Not reported	223	62	161	18	20	47	15	27	48	41	33	125	24

– = Zero or rounds to zero.

Source: U.S. Census Bureau, American Housing Survey

Table 1-11. Previous Unit of Recent Movers, Owner-Occupied Units, 2009

[Numbers in thousands.]

Characteristics	Total occupied units	Housing unit characteristics		Household characteristics				Regions			
		New construction 4 years	Manufactured/ mobile homes	Black alone	Hispanic	Elderly (65 years and over)	Below poverty level	Northeast	Midwest	South	West
Householder moved during the past year from within the United States											
Total	4,341	956	388	336	412	294	358	582	966	1,665	1,129
Structure type of previous residence											
Moved from within the United States	4,341	956	388	336	412	294	358	582	966	1,665	1,129
House	2,595	631	187	145	215	225	189	339	615	986	655
Apartment	1,208	213	60	149	144	28	86	210	233	459	306
Manufactured/mobile home	238	56	108	22	19	15	30	7	63	123	45
Other	119	25	11	9	11	11	6	9	25	27	58
Not reported	182	31	21	11	23	15	46	17	30	70	65
Tenure of previous residence											
House, apartment, manufactured/mobile home in the United States	4,041	900	356	316	379	268	306	556	911	1,568	1,006
Owner occupied	2,032	538	185	96	177	222	150	284	475	811	463
Renter occupied	2,009	362	171	220	201	46	156	272	436	757	544
Persons—previous residence											
House, apartment, manufactured/mobile home in the United States	4,041	900	356	316	379	268	306	556	911	1,568	1,006
1 person	579	127	25	67	31	73	64	64	107	244	163
2 persons	1,420	316	145	110	77	167	68	187	293	594	346
3 persons	778	165	75	46	82	14	46	107	219	283	169
4 persons	654	162	50	48	64	6	42	110	155	241	147
5 persons	353	92	19	32	67	–	43	64	75	105	109
6 persons	122	25	24	4	31	5	15	11	28	46	38
7 persons or more	98	3	16	–	25	3	22	7	24	37	31
Not reported	38	10	3	9	2	2	6	6	11	18	3
Previous home owned or rented by someone who moved here											
House, apartment, manufactured/mobile home in the United States	4,041	900	356	316	379	268	306	556	911	1,568	1,006
Owned or rented by a mover	3,420	801	238	268	312	234	226	488	733	1,309	890
Owned or rented by other	540	90	95	44	62	20	74	61	167	207	105
By a relative	303	31	58	24	42	3	45	37	91	102	72
By a nonrelative	238	59	37	21	20	16	30	24	76	104	33
Not reported	–	–	–	–	–	–	–	–	–	–	–
Not reported	80	9	24	4	4	14	6	6	10	52	12
Change in housing costs											
House, apartment, manufactured/mobile home in the United States	4,041	900	356	316	379	268	306	556	911	1,568	1,006
Increased with move	2,455	648	128	220	214	94	124	364	564	918	609
Decreased	801	94	148	35	114	50	97	87	173	354	186
Stayed about the same	663	127	65	54	38	88	62	86	153	246	179
Don't know	60	19	–	4	9	16	14	10	9	19	22
Not reported	62	11	15	3	4	20	9	9	12	30	11

– = Zero or rounds to zero.

Source: U.S. Census Bureau, American Housing Survey

Table 1-12. Previous Unit of Recent Movers, Renter-Occupied Units, 2009

[Numbers in thousands.]

Characteristics	Total occupied units	Housing unit characteristics		Household characteristics				Regions			
		New construction 4 years	Manufactured/ mobile homes	Black alone	Hispanic	Elderly (65 years and over)	Below poverty level	Northeast	Midwest	South	West
Householder moved during the past year from within the United States											
Total	12,422	555	538	2,565	2,273	574	3,341	1,608	2,720	4,920	3,173
Structure type of previous residence											
Moved from within the United States	12,422	555	538	2,565	2,273	574	3,341	1,608	2,720	4,920	3,173
House	5,936	266	250	1,101	996	261	1,518	652	1,341	2,406	1,538
Apartment	5,228	229	96	1,232	1,109	233	1,403	848	1,129	1,914	1,337
Manufactured/mobile home	545	23	175	56	79	44	208	23	97	311	114
Other	380	28	5	63	46	26	125	47	99	123	111
Not reported	331	10	11	114	43	10	87	38	53	167	72
Tenure of previous residence											
House, apartment, manufactured/mobile home in the United States	11,710	518	522	2,388	2,184	537	3,129	1,523	2,568	4,630	2,990
Owner occupied	2,991	163	136	456	392	208	681	344	691	1,215	740
Renter occupied	8,719	355	385	1,932	1,793	329	2,449	1,179	1,877	3,415	2,249
Persons—previous residence											
House, apartment, manufactured/mobile home in the United States	11,710	518	522	2,388	2,184	537	3,129	1,523	2,568	4,630	2,990
1 person	1,835	107	47	371	201	297	457	272	463	699	402
2 persons	2,970	133	102	486	386	170	522	442	611	1,174	743
3 persons	2,480	96	116	520	454	40	689	321	569	949	640
4 persons	2,080	102	118	446	466	9	595	227	463	854	536
5 persons	1,055	29	79	246	253	6	373	114	221	433	287
6 persons	589	28	26	133	188	7	256	58	111	238	182
7 persons or more	469	12	24	132	184	1	198	47	103	182	137
Not reported	232	10	10	56	53	8	39	41	27	101	63
Previous home owned or rented by someone who moved here											
House, apartment, manufactured/mobile home in the United States	11,710	518	522	2,388	2,184	537	3,129	1,523	2,568	4,630	2,990
Owned or rented by a mover	8,513	411	389	1,700	1,567	482	2,115	1,084	1,841	3,380	2,208
Owned or rented by other	2,923	102	116	639	566	51	959	380	684	1,126	733
By a relative	1,773	54	66	424	306	32	588	201	420	705	446
By a nonrelative	1,149	48	49	214	260	19	371	177	264	421	287
Not reported	1	–	–	1	–	–	–	1	–	–	–
Not reported	274	5	17	49	52	4	55	60	42	124	48
Change in housing costs											
House, apartment, manufactured/mobile home in the United States	11,710	518	522	2,388	2,184	537	3,129	1,523	2,568	4,630	2,990
Increased with move	5,135	265	141	1,046	927	198	1,290	696	1,161	1,922	1,356
Decreased	3,719	125	187	738	703	184	990	463	796	1,453	1,008
Stayed about the same	2,444	118	161	523	496	135	745	274	541	1,065	564
Don't know	250	3	28	38	47	14	66	59	49	96	47
Not reported	161	7	5	44	11	7	39	32	21	94	14

– = Zero or rounds to zero.

Source: U.S. Census Bureau, American Housing Survey

Table 1-13. Reasons for Move and Choice of Current Residence, Occupied Units, 2009

[Numbers in thousands.]

Characteristics	Total occupied units	Tenure		Housing unit characteristics		Household characteristics				Regions			
		Owner	Renter	New construction 4 years	Manufactured/ mobile homes	Black alone	Hispanic	Elderly (65 years or over)	Below poverty level	Northeast	Midwest	South	West
Respondent moved during past year													
Total	17,463	4,623	12,840	1,529	960	2,965	2,832	920	3,870	2,294	3,809	6,858	4,502
Reasons for leaving previous unit[1]													
Private displacement	442	49	393	16	33	50	77	28	114	72	59	162	149
Owner to move into unit	142	13	129	8	11	9	27	2	33	17	24	56	45
To be converted to condominium or cooperative	25	4	20	–	–	–	–	–	14	14	–	3	7
Closed for repairs	19	2	17	–	–	1	6	4	5	1	2	2	15
Other	254	29	225	9	22	38	44	20	62	40	34	99	82
Not reported	2	–	2	–	–	2	–	2	–	–	–	2	–
Government displacement	161	22	138	19	7	30	46	10	52	13	39	49	60
Government wanted building or land	29	8	21	7	3	10	10	4	14	1	4	10	13
Unit unfit for occupancy	13	–	13	–	4	3	–	–	7	–	3	8	2
Other	119	15	105	12	–	18	36	5	30	11	32	31	44
Not reported	–	–	–	–	–	–	–	–	–	–	–	–	–
Disaster loss (fire, flood, etc.)	155	24	132	9	17	38	23	10	66	15	23	108	10
New job or job transfer	1,734	408	1,326	215	23	213	238	22	137	172	345	783	434
To be closer to work/school/other	2,026	315	1,711	121	95	286	340	43	494	271	438	763	553
Other, financial/employment related	829	139	690	50	60	159	199	38	214	107	182	246	294
To establish own household	2,163	719	1,445	197	155	385	325	33	502	248	554	826	535
Needed larger house or apartment	1,951	589	1,362	233	74	401	402	43	358	286	447	763	455
Married	256	115	141	23	11	29	37	–	21	31	52	94	80
Widowed, divorced, or separated	446	154	292	29	39	58	39	53	99	68	132	157	88
Other, family/person related	1,649	431	1,218	99	119	205	218	204	395	254	384	630	381
Wanted better home	1,790	511	1,279	229	62	362	285	88	410	240	460	685	405
Change from owner to renter	180	X	180	12	7	27	35	10	15	21	32	86	41
Change from renter to owner	775	775	X	105	53	79	89	2	19	86	152	278	259
Wanted lower rent or maintenance	1,223	103	1,120	36	68	238	252	77	339	165	267	480	311
Other housing related reasons	1,052	224	828	99	55	212	142	85	272	153	238	381	279
Evicted from residence	191	21	169	3	33	37	45	16	79	16	43	82	49
Other	2,376	545	1,831	236	114	399	366	254	551	348	490	868	669
Not reported	718	246	472	44	52	167	88	55	194	99	104	359	156
Main reason for leaving previous unit													
All reported reasons equal	653	203	450	58	38	89	114	37	114	120	188	205	141
Private displacement	123	5	118	5	9	18	30	–	30	28	9	35	51
Government displacement	53	8	45	7	3	8	13	4	20	1	10	19	21
Disaster loss (fire, flood, etc.)	149	24	126	9	13	37	21	10	61	15	21	104	10
New job or job transfer	1,590	370	1,220	207	19	191	215	22	125	157	314	719	400
To be closer to work/school/other	1,634	217	1,416	97	75	237	275	38	432	211	342	629	452
Other, financial/employment related	646	119	527	47	52	125	157	28	176	76	149	191	229
To establish own household	1,876	594	1,282	174	146	353	297	23	469	204	484	721	467
Needed larger house or apartment	1,534	431	1,103	185	58	328	333	33	296	242	329	600	363
Married, widowed, divorced, or separated	912	284	628	59	63	113	92	44	148	118	224	327	243
Other, family/personal related	1,372	368	1,004	85	102	183	188	180	347	225	315	529	303
Wanted better home	1,186	305	881	140	37	257	195	66	292	160	294	465	266
Change from owner to renter or renter to owner	804	685	120	98	44	86	91	9	28	86	143	307	269
Wanted lower rent or maintenance	927	60	867	22	49	190	196	54	274	115	185	384	244
Other housing related reasons	782	168	614	70	48	155	109	57	226	118	187	284	192
Evicted from residence	126	14	112	3	29	18	35	8	50	11	24	47	43
Other	2,032	484	1,548	202	101	362	314	224	488	277	418	788	548
Not reported	1,065	286	779	62	77	215	159	84	294	129	171	504	261
Choice of present neighborhood[1]													
Convenient to job	5,207	1,138	4,069	501	178	778	842	69	666	717	1,024	2,185	1,281
Convenient to friends or relatives	4,039	1,030	3,009	247	325	646	738	336	1,002	595	1,017	1,459	967
Convenient to leisure activities	1,352	380	972	148	44	158	146	53	192	192	302	455	403
Convenient to public transportation	928	176	753	63	19	195	179	35	235	188	166	289	285
Good schools	2,008	637	1,370	166	53	334	392	12	525	285	409	751	563
Other public services	673	129	544	63	12	130	124	64	174	88	145	248	192
Looks/design of neighborhood	3,288	1,242	2,046	419	128	509	501	169	507	386	769	1,280	852
House was most important consideration	2,761	1,238	1,523	358	142	421	392	122	489	346	656	993	767
Other	3,806	875	2,931	314	243	686	510	244	1,084	472	801	1,555	978
Not reported	757	264	493	60	62	161	99	71	208	106	116	372	163
Main reason for choice of present neighborhood													
All reported reasons equal	1,905	551	1,354	183	78	284	269	99	356	302	406	695	502
Convenient to job	3,535	611	2,924	342	116	521	637	35	431	460	655	1,511	909
Convenient to friends or relatives	2,485	570	1,915	131	270	432	459	255	765	314	650	934	586
Convenient to leisure activities	331	87	244	29	18	18	30	12	51	44	89	97	102
Convenient to public transportation	266	29	237	6	3	73	61	11	94	54	51	78	83

Table 1-13. Reasons for Move and Choice of Current Residence, Occupied Units, 2009—*Continued*

[Numbers in thousands.]

Characteristics	Total occupied units	Tenure		Housing unit characteristics		Household characteristics				Regions			
		Owner	Renter	New construction 4 years	Manufactured/ mobile homes	Black alone	Hispanic	Elderly (65 years or over)	Below poverty level	Northeast	Midwest	South	West
Good schools	1,087	289	798	79	26	190	213	11	294	175	215	411	287
Other public services	221	36	185	20	3	66	48	38	70	30	57	80	54
Looks/design of neighborhood	1,798	635	1,163	215	79	316	299	99	284	188	426	717	467
House was most important consideration	1,765	801	964	203	100	285	277	89	337	211	451	592	510
Other	3,313	750	2,563	261	209	620	440	201	980	410	693	1,371	839
Not reported	757	264	493	60	62	161	99	71	208	106	116	372	163
Neighborhood search													
Looked at just this neighborhood	7,490	1,590	5,900	519	642	1,191	1,401	532	1,929	1,079	1,571	2,948	1,893
Looked at other neighborhood(s)	9,335	2,802	6,533	966	272	1,619	1,347	327	1,775	1,132	2,143	3,592	2,468
Not reported	638	231	407	44	47	155	85	62	166	83	95	318	142
Choice of present home[1]													
Financial reasons	6,261	1,444	4,817	385	455	1,046	1,064	222	1,551	777	1,457	2,384	1,643
Room layout/design	4,633	1,618	3,015	659	139	744	689	255	772	664	1,016	1,734	1,218
Kitchen	758	321	437	87	41	95	138	32	160	138	190	248	183
Size	3,677	1,091	2,586	383	152	656	660	155	720	488	883	1,388	917
Exterior appearance	1,619	657	963	189	72	230	242	107	258	227	316	638	438
Yard/trees/view	1,987	856	1,131	152	72	199	232	105	266	286	471	759	471
Quality of construction	1,346	674	671	293	41	139	165	82	168	194	328	476	348
Only one available	871	107	764	23	73	171	141	73	273	129	171	353	219
Other	3,286	741	2,545	230	178	478	466	223	713	442	656	1,245	943
Not reported	824	284	540	74	62	185	110	71	207	115	129	407	174
Main reason for choice of present home													
All reported reasons equal	2,256	808	1,448	257	104	304	315	135	391	349	557	807	544
Financial reasons	4,854	1,008	3,846	248	390	852	886	162	1,294	575	1,139	1,864	1,277
Room layout/design	2,540	797	1,743	405	66	467	386	136	455	336	526	995	682
Kitchen	98	33	65	5	1	22	22	6	30	20	28	26	24
Size	1,775	377	1,398	130	59	378	371	57	386	237	423	700	416
Exterior appearance	475	125	350	42	19	87	91	38	91	58	81	215	121
Yard/trees/view	699	287	412	43	31	60	71	46	92	97	151	275	176
Quality of construction	417	186	231	112	15	53	57	15	65	62	91	168	96
Only one available	684	76	608	15	60	135	117	60	218	93	128	277	187
Other	2,834	636	2,198	198	153	423	406	193	633	352	556	1,125	801
Not reported	830	290	540	74	62	185	110	71	213	115	129	407	180
Home search													
Now in house	8,129	3,929	4,200	1,084	X	1,143	1,104	368	1,248	934	1,702	3,383	2,110
Did not look at apartments	6,318	3,430	2,888	934	X	816	831	301	851	648	1,328	2,668	1,674
Looked at apartments too	1,467	305	1,162	118	X	260	238	38	320	232	320	576	339
Search not reported	344	194	150	31	X	67	35	29	77	54	54	139	97
Now in manufactured/mobile home	960	410	551	32	960	67	150	60	305	50	209	513	188
Did not look at apartments	663	304	360	22	663	50	110	43	180	32	116	383	133
Looked at apartments too	250	69	181	7	250	17	37	3	112	18	89	100	43
Search not reported	47	37	10	3	47	–	3	15	13	–	4	31	12
Now in apartment	8,374	285	8,090	413	X	1,756	1,579	491	2,318	1,310	1,898	2,962	2,204
Did not look at houses	5,907	181	5,726	255	X	1,195	1,132	427	1,643	959	1,444	2,029	1,475
Looked at houses too	2,148	92	2,056	145	X	465	396	37	573	303	404	785	656
Search not reported	319	12	308	13	X	96	51	27	102	48	50	148	73
Recent mover comparison to previous home													
Better home	9,209	3,017	6,192	1,121	446	1,583	1,519	407	1,905	1,195	2,020	3,666	2,328
Worse home	3,102	426	2,676	103	209	484	439	128	764	434	686	1,140	843
About the same	4,418	920	3,498	242	253	757	784	311	1,018	572	988	1,708	1,150
Not reported	734	261	474	64	53	142	90	74	183	93	116	344	181
Recent mover comparison to previous neighborhood													
Better neighborhood	7,206	2,253	4,953	790	409	1,254	1,226	351	1,515	887	1,492	2,978	1,849
Worse neighborhood	2,303	347	1,955	103	84	409	310	64	609	306	517	865	615
About the same	6,471	1,555	4,916	507	348	1,054	1,061	384	1,394	886	1,525	2,387	1,674
Same neighborhood	699	179	520	63	67	97	145	47	151	104	133	269	192
Not reported	786	290	496	66	53	151	91	74	200	111	142	360	173

– = Zero or rounds to zero.
X = Not applicable.
[1] = Figures may not add to total because more than one category may apply to a unit.

Source: U.S. Census Bureau, American Housing Survey

Table 1-14. Reasons for Move and Choice of Current Residence, Owner-Occupied Units, 2009

[Numbers in thousands.]

Characteristics	Total occupied units	Housing unit characteristics		Household characteristics				Regions			
		New construction 4 years	Manufactured/ mobile homes	Black alone	Hispanic	Elderly (65 years and over)	Below poverty level	Northeast	Midwest	South	West
Respondent moved during past year											
Total	4,623	965	410	353	451	342	401	603	1,030	1,802	1,188
Reasons for leaving previous unit[1]											
Private displacement	49	–	23	1	5	10	3	5	16	12	16
Owner to move into unit	13	–	7	–	3	2	–	3	7	–	3
To be converted to condominium or cooperative	4	–	–	–	–	–	–	–	–	–	4
Closed for repairs	2	–	–	–	–	–	–	–	–	–	2
Other	29	–	16	1	2	8	3	1	9	12	6
Not reported	–	–	–	–	–	–	–	–	–	–	–
Government displacement	22	11	3	8	8	2	3	–	3	14	5
Government wanted building or land	8	2	3	2	–	2	3	–	–	8	–
Unit unfit for occupancy	–	–	–	–	–	–	–	–	–	–	–
Other	15	9	–	6	8	–	–	–	3	6	5
Not reported	–	–	–	–	–	–	–	–	–	–	–
Disaster loss (fire, flood, etc.)	24	9	4	–	3	–	3	4	3	16	–
New job or job transfer	408	105	2	27	27	9	14	41	107	193	67
To be closer to work/school/other	315	65	25	24	32	20	28	33	76	130	76
Other, financial/employment related	139	27	6	8	33	13	28	5	40	36	59
To establish own household	719	151	73	73	91	6	62	90	183	258	189
Needed larger house or apartment	589	165	21	65	62	18	11	94	158	202	135
Married	115	20	8	8	4	–	3	12	29	48	26
Widowed, divorced, or separated	154	25	22	12	8	16	22	26	50	46	32
Other, family/person related	431	54	60	9	23	71	44	75	89	158	109
Wanted better home	511	157	25	45	59	25	36	67	138	196	109
Change from owner to renter	X	X	X	X	X	X	X	X	X	X	X
Change from renter to owner	775	105	53	79	89	2	19	86	152	278	259
Wanted lower rent or maintenance	103	10	22	3	17	18	15	22	22	33	26
Other housing related reasons	224	55	20	16	13	27	16	46	55	76	47
Evicted from residence	21	–	11	–	3	3	–	1	5	6	9
Other	545	144	49	47	24	98	43	79	101	239	126
Not reported	246	32	37	15	20	40	63	24	34	114	73
Main reason for leaving previous unit											
All reported reasons equal	203	36	15	16	20	13	6	35	68	63	37
Private displacement	5	–	3	–	2	–	3	–	–	2	3
Government displacement	8	2	3	2	–	2	3	–	–	8	–
Disaster loss (fire, flood, etc.)	24	9	4	–	3	–	3	4	3	16	–
New job or job transfer	370	101	2	18	27	9	14	36	94	177	64
To be closer to work/school/other	217	41	15	19	26	17	28	18	52	94	54
Other, financial/employment related	119	27	6	8	32	10	27	2	36	36	45
To establish own household	594	138	65	59	81	5	60	70	147	218	158
Needed larger house or apartment	431	129	17	35	46	15	10	72	107	148	103
Married, widowed, divorced, or separated	284	41	39	20	14	13	29	37	80	99	69
Other, family/personal related	368	44	55	9	20	63	38	71	72	133	91
Wanted better home	305	103	12	19	40	22	34	41	65	124	76
Change from owner to renter or renter to owner	685	88	41	70	70	2	17	70	120	255	239
Wanted lower rent or maintenance	60	3	13	3	11	10	11	11	10	18	20
Other housing related reasons	168	39	13	9	12	20	16	38	47	55	29
Evicted from residence	14	–	7	–	3	–	–	1	1	6	6
Other	484	128	47	46	20	93	39	69	78	224	113
Not reported	286	35	54	19	23	48	63	29	48	127	81
Choice of present neighborhood[1]											
Convenient to job	1,138	288	45	81	90	24	57	175	249	479	236
Convenient to friends or relatives	1,030	148	127	46	120	106	90	168	264	355	242
Convenient to leisure activities	380	81	23	7	26	25	20	42	103	127	107
Convenient to public transportation	176	34	6	13	15	5	16	40	27	58	51
Good schools	637	110	22	39	81	7	57	105	144	230	158
Other public services	129	30	8	4	10	13	6	16	39	34	41
Looks/design of neighborhood	1,242	295	76	90	133	72	49	165	292	465	319
House was most important consideration	1,238	265	80	107	123	64	87	174	313	416	336
Other	875	211	120	88	61	78	93	91	156	421	207
Not reported	264	43	37	15	23	55	66	24	36	121	83

Table 1-14. Reasons for Move and Choice of Current Residence, Owner-Occupied Units, 2009—*Continued*

[Numbers in thousands.]

Characteristics	Total occupied units	Housing unit characteristics		Household characteristics				Regions			
		New construction 4 years	Manufactured/ mobile homes	Black alone	Hispanic	Elderly (65 years and over)	Below poverty level	Northeast	Midwest	South	West
Main reason for choice of present neighborhood											
All reported reasons equal	551	108	38	22	50	33	39	89	117	202	143
Convenient to job	611	183	15	44	64	6	45	98	104	280	129
Convenient to friends or relatives	570	79	102	36	61	79	51	80	141	221	128
Convenient to leisure activities	87	15	6	–	7	11	8	1	28	28	30
Convenient to public transportation	29	–	–	4	4	1	3	6	1	12	10
Good schools	289	48	7	24	35	6	16	51	62	116	60
Other public services	36	12	3	4	5	6	–	1	10	5	20
Looks/design of neighborhood	635	145	41	55	74	46	30	71	171	216	176
House was most important consideration	801	153	59	75	70	41	52	111	221	247	222
Other	750	179	102	74	59	58	91	71	138	355	186
Not reported	264	43	37	15	23	55	66	24	36	121	83
Neighborhood search											
Looked at just this neighborhood	1,590	314	249	98	181	170	224	247	328	644	370
Looked at other neighborhood(s)	2,802	619	124	239	250	133	117	337	669	1,046	750
Not reported	231	32	37	16	20	39	60	19	32	112	67
Choice of present home[1]											
Financial reasons	1,444	240	170	99	138	63	160	171	337	549	387
Room layout/design	1,618	459	84	95	165	91	88	209	347	618	444
Kitchen	321	50	23	20	46	13	41	60	66	111	84
Size	1,091	263	75	90	130	57	72	134	272	411	273
Exterior appearance	657	119	38	41	67	51	47	104	127	262	164
Yard/trees/view	856	111	38	36	84	47	51	153	204	317	181
Quality of construction	674	205	29	37	65	41	59	97	156	256	165
Only one available	107	13	18	2	12	16	6	21	17	38	31
Other	741	115	69	66	46	61	59	104	170	281	186
Not reported	284	60	37	16	26	50	56	33	34	131	87
Main reason for choice of present home											
All reported reasons equal	808	178	49	45	75	45	36	105	214	297	192
Financial reasons	1,008	143	150	82	114	48	135	97	236	393	282
Room layout/design	797	276	38	64	81	55	37	89	160	313	234
Kitchen	33	–	1	7	7	–	10	11	12	10	–
Size	377	75	24	50	44	21	27	53	106	123	96
Exterior appearance	125	14	6	11	21	17	10	15	21	65	24
Yard/trees/view	287	30	12	7	17	22	9	67	47	105	68
Quality of construction	186	85	15	12	14	13	18	33	39	86	28
Only one available	76	10	18	–	9	14	3	15	11	24	26
Other	636	94	60	59	42	56	55	87	149	254	146
Not reported	290	60	37	16	26	50	62	33	34	131	92
Home search											
Now in house	3,929	893	X	314	400	249	285	505	864	1,538	1,023
Did not look at apartments	3,430	796	X	273	358	203	213	412	767	1,366	884
Looked at apartments too	305	68	X	25	24	18	24	70	70	90	75
Search not reported	194	29	X	16	17	28	48	22	27	82	63
Now in manufactured/mobile home	410	29	410	9	37	52	76	31	121	181	76
Did not look at apartments	304	22	304	9	25	37	37	23	79	149	53
Looked at apartments too	69	3	69	–	10	–	26	8	37	12	11
Search not reported	37	3	37	–	3	15	13	–	4	20	12
Now in apartment	285	44	X	31	14	42	40	67	45	83	89
Did not look at houses	181	22	X	17	9	36	29	48	39	46	49
Looked at houses too	92	19	X	13	4	2	7	16	5	31	40
Search not reported	12	3	X	–	–	3	5	3	2	7	–
Recent mover comparison to previous home											
Better home	3,017	756	211	253	291	131	187	385	660	1,206	765
Worse home	426	40	80	18	45	38	47	63	89	178	97
About the same	920	122	82	74	85	122	108	130	244	310	235
Not reported	261	47	36	8	29	50	59	25	37	107	91
Recent mover comparison to previous neighborhood											
Better neighborhood	2,253	544	149	187	232	125	143	286	439	977	551
Worse neighborhood	347	42	34	19	30	18	41	31	87	134	96
About the same	1,555	279	141	132	140	141	134	236	412	501	406
Same neighborhood	179	49	50	5	18	13	17	16	39	80	44
Not reported	290	52	36	9	32	46	66	35	53	111	92

– = Zero or rounds to zero.
X = Not applicable.
[1] = Figures may not add to total because more than one category may apply to a unit.

Source: U.S. Census Bureau, American Housing Survey

Table 1-15. Reasons for Move and Choice of Current Residence, Renter-Occupied Units, 2009

[Numbers in thousands.]

Characteristics	Total occupied units	Housing unit characteristics		Household characteristics				Regions			
		New construction 4 years	Manufactured/ mobile homes	Black alone	Hispanic	Elderly (65 years and over)	Below poverty level	Northeast	Midwest	South	West
Respondent moved during past year											
Total	12,840	564	551	2,613	2,381	577	3,469	1,690	2,780	5,056	3,314
Reasons for leaving previous unit[1]											
Private displacement	393	16	10	49	72	17	111	67	44	150	133
Owner to move into unit	129	8	4	9	24	–	33	14	17	56	43
To be converted to condominium or cooperative	20	–	–	–	–	–	14	14	–	3	3
Closed for repairs	17	–	–	1	6	4	5	1	2	2	12
Other	225	9	6	36	42	11	59	38	25	87	75
Not reported	2	–	–	2	–	2	–	–	–	2	–
Government displacement	138	8	4	22	38	7	49	13	36	36	54
Government wanted building or land	21	5	–	7	10	2	12	1	4	3	13
Unit unfit for occupancy	13	–	4	3	–	–	7	–	3	8	2
Other	105	3	–	12	28	5	30	11	29	26	39
Not reported	–	–	–	–	–	–	–	–	–	–	–
Disaster loss (fire, flood, etc.)	132	–	13	38	20	10	64	11	20	91	10
New job or job transfer	1,326	111	20	187	211	12	122	130	238	590	367
To be closer to work/school/other	1,711	56	70	261	308	24	466	238	363	633	477
Other, financial/employment related	690	23	53	151	166	25	186	102	142	210	235
To establish own household	1,445	46	81	313	234	27	440	159	372	568	346
Needed larger house or apartment	1,362	69	53	335	340	25	347	192	289	561	320
Married	141	3	3	21	33	–	18	18	23	46	54
Widowed, divorced, or separated	292	5	17	46	31	37	77	42	83	111	56
Other, family/person related	1,218	45	59	196	196	133	351	179	295	472	272
Wanted better home	1,279	71	37	317	226	63	373	172	322	489	296
Change from owner to renter	180	12	7	27	35	10	15	21	32	86	41
Change from renter to owner	X	X	X	X	X	X	X	X	X	X	X
Wanted lower rent or maintenance	1,120	25	45	235	235	59	324	143	245	447	285
Other housing related reasons	828	45	34	197	129	58	256	107	184	305	233
Evicted from residence	169	3	22	37	42	13	79	15	37	76	40
Other	1,831	93	65	351	342	156	509	270	389	630	543
Not reported	472	12	15	152	68	15	131	74	70	245	83
Main reason for leaving previous unit											
All reported reasons equal	450	22	24	73	94	24	107	85	120	141	104
Private displacement	118	5	6	18	27	–	27	28	9	33	48
Government displacement	45	5	–	5	13	2	17	1	10	12	21
Disaster loss (fire, flood, etc.)	126	–	9	37	19	10	59	11	18	87	10
New job or job transfer	1,220	106	17	173	188	12	110	122	220	542	336
To be closer to work/school/other	1,416	56	60	217	249	21	404	193	290	535	398
Other, financial/employment related	527	19	46	117	124	18	148	74	113	156	184
To establish own household	1,282	35	81	294	216	19	409	134	337	503	309
Needed larger house or apartment	1,103	56	41	293	287	18	286	170	222	452	259
Married, widowed, divorced, or separated	628	18	24	93	78	31	119	82	144	228	174
Other, family/personal related	1,004	41	47	174	168	117	310	154	243	396	212
Wanted better home	881	37	25	238	155	44	258	119	230	342	190
Change from owner to renter or renter to owner	120	10	3	16	20	6	11	16	22	52	30
Wanted lower rent or maintenance	867	19	36	187	185	44	263	104	174	366	223
Other housing related reasons	614	30	34	147	96	37	210	80	140	230	163
Evicted from residence	112	3	22	18	32	8	50	10	24	41	37
Other	1,548	74	54	315	293	131	449	208	341	564	436
Not reported	779	26	23	196	136	36	231	100	123	377	179
Choice of present neighborhood[1]											
Convenient to job	4,069	213	133	698	752	45	609	542	775	1,706	1,046
Convenient to friends or relatives	3,009	99	198	600	617	230	913	427	753	1,104	725
Convenient to leisure activities	972	67	21	151	121	28	172	149	199	328	296
Convenient to public transportation	753	29	13	182	164	31	218	148	140	231	234
Good schools	1,370	56	31	295	310	5	468	179	265	521	405
Other public services	544	32	5	126	114	51	168	72	107	214	151
Looks/design of neighborhood	2,046	124	52	419	368	98	458	221	477	815	533
House was most important consideration	1,523	92	63	314	269	58	402	172	343	577	431
Other	2,931	102	122	598	449	166	992	381	644	1,135	771
Not reported	493	18	25	146	76	16	142	82	80	251	80

Table 1-15. Reasons for Move and Choice of Current Residence, Renter-Occupied Units, 2009—*Continued*

[Numbers in thousands.]

Characteristics	Total occupied units	Housing unit characteristics		Household characteristics				Regions			
		New construction 4 years	Manufactured/ mobile homes	Black alone	Hispanic	Elderly (65 years and over)	Below poverty level	Northeast	Midwest	South	West
Main reason for choice of present neighborhood											
All reported reasons equal	1,354	74	40	262	219	66	317	213	289	493	359
Convenient to job	2,924	159	101	477	573	29	386	362	551	1,231	781
Convenient to friends or relatives	1,915	52	168	396	398	176	714	235	509	714	457
Convenient to leisure activities	244	14	12	18	23	1	42	42	60	69	72
Convenient to public transportation	237	6	3	69	57	10	91	48	50	67	73
Good schools	798	31	18	166	179	5	278	124	153	295	226
Other public services	185	7	–	63	43	32	70	30	47	74	34
Looks/design of neighborhood	1,163	70	38	260	224	53	254	117	255	501	290
House was most important consideration	964	50	41	210	208	47	285	100	230	346	288
Other	2,563	82	106	546	381	143	889	339	555	1,016	653
Not reported	493	18	25	146	76	16	142	82	80	251	80
Neighborhood search											
Looked at just this neighborhood	5,900	206	392	1,093	1,219	361	1,705	832	1,242	2,304	1,522
Looked at other neighborhood(s)	6,533	347	148	1,380	1,097	194	1,658	795	1,474	2,546	1,718
Not reported	407	12	10	140	65	22	106	64	63	206	74
Choice of present home[1]											
Financial reasons	4,817	146	285	946	926	159	1,390	606	1,120	1,835	1,256
Room layout/design	3,015	200	55	649	524	163	684	455	669	1,117	774
Kitchen	437	37	18	75	93	20	119	78	123	137	99
Size	2,586	120	78	566	530	97	648	354	611	977	644
Exterior appearance	963	70	35	189	176	55	210	123	189	376	275
Yard/trees/view	1,131	41	34	163	148	59	215	134	266	442	290
Quality of construction	671	88	12	102	100	40	108	97	172	220	183
Only one available	764	10	54	169	129	57	266	107	155	315	187
Other	2,545	115	109	412	421	161	655	338	485	964	757
Not reported	540	14	25	169	84	22	151	82	95	276	87
Main reason for choice of present home											
All reported reasons equal	1,448	80	55	259	240	89	355	244	343	510	351
Financial reasons	3,846	105	241	770	771	115	1,160	479	902	1,470	995
Room layout/design	1,743	129	27	404	304	81	418	247	367	682	448
Kitchen	65	5	–	15	15	6	21	9	16	16	24
Size	1,398	55	35	328	328	36	359	184	317	577	320
Exterior appearance	350	27	13	76	71	20	82	43	60	150	97
Yard/trees/view	412	13	20	53	54	24	83	30	104	170	108
Quality of construction	231	27	–	41	43	2	47	29	51	82	68
Only one available	608	5	42	135	108	46	214	78	117	253	161
Other	2,198	104	92	363	364	137	578	266	407	871	655
Not reported	540	14	25	169	84	22	151	82	95	276	87
Home search											
Now in house	4,200	191	X	829	704	119	963	429	838	1,845	1,087
Did not look at apartments	2,888	138	X	543	473	98	638	235	561	1,302	790
Looked at apartments too	1,162	50	X	235	213	20	295	162	250	486	263
Search not reported	150	3	X	51	17	1	29	32	27	57	34
Now in manufactured/mobile home	551	4	551	58	112	9	229	19	89	332	111
Did not look at apartments	360	–	360	41	85	6	143	9	37	234	80
Looked at apartments too	181	4	181	17	27	3	86	10	52	88	32
Search not reported	10	–	10	–	–	–	–	–	–	10	–
Now in apartment	8,090	369	X	1,725	1,565	449	2,277	1,242	1,853	2,879	2,116
Did not look at houses	5,726	233	X	1,177	1,123	391	1,614	911	1,405	1,983	1,427
Looked at houses too	2,056	127	X	451	392	35	566	287	400	754	616
Search not reported	308	9	X	96	51	23	97	44	48	142	73
Recent mover comparison to previous home											
Better home	6,192	365	235	1,330	1,228	276	1,718	810	1,359	2,460	1,563
Worse home	2,676	63	129	466	394	90	718	371	597	961	746
About the same	3,498	120	171	683	699	189	909	442	743	1,398	915
Not reported	474	16	16	134	61	23	124	67	79	237	90
Recent mover comparison to previous neighborhood											
Better neighborhood	4,953	246	260	1,067	994	226	1,372	601	1,053	2,001	1,298
Worse neighborhood	1,955	62	49	389	280	46	568	275	431	731	519
About the same	4,916	228	207	922	921	243	1,260	650	1,112	1,885	1,268
Same neighborhood	520	14	18	92	127	34	134	88	94	189	149
Not reported	496	15	16	142	60	28	134	76	89	250	81

– = Zero or rounds to zero.
X = Not applicable.
[1] = Figures may not add to total because more than one category may apply to a unit.

Source: U.S. Census Bureau, American Housing Survey

Table 1-16. Income Characteristics, Occupied Units, 2009

[Numbers in thousands, except as noted.]

Characteristics	Total occupied units	Tenure		Housing unit characteristics		Household characteristics				Regions			
		Owner	Renter	New construction 4 years	Manufactured/ mobile homes	Black alone	Hispanic	Elderly (65 years or over)	Below poverty level	Northeast	Midwest	South	West
Total	111,806	76,428	35,378	4,771	6,839	13,993	12,739	23,095	15,739	20,451	25,368	41,586	24,401
Household income													
Less than $5,000	5,849	2,539	3,310	152	446	1,553	726	1,661	5,849	1,080	1,244	2,430	1,094
$5,000 to $9,999	4,683	1,884	2,799	117	445	1,123	585	1,653	4,683	843	1,141	1,898	801
$10,000 to $14,999	5,963	2,788	3,175	74	594	1,101	782	2,554	2,861	973	1,400	2,434	1,157
$15,000 to $19,999	6,062	3,123	2,940	183	644	1,014	884	2,334	1,106	1,046	1,281	2,598	1,137
$20,000 to $24,999	5,961	3,110	2,850	147	650	1,012	973	1,918	685	985	1,450	2,386	1,140
$25,000 to $29,999	7,637	4,507	3,131	214	585	1,193	1,133	2,374	448	1,421	1,641	3,097	1,479
$30,000 to $34,999	5,966	3,600	2,366	190	586	881	891	1,424	73	911	1,417	2,403	1,235
$35,000 to $39,999	5,593	3,482	2,111	189	434	650	732	1,344	15	906	1,306	2,274	1,106
$40,000 to $49,999	10,290	6,852	3,438	364	816	1,286	1,317	2,099	19	1,714	2,500	3,894	2,182
$50,000 to $59,999	8,654	6,328	2,326	338	512	882	984	1,401	–	1,473	2,113	3,191	1,877
$60,000 to $79,999	13,780	10,535	3,244	728	593	1,259	1,452	1,740	–	2,442	3,344	4,797	3,197
$80,000 to $99,999	10,073	8,409	1,663	622	269	843	970	967	–	1,859	2,423	3,403	2,388
$100,000 to $119,999	6,840	6,007	833	438	107	495	517	574	–	1,522	1,443	2,182	1,693
$120,000 or more	14,456	13,264	1,192	1,016	159	702	792	1,050	–	3,277	2,665	4,600	3,914
Median (dollars)	47,000	60,000	28,400	70,200	30,000	30,000	37,000	27,000	7,688	50,100	46,309	42,000	53,300
As percent of poverty level:													
Less than 50 percent	7,499	3,138	4,361	208	589	2,038	1,112	1,820	7,499	1,346	1,562	3,140	1,449
50 to 99 percent	8,240	3,267	4,973	161	904	1,826	1,604	2,089	8,240	1,286	1,823	3,555	1,577
100 to 149 percent	10,449	5,456	4,993	261	1,045	1,771	1,859	3,227	X	1,649	2,286	4,341	2,173
150 to 199 percent	10,953	6,692	4,262	402	955	1,653	1,617	3,353	X	2,023	2,485	4,378	2,067
200 percent or more	74,665	57,875	16,790	3,740	3,347	6,705	6,547	12,605	X	14,147	17,212	26,172	17,133
Income of families and primary individuals													
Less than $5,000	6,728	2,714	4,014	171	495	1,661	915	1,687	6,219	1,210	1,415	2,745	1,357
$5,000 to $9,999	5,176	2,024	3,152	121	517	1,176	687	1,690	4,712	898	1,286	2,074	918
$10,000 to $14,999	6,377	2,941	3,436	70	660	1,128	814	2,590	2,679	1,017	1,509	2,577	1,274
$15,000 to $19,999	6,345	3,293	3,053	186	675	1,040	958	2,373	1,008	1,109	1,346	2,713	1,178
$20,000 to $24,999	6,310	3,204	3,106	180	677	1,024	1,073	1,908	608	1,066	1,534	2,474	1,236
$25,000 to $29,999	7,943	4,725	3,218	241	591	1,206	1,164	2,383	414	1,472	1,734	3,194	1,543
$30,000 to $34,999	6,105	3,710	2,396	205	585	920	843	1,414	72	946	1,464	2,467	1,228
$35,000 to $39,999	5,578	3,567	2,011	187	403	659	710	1,326	10	932	1,271	2,259	1,116
$40,000 to $49,999	10,132	6,985	3,146	409	782	1,222	1,227	2,061	16	1,703	2,465	3,798	2,166
$50,000 to $59,999	8,367	6,278	2,089	339	468	815	949	1,391	–	1,482	2,025	3,039	1,822
$60,000 to $79,999	13,096	10,346	2,751	696	506	1,219	1,346	1,731	–	2,332	3,127	4,596	3,042
$80,000 to $99,999	9,509	8,100	1,409	594	250	798	870	962	–	1,768	2,250	3,204	2,287
$100,000 to $119,999	6,458	5,790	668	426	96	451	474	565	–	1,431	1,369	2,044	1,614
$120,000 or more	13,680	12,751	929	945	134	674	710	1,013	–	3,085	2,574	4,401	3,621
Median (dollars)	44,200	57,000	25,030	65,200	27,084	28,000	34,000	26,500	7,200	48,500	43,842	40,000	50,000
Income sources of families and primary individuals[1]													
Wages and salaries	82,121	56,438	25,683	4,037	4,600	9,915	10,284	6,126	5,880	14,703	18,712	30,465	18,242
Wages and salaries were majority of income	73,826	49,803	24,023	3,691	4,112	9,121	9,612	3,284	5,067	13,335	16,775	27,413	16,304
2 or more people each earned over 20 percent of wages and salaries	14,814	11,622	3,191	687	850	1,445	1,716	1,552	329	2,746	3,450	5,468	3,149
Self-employment	12,966	10,387	2,578	659	550	884	1,154	1,396	917	2,112	2,929	4,487	3,437
Interest	24,637	21,120	3,517	1,062	642	1,092	1,057	7,961	1,128	5,064	6,197	7,993	5,382
Dividends	9,969	8,868	1,100	410	172	364	263	3,362	281	2,029	2,434	3,213	2,293
Rental income	5,613	5,127	487	344	134	333	486	1,470	242	1,110	1,260	1,718	1,525
Social Security or Railroad Retirement	28,043	22,201	5,843	638	2,168	2,919	1,931	20,975	4,501	5,406	6,481	10,649	5,507
Retirement or survivor pensions	15,878	13,755	2,122	453	906	1,465	749	10,550	943	3,073	3,865	5,680	3,260
Supplementary Security Income (SSI)	4,430	2,081	2,350	95	459	1,102	704	1,334	2,095	817	870	1,710	1,033
Child support or alimony	4,272	2,350	1,922	204	242	789	559	158	907	660	1,159	1,649	804
Public assistance or public welfare	2,049	559	1,490	47	210	672	413	236	1,252	434	455	570	589
Food stamp benefits	6,593	1,544	5,050	145	791	2,192	1,220	954	5,071	1,187	1,676	2,728	1,002
Disability payments, workers' compensation, veterans' disability, other disability	5,028	3,421	1,606	191	467	856	454	948	857	968	1,103	1,882	1,074
Other income (VA payments, unemployment, royalty, estates, and more)	7,426	5,056	2,370	322	508	820	704	862	847	1,354	2,159	2,028	1,886
Food stamps													
Income of $25,000 or less	32,692	15,042	17,650	788	3,182	6,353	4,787	10,516	15,397	5,625	7,446	13,352	6,269
Family members received food stamps	6,593	1,544	5,050	145	791	2,192	1,220	954	5,071	1,187	1,676	2,728	1,002
Did not receive food stamps	24,021	12,429	11,592	583	2,280	3,721	3,366	8,993	9,144	4,033	5,394	9,667	4,927
Not reported	2,077	1,069	1,009	60	111	440	200	569	1,183	405	375	956	341

– = Zero or rounds to zero.
X = Not applicable.
[1] = Figures may not add to total because more than one category may apply to a unit.

Source: U.S. Census Bureau, American Housing Survey

Table 1-17. Income Characteristics, Owner-Occupied Units, 2009

[Numbers in thousands, except as noted.]

Characteristics	Total occupied units	Housing unit characteristics		Household characteristics				Regions			
		New construction 4 years	Manufactured/ mobile homes	Black alone	Hispanic	Elderly (65 years and over)	Below poverty level	Northeast	Midwest	South	West
Total	76,428	3,830	5,418	6,547	6,439	18,472	6,405	13,378	18,249	29,193	15,607
Household income											
Less than $5,000	2,539	68	327	404	234	1,058	2,539	369	516	1,147	508
$5,000 to $9,999	1,884	59	280	294	147	952	1,884	286	377	905	316
$10,000 to $14,999	2,788	31	426	382	212	1,679	1,066	393	679	1,320	397
$15,000 to $19,999	3,123	127	491	299	294	1,776	364	514	678	1,410	521
$20,000 to $24,999	3,110	92	468	335	401	1,476	276	490	833	1,305	482
$25,000 to $29,999	4,507	142	458	458	424	2,024	209	794	1,067	1,899	747
$30,000 to $34,999	3,600	117	494	393	437	1,208	47	461	934	1,580	625
$35,000 to $39,999	3,482	132	356	325	353	1,140	10	517	891	1,481	593
$40,000 to $49,999	6,852	268	721	676	645	1,842	11	1,035	1,791	2,783	1,243
$50,000 to $59,999	6,328	283	416	541	573	1,287	–	1,026	1,665	2,453	1,184
$60,000 to $79,999	10,535	636	524	815	938	1,595	–	1,758	2,764	3,775	2,239
$80,000 to $99,999	8,409	538	243	617	700	899	–	1,485	2,163	2,902	1,859
$100,000 to $119,999	6,007	387	87	383	419	540	–	1,290	1,323	1,973	1,421
$120,000 or more	13,264	950	127	625	663	995	–	2,962	2,570	4,260	3,472
Median (dollars)	60,000	78,000	32,000	44,793	50,000	30,400	7,130	68,000	57,000	52,000	70,000
As percent of poverty level:											
Less than 50 percent	3,138	101	399	495	321	1,190	3,138	431	642	1,431	634
50 to 99 percent	3,267	80	610	529	489	1,258	3,267	445	668	1,658	497
100 to 149 percent	5,456	151	776	622	745	2,258	X	729	1,311	2,508	909
150 to 199 percent	6,692	307	772	734	708	2,691	X	1,180	1,620	2,790	1,103
200 percent or more	57,875	3,191	2,861	4,168	4,176	11,074	X	10,594	14,009	20,806	12,465
Income of families and primary individuals											
Less than $5,000	2,714	70	354	407	263	1,081	2,602	402	552	1,211	549
$5,000 to $9,999	2,024	65	318	311	161	977	1,880	298	423	977	327
$10,000 to $14,999	2,941	31	463	389	226	1,711	1,032	412	720	1,367	442
$15,000 to $19,999	3,293	135	518	310	329	1,800	354	539	734	1,473	547
$20,000 to $24,999	3,204	116	484	341	419	1,474	263	516	847	1,319	522
$25,000 to $29,999	4,725	159	467	467	463	2,036	210	831	1,128	1,982	784
$30,000 to $34,999	3,710	123	497	409	416	1,205	49	469	958	1,653	629
$35,000 to $39,999	3,567	132	350	333	358	1,125	8	534	897	1,511	625
$40,000 to $49,999	6,985	321	714	670	640	1,807	7	1,056	1,828	2,808	1,293
$50,000 to $59,999	6,278	284	378	526	577	1,278	–	1,050	1,672	2,385	1,171
$60,000 to $79,999	10,346	604	452	831	929	1,586	–	1,753	2,671	3,707	2,215
$80,000 to $99,999	8,100	500	222	586	649	888	–	1,447	2,045	2,785	1,822
$100,000 to $119,999	5,790	385	85	360	394	539	–	1,237	1,277	1,888	1,388
$120,000 or more	12,751	903	114	607	615	967	–	2,834	2,497	4,128	3,293
Median (dollars)	57,000	75,000	30,001	43,600	48,001	30,000	7,000	65,000	55,000	50,000	66,400
Income sources of families and primary individuals[1]											
Wages and salaries	56,438	3,282	3,598	4,842	5,249	5,198	1,878	9,876	13,768	21,209	11,585
Wages and salaries were majority of income	49,803	2,978	3,161	4,392	4,795	2,713	1,525	8,830	12,169	18,739	10,065
2 or more people each earned over 20 percent of wages and salaries	11,622	621	709	907	939	1,352	116	2,097	2,890	4,350	2,285
Self-employment	10,387	574	472	505	736	1,269	480	1,676	2,495	3,618	2,599
Interest	21,120	957	608	807	827	7,088	770	4,272	5,439	6,979	4,430
Dividends	8,868	383	159	295	221	3,033	206	1,770	2,234	2,874	1,990
Rental income	5,127	329	129	284	430	1,392	200	1,010	1,195	1,558	1,363
Social Security or Railroad Retirement	22,201	518	1,887	1,826	1,326	17,046	2,635	3,962	5,068	8,842	4,328
Retirement or survivor pensions	13,755	398	853	1,108	612	9,121	682	2,505	3,364	5,051	2,836
Supplementary Security Income (SSI)	2,081	68	325	397	303	719	583	299	404	910	468
Child support or alimony	2,350	135	164	258	239	137	213	380	694	848	428
Public assistance or public welfare	559	35	131	117	99	115	196	86	123	194	156
Food stamp benefits	1,544	51	471	365	229	360	1,105	177	388	776	204
Disability payments, workers' compensation, veterans' disability, other disability	3,421	157	400	422	253	753	328	610	784	1,318	709
Other income (VA payments, unemployment, royalty, estates, and more)	5,056	258	365	361	386	728	377	921	1,587	1,360	1,188
Food stamps											
Income of $25,000 or less	15,042	446	2,256	1,867	1,502	7,268	6,197	2,295	3,500	6,744	2,502
Family members received food stamps	1,544	51	471	365	229	360	1,105	177	388	776	204
Did not receive food stamps	12,429	364	1,706	1,368	1,191	6,496	4,497	1,974	2,902	5,444	2,109
Not reported	1,069	31	79	135	82	413	595	145	210	524	190

– = Zero or rounds to zero.
X = Not applicable.
[1] = Figures may not add to total because more than one category may apply to a unit.

Source: U.S. Census Bureau, American Housing Survey

Table 1-18. Income Characteristics, Renter-Occupied Units, 2009

[Numbers in thousands, except as noted.]

Characteristics	Total occupied units	Housing unit characteristics		Household characteristics				Regions			
		New construction 4 years	Manufactured/ mobile homes	Black alone	Hispanic	Elderly (65 years and over)	Below poverty level	Northeast	Midwest	South	West
Total	35,378	941	1,421	7,446	6,300	4,623	9,334	7,073	7,119	12,392	8,794
Household income											
Less than $5,000	3,310	85	119	1,148	492	603	3,310	711	729	1,283	586
$5,000 to $9,999	2,799	57	164	829	438	701	2,799	557	763	993	486
$10,000 to $14,999	3,175	42	168	719	570	875	1,795	580	721	1,115	760
$15,000 to $19,999	2,940	56	153	715	590	558	742	532	603	1,188	616
$20,000 to $24,999	2,850	55	182	677	572	442	409	495	617	1,080	658
$25,000 to $29,999	3,131	72	126	734	710	351	239	626	574	1,198	733
$30,000 to $34,999	2,366	73	92	488	453	216	26	450	483	823	610
$35,000 to $39,999	2,111	57	79	325	379	204	5	389	415	793	513
$40,000 to $49,999	3,438	96	96	610	672	257	9	679	710	1,111	939
$50,000 to $59,999	2,326	55	96	342	412	115	–	448	449	737	693
$60,000 to $79,999	3,244	93	68	444	515	145	–	684	581	1,022	958
$80,000 to $99,999	1,663	84	26	226	270	68	–	374	260	501	528
$100,000 to $119,999	833	51	21	113	98	34	–	231	120	209	272
$120,000 or more	1,192	66	32	76	129	55	–	315	94	340	442
Median (dollars)	28,400	37,000	23,000	21,280	27,000	15,744	8,000	30,000	25,200	25,670	34,000
As percent of poverty level:											
Less than 50 percent	4,361	107	190	1,543	791	630	4,361	916	920	1,709	816
50 to 99 percent	4,973	80	294	1,298	1,115	832	4,973	841	1,155	1,896	1,081
100 to 149 percent	4,993	109	269	1,149	1,114	969	X	920	975	1,833	1,264
150 to 199 percent	4,262	95	183	919	909	662	X	843	865	1,588	965
200 percent or more	16,790	549	486	2,538	2,371	1,531	X	3,553	3,203	5,366	4,668
Income of families and primary individuals											
Less than $5,000	4,014	101	141	1,254	652	606	3,618	808	864	1,534	808
$5,000 to $9,999	3,152	56	199	865	526	714	2,832	601	863	1,097	591
$10,000 to $14,999	3,436	38	198	740	587	879	1,647	606	788	1,211	832
$15,000 to $19,999	3,053	51	157	730	629	574	654	570	612	1,240	630
$20,000 to $24,999	3,106	63	193	683	653	435	345	550	687	1,155	714
$25,000 to $29,999	3,218	82	123	739	701	346	204	641	606	1,212	759
$30,000 to $34,999	2,396	82	88	511	427	209	23	477	506	814	599
$35,000 to $39,999	2,011	56	53	326	352	201	2	398	374	748	491
$40,000 to $49,999	3,146	87	67	552	587	255	9	647	636	990	873
$50,000 to $59,999	2,089	54	90	289	372	113	–	432	353	654	651
$60,000 to $79,999	2,751	92	54	388	417	145	–	578	456	889	828
$80,000 to $99,999	1,409	94	27	212	221	75	–	321	204	419	465
$100,000 to $119,999	668	41	11	91	80	27	–	194	92	156	226
$120,000 or more	929	42	20	67	96	46	–	251	77	273	328
Median (dollars)	25,030	34,000	20,000	20,000	25,000	15,600	7,378	26,100	22,800	24,400	30,000
Income sources of families and primary individuals[1]											
Wages and salaries	25,683	755	1,002	5,073	5,035	928	4,002	4,827	4,944	9,255	6,656
Wages and salaries were majority of income	24,023	712	951	4,728	4,817	571	3,542	4,504	4,606	8,674	6,239
2 or more people each earned over 20 percent of wages and salaries	3,191	66	141	538	777	200	213	649	560	1,118	864
Self-employment	2,578	85	79	380	418	127	436	436	434	870	838
Interest	3,517	105	35	285	230	873	357	792	759	1,015	952
Dividends	1,100	27	14	69	42	329	75	259	200	339	303
Rental income	487	15	5	49	56	78	43	100	65	160	162
Social Security or Railroad Retirement	5,843	121	281	1,093	605	3,929	1,866	1,444	1,413	1,808	1,179
Retirement or survivor pensions	2,122	55	54	357	137	1,430	262	568	501	629	425
Supplementary Security Income (SSI)	2,350	27	133	705	400	615	1,513	518	466	800	565
Child support or alimony	1,922	69	78	532	319	22	695	281	465	800	376
Public assistance or public welfare	1,490	13	79	555	314	121	1,056	348	333	377	433
Food stamp benefits	5,050	94	320	1,827	992	594	3,966	1,010	1,289	1,952	798
Disability payments, workers' compensation, veterans' disability, other disability	1,606	34	67	434	202	195	530	358	319	564	365
Other income (VA payments, unemployment, royalty, estates, and more)	2,370	64	143	460	319	134	470	433	572	667	698

Table 1-18. Income Characteristics, Renter-Occupied Units, 2009—*Continued*

[Numbers in thousands, except as noted.]

Characteristics	Total occupied units	Housing unit characteristics		Household characteristics				Regions			
		New construction 4 years	Manufactured/ mobile homes	Black alone	Hispanic	Elderly (65 years and over)	Below poverty level	Northeast	Midwest	South	West
Food stamps											
Income of $25,000 or less	17,650	341	926	4,486	3,284	3,248	9,201	3,329	3,946	6,608	3,767
Family members received food stamps	5,050	94	320	1,827	992	594	3,966	1,010	1,289	1,952	798
Did not receive food stamps	11,592	219	574	2,353	2,174	2,497	4,647	2,059	2,492	4,223	2,818
Not reported	1,009	28	33	306	119	156	588	261	165	432	150
Rent reductions											
No subsidy	28,706	758	1,311	5,055	5,231	3,097	5,911	5,288	5,734	10,171	7,514
Rent control	529	9	–	75	136	101	99	193	–	25	310
No rent control	28,067	746	1,307	4,967	5,079	2,986	5,796	5,081	5,713	10,096	7,177
Reduced by owner	1,996	38	221	208	250	375	505	401	389	751	455
Not reduced by owner	26,063	708	1,086	4,756	4,827	2,609	5,287	4,674	5,324	9,345	6,720
Owner reduction not reported	8	–	–	2	2	2	4	6	–	–	2
Rent control not reported	110	4	5	13	17	10	16	14	20	49	26
Owned by public housing authority	1,679	20	–	659	250	476	1,005	499	432	499	250
Government subsidy	3,185	117	41	1,233	520	808	1,947	800	677	1,007	700
Other income verification	988	30	22	260	208	163	248	269	162	352	205
Subsidy not reported	820	15	46	240	91	78	223	217	114	363	125

– = Zero or rounds to zero.
X = Not applicable.
[1] = Figures may not add to total because more than one category may apply to a unit.

Source: U.S. Census Bureau, American Housing Survey

Table 1-19. Characteristics of Occupied Housing Units, United States and Puerto Rico, 2010

[Numbers in thousands, percent.]

State/Territory	Population in occupied housing units	Occupied housing units								
					Average household size			Percent		
		Total	Owner	Renter	Total	Owner	Renter	Owner	1-person households	With householder 65 years and over
United States	300,758.2	116,716.3	75,986.1	40,730.2	2.6	2.7	2.4	65.1	26.7	22.1
Alabama	4,663.9	1,883.8	1,312.6	571.2	2.5	2.5	2.4	69.7	27.4	23.3
Alaska	683.9	258.1	162.8	95.3	2.7	2.8	2.5	63.1	25.6	13.7
Arizona	6,252.6	2,381.0	1,571.7	809.3	2.6	2.6	2.6	66.0	26.1	23.5
Arkansas	2,837.0	1,147.1	768.2	378.9	2.5	2.5	2.4	67.0	27.1	24.0
California	36,434.1	12,577.5	7,035.4	5,542.1	2.9	3.0	2.8	55.9	23.3	20.4
Colorado	4,913.3	1,972.9	1,293.1	679.8	2.5	2.6	2.3	65.5	27.9	18.1
Connecticut	3,455.9	1,371.1	925.3	445.8	2.5	2.6	2.3	67.5	27.3	23.4
Delaware	873.5	342.3	246.7	95.6	2.6	2.6	2.5	72.1	25.6	24.1
District of Columbia	561.7	266.7	112.1	154.7	2.1	2.2	2.0	42.0	44.0	18.5
Florida	18,379.6	7,420.8	4,999.0	2,421.8	2.5	2.5	2.5	67.4	27.2	27.7
Georgia	9,434.5	3,585.6	2,354.4	1,231.2	2.6	2.7	2.6	65.7	25.4	18.5
Hawaii	1,317.4	455.3	262.7	192.7	2.9	3.0	2.7	57.7	23.3	24.8
Idaho	1,538.6	579.4	404.9	174.5	2.7	2.7	2.6	69.9	23.8	21.9
Illinois	12,528.9	4,837.0	3,263.6	1,573.3	2.6	2.7	2.4	67.5	27.8	21.6
Indiana	6,296.9	2,502.2	1,748.0	754.2	2.5	2.6	2.3	69.9	26.9	21.9
Iowa	2,948.2	1,221.6	880.6	340.9	2.4	2.5	2.1	72.1	28.4	24.1
Kansas	2,774.0	1,112.1	753.5	358.6	2.5	2.6	2.3	67.8	27.8	22.0
Kentucky	4,213.5	1,720.0	1,181.3	538.7	2.5	2.5	2.3	68.7	27.5	22.4
Louisiana	4,405.9	1,728.4	1,162.3	566.1	2.6	2.6	2.4	67.2	26.9	21.4
Maine	1,292.8	557.2	397.4	159.8	2.3	2.4	2.0	71.3	28.6	24.7
Maryland	5,635.2	2,156.4	1,455.8	700.6	2.6	2.7	2.4	67.5	26.1	20.7
Massachusetts	6,308.7	2,547.1	1,587.2	959.9	2.5	2.7	2.2	62.3	28.7	22.7
Michigan	9,654.6	3,872.5	2,793.3	1,079.2	2.5	2.6	2.3	72.1	27.9	23.4
Minnesota	5,168.5	2,087.2	1,523.9	563.4	2.5	2.6	2.2	73.0	28.0	21.3
Mississippi	2,875.3	1,115.8	777.1	338.7	2.6	2.6	2.5	69.6	26.3	22.8
Missouri	5,814.8	2,375.6	1,633.6	742.0	2.5	2.5	2.3	68.8	28.3	23.1
Montana	960.6	409.6	278.4	131.2	2.4	2.4	2.2	68.0	29.7	23.8
Nebraska	1,775.2	721.1	484.7	236.4	2.5	2.6	2.2	67.2	28.7	22.5
Nevada	2,664.4	1,006.3	591.5	414.8	2.7	2.7	2.6	58.8	25.7	20.2
New Hampshire	1,276.4	519.0	368.3	150.7	2.5	2.6	2.1	71.0	25.6	21.6
New Jersey	8,605.0	3,214.4	2,102.5	1,111.9	2.7	2.8	2.5	65.4	25.2	23.1
New Mexico	2,016.6	791.4	542.1	249.3	2.6	2.6	2.4	68.5	28.0	22.6
New York	18,792.4	7,317.8	3,897.8	3,419.9	2.6	2.7	2.4	53.3	29.1	22.8
North Carolina	9,278.2	3,745.2	2,497.9	1,247.3	2.5	2.5	2.4	66.7	27.0	21.5
North Dakota	647.5	281.2	183.9	97.2	2.3	2.5	2.0	65.4	31.5	22.8
Ohio	11,230.2	4,603.4	3,111.1	1,492.4	2.4	2.5	2.2	67.6	28.9	23.2
Oklahoma	3,639.3	1,460.5	981.8	478.7	2.5	2.5	2.4	67.2	27.5	22.9
Oregon	3,744.4	1,518.9	944.5	574.5	2.5	2.5	2.4	62.2	27.4	22.8
Pennsylvania	12,276.3	5,018.9	3,491.7	1,527.2	2.5	2.6	2.2	69.6	28.6	25.2
Rhode Island	1,009.9	413.6	251.0	162.6	2.4	2.6	2.2	60.7	29.6	23.6
South Carolina	4,486.2	1,801.2	1,248.8	552.4	2.5	2.5	2.5	69.3	26.5	23.1
South Dakota	780.1	322.3	219.6	102.7	2.4	2.5	2.2	68.1	29.4	23.5
Tennessee	6,192.6	2,493.6	1,700.6	793.0	2.5	2.5	2.4	68.2	26.9	22.5
Texas	24,564.4	8,922.9	5,685.4	3,237.6	2.8	2.9	2.5	63.7	24.2	18.4
Utah	2,717.7	877.7	618.1	259.6	3.1	3.2	2.8	70.4	18.7	18.0
Vermont	600.4	256.4	181.4	75.0	2.3	2.5	2.1	70.7	28.2	23.1
Virginia	7,761.2	3,056.1	2,055.2	1,000.9	2.5	2.6	2.4	67.2	26.0	20.6
Washington	6,585.2	2,620.1	1,673.9	946.2	2.5	2.6	2.4	63.9	27.2	20.3
West Virginia	1,803.6	763.8	561.0	202.8	2.4	2.4	2.2	73.4	28.4	26.3
Wisconsin	5,536.8	2,279.8	1,551.6	728.2	2.4	2.6	2.2	68.1	28.2	22.3
Wyoming	549.9	226.9	157.1	69.8	2.4	2.5	2.3	69.2	28.0	20.3
Puerto Rico	3,687.8	1,376.5	986.2	390.4	2.7	2.7	2.6	71.6	23.8	26.3

Source: U.S. Census Bureau, American Community Survey

Table 1-20. Characteristics of Occupied Housing Units, Regions, Divisions, States, and Puerto Rico, 2010

[Numbers in thousands, percent.]

State/Territory	Population in occupied housing units	Occupied housing units								
		Total	Owner	Renter	Average household size			Percent		
					Total	Owner	Renter	Owner	1-person households	With householder 65 years and over
United States	300,758.2	116,716.3	75,986.1	40,730.2	2.58	2.65	2.44	65.1	26.7	22.1
Northeast Region	53,617.9	21,215.4	13,202.6	8,012.9	2.53	2.66	2.32	62.2	28.1	23.5
New England Division	13,944.2	5,664.4	3,710.5	1,953.9	2.46	2.61	2.19	65.5	28.1	23.0
Maine	1,292.8	557.2	397.4	159.8	2.32	2.43	2.04	71.3	28.6	24.7
New Hampshire	1,276.4	519.0	368.3	150.7	2.46	2.59	2.14	71.0	25.6	21.6
Vermont	600.4	256.4	181.4	75.0	2.34	2.45	2.08	70.7	28.2	23.1
Massachusetts	6,308.7	2,547.1	1,587.2	959.9	2.48	2.66	2.18	62.3	28.7	22.7
Rhode Island	1,009.9	413.6	251.0	162.6	2.44	2.59	2.21	60.7	29.6	23.6
Connecticut	3,455.9	1,371.1	925.3	445.8	2.52	2.64	2.27	67.5	27.3	23.4
Middle Atlantic Division	39,673.7	15,551.0	9,492.0	6,059.0	2.55	2.68	2.36	61.0	28.1	23.6
New York	18,792.4	7,317.8	3,897.8	3,419.9	2.57	2.71	2.41	53.3	29.1	22.8
New Jersey	8,605.0	3,214.4	2,102.5	1,111.9	2.68	2.79	2.47	65.4	25.2	23.1
Pennsylvania	12,276.3	5,018.9	3,491.7	1,527.2	2.45	2.57	2.16	69.6	28.6	25.2
Midwest Region	65,155.8	26,216.0	18,147.4	8,068.5	2.49	2.58	2.26	69.2	28.1	22.6
East North Central Division	45,247.3	18,094.8	12,467.6	5,627.3	2.50	2.60	2.29	68.9	28.0	22.5
Ohio	11,230.2	4,603.4	3,111.1	1,492.4	2.44	2.54	2.24	67.6	28.9	23.2
Indiana	6,296.9	2,502.2	1,748.0	754.2	2.52	2.60	2.33	69.9	26.9	21.9
Illinois	12,528.9	4,837.0	3,263.6	1,573.3	2.59	2.69	2.38	67.5	27.8	21.6
Michigan	9,654.6	3,872.5	2,793.3	1,079.2	2.49	2.57	2.29	72.1	27.9	23.4
Wisconsin	5,536.8	2,279.8	1,551.6	728.2	2.43	2.56	2.16	68.1	28.2	22.3
West North Central Division	19,908.4	8,121.1	5,679.9	2,441.2	2.45	2.56	2.20	69.9	28.4	22.6
Minnesota	5,168.5	2,087.2	1,523.9	563.4	2.48	2.59	2.16	73.0	28.0	21.3
Iowa	2,948.2	1,221.6	880.6	340.9	2.41	2.52	2.14	72.1	28.4	24.1
Missouri	5,814.8	2,375.6	1,633.6	742.0	2.45	2.54	2.25	68.8	28.3	23.1
North Dakota	647.5	281.2	183.9	97.2	2.30	2.48	1.96	65.4	31.5	22.8
South Dakota	780.1	322.3	219.6	102.7	2.42	2.53	2.18	68.1	29.4	23.5
Nebraska	1,775.2	721.1	484.7	236.4	2.46	2.58	2.21	67.2	28.7	22.5
Kansas	2,774.0	1,112.1	753.5	358.6	2.49	2.60	2.27	67.8	27.8	22.0
South Region	111,605.8	43,609.9	29,099.9	14,510.0	2.56	2.61	2.46	66.7	26.4	22.0
South Atlantic Division	58,213.7	23,138.0	15,530.8	7,607.2	2.52	2.55	2.45	67.1	26.8	23.1
Delaware	873.5	342.3	246.7	95.6	2.55	2.58	2.48	72.1	25.6	24.1
Maryland	5,635.2	2,156.4	1,455.8	700.6	2.61	2.71	2.42	67.5	26.1	20.7
District of Columbia	561.7	266.7	112.1	154.7	2.11	2.20	2.04	42.0	44.0	18.5
Virginia	7,761.2	3,056.1	2,055.2	1,000.9	2.54	2.60	2.41	67.2	26.0	20.6
West Virginia	1,803.6	763.8	561.0	202.8	2.36	2.43	2.18	73.4	28.4	26.3
North Carolina	9,278.2	3,745.2	2,497.9	1,247.3	2.48	2.52	2.40	66.7	27.0	21.5
South Carolina	4,486.2	1,801.2	1,248.8	552.4	2.49	2.51	2.45	69.3	26.5	23.1
Georgia	9,434.5	3,585.6	2,354.4	1,231.2	2.63	2.67	2.56	65.7	25.4	18.5
Florida	18,379.6	7,420.8	4,999.0	2,421.8	2.48	2.47	2.49	67.4	27.2	27.7
East South Central Division	17,945.4	7,213.1	4,971.5	2,241.6	2.49	2.53	2.38	68.9	27.1	22.7
Kentucky	4,213.5	1,720.0	1,181.3	538.7	2.45	2.51	2.31	68.7	27.5	22.4
Tennessee	6,192.6	2,493.6	1,700.6	793.0	2.48	2.53	2.38	68.2	26.9	22.5
Alabama	4,663.9	1,883.8	1,312.6	571.2	2.48	2.52	2.37	69.7	27.4	23.3
Mississippi	2,875.3	1,115.8	777.1	338.7	2.58	2.60	2.53	69.6	26.3	22.8
West South Central Division	35,446.7	13,258.8	8,597.6	4,661.3	2.67	2.77	2.50	64.8	25.2	19.8
Arkansas	2,837.0	1,147.1	768.2	378.9	2.47	2.51	2.40	67.0	27.1	24.0
Louisiana	4,405.9	1,728.4	1,162.3	566.1	2.55	2.61	2.43	67.2	26.9	21.4
Oklahoma	3,639.3	1,460.5	981.8	478.7	2.49	2.54	2.38	67.2	27.5	22.9
Texas	24,564.4	8,922.9	5,685.4	3,237.6	2.75	2.87	2.54	63.7	24.2	18.4
West Region	70,378.8	25,675.0	15,536.1	10,138.9	2.74	2.79	2.67	60.5	24.8	20.7
Mountain Division	21,613.7	8,245.1	5,456.9	2,788.2	2.62	2.67	2.52	66.2	25.9	20.9
Montana	960.6	409.6	278.4	131.2	2.35	2.42	2.18	68.0	29.7	23.8
Idaho	1,538.6	579.4	404.9	174.5	2.66	2.70	2.56	69.9	23.8	21.9
Wyoming	549.9	226.9	157.1	69.8	2.42	2.50	2.26	69.2	28.0	20.3
Colorado	4,913.3	1,972.9	1,293.1	679.8	2.49	2.57	2.34	65.5	27.9	18.1
New Mexico	2,016.6	791.4	542.1	249.3	2.55	2.60	2.43	68.5	28.0	22.6
Arizona	6,252.6	2,381.0	1,571.7	809.3	2.63	2.63	2.62	66.0	26.1	23.5
Utah	2,717.7	877.7	618.1	259.6	3.10	3.21	2.82	70.4	18.7	18.0
Nevada	2,664.4	1,006.3	591.5	414.8	2.65	2.66	2.63	58.8	25.7	20.2
Pacific Division	48,765.0	17,429.9	10,079.2	7,350.7	2.80	2.85	2.72	57.8	24.3	20.6
Washington	6,585.2	2,620.1	1,673.9	946.2	2.51	2.61	2.35	63.9	27.2	20.3
Oregon	3,744.4	1,518.9	944.5	574.5	2.47	2.53	2.36	62.2	27.4	22.8
California	36,434.1	12,577.5	7,035.4	5,542.1	2.90	2.95	2.83	55.9	23.3	20.4
Alaska	683.9	258.1	162.8	95.3	2.65	2.76	2.47	63.1	25.6	13.7
Hawaii	1,317.4	455.3	262.7	192.7	2.89	3.02	2.72	57.7	23.3	24.8
Puerto Rico	3,687.8	1,376.5	986.2	390.4	2.68	2.70	2.63	71.6	23.8	26.3

Table 1-21. General Occupancy and Racial Characteristics of Housing, United States, 2010

[Numbers in thousands, percent.]

Characteristics	Number	Percent
Occupancy status		
Total housing units	131,704.0	100.0
Occupied housing units	116,716.0	88.6
Vacant housing units	14,988.0	11.4
Tenure		
Occupied housing units	116,716.0	100.0
Owner occupied	75,986.0	65.1
Occupied with a mortgage or loan	52,979.0	45.4
Owned free and clear	23,006.0	19.7
Renter occupied	40,730.0	34.9
Vacancy status		
Vacant housing units	14,988.0	100.0
For rent	4,137.0	27.6
Rented, not occupied	206.0	1.4
For sale only	1,896.0	12.7
Sold, not occupied	421.0	2.8
For seasonal, recreational, or occasional use	4,649.0	31.0
For migratory workers	24.0	0.2
Other vacant	3,652.0	24.4
Tenure by Hispanic or Latino origin of householder by race of householder		
Occupied housing units	116,716.0	100.0
Owner-occupied units	75,986.0	65.1
Not Hispanic or Latino	69,617.0	59.6
White alone	59,483.0	51.0
Black or African American alone	6,156.0	5.3
American Indian and Alaska native alone	434.0	0.4
Asian alone	2,662.0	2.3
Native Hawaiian and Other Pacific Islander alone	57.0	0.0
Some other race alone	72.0	0.1
Two or more races	751.0	0.6
Hispanic or Latino	6,368.0	5.5
White alone	3,962.0	3.4
Black or African American alone	105.0	0.1
American Indian and Alaska native alone	75.0	0.1
Asian alone	26.0	0.0
Native Hawaiian and Other Pacific Islander alone	4.0	0.0
Some other race alone	1,903.0	1.6
Two or more races	290.0	0.2
Renter-occupied units	40,730.0	34.9
Not Hispanic or Latino	33,637.0	28.8
White alone	22,849.0	19.6
Black or African American alone	7,639.0	6.5
American Indian and Alaska native alone	325.0	0.3
Asian alone	1,917.0	1.6
Native Hawaiian and Other Pacific Islander alone	72.0	0.1
Some other race alone	85.0	0.1
Two or more races	748.0	0.6
Hispanic or Latino	7,092.0	6.1
White alone	3,458.0	3.0
Black or African American alone	229.0	0.2
American Indian and Alaska native alone	105.0	0.1
Asian alone	25.0	0.0
Native Hawaiian and Other Pacific Islander alone	9.0	0.0
Some other race alone	2,855.0	2.4
Two or more races	409.0	0.4

Source: U.S. Census Bureau

Table 1-22. Selected Demographic and Housing Characteristics, 2010 American Community Survey, 1-, 3-, and 5-Year Estimates

[Numbers in thousands, percent.]

Characteristics	United States											
	1-year estimates				3-year estimates				5-year-estimates			
	Estimate	Estimate margin of error (+/-)	Percent	Percent margin of error (+/-)	Estimate	Estimate margin of error (+/-)	Percent	Percent margin of error (+/-)	Estimate	Estimate margin of error (+/-)	Percent	Percent margin of error (+/-)
Sex and age												
Total population	309,349.7	*****	100.0	X	306,738.4	*****	100.0	X	303,965.3	*****	100.0	X
Male	152,089.5	27.3	49.2	0.1	150,770.8	10.5	49.2	0.1	149,398.7	6.5	49.1	0.1
Female	157,260.2	27.3	50.8	0.1	155,967.7	10.5	50.8	0.1	154,566.5	6.5	50.9	0.1
Under 5 years	20,133.9	20.6	6.5	0.1	20,204.4	5.9	6.6	0.1	20,131.4	4.3	6.6	0.1
5 to 9 years	20,391.5	54.3	6.6	0.1	20,250.7	27.2	6.6	0.1	20,116.7	25.8	6.6	0.1
10 to 14 years	20,768.3	48.9	6.7	0.1	20,637.9	27.2	6.7	0.1	20,643.7	28.1	6.8	0.1
15 to 19 years	22,104.2	38.0	7.1	0.1	22,219.3	13.9	7.2	0.1	22,132.7	10.0	7.3	0.1
20 to 24 years	21,662.8	39.9	7.0	0.1	21,373.0	16.3	7	0.1	21,214.1	9.0	7.0	0.1
25 to 34 years	40,972.1	42.2	13.2	0.1	40,596.1	13.0	13.2	0.1	40,191.0	8.4	13.2	0.1
35 to 44 years	41,192.3	31.0	13.3	0.1	41,661.2	12.3	13.6	0.1	42,206.1	7.4	13.9	0.1
45 to 54 years	44,929.0	32.0	14.5	0.1	44,753.3	13.9	14.6	0.1	44,302.7	8.1	14.6	0.1
55 to 59 years	19,682.7	52.6	6.4	0.1	19,171.3	25.8	6.3	0.1	18,817.7	23.6	6.2	0.1
60 to 64 years	17,079.3	53.1	5.5	0.1	16,269.5	26.1	5.3	0.1	15,459.7	23.3	5.1	0.1
65 to 74 years	21,854.0	15.2	7.1	0.1	21,199.5	6.5	6.9	0.1	20,493.5	4.0	6.7	0.1
75 to 84 years	13,019.1	30.8	4.2	0.1	13,039.9	17.5	4.3	0.1	13,079.8	11.9	4.3	0.1
85 years and over	5,560.4	29.3	1.8	0.1	5,362.3	16.4	1.7	0.1	5,176.1	11.3	1.7	0.1
Median age	37.2	0.1	X	X	37.0	0.1	X	X	36.9	0.0	X	X
18 years and over	235,184.3	32.0	76.0	0.1	232,605.9	12.0	75.8	0.1	229,932.2	8.5	75.6	0.1
21 years and over	221,221.9	80.7	71.5	0.1	218,808.1	32.3	71.3	0.1	216,369.6	27.0	71.2	0.1
62 years and over	50,290.3	47.9	16.3	0.1	48,645.7	22.0	15.9	0.1	47,432.2	17.4	15.6	0.1
65 years and over	40,433.5	19.5	13.1	0.1	39,601.7	7.1	12.9	0.1	38,749.4	4.3	12.7	0.1
18 years and over	235,184.3	32.0	X	X	232,605.9	12.0	X	X	229,932.2	8.5	X	X
Male	114,105.9	21.4	48.5	0.1	112,839.5	8.9	48.5	0.1	111,508.2	6.4	48.5	0.1
Female	121,078.4	22.3	51.5	0.1	119,766.4	7.8	51.5	0.1	118,423.9	5.6	51.5	0.1
65 years and over	40,433.5	19.5	X	X	39,601.7	7.1	X	X	38,749.4	4.3	X	X
Male	17,433.6	10.9	43.1	0.1	17,010.1	4.0	43	0.1	16,563.1	2.6	42.7	0.1
Female	22,999.9	13.7	56.9	0.1	22,591.6	5.1	57	0.1	22,186.3	2.8	57.3	0.1
Race												
Total population	309,349.7	*****	100.0	X	306,738.4	*****	100.0	X	303,965.3	*****	100.0	X
One race	300,951.3	78.5	97.3	0.1	298,962.6	49.2	97.5	0.1	296,635.9	69.1	97.6	0.1
Two or more races	8,398.4	78.5	2.7	0.1	7,775.9	49.2	2.5	0.1	7,329.4	69.1	2.4	0.1
One race	300,951.3	78.5	97.3	0.1	298,962.6	49.2	97.5	0.1	296,635.9	69.1	97.6	0.1
White	229,397.5	133.3	74.2	0.1	227,877.2	60.3	74.3	0.1	224,895.7	44.8	74.0	0.1
Black or African American	38,874.6	51.6	12.6	0.1	38,463.5	28.0	12.5	0.1	37,978.8	20.4	12.5	0.1
American Indian and Alaska Native	2,553.6	28.6	0.8	0.1	2,508.1	16.0	0.8	0.1	2,480.5	14.3	0.8	0.1
Cherokee tribal grouping	285.5	9.6	0.1	0.1	272.2	5.1	0.1	0.1	282.8	4.6	0.1	0.1
Chippewa tribal grouping	115.9	5.7	0.0	0.1	114.7	3.1	0	0.1	115.0	2.3	0.0	0.1
Navajo tribal grouping	308.0	10.3	0.1	0.1	303.2	5.1	0.1	0.1	298.2	4.1	0.1	0.1
Sioux tribal grouping	131.0	5.8	0.0	0.1	123.0	3.2	0	0.1	119.2	2.5	0.0	0.1
Asian	14,728.3	30.2	4.8	0.1	14,537.1	20.5	4.7	0.1	14,185.5	18.5	4.7	0.1
Asian Indian	2,765.2	35.0	0.9	0.1	2,757.4	21.9	0.9	0.1	2,713.8	18.3	0.9	0.1
Chinese	3,456.9	45.4	1.1	0.1	3,371.5	22.6	1.1	0.1	3,294.6	18.4	1.1	0.1
Filipino	2,512.7	31.1	0.8	0.1	2,569.3	22.9	0.8	0.1	2,523.4	17.9	0.8	0.1
Japanese	774.6	19.3	0.3	0.1	792.2	10.8	0.3	0.1	817.1	10.1	0.3	0.1
Korean	1,456.1	33.1	0.5	0.1	1,420.3	17.5	0.5	0.1	1,399.6	14.3	0.5	0.1
Vietnamese	1,625.4	33.8	0.5	0.1	1,557.4	19.8	0.5	0.1	1,547.9	16.0	0.5	0.1
Other Asian	2,137.5	45.5	0.7	0.1	2,069.0	24.8	0.7	0.1	1,889.1	18.6	0.6	0.1
Native Hawaiian and Other Pacific Islander	507.9	9.5	0.2	0.1	500.4	5.6	0.2	0.1	491.7	4.7	0.2	0.1
Native Hawaiian	157.0	9.4	0.1	0.1	157.2	4.6	0.1	0.1	158.2	4.2	0.1	0.1
Guamanian or Chamorro	72.8	6.2	0.0	0.1	66.8	3.7	0	0.1	77.0	3.6	0.0	0.1
Samoan	114.8	9.7	0.0	0.1	111.6	5.5	0	0.1	96.4	4.6	0.0	0.1
Other Pacific Islander	163.3	11.6	0.1	0.1	164.8	6.3	0.1	0.1	160.1	4.8	0.1	0.1
Some other race	14,889.4	118.7	4.8	0.1	15,076.3	62.7	4.9	0.1	16,603.8	63.8	5.5	0.1
Two or more races	8,398.4	78.5	2.7	0.1	7,775.9	49.2	2.5	0.1	7,329.4	69.1	2.4	0.1
White and Black or African American	2,028.5	36.4	0.7	0.1	1,870.6	20.6	0.6	0.1	1,677.2	18.6	0.6	0.1
White and American Indian and Alaska Native	1,705.5	23.2	0.6	0.1	1,718.5	11.7	0.6	0.1	1,627.9	9.8	0.5	0.1
White and Asian	1,558.9	28.7	0.5	0.1	1,411.0	19.1	0.5	0.1	1,302.3	19.7	0.4	0.1
Black and African American and American Indian and Alaska Native	289.3	14.5	0.1	0.1	283.4	7.8	0.1	0.1	273.5	5.9	0.1	0.1

Table 1-22. Selected Demographic and Housing Characteristics, 2010 American Community Survey, 1-, 3-, and 5-Year Estimates—*Continued*

[Numbers in thousands, percent.]

Characteristics	United States											
	1-year estimates				3-year estimates				5-year-estimates			
	Estimate	Estimate margin of error (+/-)	Percent	Percent margin of error (+/-)	Estimate	Estimate margin of error (+/-)	Percent	Percent margin of error (+/-)	Estimate	Estimate margin of error (+/-)	Percent	Percent margin of error (+/-)
Race alone or in combination with one or more other races												
Total population	309,349.7	*****	100.0	X	306,738.4	*****	100.0	X	303,965.3	*****	100.0	X
White	236,475.2	140.7	76.4	0.1	234,547.2	71.8	76.5	0.1	231,170.2	69.2	76.1	0.1
Black or African American	42,042.7	47.3	13.6	0.1	41,370.7	21.2	13.5	0.1	40,633.1	18.4	13.4	0.1
American Indian and Alaska Native	5,066.8	40.2	1.6	0.1	4,951.7	20.8	1.6	0.1	4,787.4	18.7	1.6	0.1
Asian	17,242.3	27.3	5.6	0.1	16,714.9	12.7	5.4	0.1	16,198.6	14.5	5.3	0.1
Native Hawaiian and Other Pacific Islander	1,167.1	20.7	0.4	0.1	1,018.3	9.7	0.3	0.1	973.3	7.4	0.3	0.1
Some other race	16,534.5	126.5	5.3	0.1	16,580.1	61.3	5.4	0.1	18,134.0	51.0	6.0	0.1
Hispanic or Latino and race												
Total population	309,349.7	*****	100.0	X	306,738.4	*****	100.0	X	303,965.3	*****	100.0	X
Hispanic or Latino (of any race)	50,740.1	10.7	16.4	0.1	49,276.2	3.0	16.1	0.1	47,727.5	2.7	15.7	0.1
Mexican	32,929.7	77.0	10.6	0.1	32,037.8	44.2	10.4	0.1	30,731.9	49.7	10.1	0.1
Puerto Rican	4,691.9	57.3	1.5	0.1	4,591.3	31.2	1.5	0.1	4,455.1	25.5	1.5	0.1
Cuban	1,873.6	36.7	0.6	0.1	1,758.3	20.9	0.6	0.1	1,690.1	14.0	0.6	0.1
Other Hispanic or Latino	11,244.9	86.8	3.6	0.1	10,888.7	49.1	3.5	0.1	10,850.4	44.8	3.6	0.1
Not Hispanic or Latino	258,609.6	10.7	83.6	0.1	257,462.2	3.0	83.9	0.1	256,237.7	2.7	84.3	0.1
White alone	196,929.4	20.4	63.7	0.1	196,747.1	12.4	64.1	0.1	196,572.8	9.8	64.7	0.1
Black or African American alone	37,897.5	47.3	12.3	0.1	37,504.5	25.6	12.2	0.1	37,122.4	23.6	12.2	0.1
American Indian and Alaska Native alone	2,074.5	18.4	0.7	0.1	2,032.2	10.3	0.7	0.1	2,048.8	7.9	0.7	0.1
Asian alone	14,566.3	30.8	4.7	0.1	14,381.2	20.5	4.7	0.1	14,022.0	20.4	4.6	0.1
Native Hawaiian and Other Pacific Islander alone	474.8	9.5	0.2	0.1	470.8	5.2	0.2	0.1	458.8	4.2	0.2	0.1
Some other race alone	558.2	23.0	0.2	0.1	643.5	13.4	0.2	0.1	685.7	11.0	0.2	0.1
Two or more races	6,108.9	55.2	2.0	0.1	5,682.9	35.2	1.9	0.1	5,327.3	40.5	1.8	0.1
Two races including "some other race"	303.4	14.5	0.1	0.1	258.9	6.8	0.1	0.1	248.6	6.1	0.1	0.1
Two races excluding "some other race"	5,805.5	53.0	1.9	0.1	5,424.0	33.9	1.8	0.1	5,078.7	36.9	1.7	0.1
Total housing units	131,791.1	5.7	X	X	131,210.6	6.1	X	X	130,038.1	11.2	X	X

X = Not applicable.
***** = Estimate is controlled. A statistical test for sampling variability is not appropriate.

Source: U.S. Census Bureau, American Community Survey

Table 1-23. Race, Hispanic or Latino, Age, and Housing Occupancy, 2010 Census National Summary File of Redistricting, 2010

[Numbers in thousands, percent.]

Characteristics	Total		18 years and over	
	Number	Percent	Number	Percent
Population				
Total population	308,745.5	100.0	234,564.1	100.0
Race				
One race	299,736.5	97.1	229,723.4	97.9
White	223,553.3	72.4	175,134.9	74.7
Black or African American	38,929.3	12.6	28,088.0	12.0
American Indian and Alaska Native	2,932.2	0.9	2,043.9	0.9
Asian	14,674.3	4.8	11,422.6	4.9
Native Hawaiian and Other Pacific Islander	540.0	0.2	382.4	0.2
Some other race	19,107.4	6.2	12,651.6	5.4
Two or more races	9,009.1	2.9	4,840.7	2.1
Hispanic or Latino and race				
Hispanic or Latino (of any race)	50,477.6	16.3	33,346.7	14.2
Not Hispanic or Latino	258,267.9	83.7	201,217.4	85.8
One race	252,301.5	81.7	198,040.5	84.4
White	196,817.6	63.7	157,101.0	67.0
Black or African American	37,685.8	12.2	27,323.7	11.6
American Indian and Alaska Native	2,247.1	0.7	1,599.8	0.7
Asian	14,465.1	4.7	11,289.0	4.8
Native Hawaiian and Other Pacific Islander	481.6	0.2	346.0	0.1
Some other race	604.3	0.2	381.0	0.2
Two or more races	5,966.5	1.9	3,176.9	1.4
Housing units				
Total housing units	131,704.7	100.0	X	X
Occupancy status				
Occupied housing units	116,716.3	88.6	X	X
Vacant housing units	14,988.4	11.4	X	X

X = Not applicable.

Source: U.S. Census Bureau, 2010 Census

Table 1-24. General Housing Characteristics, United States and Puerto Rico, 2010

[Numbers in thousands, percent.]

State and territory	Total housing units	Occupied housing units	Vacant housing units				Vacancy rate	
			Total	Percent			Homeowner[1]	Rental[2]
				For sale	For rent	Seasonal, recreational, or occasional use		
United States	131,704.7	116,716.3	14,988.4	12.7	27.6	31.0	2.4	9.2
Alabama	2,171.9	1,883.8	288.1	12.5	27.5	22.2	2.6	12.1
Alaska	307.0	258.1	48.9	5.9	13.8	57.0	1.7	6.6
Arizona	2,844.5	2,381.0	463.5	13.9	26.0	39.8	3.9	12.9
Arkansas	1,316.3	1,147.1	169.2	10.9	27.4	22.5	2.3	10.9
California	13,680.1	12,577.5	1,102.6	14.0	34.0	27.5	2.1	6.3
Colorado	2,212.9	1,972.9	240.0	13.6	24.0	42.5	2.5	7.8
Connecticut	1,487.9	1,371.1	116.8	13.3	34.2	25.4	1.6	8.2
Delaware	405.9	342.3	63.6	9.4	17.9	56.5	2.4	10.6
District of Columbia	296.7	266.7	30.0	13.1	44.6	11.8	3.4	7.9
Florida	8,989.6	7,420.8	1,568.8	12.6	23.7	41.9	3.8	13.2
Georgia	4,088.8	3,585.6	503.2	16.7	34.7	16.2	3.4	12.3
Hawaii	519.5	455.3	64.2	6.7	25.6	46.9	1.6	7.8
Idaho	667.8	579.4	88.4	14.5	18.5	47.1	3.1	8.5
Illinois	5,296.7	4,837.0	459.7	18.0	34.6	10.3	2.5	9.1
Indiana	2,795.5	2,502.2	293.4	15.8	31.7	15.5	2.6	10.9
Iowa	1,336.4	1,221.6	114.8	16.0	27.7	18.3	2.0	8.5
Kansas	1,233.2	1,112.1	121.1	13.4	33.4	10.5	2.1	10.1
Kentucky	1,927.2	1,720.0	207.2	13.2	27.5	18.6	2.2	9.5
Louisiana	1,965.0	1,728.4	236.6	9.1	28.3	17.9	1.8	10.5
Maine	721.8	557.2	164.6	5.9	9.6	71.9	2.4	8.9
Maryland	2,378.8	2,156.4	222.4	14.8	27.8	25.1	2.2	8.1
Massachusetts	2,808.3	2,547.1	261.2	9.6	25.5	44.3	1.5	6.5
Michigan	4,532.2	3,872.5	659.7	11.7	21.5	39.9	2.7	11.5
Minnesota	2,347.2	2,087.2	260.0	11.8	18.5	50.2	2.0	7.8
Mississippi	1,274.7	1,115.8	159.0	10.6	28.1	18.2	2.1	11.6
Missouri	2,712.7	2,375.6	337.1	13.1	27.6	23.8	2.6	11.1
Montana	482.8	409.6	73.2	8.1	13.8	52.6	2.1	7.1
Nebraska	796.8	721.1	75.7	12.1	32.3	18.3	1.8	9.3
Nevada	1,173.8	1,006.3	167.6	19.7	37.0	19.5	5.2	13.0
New Hampshire	614.8	519.0	95.8	7.9	13.9	66.7	2.0	8.1
New Jersey	3,553.6	3,214.4	339.2	11.6	27.2	39.8	1.8	7.6
New Mexico	901.4	791.4	110.0	10.0	20.1	33.3	2.0	8.1
New York	8,108.1	7,317.8	790.3	9.8	25.3	36.6	1.9	5.5
North Carolina	4,327.5	3,745.2	582.4	12.3	26.9	32.9	2.8	11.1
North Dakota	317.5	281.2	36.3	7.5	20.4	31.6	1.5	7.1
Ohio	5,127.5	4,603.4	524.1	14.9	35.1	11.2	2.4	10.9
Oklahoma	1,664.4	1,460.5	203.9	11.1	29.1	17.3	2.2	11.0
Oregon	1,675.6	1,518.9	156.6	15.4	25.7	35.4	2.5	6.5
Pennsylvania	5,567.3	5,018.9	548.4	11.8	24.7	29.5	1.8	8.1
Rhode Island	463.4	413.6	49.8	10.4	31.7	34.3	2.0	8.8
South Carolina	2,137.7	1,801.2	336.5	10.9	27.6	33.4	2.8	14.3
South Dakota	363.4	322.3	41.2	9.0	25.2	32.3	1.6	9.1
Tennessee	2,812.1	2,493.6	318.6	14.8	30.9	19.1	2.7	11.0
Texas	9,977.4	8,922.9	1,054.5	11.5	37.4	19.8	2.1	10.8
Utah	979.7	877.7	102.0	14.3	19.8	47.0	2.3	7.2
Vermont	322.5	256.4	66.1	5.4	8.5	75.9	1.9	6.9
Virginia	3,364.9	3,056.1	308.9	14.5	26.7	26.1	2.1	7.6
Washington	2,885.7	2,620.1	265.6	15.6	27.2	33.9	2.4	7.0
West Virginia	881.9	763.8	118.1	8.8	16.5	32.4	1.8	8.7
Wisconsin	2,624.4	2,279.8	344.6	9.9	18.4	56.0	2.2	8.0
Wyoming	261.9	226.9	35.0	9.6	20.9	42.6	2.1	9.4
Puerto Rico	1,636.9	1,376.5	260.4	10.8	16.6	22.9	2.8	9.9

[1] = The homeowner vacancy rate is the proportion of the homeowner inventory that is vacant "for sale." It is computed by dividing the number of vacant units "for sale only" by the sum of the owner-occupied units, vacant units that are "for sale only," and vacant units that have been sold but not yet occupied, and then multiplying by 100. This measure is rounded to the nearest tenth.

[2] = The rental vacancy rate is the proportion of the rental inventory that is vacant "for rent." It is computed by dividing the total number of vacant units "for rent" by the sum of the renter-occupied units, vacant units that are "for rent," and vacant units that have been rented but not yet occupied; and then multiplying by 100. This measure is rounded to the nearest tenth

Source: U.S. Census Bureau, 2010 Census

Table 1-25. General Housing Characteristics, States, Regions, and Puerto Rico, 2010

[Numbers in thousands, percent.]

State and region	Total housing units	Occupied housing units	Vacant housing units				Vacancy rate	
			Total	Percent				
				For sale	For rent	Seasonal, recreational, or occasional use	Homeowner[1]	Rental[2]
United States	131,704.7	116,716.3	14,988.4	12.7	27.6	31.0	2.4	9.2
Region and division								
Northeast Region	23,647.6	21,215.4	2,432.2	10.2	24.0	40.3	1.8	6.8
New England Division	6,418.7	5,664.4	754.3	8.8	20.8	52.3	1.8	7.4
Middle Atlantic Division	17,229.0	15,551.0	1,678.0	10.8	25.5	34.9	1.9	6.6
Midwest Region	29,483.6	26,216.0	3,267.7	13.6	27.4	27.3	2.4	10.0
East North Central Division	20,376.4	18,094.8	2,281.5	14.0	28.1	26.6	2.5	10.2
West North Central Division	9,107.3	8,121.1	986.2	12.7	25.9	28.7	2.1	9.4
South Region	49,980.8	43,609.9	6,370.9	12.6	28.7	27.8	2.7	11.1
South Atlantic Division	26,871.9	23,138.0	3,733.8	13.1	26.4	33.7	3.0	11.4
East South Central Division	8,185.9	7,213.1	972.8	13.1	28.7	19.8	2.5	11.0
West South Central Division	14,923.1	13,258.8	1,664.3	11.1	34.1	19.5	2.1	10.8
West Region	28,592.6	25,675.0	2,917.6	13.9	28.3	34.4	2.5	7.5
Mountain Division	9,524.8	8,245.1	1,279.7	13.9	24.7	39.0	3.1	10.1
Pacific Division	19,067.8	17,429.9	1,637.9	13.9	31.1	30.9	2.2	6.5
Division and state								
New England Division	6,418.7	5,664.4	754.3	8.8	20.8	52.3	1.8	7.4
Maine	721.8	557.2	164.6	5.9	9.6	71.9	2.4	8.9
New Hampshire	614.8	519.0	95.8	7.9	13.9	66.7	2.0	8.1
Vermont	322.5	256.4	66.1	5.4	8.5	75.9	1.9	6.9
Massachusetts	2,808.3	2,547.1	261.2	9.6	25.5	44.3	1.5	6.5
Rhode Island	463.4	413.6	49.8	10.4	31.7	34.3	2.0	8.8
Connecticut	1,487.9	1,371.1	116.8	13.3	34.2	25.4	1.6	8.2
Middle Atlantic Division	17,229.0	15,551.0	1,678.0	10.8	25.5	34.9	1.9	6.6
New York	8,108.1	7,317.8	790.3	9.8	25.3	36.6	1.9	5.5
New Jersey	3,553.6	3,214.4	339.2	11.6	27.2	39.8	1.8	7.6
Pennsylvania	5,567.3	5,018.9	548.4	11.8	24.7	29.5	1.8	8.1
East North Central Division	20,376.4	18,094.8	2,281.5	14.0	28.1	26.6	2.5	10.2
Ohio	5,127.5	4,603.4	524.1	14.9	35.1	11.2	2.4	10.9
Indiana	2,795.5	2,502.2	293.4	15.8	31.7	15.5	2.6	10.9
Illinois	5,296.7	4,837.0	459.7	18.0	34.6	10.3	2.5	9.1
Michigan	4,532.2	3,872.5	659.7	11.7	21.5	39.9	2.7	11.5
Wisconsin	2,624.4	2,279.8	344.6	9.9	18.4	56.0	2.2	8.0
West North Central Division	9,107.3	8,121.1	986.2	12.7	25.9	28.7	2.1	9.4
Minnesota	2,347.2	2,087.2	260.0	11.8	18.5	50.2	2.0	7.8
Iowa	1,336.4	1,221.6	114.8	16.0	27.7	18.3	2.0	8.5
Missouri	2,712.7	2,375.6	337.1	13.1	27.6	23.8	2.6	11.1
North Dakota	317.5	281.2	36.3	7.5	20.4	31.6	1.5	7.1
South Dakota	363.4	322.3	41.2	9.0	25.2	32.3	1.6	9.1
Nebraska	796.8	721.1	75.7	12.1	32.3	18.3	1.8	9.3
Kansas	1,233.2	1,112.1	121.1	13.4	33.4	10.5	2.1	10.1
South Atlantic Division	26,871.9	23,138.0	3,733.8	13.1	26.4	33.7	3.0	11.4
Delaware	405.9	342.3	63.6	9.4	17.9	56.5	2.4	10.6
Maryland	2,378.8	2,156.4	222.4	14.8	27.8	25.1	2.2	8.1
District of Columbia	296.7	266.7	30.0	13.1	44.6	11.8	3.4	7.9
Virginia	3,364.9	3,056.1	308.9	14.5	26.7	26.1	2.1	7.6
West Virginia	881.9	763.8	118.1	8.8	16.5	32.4	1.8	8.7
North Carolina	4,327.5	3,745.2	582.4	12.3	26.9	32.9	2.8	11.1
South Carolina	2,137.7	1,801.2	336.5	10.9	27.6	33.4	2.8	14.3
Georgia	4,088.8	3,585.6	503.2	16.7	34.7	16.2	3.4	12.3
Florida	8,989.6	7,420.8	1,568.8	12.6	23.7	41.9	3.8	13.2
East South Central Division	8,185.9	7,213.1	972.8	13.1	28.7	19.8	2.5	11.0
Kentucky	1,927.2	1,720.0	207.2	13.2	27.5	18.6	2.2	9.5
Tennessee	2,812.1	2,493.6	318.6	14.8	30.9	19.1	2.7	11.0
Alabama	2,171.9	1,883.8	288.1	12.5	27.5	22.2	2.6	12.1
Mississippi	1,274.7	1,115.8	159.0	10.6	28.1	18.2	2.1	11.6
West South Central Division	14,923.1	13,258.8	1,664.3	11.1	34.1	19.5	2.1	10.8
Arkansas	1,316.3	1,147.1	169.2	10.9	27.4	22.5	2.3	10.9
Louisiana	1,965.0	1,728.4	236.6	9.1	28.3	17.9	1.8	10.5
Oklahoma	1,664.4	1,460.5	203.9	11.1	29.1	17.3	2.2	11.0
Texas	9,977.4	8,922.9	1,054.5	11.5	37.4	19.8	2.1	10.8

Table 1-25. General Housing Characteristics, States, Regions, and Puerto Rico, 2010—*Continued*

[Numbers in thousands, percent.]

State and region	Total housing units	Occupied housing units	Vacant housing units				Vacancy rate	
			Total	Percent			Homeowner[1]	Rental[2]
				For sale	For rent	Seasonal, recreational, or occasional use		
Mountain Division	9,524.8	8,245.1	1,279.7	13.9	24.7	39.0	3.1	10.1
Montana	482.8	409.6	73.2	8.1	13.8	52.6	2.1	7.1
Idaho	667.8	579.4	88.4	14.5	18.5	47.1	3.1	8.5
Wyoming	261.9	226.9	35.0	9.6	20.9	42.6	2.1	9.4
Colorado	2,212.9	1,972.9	240.0	13.6	24.0	42.5	2.5	7.8
New Mexico	901.4	791.4	110.0	10.0	20.1	33.3	2.0	8.1
Arizona	2,844.5	2,381.0	463.5	13.9	26.0	39.8	3.9	12.9
Utah	979.7	877.7	102.0	14.3	19.8	47.0	2.3	7.2
Nevada	1,173.8	1,006.3	167.6	19.7	37.0	19.5	5.2	13.0
Pacific Division	19,067.8	17,429.9	1,637.9	13.9	31.1	30.9	2.2	6.5
Washington	2,885.7	2,620.1	265.6	15.6	27.2	33.9	2.4	7.0
Oregon	1,675.6	1,518.9	156.6	15.4	25.7	35.4	2.5	6.5
California	13,680.1	12,577.5	1,102.6	14.0	34.0	27.5	2.1	6.3
Alaska	307.0	258.1	48.9	5.9	13.8	57.0	1.7	6.6
Hawaii	519.5	455.3	64.2	6.7	25.6	46.9	1.6	7.8
Puerto Rico	1,636.9	1,376.5	260.4	10.8	16.6	22.9	2.8	9.9

[1] = The homeowner vacancy rate is the proportion of the homeowner inventory that is vacant "for sale." It is computed by dividing the number of vacant units "for sale only" by the sum of the owner-occupied units, vacant units that are "for sale only," and vacant units that have been sold but not yet occupied, and then multiplying by 100. This measure is rounded to the nearest tenth.

[2] = The rental vacancy rate is the proportion of the rental inventory that is vacant "for rent." It is computed by dividing the total number of vacant units "for rent" by the sum of the renter-occupied units, vacant units that are "for rent," and vacant units that have been rented but not yet occupied; and then multiplying by 100. This measure is rounded to the nearest tenth

Source: U.S. Census Bureau, 2010 Census

Table 1-26. Population and Housing Occupancy Status, United States and Puerto Rico, 2010

[Numbers in thousands.]

State and territory	Total population	Housing units		
		Total	Occupied	Vacant
United States	308,745.5	131,704.7	116,716.3	14,988.4
Alabama	4,779.7	2,171.9	1,883.8	288.1
Alaska	710.2	307.0	258.1	48.9
Arizona	6,392.0	2,844.5	2,381.0	463.5
Arkansas	2,915.9	1,316.3	1,147.1	169.2
California	37,254.0	13,680.1	12,577.5	1,102.6
Colorado	5,029.2	2,212.9	1,972.9	240.0
Connecticut	3,574.1	1,487.9	1,371.1	116.8
Delaware	897.9	405.9	342.3	63.6
District of Columbia	601.7	296.7	266.7	30.0
Florida	18,801.3	8,989.6	7,420.8	1,568.8
Georgia	9,687.7	4,088.8	3,585.6	503.2
Hawaii	1,360.3	519.5	455.3	64.2
Idaho	1,567.6	667.8	579.4	88.4
Illinois	12,830.6	5,296.7	4,837.0	459.7
Indiana	6,483.8	2,795.5	2,502.2	293.4
Iowa	3,046.4	1,336.4	1,221.6	114.8
Kansas	2,853.1	1,233.2	1,112.1	121.1
Kentucky	4,339.4	1,927.2	1,720.0	207.2
Louisiana	4,533.4	1,965.0	1,728.4	236.6
Maine	1,328.4	721.8	557.2	164.6
Maryland	5,773.6	2,378.8	2,156.4	222.4
Massachusetts	6,547.6	2,808.3	2,547.1	261.2
Michigan	9,883.6	4,532.2	3,872.5	659.7
Minnesota	5,303.9	2,347.2	2,087.2	260.0
Mississippi	2,967.3	1,274.7	1,115.8	159.0
Missouri	5,988.9	2,712.7	2,375.6	337.1
Montana	989.4	482.8	409.6	73.2
Nebraska	1,826.3	796.8	721.1	75.7
Nevada	2,700.6	1,173.8	1,006.3	167.6
New Hampshire	1,316.5	614.8	519.0	95.8
New Jersey	8,791.9	3,553.6	3,214.4	339.2
New Mexico	2,059.2	901.4	791.4	110.0
New York	19,378.1	8,108.1	7,317.8	790.3
North Carolina	9,535.5	4,327.5	3,745.2	582.4
North Dakota	672.6	317.5	281.2	36.3
Ohio	11,536.5	5,127.5	4,603.4	524.1
Oklahoma	3,751.4	1,664.4	1,460.5	203.9
Oregon	3,831.1	1,675.6	1,518.9	156.6
Pennsylvania	12,702.4	5,567.3	5,018.9	548.4
Rhode Island	1,052.6	463.4	413.6	49.8
South Carolina	4,625.4	2,137.7	1,801.2	336.5
South Dakota	814.2	363.4	322.3	41.2
Tennessee	6,346.1	2,812.1	2,493.6	318.6
Texas	25,145.6	9,977.4	8,922.9	1,054.5
Utah	2,763.9	979.7	877.7	102.0
Vermont	625.7	322.5	256.4	66.1
Virginia	8,001.0	3,364.9	3,056.1	308.9
Washington	6,724.5	2,885.7	2,620.1	265.6
West Virginia	1,853.0	881.9	763.8	118.1
Wisconsin	5,687.0	2,624.4	2,279.8	344.6
Wyoming	563.6	261.9	226.9	35.0
Puerto Rico	3,725.8	1,636.9	1,376.5	260.4

Source: U.S. Census Bureau, 2010 Census

Table 1-27. Population and Housing Occupancy Status, States, Regions, and Puerto Rico, 2010

[Numbers in thousands.]

State and region	Total population	Housing units		
		Total	Occupied	Vacant
United States	308,745.5	131,704.7	116,716.3	14,988.4
Region and division				
Northeast Region	55,317.2	23,647.6	21,215.4	2,432.2
New England Division	14,444.9	6,418.7	5,664.4	754.3
Middle Atlantic Division	40,872.4	17,229.0	15,551.0	1,678.0
Midwest Region	66,927.0	29,483.6	26,216.0	3,267.7
East North Central Division	46,421.6	20,376.4	18,094.8	2,281.5
West North Central Division	20,505.4	9,107.3	8,121.1	986.2
South Region	114,555.7	49,980.8	43,609.9	6,370.9
South Atlantic Division	59,777.0	26,871.9	23,138.0	3,733.8
East South Central Division	18,432.5	8,185.9	7,213.1	972.8
West South Central Division	36,346.2	14,923.1	13,258.8	1,664.3
West Region	71,945.6	28,592.6	25,675.0	2,917.6
Mountain Division	22,065.5	9,524.8	8,245.1	1,279.7
Pacific Division	49,880.1	19,067.8	17,429.9	1,637.9
Division and state				
New England Division	14,444.9	6,418.7	5,664.4	754.3
Maine	1,328.4	721.8	557.2	164.6
New Hampshire	1,316.5	614.8	519.0	95.8
Vermont	625.7	322.5	256.4	66.1
Massachusetts	6,547.6	2,808.3	2,547.1	261.2
Rhode Island	1,052.6	463.4	413.6	49.8
Connecticut	3,574.1	1,487.9	1,371.1	116.8
Middle Atlantic Division	40,872.4	17,229.0	15,551.0	1,678.0
New York	19,378.1	8,108.1	7,317.8	790.3
New Jersey	8,791.9	3,553.6	3,214.4	339.2
Pennsylvania	12,702.4	5,567.3	5,018.9	548.4
East North Central Division	46,421.6	20,376.4	18,094.8	2,281.5
Ohio	11,536.5	5,127.5	4,603.4	524.1
Indiana	6,483.8	2,795.5	2,502.2	293.4
Illinois	12,830.6	5,296.7	4,837.0	459.7
Michigan	9,883.6	4,532.2	3,872.5	659.7
Wisconsin	5,687.0	2,624.4	2,279.8	344.6
West North Central Division	20,505.4	9,107.3	8,121.1	986.2
Minnesota	5,303.9	2,347.2	2,087.2	260.0
Iowa	3,046.4	1,336.4	1,221.6	114.8
Missouri	5,988.9	2,712.7	2,375.6	337.1
North Dakota	672.6	317.5	281.2	36.3
South Dakota	814.2	363.4	322.3	41.2
Nebraska	1,826.3	796.8	721.1	75.7
Kansas	2,853.1	1,233.2	1,112.1	121.1
South Atlantic Division	59,777.0	26,871.9	23,138.0	3,733.8
Delaware	897.9	405.9	342.3	63.6
Maryland	5,773.6	2,378.8	2,156.4	222.4
District of Columbia	601.7	296.7	266.7	30.0
Virginia	8,001.0	3,364.9	3,056.1	308.9
West Virginia	1,853.0	881.9	763.8	118.1
North Carolina	9,535.5	4,327.5	3,745.2	582.4
South Carolina	4,625.4	2,137.7	1,801.2	336.5
Georgia	9,687.7	4,088.8	3,585.6	503.2
Florida	18,801.3	8,989.6	7,420.8	1,568.8
East South Central Division	18,432.5	8,185.9	7,213.1	972.8
Kentucky	4,339.4	1,927.2	1,720.0	207.2
Tennessee	6,346.1	2,812.1	2,493.6	318.6
Alabama	4,779.7	2,171.9	1,883.8	288.1
Mississippi	2,967.3	1,274.7	1,115.8	159.0
West South Central Division	36,346.2	14,923.1	13,258.8	1,664.3
Arkansas	2,915.9	1,316.3	1,147.1	169.2
Louisiana	4,533.4	1,965.0	1,728.4	236.6
Oklahoma	3,751.4	1,664.4	1,460.5	203.9
Texas	25,145.6	9,977.4	8,922.9	1,054.5
Mountain Division	22,065.5	9,524.8	8,245.1	1,279.7
Montana	989.4	482.8	409.6	73.2
Idaho	1,567.6	667.8	579.4	88.4
Wyoming	563.6	261.9	226.9	35.0
Colorado	5,029.2	2,212.9	1,972.9	240.0
New Mexico	2,059.2	901.4	791.4	110.0
Arizona	6,392.0	2,844.5	2,381.0	463.5
Utah	2,763.9	979.7	877.7	102.0
Nevada	2,700.6	1,173.8	1,006.3	167.6
Pacific Division	49,880.1	19,067.8	17,429.9	1,637.9
Washington	6,724.5	2,885.7	2,620.1	265.6
Oregon	3,831.1	1,675.6	1,518.9	156.6
California	37,254.0	13,680.1	12,577.5	1,102.6
Alaska	710.2	307.0	258.1	48.9
Hawaii	1,360.3	519.5	455.3	64.2
Puerto Rico	3,725.8	1,636.9	1,376.5	260.4

Source: U.S. Census Bureau, 2010 Census

Table 1-28. Characteristics of the Group Quarters Population by Group Quarters Type, 2010 American Community Survey, 1-Year Estimates

[Numbers in thousands, percent, dollars.]

Characteristics	United States									
	Total population		Total group quarters population		Adult correctional facilities		Nursing facilities/ skilled nursing facilities		College/university housing	
	Estimate	Margin of error (+/-)	Estimate	Margin of error (+/-)	Estimate	Margin of error (+/-)	Estimate	Margin of error (+/-)	Estimate	Margin of error (+/-)
Total population	309,349.7	*****	7,987.3	*****	2,267.7	5.7	1,502.2	7.1	2,520.1	8,355.0
Sex and age, percent (except where noted)										
Male	49.2	0.1	60.9	0.4	90.7	0.6	33.6	0.7	47.0	0.9
Female	50.8	0.1	39.1	0.4	9.3	0.6	66.4	0.7	53.0	0.9
Under 15 years	19.8	0.1	0.8	0.1	X	X	X	X	X	X
15 to 17 years	4.2	0.1	2.0	0.1	0.4	0.1	X	X	1.3	0.1
18 to 24 years	10.0	0.1	41.0	0.3	18.0	0.4	0.4	0.1	96.3	0.3
25 to 34 years	13.2	0.1	12.7	0.2	32.8	0.5	0.8	0.1	1.7	0.2
35 to 44 years	13.3	0.1	9.7	0.1	24.9	0.4	1.5	0.2	0.2	0.1
45 to 54 years	14.5	0.1	8.7	0.2	17.3	0.3	4.3	0.2	0.2	0.1
55 to 64 years	11.9	0.1	5.5	0.1	5.3	0.2	9.3	0.4	0.2	0.1
65 to 74 years	7.1	0.1	4.0	0.1	1.1	0.1	13.9	0.4	0.0	0.1
75 to 84 years	4.2	0.1	6.5	0.1	0.2	0.1	28.2	0.5	X	X
85 years and over	1.8	0.1	9.1	0.2	0.0	0.1	41.6	0.7	X	X
Under 18 years, total	74,165.4	32.0	221.6	10.3	9.1	1.4	X	X	33.9	3.6
Male	51.2	0.1	67.9	2.5	89.3	3.9	X	X	37.5	4.7
Female	48.8	0.1	32.1	2.5	10.7	3.9	X	X	62.5	4.7
65 years and over, total	40,433.5	19.5	1,564.6	23.5	29.3	2.2	1,257.8	10.9	N	N
Male	43.1	0.1	31.9	0.6	96.5	1.3	29.4	0.6	N	N
Female	56.9	0.1	68.1	0.6	3.5	1.3	70.6	0.6	N	N
Median age (years)	37.2	0.1	29.4	0.2	34.5	0.2	82.7	0.3	19.6	0.1
Race and Hispanic origin or Latino, percent (except where noted)										
One race, total	300,951.3	78.5	7,755.2	7.5	2,187.1	6.6	1,492.3	7.1	2,431.8	9.4
White	76.2	0.1	69.0	0.4	50.8	0.6	83.2	0.6	77.2	0.8
Black or African American	12.9	0.1	22.6	0.4	40.1	0.5	13.4	0.5	12.8	0.7
American Indian and Alaska Native	0.8	0.1	1.2	0.1	2.0	0.2	0.5	0.1	0.4	0.1
Asian	4.9	0.1	3.5	0.2	0.9	0.1	1.5	0.2	7.7	0.4
Native Hawaiian and Other Pacific Islander	0.2	0.1	0.2	0.1	0.2	0.1	0.1	0.1	0.1	0.1
Some other race	4.9	0.1	3.5	0.2	6.0	4.0	1.3	0.2	1.8	0.1
Two or more races, total	8,398.4	78.5	232.2	7.5	80.6	4.0	10.0	1.4	88.3	4.8
Hispanic or Latino (of any race)	16.4	0.1	11.6	0.2	19.8	0.4	4.9	0.3	7.1	0.3
Not Hispanic or Latino	83.6	0.1	88.4	0.2	80.2	0.4	95.1	0.3	92.9	0.3
White alone, Not Hispanic or Latino	63.7	0.1	60.0	0.4	37.0	0.6	79.2	0.6	70.1	0.7
Marital status, percent (except where noted)										
Population 15 years and over, total	248,055.9	35.6	7,922.0	7.3	2,267.7	5.7	1,502.2	7.1	2,520.1	8.4
Now married, except separated	48.8	0.1	10.0	0.2	15.1	0.3	18.4	0.4	0.6	0.1
Widowed	6.0	0.1	11.3	0.2	1.5	0.1	49.3	0.6	0.1	0.1
Divorced	10.9	0.1	9.4	0.1	16.8	0.3	13.2	0.4	0.2	0.1
Separated	2.2	0.1	2.3	0.1	5.1	0.2	1.7	0.1	0.1	0.1
Never married	32.1	0.1	66.9	0.3	61.4	0.5	17.4	0.5	99.0	0.2
School enrollment, percent (except where noted)										
Population 3 years and over enrolled in school, total	82,724.2	89.4	2,992.7	15.8	187.2	7.4	4.3	1.7	2,507.8	9.5
Nursery school through 12th grade	71.7	0.1	10.0	0.3	56.7	1.8	60.2	17.6	0.0	0.1
College or graduate school	28.3	0.1	90.0	0.3	43.3	1.8	39.8	17.6	100.0	0.1
Educational attainment, percent (except where noted)										
Population 25 years and over, total	204,288.9	73.0	4,491.7	23.0	1,849.3	9.6	1,496.6	7.1	59.1	7.9
High school graduate or higher	85.6	0.1	65.7	0.4	64.5	0.6	65.5	0.5	97.6	1.4
Bachelor's degree or higher	28.2	0.1	8.9	0.3	3.2	0.2	10.5	0.4	57.0	5.3
Veteran status, percent (except where noted)										
Civilian population 18 years and over, total	234,137.3	30.0	7,442.4	14.7	2,258.6	5.9	1,502.2	7.1	2,484.6	8.5
Civilian veteran	9.3	0.1	6.6	0.2	6.9	0.3	14.4	0.5	0.3	0.1
Disability status, percent (except where noted)										
Population, total	309,349.7	*****	7,987.3	*****	2,267.7	5.7	1,502.2	7.1	2,520.1	8.4
With a disability	12.4	0.1	35.6	0.3	23.9	0.5	96.0	0.5	3.4	0.2
Population 18 to 64 years, total	194,750.8	26.3	6,201.1	24.3	2,229.3	5.9	244.4	9.5	2,485.6	8.6
With a disability	10.2	0.1	21.2	0.3	23.5	0.5	90.8	2.1	3.4	0.2
No disability	89.8	0.1	78.8	0.3	76.5	0.5	9.2	2.1	96.6	0.2
Population 65 years and over, total	40,433.5	19.5	1,564.6	23.5	29.3	2.2	1,257.9	10.9	N	N
With a disability	38.6	0.1	93.9	0.3	56.4	3.6	97.0	0.2	N	N
Residence 1 year ago, percent (except where noted)										
Population 1 year and over, total	305,628.6	29.8	7,984.5	1.1	2,267.7	5.7	1,502.2	7.1	2,520.1	8.4
Same address	84.6	0.1	51.2	0.5	45.6	0.8	72.5	0.7	41.3	0.9
Different address in the U.S.	14.8	0.1	47.2	0.5	53.9	0.8	27.4	0.7	56.1	0.9
Same county	9.4	0.1	16.1	0.3	19.5	0.8	19.4	0.6	12.1	0.5
Different county	5.4	0.1	31.1	0.4	34.3	0.7	8.0	0.4	44.0	0.9
Same state	3.2	0.1	21.5	0.4	29.7	0.7	6.6	0.3	28.0	0.7
Different state	2.2	0.1	9.6	0.3	4.6	0.2	1.4	0.1	16.0	0.6
Abroad	0.6	0.1	1.5	0.1	0.6	0.1	0.1	0.1	2.6	0.2

Table 1-28. Characteristics of the Group Quarters Population by Group Quarters Type, 2010 American Community Survey, 1-Year Estimates—*Continued*

[Numbers in thousands, percent, dollars.]

Characteristics	United States									
	Total population		Total group quarters population		Adult correctional facilities		Nursing facilities/ skilled nursing facilities		College/university housing	
	Estimate	Margin of error (+/-)	Estimate	Margin of error (+/-)	Estimate	Margin of error (+/-)	Estimate	Margin of error (+/-)	Estimate	Margin of error (+/-)
Place of birth, citizenship status and year of entry, percent (except where noted)										
Population, total	309,349.7	*****	7,987.3	*****	2,267.7	5.7	1,502.2	7.1	2,520.1	8.4
Native population, total	269,393.8	115.2	7,381.6	16.7	2,071.7	7.6	1,411.0	8.0	2,342.9	13.2
Male	49.2	0.1	60.5	0.4	90.3	0.6	33.5	0.7	46.7	0.9
Female	50.8	0.1	39.5	0.4	9.7	0.6	66.5	0.7	53.3	0.9
Foreign-born population, total	39,955.9	115.2	605.7	16.7	196.0	5.8	91.2	4.1	177.2	9.6
Male	49.1	0.1	66.1	1.2	95.2	0.6	34.7	2.2	51.9	2.0
Female	50.9	0.1	33.9	1.2	4.8	0.6	65.3	2.2	48.1	2.0
Naturalized U.S. citizen population, total	17,476.1	81.7	204.1	8.8	28.4	2.4	69.5	3.5	45.6	3.7
Male	45.8	0.1	50.8	1.7	92.1	2.1	31.5	2.2	51.7	3.8
Female	54.2	0.1	49.2	1.7	7.9	2.1	68.5	2.2	48.3	3.8
Not a U.S. citizen, total	22,479.8	120.4	401.7	14.0	167.5	5.5	21.7	2.2	131.6	9.0
Male	51.6	0.1	73.8	1.5	95.7	0.7	45.2	4.7	51.9	2.3
Female	48.4	0.1	26.2	1.5	4.3	0.7	54.8	4.7	48.1	2.3
Entered 2000 or later	34.7	0.2	51.9	1.3	39.5	1.6	40.7	2.6	73.3	2.1
Entered 1990 to 1999	27.2	0.2	21.3	0.9	26.2	1.3	6.4	1.2	25.0	2.2
Entered before 1990	38.1	0.2	26.8	1.1	34.4	1.2	52.9	2.4	1.7	0.6
World region of birth of foreign birth, percent (except where noted)										
Foreign-born population, excluding population born at sea, total	39,955.7	115.1	605.7	16.7	196.0	5.8	91.2	4.1	177.2	9.6
Europe	12.1	0.1	13.7	0.8	3.0	0.4	32.4	2.0	15.6	1.5
Asia	28.2	0.1	26.9	1.2	7.5	0.8	22.4	2.0	52.6	2.3
Latin America	53.1	0.1	49.7	1.3	86.1	1.1	36.4	2.6	15.7	1.6
Other	6.6	0.1	9.7	0.6	3.5	0.5	8.7	1.2	16.1	1.3
Language spoken at home and ability to speak English, percent (except where noted)										
Population 5 years and over, total	289,215.7	20.6	7,975.0	2.9	2,267.7	5.7	1,502.2	7.1	2,520.1	8.4
English only	79.4	0.1	84.9	0.3	79.8	0.3	90.1	0.4	86.5	0.4
Language other than English	20.6	0.1	15.1	0.3	20.2	0.3	9.9	0.4	13.5	0.4
Speak English less than "very well"	8.7	0.1	5.2	0.2	7.6	0.2	5.1	0.3	2.6	0.2
Employment status, percent (except where noted)										
Population 16 years and over, total	243,832.9	46.3	7,895.3	7.4	X	X	X	X	2,520.1	8.4
In labor force	64.4	0.1	20.0	0.3	X	X	X	X	36.7	0.7
Civilian labor force	63.9	0.1	15.9	0.3	X	X	X	X	36.6	0.7
Employed	57.0	0.1	12.9	0.3	X	X	X	X	30.1	0.7
Unemployed	6.9	0.1	3.0	0.1	X	X	X	X	6.5	0.3
Percent of civilian labor force	10.8	0.1	18.9	0.7	X	X	X	X	17.8	0.7
Armed Forces	0.4	0.1	4.1	0.1	X	X	X	X	0.1	0.1
Not in labor force	35.6	0.1	80.0	0.3	X	X	X	X	63.3	0.7
Occupation, percent (except where noted)										
Civilian employed population 16 years and over, total	139,033.9	147.6	1,015.2	25.7	X	X	X	X	758.9	17.6
Management, business, science, and arts occupations	35.9	0.1	24.2	0.9	X	X	X	X	25.8	1.0
Service occupations	18.0	0.1	30.4	1.1	X	X	X	X	32.6	1.1
Sales and office occupations	25.0	0.1	29.5	1.0	X	X	X	X	35.5	1.0
Natural resources, construction, extraction, and maintenance occupations	9.1	0.1	5.8	0.8	X	X	X	X	2.1	0.2
Production, transportation, and material moving occupations	11.9	0.1	10.1	0.6	X	X	X	X	4.0	0.3
Income and benefits in the past 12 months (in 2010 inflation-adjusted dollars)										
Individuals, total	309,349.7	*****	7987.3	*****	2,267.7	5.7	1,520.1	7.1	2,520.1	8.4
Per capita income (dollars)	26,059.0	51	7,624	195	4,750	126	13,457	248	3,707	289
With earnings										
Male, total	83,278,579.0	82,714	2,011,792	29,396	618,447	12,736	12,556	2,967	838,260	20,024
Female, total	75,606,300.0	94,787	1,245,087	24,550	74,278	6,473	7,492	1,278	988,173	21,006
Mean earnings (dollars)										
Male, total	47,877.0	111	11,174	396	13,794	397	18,050	6,744	4,407	151
Female, total	32,087.0	64	5,609	181	10,769	889	17,569	3,121	3,645	90
Median earnings (dollars)										
Male, total	33,276.0	145	5,437	124	7,596	335	7,051	2,022	2,937	75
Female, total	24,157.0	77	3,033	83	6,350	500	9,600	3,753	2500 ^	***
With Food Stamp/SNAP benefits	X	X	546.8	19.9	231.1	9.0	26.0	3.7	25.6	2.8

N = Data for this geographic area cannot be displayed because the number of sample cases is too small.
X = Not applicable.
^ = Either no sample observations or too few sample observations were available to compute an estimate, or a ratio of medians cannot be calculated because one or both of the median estimates falls in the lowest interval or upper interval of an open-ended distribution.
*** = The median falls in the lowest interval or upper interval of an open-ended distribution. A statistical test is not appropriate.
***** = Estimate is controlled. A statistical test for sampling variability is not appropriate.

Source: U.S. Census Bureau, American Community Survey

Table 1-29. Characteristics of the Group Quarters Population by Group Quarters Type, 2010 American Community Survey, 3-Year Estimates

[Numbers in thousands, percent, dollars.]

Characteristics	United States									
	Total population		Total group quarters population		Adult correctional facilities		Nursing facilities/ skilled nursing facilities		College/university housing	
	Estimate	Margin of error (+/-)	Estimate	Margin of error (+/-)	Estimate	Margin of error (+/-)	Estimate	Margin of error (+/-)	Estimate	Margin of error (+/-)
Total population	306,738.4	*****	8,005.7	*****	2,261.9	2.2	1,524.2	1.2	2,509.1	2.1
Sex and age, percent (except where noted)										
Male	49.2	0.1	60.3	0.2	90.6	0.3	32.5	0.4	46.6	0.5
Female	50.8	0.1	39.7	0.2	9.4	0.3	67.5	0.4	53.4	0.5
Under 15 years	19.9	0.1	0.9	0.1	X	X	X	X	X	X
15 to 17 years	4.3	0.1	2.0	0.1	0.5	0.1	X	X	1.5	0.1
18 to 24 years	10.0	0.1	40.6	0.1	18.1	0.2	0.2	0.1	96.1	0.2
25 to 34 years	13.2	0.1	12.6	0.1	32.7	0.2	0.8	0.1	1.9	0.1
35 to 44 years	13.6	0.1	10.1	0.1	25.7	0.2	1.6	0.1	0.2	0.1
45 to 54 years	14.6	0.1	8.8	0.1	17.0	0.2	4.6	0.2	0.2	0.1
55 to 64 years	11.6	0.1	5.2	0.1	5.0	0.1	8.5	0.2	0.1	0.1
65 to 74 years	6.9	0.1	3.9	0.1	1.0	0.1	13.4	0.2	0.0	0.1
75 to 84 years	4.3	0.1	6.6	0.1	0.2	0.1	28.5	0.3	X	X
85 years and over	1.7	0.1	9.4	0.1	0.0	0.1	42.4	0.4	X	X
Under 18 years, total	74,132.6	12.0	232.8	5.8	10.2	0.9	X	X	38.4	3.4
Male	51.2	0.1	65.3	1.4	94.0	1.7	X	X	41.1	4.4
Female	48.8	0.1	34.7	1.4	6.0	1.7	X	X	58.9	4.4
65 years and over, total	39,601.7	7.1	1,586.3	11.2	26.4	1.2	1,284.9	5.5	0.3	0.2
Male	43.0	0.1	30.8	0.3	96.7	0.7	28.4	0.3	30.8	38.3
Female	57.0	0.1	69.2	0.3	3.3	0.7	71.6	0.3	69.2	38.3
Median age (years)	37.0	0.1	29.6	0.2	34.6	0.2	83.0	0.2	19.6	0.1
Race and Hispanic origin or Latino, percent (except where noted)										
One race, total	298,962.6	49.2	7,788.9	5.5	2,186.2	3.7	1,513.6	1.5	2,432.7	4.1
White	76.2	0.1	68.9	0.2	49.5	0.4	83.8	0.3	77.1	0.4
Black or African American	12.9	0.1	22.5	0.2	40.6	0.3	12.8	0.2	12.6	0.4
American Indian and Alaska Native	0.8	0.1	1.1	0.1	2.0	0.1	0.5	0.1	0.5	0.1
Asian	4.9	0.1	3.5	0.1	0.9	0.1	1.5	0.1	7.6	0.2
Native Hawaiian and Other Pacific Islander	0.2	0.1	0.2	0.1	0.2	0.1	0.1	0.1	0.2	0.1
Some other race	5.0	0.1	3.8	0.1	6.8	0.2	1.3	0.1	2.0	0.1
Two or more races, total	7,77.9	49.2	216.8	5.5	75.6	2.6	10.6	0.7	76.4	3.4
Hispanic or Latino (of any race)	16.1	0.1	11.4	0.1	19.7	0.2	4.5	0.1	6.7	0.2
Not Hispanic or Latino	83.9	0.1	88.6	0.1	80.3	0.2	95.5	0.1	93.3	0.2
White alone, Not Hispanic or Latino	64.1	0.1	60.5	0.2	36.6	0.3	80.2	0.3	70.7	0.4
Marital status, percent (except where noted)										
Population 15 years and over, total	245,645.5	13.6	7,936.0	4.9	2,261.9	2.2	1,524.2	1.2	2,509.1	2.1
Now married, except separated	49.6	0.1	10.4	0.1	16.1	0.2	18.1	0.2	0.8	0.1
Widowed	6.1	0.1	11.7	0.1	1.6	0.1	50.3	0.4	0.1	0.1
Divorced	10.7	0.1	9.4	0.1	17.1	0.2	12.5	0.2	0.2	0.1
Separated	2.2	0.1	2.3	0.1	5.2	0.1	1.5	0.1	0.1	0.1
Never married	31.6	0.1	66.1	0.2	60.0	0.3	17.5	0.4	98.9	0.1
School enrollment, percent (except where noted)										
Population 3 years and over enrolled in school, total	81,644.4	56.1	2,978.9	8.3	187.6	4.1	3.6	0.6	2,498.7	2.9
Nursery school through 12th grade	72.6	0.1	10.4	0.2	58.8	1.1	65.0	9.4	0.1	0.1
College or graduate school	27.4	0.1	89.6	0.2	41.2	1.1	35.0	9.4	99.9	0.1
Educational attainment, percent (except where noted)										
Population 25 years and over, total	202,053.2	26.6	4,525.5	11.9	1,842.3	4.1	1,520.6	1.2	59.2	4.0
High school graduate or higher	85.3	0.1	64.6	0.2	63.5	0.3	63.9	0.4	97.4	1.1
Bachelor's degree or higher	28.0	0.1	8.9	0.2	3.2	0.1	10.3	0.2	57.4	2.9
Veteran status, percent (except where noted)										
Civilian population 18 years and over, total	231,412.4	13.0	7,461.0	7,586.0	2,251.7	2.3	1,524.2	1.2	2,469.6	4.1
Civilian veteran	9.6	0.1	6.8	0.1	7.3	0.2	13.5	0.3	0.4	0.1
Disability status, percent (except where noted)										
Population, total	306,738.4	*****	8,005.7	*****	2,261.9	2.2	1,524.2	1.2	2,509.1	2.1
With a disability	12.5	0.1	36.3	0.2	24.6	0.3	96.3	0.2	3.8	0.1
Population 18 to 64 years, total	193,004.2	9.1	6,186.6	12.8	2,225.3	2.5	239.3	5.5	2,470.5	4.1
With a disability	10.3	0.1	21.9	0.2	24.2	0.3	92.8	0.9	3.8	0.1
No disability	89.7	0.1	78.1	0.2	75.8	0.3	7.2	0.9	96.2	0.1
Population 65 years and over, total	39,601.7	7.1	1,586.3	112.3	26.4	1.2	1,284.9	5.5	0.3	0.2
With a disability	39.2	0.1	93.8	0.3	57.4	2.3	97.0	0.2	N	N
Residence one year ago, percent (except where noted)										
Population 1 year and over, total	302,880.3	17.4	8,002.1	0.8	2,261.9	2.2	1,524.2	1.2	2,509.1	2.1
Same address	84.5	0.1	50.0	0.3	43.3	0.4	71.4	0.3	40.8	0.5
Different address in the U.S.	14.9	0.1	48.3	0.3	55.7	0.4	28.5	0.3	56.6	0.5
Same county	9.4	0.1	16.5	0.2	19.8	0.3	20.1	0.3	12.3	0.3
Different county	5.5	0.1	31.8	0.3	35.9	0.3	8.4	0.2	44.3	0.6
Same state	3.2	0.1	21.9	0.2	31.2	0.3	7.1	0.2	27.9	0.4
Different state	2.3	0.1	9.9	0.2	4.8	0.1	1.4	0.1	16.4	0.4
Abroad	0.6	0.1	1.7	0.1	0.9	0.1	0.1	0.1	2.5	0.1

Table 1-29. Characteristics of the Group Quarters Population by Group Quarters Type, 2010 American Community Survey, 3-Year Estimates—*Continued*

[Numbers in thousands, percent, dollars.]

Characteristics	United States									
	Total population		Total group quarters population		Adult correctional facilities		Nursing facilities/ skilled nursing facilities		College/university housing	
	Estimate	Margin of error (+/-)	Estimate	Margin of error (+/-)	Estimate	Margin of error (+/-)	Estimate	Margin of error (+/-)	Estimate	Margin of error (+/-)
Population, total	306,738.4	*****	8,005.7	*****	2,261.9	2.2	1,524,183	1.2	2,509.1	2.1
Native population, total	267,399.2	75.7	7,383.4	10.7	2,063.6	4.8	1,431,376	2.7	2,326.5	4.2
Male	49.1	0.1	59.8	0.2	90.2	0.3	32.4	0.4	46.2	0.6
Female	50.9	0.1	40.2	0.2	9.8	0.3	67.6	0.4	53.8	0.6
Foreign-born population, total	39,339.3	75.7	622.3	10.7	198.3	4.6	92.8	2.5	182.7	3.9
Male	49.2	0.1	66.6	0.6	94.8	0.4	34.3	1.2	51.6	1.2
Female	50.8	0.1	33.4	0.6	5.2	0.4	65.7	1.2	48.4	1.2
Naturalized U.S. citizen population, total	17,054.9	47,263.0	202,300	4,790.0	27,970	1,311.0	72,967	2,358.0	45,035	2,061.0
Male	45.8	0.1	50.4	1.0	90.5	1.4	32.0	1.2	49.7	2.1
Female	54.2	0.1	49.6	1.0	9.5	1.4	68.0	1.2	50.3	2.1
Not a U.S. citizen, total	22,284.4	79,601.0	420,003	9,952.0	170,300	4,374.0	19,840	1,222.0	137,616	3,956.0
Male	51.9	0.1	74.4	0.7	95.5	0.4	42.8	3.9	52.2	1.5
Female	48.1	0.1	25.6	0.7	4.5	0.4	57.2	3.9	47.8	1.5
Entered 2000 or later	32.4	0.1	43.1	0.9	33.1	1.0	16.0	1.2	69.1	1.3
Entered 1990 to 1999	27.8	0.1	23.4	0.5	28.6	0.8	6.7	0.7	27.2	1.2
Entered before 1990	39.8	0.1	33.5	0.7	38.2	1.0	77.3	1.2	3.7	0.5
World region of birth of foreign birth, percent (except where noted)										
Foreign-born population, excluding population born at sea, total	39,339.1	75,677.0	622,303	10,670.0	198,270	4,599.0	92,807	2,451.0	182,651	3,946.0
Europe	12.3	0.1	14.0	0.5	3.3	0.3	34.2	1.3	15.4	0.8
Asia	28.2	0.1	26.4	0.8	7.8	0.4	22.1	1.3	52.1	1.2
Latin America	53.0	0.1	50.3	0.9	85.5	0.6	34.9	1.3	16.9	0.8
Other	6.5	0.1	9.3	0.4	3.5	0.3	8.8	0.8	15.7	0.8
Language spoken at home and ability to speak English, percent (except where noted)										
Population 5 years and over, total	286,534.1	5,846.0	7,991.0	1.9	2,261.9	2.2	1,524.2	1.2	2,509.1	2.1
English only	79.6	0.1	84.7	0.1	79.3	0.2	90.2	0.2	86.4	0.2
Language other than English	20.4	0.1	15.3	0.1	20.7	0.2	9.8	0.2	13.6	0.2
Speak English less than "very well"	8.7	0.1	5.3	0.1	7.7	0.2	5.0	0.2	2.8	0.1
Employment status, percent (except where noted)										
Population 16 years and over, total	241,366.7	18.0	7,909.3	5.0	X	X	X	X	2,509.1	2.1
In labor force	65.1	0.1	20.5	0.2	X	X	X	X	38.2	0.4
Civilian labor force	64.6	0.1	16.5	0.2	X	X	X	X	38.2	0.4
Employed	58.8	0.1	13.7	0.2	X	X	X	X	32.1	0.4
Unemployed	5.8	0.1	2.8	0.1	X	X	X	X	6.1	0.2
Percent of civilian labor force	9.0	0.1	17.2	0.5	X	X	X	X	16.0	0.4
Armed Forces	0.5	0.1	4.0	0.1	X	X	X	X	0.0	0.1
Not in labor force	34.9	0.1	79.5	0.2	X	X	X	X	61.8	0.4
Occupation, percent (except where noted)										
Civilian employed population 16 years and over, total	141,848,097	86.9	1,079.9	14.6	X	X	X	X	804.4	9.5
Management, business, science, and arts occupations	35.6	0.1	23.4	0.5	X	X	X	X	25.0	0.7
Service occupations	17.6	0.1	30.2	0.6	X	X	X	X	32.5	0.7
Sales and office occupations	25.2	0.1	30.3	0.5	X	X	X	X	36.2	0.6
Natural resources, construction, extraction, and maintenance occupations	9.5	0.1	6.4	0.6	X	X	X	X	2.4	0.2
Production, transportation, and material moving occupations	12.1	0.1	9.8	0.4	X	X	X	X	3.9	0.2
Income and benefits in the past 12 months (in 2010 inflation-adjusted dollars)										
Individuals, total	306,738.4	*****	8,005.7	*****	2,261.9	2.2	1,524.2	1.2	2,509.1	2.1
Per capita income (dollars)	26,942	40.0	7,737	102.0	5,392	93.0	13,028	266.0	3,764	131.0
With earnings										
Male, total	85,147.8	54.2	2,123.4	14.9	679.9	8.3	11.3	1.4	869.4	12.0
Female, total	76,821.1	57.2	1,313.1	14.3	83.8	3.2	7.5	0.7	1,041.8	11.5
Mean earnings (dollars)										
Male, total	49,044	76.0	11,430	195.0	14,311	232.0	24,263	11,246.0	4,723	106.0
Female, total	32,054	36.0	5,699	90.0	10,494	479.0	16,532	1,669.0	3,792	50.0
Median earnings (dollars)										
Male, total	34,772	83.0	5,824	87.0	8,593	197.0	8,594	1,659.0	3,214	48.0
Female, total	24,166	36.0	3,258	42.0	6,469	306.0	9,182	2,337.0	2,713	48.0
With Food Stamp/SNAP benefits	X	X	496.5	9.6	194.3	5.0	23.5	1.8	26.0	1.9

N = Data for this geographic area cannot be displayed because the number of sample cases is too small.
X = Not applicable.
**** = Estimate is controlled. A statistical test for sampling variability is not appropriate.

Source: U.S. Census Bureau, American Community Survey

Table 1-30. Characteristics of the Group Quarters Population by Group Quarters Type, 2010 American Community Survey, 5-Year Estimates

[Numbers in thousands, percent, dollars.]

Characteristics	United States									
	Total population		Total group quarters population		Adult correctional facilities		Nursing facilities/ skilled nursing facilities		College/university housing	
	Estimate	Margin of error (+/-)	Estimate	Margin of error (+/-)	Estimate	Margin of error (+/-)	Estimate	Margin of error (+/-)	Estimate	Margin of error (+/-)
Total population	306,738.4	*****	8,005.7	*****	2,261.9	2.2	1,524.2	1.2	2,509.1	2.1
Sex and age, percent (except where noted)										
Male	49.2	0.1	60.3	0.2	90.6	0.3	32.5	0.4	46.6	0.5
Female	50.8	0.1	39.7	0.2	9.4	0.3	67.5	0.4	53.4	0.5
Under 15 years	19.9	0.1	0.9	0.1	X	X	X	X	X	X
15 to 17 years	4.3	0.1	2.0	0.1	0.5	0.1	X	X	1.5	0.1
18 to 24 years	10.0	0.1	40.6	0.1	18.1	0.2	0.2	0.1	96.1	0.2
25 to 34 years	13.2	0.1	12.6	0.1	32.7	0.2	0.8	0.1	1.9	0.1
35 to 44 years	13.6	0.1	10.1	0.1	25.7	0.2	1.6	0.1	0.2	0.1
45 to 54 years	14.6	0.1	8.8	0.1	17.0	0.2	4.6	0.2	0.2	0.1
55 to 64 years	11.6	0.1	5.2	0.1	5.0	0.1	8.5	0.2	0.1	0.1
65 to 74 years	6.9	0.1	3.9	0.1	1.0	0.1	13.4	0.2	0.0	0.1
75 to 84 years	4.3	0.1	6.6	0.1	0.2	0.1	28.5	0.3	X	X
85 years and over	1.7	0.1	9.4	0.1	0.0	0.1	42.4	0.4	X	X
Under 18 years, total	74,132.6	12.0	232.8	5.8	10.2	0.9	X	X	38.4	3.4
Male	51.2	0.1	65.3	1.4	94.0	1.7	X	X	41.1	4.4
Female	48.8	0.1	34.7	1.4	6.0	1.7	X	X	58.9	4.4
65 years and over, total	39,601.7	7.1	1,586.3	11.2	26.4	1.2	1,284.9	5.5	0.3	0.2
Male	43.0	0.1	30.8	0.3	96.7	0.7	28.4	0.3	30.8	38.3
Female	57.0	0.1	69.2	0.3	3.3	0.7	71.6	0.3	69.2	38.3
Median age (years)	37.0	0.1	29.6	0.2	34.6	0.2	83.0	0.2	19.6	0.1
Race and Hispanic origin or Latino, percent (except where noted)										
One race, total	298,962.6	49.2	7,788.9	5.5	2,186.2	3.7	1,513.6	1.5	2,432.7	4.1
White	76.2	0.1	68.9	0.2	49.5	0.4	83.8	0.3	77.1	0.4
Black or African American	12.9	0.1	22.5	0.2	40.6	0.3	12.8	0.2	12.6	0.4
American Indian and Alaska Native	0.8	0.1	1.1	0.1	2.0	0.1	0.5	0.1	0.5	0.1
Asian	4.9	0.1	3.5	0.1	0.9	0.1	1.5	0.1	7.6	0.2
Native Hawaiian and Other Pacific Islander	0.2	0.1	0.2	0.1	0.2	0.1	0.1	0.1	0.2	0.1
Some other race	5.0	0.1	3.8	0.1	6.8	0.2	1.3	0.1	2.0	0.1
Two or more races, total	7,775.9	49.2	216.8	5.5	7.6	2.6	10.6	0.7	76.4	3.4
Hispanic or Latino (of any race)	16.1	0.1	11.4	0.1	19.7	0.2	4.5	0.1	6.7	0.2
Not Hispanic or Latino	83.9	0.1	88.6	0.1	80.3	0.2	95.5	0.1	93.3	0.2
White alone, Not Hispanic or Latino	64.1	0.1	60.5	0.2	36.6	0.3	80.2	0.3	70.7	0.4
Marital status, percent (except where noted)										
Population 15 years and over, total	245,645.5	13.6	7,936.0	4.9	2,261.9	2.2	1,524.2	1.2	2,509.1	2.1
Now married, except separated	49.6	0.1	10.4	0.1	16.1	0.2	18.1	0.2	0.8	0.1
Widowed	6.1	0.1	11.7	0.1	1.6	0.1	50.3	0.4	0.1	0.1
Divorced	10.7	0.1	9.4	0.1	17.1	0.2	12.5	0.2	0.2	0.1
Separated	2.2	0.1	2.3	0.1	5.2	0.1	1.5	0.1	0.1	0.1
Never married	31.6	0.1	66.1	0.2	60.0	0.3	17.5	0.4	98.9	0.1
School enrollment, percent (except where noted)										
Population 3 years and over enrolled in school, total	81,644.4	56.1	2,978.9	8.3	187.6	4.1	3.6	0.6	2,498.7	2.9
Nursery school through 12th grade	72.6	0.1	10.4	0.2	58.8	1.1	65.0	9.4	0.1	0.1
College or graduate school	27.4	0.1	89.6	0.2	41.2	1.1	35.0	9.4	99.9	0.1
Educational attainment, percent (except where noted)										
Population 25 years and over, total	202,053.2	26.6	4,525.5	11.9	1,842.3	4.1	1,520.6	1.2	59.2	4.0
High school graduate or higher	85.3	0.1	64.6	0.2	63.5	0.3	63.9	0.4	97.4	1.1
Bachelor's degree or higher	28.0	0.1	8.9	0.2	3.2	0.1	10.3	0.2	57.4	2.9
Veteran status, percent (except where noted)										
Civilian population 18 years and over, total	231,412.4	13.0	7,461.0	7.6	2,251.7	2.3	1,524.2	1.2	2,469.6	4.1
Civilian veteran	9.6	0.1	6.8	0.1	7.3	0.2	13.5	0.3	0.4	0.1
Disability status, percent (except where noted)										
Population, total	306,738.4	*****	8,005.7	*****	2,261.9	2.2	1,524.2	1.2	2,509.1	2.1
With a disability	12.5	0.1	36.3	0.2	24.6	0.3	96.3	0.2	3.8	0.1
Population 18 to 64 years, total	193,004.2	9.1	6,186.6	12.8	2,225.3	2.5	239.3	5.5	2,470.5	4.1
With a disability	10.3	0.1	21.9	0.2	24.2	0.3	92.8	0.9	3.8	0.1
No disability	89.7	0.1	78.1	0.2	75.8	0.3	7.2	0.9	96.2	0.1
Population 65 years and over, total	39,601.7	7.1	1,586.3	11,233.0	26.4	1.2	1,284.9	5.5	0.3	0.2
With a disability	39.2	0.1	93.8	0.3	57.4	2.3	97.0	0.2	N	N
Residence one year ago, percent (except where noted)										
Population 1 year and over, total	302,880.3	17.4	8,002.1	0.8	2,261.9	2.2	1,524.2	1.2	2,509.1	2.1
Same address	84.5	0.1	50.0	0.3	43.3	0.4	71.4	0.3	40.8	0.5
Different address in the U.S.	14.9	0.1	48.3	0.3	55.7	0.4	28.5	0.3	56.6	0.5
Same county	9.4	0.1	16.5	0.2	19.8	0.3	20.1	0.3	12.3	0.3
Different county	5.5	0.1	31.8	0.3	35.9	0.3	8.4	0.2	44.3	0.6
Same state	3.2	0.1	21.9	0.2	31.2	0.3	7.1	0.2	27.9	0.4
Different state	2.3	0.1	9.9	0.2	4.8	0.1	1.4	0.1	16.4	0.4
Abroad	0.6	0.1	1.7	0.1	0.9	0.1	0.1	0.1	2.5	0.1

Table 1-30. Characteristics of the Group Quarters Population by Group Quarters Type, 2010 American Community Survey, 5-Year Estimates—*Continued*

[Numbers in thousands, percent, dollars.]

Characteristics	United States									
	Total population		Total group quarters population		Adult correctional facilities		Nursing facilities/ skilled nursing facilities		College/university housing	
	Estimate	Margin of error (+/-)	Estimate	Margin of error (+/-)	Estimate	Margin of error (+/-)	Estimate	Margin of error (+/-)	Estimate	Margin of error (+/-)
Population, total	306,738.4	*****	8,005.7	*****	2,261.9	2.2	1,524.2	1.2	2,509.1	2.1
Native population, total	267,399.2	75.7	7,383.4	10.7	2,063.6	4.8	1,431.4	2.7	2,326.5	4.2
Male	49.1	0.1	59.8	0.2	90.2	0.3	32.4	0.4	46.2	0.6
Female	50.9	0.1	40.2	0.2	9.8	0.3	67.6	0.4	53.8	0.6
Foreign-born population, total	39,339.3	75.7	622.3	10.7	198.3	4.6	92.8	2.5	182.7	3.9
Male	49.2	0.1	66.6	0.6	94.8	0.4	34.3	1.2	51.6	1.2
Female	50.8	0.1	33.4	0.6	5.2	0.4	65.7	1.2	48.4	1.2
Naturalized U.S. citizen population, total	17,054.9	47.3	202.3	4.8	28.0	1.3	73.0	2.4	45.0	2.1
Male	45.8	0.1	50.4	1.0	90.5	1.4	32.0	1.2	49.7	2.1
Female	54.2	0.1	49.6	1.0	9.5	1.4	68.0	1.2	50.3	2.1
Not a U.S. citizen, total	22,284.4	79.6	420.0	10.0	170.3	4.4	19.8	1.2	137.6	4.0
Male	51.9	0.1	74.4	0.7	95.5	0.4	42.8	3.9	52.2	1.5
Female	48.1	0.1	25.6	0.7	4.5	0.4	57.2	3.9	47.8	1.5
Entered 2000 or later	32.4	0.1	43.1	0.9	33.1	1.0	16.0	1.2	69.1	1.3
Entered 1990 to 1999	27.8	0.1	23.4	0.5	28.6	0.8	6.7	0.7	27.2	1.2
Entered before 1990	39.8	0.1	33.5	0.7	38.2	1.0	77.3	1.2	3.7	0.5
World region of birth of foreign birth, percent (except where noted)										
Foreign-born population, excluding population born at sea, total	39,339.1	75.7	622.3	10.7	198.3	4.6	92.8	2.5	182.7	3.9
Europe	12.3	0.1	14.0	0.5	3.3	0.3	34.2	1.3	15.4	0.8
Asia	28.2	0.1	26.4	0.8	7.8	0.4	22.1	1.3	52.1	1.2
Latin America	53.0	0.1	50.3	0.9	85.5	0.6	34.9	1.3	16.9	0.8
Other	6.5	0.1	9.3	0.4	3.5	0.3	8.8	0.8	15.7	0.8
Language spoken at home and ability to speak English, percent (except where noted)										
Population 5 years and over, total	286,534.1	5.8	7,991.0	1.9	2,261.9	2.2	1,524.2	1.2	2,509.1	2.1
English only	79.6	0.1	84.7	0.1	79.3	0.2	90.2	0.2	86.4	0.2
Language other than English	20.4	0.1	15.3	0.1	20.7	0.2	9.8	0.2	13.6	0.2
Speak English less than "very well"	8.7	0.1	5.3	0.1	7.7	0.2	5.0	0.2	2.8	0.1
Employment status, percent (except where noted)										
Population 16 years and over, total	241,366.7	18.0	7,909.3	5.0	X	X	X	X	2,509.1	2.1
In labor force	65.1	0.1	20.5	0.2	X	X	X	X	38.2	0.4
Civilian labor force	64.6	0.1	16.5	0.2	X	X	X	X	38.2	0.4
Employed	58.8	0.1	13.7	0.2	X	X	X	X	32.1	0.4
Unemployed	5.8	0.1	2.8	0.1	X	X	X	X	6.1	0.2
Percent of civilian labor force	9.0	0.1	17.2	0.5	X	X	X	X	16.0	0.4
Armed Forces	0.5	0.1	4.0	0.1	X	X	X	X	0.0	0.1
Not in labor force	34.9	0.1	79.5	0.2	X	X	X	X	61.8	0.4
Occupation, percent (except where noted)										
Civilian employed population 16 years and over, total	141,848.1	86.9	1,079.9	14.6	X	X	X	X	804.4	9.5
Management, business, science, and arts occupations	35.6	0.1	23.4	0.5	X	X	X	X	25.0	0.7
Service occupations	17.6	0.1	30.2	0.6	X	X	X	X	32.5	0.7
Sales and office occupations	25.2	0.1	30.3	0.5	X	X	X	X	36.2	0.6
Natural resources, construction, extraction, and maintenance occupations	9.5	0.1	6.4	0.6	X	X	X	X	2.4	0.2
Production, transportation, and material moving occupations	12.1	0.1	9.8	0.4	X	X	X	X	3.9	0.2
Income and benefits in the past 12 months (in 2010 inflation-adjusted dollars)										
Individuals, total	306,738.4	*****	8,005.7	*****	2,261.9	2.2	1,524.2	1.2	2,509.1	2.1
Per capita income (dollars)	26,942	40.0	7,737	102.0	5,392	93.0	13,028	266.0	3,764	131.0
With earnings										
Male, total	85,147.8	54.2	2,123.4	14.9	679.9	8.3	11.3	1.4	869.4	12.0
Female, total	76,821.1	57.2	1,313.1	14.3	83.8	3.2	7.5	0.7	1,041.8	11.5
Mean earnings (dollars)										
Male, total	49,044	76	11,430	195	14,311	232	24,263	11,246	4,723	106
Female, total	32,054	36	5,699	90	10,494	479	16,532	1,669	3,792	50
Median earnings (dollars)										
Male, total	34,772	83	5,824	87	8,593	197	8,594	1,659	3,214	48
Female, total	24,166	36	3,258	42	6,469	306	9,182	2,337	2,713	48
With Food Stamp/SNAP benefits	X	X	496.5	9.6	194.3	5.0	23.5	1.8	26.0	1.9

X = Not applicable.
**** = Estimate is controlled. A statistical test for sampling variability is not appropriate.

Source: U.S. Census Bureau, American Community Survey

Table 1-31. Selected Population Profile of the United States, 2010 American Community Survey, 1-Year Estimates

[Numbers in thousands, percent, except as noted.]

Characteristics	United States	
	Estimate	Margin of error (+/-)
Total number of races reporting		
Total population	309,349.7	*****
One race	97.3	0.1
Two races	2.5	0.1
Three races	0.2	0.1
Four or more races	0.0	0.1
Sex and age		
Total population	309,349.7	*****
Male	49.2	0.1
Female	50.8	0.1
Under 5 years	6.5	0.1
5 to 17 years	17.5	0.1
18 to 24 years	10.0	0.1
25 to 34 years	13.2	0.1
35 to 44 years	13.3	0.1
45 to 54 years	14.5	0.1
55 to 64 years	11.9	0.1
65 to 74 years	7.1	0.1
75 years and over	6.0	0.1
Median age (years)	37.2	0.1
18 years and over	76.0	0.1
21 years and over	71.5	0.1
62 years and over	16.3	0.1
65 years and over	13.1	0.1
Under 18 years	74,165.4	32.0
Male	51.2	0.1
Female	48.8	0.1
18 years and over	235,184.3	32.0
Male	48.5	0.1
Female	51.5	0.1
18 to 34 years	71,867.5	42.9
Male	50.6	0.1
Female	49.4	0.1
35 to 64 years	122,883.3	55.6
Male	49.1	0.1
Female	50.9	0.1
65 years and over	40,433.5	19.5
Male	43.1	0.1
Female	56.9	0.1
Relationship		
Population in households	301,362.4	*****
Householder or spouse	56.5	0.1
Child	30.6	0.1
Other relatives	7.2	0.1
Nonrelatives	5.8	0.1
Unmarried partner	2.3	0.1
Households by type		
Households	114,567.4	163.2
Family households	66.4	0.1
With own children under 18 years	29.7	0.1
Married-couple family	48.6	0.1
With own children under 18 years	20.0	0.1
Female householder, no husband present	13.1	0.1
With own children under 18 years	7.4	0.1
Nonfamily households	33.6	0.1
Male householder	15.5	0.1
Living alone	12.1	0.1
Not living alone	3.4	0.1
Female householder	18.0	0.1
Living alone	15.3	0.1
Not living alone	2.7	0.1
Average household size (number)	2.63	0.0
Average family size (number)	3.23	0.0
Marital status		
Population 15 years and over	248,055.9	35.6
Now married, except separated	48.8	0.1
Widowed	6.0	0.1
Divorced	10.9	0.1
Separated	2.2	0.1
Never married	32.1	0.1

Table 1-31. Selected Population Profile of the United States, 2010 American Community Survey, 1-Year Estimates—*Continued*

[Numbers in thousands, percent, except as noted.]

Characteristics	United States	
	Estimate	Margin of error (+/-)
Male, 15 years and over	120,742.6	25.8
Now married, except separated	50.5	0.1
Widowed	2.5	0.1
Divorced	9.6	0.1
Separated	1.9	0.1
Never married	35.4	0.1
Female, 15 years and over	127,313.3	27.9
Now married, except separated	47.1	0.1
Widowed	9.3	0.1
Divorced	12.1	0.1
Separated	2.5	0.1
Never married	29.0	0.1
School enrollment		
Population, 3 years and over, enrolled in school	82,724.2	89.4
Nursery school, preschool	6.0	0.1
Kindergarten	5.1	0.1
Elementary school (grades 1-8)	39.8	0.1
High school (grades 9-12)	20.8	0.1
College or graduate school	28.3	0.1
Male, 3 years and over, enrolled in school	40,704.6	62.2
Percent enrolled in kindergarten through grade 12	68.6	0.1
Percent enrolled in college or graduate school	25.1	0.1
Female, 3 years and over, enrolled in school	42,019.7	64.0
Percent enrolled in kindergarten through grade 12	62.8	0.1
Percent enrolled in college or graduate school	31.5	0.1
Educational attainment		
Population, 25 years and over	204,288.9	73.0
Less than a high school diploma	14.4	0.1
High school graduate (includes equivalency)	28.5	0.1
Some college or associate's degree	28.9	0.1
Bachelor's degree	17.7	0.1
Graduate or professional degree	10.4	0.1
High school graduate or higher	85.6	0.1
Male, high school graduate or higher	84.8	0.1
Female, high school graduate or higher	86.3	0.1
Bachelor's degree or higher	28.2	0.1
Male, bachelor's degree or higher	28.5	0.1
Female, bachelor's degree or higher	27.9	0.1
Fertility		
Women, 15 to 50 years	76,352.0	34.6
Women, 15 to 50 years, who had a birth in the past 12 months	4,168.7	39.1
Unmarried women, 15 to 50 years, who had a birth in the past 12 months	1,501.9	23.4
As a percent of all women with a birth in the past 12 months	36.0	0.4
Responsibility for grandchildren under 18 years		
Population, 30 years and over	183,336.4	62.7
Living with grandchildren (rent)	3.8	0.1
Responsible for grandchild (rent)	39.1	0.3
Veteran status		
Civilian population, 18 years and over	234,137.3	30.0
Civilian veteran	9.3	0.1
Disability status		
Total civilian noninstitutionalized population	304,287.8	15.2
With a disability	11.9	0.1
Civilian noninstitutionalized population, under 18 years	74,017.5	32.7
With a disability	4.0	0.1
Civilian noninstitutionalized population, 18 to 64 years	191,138.1	27.9
With a disability	10.0	0.1
Civilian noninstitutionalized population, 65 years and over	39,132.3	22.5
With a disability	36.7	0.1
Residence 1 year ago		
Population, 1 year and over	305,628.6	29.8
Same house	84.6	0.1
Different house in the U.S.	14.8	0.1
Same county	9.4	0.1
Different county	5.4	0.1
Same state	3.2	0.1
Different state	2.2	0.1
Abroad	0.6	0.1

Table 1-31. Selected Population Profile of the United States, 2010 American Community Survey, 1-Year Estimates—*Continued*

[Numbers in thousands, percent, except as noted.]

Characteristics	United States	
	Estimate	Margin of error (+/-)
Place of birth, citizenship status, and year of entry		
Native	269,393.8	115.2
Male	49.2	0.1
Female	50.8	0.1
Foreign born	39,955.9	115.2
Male	49.1	0.1
Female	50.9	0.1
Foreign born, naturalized U.S. citizen	17,476.1	81.7
Male	45.8	0.1
Female	54.2	0.1
Foreign born, not a U.S. citizen	22,479.8	120.4
Male	51.6	0.1
Female	48.4	0.1
Population born outside of U.S.	39,955.9	115.2
Entered 2000 or later	34.7	0.2
Entered 1990 to 1999	27.2	0.2
Entered before 1990	38.1	0.2
World region of birth of foreign born		
Foreign-born population, excluding population born at sea	39,955.7	115.1
Europe	12.1	0.1
Asia	28.2	0.1
Africa	4.0	0.1
Oceania	0.5	0.1
Latin America	53.1	0.1
North America	2.0	0.1
Language spoken at home and ability to speak English		
Population, 5 years and over	289,215.7	20.6
English only	79.4	0.1
Language other than English	20.6	0.1
Speak English less than "very well"	8.7	0.1
Employment status		
Population, 16 years and over	243,832.9	46.3
In labor force	64.4	0.1
Civilian labor force	63.9	0.1
Employed	57.0	0.1
Unemployed	6.9	0.1
Percent of civilian labor force	10.8	0.1
Armed Forces	0.4	0.1
Not in labor force	35.6	0.1
Females, 16 years and over	125,271.8	35.5
In labor force	59.3	0.1
Civilian labor force	59.1	0.1
Employed	53.2	0.1
Unemployed	5.9	0.1
Percent of civilian labor force	10.0	0.1
Commuting to work		
Workers, 16 years and over	136,941.0	
Car, truck or van - drove alone	76.6	148.1
Car, truck or van - carpooled	9.7	0.1
Public transportation (excluding taxicab)	4.9	0.1
Walked	2.8	0.1
Other means	1.7	0.1
Worked at home	4.3	0.1
		0.1
Mean travel time to work (minutes)	25.3	0.1
Occupation		
Civilian employed population, 16 years and over	139,033.9	14.8
Management, business, science, and arts	35.9	0.1
Service	18.0	0.1
Sales and office	25.0	0.1
Natural resources, construction, and maintenance	9.1	0.1
Production, transportation, and material moving	11.9	0.1
Male civilian employed population, 16 years and over	72,375.4	97.0
Management, business, science, and arts	32.8	0.1
Service	15.0	0.1
Sales and office	17.8	0.1
Natural resources, construction, and maintenance	16.7	0.1
Production, transportation, and material moving	17.7	0.1
Female civilian employed population, 16 years and over	66,658,487	92.7
Management, business, science, and arts	39.4	0.1
Service	21.3	0.1
Sales and office	32.7	0.1
Natural resources, construction, and maintenance	0.9	0.1
Production, transportation, and material moving	5.7	0.1

Table 1-31. Selected Population Profile of the United States, 2010 American Community Survey, 1-Year Estimates—*Continued*

[Numbers in thousands, percent, except as noted.]

Characteristics	United States	
	Estimate	Margin of error (+/-)
Industry		
Civilian employed population, 16 years and over	139,033.9	147.6
Agriculture, forestry, fishing, and hunting; and mining	1.9	0.1
Construction	6.2	0.1
Manufacturing	10.4	0.1
Wholesale trade	2.8	0.1
Retail trade	11.7	0.1
Transportation and warehousing; and utilities	4.9	0.1
Information	2.2	0.1
Finance and insurance; and real estate and rental and leasing	6.7	0.1
Professional, scientific, and management; and administrative and waste management	10.6	0.1
Educational services; and health care and social assistance	23.2	0.1
Arts, entertainment, and recreation; and accommodation and food services	9.2	0.1
Other services (except public administration)	5.0	0.1
Public administration	5.2	0.1
Class of worker		
Civilian employed population, 16 years and over	139,033.9	147.6
Private wage and salary workers	78.3	0.1
Government workers	15.3	0.1
Self-employed workers in own not incorporated business	6.3	0.1
Unpaid family workers	0.1	0.1
Income in the past 12 months, in 2010 inflation-adjusted dollars		
Households	114,567.4	163.2
Median household income (dollars)	50,046	64.0
With earnings	78.3	0.1
Mean earnings (dollars)	69,506	115.0
With Social Security income	28.4	0.1
Mean Social Security income (dollars)	16,236	21.0
With Supplemental Security income	5.1	0.1
Mean Supplemental Security income (dollars)	8,775	34.0
With cash public assistance income	2.9	0.1
Mean cash public assistance income (dollars)	3,936	37.0
With retirement income	17.5	0.1
Mean retirement income (dollars)	22,006	92.0
With Food Stamp/SNAP benefits	11.9	0.1
Families	76,089.0	141.3
Median family income (dollars)	60,609	93.0
Married-couple family	73.2	0.1
Median income (dollars)	72,596	149.0
Male householder, no spouse present, with family	7.1	0.1
Median income (dollars)	41,474	242.0
Female householder, no spouse present, with family	19.7	0.1
Median income (dollars)	30,085	121.0
Individuals	309,349.7	*****
Per capita income (dollars)	26,059	51.0
With earnings for full-time, year-round workers		
Male	54,540.8	82.0
Female	41,906.8	81.3
Mean earnings (dollars) for full-time, year round workers		
Male	62,407	154.0
Female	45,097	103.0
Median earnings (dollars) for full-time, year round workers		
Male	46,500	78.0
Female	36,551	65.0
Health insurance coverage		
Civilian noninstitutionalized population	304,287.8	15.2
With private health insurance	65.8	0.1
With public coverage	29.7	0.1
No health insurance coverage	15.5	0.1
Poverty rates for families and people for whom poverty status is determined		
All families	11.3	0.1
With related children under 18 years	17.9	0.1
With related children under 5 years only	19.3	0.2
Married-couple families	5.6	0.1
With related children under 18 years	8.4	0.1
With related children under 5 years only	7.6	0.2
Female householder, no spouse present, with family	30.3	0.2
With related children under 18 years	39.6	0.3
With related children under 5 years only	47.7	0.7

Table 1-31. Selected Population Profile of the United States, 2010 American Community Survey, 1-Year Estimates—*Continued*

[Numbers in thousands, percent, except as noted.]

Characteristics	United States	
	Estimate	Margin of error (+/-)
All people	15.3	0.1
Under 18 years	21.6	0.2
Related children under 18 years	21.2	0.2
Related children under 5 years	25.0	0.2
Related children 5 to 17 years	19.8	0.2
18 years and over	13.3	0.1
18 to 64 years	14.2	0.1
65 years and over	9.0	0.1
People in families	12.8	0.1
Unrelated individuals 15 years and over	26.2	0.1
Housing tenure		
Occupied housing units	114,567.4	163.2
Owner-occupied housing units	65.4	0.1
Renter-occupied housing units	34.6	0.1
Average household size of owner-occupied unit (number)	2.70	0.0
Average household size of renter-occupied unit (number)	2.50	0.0
Units in structure		
Occupied housing units	114,567.4	163.2
1-unit, detached or attached	69.0	0.1
2 to 4 units	7.9	0.1
5 or more units	17.0	0.1
Mobile home, boat, RV, van, etc.	6.1	0.1
Year structure built		
Occupied housing units	114,567.4	163.2
Built 2000 or later	14.8	0.1
Built 1990 to 1999	14.1	0.1
Built 1980 to 1989	13.9	0.1
Built 1960 to 1979	27.2	0.1
Built 1940 to 1959	16.7	0.1
Built 1939 or earlier	13.2	0.1
Vehicles available		
Occupied housing units	114,567.4	163.2
None	9.1	0.1
1 or more	90.9	0.1
House heating fuel		
Occupied housing units	114,567.4	163.2
Gas	54.5	0.1
Electricity	35.4	0.1
All other fuels	9.1	0.1
No fuel used	0.9	0.1
Selected housing characteristics		
Occupied housing units	114,567.4	163.2
No telephone service available	2.5	0.1
1.01 or more occupants per room	3.4	0.1
Selected monthly owner costs as a percentage of household income in the past 12 months		
Housing units with a mortgage (excluding units where SMOC cannot be computed)	50,082.8	14.5
Less than 30 percent	62.0	0.1
30 percent or more	38.0	0.1
Owner characteristics		
Owner-occupied housing units	74,873.4	21.6
Median value (dollars)	179,900	292.0
Median selected monthly owner costs with a mortgage (dollars)	1,496	3.0
Median selected monthly owner costs without a mortgage (dollars)	431	1.0
Gross rent as a percentage of household income in the past 12 months		
Occupied units paying rent (excluding units where GRAPI cannot be computed)	36,656.5	91.1
Less than 30 percent	47.0	0.1
30 percent or more	53.0	0.1
Gross rent		
Occupied units paying rent	37,521,157	92.2
Median gross rent (dollars)	855	2.0

***** = Estimate is controlled. A statistical test for sampling variability is not appropriate.

Source: U.S. Census Bureau, American Community Survey

Table 1-32. Mortgage Status by Age of Householder, Owner-Occupied Housing Units, 2010 American Community Survey, 1-, 3-, and 5-Year Estimates

[Numbers in thousands.]

Characteristics	United States					
	1-year estimates		3-year estimates		5-year estimates	
	Estimate	Margin of error (+/-)	Estimate	Margin of error (+/-)	Estimate	Margin of error (+/-)
Total	74,873.4	216.1	75,557.7	165.3	76,089.7	362.8
Housing units with a mortgage	50,339.5	146.0	51,197.5	120.7	51,696.8	255.2
Householder 15 to 34 years	7,134.2	58.9	7,553.2	42.4	7,954.6	80.0
Householder 35 to 44 years	11,652.2	46.0	12,303.4	37.6	12,859.2	80.6
Householder 45 to 54 years	14,178.7	48.7	14,469.8	33.1	14,588.2	52.1
Householder 55 to 59 years	5,991.2	30.2	5,967.6	18.0	5,935.3	23.2
Householder 60 to 64 years	4,836.4	32.1	4,625.9	18.0	4,382.2	13.6
Householder 65 to 74 years	4,752.7	28.2	4,537.6	15.6	4,305.2	18.2
Householder 75 years and over	1,794.2	17.2	1,740.0	10.2	1,672.2	9.8
Housing units without a mortgage	24,533.9	94.7	24,360.2	56.3	24,392.8	111.6
Householder 15 to 34 years	927.8	17.4	893.1	10.0	919.9	11.8
Householder 35 to 44 years	1,513.2	19.5	1,508.5	10.1	1,566.4	10.4
Householder 45 to 54 years	3,491.5	27.5	3,498.7	14.9	3,530.9	18.9
Householder 55 to 59 years	2,535.3	23.4	2,479.1	11.8	2,493.0	12.7
Householder 60 to 64 years	3,066.9	24.5	2,963.8	12.3	2,887.4	10.3
Householder 65 to 74 years	5,964.6	31.7	5,937.0	18.5	5,884.2	27.2
Householder 75 years and over	7,034.6	34.2	7,079.9	21.5	7,111.0	41.0

Source: U.S. Census Bureau, American Community Survey

Table 1-33. Tenure, Household Size, and Age of Householder, 2010

[Numbers in thousands, percent.]

Characteristics	Number	Percent
Tenure		
Occupied housing units	116,716.3	100.0
Owned with a mortgage or loan	52,979.4	45.4
Owned free and clear	23,006.6	19.7
Renter occupied	40,730.2	34.9
Tenure by household size		
Owner-occupied housing units	75,986.1	100.0
1-person household	16,453.6	21.7
2-person household	27,618.6	36.3
3- person household	12,517.6	16.5
4-person household	10,998.8	14.5
5-person household	5,057.8	6.7
6-person household	1,965.8	2.6
7-person household or more	1,374.0	1.8
Renter-occupied housing units	40,730.2	100.0
1-person household	14,751.3	36.2
2-person household	10,624.0	26.1
3- person household	6,240.4	15.3
4-person household	4,626.5	11.4
5-person household	2,480.9	6.1
6-person household	1,108.9	2.7
7-person household or more	898.2	2.2
Tenure by age of householder		
Owner-occupied housing units	75,986.1	100.0
15 to 24 years	869.6	1.1
25 to 34 years	7,547.4	9.9
35 to 44 years	13,255.6	17.4
45 to 54 years	17,804.1	23.4
55 to 64 years	16,502.7	21.7
65 years and over	20,006.6	26.3
65 to 74 years	10,834.0	14.3
75 to 84 years	6,789.0	8.9
85 years and over	2,383.6	3.1
Renter-occupied housing units	40,730.2	11.1
15 to 24 years	4,531.2	25.6
25 to 34 years	10,410.0	19.7
35 to 44 years	8,035.3	17.4
45 to 54 years	7,103.0	11.9
55 to 64 years		
		14.3
65 years and over	5,813.2	6.6
65 to 74 years	2,670.5	4.7
75 to 84 years	1,927.4	3.0
85 years and over	1,215.3	2.7

Source: U.S. Census Bureau, 2010 Census

Table 1-34. Nonfamily Households, by Sex of Householder and by Living Alone, 2010 American Community Survey, 1-, 3-, and 5-Year Estimates

[Numbers in thousands.]

Characteristics	United States					
	1-year estimates		3-year estimates		5-year estimates	
	Estimate	Margin of error (+/-)	Estimate	Margin of error (+/-)	Estimate	Margin of error (+/-)
Total	38,478.4	96.9	38,334.0	58.7	37,981.7	38.6
Male householder	17,810.7	71.0	17,756.6	34.6	17,572.6	40.6
Living alone	13,884.6	64.0	13,841.2	28.3	13,694.6	24.5
Householder 15 to 64 years	10,760.5	57.6	10,800.8	25.6	10,745.7	42.9
Householder 65 years and over	3,124.2	24.2	3,040.4	17.3	2,948.9	32.5
Not living alone	3,926.1	39.4	3,915.4	23.4	3,878.1	29.9
Householder 15 to 64 years	3,633.3	38.9	3,639.6	23.2	3,604.4	30.5
Householder 65 years and over	292.8	7.0	275.8	4.0	273.6	3.6
Female householder	20,667.6	77.7	20,577.4	46.1	20,409.0	56.3
Living alone	17,518.7	74.2	17,519.9	45.9	17,420.6	66.1
Householder 15 to 64 years	9,734.4	50.4	9,763.9	31.3	9,692.5	28.6
Householder 65 years and over	7,784.3	40.4	7,756.0	31.3	7,728.1	83.7
Not living alone	3,148.9	27.2	3,057.4	16.4	2,988.4	16.8
Householder 15 to 64 years	2,854.8	26.1	2,781.5	16.1	2,726.4	16.1
Householder 65 years and over	294.1	8.2	275.9	4.3	262.1	3.1

Source: U.S. Census Bureau, 2010 American Community Survey

Table 1-35. Poverty Status in the Past 12 Months, by Household Type and Age of Householder, 2010 American Community Survey, 1-, 3-, and 5-Year Estimates

[Numbers in thousands.]

Characteristics	United States					
	1-year estimates		3-year estimates		5-year estimates	
	Estimate	Margin of error (+/-)	Estimate	Margin of error (+/-)	Estimate	Margin of error (+/-)
Total	114,567.4	163.2	114,596.9	112.1	114,236.0	248.1
Income in the past 12 months below poverty level	16,065.2	49.7	15,358.2	37.5	14,865.3	33.0
Family households	8,579.9	42.4	8,000.7	28.8	7,685.3	27.3
Married-couple family	3,125.8	28.0	2,897.8	14.6	2,773.7	13.2
Householder under 25 years	160.1	6.3	151.5	4.3	153.8	3.1
Householder 25 to 44 years	1,533.9	20.5	1,390.5	9.7	1,324.0	8.8
Householder 45 to 64 years	1,060.4	16.2	961.3	9.8	905.2	6.7
Householder 65 years and over	371.4	7.8	394.5	4.2	390.7	4.6
Other family	5,454.2	38.2	5,102.9	23.9	4,911.7	23.9
Male householder, no spouse present	911.5	17.1	817.7	8.6	760.1	7.5
Householder under 25 years	120.9	6.6	115.7	3.4	113.2	3.2
Householder 25 to 44 years	466.5	11.8	419.3	7.0	386.8	5.3
Householder 45 to 64 years	271.2	9.2	235.1	4.2	215.3	4.1
Householder 65 years and over	52.8	3.6	47.6	1.8	44.8	1.5
Female householder, no spouse present	4,542.7	35.5	4,285.2	21.6	4,151.6	20.3
Householder under 25 years	569.9	11.7	568.1	8.2	574.6	6.5
Householder 25 to 44 years	2,720.6	29.5	2,554.5	17.2	2,475.9	18.2
Householder 45 to 64 years	1,022.0	15.0	939.7	8.1	886.7	7.3
Householder 65 years and over	230.3	8.1	222.9	4.4	214.3	3.4
Nonfamily households	7,485.3	42.9	7,357.5	24.8	7,180.0	18.2
Male householder	3,160.5	27.9	3,038.7	16.1	2,913.6	12.6
Householder under 25 years	568.8	11.3	572.0	7.6	574.3	5.9
Householder 25 to 44 years	837.2	16.7	789.6	8.2	754.6	8.4
Householder 45 to 64 years	1,280.6	19.5	1,187.6	10.9	1,110.6	9.8
Householder 65 years and over	473.9	10.6	489.6	5.5	474.1	4.6
Female householder	4,324.8	36.7	4,318.8	19.6	4,266.3	16.5
Householder under 25 years	684.7	14.4	679.4	8.0	676.7	7.0
Householder 25 to 44 years	653.7	15.9	623.8	8.6	615.6	7.1
Householder 45 to 64 years	1,513.5	20.8	1,456.8	10.3	1,411.3	10.3
Householder 65 years and over	1,472.9	18.3	1,558.7	9.6	1,562.8	13.5
Income in the past 12 months at or above poverty level	98,502.2	164.5	99,238.8	123.5	99,370.7	270.1
Family households	67,509.1	142.2	68,262.3	111.3	68,569.0	252.1
Married-couple family	52,579.0	148.8	53,421.6	128.3	53,881.7	296.6
Householder under 25 years	694.1	16.4	783.0	10.5	853.2	11.5
Householder 25 to 44 years	17,825.6	70.9	18,615.7	71.5	19,282.8	173.5
Householder 45 to 64 years	23,629.7	61.5	23,770.8	54.4	23,713.6	126.7
Householder 65 years and over	10,429.6	43.2	10,252.2	17.0	10,032.1	16.6
Other family	14,930.1	65.1	14,840.7	42.2	14,687.3	49.4
Male householder, no spouse present	4,474.3	37.1	4,469.0	21.7	4,454.9	26.9
Householder under 25 years	271.7	9.3	297.9	5.9	318.0	4.3
Householder 25 to 44 years	1,943.7	24.7	2,003.3	15.1	2,027.1	16.9
Householder 45 to 64 years	1,745.0	21.0	1,681.6	13.9	1,636.9	12.1
Householder 65 years and over	513.9	9.6	486.2	5.6	472.9	4.6
Female householder, no spouse present	10,455.8	49.2	10,371.7	31.9	10,232.4	28.8
Householder under 25 years	339.7	10.2	371.1	5.9	386.7	5.3
Householder 25 to 44 years	4,166.4	33.3	4,234.1	20.9	4,247.1	21.0
Householder 45 to 64 years	4,169.0	32.4	4,042.9	17.2	3,926.8	16.5
Householder 65 years and over	1,780.7	18.2	1,723.6	11.5	1,671.8	8.8
Nonfamily households	30,993.1	92.1	30,976.4	52.6	30,801.7	38.9
Male householder	14,650.3	64.5	14,717.8	29.8	14,659.0	36.4
Householder under 25 years	795.9	15.8	902.3	9.5	954.4	9.2
Householder 25 to 44 years	5,407.8	40.7	5,586.3	23.2	5,669.2	36.7
Householder 45 to 64 years	5,503.5	37.9	5,402.7	19.8	5,287.0	32.9
Householder 65 years and over	2,943.1	24.2	2,826.6	16.4	2,748.4	30.8
Female householder	16,342.8	67.9	16,258.6	42.4	16,142.7	50.7
Householder under 25 years	695.4	14.0	757.7	8.9	793.1	9.4
Householder 25 to 44 years	3,497.9	32.1	3,548.9	18.5	3,540.5	17.5
Householder 45 to 64 years	5,544.0	32.7	5,478.8	19.5	5,381.7	25.9
Householder 65 years and over	6,605.5	36.1	6,473.3	27.8	6,427.4	72.1

Source: U.S. Census Bureau, 2010 American Community Survey

Table 1-36. Household Population and Household Type, by Tenure, 2010

[Numbers in thousands, percent, except where noted.]

Characteristics	Number	Percent
Household population		
Occupied housing units	116,716.3	100.0
Owner-occupied housing units	75,986.1	65.1
Population in owner-occupied housing units	201,278.5	X
Average household size of owner-occupied housing units (number)	2.65	X
Renter-occupied housing units	40,730.2	34.9
Population in renter-occupied housing units	99,479.7	X
Average household size of renter-occupied housing units (number)	2.44	X
Household type		
Owner-occupied housing units	75,986.1	100.0
Family households	56,206.3	74.0
Householder 15 to 64 years	43,821.0	57.7
Householder 65 years and over	12,385.3	16.3
Husband-wife family	45,800.9	60.3
Male householder, no spouse present	3,126.9	4.1
Female householder, no spouse present	7,278.5	9.6
Nonfamily households	19,779.8	26.0
Householder 15 to 64 years	12,158.5	16.0
Householder 65 years and over	7,621.3	10.0
Male householder	8,727.3	11.5
Living alone	6,828.3	9.0
65 years and over	2,020.4	2.7
Living with others	1,899.0	2.5
Female householder	11,052.5	14.5
Living alone	9,625.2	12.7
65 years and over	5,068.3	6.7
Living with others	1,427.3	1.9
Renter-occupied housing units	40,730.2	100.0
Family households	21,332.0	52.4
Householder 15 to 64 years	19,608.1	48.1
Householder 65 years and over	1,724.0	4.2
Husband-wife family	10,709.5	26.3
Male householder, no spouse present	2,650.6	6.5
Female householder, no spouse present	7,971.9	19.6
Nonfamily households	19,398.2	47.6
Householder 15 to 64 years	15,308.9	37.6
Householder 65 years and over	4,089.3	10.0
Male householder	9,731.9	23.9
Living alone	7,078.0	17.4
65 years and over	1,151.3	2.8
Living with others	2,654.0	6.5
Female householder	9,666.2	23.7
Living alone	7,673.4	18.8
65 years and over	2,755.6	6.8
Living with others	1,992.9	4.9

X = Not applicable.
Source: U.S. Census Bureau, 2010 Census

Table 1-37. Age, Race, and Hispanic Origin of Householder, by Household Income in the Past 12 Months (in 2010 Inflation-Adjusted Dollars), 2010 American Community Survey, 1-Year Estimates

[Numbers in thousands.]

Characteristics	United States									
	Total population		White alone		Black or African American alone		American Indian and Alaska Native alone		Asian alone	
	Estimate	Margin of error (+/-)	Estimate	Margin of error (+/-)	Estimate	Margin of error (+/-)	Estimate	Margin of error (+/-)	Estimate	Margin of error (+/-)
Total households	114,567.4	163.2	89,549.2	89,549.2	13,738.5	41.8	813.2	15.5	4,582.8	24.0
Householder under 25 years	4,901.2	42.7	3,542.9	3,542.9	701.1	14.0	44.8	3.6	199.1	8.4
Less than $10,000	1,121.0	17.9	714.3	714.3	238.4	9.3	10.0	1.7	77.0	5.1
$10,000 to $14,999	486.3	13.3	336.8	336.8	89.2	5.5	4.9	1.3	15.0	2.3
$15,000 to $19,999	461.4	12.5	326.4	326.4	78.9	5.3	4.1	1.1	11.1	2.2
$20,000 to $24,999	443.9	13.1	318.2	318.2	66.3	4.9	6.4	1.4	11.7	1.7
$25,000 to $29,999	366.2	10.5	273.0	273.0	48.1	4.0	4.1	0.9	9.3	1.8
$30,000 to $34,999	349.3	12.3	264.0	264.0	41.3	3.7	2.7	1.0	10.8	1.9
$35,000 to $39,999	281.0	9.7	213.8	213.8	31.8	3.5	2.5	0.9	8.0	1.6
$40,000 to $44,999	263.0	8.8	207.8	207.8	20.4	2.6	2.1	0.8	8.3	1.4
$45,000 to $49,999	192.7	9.1	150.7	150.7	17.8	3.1	1.5	0.6	5.4	1.4
$50,000 to $59,999	306.4	9.9	245.3	245.3	24.3	3.1	2.8	1.0	9.8	1.9
$60,000 to $74,999	287.4	9.9	227.2	227.2	21.9	2.8	1.5	0.6	11.5	1.8
$75,000 to $99.999	204.9	7.8	159.8	159.8	13.8	2.3	1.4	0.7	10.9	2.0
$100,000 to $124,999	76.2	5.4	58.7	58.7	4.6	1.3	0.4	0.3	5.3	1.2
$125,000 to $149,999	28.9	2.6	23.6	23.6	1.6	0.7	0.1	0.1	1.5	0.5
$150,000 to $199,999	20.7	2.5	15.6	15.6	1.3	0.6	0.1	0.1	2.1	0.8
$200,000 or more	11.8	1.9	7.8	7.8	1.4	0.7	0.3	0.3	1.5	0.8
Householder 25 to 44 years	39,053.2	70.7	28,382.7	28,382.7	5,285.3	26.5	306.1	9.7	2,091.5	17.4
Less than $10,000	2,638.0	27.8	1,498.6	1,498.6	751.7	17.2	39.1	3.2	107.5	6.3
$10,000 to $14,999	1,640.8	24.3	1,013.2	1,013.2	380.4	13.1	20.9	2.1	52.5	3.9
$15,000 to $19,999	1,723.5	23.2	1,081.3	1,081.3	365.3	12.7	21.1	2.4	55.7	4.0
$20,000 to $24,999	2,025.7	24.2	1,300.5	1,300.5	392.5	11.8	23.0	2.9	82.0	4.9
$25,000 to $29,999	1,895.2	23.9	1,262.6	1,262.6	346.9	10.2	19.7	2.1	61.7	3.9
$30,000 to $34,999	2,127.0	24.2	1,461.5	1,461.5	366.4	10.5	22.0	2.3	75.8	4.7
$35,000 to $39,999	1,987.6	21.6	1,403.5	1,403.5	309.8	9.6	18.8	2.4	71.4	4.4
$40,000 to $44,999	2,045.4	28.2	1,463.8	1,463.8	297.3	10.9	18.7	2.3	87.1	4.7
$45,000 to $49,999	1,793.4	24.2	1,322.5	1,322.5	231.8	8.0	13.6	1.8	73.8	4.7
$50,000 to $59,999	3,456.2	29.5	2,592.1	2,592.1	425.9	12.0	26.0	2.7	152.9	6.8
$60,000 to $74,999	4,483.9	35.7	3,451.5	3,451.5	466.9	13.0	28.4	2.5	231.6	8.5
$75,000 to $99.999	5,298.2	42.1	4,196.6	4,196.6	465.7	13.6	24.5	2.5	306.2	9.2
$100,000 to $124,999	3,265.8	29.6	2,617.5	2,617.5	230.0	8.9	15.3	2.1	235.6	8.1
$125,000 to $149,999	1,741.2	20.0	1,392.2	1,392.2	110.1	6.4	6.3	1.4	152.1	5.9
$150,000 to $199,999	1,602.8	20.3	1,257.6	1,257.6	91.0	5.5	5.7	1.3	183.1	7.1
$200,000 or more	1,328.5	17.1	1,067.9	1,067.9	53.5	3.8	2.7	0.8	162.3	5.7
Householder 45 to 64 years	45,738.9	72.0	36,180.7	36,180.7	5,535.2	25.0	346.4	10.3	1,701.2	14.4
Less than $10,000	3,048.7	26.3	2,010.3	2,010.3	730.0	14.0	48.3	3.3	81.4	5.0
$10,000 to $14,999	2,001.7	20.5	1,384.4	1,384.4	420.2	10.8	25.9	2.6	48.0	3.5
$15,000 to $19,999	1,891.9	19.3	1,345.4	1,345.4	350.7	10.3	24.0	2.4	56.9	4.0
$20,000 to $24,999	2,029.1	19.4	1,479.1	1,479.1	349.0	9.3	19.4	2.3	66.2	4.1
$25,000 to $29,999	1,938.0	27.3	1,434.8	1,434.8	313.6	8.1	21.6	2.2	59.3	3.5
$30,000 to $34,999	2,096.5	19.9	1,569.1	1,569.1	324.9	10.0	17.4	2.0	65.3	4.1
$35,000 to $39,999	1,966.5	19.8	1,491.1	1,491.1	284.6	9.3	19.6	2.1	63.3	3.9
$40,000 to $44,999	2,053.3	21.9	1,582.3	1,582.3	278.1	10.1	17.7	2.1	68.6	4.1
$45,000 to $49,999	1,858.4	20.4	1,457.4	1,457.4	239.6	8.1	15.9	2.1	53.7	4.2
$50,000 to $59,999	3,694.0	34.1	2,932.7	2,932.7	439.1	10.4	29.1	2.3	123.4	5.9
$60,000 to $74,999	4,910.3	30.4	3,991.6	3,991.6	514.0	11.6	31.2	2.9	168.5	6.3
$75,000 to $99.999	6,095.2	38.0	5,076.8	5,076.8	536.2	12.7	33.7	2.9	227.8	7.2
$100,000 to $124,999	4,295.0	32.1	3,636.9	3,636.9	323.0	9.4	17.4	1.9	185.3	6.7
$125,000 to $149,999	2,577.2	24.2	2,200.0	2,200.0	177.8	7.3	9.5	1.2	119.4	4.8
$150,000 to $199,999	2,662.0	21.7	2,279.0	2,279.0	156.0	6.4	9.2	1.8	153.2	5.2
$200,000 or more	2,621.0	25.8	2,309.8	2,309.8	98.4	4.9	6.4	1.1	160.8	5.9
Householder 65 years and over	24,874.1	55.6	21,442.8	21,442.8	2,216.9	17.2	116.0	4.6	591.0	9.2
Less than $10,000	1,949.4	19.9	1,436.2	1,436.2	356.1	9.1	16.4	1.7	69.7	4.1
$10,000 to $14,999	2,540.1	21.4	2,074.7	2,074.7	322.2	9.2	14.8	1.7	63.7	3.5
$15,000 to $19,999	2,378.6	23.7	2,029.6	2,029.6	234.0	7.5	12.2	1.7	51.6	3.3
$20,000 to $24,999	2,211.2	17.2	1,912.4	1,912.4	200.3	6.2	11.3	1.4	38.9	3.0
$25,000 to $29,999	1,886.6	20.4	1,656.3	1,656.3	157.2	6.2	8.7	1.2	29.3	2.5
$30,000 to $34,999	1,664.5	19.0	1,471.5	1,471.5	128.0	5.8	8.0	1.2	26.8	2.4
$35,000 to $39,999	1,458.9	20.3	1,294.4	1,294.4	107.4	4.8	6.0	1.1	24.7	2.2
$40,000 to $44,999	1,290.0	15.3	1,147.3	1,147.3	90.4	4.3	6.0	0.9	22.1	2.1
$45,000 to $49,999	1,122.3	14.6	996.5	996.5	80.8	3.6	4.1	0.9	21.2	2.3
$50,000 to $59,999	1,819.7	18.0	1,613.8	1,613.8	132.6	5.8	7.5	1.2	34.7	2.9
$60,000 to $74,999	1,982.9	20.3	1,763.4	1,763.4	136.6	5.2	6.4	1.0	43.6	3.2
$75,000 to $99.999	1,928.1	16.6	1,707.0	1,707.0	127.1	4.8	7.4	1.3	52.8	2.9
$100,000 to $124,999	1,014.0	12.2	895.9	895.9	65.1	3.8	2.9	0.9	34.8	2.8
$125,000 to $149,999	546.6	9.1	479.2	479.2	32.7	2.4	2.4	0.9	23.5	2.4
$150,000 to $199,999	524.5	10.1	462.6	462.6	27.5	2.7	1.1	0.4	26.0	2.2
$200,000 or more	556.7	11.4	502.0	502.0	18.9	1.8	0.8	0.4	27.4	2.5

Source: U.S. Census Bureau, 2010 American Community Survey

Table 1-37. Age, Race, and Hispanic Origin of Householder, by Household Income in the Past 12 Months (in 2010 Inflation-Adjusted Dollars), 2010 American Community Survey, 1-Year Estimates—*Continued*

[Numbers in thousands.]

Characteristics	United States									
	Native Hawaiian and Other Pacific Islander alone		Some other race alone		Two or more races		White alone, not Hispanic or Latino		Hispanic or Latino	
	Estimate	Margin of error (+/-)	Estimate	Margin of error (+/-)	Estimate	Margin of error (+/-)	Estimate	Margin of error (+/-)	Estimate	Margin of error (+/-)
Total households	130.8	4.5	3,830.8	30.7	1,922.1	29.3	80,856.7	85.2	13,269.1	52.4
Householder under 25 years	8.0	1.6	257.6	9.8	147.9	7.4	3,039.3	31.7	818.9	15.3
Less than $10,000	1.3	0.7	44.1	3.6	36.0	3.5	626.5	12.0	146.0	6.3
$10,000 to $14,999	0.5	0.4	25.1	2.8	14.8	2.1	287.1	9.9	81.7	5.3
$15,000 to $19,999	0.2	0.2	25.3	2.8	15.4	2.3	272.7	9.4	84.6	5.0
$20,000 to $24,999	1.3	0.8	26.7	3.1	13.4	2.0	268.7	9.6	80.9	5.1
$25,000 to $29,999	1.1	0.8	18.9	2.3	11.7	2.0	231.2	8.4	64.2	4.7
$30,000 to $34,999	0.9	0.5	21.3	2.4	8.4	1.7	224.7	9.1	64.9	4.9
$35,000 to $39,999	0.5	0.4	16.4	2.5	8.0	1.7	184.4	7.8	49.1	3.4
$40,000 to $44,999	0.3	0.2	16.1	2.0	7.9	1.5	180.9	7.3	46.1	4.3
$45,000 to $49,999	0.1	0.1	12.7	2.2	4.6	1.3	126.4	5.9	38.5	4.0
$50,000 to $59,999	0.5	0.3	15.2	2.4	8.5	1.6	210.8	6.8	53.0	4.0
$60,000 to $74,999	0.4	0.4	16.0	2.0	8.8	1.8	194.4	8.1	53.7	3.8
$75,000 to $99.999	0.4	0.4	12.0	2.0	6.7	1.6	138.8	6.4	34.1	3.6
$100,000 to $124,999	0.5	0.4	5.2	1.3	1.6	0.7	50.8	4.3	13.3	2.1
$125,000 to $149,999	0.0	0.0	1.2	0.6	0.9	0.5	20.7	2.2	4.4	1.1
$150,000 to $199,999	0.0	0.3	0.8	0.4	1.0	0.5	13.8	2.0	2.9	0.9
$200,000 or more	0.0	0.3	0.5	0.3	0.3	0.3	7.3	1.5	1.5	0.6
Householder 25 to 44 years	62.3	3.7	2,078.8	23.6	846.5	17.8	24,189.0	46.3	6,624.0	35.2
Less than $10,000	4.0	1.0	161.2	7.7	76.0	5.0	1,210.6	17.9	485.0	12.8
$10,000 to $14,999	3.0	1.2	128.3	7.0	42.5	3.3	771.4	14.1	391.5	13.2
$15,000 to $19,999	2.7	0.8	153.5	7.5	43.9	3.9	799.4	13.4	458.9	12.1
$20,000 to $24,999	3.9	1.1	174.2	8.2	49.6	4.5	979.0	16.6	521.6	16.0
$25,000 to $29,999	3.4	1.0	155.5	7.4	45.5	3.8	974.3	17.8	466.6	11.8
$30,000 to $34,999	2.8	0.9	153.3	7.2	45.1	3.6	1,163.3	16.4	475.3	12.5
$35,000 to $39,999	3.0	1.0	139.3	6.6	41.7	3.5	1,135.8	16.7	424.8	11.8
$40,000 to $44,999	4.1	1.4	129.3	5.2	45.1	3.3	1,219.5	19.4	392.5	12.1
$45,000 to $49,999	3.4	1.1	108.4	6.0	39.8	3.3	1,100.1	18.7	350.9	11.2
$50,000 to $59,999	4.0	1.1	180.0	8.1	75.4	4.8	2,222.9	25.6	579.7	12.3
$60,000 to $74,999	6.9	1.3	208.4	7.6	90.3	5.0	3,025.5	27.2	668.6	13.7
$75,000 to $99.999	8.1	1.8	192.7	8.0	104.4	5.3	3,754.7	29.9	669.6	15.5
$100,000 to $124,999	5.3	1.3	99.1	5.2	62.9	4.3	2,384.5	23.8	353.7	10.6
$125,000 to $149,999	3.4	1.1	45.3	3.5	31.7	2.8	1,281.9	16.3	164.9	7.4
$150,000 to $199,999	2.5	1.0	32.3	3.3	30.5	2.9	1,160.5	17.3	136.2	5.5
$200,000 or more	1.8	1.0	18.0	2.6	22.2	2.5	1,005.5	12.9	84.2	5.2
Householder 45 to 64 years	49.7	3.3	1,237.2	17.9	688.4	15.7	33,251.0	41.0	4,421.4	25.3
Less than $10,000	2.5	0.7	109.9	6.1	66.3	4.6	1,800.0	20.0	347.0	9.4
$10,000 to $14,999	1.4	0.6	76.7	4.9	45.0	3.3	1,229.5	16.3	250.4	9.1
$15,000 to $19,999	1.4	0.6	76.7	5.1	36.7	3.5	1,182.5	14.6	255.4	7.6
$20,000 to $24,999	2.2	0.9	78.0	4.7	35.2	2.7	1,307.8	13.6	267.0	8.8
$25,000 to $29,999	1.4	0.6	71.5	5.3	35.8	2.8	1,268.3	18.9	253.5	9.6
$30,000 to $34,999	2.5	0.8	83.3	5.7	33.9	2.9	1,407.2	17.5	261.1	10.0
$35,000 to $39,999	1.8	0.7	74.0	5.1	31.9	2.9	1,334.6	15.2	244.4	8.1
$40,000 to $44,999	2.3	0.9	70.1	4.6	34.3	3.1	1,438.3	19.2	230.0	7.6
$45,000 to $49,999	3.0	0.9	59.1	4.9	29.7	2.7	1,314.1	15.8	213.8	9.5
$50,000 to $59,999	4.2	1.0	113.3	5.2	52.1	3.3	2,672.8	26.0	396.1	10.2
$60,000 to $74,999	6.3	1.2	131.1	6.8	67.6	3.7	3,666.4	23.3	477.0	12.5
$75,000 to $99.999	8.3	1.5	133.4	5.6	79.1	4.2	4,737.7	31.0	495.2	10.2
$100,000 to $124,999	4.6	1.2	76.5	4.9	51.3	3.4	3,419.7	26.7	309.8	8.8
$125,000 to $149,999	2.9	0.9	37.7	3.1	29.9	2.8	2,078.6	21.1	167.9	7.1
$150,000 to $199,999	2.4	0.8	29.9	3.0	32.4	2.7	2,167.9	19.6	147.7	6.3
$200,000 or more	2.4	0.6	15.9	2.1	27.2	2.8	2,225.8	20.6	105.2	6.3
Householder 65 years and over	10.9	1.4	257.2	8.5	239.4	8.3	20,377.4	40.1	1,404.8	15.5
Less than $10,000	0.6	0.3	42.8	3.5	27.6	2.8	1,276.5	16.4	219.0	7.0
$10,000 to $14,999	0.9	0.4	35.1	2.8	28.7	2.9	1,926.1	18.1	195.2	6.7
$15,000 to $19,999	0.8	0.4	26.3	2.7	24.1	2.4	1,917.8	20.5	147.1	6.1
$20,000 to $24,999	1.0	0.6	25.5	2.8	21.9	2.2	1,822.9	14.8	121.9	4.8
$25,000 to $29,999	0.8	0.4	17.3	2.2	16.9	1.9	1,582.9	20.0	95.5	4.2
$30,000 to $34,999	0.7	0.3	14.3	2.0	15.1	1.6	1,406.6	17.0	83.9	4.8
$35,000 to $39,999	0.4	0.2	13.0	1.7	12.9	1.7	1,241.1	18.5	69.3	4.4
$40,000 to $44,999	0.5	0.3	12.2	1.9	11.5	1.6	1,099.2	14.1	63.3	3.4
$45,000 to $49,999	0.7	0.4	9.4	1.6	9.6	1.6	958.5	12.7	50.3	3.5
$50,000 to $59,999	1.0	0.4	16.9	2.0	13.2	1.6	1,548.7	15.9	85.6	4.5
$60,000 to $74,999	0.7	0.3	15.7	1.8	16.5	1.9	1,690.0	18.2	94.4	4.5
$75,000 to $99.999	0.9	0.5	14.2	1.7	18.7	2.1	1,645.2	15.7	81.5	4.1
$100,000 to $124,999	0.8	0.4	6.7	1.3	7.7	1.3	862.2	9.3	42.6	3.0
$125,000 to $149,999	0.6	0.3	3.0	0.8	5.3	1.1	463.5	9.4	20.1	2.0
$150,000 to $199,999	0.3	0.2	2.5	0.8	4.6	1.1	447.2	9.6	18.8	2.1
$200,000 or more	0.1	0.2	2.1	0.9	5.3	1.0	489.0	10.1	16.3	2.1

Table 1-38. Age, Race, and Hispanic Origin of Householder, by Household Income in the Past 12 Months (in 2010 Inflation-Adjusted Dollars), 2010 American Community Survey, 3-Year Estimates

[Numbers in thousands.]

Characteristics	United States									
	Total population		White alone		Black or African American alone		American Indian and Alaska Native alone		Asian alone	
	Estimate	Margin of error (+/-)	Estimate	Margin of error (+/-)	Estimate	Margin of error (+/-)	Estimate	Margin of error (+/-)	Estimate	Margin of error (+/-)
Total households	114,596.9	112.1	89,594.3	83.4	13,735.3	24.9	803.6	7.2	4,582.4	12,071
Householder under 25 years	5,198.8	22.4	3,761.5	18.5	745.6	8.9	47.9	1.7	209.5	4,503
Less than $10,000	1,096.8	11.9	699.0	8.6	239.0	5.2	11.4	1.0	72.2	2,521
$10,000 to $14,999	496.9	6.8	342.5	6.3	95.4	3.2	4.8	0.7	15.2	1,283
$15,000 to $19,999	472.1	7.2	328.8	5.6	83.1	3.3	4.8	0.8	12.7	1,252
$20,000 to $24,999	466.4	6.4	334.4	5.8	71.5	3.0	5.2	0.6	12.8	1,193
$25,000 to $29,999	392.4	6.4	289.0	5.4	53.5	2.6	4.5	0.7	10.0	864
$30,000 to $34,999	378.4	6.6	283.1	5.4	44.8	2.5	3.1	0.5	11.7	1,123
$35,000 to $39,999	310.1	6.0	240.1	5.0	33.3	2.2	2.7	0.5	8.7	993
$40,000 to $44,999	282.0	5.8	220.0	4.9	25.8	1.8	2.3	0.4	9.3	887
$45,000 to $49,999	218.2	4.5	171.2	4.1	19.4	1.6	1.4	0.3	6.5	808
$50,000 to $59,999	351.7	6.6	278.5	5.5	28.1	2.0	2.9	0.6	12.1	961
$60,000 to $74,999	329.8	6.2	261.4	5.1	24.0	1.8	2.0	0.4	13.7	1,274
$75,000 to $99.999	240.3	5.9	190.4	4.9	17.1	1.6	1.5	0.3	10.8	1,091
$100,000 to $124,999	89.5	3.0	68.0	2.2	5.5	0.8	0.7	0.3	6.8	856
$125,000 to $149,999	35.8	1.6	27.7	1.7	2.5	0.5	0.3	0.1	2.7	522
$150,000 to $199,999	24.4	1.7	18.4	1.4	1.3	0.3	0.1	0.1	2.3	432
$200,000 or more	13.7	1.2	9.2	1.0	1.5	0.5	0.2	0.1	1.7	434
Householder 25 to 44 years	39,766.1	42.5	28,923.7	35.7	5,368.5	14.7	310.1	4.5	2,127.3	10,108
Less than $10,000	2,434.7	18.2	1,373.0	12.4	700.6	9.4	35.0	1.6	104.7	3,507
$10,000 to $14,999	1,545.4	12.0	945.8	10.4	364.8	5.6	19.7	1.3	51.2	2,581
$15,000 to $19,999	1,677.1	14.0	1,035.7	10.8	365.1	6.9	19.8	1.4	57.0	2,290
$20,000 to $24,999	1,942.1	14.2	1,246.9	11.9	380.2	6.6	21.9	1.4	74.9	2,890
$25,000 to $29,999	1,906.1	13.8	1,255.0	10.4	362.8	6.3	20.1	1.3	63.6	2,343
$30,000 to $34,999	2,119.6	15.2	1,448.8	11.4	369.5	6.3	21.7	1.6	73.7	2,608
$35,000 to $39,999	1,998.6	13.6	1,394.5	11.4	321.9	6.1	18.5	1.3	74.9	2,802
$40,000 to $44,999	2,076.4	13.3	1,484.5	9.8	305.5	5.8	17.2	1.2	85.1	2,931
$45,000 to $49,999	1,834.6	14.2	1,344.5	12.2	244.2	6.0	15.0	1.0	75.7	2,859
$50,000 to $59,999	3,569.8	18.4	2,680.1	15.6	438.2	7.0	26.7	1.8	152.3	3,806
$60,000 to $74,999	4,682.4	21.0	3,592.5	15.9	497.7	7.8	30.9	1.6	237.4	4,396
$75,000 to $99.999	5,576.2	24.4	4,408.7	20.5	491.6	7.0	30.4	1.6	316.9	5,204
$100,000 to $124,999	3,446.7	17.7	2,748.7	16.3	255.1	5.8	17.0	1.2	251.7	4,537
$125,000 to $149,999	1,828.0	11.4	1,460.5	10.4	122.0	3.1	7.6	0.9	155.1	3,696
$150,000 to $199,999	1,686.7	10.9	1,332.7	8.8	92.7	3.3	5.2	0.6	186.4	3,367
$200,000 or more	1,441.7	10.2	1,171.9	9.7	56.6	2.4	3.2	0.5	166.7	3,302
Householder 45 to 64 years	45,157.0	35.6	35,798.6	27.1	5,439.6	14.9	332.0	4.5	1,676.0	7,670
Less than $10,000	2,870.9	14.2	1,883.0	12.3	701.9	7.9	43.1	1.8	75.8	3,191
$10,000 to $14,999	1,852.7	13.4	1,280.9	11.0	387.5	6.1	24.2	1.4	47.8	1,688
$15,000 to $19,999	1,752.6	13.4	1,237.5	10.8	335.3	6.0	20.7	1.2	53.1	2,123
$20,000 to $24,999	1,913.2	14.1	1,386.8	12.4	332.5	5.8	19.6	1.3	64.2	2,168
$25,000 to $29,999	1,864.1	12.0	1,370.7	10.3	314.0	5.6	17.6	1.1	57.3	2,115
$30,000 to $34,999	2,024.5	11.8	1,516.6	10.2	315.7	5.4	17.4	1.1	66.0	2,486
$35,000 to $39,999	1,908.8	12.0	1,448.8	10.3	279.8	4.3	18.6	1.2	59.6	2,195
$40,000 to $44,999	2,003.4	13.1	1,548.8	11.7	272.8	5.0	16.8	1.1	63.8	2,316
$45,000 to $49,999	1,817.2	12.6	1,423.1	9.4	234.8	4.5	14.3	1.0	55.6	1,994
$50,000 to $59,999	3,682.7	16.5	2,929.6	14.7	439.8	6.0	26.7	1.2	120.0	3,344
$60,000 to $74,999	4,871.9	17.3	3,963.3	15.6	511.0	7.2	32.7	1.6	162.6	3,282
$75,000 to $99.999	6,190.7	21.8	5,150.1	19.5	554.9	7.0	34.6	1.5	225.3	3,520
$100,000 to $124,999	4,349.9	17.0	3,679.0	14.2	327.5	5.2	19.8	1.3	188.8	3,683
$125,000 to $149,999	2,619.3	13.4	2,238.6	12.6	176.6	4.1	9.7	0.8	123.0	2,894
$150,000 to $199,999	2,718.9	12.5	2,337.0	11.2	157.8	4.0	9.1	0.8	149.8	2,836
$200,000 or more	2,716.3	15.4	2,404.7	14.1	97.7	2.7	6.9	0.6	163.1	2,901
Householder 65 years and over	24,475.1	44.9	21,110.5	35.2	2,181.6	8.3	113.6	2.5	569.6	5,078
Less than $10,000	2,076.3	11.8	1,530.2	9.6	382.7	4.8	17.6	1.0	69.8	1,954
$10,000 to $14,999	2,530.6	14.0	2,061.6	11.7	319.6	4.4	16.2	1.0	63.5	2,004
$15,000 to $19,999	2,294.8	13.7	1,959.0	12.1	224.5	4.3	12.3	0.7	48.3	1,967
$20,000 to $24,999	2,117.6	11.0	1,841.7	10.8	188.9	3.5	10.4	0.8	33.8	1,575
$25,000 to $29,999	1,820.3	10.4	1,602.5	9.9	147.8	3.1	7.8	0.7	28.4	1,467
$30,000 to $34,999	1,609.3	8.4	1,426.6	7.7	121.6	3.1	7.0	0.7	24.8	1,349
$35,000 to $39,999	1,417.8	8.9	1,257.6	8.1	105.2	2.7	5.8	0.6	23.4	1,133
$40,000 to $44,999	1,258.3	9.1	1,119.9	7.7	89.7	2.8	5.1	0.5	21.4	1,151
$45,000 to $49,999	1,093.7	6.4	973.7	6.1	77.7	2.3	4.4	0.5	19.4	1,165
$50,000 to $59,999	1,794.3	10.2	1,598.0	9.7	125.4	3.0	6.9	0.7	33.2	1,260
$60,000 to $74,999	1,922.9	10.2	1,708.4	9.8	134.1	2.8	6.3	0.6	42.5	1,598
$75,000 to $99.999	1,877.8	9.9	1,666.5	9.1	123.9	2.4	6.7	0.8	49.5	1,709
$100,000 to $124,999	1,008.5	7.9	890.4	7.8	64.0	1.9	3.2	0.5	35.7	1,613
$125,000 to $149,999	549.1	5.5	484.6	5.4	31.5	1.3	1.7	0.4	23.2	1,110
$150,000 to $199,999	527.4	5.6	466.8	4.7	26.5	1.5	1.1	0.2	25.8	1,334
$200,000 or more	576.5	5.6	523.0	5.1	18.5	1.1	1.0	0.2	26.9	1,364

Source: U.S. Census Bureau, 2010 American Community Survey

Table 1-38. Age, Race, and Hispanic Origin of Householder, by Household Income in the Past 12 Months (in 2010 Inflation-Adjusted Dollars), 2010 American Community Survey, 3-Year Estimates—*Continued*

[Numbers in thousands.]

Characteristics	United States									
	Native Hawaiian and Other Pacific Islander alone		Some other race alone		Two or more races		White alone, not Hispanic or Latino		Hispanic or Latino	
	Estimate	Margin of error (+/-)	Estimate	Margin of error (+/-)	Estimate	Margin of error (+/-)	Estimate	Margin of error (+/-)	Estimate	Margin of error (+/-)
Total households	134.8	3.0	3,976.8	15.8	1,769.8	16.2	81,127.1	70.3	13,127.5	26.3
Householder under 25 years	9.2	1.2	283.5	5.0	141.6	3.7	3,233.6	17.0	866.9	8.8
Less than $10,000	2.0	0.5	41.5	2.0	31.7	1.9	614.7	7.8	138.2	4.2
$10,000 to $14,999	0.6	0.3	25.7	1.5	12.8	1.1	291.4	5.8	82.1	2.7
$15,000 to $19,999	0.7	0.3	28.7	1.9	13.3	1.1	276.6	5.2	86.2	2.4
$20,000 to $24,999	0.8	0.3	28.1	1.5	13.7	1.3	280.7	5.1	87.0	2.7
$25,000 to $29,999	0.8	0.3	23.6	1.7	11.1	1.0	244.9	5.1	71.6	2.9
$30,000 to $34,999	0.7	0.4	25.0	1.8	10.0	1.1	242.1	4.7	70.5	3.1
$35,000 to $39,999	0.5	0.2	17.3	1.4	7.4	0.9	206.5	4.7	53.4	2.2
$40,000 to $44,999	0.5	0.2	17.2	1.3	7.0	1.0	191.3	4.5	48.5	2.2
$45,000 to $49,999	0.2	0.1	14.1	1.1	5.3	0.7	147.3	3.7	40.2	2.3
$50,000 to $59,999	0.5	0.2	20.5	1.3	9.2	0.9	241.1	4.8	61.7	2.5
$60,000 to $74,999	0.9	0.4	18.8	1.5	9.0	1.1	225.3	4.6	58.9	2.6
$75,000 to $99.999	0.4	0.2	13.4	1.3	6.7	0.9	165.0	4.9	40.9	2.2
$100,000 to $124,999	0.3	0.1	6.1	0.9	2.2	0.5	58.7	2.0	16.0	1.4
$125,000 to $149,999	0.2	0.1	1.6	0.4	0.9	0.4	23.7	1.5	6.1	0.8
$150,000 to $199,999	0.1	0.1	1.2	0.3	1.0	0.3	16.1	1.4	3.9	0.7
$200,000 or more	0.0	0.1	0.8	0.3	0.3	0.2	8.4	0.9	1.8	0.5
Householder 25 to 44 years	63.0	2.3	2,186.4	13.5	787.0	9.2	24,801.8	26.7	6,632.1	18.3
Less than $10,000	3.1	0.5	155.0	4.5	63.2	2.3	1,114.2	11.6	445.5	7.0
$10,000 to $14,999	2.2	0.5	124.8	3.6	36.8	1.7	718.8	8.4	371.5	7.0
$15,000 to $19,999	2.7	0.6	157.2	4.5	39.5	1.8	764.3	8.2	448.7	6.6
$20,000 to $24,999	3.2	0.6	172.7	4.8	42.3	1.8	931.0	9.9	511.5	8.2
$25,000 to $29,999	3.3	0.7	159.3	4.8	42.0	2.1	971.1	9.9	463.6	7.4
$30,000 to $34,999	3.1	0.6	160.4	4.4	42.3	1.9	1,162.2	11.0	467.7	7.4
$35,000 to $39,999	3.5	0.6	145.5	3.9	39.9	1.7	1,135.8	10.2	423.3	6.2
$40,000 to $44,999	4.2	0.7	137.3	4.1	42.6	2.0	1,238.6	9.1	402.0	6.3
$45,000 to $49,999	3.3	0.6	116.0	3.4	35.9	1.7	1,130.6	11.2	346.7	5.1
$50,000 to $59,999	5.7	1.0	194.3	5.0	72.5	2.9	2,308.2	14.4	593.9	8.2
$60,000 to $74,999	7.7	1.0	228.9	4.9	87.4	2.7	3,162.2	14.0	692.6	8.7
$75,000 to $99.999	8.5	1.1	219.6	4.2	100.6	2.9	3,965.3	18.1	696.7	7.3
$100,000 to $124,999	5.2	0.7	109.4	3.2	59.6	2.5	2,512.8	15.4	364.6	5.3
$125,000 to $149,999	3.5	0.5	47.9	2.3	31.4	1.5	1,343.1	9.7	173.4	3.7
$150,000 to $199,999	2.2	0.5	38.0	1.8	29.5	1.6	1,237.0	8.1	141.1	3.8
$200,000 or more	1.6	0.5	20.0	1.6	21.6	1.4	1,106.5	9.4	89.2	2.9
Householder 45 to 64 years	50.3	1.7	1,236.2	9.1	624.3	7.4	33,000.7	24.6	4,263.9	14.4
Less than $10,000	2.8	0.6	104.9	3.1	59.4	1.8	1,682.9	11.3	329.5	5.5
$10,000 to $14,999	1.7	0.4	74.0	3.0	36.6	1.8	1,136.0	10.5	235.1	4.5
$15,000 to $19,999	1.7	0.4	71.9	3.0	32.3	1.5	1,087.9	9.6	234.5	5.2
$20,000 to $24,999	2.0	0.4	76.5	2.6	31.7	1.7	1,223.8	11.4	254.7	4.4
$25,000 to $29,999	1.9	0.4	73.0	3.1	29.5	1.7	1,213.9	8.9	243.2	5.5
$30,000 to $34,999	2.1	0.5	75.7	3.0	31.0	1.4	1,357.8	9.7	248.3	5.2
$35,000 to $39,999	2.1	0.5	71.0	2.9	29.0	1.5	1,300.9	9.9	231.1	4.3
$40,000 to $44,999	2.3	0.5	69.3	2.6	29.6	1.7	1,407.3	11.2	224.4	5.4
$45,000 to $49,999	2.1	0.4	60.9	2.6	26.3	1.4	1,291.7	9.2	202.4	4.9
$50,000 to $59,999	4.2	0.6	113.3	3.0	49.0	2.1	2,680.2	13.8	383.0	6.2
$60,000 to $74,999	6.1	0.7	133.4	4.1	62.9	2.0	3,661.9	13.8	455.7	7.5
$75,000 to $99.999	7.9	0.9	140.3	3.7	77.4	2.4	4,815.6	18.3	499.1	7.4
$100,000 to $124,999	5.4	0.7	80.8	3.0	48.6	1.9	3,471.0	14.3	302.5	4.7
$125,000 to $149,999	3.2	0.4	40.4	2.1	27.7	1.4	2,120.5	12.3	166.3	3.1
$150,000 to $199,999	3.0	0.4	33.4	2.1	28.8	1.4	2,228.8	10.7	148.5	4.0
$200,000 or more	1.9	0.4	17.6	1.3	24.4	1.3	2,320.6	13.4	105.6	3.0
Householder 65 years and over	12.3	0.7	270.6	4.5	216.9	4.0	20,091.1	30.6	1,364.6	8.7
Less than $10,000	0.7	0.2	50.2	1.9	25.1	1.3	1,365.3	8.9	231.0	3.9
$10,000 to $14,999	1.0	0.3	41.3	2.1	27.5	1.2	1,922.5	11.4	191.1	3.4
$15,000 to $19,999	0.7	0.2	28.2	1.6	21.7	1.1	1,855.0	12.0	140.1	3.5
$20,000 to $24,999	0.8	0.2	23.5	1.4	18.4	1.1	1,755.8	10.6	114.9	3.1
$25,000 to $29,999	0.9	0.3	17.6	1.0	15.4	1.0	1,532.7	9.2	92.0	2.8
$30,000 to $34,999	0.5	0.2	15.4	1.0	13.4	0.9	1,365.8	7.4	80.8	2.1
$35,000 to $39,999	0.7	0.2	13.2	1.2	11.8	0.8	1,207.8	8.4	66.0	2.1
$40,000 to $44,999	0.9	0.2	11.2	1.0	10.1	0.8	1,074.5	7.6	59.3	2.1
$45,000 to $49,999	0.7	0.2	9.4	0.9	8.4	0.6	935.8	5.8	49.9	2.0
$50,000 to $59,999	1.1	0.3	16.3	1.2	13.3	1.0	1,536.7	9.5	81.0	2.5
$60,000 to $74,999	1.0	0.3	15.6	1.1	14.9	0.9	1,642.7	9.0	85.5	2.5
$75,000 to $99.999	1.5	0.4	13.0	1.2	16.5	1.0	1,606.6	9.0	77.6	2.3
$100,000 to $124,999	0.7	0.2	7.2	0.7	7.3	0.8	859.0	7.5	40.4	1.9
$125,000 to $149,999	0.6	0.2	3.4	0.4	4.3	0.5	468.5	5.3	20.8	1.3
$150,000 to $199,999	0.3	0.1	2.9	0.4	4.0	0.6	452.3	4.8	18.5	1.2
$200,000 or more	0.2	0.1	2.1	0.4	4.7	0.6	510.2	5.1	15.6	1.0

Table 1-39. Age, Race, and Hispanic Origin of Householder, by Household Income in the Past 12 Months (in 2010 Inflation-Adjusted Dollars), 2010 American Community Survey, 5-Year Estimates

[Numbers in thousands.]

Characteristics	United States									
	Total population		White alone		Black or African American alone		American Indian and Alaska Native alone		Asian alone	
	Estimate	Margin of error (+/-)	Estimate	Margin of error (+/-)	Estimate	Margin of error (+/-)	Estimate	Margin of error (+/-)	Estimate	Margin of error (+/-)
Total households	114,236.0	248.1	89,046.1	180.6	13,620.0	30.9	804.0	6.8	4,501.4	15.9
Householder under 25 years	5,397.9	38.0	3,887.8	30.0	769.2	7.2	50.3	1.7	211.5	3.7
Less than $10,000	1,101.1	11.5	697.3	8.5	242.7	4.0	11.2	0.8	72.1	2.0
$10,000 to $14,999	500.6	6.0	343.2	4.9	95.0	3.2	5.2	0.5	15.1	0.9
$15,000 to $19,999	486.7	5.8	337.3	5.2	85.0	2.3	4.7	0.6	13.0	0.9
$20,000 to $24,999	472.9	6.1	336.1	4.8	71.9	2.6	5.5	0.6	13.3	0.9
$25,000 to $29,999	416.8	6.1	305.3	4.7	55.7	1.8	4.8	0.5	10.4	0.8
$30,000 to $34,999	397.2	5.2	297.7	4.4	47.0	1.6	3.4	0.5	11.9	0.9
$35,000 to $39,999	325.4	5.1	247.6	4.6	35.7	1.4	3.0	0.4	9.6	0.9
$40,000 to $44,999	299.7	4.3	231.7	3.6	28.2	1.3	2.6	0.4	9.1	0.9
$45,000 to $49,999	237.0	3.9	186.9	3.2	20.3	1.1	1.6	0.3	6.2	0.7
$50,000 to $59,999	374.6	5.7	294.5	5.2	31.1	1.5	2.8	0.4	12.0	0.9
$60,000 to $74,999	351.3	5.0	275.4	4.5	27.0	1.5	2.4	0.3	14.0	0.9
$75,000 to $99,999	259.6	3.8	203.9	3.1	17.9	1.2	1.7	0.3	11.2	0.8
$100,000 to $124,999	96.5	2.4	73.3	2.0	6.1	0.6	0.6	0.2	6.4	0.7
$125,000 to $149,999	37.5	1.5	28.2	1.4	2.7	0.5	0.3	0.1	3.0	0.3
$150,000 to $199,999	25.6	1.3	18.6	1.1	1.6	0.3	0.1	0.1	2.4	0.3
$200,000 or more	15.5	0.9	10.6	0.8	1.3	0.3	0.3	0.1	1.8	0.3
Householder 25 to 44 years	40,323.6	74.4	29,197.7	52.4	5,416.3	12.9	315.1	3.3	2,114.5	8.9
Less than $10,000	2,365.5	14.3	1,314.6	11.3	684.7	6.7	36.5	1.1	103.2	2.6
$10,000 to $14,999	1,491.1	10.6	896.0	8.6	357.2	4.9	20.9	1.2	49.9	1.6
$15,000 to $19,999	1,647.1	12.8	1,003.4	10.4	362.7	5.4	19.7	1.2	57.0	1.7
$20,000 to $24,999	1,876.3	10.7	1,184.0	8.5	373.8	4.7	21.5	1.0	71.7	2.1
$25,000 to $29,999	1,936.0	11.3	1,252.3	9.7	371.0	4.9	20.7	0.9	67.3	2.0
$30,000 to $34,999	2,126.8	11.6	1,435.8	9.5	371.9	4.3	21.3	1.1	76.5	2.1
$35,000 to $39,999	2,015.9	11.2	1,393.4	9.5	324.3	4.4	18.4	1.0	74.3	2.1
$40,000 to $44,999	2,111.1	10.9	1,496.6	9.4	309.9	4.3	17.8	0.9	86.1	2.2
$45,000 to $49,999	1,851.2	9.4	1,343.3	7.9	246.6	4.5	15.5	1.0	75.6	2.1
$50,000 to $59,999	3,654.0	15.0	2,718.4	12.4	451.4	5.9	26.9	1.2	153.9	3.1
$60,000 to $74,999	4,765.1	19.0	3,637.3	16.1	508.4	5.1	30.5	1.2	232.8	3.6
$75,000 to $99,999	5,810.1	35.8	4,579.9	28.6	508.1	5.3	32.4	1.2	320.0	4.8
$100,000 to $124,999	3,540.1	26.3	2,822.8	21.5	263.0	4.4	16.4	0.9	246.2	3.4
$125,000 to $149,999	1,899.2	16.2	1,518.4	13.5	126.4	3.0	7.5	0.6	154.6	2.8
$150,000 to $199,999	1,737.2	15.0	1,377.1	12.8	98.0	2.3	5.3	0.5	182.6	3.1
$200,000 or more	1,496.7	13.8	1,224.5	11.6	59.0	1.8	3.9	0.5	162.7	2.9
Householder 45 to 64 years	44,475.1	41.2	35,233.0	25.5	5,301.3	12.2	327.5	4.0	1,626.5	6.4
Less than $10,000	2,740.5	15.2	1,784.1	13.2	676.9	5.1	42.3	1.3	69.8	2.0
$10,000 to $14,999	1,756.6	11.3	1,209.1	9.4	366.8	4.4	23.1	1.0	45.2	1.5
$15,000 to $19,999	1,689.7	10.3	1,185.3	9.3	324.2	3.9	20.1	0.9	51.1	1.4
$20,000 to $24,999	1,808.5	10.5	1,302.6	9.0	317.0	4.3	18.7	0.9	58.3	1.8
$25,000 to $29,999	1,824.4	10.4	1,336.7	9.2	301.9	3.9	17.6	0.8	58.1	1.7
$30,000 to $34,999	1,967.3	11.3	1,468.3	9.2	307.5	4.1	17.8	0.8	60.8	1.9
$35,000 to $39,999	1,862.3	9.9	1,412.5	8.5	272.1	4.1	17.0	0.8	55.4	1.6
$40,000 to $44,999	1,964.5	9.8	1,514.8	8.0	266.5	4.2	17.0	0.9	60.5	1.7
$45,000 to $49,999	1,785.7	8.2	1,394.6	7.0	230.5	3.0	14.1	0.7	55.2	1.7
$50,000 to $59,999	3,642.5	11.8	2,893.0	10.4	430.0	4.2	26.2	1.1	117.4	2.1
$60,000 to $74,999	4,793.7	13.3	3,887.2	12.5	503.0	4.9	31.5	1.1	159.5	2.7
$75,000 to $99,999	6,211.3	22.1	5,153.7	17.3	556.9	6.3	35.2	1.1	223.7	3.2
$100,000 to $124,999	4,341.1	21.4	3,672.1	17.6	323.1	4.2	20.2	0.7	183.5	3.0
$125,000 to $149,999	2,646.1	16.2	2,259.7	13.3	176.9	3.0	10.8	0.6	123.3	2.0
$150,000 to $199,999	2,722.2	17.5	2,343.9	14.9	153.6	3.2	9.1	0.6	148.2	2.8
$200,000 or more	2,718.8	16.7	2,415.6	14.2	94.5	2.5	6.8	0.5	156.3	2.2
Householder 65 years and over	24,039.3	107.1	20,727.7	87.9	2,133.3	11.9	111.1	2.0	548.8	5.8
Less than $10,000	2,067.2	15.0	1,518.0	11.8	384.5	4.3	17.5	0.7	66.7	1.7
$10,000 to $14,999	2,546.5	21.4	2,078.8	18.0	316.0	4.3	16.2	0.8	61.7	1.7
$15,000 to $19,999	2,284.3	17.7	1,949.7	16.5	222.5	2.8	12.7	0.6	45.9	1.5
$20,000 to $24,999	2,075.3	14.3	1,806.5	12.7	181.8	3.2	9.9	0.5	32.7	1.2
$25,000 to $29,999	1,796.5	12.7	1,581.6	11.8	143.9	2.5	7.9	0.5	27.9	1.2
$30,000 to $34,999	1,579.0	11.1	1,400.6	9.5	118.2	2.2	6.5	0.5	23.9	1.0
$35,000 to $39,999	1,383.2	8.8	1,227.1	7.6	101.6	2.2	5.2	0.4	23.0	0.8
$40,000 to $44,999	1,233.0	7.3	1,096.8	6.1	87.3	2.0	4.7	0.4	21.2	1.0
$45,000 to $49,999	1,063.8	7.1	947.6	6.4	74.8	1.5	4.1	0.4	18.7	0.8
$50,000 to $59,999	1,750.6	8.7	1,558.0	7.7	121.4	2.5	6.7	0.5	32.7	1.2
$60,000 to $74,999	1,869.9	8.6	1,662.1	7.3	128.2	2.9	6.2	0.4	40.9	1.1
$75,000 to $99,999	1,816.2	8.5	1,612.1	7.5	118.5	2.2	6.7	0.4	47.8	1.7
$100,000 to $124,999	969.5	5.3	854.9	5.0	61.8	1.8	2.8	0.3	34.1	1.2
$125,000 to $149,999	535.8	4.0	473.0	3.7	30.4	1.0	1.7	0.3	22.4	1.0
$150,000 to $199,999	508.8	4.3	450.4	3.9	25.5	1.0	1.2	0.2	24.1	0.9
$200,000 or more	559.9	4.0	510.5	3.7	17.1	0.8	1.0	0.2	25.0	1.0

Source: U.S. Census Bureau, 2010 American Community Survey

Table 1-39. Age, Race, and Hispanic Origin of Householder, by Household Income in the Past 12 Months (in 2010 Inflation-Adjusted Dollars), 2010 American Community Survey, 5-Year Estimates—*Continued*

[Numbers in thousands.]

Characteristics	United States									
	Native Hawaiian and Other Pacific Islander alone		Some other race alone		Two or more races		White alone, not Hispanic or Latino		Hispanic or Latino	
	Estimate	Margin of error (+/-)	Estimate	Margin of error (+/-)	Estimate	Margin of error (+/-)	Estimate	Margin of error (+/-)	Estimate	Margin of error (+/-)
Total households	134.6	2.1	4,444.8	12.2	1,685.2	21.1	81,235.6	158.3	12,871.6	41.0
Householder under 25 years	9.9	0.7	328.8	4.8	140.4	3.4	3,377.8	28.6	891.2	8.4
Less than $10,000	1.7	0.4	45.7	2.1	30.4	1.3	617.8	7.8	135.9	3.5
$10,000 to $14,999	0.6	0.2	28.8	1.5	12.6	1.0	296.9	4.5	80.0	2.5
$15,000 to $19,999	0.8	0.3	32.7	1.5	13.3	0.8	286.2	4.8	88.7	2.4
$20,000 to $24,999	1.0	0.3	32.1	1.5	13.1	0.9	287.0	4.7	86.4	2.3
$25,000 to $29,999	0.8	0.3	28.4	1.3	11.4	1.0	261.3	4.5	76.7	2.4
$30,000 to $34,999	0.8	0.3	26.6	1.2	9.8	0.7	258.7	4.3	69.8	1.9
$35,000 to $39,999	0.6	0.2	20.8	1.2	8.2	0.7	215.9	4.0	55.2	1.9
$40,000 to $44,999	0.5	0.2	20.4	1.0	7.0	0.7	202.7	3.3	52.3	2.0
$45,000 to $49,999	0.3	0.1	16.1	1.0	5.5	0.6	163.2	3.0	41.7	1.7
$50,000 to $59,999	0.8	0.2	24.2	1.2	9.1	0.7	257.6	4.5	64.9	2.0
$60,000 to $74,999	0.8	0.3	22.4	1.4	9.2	0.7	240.1	4.0	61.7	2.1
$75,000 to $99.999	0.6	0.2	17.9	1.1	6.5	0.6	177.9	3.1	45.8	1.4
$100,000 to $124,999	0.3	0.2	7.5	0.7	2.3	0.4	62.9	1.8	18.4	1.1
$125,000 to $149,999	0.1	0.1	2.3	0.4	0.8	0.2	24.2	1.3	6.6	0.7
$150,000 to $199,999	0.1	0.1	1.8	0.3	0.9	0.2	16.1	1.0	4.5	0.5
$200,000 or more	0.0	0.1	1.1	0.2	0.4	0.1	9.2	0.7	2.6	0.4
Householder 25 to 44 years	63.3	1.6	2,467.3	9.3	749.4	11.2	25,375.6	45.1	6,582.5	18.2
Less than $10,000	3.1	0.4	164.9	2.9	58.6	1.8	1,082.2	10.1	425.3	5.8
$10,000 to $14,999	2.1	0.4	130.9	2.6	34.1	1.3	696.1	7.3	347.5	4.4
$15,000 to $19,999	2.4	0.4	166.5	3.3	35.4	1.3	751.0	8.0	436.2	6.3
$20,000 to $24,999	3.4	0.5	183.1	3.3	38.7	1.4	903.1	7.3	482.8	5.4
$25,000 to $29,999	3.3	0.4	181.7	3.9	39.7	1.4	985.9	8.6	466.1	5.2
$30,000 to $34,999	3.2	0.4	177.8	2.8	40.4	1.5	1,168.4	8.9	463.9	5.2
$35,000 to $39,999	3.5	0.5	163.2	3.3	38.9	1.5	1,153.1	8.9	420.4	5.1
$40,000 to $44,999	3.9	0.6	155.1	3.1	41.7	1.6	1,268.5	9.0	400.5	4.7
$45,000 to $49,999	3.3	0.4	131.9	2.7	35.2	1.4	1,146.2	7.4	344.5	4.8
$50,000 to $59,999	5.7	0.7	229.4	4.4	68.4	2.1	2,368.4	11.5	605.4	6.4
$60,000 to $74,999	8.3	0.7	264.7	3.9	83.2	2.6	3,237.9	15.3	694.9	6.6
$75,000 to $99.999	9.0	0.6	261.7	4.2	99.0	3.0	4,161.7	25.6	712.5	8.0
$100,000 to $124,999	5.1	0.5	128.4	2.6	58.1	2.0	2,599.6	19.8	369.0	5.2
$125,000 to $149,999	3.4	0.5	59.2	1.8	29.8	1.2	1,405.8	12.6	180.0	3.5
$150,000 to $199,999	2.2	0.3	44.4	1.5	27.7	1.2	1,287.0	11.6	141.1	3.0
$200,000 or more	1.5	0.3	24.6	1.2	20.6	1.0	1,160.6	10.8	92.4	2.4
Householder 45 to 64 years	49.3	1.3	1,345.2	7.3	592.4	6.9	32,700.2	20.6	4,082.3	13.8
Less than $10,000	2.6	0.3	109.1	2.3	55.6	1.8	1,606.5	12.2	308.5	4.2
$10,000 to $14,999	1.6	0.3	75.5	1.8	35.3	1.4	1,081.4	8.9	217.3	3.3
$15,000 to $19,999	1.8	0.3	77.3	2.2	29.9	1.1	1,050.1	9.1	224.5	3.8
$20,000 to $24,999	1.8	0.3	80.8	2.2	29.3	1.3	1,158.6	8.7	237.3	3.8
$25,000 to $29,999	2.1	0.4	80.4	2.3	27.6	1.0	1,195.8	8.5	232.8	3.4
$30,000 to $34,999	1.9	0.3	81.7	2.2	29.3	1.2	1,325.0	8.8	237.1	4.0
$35,000 to $39,999	2.3	0.3	76.1	2.1	27.0	1.2	1,277.2	7.9	221.8	3.5
$40,000 to $44,999	2.1	0.4	75.7	2.0	28.1	1.1	1,384.9	7.8	216.6	3.7
$45,000 to $49,999	1.7	0.2	64.8	1.9	24.8	1.0	1,275.8	6.6	192.6	3.0
$50,000 to $59,999	4.3	0.4	124.3	2.4	47.2	1.2	2,668.8	10.2	366.3	4.9
$60,000 to $74,999	5.9	0.5	146.5	3.0	60.1	1.8	3,616.6	10.6	436.7	5.3
$75,000 to $99.999	7.4	0.6	160.8	3.0	73.5	1.9	4,846.5	15.7	489.8	5.3
$100,000 to $124,999	5.1	0.5	89.8	2.0	47.4	1.6	3,483.0	16.3	291.7	4.2
$125,000 to $149,999	3.4	0.4	45.5	1.7	26.6	1.1	2,149.7	12.4	162.2	3.2
$150,000 to $199,999	3.2	0.4	36.7	1.4	27.5	1.1	2,242.4	14.1	144.9	2.8
$200,000 or more	2.1	0.3	20.2	1.1	23.2	1.0	2,337.8	13.5	101.9	2.5
Householder 65 years and over	12.0	0.7	303.5	3.7	202.9	3.6	19,782.0	80.6	1,315.7	10.6
Less than $10,000	0.6	0.1	56.1	1.7	23.7	1.0	1,364.9	10.5	222.6	3.6
$10,000 to $14,999	0.9	0.2	46.6	1.6	26.2	1.1	1,949.1	16.9	186.5	3.4
$15,000 to $19,999	0.7	0.2	32.6	1.3	20.2	0.9	1,851.2	16.0	137.9	2.0
$20,000 to $24,999	0.7	0.2	26.5	1.2	17.1	0.9	1,725.9	12.1	112.2	2.2
$25,000 to $29,999	0.8	0.2	19.5	0.9	15.0	0.7	1,516.7	11.3	88.5	2.0
$30,000 to $34,999	0.5	0.1	16.8	1.0	12.6	0.7	1,345.4	9.3	75.9	2.0
$35,000 to $39,999	0.8	0.2	14.4	0.9	11.2	0.6	1,181.3	7.2	63.0	1.8
$40,000 to $44,999	0.7	0.2	12.9	0.8	9.4	0.6	1,056.0	5.9	56.1	1.4
$45,000 to $49,999	0.6	0.1	10.5	0.6	7.5	0.6	912.7	6.1	47.6	1.4
$50,000 to $59,999	1.0	0.2	18.0	0.8	12.7	0.7	1,500.4	7.0	78.9	1.8
$60,000 to $74,999	1.0	0.2	17.3	0.9	14.3	0.6	1,601.1	7.2	82.1	2.0
$75,000 to $99.999	1.5	0.3	15.0	0.9	14.6	0.8	1,556.6	7.1	74.4	1.9
$100,000 to $124,999	0.8	0.2	7.8	0.6	7.1	0.5	826.6	4.8	38.1	1.1
$125,000 to $149,999	0.7	0.2	4.1	0.4	3.5	0.4	458.4	3.6	19.8	1.0
$150,000 to $199,999	0.3	0.1	3.5	0.4	3.8	0.4	437.2	3.9	17.6	0.8
$200,000 or more	0.3	0.1	2.1	0.3	3.9	0.4	498.5	3.8	14.5	0.8

Table 1-40. Median and Aggregate Household Income in the Past 12 Months (in 2010 Inflation-Adjusted Dollars), by Age of Householder, 2010 American Community Survey, 1-, 3- and 5-Year Estimates

[Dollars, except as noted.]

Characteristics	United States					
	1-year estimates		3-year estimates		5-year estimates	
	Estimate	Margin of error (+/-)	Estimate	Margin of error (+/-)	Estimate	Margin of error (+/-)
Median household income in the past 12 months						
Median total income (in 2010 inflation-adjusted dollars)	50,046	64	51,222	46	51,914	89
Householder under 25 years	24,143	268	25,732	136	26,465	100
Householder 25 to 44 years	54,024	156	56,068	111	57,132	213
Householder 45 to 64 years	60,683	125	62,228	82	63,398	205
Householder 65 years and over	34,381	97	34,303	52	33,906	80
Aggregate household income in the past 12 months (thousands of dollars)	7,820,269,222.8	17,953,159.9	8,035,025,284.9	14,220,551.1	8,097,400,587.5	31,165,820.1
Householder under 25 years	152,870,873.1	1,768,064.0	170,606,788.6	994,098.5	181,093,174.1	1,176,963.8
Householder 25 to 44 years	2,701,091,191.0	7,857,856.4	2,839,594,083.5	6,294,082.5	2,926,718,894.0	14,065,013.9
Householder 45 to 64 years	3,685,020,944.1	11,221,124.1	3,752,673,957.7	7,468,902.9	3,750,937,436.8	13,145,853.3
Householder 65 years and over	1,281,286,214.6	5,822,660.3	1,272,150,455.1	3,147,953.3	1,238,651,082.6	4,443,169.4

Source: U.S. Census Bureau, 2010 American Community Survey

Table 1-41. Tenure, by Household Size, by Age of Householder, 2010 American Community Survey, 1-, 3-, and 5-Year Estimates

[Numbers in thousands.]

Characteristics	United States					
	1-year estimates		3-year estimates		5-year estimates	
	Estimate	Margin of error (+/-)	Estimate	Margin of error (+/-)	Estimate	Margin of error (+/-)
Total	114,567.4	163.2	114,596.9	112.1	114,236.0	248.1
Owner-occupied units	74,873.4	216.1	75,557.7	165.3	76,089.7	362.8
1-person household	16,729.6	84.8	16,759.2	50.7	16,716.9	71.5
Householder 15 to 54 years	5,685.6	45.9	5,855.1	21.0	5,978.8	22.1
Householder 55 to 64 years	3,848.8	31.3	3,718.4	15.6	3,609.6	15.6
Householder 65 to 74 years	3,117.8	25.8	3,081.3	19.1	3,010.6	39.9
Householder 75 years and over	4,077.5	28.9	4,104.4	21.9	4,117.9	50.3
2-person or more household	58,143.8	165.3	58,798.4	132.0	59,372.7	296.2
Householder 15 to 54 years	33,211.8	122.1	34,371.7	112.3	35,440.4	252.0
Householder 55 to 64 years	12,581.0	41.5	12,318.1	23.8	12,088.4	48.7
Householder 65 to 74 years	7,599.5	28.6	7,393.2	12.9	7,178.7	9.1
Householder 75 years and over	4,751.4	25.1	4,715.4	13.2	4,665.3	9.9
Owner-occupied units	39,694.0	91.9	39,039.3	74.5	38,146.3	120.2
1-person household	14,673.7	55.1	14,601.9	36.5	14,398.3	25.5
Householder 15 to 54 years	8,529.8	46.0	8,677.0	28.7	8,650.2	31.9
Householder 55 to 64 years	2,430.7	22.7	2,314.2	14.5	2,199.6	15.5
Householder 65 to 74 years	1,559.1	19.7	1,501.9	11.1	1,448.7	12.4
Householder 75 years and over	2,154.2	20.0	2,108.8	11.8	2,099.8	18.0
2-person or more household	25,020.3	87.0	24,437.4	69.5	23,748.1	109.1
Householder 15 to 54 years	21,172.4	77.1	20,781.3	62.0	20,273.1	92.3
Householder 55 to 64 years	2,233.3	25.9	2,086.1	13.2	1,956.6	14.2
Householder 65 to 74 years	940.7	13.9	908.3	8.7	868.1	6.4
Householder 75 years and over	674.0	10.9	661.7	6.5	650.2	4.6

Source: U.S. Census Bureau, 2010 American Community Survey

Table 1-42. Grandparents Living with Own Grandchildren Under 18 Years, by Responsibility for Children, Age of Grandparent, and Units in Structure, 2010 American Community Survey, 1-, 3-, and 5-Year Estimates

[Numbers in thousands.]

Characteristics	United States					
	1-year estimates		3-year estimates		5-year estimates	
	Estimate	Margin of error (+/-)	Estimate	Margin of error (+/-)	Estimate	Margin of error (+/-)
Total	7,008.5	61.7	6,727.8	32.0	6,445.9	30.2
In 1-unit structures	5,533.8	53.1	5,330.5	28.7	5,105.2	21.0
Grandparent responsible for own grandchildren under 18 years	2,105.4	30.9	2,096.0	13.6	2,032.6	12.4
30 to 59 years	1,371.5	25.0	1,371.9	11.3	1,332.4	11.0
60 years and over	733.9	15.5	724.1	8.4	700.3	5.8
Grandparent not responsible for own grandchildren under 18 years	3,428.3	36.8	3,234.5	24.3	3,072.6	19.0
In 2-unit or more structures	945.3	21.3	890.3	11.4	851.7	11.0
Grandparent responsible for own grandchildren under 18 years	359.4	13.3	357.8	7.2	348.0	5.9
30 to 59 years	256.9	11.2	257.2	5.9	248.4	4.8
60 years and over	102.5	5.5	100.6	3.5	99.6	2.5
Grandparent not responsible for own grandchildren under 18 years	585.9	16.5	532.4	8.5	503.7	8.1
In mobile homes and all other types of units	529.4	16.8	507.1	8.5	488.9	6.3
Grandparent responsible for own grandchildren under 18 years	273.0	11.5	267.5	6.0	259.7	3.8
30 to 59 years	194.1	9.8	193.7	5.7	188.5	3.3
60 years and over	79.0	5.3	73.8	2.4	71.2	2.0
Grandparent not responsible for own grandchildren under 18 years	256.4	11.1	239.6	5.8	229.3	4.4

Source: U.S. Census Bureau, 2010 American Community Survey

Table 1-43. Household Type, by Units in Structure, 2010 American Community Survey, 1-, 3-, and 5-Year Estimates

[Numbers in thousands.]

Characteristics	United States					
	1-year estimates		3-year estimates		5-year estimates	
	Estimate	Margin of error (+/-)	Estimate	Margin of error (+/-)	Estimate	Margin of error (+/-)
Total	114,567.4	163.2	114,596.9	112.1	114,236.0	248.1
Family households	76,089.0	141.3	76,263.0	103.7	76,254.3	230.8
Married-couple family	55,704.8	151.6	56,319.4	127.8	56,655.4	293.6
1-unit structure	46,463.0	144.0	46,984.7	129.3	47,251.7	291.6
2-unit or more structure	6,278.1	48.5	6,322.4	23.6	6,325.7	13.8
Mobile homes and all other types of units	2,963.7	26.8	3,012.2	13.7	3,078.0	10.8
Other family	20,384.3	77.7	19,943.6	52.2	19,598.9	67.8
Male householder, no spouse present	5,385.8	41.9	5,286.7	23.1	5,215.0	30.5
1-unit structure	3,501.4	34.7	3,431.3	17.3	3,373.3	20.7
2-unit or more structure	1,432.8	22.9	1,412.2	12.7	1,397.2	12.1
Mobile homes and all other types of units	451.6	11.6	443.3	6.3	444.5	5.4
Female householder, no spouse present	14,998.5	60.8	14,656.9	39.0	14,384.0	42.6
1-unit structure	9,117.6	47.0	8,905.8	27.9	8,726.6	24.6
2-unit or more structure	4,811.8	33.6	4,702.4	20.3	4,625.6	19.8
Mobile homes and all other types of units	1,069.0	14.8	1,048.7	10.6	1,031.8	9.4
Nonfamily households	38,478.4	96.9	38,334.0	58.7	37,981.7	38.6
1-unit structure	19,998.7	86.5	19,788.5	44.2	19,533.4	34.5
2-unit or more structure	15,983.3	52.1	16,018.7	38.3	15,900.4	25.7
Mobile homes and all other types of units	2,496.4	23.3	2,526.7	13.8	2,547.8	11.0

Source: U.S. Census Bureau, 2010 American Community Survey

Table 1-44. Units in Structure, by Race and Hispanic Origin of Householder, 2010 American Community Survey, 1-, 3-, and 5-Year Estimates

[Numbers in thousands.]

Characteristics	United States						White alone householder					
	1-year estimates		3-year estimates		5-year estimates		1-year estimates		3-year estimates		5-year estimates	
	Estimate	Margin of error (+/-)	Estimate	Margin of error (+/-)	Estimate	Margin of error (+/-)	Estimate	Margin of error (+/-)	Estimate	Margin of error (+/-)	Estimate	Margin of error (+/-)
Total units	131,791.1	5.7	131,210.6	6.1	130,038.1	11.2	89,549.2	107.6	89,594.3	83.4	89,046.1	180.6
1, detached	80.965.7	113.5	80,772.1	78.5	80,135.9	124.0	60,140.6	126.9	60,177.5	94.7	59,849.0	186.0
1, attached	7,661.9	35.4	7,551.8	21.7	7,461.6	25.5	4,851.0	28.0	4,800.8	17.1	4,752.2	23.1
2	5.049.2	40.4	5,080.4	21.7	5,043.90	31.9	2,785.50	25.2	2,831.7	17.8	2,814.9	16.0
3 or 4	5.847.8	40.6	5,868.6	27.6	5,817.3	25.8	3,167.1	30.3	3,204.8	19.2	3,178.1	11.9
5 to 9	6,338.4	40.2	6,363.8	25.2	6,293.0	31.7	3,406.8	27.7	3,454.6	20.6	3,414,0	14.5
10 to 19	5,930.8	42.3	5,959.6	30.3	5,876.2	33.3	3,089.8	31.7	3,119.3	17.6	3,095.5	15.2
20 to 49	4,740.5	34.2	4,600.5	26.8	4,516.3	15.1	2,558.6	25.6	2,495.4	13.6	2,462.0	10.0
50 or more	6,509.8	37.0	6,267.9	19.4	6,101.9	22.9	3,610.5	28.4	3,512.2	16.4	3,450.8	22.5
Mobile home	8,636.7	49.0	8,636.7	30.9	8,684.4	39.3	5,845.2	33.1	5,903.8	20.4	5,937.2	19.8
Boat, RV, van, etc.	110.2	4.9	109.2	3.1	107.5	2.4	94.1	5.2	94.2	3.0	92.4	2.3

Source: U.S. Census Bureau, 2010 American Community Survey

Characteristics	Black or African American alone householder						American Indian and Alaska Native alone householder					
	1-year estimates		3-year estimates		5-year estimates		1-year estimates		3-year estimates		5-year estimates	
	Estimate	Margin of error (+/-)	Estimate	Margin of error (+/-)	Estimate	Margin of error (+/-)	Estimate	Margin of error (+/-)	Estimate	Margin of error (+/-)	Estimate	Margin of error (+/-)
Total units	13,738.5	41.8	13,735.3	24.9	13,620.0	30.9	813.2	15.5	803.6	7.2	804.0	6.8
1, detached	6,529.2	40.2	6,581.6	21.3	6,551.6	29.7	493.4	11.5	486.8	6.6	486.0	6.4
1, attached	1,150.1	18.8	1,139.5	8.2	1,124.2	8.7	33.9	3.2	30.7	1.6	30.6	1.3
2	826.8	15.6	836.6	7.6	828.3	6.9	29.8	2.6	30.2	1.4	30.6	1.2
3 or 4	937.3	15.7	956.5	11.7	948.0	6.3	41.5	3.2	38.6	1.7	38.6	1.4
5 to 9	1,097.3	18.8	1,093.2	11.5	1,092.9	8.6	36.6	2.7	38.7	1.6	38.1	1.2
10 to 19	1,010.1	20.1	1,006.5	12.4	986.6	8.8	33.2	3.2	34.1	1.8	32.9	1.4
20 to 49	676.1	14.6	652.9	7.9	637.0	5.0	23.8	2.6	21.9	1.3	21.9	1.0
50 or more	952.0	13.4	922.0	8.6	895.7	7.6	22.8	2.9	22.6	1.4	22.5	1.1
Mobile home	553.3	10.7	540.6	6.5	550.0	4.2	96.6	4.2	98.3	2.5	101.0	1.9
Boat, RV, van, etc.	6.6	1.6	5.9	0.8	5.5	0.7	1.7	0.6	1.6	0.3	1.6	0.2

Characteristics	Asian alone householder						Native Hawaiian and Other Pacific Islander alone householder					
	1-year estimates		3-year estimates		5-year estimates		1-year estimates		3-year estimates		5-year estimates	
	Estimate	Margin of error (+/-)	Estimate	Margin of error (+/-)	Estimate	Margin of error (+/-)	Estimate	Margin of error (+/-)	Estimate	Margin of error (+/-)	Estimate	Margin of error (+/-)
Total units	4,582.8	24.0	4,582.4	12.1	4,501.4	15.9	130.8	4.5	134.8	3.0	134.6	2.1
1, detached	2,332.5	18.9	2,325.5	11.3	2,287.1	12.4-	74.1	3.7	75.8	2.5	75.2	1.7
1, attached	409.5	8.0	404.0	6.1	397.7	5.0	8.5	1.5	8.2	0.9	8.3	0.7
2	183.7	6.9	177.5	4.2	171.2	2.9	4.1	1.0	4.9	0.7	4.5	0.6
3 or 4	256.4	6.8	256.5	4.4	249.4	3.3	9.8	1.7	9.0	1.0	8.9	0.8
5 to 9	283.2	8.6	293.4	4.7	292.9	3.5	11.3	2.1	11.0	1.0	11.1	0.8
10 to 19	310.8	11.2	322.5	5.5	318.6	3.9	8.0	1.6	9.9	0.9	10.0	0.7
20 to 49	275.4	9.3	282.1	5.5	277.4	3.7	5.4	1.2	6.2	0.9	6.4	0.7
50 or more	489.3	11.0	478.5	5.9	463.7	5.3	6.4	1.5	6.5	0.7	6.3	0.7
Mobile home	40.0	2.9	40.8	1.7	41.6	1.3	3.0	1.0	3.0	0.5	3.7	0.5
Boat, RV, van, etc.	2.1	0.8	1.8	0.5	1.8	0.3	0.9	0.2	0.2	0.2	0.1	0.1

Table 1-44. Units in Structure, by Race and Hispanic Origin of Householder, 2010 American Community Survey, 1-, 3-, and 5-Year Estimates—*Continued*

[Numbers in thousands.]

Characteristics	Some other race alone householder						Two or more races householder					
	1-year estimates		3-year estimates		5-year estimates		1-year estimates		3-year estimates		5-year estimates	
	Estimate	Margin of error (+/-)	Estimate	Margin of error (+/-)	Estimate	Margin of error (+/-)	Estimate	Margin of error (+/-)	Estimate	Margin of error (+/-)	Estimate	Margin of error (+/-)
Total units	3,830.8	30.7	3,976.8	15.8	4,444.8	12.2	1,922.1	29.3	1,769.8	16.2	1,685.2	21.1
1, detached	1,682.1	24.3	1,774.9	11.5	2,038.6	10.5	1,013.4	19.6	948.6	11.5	906.4	13.8
1, attached	230.5	7.1	239.4	4.9	269.0	3.7	132.0	6.6	116.9	3.6	109.1	2.8
2	258.5	9.2	258.4	5.2	286.1	4.5	89.0	5.1	79.3	2.5	73.3	2.0
3 or 4	322.9	9.9	328.8	5.9	362.7	5.4	120.4	5.9	107.8	3.1	103.6	2.3
5 to 9	289.5	10.4	296.8	6.2	327.3	4.6	127.6	6.4	116.0	3.1	108.7	2.6
10 to 19	274.7	10.1	291.5	5.2	313.8	4.8	114.3	6.7	106.2	3.3	101.7	2.6
20 to 49	270.6	8.8	272.6	5.6	290.1	3.8	95.5	5.4	85.0	2.7	80.3	2.1
50 or more	265.3	9.3	274.7	5.8	291.3	3.9	128.2	6.7	108.9	2.7	101.1	2.7
Mobile home	233.5	8.4	236.7	5.3	262.4	4.1	99.0	5.1	98.5	2.8	98.6	2.3
Boat, RV, van, etc.	3.2	1.0	3.0	0.5	3.5	0.5	2.6	0.8	2.6	0.5	2.4	0.3

Characteristics	White alone, not Hispanic or Latino householder						Hispanic or Latino householder					
	1-year estimates		3-year estimates		5-year estimates		1-year estimates		3-year estimates		5-year estimates	
	Estimate	Margin of error (+/-)	Estimate	Margin of error (+/-)	Estimate	Margin of error (+/-)	Estimate	Margin of error (+/-)	Estimate	Margin of error (+/-)	Estimate	Margin of error (+/-)
Total units	80,856.7	85.2	81,127.1	70.3	81,235.6	158.3	13,269.1	52.4	13,127.5	26.3	12,871.6	41.0
1, detached	55,447.4	110.4	55,633.3	82.4	55,668.4	165.9	6,680.0	41.7	6,604.8	26.8	6,489.6	37.1
1, attached	4,335.7	25.6	4,295.6	16.7	4,280.8	19.0	808.3	15.2	800.0	8.2	789.3	9.4
2	2,383.0	25.3	2,431.4	16.4	2,455.7	14.5	701.5	12.9	694.9	7.2	675.4	6.7
3 or 4	2,639.9	25.5	2,680.8	18.2	2,697.9	10.3	907.9	16.9	906.9	9.5	887.8	7.7
5 to 9	2,842.7	24.3	2,892.8	17.4	2,895.0	12.7	917.8	17.5	911.1	10.4	893.6	7.6
10 to 19	2,550.5	26.7	2.584.2	15.7	2,591.7	13.0	864.5	17.6	873.5	10.5	859.1	7.9
20 to 49	2,137.7	25.3	2,094.4	13.1	2,087.0	8.6	749.4	13.0	726.4	8.6	710.8	6.0
50 or more	3,148.1	24.7	3,067.2	13.7	3,036.5	18.9	801.6	14.8	788.9	8.9	764.7	7.6
Mobile home	5,285.1	31.7	5,359.7	19.8	5,436.2	18.7	826.7	15.6	810.6	8.3	791.1	5.7
Boat, RV, van, etc.	86.6	5.0	87.6	3.0	86.4	2.1	11.4	1.9	10.3	0.9	10.2	0.8

Table 1-45. Family Net Worth, by Selected Characteristics of Families, 1989–2010

[Thousands of 2010 dollars.]

Characteristics	From internal Federal Reserve Board data															
	1989		1992		1995		1998		2001		2004		2007		2010	
	Median	Mean	Median	Mean	Median	Mean	Median	Mean	Median	Mean	Median	Mean	Median	Mean	Median	Mean
All families	79.1	313.6	75.1	282.9	81.9	300.4	95.6	377.3	106.1	487.0	107.2	517.1	126.4	584.6	77.3	498.8
Percentile of income																
Less than 20	3.0	41.6	6.0	49.9	8.5	62.9	7.8	63.7	9.6	64.7	8.6	83.6	8.5	110.3	6.2	116.8
20–39.9	40.6	110.9	42.1	97.3	47.5	112.0	44.2	128.2	45.9	141.2	38.8	139.8	39.6	141.3	25.6	127.9
40–59.9	70.2	170.9	60.0	153.4	65.7	144.9	71.2	168.7	78.0	199.4	82.8	224.0	92.3	220.6	65.9	199.0
60–79.9	112.1	229.4	114.8	213.5	107.7	228.5	149.8	275.3	176.8	360.7	184.0	392.9	215.7	393.9	128.6	294.0
80–89.9	222.6	375.1	175.4	343.3	181.4	364.7	251.4	434.8	322.4	560.3	360.9	563.7	373.2	638.1	286.6	567.3
90–100	655.2	1,654.9	551.4	1,456.8	503.6	1,541.8	603.4	2,065.9	1,021.5	2,777.1	1,069.7	2,925.2	1,172.3	3,474.7	1,194.3	2,944.3
Age of head (years)																
Less than 35	13.2	79.0	14.0	68.8	17.0	61.2	12.2	85.2	14.3	111.2	16.3	84.6	12.4	111.1	9.3	65.3
35–44	95.2	249.0	67.7	202.1	74.0	203.6	84.6	262.1	95.1	318.6	79.9	345.2	92.4	341.9	42.1	217.4
45–54	166.5	466.2	118.6	407.6	134.4	420.2	140.9	485.3	164.9	595.9	167.1	625.8	193.7	694.6	117.9	573.0
55–64	165.0	519.1	172.8	512.4	163.5	543.2	170.6	710.6	227.2	898.6	290.0	976.4	266.2	986.7	179.4	880.5
65–74	129.3	471.9	149.6	434.4	157.2	493.9	195.4	622.6	217.8	831.4	218.8	795.1	250.8	1,064.1	206.7	848.4
75 or more	122.2	407.4	131.7	324.7	131.7	365.8	167.5	414.6	190.3	574.8	187.7	607.7	223.7	668.8	216.8	677.9
Family structure																
Single with child(ren)	12.2	106.7	12.9	82.1	17.0	103.0	21.5	136.6	16.2	117.4	24.0	149.9	24.4	187.4	15.5	143.7
Single, no child, age less than 55 years	13.7	122.4	22.6	107.4	24.8	102.8	20.6	123.0	24.0	185.5	24.2	179.8	26.3	217.2	14.6	117.5
Single, no child, age 55 years or more	69.0	206.9	88.2	236.5	100.2	280.3	116.4	328.2	111.9	355.8	134.0	405.8	150.7	408.9	102.0	391.6
Couple with child(ren)	104.6	339.0	91.7	312.0	93.3	304.7	116.2	398.6	139.3	540.1	140.6	580.5	147.5	629.1	86.7	555.7
Couple, no child	187.3	585.5	157.8	481.0	163.4	511.8	198.1	643.5	217.1	790.1	240.2	868.2	236.2	998.6	205.7	864.8
Education of head																
No high school diploma	40.7	140.1	28.3	106.3	32.1	119.3	28.1	105.2	31.3	127.5	23.7	157.1	34.8	149.7	16.1	110.7
High school diploma	62.1	187.9	58.3	169.4	73.5	188.3	72.1	210.5	71.1	222.0	79.1	227.2	84.3	263.8	56.7	218.1
Some college	77.5	314.4	87.5	260.0	66.3	267.4	98.5	317.3	89.8	352.1	79.8	355.7	88.8	384.5	50.9	272.2
College degree	187.3	610.0	149.8	515.5	147.9	545.8	195.3	705.8	262.2	976.6	260.2	982.3	298.6	1,154.5	195.2	977.7
Race or ethnicity of respondent																
White non-Hispanic	120.0	383.6	105.7	337.2	108.5	355.5	127.8	450.6	150.4	599.0	162.2	648.3	179.4	727.4	130.5	654.5
Nonwhite or Hispanic	11.3	106.0	18.2	117.5	22.4	109.3	22.2	134.1	22.0	144.1	28.5	176.2	29.7	240.3	20.4	175.9
Current work status of head																
Working for someone else	64.1	191.8	59.9	185.6	69.6	194.2	70.4	224.5	79.7	276.9	77.4	310.7	98.5	369.1	55.2	298.8
Self-employed	286.1	1,099.0	218.7	909.6	220.7	993.0	331.4	1,235.2	431.7	1,546.5	402.2	1,639.9	407.3	2,057.4	285.6	1,743.7
Retired	111.5	308.2	106.8	287.7	114.9	318.9	150.8	410.2	141.0	556.4	160.9	539.8	169.9	569.1	151.1	485.3
Other not working	1.3	66.2	5.0	80.5	5.1	80.7	4.7	98.7	9.4	218.4	13.6	186.7	6.0	130.1	11.9	137.5
Current occupation of head																
Managerial or professional	183.1	640.0	153.6	569.9	156.6	610.2	176.5	722.8	242.1	942.4	227.3	995.6	258.8	1,174.8	167.3	1,047.0
Technical, sales, or services	45.8	220.5	55.3	207.7	52.8	229.8	54.4	257.7	57.3	244.7	51.7	284.8	77.0	325.8	32.6	219.1
Other occupation	62.4	181.5	49.7	132.6	63.9	158.3	66.7	168.7	58.9	167.1	65.0	169.8	68.4	201.3	46.6	162.8
Retired or other not working	74.5	257.8	75.8	238.6	88.3	270.5	109.2	357.9	118.2	501.4	127.9	485.0	135.6	500.6	93.5	410.4
Region																
Northeast	147.3	363.7	97.2	319.6	117.3	355.5	125.8	404.8	114.3	556.3	186.1	655.0	167.1	684.6	119.9	615.2
Midwest	88.6	316.1	86.3	262.7	92.9	282.1	107.1	332.2	130.3	418.3	132.4	503.8	112.7	491.2	68.4	399.8
South	59.5	221.8	52.4	213.6	62.5	264.3	81.7	356.5	90.4	461.4	73.4	401.0	102.0	525.9	68.2	440.8
West	77.3	414.3	108.4	385.8	77.5	329.2	81.8	437.2	109.0	541.8	109.3	605.3	164.1	695.4	73.4	599.9
Urban/city																
Metropolitan statistical area (MSA)	78.3	334.9	80.3	316.5	84.0	320.4	96.7	409.0	108.0	525.0	120.1	582.0	138.8	652.6	78.4	553.6
Non-MSA	83.4	223.1	58.8	134.8	72.3	184.1	92.1	193.1	98.0	250.1	68.2	203.5	82.0	253.9	74.5	236.1
Housing status																
Owner	169.2	454.3	149.9	409.5	147.5	430.4	176.2	540.0	211.5	687.2	212.6	720.9	246.0	817.6	174.5	713.4
Renter or other	3.3	64.8	4.9	58.7	6.9	62.0	5.7	57.9	5.9	67.7	4.6	62.3	5.4	74.7	5.1	57.2
Percentile of net worth																
Less than 25	.3	–1.0	.8	–.9	1.3	–.2	.7	–2.5	1.4	.1	2.0	–1.6	1.3	–2.3	†	–12.8
25–49.9	35.5	38.7	35.8	38.5	40.0	43.3	43.6	47.9	50.1	54.4	50.2	54.2	56.8	60.9	32.2	35.6
50–74.9	146.1	150.1	132.8	137.3	134.7	141.1	160.7	171.5	193.6	204.9	196.7	213.7	230.8	238.6	157.2	168.9
75–89.9	354.6	381.1	309.4	331.4	313.3	338.0	413.6	429.6	528.0	553.5	586.7	608.4	601.2	616.7	482.7	527.9
90–100	1,161.3	2,094.6	1,007.9	1,894.2	967.8	2,035.8	1,195.6	2,586.1	1,602.6	3,390.0	1,645.5	3,591.1	1,991.9	4,176.9	1,864.1	3,716.4

Note: For questions on income, respondents were asked to base their answers on the calendar year preceding the interview.
† = Less than 0.05 ($50).

Table 1-45. Family Net Worth, by Selected Characteristics of Families, 1989–2010—*Continued*

[Thousands of 2010 dollars.]

Characteristics	From public data															
	1989		1992		1995		1998		2001		2004		2007		2010	
	Median	Mean	Median	Mean	Median	Mean	Median	Mean	Median	Mean	Median	Mean	Median	Mean	Median	Mean
All families	79.4	319.4	75.4	283.6	81.9	301.9	95.6	378.3	106.3	487.2	107.1	516.8	126.8	583.5	77.0	494.9
Percentile of income																
Less than 20	3.2	41.7	6.0	50.5	8.4	63.2	7.7	66.1	9.7	65.3	8.5	82.3	9.2	110.9	6.1	116.9
20–39.9	41.8	114.8	42.1	98.3	49.1	113.7	46.2	130.3	47.2	144.8	39.6	141.8	39.6	140.9	27.7	130.0
40–59.9	71.0	173.1	60.0	153.8	64.9	143.8	71.2	167.7	78.1	200.1	83.4	225.2	92.6	220.7	64.9	197.1
60–79.9	113.9	230.4	114.3	211.8	106.8	226.3	149.0	272.3	173.5	361.6	184.1	390.3	214.5	390.5	127.1	292.4
80–89.9	226.2	377.2	181.7	345.6	181.7	366.3	252.1	439.7	321.4	555.1	361.3	567.3	374.6	643.4	288.9	569.6
90–100	666.2	1,696.5	553.1	1,461.0	505.8	1,557.9	603.3	2,070.5	1,022.6	2,770.4	1,064.9	2,921.0	1,173.5	3,464.2	1,190.0	2,906.6
Age of head (years)																
Less than 35	13.7	84.0	14.1	68.8	17.0	61.3	12.1	89.5	14.3	104.3	16.3	84.8	12.3	111.1	9.3	65.1
35–44	95.4	250.5	67.8	202.1	73.8	204.0	84.7	261.9	96.2	318.6	79.9	344.9	92.9	342.1	42.4	216.6
45–54	165.5	475.7	118.7	407.8	131.3	425.9	140.9	484.9	164.6	602.9	167.0	626.2	193.8	694.9	117.2	570.1
55–64	165.6	519.8	172.5	514.5	163.6	542.0	170.6	711.6	227.0	903.0	290.0	974.9	265.8	981.0	178.7	878.9
65–74	130.9	492.8	149.6	436.8	157.2	495.9	195.4	622.6	218.1	829.1	218.9	796.3	250.8	1,061.7	206.7	842.5
75 or more	122.4	407.3	131.8	324.8	131.7	368.3	167.8	414.0	191.6	573.7	187.7	605.5	223.4	669.7	216.9	658.2
Family structure																
Single with child(ren)	11.8	107.1	12.9	80.4	17.0	103.1	21.5	139.9	16.0	116.7	23.7	150.4	25.9	186.8	15.7	143.2
Single, no child, age less than 55 years	13.9	126.5	22.7	107.2	24.6	102.9	20.7	122.5	23.9	183.0	24.9	180.0	26.3	217.8	14.7	118.2
Single, no child, age 55 years or more	68.6	206.9	88.8	237.1	100.2	280.4	116.1	328.0	112.0	357.5	134.9	403.6	150.8	408.9	101.3	381.5
Couple with child(ren)	105.6	343.1	91.4	313.4	93.3	307.1	116.1	401.2	139.8	541.1	140.6	581.2	147.6	628.0	86.4	552.1
Couple, no child	188.9	600.9	156.7	478.7	164.0	514.4	198.0	643.3	215.4	789.9	240.0	866.7	234.6	995.1	205.0	860.3
Education of head																
No high school diploma	40.8	140.3	28.4	106.3	32.6	118.8	28.0	105.2	31.1	129.1	23.7	156.7	34.7	149.7	16.3	110.6
High school diploma	61.9	189.9	58.2	169.4	73.3	188.8	72.2	210.4	71.1	222.1	78.7	227.1	84.3	263.8	56.7	216.4
Some college	78.7	314.4	87.7	261.2	67.0	267.9	99.5	318.6	89.5	344.4	79.5	355.2	88.6	384.6	50.9	272.2
College degree	190.6	626.3	150.6	516.8	148.0	550.2	195.2	708.3	262.7	980.4	260.8	982.0	298.2	1,151.5	193.5	969.7
Race or ethnicity of respondent																
White non-Hispanic	121.7	390.2	105.7	338.1	108.8	357.5	128.0	451.9	150.6	599.2	162.2	647.8	179.7	725.9	129.8	649.2
Nonwhite or Hispanic	10.6	109.2	18.2	117.6	22.0	109.2	22.1	134.0	22.1	144.1	28.6	176.5	29.5	240.3	20.5	175.5
Current work status of head																
Working for someone else	64.6	193.3	60.0	186.3	70.1	195.1	69.9	225.7	80.1	279.4	77.5	310.7	98.1	368.7	55.1	297.7
Self-employed	285.9	1,120.8	222.9	911.8	221.1	1,000.0	331.3	1,231.9	428.9	1,529.9	400.2	1,638.2	407.6	2,049.2	284.5	1,719.4
Retired	114.1	314.2	106.9	287.6	115.0	320.0	151.1	404.0	141.5	558.8	160.9	539.4	168.9	569.5	150.5	484.1
Other not working	1.0	78.6	5.0	80.5	5.2	80.8	4.8	143.9	9.6	218.4	13.4	186.6	6.0	129.5	11.9	134.7
Current occupation of head																
Managerial or professional	188.5	647.3	154.3	572.0	156.9	616.4	177.1	726.1	242.7	942.5	227.1	994.9	259.0	1,170.8	166.3	1,035.9
Technical, sales, or services	47.1	220.4	55.5	208.3	52.3	226.7	55.1	257.1	56.7	242.1	52.2	284.8	77.4	325.9	32.5	218.4
Other occupation	62.3	188.1	49.7	132.6	64.7	160.1	66.4	167.8	60.9	167.1	65.4	169.9	67.8	201.3	46.6	162.4
Retired or other not working	74.2	265.1	75.8	238.5	88.2	271.4	109.8	358.7	118.4	503.5	127.4	484.7	135.2	500.8	93.4	409.4
Housing status																
Owner	169.7	459.8	150.2	410.5	147.1	432.6	176.3	541.7	211.6	687.5	212.5	720.5	246.2	816.1	173.0	708.0
Renter or other	3.4	71.2	4.9	58.7	6.8	62.1	5.6	57.7	5.9	67.5	4.7	62.4	5.3	74.7	5.1	56.7
Percentile of net worth																
Less than 25	.2	–.9	.8	–.9	1.3	–.2	.7	–2.5	1.5	.1	2.0	–1.5	1.4	–2.2	†	–12.1
25–49.9	35.4	39.0	35.8	38.6	40.1	43.4	43.8	48.0	50.2	54.5	50.2	54.3	56.8	60.9	32.3	35.6
50–74.9	147.2	151.3	133.3	137.6	134.7	141.1	161.1	171.7	193.5	205.2	196.9	213.9	231.1	238.6	156.8	168.1
75–89.9	357.0	384.1	309.9	332.1	314.0	338.1	414.8	430.4	528.7	554.3	586.7	608.6	600.3	616.8	479.9	525.0
90–100	1,165.5	2,140.9	1,012.7	1,899.2	969.3	2,050.0	1,200.9	2,593.7	1,613.6	3,388.7	1,644.9	3,588.5	1,992.6	4,166.4	1,863.8	3,681.9

Note: For questions on income, respondents were asked to base their answers on the calendar year preceding the interview.
† = Less than 0.05 ($50).

Source: Federal Reserve Board, Survey of Consumer Finances

Table 1-46. Family Holdings of Nonfinancial Assets and of Any Asset, Selected Characteristics of Families and Types of Assets, Federal Reserve Internal Data, 2010

[Percent, thousands of 2010 dollars.]

Characteristics	Percentage of families holding asset							
	Vehicles	Primary residence	Other residential property	Equity in nonresidential property	Business equity	Other	Any nonfinancial asset	Any asset
All families	86.7	67.3	14.3	7.7	13.3	7.0	91.3	97.4
Percentile of income								
Less than 20	64.9	37.2	4.4	3.9	5.1	2.7	72.0	89.9
20–39.9	85.4	55.9	7.4	5.2	6.6	4.4	90.7	98.0
40–59.9	91.8	71.1	11.6	6.3	10.6	7.3	96.0	99.5
60–79.9	95.4	80.7	16.0	7.9	15.5	9.3	98.6	99.9
80–89.9	96.4	90.6	22.8	11.4	19.3	10.8	99.4	100.0
90–100	95.7	92.4	42.1	18.8	37.6	12.3	99.4	100.0
Age of head (years)								
Less than 35	79.4	37.5	4.5	2.3	8.4	6.1	82.8	95.5
35–44	88.9	63.8	9.7	3.9	11.2	4.2	92.7	97.4
45–54	91.0	75.2	17.0	7.5	16.8	6.6	94.7	98.3
55–64	90.3	78.1	22.1	12.6	19.6	9.6	94.4	98.3
65–74	86.5	82.6	22.8	11.0	15.9	11.1	92.6	97.1
75 or more	83.4	81.9	14.6	13.4	6.0	6.0	93.0	98.7
Family structure								
Single with child(ren)	79.1	52.0	6.2	4.0	5.1	3.9	84.5	94.6
Single, no child, age less than 55 years	74.6	40.1	6.3	2.4	7.4	5.7	80.6	95.3
Single, no child, age 55 years or more	76.3	66.7	11.8	8.2	6.6	8.0	86.8	96.6
Couple with child(ren)	94.8	75.6	15.5	7.1	17.0	5.9	97.0	99.0
Couple, no child	93.2	79.7	22.6	12.8	19.5	10.0	96.3	98.5
Education of head								
No high school diploma	76.2	54.3	5.0	3.3	5.2	1.3	82.2	92.5
High school diploma	85.8	64.7	10.0	6.9	10.9	5.5	90.5	96.5
Some college	85.4	61.5	11.7	6.4	11.2	7.6	89.6	98.2
College degree	91.5	76.6	22.4	10.4	18.9	9.9	95.9	99.5
Race or ethnicity of respondent								
White non-Hispanic	90.9	75.3	16.5	9.4	15.6	8.8	94.9	99.1
Nonwhite or Hispanic	78.1	50.6	9.9	4.2	8.3	3.3	84.0	94.1
Current work status of head								
Working for someone else	89.9	64.8	11.9	5.5	6.6	6.4	92.8	98.3
Self-employed	88.5	78.4	28.3	17.5	71.1	12.0	96.4	98.8
Retired	82.4	74.6	15.0	9.6	4.5	6.8	89.2	96.3
Other not working	72.8	43.0	8.7	2.8	4.1	4.8	78.6	92.5
Current occupation of head								
Managerial or professional	91.0	76.1	22.9	10.7	25.9	9.6	95.7	99.7
Technical, sales, or services	86.7	56.0	9.7	5.1	9.6	5.1	90.1	97.7
Other occupation	91.1	66.6	8.4	5.6	13.8	6.7	93.8	97.1
Retired or other not working	80.3	67.8	13.7	8.1	4.4	6.3	86.9	95.5
Region								
Northeast	78.5	65.0	15.3	5.9	11.1	5.5	85.6	95.1
Midwest	90.1	73.3	11.0	7.6	13.0	5.8	93.8	98.0
South	87.5	67.6	14.1	9.4	12.5	6.6	92.1	97.5
West	88.8	62.5	17.4	6.4	16.6	10.2	92.4	98.7
Urban/city								
Metropolitan statistical area (MSA)	86.0	65.9	14.9	7.2	13.4	6.9	90.6	97.4
Non-MSA	90.2	73.9	11.9	10.1	12.3	7.8	95.0	97.8
Housing status								
Owner	93.9	100.0	19.1	10.5	17.0	8.4	100.0	100.0
Renter or other	71.9	*	4.6	1.9	5.5	4.2	73.6	92.2
Percentile of net worth								
Less than 25	67.4	21.8	2.8	0.8	2.9	2.5	69.7	89.8
25–49.9	91.6	61.3	4.6	2.1	6.1	4.9	96.8	100.0
50–74.9	93.2	90.1	13.0	7.8	12.9	7.3	99.2	100.0
75–89.9	94.3	95.3	27.1	14.9	20.8	9.2	99.6	100.0
90–100	95.2	97.1	51.7	27.9	46.6	19.7	99.9	100.0

Table 1-46. Family Holdings of Nonfinancial Assets and of Any Asset, Selected Characteristics of Families and Types of Assets, Federal Reserve Internal Data, 2010—*Continued*

[Percent, thousands of 2010 dollars.]

Characteristics	Median value of holdings for families holding asset							
	Vehicles	Primary residence	Other residential property	Equity in nonresidential property	Business equity	Other	Any nonfinancial asset	Any asset
All families	15.3	170.0	120.0	65.0	78.7	15.0	154.6	187.2
Percentile of income								
Less than 20	5.8	89.0	82.0	36.0	25.0	5.3	23.6	15.2
20–39.9	9.3	110.0	70.0	60.0	25.3	5.0	74.3	75.5
40–59.9	13.8	135.0	82.0	60.0	44.7	10.0	131.2	159.8
60–79.9	20.1	175.0	71.0	50.0	50.0	13.0	198.3	267.0
80–89.9	27.9	250.0	120.0	58.0	82.4	22.0	311.1	448.4
90–100	35.8	475.0	320.0	200.0	455.0	35.0	756.4	1,486.7
Age of head (years)								
Less than 35	12.4	140.0	72.0	24.0	30.0	5.0	34.2	35.7
35–44	16.5	170.0	75.0	50.0	50.0	10.0	142.8	156.3
45–54	18.4	200.0	103.5	50.0	80.0	15.0	191.4	248.4
55–64	17.8	185.0	165.0	102.0	100.0	20.0	206.6	286.6
65–74	16.0	165.0	125.0	60.0	100.0	28.1	199.8	281.7
75 or more	10.6	150.0	125.0	65.0	220.9	26.0	168.2	237.7
Family structure								
Single with child(ren)	9.7	134.0	100.0	50.0	20.0	15.0	79.0	70.0
Single, no child, age less than 55 years	9.6	135.2	70.0	75.0	43.0	7.0	56.9	50.1
Single, no child, age 55 years or more	7.5	130.0	151.0	50.0	80.3	15.0	115.5	143.9
Couple with child(ren)	21.3	190.0	120.0	60.0	75.0	12.0	193.4	233.9
Couple, no child	20.3	180.0	120.0	75.0	109.0	20.0	209.0	306.7
Education of head								
No high school diploma	9.7	95.0	75.0	30.0	27.8	5.0	59.0	47.8
High school diploma	13.3	130.0	62.5	58.0	64.1	8.0	122.2	138.4
Some college	14.5	150.0	66.0	35.0	110.0	14.4	136.2	150.1
College degree	19.5	250.0	190.0	100.0	88.0	20.0	251.5	352.6
Race or ethnicity of respondent								
White non-Hispanic	16.7	175.0	140.0	75.0	97.2	15.0	183.5	238.9
Nonwhite or Hispanic	12.3	139.0	70.0	50.0	43.0	10.0	86.0	76.8
Current work status of head								
Working for someone else	16.3	170.0	96.0	50.0	25.0	10.0	142.7	165.7
Self-employed	21.7	270.0	250.0	132.0	100.0	30.0	370.0	440.2
Retired	11.7	150.0	100.0	62.5	125.5	25.0	155.9	198.0
Other not working	10.7	135.0	60.0	46.6	37.6	10.0	56.7	41.0
Current occupation of head								
Managerial or professional	20.8	250.0	200.0	100.0	102.0	23.0	260.0	347.5
Technical, sales, or services	12.7	153.0	70.0	50.0	27.0	8.0	107.6	115.5
Other occupation	17.2	130.0	57.0	50.0	51.5	8.0	125.0	147.2
Retired or other not working	11.5	150.0	98.0	62.0	81.6	22.0	139.9	163.3
Region								
Northeast	16.2	260.0	154.0	65.0	70.0	30.0	220.4	260.0
Midwest	13.6	135.0	86.5	70.0	100.0	10.0	142.1	174.9
South	15.4	141.7	100.0	50.0	80.3	15.0	134.3	153.1
West	16.3	230.0	170.0	159.4	52.8	15.0	189.1	216.8
Urban/city								
Metropolitan statistical area (MSA)	15.5	181.0	135.0	70.0	73.6	15.0	168.0	199.9
Non-MSA	14.4	100.0	75.0	60.0	104.5	12.5	111.6	140.1
Housing status								
Owner	18.8	170.0	120.0	70.0	95.0	20.0	217.0	296.2
Renter or other	8.5	*	120.0	22.5	25.0	5.3	9.7	12.6
Percentile of net worth								
Less than 25	6.9	117.0	60.0	3.0	1.2	5.0	9.4	7.4
25–49.9	11.7	95.5	25.0	10.0	11.6	5.0	60.0	69.1
50–74.9	17.7	150.0	48.0	30.0	40.0	13.0	181.6	240.3
75–89.9	22.7	250.0	120.0	65.0	125.0	20.6	360.7	583.8
90–100	32.7	531.5	350.0	250.0	600.0	50.0	1,114.3	2,082.8

Table 1-46. Family Holdings of Nonfinancial Assets and of Any Asset, Selected Characteristics of Families and Types of Assets, Federal Reserve Internal Data, 2010—*Continued*

[Percent, thousands of 2010 dollars.]

Characteristics	Mean value of holdings for families holding asset[1]							
	Vehicles	Primary residence	Other residential property	Equity in nonresidential property	Business equity	Other	Any nonfinancial asset	Any asset
All families	22.1	261.2	288.9	321.6	788.3	66.5	405.5	612.3
Percentile of income								
Less than 20	10.9	136.5	229.5	398.5	541.8	25.0	155.9	159.0
20–39.9	12.0	147.2	125.1	135.1	187.3	34.7	135.3	166.1
40–59.9	17.9	170.6	144.6	170.0	186.6	52.7	196.5	272.2
60–79.9	23.6	214.8	159.0	128.6	207.8	41.9	271.3	406.9
80–89.9	31.1	304.9	202.2	244.1	308.7	52.0	447.8	736.3
90–100	51.4	677.3	582.9	703.3	2,127.9	173.8	1,887.7	3,264.0
Age of head (years)								
Less than 35	16.7	170.4	121.0	117.5	249.4	17.9	129.9	141.3
35–44	21.0	238.1	173.6	132.2	442.0	28.3	262.4	356.2
45–54	26.8	294.3	281.7	240.7	895.5	49.6	491.3	725.8
55–64	25.7	306.1	342.5	414.8	911.3	98.9	612.4	1,006.5
65–74	24.9	271.4	322.3	417.8	970.3	95.5	572.0	947.1
75 or more	14.7	232.0	348.0	347.6	1,590.0	104.6	433.6	714.6
Family structure								
Single with child(ren)	12.7	187.2	229.4	212.4	182.2	52.6	167.6	218.2
Single, no child, age less than 55 years	15.0	179.3	136.7	210.6	241.2	22.8	143.7	188.0
Single, no child, age 55 years or more	12.4	197.0	253.6	290.9	619.3	88.2	279.9	441.9
Couple with child(ren)	27.0	301.5	316.6	299.1	846.4	57.0	485.9	717.1
Couple, no child	27.6	291.1	307.8	374.4	949.1	79.7	590.1	981.7
Education of head								
No high school diploma	14.0	125.8	186.0	418.4	270.5	19.1	141.6	150.2
High school diploma	18.7	168.8	130.5	205.7	460.6	29.8	225.5	285.7
Some college	20.9	214.7	188.1	176.4	515.1	52.7	273.4	361.5
College degree	27.7	377.7	383.3	422.3	1,075.7	91.2	685.8	1,146.1
Race or ethnicity of respondent								
White non-Hispanic	23.8	279.7	316.8	350.5	895.2	73.5	489.1	772.2
Nonwhite or Hispanic	18.0	204.1	192.8	185.8	372.6	28.5	209.8	263.4
Current work status of head								
Working for someone else	21.7	239.8	225.0	149.9	332.1	36.6	252.4	415.4
Self-employed	33.7	448.1	495.1	658.9	1,036.8	141.2	1,443.9	1,962.8
Retired	19.3	224.0	250.7	266.8	662.3	78.3	315.7	543.5
Other not working	14.4	195.2	143.5	292.2	216.5	30.0	159.6	209.8
Current occupation of head								
Managerial or professional	29.3	388.3	404.6	466.2	1,163.7	100.7	809.8	1,234.3
Technical, sales, or services	18.3	217.1	187.7	186.4	331.9	35.8	220.5	311.7
Other occupation	21.4	160.4	104.2	188.9	233.7	15.2	190.6	249.7
Retired or other not working	18.3	220.0	236.0	268.7	571.7	70.3	285.3	473.8
Region								
Northeast	23.0	355.5	358.2	260.3	871.3	116.6	493.0	759.1
Midwest	20.5	188.2	246.0	289.5	704.4	36.4	318.8	496.1
South	22.3	214.5	221.5	255.7	867.1	67.5	361.5	535.0
West	22.8	351.6	358.2	567.1	709.6	60.8	501.4	740.5
Urban/city								
Metropolitan statistical area (MSA)	22.6	288.3	312.5	357.5	866.6	72.8	445.1	678.4
Non-MSA	19.8	145.4	148.1	197.8	379.3	40.0	224.5	296.9
Housing status								
Owner	25.9	261.2	297.2	340.3	874.9	78.3	533.7	851.2
Renter or other	12.1	*	218.1	113.0	236.1	18.5	47.1	79.3
Percentile of net worth								
Less than 25	10.8	139.0	80.6	–34.3	12.4	5.3	57.4	49.7
25–49.9	15.2	109.6	44.1	17.4	24.9	8.2	88.3	100.4
50–74.9	21.5	173.6	77.7	46.6	60.5	28.5	201.7	261.4
75–89.9	27.5	291.4	162.3	128.2	190.2	46.1	411.9	642.8
90–100	52.4	727.7	604.9	752.3	2,063.3	171.9	2,277.9	3,986.5

Note: For questions on income, respondents were asked to base their answers on the calendar year preceding the interview.
* = Ten or fewer observations.
[1] = These estimates have not been reviewed for robustness and may be sensitive to outliers.

Source: Federal Reserve Board, Survey of Consumer Finances

Table 1-47. Family Holdings of Nonfinancial Assets and of Any Asset, Selected Characteristics of Families and Types of Assets, Public Data, 2010

[Percent, thousands of 2010 dollars.]

Characteristics	Percentage of families holding asset							
	Vehicles	Primary residence	Other residential property	Equity in nonresidential property	Business equity	Other	Any nonfinancial asset	Any asset
All families	86.7	67.3	14.4	7.6	13.2	6.5	91.3	97.4
Percentile of income								
Less than 20	64.9	37.3	4.5	3.9	5.1	2.4	71.8	89.8
20–39.9	85.5	56.1	7.6	5.2	6.5	4.0	90.8	98.0
40–59.9	91.7	70.9	11.3	6.3	10.8	6.6	96.0	99.5
60–79.9	95.5	80.6	16.1	7.7	15.4	8.6	98.6	99.9
80–89.9	96.1	91.1	22.9	11.2	19.2	10.2	99.4	100.0
90–100	95.9	92.0	41.7	18.7	37.7	11.3	99.4	100.0
Age of head (years)								
Less than 35	79.4	37.5	4.6	2.3	8.4	6.1	82.8	95.5
35–44	88.9	63.8	9.7	3.9	11.1	3.9	92.6	97.4
45–54	91.0	75.2	17.0	7.4	16.8	6.4	94.7	98.3
55–64	90.3	78.1	22.1	12.3	19.6	8.8	94.4	98.3
65–74	86.5	82.6	22.8	11.0	15.8	9.2	92.6	97.1
75 or more	83.4	81.9	14.8	13.5	6.0	5.1	93.0	98.7
Family structure								
Single with child(ren)	79.0	52.1	6.2	3.9	5.2	3.6	84.4	94.6
Single, no child, age less than 55 years	74.6	40.2	6.2	2.5	7.4	5.5	80.6	95.3
Single, no child, age 55 years or more	76.3	66.6	11.9	8.2	6.6	7.5	86.8	96.6
Couple with child(ren)	94.8	75.6	15.5	7.0	17.0	5.5	97.0	99.0
Couple, no child	93.2	79.7	22.8	12.6	19.4	8.8	96.3	98.5
Education of head								
No high school diploma	76.2	54.3	5.0	3.3	5.2	1.3	82.2	92.5
High school diploma	85.8	64.7	10.0	6.9	10.8	4.7	90.5	96.5
Some college	85.4	61.5	12.0	6.1	11.2	7.1	89.6	98.2
College degree	91.5	76.6	22.4	10.3	18.9	9.4	95.9	99.5
Race or ethnicity of respondent								
White non-Hispanic	90.9	75.3	16.6	9.3	15.6	8.1	94.9	99.1
Nonwhite or Hispanic	78.1	50.6	9.9	4.2	8.3	3.1	84.0	94.1
Current work status of head								
Working for someone else	89.9	64.8	11.9	5.4	6.6	6.1	92.8	98.3
Self-employed	88.5	78.4	28.4	17.4	71.1	10.3	96.3	98.8
Retired	82.2	74.5	15.1	9.6	4.5	6.0	89.1	96.3
Other not working	73.2	43.3	8.8	2.5	4.1	4.6	78.8	92.5
Current occupation of head								
Managerial or professional	91.0	76.1	22.8	10.6	25.9	8.9	95.7	99.7
Technical, sales, or services	86.7	56.0	9.7	5.1	9.6	5.0	90.1	97.7
Other occupation	91.1	66.6	8.4	5.4	13.8	5.9	93.8	97.1
Retired or other not working	80.3	67.8	13.7	8.1	4.4	5.7	86.9	95.5
Housing status								
Owner	93.9	100.0	19.2	10.3	17.0	7.7	100.0	100.0
Renter or other	71.9	*	4.5	2.0	5.5	4.0	73.5	92.2
Percentile of net worth								
Less than 25	67.4	21.8	2.7	.9	2.9	2.5	69.6	89.8
25–49.9	91.6	61.4	4.7	2.0	6.1	4.5	96.8	100.0
50–74.9	93.2	90.0	13.1	7.7	12.9	6.9	99.2	100.0
75–89.9	94.3	95.2	26.9	14.5	20.6	8.2	99.6	100.0
90–100	95.2	97.1	52.2	27.9	46.6	17.8	99.9	100.0

Table 1-47. Family Holdings of Nonfinancial Assets and of Any Asset, Selected Characteristics of Families and Types of Assets, Public Data, 2010—*Continued*

[Percent, thousands of 2010 dollars.]

Characteristics	Median value of holdings for families holding asset							
	Vehicles	Primary residence	Other residential property	Equity in nonresidential property	Business equity	Other	Any nonfinancial asset	Any asset
All families	15.0	170.0	120.0	65.0	78.0	15.0	154.2	186.4
Percentile of income								
Less than 20	5.8	89.0	60.0	36.0	23.7	5.3	24.0	15.0
20–39.9	9.3	110.0	72.0	45.0	25.5	5.0	74.3	76.2
40–59.9	13.9	135.0	85.0	60.0	40.0	10.0	131.0	159.5
60–79.9	20.0	175.0	72.5	50.0	50.0	13.0	197.1	266.5
80–89.9	28.0	250.0	120.0	58.0	85.0	22.0	311.1	449.0
90–100	36.0	475.0	320.0	200.0	450.0	35.0	756.5	1,486.0
Age of head (years)								
Less than 35	12.2	140.0	72.5	24.0	30.0	5.0	34.0	35.8
35–44	16.6	170.0	75.0	50.0	50.0	10.0	142.9	156.4
45–54	18.3	198.0	100.0	50.0	80.0	17.0	190.9	246.4
55–64	17.9	185.0	165.0	115.0	100.0	23.0	206.1	283.3
65–74	16.0	165.0	125.0	60.0	100.0	34.0	199.1	278.5
75 or more	10.4	150.0	125.0	62.5	222.0	25.0	167.8	237.5
Family structure								
Single with child(ren)	9.7	130.0	100.0	50.0	20.0	15.0	79.0	70.2
Single, no child, age less than 55 years	9.6	140.0	72.0	75.0	43.0	8.5	57.0	50.0
Single, no child, age 55 years or more	7.5	130.0	151.0	50.0	65.0	15.0	115.0	143.8
Couple with child(ren)	21.4	189.0	125.0	60.0	75.0	11.8	193.2	233.3
Couple, no child	20.3	180.0	120.0	80.0	108.0	20.0	208.0	304.8
Education of head								
No high school diploma	9.6	95.0	75.0	30.0	28.0	5.0	59.0	47.8
High school diploma	13.1	130.0	65.0	56.0	63.8	8.0	122.0	138.1
Some college	14.6	150.0	68.8	35.0	110.0	15.0	135.0	150.5
College degree	19.4	250.0	190.0	100.0	88.0	20.0	251.4	351.5
Race or ethnicity of respondent								
White non-Hispanic	16.8	175.0	140.0	72.5	95.0	15.0	183.0	237.7
Nonwhite or Hispanic	12.1	139.0	70.0	49.5	43.0	9.0	86.0	76.9
Current work status of head								
Working for someone else	16.1	170.0	96.0	50.0	25.0	10.0	142.5	165.5
Self-employed	21.8	269.0	250.0	137.0	100.0	40.0	369.1	447.4
Retired	12.0	150.0	100.0	60.8	125.5	25.0	155.4	197.3
Other not working	10.6	135.0	60.0	14.2	38.0	12.0	55.5	41.4
Current occupation of head								
Managerial or professional	21.0	250.0	200.0	100.0	102.0	23.0	260.1	347.0
Technical, sales, or services	12.7	153.0	75.0	50.0	27.0	8.0	108.0	115.4
Other occupation	17.0	130.0	58.0	50.0	51.5	8.0	125.1	147.3
Retired or other not working	11.6	150.0	98.0	60.0	82.0	22.0	139.8	163.2
Housing status								
Owner	18.9	170.0	120.0	70.0	95.0	20.0	215.5	295.8
Renter or other	8.5	*	125.0	21.0	25.0	5.3	9.7	12.6
Percentile of net worth								
Less than 25	6.9	120.0	60.0	3.3	1.2	5.0	9.3	7.4
25–49.9	12.0	95.0	22.0	12.5	11.6	5.0	59.7	69.1
50–74.9	17.6	150.0	50.0	30.0	40.0	13.0	181.0	239.6
75–89.9	22.8	250.0	120.0	65.0	125.0	21.0	355.8	579.0
90–100	33.0	537.0	350.0	245.0	600.0	50.0	1,114.3	2,082.0

Table 1-47. Family Holdings of Nonfinancial Assets and of Any Asset, Selected Characteristics of Families and Types of Assets, Public Data, 2010—*Continued*

[Percent, thousands of 2010 dollars.]

Characteristics	Mean value of holdings for families holding asset[1]							
	Vehicles	Primary residence	Other residential property	Equity in nonresidential property	Business equity	Other	Any nonfinancial asset	Any asset
All families	22.1	260.9	288.8	322.3	781.2	64.2	403.4	608.1
Percentile of income								
Less than 20	10.8	136.7	224.5	412.0	549.5	24.9	156.7	159.0
20–39.9	12.1	147.3	130.8	122.8	195.4	37.4	136.1	167.7
40–59.9	17.8	170.4	147.5	166.9	180.7	55.1	195.1	269.7
60–79.9	23.6	214.0	158.6	128.2	209.1	36.4	269.6	405.4
80–89.9	31.2	305.4	203.1	247.4	308.8	51.6	449.8	739.4
90–100	51.3	677.6	584.7	707.0	2,094.6	164.4	1,870.5	3,224.4
Age of head (years)								
Less than 35	16.7	170.3	120.6	117.7	248.2	17.6	129.7	141.1
35–44	21.0	237.9	173.8	132.1	436.9	28.5	261.6	355.1
45–54	26.8	294.2	281.4	244.5	891.3	47.4	489.9	722.0
55–64	25.7	305.6	342.5	421.4	912.0	98.9	610.8	1,004.8
65–74	24.8	271.0	321.8	418.8	953.2	105.1	567.2	940.9
75 or more	14.7	231.7	349.3	335.9	1,534.2	84.9	426.9	694.5
Family structure								
Single with child(ren)	12.7	185.9	230.0	220.8	182.0	55.5	167.3	217.8
Single, no child, age less than 55 years	14.9	180.7	138.6	203.9	240.5	23.5	144.4	188.4
Single, no child, age 55 years or more	12.4	196.5	257.8	278.9	574.3	83.2	274.5	431.2
Couple with child(ren)	27.0	301.2	317.3	302.1	841.9	54.7	484.4	713.1
Couple, no child	27.5	291.0	304.9	378.9	944.9	77.7	587.1	976.8
Education of head								
No high school diploma	14.0	125.7	185.7	417.8	270.0	18.9	141.5	150.1
High school diploma	18.7	168.7	131.2	203.9	459.2	23.8	224.6	283.7
Some college	20.9	214.7	190.1	172.6	518.5	54.3	273.5	361.4
College degree	27.6	377.5	383.2	425.1	1,062.5	87.4	681.7	1,137.7
Race or ethnicity of respondent								
White non-Hispanic	23.8	279.5	316.2	352.5	887.0	70.7	486.5	766.5
Nonwhite or Hispanic	18.0	203.8	193.5	184.0	370.3	29.1	209.2	262.8
Current work status of head								
Working for someone else	21.7	239.6	224.7	151.7	331.2	35.4	251.8	414.1
Self-employed	33.6	448.3	493.0	663.4	1,024.7	146.2	1,433.9	1,937.3
Retired	19.3	223.6	252.4	261.2	664.8	73.2	314.4	542.0
Other not working	14.4	194.9	143.4	309.5	220.6	31.6	159.3	207.3
Current occupation of head								
Managerial or professional	29.3	388.1	404.5	468.6	1,151.5	97.5	804.8	1,222.7
Technical, sales, or services	18.3	217.1	186.7	188.2	326.8	35.9	219.8	310.8
Other occupation	21.4	160.4	104.9	192.5	233.5	15.5	190.6	249.2
Retired or other not working	18.3	219.6	237.4	264.4	576.9	66.1	284.3	472.6
Housing status								
Owner	25.8	260.9	296.3	343.1	867.8	75.7	531.0	845.3
Renter or other	12.1	*	222.5	106.9	230.0	18.9	46.6	78.8
Percentile of net worth								
Less than 25	10.7	139.8	84.2	−13.3	11.6	5.3	57.9	50.0
25–49.9	15.3	109.3	43.2	18.0	25.0	8.4	88.2	100.2
50–74.9	21.5	173.3	78.8	44.7	60.2	28.9	201.2	260.7
75–89.9	27.5	290.3	162.1	129.6	190.9	44.1	409.4	639.3
90–100	52.3	727.9	599.9	747.4	2,038.4	168.0	2,262.8	3,951.3

Note: For questions on income, respondents were asked to base their answers on the calendar year preceding the interview.
* = Ten or fewer observations.
[1] = These estimates have not been reviewed for robustness and may be sensitive to outliers.

Source: Federal Reserve Board, Survey of Consumer Finances

PART II
FINANCIAL CHARACTERISTICS

PART II: FINANCIAL CHARACTERISTICS

Figure 2-1. Rental and Homeowner Vacancy Rates, Housing Vacancies and Homeownership Survey, Second Quarter 2008 and 2012

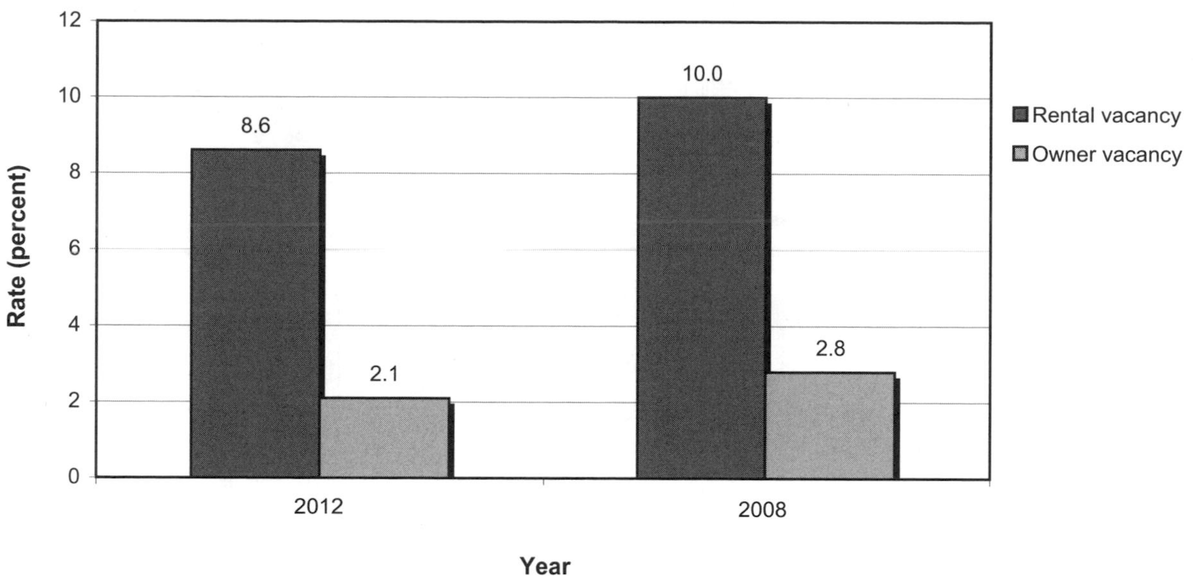

- Rental and homeowner vacancy rates have come down somewhat from their 2008 levels, reaching 8.6 and 2.1 percent, respectively, in the second quarter of 2012. (Table 2-31)
- According to the 2009 American Housing Survey, in all occupied units, a majority of householders spent between 5 and 29 percent of their monthly income on household expenses. (Table 2-1)
- The median value of owner-occupied units in the United States was $179,000 in 2010. Among the states, Puerto Rico, and the District of Columbia, median prices ranged from $95,100 in West Virginia to $525,400 in Hawaii. (Table 2-29a, 1-year ACS estimates)
- In the second quarter of 2012, homeownership rates were observed at 65.5 percent, down from 67.2 percent in the second quarter of 2000 but greater than the 63.7 percent observed in the second quarter of 1990. (Table 2-37)

Table 2-1. Selected Housing Costs, Occupied Units, 2009

[Numbers in thousands, except as noted.]

Characteristics	Total occupied units	Tenure		Housing unit characteristics		Household characteristics				Regions			
		Owner	Renter	New construction 4 years	Manufactured/ mobile homes	Black alone	Hispanic	Elderly (65 years or over)	Below poverty level	Northeast	Midwest	South	West
Total	111,806	76,428	35,378	4,771	6,839	13,993	12,739	23,095	15,739	20,451	25,368	41,586	24,401
Monthly housing costs													
Less than $100	723	475	248	7	259	154	88	212	315	99	117	265	242
$100 to $199	2,889	2,161	728	60	927	538	297	1,168	1,171	282	580	1,454	573
$200 to $249	3,114	2,376	738	118	783	414	294	1,483	1,045	393	631	1,629	460
$250 to $299	3,619	2,976	643	67	513	474	359	1,565	885	330	789	1,805	696
$300 to $349	3,570	2,989	581	84	435	467	274	1,657	713	487	859	1,666	557
$350 to $399	3,811	3,033	778	79	347	389	343	1,603	704	518	1,061	1,611	621
$400 to $449	3,823	2,830	993	83	275	450	376	1,509	730	536	1,083	1,575	629
$450 to $499	3,578	2,478	1,101	83	278	439	328	1,294	703	537	1,061	1,398	582
$500 to $599	7,392	4,407	2,985	176	488	1,091	766	2,145	1,344	1,376	1,931	2,929	1,157
$600 to $699	7,542	3,735	3,808	129	502	1,279	902	1,761	1,361	1,362	2,007	3,045	1,130
$700 to $799	7,306	3,597	3,709	186	515	1,133	889	1,406	1,215	1,256	1,893	2,928	1,228
$800 to $999	13,200	7,139	6,060	347	580	2,014	1,921	1,980	1,735	2,409	3,260	5,042	2,489
$1,000 to $1,249	12,933	8,156	4,777	541	373	1,784	1,604	1,598	1,268	2,594	3,056	4,646	2,637
$1,250 to $1,499	9,459	6,828	2,631	522	178	1,000	1,091	902	619	1,803	2,182	3,188	2,286
$1,500 to $1,999	11,692	9,445	2,247	832	78	980	1,379	1,010	619	2,444	2,397	3,450	3,401
$2,000 to $2,499	6,140	5,422	718	512	10	466	633	500	260	1,476	1,037	1,763	1,864
$2,500 or more	8,980	8,383	596	923	51	572	958	820	328	2,208	1,027	2,248	3,496
No cash rent	2,037	X	2,037	23	248	348	239	481	722	341	398	945	352
Median (dollars; excludes no cash rent)	909	1,000	808	1,451	404	799	935	534	590	1,038	829	800	1,145
Monthly housing costs as percent of current income[1]													
Less than 5 percent	3,065	2,903	162	99	491	148	206	617	25	413	571	1,276	805
5 to 9 percent	10,334	9,614	721	356	1,190	722	644	2,737	70	1,534	2,362	4,538	1,899
10 to 14 percent	13,111	11,147	1,964	420	1,075	1,137	967	3,103	156	2,351	3,380	5,216	2,164
15 to 19 percent	14,210	10,986	3,224	514	683	1,367	1,169	2,644	302	2,543	3,850	5,195	2,622
20 to 24 percent	13,271	9,589	3,682	728	573	1,451	1,319	2,295	350	2,426	3,215	4,817	2,813
25 to 29 percent	10,775	7,167	3,608	652	512	1,333	1,202	1,975	628	2,059	2,432	3,775	2,510
30 to 34 percent	8,116	5,160	2,956	382	340	1,139	1,185	1,394	642	1,563	1,898	2,755	1,899
35 to 39 percent	6,071	3,753	2,317	296	238	955	759	1,130	564	1,143	1,365	2,105	1,458
40 to 49 percent	7,851	4,529	3,322	449	345	1,157	1,256	1,513	995	1,506	1,505	2,794	2,047
50 to 59 percent	4,859	2,649	2,210	191	226	811	825	972	975	967	932	1,717	1,244
60 to 69 percent	3,099	1,676	1,423	141	148	508	537	670	804	590	625	1,039	845
70 to 99 percent	4,795	2,380	2,415	184	226	844	864	1,047	1,793	988	853	1,642	1,311
100 percent or more[2]	8,091	4,016	4,076	258	422	1,604	1,248	2,338	5,816	1,684	1,618	2,871	1,918
Zero or negative income	2,119	859	1,261	78	123	471	319	177	1,897	342	364	898	515
No cash rent	2,037	X	2,037	23	248	348	239	481	722	341	398	945	352
Median (dollars; excludes 2 previous lines)	24	21	34	26	18	31	32	24	84	26	23	23	27
Median (dollars; excludes 3 lines before medians)	23	20	31	25	17	28	29	21	49	24	21	22	25
Rent paid by lodgers													
Lodgers in housing units	977	372	606	39	74	63	282	44	129	147	162	361	306
Less than $200 per month	174	71	104	7	35	20	67	5	30	20	37	78	40
$200 to $299	118	34	84	3	19	10	42	11	13	2	19	66	32
$300 to $399	159	66	93	10	10	7	50	3	20	25	32	46	56
$400 to $499	164	65	99	7	3	6	36	8	17	29	23	59	53
$500 to $599	95	28	67	2	3	3	25	2	20	9	21	37	28
$600 to $799	93	35	58	–	–	–	29	–	3	14	14	39	26
$800 or more per month	106	32	74	6	–	8	28	4	14	35	4	13	55
Not reported	68	40	28	3	5	9	5	12	11	13	13	24	17
Median (dollars)	400	350	400	Z	156	250	350	Z	325	450	325	350	400
Monthly cost paid for electricity													
Electricity used	111,746	76,378	35,368	4,763	6,839	13,993	12,739	23,093	15,727	20,431	25,342	41,572	24,401
Less than $25	1,701	442	1,259	34	52	203	324	450	402	194	527	77	903
$25 to $49	9,851	4,425	5,426	224	377	1,157	1,549	2,482	1,967	2,333	2,767	990	3,762
$50 to $74	17,551	11,016	6,535	528	895	2,069	2,131	4,448	2,778	4,140	4,887	3,719	4,805
$75 to $99	18,444	12,975	5,469	728	1,062	2,086	2,095	3,859	2,363	3,599	4,946	5,829	4,070
$100 to $149	27,826	21,237	6,589	1,505	1,928	3,287	2,826	5,236	3,180	4,337	6,354	12,534	4,600
$150 to $199	14,959	12,164	2,795	844	1,221	1,828	1,428	2,520	1,618	2,052	2,562	8,019	2,325
$200 or more	14,451	12,110	2,341	730	1,067	2,171	1,455	2,237	1,496	2,372	1,829	8,150	2,099
Median (dollars)	107	117	84	124	122	112	98	96	93	94	93	135	85
Included in rent, other fee, or obtained free	6,964	2,010	4,954	170	237	1,192	931	1,861	1,924	1,402	1,470	2,255	1,836

Table 2-1. Selected Housing Costs, Occupied Units, 2009—*Continued*

[Numbers in thousands, except as noted.]

Characteristics	Total occupied units	Tenure		Housing unit characteristics		Household characteristics				Regions			
		Owner	Renter	New construction 4 years	Manufactured/ mobile homes	Black alone	Hispanic	Elderly (65 years or over)	Below poverty level	Northeast	Midwest	South	West
Monthly cost paid for piped gas													
Piped gas used	67,886	46,700	21,186	2,507	1,723	8,838	8,701	13,548	8,940	13,048	19,005	17,083	18,750
Less than $25	3,856	1,410	2,447	118	104	450	982	724	796	635	289	920	2,013
$25 to $49	12,402	7,933	4,469	542	476	1,427	2,292	2,464	1,833	1,006	2,297	3,555	5,544
$50 to $74	14,777	11,196	3,581	601	455	1,605	1,993	2,803	1,599	1,320	3,858	4,024	5,575
$75 to $99	10,648	8,595	2,054	422	253	1,291	918	2,123	1,073	1,747	3,522	3,205	2,174
$100 to $149	11,578	9,694	1,884	482	185	1,297	810	2,439	1,002	3,196	4,546	2,534	1,302
$150 to $199	4,341	3,698	643	112	51	714	275	903	414	1,525	1,638	812	366
$200 or more	3,200	2,682	518	107	30	659	237	673	360	1,268	1,042	621	269
Median (dollars)	73	80	55	70	58	79	54	75	63	106	89	70	54
Included in rent, other fee, or obtained free	7,082	1,494	5,588	123	169	1,394	1,194	1,420	1,863	2,352	1,814	1,410	1,507
Average monthly cost paid for fuel oil													
Fuel oil used	9,208	6,409	2,800	74	249	912	818	2,369	1,172	7,274	694	1,019	222
Less than $25	228	176	52	–	18	15	4	49	47	102	64	54	9
$25 to $49	395	325	70	6	20	23	17	85	54	219	68	96	12
$50 to $74	581	490	91	3	40	52	40	165	81	374	63	118	26
$75 to $99	825	725	100	5	40	45	22	252	103	546	89	158	32
$100 to $149	1,566	1,403	163	12	72	64	81	448	137	1,072	182	249	62
$150 to $199	1,161	1,052	108	7	32	58	51	295	78	965	57	117	22
$200 or more	1,848	1,701	146	16	10	107	76	504	107	1,671	71	90	15
Median (dollars)	133	133	100	138	96	125	125	125	100	154	100	100	100
Included in rent, other fee, or obtained free	2,604	536	2,068	26	17	547	528	571	564	2,325	99	135	45
Property insurance													
Property insurance paid	81,711	72,313	9,397	4,116	4,330	7,484	6,372	18,829	6,553	14,462	20,152	30,222	16,874
Median per month (dollars)	50	55	16	52	38	45	50	50	39	51	44	52	54
Monthly costs paid for selected utilities and fuels													
Water paid separately	62,789	53,552	9,237	3,007	3,111	6,889	6,281	13,128	6,283	9,350	14,380	25,721	13,338
Median (dollars)	35	38	29	35	30	33	40	33	30	37	33	33	43
Trash paid separately	52,525	44,974	7,551	2,686	2,481	4,525	5,193	10,922	4,957	5,357	13,125	20,327	13,716
Median (dollars)	21	21	20	21	17	22	27	20	20	21	19	21	25
Bottled gas paid separately	6,632	5,902	730	376	977	394	337	1,716	752	1,176	1,632	3,012	812
Median (dollars)	62	63	54	64	53	56	44	62	57	63	76	59	52
Other fuel paid separately	3,786	3,117	669	85	510	248	244	689	403	1,280	500	1,079	926
Median (dollars)	25	25	25	33	33	25	25	27	30	50	21	17	21

– = Zero or rounds to zero.
X = Not applicable.
Z = Sample too small.
[1] = Beginning with 1989, this item uses current income in its calculation.
[2] = May reflect a temporary situation, living off savings, or response error.

Source: U.S. Census Bureau, American Housing Survey

Table 2-2. Selected Housing Costs, Owner-Occupied Units, 2009

[Numbers in thousands except as noted.]

Characteristics	Total occupied units	Housing unit characteristics		Household characteristics				Regions			
		New construction 4 years	Manufactured/ mobile homes	Black alone	Hispanic	Elderly (65 years and over)	Below poverty level	Northeast	Midwest	South	West
Total	76,428	3,830	5,418	6,547	6,439	18,472	6,405	13,378	18,249	29,193	15,607
Monthly housing costs											
Less than $100	475	3	257	63	47	170	128	43	61	182	190
$100 to $199	2,161	36	919	259	207	949	598	149	369	1,186	457
$200 to $249	2,376	101	759	197	171	1,194	540	158	442	1,442	334
$250 to $299	2,976	65	494	270	281	1,393	494	207	645	1,584	539
$300 to $349	2,989	74	408	301	198	1,491	431	328	708	1,481	472
$350 to $399	3,033	72	267	199	246	1,406	387	325	841	1,355	513
$400 to $449	2,830	69	214	252	219	1,293	337	376	815	1,205	434
$450 to $499	2,478	62	194	218	152	1,102	273	361	713	986	418
$500 to $599	4,407	127	289	396	279	1,756	439	898	1,130	1,715	663
$600 to $699	3,735	86	283	405	224	1,324	338	784	962	1,547	442
$700 to $799	3,597	97	320	363	246	1,040	338	698	998	1,451	449
$800 to $999	7,139	196	397	678	664	1,462	555	1,239	2,073	2,824	1,003
$1,000 to $1,249	8,156	366	333	743	619	1,219	436	1,440	2,388	3,109	1,219
$1,250 to $1,499	6,828	422	156	570	567	748	286	1,139	1,910	2,454	1,326
$1,500 to $1,999	9,445	719	77	718	918	814	375	1,877	2,223	2,949	2,396
$2,000 to $2,499	5,422	466	10	381	501	420	174	1,316	988	1,615	1,502
$2,500 or more	8,383	870	41	537	900	692	275	2,039	982	2,111	3,251
No cash rent	X	X	X	X	X	X	X	X	X	X	X
Median (dollars; excludes no cash rent)	1,000	1,572	332	901	1,113	512	502	1,196	937	827	1,389
Median monthly housing costs for owners (dollars)											
Monthly costs including all mortgages plus maintenance costs	1,049	1,607	370	959	1,177	548	541	1,255	981	881	1,438
Monthly costs excluding second and subsequent mortgages and maintenance costs	984	1,538	332	882	1,080	511	501	1,173	915	819	1,340
Monthly housing costs as percent of current income[1]											
Less than 5 percent	2,903	92	488	133	171	594	8	364	550	1,231	758
5 to 9 percent	9,614	334	1,134	617	561	2,658	49	1,358	2,237	4,283	1,736
10 to 14 percent	11,147	361	973	842	711	2,932	109	1,923	2,910	4,601	1,713
15 to 19 percent	10,986	437	607	814	719	2,410	215	1,911	3,112	4,062	1,902
20 to 24 percent	9,589	635	467	754	716	1,966	191	1,693	2,478	3,584	1,834
25 to 29 percent	7,167	514	398	625	586	1,481	262	1,336	1,648	2,604	1,578
30 to 34 percent	5,160	299	248	488	579	1,024	282	925	1,289	1,763	1,182
35 to 39 percent	3,753	225	168	429	370	818	242	717	834	1,277	925
40 to 49 percent	4,529	358	219	468	551	1,119	434	856	992	1,598	1,084
50 to 59 percent	2,649	129	151	268	332	675	317	566	510	916	657
60 to 69 percent	1,676	109	83	192	229	443	285	343	380	553	401
70 to 99 percent	2,380	142	137	300	324	664	548	493	416	812	658
100 percent or more[2]	4,016	157	263	516	486	1,577	2,660	776	747	1,546	947
Zero or negative income	859	39	82	102	103	109	803	118	146	363	232
No cash rent	X	X	X	X	X	X	X	X	X	X	X
Median (dollars; excludes 2 previous lines)	21	25	15	25	27	21	89	23	20	20	24
Median (dollars; excludes 3 lines before medians)	20	24	14	23	25	19	42	21	19	19	22
Rent paid by lodgers											
Lodgers in housing units	372	22	47	13	70	34	32	41	79	150	101
Less than $200 per month	71	2	23	2	16	5	11	9	13	29	21
$200 to $299	34	3	12	1	10	4	4	1	7	20	6
$300 to $399	66	7	5	–	12	3	3	9	17	16	25
$400 to $499	65	4	3	6	10	8	5	13	18	23	12
$500 to $599	28	2	–	–	7	2	4	–	6	22	–
$600 to $799	35	–	–	–	7	–	1	1	8	20	7
$800 or more per month	32	–	–	–	8	1	5	7	3	6	16
Not reported	40	3	5	4	–	12	–	2	8	15	15
Median (dollars)	350	Z	Z	Z	350	Z	Z	Z	325	400	347
Monthly cost paid for electricity											
Electricity used	76,378	3,822	5,418	6,547	6,439	18,470	6,397	13,364	18,223	29,183	15,607
Less than $25	442	12	43	23	65	190	72	65	116	28	234
$25 to $49	4,425	144	292	288	489	1,622	609	945	1,363	477	1,640
$50 to $74	11,016	385	728	762	964	3,600	1,155	2,611	3,397	1,994	3,014
$75 to $99	12,975	540	833	904	1,093	3,289	1,078	2,559	3,889	3,582	2,944
$100 to $149	21,237	1,251	1,545	1,806	1,684	4,728	1,580	3,311	5,237	9,145	3,543
$150 to $199	12,164	742	1,003	1,178	913	2,355	895	1,732	2,187	6,397	1,849
$200 or more	12,110	674	849	1,381	1,088	2,105	816	2,018	1,530	6,791	1,770
Median (dollars)	117	129	123	133	115	102	105	105	100	145	97
Included in rent, other fee, or obtained free	2,010	75	125	206	144	581	192	123	504	770	613

Table 2-2. Selected Housing Costs, Owner-Occupied Units, 2009—*Continued*

[Numbers in thousands except as noted.]

Characteristics	Total occupied units	Housing unit characteristics		Household characteristics				Regions			
		New construction 4 years	Manufactured/ mobile homes	Black alone	Hispanic	Elderly (65 years and over)	Below poverty level	Northeast	Midwest	South	West
Monthly cost paid for piped gas											
Piped gas used	46,700	2,125	1,306	4,263	4,486	10,939	3,443	7,819	13,959	12,638	12,284
Less than $25	1,410	81	50	100	250	375	185	169	112	547	581
$25 to $49	7,933	439	370	581	1,208	2,001	766	475	1,573	2,494	3,391
$50 to $74	11,196	511	339	834	1,314	2,495	796	598	2,959	3,156	4,481
$75 to $99	8,595	394	211	801	641	1,912	583	1,235	2,854	2,656	1,850
$100 to $149	9,694	440	144	876	543	2,243	519	2,523	3,845	2,192	1,133
$150 to $199	3,698	102	47	501	192	856	250	1,300	1,403	685	309
$200 or more	2,682	99	23	421	159	621	173	1,094	851	490	247
Median (dollars)	80	75	60	91	61	79	71	118	92	73	59
Included in rent, other fee, or obtained free	1,494	59	121	149	179	437	170	426	360	417	291
Average monthly cost paid for fuel oil											
Fuel oil used	6,409	55	212	373	229	1,887	513	4,846	550	845	167
Less than $25	176	–	15	13	2	46	30	90	39	44	3
$25 to $49	325	6	16	12	3	80	37	179	63	74	10
$50 to $74	490	1	34	43	22	162	65	307	60	101	22
$75 to $99	725	5	40	33	16	237	79	480	81	139	26
$100 to $149	1,403	12	67	52	60	427	108	945	164	241	52
$150 to $199	1,052	7	27	50	35	276	62	886	50	95	22
$200 or more	1,701	16	6	93	55	476	92	1,540	64	82	15
Median (dollars)	133	Z	96	142	133	125	100	167	100	100	117
Included in rent, other fee, or obtained free	536	9	6	77	35	182	39	419	30	68	18
Property insurance											
Property insurance paid	72,313	3,749	4,173	5,972	5,615	17,351	5,220	12,930	17,676	26,972	14,736
Median per month (dollars)	55	56	38	54	54	50	48	58	50	58	58
Monthly costs paid for selected utilities and fuels											
Water paid separately	53,552	2,686	2,566	5,033	4,892	12,366	4,136	8,710	12,504	20,914	11,424
Median (dollars)	38	38	30	35	45	33	33	38	35	35	46
Trash paid separately	44,974	2,458	2,068	3,267	4,063	10,253	3,282	4,921	11,498	16,876	11,679
Median (dollars)	21	21	17	23	29	20	21	21	20	21	25
Bottled gas paid separately	5,902	349	804	320	231	1,626	589	1,057	1,485	2,662	698
Median (dollars)	63	64	54	56	43	62	62	64	76	59	57
Other fuel paid separately	3,117	79	414	165	173	631	243	1,189	391	828	709
Median (dollars)	25	33	33	25	25	25	30	42	21	17	21
Cost and ownership sharing											
Ownership shared by person not living here	2,527	93	193	279	289	666	472	481	535	906	604
Costs shared by person not living here	476	31	21	38	56	73	130	121	66	127	162
Costs not shared	2,035	63	173	237	233	593	339	354	467	775	439
Cost sharing not reported	16	–	–	3	–	–	3	6	2	5	3
Ownership not shared	72,124	3,643	5,135	6,105	6,050	17,438	5,660	12,566	17,424	27,470	14,664
Costs shared by person not living here	1,008	53	115	116	109	153	142	169	191	493	156
Costs not shared	70,949	3,589	5,016	5,980	5,942	17,241	5,481	12,357	17,212	26,881	14,499
Cost sharing not reported	167	–	4	9	–	44	36	41	21	96	9
Ownership sharing not reported	1,777	94	90	163	100	368	274	331	290	817	339
Monthly payment for principal and interest											
One or more regular mortgages	47,945	3,197	2,039	4,242	4,410	4,936	2,589	8,237	11,775	17,118	10,815
Less than $100	1,327	140	132	131	120	229	118	279	265	580	203
$100 to $199	1,072	49	162	171	82	236	167	208	290	438	136
$200 to $249	776	42	139	88	50	166	96	145	208	321	102
$250 to $299	981	27	156	143	77	168	121	127	307	471	75
$300 to $349	1,323	40	156	189	98	280	94	260	413	516	134
$350 to $399	1,550	49	219	163	159	292	205	191	467	724	168
$400 to $449	1,631	16	200	194	119	228	135	219	558	718	136
$450 to $499	1,707	49	79	173	123	269	161	282	561	674	189
$500 to $599	3,816	75	251	388	331	482	220	511	1,239	1,647	420
$600 to $699	3,859	159	165	365	367	442	157	540	1,143	1,580	596
$700 to $799	3,443	185	157	314	271	305	198	493	1,084	1,372	493
$800 to $999	6,162	377	125	508	479	513	212	1,016	1,648	2,372	1,126
$1,000 to $1,249	5,879	478	56	438	540	405	247	1,054	1,443	1,897	1,485
$1,250 to $1,499	4,059	371	23	306	398	265	144	796	810	1,247	1,207
$1,500 to $1,999	4,786	489	8	300	525	305	129	1,019	759	1,325	1,682
$2,000 or more	5,574	649	11	370	672	352	185	1,097	578	1,236	2,663
Median (dollars)	878	1,198	403	739	977	625	583	966	736	760	1,275

Table 2-2. Selected Housing Costs, Owner-Occupied Units, 2009—*Continued*

[Numbers in thousands except as noted.]

Characteristics	Total occupied units	Housing unit characteristics		Household characteristics				Regions			
		New construction 4 years	Manufactured/ mobile homes	Black alone	Hispanic	Elderly (65 years and over)	Below poverty level	Northeast	Midwest	South	West
Average monthly cost paid for real estate taxes											
Less than $25	7,751	423	2,688	1,210	631	2,700	1,558	479	1,056	5,107	1,110
$25 to $49	6,017	214	1,071	680	456	1,964	816	361	1,232	3,495	929
$50 to $74	6,565	240	654	721	578	1,886	718	483	1,508	3,455	1,119
$75 to $99	5,883	231	238	547	536	1,612	537	573	1,478	2,575	1,257
$100 to $124	6,494	272	225	543	641	1,567	541	629	1,828	2,585	1,452
$125 to $149	4,880	193	122	400	410	1,124	304	593	1,518	1,680	1,089
$150 to $199	9,140	434	147	699	873	2,124	593	1,442	2,677	2,904	2,117
$200 to $299	11,727	605	136	756	953	2,317	567	2,581	3,216	3,313	2,617
$300 to $399	6,171	379	29	327	487	1,107	237	1,783	1,581	1,411	1,397
$400 to $499	3,655	257	37	221	305	674	154	1,264	768	864	759
$500 to $599	2,884	181	20	183	204	476	130	1,103	532	598	652
$600 or more	5,260	401	51	261	366	921	250	2,088	854	1,207	1,110
Median (dollars)	150	183	25	100	146	114	77	280	154	99	167
Annual taxes paid per $1,000 value											
Less than $5	12,710	804	1,606	1,440	1,011	4,686	1,684	796	1,227	7,266	3,422
$5 to $9	21,383	1,057	904	1,694	1,621	4,995	1,555	2,129	3,355	9,467	6,431
$10 to $14	17,473	854	769	1,343	1,309	3,756	1,215	3,417	5,018	5,539	3,499
$15 to $19	9,992	407	458	717	871	1,999	598	2,798	3,830	2,376	988
$20 to $24	6,058	301	287	493	607	1,134	406	1,777	2,191	1,692	399
$25 or more	8,812	408	1,394	859	1,021	1,902	947	2,462	2,628	2,854	868
Median (dollars)	10	10	10	10	11	9	9	15	14	8	8
Routine maintenance in last year											
Less than $25 per month	29,139	2,479	3,127	2,682	2,378	8,948	2,972	3,809	7,554	11,986	5,791
$25 to $49	17,691	509	1,092	1,475	1,461	3,503	1,104	3,032	4,333	6,513	3,814
$50 to $74	2,887	48	133	288	341	593	205	567	640	1,087	593
$75 to $99	7,768	198	235	470	643	1,199	399	1,701	1,735	2,787	1,545
$100 to $149	2,655	73	69	271	202	478	160	583	563	981	529
$150 to $199	3,460	48	93	281	297	549	160	840	680	1,151	789
$200 or more per month	3,885	46	128	352	413	692	247	907	773	1,322	883
Not reported	8,942	430	540	728	705	2,509	1,157	1,939	1,973	3,366	1,664
Median (dollars)	29	4	17	25	29	17	17	42	25	25	33
Condominium and cooperative fees											
Fee paid by owners	4,790	302	X	296	425	1,386	374	1,149	982	1,328	1,331
Less than $50 per month	206	8	X	24	37	51	10	46	19	82	59
$50 to $99	254	33	X	12	32	66	32	23	57	87	87
$100 to $149	536	53	X	14	56	118	40	105	172	131	127
$150 to $199	685	74	X	37	67	147	45	122	175	192	196
$200 to $299	1,016	55	X	44	95	279	48	173	241	265	337
$300 to $499	838	44	X	51	65	275	65	176	114	253	296
$500 or more per month	445	19	X	27	8	174	16	205	62	85	92
Not reported	810	16	X	87	64	276	119	299	142	232	137
Median (dollars)	220	180	X	220	187	252	200	270	198	215	230
Other housing costs per month											
Homeowner association fee paid	9,397	1,409	–	732	675	1,651	337	581	1,614	4,797	2,405
Median (dollars)	33	42	Z	31	36	42	33	58	17	33	47
Manufactured/mobile home park fee paid	310	–	310	6	40	120	64	15	63	158	73
Median (dollars)	120	Z	120	Z	Z	105	120	Z	240	25	250
Land rent fee paid	85	4	7	9	2	19	10	10	19	33	23
Median (dollars)	33	Z	Z	Z	Z	Z	Z	Z	Z	Z	Z
Government subsidy for repairs											
Units with major repairs in the last 2 years	43,019	1,453	2,874	3,446	3,659	9,280	3,010	7,366	11,136	15,742	8,775
Received low interest loan or grant	796	14	77	113	107	203	120	166	189	265	175
No low interest loan or grant	42,002	1,417	2,792	3,318	3,532	9,045	2,871	7,176	10,882	15,382	8,563
Not reported	221	22	6	15	20	32	19	24	65	96	36

– = Zero or rounds to zero.
X = Not applicable.
Z = Sample too small.
[1] = Beginning with 1989, this item uses current income in its calculation.
[2] = May reflect a temporary situation, living off savings, or response error.

Source: U.S. Census Bureau, American Housing Survey

Table 2-3. Selected Housing Costs, Renter-Occupied Units, 2009

[Numbers in thousands, except as noted.]

Characteristics	Total occupied units	Housing unit characteristics		Household characteristics				Regions			
		New construction 4 years	Manufactured/ mobile homes	Black alone	Hispanic	Elderly (65 years and over)	Below poverty level	Northeast	Midwest	South	West
Total	35,378	941	1,421	7,446	6,300	4,623	9,334	7,073	7,119	12,392	8,794
Monthly housing costs											
Less than $100	248	5	3	91	41	42	186	56	56	83	52
$100 to $199	728	24	8	279	91	219	573	134	211	268	116
$200 to $249	738	17	24	218	122	289	505	235	189	187	126
$250 to $299	643	2	19	204	78	172	390	122	143	221	156
$300 to $349	581	10	26	166	76	166	282	159	151	185	86
$350 to $399	778	6	80	191	96	197	317	193	220	256	109
$400 to $449	993	14	61	198	157	216	393	160	267	370	195
$450 to $499	1,101	21	83	222	176	192	430	175	348	413	164
$500 to $599	2,985	49	200	696	487	389	906	477	800	1,714	493
$600 to $699	3,808	43	219	874	678	438	1,023	578	1,044	1,498	688
$700 to $799	3,709	89	195	770	644	366	877	558	895	1,477	779
$800 to $999	6,060	151	183	1,337	1,257	517	1,180	1,170	1,187	2,218	1,486
$1,000 to $1,249	4,777	174	40	1,041	985	379	833	1,154	668	1,537	1,417
$1,250 to $1,499	2,631	100	22	430	523	154	333	664	272	734	960
$1,500 to $1,999	2,247	114	2	262	461	196	244	567	174	501	1,005
$2,000 to $2,499	718	46	–	86	132	80	87	160	48	147	363
$2,500 or more	596	53	10	35	58	129	53	169	45	137	245
No cash rent	2,037	23	248	348	239	481	722	341	398	945	352
Median (dollars; excludes no cash rent)	808	1,045	623	746	854	640	629	877	691	764	956
Monthly housing costs as percent of current income[1]											
Less than 5 percent	162	7	3	15	35	23	17	50	21	45	47
5 to 9 percent	721	22	55	105	83	79	21	176	126	256	163
10 to 14 percent	1,964	60	102	295	256	170	47	428	470	615	451
15 to 19 percent	3,224	77	77	553	450	235	87	632	738	1,133	720
20 to 24 percent	3,682	93	105	697	603	329	159	733	736	1,234	979
25 to 29 percent	3,608	138	114	708	615	494	366	722	783	1,170	932
30 to 34 percent	2,956	82	92	651	606	370	360	638	609	992	717
35 to 39 percent	2,317	71	69	525	388	312	322	426	531	828	532
40 to 49 percent	3,322	91	126	689	704	394	561	650	513	1,196	963
50 to 59 percent	2,210	62	75	542	493	298	658	401	422	800	587
60 to 69 percent	1,423	32	65	316	308	227	519	247	245	487	444
70 to 99 percent	2,415	42	89	544	540	383	1,245	495	437	830	653
100 percent or more[2]	4,076	102	159	1,089	762	761	3,156	908	871	1,325	971
Zero or negative income	1,261	40	41	369	216	68	1,094	224	217	536	283
No cash rent	2,037	23	248	348	239	481	722	341	398	945	352
Median (dollars; excludes 2 previous lines)	34	31	36	38	38	40	82	33	32	35	35
Median (dollars; excludes 3 lines before medians)	31	29	31	33	33	34	53	30	29	31	31
Rent paid by lodgers											
Lodgers in housing units	606	17	26	50	211	10	97	106	84	211	205
Less than $200 per month	104	5	12	17	51	–	19	11	24	49	19
$200 to $299	84	–	7	9	32	7	10	1	11	46	26
$300 to $399	93	3	5	7	38	–	18	16	15	30	32
$400 to $499	99	3	–	–	26	–	12	16	5	35	42
$500 to $599	67	–	3	3	18	–	16	9	15	15	28
$600 to $799	58	–	–	–	22	–	3	13	6	20	19
$800 or more per month	74	6	–	8	20	3	9	27	1	7	38
Not reported	28	–	–	5	5	–	11	11	5	9	2
Median (dollars)	400	Z	Z	Z	332	Z	350	500	300	300	450
Monthly cost paid for electricity											
Electricity used	35,368	941	1,421	7,446	6,300	4,623	9,330	7,067	7,119	12,389	8,794
Less than $25	1,259	22	9	181	259	260	330	129	411	49	670
$25 to $49	5,426	80	85	869	1,060	860	1,358	1,389	1,403	513	2,122
$50 to $74	6,535	144	167	1,307	1,167	848	1,623	1,529	1,490	1,725	1,791
$75 to $99	5,469	188	229	1,182	1,002	570	1,284	1,040	1,057	2,248	1,125
$100 to $149	6,589	254	383	1,480	1,142	508	1,600	1,026	1,118	3,388	1,057
$150 to $199	2,795	102	218	651	515	165	723	320	376	1,622	477
$200 or more	2,341	56	218	790	368	132	680	354	299	1,359	329
Median (dollars)	84	98	118	94	82	64	84	71	70	111	62
Included in rent, other fee, or obtained free	4,954	94	112	986	787	1,280	1,732	1,279	966	1,485	1,224

Table 2-3. Selected Housing Costs, Renter-Occupied Units, 2009—*Continued*

[Numbers in thousands, except as noted.]

Characteristics	Total occupied units	Housing unit characteristics		Household characteristics				Regions			
		New construction 4 years	Manufactured/ mobile homes	Black alone	Hispanic	Elderly (65 years and over)	Below poverty level	Northeast	Midwest	South	West
Monthly cost paid for piped gas											
Piped gas used	21,186	381	417	4,575	4,215	2,610	5,497	5,230	5,046	4,444	6,466
Less than $25	2,447	36	54	350	732	349	612	466	176	373	1,432
$25 to $49	4,469	103	107	847	1,083	462	1,067	531	725	1,060	2,153
$50 to $74	3,581	90	116	771	679	309	803	722	898	867	1,094
$75 to $99	2,054	28	41	490	277	211	490	513	667	550	324
$100 to $149	1,884	43	41	421	268	197	483	673	701	342	168
$150 to $199	643	10	4	213	83	48	163	225	234	127	57
$200 or more	518	7	6	238	78	51	187	174	191	130	23
Median (dollars)	55	54	54	64	44	50	56	71	74	56	37
Included in rent, other fee, or obtained free	5,588	64	48	1,245	1,014	982	1,693	1,927	1,454	993	1,215
Average monthly cost paid for fuel oil											
Fuel oil used	2,800	19	37	539	589	482	659	2,428	144	174	55
Less than $25	52	–	2	2	2	3	17	11	25	10	6
$25 to $49	70	–	4	11	13	5	16	40	5	23	3
$50 to $74	91	3	6	9	17	3	15	68	3	17	4
$75 to $99	100	–	–	12	6	15	25	66	9	19	6
$100 to $149	163	–	5	12	21	20	30	127	19	8	10
$150 to $199	108	–	5	9	16	19	16	79	8	22	–
$200 or more	146	–	4	14	21	28	15	131	7	8	–
Median (dollars)	100	Z	Z	100	125	150	83	125	75	83	Z
Included in rent, other fee, or obtained free	2,068	17	11	471	493	389	525	1,905	69	67	27
Property insurance											
Property insurance paid	9,397	367	157	1,512	757	1,478	1,333	1,532	2,476	3,250	2,138
Median per month (dollars)	16	17	17	17	17	14	15	17	13	16	17
Monthly costs paid for selected utilities and fuels											
Water paid separately	9,237	321	545	1,857	1,389	762	2,148	640	1,877	4,807	1,913
Median (dollars)	29	25	27	29	29	25	25	33	28	26	33
Trash paid separately	7,551	228	414	1,258	1,129	669	1,675	436	1,627	3,451	2,037
Median (dollars)	20	20	17	21	20	19	19	18	17	20	23
Bottled gas paid separately	730	27	173	74	106	90	163	119	147	350	115
Median (dollars)	54	Z	44	54	44	43	53	48	64	54	41
Other fuel paid separately	669	6	96	83	71	58	160	90	109	252	218
Median (dollars)	25	Z	25	19	15	33	Z	67	29	17	21

– = Zero or rounds to zero.
Z = Sample too small.
[1] = Beginning with 1989, this item uses current income in its calculation.
[2] = May reflect a temporary situation, living off savings, or response error.

Source: U.S. Census Bureau, American Housing Survey

Table 2-4. Value, Purchase Price, and Source of Down Payment, Owner-Occupied Units, 2009

[Numbers in thousands, except as noted.]

Characteristics	Total occupied units	Housing unit characteristics		Household characteristics				Regions			
		New construction 4 years	Manufactured/ mobile homes	Black alone	Hispanic	Elderly (65 years and over)	Below poverty level	Northeast	Midwest	South	West
Total	76,428	3,830	5,418	6,547	6,439	18,472	6,405	13,378	18,249	29,193	15,607
Value											
Less than $10,000	1,696	17	1,256	157	203	360	400	209	323	783	381
$10,000 to $19,999	1,311	64	1,001	129	115	364	259	154	307	660	190
$20,000 to $29,999	1,073	18	581	157	96	321	248	134	251	577	110
$30,000 to $39,999	1,187	47	429	121	120	351	241	174	261	620	131
$40,000 to $59,999	3,155	77	611	501	347	1,090	566	410	968	1,468	309
$60,000 to $79,999	5,261	159	584	690	496	1,561	634	633	1,841	2,341	447
$80,000 to $99,999	6,002	118	290	795	594	1,624	684	754	1,958	2,882	409
$100,000 to $119,999	4,980	122	214	551	431	1,397	468	524	1,728	2,281	447
$120,000 to $149,999	7,629	310	251	693	625	1,680	504	836	2,487	3,573	732
$150,000 to $199,999	11,141	644	158	882	866	2,483	775	1,682	3,162	4,494	1,803
$200,000 to $299,999	13,494	984	34	893	1,114	2,942	735	2,640	2,857	4,549	3,447
$300,000 to $399,999	7,924	512	5	463	701	1,681	393	2,025	1,087	2,390	2,421
$400,000 to $499,999	4,200	288	–	236	285	884	202	1,342	415	993	1,449
$500,000 to $749,999	4,577	290	2	211	313	1,069	202	1,268	400	980	1,930
$750,000 or more	2,798	179	1	67	133	666	94	591	204	602	1,402
Median (dollars)	170,000	220,000	25,000	120,000	150,000	150,000	100,000	230,000	134,000	140,000	270,000
Ratio of value to current income											
Less than 1.5	15,304	512	3,528	1,443	1,183	2,230	505	2,245	4,561	6,660	1,839
1.5 to 1.9	9,070	461	447	737	746	1,258	63	1,377	2,816	3,684	1,193
2.0 to 2.4	8,281	516	277	668	589	1,170	161	1,342	2,369	3,245	1,325
2.5 to 2.9	7,123	499	157	612	607	1,243	99	1,225	1,814	2,652	1,432
3.0 to 3.9	10,044	666	271	874	892	2,093	229	1,732	2,260	3,781	2,270
4.0 to 4.9	5,844	317	169	413	548	1,626	217	1,080	1,055	2,004	1,706
5.0 to 6.9	7,220	368	157	560	634	2,560	477	1,469	1,368	2,525	1,858
7.0 to 8.9	3,486	168	66	258	359	1,428	324	692	545	1,152	1,098
9.0 to 10.9	1,975	56	29	176	165	957	317	464	285	702	523
11 or more	7,222	226	235	704	613	3,799	3,210	1,635	1,031	2,426	2,131
Zero or negative income	859	39	82	102	103	109	803	118	146	363	232
Median (number)	2.8	2.9	0.8	2.7	3.0	4.7	15.0	3.2	2.3	2.6	3.8
Other activities on property											
Medical or commercial establishment	652	19	25	38	32	142	44	199	162	206	86
Neither	75,776	3,811	5,393	6,509	6,407	18,330	6,361	13,179	18,088	28,987	15,521
Year unit acquired											
2005 to 2009	19,482	3,830	1,539	1,600	1,892	1,527	1,405	2,769	4,452	7,949	4,312
2000 to 2004	17,794	X	1,474	1,448	1,867	2,245	1,376	2,841	4,165	6,749	4,039
1995 to 1999	11,722	X	1,264	1,106	961	2,151	858	2,038	2,791	4,534	2,359
1990 to 1994	7,681	X	506	612	577	1,727	581	1,371	1,954	2,870	1,485
1985 to 1989	5,501	X	304	418	391	1,610	477	1,105	1,363	1,992	1,041
1980 to 1984	3,166	X	150	290	202	1,145	345	737	715	1,184	531
1975 to 1979	3,763	X	96	338	190	1,895	371	778	1,002	1,318	665
1970 to 1974	2,545	X	60	275	152	1,753	312	552	616	1,011	366
1960 to 1969	3,102	X	21	326	140	2,817	379	755	785	1,056	506
1950 to 1959	1,405	X	2	118	58	1,361	256	343	351	450	261
1940 to 1949	237	X	2	13	10	225	38	77	51	73	36
1939 or earlier	29	X	X	3	–	15	8	12	3	8	6
Median (year)	1999	2007	2000	1999	2001	1985	1997	1997	1999	2000	2000
First-time owners											
First home ever owned	31,676	1,066	2,196	4,155	3,639	5,851	3,102	6,761	7,362	11,616	5,938
Not first home	43,233	2,648	3,128	2,233	2,741	12,366	3,061	6,243	10,625	16,995	9,370
Not reported	1,519	117	94	158	59	255	243	374	263	583	300
Purchase price											
Home purchased or built	71,877	3,706	5,076	5,904	6,148	17,250	5,532	12,346	17,380	27,307	14,843
Less than $10,000	2,799	13	912	270	331	1,432	625	460	694	1,265	381
$10,000 to $19,999	4,229	8	863	512	320	2,528	631	747	1,174	1,684	625
$20,000 to $29,999	3,648	12	750	357	270	1,697	421	683	979	1,515	472
$30,000 to $39,999	3,489	44	510	380	252	1,339	394	682	958	1,429	421
$40,000 to $49,999	3,002	17	427	254	244	957	292	511	850	1,239	403
$50,000 to $59,999	3,076	23	279	365	226	855	293	459	945	1,335	337
$60,000 to $69,999	3,126	29	258	269	310	735	264	450	921	1,343	411
$70,000 to $79,999	2,968	37	190	332	270	673	238	412	805	1,333	418
$80,000 to $99,999	5,662	136	236	531	562	931	300	780	1,569	2,426	887
$100,000 to $119,999	4,288	109	126	341	370	684	254	643	1,210	1,685	751

Table 2-4. Value, Purchase Price, and Source of Down Payment, Owner-Occupied Units, 2009—*Continued*

[Numbers in thousands, except as noted.]

Characteristics	Total occupied units	Housing unit characteristics		Household characteristics				Regions			
		New construction 4 years	Manufactured/ mobile homes	Black alone	Hispanic	Elderly (65 years and over)	Below poverty level	Northeast	Midwest	South	West
$120,000 to $149,999	6,691	262	97	532	594	991	317	962	1,806	2,647	1,275
$150,000 to $199,999	8,055	602	19	490	805	1,152	312	1,408	1,939	2,755	1,953
$200,000 to $249,999	5,029	521	9	263	374	577	203	886	1,006	1,680	1,457
$250,000 to $299,999	3,024	335	–	163	240	375	89	553	565	1,004	902
$300,000 or more	8,594	1,266	3	353	765	911	287	1,766	1,032	2,238	3,558
Not reported	4,196	293	399	491	214	1,416	612	944	928	1,729	595
Median (dollars)	107,500	240,000	27,000	78,000	110,000	49,000	50,000	115,000	89,900	91,500	165,000
Received as inheritance or gift	3,388	16	292	526	235	1,032	676	729	683	1,411	564
Not reported	1,163	108	50	117	56	189	197	303	186	475	200
Down payment											
Home purchased or built	71,877	3,706	5,076	5,904	6,148	17,250	5,532	12,346	17,380	27,307	14,843
Percent of purchase price											
No down payment	8,346	602	893	883	797	1,785	889	871	2,049	3,808	1,619
Less than 3 percent	5,034	239	274	663	606	967	437	622	1,185	2,232	996
3-5 percent	7,289	401	295	961	972	858	427	1,031	1,703	2,985	1,570
6-10 percent	9,895	504	566	1,017	1,057	1,547	531	1,617	2,427	3,762	2,088
11-15 percent	3,946	173	294	305	389	750	243	796	910	1,393	846
16-20 percent	8,200	452	258	347	549	1,332	304	1,521	2,038	2,645	1,995
21-40 percent	7,999	384	402	272	450	1,847	433	1,682	2,006	2,405	1,906
41-99 percent	4,478	227	260	130	222	1,569	280	1,007	1,167	1,336	969
Bought outright	6,377	257	1,081	297	393	3,199	827	990	1,503	2,682	1,201
Not reported	10,308	467	754	1,031	712	3,395	1,158	2,209	2,391	4,055	1,653
Major source of down payment											
Home purchased or built	71,877	3,706	5,076	5,904	6,148	17,250	5,532	12,346	17,380	27,307	14,843
Sale of previous home	21,946	1,330	962	711	1,203	6,381	1,133	3,387	5,861	7,760	4,938
Savings or cash on hand	31,437	1,193	2,152	3,357	3,299	6,894	2,399	6,474	7,094	11,680	6,189
Sale of other investment	750	42	53	22	61	219	59	106	150	247	246
Borrowing, other than mortgage on this property	2,409	88	264	247	262	590	263	385	589	959	477
Inheritance or gift	1,358	44	72	77	92	226	133	271	355	390	343
Land where building built used for financing	639	83	93	57	37	131	39	64	142	378	55
Other	3,125	145	383	344	293	573	337	430	786	1,279	630
No down payment	8,346	602	893	883	797	1,785	889	871	2,049	3,808	1,619
Not reported	1,867	181	205	205	104	451	281	359	354	808	347
How acquired											
First occupant in single-family unit built 1990 or later	8,811	2,627	X	679	720	1,326	364	891	2,080	4,089	1,751
Already built	3,022	1,015	X	323	307	396	87	240	595	1,396	791
Sales agreement	2,395	731	X	216	241	356	76	272	513	1,107	502
Contractor	2,113	481	X	87	118	413	88	248	653	974	238
Built it oneself	1,176	337	X	43	54	150	113	123	301	555	198
Received as inheritance or gift	11	3	X	3	–	1	–	1	6	3	–
Not reported	94	61	X	8	–	10	1	8	12	53	21

– = Zero or rounds to zero.
X = Not applicable.

Source: U.S. Census Bureau, American Housing Survey

Table 2-5. Mortgage Characteristics, Owner-Occupied Units, 2009

[Numbers in thousands, except as noted.]

Characteristics	Total occupied units	Housing unit characteristics		Household characteristics				Regions			
		New construction 4 years	Manufactured/ mobile homes	Black alone	Hispanic	Elderly (65 years and over)	Below poverty level	Northeast	Midwest	South	West
Total	76,428	3,830	5,418	6,547	6,439	18,472	6,405	13,378	18,249	29,193	15,607
Mortgages currently on property[1]											
None, owned free and clear	24,206	499	3,237	2,073	1,752	12,071	3,466	4,122	5,566	10,502	4,015
Reverse mortgage	252	3	11	17	24	241	36	33	33	106	80
Regular and/or home-equity mortgage[2]	50,300	3,251	2,107	4,338	4,525	5,804	2,710	8,839	12,357	17,900	11,203
Regular mortgage	46,703	3,174	2,002	4,153	4,325	4,604	2,509	7,848	11,461	16,753	10,640
Home-equity lump-sum mortgage	4,022	154	57	241	300	522	156	984	1,139	1,084	816
Home-equity line of credit	9,184	297	106	426	579	1,527	334	1,935	2,408	2,681	2,160
Line of credit not reported, no regular or lump sum	1,670	78	64	120	139	356	193	384	294	684	308
Number of regular mortgages and home-equity mortgages											
1 mortgage	35,274	2,391	1,830	3,329	3,307	4,322	1,940	6,067	8,650	12,984	7,573
2 mortgages	10,896	621	98	646	928	833	321	2,003	2,835	3,288	2,770
3 mortgages or more	801	20	2	43	67	76	25	121	255	192	233
Number not reported	5,000	297	240	440	361	928	617	1,033	910	2,121	936
Types of mortgages											
Regular and home-equity lump sum	2,779	131	20	152	215	189	76	595	825	719	640
With home-equity line of credit	429	11	2	16	40	52	10	71	151	99	108
No home-equity line of credit	2,341	120	17	135	173	137	65	519	672	620	530
Home-equity line of credit not reported	10	–	–	2	2	–	1	5	2	–	2
Regular, no home-equity lump sum	43,923	3,043	1,982	4,001	4,110	4,415	2,433	7,253	10,637	16,034	10,000
With home-equity line of credit	6,153	230	36	294	407	527	189	1,178	1,615	1,733	1,627
No home-equity line of credit	34,513	2,594	1,773	3,390	3,486	3,330	1,835	5,453	8,422	12,882	7,757
Home-equity line of credit not reported	3,258	219	173	317	217	558	409	622	600	1,419	616
Home-equity lump sum, no regular	1,243	22	37	89	85	333	80	389	314	365	175
With home-equity line of credit	248	2	–	20	17	80	14	84	61	65	37
No home-equity line of credit	989	20	37	69	68	252	67	301	251	299	138
Home-equity line of credit not reported	6	–	–	–	–	–	–	4	2	–	–
No regular or home-equity lump sum	28,483	634	3,379	2,305	2,029	13,535	3,816	5,141	6,474	12,076	4,792
With home-equity line of credit	2,355	54	68	96	115	867	121	602	581	783	388
No home-equity line of credit	24,458	501	3,247	2,089	1,776	12,312	3,502	4,155	5,599	10,609	4,096
Home-equity line of credit not reported	1,670	78	64	120	139	356	193	384	294	684	308
Owners with one or more regular or lump-sum home-equity mortgages											
Total	47,945	3,197	2,039	4,242	4,410	4,936	2,589	8,237	11,775	17,118	10,815
Land contract											
Units with one regular mortgage only	32,024	2,316	1,725	3,165	3,127	3,232	1,767	5,195	7,842	11,926	7,060
Mortgage is a land contract	3,488	309	250	367	542	351	185	528	400	1,646	915
Not a land contract	27,694	1,930	1,423	2,711	2,521	2,781	1,510	4,467	7,297	9,987	5,942
Not reported	842	78	52	86	65	100	71	200	146	293	204
Type of primary mortgage											
FHA	6,272	457	112	1,038	801	443	352	645	1,300	2,897	1,430
VA	3,660	273	207	316	312	356	140	554	858	1,442	805
RHS/RD	435	63	36	51	51	49	41	43	138	153	101
Other types	34,021	2,161	1,490	2,449	3,001	3,463	1,603	6,332	8,851	11,049	7,789
Don't know	98	8	18	26	10	18	12	10	23	47	19
Not reported	3,460	235	176	363	236	608	441	653	606	1,530	671
Lower cost state and local mortgages											
State or local program used	2,709	219	123	428	382	176	203	430	637	1,131	512
Not used	41,789	2,744	1,724	3,440	3,765	4,164	1,937	7,171	10,490	14,481	9,648
Not reported	3,447	233	192	374	263	597	449	637	649	1,506	656
Mortgage origination											
Placed new mortgage(s)	47,616	3,188	2,007	4,212	4,344	4,891	2,556	8,205	11,710	16,986	10,716
Primary obtained when property acquired	35,884	3,005	1,744	3,436	3,570	3,010	2,075	6,188	8,436	13,745	7,515
Obtained later	11,733	183	263	776	773	1,881	481	2,017	3,274	3,241	3,201
Assumed	259	8	28	19	51	40	25	24	58	110	67
Wrap-around	27	–	4	4	8	–	3	4	4	9	10
Combination of the above	43	–	–	7	8	5	6	4	4	14	22
Payment plan of primary mortgage											
Fixed payment, self-amortizing	40,055	2,664	1,713	3,472	3,686	3,820	1,861	6,935	10,048	14,259	8,813
Adjustable rate mortgage	1,942	80	58	201	238	187	97	271	464	634	573
Adjustable term mortgage	80	14	3	3	5	26	15	14	31	28	7
Graduated payment mortgage	523	48	–	48	62	26	17	62	126	86	249
Balloon	220	10	14	5	16	21	13	22	86	49	64
Other	6	–	3	–	–	3	–	–	–	3	4
Combination of the above	169	9	–	9	14	21	5	11	30	47	81
Not reported	4,950	373	248	504	390	832	581	923	991	2,012	1,024

Table 2-5. Mortgage Characteristics, Owner-Occupied Units, 2009—*Continued*

[Numbers in thousands, except as noted.]

Characteristics	Total occupied units	Housing unit characteristics		Household characteristics				Regions			
		New construction 4 years	Manufactured/ mobile homes	Black alone	Hispanic	Elderly (65 years and over)	Below poverty level	Northeast	Midwest	South	West
Payment plan of secondary mortgage											
Units with two or more mortgages	5,520	418	67	404	601	309	159	883	1,467	1,744	1,427
Fixed payment, self-amortizing	4,514	359	58	342	482	221	117	756	1,171	1,482	1,104
Adjustable rate mortgage	393	15	–	32	53	32	16	39	135	100	119
Adjustable term mortgage	71	1	–	1	3	15	3	12	24	26	9
Graduated payment mortgage	71	10	–	3	16	6	–	9	14	13	35
Balloon	143	20	4	6	8	12	4	11	39	38	55
Other	2	–	–	–	–	–	–	–	2	–	–
Combination of the above	101	9	–	–	4	1	6	19	24	22	35
Not reported	225	4	5	20	34	22	13	37	57	63	69
Lenders of primary and secondary mortgages											
Only borrowed from firm(s)	43,467	2,897	1,707	3,762	4,023	4,231	2,063	7,475	10,941	15,158	9,894
Only borrowed from seller	283	4	73	19	41	15	19	29	90	128	36
Only borrowed from other individual(s)	238	28	48	28	33	41	16	23	50	85	80
Borrowed from a firm and seller	17	–	–	–	–	–	–	3	3	8	3
Borrowed from a firm and other individual	36	–	–	–	9	–	–	–	16	9	12
Borrowed from seller and other individual	–	–	–	–	–	–	–	–	–	–	–
One or both sources not reported	3,904	267	211	434	306	649	492	707	676	1,731	790
Items included in primary mortgage payment[2]											
Principal and interest only	13,050	758	894	950	1,066	1,948	710	2,171	3,337	4,110	3,431
Property taxes	28,542	1,986	558	2,538	2,829	2,029	1,230	4,874	7,265	10,201	6,202
Property insurance	26,595	1,855	820	2,453	2,674	1,809	1,183	4,037	6,671	10,119	5,769
Private mortgage insurance	6,205	599	137	795	604	297	258	982	1,629	2,430	1,164
Other	376	52	12	33	36	30	14	86	82	143	66
Not reported	5,224	347	268	530	434	830	599	1,021	994	2,135	1,074
Year primary mortgage originated											
2005 to 2009	21,064	3,192	779	1,671	1,878	1,393	939	3,147	5,145	7,558	5,213
2000 to 2004	14,175	5	545	1,105	1,459	1,286	762	2,444	3,631	4,868	3,233
1995 to 1999	6,152	X	544	651	516	715	396	1,200	1,457	2,328	1,167
1990 to 1994	2,953	X	83	326	302	414	169	651	676	1,057	569
1985 to 1989	1,808	X	41	191	150	389	139	401	431	629	347
1980 to 1984	767	X	27	119	52	239	53	183	174	307	103
1975 to 1979	564	X	15	83	30	188	56	115	153	201	94
1970 to 1974	434	X	6	93	18	292	73	83	103	165	83
1969 or earlier	28	X	–	2	5	20	1	13	5	6	5
Median (year)	2004	2007	2002	2003	2004	2000	2003	2003	2004	2004	2004
Term of primary mortgage at origination or assumption											
Less than 8 years	695	32	120	52	66	101	58	91	182	231	191
8 to 12 years	1,159	42	167	62	111	182	101	242	327	425	165
13 to 17 years	5,501	217	370	243	340	629	254	953	1,517	2,024	1,007
18 to 22 years	2,421	89	289	209	144	333	181	485	666	908	362
23 to 27 years	929	33	114	89	37	134	52	166	262	409	91
28 to 32 years	35,845	2,743	940	3,363	3,562	3,023	1,760	6,031	8,491	12,645	8,677
33 years or more	1,251	19	35	216	145	490	167	246	294	431	280
Variable	145	22	3	8	6	45	15	23	36	43	43
Median (years)	30	30	25	30	30	30	30	30	30	30	30
Remaining years mortgaged											
Less than 8 years	6,160	53	535	607	431	1,363	496	1,276	1,506	2,378	1,001
8 to 12 years	5,188	97	312	348	368	813	313	974	1,404	1,831	978
13 to 17 years	5,077	162	277	463	436	630	285	998	1,291	1,787	1,001
18 to 22 years	6,568	63	393	755	699	640	373	1,186	1,590	2,427	1,366
23 to 27 years	14,948	971	310	1,201	1,632	974	703	2,369	3,732	5,187	3,660
28 to 32 years	9,569	1,808	200	837	778	448	380	1,369	2,137	3,393	2,670
33 years or more	164	16	8	22	57	8	21	21	37	30	76
Variable	271	26	3	9	10	62	19	44	78	85	64
Median (years)	23	28	16	22	24	14	21	21	23	23	24
Current interest rate											
Less than 5 percent	6,220	470	225	341	440	719	246	1,090	1,596	2,021	1,512
5 to 5.9 percent	17,659	1,070	393	1,170	1,341	1,604	804	3,248	4,295	5,632	4,484
6 to 6.9 percent	15,940	1,228	504	1,502	1,571	1,601	854	2,678	4,008	5,860	3,394
7 to 7.9 percent	4,619	269	318	584	595	537	341	704	1,098	1,930	887
8 to 8.9 percent	1,772	80	228	312	251	230	125	243	427	801	302
9 percent or more	1,735	80	371	332	212	244	219	274	351	873	236
Not reported	–	–	–	–	–	–	–	–	–	–	–
Median (percent)	6.0	6.0	6.5	6.2	6.0	6.0	6.0	5.9	5.9	6.0	5.8

Table 2-5. Mortgage Characteristics, Owner-Occupied Units, 2009—*Continued*

[Numbers in thousands, except as noted.]

Characteristics	Total occupied units	Housing unit characteristics		Household characteristics				Regions			
		New construction 4 years	Manufactured/ mobile homes	Black alone	Hispanic	Elderly (65 years and over)	Below poverty level	Northeast	Midwest	South	West
Total outstanding principal amount											
Less than $10,000	2,797	24	423	382	217	813	320	525	701	1,218	353
$10,000 to $19,999	1,972	95	327	210	128	410	158	386	522	838	226
$20,000 to $29,999	1,877	32	246	236	148	394	162	354	566	732	225
$30,000 to $39,999	1,978	32	191	249	185	345	241	343	536	854	245
$40,000 to $49,999	2,338	37	171	224	189	315	174	424	734	864	316
$50,000 to $59,999	2,328	39	73	266	228	307	171	334	733	967	294
$60,000 to $69,999	2,504	73	140	257	298	259	201	350	756	1,027	370
$70,000 to $79,999	2,484	124	140	228	202	213	127	371	785	979	349
$80,000 to $99,999	4,420	161	165	426	389	433	217	719	1,343	1,662	696
$100,000 to $119,999	3,751	212	64	349	315	243	146	604	1,096	1,440	611
$120,000 to $149,999	5,029	314	48	320	427	335	168	741	1,332	1,879	1,076
$150,000 to $199,999	5,926	587	42	440	547	325	185	1,090	1,319	1,950	1,567
$200,000 to $249,999	3,575	447	3	248	377	177	121	714	664	965	1,232
$250,000 to $299,999	2,267	273	–	123	234	131	69	428	238	657	944
$300,000 or more	4,700	745	8	284	525	239	128	855	450	1,085	2,310
Not reported	–	–	–	–	–	–	–	–	–	–	–
Median (dollars)	106,909	189,805	31,214	83,099	114,364	55,911	63,675	110,806	88,069	93,171	170,531
Current total loan as percent of value											
Less than 20 percent	6,174	94	240	647	413	1,629	474	1,489	1,316	2,072	1,297
20 to 39 percent	7,478	167	219	616	618	1,032	383	1,669	1,488	2,557	1,763
40 to 59 percent	8,524	330	229	634	672	859	478	1,635	2,090	2,973	1,826
60 to 79 percent	9,924	647	295	740	836	601	439	1,536	2,684	3,713	1,991
80 to 89 percent	5,128	521	195	451	433	266	248	732	1,453	1,956	987
90 to 99 percent	4,928	671	170	504	516	226	212	556	1,346	1,873	1,154
100 percent or more	5,789	766	691	650	922	324	355	620	1,398	1,974	1,797
Not reported	–	–	–	–	–	–	–	–	–	–	–
Median (percent)	63.0	86.0	82.0	66.0	72.0	35.0	58.0	51.0	67.0	65.0	65.0
Reason primary mortgage refinanced											
Units with a refinanced primary mortgage[2]	12,220	224	269	792	947	1,337	429	1,950	3,337	3,321	3,613
To get lower interest rate	9,228	174	172	563	666	832	246	1,505	2,595	2,490	2,638
To reduce the monthly payment	1,552	32	43	99	142	177	59	215	413	469	456
To increase payment period	180	4	9	4	16	6	11	32	47	27	74
To reduce payment period	573	5	9	25	40	37	19	67	158	188	160
To renew or extend a loan that has fallen due	123	3	2	7	15	20	8	21	38	35	29
To receive cash	1,587	16	32	147	153	265	72	265	333	443	546
Other reason	1,655	32	58	96	170	211	65	234	466	403	551
Cash received in primary mortgage refinance											
Received refinance cash	1,587	16	32	147	153	265	72	265	333	443	546
Less than $10,000	125	–	8	30	6	23	9	12	23	61	29
$10,000 to $19,999	231	3	15	25	26	25	9	13	90	75	53
$20,000 to $29,999	226	3	–	15	12	22	14	34	51	52	89
$30,000 to $39,999	157	–	–	16	22	20	8	32	20	46	59
$40,000 to $49,999	93	–	4	2	7	8	–	11	20	23	39
$50,000 to $59,999	99	–	–	5	8	23	2	22	15	22	41
$60,000 to $69,999	46	–	–	–	9	14	–	3	10	8	25
$70,000 to $79,999	25	2	–	–	8	1	–	8	3	6	8
$80,000 to $99,999	93	4	–	3	5	15	6	12	16	25	40
$100,000 to $119,999	90	–	–	4	12	16	5	11	5	18	57
$120,000 to $149,999	30	–	–	–	3	8	8	6	5	10	10
$150,000 or more	95	4	–	5	21	24	–	19	10	34	32
Not reported	276	–	5	41	15	65	10	82	65	63	65
Median (dollars)	30,000	Z	Z	18,000	40,000	50,000	25,000	37,500	20,000	30,000	40,000
Percent of primary mortgage refinance cash used for home additions, improvements, or repairs											
Received refinance cash	1,587	16	32	147	153	265	72	265	333	443	546
Zero percent	647	10	21	56	63	113	34	85	116	242	204
1 to 9 percent	53	–	3	10	5	8	8	9	13	13	17
10 to 19 percent	69	–	3	4	6	16	3	14	5	19	31
20 to 29 percent	53	–	–	3	13	6	5	7	3	16	27
30 to 39 percent	18	–	–	3	3	5	–	1	8	6	3
40 to 49 percent	16	–	–	3	5	7	–	2	2	3	8
50 to 59 percent	99	–	–	5	6	13	7	16	17	27	39
60 to 69 percent	12	–	–	–	2	3	–	5	4	–	2
70 to 79 percent	53	–	–	8	11	6	3	11	6	11	24
80 to 89 percent	22	–	–	4	10	7	–	1	8	5	7
90 to 99 percent	46	–	–	4	2	5	–	21	8	6	11
100 percent	426	6	6	31	24	55	3	74	124	67	161
Not reported	73	–	–	15	2	21	8	18	17	27	11
Median	15.0	Z	Z	7.0	20.0	10.0	–	50.0	50.0	–	25.0

Table 2-5. Mortgage Characteristics, Owner-Occupied Units, 2009—*Continued*

[Numbers in thousands, except as noted.]

Characteristics	Total occupied units	Housing unit characteristics: New construction 4 years	Housing unit characteristics: Manufactured/ mobile homes	Household characteristics: Black alone	Household characteristics: Hispanic	Household characteristics: Elderly (65 years and over)	Household characteristics: Below poverty level	Regions: Northeast	Regions: Midwest	Regions: South	Regions: West
Percent of nonrefinanced primary mortgage, including home-equity lump sum, used for home purchase and improvement											
Units with a nonrefinanced primary mortgage	31,898	2,739	1,555	3,062	3,153	2,916	1,682	5,579	7,729	12,165	6,425
Zero percent	5,901	468	341	681	687	765	381	927	1,162	2,378	1,435
1 to 9 percent	748	80	82	89	110	96	42	131	134	277	207
10 to 19 percent	205	10	5	29	31	31	5	37	34	95	40
20 to 29 percent	151	6	9	8	10	33	10	29	39	51	33
30 to 39 percent	76	11	15	–	4	35	–	21	13	18	23
40 to 49 percent	49	6	–	11	3	9	3	9	5	31	5
50 to 59 percent	158	5	7	8	21	25	23	44	28	66	21
60 to 69 percent	56	5	8	1	10	18	5	11	4	24	17
70 to 79 percent	121	7	13	7	6	20	13	15	29	39	38
80 to 89 percent	223	22	4	14	32	19	10	42	31	67	84
90 to 99 percent	221	14	3	15	20	7	7	49	68	69	35
100 percent	22,611	2,031	1,016	1,975	2,040	1,663	1,039	3,960	5,944	8,512	4,195
Not reported	1,376	75	52	223	177	196	144	304	239	539	293
Median (percent)	100.0	100.0	100.0	100.0	100.0	100.0	100.0	100.0	100.0	100.0	100.0
Owners with one or more home-equity line-of-credit mortgages											
Total	9,184	297	106	426	579	1,527	334	1,935	2,408	2,681	2,160
Total home-equity line-of-credit limit											
Less than $10,000	295	11	7	18	25	40	19	55	76	105	59
$10,000 to $19,999	766	15	10	42	56	115	23	141	266	241	119
$20,000 to $29,999	1,014	28	11	66	43	126	34	210	329	288	187
$30,000 to $39,999	794	45	7	41	39	122	26	129	269	248	148
$40,000 to $49,999	490	16	23	15	49	54	6	86	155	141	109
$50,000 to $59,999	915	30	8	53	52	163	30	204	207	320	184
$60,000 to $69,999	404	10	2	27	20	48	10	93	114	94	104
$70,000 to $79,999	328	11	–	–	25	45	16	77	63	81	106
$80,000 to $99,999	336	14	4	13	30	62	2	84	69	102	81
$100,000 to $119,999	836	14	–	24	48	183	30	181	167	243	244
$120,000 to $149,999	254	10	–	9	13	50	6	62	54	67	71
$150,000 or more	1,013	40	–	16	39	193	34	257	158	203	394
Not reported	1,739	54	33	103	140	325	98	358	481	547	354
Median (dollars)	50,000	50,000	40,000	39,000	50,000	50,000	50,000	50,000	40,000	50,000	68,000
Total outstanding line-of-credit loans											
Outstanding loan(s)	5,306	148	37	185	277	789	171	1,179	1,395	1,431	1,301
Less than $10,000	837	16	10	31	36	160	28	174	289	265	109
$10,000 to $19,999	982	9	5	27	45	166	23	199	312	287	183
$20,000 to $29,999	748	19	5	22	28	87	10	162	195	222	168
$30,000 to $39,999	460	15	–	29	16	63	6	106	137	99	117
$40,000 to $49,999	354	14	–	16	23	47	17	70	100	88	96
$50,000 to $59,999	227	14	7	3	22	38	8	61	42	62	62
$60,000 to $69,999	237	7	4	8	24	26	2	44	43	63	87
$70,000 to $79,999	151	1	3	5	10	29	3	36	29	30	56
$80,000 to $99,999	264	9	2	13	20	49	10	44	44	74	102
$100,000 to $119,999	159	3	–	2	9	21	3	48	17	40	54
$120,000 to $149,999	111	2	–	2	14	12	6	17	9	39	45
$150,000 or more	245	12	–	3	13	24	19	61	47	35	102
Not reported	523	25	–	24	17	68	34	152	132	124	115
Median (dollars)	26,000	40,000	Z	30,000	40,000	21,659	40,000	27,000	20,000	23,000	40,000
Current line-of-credit interest rate											
Outstanding loan(s)	5,306	148	37	185	277	789	171	1,179	1,395	1,431	1,301
Less than 3 percent	475	4	3	20	30	81	5	145	92	138	99
3 to 3.9 percent	940	22	2	12	44	180	23	261	223	223	233
4 to 4.9 percent	760	32	7	15	43	114	28	136	192	201	231
5 to 5.9 percent	650	9	5	39	33	104	21	132	217	181	120
6 to 6.9 percent	515	17	2	14	44	75	31	90	125	164	137
7 to 7.9 percent	356	17	3	15	13	34	3	52	106	115	83
8 percent or more	340	11	6	18	21	24	7	34	120	96	90
Not reported	1,271	35	9	52	48	179	53	329	320	314	307
Median (percent)	4.5	4.5	Z	5.5	4.8	4.3	5.0	4.0	5.0	4.9	4.5

Table 2-5. Mortgage Characteristics, Owner-Occupied Units, 2009—*Continued*

[Numbers in thousands, except as noted.]

Characteristics	Total occupied units	Housing unit characteristics		Household characteristics				Regions			
		New construction 4 years	Manufactured/ mobile homes	Black alone	Hispanic	Elderly (65 years and over)	Below poverty level	Northeast	Midwest	South	West
Line-of-credit monthly payment											
Outstanding loan(s)	5,306	148	37	185	277	789	171	1,179	1,395	1,431	1,301
Less than $100	532	16	–	17	21	100	9	128	156	138	110
$100 to $199	1,010	34	5	48	68	163	53	176	303	297	234
$200 to $249	635	25	12	16	32	80	13	96	196	194	150
$250 to $299	330	5	–	12	6	53	7	75	78	91	86
$300 to $349	414	10	4	9	19	56	17	89	101	109	115
$350 to $399	180	5	–	9	18	23	7	45	26	53	55
$400 to $449	239	3	–	10	18	26	3	41	61	84	52
$450 to $499	110	–	5	3	10	12	2	29	30	19	33
$500 to $599	414	–	–	12	17	43	12	97	97	125	96
$600 to $699	183	6	–	3	17	38	2	37	35	42	69
$700 to $799	109	3	3	7	10	16	7	20	27	27	35
$800 to $999	146	10	–	6	4	22	8	29	41	30	46
$1,000 or more	457	9	–	18	21	80	10	126	127	101	103
Not reported	546	22	7	16	17	76	20	190	117	122	118
Median (dollars)	260	220	Z	250	300	250	255	300	240	250	300
Line-of-credit amount used for home additions, improvements, or repairs											
Outstanding loan(s)	5,306	148	37	185	277	789	171	1,179	1,395	1,431	1,301
Yes	2,695	28	20	69	137	328	79	637	692	646	720
No	2,569	117	17	111	140	449	92	529	696	770	574
Not reported	41	4	–	6	–	12	–	13	7	15	6

– = Zero or rounds to zero.
X = Not applicable.
Z = Sample too small.
[1] = Regular mortgages include all mortgages not classified as home-equity or reverse.
[2] = Figures may not add to total because more than one category may apply to a unit.

Source: U.S. Census Bureau, American Housing Survey

Table 2-6. New Privately Owned Housing Units, Authorized, Annual Unadjusted Data for the United States, 2000–2011

[Numbers in thousands, except as noted.]

Characteristics	Total housing units	1 unit	2 units	3 and 4 units	5 units or more
Annual data					
20,000-place series					
2011	624.1	418.5	11.1	10.4	184.0
2010	604.6	447.3	10.8	11.2	135.3
2009	583.0	441.1	10.7	10.0	121.1
2008	905.4	575.6	16.8	17.6	295.4
2007	1,398.4	979.9	28.1	31.5	359.0
2006	1,838.9	1,378.2	35.3	41.3	384.1
2005	2,155.3	1,682.0	39.3	44.7	389.3
2004	2,070.1	1,613.4	43.0	47.4	366.2
19,000-place series					
2003	1,889.2	1,460.9	40.9	41.6	345.8
2002	1,747.7	1,332.6	37.2	36.5	341.4
2001	1,636.7	1,235.6	31.8	34.2	335.2
2000	1,592.3	1,198.1	30.6	34.3	329.3
Year to date, April 2012	230.2	150.9	3.2	3.6	72.5
Year to date, April 2011	179.0	127.8	2.9	2.8	45.5
Percent change, 2011 to 2012	29%	18%	9%	27%	59%
Percent change, 2010 to 2011	3%	-6%	3%	-7%	36%
Monthly data					
20,000-place series					
2012					
January	46.3	29.9	0.6	0.7	15.1
February	51.9	35.1	0.7	0.9	15.2
March	67.4	42.2	0.8	1.1	23.2
April	62.5	43.9	1.0	0.8	16.8
2011					
January	36.3	26.2	0.5	0.8	8.7
February	37.7	26.5	0.6	0.5	10.0
March	54.4	37.8	1.0	0.5	15.1
April	50.7	37.2	0.9	1.0	11.6
May	57.3	39.7	1.0	0.9	15.8
June	63.8	41.5	1.2	0.9	20.3
July	52.6	35.9	1.1	0.9	14.8
August	62.6	41.6	1.3	1.4	18.4
September	53.2	36.3	0.9	0.9	15.1
October	52.0	34.4	0.9	1.0	15.7
November	51.9	31.6	1.1	0.7	18.5
December	51.6	29.8	0.7	1.0	20.0
2010					
January	40.4	31.4	0.7	0.6	7.6
February	45.3	35.4	0.7	0.7	8.5
March	64.1	50.9	1.0	1.1	11.0
April	58.9	46.1	0.8	0.7	11.2
May	51.1	39.9	0.9	0.8	9.5
June	59.2	42.9	1.1	1.0	14.2
July	51.6	37.5	0.9	0.9	12.2
August	53.7	37.2	1.0	1.0	14.5
September	48.5	34.3	0.9	1.4	11.9
October	43.5	31.5	1.0	0.9	10.1
November	40.9	29.6	0.8	0.9	9.6
December	47.6	30.6	0.9	1.1	15.0
2009					
January	37.6	22.1	0.7	0.8	14.0
February	39.2	26.3	0.7	0.6	11.6
March	45.4	32.7	1.0	0.9	10.7
April	47.8	37.8	1.0	0.7	8.3
May	49.5	39.5	0.8	0.9	8.3
June	61.3	47.0	1.0	1.4	11.9
July	56.1	46.9	0.8	0.9	7.5
August	54.0	42.9	1.0	0.8	9.3
September	52.9	40.7	1.0	0.8	10.4
October	47.9	38.6	0.9	0.4	8.0
November	42.1	31.9	1.2	0.9	8.1
December	49.2	34.7	0.7	0.7	13.1
2008					
January	77.4	48.0	1.6	1.4	26.4
February	75.0	48.0	1.5	1.5	24.0
March	79.1	54.1	1.4	1.7	21.7
April	91.5	63.4	1.8	1.8	24.5
May	92.3	61.9	1.5	1.7	27.3
June	110.6	59.4	1.6	1.5	48.0

Table 2-6. New Privately Owned Housing Units, Authorized, Annual Unadjusted Data for the United States, 2000–2011—*Continued*

[Numbers in thousands, except as noted.]

Characteristics	Total housing units	1 unit	2 units	3 and 4 units	5 units or more
July	85.9	55.7	1.6	1.6	26.9
August	76.3	48.0	1.4	1.5	25.4
September	70.9	45.9	1.6	1.7	21.7
October	63.7	40.4	1.3	1.4	20.6
November	41.5	26.2	0.6	0.9	13.8
December	41.2	24.6	0.8	0.8	15.1
2007					
January	114.1	80.3	2.1	2.9	28.8
February	112.1	79.4	2.2	2.7	27.9
March	139.4	103.4	3.2	3.1	29.8
April	130.9	98.6	2.7	2.4	27.2
May	146.0	106.6	3.0	3.1	33.3
June	135.6	97.2	2.5	2.7	33.3
July	122.5	89.8	2.4	2.9	27.5
August	126.0	87.5	2.4	2.8	33.3
September	100.5	66.6	1.9	2.1	30.0
October	103.8	70.7	2.1	2.2	28.8
November	89.5	54.7	1.9	2.4	30.5
December	77.8	45.2	1.8	2.2	28.7
2006					
January	152.6	114.3	3.0	3.6	31.7
February	151.0	115.6	2.6	3.1	29.7
March	194.2	146.7	3.5	4.0	40.0
April	168.6	130.8	2.5	3.7	31.5
May	184.4	144.5	3.6	4.2	32.1
June	184.2	139.3	3.2	3.8	38.0
July	148.0	111.6	3.1	3.6	29.7
August	161.2	121.5	3.7	3.7	32.3
September	136.6	97.7	2.9	3.2	32.8
October	133.1	98.0	3.0	3.0	29.1
November	111.4	82.2	2.2	2.4	24.6
December	113.6	76.0	2.0	3.0	32.6
2005					
January	139.7	106.9	2.0	2.5	28.3
February	149.4	114.8	3.0	2.9	28.6
March	190.5	150.6	3.2	4.1	32.6
April	193.2	152.7	3.2	3.5	33.9
May	193.1	156.0	3.5	3.8	29.7
June	211.9	166.2	4.0	4.7	37.1
July	185.5	145.9	3.5	4.1	31.9
August	208.0	161.9	3.8	4.6	37.7
September	193.7	151.3	3.9	4.0	34.6
October	176.0	139.1	3.5	3.6	29.8
November	162.9	124.0	2.9	3.6	32.3
December	151.3	112.5	2.7	3.3	32.7
2004					
January	132.0	103.4	2.9	2.9	22.8
February	137.1	108.4	2.7	2.9	23.1
March	190.7	154.8	4.0	5.2	26.6
April	192.5	155.0	4.0	4.6	28.9
May	188.4	150.2	3.7	3.7	30.8
June	197.1	159.3	3.9	4.7	29.2
July	185.9	145.3	3.8	4.8	32.1
August	185.2	145.6	3.9	3.8	31.9
September	174.9	134.5	3.3	3.5	33.6
October	174.5	128.5	3.8	3.8	38.4
November	156.4	114.6	4.0	3.6	34.2
December	155.2	113.8	3.0	3.8	34.6
19,000-place series					
2003					
January	126.4	98.0	2.6	3.0	22.8
February	128.5	93.9	2.5	2.7	29.3
March	148.4	117.7	3.1	3.0	24.7
April	167.6	134.2	4.0	4.0	25.4
May	169.5	132.1	3.8	3.6	30.0
June	175.8	138.3	3.8	3.7	29.9
July	173.0	138.6	3.4	3.2	27.9
August	169.9	131.0	3.5	3.7	31.7
September	169.1	130.5	4.0	4.5	30.2
October	182.8	138.1	3.9	3.9	37.0
November	130.5	99.2	3.6	3.3	24.4
December	147.9	109.6	2.8	3.1	32.4

Table 2-6. New Privately Owned Housing Units, Authorized, Annual Unadjusted Data for the United States, 2000–2011—*Continued*

[Numbers in thousands, except as noted.]

Characteristics	Total housing units	1 unit	2 units	3 and 4 units	5 units or more
2002					
January	115.7	88.7	2.3	2.3	22.4
February	122.5	95.5	2.0	2.3	22.6
March	143.2	111.0	2.8	3.0	26.5
April	156.0	125.4	3.5	2.9	24.3
May	164.2	127.1	3.4	3.0	30.7
June	158.0	118.9	3.2	4.5	31.3
July	159.3	122.4	3.1	2.9	30.9
August	153.7	119.8	3.3	3.2	27.3
September	149.5	110.1	4.1	3.8	31.4
October	162.9	123.0	3.6	3.3	32.9
November	126.8	96.0	2.9	2.3	25.6
December	135.8	94.6	2.8	2.8	35.5
2001					
January	117.0	85.6	1.8	1.9	27.6
February	114.3	85.1	2.3	2.3	24.6
March	147.7	112.7	2.6	3.3	29.1
April	148.6	116.5	2.8	3.0	26.2
May	159.8	124.4	3.1	3.4	28.9
June	153.9	119.2	3.4	4.4	27.0
July	140.6	110.2	2.6	2.5	25.3
August	151.4	116.2	3.0	3.2	29.0
September	125.2	92.4	2.3	2.2	28.2
October	140.2	104.4	3.1	2.9	29.8
November	124.4	89.2	2.4	2.4	30.4
December	113.6	79.7	2.2	2.7	29.0
2000					
January	107.3	78.3	1.8	1.8	25.3
February	121.8	89.1	2.5	2.4	27.8
March	153.7	119.0	2.8	3.0	28.9
April	138.9	107.6	2.5	2.6	26.1
May	148.9	119.3	2.7	3.7	23.2
June	155.1	114.5	3.2	3.2	34.3
July	129.8	98.8	2.3	2.3	26.5
August	146.8	111.6	3.0	3.4	28.9
September	131.4	95.8	2.3	3.5	29.8
October	134.8	102.8	3.0	3.5	25.5
November	121.0	87.7	2.5	2.8	28.0
December	102.9	73.7	2.0	2.1	25.2

Source: U.S. Census Bureau, Building Permits Survey

Table 2-7. New Privately Owned Housing Units, Authorized, Unadjusted Data for the Northeast and Midwest Regions, 1991–2011

[Numbers in thousands, except as noted.]

Characteristics	Northeast			Midwest		
	Total housing units	1 unit	2 units or more	Total housing units	1 unit	2 units or more
Annual data						
20,000-place series						
2011	68.5	39.0	29.5	102.7	70.5	32.2
2010	73.8	49.1	24.7	103.5	75.4	28.1
2009	68.5	45.8	22.7	100.3	74.9	25.5
2008	119.0	58.0	61.0	137.7	93.2	44.5
2007	150.6	83.7	66.9	211.7	153.8	58.0
2006	174.6	103.4	71.2	279.4	209.3	70.1
2005	203.8	126.6	77.2	353.9	278.7	75.2
2004	197.0	131.8	65.2	370.5	295.5	74.9
19,000-place series						
2003	182.4	124.4	58.0	371.0	287.3	83.7
2002	173.7	126.6	47.2	352.4	263.4	88.9
2001	159.8	117.7	42.1	333.6	252.5	81.1
2000	165.1	122.3	42.8	323.8	245.4	78.5
1999	164.9	127.1	37.8	345.4	262.1	83.3
1998	159.4	124.1	35.3	327.2	247.8	79.4
1997	141.9	111.2	30.7	299.8	220.0	79.8
1996	136.9	108.8	28.1	317.8	236.6	81.2
1995	124.2	104.5	19.7	296.6	220.5	76.1
1994	138.5	119.1	19.4	305.2	233.6	71.6
17,000-place series						
1994	133.9	114.9	19.0	299.1	228.3	70.7
1993	133.5	113.7	19.8	276.6	218.4	58.3
1992	124.8	108.5	16.3	259.0	204.4	54.6
1991	109.8	91.8	18.0	215.4	168.1	47.3
Year to date, April 2012	23.2	12.6	10.6	32.2	22.8	9.4
Year to date, April 2011	17.8	11.5	6.3	26.3	18.8	7.6
Percent change, 2011 to 2012	30%	10%	67%	22%	22%	24%
Percent change, 2010 to 2011	-7%	-21%	19%	-1%	-6%	14%
Monthly data						
19,000-Place Series						
2012						
January	4.8	2.2	2.5	5.0	3.3	1.7
February	5.5	2.7	2.9	6.5	4.6	1.9
March	5.8	3.6	2.2	10.3	7.3	3.1
April	7.6	4.0	3.6	10.6	7.8	2.8
2011						
January	4.5	3.0	1.6	4.5	2.7	1.8
February	3.6	2.1	1.5	4.5	3.3	1.2
March	4.7	3.1	1.6	8.1	6.0	2.2
April	5.0	3.3	1.6	9.2	6.8	2.4
May	7.3	3.6	3.7	9.9	7.1	2.8
June	8.2	3.7	4.6	10.1	7.3	2.8
July	5.1	3.5	1.7	9.1	6.3	2.8
August	6.0	3.4	2.6	11.3	7.6	3.7
September	6.0	3.6	2.4	10.5	6.8	3.6
October	5.8	3.6	2.2	10.0	6.4	3.6
November	6.5	3.5	3.0	8.4	5.2	3.3
December	5.7	2.8	3.0	7.1	4.1	3.0
2010						
January	4.2	3.0	1.2	4.6	3.5	1.1
February	4.9	3.5	1.4	5.7	4.6	1.0
March	5.7	4.2	1.6	9.8	7.9	1.9
April	6.5	4.3	2.2	11.4	8.6	2.8
May	5.8	4.4	1.4	9.7	7.3	2.4
June	8.6	4.8	3.9	10.0	7.9	2.1
July	5.8	4.0	1.7	9.8	6.8	3.0
August	6.4	4.1	2.3	9.7	6.6	3.0
September	6.3	4.1	2.2	9.0	6.4	2.6
October	5.6	3.7	1.9	10.2	6.5	3.7
November	5.1	3.8	1.3	7.4	5.8	1.6
December	8.9	5.3	3.6	6.3	3.6	2.7

Table 2-7. New Privately Owned Housing Units, Authorized, Unadjusted Data for the Northeast and Midwest Regions, 1991–2011—*Continued*

[Numbers in thousands, except as noted.]

Characteristics	Northeast			Midwest		
	Total housing units	1 unit	2 units or more	Total housing units	1 unit	2 units or more
2009						
January	3.6	2.5	1.1	4.5	2.3	2.2
February	4.2	2.0	2.1	4.7	3.5	1.2
March	4.6	3.0	1.6	6.9	4.8	2.0
April	5.3	3.7	1.6	8.0	6.6	1.4
May	5.4	4.0	1.4	9.0	7.7	1.3
June	7.0	4.6	2.3	10.6	8.4	2.2
July	6.3	4.8	1.5	11.0	8.5	2.5
August	6.3	4.3	1.9	9.6	8.0	1.7
September	6.4	4.5	1.9	10.2	7.5	2.7
October	6.2	4.5	1.6	10.0	7.4	2.6
November	5.6	3.7	1.9	8.2	5.7	2.5
December	7.8	4.0	3.8	7.6	4.6	3.0
2008						
January	8.2	4.4	3.9	10.1	5.8	4.3
February	6.6	4.0	2.6	7.9	5.2	2.7
March	8.6	5.0	3.6	9.8	7.3	2.5
April	10.0	6.0	4.0	15.7	11.2	4.5
May	12.9	5.9	7.1	14.2	11.1	3.1
June	30.1	5.5	24.6	14.5	10.0	4.5
July	10.0	5.9	4.2	14.4	9.9	4.6
August	7.4	5.6	1.8	13.1	8.1	5.0
September	8.4	5.2	3.2	13.0	8.6	4.4
October	7.0	4.6	2.4	12.4	8.1	4.3
November	5.0	3.1	2.0	7.3	4.9	2.3
December	4.7	2.9	1.8	5.5	3.2	2.3
2007						
January	12.0	6.1	5.9	14.5	9.0	5.5
February	8.2	4.4	3.8	12.1	8.1	4.0
March	12.8	7.4	5.4	19.4	14.7	4.8
April	14.4	8.3	6.0	20.9	16.2	4.7
May	14.1	9.0	5.1	23.7	18.3	5.4
June	15.5	8.4	7.1	21.5	16.4	5.1
July	14.5	8.3	6.3	19.9	14.8	5.1
August	14.3	8.4	5.8	19.0	14.7	4.1
September	11.2	6.4	4.7	17.7	12.2	5.0
October	13.7	7.2	6.5	18.0	13.2	4.9
November	10.1	5.2	4.9	14.9	9.9	5.0
December	9.8	4.6	5.2	10.0	6.2	3.8
2006						
January	12.6	7.6	5.1	18.5	13.3	5.1
February	11.9	6.9	4.9	20.7	14.5	6.3
March	17.2	10.4	6.8	27.3	21.3	6.0
April	15.6	10.0	5.6	25.4	21.2	4.2
May	16.5	10.4	6.2	29.7	23.7	6.0
June	17.7	10.5	7.2	28.5	21.4	7.1
July	15.8	8.8	7.0	24.6	18.5	6.1
August	16.0	9.5	6.5	27.3	19.3	8.0
September	13.9	8.0	5.9	22.2	16.3	5.9
October	13.6	8.7	4.9	22.7	17.2	5.5
November	11.7	6.6	5.0	17.8	12.9	4.8
December	12.1	6.0	6.1	14.7	9.6	5.1
2005						
January	11.4	6.8	4.6	16.4	12.7	3.7
February	11.5	6.9	4.6	21.4	16.5	5.0
March	15.1	9.6	5.5	29.7	23.9	5.8
April	18.0	11.0	7.0	35.0	27.7	7.2
May	19.9	12.7	7.2	34.3	27.7	6.6
June	22.1	13.0	9.1	34.8	28.4	6.5
July	18.3	12.1	6.2	32.7	26.0	6.7
August	20.1	13.0	7.1	35.3	27.5	7.8
September	18.6	12.7	5.9	32.3	25.8	6.5
October	16.8	11.2	5.7	32.9	25.9	7.0
November	17.1	9.7	7.3	28.4	21.6	6.8
December	15.0	8.0	6.9	20.5	14.8	5.7

Table 2-7. New Privately Owned Housing Units, Authorized, Unadjusted Data for the Northeast and Midwest Regions, 1991–2011—*Continued*

[Numbers in thousands, except as noted.]

Characteristics	Northeast			Midwest		
	Total housing units	1 unit	2 units or more	Total housing units	1 unit	2 units or more
2004						
January	11.2	7.5	3.7	18.0	14.7	3.4
February	10.7	7.4	3.3	20.5	17.1	3.4
March	17.4	12.7	4.8	33.4	27.4	6.1
April	18.5	13.9	4.5	36.9	30.4	6.5
May	18.8	12.9	5.9	33.7	28.2	5.5
June	21.3	14.3	7.1	34.7	29.6	5.1
July	18.5	12.1	6.4	32.7	27.2	5.6
August	16.5	11.2	5.3	36.8	28.9	7.9
September	17.6	10.8	6.7	35.1	26.6	8.5
October	15.6	10.4	5.2	34.3	25.6	8.7
November	16.5	10.1	6.4	28.0	21.1	6.9
December	14.4	8.5	5.9	26.4	19.0	7.4
17,000-place series						
2003						
January	10.5	7.2	3.3	19.1	14.4	4.7
February	9.6	5.9	3.7	18.4	14.1	4.4
March	12.6	9.1	3.5	27.2	22.0	5.2
April	16.0	11.4	4.7	35.1	28.1	7.0
May	17.0	12.1	4.9	34.4	28.0	6.4
June	16.9	12.2	4.8	37.2	28.8	8.4
July	17.9	12.9	5.0	36.1	29.2	6.9
August	18.2	11.4	6.8	35.0	26.6	8.3
September	15.7	11.7	4.0	37.1	28.2	8.9
October	18.8	12.5	6.3	37.9	29.8	8.1
November	14.1	9.3	4.8	27.9	20.1	7.8
December	15.1	8.8	6.2	25.5	18.0	7.5
2002						
January	10.5	7.8	2.8	18.7	14.1	4.6
February	11.7	8.0	3.7	20.4	15.5	5.0
March	11.9	9.5	2.4	27.3	20.9	6.4
April	15.5	12.1	3.4	33.6	26.9	6.6
May	17.9	12.5	5.5	34.6	26.8	7.8
June	16.8	11.9	4.9	31.9	24.4	7.4
July	17.3	12.3	5.0	33.8	24.9	8.9
August	15.5	11.2	4.3	31.8	23.8	8.0
September	15.2	11.2	4.0	32.1	23.1	9.0
October	16.2	12.0	4.3	36.2	26.0	10.2
November	12.4	9.1	3.3	25.2	19.7	5.5
December	12.6	9.0	3.6	26.7	17.2	9.5
2001						
January	9.0	6.9	2.2	17.8	13.0	4.8
February	10.6	6.6	4.0	19.1	14.0	5.1
March	12.9	9.3	3.6	28.7	22.6	6.1
April	14.1	10.4	3.7	31.5	24.9	6.7
May	15.3	12.3	3.0	34.7	27.5	7.2
June	15.1	11.5	3.6	33.0	25.9	7.0
July	15.0	11.1	3.9	31.1	24.2	7.0
August	15.8	11.8	4.0	31.2	24.7	6.5
September	12.2	9.6	2.6	27.0	19.8	7.2
October	15.3	11.3	4.0	30.8	22.6	8.2
November	13.0	8.9	4.0	27.4	18.9	8.4
December	11.4	8.0	3.4	21.4	14.4	7.0
2000						
January	10.9	6.9	3.9	17.3	12.9	4.4
February	10.4	7.4	3.0	21.9	15.4	6.5
March	15.1	11.6	3.5	32.9	25.2	7.6
April	14.7	10.9	3.8	32.3	25.5	6.8
May	15.9	12.9	3.0	33.2	25.9	7.3
June	16.6	12.2	4.3	31.3	24.1	6.7
July	14.1	10.6	3.5	28.0	21.3	6.7
August	15.3	11.4	3.9	30.8	23.4	7.4
September	14.2	10.2	4.0	26.6	20.2	6.4
October	14.1	11.2	2.9	31.3	22.6	8.8
November	13.5	9.3	4.1	23.0	17.5	5.5
December	10.3	7.5	2.7	15.2	11.2	4.0

Source: U.S. Census Bureau, Building Permits Survey

Table 2-8. New Privately Owned Housing Units, Authorized, Unadjusted Data for the South and West Regions, 1991–2011

[Numbers in thousands, except as noted.]

Characteristics	South			West		
	Total housing units	1 unit	2 units or more	Total housing units	1 unit	2 units or more
Annual data						
20,000-place series						
2011	320.7	227.1	93.5	132.2	81.9	50.3
2010	299.1	232.3	66.8	128.2	90.6	37.6
2009	297.4	231.8	65.7	116.7	88.7	28.0
2008	451.9	304.3	147.5	196.7	120.0	76.8
2007	692.2	507.5	184.6	343.9	234.9	109.0
2006	929.7	726.2	203.5	455.2	339.3	115.9
2005	1,039.0	826.8	212.3	558.6	450.0	108.6
2004	960.8	756.1	204.6	541.9	430.0	111.9
19,000-place series						
2003	849.3	670.1	179.1	486.5	379.0	107.4
2002	790.7	606.5	184.3	430.9	336.2	94.7
2001	730.3	556.9	173.4	413.0	308.5	104.5
2000	701.9	529.7	172.2	401.5	300.7	100.8
1999	748.9	550.4	198.6	404.3	307.1	97.3
1998	724.5	521.9	202.6	401.2	293.8	107.4
1997	635.9	464.2	171.7	363.5	267.1	96.4
1996	623.4	468.5	154.9	347.4	255.6	91.8
1995	583.2	430.3	152.9	328.5	241.9	86.5
1994	585.5	453.0	132.5	342.4	262.8	79.7
17,000-place series						
1994	560.5	430.6	129.9	340.3	260.8	79.5
1993	500.7	419.5	81.2	288.2	235.0	53.2
1992	442.5	382.2	60.2	268.6	215.6	53.0
1991	375.7	308.4	67.2	247.9	185.2	62.7
Year to date, April 2012	124.8	84.3	40.5	50.0	31.3	18.8
Year to date, April 2011	98.6	72.7	25.9	36.3	24.8	11.5
Percent change, 2011 to 2012	27%	16%	56%	38%	26%	63%
Percent change, 2010 to 2011	7%	-2%	40%	3%	-10%	34%
Monthly data						
19,000-place series						
2012						
January	28.4	18.3	10.1	8.2	6.1	2.1
February	28.9	21.1	7.8	11.1	6.8	4.3
March	34.3	22.5	11.8	17.0	8.9	8.1
April	30.5	22.4	8.1	13.7	9.6	4.1
2011						
January	20.3	15.3	5.0	7.0	5.3	1.7
February	22.6	16.2	6.4	6.9	5.0	1.9
March	30.2	21.6	8.6	11.4	7.1	4.3
April	25.5	19.6	5.9	11.0	7.4	3.6
May	27.6	20.9	6.6	12.6	8.0	4.6
June	31.1	21.9	9.3	14.3	8.5	5.7
July	27.6	18.9	8.8	10.8	7.2	3.6
August	31.4	22.3	9.1	13.8	8.1	5.7
September	25.4	18.9	6.5	11.3	6.8	4.5
October	26.1	17.8	8.3	10.1	6.5	3.6
November	25.6	16.9	8.7	11.4	6.0	5.4
December	27.2	16.9	10.3	11.5	6.0	5.5
2010						
January	22.2	18.1	4.0	9.4	6.8	2.7
February	23.8	19.7	4.1	10.9	7.5	3.3
March	34.8	28.4	6.4	13.8	10.4	3.3
April	29.3	24.2	5.0	11.7	9.0	2.8
May	25.8	20.5	5.3	9.9	7.8	2.1
June	28.6	21.3	7.3	12.0	8.9	3.0
July	26.0	19.2	6.9	10.0	7.6	2.4
August	26.2	19.2	7.0	11.4	7.3	4.1
September	23.6	17.0	6.7	9.6	6.9	2.7
October	19.0	15.0	3.9	8.6	6.2	2.4
November	19.9	14.8	5.2	8.4	5.3	3.2
December	19.9	14.8	5.1	12.5	6.9	5.6

Table 2-8. New Privately Owned Housing Units, Authorized, Unadjusted Data for the South and West Regions, 1991–2011—*Continued*

[Numbers in thousands, except as noted.]

Characteristics	South			West		
	Total housing units	1 unit	2 units or more	Total housing units	1 unit	2 units or more
2009						
January	21.3	13.1	8.2	8.1	4.1	4.0
February	22.9	16.3	6.6	7.4	4.5	2.9
March	24.7	18.9	5.8	9.1	6.0	3.1
April	24.5	19.5	5.0	10.0	8.0	2.0
May	24.9	19.5	5.4	10.1	8.2	2.0
June	31.6	24.1	7.5	12.1	9.9	2.2
July	26.7	23.9	2.8	12.2	9.8	2.4
August	27.5	21.9	5.6	10.6	8.7	1.9
September	25.6	20.4	5.1	10.8	8.3	2.5
October	22.3	18.9	3.4	9.4	7.6	1.8
November	20.9	16.4	4.5	7.4	6.2	1.2
December	24.4	18.7	5.8	9.4	7.4	2.0
2008						
January	44.0	28.6	15.3	15.1	9.2	5.9
February	41.4	28.9	12.5	19.2	9.9	9.3
March	44.5	30.6	13.9	16.2	11.2	4.9
April	45.7	33.0	12.8	20.1	13.2	6.9
May	42.9	31.3	11.6	22.2	13.6	8.7
June	43.2	30.0	13.2	22.9	13.9	9.0
July	43.9	28.2	15.7	17.5	11.7	5.8
August	39.7	24.4	15.3	16.0	10.0	6.1
September	34.5	22.8	11.7	15.0	9.3	5.7
October	30.3	20.0	10.3	14.0	7.7	6.3
November	19.3	13.1	6.2	9.9	5.1	4.8
December	22.4	13.5	8.9	8.6	5.0	3.6
2007						
January	60.0	45.0	15.0	27.5	20.2	7.3
February	61.6	46.4	15.2	30.2	20.5	9.8
March	70.8	54.5	16.3	36.5	26.8	9.6
April	64.1	49.8	14.3	31.6	24.2	7.3
May	73.1	53.1	20.1	35.1	26.2	8.8
June	65.6	47.9	17.7	33.0	24.4	8.5
July	59.3	44.8	14.6	28.8	21.9	6.8
August	59.1	44.3	13.9	33.5	20.1	12.0
September	47.8	33.7	12.6	23.8	14.3	9.2
October	45.9	34.5	11.5	26.2	15.9	10.3
November	44.3	28.8	15.5	20.2	10.8	9.4
December	40.4	24.9	15.6	17.6	9.6	8.1
2006						
January	83.7	64.3	19.3	37.8	29.0	8.8
February	78.2	64.5	13.6	40.3	29.7	10.6
March	101.6	78.5	23.1	48.1	36.6	11.6
April	85.0	65.9	19.1	42.6	33.7	9.0
May	89.8	73.5	16.3	48.4	36.9	11.4
June	89.6	70.7	18.9	48.5	36.7	11.8
July	73.2	57.6	15.7	34.4	26.7	7.7
August	80.1	63.6	16.5	37.8	29.1	8.7
September	65.7	50.2	15.6	34.7	23.2	11.5
October	66.2	50.7	15.5	30.6	21.4	9.2
November	56.7	43.8	13.0	25.3	18.8	6.4
December	59.9	42.8	17.0	26.9	17.6	9.3
2005						
January	75.0	58.6	16.3	36.9	28.7	8.1
February	76.3	60.2	16.1	40.1	31.3	8.8
March	94.8	75.3	19.5	50.7	41.8	8.9
April	90.7	73.8	16.9	49.4	40.1	9.2
May	89.3	72.9	16.4	49.3	42.7	6.6
June	99.2	79.2	20.0	55.5	45.6	9.9
July	86.5	68.7	17.8	48.0	39.1	8.9
August	101.3	79.7	21.6	51.3	41.7	9.6
September	88.9	70.7	18.2	53.9	42.2	11.7
October	82.6	66.4	16.2	43.7	35.6	8.1
November	76.6	61.9	14.7	40.8	30.8	10.0
December	77.8	59.3	18.5	38.1	30.4	7.7

Table 2-8. New Privately Owned Housing Units, Authorized, Unadjusted Data for the South and West Regions, 1991–2011—*Continued*

[Numbers in thousands, except as noted.]

Characteristics	South			West		
	Total housing units	1 unit	2 units or more	Total housing units	1 unit	2 units or more
2004						
January	68.0	53.2	14.7	34.9	28.0	6.8
February	70.0	55.0	15.1	35.9	29.0	6.9
March	89.9	73.7	16.2	49.9	41.0	8.9
April	87.7	70.2	17.5	49.5	40.5	9.0
May	87.4	68.0	19.3	48.5	41.0	7.5
June	87.6	73.0	14.7	53.5	42.5	11.0
July	85.1	66.5	18.7	49.6	39.6	10.0
August	85.8	67.7	18.1	46.2	37.9	8.3
September	75.4	60.6	14.8	46.8	36.5	10.3
October	82.7	60.2	22.5	41.9	32.4	9.5
November	69.7	52.8	16.9	42.3	30.7	11.7
December	71.5	55.4	16.1	42.9	31.0	12.0
17,000-place series						
2003						
January	62.3	48.4	13.9	34.5	27.8	6.6
February	61.8	47.3	14.5	38.6	26.7	11.9
March	69.8	55.8	14.0	38.7	30.7	8.0
April	74.1	60.3	13.7	42.4	34.3	8.0
May	74.4	58.7	15.7	43.7	33.3	10.4
June	77.3	62.2	15.1	44.3	35.1	9.2
July	75.3	61.1	14.2	43.7	35.4	8.3
August	75.7	60.5	15.2	41.0	32.5	8.6
September	73.9	57.7	16.3	42.4	32.9	9.5
October	79.4	61.1	18.3	46.7	34.7	12.0
November	56.3	44.7	11.6	32.2	25.1	7.1
December	69.0	52.3	16.8	38.3	30.5	7.8
2002						
January	58.9	45.9	13.0	27.6	21.0	6.6
February	62.0	49.6	12.4	28.3	22.5	5.8
March	69.1	52.7	16.4	34.8	27.9	7.0
April	69.2	55.6	13.7	37.8	30.8	7.0
May	71.7	55.3	16.4	40.0	32.5	7.4
June	69.6	52.0	17.6	39.8	30.6	9.2
July	70.6	54.0	16.6	37.6	31.1	6.5
August	68.7	54.3	14.4	37.6	30.4	7.2
September	63.6	48.0	15.6	38.5	27.7	10.8
October	68.6	52.3	16.3	41.9	32.8	9.1
November	55.6	42.8	12.8	33.5	24.4	9.2
December	63.0	44.1	19.0	33.4	24.3	9.1
2001						
January	56.1	42.0	14.1	34.1	23.7	10.4
February	55.1	42.1	13.0	29.5	22.3	7.2
March	67.1	51.3	15.8	38.9	29.4	9.5
April	65.2	51.8	13.4	37.7	29.4	8.3
May	70.2	53.6	16.6	39.6	31.0	8.6
June	65.4	52.2	13.1	40.5	29.5	11.0
July	61.1	47.9	13.2	33.4	27.0	6.4
August	65.6	51.1	14.5	38.8	28.5	10.3
September	54.3	40.0	14.3	31.7	23.0	8.7
October	60.2	46.0	14.2	33.9	24.6	9.3
November	57.4	41.1	16.3	26.7	20.3	6.5
December	52.7	37.7	15.1	28.1	19.6	8.5
2000						
January	50.9	38.6	12.3	28.2	19.9	8.4
February	59.0	45.2	13.8	30.6	21.1	9.4
March	68.7	54.0	14.7	37.0	28.2	8.8
April	58.2	44.5	13.7	33.6	26.6	7.0
May	64.2	50.8	13.4	35.6	29.6	6.0
June	66.1	49.1	17.0	41.0	29.1	12.0
July	55.6	42.6	13.0	32.0	24.3	7.7
August	62.5	48.5	14.0	38.3	28.2	10.0
September	58.3	40.8	17.5	32.2	24.5	7.6
October	57.3	43.8	13.6	32.0	25.2	6.8
November	54.0	38.4	15.6	30.5	22.4	8.1
December	47.0	33.4	13.6	30.5	21.5	9.0

Source: U.S. Census Bureau, Building Permits Survey

Table 2-9. New Privately Owned Housing Units Authorized by Building Permits in Permit-Issuing Places, Annual Data, 1959–2011

[Numbers in thousands.]

Characteristics	Total	In structures with			Region							
		1 unit	2 to 4 units	5 units or more	Northeast		Midwest		South		West	
					Total	1 unit	Total	1 unit	Total	1 unit	Total	1 unit
20,000-place series												
2011	624.1	418.5	21.6	184.0	68.5	39.0	102.7	70.5	320.7	227.1	132.2	81.9
2010	604.6	447.3	22.0	135.3	73.8	49.1	103.5	75.4	299.1	232.3	128.2	90.6
2009	583.0	441.1	20.7	121.1	68.5	45.8	100.3	74.9	297.4	231.8	116.7	88.7
2008	905.4	575.6	34.4	295.4	119.0	58.0	137.7	93.2	451.9	304.3	196.7	120.0
2007	1,398.4	979.9	59.6	359.0	150.6	83.7	211.7	153.8	692.2	507.5	343.9	234.9
2006	1,838.9	1,378.2	76.6	384.1	174.6	103.4	279.4	209.3	929.7	726.2	455.2	339.3
2005	2,155.3	1,682.0	84.0	389.3	203.8	126.6	353.9	278.7	1,039.0	826.8	558.6	450.0
2004	2,070.1	1,613.4	90.4	366.2	197.0	131.8	370.5	295.5	960.8	756.1	541.9	430.0
19,000-place series												
2003	1,889.2	1,460.9	82.5	345.8	182.4	124.4	371.0	287.3	849.3	670.1	486.5	379.0
2002	1,747.7	1,332.6	73.7	341.4	173.7	126.6	352.4	263.4	790.7	606.5	430.9	336.2
2001	1,636.7	1,235.6	66.0	335.2	159.8	117.7	333.6	252.5	730.3	556.9	413.0	308.5
2000	1,592.3	1,198.1	64.9	329.3	165.1	122.3	323.8	245.4	701.9	529.7	401.5	300.7
1999	1,663.5	1,246.7	65.8	351.1	164.9	127.1	345.4	262.1	748.9	550.4	404.3	307.1
1998	1,612.3	1,187.6	69.2	355.5	159.4	124.1	327.2	247.8	724.5	521.9	401.2	293.8
1997	1,441.1	1,062.4	68.4	310.3	141.9	111.2	299.8	220.0	635.9	464.2	363.5	267.1
1996	1,425.6	1,069.5	65.8	290.3	136.9	108.8	317.8	236.6	623.4	468.5	347.4	255.6
1995	1,332.5	997.3	63.8	271.5	124.2	104.5	296.6	220.5	583.2	430.3	328.5	241.9
1994	1,371.6	1,068.5	62.2	241.0	138.5	119.1	305.2	233.6	585.5	453.0	342.4	262.8
17,0000-place series												
1993	1,199.1	986.5	52.4	160.2	133.5	113.7	276.6	218.4	500.7	419.5	288.2	235.0
1992	1,094.9	910.7	45.8	138.4	124.8	108.5	259.0	204.4	442.5	382.2	268.6	215.6
1991	948.8	753.5	43.1	152.1	109.8	91.8	215.4	168.1	375.7	308.4	247.9	185.2
1990	1,110.8	793.9	54.3	262.6	125.8	96.5	233.8	165.7	426.2	318.1	324.9	213.7
1989	1,338.4	931.7	66.9	339.8	179.0	129.7	252.1	172.1	505.3	361.5	402.1	268.4
1988	1,455.6	993.8	75.7	386.1	230.2	166.0	266.3	177.8	543.5	391.6	415.6	258.3
1987	1,534.8	1,024.4	89.3	421.1	271.8	194.0	282.3	180.3	574.7	413.1	406.0	236.9
1986	1,769.4	1,077.6	108.4	583.5	283.3	203.8	290.0	167.5	686.5	443.2	509.7	263.1
1985	1,733.3	956.6	120.1	656.6	259.7	173.5	237.0	128.6	752.6	428.9	483.9	225.7
1984	1,681.8	922.4	142.6	616.8	200.8	141.2	211.7	121.5	812.1	432.3	457.3	227.4
16,000-place series												
1983	1,605.2	901.5	133.7	570.1	164.1	112.3	187.8	117.4	862.9	443.0	390.4	228.6
1982	1,000.5	546.4	88.3	365.8	106.7	65.7	126.3	67.6	543.5	281.1	224.1	132.0
1981	985.5	564.3	101.8	319.4	109.8	65.7	133.3	78.3	491.1	270.7	251.3	149.5
1980	1,190.6	710.4	114.5	365.7	117.9	75.7	192.0	107.9	561.9	333.0	318.9	193.7
1979	1,551.8	981.5	125.4	444.8	166.9	110.2	289.1	182.4	628.0	392.1	467.7	296.7
1978	1,800.5	1,182.6	130.6	487.3	194.4	132.9	388.0	260.8	667.6	439.3	550.5	349.6
14,000-place series												
1977	1,690.0	1,126.1	121.3	442.7	181.9	126.8	402.4	269.3	561.1	370.1	544.6	359.9
1976	1,296.2	893.6	93.1	309.5	152.4	111.2	326.1	219.4	401.7	292.6	416.0	270.5
1975	939.2	675.5	63.8	199.8	129.5	92.6	241.5	169.3	292.7	222.8	275.5	190.8
1974	1,074.4	643.8	64.4	366.2	165.4	97.2	241.3	154.5	390.1	223.7	277.6	168.4
1973	1,819.5	882.1	117.0	820.5	271.9	141.6	361.4	197.5	763.2	323.9	423.1	219.0
1972	2,218.9	1,033.1	148.6	1,037.2	333.3	147.3	440.8	230.1	905.4	391.5	539.3	264.3
13,000-place series												
1971	1,924.6	906.1	132.9	885.7	303.6	127.3	421.1	208.1	725.4	338.6	474.6	232.1
1970	1,351.5	646.8	88.1	616.7	218.3	93.1	287.4	148.1	502.9	246.5	342.9	159.1
1969	1,322.3	624.8	85.2	612.4	215.8	104.7	317.0	149.9	470.5	215.6	319.0	154.6
1968	1,353.4	694.7	84.3	574.4	234.8	119.2	350.1	182.1	477.3	233.9	291.1	159.5
1967	1,141.0	650.6	73.0	417.5	222.6	119.6	309.8	176.0	390.8	225.0	217.8	130.0
12,000-place series												
1966	971.9	563.2	61.0	347.7	209.8	113.9	250.9	148.6	331.1	186.0	180.2	114.7
1965	1,240.6	709.9	84.7	445.9	252.7	137.4	310.5	181.7	408.3	236.5	269.1	154.3
1964[1]	1,285.8	720.1	100.8	464.9	243.4	130.1	286.9	175.9	401.4	240.8	354.2	173.3
1963[1]	1,334.7	750.2	118.9	465.6	239.4	129.0	268.8	174.0	403.2	245.1	423.3	202.3
10,000-place series												
1962[1]	1,186.6	716.2	87.1	383.3	242.5	125.5	238.3	164.0	342.8	232.2	363.0	194.6
1961[1]	1,064.2	722.8	67.6	273.8	229.4	124.6	226.1	171.8	299.4	236.2	309.4	190.2
1960[1]	997.6	745.9	64.5	187.1	199.1	129.6	228.0	186.3	284.1	237.6	286.3	192.4
1959[1]	1,208.0	938.0	77.0	193.0	222.0	NA	286.0	NA	356.0	NA	344.0	NA

NA = Not available.
[1]Derived rounded estimates previously shown in this table have been replaced with actual estimates.

Source: U.S. Census Bureau, Building Permits Survey

Table 2-10. New Privately Owned Housing Units Authorized by Building Permits in Permit-Issuing Places, Not Seasonally Adjusted, 1959–2012

[Numbers in thousands.]

Characteristics	Total	In structures with			Region							
		1 unit	2 to 4 units	5 units or more	Northeast		Midwest		South		West	
					Total	1 unit	Total	1 unit	Total	1 unit	Total	1 unit
20,000-place series												
2012												
January	46.3	29.9	1.3	15.1	4.8	2.2	5.0	3.3	28.4	18.3	8.2	6.1
February	51.9	35.1	1.7	15.2	5.5	2.7	6.5	4.6	28.9	21.1	11.1	6.8
March	67.4	42.2	2.0	23.2	5.8	3.6	10.3	7.3	34.3	22.5	17.0	8.9
April	62.5	43.9	1.8	16.8	7.6	4.0	10.6	7.8	30.5	22.4	13.7	9.6
May	75.4	49.6	2.0	23.8	7.3	4.4	12.3	9.1	38.6	24.9	17.2	11.3
2011												
January	36.3	26.2	1.3	8.7	4.5	3.0	4.5	2.7	20.3	15.3	7.0	5.3
February	37.7	26.5	1.1	10.0	3.6	2.1	4.5	3.3	22.6	16.2	6.9	5.0
March	54.4	37.8	1.5	15.1	4.7	3.1	8.1	6.0	30.2	21.6	11.4	7.1
April	50.7	37.2	1.9	11.6	5.0	3.3	9.2	6.9	25.5	19.6	11.0	7.4
May	57.3	39.7	1.8	15.8	7.3	3.6	9.9	7.2	27.6	20.9	12.6	8.0
June	63.8	41.5	2.1	20.3	8.2	3.7	10.1	7.4	31.1	21.9	14.3	8.5
July	52.6	35.9	1.9	14.8	5.1	3.5	9.1	6.4	27.6	18.9	10.8	7.2
August	62.6	41.6	2.6	18.4	6.0	3.4	11.3	7.8	31.4	22.3	13.8	8.1
September	53.2	36.3	1.9	15.1	6.0	3.6	10.5	7.0	25.4	18.9	11.3	6.8
October	52.0	34.4	2.0	15.7	5.8	3.6	10.0	6.5	26.1	17.8	10.1	6.5
November	51.9	31.6	1.8	18.5	6.5	3.5	8.4	5.3	25.6	16.9	11.4	6.0
December	51.6	29.8	1.8	20.0	5.7	2.8	7.1	4.2	27.2	16.9	11.5	6.0
2010												
January	40.4	31.4	1.3	7.6	4.2	3.0	4.6	3.5	22.2	18.1	9.4	6.8
February	45.3	35.4	1.4	8.5	4.9	3.5	5.7	4.6	23.8	19.7	10.9	7.5
March	64.1	50.9	2.2	11.0	5.7	4.2	9.8	7.9	34.8	28.4	13.8	10.4
April	58.9	46.1	1.6	11.2	6.5	4.3	11.4	8.6	29.3	24.2	11.7	9.0
May	51.1	39.9	1.7	9.5	5.8	4.4	9.7	7.3	25.8	20.5	9.9	7.8
June	59.2	42.9	2.1	14.2	8.6	4.8	10.0	7.9	28.6	21.3	12.0	8.9
July	51.6	37.5	1.8	12.2	5.8	4.0	9.8	6.8	26.0	19.2	10.0	7.6
August	53.7	37.2	1.9	14.5	6.4	4.1	9.7	6.6	26.2	19.2	11.4	7.3
September	48.5	34.3	2.3	11.9	6.3	4.1	9.0	6.4	23.6	17.0	9.6	6.9
October	43.5	31.5	1.9	10.1	5.6	3.7	10.2	6.5	19.0	15.0	8.6	6.2
November	40.9	29.6	1.7	9.6	5.1	3.8	7.4	5.8	19.9	14.8	8.4	5.3
December	47.6	30.6	2.0	15.0	8.9	5.3	6.3	3.6	19.9	14.8	12.5	6.9
2009												
January	37.6	22.1	1.5	14.0	3.6	2.5	4.5	2.3	21.3	13.1	8.1	4.1
February	39.2	26.3	1.3	11.6	4.2	2.0	4.7	3.5	22.9	16.3	7.4	4.5
March	45.4	32.7	2.0	10.7	4.6	3.0	6.9	4.8	24.7	18.9	9.1	6.0
April	47.8	37.8	1.7	8.3	5.3	3.7	8.0	6.6	24.5	19.5	10.0	8.0
May	49.5	39.5	1.7	8.3	5.4	4.0	9.0	7.7	24.9	19.5	10.1	8.2
June	61.3	47.0	2.4	11.9	7.0	4.6	10.6	8.4	31.6	24.1	12.1	9.9
July	56.1	46.9	1.7	7.5	6.3	4.8	11.0	8.5	26.7	23.9	12.2	9.8
August	54.0	42.9	1.7	9.3	6.3	4.3	9.6	8.0	27.5	21.9	10.6	8.7
September	52.9	40.7	1.8	10.4	6.4	4.5	10.2	7.5	25.6	20.4	10.8	8.3
October	47.9	38.6	1.3	8.0	6.2	4.5	10.0	7.4	22.3	18.9	9.4	7.6
November	42.1	31.9	2.1	8.1	5.6	3.7	8.2	5.7	20.9	16.4	7.4	6.2
December	49.2	34.7	1.4	13.1	7.8	4.0	7.6	4.6	24.4	18.7	9.4	7.4
2008												
January	77.4	48.0	3.0	26.4	8.2	4.4	10.1	5.8	44.0	28.6	15.1	9.2
February	75.0	48.0	3.0	24.0	6.6	4.0	7.9	5.2	41.4	28.9	19.2	9.9
March	79.1	54.1	3.2	21.7	8.6	5.0	9.8	7.3	44.5	30.6	16.2	11.2
April	91.5	63.4	3.6	24.5	10.0	6.0	15.7	11.2	45.7	33.0	20.1	13.2
May	92.3	61.9	3.2	27.3	12.9	5.9	14.2	11.1	42.9	31.3	22.2	13.6
June	110.6	59.4	3.1	48.0	30.1	5.5	14.5	10.0	43.2	30.0	22.9	13.9
July	85.9	55.7	3.3	26.9	10.0	5.9	14.4	9.9	43.9	28.2	17.5	11.7
August	76.3	48.0	2.9	25.4	7.4	5.6	13.1	8.1	39.7	24.4	16.0	10.0
September	70.9	45.9	3.4	21.7	8.4	5.2	13.0	8.6	34.5	22.8	15.0	9.3
October	63.7	40.4	2.7	20.6	7.0	4.6	12.4	8.1	30.3	20.0	14.0	7.7
November	41.5	26.2	1.5	13.8	5.0	3.1	7.3	4.9	19.3	13.1	9.9	5.1
December	41.2	24.6	1.5	15.1	4.7	2.9	5.5	3.2	22.4	13.5	8.6	5.0
2007												
January	114.1	80.3	5.0	28.8	12.0	6.1	14.5	9.0	60.0	45.0	27.5	20.2
February	112.1	79.4	4.9	27.9	8.2	4.4	12.1	8.1	61.6	46.4	30.2	20.5
March	139.4	103.4	6.3	29.8	12.8	7.4	19.4	14.7	70.8	54.5	36.5	26.8
April	130.9	98.6	5.2	27.2	14.4	8.3	20.9	16.2	64.1	49.8	31.6	24.2
May	146.0	106.6	6.1	33.3	14.1	9.0	23.7	18.3	73.1	53.1	35.1	26.2
June	135.6	97.2	5.2	33.3	15.5	8.4	21.5	16.4	65.6	47.9	33.0	24.4
July	122.5	89.8	5.2	27.5	14.5	8.3	19.9	14.8	59.3	44.8	28.8	21.9
August	126.0	87.5	5.2	33.3	14.3	8.4	19.0	14.7	59.1	44.3	33.5	20.1
September	100.5	66.6	3.9	30.0	11.2	6.4	17.7	12.2	47.8	33.7	23.8	14.3
October	103.8	70.7	4.3	28.8	13.7	7.2	18.0	13.2	45.9	34.5	26.2	15.9
November	89.5	54.7	4.3	30.5	10.1	5.2	14.9	9.9	44.3	28.8	20.2	10.8
December	77.8	45.2	4.0	28.7	9.8	4.6	10.0	6.2	40.4	24.9	17.6	9.6

Table 2-10. New Privately Owned Housing Units Authorized by Building Permits in Permit-Issuing Places, Not Seasonally Adjusted, 1959–2012—*Continued*

[Numbers in thousands.]

Characteristics	Total	In structures with			Region							
		1 unit	2 to 4 units	5 units or more	Northeast		Midwest		South		West	
					Total	1 unit	Total	1 unit	Total	1 unit	Total	1 unit
2006												
January	152.6	114.3	6.6	31.7	12.6	7.6	18.5	13.3	83.7	64.3	37.8	29.0
February	151.0	115.6	5.7	29.7	11.9	6.9	20.7	14.5	78.2	64.5	40.3	29.7
March	194.2	146.7	7.5	40.0	17.2	10.4	27.3	21.3	101.6	78.5	48.1	36.6
April	168.6	130.8	6.3	31.5	15.6	10.0	25.4	21.2	85.0	65.9	42.6	33.7
May	184.4	144.5	7.8	32.1	16.5	10.4	29.7	23.7	89.8	73.5	48.4	36.9
June	184.2	139.3	7.0	38.0	17.7	10.5	28.5	21.4	89.6	70.7	48.5	36.7
July	148.0	111.6	6.7	29.7	15.8	8.8	24.6	18.5	73.2	57.6	34.4	26.7
August	161.2	121.5	7.4	32.3	16.0	9.5	27.3	19.3	80.1	63.6	37.8	29.1
September	136.6	97.7	6.0	32.8	13.9	8.0	22.2	16.3	65.7	50.2	34.7	23.2
October	133.1	98.0	6.0	29.1	13.6	8.7	22.7	17.2	66.2	50.7	30.6	21.4
November	111.4	82.2	4.6	24.6	11.7	6.6	17.8	12.9	56.7	43.8	25.3	18.8
December	113.6	76.0	5.0	32.6	12.1	6.0	14.7	9.6	59.9	42.8	26.9	17.6
2005												
January	139.7	106.9	4.5	28.3	11.4	6.8	16.4	12.7	75.0	58.6	36.9	28.7
February	149.4	114.8	5.9	28.6	11.5	6.9	21.4	16.5	76.3	60.2	40.2	31.3
March	190.5	150.6	7.3	32.6	15.1	9.6	29.7	23.9	94.8	75.3	50.9	41.8
April	193.2	152.7	6.7	33.9	18.0	11.0	35.0	27.7	90.7	73.8	49.6	40.1
May	193.1	156.0	7.4	29.7	19.9	12.7	34.3	27.7	89.3	72.9	49.5	42.7
June	211.9	166.2	8.7	37.1	22.1	13.0	34.8	28.4	99.2	79.2	55.8	45.6
July	185.5	145.9	7.6	31.9	18.3	12.1	32.7	26.0	86.5	68.7	48.0	39.1
August	208.0	161.9	8.4	37.7	20.1	13.0	35.3	27.5	101.3	79.7	51.3	41.7
September	193.7	151.3	7.8	34.6	18.6	12.7	32.3	25.8	88.9	70.7	53.9	42.2
October	176.0	139.1	7.1	29.8	16.8	11.2	32.9	25.9	82.6	66.4	43.7	35.6
November	162.9	124.0	6.5	32.3	17.1	9.7	28.4	21.6	76.6	61.9	40.8	30.8
December	151.3	112.5	6.1	32.7	15.0	8.0	20.5	14.8	77.8	59.3	38.1	30.4
2004												
January	132.0	103.4	5.8	22.8	11.2	7.5	18.0	14.7	68.0	53.2	34.9	28.0
February	137.1	108.4	5.6	23.1	10.7	7.4	20.5	17.1	70.0	55.0	35.9	29.0
March	190.7	154.8	9.3	26.6	17.4	12.7	33.4	27.4	89.9	73.7	49.9	41.0
April	192.5	155.0	8.6	28.9	18.5	13.9	36.9	30.4	87.7	70.2	49.5	40.5
May	188.4	150.2	7.4	30.8	18.8	12.9	33.7	28.2	87.4	68.0	48.5	41.0
June	197.1	159.3	8.6	29.2	21.3	14.3	34.7	29.6	87.6	73.0	53.5	42.5
July	185.9	145.3	8.6	32.1	18.5	12.1	32.7	27.2	85.1	66.5	49.6	39.6
August	185.2	145.6	7.7	31.9	16.5	11.2	36.8	28.9	85.8	67.7	46.2	37.9
September	174.9	134.5	6.8	33.6	17.6	10.8	35.1	26.6	75.4	60.6	46.8	36.5
October	174.5	128.5	7.6	38.4	15.6	10.4	34.3	25.6	82.7	60.2	41.9	32.4
November	156.4	114.6	7.6	34.2	16.5	10.1	28.0	21.1	69.7	52.8	42.3	30.7
December	155.2	113.8	6.8	34.6	14.4	8.5	26.4	19.0	71.5	55.4	42.9	31.0
19,000-place series												
2003												
January	126.4	98.0	5.6	22.8	10.5	7.2	19.1	14.4	62.3	48.4	34.5	27.8
February	128.5	93.9	5.2	29.3	9.6	5.9	18.4	14.1	61.8	47.3	38.6	26.7
March	148.4	117.7	6.0	24.7	12.6	9.1	27.2	22.0	69.8	55.8	38.7	30.7
April	167.6	134.2	8.0	25.4	16.0	11.4	35.1	28.1	74.1	60.3	42.4	34.3
May	169.5	132.1	7.5	30.0	17.0	12.1	34.4	28.0	74.4	58.7	43.7	33.3
June	175.8	138.3	7.6	29.9	16.9	12.2	37.2	28.8	77.3	62.2	44.3	35.1
July	173.0	138.6	6.5	27.9	17.9	12.9	36.1	29.2	75.3	61.1	43.7	35.4
August	169.9	131.0	7.2	31.7	18.2	11.4	35.0	26.6	75.7	60.5	41.0	32.5
September	169.1	130.5	8.4	30.2	15.7	11.7	37.1	28.2	73.9	57.7	42.4	32.9
October	182.8	138.1	7.7	37.0	18.8	12.5	37.9	29.8	79.4	61.1	46.7	34.7
November	130.5	99.2	6.9	24.4	14.1	9.3	27.9	20.1	56.3	44.7	32.2	25.1
December	147.9	109.6	5.9	32.4	15.1	8.8	25.5	18.0	69.0	52.3	38.3	30.5
2002												
January	115.7	88.7	4.5	22.4	10.5	7.8	18.7	14.1	58.9	45.9	27.6	21.0
February	122.5	95.5	4.4	22.6	11.7	8.0	20.4	15.5	62.0	49.6	28.3	22.5
March	143.2	111.0	5.8	26.5	11.9	9.5	27.3	20.9	69.1	52.7	34.8	27.9
April	156.0	125.4	6.4	24.3	15.5	12.1	33.6	26.9	69.2	55.6	37.8	30.8
May	164.2	127.1	6.4	30.7	17.9	12.5	34.6	26.8	71.7	55.3	40.0	32.5
June	158.0	118.9	7.8	31.3	16.8	11.9	31.9	24.4	69.6	52.0	39.8	30.6
July	159.3	122.4	6.0	30.9	17.3	12.3	33.8	24.9	70.6	54.0	37.6	31.1
August	153.7	119.8	6.6	27.3	15.5	11.2	31.8	23.8	68.7	54.3	37.6	30.4
September	149.5	110.1	8.0	31.4	15.2	11.2	32.1	23.1	63.6	48.0	38.5	27.7
October	162.9	123.0	7.0	32.9	16.2	12.0	36.2	26.0	68.6	52.3	41.9	32.8
November	126.8	96.0	5.3	25.6	12.4	9.1	25.2	19.7	55.6	42.8	33.5	24.4
December	135.8	94.6	5.6	35.5	12.6	9.0	26.7	17.2	63.0	44.1	33.4	24.3

Table 2-10. New Privately Owned Housing Units Authorized by Building Permits in Permit-Issuing Places, Not Seasonally Adjusted, 1959–2012—*Continued*

[Numbers in thousands.]

Characteristics	Total	In structures with			Region							
		1 unit	2 to 4 units	5 units or more	Northeast		Midwest		South		West	
					Total	1 unit	Total	1 unit	Total	1 unit	Total	1 unit
2001												
January	117.0	85.6	3.8	27.6	9.0	6.9	17.8	13.0	56.1	42.0	34.1	23.7
February	114.3	85.1	4.7	24.6	10.6	6.6	19.1	14.0	55.1	42.1	29.5	22.3
March	147.7	112.7	5.9	29.1	12.9	9.3	28.7	22.6	67.1	51.3	38.9	29.4
April	148.6	116.5	5.8	26.2	14.1	10.4	31.5	24.9	65.2	51.8	37.7	29.4
May	159.8	124.4	6.5	28.9	15.3	12.3	34.7	27.5	70.2	53.6	39.6	31.0
June	153.9	119.2	7.8	27.0	15.1	11.5	33.0	25.9	65.4	52.2	40.5	29.5
July	140.6	110.2	5.1	25.3	15.0	11.1	31.1	24.2	61.1	47.9	33.4	27.0
August	151.4	116.2	6.2	29.0	15.8	11.8	31.2	24.7	65.6	51.1	38.8	28.5
September	125.2	92.4	4.6	28.2	12.2	9.6	27.0	19.8	54.3	40.0	31.7	23.0
October	140.2	104.4	5.9	29.8	15.3	11.3	30.8	22.6	60.2	46.0	33.9	24.6
November	124.4	89.2	4.8	30.4	13.0	8.9	27.4	18.9	57.4	41.1	26.7	20.3
December	113.6	79.7	4.9	29.0	11.4	8.0	21.4	14.4	52.7	37.7	28.1	19.6
2000												
January	107.3	78.3	3.7	25.3	10.9	6.9	17.3	12.9	50.9	38.6	28.2	19.9
February	121.8	89.1	5.0	27.8	10.4	7.4	21.9	15.4	59.0	45.2	30.6	21.1
March	153.7	119.0	5.8	28.9	15.1	11.6	32.9	25.2	68.7	54.0	37.0	28.2
April	138.9	107.6	5.1	26.1	14.7	10.9	32.3	25.5	58.2	44.5	33.6	26.6
May	148.9	119.3	6.5	23.2	15.9	12.9	33.2	25.9	64.2	50.8	35.6	29.6
June	155.1	114.5	6.3	34.3	16.6	12.2	31.3	24.1	66.1	49.1	41.0	29.1
July	129.8	98.8	4.5	26.5	14.1	10.6	28.0	21.3	55.6	42.6	32.0	24.3
August	146.8	111.6	6.4	28.9	15.3	11.4	30.8	23.4	62.5	48.5	38.3	28.2
September	131.4	95.8	5.8	29.8	14.2	10.2	26.6	20.2	58.3	40.8	32.2	24.5
October	134.8	102.8	6.5	25.5	14.1	11.2	31.3	22.6	57.3	43.8	32.0	25.2
November	121.0	87.7	5.3	28.0	13.5	9.3	23.0	17.5	54.0	38.4	30.5	22.4
December	102.9	73.7	4.1	25.2	10.3	7.5	15.2	11.2	47.0	33.4	30.5	21.5
1999												
January	105.7	74.2	4.3	27.1	9.2	6.8	13.6	10.3	55.3	37.7	27.7	19.4
February	114.7	86.6	4.5	23.7	9.7	7.7	18.9	14.8	58.7	43.3	27.4	20.8
March	154.6	118.9	6.0	29.8	14.4	10.7	32.0	24.2	70.4	54.2	37.9	29.8
April	151.8	119.9	6.0	25.9	15.5	12.7	34.3	27.4	66.2	51.2	35.8	28.6
May	145.1	115.9	4.9	24.3	14.7	12.6	33.4	25.5	60.5	49.2	36.5	28.7
June	169.3	128.0	6.4	34.9	18.7	13.2	34.5	27.2	71.4	52.9	44.8	34.5
July	149.1	114.6	5.2	29.2	15.1	12.3	30.4	24.6	66.3	49.1	37.2	28.6
August	151.9	112.6	5.9	33.3	15.5	12.1	33.4	25.2	68.5	49.3	34.4	26.1
September	137.3	103.1	5.8	28.3	13.4	10.4	32.2	24.0	58.3	43.9	33.4	24.8
October	137.6	97.6	5.8	34.2	12.8	10.0	31.3	23.2	62.3	41.6	31.2	22.8
November	125.6	90.3	5.7	29.6	13.6	9.6	29.4	20.0	55.0	40.0	27.6	20.6
December	120.9	84.8	5.2	30.9	12.3	8.9	22.1	15.6	55.9	38.0	30.6	22.3
1998												
January	96.2	70.1	4.0	22.1	9.7	7.0	14.7	10.9	46.3	34.4	25.4	17.8
February	107.4	78.1	4.8	24.4	8.9	7.2	19.7	14.3	51.2	37.5	27.5	19.1
March	140.9	105.1	6.0	29.9	12.1	10.2	26.8	20.4	68.4	47.7	33.6	26.8
April	146.3	113.6	5.4	27.3	13.2	11.4	31.0	25.2	63.6	48.0	38.5	29.0
May	138.2	107.3	5.4	25.5	13.3	11.2	30.7	24.4	62.5	45.9	31.8	25.8
June	153.4	115.8	7.5	30.1	16.0	12.8	31.6	25.2	65.0	48.6	40.8	29.2
July	149.3	111.2	6.4	31.7	15.4	11.9	29.7	23.4	66.1	47.7	38.0	28.2
August	144.7	104.4	6.1	34.1	14.3	11.1	28.9	21.8	67.1	46.5	34.4	25.1
September	141.7	102.5	6.4	32.9	14.7	11.0	30.3	22.1	62.2	44.0	34.7	25.4
October	149.8	103.8	6.8	39.3	15.7	11.1	32.4	23.6	65.8	44.0	35.9	25.1
November	119.9	86.6	4.7	28.6	13.4	9.8	24.9	18.9	51.2	37.2	30.3	20.7
December	124.5	89.0	5.7	29.8	12.7	9.5	26.5	17.6	55.1	40.6	30.2	21.3
1997												
January	88.1	65.8	3.9	18.5	9.1	6.5	13.2	9.2	43.3	33.6	22.5	16.4
February	94.1	70.3	4.1	19.7	9.1	5.8	15.7	11.4	44.6	34.3	24.6	18.8
March	120.1	88.7	5.4	26.0	11.8	8.7	24.3	18.0	55.4	39.7	28.7	22.3
April	137.2	104.4	6.6	26.2	12.6	10.4	32.0	24.3	61.5	45.0	31.2	24.8
May	131.6	101.3	5.8	24.6	12.8	11.0	29.4	22.9	55.8	42.3	33.5	25.1
June	133.6	100.9	6.6	26.2	14.0	11.0	29.2	22.3	57.1	42.4	33.3	25.2
July	133.7	99.8	6.7	27.2	13.5	11.1	27.8	21.6	58.7	41.8	33.7	25.3
August	126.0	91.8	5.5	28.7	12.9	9.8	28.3	20.0	53.4	38.9	31.4	23.1
September	134.4	95.6	6.1	32.7	12.4	10.1	28.8	20.7	57.4	40.0	35.7	24.8
October	135.5	97.5	7.6	30.4	12.5	10.7	29.5	20.7	58.0	41.4	35.5	24.8
November	100.4	72.5	4.5	23.3	10.6	8.1	21.3	14.8	44.0	32.0	24.5	17.7
December	106.4	73.9	5.7	26.8	10.7	8.0	20.3	14.1	46.5	32.9	28.9	18.9
1996												
January	88.3	66.0	3.8	18.5	5.5	4.5	14.3	10.4	44.0	33.7	24.5	17.4
February	96.0	74.4	4.0	17.6	6.1	5.4	17.1	13.7	46.4	37.2	26.4	18.1
March	120.4	95.7	4.9	19.8	10.8	8.9	26.6	20.2	52.0	43.3	31.1	23.3
April	140.1	109.9	6.9	23.3	14.0	10.9	33.9	26.7	60.3	47.1	31.9	25.1
May	140.5	109.2	6.2	25.1	14.2	11.8	32.8	26.1	61.8	46.0	31.8	25.4
June	131.4	100.7	6.1	24.7	13.1	10.7	29.4	23.4	55.6	42.2	33.4	24.4
July	135.1	101.9	5.8	27.5	13.4	11.1	33.1	24.6	54.7	41.6	33.8	24.5
August	129.1	97.6	5.5	26.0	14.0	10.6	30.3	22.6	55.4	41.3	29.4	23.2
September	121.1	85.9	6.1	29.1	12.2	9.6	27.8	20.1	51.4	35.7	29.8	20.5
October	123.7	90.8	7.0	25.9	13.4	10.0	30.8	21.4	49.6	38.1	29.9	21.3
November	100.7	71.5	5.3	23.9	10.8	8.3	23.1	15.3	44.9	31.7	21.9	16.3
December	99.2	66.0	4.2	29.1	9.4	7.0	18.7	12.1	47.4	30.7	23.6	16.2

Table 2-10. New Privately Owned Housing Units Authorized by Building Permits in Permit-Issuing Places, Not Seasonally Adjusted, 1959–2012—*Continued*

[Numbers in thousands.]

Characteristics	Total	In structures with			Region							
		1 unit	2 to 4 units	5 units or more	Northeast		Midwest		South		West	
					Total	1 unit	Total	1 unit	Total	1 unit	Total	1 unit
1995												
January	78.0	58.2	3.8	16.1	7.4	6.2	12.3	8.6	40.1	29.1	18.3	14.3
February	80.4	59.8	3.3	17.3	5.6	4.7	13.7	10.4	38.7	28.9	22.5	15.8
March	111.5	85.1	5.8	20.5	10.5	8.8	23.8	18.5	52.7	39.1	24.5	18.8
April	109.7	83.1	5.3	21.3	11.5	9.5	25.2	19.4	46.6	34.9	26.5	19.3
May	122.8	95.9	5.8	21.1	12.4	11.0	29.3	22.7	51.0	39.1	30.1	23.1
June	129.3	97.4	6.6	25.3	12.4	10.6	29.7	23.1	53.3	39.7	33.9	24.1
July	115.6	88.3	4.8	22.5	10.7	9.4	27.3	20.9	48.4	36.9	29.2	21.1
August	133.5	101.4	6.0	26.1	12.3	10.6	31.9	23.5	55.9	42.1	33.5	25.2
September	124.1	90.1	5.9	28.1	11.2	9.4	28.9	20.5	55.0	39.4	29.1	20.8
October	122.2	90.8	6.4	25.0	11.9	9.8	31.9	22.1	51.5	37.7	27.0	21.2
November	107.8	78.4	5.9	23.5	10.5	8.0	24.9	18.2	46.3	33.3	26.2	18.9
December	97.4	68.8	3.9	24.7	8.0	6.6	17.8	12.5	43.8	30.1	27.8	19.5
1994												
January	80.7	63.4	3.8	13.4	5.0	4.5	12.2	9.6	40.6	31.7	22.8	17.6
February	81.7	69.2	3.6	8.9	5.3	4.8	13.9	11.6	40.1	34.2	22.5	18.6
March	126.4	104.0	5.5	16.8	10.3	8.8	27.1	22.6	56.4	46.0	32.5	26.7
April	127.6	102.0	5.6	20.0	12.6	11.0	29.6	24.2	54.4	42.2	31.1	24.5
May	131.4	107.7	5.9	17.8	14.3	12.8	32.8	25.7	52.9	43.2	31.4	25.9
June	138.8	109.2	6.1	23.5	15.6	13.3	31.6	25.4	54.6	43.4	37.0	27.1
July	114.8	90.9	4.8	19.1	14.7	12.8	27.3	21.2	46.2	35.9	26.6	21.0
August	131.5	100.9	5.7	24.9	14.2	11.9	30.7	22.8	54.1	42.1	32.5	24.2
September	127.2	91.5	5.3	30.3	12.3	10.5	28.3	20.8	54.3	38.2	32.2	22.0
October	117.0	85.9	6.2	24.9	11.9	10.2	29.9	20.1	46.1	34.3	29.2	21.3
November	100.5	74.8	5.4	20.3	11.5	9.8	23.0	16.8	43.4	31.0	22.6	17.2
December	94.2	68.9	4.2	21.0	10.8	8.7	18.8	12.8	42.6	30.9	22.0	16.5
17,000-place series												
1993												
January	67.1	55.1	2.6	9.3	6.9	6.0	11.4	9.2	32.9	27.4	15.9	12.6
February	73.1	61.3	3.3	8.4	7.1	5.9	13.3	10.6	35.6	30.5	17.1	14.3
March	99.1	84.2	4.1	10.9	9.1	7.9	22.5	17.9	41.5	36.4	26.0	22.0
April	107.3	91.5	4.8	10.9	11.4	10.3	24.8	21.0	45.4	38.8	25.7	21.3
May	101.7	85.2	4.2	12.3	12.3	10.9	26.1	20.7	39.8	34.2	23.4	19.4
June	117.8	97.0	5.3	15.5	14.0	11.6	28.5	22.6	45.0	38.3	30.3	24.4
July	104.5	88.2	4.4	11.9	12.1	10.7	24.6	20.2	42.2	36.7	25.5	20.5
August	111.9	91.0	4.9	16.0	12.4	10.5	27.1	21.1	45.8	38.0	26.6	21.4
September	111.5	89.8	5.1	16.6	12.3	10.9	27.3	20.7	45.0	36.4	26.8	21.8
October	107.0	87.9	5.1	13.9	13.2	11.3	27.3	21.1	41.9	35.4	24.6	20.1
November	98.1	80.5	4.5	13.0	11.4	9.5	24.2	18.4	39.4	33.8	23.1	18.7
December	100.1	74.8	3.9	21.4	11.4	8.3	19.4	14.6	46.1	33.5	23.3	18.4
1992												
January	67.9	55.2	2.6	10.1	6.9	5.4	11.9	9.5	31.6	26.4	17.5	13.8
February	72.6	61.1	2.8	8.7	6.6	5.5	15.5	12.1	32.0	28.7	18.5	14.8
March	97.7	82.4	3.8	11.6	10.3	9.0	22.7	18.5	42.0	35.9	22.8	18.9
April	103.9	88.0	4.0	11.9	11.6	10.3	25.7	20.7	41.0	35.9	25.7	21.0
May	97.1	82.7	4.0	10.5	12.0	10.8	26.1	20.7	36.7	32.8	22.3	18.5
June	109.2	91.6	4.8	12.8	13.0	11.0	25.8	21.3	43.3	37.2	27.2	22.1
July	101.1	83.3	3.7	14.1	12.4	10.6	24.9	19.4	39.0	34.1	24.8	19.1
August	93.0	76.6	4.7	11.8	11.1	9.8	23.2	18.2	35.6	30.6	23.1	18.1
September	99.2	80.1	3.9	15.2	11.5	9.6	25.4	19.0	38.7	32.9	23.7	18.6
October	97.1	80.3	4.5	12.3	10.9	9.9	23.8	19.2	39.3	32.3	23.1	18.8
November	76.4	63.8	3.5	9.1	10.0	8.9	18.0	13.5	30.0	26.8	18.3	14.6
December	79.5	65.8	3.4	10.3	8.5	7.6	16.1	12.3	33.5	28.8	21.4	17.2
1991												
January	51.5	37.6	2.4	11.5	5.1	3.7	8.5	5.3	23.0	18.5	14.9	10.0
February	54.1	43.5	2.9	7.8	4.9	3.9	9.5	7.7	25.0	20.7	14.7	11.3
March	78.7	61.2	3.9	13.6	8.2	6.4	16.3	12.9	31.9	26.3	22.3	15.5
April	90.9	75.7	4.3	10.9	11.0	9.5	22.4	18.5	34.9	29.9	22.7	17.8
May	98.3	78.1	3.9	16.3	11.0	9.7	23.8	19.1	37.0	30.5	26.5	18.8
June	93.2	73.9	4.5	14.9	10.7	9.3	21.6	17.5	35.4	28.4	25.4	18.7
July	91.3	74.9	3.6	12.8	10.9	9.1	22.8	18.0	34.7	29.4	22.9	18.3
August	84.9	69.9	3.8	11.3	10.7	9.3	20.7	16.8	32.5	27.6	21.0	16.1
September	80.6	64.2	3.6	12.8	9.2	8.0	19.4	15.2	32.8	26.3	19.1	14.8
October	89.8	70.4	3.9	15.4	12.0	9.8	22.5	16.7	32.9	27.4	22.5	16.5
November	67.1	52.6	3.3	11.1	8.9	7.3	15.1	11.3	26.8	21.1	16.3	13.0
December	68.5	51.7	3.0	13.7	7.2	5.9	12.9	9.0	28.8	22.2	19.7	14.6

Table 2-10. New Privately Owned Housing Units Authorized by Building Permits in Permit-Issuing Places, Not Seasonally Adjusted, 1959–2012—*Continued*

[Numbers in thousands.]

Characteristics	Total	In structures with			Region							
		1 unit	2 to 4 units	5 units or more	Northeast		Midwest		South		West	
					Total	1 unit	Total	1 unit	Total	1 unit	Total	1 unit
1990												
January	112.6	60.7	5.2	46.7	10.5	6.6	21.3	8.9	50.3	26.6	30.4	18.7
February	82.8	60.7	4.1	18.1	9.1	6.6	13.4	9.8	32.8	26.1	27.5	18.1
March	111.0	82.8	4.8	23.4	12.0	10.0	20.5	16.1	43.3	33.6	35.2	23.1
April	105.8	79.2	5.1	21.5	11.8	9.4	24.6	18.5	38.4	29.8	31.1	21.5
May	107.9	83.1	5.1	19.7	13.2	10.4	24.0	18.6	39.4	31.7	31.4	22.4
June	111.6	79.7	4.5	27.3	12.5	9.8	23.5	17.8	40.9	30.4	34.6	21.6
July	96.2	70.9	5.2	20.0	10.8	8.8	21.8	16.3	35.0	26.8	28.6	19.1
August	99.8	72.5	5.8	21.6	11.2	8.4	22.0	16.2	37.1	28.9	29.5	18.9
September	79.2	57.7	3.9	17.5	9.4	6.8	19.4	13.1	29.4	23.5	20.9	14.3
October	82.5	62.5	4.2	15.8	10.9	8.4	19.0	13.9	30.4	24.6	22.2	15.6
November	67.8	47.0	3.1	17.7	8.1	6.5	14.6	9.9	27.4	19.7	17.7	11.0
December	53.6	37.1	3.2	13.3	6.3	4.7	9.6	6.4	21.9	16.4	15.8	9.6
1989												
January	88.5	60.9	4.2	23.4	11.7	8.1	11.4	7.6	39.4	28.3	26.0	16.9
February	86.0	58.9	5.4	21.7	9.6	6.9	12.5	7.7	37.2	26.2	26.8	18.2
March	116.4	84.1	6.0	26.3	15.6	10.8	21.3	15.2	44.8	34.4	34.6	23.8
April	122.9	87.5	5.7	29.7	18.4	14.0	24.8	17.8	45.4	32.3	34.3	23.5
May	135.2	93.6	7.1	34.6	18.2	14.1	26.7	19.0	50.1	34.5	40.2	26.0
June	137.2	92.0	6.2	39.0	18.7	13.3	25.9	18.0	50.8	34.2	41.8	26.4
July	108.3	79.0	5.7	23.6	14.6	10.8	21.5	16.3	38.4	29.2	33.8	22.7
August	125.6	89.2	6.6	29.8	17.5	12.4	26.0	17.2	46.6	34.3	35.4	25.4
September	110.7	78.6	5.4	26.7	15.4	11.0	23.1	15.9	40.7	30.4	31.5	21.4
October	116.5	81.2	5.5	29.8	15.4	10.7	26.0	17.2	40.3	29.1	34.8	24.1
November	98.9	69.2	4.7	25.0	12.7	9.6	20.2	12.9	36.5	27.0	29.5	19.7
December	92.3	57.4	4.4	30.5	11.0	8.2	12.7	7.3	35.0	21.7	33.5	20.2
1988												
January	71.7	50.5	3.9	17.3	12.3	7.9	8.4	5.6	28.9	21.7	22.1	15.3
February	93.3	63.0	4.9	25.5	12.6	8.4	11.7	7.9	43.3	30.4	25.7	16.3
March	140.4	98.2	7.7	34.5	24.6	18.5	23.8	17.0	54.5	39.6	37.6	23.2
April	135.3	93.1	6.5	35.8	23.7	16.1	27.5	19.1	47.5	35.8	36.7	22.1
May	138.7	98.7	7.2	32.9	24.3	17.6	28.2	19.8	48.4	36.4	37.8	24.9
June	153.9	105.9	7.6	40.4	24.9	18.2	30.2	20.1	56.0	39.8	42.8	27.9
July	121.7	85.3	6.3	30.1	20.5	15.2	23.7	16.4	43.7	31.9	33.8	21.9
August	137.3	95.9	6.5	34.9	21.3	15.9	25.0	18.0	50.2	37.5	40.8	24.5
September	127.9	85.1	6.7	36.0	18.4	13.8	25.3	16.2	46.1	32.9	38.0	22.2
October	124.0	82.9	7.2	33.9	19.1	13.7	23.6	15.7	44.2	31.0	37.1	22.5
November	110.0	71.8	5.8	32.5	14.9	11.4	18.8	12.1	42.4	28.1	33.9	20.2
December	101.4	63.4	5.4	32.5	13.6	9.4	20.1	10.1	38.3	26.5	29.4	17.5
1987												
January	101.0	62.4	6.0	32.6	14.2	9.0	13.6	7.8	41.0	28.1	32.2	17.6
February	102.0	69.5	6.6	25.8	14.6	10.7	15.8	10.3	43.8	31.1	27.8	17.4
March	152.1	103.5	8.6	39.9	25.4	18.2	25.7	17.2	59.7	42.4	41.3	25.7
April	157.9	107.6	9.0	41.3	28.5	20.5	31.6	20.3	58.1	42.4	39.8	24.4
May	137.3	96.6	8.1	32.6	25.9	19.2	28.0	18.5	49.6	38.2	33.9	20.8
June	157.5	107.7	8.7	41.1	28.6	21.1	29.3	19.8	58.1	42.8	41.6	24.1
July	142.0	95.8	7.9	38.4	27.5	20.1	27.3	18.2	48.7	36.3	38.6	21.1
August	128.9	87.6	7.1	34.2	23.3	16.4	23.0	16.0	48.5	35.1	34.1	20.1
September	136.5	86.6	7.8	42.1	24.4	17.2	28.2	16.5	49.1	33.8	34.7	19.0
October	124.0	81.7	7.3	35.1	22.5	16.1	26.4	15.6	45.1	32.4	30.0	17.5
November	102.2	65.5	6.1	30.6	19.4	13.4	19.3	11.7	38.3	25.9	25.3	14.6
December	93.4	59.7	6.1	27.6	17.8	12.1	13.9	8.4	34.8	24.7	26.9	14.5
1986												
January	118.3	65.3	8.4	44.5	14.1	8.8	11.4	5.7	58.6	34.5	34.2	16.4
February	111.1	61.1	7.1	42.9	11.6	7.9	11.7	6.3	55.7	31.0	32.0	15.9
March	152.8	89.3	8.8	54.7	20.1	14.6	21.0	12.5	65.3	40.8	46.5	21.4
April	182.2	114.8	10.7	56.7	28.9	22.4	32.8	18.8	70.2	46.7	50.4	26.9
May	170.2	109.3	10.9	49.9	28.7	21.0	30.7	19.1	62.5	43.7	48.3	25.5
June	173.7	110.8	10.1	52.7	28.4	21.1	29.5	18.4	66.5	44.2	49.2	27.2
July	167.1	106.2	9.6	51.4	29.9	22.0	30.6	18.1	62.0	41.4	44.7	24.7
August	146.5	91.3	9.2	45.9	25.7	18.9	27.9	16.5	53.0	34.9	39.9	21.0
September	153.7	94.8	9.3	49.6	30.2	20.4	27.8	16.3	54.4	36.5	41.3	21.7
October	150.2	93.5	10.1	46.7	26.7	19.5	26.8	15.8	54.3	35.9	42.5	22.3
November	110.3	66.4	6.4	37.5	18.5	14.1	21.3	10.9	40.9	25.7	29.6	15.7
December	133.4	74.7	7.7	51.0	20.5	13.1	18.6	9.1	43.2	28.0	51.1	24.5
1985												
January	106.4	55.8	8.6	41.9	13.8	8.1	7.4	3.9	53.9	28.9	31.3	15.0
February	104.4	58.1	6.6	39.7	12.3	8.2	7.4	4.2	50.2	28.6	34.6	17.0
March	146.0	85.9	11.5	48.6	19.8	13.4	17.5	11.2	68.3	41.3	40.5	20.0
April	160.8	93.9	11.0	55.9	24.3	18.0	23.1	13.7	70.3	41.4	43.2	20.9
May	168.9	96.8	11.7	60.4	27.3	18.6	26.2	15.1	71.0	41.2	44.4	21.8
June	156.5	89.0	11.5	56.0	24.8	16.2	23.7	13.4	64.5	38.3	43.6	21.0
July	158.4	92.1	10.4	55.9	23.3	16.0	25.5	14.8	66.4	40.3	43.1	20.9
August	159.5	90.0	11.0	58.6	25.2	17.2	25.2	13.6	64.3	37.5	44.8	21.6
September	168.8	81.3	11.6	76.0	23.7	15.3	23.9	12.5	65.4	35.4	55.8	18.1
October	157.5	89.7	10.5	57.3	27.5	17.4	24.6	13.0	64.5	37.9	40.9	21.4
November	118.6	64.9	8.0	45.6	20.1	14.4	15.8	7.9	51.5	28.7	31.1	14.0
December	127.5	59.1	7.7	60.7	17.6	10.6	16.7	5.3	62.5	29.3	30.7	13.9

Table 2-10. New Privately Owned Housing Units Authorized by Building Permits in Permit-Issuing Places, Not Seasonally Adjusted, 1959–2012—*Continued*

[Numbers in thousands.]

Characteristics	Total	In structures with			Region							
		1 unit	2 to 4 units	5 units or more	Northeast		Midwest		South		West	
					Total	1 unit	Total	1 unit	Total	1 unit	Total	1 unit
1984												
January	114.1	60.2	9.4	44.5	8.1	5.2	8.8	4.9	64.2	33.2	33.0	16.9
February	130.1	72.6	10.7	46.8	10.0	6.9	11.9	7.0	71.9	39.0	36.3	19.6
March	152.3	88.6	14.4	49.3	14.8	10.5	14.8	9.5	78.0	45.2	44.7	23.3
April	161.0	92.3	13.7	55.0	17.8	13.8	21.7	13.7	78.5	41.7	43.1	23.2
May	169.4	98.2	14.1	57.1	22.3	16.3	22.8	15.3	78.6	43.0	45.6	23.6
June	172.3	90.3	14.1	67.9	19.4	14.8	22.7	13.6	80.4	40.0	49.7	21.9
July	141.5	79.1	12.2	50.2	17.5	13.5	21.0	11.6	64.4	35.3	38.6	18.6
August	142.6	80.7	12.3	49.7	18.7	14.0	19.8	11.5	65.3	35.9	38.9	19.3
September	131.9	70.8	10.9	50.2	19.3	12.1	18.3	9.8	60.7	32.6	33.7	16.4
October	137.3	75.8	12.1	49.3	19.8	13.8	20.3	10.8	61.9	34.1	35.2	17.1
November	122.9	62.7	10.1	50.1	18.0	11.2	17.9	8.5	56.0	28.2	31.0	14.7
December	106.5	51.2	8.6	46.7	15.1	9.0	11.7	5.2	52.4	24.1	27.4	12.9
16,000-place series												
1983												
January	83.7	48.5	6.8	28.5	6.4	3.7	5.9	3.4	51.4	29.0	20.1	12.4
February	93.4	50.9	7.3	35.2	7.8	3.4	6.4	4.6	56.9	29.2	22.3	13.6
March	135.5	79.2	11.6	44.7	11.3	8.2	14.2	9.9	82.1	43.7	27.8	17.4
April	138.8	81.6	12.1	45.2	13.5	9.2	16.6	11.2	75.1	40.0	33.7	21.1
May	150.7	93.0	11.6	46.1	15.2	11.7	19.5	13.5	78.4	44.4	37.6	23.4
June	173.2	101.2	13.7	58.4	18.4	13.0	21.4	14.3	88.2	45.5	45.3	28.4
July	148.6	82.3	11.4	54.9	16.3	11.5	17.2	11.7	78.5	38.5	36.6	20.5
August	155.5	85.9	12.5	57.2	18.0	12.2	20.8	12.5	79.2	40.2	37.6	20.9
September	149.5	77.8	12.6	59.1	17.9	11.4	20.8	11.4	73.8	35.9	37.0	19.0
October	142.6	76.5	13.3	52.8	15.5	11.1	20.0	11.0	73.7	35.7	33.3	18.8
November	124.7	68.3	11.4	45.1	12.3	9.1	15.7	8.8	68.0	33.9	28.8	16.4
December	108.9	56.5	9.4	43.0	11.4	7.8	9.4	4.9	57.7	27.1	30.3	16.7
1982												
January	47.6	25.4	4.2	18.0	3.0	1.7	2.5	1.4	31.8	15.9	10.3	6.4
February	52.4	27.9	4.6	19.9	3.8	1.8	3.1	1.7	34.3	17.5	11.2	6.9
March	81.0	44.0	7.4	29.6	7.8	4.8	8.0	4.3	47.7	24.4	17.5	10.4
April	82.7	46.6	6.9	29.2	8.8	6.2	10.5	6.4	46.1	23.5	17.2	10.6
May	82.2	45.8	8.5	27.9	10.2	6.2	13.5	6.9	40.4	22.4	18.1	10.3
June	89.4	50.6	8.3	30.5	10.2	6.3	12.3	7.1	46.1	24.5	20.7	12.8
July	92.2	46.8	7.3	38.1	9.2	6.0	13.5	6.3	45.7	21.9	23.8	12.7
August	82.4	47.6	7.9	26.8	10.4	6.1	11.3	6.9	43.3	23.7	17.4	10.9
September	101.2	52.4	9.5	39.3	12.1	6.8	16.4	7.7	51.4	26.3	21.2	11.7
October	99.7	55.5	8.1	36.1	12.3	7.6	14.5	7.7	51.2	27.0	21.8	13.2
November	93.2	54.8	7.6	30.7	10.8	7.2	11.8	6.7	49.9	28.0	20.6	13.0
December	96.5	48.9	7.9	39.7	7.9	5.1	8.9	4.5	55.5	26.2	24.2	13.1
1981												
January	72.8	39.6	8.6	24.7	5.1	2.4	6.7	3.5	42.3	22.2	18.8	11.4
February	74.4	42.9	7.2	24.4	4.9	2.7	7.0	3.5	43.0	24.4	19.6	12.2
March	103.3	61.2	10.1	32.0	10.0	5.7	15.3	8.1	52.9	31.0	25.1	16.4
April	113.3	69.3	11.5	32.4	11.8	8.0	16.3	10.2	54.2	33.0	31.0	18.2
May	102.3	61.0	9.2	32.1	10.5	7.4	14.1	9.1	48.0	26.9	29.7	17.7
June	95.4	56.3	10.2	28.9	11.0	7.1	14.4	9.0	43.4	25.1	26.6	15.2
July	85.9	52.6	8.7	24.6	11.3	7.2	12.1	8.3	40.6	23.9	21.9	13.2
August	75.9	45.2	7.8	22.8	10.5	7.3	10.5	6.7	36.0	20.1	18.9	11.2
September	82.5	41.8	7.9	32.8	10.2	5.2	12.6	6.6	40.0	19.3	19.7	10.7
October	66.8	35.6	8.4	22.8	10.6	5.9	10.8	5.7	29.8	15.2	15.7	8.8
November	54.9	29.2	6.1	19.6	6.9	4.0	8.0	4.3	28.4	14.0	11.6	6.9
December	58.1	29.6	6.1	22.3	7.1	3.0	5.5	3.3	32.6	15.7	12.8	7.7
1980												
January	76.8	45.2	7.2	24.4	5.2	4.0	8.3	3.9	40.0	24.1	23.3	13.2
February	77.9	47.0	7.2	23.6	5.6	3.4	8.1	4.0	39.6	25.0	24.6	14.6
March	83.2	49.1	8.2	25.9	9.7	6.0	10.4	6.1	40.6	23.1	22.5	14.0
April	77.3	48.4	6.4	22.6	8.2	5.6	12.6	8.3	36.8	22.3	19.8	12.2
May	79.0	49.6	7.5	21.9	9.6	5.7	13.5	9.0	36.1	22.8	19.8	12.1
June	103.1	61.2	8.9	33.0	11.3	6.5	15.9	9.7	48.4	28.8	27.6	16.2
July	115.5	74.6	10.5	30.5	11.5	7.8	20.5	11.9	51.5	33.5	32.1	21.4
August	118.2	75.3	11.5	31.4	11.2	7.9	20.2	12.0	53.0	33.6	33.8	21.8
September	144.3	80.2	14.1	50.0	14.0	8.5	26.7	13.5	68.2	36.6	35.3	21.5
October	129.3	76.3	14.0	39.1	14.1	8.5	26.5	14.0	56.5	34.7	32.1	19.1
November	96.8	55.3	10.7	30.9	9.6	6.5	17.2	9.5	44.7	25.0	25.5	14.3
December	89.2	48.2	8.4	32.6	8.0	5.6	12.2	5.9	46.5	23.5	22.5	13.2

Table 2-10. New Privately Owned Housing Units Authorized by Building Permits in Permit-Issuing Places, Not Seasonally Adjusted, 1959–2012—*Continued*

[Numbers in thousands.]

Characteristics	Total	In structures with			Region							
		1 unit	2 to 4 units	5 units or more	Northeast		Midwest		South		West	
					Total	1 unit	Total	1 unit	Total	1 unit	Total	1 unit
1979												
January	88.1	54.9	7.5	25.7	9.8	4.8	7.8	4.6	40.7	25.9	29.8	19.6
February	91.7	56.4	6.6	28.7	6.7	4.5	10.5	6.3	42.1	25.5	32.4	20.2
March	151.3	101.5	11.9	37.9	12.9	10.0	26.0	17.5	69.0	43.2	43.4	30.8
April	147.1	102.2	11.4	33.5	14.8	12.2	31.1	22.4	54.8	36.4	46.4	31.2
May	164.1	110.0	11.7	42.4	17.9	13.6	36.4	24.7	61.6	39.9	48.2	31.9
June	156.3	100.8	11.8	43.6	18.1	11.8	33.6	22.1	58.4	37.0	46.2	29.9
July	138.9	93.0	11.5	34.4	15.1	11.3	27.5	18.8	51.4	34.9	44.9	28.1
August	151.9	97.1	13.3	41.5	15.4	11.2	29.9	18.4	59.2	38.7	47.3	28.8
September	140.7	79.4	11.7	49.7	18.3	9.6	29.5	15.8	54.8	31.7	38.1	22.3
October	140.5	83.3	13.2	43.9	14.3	8.9	28.6	16.3	59.1	34.4	38.5	23.8
November	99.6	57.7	8.0	33.8	12.9	7.5	16.9	9.6	42.1	24.3	27.7	16.5
December	81.6	45.1	6.9	29.6	10.6	4.9	11.4	6.2	34.8	20.3	24.8	13.7
1978												
January	97.2	62.9	6.6	27.7	10.1	5.5	11.7	8.2	41.4	26.8	34.0	22.7
February	105.7	67.9	7.9	29.9	6.7	3.7	16.2	10.1	44.5	30.5	38.3	24.0
March	166.5	110.1	12.9	43.5	14.5	9.2	35.1	23.8	63.6	44.0	53.3	33.4
April	175.3	119.7	11.1	44.5	17.3	13.7	40.3	29.5	67.7	44.0	50.0	32.6
May	177.9	124.3	11.9	41.7	18.7	14.8	43.9	31.7	61.9	43.3	53.4	34.3
June	200.2	130.4	16.1	53.7	21.2	14.6	42.3	30.5	62.0	40.9	74.7	43.5
July	151.9	100.9	9.4	41.6	19.2	12.9	35.4	23.7	53.3	35.5	44.0	28.7
August	159.3	107.3	10.8	41.2	20.7	13.7	38.6	26.4	56.8	38.4	43.2	28.8
September	152.4	96.6	11.1	44.7	18.7	12.3	38.3	23.1	55.0	34.6	40.4	26.5
October	160.7	104.0	12.9	43.8	17.2	12.5	38.2	24.5	60.5	38.6	44.8	28.6
November	138.0	87.5	11.0	39.5	16.6	10.9	29.5	18.0	54.5	34.2	37.4	24.6
December	115.4	71.0	8.9	35.5	13.5	9.1	18.5	11.6	46.4	28.5	37.0	22.0
14,000-place series												
1977												
January	80.2	52.6	6.6	21.0	6.9	3.2	11.0	6.8	29.0	19.8	33.2	22.6
February	97.3	67.2	7.4	22.7	5.8	4.4	15.2	10.8	36.6	25.8	39.6	26.1
March	158.2	110.5	11.2	36.5	18.8	13.6	35.5	25.6	51.4	35.3	52.4	36.1
April	161.2	108.2	10.9	42.0	17.0	12.6	43.1	29.3	51.5	33.9	49.6	32.5
May	162.3	112.4	11.0	38.9	17.5	13.1	43.8	30.6	51.7	35.7	49.4	33.1
June	175.9	117.2	11.2	47.5	22.5	14.4	45.3	31.0	55.4	36.7	52.8	35.2
July	145.7	99.7	10.7	35.2	15.0	11.7	37.0	25.7	47.3	31.7	46.3	30.7
August	164.5	110.1	11.8	42.7	18.2	13.3	42.8	28.3	54.6	35.2	48.9	33.3
September	144.2	97.2	10.4	36.6	16.1	11.9	36.0	24.3	47.5	30.9	44.6	30.1
October	146.1	94.9	11.0	40.2	17.3	11.0	35.9	24.3	48.7	31.2	44.3	28.4
November	135.9	87.6	11.3	37.0	13.9	10.0	34.0	21.1	44.1	28.1	43.9	28.4
December	118.4	68.4	7.9	42.2	12.8	7.6	22.6	11.5	43.4	25.8	39.5	23.4
1976												
January	67.6	46.3	4.9	16.5	6.2	4.0	10.8	7.2	25.2	19.1	25.3	15.9
February	73.4	53.6	5.4	14.5	6.3	4.8	14.1	10.3	28.9	22.7	24.1	15.8
March	110.6	81.4	7.9	21.3	13.0	10.0	28.0	20.1	36.4	28.3	33.2	22.9
April	117.0	87.3	7.9	21.7	14.2	11.4	31.9	24.2	35.2	27.3	35.6	24.3
May	112.7	81.3	7.9	23.5	13.5	10.8	30.8	22.5	35.5	25.7	32.9	22.3
June	122.7	89.1	8.0	25.5	13.8	11.7	34.2	23.8	36.6	27.6	38.2	26.0
July	113.7	82.5	7.6	23.6	13.9	10.7	28.7	20.5	34.2	26.1	37.0	25.2
August	116.9	80.6	8.3	28.0	15.6	10.5	29.0	20.3	34.4	25.7	37.9	24.1
September	125.8	78.5	9.3	37.9	14.5	10.6	35.3	21.0	38.5	24.8	37.6	22.2
October	117.5	77.4	9.1	31.0	15.5	10.0	33.7	20.7	32.3	23.4	36.0	23.4
November	114.0	73.8	9.1	31.0	13.7	9.6	28.9	17.7	32.0	22.0	39.5	24.5
December	104.2	61.8	7.6	34.7	12.2	7.2	20.7	10.9	32.5	19.8	38.8	23.8
1975												
January	43.5	29.8	2.9	10.8	4.6	3.4	8.5	4.7	17.2	11.9	13.4	9.8
February	45.2	32.5	3.8	8.9	5.0	3.8	8.2	5.8	17.1	12.4	14.8	10.6
March	60.5	45.5	3.8	11.2	8.6	6.3	13.6	10.5	19.3	15.7	19.0	13.1
April	89.3	65.2	6.4	17.7	13.3	9.0	23.1	16.8	28.0	22.5	25.0	17.0
May	91.2	68.2	5.7	17.3	13.3	10.3	25.6	18.2	26.0	21.5	26.4	18.3
June	94.0	68.4	6.0	19.6	12.5	9.8	25.0	17.9	29.1	21.5	27.4	19.1
July	98.7	69.5	7.2	22.1	13.3	8.9	28.8	19.2	28.3	21.9	28.3	19.4
August	85.3	63.8	5.0	16.6	12.7	8.9	22.0	16.9	25.9	20.4	24.6	17.7
September	90.6	65.5	5.9	19.3	12.9	9.0	23.6	17.4	27.6	20.3	26.5	18.7
October	95.2	68.0	7.1	20.1	12.8	9.6	27.3	18.9	28.2	21.1	27.0	18.3
November	73.2	51.5	5.4	16.3	10.8	7.3	19.5	13.2	22.1	16.9	20.8	14.1
December	72.5	47.6	5.0	19.9	9.8	6.3	16.3	9.7	24.0	16.7	22.4	14.7
1974												
January	87.5	38.7	6.0	42.8	11.5	5.3	13.3	5.9	42.1	17.7	20.6	9.8
February	86.7	44.8	5.5	36.4	9.7	5.2	13.6	8.1	41.7	19.8	21.7	11.7
March	120.1	66.5	7.7	45.9	15.7	9.7	26.2	15.4	47.5	24.2	30.7	17.3
April	130.9	76.8	8.0	46.1	18.0	10.6	27.6	19.7	48.2	26.1	37.2	20.3
May	116.5	73.3	7.5	35.8	17.2	11.3	28.3	18.5	40.4	24.6	30.6	18.9
June	102.2	63.7	5.8	32.6	16.0	11.1	24.8	15.4	34.6	20.7	26.8	16.5
July	95.5	61.7	5.8	28.1	14.6	10.3	23.2	16.4	33.2	19.6	24.6	15.4
August	81.7	56.6	4.5	20.5	12.4	8.5	20.7	14.5	26.7	18.6	21.9	15.1
September	66.8	46.9	3.4	16.5	11.4	7.6	18.3	12.8	20.4	14.2	16.7	12.3
October	71.1	48.2	4.1	18.9	13.1	7.4	20.5	13.3	20.8	15.4	16.7	12.1
November	55.1	36.4	2.9	15.8	11.1	6.1	14.0	8.7	16.5	11.8	13.5	9.8
December	60.3	30.3	3.2	26.8	14.8	4.2	10.9	5.9	18.1	10.9	16.5	9.3

Table 2-10. New Privately Owned Housing Units Authorized by Building Permits in Permit-Issuing Places, Not Seasonally Adjusted, 1959–2012—*Continued*

[Numbers in thousands.]

Characteristics	Total	In structures with			Region							
		1 unit	2 to 4 units	5 units or more	Northeast		Midwest		South		West	
					Total	1 unit	Total	1 unit	Total	1 unit	Total	1 unit
1973												
January	152.1	64.9	10.2	77.0	19.1	9.4	23.6	10.2	72.7	29.6	36.6	15.7
February	145.7	66.2	9.0	70.5	15.6	7.8	24.7	13.7	70.1	28.4	35.4	16.2
March	184.4	91.6	11.9	80.9	28.0	14.3	33.9	20.7	75.4	34.6	47.1	22.1
April	185.4	94.9	11.8	78.7	28.5	16.0	38.3	21.4	74.9	32.6	43.7	24.9
May	191.7	102.2	12.7	76.8	26.0	15.3	42.7	24.1	78.9	37.4	44.1	25.3
June	193.7	92.0	11.9	89.8	29.8	15.1	35.0	21.9	87.3	31.4	41.6	23.7
July	157.3	82.6	11.7	63.0	25.2	14.0	35.3	19.4	60.3	28.0	36.6	21.2
August	162.9	78.0	10.4	74.5	28.2	12.9	35.7	17.9	62.2	27.0	36.8	20.2
September	125.2	61.7	7.9	55.6	18.4	10.5	25.6	14.4	50.3	21.0	31.0	15.8
October	122.9	60.4	7.8	54.8	19.4	11.2	27.8	15.4	49.0	20.4	26.8	13.5
November	107.2	49.9	6.1	51.1	19.5	8.8	23.4	12.0	44.4	18.8	19.8	10.3
December	91.1	37.8	5.6	47.7	14.3	6.3	15.5	6.6	37.7	14.8	23.6	10.1
1972												
January	137.3	61.8	9.1	66.5	18.5	6.8	18.6	9.1	61.5	28.9	38.7	16.9
February	148.1	64.8	9.4	73.9	18.6	6.4	21.4	11.0	63.7	28.4	44.5	19.0
March	191.1	94.2	12.8	84.0	24.6	12.1	36.1	19.9	80.7	36.8	49.7	25.4
April	191.8	95.0	12.9	83.9	29.7	14.1	43.4	24.2	74.1	34.7	44.6	22.0
May	206.9	103.2	14.6	89.2	29.5	15.5	47.4	27.1	78.9	35.4	51.2	25.2
June	214.6	104.1	14.5	96.1	31.1	14.6	47.1	26.2	84.0	35.2	52.4	28.2
July	179.6	89.1	12.0	78.6	27.2	12.9	37.4	21.1	72.3	33.0	42.8	22.1
August	206.4	101.1	13.6	91.7	32.7	15.4	43.9	23.5	81.5	36.1	48.4	26.2
September	190.6	84.6	12.5	93.5	25.8	12.8	42.0	20.0	82.8	31.3	40.0	20.5
October	201.1	98.1	15.4	87.6	31.4	15.2	39.2	20.4	82.9	36.8	47.6	25.7
November	176.8	76.5	11.6	88.7	33.7	12.5	34.3	15.6	69.8	30.4	39.1	18.0
December	174.6	60.8	10.2	103.5	30.6	9.2	30.2	12.0	73.4	24.6	40.4	15.0
13,000-place series												
1971												
January	98.8	44.1	7.0	47.7	12.7	3.7	16.0	7.6	45.6	21.2	24.5	11.6
February	104.1	48.1	7.8	48.1	10.5	4.2	15.0	8.1	47.6	20.7	31.1	15.2
March	157.6	78.8	10.9	68.0	22.9	10.3	34.8	16.7	60.7	30.2	39.3	21.4
April	175.3	89.6	11.1	74.6	25.5	12.9	41.3	22.2	62.0	32.0	46.6	22.5
May	180.9	90.2	11.8	78.9	30.3	13.9	40.9	22.0	66.6	31.2	43.0	23.1
June	186.0	93.2	13.7	79.1	30.2	14.4	44.0	22.4	67.7	33.8	44.2	22.7
July	177.6	86.0	11.5	80.0	30.1	13.3	39.2	19.6	65.1	31.4	43.2	21.7
August	174.5	82.7	13.2	78.5	31.2	13.0	39.1	20.2	60.3	29.4	43.8	20.1
September	168.6	78.1	12.3	78.1	29.4	10.8	38.1	19.3	63.0	29.3	38.1	18.6
October	169.0	76.0	11.4	81.6	29.3	11.3	38.2	18.7	61.5	26.0	40.0	20.0
November	165.1	73.3	11.6	80.3	28.0	10.6	38.3	17.2	61.0	27.8	37.7	17.7
December	167.1	65.9	10.4	90.7	23.5	8.8	36.2	14.1	64.4	25.6	43.0	17.4
1970												
January	67.5	27.7	4.8	35.0	7.0	2.8	10.0	4.0	30.3	12.3	20.1	8.5
February	72.9	34.4	5.0	33.5	10.0	3.7	12.3	6.0	30.8	14.7	19.8	10.0
March	99.5	50.8	6.1	42.6	14.7	7.3	22.7	11.3	37.0	19.3	25.1	12.9
April	125.5	63.5	6.7	55.3	19.5	9.1	24.6	14.4	45.0	22.3	36.3	17.7
May	122.0	58.3	7.0	56.7	18.2	9.0	24.6	13.9	48.9	21.8	30.3	13.5
June	129.0	62.7	8.2	58.1	22.8	9.4	30.6	15.8	46.9	23.6	28.7	14.0
July	118.3	59.6	7.3	51.5	20.9	8.7	28.9	14.7	41.2	22.4	27.3	13.8
August	113.7	58.3	8.5	47.0	19.4	9.0	26.5	13.9	39.3	22.2	28.5	13.2
September	121.0	60.9	10.1	50.0	18.3	9.4	25.8	15.0	45.2	22.8	31.7	13.6
October	136.3	62.2	8.5	65.7	24.0	9.7	30.0	15.5	46.9	22.3	35.4	14.6
November	113.1	51.3	8.1	53.7	21.2	8.0	26.2	12.3	41.2	18.8	24.5	12.3
December	132.6	57.1	7.7	67.7	22.3	7.0	25.0	11.2	50.1	24.0	35.2	15.0
1969												
January	94.1	39.8	5.5	48.8	11.8	NA	19.3	NA	40.0	NA	23.1	NA
February	96.2	42.5	6.7	47.0	12.5	NA	22.0	NA	40.4	NA	21.3	NA
March	121.7	58.5	8.3	54.9	20.2	NA	30.8	NA	44.0	NA	26.6	NA
April	149.3	69.7	8.4	71.3	26.8	NA	37.0	NA	48.7	NA	36.8	NA
May	128.6	64.5	7.5	56.5	22.9	NA	29.0	NA	45.7	NA	30.9	NA
June	125.5	61.7	7.9	55.9	21.2	NA	31.0	NA	41.5	NA	31.7	NA
July	114.0	55.2	7.5	51.3	19.4	NA	28.3	NA	38.3	NA	27.9	NA
August	106.1	50.3	6.9	48.9	17.5	NA	25.4	NA	38.0	NA	25.1	NA
September	106.8	51.3	6.6	48.9	17.4	NA	25.7	NA	37.1	NA	26.6	NA
October	111.1	53.5	7.6	50.1	19.7	NA	28.3	NA	35.6	NA	27.5	NA
November	84.4	40.1	6.2	38.1	13.4	NA	20.7	NA	30.5	NA	19.9	NA
December	85.9	38.8	6.1	40.9	12.8	NA	19.3	NA	30.7	NA	23.0	NA

Table 2-10. New Privately Owned Housing Units Authorized by Building Permits in Permit-Issuing Places, Not Seasonally Adjusted, 1959–2012—*Continued*

[Numbers in thousands.]

Characteristics	Total	In structures with			Region							
		1 unit	2 to 4 units	5 units or more	Northeast		Midwest		South		West	
					Total	1 unit	Total	1 unit	Total	1 unit	Total	1 unit
1968												
January	74.4	38.9	5.6	29.9	8.7	NA	15.8	NA	31.7	NA	18.2	NA
February	90.2	44.7	6.4	39.1	11.7	NA	20.5	NA	37.1	NA	20.9	NA
March	117.5	61.4	7.1	49.1	24.0	NA	28.2	NA	40.0	NA	25.3	NA
April	134.8	72.0	7.8	55.0	27.4	NA	35.8	NA	43.5	NA	28.1	NA
May	132.8	70.7	7.9	54.1	22.0	NA	39.0	NA	44.1	NA	27.7	NA
June	116.2	60.2	7.3	48.7	23.9	NA	29.2	NA	40.3	NA	22.8	NA
July	120.1	64.3	6.4	49.4	20.6	NA	30.7	NA	42.8	NA	26.0	NA
August	115.7	62.2	6.8	46.7	22.4	NA	30.1	NA	38.5	NA	24.7	NA
September	118.2	60.8	7.1	50.3	19.5	NA	33.9	NA	40.3	NA	24.6	NA
October	129.9	65.0	7.6	57.3	23.7	NA	35.0	NA	45.2	NA	26.0	NA
November	106.1	51.9	7.2	47.1	15.7	NA	31.4	NA	35.1	NA	23.9	NA
December	97.3	42.5	7.3	47.7	15.0	NA	20.5	NA	38.7	NA	23.2	NA
1967												
January	58.5	31.5	3.8	23.2	14.1	NA	10.5	NA	23.3	NA	10.6	NA
February	57.0	34.2	3.8	19.0	9.9	NA	11.6	NA	23.4	NA	12.2	NA
March	91.4	56.0	6.0	29.4	15.6	NA	23.3	NA	34.7	NA	17.9	NA
April	99.5	59.2	5.5	34.8	22.6	NA	27.8	NA	31.8	NA	17.3	NA
May	111.2	67.6	6.3	37.2	20.7	NA	30.1	NA	39.6	NA	20.7	NA
June	115.5	68.5	7.3	39.7	24.0	NA	31.3	NA	38.8	NA	21.4	NA
July	97.1	58.1	6.0	33.0	19.4	NA	28.2	NA	31.3	NA	18.2	NA
August	110.6	64.7	7.0	38.9	21.1	NA	31.8	NA	34.7	NA	23.0	NA
September	103.4	57.6	6.6	39.1	19.9	NA	31.6	NA	33.0	NA	19.0	NA
October	111.8	61.2	7.8	42.9	21.5	NA	33.6	NA	36.0	NA	20.7	NA
November	99.8	51.6	7.1	41.1	18.6	NA	28.7	NA	34.3	NA	18.2	NA
December	85.2	40.2	5.9	39.2	15.3	NA	21.3	NA	30.0	NA	18.6	NA
12,000-place series												
1966												
January	76.0	39.1	5.7	31.2	13.8	NA	15.2	NA	29.8	NA	17.3	NA
February	73.1	38.1	4.8	30.3	11.7	NA	15.8	NA	28.7	NA	16.9	NA
March	117.8	69.6	8.4	39.8	25.0	NA	31.8	NA	39.0	NA	22.1	NA
April	114.1	66.2	7.1	40.8	26.2	NA	30.7	NA	36.5	NA	20.7	NA
May	107.0	60.5	6.2	40.3	22.9	NA	29.1	NA	35.4	NA	19.6	NA
June	95.0	58.8	5.6	30.6	21.4	NA	25.6	NA	31.1	NA	16.8	NA
July	77.4	47.3	4.6	25.6	19.0	NA	19.9	NA	24.4	NA	14.1	NA
August	79.3	46.9	4.5	27.9	19.8	NA	20.9	NA	25.9	NA	12.7	NA
September	65.9	40.2	3.7	21.9	13.8	NA	19.9	NA	21.1	NA	11.0	NA
October	61.3	36.9	3.8	20.6	12.3	NA	17.3	NA	20.8	NA	10.9	NA
November	56.1	32.7	3.6	19.9	13.8	NA	14.7	NA	18.6	NA	9.0	NA
December	48.9	27.1	3.0	18.8	10.2	NA	10.0	NA	19.8	NA	9.0	NA
1965												
January	74.3	39.2	6.3	28.7	9.8	NA	15.1	NA	29.2	NA	20.2	NA
February	75.4	41.4	5.4	28.7	10.3	NA	13.1	NA	29.7	NA	22.3	NA
March	115.7	65.6	8.5	41.6	22.7	NA	23.2	NA	38.7	NA	31.1	NA
April	120.6	73.2	8.9	38.6	24.8	NA	32.9	NA	36.8	NA	26.2	NA
May	115.0	69.3	7.3	38.4	23.8	NA	31.8	NA	34.6	NA	24.8	NA
June	122.0	71.3	7.9	42.7	26.7	NA	32.5	NA	39.2	NA	23.6	NA
July	108.6	64.9	7.4	36.3	21.3	NA	31.6	NA	34.2	NA	21.5	NA
August	108.9	64.6	7.2	37.0	23.9	NA	29.2	NA	33.1	NA	22.8	NA
September	104.2	60.3	7.1	36.7	22.9	NA	28.2	NA	32.8	NA	20.3	NA
October	105.7	61.5	6.4	37.8	23.4	NA	26.6	NA	36.0	NA	19.6	NA
November	99.3	54.0	6.3	39.0	23.0	NA	23.8	NA	31.5	NA	20.9	NA
December	90.1	44.5	6.2	39.5	20.2	NA	22.3	NA	31.7	NA	15.8	NA
1964												
January	86.4	42.7	8.8	34.8	9.6	NA	14.2	NA	30.6	NA	32.0	NA
February	90.9	48.5	8.9	33.5	12.8	NA	16.2	NA	29.4	NA	32.5	NA
March	119.2	67.6	10.0	41.6	22.6	NA	25.6	NA	37.8	NA	33.2	NA
April	128.8	73.1	10.1	45.7	25.2	NA	28.9	NA	38.7	NA	36.1	NA
May	122.9	70.9	9.1	42.9	23.4	NA	28.7	NA	35.8	NA	35.0	NA
June	124.8	72.3	9.4	43.0	26.8	NA	29.2	NA	36.2	NA	32.5	NA
July	119.5	68.2	8.8	42.5	22.2	NA	27.2	NA	37.3	NA	32.9	NA
August	108.4	61.1	7.3	40.0	21.7	NA	25.8	NA	34.5	NA	26.4	NA
September	107.6	61.9	7.5	38.2	21.0	NA	27.7	NA	33.3	NA	25.6	NA
October	106.6	60.8	8.4	37.5	20.2	NA	27.5	NA	33.2	NA	25.7	NA
November	90.6	50.8	7.0	32.9	18.9	NA	21.7	NA	29.3	NA	20.7	NA
December	80.0	42.2	5.6	32.2	19.1	NA	14.2	NA	25.2	NA	21.5	NA

Table 2-10. New Privately Owned Housing Units Authorized by Building Permits in Permit-Issuing Places, Not Seasonally Adjusted, 1959–2012—*Continued*

[Numbers in thousands.]

Characteristics	Total	In structures with			Region							
		1 unit	2 to 4 units	5 units or more	Northeast		Midwest		South		West	
					Total	1 unit	Total	1 unit	Total	1 unit	Total	1 unit
1963												
January	84.4	43.3	8.1	33.0	11.8	NA	9.5	NA	28.2	NA	35.0	NA
February	78.7	43.4	7.1	28.2	11.6	NA	9.0	NA	26.8	NA	31.2	NA
March	108.8	63.8	11.3	33.6	18.5	NA	20.4	NA	32.6	NA	37.2	NA
April	131.5	82.1	10.8	38.6	25.2	NA	30.9	NA	37.5	NA	37.8	NA
May	138.7	78.8	11.3	48.7	26.1	NA	30.5	NA	39.2	NA	42.9	NA
June	118.7	71.0	11.8	35.9	19.7	NA	28.5	NA	33.2	NA	37.2	NA
July	121.9	72.8	10.4	38.7	20.9	NA	26.9	NA	37.1	NA	37.0	NA
August	115.0	68.1	8.8	38.1	20.5	NA	25.4	NA	33.5	NA	35.6	NA
September	114.7	65.4	10.3	39.0	22.4	NA	24.3	NA	34.6	NA	33.4	NA
October	127.8	69.7	11.6	46.4	24.8	NA	26.9	NA	37.7	NA	38.3	NA
November	98.6	51.0	9.2	38.4	18.8	NA	22.0	NA	30.4	NA	27.4	NA
December	96.1	40.8	8.2	47.0	19.1	NA	14.5	NA	32.2	NA	30.3	NA
10,000-place series												
1962												
January	73.2	44.3	5.9	23.0	12.9	NA	9.2	NA	24.4	NA	26.7	NA
February	74.6	45.1	5.1	24.4	14.1	NA	11.9	NA	24.4	NA	24.3	NA
March	101.4	63.3	8.4	29.7	19.8	NA	18.7	NA	31.4	NA	31.5	NA
April	120.8	75.2	8.1	37.5	30.2	NA	24.8	NA	30.7	NA	35.1	NA
May	117.5	75.2	9.3	33.0	23.7	NA	26.8	NA	33.1	NA	34.0	NA
June	107.0	67.8	6.9	32.3	21.7	NA	25.6	NA	28.7	NA	31.0	NA
July	105.8	66.8	7.3	31.7	20.2	NA	24.2	NA	30.3	NA	31.2	NA
August	111.0	68.8	7.1	35.1	21.9	NA	22.5	NA	32.3	NA	34.3	NA
September	95.2	57.5	6.6	31.1	17.9	NA	21.8	NA	27.8	NA	27.8	NA
October	107.6	62.9	7.8	36.8	23.1	NA	22.5	NA	30.8	NA	31.1	NA
November	94.5	51.1	7.1	36.3	20.6	NA	17.8	NA	27.6	NA	28.5	NA
December	78.0	38.3	7.3	32.4	16.6	NA	12.5	NA	21.3	NA	27.6	NA
1961												
January	59.7	41.1	4.1	14.4	7.9	NA	9.9	NA	19.8	NA	22.1	NA
February	58.8	40.2	4.2	14.5	8.3	NA	11.7	NA	18.6	NA	20.2	NA
March	92.7	64.8	6.2	21.6	16.9	NA	19.9	NA	28.0	NA	27.9	NA
April	94.0	65.8	6.4	21.7	20.5	NA	21.4	NA	26.3	NA	25.8	NA
May	105.3	74.0	6.4	24.8	23.3	NA	24.6	NA	28.3	NA	29.1	NA
June	104.5	72.4	6.3	25.9	21.7	NA	24.7	NA	28.0	NA	30.1	NA
July	92.8	66.3	4.8	21.8	20.5	NA	21.4	NA	25.7	NA	25.3	NA
August	108.6	71.1	6.1	31.3	28.9	NA	21.9	NA	29.3	NA	28.5	NA
September	90.4	62.1	5.8	22.6	19.0	NA	20.9	NA	25.8	NA	24.7	NA
October	98.3	67.0	6.8	24.5	21.8	NA	21.1	NA	27.5	NA	27.9	NA
November	87.4	56.2	5.5	25.7	21.1	NA	17.5	NA	23.3	NA	25.6	NA
December	71.7	41.8	4.9	25.1	19.5	NA	11.1	NA	18.9	NA	22.2	NA
1960												
January	62.6	46.8	4.4	11.5	10.7	NA	10.0	NA	22.6	NA	19.2	NA
February	68.1	52.7	4.9	10.5	10.2	NA	12.2	NA	23.2	NA	22.5	NA
March	89.0	67.7	6.3	15.0	14.0	NA	16.4	NA	27.1	NA	31.5	NA
April	101.1	78.7	5.7	16.8	20.1	NA	26.1	NA	27.3	NA	27.7	NA
May	103.4	76.1	6.0	21.4	22.9	NA	25.6	NA	28.3	NA	26.7	NA
June	94.8	75.8	6.2	12.8	18.0	NA	24.2	NA	26.2	NA	26.5	NA
July	86.3	65.8	5.7	14.7	19.3	NA	21.1	NA	22.4	NA	23.5	NA
August	93.7	70.0	5.7	18.0	20.1	NA	22.5	NA	24.8	NA	26.2	NA
September	84.9	62.3	5.2	17.4	18.1	NA	20.6	NA	22.5	NA	23.7	NA
October	81.6	59.6	4.9	17.0	17.4	NA	20.6	NA	21.3	NA	22.3	NA
November	73.9	51.8	5.4	16.7	17.0	NA	16.6	NA	20.3	NA	20.0	NA
December	58.7	38.7	4.4	15.6	11.2	NA	12.3	NA	17.2	NA	17.9	NA
1959												
January	75.7	55.7	5.2	14.8	11.4	NA	11.8	NA	26.8	NA	25.6	NA
February	79.0	59.9	5.2	13.9	13.2	NA	12.7	NA	29.4	NA	23.8	NA
March	119.0	91.3	8.4	19.3	22.4	NA	25.9	NA	34.8	NA	35.8	NA
April	127.9	99.7	8.0	20.2	23.4	NA	34.7	NA	36.0	NA	33.8	NA
May	120.8	93.5	7.5	19.7	23.0	NA	30.0	NA	32.3	NA	35.4	NA
June	120.9	94.9	7.8	18.2	24.0	NA	33.0	NA	31.7	NA	32.2	NA
July	112.3	90.2	6.2	15.8	20.6	NA	30.8	NA	32.7	NA	28.2	NA
August	106.4	85.4	5.9	15.2	18.4	NA	26.5	NA	30.4	NA	31.2	NA
September	102.5	80.3	6.2	16.0	19.9	NA	27.0	NA	29.6	NA	25.9	NA
October	94.6	74.4	6.4	13.7	19.1	NA	23.0	NA	25.4	NA	27.1	NA
November	75.8	57.8	5.4	12.6	14.2	NA	16.8	NA	23.4	NA	21.5	NA
December	73.5	55.1	4.9	13.5	12.8	NA	13.5	NA	23.3	NA	23.9	NA

NA = Not available.

Source: U.S. Census Bureau, Building Permits Survey

Table 2-11. Seasonal Indexes Used to Adjust Housing Units Authorized in Permit-Issuing Places, 1996–2012

[Numbers in thousands.]

Characteristics	United States[1]	In structures with						All units			
		1 unit				2 to 4 units	5 units or more	Northeast	Midwest	South	West
		Northeast	Midwest	South	West						
20,000-place series											
2012											
January	81.2	72.8	52.4	89.4	77.2	80.4	85.4	74.2	59.7	91.3	77.9
February	88.1	70.5	69.2	97.0	87.4	83.2	89.2	81.4	65.0	95.6	91.2
March	105.1	97.4	103.2	112.0	109.9	105.5	99.1	87.5	98.3	114.2	111.9
April	103.7	108.5	122.3	108.7	108.9	100.2	89.0	106.2	111.8	103.3	102.2
May	115.4	122.7	133.0	117.3	123.2	109.3	104.9	112.7	125.0	113.3	119.2
2011											
January	76.9	69.5	49.9	85.2	73.6	73.9	82.3	71.4	56.4	86.5	76.5
February	84.3	67.4	66.7	93.0	82.7	81.5	85.2	77.0	62.6	92.6	87.0
March	110.7	102.1	108.4	116.7	115.1	110.2	103.0	93.1	103.3	118.1	113.7
April	105.2	108.8	124.4	108.7	109.6	103.1	89.7	99.7	114.0	104.5	108.1
May	110.2	118.0	125.4	112.1	115.3	108.3	99.1	110.6	119.6	108.1	111.3
June	121.0	120.7	126.3	116.5	126.7	113.6	122.6	139.5	120.2	115.9	124.6
July	100.7	109.2	108.3	100.7	104.0	98.9	95.4	98.6	110.9	101.9	99.7
August	116.4	118.1	121.9	114.0	116.5	114.1	117.0	115.3	123.3	112.9	117.6
September	103.7	109.4	111.2	97.5	101.0	107.7	108.0	105.7	112.8	98.4	102.2
October	93.5	102.4	105.7	87.7	92.2	100.2	94.4	102.0	106.9	84.8	88.3
November	87.8	91.7	87.0	83.2	81.6	96.3	94.5	97.5	94.6	85.2	84.1
December	88.3	80.6	64.0	82.4	80.2	89.4	107.8	88.3	74.4	89.1	86.9
2010											
January	76.2	71.7	49.8	83.3	72.9	80.5	85.3	70.7	58.5	86.2	80.3
February	83.6	67.2	67.1	92.9	82.9	82.0	85.5	76.9	62.7	92.6	87.6
March	111.9	102.3	108.0	116.9	115.8	112.1	102.8	95.3	101.5	116.8	115.1
April	110.9	113.7	130.4	113.8	113.6	107.9	94.5	104.4	118.0	109.7	110.8
May	106.7	111.2	119.2	107.0	110.9	99.0	94.7	106.1	111.8	102.4	107.8
June	121.0	122.2	126.7	116.7	128.1	117.9	122.4	137.1	124.5	117.3	124.6
July	106.9	113.9	115.5	106.2	110.1	103.6	99.6	104.3	115.9	106.1	105.9
August	111.0	113.6	115.3	109.2	109.6	111.7	111.7	108.6	119.0	110.4	108.5
September	103.3	108.6	110.9	97.2	101.9	101.8	108.3	109.1	111.6	97.0	101.1
October	93.4	103.1	104.6	86.9	91.5	101.7	93.7	99.3	107.8	84.2	89.7
November	87.7	91.4	88.1	84.2	81.0	99.1	94.6	96.9	94.7	86.2	83.8
December	90.4	84.2	66.4	85.3	83.8	92.6	112.3	93.8	76.4	91.7	90.3
2009											
January	82.8	74.5	52.9	87.8	77.2	82.4	90.6	74.6	61.2	90.4	84.7
February	84.3	64.5	68.0	91.7	83.9	79.2	86.3	67.8	63.3	92.3	89.8
March	106.1	96.3	103.7	112.6	108.1	110.9	98.1	92.1	97.9	115.1	106.7
April	110.1	110.1	130.8	113.5	115.3	97.9	91.0	110.8	117.0	108.8	109.3
May	106.9	110.4	118.8	106.7	110.3	102.8	95.8	100.4	113.6	104.2	107.3
June	122.4	123.0	127.9	118.8	128.8	119.3	120.7	130.7	124.8	117.5	122.5
July	113.2	119.2	120.1	112.3	115.6	109.7	103.1	117.2	120.5	108.8	111.1
August	105.1	108.2	106.0	104.0	104.5	101.6	106.2	107.0	108.8	104.4	102.4
September	104.3	111.3	110.7	98.6	101.8	111.7	110.3	108.6	115.0	98.4	103.3
October	98.6	108.0	111.5	92.3	96.1	96.2	101.4	107.0	111.4	86.7	96.4
November	81.1	87.4	82.8	77.9	75.7	96.7	85.1	92.4	89.0	81.4	78.5
December	88.9	89.8	67.3	83.9	83.9	92.9	114.3	92.4	78.4	92.0	88.0
2008											
January	84.9	75.8	58.2	89.5	81.0	84.5	92.3	76.1	67.5	93.3	85.9
February	88.8	68.9	69.1	94.9	85.6	86.0	93.4	71.3	64.5	95.4	95.0
March	98.1	90.5	94.2	105.0	101.1	103.6	91.0	91.6	90.9	105.1	100.9
April	109.0	113.6	124.3	112.2	116.9	107.2	95.8	109.7	117.0	109.0	109.8
May	111.3	116.6	128.4	112.7	120.2	107.4	100.4	109.9	116.3	109.9	115.1
June	112.5	116.8	121.7	114.1	124.9	108.7	106.7	121.9	117.9	112.4	116.4
July	111.9	122.8	124.6	113.1	118.4	110.6	102.4	119.4	124.4	109.3	109.1
August	106.7	111.2	110.1	105.0	103.2	103.2	108.1	104.0	110.4	106.5	103.1
September	106.7	112.9	111.9	100.6	101.4	110.7	112.1	111.0	115.8	99.2	103.6
October	103.8	113.3	115.6	98.9	98.9	97.8	105.8	108.9	113.6	93.7	102.0
November	79.5	79.5	78.6	74.3	71.0	90.4	89.0	85.9	89.4	78.7	74.3
December	89.3	83.2	67.3	84.2	81.9	93.2	107.3	93.6	78.4	91.6	89.1
2007											
January	84.2	74.5	60.8	89.7	81.9	87.0	90.2	78.3	65.0	91.5	84.6
February	84.2	65.3	63.5	91.8	83.2	82.4	85.4	68.1	65.6	90.7	86.9
March	104.8	98.1	98.7	112.3	108.3	109.3	93.9	94.1	96.4	110.4	107.6
April	106.9	111.9	118.1	110.4	110.7	102.8	92.6	107.8	112.5	105.7	104.5
May	117.4	121.5	132.7	118.7	125.5	113.0	103.5	114.3	124.4	112.8	116.4
June	115.7	117.0	120.6	113.6	122.6	108.4	112.6	121.6	117.1	111.3	119.3
July	108.0	117.8	117.1	107.1	109.6	110.7	101.0	115.6	115.8	107.3	102.7
August	114.5	120.3	118.4	113.1	113.3	110.3	114.6	114.6	117.3	113.7	112.9
September	95.7	99.3	102.8	89.5	93.6	93.9	101.2	98.1	104.3	91.2	95.6
October	104.5	112.7	118.5	98.6	99.8	102.0	107.7	111.8	116.3	98.5	103.8
November	87.8	88.7	88.0	81.5	78.7	96.7	97.3	92.6	95.1	85.0	86.7
December	81.3	75.5	63.7	75.0	74.2	83.9	98.3	85.5	70.1	82.3	80.8

Table 2-11. Seasonal Indexes Used to Adjust Housing Units Authorized in Permit-Issuing Places, 1996–2012—*Continued*

[Numbers in thousands.]

Characteristics	United States[1]	In structures with						All units			
		1 unit				2 to 4 units	5 units or more	Northeast	Midwest	South	West
		Northeast	Midwest	South	West						
2006											
January	82.8	71.3	60.4	89.6	80.2	78.4	90.1	71.9	63.1	91.8	80.5
February	84.6	66.5	65.5	92.3	86.1	80.4	86.3	69.5	70.3	91.3	87.8
March	110.0	104.1	105.3	116.4	115.6	108.3	99.2	99.0	101.8	114.9	113.2
April	101.3	104.5	111.8	103.0	104.8	96.4	89.1	101.8	108.0	100.4	99.6
May	116.1	123.7	128.4	115.2	122.5	114.6	103.0	117.5	123.0	112.5	116.2
June	118.4	124.7	124.7	116.7	122.6	116.4	113.4	124.2	120.3	116.3	121.7
July	100.7	109.0	108.8	99.2	103.5	103.1	94.2	109.9	106.3	97.9	99.3
August	112.3	117.2	119.6	112.3	112.1	114.6	107.0	114.8	119.8	109.5	108.8
September	99.0	101.8	105.6	93.2	95.5	100.6	108.0	101.6	107.3	94.1	102.5
October	101.7	109.9	114.1	96.5	95.4	104.3	106.8	105.9	113.7	97.5	97.8
November	87.1	88.9	90.3	83.8	82.3	94.3	94.3	95.6	91.2	85.1	85.9
December	83.2	76.4	64.3	79.4	76.3	85.2	106.3	84.9	72.0	86.7	83.2
2005											
January	78.4	66.4	57.4	85.2	78.3	71.5	83.1	68.9	58.7	85.2	79.1
February	84.8	66.8	69.1	92.3	85.6	80.1	87.0	69.7	69.7	91.8	86.7
March	110.9	103.7	109.1	116.5	116.3	109.3	97.3	98.7	104.5	114.1	111.3
April	107.8	109.3	118.3	108.6	110.5	106.3	96.5	107.1	113.3	106.6	108.1
May	111.1	121.1	121.5	110.0	113.8	109.3	99.0	115.3	116.8	108.9	107.7
June	116.8	122.6	121.9	114.7	122.1	119.9	109.0	123.5	117.5	111.9	122.8
July	101.0	108.7	107.9	98.8	100.8	95.7	99.5	108.3	106.4	100.0	99.6
August	112.5	114.9	117.8	112.1	112.1	115.7	108.7	116.1	121.2	110.0	110.0
September	102.7	108.2	108.6	97.6	100.6	106.5	110.1	105.3	109.4	99.6	104.8
October	97.3	103.4	107.0	92.7	92.6	102.2	103.9	101.2	109.3	93.8	94.6
November	88.1	93.2	90.1	85.2	83.0	95.1	95.7	96.6	95.4	86.1	85.4
December	85.7	79.0	70.2	84.2	82.6	86.7	104.8	87.1	76.2	88.3	88.4
2004											
January	81.2	68.8	61.0	89.9	82.3	74.6	85.4	70.3	59.5	90.7	83.4
February	83.7	67.7	69.1	91.5	83.8	78.6	87.9	68.5	70.2	92.0	83.5
March	110.8	101.6	106.9	116.6	114.0	109.8	100.6	100.8	106.1	113.3	111.7
April	111.6	115.4	122.5	112.9	113.2	110.5	96.8	110.9	116.1	110.3	110.1
May	105.1	113.8	113.4	103.7	108.8	100.0	95.8	111.6	109.1	102.2	104.5
June	117.1	123.5	122.9	115.0	119.8	125.5	108.8	124.1	119.4	113.3	121.2
July	105.6	114.0	112.8	104.4	107.9	98.1	99.7	112.3	108.9	104.2	105.9
August	108.1	112.8	113.4	107.7	105.8	110.9	105.3	110.3	115.4	107.7	104.1
September	102.8	106.7	108.5	97.0	104.1	103.6	107.6	105.7	110.0	97.1	106.6
October	99.9	103.3	107.6	93.6	93.3	105.5	110.4	102.4	111.2	97.0	95.3
November	90.3	94.6	90.7	87.0	84.3	100.4	98.8	97.5	98.1	88.3	86.9
December	89.5	82.4	76.3	86.6	87.8	89.9	109.5	90.5	80.4	90.4	92.6
19,000-place series											
2003											
January	83.9	71.3	62.8	92.9	85.3	75.3	90.4	73.7	61.4	92.5	85.5
February	83.1	66.7	68.4	91.4	83.6	79.0	84.4	69.9	67.3	91.8	84.4
March	101.3	93.9	99.0	107.3	104.8	97.4	91.5	92.3	96.3	104.6	102.7
April	111.5	114.5	124.1	112.2	116.0	112.6	93.2	110.7	118.1	107.6	110.5
May	110.9	119.5	120.9	110.5	113.6	108.8	98.8	115.3	115.8	109.2	109.7
June	112.5	119.2	117.6	110.4	114.2	114.3	107.2	119.4	116.4	108.9	117.2
July	110.2	119.2	117.8	108.2	113.4	101.0	101.6	115.9	114.6	106.5	108.7
August	103.7	105.7	107.6	102.6	100.6	103.1	105.1	107.3	108.6	103.1	101.0
September	103.5	107.8	109.8	98.1	101.2	110.8	107.8	104.7	114.4	100.2	103.6
October	109.0	112.4	115.0	101.8	103.6	116.2	121.3	113.0	119.8	104.6	106.1
November	81.6	85.9	81.5	77.3	76.7	86.7	94.2	89.1	85.3	80.0	78.8
December	89.3	83.7	75.3	86.7	88.5	92.8	107.3	89.9	82.5	89.4	93.5
2002											
January	83.4	70.1	63.7	92.7	86.4	78.2	86.4	72.9	64.4	90.9	85.7
February	82.2	65.4	65.6	92.2	82.6	79.5	84.7	65.9	66.4	91.3	84.2
March	101.6	94.4	98.7	106.9	103.5	97.4	96.2	95.3	97.1	107.0	101.4
April	112.2	115.6	126.2	114.8	114.4	113.1	92.1	112.2	120.3	109.9	109.3
May	114.8	124.8	125.3	113.9	118.5	108.4	103.3	119.4	119.5	111.9	112.9
June	107.9	112.3	114.2	104.4	110.3	113.8	103.9	115.8	111.3	103.2	115.3
July	110.0	118.8	117.5	108.3	112.9	102.9	102.6	116.9	114.9	106.2	109.1
August	108.8	112.5	112.9	108.3	106.9	108.9	107.0	112.7	111.4	107.2	107.0
September	99.5	103.4	103.1	92.8	96.3	103.3	109.3	99.6	106.8	96.8	98.9
October	108.7	112.7	117.1	101.8	105.5	117.3	114.2	113.4	121.7	103.9	106.7
November	85.9	89.9	86.0	82.7	80.3	91.1	96.0	92.8	89.8	85.4	82.3
December	85.9	81.0	72.1	83.1	82.7	86.7	104.0	84.9	79.4	87.9	86.4

Table 2-11. Seasonal Indexes Used to Adjust Housing Units Authorized in Permit-Issuing Places, 1996–2012—*Continued*

[Numbers in thousands.]

Characteristics	United States[1]	In structures with						All units			
		1 unit				2 to 4 units	5 units or more	Northeast	Midwest	South	West
		Northeast	Midwest	South	West						
2001											
January	82.7	70.1	62.6	91.3	85.4	75.2	85.8	71.3	63.8	90.0	84.7
February	82.8	66.7	66.4	92.8	82.1	79.9	85.8	66.5	68.4	90.8	84.1
March	106.8	99.5	104.9	113.6	110.4	102.0	97.7	98.9	102.5	111.3	107.3
April	107.0	111.0	119.9	108.5	109.2	105.9	91.0	107.0	114.7	105.0	105.0
May	115.1	124.9	128.7	115.6	120.4	111.5	97.1	120.4	124.8	111.3	112.6
June	113.6	120.3	118.8	109.9	116.1	116.0	110.2	120.5	113.3	109.0	119.5
July	105.6	113.8	112.3	103.9	105.6	99.2	101.0	112.8	111.5	104.0	103.0
August	112.5	117.2	115.5	110.6	111.0	112.7	112.8	116.7	113.6	110.0	111.0
September	96.0	97.3	99.4	89.0	93.5	99.8	106.3	98.5	101.2	93.5	96.5
October	107.4	112.1	114.9	101.0	104.7	119.0	111.9	111.4	120.1	102.8	107.1
November	90.4	92.5	88.9	87.6	82.9	95.0	101.6	96.5	92.6	90.8	84.8
December	81.2	76.6	68.8	77.8	79.9	83.4	98.2	79.6	74.5	81.6	84.9
2000											
January	74.6	64.4	55.3	82.8	77.5	67.8	78.7	65.8	54.7	81.9	76.4
February	86.4	69.1	70.5	97.7	85.5	83.8	87.5	70.2	71.0	95.4	87.4
March	111.7	105.8	108.7	117.6	115.7	108.7	103.9	104.4	107.6	115.4	112.0
April	104.3	107.4	117.2	104.4	107.5	101.4	91.0	105.8	112.0	101.8	102.4
May	115.8	126.4	128.8	116.3	121.1	111.5	95.7	117.6	125.1	110.7	113.6
June	118.4	124.4	123.7	114.8	119.7	121.6	116.0	124.9	119.4	115.4	124.4
	101.0	108.7	108.2	98.9	103.6	94.3	95.2	106.4	105.6	96.4	102.2
July											
August	113.5	116.6	119.4	111.8	113.0	113.1	111.3	118.5	121.0	109.6	112.6
September	100.4	100.6	102.2	93.5	96.5	102.8	113.8	101.8	106.2	99.9	100.0
October	102.5	106.9	110.5	96.8	97.1	115.0	107.2	107.1	115.5	100.2	99.1
November	89.9	92.9	88.1	86.7	84.8	95.9	98.8	97.1	94.9	88.0	85.4
December	80.1	75.6	66.6	76.7	76.9	82.1	99.6	80.0	67.9	82.9	82.5
1999											
January	73.2	62.8	47.5	81.4	74.4	64.9	83.0	65.8	50.8	82.4	75.3
February	80.0	64.6	52.4	91.7	81.0	78.5	78.7	67.0	66.3	88.5	83.1
March	111.4	106.2	110.0	118.6	117.4	108.5	99.0	103.4	109.7	114.3	111.4
April	113.8	118.0	63.8	113.9	113.5	110.2	100.8	112.8	120.8	113.7	109.7
May	106.1	117.0	119.8	105.7	110.4	100.0	88.7	109.1	114.9	101.6	103.6
June	119.4	124.8	68.4	114.3	124.2	121.5	115.8	127.9	122.6	112.8	126.1
July	106.3	113.6	114.4	104.1	106.7	99.9	101.8	111.4	107.9	103.1	107.8
August	109.1	111.7	115.2	106.8	105.4	107.7	110.3	112.9	116.9	108.0	105.3
September	106.2	105.3	109.8	99.3	103.9	109.3	117.5	105.9	115.8	103.4	106.4
October	100.1	102.8	105.8	93.0	93.7	111.1	108.3	104.3	108.8	96.3	96.0
November	90.2	93.0	90.1	87.6	84.1	100.2	96.1	96.0	92.9	89.1	84.8
December	86.2	81.5	69.3	84.2	85.1	89.1	104.6	84.5	72.6	89.3	90.9
1998											
January	74.2	63.6	50.2	85.1	76.4	68.4	81.2	66.8	52.6	84.8	77.9
February	78.2	60.7	63.9	90.5	81.1	77.3	77.3	63.2	63.4	87.4	82.3
March	105.4	97.3	105.0	112.0	110.5	102.1	96.3	99.2	103.5	111.4	104.3
April	113.5	116.3	133.7	114.7	116.6	112.9	98.3	113.2	122.9	111.1	112.3
May	106.7	119.3	119.9	105.5	108.4	98.2	94.6	113.1	114.3	103.4	103.2
June	118.7	126.6	129.2	115.4	122.3	123.8	109.3	125.3	121.9	114.4	125.3
July	111.3	120.4	118.5	108.6	113.4	102.9	107.7	116.7	113.5	107.7	112.7
August	105.0	107.5	110.5	102.6	103.5	102.8	106.1	108.2	111.4	100.9	103.0
September	107.9	106.8	110.4	99.7	103.8	111.1	122.5	107.4	113.2	104.7	106.5
October	104.6	108.2	66.9	98.4	99.6	116.0	109.0	108.6	115.1	100.2	103.0
November	86.0	90.3	84.8	82.5	80.3	93.7	94.0	92.1	90.3	85.5	80.3
December	85.7	83.1	69.7	85.1	84.1	91.1	102.1	86.3	78.8	89.5	90.6
1997											
January	76.5	64.4	51.5	88.0	78.3	73.3	81.6	68.2	53.7	88.3	80.3
February	78.1	59.9	63.3	89.6	80.7	76.4	76.4	62.9	62.5	87.7	81.4
March	100.4	91.8	99.0	106.9	105.9	98.4	91.8	92.9	97.9	103.8	103.4
April	115.9	119.0	127.9	115.7	116.6	114.7	105.9	116.5	122.2	113.3	111.2
May	111.7	122.8	127.0	111.3	112.7	106.3	97.3	116.4	121.5	108.0	106.9
June	114.4	118.6	120.7	108.8	117.6	117.0	112.7	118.5	116.3	109.6	118.6
July	111.5	122.1	64.4	109.2	113.0	106.9	103.5	118.3	116.1	106.7	112.2
August	104.4	109.4	63.8	101.0	102.1	101.2	106.7	110.0	110.5	102.7	101.4
September	107.9	108.6	112.0	101.7	104.1	109.3	116.8	108.1	114.1	105.9	108.3
October	108.5	112.6	113.9	102.4	105.7	120.8	112.0	113.4	120.2	103.6	109.7
November	82.0	88.0	81.0	78.8	77.1	88.1	89.2	89.1	85.4	80.4	77.0
December	87.7	81.9	71.1	85.5	86.0	88.3	107.9	85.4	78.5	88.8	90.5

Table 2-11. Seasonal Indexes Used to Adjust Housing Units Authorized in Permit-Issuing Places, 1996–2012—*Continued*

[Numbers in thousands.]

Characteristics	United States[1]	In structures with						All units			
		1 unit				2 to 4 units	5 units or more	Northeast	Midwest	South	West
		Northeast	Midwest	South	West						
1996											
January	76.4	62.3	52.0	87.7	79.3	72.6	81.1	67.9	54.7	86.4	79.8
February	81.1	61.8	67.0	93.6	84.3	80.2	76.9	63.0	64.2	90.1	85.0
March	100.6	95.8	99.7	107.5	103.8	98.3	88.3	95.5	97.0	106.6	103.0
April	114.9	121.5	127.8	116.6	114.3	114.0	99.3	117.0	123.1	114.3	110.4
May	115.7	129.7	64.5	113.8	117.7	111.6	102.1	123.6	125.9	112.5	112.7
June	110.4	117.8	117.5	104.9	112.7	114.0	107.3	117.8	113.5	103.2	113.3
July	111.8	120.7	121.5	108.3	113.2	103.6	106.6	117.2	117.3	106.2	113.0
August	109.6	112.8	115.9	107.8	108.9	105.8	107.9	113.7	116.4	105.5	107.3
September	104.4	102.1	104.9	95.8	99.6	106.0	122.4	101.5	109.0	102.3	102.2
October	109.3	113.1	84.7	103.2	107.0	123.9	110.9	113.8	121.5	102.5	108.9
November	85.6	89.9	83.2	83.7	79.4	93.2	91.6	91.8	88.6	84.5	81.5
December	84.4	75.7	68.4	80.8	82.3	79.8	104.6	79.5	72.4	89.9	85.0

Note: These seasonal indexes include trading-day adjustment factors. Previous derived rounded estimates have been replaced with actual estimates.
[1]Implicit seasonal index - The ratio of the unadjusted number of housing units authorized to the seasonally adjusted housing units authorized.

Source: U.S. Census Bureau, Building Permits Survey

Table 2-12. New Privately Owned Housing Units Authorized by Building Permits in Permit-Issuing Places, Seasonally Adjusted Annual Rate, 1960–2012

[Numbers in thousands.]

Characteristics	Total	In structures with			Region							
		1 unit	2 to 4 units	5 units or more	Northeast		Midwest		South		West	
					Total	1 unit	Total	1 unit	Total	1 unit	Total	1 unit
20,000-place series												
2012												
January	684	452	20	212	78	37	101	75	377	245	128	95
February	707	478	25	204	82	46	119	79	361	260	145	93
March	769	466	22	281	81	44	130	84	371	241	187	97
April	723	475	22	226	88	45	114	76	359	248	162	106
May	784	490	22	272	78	43	119	82	412	255	175	110
2011												
January	566	417	21	128	76	51	97	65	283	215	110	86
February	536	379	16	141	57	37	88	60	295	209	96	73
March	590	398	16	176	61	36	96	66	311	222	122	74
April	578	401	22	155	61	37	97	66	296	217	124	81
May	624	412	21	191	79	36	100	69	308	224	137	83
June	633	412	23	198	71	36	101	70	323	225	138	81
July	627	417	24	186	64	38	100	71	331	225	132	83
August	645	429	27	189	62	35	110	76	332	234	141	84
September	616	428	21	167	67	39	110	75	307	233	132	81
October	667	444	24	199	66	42	109	74	359	244	133	84
November	709	451	23	235	80	46	107	73	360	244	162	88
December	701	454	24	223	76	41	112	78	358	246	155	89
2010												
January	636	504	21	111	75	50	99	85	313	257	149	112
February	650	510	20	120	78	63	110	83	312	255	150	109
March	687	536	23	128	72	49	115	87	357	292	143	108
April	637	476	18	143	75	46	116	79	319	256	127	95
May	575	435	20	120	64	47	102	73	299	230	110	85
June	587	425	23	139	77	47	97	74	296	220	117	84
July	579	411	21	147	67	42	102	70	297	217	113	82
August	580	402	22	156	71	43	98	69	284	210	127	80
September	563	404	28	131	68	45	95	69	288	209	112	81
October	558	408	21	129	67	44	112	75	266	208	113	81
November	560	418	20	122	64	50	95	79	280	211	121	78
December	632	447	25	160	113	76	98	65	257	208	164	98
2009												
January	545	337	23	185	59	41	89	53	282	179	115	64
February	558	377	20	161	74	38	89	61	296	213	99	65
March	513	361	21	131	61	38	86	55	262	201	104	67
April	521	391	21	109	58	41	83	61	270	206	110	83
May	556	431	21	104	64	44	95	78	285	220	112	89
June	601	458	25	118	63	45	100	78	320	243	118	92
July	595	489	19	87	64	48	109	85	292	255	130	101
August	616	491	20	105	70	48	106	90	316	253	124	100
September	609	477	19	113	70	49	105	81	309	249	125	98
October	583	472	16	95	67	51	104	80	299	246	113	95
November	623	483	26	114	74	50	114	82	318	253	117	98
December	664	508	18	138	101	53	116	82	319	267	128	106
2008												
January	1,094	708	42	344	131	69	181	119	570	384	212	136
February	1,014	664	41	309	110	70	145	90	518	365	241	139
March	967	642	38	287	116	66	133	93	521	350	197	133
April	1,008	661	41	306	111	64	163	108	511	353	223	136
May	995	633	36	326	142	60	148	104	471	333	234	136
June	1,180	605	35	540	306	57	153	99	477	315	244	134
July	921	571	34	316	101	57	140	95	486	300	194	119
August	858	543	33	282	85	60	142	88	445	279	186	116
September	797	529	36	232	88	55	132	92	408	272	169	110
October	736	469	33	234	75	49	126	84	375	242	160	94
November	626	420	20	186	71	47	98	75	297	212	160	86
December	554	364	21	169	61	42	84	56	293	192	116	74
2007												
January	1,626	1,174	70	382	184	98	267	178	785	602	390	296
February	1,598	1,136	70	392	144	81	222	154	815	606	417	295
March	1,596	1,147	69	380	164	90	244	178	777	582	411	297
April	1,470	1,058	60	352	159	89	222	164	727	542	362	263
May	1,493	1,042	64	387	145	88	226	166	766	537	356	251
June	1,407	995	57	355	153	87	219	163	705	506	330	239
July	1,361	978	57	326	151	84	207	152	666	502	337	240
August	1,321	916	57	348	150	84	194	149	622	470	355	213
September	1,261	855	50	356	136	77	202	143	626	452	297	183
October	1,192	821	50	321	146	77	185	133	559	420	302	191
November	1,224	795	52	377	131	71	188	135	625	424	280	165
December	1,149	742	57	350	136	73	169	116	584	398	260	155

Table 2-12. New Privately Owned Housing Units Authorized by Building Permits in Permit-Issuing Places, Seasonally Adjusted Annual Rate, 1960–2012—*Continued*

[Numbers in thousands.]

Characteristics	Total	In structures with			Region							
		1 unit	2 to 4 units	5 units or more	Northeast		Midwest		South		West	
					Total	1 unit	Total	1 unit	Total	1 unit	Total	1 unit
2006												
January	2,212	1,689	101	422	211	128	350	265	1,090	862	561	434
February	2,141	1,643	85	413	205	125	354	265	1,030	839	552	414
March	2,118	1,551	83	484	211	120	323	242	1,070	810	514	379
April	1,998	1,496	78	424	184	115	283	228	1,017	768	514	385
May	1,905	1,450	81	374	167	100	288	222	953	766	497	362
June	1,867	1,393	72	402	172	101	286	206	929	727	480	359
July	1,763	1,307	78	378	172	97	277	204	898	696	416	310
August	1,722	1,282	77	363	166	97	272	194	871	680	413	311
September	1,655	1,218	72	365	164	94	248	186	837	646	406	292
October	1,570	1,175	69	326	152	95	238	181	808	630	372	269
November	1,535	1,163	58	314	147	90	234	172	801	627	353	274
December	1,638	1,198	72	368	172	94	246	179	831	648	389	277
2005												
January	2,139	1,654	76	409	197	122	334	266	1,051	826	557	440
February	2,114	1,630	89	395	197	123	368	286	995	783	554	438
March	2,062	1,580	80	402	183	111	340	263	993	775	546	431
April	2,150	1,654	75	421	202	121	371	281	1,025	816	552	436
May	2,085	1,644	81	360	206	125	351	274	979	795	549	450
June	2,178	1,683	87	408	215	127	355	279	1,064	829	544	448
July	2,203	1,722	96	385	205	134	371	289	1,045	834	582	465
August	2,219	1,716	87	416	207	136	350	281	1,104	853	558	446
September	2,263	1,798	88	377	213	141	356	285	1,075	869	619	503
October	2,170	1,742	84	344	200	130	361	291	1,056	860	553	461
November	2,218	1,730	82	406	213	125	359	288	1,071	872	575	445
December	2,120	1,661	84	375	208	122	325	253	1,066	845	521	441
2004												
January	1,952	1,539	93	320	191	131	362	288	898	711	501	409
February	1,966	1,564	87	315	187	131	351	297	913	721	515	415
March	2,066	1,648	100	318	207	150	376	307	949	759	534	432
April	2,070	1,617	94	359	200	145	380	297	952	746	538	429
May	2,150	1,675	89	386	202	136	370	299	1,022	787	556	453
June	2,020	1,615	83	322	207	139	350	289	931	761	532	426
July	2,112	1,620	106	386	198	127	363	289	986	764	565	440
August	2,056	1,609	83	364	180	119	384	306	958	754	534	430
September	2,041	1,586	80	375	200	122	383	294	931	749	527	421
October	2,097	1,593	87	417	183	121	368	285	1,020	771	526	416
November	2,079	1,572	92	415	203	128	343	279	948	728	585	437
December	2,082	1,613	90	379	190	124	392	298	946	768	554	423
19,000-place series												
2003												
January	1,808	1,416	89	303	169	122	367	276	796	626	476	392
February	1,854	1,357	80	417	166	106	330	247	808	621	550	383
March	1,757	1,359	74	324	164	116	339	267	801	624	453	352
April	1,803	1,391	85	327	172	119	354	272	820	645	457	355
May	1,835	1,389	82	364	177	121	358	278	820	638	480	352
June	1,875	1,461	79	335	171	122	387	294	859	676	458	369
July	1,885	1,478	77	330	184	130	376	297	845	677	480	374
August	1,966	1,521	83	362	204	129	388	297	885	708	489	387
September	1,961	1,533	92	336	181	130	393	308	892	705	495	390
October	2,012	1,566	80	366	200	134	378	311	907	719	527	402
November	1,918	1,513	94	311	190	130	393	296	845	694	490	393
December	1,987	1,549	76	362	200	126	370	286	926	723	491	414
2002												
January	1,665	1,285	69	311	171	133	344	266	768	594	382	292
February	1,787	1,401	66	320	211	146	367	283	808	645	401	327
March	1,691	1,289	72	330	151	120	341	254	783	592	416	323
April	1,669	1,285	68	316	165	125	334	256	755	581	415	323
May	1,716	1,289	71	356	180	120	346	257	767	583	423	329
June	1,758	1,314	82	362	176	127	347	257	817	597	418	333
July	1,738	1,307	69	362	177	124	352	254	796	598	413	331
August	1,695	1,317	72	306	165	120	341	253	768	602	421	342
September	1,803	1,366	92	345	184	130	361	269	790	621	468	346
October	1,799	1,382	71	346	172	127	359	267	795	615	473	373
November	1,771	1,382	70	319	161	122	338	275	782	621	490	364
December	1,896	1,409	78	409	177	134	402	286	856	636	461	353

Table 2-12. New Privately Owned Housing Units Authorized by Building Permits in Permit-Issuing Places, Seasonally Adjusted Annual Rate, 1960–2012—*Continued*

[Numbers in thousands.]

Characteristics	Total	In structures with			Region							
		1 unit	2 to 4 units	5 units or more	Northeast		Midwest		South		West	
					Total	1 unit	Total	1 unit	Total	1 unit	Total	1 unit
2001												
January	1,699	1,251	61	387	150	117	330	249	740	551	479	334
February	1,656	1,242	69	345	189	118	330	253	721	545	416	326
March	1,659	1,232	69	358	158	113	336	259	728	541	437	319
April	1,666	1,259	65	342	158	112	333	249	744	575	431	323
May	1,665	1,240	69	356	153	118	334	256	756	557	422	309
June	1,626	1,252	81	293	151	115	350	262	719	570	406	305
July	1,598	1,235	62	301	160	117	338	258	709	554	391	306
August	1,615	1,241	65	309	161	121	328	257	711	555	415	308
September	1,565	1,192	54	319	149	118	321	239	699	539	396	296
October	1,566	1,185	60	321	166	121	310	236	707	546	383	282
November	1,651	1,229	62	360	161	116	354	256	757	563	379	294
December	1,680	1,251	73	356	171	125	341	251	772	579	396	296
2000												
January	1,727	1,277	64	386	192	129	377	280	726	560	432	308
February	1,692	1,241	70	381	176	128	366	262	735	555	415	296
March	1,651	1,253	65	333	174	132	366	278	715	551	396	292
April	1,597	1,192	61	344	167	122	347	261	688	512	395	297
May	1,543	1,182	70	291	162	123	317	242	691	524	373	293
June	1,572	1,156	61	355	160	117	318	234	694	513	400	292
July	1,542	1,152	57	333	159	117	317	236	691	517	375	282
August	1,552	1,173	68	311	155	118	305	235	684	520	408	300
September	1,570	1,189	67	314	169	122	304	238	708	524	389	305
October	1,577	1,224	68	285	160	126	330	245	695	542	392	311
November	1,614	1,208	66	340	165	120	290	239	733	532	426	317
December	1,543	1,180	60	303	154	120	268	202	678	522	443	336
1999												
January	1,732	1,259	81	392	167	129	321	261	804	556	440	313
February	1,720	1,291	68	361	176	144	343	272	802	567	399	308
March	1,665	1,239	65	361	167	121	350	264	740	549	408	305
April	1,600	1,227	65	308	166	130	341	256	700	539	393	302
May	1,640	1,254	58	328	160	129	347	255	712	558	421	312
June	1,702	1,276	64	362	175	127	338	259	762	556	427	334
July	1,682	1,276	62	344	162	130	337	258	770	566	413	322
August	1,671	1,243	66	362	166	130	344	262	767	554	394	297
September	1,551	1,198	64	289	154	119	336	262	682	531	379	286
October	1,649	1,208	63	378	146	116	343	263	772	537	388	292
November	1,672	1,233	69	370	169	124	378	267	737	548	388	294
December	1,683	1,257	71	355	174	131	362	270	746	541	401	315
1998												
January	1,555	1,158	71	326	173	132	336	261	655	485	391	280
February	1,647	1,191	77	379	170	142	373	268	703	498	401	283
March	1,605	1,162	71	372	149	126	316	234	747	511	393	291
April	1,547	1,157	57	333	140	118	304	239	690	502	413	298
May	1,554	1,165	66	323	142	113	321	244	723	522	368	286
June	1,551	1,148	73	330	155	122	314	234	687	505	395	287
July	1,610	1,181	76	353	158	118	313	237	735	527	404	299
August	1,654	1,196	72	386	157	124	309	237	790	544	398	291
September	1,577	1,187	68	322	162	123	319	241	708	529	388	294
October	1,719	1,217	70	432	174	123	338	255	789	536	418	303
November	1,672	1,248	59	365	174	130	330	267	717	541	451	310
December	1,742	1,317	75	350	179	137	408	302	750	573	405	305
1997												
January	1,382	1,046	64	272	160	121	295	215	590	458	337	252
February	1,445	1,070	65	310	173	116	301	216	609	459	362	279
March	1,436	1,031	66	339	153	114	300	218	647	446	336	253
April	1,421	1,054	70	297	129	105	312	228	646	466	334	255
May	1,414	1,046	65	303	132	107	289	216	618	456	375	267
June	1,402	1,057	67	278	141	111	301	222	624	467	336	257
July	1,440	1,050	74	316	136	109	287	214	658	459	359	268
August	1,449	1,061	65	323	141	107	309	221	626	462	373	271
September	1,494	1,091	67	336	138	112	304	221	654	472	398	286
October	1,499	1,098	76	325	134	114	297	218	677	485	391	281
November	1,469	1,093	62	314	141	110	297	220	652	487	379	276
December	1,456	1,080	77	299	149	117	307	238	621	461	379	264

Table 2-12. New Privately Owned Housing Units Authorized by Building Permits in Permit-Issuing Places, Seasonally Adjusted Annual Rate, 1960–2012—*Continued*

[Numbers in thousands.]

Characteristics	Total	In structures with			Region							
		1 unit	2 to 4 units	5 units or more	Northeast		Midwest		South		West	
					Total	1 unit	Total	1 unit	Total	1 unit	Total	1 unit
1996												
January	1,387	1,051	63	273	97	87	313	240	610	461	367	263
February	1,420	1,085	60	275	116	105	318	246	615	477	371	257
March	1,437	1,108	60	269	137	111	335	244	596	484	369	269
April	1,463	1,108	74	281	145	108	333	251	636	485	349	264
May	1,457	1,096	66	295	139	109	314	243	663	485	341	259
June	1,429	1,089	64	276	132	109	307	239	640	482	350	259
July	1,450	1,074	67	309	137	110	338	243	617	461	358	260
August	1,413	1,061	63	289	147	113	312	234	627	459	327	255
September	1,392	1,037	70	285	143	113	303	229	598	447	348	248
October	1,358	1,010	68	280	142	106	305	222	581	443	330	239
November	1,412	1,031	68	313	140	111	313	220	636	454	323	246
December	1,411	1,015	62	334	142	111	309	212	629	455	331	237
1995												
January	1,282	967	66	249	139	121	285	206	567	412	291	228
February	1,254	916	52	286	112	96	274	201	536	391	332	228
March	1,226	914	64	248	128	106	274	206	558	404	266	198
April	1,259	925	60	274	129	106	278	202	539	396	313	221
May	1,271	958	61	252	121	103	278	209	546	410	326	236
June	1,305	982	64	259	119	101	295	218	565	424	326	239
July	1,354	1,019	61	274	117	101	303	225	598	443	336	250
August	1,386	1,045	63	278	121	107	310	233	600	444	355	261
September	1,421	1,079	68	274	128	108	315	234	638	487	340	250
October	1,400	1,052	65	283	128	106	322	235	634	458	316	253
November	1,430	1,060	70	300	126	101	314	241	622	454	368	264
December	1,442	1,091	62	289	129	105	300	232	618	460	395	294
1994												
January	1,390	1,112	68	210	102	99	298	246	599	472	391	295
February	1,269	1,065	56	148	112	98	278	227	545	466	334	274
March	1,342	1,078	61	203	121	103	305	243	576	460	340	272
April	1,392	1,084	62	246	135	117	306	237	600	462	351	268
May	1,396	1,110	66	220	143	124	315	240	592	471	346	275
June	1,357	1,067	58	232	146	126	301	232	565	450	345	259
July	1,335	1,041	60	234	161	137	300	228	567	429	307	247
August	1,377	1,054	60	263	143	121	303	225	589	452	342	256
September	1,412	1,056	60	296	135	118	295	228	608	450	374	260
October	1,397	1,042	68	287	131	113	318	226	591	438	357	265
November	1,340	1,014	66	260	137	119	298	229	590	426	315	240
December	1,396	1,086	62	248	167	129	323	246	603	466	303	245
17,000-place series												
1993												
January	1,177	989	47	141	142	132	281	246	485	404	269	207
February	1,148	953	52	143	143	121	267	210	486	414	252	208
March	1,056	881	44	131	108	95	253	193	423	366	272	227
April	1,104	922	52	130	117	104	240	192	475	406	272	220
May	1,112	911	48	153	128	109	257	200	458	387	269	215
June	1,130	932	51	147	129	107	266	204	455	391	280	230
July	1,174	977	53	144	127	110	261	208	500	427	286	232
August	1,230	1,000	52	178	130	111	281	220	522	428	297	241
September	1,251	1,028	59	164	137	122	286	224	514	426	314	256
October	1,287	1,071	58	158	146	126	299	240	541	457	301	248
November	1,357	1,125	58	174	141	119	329	261	557	475	330	270
December	1,461	1,161	55	245	171	122	326	278	646	492	318	269
1992												
January	1,077	893	44	140	127	111	263	215	422	361	265	206
February	1,146	951	43	152	129	109	311	244	432	384	274	214
March	1,082	897	44	141	123	107	265	209	445	376	249	205
April	1,054	868	43	143	118	102	243	186	425	367	268	213
May	1,056	885	45	126	125	109	258	200	419	371	254	205
June	1,057	888	46	123	122	104	242	194	437	380	256	210
July	1,089	884	42	163	129	109	252	191	441	378	267	206
August	1,075	883	53	139	124	110	254	198	425	362	272	213
September	1,114	914	44	156	127	107	262	204	447	385	278	218
October	1,132	944	50	138	116	107	254	210	485	402	277	225
November	1,118	945	48	125	134	118	260	209	448	396	276	222
December	1,176	1,017	45	114	129	111	280	235	478	421	289	250

Table 2-12. New Privately Owned Housing Units Authorized by Building Permits in Permit-Issuing Places, Seasonally Adjusted Annual Rate, 1960–2012—*Continued*

[Numbers in thousands.]

Characteristics	Total	In structures with			Region							
		1 unit	2 to 4 units	5 units or more	Northeast		Midwest		South		West	
					Total	1 unit	Total	1 unit	Total	1 unit	Total	1 unit
1991												
January	786	587	41	158	92	72	180	116	297	250	217	149
February	853	680	42	131	96	78	196	157	341	281	220	164
March	911	694	46	171	103	80	203	153	353	287	252	174
April	916	742	46	128	108	91	208	163	364	307	236	181
May	991	763	39	189	107	91	218	169	391	314	275	189
June	964	763	48	153	109	93	218	171	378	308	259	191
July	973	787	41	145	111	92	225	175	391	325	246	195
August	944	772	40	132	114	99	217	175	375	315	238	183
September	974	788	44	142	109	96	213	175	409	328	243	189
October	991	787	41	163	122	102	229	176	384	323	256	186
November	984	789	46	149	122	98	221	178	398	317	243	196
December	1,061	860	41	160	113	95	240	193	432	349	276	223
1990												
January	1,748	989	85	674	193	135	462	209	656	367	437	278
February	1,329	963	60	306	183	138	281	200	455	360	410	265
March	1,246	912	56	278	150	122	250	187	459	353	387	250
April	1,136	818	58	260	119	93	241	173	428	321	348	231
May	1,067	793	51	223	126	95	219	161	410	318	312	219
June	1,108	795	48	265	122	95	227	167	421	319	338	214
July	1,078	775	59	244	115	92	225	162	416	310	322	211
August	1,069	764	62	243	115	86	222	160	410	313	322	205
September	976	721	48	207	113	83	217	153	373	298	273	187
October	925	708	46	171	113	88	194	148	361	292	257	180
November	941	682	41	218	108	86	202	151	378	284	253	161
December	861	655	45	161	101	80	187	146	340	274	233	155
1989												
January	1,466	1,040	71	355	234	173	280	200	556	409	396	258
February	1,383	943	82	358	198	148	268	171	518	363	399	261
March	1,214	860	67	287	178	119	243	163	441	335	352	243
April	1,376	948	67	361	202	150	253	173	525	362	396	263
May	1,381	910	72	399	175	130	250	166	536	353	420	261
June	1,322	882	64	376	176	123	241	161	507	344	398	254
July	1,283	913	67	303	165	117	234	170	483	358	401	268
August	1,334	935	70	329	179	126	261	168	514	370	380	271
September	1,314	948	62	304	171	127	248	177	504	374	391	270
October	1,365	953	61	351	167	118	277	189	500	359	421	287
November	1,344	986	64	294	169	124	269	189	489	384	417	289
December	1,422	983	63	376	169	135	233	163	526	357	494	328
1988												
January	1,244	899	68	277	255	181	221	150	422	326	346	242
February	1,438	991	73	374	248	182	256	171	568	409	366	229
March	1,525	1,039	84	402	298	214	277	193	551	393	399	239
April	1,429	952	73	404	244	163	268	177	518	379	399	233
May	1,444	988	76	380	241	167	268	176	533	387	402	258
June	1,485	1,009	77	399	235	167	278	177	564	399	408	266
July	1,439	980	75	384	229	163	257	170	552	389	401	258
August	1,460	1,002	70	388	216	158	248	175	556	407	440	262
September	1,436	975	74	387	190	148	259	171	542	388	445	268
October	1,516	1,023	82	411	218	159	260	180	568	400	470	284
November	1,508	1,018	76	414	199	150	249	177	575	399	485	292
December	1,501	1,050	75	376	201	150	347	215	545	413	408	272
1987												
January	1,690	1,088	100	502	286	NA	351	NA	570	NA	483	NA
February	1,689	1,195	103	391	306	NA	371	NA	603	NA	409	NA
March	1,704	1,132	97	475	317	NA	319	NA	625	NA	443	NA
April	1,601	1,057	97	447	287	NA	298	NA	604	NA	412	NA
May	1,500	1,006	91	403	267	NA	278	NA	576	NA	379	NA
June	1,522	1,015	86	421	272	NA	268	NA	587	NA	395	NA
July	1,516	996	88	432	279	NA	266	NA	553	NA	418	NA
August	1,511	1,008	85	418	259	NA	252	NA	598	NA	402	NA
September	1,514	989	85	440	248	NA	284	NA	577	NA	405	NA
October	1,447	960	78	409	244	NA	279	NA	554	NA	370	NA
November	1,457	973	83	401	270	NA	267	NA	542	NA	378	NA
December	1,345	950	81	314	254	NA	232	NA	479	NA	380	NA

Table 2-12. New Privately Owned Housing Units Authorized by Building Permits in Permit-Issuing Places, Seasonally Adjusted Annual Rate, 1960–2012—*Continued*

[Numbers in thousands.]

Characteristics	Total	In structures with			Region							
		1 unit	2 to 4 units	5 units or more	Northeast		Midwest		South		West	
					Total	1 unit	Total	1 unit	Total	1 unit	Total	1 unit
1986												
January	1,847	1,064	131	652	277	NA	288	NA	786	NA	496	NA
February	1,767	1,017	113	637	253	NA	288	NA	754	NA	472	NA
March	1,780	1,014	100	666	265	NA	272	NA	717	NA	526	NA
April	1,858	1,127	115	616	299	NA	314	NA	728	NA	517	NA
May	1,797	1,089	119	589	285	NA	296	NA	698	NA	518	NA
June	1,790	1,107	106	577	284	NA	289	NA	724	NA	493	NA
July	1,780	1,102	107	571	302	NA	297	NA	701	NA	480	NA
August	1,726	1,056	109	561	284	NA	304	NA	662	NA	476	NA
September	1,686	1,077	101	508	304	NA	273	NA	631	NA	478	NA
October	1,675	1,050	107	518	273	NA	264	NA	633	NA	505	NA
November	1,644	1,027	93	524	265	NA	295	NA	607	NA	4//	NA
December	1,903	1,184	105	614	292	NA	313	NA	591	NA	707	NA
1985												
January	1,660	905	134	621	285	NA	189	NA	723	NA	463	NA
February	1,662	969	104	589	272	NA	191	NA	688	NA	511	NA
March	1,727	997	136	594	266	NA	235	NA	762	NA	464	NA
April	1,664	927	118	619	259	NA	228	NA	729	NA	448	NA
May	1,709	921	124	664	260	NA	243	NA	759	NA	447	NA
June	1,716	945	127	644	263	NA	243	NA	752	NA	458	NA
July	1,697	955	117	625	240	NA	244	NA	746	NA	467	NA
August	1,808	1,001	123	684	262	NA	256	NA	780	NA	510	NA
September	1,916	963	128	825	241	NA	238	NA	776	NA	661	NA
October	1,743	997	108	638	271	NA	242	NA	749	NA	481	NA
November	1,692	950	112	630	273	NA	209	NA	730	NA	480	NA
December	1,794	967	109	718	247	NA	279	NA	836	NA	432	NA
1984												
January	1,816	1,003	148	665	175	NA	246	NA	890	NA	505	NA
February	1,987	1,141	165	681	229	NA	292	NA	952	NA	514	NA
March	1,725	971	161	593	188	NA	195	NA	831	NA	511	NA
April	1,776	968	156	652	194	NA	231	NA	872	NA	479	NA
May	1,741	945	152	644	211	NA	211	NA	849	NA	470	NA
June	1,814	931	148	735	194	NA	221	NA	894	NA	505	NA
July	1,605	863	141	601	187	NA	215	NA	777	NA	426	NA
August	1,530	849	131	550	186	NA	190	NA	741	NA	413	NA
September	1,523	874	125	524	206	NA	181	NA	734	NA	402	NA
October	1,490	834	123	533	192	NA	188	NA	710	NA	400	NA
November	1,643	862	127	654	227	NA	220	NA	751	NA	445	NA
December	1,626	878	132	616	237	NA	214	NA	746	NA	429	NA
16,000-place series												
1983												
January	1,426	863	113	450	148	NA	181	NA	765	NA	332	NA
February	1,471	823	118	530	184	NA	164	NA	792	NA	331	NA
March	1,475	854	125	496	143	NA	177	NA	843	NA	312	NA
April	1,566	874	141	551	157	NA	176	NA	860	NA	373	NA
May	1,669	959	139	571	155	NA	194	NA	915	NA	405	NA
June	1,769	1,025	144	600	183	NA	201	NA	945	NA	440	NA
July	1,795	960	142	693	187	NA	188	NA	1,000	NA	420	NA
August	1,713	923	138	652	187	NA	207	NA	917	NA	402	NA
September	1,585	878	137	570	174	NA	189	NA	821	NA	401	NA
October	1,716	934	152	630	171	NA	202	NA	926	NA	417	NA
November	1,668	942	147	579	158	NA	192	NA	910	NA	408	NA
December	1,627	939	145	543	179	NA	180	NA	823	NA	445	NA
1982												
January	794	444	71	279	72	NA	79	NA	472	NA	171	NA
February	808	445	73	290	87	NA	77	NA	473	NA	171	NA
March	891	473	78	340	95	NA	101	NA	492	NA	203	NA
April	888	467	75	346	98	NA	108	NA	502	NA	180	NA
May	953	487	104	362	114	NA	145	NA	490	NA	204	NA
June	913	506	86	321	101	NA	116	NA	492	NA	204	NA
July	1,044	506	84	454	97	NA	152	NA	540	NA	255	NA
August	926	523	88	315	109	NA	114	NA	509	NA	194	NA
September	1,042	584	97	361	113	NA	141	NA	558	NA	230	NA
October	1,149	657	86	406	127	NA	141	NA	615	NA	266	NA
November	1,229	737	95	397	133	NA	144	NA	661	NA	291	NA
December	1,351	755	115	481	114	NA	163	NA	745	NA	329	NA

Table 2-12. New Privately Owned Housing Units Authorized by Building Permits in Permit-Issuing Places, Seasonally Adjusted Annual Rate, 1960–2012—*Continued*

[Numbers in thousands.]

Characteristics	Total	In structures with			Region							
		1 unit	2 to 4 units	5 units or more	Northeast		Midwest		South		West	
					Total	1 unit	Total	1 unit	Total	1 unit	Total	1 unit
1981												
January	1,221	693	140	388	111	NA	199	NA	608	NA	303	NA
February	1,199	702	117	380	120	NA	179	NA	603	NA	297	NA
March	1,183	690	113	380	126	NA	196	NA	565	NA	296	NA
April	1,190	686	126	378	129	NA	164	NA	575	NA	322	NA
May	1,173	654	110	409	111	NA	145	NA	578	NA	339	NA
June	976	565	107	304	109	NA	137	NA	466	NA	264	NA
July	935	543	99	293	118	NA	121	NA	469	NA	227	NA
August	889	512	90	287	115	NA	114	NA	439	NA	221	NA
September	847	461	80	306	95	NA	110	NA	428	NA	214	NA
October	731	401	85	245	105	NA	100	NA	343	NA	183	NA
November	748	411	78	259	87	NA	100	NA	395	NA	166	NA
December	796	458	86	252	90	NA	103	NA	431	NA	172	NA
1980												
January	1,280	786	113	381	126	NA	232	NA	563	NA	359	NA
February	1,199	733	108	358	131	NA	191	NA	529	NA	348	NA
March	988	576	95	317	123	NA	131	NA	462	NA	272	NA
April	808	476	68	264	89	NA	125	NA	393	NA	201	NA
May	861	508	87	266	105	NA	135	NA	403	NA	218	NA
June	1,118	650	100	368	120	NA	161	NA	545	NA	292	NA
July	1,259	772	119	368	118	NA	217	NA	584	NA	340	NA
August	1,367	846	135	386	122	NA	221	NA	632	NA	392	NA
September	1,484	881	145	458	136	NA	239	NA	722	NA	387	NA
October	1,366	824	134	408	135	NA	240	NA	631	NA	360	NA
November	1,383	819	142	422	127	NA	221	NA	654	NA	381	NA
December	1,249	745	123	381	114	NA	211	NA	621	NA	303	NA
1979												
January	1,461	959	117	385	190	NA	213	NA	591	NA	467	NA
February	1,492	935	101	456	164	NA	260	NA	593	NA	475	NA
March	1,720	1,139	134	447	157	NA	320	NA	753	NA	490	NA
April	1,597	1,062	127	408	159	NA	314	NA	621	NA	503	NA
May	1,684	1,067	128	489	177	NA	341	NA	660	NA	506	NA
June	1,640	1,041	131	468	181	NA	330	NA	639	NA	490	NA
July	1,534	989	130	415	161	NA	287	NA	599	NA	487	NA
August	1,591	989	141	461	152	NA	297	NA	640	NA	502	NA
September	1,638	965	134	539	201	NA	303	NA	660	NA	474	NA
October	1,481	901	132	448	142	NA	263	NA	643	NA	433	NA
November	1,276	770	96	410	151	NA	203	NA	554	NA	368	NA
December	1,254	777	119	358	152	NA	224	NA	517	NA	361	NA
1978												
January	1,740	1,186	113	441	193	NA	351	NA	649	NA	547	NA
February	1,736	1,112	124	500	167	NA	406	NA	620	NA	543	NA
March	1,799	1,160	134	505	174	NA	408	NA	647	NA	570	NA
April	1,948	1,279	128	541	204	NA	415	NA	771	NA	558	NA
May	1,766	1,178	126	462	184	NA	387	NA	644	NA	551	NA
June	1,983	1,254	169	560	192	NA	384	NA	648	NA	759	NA
July	1,786	1,146	118	522	218	NA	399	NA	656	NA	513	NA
August	1,691	1,113	118	460	202	NA	388	NA	635	NA	466	NA
September	1,751	1,150	125	476	203	NA	391	NA	654	NA	503	NA
October	1,781	1,182	130	469	183	NA	383	NA	683	NA	532	NA
November	1,795	1,176	134	485	201	NA	363	NA	725	NA	506	NA
December	1,818	1,247	140	431	212	NA	372	NA	699	NA	535	NA
14,000-place series												
1977												
January	1,466	996	116	354	136	NA	326	NA	457	NA	547	NA
February	1,560	1,091	114	355	140	NA	351	NA	508	NA	561	NA
March	1,660	1,140	114	406	212	NA	393	NA	514	NA	541	NA
April	1,660	1,089	113	458	177	NA	418	NA	547	NA	518	NA
May	1,668	1,107	114	447	181	NA	407	NA	556	NA	524	NA
June	1,752	1,121	118	513	239	NA	414	NA	571	NA	528	NA
July	1,687	1,125	129	433	165	NA	412	NA	571	NA	539	NA
August	1,780	1,156	134	490	176	NA	446	NA	613	NA	545	NA
September	1,674	1,137	119	418	171	NA	381	NA	568	NA	554	NA
October	1,758	1,159	123	476	204	NA	381	NA	610	NA	563	NA
November	1,771	1,176	142	453	166	NA	414	NA	597	NA	594	NA
December	1,754	1,161	119	474	182	NA	402	NA	620	NA	550	NA

Table 2-12. New Privately Owned Housing Units Authorized by Building Permits in Permit-Issuing Places, Seasonally Adjusted Annual Rate, 1960–2012—*Continued*

[Numbers in thousands.]

Characteristics	Total	In structures with			Region							
		1 unit	2 to 4 units	5 units or more	Northeast		Midwest		South		West	
					Total	1 unit	Total	1 unit	Total	1 unit	Total	1 unit
1976												
January	1,195	855	80	260	136	NA	284	NA	374	NA	401	NA
February	1,190	865	84	241	141	NA	318	NA	385	NA	346	NA
March	1,164	838	82	244	143	NA	313	NA	365	NA	343	NA
April	1,132	832	77	223	139	NA	288	NA	357	NA	348	NA
May	1,194	830	83	281	144	NA	297	NA	396	NA	357	NA
June	1,188	846	83	259	132	NA	307	NA	370	NA	379	NA
July	1,245	877	83	285	151	NA	300	NA	388	NA	406	NA
August	1,309	878	101	330	163	NA	315	NA	395	NA	436	NA
September	1,481	917	112	452	159	NA	391	NA	469	NA	462	NA
October	1,425	967	109	349	163	NA	364	NA	421	NA	477	NA
November	1,531	1,029	115	387	166	NA	366	NA	449	NA	550	NA
December	1,511	1,028	113	370	170	NA	351	NA	462	NA	528	NA
1975												
January	726	527	45	154	97	NA	191	NA	235	NA	203	NA
February	729	528	56	145	112	NA	177	NA	223	NA	217	NA
March	709	532	43	134	103	NA	168	NA	215	NA	223	NA
April	866	616	63	187	133	NA	211	NA	283	NA	239	NA
May	914	657	58	199	135	NA	238	NA	272	NA	269	NA
June	946	671	64	211	126	NA	235	NA	310	NA	275	NA
July	1,020	697	71	252	139	NA	283	NA	306	NA	292	NA
August	994	726	62	206	135	NA	251	NA	316	NA	292	NA
September	1,064	763	69	232	148	NA	262	NA	334	NA	320	NA
October	1,096	786	84	226	139	NA	278	NA	341	NA	338	NA
November	1,110	805	79	226	141	NA	285	NA	347	NA	337	NA
December	1,091	810	73	208	139	NA	285	NA	349	NA	318	NA
1974												
January	1,331	675	87	569	212	NA	279	NA	540	NA	300	NA
February	1,360	727	86	547	206	NA	292	NA	543	NA	319	NA
March	1,440	786	89	565	201	NA	338	NA	544	NA	357	NA
April	1,254	714	79	461	178	NA	247	NA	485	NA	344	NA
May	1,138	667	71	400	177	NA	250	NA	415	NA	296	NA
June	1,086	657	64	365	167	NA	246	NA	386	NA	287	NA
July	1,002	621	57	324	146	NA	225	NA	372	NA	259	NA
August	917	614	55	248	131	NA	226	NA	314	NA	246	NA
September	840	578	42	220	139	NA	218	NA	264	NA	219	NA
October	824	560	48	216	144	NA	217	NA	253	NA	210	NA
November	783	543	42	198	131	NA	193	NA	243	NA	216	NA
December	869	535	49	285	179	NA	188	NA	266	NA	236	NA
1973												
January	2,271	1,108	149	1,015	357	NA	472	NA	910	NA	532	NA
February	2,226	1,074	137	1,015	317	NA	500	NA	905	NA	504	NA
March	2,062	992	134	936	341	NA	406	NA	817	NA	498	NA
April	1,908	938	128	842	299	NA	372	NA	813	NA	424	NA
May	1,931	957	126	848	267	NA	393	NA	824	NA	447	NA
June	2,051	932	126	992	307	NA	337	NA	963	NA	444	NA
July	1,819	897	128	794	279	NA	382	NA	735	NA	422	NA
August	1,809	825	114	870	284	NA	381	NA	735	NA	409	NA
September	1,704	812	104	788	242	NA	326	NA	693	NA	443	NA
October	1,411	689	90	632	207	NA	298	NA	582	NA	324	NA
November	1,402	691	82	630	217	NA	294	NA	599	NA	292	NA
December	1,288	665	84	540	197	NA	247	NA	520	NA	324	NA
1972												
January	2,238	1,115	145	978	372	NA	416	NA	852	NA	597	NA
February	2,169	992	136	1,042	350	NA	416	NA	802	NA	601	NA
March	2,105	1,000	140	965	290	NA	404	NA	873	NA	538	NA
April	2,139	1,008	154	977	333	NA	455	NA	872	NA	480	NA
May	2,067	961	149	957	308	NA	447	NA	785	NA	527	NA
June	2,183	1,018	149	1,017	301	NA	445	NA	889	NA	549	NA
July	2,195	1,027	142	1,027	311	NA	423	NA	932	NA	530	NA
August	2,263	1,074	145	1,043	322	NA	460	NA	953	NA	528	NA
September	2,393	1,050	149	1,194	318	NA	507	NA	1,044	NA	523	NA
October	2,354	1,150	180	1,024	341	NA	435	NA	1,009	NA	569	NA
November	2,234	1,033	145	1,056	366	NA	412	NA	909	NA	548	NA
December	2,419	1,034	150	1,235	426	NA	461	NA	1,010	NA	522	NA

Table 2-12. New Privately Owned Housing Units Authorized by Building Permits in Permit-Issuing Places, Seasonally Adjusted Annual Rate, 1960–2012—*Continued*

[Numbers in thousands.]

Characteristics	Total	In structures with			Region							
		1 unit	2 to 4 units	5 units or more	Northeast		Midwest		South		West	
					Total	1 unit	Total	1 unit	Total	1 unit	Total	1 unit
13,000-place series												
1971												
January	1,643	796	111	736	264	NA	366	NA	635	NA	378	NA
February	1,588	776	118	694	202	NA	308	NA	632	NA	446	NA
March	1,759	844	120	795	273	NA	395	NA	659	NA	432	NA
April	1,745	865	122	758	251	NA	400	NA	655	NA	439	NA
May	1,972	939	133	900	342	NA	430	NA	720	NA	480	NA
June	1,903	923	145	835	293	NA	420	NA	716	NA	474	NA
July	2,069	960	140	969	333	NA	435	NA	790	NA	511	NA
August	2,004	911	143	950	331	NA	426	NA	740	NA	507	NA
September	1,996	907	141	948	344	NA	427	NA	758	NA	467	NA
October	2,026	918	134	974	318	NA	431	NA	776	NA	501	NA
November	2,079	969	137	973	316	NA	458	NA	794	NA	511	NA
December	2,133	994	135	1,004	313	NA	476	NA	821	NA	523	NA
1970												
January	1,062	486	73	503	150	NA	216	NA	407	NA	289	NA
February	1,118	558	73	487	192	NA	240	NA	401	NA	285	NA
March	1,132	557	68	507	177	NA	258	NA	410	NA	287	NA
April	1,224	611	75	538	181	NA	235	NA	466	NA	342	NA
May	1,328	602	81	645	200	NA	259	NA	528	NA	341	NA
June	1,322	623	85	614	217	NA	298	NA	494	NA	313	NA
July	1,324	648	87	589	226	NA	309	NA	480	NA	309	NA
August	1,394	684	100	610	221	NA	311	NA	513	NA	349	NA
September	1,426	702	121	603	208	NA	287	NA	549	NA	382	NA
October	1,564	717	97	750	249	NA	322	NA	569	NA	424	NA
November	1,502	710	99	693	265	NA	330	NA	564	NA	343	NA
December	1,767	854	97	816	314	NA	350	NA	669	NA	434	NA
1969												
January	1,459	683	82	694	239	NA	388	NA	517	NA	315	NA
February	1,495	707	97	691	243	NA	423	NA	525	NA	304	NA
March	1,438	665	97	676	254	NA	366	NA	507	NA	311	NA
April	1,441	662	89	690	242	NA	351	NA	502	NA	346	NA
May	1,328	634	84	610	242	NA	290	NA	470	NA	326	NA
June	1,349	642	86	621	211	NA	322	NA	456	NA	360	NA
July	1,278	595	89	594	209	NA	304	NA	448	NA	317	NA
August	1,317	591	83	643	198	NA	299	NA	507	NA	313	NA
September	1,263	591	78	594	199	NA	286	NA	456	NA	322	NA
October	1,216	589	83	544	198	NA	289	NA	413	NA	316	NA
November	1,191	585	81	525	178	NA	276	NA	442	NA	295	NA
December	1,155	587	77	491	184	NA	271	NA	409	NA	291	NA
1968												
January	1,179	679	81	419	181	NA	333	NA	414	NA	251	NA
February	1,342	711	89	542	224	NA	381	NA	460	NA	277	NA
March	1,370	691	80	599	297	NA	332	NA	454	NA	287	NA
April	1,286	675	81	530	243	NA	330	NA	446	NA	267	NA
May	1,297	665	83	549	218	NA	369	NA	435	NA	275	NA
June	1,300	654	83	563	250	NA	317	NA	464	NA	269	NA
July	1,344	689	75	580	222	NA	327	NA	502	NA	293	NA
August	1,357	700	79	578	245	NA	336	NA	481	NA	295	NA
September	1,464	738	88	638	234	NA	393	NA	522	NA	315	NA
October	1,421	717	84	620	242	NA	358	NA	521	NA	300	NA
November	1,436	729	90	617	204	NA	400	NA	490	NA	342	NA
December	1,389	688	94	607	224	NA	316	NA	533	NA	316	NA
1967												
January	995	577	56	362	289	NA	234	NA	322	NA	150	NA
February	907	564	56	287	200	NA	229	NA	310	NA	168	NA
March	955	570	61	324	172	NA	248	NA	354	NA	181	NA
April	1,035	606	61	368	220	NA	276	NA	356	NA	183	NA
May	1,076	636	66	374	204	NA	277	NA	393	NA	202	NA
June	1,169	673	76	420	226	NA	306	NA	406	NA	231	NA
July	1,177	675	77	425	228	NA	329	NA	396	NA	224	NA
August	1,229	697	80	452	220	NA	337	NA	407	NA	265	NA
September	1,279	701	81	497	243	NA	363	NA	429	NA	244	NA
October	1,280	707	90	483	233	NA	361	NA	433	NA	253	NA
November	1,297	695	86	516	228	NA	356	NA	462	NA	251	NA
December	1,315	701	83	531	240	NA	359	NA	441	NA	275	NA

Table 2-12. New Privately Owned Housing Units Authorized by Building Permits in Permit-Issuing Places, Seasonally Adjusted Annual Rate, 1960–2012—*Continued*

[Numbers in thousands.]

Characteristics	Total	In structures with			Region							
		1 unit	2 to 4 units	5 units or more	Northeast		Midwest		South		West	
					Total	1 unit	Total	1 unit	Total	1 unit	Total	1 unit
12,000-place series												
1966												
January	1,325	739	89	497	304	NA	338	NA	430	NA	253	NA
February	1,159	631	71	457	234	NA	317	NA	382	NA	226	NA
March	1,234	711	84	439	273	NA	344	NA	395	NA	222	NA
April	1,145	647	73	425	245	NA	291	NA	394	NA	215	NA
May	1,078	589	68	421	234	NA	275	NA	369	NA	200	NA
June	956	574	58	324	204	NA	246	NA	327	NA	179	NA
July	932	544	58	330	226	NA	228	NA	306	NA	172	NA
August	877	505	51	321	208	NA	220	NA	305	NA	144	NA
September	774	467	44	263	159	NA	218	NA	261	NA	136	NA
October	739	446	47	246	141	NA	197	NA	261	NA	140	NA
November	736	442	44	250	170	NA	189	NA	251	NA	126	NA
December	743	458	44	241	151	NA	176	NA	285	NA	131	NA
1965												
January	1,264	728	94	442	221	NA	338	NA	420	NA	285	NA
February	1,185	687	79	419	219	NA	270	NA	404	NA	292	NA
March	1,211	674	82	455	251	NA	253	NA	391	NA	316	NA
April	1,162	684	87	391	223	NA	300	NA	376	NA	263	NA
May	1,207	707	82	418	252	NA	309	NA	381	NA	265	NA
June	1,241	696	86	459	258	NA	308	NA	419	NA	256	NA
July	1,237	709	89	439	240	NA	345	NA	402	NA	250	NA
August	1,249	724	86	439	261	NA	320	NA	397	NA	271	NA
September	1,227	701	87	439	264	NA	306	NA	403	NA	254	NA
October	1,279	749	77	453	273	NA	305	NA	448	NA	253	NA
November	1,306	737	79	490	279	NA	308	NA	424	NA	295	NA
December	1,315	741	85	489	273	NA	380	NA	441	NA	221	NA
1964												
January	1,296	708	114	474	198	NA	298	NA	401	NA	399	NA
February	1,442	820	131	491	269	NA	343	NA	405	NA	425	NA
March	1,313	737	99	477	262	NA	297	NA	398	NA	356	NA
April	1,264	688	99	477	232	NA	264	NA	398	NA	370	NA
May	1,299	727	104	468	244	NA	279	NA	399	NA	377	NA
June	1,280	710	103	467	264	NA	269	NA	391	NA	356	NA
July	1,304	709	104	491	244	NA	276	NA	414	NA	370	NA
August	1,306	714	94	498	250	NA	295	NA	434	NA	327	NA
September	1,265	713	92	460	241	NA	299	NA	401	NA	324	NA
October	1,230	705	98	427	223	NA	301	NA	392	NA	314	NA
November	1,254	731	93	430	243	NA	295	NA	411	NA	305	NA
December	1,164	699	75	390	248	NA	252	NA	367	NA	297	NA
1963												
January	1,248	695	104	449	245	NA	201	NA	370	NA	432	NA
February	1,212	699	103	410	233	NA	193	NA	375	NA	411	NA
March	1,258	738	116	404	230	NA	251	NA	361	NA	416	NA
April	1,288	777	104	407	230	NA	285	NA	382	NA	391	NA
May	1,350	740	117	493	247	NA	270	NA	406	NA	427	NA
June	1,345	771	143	431	213	NA	285	NA	399	NA	448	NA
July	1,321	752	126	443	226	NA	268	NA	409	NA	418	NA
August	1,310	756	107	447	224	NA	277	NA	392	NA	417	NA
September	1,413	784	132	497	268	NA	274	NA	428	NA	443	NA
October	1,414	771	132	511	261	NA	281	NA	425	NA	447	NA
November	1,357	735	126	496	235	NA	299	NA	422	NA	401	NA
December	1,423	714	115	594	243	NA	274	NA	476	NA	430	NA
10,000-place series												
1962												
January	1,122	717	82	323	269	NA	199	NA	323	NA	331	NA
February	1,194	741	81	372	275	NA	253	NA	339	NA	327	NA
March	1,134	706	83	345	243	NA	223	NA	330	NA	338	NA
April	1,235	746	83	406	290	NA	236	NA	327	NA	382	NA
May	1,142	710	96	336	220	NA	238	NA	341	NA	343	NA
June	1,154	704	79	371	233	NA	241	NA	329	NA	351	NA
July	1,189	717	92	380	226	NA	251	NA	346	NA	366	NA
August	1,200	725	84	391	228	NA	233	NA	359	NA	380	NA
September	1,223	718	88	417	222	NA	258	NA	355	NA	388	NA
October	1,181	690	86	405	241	NA	234	NA	347	NA	359	NA
November	1,236	700	95	441	242	NA	233	NA	364	NA	397	NA
December	1,236	702	106	428	231	NA	249	NA	346	NA	410	NA

Table 2-12. New Privately Owned Housing Units Authorized by Building Permits in Permit-Issuing Places, Seasonally Adjusted Annual Rate, 1960–2012—*Continued*

[Numbers in thousands.]

Characteristics	Total	In structures with			Region							
		1 unit	2 to 4 units	5 units or more	Northeast		Midwest		South		West	
					Total	1 unit	Total	1 unit	Total	1 unit	Total	1 unit
1961												
January	969	703	59	207	172	NA	236	NA	275	NA	286	NA
February	961	673	63	225	176	NA	251	NA	258	NA	276	NA
March	1,000	699	59	242	201	NA	229	NA	282	NA	288	NA
April	1,002	687	69	246	205	NA	213	NA	292	NA	292	NA
May	1,027	706	66	255	219	NA	222	NA	290	NA	296	NA
June	1,070	716	69	285	221	NA	220	NA	305	NA	324	NA
July	1,083	741	64	278	237	NA	228	NA	308	NA	310	NA
August	1,159	747	71	341	301	NA	225	NA	319	NA	314	NA
September	1,098	738	72	288	226	NA	235	NA	315	NA	322	NA
October	1,123	766	76	281	235	NA	228	NA	325	NA	335	NA
November	1,152	768	74	310	252	NA	231	NA	314	NA	355	NA
December	1,161	774	72	315	275	NA	227	NA	321	NA	338	NA
1960												
January	1,092	846	67	179	246	NA	253	NA	331	NA	262	NA
February	1,088	868	71	149	232	NA	256	NA	305	NA	295	NA
March	955	729	60	166	166	NA	189	NA	273	NA	327	NA
April	1,016	778	57	181	189	NA	244	NA	286	NA	297	NA
May	1,052	758	63	231	224	NA	240	NA	302	NA	286	NA
June	958	749	68	141	176	NA	213	NA	285	NA	284	NA
July	999	732	77	190	219	NA	224	NA	268	NA	288	NA
August	994	732	65	197	208	NA	230	NA	270	NA	286	NA
September	984	704	63	217	205	NA	220	NA	264	NA	295	NA
October	972	711	58	203	196	NA	232	NA	263	NA	281	NA
November	979	707	71	201	205	NA	223	NA	274	NA	277	NA
December	951	688	65	198	169	NA	238	NA	280	NA	264	NA

NA = Not available.

Source: U.S. Census Bureau, Building Permits Survey

Table 2-13. New Privately Owned Housing Units, Authorized, Unadjusted Data for the United States, Valuation, 2000–2011

[Dollars in millions, except as noted.]

Characteristics	Total housing units	1 unit	2 units	3 and 4 units	5 units or more
Annual data					
20,000-place series					
2011	105,268.5	86,326.8	1,197.4	1,069.2	16,675.1
2010	101,943.1	87,124.2	1,124.4	1,206.5	12,487.9
2009	95,410.3	82,357.3	1,098.0	1,006.0	10,949.0
2008	141,623.5	110,687.4	1,818.2	1,715.5	27,402.4
2007	225,236.6	183,679.2	2,867.8	3,012.7	35,677.0
2006	291,314.5	245,687.0	3,493.8	3,986.4	38,147.3
2005	329,254.5	284,452.3	3,828.2	4,039.6	36,934.4
2004	292,413.7	255,511.3	3,921.9	4,029.3	28,951.2
19,000-place series					
2003	249,693.1	218,228.6	3,805.5	3,316.4	24,342.6
2002	219,188.7	190,433.1	3,116.8	2,837.1	22,801.6
2001	196,247.6	170,010.8	2,546.6	2,563.4	21,123.1
2000	185,743.7	160,623.5	2,376.2	2,497.2	20,246.7
Year to date, April 2012	38,663.6	31,367.1	338.2	338.3	6,620.0
Year to date, April 2011	30,796.2	26,302.8	323.6	283.6	3,886.2
Percent change, 2011 to 2012	26%	19%	5%	19%	70%
Percent change, 2010 to 2011	3%	-1%	6%	-11%	34%
Monthly data					
20,000-place series					
2012					
January	7,548.5	6,200.7	72.6	57.8	1,217.4
February	8,719.2	7,195.4	77.1	98.9	1,347.9
March	11,105.7	8,689.6	84.7	110.4	2,220.9
April	10,943.8	9,277.9	106.5	72.6	1,486.9
2011					
January	6,417.3	5,536.2	69.5	94.5	717.2
February	6,378.2	5,417.8	66.6	46.6	847.1
March	9,194.5	7,728.1	109.8	56.1	1,300.6
April	8,806.2	7,620.7	77.7	86.5	1,021.3
May	9,601.0	8,032.8	103.9	74.5	1,389.8
June	10,344.5	8,562.4	108.7	94.2	1,579.2
July	8,699.6	7,372.2	103.3	89.4	1,134.7
August	10,400.7	8,373.4	122.9	160.4	1,744.0
September	9,076.5	7,483.4	82.5	85.6	1,425.0
October	8,508.1	7,107.1	82.0	97.4	1,221.7
November	8,643.7	6,575.5	104.3	76.7	1,887.2
December	7,980.8	6,002.5	80.7	117.2	1,780.4
2010					
January	6,596.8	5,932.8	66.5	66.1	531.4
February	7,379.4	6,537.7	71.6	72.6	697.4
March	10,735.6	9,472.8	97.3	107.4	1,058.1
April	9,796.0	8,591.0	80.8	116.0	1,008.1
May	8,825.3	7,685.3	89.8	86.9	963.3
June	9,908.8	8,307.5	105.1	136.4	1,359.9
July	8,492.0	7,368.5	86.1	97.2	940.2
August	8,636.0	7,319.7	91.1	123.6	1101.6
September	8,250.2	6,897.0	91.6	131.6	1130.0
October	7,422.7	6,389.9	93.5	88.8	850.5
November	7,122.2	6,056.0	81.2	83.8	901.2
December	7,941.3	6,259.1	89.0	103.6	1,489.7
2009					
January	5,425.7	4,187.1	68.4	69.1	1,101.0
February	5,961.9	4,739.0	62.6	56.8	1,103.5
March	7,282.3	5,977.2	86.3	220.8	998.0
April	7,884.3	6,901.6	101.6	85.0	796.1
May	8,136.1	7,145.0	78.5	104.2	808.5
June	9,734.5	8,646.2	91.4	115.6	881.3
July	9,259.8	8,468.4	72.3	89.5	629.5
August	9,006.8	7,842.1	95.5	71.6	997.7
September	8,916.4	7,776.3	100.5	82.1	957.5
October	8,109.4	7,270.5	90.5	56.2	692.2
November	7,028.0	6,156.3	94.8	103.4	673.5
December	7,780.8	6,537.7	73.1	86.1	1,083.9

Table 2-13. New Privately Owned Housing Units, Authorized, Unadjusted Data for the United States, Valuation, 2000–2011—*Continued*

[Dollars in millions, except as noted.]

Characteristics	Total housing units	1 unit	2 units	3 and 4 units	5 units or more
2008					
January	11,957.3	9,127.8	148.0	111.3	2,570.3
February	11,613.0	9,088.1	155.3	126.8	2,242.8
March	12,668.7	10,332.1	173.3	170.5	1,992.8
April	14,927.7	12,057.0	194.1	169.7	2,506.9
May	14,561.3	11,691.1	127.9	153.7	2,588.6
June	15,646.5	11,380.6	167.7	148.7	3,949.5
July	13,128.1	10,535.7	152.2	140.8	2,299.4
August	11,613.7	9,228.6	140.6	132.6	2,111.9
September	11,206.0	8,606.8	160.0	193.6	2,245.6
October	9,765.1	7,840.8	128.9	123.2	1,672.1
November	6,389.2	5,029.8	69.0	89.1	1,201.3
December	6,155.9	4,693.6	85.2	65.4	1,311.7
2007					
January	17,793.8	14,542.1	213.6	294.9	2,743.1
February	17,293.1	14,309.2	204.0	249.9	2,530.0
March	21,989.5	18,519.3	310.8	298.3	2,861.2
April	21,346.8	18,152.0	264.5	245.3	2,685.0
May	23,341.6	19,601.8	296.0	282.2	3,161.6
June	21,744.3	18,110.2	247.7	244.8	3,141.7
July	20,064.2	16,978.9	240.2	273.1	2,572.0
August	20,140.4	16,358.0	241.1	301.4	3,240.0
September	16,261.5	12,705.2	181.0	179.3	3,196.0
October	17,005.4	13,593.0	198.8	192.5	3,021.1
November	13,710.8	10,466.0	187.5	215.7	2,841.7
December	11,688.8	8,675.0	170.0	201.8	2,642.0
2006					
January	23,438.3	19,764.8	288.5	322.6	3,062.4
February	23,699.3	20,158.6	257.7	298.6	2,984.4
March	30,220.9	25,595.9	330.7	395.3	3,898.9
April	27,012.4	23,190.0	259.4	341.8	3,221.1
May	29,267.5	25,448.7	367.9	395.4	3,055.4
June	29,213.1	24,809.0	301.2	415.4	3,687.5
July	23,539.6	19,924.1	283.6	337.8	2,994.1
August	25,571.3	21,746.3	364.3	407.4	3,053.3
September	21,713.6	17,880.9	281.0	321.9	3,229.9
October	21,222.0	17,766.6	299.0	302.4	2,854.0
November	18,078.5	15,300.5	220.2	249.1	2,308.7
December	17,423.9	13,987.9	211.1	282.1	2,942.8
2005					
January	20,416.8	17,498.5	216.0	219.8	2,482.5
February	22,158.4	19,065.4	281.7	275.4	2,535.8
March	28,600.3	24,918.6	321.5	365.8	2,994.4
April	29,081.8	25,551.0	314.7	307.4	2,908.7
May	29,595.4	26,087.4	351.6	352.3	2,804.1
June	32,303.1	28,099.6	366.5	417.0	3,420.0
July	28,350.1	24,554.8	343.7	339.4	3,112.3
August	31,370.8	27,296.5	366.9	396.9	3,310.6
September	30,299.6	26,248.1	375.4	357.8	3,318.3
October	27,545.5	23,992.6	330.8	332.1	2,889.9
November	25,131.4	21,554.4	273.9	312.7	2,990.4
December	23,725.9	19,645.6	274.3	304.6	3,501.5
2004					
January	18,112.7	15,791.0	257.8	238.8	1,825.2
February	19,061.2	16,635.3	257.4	242.2	1,926.4
March	26,627.3	23,804.7	378.0	379.7	2,064.9
April	27,312.5	24,287.6	375.1	404.5	2,245.4
May	26,317.0	23,402.3	361.6	318.8	2,234.3
June	28,176.8	25,019.5	385.7	417.2	2,354.4
July	26,543.2	23,150.4	379.5	425.9	2,587.5
August	26,410.0	23,354.4	372.3	310.2	2,373.1
September	24,477.0	21,504.3	320.6	309.0	2,343.1
October	24,408.2	20,826.6	357.2	337.3	2,887.1
November	22,302.6	18,845.3	372.0	323.7	2,761.6
December	22,070.7	18,609.7	279.9	350.5	2,830.5

Table 2-13. New Privately Owned Housing Units, Authorized, Unadjusted Data for the United States, Valuation, 2000–2011—*Continued*

[Dollars in millions, except as noted.]

Characteristics	Total housing units	1 unit	2 units	3 and 4 units	5 units or more
19,000-place series					
2003					
January	16,272.6	14,285.5	208.3	241.8	1,537.1
February	15,933.6	13,534.7	206.3	210.3	1,982.2
March	19,240.7	17,078.3	246.4	237.8	1,678.2
April	21,893.7	19,579.6	346.5	314.7	1,652.8
May	21,974.7	19,287.3	345.2	293.6	2,048.7
June	22,850.0	20,197.5	341.6	322.2	1,988.8
July	22,860.5	20,343.8	296.0	259.7	1,961.0
August	22,367.8	19,545.5	324.7	295.5	2,202.0
September	22,244.2	19,497.7	371.8	333.9	2,040.8
October	24,215.9	20,890.4	371.8	317.7	2,636.0
November	17,505.5	15,146.6	316.5	269.2	1,773.2
December	19,701.2	16,960.1	258.6	253.9	2,228.6
2002					
January	14,064.4	12,240.6	196.8	166.6	1,460.4
February	14,966.5	13,129.5	167.6	175.5	1,494.0
March	17,545.0	15,498.1	233.8	224.1	1,589.0
April	19,760.0	17,667.5	294.5	212.4	1,585.5
May	20,539.9	18,044.6	297.8	219.1	1,978.4
June	19,469.0	16,780.0	261.6	322.8	2,104.7
July	19,878.1	17,360.7	248.7	228.5	2,040.2
August	19,243.7	16,967.5	284.2	262.2	1,729.8
September	18,380.4	15,593.8	314.8	302.5	2,169.3
October	20,494.9	17,707.3	300.4	261.0	2,226.2
November	16,148.0	14,043.0	236.1	176.4	1,692.4
December	16,219.2	13,662.5	207.7	217.4	2,131.6
2001					
January	13,759.0	11,750.2	134.1	125.8	1,748.9
February	13,384.9	11,536.1	171.7	174.1	1,502.9
March	17,326.0	15,198.4	201.4	220.1	1,706.0
April	17,949.1	15,844.6	234.0	221.6	1,648.9
May	19,314.1	16,953.7	252.5	273.8	1,834.1
June	18,384.1	16,222.8	259.8	277.5	1,623.9
July	17,079.4	15,071.3	228.4	208.5	1,571.2
August	17,977.5	15,803.3	254.7	262.0	1,657.6
September	14,708.7	12,625.7	205.0	187.4	1,690.6
October	16,475.4	14,133.4	257.1	238.2	1,846.7
November	14,338.4	12,102.2	209.4	196.4	1,830.4
December	13,107.9	10,981.1	181.4	226.0	1,715.9
2000					
January	11,371.6	9,744.8	117.8	138.9	1,370.1
February	12,664.1	10,894.2	172.7	153.0	1,444.1
March	16,686.7	14,909.5	186.9	204.3	1,386.1
April	15,565.3	13,664.0	177.9	176.6	1,547.9
May	16,799.1	15,097.5	182.1	208.1	1,311.3
June	17,330.4	14,887.6	222.6	213.8	2,006.4
July	14,831.8	12,806.9	164.8	160.1	1,700.0
August	16,486.1	14,374.5	223.8	252.1	1,635.7
September	14,808.4	12,678.4	171.7	228.9	1,729.4
October	15,560.6	13,543.2	238.2	249.9	1,529.3
November	13,977.0	11,720.0	183.8	209.4	1,863.8
December	11,690.3	9,931.9	137.0	138.0	1,483.4

Source: U.S. Census Bureau, Building Permits Survey

Table 2-14. New Privately Owned Housing Units, Authorized, Unadjusted Data for the Northeast and Midwest Regions, Valuation, 1991–2011

[Dollars in millions, except as noted.]

Characteristics	Northeast			Midwest		
	Total housing units	1 unit	2 units or more	Total housing units	1 unit	2 units or more
Annual data						
20,000-place series						
2011	11,603.3	8,712.2	2,891.1	16,845.4	14,169.5	2,676.0
2010	12,543.0	10,129.0	2,413.9	16,921.3	14,361.9	2,559.4
2009	11,768.0	9,299.2	2,468.8	15,918.6	13,823.7	2,094.9
2008	17,955.0	12,163.3	5,791.7	21,774.2	17,917.2	3,857.0
2007	23,245.4	16,961.4	6,284.0	34,108.9	29,173.3	4,935.6
2006	25,905.9	19,839.8	6,066.2	44,112.5	38,163.5	5,949.0
2005	29,388.3	23,122.2	6,266.0	54,681.7	48,328.4	6,353.3
2004	27,317.7	22,049.8	5,267.9	54,031.7	48,203.9	5,827.8
19,000-place series						
2003	23,852.4	19,391.2	4,461.2	50,571.1	44,419.2	6,151.9
2002	22,187.1	18,671.2	3,515.9	45,169.0	38,747.3	6,421.7
2001	19,638.6	16,615.3	3,023.2	40,952.7	35,845.3	5,107.4
2000	19,425.5	16,432.4	2,993.0	38,162.0	33,530.4	4,631.6
1999	18,386.1	16,092.5	2,293.6	38,993.4	34,117.7	4,875.7
1998	16,712.6	14,745.0	1,967.6	34,844.7	30,563.1	4,281.6
1997	14,137.2	12,566.2	1,571.0	30,261.9	26,150.5	4,111.4
1996	13,210.7	11,827.3	1,383.4	30,837.5	26,974.5	3,863.0
1995	12,005.6	11,003.4	1,002.1	27,538.6	24,147.4	3,391.2
1994	13,193.8	12,260.0	933.8	28,157.1	25,063.9	3,093.3
17,000-place series						
1994	12,844.3	11,935.5	908.8	27,648.8	24,598.2	3,050.6
1993	12,202.0	11,260.0	942.0	25,031.8	22,594.4	2,437.5
1992	11,215.9	10,442.4	773.4	22,385.8	20,213.6	2,172.2
1991	9,327.2	8,421.9	905.3	17,622.9	15,822.6	1,800.3
Year to date, April 2012	3,644.1	2,665.3	978.8	5,473.2	4,646.5	826.7
Year to date, April 2011	3,207.5	2,504.0	703.5	4,315.6	3,773.1	542.5
Percent change, 2011 to 2012	14%	6%	39%	27%	23%	52%
Percent change, 2010 to 2011	-7%	-14%	20%	0%	-1%	5%
Monthly data						
20,000-place series						
2012						
January	668.9	484.3	184.6	840.2	702.2	138.0
February	801.4	546.3	255.1	1,035.8	877.7	158.1
March	947.3	760.1	187.2	1,767.7	1,451.3	316.4
April	1,224.0	849.5	374.5	1,872.5	1,625.5	247.0
2011						
January	876.6	690.4	186.2	678.1	551.6	126.5
February	603.6	451.6	152.0	748.7	664.9	83.8
March	897.7	672.9	224.9	1,333.0	1,184.7	148.3
April	829.6	689.1	140.5	1,555.8	1,371.8	183.9
May	1,068.4	768.6	299.8	1,663.1	1,463.2	199.8
June	1,180.4	813.6	366.8	1,736.1	1,486.4	249.7
July	893.0	737.6	155.3	1,455.9	1,260.8	195.1
August	983.9	749.8	234.0	1,801.1	1,553.6	247.6
September	977.6	792.6	185.0	1,722.6	1,365.4	357.1
October	934.2	739.2	194.9	1,557.1	1,316.8	240.2
November	1,098.8	752.3	346.5	1,389.8	1,086.8	303.0
December	868.7	577.3	291.4	1,049.6	862.4	187.3
2010						
January	719.3	598.3	121.0	713.2	651.1	62.1
February	788.1	666.3	121.8	933.9	846.8	87.1
March	984.7	854.4	130.3	1,590.0	1,437.0	153.1
April	1,094.5	846.7	247.7	1,779.9	1,570.6	209.3
May	1,020.9	879.2	141.7	1,752.5	1,379.9	372.6
June	1,326.7	953.2	373.6	1,708.5	1,498.2	210.3
July	1,019.8	818.4	201.4	1,447.3	1,261.5	185.8
August	1,042.7	856.6	186.1	1,500.1	1,283.5	216.5
September	1,106.9	836.4	270.6	1,440.5	1,219.6	220.9
October	1,016.9	829.7	187.3	1,561.4	1,291.5	269.9
November	987.5	842.3	145.2	1,259.0	1,139.4	119.6
December	1,465.6	1,065.3	400.3	943.4	746.4	196.9

Table 2-14. New Privately Owned Housing Units, Authorized, Unadjusted Data for the Northeast and Midwest Regions, Valuation, 1991–2011—*Continued*

[Dollars in millions, except as noted.]

Characteristics	Northeast			Midwest		
	Total housing units	1 unit	2 units or more	Total housing units	1 unit	2 units or more
2009						
January	557.8	457.7	100.1	595.7	445.6	150.1
February	707.7	409.9	297.8	683.7	616.7	67.1
March	870.3	591.4	278.9	1,062.8	876.6	186.2
April	856.3	692.1	164.2	1,301.4	1,198.8	102.5
May	978.7	771.5	207.2	1,465.2	1,375.4	89.8
June	1,059.7	862.8	196.9	1,683.7	1,508.4	175.3
July	1,026.0	905.9	120.0	1,696.5	1,508.3	188.2
August	1,031.0	840.8	190.2	1,542.2	1,407.5	134.7
September	1,080.2	903.7	176.5	1,710.2	1,390.6	319.7
October	1,050.1	935.4	114.7	1,582.9	1,378.2	204.7
November	961.6	776.1	185.5	1,313.8	1,102.3	211.6
December	1,154.3	770.3	384.0	1,085.7	858.2	227.5
2008						
January	1,332.9	920.5	412.4	1,470.1	1,116.3	353.8
February	1,064.0	803.1	260.9	1,327.4	1,055.1	272.3
March	1,343.6	961.9	381.7	1,647.9	1,464.7	183.2
April	1,657.2	1,158.9	498.2	2,650.4	2,149.7	500.6
May	1,853.5	1,216.3	637.2	2,457.9	2,102.4	355.5
June	3,067.5	1,121.2	1,946.3	2,208.5	1,925.8	282.7
July	1,529.8	1,128.5	401.3	2,215.2	1,889.2	326.0
August	1,315.8	1,122.0	193.9	1,955.5	1,597.4	358.1
September	1,484.3	1,052.9	431.4	1,963.0	1,630.8	332.2
October	1,176.7	947.3	229.4	1,907.6	1,541.1	366.5
November	859.7	642.2	217.5	1,114.6	961.8	152.8
December	720.1	542.0	178.0	887.3	648.5	238.8
2007						
January	1,751.5	1,176.6	574.9	2,296.7	1,793.9	502.8
February	1,187.3	875.6	311.7	1,940.2	1,627.7	312.5
March	1,898.1	1,416.6	481.5	3,261.9	2,854.3	407.6
April	2,193.8	1,594.8	598.9	3,500.4	3,112.6	387.9
May	2,209.4	1,770.8	438.6	3,915.6	3,479.6	435.9
June	2,306.5	1,635.5	671.0	3,502.0	3,106.8	395.2
July	2,265.8	1,665.5	600.3	3,255.9	2,801.6	454.3
August	2,281.0	1,669.5	600.9	3,163.5	2,813.8	349.9
September	1,804.7	1,355.1	460.5	2,718.3	2,287.1	409.3
October	2,211.1	1,557.4	653.7	2,950.9	2,552.0	398.9
November	1,534.6	1,136.1	398.5	2,345.0	1,949.5	395.4
December	1,486.5	979.4	507.1	1,538.7	1,224.4	314.3
2006						
January	1,850.4	1,431.4	418.9	2,973.4	2,569.0	404.4
February	1,681.7	1,272.3	409.3	3,291.0	2,777.2	513.7
March	2,526.1	1,917.4	608.8	4,498.9	4,047.2	451.7
April	2,397.4	1,841.1	556.4	4,238.7	3,885.3	353.4
May	2,460.4	1,971.4	488.9	4,867.6	4,334.8	532.8
June	2,582.0	2,019.9	562.1	4,580.4	3,982.2	598.2
July	2,183.7	1,692.4	491.3	3,926.3	3,383.7	542.6
August	2,336.9	1,810.6	526.3	4,245.0	3,579.0	666.0
September	2,133.5	1,539.1	594.4	3,616.7	3,103.3	513.3
October	2,147.4	1,746.5	400.9	3,638.6	3,214.1	424.6
November	1,807.6	1,368.5	439.0	2,908.9	2,498.0	411.0
December	1,785.4	1,246.9	538.5	2,360.3	1,926.1	434.3
2005						
January	1,701.4	1,318.5	382.8	2,578.2	2,309.3	268.9
February	1,587.9	1,185.0	402.8	3,258.0	2,902.9	355.1
March	2,087.0	1,677.0	409.9	4,631.1	4,213.8	417.3
April	2,428.1	1,918.0	510.1	5,468.5	4,867.0	601.4
May	2,887.0	2,248.9	638.1	5,404.5	4,863.1	541.3
June	3,067.3	2,325.9	741.4	5,544.0	5,015.9	528.0
July	2,633.8	2,166.2	467.5	5,071.8	4,499.7	572.1
August	2,828.7	2,293.0	535.7	5,450.0	4,808.8	641.2
September	2,711.8	2,259.2	452.6	4,986.7	4,489.1	497.6
October	2,521.2	2,073.6	447.6	5,154.8	4,565.7	589.0
November	2,391.9	1,827.6	564.3	4,666.4	3,936.1	730.4
December	2,036.7	1,508.3	528.3	3,284.7	2,820.8	463.9

Table 2-14. New Privately Owned Housing Units, Authorized, Unadjusted Data for the Northeast and Midwest Regions, Valuation, 1991–2011—*Continued*

[Dollars in millions, except as noted.]

Characteristics	Northeast			Midwest		
	Total housing units	1 unit	2 units or more	Total housing units	1 unit	2 units or more
2004						
January	1,403.8	1,157.3	246.4	2,681.4	2,371.7	309.7
February	1,410.3	1,155.8	254.5	3,047.5	2,779.9	267.6
March	2,382.2	1,999.5	382.7	4,903.7	4,427.9	475.8
April	2,578.5	2,230.1	348.4	5,508.1	5,024.1	484.0
May	2,559.9	2,096.4	463.5	5,033.4	4,641.5	391.9
June	2,816.1	2,280.3	535.8	5,372.1	4,920.4	451.7
July	2,613.6	2,014.4	599.2	5,017.4	4,559.0	458.5
August	2,358.9	1,916.2	442.7	5,348.7	4,751.0	597.8
September	2,355.2	1,838.4	516.8	5,050.0	4,424.4	625.6
October	2,177.2	1,767.8	409.4	4,979.4	4,348.9	630.4
November	2,215.9	1,698.4	517.4	4,269.9	3,723.4	546.6
December	1,997.2	1,542.9	454.3	3,852.8	3,274.7	578.2
19,000-place series						
2003						
January	1,293.0	1,079.8	213.3	2,502.6	2,179.2	323.4
February	1,166.6	892.2	274.4	2,481.1	2,176.0	305.1
March	1,620.2	1,356.0	264.3	3,698.8	3,364.8	334.0
April	2,003.5	1,663.5	339.9	4,700.7	4,199.7	501.0
May	2,146.9	1,735.7	411.2	4,537.1	4,108.1	429.0
June	2,138.9	1,769.8	369.1	4,834.2	4,250.9	583.2
July	2,185.0	1,852.0	333.0	4,867.1	4,356.9	510.2
August	2,180.1	1,681.9	498.3	4,688.3	4,098.8	589.5
September	2,097.7	1,783.1	314.6	4,917.1	4,258.7	658.4
October	2,507.6	1,915.6	592.0	5,144.8	4,584.5	560.3
November	1,796.2	1,441.2	355.0	3,748.0	3,176.1	571.9
December	1,852.9	1,411.5	441.4	3,486.4	2,914.7	571.8
2002						
January	1,284.9	1,087.5	197.4	2,374.4	2,034.4	340.1
February	1,348.7	1,092.2	256.5	2,587.6	2,234.3	353.3
March	1,518.7	1,331.4	187.3	3,411.5	3,038.2	373.3
April	1,990.5	1,734.2	256.3	4,295.1	3,859.6	435.5
May	2,221.0	1,802.4	418.6	4,404.8	3,898.4	506.5
June	2,000.1	1,658.7	341.5	3,973.3	3,507.7	465.6
July	2,131.7	1,749.8	381.9	4,156.4	3,576.7	579.7
August	1,935.2	1,606.9	328.3	3,946.6	3,424.4	522.2
September	1,893.1	1,621.9	271.2	3,994.6	3,358.4	636.1
October	2,090.1	1,773.6	316.5	4,395.1	3,790.0	605.1
November	1,632.8	1,400.6	232.2	3,276.7	2,908.3	368.4
December	1,593.0	1,334.6	258.3	3,155.5	2,577.7	577.8
2001						
January	1,137.8	968.1	169.7	2,161.3	1,873.1	288.2
February	1,172.0	905.2	266.7	2,290.0	1,990.3	299.7
March	1,518.9	1,263.5	255.4	3,523.7	3,161.5	362.3
April	1,679.9	1,416.7	263.2	3,864.4	3,455.1	409.3
May	1,904.6	1,662.3	242.3	4,180.1	3,748.6	431.4
June	1,811.5	1,562.6	248.8	4,018.2	3,589.8	428.4
July	1,785.7	1,516.7	269.0	3,724.8	3,308.7	416.1
August	1,887.9	1,632.3	255.6	3,780.9	3,375.6	405.3
September	1,526.3	1,330.7	195.6	3,142.6	2,700.4	442.3
October	1,788.5	1,519.3	269.1	3,613.5	3,126.5	486.9
November	1,561.5	1,265.1	296.3	3,206.2	2,667.1	539.2
December	1,363.2	1,157.0	206.2	2,488.6	2,055.6	433.0
2000						
January	1,126.3	877.6	248.7	1,905.9	1,677.3	228.6
February	1,048.4	889.6	158.7	2,329.9	2,026.0	303.9
March	1,620.0	1,430.0	190.0	3,645.5	3,233.2	412.3
April	1,634.6	1,392.7	241.8	3,705.8	3,305.3	400.5
May	1,737.4	1,543.4	194.0	3,788.8	3,382.5	406.3
June	1,788.3	1,536.3	252.0	3,592.7	3,187.3	405.4
July	1,601.7	1,359.4	242.3	3,210.6	2,790.9	419.8
August	1,642.0	1,439.1	202.9	3,534.6	3,108.4	426.2
September	1,606.7	1,345.3	261.4	3,175.1	2,765.0	410.2
October	1,636.4	1,450.9	185.5	3,542.8	3,015.5	527.4
November	1,548.8	1,248.7	300.1	2,813.9	2,433.7	380.2
December	1,196.2	1,039.2	157.1	1,748.5	1,499.1	249.4

Source: U.S. Census Bureau, Building Permits Survey

Table 2-15. New Privately Owned Housing Units, Authorized, Unadjusted Data for the South and West Regions, Valuation, 1991–2011

[Millions of dollars, except as noted.]

Characteristics	South			West		
	Total housing units	1 unit	2 units or more	Total housing units	1 unit	2 units or more
Annual data						
20,000-place series						
2011	50,769.1	43,549.8	7,219.3	26,050.7	19,895.4	6,155.3
2010	47,397.1	42,067.9	5,329.2	25,081.7	20,565.4	4,516.3
2009	45,085.5	39,830.9	5,254.5	22,638.2	19,403.4	3,234.8
2008	65,827.4	53,778.0	12,049.4	36,066.8	26,828.9	9,238.0
2007	104,665.1	87,930.4	16,734.7	63,217.2	49,614.1	13,603.1
2006	140,059.7	119,898.6	20,161.1	81,236.3	67,785.1	13,451.2
2005	148,595.9	128,004.0	20,591.8	96,588.6	84,997.6	11,591.0
2004	124,514.7	108,655.1	15,859.5	86,549.6	76,602.4	9,947.1
19,000-place series						
2003	102,312.8	90,063.8	12,249.0	72,956.8	64,354.4	8,602.4
2002	89,336.9	78,021.3	11,315.6	62,495.7	54,993.3	7,502.4
2001	79,447.4	69,077.8	10,369.6	56,209.0	48,472.4	7,736.6
2000	74,287.3	64,186.5	10,100.8	53,869.0	46,474.2	7,394.8
1999	73,074.3	62,698.2	10,376.1	50,791.9	44,215.0	6,576.9
1998	66,779.8	56,831.8	9,948.0	46,928.7	40,100.8	6,827.9
1997	55,879.7	47,745.4	8,134.3	40,725.5	34,732.4	5,993.1
1996	53,078.9	46,007.7	7,071.2	37,048.7	31,725.6	5,323.1
1995	47,518.2	40,830.6	6,687.6	33,748.3	28,757.2	4,991.2
1994	47,327.5	41,888.9	5,438.6	34,599.9	30,081.2	4,518.7
17,000-place series						
1994	45,541.6	40,210.3	5,331.4	34,395.0	29,888.0	4,507.0
1993	40,808.0	37,484.2	3,323.8	28,759.1	25,780.0	2,979.0
1992	35,098.0	32,696.7	2,401.3	26,839.3	23,718.7	3,120.6
1991	27,534.7	25,174.2	2,360.5	24,287.3	20,304.1	3,983.2
Year to date, April 2012	19,630.8	16,422.9	3,207.9	9,915.4	7,632.3	2,283.1
Year to date, April 2011	15,541.4	13,748.0	1,793.5	7,731.6	6,277.7	1,453.9
Percent change, 2011 to 2012	2631%	1946%	7887%	2825%	2158%	5703%
Percent change, 2010 to 2011	711%	352%	3547%	386%	-326%	3629%
Monthly data						
19,000-place series						
2012						
January	4,340.7	3,546.1	794.7	1,698.6	1,468.2	230.5
February	4,755.1	4,128.5	626.6	2,126.9	1,642.9	484.1
March	5,246.7	4,353.3	893.4	3,144.0	2,125.0	1,019.0
April	5,031.7	4,432.6	599.1	2,815.7	2,370.3	445.4
2011						
January	3,288.6	2,908.3	380.3	1,574.0	1,385.9	188.2
February	3,497.9	3,043.3	454.6	1,528.1	1,258.0	270.1
March	4,628.2	4,086.3	541.9	2,335.5	1,784.2	551.3
April	4,126.8	3,710.1	416.7	2,294.0	1,849.7	444.3
May	4,307.1	3,847.9	459.2	2,562.5	1,953.1	609.4
June	4,731.6	4,133.6	598.0	2,696.4	2,128.8	567.6
July	4,260.7	3,612.5	648.2	2,090.0	1,761.3	328.7
August	4,766.6	4,045.2	721.3	2,849.1	2,024.8	824.3
September	4,090.4	3,551.1	539.2	2,286.0	1,774.2	511.8
October	3,997.9	3,455.1	542.7	2,019.1	1,596.0	423.1
November	4,068.2	3,232.9	835.3	2,087.0	1,503.5	583.4
December	3,987.6	3,122.1	865.5	2,074.9	1,440.7	634.2
2010						
January	3,443.6	3,202.5	241.1	1,720.7	1,481.0	239.7
February	3,665.4	3,384.4	281.0	1,992.0	1,640.1	351.8
March	5,513.5	4,959.2	554.4	2,647.3	2,222.2	425.1
April	4,518.4	4,114.4	403.9	2,403.2	2,059.2	344.0
May	3,973.2	3,605.1	368.1	2,078.7	1,821.0	257.7
June	4,383.9	3,748.6	635.2	2,489.8	2,107.5	382.3
July	3,954.2	3,499.6	454.6	2,070.7	1,788.9	281.8
August	3,936.3	3,471.9	464.4	2,156.9	1,707.6	449.2
September	3,665.9	3,157.6	508.4	2,036.8	1,683.4	353.3
October	3,090.9	2,782.9	308.0	1,753.4	1,485.8	267.6
November	3,196.7	2,776.6	420.1	1,679.0	1,297.7	381.3
December	3,113.7	2,769.5	344.2	2,418.6	1,677.8	740.8

Table 2-15. New Privately Owned Housing Units, Authorized, Unadjusted Data for the South and West Regions, Valuation, 1991–2011—*Continued*

[Millions of dollars, except as noted.]

Characteristics	South			West		
	Total housing units	1 unit	2 units or more	Total housing units	1 unit	2 units or more
2009						
January	2,865.0	2,333.8	531.2	1,407.1	950.0	457.1
February	3,205.0	2,708.3	496.7	1,365.4	1,004.1	361.3
March	3,561.6	3,145.2	416.4	1,787.6	1,363.9	423.7
April	3,694.5	3,288.8	405.7	2,032.1	1,721.9	310.2
May	3,733.0	3,252.3	480.6	1,959.3	1,745.8	213.5
June	4,598.0	4,100.8	497.2	2,393.2	2,174.2	219.0
July	4,274.2	4,031.9	242.3	2,263.1	2,022.2	240.9
August	4,364.4	3,736.0	628.4	2,069.3	1,857.8	211.5
September	3,956.2	3,587.6	368.6	2,169.8	1,894.4	275.4
October	3,551.4	3,283.0	268.4	1,925.0	1,673.8	251.2
November	3,255.3	2,918.8	336.6	1,497.2	1,359.2	138.1
December	3,638.5	3,228.6	410.0	1,902.3	1,680.7	221.6
2008						
January	6,506.0	5,023.3	1,482.7	2,648.4	2,067.8	580.6
February	6,056.6	5,048.4	1,008.2	3,165.1	2,181.6	983.5
March	6,501.2	5,380.6	1,120.6	3,176.0	2,524.8	651.2
April	6,818.8	5,738.6	1,080.2	3,801.3	3,009.7	791.6
May	6,241.2	5,441.2	800.0	4,008.8	2,931.2	1,077.5
June	6,369.8	5,274.3	1,095.5	4,000.8	3,059.3	941.5
July	6,095.1	4,913.2	1,181.9	3,288.0	2,604.8	683.2
August	5,414.0	4,325.5	1,088.6	2,928.4	2,183.7	744.7
September	4,874.1	3,843.2	1,030.9	2,884.5	2,079.8	804.8
October	4,314.5	3,538.7	775.8	2,366.3	1,813.7	552.6
November	2,713.7	2,269.7	444.0	1,701.2	1,156.1	545.1
December	2,882.6	2,341.4	541.1	1,666.0	1,161.6	504.4
2007						
January	8,821.4	7,489.2	1,332.2	4,924.2	4,082.5	841.8
February	9,048.0	7,645.4	1,402.5	5,117.7	4,160.6	957.1
March	10,469.0	8,939.1	1,529.9	6,360.5	5,309.2	1,051.3
April	9,654.6	8,345.5	1,309.1	5,997.9	5,099.1	898.8
May	10,786.2	8,904.5	1,881.8	6,430.4	5,447.0	983.5
June	9,680.4	8,196.3	1,484.1	6,255.5	5,171.6	1,083.9
July	9,153.0	7,845.5	1,307.5	5,389.5	4,666.3	723.2
August	8,838.4	7,484.3	1,370.7	5,857.5	4,390.3	1,285.7
September	7,050.8	5,895.1	1,114.5	4,687.7	3,167.9	1,551.8
October	7,229.5	6,133.1	1,096.4	4,613.9	3,350.6	1,263.3
November	6,226.2	4,968.8	1,257.4	3,605.1	2,411.5	1,193.5
December	5,676.1	4,385.2	1,290.9	2,987.5	2,085.9	901.5
2006						
January	11,832.0	10,160.2	1,671.8	6,782.5	5,604.2	1,178.4
February	11,826.7	10,349.7	1,477.0	6,900.0	5,759.3	1,140.7
March	14,901.3	12,675.5	2,225.9	8,294.5	6,955.9	1,338.6
April	12,731.6	10,842.9	1,888.7	7,644.7	6,620.7	1,024.0
May	13,501.6	11,860.0	1,641.5	8,438.0	7,282.4	1,155.6
June	13,288.9	11,477.5	1,811.4	8,761.8	7,329.3	1,432.4
July	11,219.5	9,465.4	1,754.0	6,210.1	5,382.6	827.5
August	11,947.0	10,385.5	1,561.5	7,042.4	5,971.1	1,071.3
September	9,831.2	8,387.5	1,443.7	6,132.2	4,850.9	1,281.3
October	10,012.7	8,466.4	1,546.2	5,423.3	4,339.6	1,083.7
November	8,564.7	7,504.7	1,060.0	4,797.3	3,929.3	868.0
December	8,626.5	7,175.3	1,451.2	4,651.7	3,639.8	1,011.9
2005						
January	10,143.8	8,675.4	1,468.3	5,993.4	5,195.2	798.2
February	10,661.5	9,184.1	1,477.4	6,651.0	5,793.4	857.6
March	13,266.2	11,305.0	1,961.2	8,616.1	7,722.8	893.3
April	12,736.2	11,245.2	1,491.0	8,449.0	7,520.8	928.2
May	12,696.7	11,098.6	1,598.1	8,607.3	7,876.7	730.5
June	13,984.4	12,120.8	1,863.6	9,707.4	8,637.0	1,070.4
July	12,304.6	10,554.4	1,750.2	8,340.0	7,334.5	1,005.5
August	13,983.8	12,124.8	1,858.9	9,108.3	8,069.9	1,038.4
September	13,121.4	11,312.1	1,809.2	9,479.7	8,187.6	1,292.0
October	12,227.6	10,494.3	1,733.4	7,641.8	6,859.0	782.9
November	11,114.6	9,905.4	1,209.3	6,958.5	5,885.5	1,073.0
December	11,763.5	9,486.0	2,277.5	6,641.0	5,830.4	810.7

Table 2-15. New Privately Owned Housing Units, Authorized, Unadjusted Data for the South and West Regions, Valuation, 1991–2011—*Continued*

[Millions of dollars, except as noted.]

Characteristics	South			West		
	Total housing units	1 unit	2 units or more	Total housing units	1 unit	2 units or more
2004						
January	8,591.5	7,409.1	1,182.5	5,436.1	4,852.9	583.2
February	8,949.7	7,723.6	1,226.1	5,653.7	4,976.0	677.7
March	11,368.0	10,305.6	1,062.4	7,973.4	7,071.8	901.7
April	11,314.1	9,886.3	1,427.8	7,911.9	7,147.1	764.8
May	10,934.7	9,561.6	1,373.0	7,789.1	7,102.8	686.3
June	11,361.5	10,309.3	1,052.2	8,627.1	7,509.5	1,117.6
July	11,077.8	9,636.6	1,441.2	7,834.5	6,940.4	894.0
August	11,124.6	9,818.4	1,306.2	7,577.8	6,868.8	709.0
September	9,637.2	8,660.0	977.2	7,434.6	6,581.5	853.1
October	10,410.9	8,772.8	1,638.1	6,840.8	5,937.1	903.7
November	9,261.4	7,863.8	1,397.7	6,555.4	5,559.7	995.7
December	9,578.9	8,183.2	1,395.7	6,641.7	5,608.9	1,032.8
17,000-place series						
2003						
January	7,145.2	6,277.1	868.1	5,331.9	4,749.5	582.4
February	7,068.8	6,082.8	986.0	5,217.1	4,383.7	833.4
March	8,176.0	7,214.7	961.3	5,745.7	5,142.8	602.9
April	8,808.8	7,989.2	819.6	6,380.7	5,727.2	653.5
May	8,789.4	7,812.0	977.4	6,501.3	5,631.5	869.8
June	9,235.3	8,280.5	954.8	6,641.7	5,896.2	745.4
July	9,138.6	8,134.7	1,004.0	6,669.8	6,000.3	669.5
August	9,184.0	8,141.6	1,042.5	6,315.3	5,623.3	692.0
September	8,737.6	7,698.6	1,039.0	6,491.7	5,757.3	734.5
October	9,485.1	8,304.2	1,180.9	7,078.4	6,086.1	992.4
November	6,959.1	6,108.6	850.5	5,002.2	4,420.7	581.5
December	8,388.7	7,289.5	1,099.3	5,973.1	5,344.5	628.7
2002						
January	6,639.3	5,839.6	799.7	3,765.7	3,279.1	486.7
February	7,053.6	6,228.9	824.6	3,976.7	3,574.1	402.6
March	7,537.7	6,570.0	967.7	5,077.0	4,558.5	518.5
April	7,854.3	7,037.9	816.4	5,620.1	5,035.8	584.3
May	7,972.6	7,016.4	956.2	5,941.5	5,327.5	614.0
June	7,835.8	6,643.4	1,192.4	5,659.8	4,970.2	689.6
July	8,027.4	6,976.1	1,051.3	5,562.7	5,058.1	504.6
August	7,842.1	6,973.4	868.7	5,519.8	4,962.7	557.1
September	7,103.7	6,112.5	991.3	5,389.0	4,501.1	888.0
October	7,745.1	6,693.5	1,051.6	6,264.7	5,450.2	814.4
November	6,383.5	5,644.1	739.4	4,855.0	4,090.0	764.9
December	6,833.3	5,763.0	1,070.2	4,637.5	3,987.1	650.4
2001						
January	6,053.3	5,249.3	804.0	4,406.7	3,659.8	746.9
February	5,931.9	5,186.5	745.4	3,991.0	3,454.1	536.9
March	7,293.6	6,344.8	948.8	4,989.8	4,428.7	561.1
April	7,148.6	6,390.5	758.1	5,256.2	4,582.4	673.8
May	7,676.5	6,673.3	1,003.2	5,552.9	4,869.4	683.5
June	7,214.0	6,431.8	782.2	5,340.5	4,638.6	701.9
July	6,800.9	5,980.9	820.0	4,768.0	4,265.0	503.0
August	7,090.3	6,332.6	757.6	5,218.5	4,462.8	755.6
September	5,784.9	4,963.5	821.4	4,254.9	3,631.1	623.8
October	6,499.4	5,649.9	849.5	4,574.0	3,837.6	736.4
November	5,962.1	5,058.4	903.7	3,608.6	3,111.6	497.0
December	5,473.9	4,669.0	804.9	3,782.3	3,099.6	682.7
2000						
January	5,036.6	4,412.6	624.0	3,302.9	2,777.4	525.5
February	5,704.4	4,984.5	719.8	3,581.5	2,994.0	587.5
March	6,833.9	6,229.5	604.4	4,587.4	4,016.8	570.6
April	5,795.4	5,058.2	737.1	4,429.6	3,907.7	521.8
May	6,535.1	5,848.0	687.2	4,737.7	4,323.7	414.0
June	6,674.1	5,768.2	906.0	5,275.3	4,395.9	879.4
July	5,726.7	5,009.2	717.6	4,292.8	3,647.5	645.3
August	6,317.9	5,618.0	699.9	4,991.6	4,209.0	782.6
September	5,694.5	4,798.8	895.7	4,332.0	3,769.3	562.7
October	5,872.2	5,174.3	697.9	4,509.2	3,902.5	606.6
November	5,646.0	4,634.9	1,011.2	3,968.3	3,402.8	565.5
December	4,901.2	4,178.8	722.4	3,844.4	3,214.8	629.6

Source: U.S. Census Bureau, Building Permits Survey

Table 2-16. Contract Rent: Renter-Occupied Housing Units, 2010 American Community Survey, 1-, 3-, and 5-Year Estimates

[Numbers in thousands.]

Characteristics	United States					
	1-year estimates		3-year estimates		5-year estimates	
	Estimate	Margin of error (+/-)	Estimate	Margin of error (+/-)	Estimate	Margin of error (+/-)
Total	39,694.0	39,694.0	39,039.3	74.5	38,146.3	120.2
With cash rent	37,521.2	37,521.2	36,882.3	74.1	35,969.3	119.8
Less than $100	507.0	507.0	520.4	5.7	517.6	5.5
$100 to $149	506.6	506.6	516.3	6.4	527.6	4.9
$150 to $199	670.5	670.5	693.7	8.4	711.6	5.6
$200 to $249	833.1	833.1	848.0	8.0	854.1	6.2
$250 to $299	758.3	758.3	795.3	9.1	827.0	6.9
$300 to $349	1,100.0	1,100.0	1,153.6	11.8	1,171.4	7.4
$350 to $399	1,325.8	1,325.8	1,329.7	10.4	1,344.3	9.4
$400 to $449	1,799.3	1,799.3	1,841.2	12.0	1,880.2	12.3
$450 to $499	1,892.3	1,892.3	1,813.6	11.9	1,821.8	9.2
$500 to $549	2,286.6	2,286.6	2,292.5	15.7	2,227.0	11.9
$550 to $599	2,088.9	2,088.9	1,967.6	15.0	1,958.0	10.7
$600 to $649	2,293.0	2,293.0	2,329.0	16.4	2,317.2	12.7
$650 to $699	2,169.8	2,169.8	2,059.3	13.6	1,858.3	11.0
$700 to $749	1,973.7	1,973.7	1,991.8	14.6	1,951.5	11.5
$750 to $799	1,791.6	1,791.6	1,721.8	13.7	1,734.2	12.2
$800 to $899	3,300.5	3,300.5	3,185.4	15.7	3,108.6	16.0
$900 to $999	2,449.8	2,449.8	2,409.3	16.5	2,355.8	13.5
$1,000 to $1,249	4,208.8	4,208.8	4,101.9	24.4	3,756.4	23.0
$1,250 to $1,499	2,167.9	2,167.9	2,078.9	13.8	2,069.6	15.3
$1,500 to $1,999	2,164.4	2,164.4	2,050.3	14.2	1,898.3	15.7
$2,000 or more	1,233.4	1,233.4	1,182.8	9.9	1,078.9	9.4
No cash rent	2,172.9	2,172.9	2,156.9	14.3	2,177.0	8.6

Source: U.S. Census Bureau, American Community Survey

Table 2-17. Financial Characteristics for Housing Units With Mortgages, 2010 American Community Survey, 1-, 3-, and 5-Year Estimates

[Numbers in thousands, percent.]

Characteristics	United States					
	Owner-occupied housing units with a mortgage					
	1-year estimates		3-year estimates		5-year estimates	
	Estimate	Margin of error (+/-)	Estimate	Margin of error (+/-)	Estimate	Margin of error (+/-)
Owner-occupied housing units with a mortgage	50,339.5	146.0	51,197.5	120.7	51,696.8	255.2
Value						
Less than $50,0000	4.5	0.1	4.4	0.1	4.3	0.1
$50,000 to $99,999	13.3	0.1	12.6	0.1	12.8	0.1
$100,000 to $149,999	16.6	0.1	15.8	0.1	15.8	0.1
$150,000 to $199,999	16.2	0.1	15.7	0.1	15.1	0.1
$200,000 to $299,999	20.3	0.1	20.4	0.1	19.4	0.1
$300,000 to $499,999	17.8	0.1	18.6	0.1	19	0.1
$500,000 or more	11.1	0.1	12.4	0.1	13.6	0.1
Median (dollars)	197,300	413.0	206,500	299.0	208,900	238
Mortgage status						
With either a second mortgage or a home equity loan, but not both	21.7	0.1	23.9	0.1	24.6	0.1
Second mortgage only	5.7	0.1	6.3	0.1	6.4	0.1
Home equity loan only	16.1	0.1	17.6	0.1	18.3	0.1
Both second mortgage and home equity loan	0.9	0.1	1.0	0.1	1	0.1
No second mortgage and no home equity loan	77.4	0.1	75.2	0.1	74.3	0.1
Household income in the past 12 months (in 2010 inflation-adjusted dollars)						
Less than $10,000	2.3	0.1	2.1	0.1	2.1	0.1
$10,000 to $24,999	7.4	0.1	6.9	0.1	6.7	0.1
$25,000 to $34,999	7.1	0.1	6.9	0.1	6.8	0.1
$35,000 to $49,999	12.6	0.1	12.3	0.1	12.2	0.1
$50,000 to $74,999	21.3	0.1	21.4	0.1	21.4	0.1
$75,000 to $99,999	16.8	0.1	17.2	0.1	17.4	0.1
$100,000 to $149,999	18.9	0.1	19.3	0.1	19.5	0.1
$150,000 or more	13.5	0.1	13.9	0.1	14	0.1
Median household income (dollars)	73,892	144.0	75,423	74.0	76,105	124
Ratio of value to household income in the past 12 months						
Less than 2.0	33.1	0.1	32.2	0.1	30.4	0.1
2.0 to 2.9	24.4	0.1	24.2	0.1	23.2	0.1
3.0 to 3.9	14.5	0.1	14.8	0.1	14.9	0.1
4.0 or more	27.5	0.1	28.3	0.1	31	0.1
Not computed	0.5	0.1	0.4	0.1	0.4	0.1
Monthly housing costs						
Less than $200	0.0	0.1	0.0	0.1	0	0.1
$200 to $299	0.2	0.1	0.2	0.1	0.2	0.1
$300 to $399	0.6	0.1	0.6	0.1	0.6	0.1
$400 to $499	1.3	0.1	1.3	0.1	1.3	0.1
$500 to $599	2.2	0.1	2.2	0.1	2.2	0.1
$600 to $699	3.3	0.1	3.2	0.1	3.2	0.1
$700 to $799	4.3	0.1	4.1	0.1	4.1	0.1
$800 to $899	5.0	0.1	4.9	0.1	4.9	0.1
$900 to $999	5.6	0.1	5.4	0.1	5.4	0.1
$1,000 to $1,249	14.5	0.1	14.0	0.1	14	0.1
$1,250 to $1,499	13.3	0.1	13.1	0.1	13	0.1
$1,500 to $1,999	20.0	0.1	19.9	0.1	19.9	0.1
$2,000 or more	29.8	0.1	31.0	0.1	31.1	0.1
Median (dollars)	1,496	3.0	1,521	2.0	1,524	1

Table 2-17. Financial Characteristics for Housing Units With Mortgages, 2010 American Community Survey, 1-, 3-, and 5-Year Estimates—*Continued*

[Numbers in thousands, percent.]

Characteristics	United States					
	Owner-occupied housing units with a mortgage					
	1-year estimates		3-year estimates		5-year estimates	
	Estimate	Margin of error (+/-)	Estimate	Margin of error (+/-)	Estimate	Margin of error (+/-)
Less than 20 percent	0.0	0.1	0.0	0.1	0	0.1
20 to 29 percent	0.1	0.1	0.1	0.1	0.1	0.1
30 percent or more	6.0	0.1	5.7	0.1	5.5	0.1
$20,000 to $34,999	10.2	0.1	9.7	0.1	9.5	0.1
Less than 20 percent	0.3	0.1	0.3	0.1	0.3	0.1
20 to 29 percent	1.3	0.1	1.3	0.1	1.3	0.1
30 percent or more	8.5	0.1	8.1	0.1	7.9	0.1
$35,000 to $49,999	12.6	0.1	12.3	0.1	12.2	0.1
Less than 20 percent	1.4	0.1	1.4	0.1	1.3	0.1
20 to 29 percent	3.6	0.1	3.5	0.1	3.4	0.1
30 percent or more	7.7	0.1	7.5	0.1	7.4	0.1
$50,000 to $74,999	21.3	0.1	21.4	0.1	21.4	0.1
Less than 20 percent	5.3	0.1	5.3	0.1	5.3	0.1
20 to 29 percent	7.8	0.1	7.8	0.1	7.7	0.1
30 percent or more	8.2	0.1	8.4	0.1	8.4	0.1
$75,000 or more	49.2	0.1	50.3	0.1	50.9	0.1
Less than 20 percent	26.5	0.1	26.6	0.1	26.8	0.1
20 to 29 percent	15.3	0.1	15.6	0.1	15.8	0.1
30 percent or more	7.4	0.1	8.1	0.1	8.3	0.1
Zero or negative income	0.5	0.1	0.4	0.1	0.4	0.1
Real estate taxes						
Less than $800	13.7	0.1	14.0	0.1	14.4	0.1
$800 to $1,499	18.7	0.1	18.8	0.1	18.9	0.1
$1,500 or more	65.6	0.1	65.1	0.1	64.6	0.1
No real estate taxes paid	2.1	0.1	2.0	0.1	2.1	0.1
Median (dollars)	2,319.0	6.0	2,295	3.0	2,245	2
Percent imputed						
Mortgage status	36.7	X	36.3	X	36.4	X

X = Not applicable.

Source: U.S. Census Bureau, American Community Survey

Table 2-18. Financial Characteristics for Housing Units Without Mortgages, 2010 American Community Survey, 1-, 3-, and 5-Year Estimates

[Numbers in thousands, percent.]

Characteristics	United States					
	Owner-occupied housing units with a mortgage					
	1-year estimates		3-year estimates		5-year estimates	
	Estimate	Margin of error (+/-)	Estimate	Margin of error (+/-)	Estimate	Margin of error (+/-)
Owner-occupied housing units without a mortgage	24,533.9	94.6	24,360.2	56.3	24,392.8	111.6
Value						
Less than $50,0000	16.9	0.1	16.8	0.1	16.3	0.1
$50,000 to $99,999	19	0.1	18.6	0.1	19.2	0.1
$100,000 to $149,999	14.7	0.1	14.3	0.1	14.9	0.1
$150,000 to $199,999	13.1	0.1	12.9	0.1	12.6	0.1
$200,000 to $299,999	15.1	0.1	15	0.1	14.3	0.1
$300,000 to $499,999	12.1	0.1	12.6	0.1	12.6	0.1
$500,000 or more	9.1	0.1	9.8	0.1	10.1	0.1
Median (dollars)	147,600	538	150,800	278	148,300	252
Household income in the past 12 months (in 2010 inflation-adjusted dollars)						
Less than $10,000	6.7	0.1	6.9	0.1	6.8	0.1
$10,000 to $24,999	22.1	0.1	21.7	0.1	21.7	0.1
$25,000 to $34,999	13.3	0.1	13.1	0.1	13.1	0.1
$35,000 to $49,999	15.8	0.1	15.7	0.1	15.7	0.1
$50,000 to $74,999	17.4	0.1	17.4	0.1	17.4	0.1
$75,000 to $99,999	9.6	0.1	9.7	0.1	9.8	0.1
$100,000 to $149,999	8.6	0.1	8.7	0.1	8.7	0.1
$150,000 or more	6.5	0.1	6.8	0.1	6.8	0.1
Median household income (dollars)	41,797	120	42,359	74	42,450	53
Ratio of value to household income in the past 12 months						
Less than 2.0	32.8	0.2	32.5	0.1	30.8	0.1
2.0 to 2.9	15.6	0.1	15.5	0.1	15.3	0.1
3.0 to 3.9	11.4	0.1	11.3	0.1	11.2	0.1
4.0 or more	39.1	0.2	39.6	0.1	41.6	0.1
Not computed	1.2	0.1	1.1	0.1	1	0.1
Monthly housing costs						
Less than $100	1.3	0.1	1.3	0.1	1.3	0.1
$100 to $149	2.6	0.1	2.7	0.1	2.6	0.1
$150 to $199	4.9	0.1	5	0.1	5	0.1
$200 to $249	7.3	0.1	7.5	0.1	7.5	0.1
$250 to $299	9.2	0.1	9.2	0.1	9.2	0.1
$300 to $349	10	0.1	9.8	0.1	9.8	0.1
$350 to $399	9.7	0.1	9.5	0.1	9.6	0.1
$400 to $499	16.4	0.1	16.1	0.1	16.2	0.1
$500 to $599	11.9	0.1	11.9	0.1	11.9	0.1
$600 to $699	8.2	0.1	8.1	0.1	8.2	0.1
$700 or more	18.7	0.1	18.8	0.1	18.7	0.1
Median (dollars)	431	1	431	1	431	1

Table 2-18. Financial Characteristics for Housing Units Without Mortgages, 2010 American Community Survey, 1-, 3-, and 5-Year Estimates—*Continued*

[Numbers in thousands, percent.]

Characteristics	United States					
	Owner-occupied housing units with a mortgage					
	1-year estimates		3-year estimates		5-year estimates	
	Estimate	Margin of error (+/-)	Estimate	Margin of error (+/-)	Estimate	Margin of error (+/-)
Less than $20,000	20.1	0.1	20	0.1	20.2	0.1
Less than 20 percent	4.2	0.1	4.2	0.1	4.1	0.1
20 to 29 percent	4.6	0.1	4.5	0.1	4.6	0.1
30 percent or more	11.3	0.1	11.3	0.1	11.5	0.1
$20,000 to $34,999	20.8	0.1	20.5	0.1	20.4	0.1
Less than 20 percent	12.6	0.1	12.4	0.1	12.3	0.1
20 to 29 percent	5.1	0.1	5	0.1	5	0.1
30 percent or more	3.1	0.1	3.1	0.1	3.1	0.1
$35,000 to $49,999	15.8	0.1	15.7	0.1	15.7	0.1
Less than 20 percent	13.3	0.1	13.2	0.1	13.2	0.1
20 to 29 percent	1.9	0.1	1.8	0.1	1.9	0.1
30 percent or more	0.6	0.1	0.6	0.1	0.6	0.1
$50,000 to $74,999	17.4	0.1	17.4	0.1	17.4	0.1
Less than 20 percent	16.3	0.1	16.3	0.1	16.3	0.1
20 to 29 percent	0.9	0.1	0.9	0.1	0.9	0.1
30 percent or more	0.2	0.1	0.2	0.1	0.2	0.1
$75,000 or more	24.8	0.1	25.3	0.1	25.3	0.1
Less than 20 percent	24.4	0.1	24.9	0.1	24.9	0.1
20 to 29 percent	0.3	0.1	0.3	0.1	0.3	0.1
30 percent or more	0.1	0.1	0.1	0.1	0.1	0.1
Zero or negative income	1.2	0.1	1.1	0.1	1	0.1
Real estate taxes						
Less than $800	27.3	0.1	27.9	0.1	27.9	0.1
$800 to $1,499	19.1	0.1	19.2	0.1	19.3	0.1
$1,500 or more	46.2	0.1	45.5	0.1	45.4	0.1
No real estate taxes paid	7.3	0.1	7.4	0.1	7.4	0.1
Median (dollars)	1,497	5	1,470	3	1,467	2
Percent imputed						
Mortgage status	28.3	X	28.8	X	27.8	X

X = Not applicable.

Source: U.S. Census Bureau, American Community Survey

Table 2-19. Median Monthly Housing Costs for Owner-Occupied Housing Units With Mortgages, United States and Puerto Rico, 2010 American Community Survey, 1-, 3-, and 5-Year Estimates

[Dollars.]

State/Territory	United States					
	1-year estimates		3-year estimates		5-year estimates	
	Median	Margin of error (+/-)	Median	Margin of error (+/-)	Median	Margin of error (+/-)
United States	1,496	3	1,521	2	1,524	1
Alabama	1,130	10	1,123	5	1,110	5
Alaska	1,772	43	1,770	20	1,765	15
Arizona	1,442	12	1,499	6	1,502	6
Arkansas	987	14	977	6	979	5
California	2,242	8	2,333	5	2,345	4
Colorado	1,590	11	1,622	6	1,636	5
Connecticut	2,068	19	2,102	10	2,082	8
Delaware	1,569	30	1,588	14	1,563	14
District of Columbia	2,297	82	2,265	47	2,220	32
Florida	1,505	10	1,573	5	1,586	4
Georgia	1,390	8	1,398	5	1,398	4
Hawaii	2,240	56	2,273	29	2,225	20
Idaho	1,187	18	1,210	9	1,208	7
Illinois	1,655	8	1,688	5	1,692	5
Indiana	1,090	6	1,132	5	1,144	3
Iowa	1,140	11	1,144	6	1,147	4
Kansas	1,239	12	1,233	6	1,231	5
Kentucky	1,072	9	1,078	6	1,080	4
Louisiana	1,163	12	1,156	7	1,144	6
Maine	1,289	21	1,314	12	1,304	9
Maryland	2,016	20	2,035	11	1,992	7
Massachusetts	2,036	16	2,096	9	2,100	7
Michigan	1,288	7	1,337	4	1,365	3
Minnesota	1,503	11	1,538	5	1,549	5
Mississippi	1,043	14	1,038	8	1,028	7
Missouri	1,182	9	1,191	5	1,192	3
Montana	1,217	20	1,230	13	1,220	8
Nebraska	1,218	14	1,243	8	1,248	7
Nevada	1,638	18	1,745	14	1,777	12
New Hampshire	1,853	24	1,889	15	1,888	12
New Jersey	2,370	15	2,398	8	2,373	6
New Mexico	1,202	19	1,202	9	1,194	7
New York	1,963	14	1,965	7	1,958	5
North Carolina	1,250	8	1,246	5	1,244	4
North Dakota	1,133	22	1,144	12	1,146	9
Ohio	1,246	6	1,272	5	1,288	3
Oklahoma	1,089	12	1,081	6	1,075	5
Oregon	1,577	15	1,599	9	1,580	7
Pennsylvania	1,390	7	1,402	5	1,395	3
Rhode Island	1,837	33	1,883	17	1,878	12
South Carolina	1,177	9	1,170	6	1,167	4
South Dakota	1,151	21	1,170	10	1,168	8
Tennessee	1,161	8	1,167	5	1,163	4
Texas	1,402	6	1,404	3	1,409	2
Utah	1,433	11	1,450	7	1,440	6
Vermont	1,445	26	1,482	12	1,467	10
Virginia	1,728	13	1,744	8	1,728	6
Washington	1,736	11	1,770	8	1,752	5
West Virginia	918	15	907	8	914	6
Wisconsin	1,404	8	1,426	5	1,433	4
Wyoming	1,300	30	1,296	18	1,249	14
Puerto Rico	851	12	848	6	851	5

Source: U.S. Census Bureau, American Community Survey

Table 2-20. Percent of Mortgaged Owners Spending 30 Percent or More of Household Income on Selected Monthly Homeowner Costs, United States: Urban/Rural Areas, States, and Puerto Rico, 2010 American Community Survey, 1-, 3-, and 5-Year Estimates

[Percent.]

State/Territory	United States					
	1-year estimates		3-year estimates		5-year estimates	
	Percent	Margin of error (+/-)	Percent	Margin of error (+/-)	Percent	Margin of error (+/-)
United States	37.8	0.1	37.7	0.1	37.4	0.1
Urban and rural areas						
Urban	38.8	0.1	38.8	0.1	38.6	0.1
Rural	35.2	0.2	34.6	0.1	34.1	0.1
Inside and outside metropolitan statistical areas						
In metropolitan or micropolitan statistical area	38.1	0.1	38.0	0.1	37.7	0.1
In metropolitan statistical area	38.6	0.1	38.5	0.1	38.3	0.1
In principal city	39.8	0.2	40.0	0.1	40.0	0.1
Not in principal city	38.0	0.1	37.8	0.1	37.6	0.1
In micropolitan statistical area	33.7	0.3	32.9	0.2	32.3	0.1
In principal city	32.1	0.5	31.3	0.3	31.0	0.3
Not in principal city	34.3	0.4	33.5	0.2	32.8	0.2
Not in metropolitan or micropolitan statistical area	33.6	0.4	32.8	0.2	32.4	0.2
Alabama	32.5	0.7	30.2	0.5	29.6	0.4
Alaska	32.1	2.0	32.8	1.3	33.2	0.9
Arizona	40.9	0.7	41.1	0.4	39.9	0.4
Arkansas	27.4	1.0	27.4	0.6	27.2	0.5
California	50.9	0.4	52.1	0.2	52.1	0.2
Colorado	37.3	0.6	36.6	0.4	37.0	0.3
Connecticut	41.3	0.8	40.8	0.5	40.4	0.4
Delaware	37.1	1.7	36.3	1.0	35.2	0.8
District of Columbia	35.5	2.6	37.3	1.5	37.6	1.1
Florida	48.3	0.5	48.9	0.3	48.0	0.2
Georgia	37.9	0.5	36.1	0.3	35.4	0.3
Hawaii	50.0	2.1	49.2	1.0	47.7	0.8
Idaho	36.6	1.3	36.0	0.8	34.9	0.6
Illinois	39.7	0.5	38.9	0.3	38.7	0.2
Indiana	27.4	0.6	27.5	0.4	27.2	0.2
Iowa	24.7	0.9	24.1	0.5	24.6	0.4
Kansas	26.4	0.8	25.6	0.5	25.6	0.3
Kentucky	30.1	0.8	28.6	0.4	28.0	0.4
Louisiana	30.1	0.9	29.4	0.5	29.1	0.4
Maine	33.9	1.2	35.6	0.8	35.1	0.6
Maryland	38.0	0.8	38.8	0.4	37.7	0.3
Massachusetts	39.0	0.6	40.3	0.4	40.7	0.3
Michigan	36.2	0.5	36.2	0.3	35.8	0.2
Minnesota	33.3	0.6	33.8	0.3	33.9	0.3
Mississippi	35.2	1.2	32.9	0.6	32.8	0.5
Missouri	30.1	0.7	29.2	0.4	29.0	0.3
Montana	35.9	2.1	34.7	0.9	34.3	0.6
Nebraska	25.9	1.2	25.8	0.5	26.1	0.5
Nevada	44.7	1.4	46.9	0.7	46.9	0.5
New Hampshire	40.0	1.5	40.8	0.8	40.5	0.7
New Jersey	46.5	0.6	46.4	0.3	45.8	0.3
New Mexico	35.9	1.1	34.8	0.8	34.1	0.6
New York	41.2	0.5	41.2	0.3	41.1	0.2
North Carolina	34.3	0.6	32.9	0.3	32.1	0.3
North Dakota	19.0	1.9	21.2	1.0	21.7	0.7
Ohio	31.8	0.4	31.2	0.2	31.2	0.2
Oklahoma	28.7	0.8	26.9	0.4	26.5	0.4
Oregon	42.6	0.9	41.8	0.5	40.9	0.4
Pennsylvania	33.1	0.5	32.9	0.2	32.8	0.2
Rhode Island	43.5	1.9	42.9	1.0	42.8	0.8
South Carolina	33.8	0.8	32.4	0.5	32.2	0.4
South Dakota	25.4	2.2	26.2	0.9	26.1	0.7
Tennessee	33.1	0.9	32.5	0.4	31.9	0.3
Texas	32.5	0.4	31.7	0.3	32.0	0.2
Utah	35.4	0.9	35.2	0.6	34.3	0.5
Vermont	38.6	1.7	38.3	1.1	37.9	0.7
Virginia	35.0	0.6	35.5	0.4	35.3	0.3
Washington	40.7	0.7	41.0	0.4	40.6	0.3
West Virginia	25.5	1.2	24.9	0.7	24.8	0.5
Wisconsin	34.2	0.6	34.3	0.4	33.9	0.3
Wyoming	28.0	2.4	27.1	1.2	26.3	0.9
Puerto Rico	48.2	1.3	48.2	0.7	47.5	0.6

Source: U.S. Census Bureau, American Community Survey

Table 2-21. Percent of Renter-Occupied Units Spending 30 Percent or More of Household Income on Selected Monthly Homeowner Costs, United States: Urban/Rural Areas, States, and Puerto Rico, 2010 American Community Survey, 1-, 3-, and 5-Year Estimates

[Percent.]

State/Territory	United States					
	1-year estimates		3-year estimates		5-year estimates	
	Percent	Margin of error (+/-)	Percent	Margin of error (+/-)	Percent	Margin of error (+/-)
United States	48.9	0.1	47.8	0.1	47.0	0.1
Urban and rural areas						
Urban	50.5	0.1	49.4	0.1	48.7	0.1
Rural	38.6	0.4	36.9	0.2	35.7	0.2
Inside and outside metropolitan statistical areas						
In metropolitan or micropolitan statistical area	49.4	0.1	48.3	0.1	47.6	0.1
In metropolitan statistical area	50.0	0.1	48.9	0.1	48.1	0.1
In principal city	51.5	0.2	50.4	0.1	49.8	0.1
Not in principal city	48.2	0.2	46.9	0.1	46.1	0.1
In micropolitan statistical area	44.2	0.5	42.8	0.3	42.1	0.2
In principal city	49.0	0.7	47.5	0.4	46.9	0.3
Not in principal city	39.8	0.6	38.4	0.3	37.5	0.2
Not in metropolitan or micropolitan statistical area	38.6	0.5	37.3	0.3	36.4	0.2
Alabama	46.7	1.1	44.1	0.7	42.9	0.4
Alaska	41.5	3.0	39.4	1.4	38.6	1.0
Arizona	49.1	1.1	48.0	0.6	47.3	0.4
Arkansas	43.3	1.3	42.5	0.8	42.5	0.6
California	54.4	0.3	53.2	0.2	52.4	0.2
Colorado	49.0	1.1	48.5	0.6	48.0	0.4
Connecticut	50.5	1.1	49.5	0.6	48.8	0.6
Delaware	50.9	2.6	49.7	1.2	48.0	1.4
District of Columbia	47.5	2.2	46.8	1.3	46.4	0.9
Florida	55.6	0.6	55.2	0.4	54.2	0.3
Georgia	49.0	0.9	47.7	0.5	46.9	0.4
Hawaii	51.3	2.1	50.8	1.1	49.3	0.9
Idaho	46.9	1.9	44.3	1.0	42.2	0.9
Illinois	48.8	0.5	47.5	0.4	47.0	0.3
Indiana	46.7	1.1	45.3	0.6	44.6	0.4
Iowa	42.3	1.3	40.7	0.8	40.3	0.6
Kansas	41.8	1.6	41.0	0.8	40.7	0.6
Kentucky	43.7	1.2	41.7	0.6	41.1	0.5
Louisiana	46.4	1.4	45.3	0.6	43.9	0.5
Maine	45.1	2.3	46.3	1.1	45.1	0.9
Maryland	48.7	1.2	48.8	0.6	47.4	0.5
Massachusetts	47.8	1.0	47.3	0.5	47.8	0.4
Michigan	51.2	0.8	50.7	0.4	49.7	0.3
Minnesota	47.5	1.0	47.0	0.6	46.0	0.5
Mississippi	47.0	1.5	44.4	0.8	43.6	0.8
Missouri	45.8	0.9	43.5	0.5	43.2	0.4
Montana	39.9	1.8	39.6	1.4	39.2	1.0
Nebraska	41.0	1.5	39.4	1.0	39.3	0.7
Nevada	50.3	1.5	49.3	0.9	48.8	0.6
New Hampshire	47.7	2.3	45.6	1.2	45.5	1.0
New Jersey	51.5	0.9	49.9	0.5	49.1	0.3
New Mexico	42.4	1.9	42.3	1.1	42.4	0.9
New York	50.2	0.5	49.3	0.2	48.7	0.2
North Carolina	47.2	0.7	45.0	0.6	44.0	0.4
North Dakota	36.2	2.5	36.2	1.4	36.8	1.0
Ohio	47.9	0.7	46.1	0.4	45.7	0.3
Oklahoma	41.8	1.3	41.0	0.7	40.8	0.5
Oregon	51.2	1.0	49.2	0.7	48.0	0.6
Pennsylvania	46.3	0.7	45.0	0.3	44.4	0.3
Rhode Island	48.1	2.1	48.1	1.2	47.4	1.0
South Carolina	47.2	1.2	44.6	0.8	42.7	0.5
South Dakota	37.2	2.2	36.1	1.4	35.4	0.9
Tennessee	46.7	1.0	45.1	0.5	43.8	0.4
Texas	46.3	0.5	45.4	0.3	44.8	0.3
Utah	45.8	1.8	44.0	0.9	42.7	0.8
Vermont	49.9	3.3	48.3	1.6	47.5	1.2
Virginia	46.6	0.8	45.6	0.5	44.3	0.4
Washington	48.4	0.8	47.2	0.5	46.4	0.4
West Virginia	40.2	2.0	39.8	1.0	39.0	0.8
Wisconsin	46.5	0.9	45.0	0.5	44.2	0.4
Wyoming	34.3	3.2	34.1	1.7	31.6	1.2
Puerto Rico	30.4	1.2	32.1	0.5	32.6	0.5

Source: U.S. Census Bureau, American Community Survey

Table 2-22. Mortgage Status by Aggregate Real Estate Taxes Paid and Median Real Estate Taxes Paid, United States, 2010 American Community Survey, 1-, 3-, and 5-Year Estimates

[Dollars in thousands, except where noted.]

Characteristics	United States					
	1-year estimates		3-year estimates		5-year estimates	
	Estimate	Margin of error (+/-)	Estimate	Margin of error (+/-)	Estimate	Margin of error (+/-)
Aggregate real estate taxes paid, total	202,840,232.2	521,472.0	203,818,346.7	422,086.3	203,498,297.8	921,818.3
Aggregate real estate taxes paid for units with a mortgage	150,211,828.3	452,872.2	152,316,360.5	347,245.5	152,182,235.2	710,284.9
Aggregate real estate taxes paid for units without a mortgage	52,628,403.9	255,247.1	51,501,986.2	142,933.3	51,316,062.6	232,975.0
Median real estate taxes paid, total	2,043.0	5.0	2,018.0	4.0	1,981.0	2.0
Median real estate taxes paid for units with a mortgage	2,319.0	6.0	2,295.0	3.0	2,245.0	2.0
Median real estate taxes paid for units without a mortgage	1,497.0	5.0	1,470.0	3.0	1,467.0	2.0

Source: U.S. Census Bureau, American Community Survey

Table 2-23. Mortgage Status by Real Estate Taxes Paid, Owner-Occupied Units, 2010 American Community Survey, 1-, 3-, and 5-Year Estimates

[Numbers in thousands.]

Characteristics	United States					
	1-year estimates		3-year estimates		5-year estimates	
	Estimate	Margin of error (+/-)	Estimate	Margin of error (+/-)	Estimate	Margin of error (+/-)
Total	74,873.4	216.1	75,557.7	165.3	76,089.7	362.8
With a mortgage	50,339.50	146.0	51,197.5	120.7	51,696.8	255.2
Less than $800	6,889.90	49.9	7,178.8	32.6	7,439.3	40.7
$800 to $1,499	9,405.2	55.4	9,621.7	30.4	9,775.3	53.6
$1,500 to $1,999	5,515.8	36.0	5,614.6	23.6	5,854.4	33.8
$2,000 to $2,999	8,887.2	55.4	9,030.1	27.3	9,068.3	47.5
$3,000 or more	18,597.5	62.9	18,708.2	46.4	18,449.1	88.0
No real estate taxes paid	1,044.0	15.2	1,044.1	7.6	1,110.4	9.9
Not mortgaged	24,533.9	94.7	24,360.2	56.2	24,392.8	111.6
Less than $800	6,697.2	42.3	6,804.9	25.1	6,807.2	31.7
$800 to $1,499	4,690.9	29.7	4,668.3	17.3	4,702.7	25.3
$1,500 to $1,999	2,288.4	23.3	2,254.2	12.6	2,320.3	14.9
$2,000 to $2,999	3,297.0	26.9	3,280.0	14.6	3,280.2	17.0
$3,000 or more	5,758.0	35.9	5,557.2	17.6	5,483.5	25.8
No real estate taxes paid	1,802.4	20.1	1,795.5	9.9	1,798.9	11.4

Source: U.S. Census Bureau, American Community Survey

Table 2-24. Aggregate Gross Rent by Year Householder Moved into Unit, Renter-Occupied Units, 2010 American Community Survey, 1- and 3-Year Estimates

[Dollars in thousands.]

Characteristics	United States			
	1-year estimates		3-year estimates	
	Estimate	Margin of error (+/-)	Estimate	Margin of error (+/-)
Aggregate gross rent, total	35,790,785.3	108,916.3	34,977,026.5	78,128.0
Moved in 2000 or later	32,387,288.8	108,005.3	31,327,008.8	77,177.1
Moved in 1990 to 1999	2,321,588.4	25,737.1	2,519,032.6	15,455.0
Moved in 1970 to 1989	933,405.4	14,019.8	978,581.3	9,648.4
Moved in 1969 or earlier	148,502.7	6,392.4	152,403.9	3,729.6

Source: U.S. Census Bureau, American Community Survey

Table 2-25. Gross Rent as a Percentage of Household Income in the Past 12 Months, by Age of Householder, 2010 American Community Survey, 1-, 3-, and 5-Year Estimates

[Numbers in thousands.]

Characteristics	United States					
	1-year estimates		3-year estimates		5-year estimates	
	Estimate	Margin of error (+/-)	Estimate	Margin of error (+/-)	Estimate	Margin of error (+/-)
Total	39,694.0	91.9	39,039.3	74.5	38,146.3	120.2
Householder 15 to 24 years	4,181.1	35.9	4,417.2	18.3	4,539.1	26.1
Less than 20.0 percent	566.2	12.2	667.1	9.0	719.5	7.0
20.0 percent to 24.9 percent	395.7	10.8	437.8	6.7	460.8	4.8
25.0 percent to 29.9 percent	377.2	11.3	412.4	7.3	426.9	5.1
30.0 to 34.9 percent	321.0	9.7	343.8	6.8	353.4	4.8
35.0 percent or more	2,173.9	26.6	2,219.4	14.0	2,234.2	16.9
Not computed	347.1	11.5	336.7	6.7	344.5	5.4
Householder 25 to 34 years	10,452.1	44.3	10,362.3	30.1	10,131.4	31.6
Less than 20.0 percent	2,496.7	28.1	2,587.8	15.7	2,591.7	11.9
20.0 percent to 24.9 percent	1,399.5	20.5	1,427.4	11.7	1,405.1	10.4
25.0 percent to 29.9 percent	1,170.0	16.2	1,159.3	11.6	1,138.2	8.7
30.0 to 34.9 percent	902.7	15.7	897.4	10.2	874.8	7.0
35.0 percent or more	3,884.9	31.3	3,715.9	18.2	3,551.7	18.1
Not computed	598.2	14.3	574.4	7.9	569.8	5.7
Householder 35 to 64 years	19,732.8	75.7	19,079.0	62.5	18,409.0	136.7
Less than 20.0 percent	4,664.9	39.7	4,725.8	24.4	4,689.2	40.1
20.0 percent to 24.9 percent	2,295.5	24.4	2,273.7	14.8	2,216.2	19.6
25.0 percent to 29.9 percent	2,075.5	24.4	2,019.7	13.7	1,953.0	17.0
30.0 to 34.9 percent	1,632.1	22.6	1,578.4	12.4	1,511.7	14.8
35.0 percent or more	7,596.1	50.8	7,092.7	28.9	6,684.0	51.4
Not computed	1,468.6	19.9	1,388.7	11.5	1,354.9	11.4
Householder 65 years and over	5,327.9	31.5	5,180.7	16.6	5,066.9	23.7
Less than 20.0 percent	725.0	11.1	717.0	7.8	707.8	6.3
20.0 percent to 24.9 percent	446.4	8.8	434.3	6.7	429.0	5.0
25.0 percent to 29.9 percent	622.1	13.6	608.0	6.1	599.0	5.8
30.0 to 34.9 percent	517.8	9.8	488.2	6.9	475.1	4.8
35.0 percent or more	2,393.0	20.8	2,312.2	13.0	2,253.1	12.2
Not computed	623.6	11.4	621.0	6.7	602.9	5.2

Source: U.S. Census Bureau, American Community Survey

Table 2-26. Selected Monthly Owner Costs as a Percentage of Household Income in the Past 12 Months, by Age of Householder, 2010 American Community Survey, 1-, 3-, and 5-Year Estimates

[Numbers in thousands.]

Characteristics	United States					
	1-year estimates		3-year estimates		5-year estimates	
	Estimate	Margin of error (+/-)	Estimate	Margin of error (+/-)	Estimate	Margin of error (+/-)
Total	74,873.4	216.1	75,557.7	165.3	76,089.7	362.8
Householder 15 to 24 years	720.1	18.6	781.5	10.5	858.9	14.2
Less than 20.0 percent	224.3	10.0	238.8	4.9	255.3	4.9
20.0 percent to 24.9 percent	102.3	5.7	106.1	3.1	115.1	2.9
25.0 percent to 29.9 percent	82.1	4.3	90.3	3.2	98.2	2.6
30.0 to 34.9 percent	64.0	4.4	70.5	2.1	78.5	2.4
35.0 percent or more	231.8	8.0	260.5	4.7	296.4	5.3
Not computed	15.6	1.8	15.4	1.2	15.4	1.0
Householder 25 to 34 years	7,341.9	54.4	7,664.8	41.4	8,015.7	76.6
Less than 20.0 percent	2,530.1	27.7	2,563.4	18.4	2,644.6	29.7
20.0 percent to 24.9 percent	1,300.3	20.1	1,328.3	10.9	1,368.9	17.0
25.0 percent to 29.9 percent	987.1	17.8	1,052.6	10.6	1,101.5	13.3
30.0 to 34.9 percent	688.7	14.4	739.1	8.0	779.0	9.2
35.0 percent or more	1,791.3	22.1	1,942.0	12.6	2,083.0	15.7
Not computed	44.3	3.9	39.4	2.0	38.7	1.3
Householder 35 to 64 years	47,265.3	125.1	47,816.9	89.2	48,242.6	189.8
Less than 20.0 percent	21,177.5	78.5	21,496.4	60.2	21,785.8	121.1
20.0 percent to 24.9 percent	6,447.6	41.8	6,577.9	26.2	6,685.2	39.2
25.0 percent to 29.9 percent	4,828.3	32.4	4,927.1	17.7	5,005.4	26.7
30.0 to 34.9 percent	3,426.2	28.6	3,475.0	18.3	3,526.9	15.6
35.0 percent or more	11,014.8	53.2	11,014.4	24.1	10,933.7	19.1
Not computed	370.9	10.6	326.2	5.7	305.5	4.5
Householder 65 years and over	19,546.2	60.0	19,294.4	40.6	18,972.5	86.7
Less than 20.0 percent	10,286.5	47.5	10,221.1	25.0	10,056.6	38.6
20.0 percent to 24.9 percent	2,017.1	19.0	1,964.2	12.1	1,942.8	12.7
25.0 percent to 29.9 percent	1,527.1	14.9	1,481.0	10.4	1,463.1	10.5
30.0 to 34.9 percent	1,132.3	15.3	1,110.3	8.2	1,091.5	8.7
35.0 percent or more	4,459.5	28.1	4,402.0	17.7	4,314.3	26.8
Not computed	123.7	4.6	115.9	2.9	104.1	2.0

Source: U.S. Census Bureau, American Community Survey

Table 2-27. Aggregate Gross Rent and Aggregate Value of Housing Units, by Units in Structure, 2010 American Community Survey, 1-, 3-, and 5-Year Estimates

[Dollars in thousands.]

Characteristics	United States					
	1-year estimates		3-year estimates		5-year estimates	
	Estimate	Margin of error (+/-)	Estimate	Margin of error (+/-)	Estimate	Margin of error (+/-)
Aggregate gross rent	35,790,785.3	108,916.3	34,977,026.5	78,728.0	33,711,093.0	142,356.6
1, detached or attached	12,995,819.5	78,855.6	12,459,644.3	48,711.3	11,652,830.8	96,222.6
2 to 4	6,381,538.6	41,684.0	6,361,614.4	29,566.5	6,258,572.6	31,280.8
5 to 19	7,668,339.9	44,604.1	7,732,257.5	30,797.7	7,633,367.1	31,742.9
20 to 49	3,055,878.9	32,015.3	2,955,348.1	16,578.6	2,888,810.4	11,598.0
50 or more	4,637,876.0	43,490.6	4,441,357.3	19,668.7	4,278,547.4	24,748.9
Mobile home	1,032,946.9	13,724.2	1,007,712.7	9,351.3	981,894.4	11,374.1
Boat, RV, van, etc.	18,385.6	2,589.8	19,092.2	1,238.6	17,070.3	1,080.9
Aggregate value	18,763,216,949.1	55,070,568.8	19,807,701,846.8	41,757,637.7	20,268,727,230.0	91,979,614.9
1, detached or attached	16,026,426,178.2	49.290.034.2	16,902,336,660.8	38,030,820.2	17,319,502,927.5	80,454,835.4
1, attached	1,106,117,002.8	13,183,289.7	1,159,644,823.9	7,378,263.6	1,211,503,110.0	9,199,219.1
2	313,754,967.3	7,652,724.2	343,921,641.6	4,050,601.5	363,303,380.0	2,812,408.1
3 or 4	190,916,371.7	6,393,081.6	208,147,498.1	3,052,654.5	215,463,422.5	2,092,931.7
5 or more	760,752,431.8	13,583,619.1	813,570,849.9	8,796,931.3	772,947,067.5	5,046,745.9
Mobile home	356,761,790.8	6,265,540.0	372,323,481.5	3,617,440.8	378,425,942.5	2,073,611.1
Boat, RV, van, etc.	8,488,206.5	1,493,105.5	7,756,891.0	655,705.0	7,581,380.0	493,827.5

Source: U.S. Census Bureau, 2010 American Community Survey

Table 2-28. Gross Rent as a Percentage of Household income in the Past 12 Months, by Units in Structure, 2010 American Community Survey, 1-, 3-, and 5-Year Estimates

[Numbers in thousands.]

Characteristics	United States					
	1-year estimates		3-year estimates		5-year estimates	
	Estimate	Margin of error (+/-)	Estimate	Margin of error (+/-)	Estimate	Margin of error (+/-)
Total units	39,694.0	91.9	39,039.3	74.5	38,146.3	120.2
1, detached or attached	13,301.1	67.0	12,854.7	41.1	12,248.9	76.3
Less than 20.0 percent	2,726.4	25.3	2,749.8	17.0	2,675.1	23.5
20.0 to 24.9 percent	1,466.5	23.5	1,441.7	13.7	1,373.0	12.1
25.0 to 29.9 percent	1,261.8	15.8	1,222.9	10.5	1,157.1	10.5
30.0 to 34.9 percent	1,010.6	19.9	974.6	10.6	919.8	8.5
35.0 percent or more	5,104.9	41.1	4,776.8	23.0	4,473.5	32.5
Not computed	1,730.9	21.2	1,688.9	12.3	1,650.5	8.2
2 to 4	7,442.6	42.2	7,458.0	30.9	7,393.9	30.0
Less than 20.0 percent	1,627.2	21.5	1,720.1	13.9	1,747.3	12.6
20.0 to 24.9 percent	866.1	16.4	895.6	9.7	898.8	8.8
25.0 to 29.9 percent	795.9	15.4	792.2	8.2	790.4	7.8
30.0 to 34.9 percent	648.8	15.3	646.5	6.7	638.0	6.6
35.0 percent or more	3,170.8	29.3	3,091.0	19.5	3,010.9	15.5
Not computed	333.8	11.1	312.5	5.5	308.5	4.0
5 to 19	9,060.0	46.8	9,121.7	32.9	9,063.5	33.6
Less than 20.0 percent	2,034.9	25.2	2,147.9	14.8	2,187.7	13.5
20.0 to 24.9 percent	1,136.0	19.1	1,163.3	11.2	1,169.8	9.8
25.0 to 29.9 percent	1,037.3	16.7	1,049.5	10.3	1,048.1	8.6
30.0 to 34.9 percent	819.5	15.3	824.4	8.6	816.3	6.7
35.0 percent or more	3,694.3	26.9	3,622.1	18.6	3,529.4	15.0
Not computed	338.0	11.4	314.5	5.5	312.3	4.1
20 to 49	3,413.0	31.5	3,315.8	16.7	3,271.8	10.8
Less than 20.0 percent	729.1	16.6	733.7	9.1	742.3	7.0
20.0 to 24.9 percent	400.8	10.7	404.7	6.3	405.5	4.8
25.0 to 29.9 percent	397.4	11.6	395.2	5.5	391.0	4.7
30.0 to 34.9 percent	310.2	9.3	304.3	5.8	297.5	3.7
35.0 percent or more	1,445.2	21.7	1,357.0	12.1	1,317.7	7.7
Not computed	130.4	5.8	120.9	3.1	117.8	2.5
50 or more	4,605.6	34.8	4,440.7	17.9	4,342.9	26.9
Less than 20.0 percent	941.3	17.3	921.5	9.1	917.3	9.1
20.0 to 24.9 percent	499.4	11.2	494.9	7.1	490.9	5.7
25.0 to 29.9 percent	602.7	13.9	587.8	6.8	580.6	7.1
30.0 to 34.9 percent	464.3	10.3	439.8	6.7	426.0	4.8
35.0 percent or more	1,915.5	22.9	1,825.6	12.5	1,761.1	12.5
Not computed	182.5	8.5	171.1	3.4	167.1	3.0
Mobile home	1,836.7	23.2	1,812.5	15.3	1,790.2	18.1
Less than 20.0 percent	387.1	11.1	416.8	6.8	431.2	7.6
20.0 to 24.9 percent	165.1	6.6	170.0	4.1	170.2	3.7
25.0 to 29.9 percent	146.3	5.7	148.9	4.2	147.3	2.9
30.0 to 34.9 percent	118.5	5.4	116.0	3.5	115.1	2.9
35.0 percent or more	706.0	14.9	656.4	7.7	620.3	7.3
Not computed	313.7	10.7	304.3	5.6	306.1	4.4
Boat, RV, van, etc.	35.0	3.4	35.9	2.0	35.1	1.5
Less than 20.0 percent	6.9	1.5	7.9	1.0	7.3	0.7
20.0 to 24.9 percent	3.2	1.1	3.1	0.6	3.0	0.5
25.0 to 29.9 percent	3.5	1.2	3.0	0.6	2.4	0.4
30.0 to 34.9 percent	1.9	0.8	2.2	0.5	2.4	0.4
35.0 percent or more	11.2	1.7	11.3	1.1	10.1	0.9
Not computed	8.3	1.8	8.6	1.0	9.9	0.8

Source: U.S. Census Bureau, 2010 American Community Survey

Table 2-29. Median and Aggregate Value, by Year Structure Built, 2010 American Community Survey, 1-, 3-, and 5-Year Estimates

[Dollars in thousands, except as noted.]

Characteristics	United States					
	1-year estimates		3-year estimates		5-year estimates	
	Estimate	Margin of error (+/-)	Estimate	Margin of error (+/-)	Estimate	Margin of error (+/-)
Median value (dollars)						
Total	179,000	292	187,500	198	188,400	184
Built 2005 or later	235,200	1,280	246,500	720	251,100	724
Built 2000 to 2004	225,700	935	237,500	555	242,200	440
Built 1990 to 1999	204,000	871	214,200	500	217,200	323
Built 1980 to 1989	179,500	818	189,100	528	192,000	371
Built 1970 to 1979	163,600	471	168,400	389	168,500	292
Built 1960 to 1969	165,800	701	170,700	339	170,900	343
Built 1950 to 1959	158,500	752	164,000	467	163,900	301
Built 1940 to 1949	146,200	1,268	150,400	706	148,700	627
Built 1939 or earlier	158,600	791	161,400	506	160,000	329
Aggregate value						
Total	18,763,216,949.1	55,070,568.8	19,807,701,846.8	41,757,637.7	20,268,727,230.0	91,979,614.9
Built 2005 or later	1,611,056,727.2	19,807,266.1	1,422,877,822.2	10,629,431.7	1,138,680,767.5	9,899,505.7
Built 2000 to 2004	1,944,856,465.8	18,343,690.2	2,086,807,375.9	12,650,825.0	2,214,403,825.0	16,243,628.7
Built 1990 to 1999	2,973,441,025.6	21,521,537.1	3,212,790,411.7	13,354,248.6	3,371,753,227.5	16,061,056.8
Built 1980 to 1989	2,443,406,814.9	17,204,291.7	2,627,691,881.3	10,178,661.3	2,767,939,945.0	12,557,422.0
Built 1970 to 1979	2,462,381,902.8	16,221,209.7	2,643,903,123.3	11,221,048.9	2,779,902,267.5	11,217,634.3
Built 1960 to 1969	1,938,557,440.2	15,712,151.2	2,066,113,675.7	9,504,151.2	2,164,836,845.0	9,428,246.2
Built 1950 to 1959	2,056,693,588.2	15,352,237.7	2,202,516,276.9	9,209,014.0	2,295,116,895.0	11,233,415.7
Built 1940 to 1949	892,654,155.0	11,026,340.1	957,370,364.1	7,204,714.4	994,067,035.0	6,362,841.3
Built 1939 or earlier	2,440,168,829.5	21,472,986.8	2,587,630,915.7	13,660,327.4	2,542,026,422.5	12,359,882.2

Source: U.S. Census Bureau, 2010 American Community Survey

Table 2-29a. Median Housing Value of Owner-Occupied Housing Units, United States: Urban/Rural Areas, States, and Puerto Rico, 2010 American Community Survey, 1-, 3-, and 5-Year Estimates

[Percent.]

State/Territory	1-year estimates		3-year estimates		5-year estimates	
	Median	Margin of error (+/-)	Median	Margin of error (+/-)	Median	Margin of error (+/-)
United States	179,000	232	187,500	198	188,400	184
Urban and rural areas						
Urban	191,300	351	200,400	260	203,200	201
Rural	160,300	446	162,100	308	159,100	224
Inside and outside metropolitan statistical areas						
In metropolitan or micropolitan statistical area	188,100	403	196,200	227	197,500	211
In metropolitan statistical area	198,900	353	109,000	233	211,400	188
In principal city	185,000	604	193,700	312	196,000	273
Not in principal city	205,400	447	215,700	273	217,900	233
In micropolitan statistical area	124,400	636	124,700	292	122,000	273
In principal city	115,400	1,005	115,500	511	111,800	452
Not in principal city	129,200	975	129,800	474	126,700	431
Not in metropolitan or micropolitan statistical area	102,500	599	101,800	347	99,500	255
Alabama	123,900	1,515	121,800	740	117,600	530
Alaska	241,400	5,365	235,300	2,272	229,100	1,625
Arizona	168,800	1,273	195,400	884	215,000	681
Arkansas	106,300	1,591	105,400	843	102,300	683
California	370,900	1,528	405,800	1,110	458,500	704
Colorado	236,600	1,553	238,800	955	236,600	636
Connecticut	288,800	2,016	294,300	1,259	296,500	1,092
Delaware	243,600	3,644	248,200	2,092	242,300	1,332
District of Columbia	426,900	16,253	446,300	7,082	443,300	5,422
Florida	164,200	756	187,400	553	205,600	504
Georgia	156,200	949	162,400	492	161,400	456
Hawaii	525,400	9,714	534,900	5,484	537,400	4,237
Idaho	165,100	2,311	173,200	1,062	172,700	925
Illinois	191,800	1,301	202,000	753	202,500	529
Indiana	123,300	895	124,100	536	123,000	415
Iowa	123,400	1,227	122,000	736	119,200	475
Kansas	127,300	1,824	126,600	1,036	122,600	685
Kentucky	121,600	1,429	119,400	877	116,800	552
Louisiana	137,500	1,828	135,600	974	130,000	678
Maine	179,100	2,735	178,600	1,901	176,200	1,164
Maryland	301,400	2,878	321,400	1,365	329,400	816
Massachusetts	334,100	1,711	342,000	966	352,300	752
Michigan	123,300	733	136,600	520	144,200	325
Minnesota	194,300	1,279	202,700	753	206,200	465
Mississippi	100,100	2,117	99,800	1,081	96,500	727
Missouri	139,000	1,279	139,700	583	137,700	456
Montana	181,200	3,525	180,800	1,784	173,300	1,236
Nebraska	127,600	1,502	126,300	893	123,900	598
Nevada	174,800	2,325	220,000	1,631	254,200	1,625
New Hampshire	243,000	3,163	251,000	1,702	253,200	1,081
New Jersey	339,200	1,549	350,300	934	357,000	765
New Mexico	161,200	2,450	163,300	1,320	158,400	1,029
New York	296,500	2,478	304,100	1,387	303,900	947
North Carolina	154,200	988	154,500	610	149,100	471
North Dakota	123,000	3,132	117,200	1,438	111,300	960
Ohio	134,400	767	136,700	453	136,400	306
Oklahoma	111,400	1,236	108,500	618	104,300	508
Oregon	244,500	1,824	257,700	1,470	252,600	1,173
Pennsylvania	165,500	863	165,200	485	159,300	347
Rhode Island	254,500	4,443	271,000	1,935	279,300	1,427
South Carolina	138,100	1,274	138,300	887	134,100	699
South Dakota	129,700	3,184	127,600	1,796	122,200	1,035
Tennessee	139,000	1,433	138,600	671	134,100	467
Texas	128,100	783	127,400	429	123,500	249
Utah	217,200	1,811	225,400	1,125	218,100	840
Vermont	216,800	3,888	215,400	2,046	208,400	1,540
Virginia	249,100	1,591	256,600	1,144	255,100	1,070
Washington	271,800	1,696	287,300	986	285,400	857
West Virginia	95,100	2,307	95,400	1,081	94,500	728
Wisconsin	169,400	826	171,000	394	169,000	312
Wyoming	180,100	3,876	184,700	2,540	174,000	1,765
Puerto Rico	120,300	1,324	120,200	567	112,600	511

Source: U.S. Census Bureau, American Community Survey

Table 2-30. Median and Aggregate Gross Rent, by Year Structure Built, 2010 American Community Survey, 1-, 3-, and 5-Year Estimates

[Dollars in thousands, except as noted.]

Characteristics	United States					
	1-year estimates		3-year estimates		5-year estimates	
	Estimate	Margin of error (+/-)	Estimate	Margin of error (+/-)	Estimate	Margin of error (+/-)
Median value (dollars)						
Total	855	2	850	1	841	1
Built 2005 or later	1,032	8	1,045	5	1,043	4
Built 2000 to 2004	970	6	979	4	970	3
Built 1990 to 1999	874	4	875	3	870	3
Built 1980 to 1989	827	4	830	3	822	2
Built 1970 to 1979	800	3	795	2	789	2
Built 1960 to 1969	834	4	825	3	816	2
Built 1950 to 1959	855	4	848	3	839	2
Built 1940 to 1949	841	6	829	3	821	3
Built 1939 or earlier	845	4	840	3	832	2
Aggregate value						
Total	35,790,785.3	108,916.3	34,977,026.5	78,728.0	33,711,093.0	142,356.6
Built 2005 or later	2,794,052.9	33,327.5	2,137,108.3	16,569.0	1,590,446.9	10,180.3
Built 2000 to 2004	2,668,639.5	29,993.9	2,673,955.8	19,406.7	2,765,776.5	16,340.8
Built 1990 to 1999	4,378,076.2	38,656.0	4,284,887.8	23,815.9	4,108,169.0	21,239.4
Built 1980 to 1989	4,949,916.2	45,592.8	4,911,915.7	25,694.7	4,793,716.0	25,748.7
Built 1970 to 1979	5,930,888.8	44,343.8	5,908,382.6	26,798.1	5,769,284.1	27,561.4
Built 1960 to 1969	4,102,593.5	40,450.1	4,048,024.0	21,702.5	3,955,940.8	23,917.6
Built 1950 to 1959	3,543,998.3	33,477.2	3,549,448.4	20,988.7	3,439,854.1	22,168.1
Built 1940 to 1949	2,062,305.7	29,228.0	2,084,297.6	14,592.8	2,026,470.0	13,177.0
Built 1939 or earlier	5,360,314.2	44,487.8	5,379,006.3	23,098.6	5,261,435.6	37,830.3

Source: U.S. Census Bureau, 2010 American Community Survey

Table 2-31. Rental and Homeowner Vacancy Rates for the United States, 1965–2012

[Percent.]

Year	Rental vacancy rates				Homeowner vacancy rates			
	First quarter	Second quarter	Third quarter	Fourth quarter	First quarter	Second quarter	Third quarter	Fourth quarter
2012	8.8	8.6	X	X	2.2	2.1	X	X
2011	9.7	9.2	9.8	9.4	2.6	2.5	2.4	2.3
2010	10.6	10.6	10.3	9.4	2.6	2.5	2.5	2.7
2009	10.1	10.6	11.1	10.7	2.7	2.5	2.6	2.7
2008	10.1	10.0	9.9	10.1	2.9	2.8	2.8	2.9
2007	10.1	9.5	9.8	9.6	2.8	2.6	2.7	2.8
2006	9.5	9.6	9.9	9.8	2.1	2.2	2.5	2.7
2005	10.1	9.8	9.9	9.6	1.8	1.8	1.9	2.0
2004	10.4	10.2	10.1	10.0	1.7	1.7	1.7	1.8
2003	9.4	9.6	9.9	10.2	1.7	1.7	1.9	1.8
2002 [1]	9.1	8.4	9.0	9.3	1.7	1.7	1.7	1.7
2002	9.1	8.5	9.1	9.4	1.7	1.7	1.7	1.7
2001	8.2	8.3	8.4	8.8	1.5	1.8	1.9	1.8
2000	7.9	8.0	8.2	7.8	1.6	1.5	1.6	1.6
1999	8.2	8.1	8.2	7.9	1.8	1.6	1.6	1.6
1998	7.7	8.0	8.2	7.8	1.7	1.7	1.7	1.8
1997	7.5	7.9	7.9	7.7	1.7	1.6	1.5	1.7
1996	7.9	7.8	8.0	7.7	1.6	1.5	1.7	1.7
1995	7.4	7.7	7.7	7.7	1.5	1.6	1.5	1.6
1994	7.5	7.4	7.2	7.4	1.4	1.4	1.4	1.6
1993 [2]	7.8	7.6	7.0	6.9	1.4	1.4	1.4	1.4
1993	7.9	7.6	7.1	6.9	1.4	1.4	1.4	1.4
1992	7.4	7.7	7.3	7.1	1.5	1.6	1.6	1.5
1991	7.5	7.3	7.6	7.3	1.7	1.8	1.8	1.6
1990	7.5	7.0	7.2	7.2	1.7	1.7	1.7	1.7
1989 [3]	7.5	7.4	7.6	7.1	1.7	1.7	1.9	1.8
1989	7.3	7.3	7.3	6.8	1.5	1.6	1.8	1.6
1988	8.0	7.7	7.8	7.3	1.6	1.6	1.6	1.6
1987	7.4	7.5	8.1	7.8	1.7	1.7	1.7	1.6
1986	6.9	7.3	7.5	7.7	1.5	1.7	1.6	1.6
1985	6.3	6.2	6.8	6.7	1.8	1.9	1.8	1.6
1984	5.6	5.5	6.0	6.3	1.6	1.7	1.7	1.7
1983	5.7	5.5	5.8	5.5	1.4	1.5	1.6	1.6
1982	5.3	5.1	5.3	5.5	1.4	1.6	1.5	1.6
1981	5.2	5.0	5.0	5.0	1.3	1.3	1.5	1.4
1980	5.2	5.6	5.7	5.0	1.3	1.4	1.4	1.4
1979 [4]	5.1	5.5	5.7	5.4	1.1	1.1	1.2	1.3
1979	4.8	5.0	5.2	5.0	1.0	1.1	1.1	1.1
1978	5.0	5.1	5.0	5.0	1.0	0.9	1.0	1.1
1977	5.1	5.3	5.4	5.1	1.3	1.3	1.1	1.0
1976	5.5	5.8	5.7	5.3	1.2	1.2	1.3	1.2
1975	6.1	6.3	6.2	5.4	1.2	1.2	1.4	1.2
1974	6.2	6.3	6.2	6.0	1.2	1.1	1.2	1.3
1973	5.7	5.8	5.8	5.8	1.0	0.9	1.1	1.2
1972	5.3	5.5	5.8	5.6	1.0	1.0	0.9	1.0
1971	5.3	5.3	5.6	5.6	1.0	0.9	1.0	1.0
1970	5.4	5.4	5.3	5.2	1.0	1.0	1.1	1.1
1969	5.6	5.7	5.5	5.1	1.0	1.0	1.1	1.0
1968	6.1	6.2	5.9	5.4	1.1	1.1	1.2	1.2
1967	7.3	6.9	7.0	6.2	1.4	1.3	1.4	1.3
1966	8.3	7.4	7.4	7.7	1.5	1.5	1.4	1.3
1965	8.5	8.2	7.8	8.5	1.7	1.5	1.6	1.5

X = Not applicable.
[1] = Revised based on the 2000 Census.
[2] = Revised based on the 1990 Census.
[3] = Revised to include year-round vacant mobile homes.
[4] = Revised to reflect changes made in 1980. See Source and Accuracy Statement for more information.

Source: U.S. Census Bureau, Housing Vacancies and Homeownership Survey (CPS/HVS)

Table 2-32. Rental Vacancy Rates, Homeowner Vacancy Rates, Gross Vacancy Rates, and Homeownership Rates for Old and New Construction, 2006–2012

[Percent.]

Year/Quarter	Rental vacancy rates			Homeowner vacancy rates			Gross vacancy rates			Homeownership rates		
	Total	Old construction	New construction	Total	Old construction	New construction	Total	Old construction	New construction	Total	Old construction	New construction
First quarter 2012	8.8	8.7	9.7	2.2	2.0	2.9	13.9	14.0	13.4	65.4	64.3	73.3
Second quarter 2012	8.6	8.5	9.9	2.1	2.0	2.6	14.0	13.9	14.0	65.5	64.4	73.7
Annual 2011	9.5	9.3	11.3	2.5	2.3	3.6	14.2	14.1	14.5	66.1	65.1	74.3
First quarter 2011	9.7	9.4	12.2	2.6	2.4	3.8	14.4	14.3	15.3	66.4	65.4	74.4
Second quarter 2011	9.2	8.9	11.7	2.5	2.4	3.8	14.3	14.1	15.3	65.9	64.9	74.2
Third quarter 2011	9.8	9.6	11.5	2.4	2.3	3.3	14.2	14.2	14.0	66.3	65.2	74.5
Fourth quarter 2011	9.4	9.3	9.8	2.3	2.1	3.3	13.9	13.9	13.4	66.0	64.9	74.2
Annual 2010	10.2	9.9	14.5	2.6	2.3	4.2	14.3	14.2	15.3	66.9	65.8	75.9
First quarter 2010	10.6	10.1	16.7	2.6	2.3	4.5	14.5	14.3	16.4	67.1	65.9	77.4
Second quarter 2010	10.6	10.1	15.2	2.5	2.3	4.1	14.4	14.3	15.8	66.9	65.8	75.9
Third quarter 2010	10.3	10.0	14.1	2.5	2.3	4.0	14.4	14.3	15.1	66.9	65.9	75.2
Fourth quarter 2010	9.4	9.2	12.3	2.7	2.4	4.2	14.1	14.0	14.2	66.5	65.4	75.4
Annual 2009	10.6	10.2	15.5	2.6	2.3	4.7	14.5	14.3	16.0	67.4	66.2	77.4
First quarter 2009	10.1	9.7	14.6	2.7	2.3	5.5	14.6	14.4	16.4	67.3	66.2	77.1
Second quarter 2009	10.6	10.2	15.3	2.5	2.2	4.2	14.3	14.1	15.8	67.4	66.3	76.7
Third quarter 2009	11.1	10.6	16.9	2.6	2.3	4.5	14.5	14.3	16.0	67.6	66.4	77.7
Fourth quarter 2009	10.7	10.4	15.4	2.7	2.4	4.7	14.5	14.3	15.9	67.2	65.9	78.0
Annual 2008	10.0	9.7	14.6	2.8	2.4	6.1	14.4	14.1	16.8	67.8	66.7	78.0
First quarter 2008	10.1	9.7	15.2	2.9	2.4	6.9	14.3	14.1	17.1	67.8	66.7	78.6
Second quarter 2008	10.0	9.6	15.2	2.8	2.3	6.1	14.4	14.1	17.0	68.1	67.0	78.3
Third quarter 2008	9.9	9.6	14.3	2.8	2.4	6.0	14.3	14.0	16.5	67.9	66.9	77.5
Fourth quarter 2008	10.1	9.8	13.9	2.9	2.5	5.5	14.5	14.3	16.5	67.5	66.4	77.6
Annual 2007	9.7	9.4	14.2	2.7	2.4	5.6	13.8	13.6	16.0	68.1	67.1	79.3
First quarter 2007	10.1	9.7	17.3	2.8	2.5	5.7	13.8	13.6	16.4	68.4	67.3	80.6
Second quarter 2007	9.5	9.3	12.6	2.6	2.3	5.2	13.6	13.5	15.3	68.2	67.2	79.0
Third quarter 2007	9.8	9.6	12.8	2.7	2.3	5.7	14.0	13.8	15.9	68.2	67.1	78.6
Fourth quarter 2007	9.6	9.3	14.4	2.8	2.4	6.0	13.8	13.5	16.4	67.8	66.7	78.9
Annual 2006	9.7	9.4	14.6	2.4	2.2	4.2	13.0	12.9	14.5	68.8	67.9	79.8
First quarter 2006	9.5	9.3	14.1	2.1	1.9	3.5	12.8	12.8	13.7	68.5	67.6	80.2
Second quarter 2006	9.6	9.4	13.4	2.2	2.0	4.1	13.0	12.9	14.4	68.7	67.8	79.6
Third quarter 2006	9.9	9.5	16.1	2.5	2.2	4.8	13.1	13.0	15.4	69.0	68.1	79.0
Fourth quarter 2006	9.8	9.6	14.4	2.7	2.5	4.4	13.2	13.1	14.5	68.9	67.9	80.5

Source: U.S. Census Bureau, Housing Vacancies and Homeownership Survey (CPS/HVS)

Table 2-33. Rental and Homeowner Vacancy Rates, by Area, Second Quarter, 2011 and 2012

[Percent.]

Characteristics	Rental vacancy rates				Homeowner vacancy rates			
	Second quarter 2011	Second quarter 2012	90-percent confidence interval (+/-) [1]		Second quarter 2011	Second quarter 2012	90-percent confidence interval (+/-) [1]	
			of 2012 rate	of difference			of 2012 rate	of difference
United States	9.2	8.6	0.4	0.4	2.5	2.1	0.1	0.2
Inside metropolitan statistical areas	9.2	8.5	0.4	0.4	2.6	2.0	0.2	0.2
In principal cities	9.6	8.9	0.6	0.6	2.9	2.4	0.3	0.3
Not in principal cities (suburbs)	8.6	8.1	0.6	0.7	2.4	1.8	0.2	0.2
Outside metropolitan statistical areas	9.1	9.2	1.4	1.4	2.3	2.4	0.3	0.4
Northeast	6.8	6.7	0.7	0.8	2.3	1.7	0.3	0.4
Midwest	10.3	9.1	0.7	0.9	2.5	2.2	0.3	0.3
South	11.4	11	0.8	0.9	2.7	2.1	0.2	0.3
West	6.8	6.2	0.7	0.8	2.5	2.2	0.3	0.4

[1] = A 90-percent confidence interval is a measure of an estimate's reliability. The larger the confidence interval is, in relation to the size of the estimate, the less reliable the estimate.

Source: U.S. Census Bureau, Housing Vacancies and Homeownership Survey (CPS/HVS)

Table 2-34. Rental Vacancy Rates, by Selected Characteristics and Percent Distribution of All Units, Second Quarter 2011 and 2012

[Percent distribution.]

Characteristics	Second quarter 2011		Second quarter 2012		
	Rental vacancy rate	Percent of total	Rental vacancy rate	Percent of total	90-percent confidence interval (+/-)[1] 2012
Total rental units	9.2	100.0	8.6	100.0	0.4
Rooms in unit					
1 and 2 rooms	26.3	4.2	26.1	4.2	2.9
3 rooms	9.6	21.8	8.7	21.7	0.8
4 rooms	9.2	32.1	8.8	32.1	0.7
5 rooms	8.1	22.9	7.6	22.9	0.8
6 rooms or more	6.7	19.1	6.2	19.1	0.8
Housing units in structure					
1 unit in structure	8.5	37.0	8.1	37.0	0.6
2 to 4 units	9.2	19.8	8.5	19.7	0.9
5 to 9 units	9.5	13.1	9.6	13.2	1.1
10 units or more	10.2	30.1	9.4	30.0	0.7
2 or more units	9.7	63.0	9.1	63.0	0.5
5 or more units	10.0	43.2	9.4	43.2	0.6
Year structure built					
April 1, 2000 or later	16.6	7.8	14.6	7.6	1.8
1995 to March 31, 2000	8.7	5.9	8.9	5.9	1.6
1990 to 1994	10.3	3.7	12.2	3.8	2.3
1980 to 1989	9.5	13.2	10.0	13.4	1.1
1970 to 1979	7.7	22.5	7.6	22.6	0.8
1960 to 1969	9.5	12.5	9.0	12.5	1.1
1950 to 1959	9.8	9.2	8.6	9.1	1.3
1940 to 1949	8.5	6.5	7.2	6.5	1.4
1939 or earlier	7.8	18.8	6.4	18.6	0.8
Monthly rent, specified renter units[2]					
All specified renter units	9.7	90.8	9.3	89.6	0.4
Less than $300	4.2	3.0	2.9	2.0	0.9
$300 to $349	7.4	2.0	8.2	2.1	2.5
$350 to $399	11.0	3.3	13.5	4.1	2.9
$400 to $449	12.7	5.4	11.3	4.5	2.3
$450 to $499	13.7	7.0	13.7	6.8	2.3
$500 to $599	12.1	14.5	10.2	11.9	1.3
$600 to $699	10.8	12.3	10.2	11.7	1.3
$700 to $799	9.3	9.2	9.7	10.0	1.4
$800 or more	9.0	34.3	8.7	36.5	0.6
$800 to $899	10.1	8.3	9.7	8.4	1.5
$900 to $999	6.7	4.1	7.2	4.8	1.5
$1,000 or more	9.2	21.9	8.8	23.3	0.8
$1,000 to $1,249	8.9	9.0	8.3	9.0	1.2
$1,250 to $1,499	8.5	4.5	7.2	4.2	1.6
$1,500 or more	9.9	8.4	10.2	10.0	1.4

[1] = A 90-percent confidence interval is a measure of an estimate's reliability. The larger the confidence interval is, in relation to the size of the estimate, the less reliable the estimate.
[2] = Limited to one-family homes on less than 10 acres and no business on property (including mobile homes).

Source: U.S. Census Bureau, Housing Vacancies and Homeownership Survey (CPS/HVS)

Table 2-35. Homeowner Vacancy Rates, by Selected Characteristics and Percent Distribution of All Units, Second Quarter 2011 and 2012

[Percent distribution.]

Characteristics	Second quarter 2011		Second quarter 2012		
	Homeowner vacancy rate	Percent of total	Homeowner vacancy rate	Percent of total	90-percent confidence interval (+/-)[1] 2012
Total homeowner units	2.5	100.0	2.1	100.0	0.1
Rooms in unit					
3 rooms or less	13.9	1.7	14.3	1.7	2.3
4 rooms	5.5	8.7	4.2	8.7	0.6
5 rooms	3.0	22.7	2.2	22.6	0.3
6 rooms or more	1.7	66.9	1.4	67.1	0.1
Housing units in structure					
1 unit in structure	2.2	94.8	1.8	94.8	0.1
2 to 4 units	8.8	1.9	7.4	1.9	1.7
5 to 9 units	8.2	0.9	7.2	0.9	2.4
10 units or more	8.7	2.4	7.3	2.4	1.5
2 or more units	8.7	5.2	7.3	5.2	1.0
5 or more units	8.6	3.3	7.2	3.3	1.2
Year structure built					
April 1, 2000 or later	4.6	13.1	3.6	13.0	0.5
1995 to March 31, 2000	2.3	9.6	1.5	9.6	0.3
1990 to 1994	2.1	6.1	1.8	6.2	0.5
1980 to 1989	2.5	12.2	1.6	12.2	0.3
1970 to 1979	1.7	17.1	1.5	17.1	0.3
1960 to 1969	2.1	11.6	2.1	11.7	0.4
1950 to 1959	2.7	11.2	2.0	11.2	0.4
1940 to 1949	2.8	5.8	2.5	5.8	0.6
1939 or earlier	2.3	13.2	2.2	13.3	0.3
Value, specified owner units[2]					
All specified owner units	2.2	87.0	1.7	87.8	0.1
Less than $50,000	3.3	7.9	2.9	8.0	0.5
$50,000 to $74,999	2.4	5.9	2.6	6.5	0.5
$75,000 to $99,999	2.2	8.1	1.9	8.6	0.4
$100,000 to $149,999	3.6	13.0	1.9	14.6	0.3
$150,000 to $199,999	2.9	11.0	1.7	12.7	0.3
$200,000 or more	1.3	41.0	1.2	37.4	0.2
$200,000 to $249,999	1.8	8.3	1.3	9.0	0.3
$250,000 to $299,999	1.4	6.5	1.6	6.4	0.4
$300,000 to $399,999	1.3	9.2	0.9	8.9	0.3
$400,000 to $499,999	0.8	5.3	1.1	4.8	0.4
$500,000 or more	1.0	11.7	1.3	8.2	0.3

[1] = A 90-percent confidence interval is a measure of an estimate's reliability. The larger the confidence interval is, in relation to the size of the estimate, the less reliable the estimate.
[2] = Limited to one-family homes on less than 10 acres and no business on property (including mobile homes).

Source: U.S. Census Bureau, Housing Vacancies and Homeownership Survey (CPS/HVS)

Table 2-36. Estimates of the Total Housing Inventory for the United States, Second Quarter 2011 and 2012

[Numbers in thousands, percent.]

Characteristics	Second quarter 2011 estimate	Second quarter 2012 estimate	90-percent confidence interval (+/-)[1]		2012 percent of total
			of 2012 estimate	of difference	
All housing units	132,232	132,718	X	X	100.0
Occupied	113,391	114,200	257	234	86.0
Owner occupied	74,706	74,832	630	430	56.4
Renter occupied	38,684	39,369	559	431	29.7
Vacant	18,843	18,518	376	336	14.0
Year-round vacant	14,271	14,025	370	321	10.6
For rent	3,947	3,766	172	195	2.8
For sale only	1,959	1,595	96	127	1.2
Rented or sold, awaiting occupancy	1,017	1,052	71	99	0.8
Held off market	7,347	7,612	280	242	5.7
For occasional use	2,312	2,413	161	139	1.8
Temporarily occupied by persons with usual residence elsewhere	1,166	1,271	118	100	1.0
For other reasons	3,869	3,928	205	177	3.0
Seasonal vacant	4,571	4,493	243	214	3.4

X = Not applicable.
[1] = A 90-percent confidence interval is a measure of an estimate's reliability. The larger the confidence interval is, in relation to the size of the estimate, the less reliable the estimate.

Source: U.S. Census Bureau, Housing Vacancies and Homeownership Survey (CPS/HVS)

Table 2-37. Homeownership Rates for the United States, 1968–2012

[Percent.]

Year	First quarter	Second quarter	Third quarter	Fourth quarter
2012	65.4	65.5	X	X
2011	66.4	65.9	66.3	66.0
2010	67.1	66.9	66.9	66.5
2009	67.3	67.4	67.6	67.2
2008	67.8	68.1	67.9	67.5
2007	68.4	68.2	68.2	67.8
2006	68.5	68.7	69.0	68.9
2005	69.1	68.6	68.8	69.0
2004	68.6	69.2	69.0	69.2
2003	68.0	68.0	68.4	68.6
2002 [1]	67.8	67.6	68.0	68.3
2002	67.8	67.6	68.0	68.3
2001	67.5	67.7	68.1	68.0
2000	67.1	67.2	67.7	67.5
1999	66.7	66.6	67.0	66.9
1998	65.9	66.0	66.8	66.4
1997	65.4	65.7	66.0	65.7
1996	65.1	65.4	65.6	65.4
1995	64.2	64.7	65.0	65.1
1994	63.8	63.8	64.1	64.2
1993 [2]	63.7	63.9	64.2	64.2
1993	64.2	64.4	64.7	64.6
1992	64.0	63.9	64.3	64.4
1991	63.9	63.9	64.2	64.2
1990	64.0	63.7	64.0	64.1
1989 [3]	63.9	63.8	64.1	63.8
1989	63.9	63.9	64.0	63.8
1988	63.7	63.7	64.0	63.8
1987	63.8	63.8	64.2	64.1
1986	63.6	63.8	63.8	63.9
1985	64.1	64.1	63.9	63.5
1984	64.6	64.6	64.6	64.1
1983	64.7	64.7	64.8	64.4
1982	64.8	64.9	64.9	64.5
1981	65.6	65.3	65.6	65.2
1980	65.5	65.5	65.8	65.5
1979 [4]	64.8	64.9	65.8	65.4
1979	65.3	65.1	66.0	65.8
1978	64.8	64.4	65.2	65.4
1977	64.8	64.5	65.0	64.9
1976	64.6	64.6	64.9	64.8
1975	64.4	64.9	64.6	64.5
1974	64.8	64.8	64.6	64.4
1973	64.9	64.4	64.4	64.4
1972	64.3	64.5	64.3	64.4
1971	64.0	64.1	64.4	64.5
1970	64.3	64.0	64.4	64.0
1969	64.1	64.4	64.4	64.4
1968	63.6	64.1	64.1	63.6

X = Not applicable.
[1] = Revised based on the 2000 Census.
[2] = Revised based on the 1990 Census.
[3] = Revised to include year-round vacant mobile homes.
[4] = Revised to reflect changes made in 1980. See Source and Accuracy Statement for more information.

Source: U.S. Census Bureau, Housing Vacancies and Homeownership Survey (CPS/HVS)

Table 2-38. Homeownership Rates, by Area, Second Quarter, 2011 and 2012

[Percent.]

Characteristics	Second quarter 2011 estimate	Second quarter 2012 estimate	90-percent confidence interval (+/-)[1]	
			of 2012 estimate	of difference
United States	65.9	65.5	0.5	0.4
Inside metropolitan statistical areas	64.4	64.1	1.3	0.5
In principal cities	51.2	51.0	1.0	0.5
Not in principal cities (suburbs)	73.2	72.8	1.3	0.5
Outside metropolitan statistical areas	73.5	72.9	2.7	0.7
Northeast	63.0	63.7	0.9	0.8
Midwest	70.0	69.6	1.0	0.8
South	68.2	67.4	0.9	0.6
West	60.3	59.7	1.2	0.8

[1] = A 90-percent confidence interval is a measure of an estimate's reliability. The larger the confidence interval is, in relation to the size of the estimate, the less reliable the estimate.

Source: U.S. Census Bureau, Housing Vacancies and Homeownership Survey (CPS/HVS)

Table 2-39. Homeownership Rates by Age of Householder, Second Quarter, 2011 and 2012

[Percent.]

Age of householder	Second quarter 2011	Second quarter 2012	90-percent confidence interval (+/-)[1]	
			of 2012 estimate	of difference
United States, total	65.9	65.5	0.5	0.4
Under 25 years	21.9	21.9	1.5	1.4
25 to 29 years	34.7	33.6	1.4	1.3
30 to 34 years	49.5	47.5	1.4	1.3
35 to 39 years	60.5	57.6	1.4	1.3
40 to 44 years	66.9	66.3	1.3	1.2
45 to 49 years	70.2	69.6	1.2	1.3
50 to 54 years	74.3	73.1	1.1	1.2
55 to 59 years	76.8	76.1	0.8	0.9
60 to 64 years	79.0	78.3	0.8	0.9
65 to 69 years	81.2	81.1	1.3	1.1
70 to 74 years	83.3	83.8	1.4	1.2
75 years and over	79.4	80.8	1.1	0.9
Under 35 years	37.5	36.5	0.9	0.8
35 to 44 years	63.8	62.2	1.0	0.9
45 to 54 years	72.3	71.4	0.8	0.9
55 to 64 years	77.8	77.1	0.6	0.6
65 years and over	80.8	81.6	0.7	0.6

[1] = A 90-percent confidence interval is a measure of an estimate's reliability. The larger the confidence interval is, in relation to the size of the estimate, the less reliable the estimate.

Source: U.S. Census Bureau, Housing Vacancies and Homeownership Survey (CPS/HVS)

Table 2-40. National Characteristics of Units for Rent and Vacant for Sale Only, by Units in Structure, Second Quarter 2011 and 2012

[Percent, except as noted.]

Characteristics	Second quarter 2012 total	1-unit structures	2-unit structures or greater	Second quarter 2011 total	1-unit structures	2-unit structures or greater	90-percent confidence interval (+/-)[1] On 2012 total	On 2012 1-units	On 2012 2-units or greater
Vacant for rent, total	100.0	34.1	65.9	100.0	33.8	66.2	X	2.2	2.2
Rooms in unit, total	100.0	100.0	100.0	100.0	100.0	100.0	X	X	X
1 and 2 rooms	12.6	6.4	15.7	11.9	6.4	14.6	1.5	2.0	2.1
3 rooms	21.5	12.1	26.5	22.7	10.9	28.7	1.9	2.6	2.5
4 rooms	32.3	24.1	36.6	31.8	25.9	34.7	2.2	3.4	2.8
5 rooms or more	33.6	57.3	21.3	33.7	56.8	22.0	2.2	3.9	2.3
Median number of rooms	4.0	4.7	3.7	4.0	4.7	3.7	X	X	X
Bedrooms in unit, total	100.0	100.0	100.0	100.0	100.0	100.0	X	X	X
No bedrooms	2.7	1.8	3.2	2.9	1.5	40.0	0.8	1.1	1.0
1 bedroom	29.7	14.6	37.6	31.6	15.3	44.9	2.1	2.8	2.8
2 bedrooms	45.5	39.4	48.6	43.7	41.3	11.4	2.3	3.9	2.9
3 bedrooms or more	22.1	44.2	10.6	21.7	41.9	3.7	1.9	3.9	1.8
Duration of vacancy, total	100.0	100.0	100.0	100.0	100.0	100.0	X	X	X
Less than 1 month	23.0	20.5	24.2	21.8	20.5	22.5	2.0	3.2	2.5
1 to 2 months	18.2	15.6	19.6	17.4	15.9	18.2	1.8	2.9	2.3
2 to 4 months	16.1	14.2	17.1	16.3	15.0	17.0	1.7	2.8	2.2
4 to 6 months	11.3	11.0	11.5	12.0	12.2	11.8	1.5	2.5	1.8
6 to 12 months	14.3	17.7	12.5	15.5	15.9	15.3	1.6	3.0	1.9
1 to 2 years	9.6	12.1	8.3	9.4	10.4	8.9	1.4	2.6	1.6
2 years or more	7.5	8.9	6.8	7.6	10.1	6.3	1.2	2.3	1.4
Median (in months)	3.1	4.0	2.7	3.3	3.8	3.1	X	X	X
Year structure built, total	100.0	100.0	100.0	100.0	100.0	100.0	X	X	X
April 1, 2000 or later	12.8	12.5	12.9	13.9	14.1	13.8	1.5	2.6	1.9
1995 to March 31, 2000	6.1	5.8	6.1	5.5	5.4	5.5	1.1	1.9	1.4
1990 to 1994	5.2	5.8	5.0	4.1	4.4	3.9	1.0	1.9	1.2
1980 to 1989	15.4	15.2	15.5	13.5	12.8	13.9	1.7	2.9	2.1
1970 to 1979	19.7	18.3	20.5	18.7	15.3	20.4	1.8	3.1	2.3
1960 to 1969	12.8	12.6	13.0	12.8	11.3	13.6	1.6	2.6	1.9
1950 to 1959	9.0	9.7	8.5	9.7	13.6	7.8	1.3	2.4	1.6
1940 to 1949	5.3	5.8	5.0	6.0	7.0	5.5	1.0	1.9	1.3
1939 or earlier	13.7	14.4	13.4	15.8	16.2	15.6	1.6	2.8	1.9
Previous occupancy, total	100.0	100.0	100.0	100.0	100.0	100.0	X	X	X
Previously occupied	97.2	98.1	96.7	97.5	98.3	97.1	0.8	1.1	1.0
Not previously occupied	2.8	1.9	3.3	2.5	1.7	2.9	0.8	1.1	1.0
Monthly rent, total[2]	100.0	100.0	100.0	100.0	100.0	100.0	X	X	X
Less than $300	2.3	2.3	2.2	3.3	5.0	2.3	0.7	1.2	0.9
$300 to $349	2.3	2.6	2.2	2.2	2.6	1.9	0.7	1.3	0.9
$350 to $399	4.6	4.0	4.9	3.6	3.4	3.8	1.0	1.6	1.3
$400 to $449	5.0	5.2	5.0	6.0	5.6	6.2	1.1	1.8	1.3
$450 to $499	7.6	6.6	8.2	7.7	7.8	7.6	1.3	2.0	1.7
$500 to $599	13.3	10.9	14.7	15.9	12.8	17.6	1.7	2.5	2.2
$600 to $699	13.0	11.3	14.0	13.5	13.4	13.6	1.7	2.6	2.1
$700 to $799	11.2	11.8	10.9	10.1	9.1	10.7	1.5	2.6	1.9
$800 or more	40.7	45.5	38.0	37.8	40.3	36.3	2.4	4.0	3.0
$800 to $899	9.4	11.4	8.2	9.1	10.0	8.6	1.4	2.6	1.7
$900 to $999	5.4	6.3	4.9	4.5	4.0	4.8	1.1	2.0	1.3
$1,000 or more	26.0	27.8	24.9	24.1	26.3	22.9	2.2	3.6	2.7
$1,000 to $1,249	10.0	11.2	9.3	10.0	12.0	8.8	1.5	2.6	1.8
$1,250 to $1,499	4.7	5.9	4.1	4.9	5.6	4.5	1.0	1.9	1.2
$1,500 or more	11.2	10.7	11.5	9.2	8.7	9.6	1.5	2.5	2.0
Median (actual dollars)	716	761	692	684	696	678	X	X	X
Median (2012 constant dollars)	716	761	692	697	709	691	X	X	X
Vacant for sale, total	100.0	81.9	18.1	100.0	82.4	17.6	X	2.3	2.3
Rooms in unit, total	100.0	100.0	100.0	100.0	100.0	100.0	X	X	X
3 rooms or less	11.6	6.8	33.2	9.1	6.4	21.6	1.9	1.7	6.7
4 rooms	17.6	14.5	31.5	18.8	14.3	39.7	2.3	2.3	6.6
5 rooms	24.2	24.9	21.5	26.8	27.5	23.3	2.6	2.9	5.8
6 rooms	19.1	21.3	9.7	21.0	23.3	9.9	2.4	2.7	4.2
7 rooms or more	27.4	32.6	4.2	24.3	28.4	5.5	2.7	3.1	2.8
Median number of rooms	5.4	5.7	4.0	5.3	5.6	4.2	X	X	X
Bedrooms in unit, total	100.0	100.0	100.0	100.0	100.0	100.0	X	X	X
1 bedroom or none	11.9	7.1	33.7	9.4	6.0	25.1	2.0	1.7	6.7
2 bedrooms	28.9	25.1	45.8	31.4	26.2	55.6	2.7	2.9	7.1
3 bedrooms	42.0	47.2	18.4	43.3	48.8	17.3	3.0	3.3	5.5
4 bedrooms or more	17.2	20.5	2.1	16.0	19.0	2.0	2.3	2.7	2.0

Table 2-40. National Characteristics of Units for Rent and Vacant for Sale Only, by Units in Structure, Second Quarter 2011 and 2012—*Continued*

[Percent, except as noted.]

Characteristics	Second quarter 2012 total	1-unit structures	2-unit structures or greater	Second quarter 2011 total	1-unit structures	2-unit structures or greater	90-percent confidence interval (+/-)[1]		
							On 2012 total	On 2012 1-units	On 2012 2-units or greater
Duration of vacancy, total	100.0	100.0	100.0	100.0	100.0	100.0	X	X	X
Less than 1 month	6.7	7.3	3.8	6.0	6.7	2.9	1.5	1.7	2.7
1 to 2 months	7.9	8.4	5.9	7.2	7.3	6.4	1.6	1.8	3.3
2 to 4 months	12.0	12.5	10.1	11.3	11.5	10.5	2.0	2.2	4.3
4 to 6 months	13.4	13.4	13.5	12.7	12.8	12.2	2.1	2.3	4.9
6 to 12 months	22.4	23.2	18.8	25.2	27.2	15.7	2.5	2.8	5.5
1 to 2 years	19.7	18.9	23.3	21.2	19.9	27.4	2.4	2.6	6.0
2 years or more	17.9	16.4	24.7	16.5	14.7	24.8	2.3	2.5	6.1
Median (in months)	8.7	8.2	11.3	9.1	8.6	13.0	X	X	X
Year structure built, total	100.0	100.0	100.0	100.0	100.0	100.0	X	X	X
April 1, 2000 or later	22.5	20.8	30.1	23.7	21.8	32.2	2.5	2.7	6.5
1995 to March 31, 2000	6.8	7.0	5.9	8.6	8.8	8.2	1.5	1.7	3.3
1990 to 1994	5.5	5.9	3.8	4.9	5.3	2.9	1.4	1.6	2.7
1980 to 1989	9.4	9.5	9.3	11.7	11.2	14.0	1.8	2.0	4.1
1970 to 1979	12.7	13.2	10.0	11.4	12.4	7.0	2.0	2.3	4.3
1960 to 1969	11.7	12.7	7.3	9.6	10.2	7.3	1.9	2.2	3.7
1950 to 1959	10.9	11.5	7.6	11.7	12.6	7.9	1.9	2.1	3.8
1940 to 1949	6.8	6.3	9.7	6.3	6.1	6.7	1.5	1.6	4.2
1939 or earlier	13.7	13.1	16.3	12.0	11.6	13.7	2.1	2.3	5.2
Previous occupancy, total	100.0	100.0	100.0	100.0	100.0	100.0	X	X	X
Previously occupied	92.5	94.7	82.6	91.6	94.8	76.7	1.6	1.5	5.4
Not previously occupied	7.5	5.3	17.4	8.4	5.2	23.3	1.6	1.5	5.4
Sales price, total[3]	100.0	100.0	X	100.0	100.0	X	X	X	X
Less than $50,000	15.5	15.5	NA	14.1	14.1	NA	2.6	2.6	NA
$50,000 to $74,999	11.0	11.0	NA	7.6	7.6	NA	2.2	2.2	NA
$75,000 to $99,999	11.1	11.1	NA	9.6	9.6	NA	2.2	2.2	NA
$100,000 to $149,999	18.2	18.2	NA	24.5	24.5	NA	2.7	2.7	NA
$150,000 to $199,999	14.3	14.3	NA	16.6	16.6	NA	2.5	2.5	NA
$200,000 to $249,999	7.6	7.6	NA	8.0	8.0	NA	1.9	1.9	NA
$250,000 to $299,999	6.7	6.7	NA	4.8	4.8	NA	1.8	1.8	NA
$300,000 or more	15.7	15.7	NA	14.8	14.8	NA	2.6	2.6	NA
$300,000 to $399,999	5.2	5.2	NA	6.3	6.3	NA	1.6	1.6	NA
$400,000 to $499,999	3.5	3.5	NA	2.2	2.2	NA	1.3	1.3	NA
$500,000 or more	7.1	7.1	NA	6.4	6.4	NA	1.8	1.8	NA
Median (actual dollars)	134,600	134,600	X	138,400	138,400	X	X	X	X
Median (2012 constant dollars)	134,600	134,600	X	141,000	141,000	X	X	X	X

NA = Not available.
X = Not applicable.
[1] = A 90-percent confidence interval is a measure of an estimate's reliability. The larger the confidence interval is, in relation to the size of the estimate, the less reliable the estimate.
[2] = Excludes one-family homes on 10 acres or more.
[3] = Limited to one-family homes on less than 10 acres and no business on property (including mobile homes).

Source: U.S. Census Bureau, Housing Vacancies and Homeownership Survey (CPS/HVS)

Table 2-41. Characteristics of Vacant For-Rent and Vacant For-Sale-Only Units for the United States and Regions: Second Quarter 2012

[Percent, except as noted.]

Characteristics	United States	90-percent confidence interval (+/-)[1]	Northeast	90-percent confidence interval (+/-)[1]	Midwest	90-percent confidence interval (+/-)[1]	South	90-percent confidence interval (+/-)[1]	West	90-percent confidence interval (+/-)[1]
Vacant for rent, total	100.0	X	14.5	1.4	21.2	1.6	46.2	2.5	18.1	1.8
Units in structure, total	100.0	X	100.0	X	100.0	X	100.0	X	100.0	X
1 unit	29.8	2.1	20.2	4.1	26.3	3.8	33.0	3.5	33.2	5.1
2 units	8.3	1.3	15.2	3.7	8.3	2.4	6.5	1.9	7.3	2.8
3 and 4 units	10.8	1.4	21.1	4.2	12.8	2.8	7.2	1.9	9.5	3.2
5 to 9 units	14.6	1.6	9.5	3.0	15.5	3.1	16.5	2.8	12.5	3.6
10 units or more	32.2	2.2	32.5	4.8	34.6	4.1	30.2	3.5	33.9	5.2
Mobile homes	4.4	1.0	1.5	1.2	2.5	1.3	6.5	1.9	3.5	2.0
Rooms in unit, total	100.0	X	100.0	X	100.0	X	100.0	X	100.0	X
1 and 2 rooms	12.6	1.5	16.7	3.8	10.5	2.6	10.2	2.3	17.6	4.2
3 rooms	21.5	1.9	24.7	4.4	23.3	3.6	19.4	3.0	22.6	4.6
4 rooms	32.3	2.2	28.0	4.6	35.0	4.1	34.3	3.6	27.6	4.9
5 rooms or more	33.6	2.2	30.6	4.7	31.3	3.9	36.1	3.6	32.2	5.1
Median number of rooms	3.7	X	3.8	X	4.0	X	4.1	X	3.9	X
Bedrooms in unit, total	100.0	X	100.0	X	100.0	X	100.0	X	100.0	X
No bedrooms	2.7	0.8	1.7	1.3	3.8	1.6	1.7	1.0	4.9	2.3
1 bedroom	29.7	2.1	40.0	5.0	31.9	4.0	25.6	3.3	29.6	5.0
2 bedrooms	45.5	2.3	42.6	5.0	45.1	4.2	48.0	3.8	41.9	5.4
3 bedrooms or more	22.1	1.9	15.8	3.7	19.3	3.4	24.7	3.2	23.7	4.6
Duration of vacancy, total	100.0	X	100.0	X	100.0	X	100.0	X	100.0	X
Less than 1 month	23.0	2.0	19.6	4.1	20.5	3.4	22.4	3.1	29.8	5.0
1 to 2 months	18.2	1.8	21.3	4.2	16.0	3.1	17.2	2.8	21.0	4.4
2 to 4 months	16.1	1.7	12.8	3.4	15.4	3.1	17.5	2.9	16.0	4.0
4 to 6 months	11.3	1.5	10.8	3.2	13.5	2.9	10.3	2.3	11.6	3.5
6 to 12 months	14.3	1.6	13.6	3.5	15.4	3.1	14.7	2.7	12.6	3.6
1 to 2 years	9.6	1.4	13.4	3.5	9.9	2.5	9.9	2.2	5.3	2.4
2 years or more	7.5	1.2	8.4	2.8	9.4	2.5	7.9	2.0	3.7	2.1
Median (in months)	3.1	X	3.4	X	3.8	X	3.2	X	2.9	X
Year structure built, total	100.0	X	100.0	X	100.0	X	100.0	X	100.0	X
April 1, 2000 or later	12.8	1.5	5.7	2.4	7.5	2.2	14.6	2.7	19.9	4.4
1995 to March 31, 2000	6.1	1.1	2.6	1.6	4.3	1.7	7.1	1.9	8.2	3.0
1990 to 1994	5.2	1.0	1.3	1.1	4.3	1.7	7.5	2.0	3.7	2.0
1980 to 1989	15.4	1.7	7.5	2.7	10.0	2.6	17.8	2.9	21.8	4.5
1970 to 1979	19.7	1.8	13.2	3.5	16.1	3.1	25.0	3.3	16.0	4.0
1960 to 1969	12.8	1.6	9.5	3.0	18.3	3.3	10.6	2.3	15.0	3.9
1950 to 1959	9.0	1.3	12.8	3.4	9.3	2.5	8.3	2.1	7.2	2.8
1940 to 1949	5.3	1.0	11.2	3.2	6.6	2.1	3.6	1.4	3.2	1.9
1939 or earlier	13.7	1.6	36.1	4.9	23.8	3.6	5.5	1.7	5.0	2.4
Previous occupancy, total	100.0	X	100.0	X	100.0	X	100.0	X	100.0	X
Previously occupied	97.2	0.8	97.6	1.6	97.9	1.2	97.5	1.2	95.4	2.3
Not previously occupied	2.8	0.8	2.4	1.6	2.1	1.2	2.5	1.2	4.6	2.3
Monthly rent asked, total[2]	100.0	X	100.0	X	100.0	X	100.0	X	100.0	X
Less than $300	2.3	0.7	1.9	1.4	2.5	1.4	2.8	1.3	1.1	1.2
$300 to $349	2.3	0.7	1.9	1.4	3.3	1.6	2.4	1.2	1.5	1.4
$350 to $399	4.6	1.0	3.1	1.8	9.6	2.6	3.9	1.6	1.7	1.4
$400 to $449	5.0	1.1	2.1	1.5	7.8	2.4	6.1	1.9	2.0	1.6
$450 to $499	7.6	1.3	2.9	1.7	11.8	2.9	8.6	2.3	4.3	2.3
$500 to $599	13.3	1.7	6.7	2.6	15.0	3.2	16.3	3.0	9.7	3.3
$600 to $699	13.0	1.7	8.7	2.9	16.8	3.4	14.4	2.9	9.0	3.2
$700 to $799	11.2	1.5	11.2	3.3	9.5	2.6	12.5	2.7	10.4	3.4
$800 to $899	9.4	1.4	14.6	3.7	7.0	2.3	8.6	2.3	9.6	3.3
$900 to $999	5.4	1.1	8.8	3.0	3.2	1.6	5.0	1.8	5.9	2.6
$1,000 or more	26.0	2.2	38.1	5.1	13.5	3.1	19.5	3.2	44.8	5.6
$1,000 to $1,249	10.0	1.5	15.0	3.7	3.6	1.7	9.7	2.4	13.9	3.9
$1,250 to $1,499	4.7	1.0	8.3	2.9	1.4	1.1	3.0	1.4	9.6	3.3
$1,500 or more	11.2	1.5	14.8	3.7	8.5	2.5	6.9	2.1	21.3	4.6
Median (dollars)	716	X	878	X	599	X	669	X	911	X
Vacant for sale, total	100.0	X	14.7	2.1	24.9	2.6	39.2	3.0	21.2	2.5
Units in structure, total	100.0	X	100.0	X	100.0	X	100.0	X	100.0	X
1 unit	76.1	2.6	63.0	7.5	78.1	5.0	81.4	3.8	73.1	5.8
2 units	3.6	1.1	7.7	4.1	6.0	2.9	1.6	1.2	1.2	1.4
3 and 4 units	3.1	1.1	3.4	2.8	4.8	2.6	2.1	1.4	3.3	2.3
5 to 9 units	3.0	1.0	1.7	2.0	3.5	2.2	1.3	1.1	6.5	3.2
10 units or more	8.4	1.7	21.3	6.3	2.5	1.9	6.9	2.5	9.2	3.8
Mobile homes	5.8	1.4	3.0	2.6	5.0	2.7	6.7	2.4	6.8	3.3

Table 2-41. Characteristics of Vacant For-Rent and Vacant For-Sale-Only Units for the United States and Regions: Second Quarter 2012—*Continued*

[Percent, except as noted.]

Characteristics	United States	90-percent confidence interval (+/-)[1]	Northeast	90-percent confidence interval (+/-)[1]	Midwest	90-percent confidence interval (+/-)[1]	South	90-percent confidence interval (+/-)[1]	West	90-percent confidence interval (+/-)[1]
Rooms in unit, total	100.0	X	100.0	X	100.0	X	100.0	X	100.0	X
3 rooms or less	11.6	1.9	25.5	6.8	11.8	3.9	5.9	2.3	12.1	4.3
4 rooms	17.6	2.3	18.7	6.0	13.1	4.1	18.1	3.7	21.3	5.4
5 rooms	24.2	2.6	13.6	5.3	28.5	5.5	25.7	4.2	24.0	5.6
6 rooms	19.1	2.4	15.7	5.6	18.9	4.8	21.6	4.0	17.2	4.9
7 rooms or more	27.4	2.7	26.4	6.8	27.7	5.4	28.8	4.4	25.4	5.7
Median number of rooms	5.4	X	4.9	X	5.4	X	5.5	X	5.2	X
Bedrooms in unit, total	100.0	X	100.0	X	100.0	X	100.0	X	100.0	X
1 bedroom or none	11.9	2.0	29.8	7.1	12.8	4.1	6.2	2.4	8.6	3.7
2 bedrooms	28.9	2.7	23.4	6.6	33.7	5.7	26.6	4.3	31.8	6.1
3 bedrooms	42.0	3.0	28.9	7.0	37.7	5.9	50.4	4.9	40.7	6.4
4 bedrooms or more	17.2	2.3	17.9	5.9	15.8	4.4	16.8	3.6	19.0	5.1
Duration of vacancy, total	100.0	X	100.0	X	100.0	X	100.0	X	100.0	X
Less than 1 month	6.7	1.5	5.5	3.5	6.8	3.1	7.0	2.5	6.8	3.3
1 to 2 months	7.9	1.6	5.9	3.7	7.3	3.2	8.0	2.6	10.0	3.9
2 to 4 months	12.0	2.0	12.3	5.1	10.1	3.7	14.1	3.4	10.3	4.0
4 to 6 months	13.4	2.1	16.9	5.8	9.3	3.5	12.8	3.2	16.8	4.9
6 to 12 months	22.4	2.5	22.9	6.5	19.9	4.9	22.1	4.0	25.4	5.7
1 to 2 years	19.7	2.4	19.5	6.1	25.0	5.3	18.6	3.8	15.6	4.7
2 years or more	17.9	2.3	16.9	5.8	21.5	5.0	17.4	3.7	15.0	4.7
Median (in months)	8.7	X	8.4	X	11.0	X	8.2	X	7.4	X
Year structure built, total	100.0	X	100.0	X	100.0	X	100.0	X	100.0	X
April 1, 2000 or later	22.5	2.5	21.2	6.3	15.6	4.4	24.0	4.2	28.9	5.9
1995 to March 31, 2000	6.8	1.5	4.7	3.3	6.3	2.9	9.3	2.8	4.4	2.7
1990 to 1994	5.5	1.4	2.5	2.4	3.0	2.1	6.4	2.4	8.6	3.7
1980 to 1989	9.4	1.8	4.2	3.1	5.0	2.7	14.2	3.4	9.1	3.8
1970 to 1979	12.7	2.0	6.8	3.9	9.8	3.6	13.4	3.3	18.6	5.1
1960 to 1969	11.7	1.9	9.7	4.6	11.3	3.8	12.8	3.2	11.5	4.2
1950 to 1959	10.9	1.9	16.1	5.7	13.8	4.2	8.6	2.7	8.0	3.5
1940 to 1949	6.8	1.5	7.2	4.0	9.8	3.6	5.1	2.1	6.5	3.2
1939 or earlier	13.7	2.1	27.5	6.9	25.4	5.3	6.1	2.3	4.4	2.7
Previous occupancy, total	100.0	X	100.0	X	100.0	X	100.0	X	100.0	X
Previously occupied	92.5	1.6	86.3	5.3	97.0	2.1	92.6	2.5	91.4	3.7
Not previously occupied	7.5	1.6	13.7	5.3	3.0	2.1	7.4	2.5	8.6	3.7
Sales price, total[3]	100.0	X	100.0	X	100.0	X	100.0	X	100.0	X
Less than $50,000	15.5	2.6	8.8	6.3	21.3	5.8	14.9	3.9	12.8	5.1
$50,000 to $74,999	11.0	2.2	6.1	5.3	16.8	5.3	10.1	3.3	8.0	4.1
$75,000 to $99,999	11.1	2.2	8.8	6.3	13.4	4.8	12.3	3.6	6.8	3.8
$100,000 to $149,999	18.2	2.7	22.8	9.3	15.8	5.2	18.9	4.2	17.2	5.7
$150,000 to $199,999	14.3	2.5	10.5	6.8	10.7	4.4	16.9	4.1	15.2	5.5
$200,000 to $249,999	7.6	1.9	11.4	7.1	6.9	3.6	7.8	2.9	6.0	3.6
$250,000 to $299,999	6.7	1.8	5.3	5.0	5.5	3.2	5.8	2.5	10.4	4.6
$300,000 to $399,999	5.2	1.6	7.9	6.0	3.1	2.5	6.0	2.6	5.2	3.4
$400,000 to $499,999	3.5	1.3	6.1	5.3	2.4	2.2	2.0	1.5	6.4	3.7
$500,000 or more	7.1	1.8	12.3	7.3	4.1	2.8	5.4	2.4	12.0	4.9
Median (dollars)	134,600	X	166,700	X	97,800	X	133,200	X	167,100	X

X = Not applicable.
[1] = A 90-percent confidence interval is a measure of an estimate's reliability. The larger the confidence interval is, in relation to the size of the estimate, the less reliable the estimate.
[2] = Excludes one-family homes on 10 acres or more.
[3] = Limited to one-family homes on less than 10 acres and no business on property (including mobile homes).

Source: U.S. Census Bureau, Housing Vacancies and Homeownership Survey (CPS/HVS)

Table 2-42. Percent Distribution by Type of Unit for the United States and for Inside and Outside Metropolitan Statistical Areas, Second Quarter 2011 and 2012

[Percent.]

Characteristics	Second quarter 2012			Second quarter 2011		
	United States	Inside metropolitan statistical areas	Outside metropolitan statistical areas	United States	Inside metropolitan statistical areas	Outside metropolitan statistical areas
All housing units	100.0	100.0	100.0	100.0	100.0	100.0
Year-round vacant	10.6	10.1	12.9	10.8	10.4	12.4
For rent	2.8	3.0	2.2	3.0	3.2	2.1
For sale only	1.2	1.2	1.4	1.5	1.5	1.4
Rented or sold, awaiting occupancy	0.8	0.8	0.6	0.8	0.8	0.6
Held off market	5.7	5.1	8.7	5.6	5.0	8.3
For occasional use	1.8	1.4	3.9	1.7	1.3	3.6
Temporarily occupied by persons with usual residence elsewhere	1.0	1.0	0.9	0.9	0.9	0.7
For other reasons	3.0	2.7	3.9	2.9	2.7	4.0
Seasonal vacant	3.4	2.1	9.2	3.5	2.1	9.6
Occupied	86.0	87.8	77.9	85.7	87.5	77.9

Source: U.S. Census Bureau, Housing Vacancies and Homeownership Survey (CPS/HVS)

Table 2-43. Percent Distribution by Type of Unit for the United States and for Inside and Outside Regions, Second Quarter 2011 and 2012

[Percent.]

Characteristics	Second quarter 2012					Second quarter 2011				
	United States	Northeast	Midwest	South	West	United States	Northeast	Midwest	South	West
All housing units	100.0	100.0	100.0	100.0	100.0	100.0	100.0	100.0	100.0	100.0
Year-round vacant	10.6	8.9	9.9	12.6	9.0	10.8	9.0	10.5	12.7	9.2
For rent	2.8	2.3	2.7	3.4	2.4	3.0	2.4	3.0	3.5	2.6
For sale only	1.2	1.0	1.3	1.2	1.2	1.5	1.3	1.6	1.6	1.3
Rented or sold, awaiting occupancy	0.8	0.8	0.9	0.9	0.6	0.8	0.9	0.8	0.8	0.7
Held off market	5.7	4.8	5.0	7.1	4.9	5.6	4.5	5.1	6.9	4.6
For occasional use	1.8	1.1	0.8	2.4	2.3	1.7	1.3	0.9	2.3	2.1
Temporarily occupied by persons with usual residence elsewhere	1.0	0.9	0.9	1.1	0.8	0.9	0.7	0.9	1.1	0.6
For other reasons	3.0	2.7	3.2	3.6	1.8	2.9	2.5	3.3	3.5	2.0
Seasonal vacant	3.4	4.0	3.0	3.6	2.8	3.5	4.0	3.0	3.7	3.0
Occupied	86.0	87.1	87.1	83.8	88.1	85.7	87.0	86.5	83.6	87.8

Source: U.S. Census Bureau, Housing Vacancies and Homeownership Survey (CPS/HVS)

Table 2-44. Absorption Rates of Privately Funded, Nonsubsidized, Unfurnished Rental Apartments, 2005–2011

[Number, percent.]

Year and quarter of completion	Unfinished apartments completed		Seasonally adjusted[1], rented within 3 months		Not seasonally adjusted, rented within: 3 months		6 months		9 months		12 months	
	Total	90-percent confidence interval (+/-)[2], number of apartments	Percent	90-percent confidence interval (+/-)[2], number of apartments	Percent	90-percent confidence interval (+/-)[2], number of apartments	Percent	90-percent confidence interval (+/-)[2], number of apartments	Percent	90-percent confidence interval (+/-)[2], number of apartments	Percent	90-percent confidence interval (+/-)[2], number of apartments
2011												
January–March	21,800	1,520	56	4.5	55	4.4	76	4.8	84	4.5	88	4.2
April–June	13,000	1,520	51	10.0	52	10.2	64	11.9	68	12.6	NA	NA
July–September	25,100	3,440	67	7.8	69	8.0	77	8.2	NA	NA	NA	NA
October–December[3]	15,500	15,500	3,240	51	9.6	49	9.2	NA	NA	NA	NA	NA
2010												
January–March	27,500	2,040	64	7.8	62	7.6	80	6.7	89	5.5	93	3.7
April–June	30,100	2,090	63	4.0	63	6.5	78	4.6	86	4.4	92	2.4
July–September	16,700	3,198	63	2.3	65	3.3	81	3.0	88	2	93	1.7
October–December	14,900	2,930	56	2.3	55	2.7	78	2.9	87	2.0	92	1.7
2009												
January–March	28,400	2,320	53	2.0	51	1.9	74	2.1	83	1.4	88	1.2
April–June	47,900	3,920	48	1.8	51	1.9	69	1.9	78	1.3	88	1.2
July–September	47,300	3,870	52	2.0	51	1.9	68	1.9	82	1.4	91	1.3
October–December	39,500	1,260	50	1.2	49	1.2	74	1.1	86	1.4	92	1.3
2008												
January–March	28,500	2,330	53	2.0	51	1.9	71	2.0	81	1.4	89	1.2
April–June	37,200	3,040	48	1.8	52	2.0	71	2.0	80	1.4	86	1.2
July–September	37,300	3,050	55	2.1	53	2.0	67	1.9	77	1.3	86	1.2
October–December	43,400	3,550	45	1.7	44	1.7	66	1.9	80	1.4	88	1.2
2007												
January–March	28,200	6,370	53	5.6	51	5.4	75	4.8	89	2.4	93	1.6
April–June	26,500	2,170	53	2.0	59	2.2	76	2.1	85	1.5	90	1.3
July–September	26,100	2,140	55	2.1	53	2.0	71	2.0	82	1.4	90	1.3
October–December	24,000	1,960	57	2.2	57	2.2	76	2.1	89	1.5	94	1.3
2006												
January–March	21,600	2,140	62	3.3	60	3.2	81	2.4	90	1.5	95	0.9
April–June	28,600	2,340	61	2.4	67	2.6	83	2.3	91	1.6	95	1.3
July–September	33,800	3,010	52	2.2	52	2.2	67	2.3	80	2.0	87	1.7
October–December	32,300	3,620	54	5.2	54	5.2	75	3.7	88	2.0	94	1.6
2005												
January–March	26,100	3,350	61	3.8	59	3.7	84	2.9	93	1.9	96	1.2
April–June	30,800	4,900	65	3.6	71	3.9	88	2.0	93	1.2	97	0.7
July–September	30,500	5,340	63	5.7	59	5.8	82	2.8	91	1.7	96	0.9
October–December	25,600	2,370	63	2.9	59	2.7	81	2.0	90	1.6	95	1.2

NA = Not available.
[1] = The Census Bureau performs seasonal adjustment of a time series of estimates only given clear evidence of seasonal behavior (i.e., new construction in the Northeast is lowest in December, January, and February, when it is curtailed due to weather conditions) and only when the adjustment passes a suitable set of diagnostic tests.
[2] = A 90-percent confidence interval is a measure of an estimate's variability. The larger the confidence interval in relation to the size of the estimate, the less reliable the estimate.
[3] = Preliminary.

Source: U.S. Census Bureau, Survey of Market Absorption

Table 2-45. Characteristics of Unfurnished Apartments Completed During the Fourth Quarter of 2011 and of Those Rented Within Three Months (Preliminary), Not Seasonally Adjusted

[Number, percent, dollars.]

Characteristics	Total unfurnished apartments completed	90-percent confidence interval (+/-)[1], number of apartments	Percent of total units	90-percent confidence interval (+/-)[1], number of apartments	Percent rented within three months	90-percent confidence interval (+/-)[1], number of apartments
Total	15,500	3,240	100	X	49	9.2
Asking rent						
Less than $950	3,800	1,650	25	7.0	59	5.8
$950 to $1,049	1,800	640	12	2.7	70	2.9
$1,050 to $1,149	1,300	450	8	2.8	67	7.7
$1,150 to $1,249	500	310	3	2.0	28	23.2
$1,250 to $1,349	1,300	230	8	2.1	32	7.1
$1,350 or more	6,800	1,270	44	5.5	39	20.6
Median asking rent	1,277	90	X	X	1,081	194
Fewer than two bedrooms	6,000	1,020	39	3.4	55	11.3
Less than $950	1,500	650	10	2.8	65	3.3
$950 to $1,049	800	230	5	2.0	71	3.8
$1,050 to $1,149	600	460	4	3.0	66	12.3
$1,150 to $1,249	100	100	1	0.6	83	10.2
$1,250 to $1,349	200	160	2	1.1	71	9.8
$1,350 or more	2,800	530	18	3.0	40	23.0
Median asking rent	1,251	275	X	X	1,076	153
Two bedrooms or more	9,400	2,330	61	3.4	45	8.3
Less than $950	2,300	1,050	15	4.7	54	9.7
$950 to $1,049	1,000	680	7	3.4	69	6.2
$1,050 to $1,149	700	190	4	1.2	67	11.8
$1,150 to $1,249	400	300	2	1.9	13	13.4
$1,250 to $1,349	1,100	140	7	1.4	23	5.4
$1,350 to $1,449	200	90	1	0.7	53	14.4
$1,450 or more	3,800	850	25	3.4	38	20.4
Median asking rent	1,283	72	X	X	1,084	257
Bedrooms						
No bedroom	600	260	4	2.2	78	18.0
1 bedroom	5,400	1,100	35	2.1	52	10.6
2 bedrooms	7,700	2,050	50	3.7	41	8.8
3 bedrooms or more	1,700	450	11	2.3	61	12.5

X = Not applicable.
[1] = A 90-percent confidence interval is a measure of an estimate's variability. The larger the confidence interval in relation to the size of the estimate, the less reliable the estimate.

Source: U.S. Census Bureau, Survey of Market Absorption

Table 2-46. Characteristics of Unfurnished Apartments Completed During the Third Quarter of 2011 and of Those Rented Within 3 Months (Revised), Not Seasonally Adjusted

[Number, percent, dollars.]

Characteristics	Total unfurnished apartments completed	90-percent confidence interval (+/-)[1], number of apartments	Percent of total units	90-percent confidence interval (+/-)[1], number of apartments	Percent rented within three months	90-percent confidence interval (+/-)[1], number of apartments
Total	25,100	3,440	100	X	69	8.0
Asking rent						
Less than $950	9,000	1,300	36	4.4	68	16.4
$950 to $1,049	2,300	590	9	2.3	55	18.6
$1,050 to $1,149	4,300	1,970	17	6.7	73	4.8
$1,150 to $1,249	1,500	230	6	0.9	47	9.6
$1,250 to $1,349	1,200	490	5	2.3	65	8.4
$1,350 or more	6,800	1,960	27	6.6	78	8.2
Median asking rent	1,078	33	X	X	1,089	41
Fewer than two bedrooms	8,500	1,480	34	3.3	79	8.1
Less than $950	4,000	820	16	2.0	81	15.1
$950 to $1,049	800	230	3	0.9	74	8.7
$1,050 to $1,149	500	230	2	1.0	70	11.5
$1,150 to $1,249	200	140	1	0.6	87	9.1
$1,250 to $1,349	700	380	3	1.7	75	10.3
$1,350 or more	2,300	890	9	3.0	77	14.9
Median asking rent	971	113	X	X	963	170
Two bedrooms or more	16,600	2,340	66	3.3	64	8.2
Less than $950	5,000	800	20	3.9	58	16.0
$950 to $1,049	1,500	630	6	2.5	46	23.5
$1,050 to $1,149	3,800	1,970	15	6.8	74	4.7
$1,150 to $1,249	1,200	210	5	0.8	39	10.0
$1,250 to $1,349	500	190	2	0.9	51	8.2
$1,350 to $1,449	900	200	4	0.6	76	7.1
$1,450 or more	3,500	1,050	14	3.9	79	6.0
Median asking rent	1,095	28	X	X	1,111	32
Bedrooms						
No bedroom	800	200	3	0.6	89	6.6
1 bedroom	7,800	1,390	31	3.5	79	8.3
2 bedrooms	12,300	1,780	49	1.7	64	7.7
3 bedrooms or more	4,200	690	17	2.1	66	12.0

X = Not applicable.
[1] = A 90-percent confidence interval is a measure of an estimate's variability. The larger the confidence interval in relation to the size of the estimate, the less reliable the estimate.

Source: U.S. Census Bureau, Survey of Market Absorption

Table 2-47. Unfurnished Apartments Completed During the Fourth Quarter of 2011, by Geographic Area, Not Seasonally Adjusted

[Number, percent, dollars.]

Geographic area	Total unfurnished apartments completed	90-percent confidence interval (+/-)[1], number of apartments	Median asking rent (dollars)	90-percent confidence interval (+/-)[1], dollars	Percent of total units completed	90-percent confidence interval (+/-)[1], number of apartments	Percent rented within three months	90-percent confidence interval (+/-)[1], number of apartments
United States, total	15,500	3,240	1,277	90	100	X	49	9.2
Inside CBSA[2]	14,600	3,150	1,251	159	94	1.1	52	9.8
Inside principal city of CBSA[2]	9,000	1,590	1,097	321	58	7.1	62	8.4
Outside principal city of CBSA[2]	5,600	1,950	1,350+	X	36	7.1	35	15.6
Outside CBSA[2]	900	160	1,303	219	6	1.1	0	X
Northeast	5,100	1,250	1,350+	X	33	5.5	38	28.1
Midwest	2,300	1,010	1,258	115	15	5.0	39	14.3
South	7,100	1,740	996	78	46	5.6	60	3.2
West	1,000	330	1,229	144	6	2.2	46	17.2

X = Not applicable.
[1] = A 90-percent confidence interval is a measure of an estimate's variability. The larger the confidence interval in relation to the size of the estimate, the less reliable the estimate.
[2] = Core based statistical area.

Source: U.S. Census Bureau, Survey of Market Absorption

Table 2-48. Absorption Rates of Condominium and Cooperative Apartments, Not Seasonally Adjusted, 2005–2011

[Number, percent.]

Year and quarter of completion	Total condominium and cooperative apartments completed	90-percent confidence interval (+/-)[1], number of apartments	Percent of all completions	90-percent confidence interval (+/-)[1], percentage points	Percent absorbed in 3 months	90-percent confidence interval (+/-)[1], percentage points	Percent absorbed in 6 months	90-percent confidence interval (+/-)[1], percentage points	Percent absorbed in 9 months	90-percent confidence interval (+/-)[1], percentage points	Percent absorbed in 12 months	90-percent confidence interval (+/-)[1], percentage points
2011												
January–March	2,800	540	9	1.8	54	4.4	78	3.5	88[3]	2.5	92	1.6
April–June	2,800	870	11	3.4	54	13.8	69	15.8	84	7.9	NA	NA
July–September	2,400	760	6	1.8	79	5.7	88	3.5	NA	NA	NA	NA
October–December[2]	2,700	1,120	8	3.5	40	13.9	NA	NA	NA	NA	NA	NA
2010												
January–March	3,400	470	9	0.9	45	6.0	59	5.5	65	4.8	76	3.3
April–June	6,000	820	13	1.4	39	5.1	57	5.3	67	4.8	77	3.3
July–September	5,300	1,230	16	2.0	43	8.7	55	8.7	60	9.6	70	9.4
October–December	4,300	950	15	3.3	44	9.4	66	5.1	74	5.3	81	4.2
2009												
January–March	12,400	1,310	23	1.9	42	4.3	57	4.1	62	4.1	67	2.2
April–June	9,900	1,050	13	1.1	36	3.6	48	3.5	57	3.7	65	2.1
July–September	8,800	930	12	1.0	46	4.7	59	4.3	69	4.5	75	2.4
October–December	7,000	630	12	1.0	38	2.6	53	2.6	61	3.0	67	3.0
2008												
January–March	21,000	2,220	34	2.8	51	5.2	71	5.1	77	4.9	82	2.6
April–June	11,800	1,250	19	1.6	49	5.0	61	4.4	70	4.6	76	2.5
July–September	19,600	2,070	26	2.2	56	5.7	63	4.5	70	4.6	76	2.5
October–December	17,400	1,840	23	1.9	39	3.9	47	3.4	60	3.9	70	2.3
2007												
January–March	21,100	4,100	35	6.7	60	6.4	72	4.0	77	4.2	82	3.4
April–June	20,900	2,210	37	3.1	64	6.5	74	5.3	79	5.2	83	2.7
July–September	26,900	2,840	37	3.1	63	6.4	72	5.2	80	5.2	87	2.8
October–December	22,100	2,330	35	2.9	56	5.7	68	4.9	75	4.9	79	2.6
2006												
January–March	24,900	4,980	41	6.5	64	7.5	79	4.7	86	3.9	89	3.4
April–June	26,800	2,830	38	3.1	66	6.7	77	5.6	83	5.4	88	2.9
July–September	22,300	2,010	30	2.9	68	4.4	81	2.9	88	1.6	92	1.1
October–December	30,700	4,400	39	5.1	66	6.2	76	5.6	87	2.4	91	1.8
2005												
January–March	13,200	2,650	26	5.9	75	8.6	90	4.1	94	3.4	96	2.9
April–June	26,200	6,230	36	6.9	79	10.6	88	7.9	91	7.4	93	6.0
July–September	19,300	3,750	28	6.0	79	6.3	86	5.3	89	5.2	93	5.1
October–December	23,100	4,300	35	4.9	71	5.9	81	5.0	87	4.5	91	4.5

NA = Not available.

[1] = A 90-percent confidence interval is a measure of an estimate's variability. The larger the confidence interval in relation to the size of the estimate, the less reliable the estimate.

[2] = Preliminary.

Source: U.S. Census Bureau, Survey of Market Absorption

Table 2-49. Characteristics of Condominium Apartments Completed During the Fourth Quarter of 2011 and of Those Sold Within 3 Months (Preliminary), Not Seasonally Adjusted

[Number, percent, dollars.]

Characteristics	Total condominium apartments completed	90-percent confidence interval (+/-)[1], number of apartments	Percent of total condominiums	90-percent confidence interval (+/-)[1], percentage points	Percent sold within 3 months	90-percent confidence interval (+/-)[1], percentage points
Total	2,700	1,120	100	X	40	13.9
Asking price						
Less than $250,000	800	520	30	15.4	24	8.8
$250,000 to $299,999	200	190	8	5.1	#	#
$300,000 to $349,999	200	110	7	2.2	52	25.1
$350,000 to $399,999	200	150	9	5.3	58	10.9
$4000,000 to $449,999	300	190	12	4.9	31	21.3
$450,000 or more	900	450	34	9.7	55	19.0
Median asking price	375,400	64,300	X	X	429,300	55,700
Bedrooms						
Fewer than 2 bedrooms	800	550	31	11.9	42	25.7
2 bedrooms	1,500	700	56	11.0	32	11.1
3 bedrooms or more	300	100	13	6.1	72	7.2

# = Withheld because the estimate did not meet publication standards because of the associated confidence interval.
X = Not applicable.
[1] = A 90-percent confidence interval is a measure of an estimate's variability. The larger the confidence interval in relation to the size of the estimate, the less reliable the estimate.

Source: U.S. Census Bureau, Survey of Market Absorption

Table 2-50. Characteristics of Condominium Apartments Completed During the Third Quarter of 2011 and of Those Sold Within 3 Months (Revised), Not Seasonally Adjusted

[Number, percent, dollars.]

Characteristics	Total condominium apartments completed	90-percent confidence interval (+/-)[1], number of apartments	Percent of total condominiums	90-percent confidence interval (+/-)[1], percentage points	Percent sold within 3 months	90-percent confidence interval (+/-)[1], percentage points
Total	2,400	760	100	X	79	5.8
Asking price						
Less than $250,000	400	220	17	8.4	85	8.6
$250,000 to $299,999	200	80	8	2.8	79	8.6
$300,000 to $349,999	200	90	8	2.8	95	4.7
$350,000 to $399,999	200	90	8	2.9	76	15.1
$4000,000 to $449,999	100	50	6	2.0	57	19.5
$450,000 or more	1,300	530	54	11.1	78	7.6
Median asking price	450,000+	X	X	X	450,000+	X
Bedrooms						
Fewer than 2 bedrooms	600	330	26	9.6	72	7.9
2 bedrooms	1,100	390	47	8.8	82	5.5
3 bedrooms or more	600	310	27	10.8	81	10.1

X = Not applicable.
[1] = A 90-percent confidence interval is a measure of an estimate's variability. The larger the confidence interval in relation to the size of the estimate, the less reliable the estimate.

Source: U.S. Census Bureau, Survey of Market Absorption

Table 2-51. Condominium Apartments Completed During the Fourth Quarter of 2011, by Geographic Area, Not Seasonally Adjusted

[Number, percent, dollars.]

Geographic area	Total condominium apartments completed	90-percent confidence interval (+/-)[1], number of apartments	Median asking price, dollars	90-percent confidence interval (+/-)[1], dollars	Percent of total units completed	90-percent confidence interval (+/-)[1], percentage points	Percent sold within three months	90-percent confidence interval (+/-)[1], percentage points
United States, total	2,700	1,120	375,400	64,290	100	X	40	13.9
Inside CBSA[2]	2,600	1,060	374,100	76,240	96	5.4	38	13.4
Inside principal city of CBSA[2]	2,000	890	431,500	44,480	74	17.1	40	16.7
Outside principal city of CBSA[2]	600	530	<250,000	50,510	22	17.1	31	12.3
Outside CBSA[2]	#	#	381,300	97,849	#	#	100	–
Northeast	1,300	750	394,100	182,750	48	18.8	51	16.4
Midwest	#	#	#	#	1	0.8	32	22.6
South	900	720	312,700	27,620	33	19.8	#	#
West	500	190	403,200	62,950	19	9.1	48	20.9

– = Zero or rounds to zero.
# = Withheld because the estimate did not meet publication standards because of the associated confidence interval.
X = Not applicable.
[1] = A 90-percent confidence interval is a measure of an estimate's variability. The larger the confidence interval in relation to the size of the estimate, the less reliable the estimate.
[2] = Core based statistical area.

Source: U.S. Census Bureau, Survey of Market Absorption

Table 2-52. Characteristics of Unfurnished Apartments Completed in the Last Four Quarters and of Those Reported as Rented and Remaining for Rent in the First Quarter of 2012

[Number, dollars.]

Characteristics	Total apartments completed in the last 4 quarters	90-percent confidence interval (+/-)[1], number of apartments	Apartments completed in last 4 quarters and rented prior to 1st quarter 2012	90-percent confidence interval (+/-)[1], number of apartments	Apartments completed in last 4 quarters and rented in 1st quarter 2012	90-percent confidence interval (+/-)[1], number of apartments	Apartments completed in last 4 quarters and remaining for rent at the end of 1st quarter 2012	90-percent confidence interval (+/-)[1], number of apartments
Total	75,300	7,110	44,000	5,310	11,000	1,680	20,300	4,460
Asking rent								
Less than $950	22,000	3,720	13,900	2,310	2,900	1,040	5,100	1,960
$950 to $1,049	10,600	2,250	4,400	590	1,600	400	4,500	2,020
$1,050 to $1,149	12,500	5,380	9,300	4,480	1,700	620	1,400	440
$1,150 to $1,249	4,500	780	2,100	470	400	110	2,000	560
$1,250 to $1,349	4,800	1,400	2,600	1,030	700	200	1,500	280
$1,350 or more	21,000	2,570	11,600	2,330	3,700	1,410	5,700	1,740
Median asking rent	1,090	31	1,088	22	1,106	112	1,085	115
Bedrooms								
Fewer than 2 bedrooms	25,700	2,590	16,200	1,870	4,400	890	5,100	1,020
2 bedrooms	37,400	4,210	20,400	2,630	5,100	870	12,000	2,690
3 bedrooms or more	12,200	2,570	7,400	2,370	1,600	510	3,200	930

[1] = A 90-percent confidence interval is a measure of an estimate's variability. The larger the confidence interval in relation to the size of the estimate, the less reliable the estimate.

Source: U.S. Census Bureau, Survey of Market Absorption

Table 2-53. Characteristics of Condominium Apartments Completed in the Last Four Quarters and of Those Reported as Sold and Remaining for Sale in the First Quarter of 2012

[Number, dollars.]

Characteristics	Total condominiums completed in the last 4 quarters	90-percent confidence interval (+/-)[1], number of apartments	Condominiums completed in last 4 quarters and sold prior to 1st quarter 2012	90-percent confidence interval (+/-)[1], number of apartments	Condominiums completed in last 4 quarters and sold in 1st quarter 2012	90-percent confidence interval (+/-)[1], number of apartments	Condominiums completed in last 4 quarters and remaining for sales at the end of 1st quarter 2012	90-percent confidence interval (+/-)[1], number of apartments
Total	10,300	1820	6,000	1,060	1,800	500	2,500	960
Asking price								
Less than $250,000	2300	830	800	270	500	310	1,000	520
$250,000 to $299,999	700	260	400	130	100	30	200	190
$300,000 to $349,999	600	170	400	120	100	60	100	90
$350,000 to $399,999	900	280	600	180	200	110	200	50
$400,000 - $449,999	700	250	300	140	100	70	300	180
$450,000 or more	5,000	1080	3,500	750	800	310	800	330
Median asking price	440,300	36,350	450,000 +	X	395,500	72,350	312,300	102,490
Bedrooms								
Fewer than 2 bedrooms	2,700	750	1,500	350	500	310	600	420
2 bedrooms	5,500	1,200	2,900	630	900	350	1,700	650
3 bedrooms or more	2,100	560	1,600	490	300	80	200	60

X = Not applicable.
[1] = A 90-percent confidence interval is a measure of an estimate's variability. The larger the confidence interval in relation to the size of the estimate, the less reliable the estimate.

Source: U.S. Census Bureau, Survey of Market Absorption

Table 2-54. Apartments Completed in Buildings with Five Units or More, 2005–2011

[Number, percent.]

Year and quarter of completion	Total apartments	90-percent confidence interval (+/-)[1]	Unfurnished apartments	90-percent confidence interval (+/-)[1]	Furnished apartments	90-percent confidence interval (+/-)[1]	Condominiums and cooperatives	90-percent confidence interval (+/-)[1]	Subsidized or tax credit[2]	90-percent confidence interval (+/-)[1]	Other[3] units	90-percent confidence interval (+/-)[1]
2011												
January–March	29,800	2,080	21,800	1,520	#	#	2,800	540	4,200	980	900	540
April–June	25,500	2,980	13,000	1,520	–	–	2,800	870	8,400	1,250	1,300	500
July–September	42,700	5,850	25,100	3,440	1,100	610	2,400	760	10,900	3,360	3,200	1,330
October–December[4]	31,900	6,670	15,500	3,240	–	–	2,700	1,120	12,800	2,760	1,000	450
2010												
January–March	39,500	2,770	27,500	2,930	–	–	3,400	470	6,300	830	2,400	880
April–June	46,000	3,230	30,100	3,200	–	–	6,000	820	9,400	1,230	500	180
July–September	32,700	4,090	16,700	2,090	1,100	230	5,300	1230	8,600	2,370	900	440
October–December	28,400	3,890	14,900	2,040	–	–	4,300	950	7,100	1,480	2,100	760
2009												
January–March	53,900	2,910	28,400	2,320	Y	Y	12,400	1,310	10,400	1,050	2,700	760
April–June	74,000	3,990	47,900	3,920	100	20	9,900	1,050	13,100	1,320	3,000	840
July–September	71,000	3,830	47,300	3,870	1,700	340	8,800	930	9,100	920	4,100	1,150
October–December	60,800	2,120	39,500	1,260	100	40	7,000	630	11,700	1,180	2,500	270
2008												
January–March	62,300	3,360	28,500	2,330	100	20	21,000	2,220	11,800	1,190	1,000	340
April–June	60,700	3,280	37,200	3,040	1,200	240	11,800	1,250	9,100	920	1,400	390
July–September	76,400	4,120	37,300	3,050	1,500	300	19,600	2,070	13,100	1,320	4,900	1,380
October–December	77,200	4,170	43,400	3,550	–	–	17,400	1,840	15,100	1,520	1,300	370
2007												
January–March	60,300	6,020	28,200	6,370	100	90	21,100	4,100	10,100	2,460	800	400
April–June	56,700	3,060	26,500	2,170	200	40	20,900	2,210	7,500	760	1,500	510
July–September	72,400	3,910	26,100	2,140	800	160	26,900	2,840	14,300	1,440	4,300	1,450
October–December	63,600	3,430	24,000	1,960	200	40	22,100	2,330	14,700	1,480	2,700	910
2006												
January–March	60,900	2,850	21,600	2,140	100	40	24,900	4,980	12,700	1,140	1,600	750
April–June	70,800	3,820	28,600	2,340	1,200	240	26,800	2,830	12,700	1,280	1,600	540
July–September	73,100	3,530	33,800	3,010	1,800	330	22,300	2,010	12,500	1,850	2,800	900
October–December	78,600	6,240	32,300	3,620	200	310	30,700	4,400	14,100	3,960	1,300	880
2005												
January–March	51,700	3,880	26,100	3,350	500	270	13,200	2,650	9,900	1,990	2,000	940
April–June	72,000	8,100	30,800	4,900	1,800	1,800	26,200	6,230	10,700	2,730	2,500	1,010
July–September	68,200	5,400	30,500	5,340	2,600	1,200	19,300	3,750	10,900	2,050	4,800	2,540
October–December	66,200	4,650	25,600	2,370	400	240	23,100	4,300	12,500	1,420	4,600	2,290

– = Zero or rounds to zero.
# = Withheld because the estimate did not meet publication standards because of the associated confidence interval.
Y = Fewer than 50 units or less than one-half of 1 percent.
[1] = A 90-percent confidence interval is a measure of an estimate's variability. The larger the confidence interval in relation to the size of the estimate, the less reliable the estimate.
[2] = Beginning with completions in the second quarter of 2004, low income tax credit units were included in this category.
[3] = Other includes time-share units, continuing care retirement units, and turnkey housing (privately built for and sold to local public housing.)
[4] = Preliminary.

Source: U.S. Census Bureau, Survey of Market Absorption

Table 2-55. Value of Construction Put in Place, 2011 (Year to Date) and 2012

[Dollars in millions, percent.]

Characteristics	Seasonally adjusted							
	June 2012[1]	May 2012[2]	April 2012[2]	March 2012	February 2012	June 2011	Percent change, June 2012 from: May 2012	Percent change, June 2012 from: June 2011
Total construction	842,082	838,327	825,133	817,842	820,677	786,784	0.4	7.0
Residential	272,080	268,546	260,635	256,156	259,640	245,853	1.3	10.7
Nonresidential	570,002	569,781	564,499	561,686	561,037	540,930	0.0	5.4
Lodging	11,308	10,902	11,020	11,122	9,658	9,173	3.7	23.3
Office	35,536	35,630	35,540	35,780	34,288	35,545	-0.3	0.0
Commercial	46,801	47,727	46,596	46,425	45,896	44,777	-1.9	4.5
Health care	41,813	41,645	40,918	40,154	41,081	40,501	0.4	3.2
Educational	83,217	83,994	84,543	85,520	85,705	84,491	-0.9	-1.5
Religious	3,756	3,731	3,912	4,019	4,078	3,964	0.7	-5.2
Public safety	10,524	10,616	10,276	10,577	10,947	10,625	-0.9	-1.0
Amusement and recreation	15,982	15,761	15,566	15,820	15,812	16,354	1.4	-2.3
Transportation	36,864	35,927	34,988	32,793	33,051	35,188	2.6	4.8
Communication	17,653	16,924	16,911	17,008	16,819	17,902	4.3	-1.4
Power	90,774	93,718	94,090	94,195	95,207	76,150	-3.1	19.2
Highway and street	80,603	79,420	79,553	77,797	77,545	77,349	1.5	4.2
Sewage and waste disposal	22,797	22,425	22,325	22,915	23,660	23,184	1.7	-1.7
Water supply	12,971	13,578	13,522	13,446	13,637	13,539	-4.5	-4.2
Conservation and development	6,211	6,472	6,094	6,323	6,064	7,593	-4.0	-18.2
Manufacturing	53,194	51,310	48,647	47,791	47,590	44,596	3.7	19.3
Total private construction[3]	567,855	564,178	552,328	544,797	544,550	502,149	0.7	13.1
Residential	265,602	262,120	254,145	249,452	252,640	236,923	1.3	12.1
Nonresidential	302,252	302,058	298,183	295,345	291,910	265,226	0.1	14.0
Lodging	10,622	10,318	10,313	10,225	8,976	8,408	2.9	26.3
Office	24,901	24,796	24,294	24,552	23,306	23,366	0.4	6.6
Commercial	43,637	44,305	43,382	43,234	42,798	40,929	-1.5	6.6
Health care	30,821	30,630	30,377	29,560	30,644	28,804	0.6	7.0
Educational	17,551	17,379	17,273	17,465	16,762	14,779	1.0	18.8
Religious	3,729	3,701	3,890	3,989	4,055	3,935	0.8	-5.2
Amusement and recreation	6,542	6,478	6,571	6,414	6,366	7,308	1.0	-10.5
Transportation	11,181	11,158	10,717	9,346	8,609	9,550	0.2	17.1
Communication	17,480	16,717	16,689	16,696	16,621	17,775	4.6	-1.7
Power	82,109	84,767	85,518	85,778	85,796	64,932	-3.1	26.5
Manufacturing	52,145	50,231	47,873	46,762	46,640	43,825	3.8	19.0
Total public construction[2]	274,228	274,149	272,805	273,045	276,127	284,635	0.0	-3.7
Residential	6,478	6,426	6,490	6,704	7,000	8,931	0.8	-27.5
Nonresidential	267,750	267,723	266,315	266,341	269,127	275,704	0.0	-2.9
Office	10,635	10,835	11,246	11,229	10,982	12,179	-1.8	-12.7
Commercial	3,164	3,422	3,214	3,191	3,098	3,848	-7.5	-17.8
Health care	10,993	11,016	10,542	10,594	10,437	11,697	-0.2	-6.0
Educational	65,666	66,615	67,270	68,055	68,943	69,711	-1.4	-5.8
Public safety	10,365	10,510	10,177	10,486	10,825	10,370	-1.4	0.0
Amusement and recreation	9,440	9,283	8,995	9,407	9,446	9,046	1.7	4.4
Transportation	25,683	24,769	24,271	23,447	24,442	25,639	3.7	0.2
Power	8,666	8,951	8,572	8,417	9,410	11,218	-3.2	-22.7
Highway and street	80,430	79,261	79,397	77,687	77,484	77,318	1.5	4.0
Sewage and waste disposal	22,144	21,768	21,819	22,254	23,058	22,671	1.7	-2.3
Water supply	12,515	13,016	13,061	13,069	13,184	12,782	-3.8	-2.1
Conservation and development	6,117	6,377	6,027	6,237	5,965	7,533	-4.1	-18.8

Table 2-55. Value of Construction Put in Place, 2011 (Year to Date) and 2012—*Continued*

[Dollars in millions, percent.]

Characteristics	Not seasonally adjusted								
	June 2012	May 2012	April 2012	March 2012	February 2012	June 2011	Percent change, June 2012 from:		
							May 2012	June 2011	Percent change
Total construction	75,908	71,364	66,201	60,939	56,108	71,297	387,055	355,108	9.0
Residential	24,917	23,427	21,639	18,755	16,543	22,622	122,338	114,483	6.9
Nonresidential	50,991	47,937	44,563	42,184	39,566	48,676	264,717	240,626	10.0
Lodging	942	909	918	927	805	764	5,303	4,318	22.8
Office	3,086	3,072	2,966	2,865	2,642	3,111	17,267	16,755	3.1
Commercial	4,148	4,052	3,862	3,646	3,394	3,983	22,464	19,983	12.4
Health care	3,608	3,511	3,388	3,264	3,178	3,482	20,085	19,214	4.5
Educational	7,987	7,101	6,626	6,363	5,950	8,185	39,969	38,961	2.6
Religious	312	298	315	321	330	334	1,897	2,061	-8.0
Public safety	902	886	831	836	820	911	5,089	4,806	5.9
Amusement and recreation	1,375	1,348	1,281	1,237	1,155	1,431	7,576	7,718	-1.8
Transportation	3,220	2,981	2,787	2,435	2,329	3,085	16,168	16,385	-1.3
Communication	1,518	1,466	1,324	1,363	1,255	1,595	8,087	8,278	-2.3
Power	7,639	7,645	7,373	7,500	7,212	6,353	44,940	32,571	38.0
Highway and street	8,029	6,858	5,502	4,333	3,853	7,776	32,214	31,266	3.0
Sewage and waste disposal	2,027	1,885	1,747	1,760	1,668	2,054	10,738	10,653	0.8
Water supply	1,142	1,147	1,111	1,041	989	1,209	6,430	6,653	-3.4
Conservation and development	519	514	492	499	453	654	2,915	3,642	-20.0
Manufacturing	4,539	4,266	4,040	3,797	3,534	3,751	23,575	17,363	35.8
Total private construction[3]	50,355	48,185	45,195	41,788	38,090	44,622	262,289	226,369	15.9
Residential	24,343	22,884	21,109	18,246	16,011	21,803	119,103	110,034	8.2
Nonresidential	26,012	25,300	24,087	23,542	22,079	22,820	143,185	116,335	23.1
Lodging	885	860	859	852	748	701	4,959	4,027	23.1
Office	2,169	2,156	2,020	1,969	1,833	2,048	11,927	10,847	10.0
Commercial	3,878	3,772	3,608	3,393	3,155	3,655	20,926	18,321	14.2
Health care	2,676	2,571	2,500	2,389	2,339	2,493	14,772	13,642	8.3
Educational	1,644	1,564	1,434	1,404	1,243	1,407	8,462	6,550	29.2
Religious	309	295	313	319	328	332	1,884	2,045	-7.9
Amusement and recreation	548	549	544	537	503	613	3,194	3,234	-1.2
Transportation	956	919	843	667	598	819	4,693	4,297	9.2
Communication	1,503	1,448	1,306	1,337	1,239	1,584	7,975	8,241	-3.2
Power	6,858	6,858	6,582	6,859	6,546	5,346	40,602	27,383	48.3
Manufacturing	4,452	4,176	3,975	3,712	3,455	3,686	23,105	17,047	35.5
Total public construction[2]	25,553	23,179	21,006	19,151	18,018	26,675	124,766	128,739	-3.1
Residential	574	543	530	509	531	819	3,235	4,449	-27.3
Nonresidential	24,980	22,637	20,476	18,642	17,487	25,856	121,531	124,290	-2.2
Office	916	916	946	896	808	1,063	5,340	5,908	-9.6
Commercial	270	280	254	253	239	328	1,538	1,662	-7.5
Health care	932	940	888	875	839	990	5,313	5,571	-4.6
Educational	6,344	5,536	5,192	4,958	4,706	6,777	31,506	32,411	-2.8
Public safety	887	877	823	828	811	888	5,028	4,710	6.8
Amusement and recreation	828	799	737	700	652	818	4,382	4,484	-2.3
Transportation	2,263	2,062	1,944	1,768	1,731	2,266	11,475	12,088	-5.1
Power	782	786	791	641	666	1,007	4,338	5,187	-16.4
Highway and street	8,013	6,845	5,489	4,324	3,849	7,773	32,150	31,242	2.9
Sewage and waste disposal	1,967	1,829	1,706	1,705	1,623	2,006	10,429	10,375	0.5
Water supply	1,106	1,103	1,076	1,014	963	1,151	6,223	6,371	-2.3
Conservation and development	511	506	486	491	445	649	2,870	3,622	-20.8

[1] = Preliminary.
[2] = Revised.
[3] = Includes the following categories of private construction not shown separately: public safety, highway and street, sewage and waste disposal, water supply, and conservation and development.
[4] = Includes the following categories of public construction not shown separately: lodging, religious, communication, and manufacturing.

Source: U.S. Census Bureau, Value of Construction Put in Place

Table 2-56. Value of Private Construction Put in Place, 2011 (Year to Date) and 2012

[Dollars in millions, percent.]

Characteristics	Seasonally adjusted							
	June 2012[1]	May 2012[2]	April 2012[2]	March 2012	February 2012	June 2011	Percent change, June 2012 from: May 2012	Percent change, June 2012 from: June 2011
Total private construction[3]	567,855	564,178	552,328	544,797	544,550	502,149	0.7	13.1
Residential (including improvements)[4]	265,602	262,120	254,145	249,452	252,640	236,923	1.3	12.1
New single family	125,884	122,169	119,578	117,712	117,837	106,140	3.0	18.6
New multi-family	21,697	20,989	19,631	18,028	17,784	14,582	3.4	48.8
Nonresidential	302,252	302,058	298,183	295,345	291,910	265,226	0.1	14.0
Lodging	10,622	10,318	10,313	10,225	8,976	8,408	2.9	26.3
Office	24,901	24,796	24,294	24,552	23,306	23,366	0.4	6.6
General	22,707	22,385	22,092	22,246	20,534	20,659	1.4	9.9
Financial	1,694	1,920	1,871	1,994	2,452	2,441	-11.8	-30.6
Commercial (including farm)	43,637	44,305	43,382	43,234	42,798	40,929	-1.5	6.6
Automotive	4,979	4,346	4,085	3,924	3,822	4,828	14.6	3.1
Sales	2,944	2,442	2,201	2,056	1,915	1,972	20.6	49.3
Service/parts	1,419	1,345	1,314	1,234	1,292	2,516	5.5	-43.6
Parking	617	559	570	635	615	340	10.4	81.5
Food/beverage	5,854	6,195	5,888	5,762	5,824	5,435	-5.5	7.7
Food	2,270	2,626	2,543	2,567	2,735	3,015	-13.6	-24.7
Dining/drinking	2,553	2,490	2,242	1,964	1,815	1,704	2.5	49.8
Multi-retail	16,000	16,580	16,298	15,990	15,317	13,430	-3.5	19.1
General merchandise	3,783	4,438	4,125	4,060	3,951	3,385	-14.8	11.8
Shopping center	8,734	8,281	8,465	8,012	7,996	6,671	5.5	30.9
Shopping mall	2,623	2,890	2,590	2,572	2,235	2,495	-9.2	5.1
Other commercial	3,357	3,334	3,265	3,227	3,225	3,661	0.7	-8.3
Drug store	695	688	898	759	716	674	1.0	3.1
Building supply store	304	424	375	407	416	625	-28.3	-51.4
Other stores	1,702	1,622	1,388	1,413	1,518	1,751	4.9	-2.8
Warehouse	6,592	6,890	6,779	6,846	6,964	6,763	-4.3	-2.5
General commercial	6,188	6,490	6,331	6,477	6,563	6,477	-4.7	-4.5
Mini-storage	307	307	356	287	322	214	0.0	43.5
Health care	30,821	30,630	30,377	29,560	30,644	28,804	0.6	7.0
Hospital	21,117	20,970	20,841	20,428	20,682	20,959	0.7	0.8
Medical building	5,931	5,814	5,880	5,222	5,854	4,971	2.0	19.3
Special care	3,773	3,846	3,656	3,910	4,108	2,874	-1.9	31.3
Educational	17,551	17,379	17,273	17,465	16,762	14,779	1.0	18.8
Preschool	322	379	338	356	257	351	-15.0	-8.3
Primary/secondary	2,899	3,060	2,956	2,758	2,751	3,036	-5.3	-4.5
Higher education	11,624	11,318	11,448	11,704	11,133	8,922	2.7	30.3
Instructional	6,510	6,285	6,586	6,953	6,550	4,925	3.6	32.2
Dormitory	2,674	2,643	2,670	2,635	2,739	2,226	1.2	20.1
Sports/recreation	803	807	776	747	650	610	-0.5	31.6
Other educational	2,177	2,161	2,029	2,057	2,154	2,028	0.7	7.3
Gallery/museum	1,361	1,417	1,376	1,351	1,378	1,595	-4.0	-14.7
Religious	3,729	3,701	3,890	3,989	4,055	3,935	0.8	-5.2
House of worship	3,025	3,068	3,175	3,203	3,232	3,002	-1.4	0.8
Other religious	704	633	715	786	823	933	11.2	-24.5
Auxiliary building	554	503	567	649	607	666	10.1	-16.8
Amusement and recreation	6,542	6,478	6,571	6,414	6,366	7,308	1.0	-10.5
Theme/amusement park	266	314	311	325	310	611	-15.3	-56.5
Sports	1,040	977	909	957	1,211	1,019	6.4	2.1
Fitness	1,296	1,529	1,302	1,325	1,265	1,022	-15.2	26.8
Performance/meeting center	785	654	658	431	400	588	20.0	33.5
Social center	636	609	583	610	529	529	4.4	20.2
Movie theater/studio	237	257	299	313	323	869	-7.8	-72.7
Transportation	11,181	11,158	10,717	9,346	8,609	9,550	0.2	17.1
Air	1,125	1,074	1,140	986	1,069	801	4.7	40.4
Land	10,037	10,046	9,521	8,290	7,528	8,716	-0.1	15.2
Communication	17,480	16,717	16,689	16,696	16,621	17,775	4.6	-1.7
Power (including gas and oil)	82,109	84,767	85,518	85,778	85,796	64,932	-3.1	26.5
Electric	68,218	71,193	71,914	72,151	72,057	54,512	-4.2	25.1
Manufacturing	52,145	50,231	47,873	46,762	46,640	43,825	3.8	19.0
Food/beverage/tobacco	3,883	3,723	3,922	3,915	4,194	6,345	4.3	-38.8
Chemical	10,053	10,878	9,680	9,894	9,626	6,582	-7.6	52.7
Plastic/rubber	1,381	1,391	1,147	796	907	1,079	-0.7	28.0
Nonmetallic mineral	1,024	931	807	454	869	863	10.0	18.7
Fabricated metal	1,626	1,676	1,698	1,897	1,894	1,849	-3.0	-12.1
Computer/electronic/electrical	14,988	13,256	12,793	13,201	12,874	9,316	13.1	60.9
Transportation equipment	4,162	3,640	3,109	2,990	2,854	3,185	14.3	30.7

Table 2-56. Value of Private Construction Put in Place, 2011 (Year to Date) and 2012—*Continued*

[Dollars in millions, percent.]

Characteristics	Not seasonally adjusted								
	June 2012	May 2012	April 2012	March 2012	February 2012	June 2011	Percent change, June 2012 from:		
							May 2012	June 2011	Percent change
Total private construction[3]	50,355	48,185	45,195	41,788	38,090	44,622	262,289	226,369	15.9
Residential (including improvements)[4]	24,343	22,884	21,109	18,246	16,011	21,803	119,103	110,034	8.2
New single family	11,354	10,373	9,550	9,018	7,621	9,597	55,793	49,658	12.4
New multi-family	1,922	1,812	1,659	1,476	1,382	1,275	9,540	6,814	40.0
Nonresidential	26,012	25,300	24,087	23,542	22,079	22,820	143,185	116,335	23.1
Lodging	885	860	859	852	748	701	4,959	4,027	23.1
Office	2,169	2,156	2,020	1,969	1,833	2,048	11,927	10,847	10.0
General	1,985	1,953	1,841	1,775	1,618	1,814	10,758	9,710	10.8
Financial	143	163	151	168	189	211	973	1,058	-8.0
Commercial (including farm)	3,878	3,772	3,608	3,393	3,155	3,655	20,926	18,321	14.2
Automotive	423	364	342	319	292	412	2,035	2,013	1.1
Sales	245	204	183	171	160	164	1,115	862	29.4
Service/parts	125	114	111	96	87	218	621	960	-35.3
Parking	53	47	47	52	45	29	299	192	55.7
Food/beverage	522	511	458	422	416	479	2,712	2,276	19.2
Food	201	225	215	207	205	270	1,243	1,230	1.1
Dining/drinking	213	188	168	146	137	139	973	746	30.4
Multi-retail	1,469	1,453	1,453	1,317	1,119	1,254	7,865	6,289	25.1
General merchandise	387	415	398	336	260	351	2,030	1,595	27.3
Shopping center	765	706	723	668	619	593	4,068	3,277	24.1
Shopping mall	235	242	223	205	164	224	1,231	986	24.8
Other commercial	295	294	257	238	235	320	1,547	1,671	-7.4
Drug store	59	61	78	59	58	57	360	306	17.6
Building supply store	28	37	29	26	24	59	176	271	-35.1
Other stores	154	146	100	99	105	153	712	717	-0.7
Warehouse	582	577	535	518	506	598	3,254	2,913	11.7
General commercial	548	543	498	487	472	574	3,047	2,749	10.8
Mini-storage	26	26	30	24	27	18	161	129	24.8
Health care	2,676	2,571	2,500	2,389	2,339	2,493	14,772	13,642	8.3
Hospital	1,838	1,759	1,733	1,665	1,586	1,816	10,154	10,036	1.2
Medical building	515	500	474	414	447	430	2,806	2,394	17.2
Special care	323	312	294	310	306	248	1,811	1,213	49.3
Educational	1,644	1,564	1,434	1,404	1,243	1,407	8,462	6,550	29.2
Preschool	33	32	26	26	16	36	151	136	11.0
Primary/secondary	294	273	244	206	191	304	1,392	1,510	-7.8
Higher education	1,085	1,029	954	955	838	857	5,637	3,832	47.1
Instructional	591	565	541	573	490	468	3,225	2,024	59.3
Dormitory	275	262	234	220	205	230	1,368	1,063	28.7
Sports/recreation	78	69	63	52	48	59	358	331	8.2
Other educational	183	189	168	169	168	171	1,030	904	13.9
Gallery/museum	115	127	114	110	103	134	665	753	-11.7
Religious	309	295	313	319	328	332	1,884	2,045	-7.9
House of worship	250	242	252	254	261	253	1,514	1,580	-4.2
Other religious	59	54	61	65	68	79	370	465	-20.4
Auxiliary building	47	43	48	53	50	56	282	350	-19.4
Amusement and recreation	548	549	544	537	503	613	3,194	3,234	-1.2
Theme/amusement park	21	27	27	27	26	49	153	280	-45.4
Sports	87	83	72	81	89	85	490	565	-13.3
Fitness	109	132	105	110	96	87	644	491	31.2
Performance/meeting center	65	55	55	36	33	49	281	262	7.3
Social center	55	52	50	52	41	45	294	260	13.1
Movie theater/studio	20	23	27	27	25	76	147	323	-54.5
Transportation	956	919	843	667	598	819	4,693	4,297	9.2
Air	95	92	94	76	77	68	503	187	169.0
Land	859	825	744	586	519	748	4,169	4,068	2.5
Communication	1,503	1,448	1,306	1,337	1,239	1,584	7,975	8,241	-3.2
Power (including gas and oil)	6,858	6,858	6,582	6,859	6,546	5,346	40,602	27,383	48.3
Electric	5,640	5,713	5,471	5,778	5,464	4,435	33,838	22,009	53.7
Manufacturing	4,452	4,176	3,975	3,712	3,455	3,686	23,105	17,047	35.5
Food/beverage/tobacco	319	323	311	299	301	503	1,882	2,153	-12.6
Chemical	833	881	788	761	674	534	4,652	2,936	58.4
Plastic/rubber	121	123	92	63	67	90	536	410	30.7
Nonmetallic mineral	96	79	62	35	69	78	403	429	-6.1
Fabricated metal	136	140	142	158	158	154	878	610	43.9
Computer/electronic/electrical	1,281	1,098	1,144	1,095	963	789	6,517	3,547	83.7
Transportation equipment	347	303	259	249	238	265	1,563	1,472	6.2

[1] = Preliminary.
[2] = Revised.
[3] = Total private construction includes the following categories of construction not shown separately: public safety, highway and street, sewage and waste disposal, water supply, and conservation and development.
[4] = Private residential improvements does not include expenditures to rental, vacant, or seasonal properties.

Source: U.S. Census Bureau, Value of Construction Put in Place

Table 2-57. Value of Private Residential Construction Put in Place, Excluding Rental, Vacant, and Seasonal Residential Improvement, 1993–2012

[Dollars in millions.]

Year	Seasonally adjusted											
	January	February	March	April	May	June	July	August	September	October	November	December
2012[1]	249,566	252,640	249,452	254,145	262,120	265,602	X	X	X	X	X	X
2011	237,726	231,154	226,848	235,985	243,060	236,923	222,417	232,215	236,507	243,661	248,178	249,385
2010	255,049	240,894	242,785	251,782	244,245	241,400	233,762	229,446	231,170	236,570	235,679	229,258
2009	274,565	258,762	246,825	242,889	230,880	228,477	234,280	242,600	248,091	254,256	251,048	245,465
2008	397,751	382,369	382,574	376,718	371,838	359,774	345,129	341,260	337,704	324,161	308,871	288,761
2007	549,553	548,617	548,643	532,200	520,746	509,318	494,545	482,490	472,291	447,839	426,529	410,303
2006	663,898	672,690	676,412	640,577	633,292	615,857	605,654	596,746	589,229	577,822	564,710	563,096
2005	565,755	578,079	585,098	575,688	588,953	600,566	619,342	624,331	630,677	643,426	650,264	664,152
2004	498,940	501,283	506,668	512,559	522,311	527,780	543,194	551,556	546,516	550,981	550,608	566,488
2003	417,788	417,500	413,303	420,510	421,143	430,929	448,917	453,031	458,676	469,855	485,245	503,356
2002	377,631	385,745	385,406	398,990	394,223	401,920	404,632	398,875	394,820	397,077	401,424	411,758
2001	348,279	353,629	350,029	361,991	360,534	365,905	366,500	369,000	368,809	370,957	375,803	376,279
2000	353,065	351,933	353,452	356,188	349,907	348,133	337,374	337,583	339,048	344,095	347,301	344,139
1999	305,968	307,914	316,822	316,111	320,326	322,905	320,854	326,779	334,947	342,423	348,035	346,989
1998	276,485	279,249	291,505	288,409	292,879	296,632	296,717	299,495	305,345	308,127	307,899	302,650
1997	255,365	258,595	264,566	257,490	264,581	262,299	261,593	263,951	270,511	272,980	272,786	269,192
1996	240,958	243,695	249,952	252,836	259,296	263,085	263,549	263,618	265,677	261,444	259,668	253,234
1995	241,184	234,257	228,013	225,488	222,062	218,972	224,113	226,045	228,688	227,589	231,913	235,572
1994	238,612	236,577	235,150	244,746	244,056	244,032	245,463	243,134	242,619	234,905	239,857	241,395
1993	194,150	194,689	190,185	198,296	198,835	203,175	208,760	212,238	214,446	214,778	227,235	235,648

Year	Not seasonally adjusted											
	January	February	March	April	May	June	July	August	September	October	November	December
2012[1]	16,510	16,011	18,246	21,109	22,884	24,343	X	X	X	X	X	X
2011	15,638	14,639	16,689	19,685	21,580	21,803	20,981	22,607	21,307	23,324	20,753	17,954
2010	16,732	15,349	17,970	20,854	21,530	22,191	22,184	22,486	20,825	22,525	19,636	16,539
2009	18,331	16,775	18,504	20,207	20,116	20,918	22,440	24,154	22,260	23,848	20,724	17,636
2008	26,409	25,540	28,934	30,404	32,098	32,676	33,086	33,903	30,735	29,977	25,535	20,961
2007	36,726	36,077	42,056	43,286	45,427	46,851	47,604	47,241	42,387	40,395	35,259	29,938
2006	44,277	44,311	52,204	52,288	55,642	57,185	58,088	57,813	52,723	51,428	46,796	40,974
2005	38,202	38,375	45,075	46,904	51,352	55,376	58,820	60,119	56,883	57,619	54,698	48,477
2004	33,745	33,101	39,011	41,811	45,481	48,749	51,568	52,899	49,247	49,400	46,531	41,360
2003	28,395	27,629	31,797	34,335	36,724	39,938	42,608	43,189	41,331	42,352	41,106	36,635
2002	25,572	25,298	29,407	32,578	34,621	37,440	38,412	37,906	35,563	35,809	34,144	29,948
2001	23,658	23,092	26,762	29,537	31,711	34,180	34,537	34,862	33,350	33,515	32,062	27,147
2000	23,854	22,694	26,921	28,993	30,893	32,731	31,718	31,913	30,894	31,114	29,730	24,684
1999	20,740	19,705	24,039	25,734	28,151	30,263	30,135	30,806	30,857	31,118	29,934	24,819
1998	18,737	17,668	21,818	23,390	25,828	27,872	27,877	28,221	28,437	28,280	26,615	21,602
1997	17,346	16,289	19,659	20,769	23,350	24,520	24,481	24,896	25,412	25,269	23,683	19,022
1996	16,444	15,262	18,492	20,274	22,841	24,591	24,659	24,988	25,102	24,303	22,723	17,817
1995	16,555	14,652	16,891	17,932	19,495	20,483	20,864	21,407	21,752	21,158	20,355	16,579
1994	16,437	14,666	17,305	19,460	21,398	22,777	22,941	23,022	23,153	21,786	21,106	16,982
1993	13,430	12,141	14,007	15,762	17,390	18,953	19,600	20,071	20,498	19,926	20,002	16,401

X = Not applicable.
[1] = Revised.

Source: U.S. Census Bureau, Value of Construction Put in Place

Table 2-58. Value of Private Nonresidential Construction Put in Place, Excluding Rental, Vacant, and Seasonal Residential Improvement, 1993–2012

[Dollars in millions.]

Year	Seasonally adjusted											
	January	February	March	April	May	June	July	August	September	October	November	December
2012[1]	297,894	291,910	295,345	298,183	302,058	302,252	X	X	X	X	X	X
2011	226,833	230,390	240,277	239,268	252,261	265,226	263,373	269,278	270,704	269,141	272,231	285,171
2010	265,226	264,648	265,447	265,825	262,759	262,842	250,462	253,837	252,704	257,129	263,784	259,138
2009	378,587	379,778	382,678	367,807	363,286	352,549	342,729	332,589	321,297	307,252	297,049	286,770
2008	414,045	410,638	405,798	409,912	413,850	407,304	411,182	402,515	410,404	412,197	403,443	392,797
2007	320,249	332,339	340,354	345,178	358,048	369,495	370,632	384,672	395,532	408,729	402,136	401,961
2006	277,343	280,283	285,365	287,651	292,927	299,334	301,402	306,563	307,094	304,567	312,164	320,162
2005	250,158	251,796	251,961	254,161	255,438	252,025	253,900	257,599	263,183	265,451	269,373	272,395
2004	227,349	227,051	233,056	233,437	232,956	232,519	238,888	241,348	246,868	246,581	247,029	246,725
2003	226,819	225,646	229,653	227,092	232,573	231,498	224,707	228,595	233,700	233,121	226,077	232,151
2002	263,731	256,668	252,252	250,341	241,636	235,344	229,426	227,442	224,568	228,572	228,716	222,509
2001	278,005	270,735	280,450	278,653	281,069	284,499	279,200	274,690	270,320	268,404	260,359	264,194
2000	247,213	265,200	268,020	264,832	275,989	271,873	274,805	284,502	289,543	286,731	288,986	281,975
1999	242,862	251,260	253,110	244,859	242,211	249,433	255,008	246,083	247,860	246,803	255,740	257,380
1998	219,748	221,382	228,207	235,598	234,582	248,234	239,636	243,170	242,566	241,654	243,153	243,689
1997	208,531	206,553	202,627	206,035	207,099	209,596	218,840	219,995	222,959	223,110	218,126	218,388
1996	187,068	185,642	184,419	189,505	187,923	194,933	189,035	196,246	200,156	209,483	209,930	208,000
1995	169,788	173,462	178,944	180,257	180,694	184,210	185,753	180,948	182,754	183,887	181,715	182,144
1994	148,235	152,047	159,948	159,650	162,280	160,441	158,233	161,620	163,466	163,059	168,246	165,270
1993	150,025	149,035	148,442	144,221	148,529	147,860	145,513	149,217	150,868	151,440	156,274	159,605

Year	Not seasonally adjusted											
	January	February	March	April	May	June	July	August	September	October	November	December
2012[1]	22,166	22,079	23,542	24,087	25,300	26,012	X	X	X	X	X	X
2011	16,912	17,225	19,116	19,350	20,912	22,820	22,481	23,564	23,554	24,041	23,818	24,207
2010	19,919	19,946	21,121	21,632	21,810	22,639	21,667	22,317	22,153	23,014	23,169	22,389
2009	28,643	28,773	30,184	30,026	30,226	30,252	29,432	28,764	27,766	27,881	25,875	24,573
2008	31,742	32,085	32,509	33,647	34,669	34,839	35,094	34,574	35,276	36,753	34,458	32,923
2007	24,435	25,361	27,347	28,147	30,258	31,711	31,666	33,496	33,891	36,300	34,518	32,903
2006	21,061	21,310	22,958	23,492	24,846	26,011	25,612	26,836	26,546	26,771	26,665	25,998
2005	18,892	19,156	20,350	20,924	21,510	21,882	21,660	22,509	22,701	23,202	23,076	22,216
2004	17,230	17,349	18,785	19,366	19,545	20,290	20,602	21,102	21,415	21,456	21,055	20,079
2003	17,078	16,991	18,199	18,860	19,562	20,138	19,608	20,045	20,436	20,461	19,009	18,949
2002	19,701	19,177	19,989	20,705	20,388	20,361	20,082	20,047	19,594	20,214	19,408	18,075
2001	20,786	20,269	22,408	22,732	23,652	24,812	24,274	24,348	23,419	23,635	22,146	21,442
2000	18,219	19,895	21,397	21,479	23,254	23,729	23,855	25,432	25,423	25,166	24,549	22,895
1999	17,842	18,628	20,058	20,023	20,254	21,792	22,316	21,937	21,868	21,610	21,836	21,005
1998	16,166	16,218	17,680	19,134	19,653	21,849	21,190	22,023	21,705	21,351	20,635	19,792
1997	15,295	15,095	15,577	16,693	17,430	18,185	19,250	19,920	20,148	19,875	18,444	17,804
1996	13,630	13,471	14,075	15,448	15,886	16,897	16,612	17,809	18,036	18,743	17,970	16,947
1995	12,225	12,423	13,815	14,572	15,244	16,096	16,184	16,469	16,641	16,481	15,579	14,804
1994	10,541	10,793	12,464	13,050	13,640	13,975	13,761	14,706	14,933	14,578	14,466	13,529
1993	10,613	10,653	11,660	11,847	12,449	12,889	12,703	13,475	13,710	13,488	13,467	13,052

X = Not applicable.
[1] = Revised.

Source: U.S. Census Bureau, Value of Construction Put in Place

Table 2-59. Value of Public Construction Put in Place, 2011 (Year to Date) and 2012

[Dollars in millions, percent.]

Characteristics	Seasonally adjusted							
	June 2012[1]	May 2012[2]	April 2012[2]	March 2012	February 2012	June 2011	Percent change, June 2012 from: May 2012	Percent change, June 2012 from: June 2011
Total public construction[3]	274,228	274,149	272,805	273,045	276,127	284,635	0.0	-3.7
Residential	6,478	6,426	6,490	6,704	7,000	8,931	0.8	-27.5
Nonresidential	267,750	267,723	266,315	266,341	269,127	275,704	0.0	-2.9
Office	10,635	10,835	11,246	11,229	10,982	12,179	-1.8	-12.7
Commercial	3,164	3,422	3,214	3,191	3,098	3,848	-7.5	-17.8
Health care	10,993	11,016	10,542	10,594	10,437	11,697	-0.2	-6.0
Educational	65,666	66,615	67,270	68,055	68,943	69,711	-1.4	-5.8
Public safety	10,365	10,510	10,177	10,486	10,825	10,370	-1.4	0.0
Amusement and recreation	9,440	9,283	8,995	9,407	9,446	9,046	1.7	4.4
Transportation	25,683	24,769	24,271	23,447	24,442	25,639	3.7	0.2
Power	8,666	8,951	8,572	8,417	9,410	11,218	-3.2	-22.7
Highway and street	80,430	79,261	79,397	77,687	77,484	77,318	1.5	4.0
Sewage and waste disposal	22,144	21,768	21,819	22,254	23,058	22,671	1.7	-2.3
Water supply	12,515	13,016	13,061	13,069	13,184	12,782	-3.8	-2.1
Conservation and development	6,117	6,377	6,027	6,237	5,965	7,533	-4.1	-18.8
Total state and local construction[3]	247,821	247,304	247,320	245,918	249,417	253,816	0.2	-2.4
Residential	4,567	4,586	4,793	4,912	5,247	6,374	-0.4	-28.3
Nonresidential	243,255	242,718	242,527	241,007	244,170	247,442	0.2	-1.7
Office	6,277	6,390	6,490	6,326	6,389	7,784	-1.8	-19.4
Commercial	1,486	1,618	1,422	1,442	1,540	2,029	-8.2	-26.8
Health care	6,958	6,884	6,798	6,824	6,774	7,173	1.1	-3.0
Educational	63,315	64,336	65,139	65,855	66,706	66,806	-1.6	-5.2
Public safety	7,997	7,970	7,691	7,924	8,024	7,715	0.3	3.7
Amusement and recreation	9,115	8,908	8,707	8,980	8,954	8,329	2.3	9.4
Transportation	23,667	22,932	22,526	21,694	22,729	23,867	3.2	-0.8
Power	7,934	8,153	7,774	7,606	8,264	9,790	-2.7	-19.0
Highway and street	79,805	78,558	78,817	76,843	76,701	76,511	1.6	4.3
Sewage and waste disposal	21,228	20,974	21,040	21,238	22,051	21,568	1.2	-1.6
Water supply	12,364	12,879	12,972	12,941	13,075	12,690	-4.0	-2.6
Conservation and development	2,293	2,385	2,254	2,187	2,093	2,389	-3.9	-4.0
Total federal construction[4]	26,406	26,845	25,486	27,126	26,709	30,819	-1.6	-14.3
Residential	1,911	1,840	1,697	1,792	1,753	2,557	3.9	-25.3
Nonresidential	24,495	25,005	23,788	25,334	24,957	28,262	-2.0	-13.3
Office	4,358	4,445	4,756	4,903	4,593	4,395	-2.0	-0.8
Commercial	1,678	1,804	1,792	1,750	1,558	1,819	-7.0	-7.8
Health care	4,035	4,131	3,744	3,770	3,663	4,524	-2.3	-10.8
Educational	2,351	2,279	2,131	2,200	2,238	2,906	3.2	-19.1
Public safety	2,368	2,541	2,486	2,562	2,801	2,655	-6.8	-10.8
Amusement and recreation	325	375	287	427	492	717	-13.3	-54.7
Transportation	2,015	1,837	1,745	1,753	1,713	1,771	9.7	13.8
Power	731	798	798	811	1,146	1,428	-8.4	-48.8
Highway and street	625	703	581	844	783	808	-11.1	-22.6
Conservation and development	3,824	3,992	3,774	4,050	3,872	5,144	-4.2	-25.7

Table 2-59. Value of Public Construction Put in Place, 2011 (Year to Date) and 2012—*Continued*

[Dollars in millions, percent.]

Characteristics	Not seasonally adjusted								
	June 2012[1]	May 2012[2]	April 2012[2]	March 2012	February 2012	June 2011	Percent change, June 2012 from:		
							May 2012	June 2011	Percent change
Total public construction[3]	25,553	23,179	21,006	19,151	18,018	26,675	124,766	128,739	-3.1
Residential	574	543	530	509	531	819	3,235	4,449	-27.3
Nonresidential	24,980	22,637	20,476	18,642	17,487	25,856	121,531	124,290	-2.2
Office	916	916	946	896	808	1,063	5,340	5,908	-9.6
Commercial	270	280	254	253	239	328	1,538	1,662	-7.5
Health care	932	940	888	875	839	990	5,313	5,571	-4.6
Educational	6,344	5,536	5,192	4,958	4,706	6,777	31,506	32,411	-2.8
Public safety	887	877	823	828	811	888	5,028	4,710	6.8
Amusement and recreation	828	799	737	700	652	818	4,382	4,484	-2.3
Transportation	2,263	2,062	1,944	1,768	1,731	2,266	11,475	12,088	-5.1
Power	782	786	791	641	666	1,007	4,338	5,187	-16.4
Highway and street	8,013	6,845	5,489	4,324	3,849	7,773	32,150	31,242	2.9
Sewage and waste disposal	1,967	1,829	1,706	1,705	1,623	2,006	10,429	10,375	0.5
Water supply	1,106	1,103	1,076	1,014	963	1,151	6,223	6,371	-2.3
Conservation and development	511	506	486	491	445	649	2,870	3,622	-20.8
Total state and local construction[3]	23,334	20,964	18,962	16,938	15,981	24,035	112,141	113,949	-1.6
Residential	409	390	398	371	392	594	2,390	3,130	-23.6
Nonresidential	22,925	20,573	18,564	16,567	15,589	23,442	109,751	110,819	-1.0
Office	559	555	547	486	459	695	3,125	3,786	-17.5
Commercial	128	136	118	108	119	174	725	863	-16.0
Health care	595	591	573	544	543	615	3,388	3,435	-1.4
Educational	6,142	5,342	5,025	4,786	4,537	6,525	30,454	30,946	-1.6
Public safety	689	660	631	623	600	661	3,824	3,463	10.4
Amusement and recreation	799	770	711	668	618	751	4,200	4,146	1.3
Transportation	2,092	1,907	1,809	1,630	1,597	2,113	10,628	11,295	-5.9
Power	716	722	730	574	584	877	3,918	4,511	-13.1
Highway and street	7,959	6,785	5,457	4,281	3,813	7,700	31,888	30,937	3.1
Sewage and waste disposal	1,890	1,765	1,652	1,612	1,543	1,916	9,997	9,903	0.9
Water supply	1,093	1,092	1,070	1,003	955	1,143	6,168	6,309	-2.2
Conservation and development	195	188	166	157	149	206	1,002	938	6.8
Total federal construction[4]	2,220	2,216	2,044	2,214	2,038	2,640	12,625	14,790	-14.6
Residential	165	152	133	139	140	225	845	1,319	-35.9
Nonresidential	2,055	2,063	1,912	2,075	1,898	2,414	11,780	13,471	-12.6
Office	358	360	399	410	350	368	2,214	2,122	4.3
Commercial	142	144	136	145	120	154	812	799	1.6
Health care	337	349	315	331	296	375	1,925	2,136	-9.9
Educational	202	194	167	172	169	252	1,052	1,465	-28.2
Public safety	198	218	192	205	212	227	1,205	1,247	-3.4
Amusement and recreation	29	29	25	32	34	67	182	339	-46.3
Transportation	171	155	135	138	134	153	848	792	7.1
Power	66	64	61	67	82	130	421	677	-37.8
Highway and street	54	60	32	44	36	74	262	305	-14.1
Conservation and development	316	319	320	334	296	443	1,869	2,684	-30.4

[1] = Preliminary.
[2] = Revised.
[3] = Includes the following categories of construction not shown separately: lodging, religious, communication, and manufacturing.
[4] = Includes the following categories of federal construction not shown separately: lodging, religious, communication, sewage and waste disposal, water supply, and manufacturing.

Source: U.S. Census Bureau, Value of Construction Put in Place

Table 2-60. Value of State and Local Construction Put in Place, 2011 (Year to Date) and 2012

[Dollars in millions, percent.]

Characteristics	Seasonally adjusted							
	June 2012[1]	May 2012[2]	April 2012[2]	March 2012	February 2012	June 2011	Percent change, June 2012 from:	
							May 2012	June 2011
Total state and local construction	247,821	247,304	247,320	245,918	249,417	253,816	0.2	-2.4
Residential	4,567	4,586	4,793	4,912	5,247	6,374	-0.4	-28.3
Multi-family	3,854	3,848	4,196	4,333	4,644	5,347	0.2	-27.9
Nonresidential	243,255	242,718	242,527	241,007	244,170	247,442	0.2	-1.7
Office	6,277	6,390	6,490	6,326	6,389	7,784	-1.8	-19.4
Commercial	1,486	1,618	1,422	1,442	1,540	2,029	-8.2	-26.8
Automotive	1,107	1,014	1,033	963	1,012	938	9.2	18.0
Parking	883	787	825	747	802	728	12.2	21.3
Health care	6,958	6,884	6,798	6,824	6,774	7,173	1.1	-3.0
Hospital	5,375	5,290	5,120	5,106	5,197	5,322	1.6	1.0
Medical building	1,121	1,112	1,157	1,025	950	956	0.8	17.3
Special care	462	482	521	692	626	895	-4.1	-48.4
Educational	63,315	64,336	65,139	65,855	66,706	66,806	-1.6	-5.2
Primary/secondary	37,049	37,007	37,966	38,273	39,485	40,427	0.1	-8.4
Elementary	10,746	10,305	11,039	10,828	10,347	10,574	4.3	1.6
Middle/junior high	6,958	6,867	7,064	7,181	7,402	8,158	1.3	-14.7
Secondary	19,085	19,490	19,146	19,874	21,297	21,426	-2.1	-10.9
Higher Education	23,042	24,302	24,344	23,953	23,976	23,373	-5.2	-1.4
Instructional	12,549	12,932	13,078	13,403	13,264	12,795	-3.0	-1.9
Dormitory	3,951	4,027	4,030	4,111	4,144	3,845	-1.9	2.8
Sports/recreation	2,009	2,202	2,401	2,329	2,305	2,357	-8.8	-14.8
Infrastructure	1,848	2,295	2,051	1,395	1,301	1,109	-19.5	66.6
Other educational	2,340	2,396	2,013	2,704	2,265	1,845	-2.3	26.8
Library/archive	1,437	1,556	1,368	1,723	1,432	1,144	-7.6	25.6
Public safety	7,997	7,970	7,691	7,924	8,024	7,715	0.3	3.7
Correctional	5,549	5,393	5,146	5,187	5,366	5,263	2.9	5.4
Detention	3,654	3,586	3,428	3,460	3,277	3,506	1.9	4.2
Police/sheriff	1,894	1,808	1,719	1,727	2,089	1,758	4.8	7.7
Other public safety	2,448	2,576	2,545	2,737	2,658	2,452	-5.0	-0.2
Fire/rescue	1,688	1,722	1,622	1,825	1,862	1,564	-2.0	7.9
Amusement and recreation	9,115	8,908	8,707	8,980	8,954	8,329	2.3	9.4
Sports	840	796	964	969	1,129	1,181	5.5	-28.9
Performance/meeting center	1,785	2,020	1,909	1,997	1,988	1,836	-11.6	-2.8
Convention center	1,373	1,420	1,461	1,384	1,394	1,025	-3.3	34.0
Social center	1,047	1,084	1,073	1,149	1,136	907	-3.4	15.4
Neighborhood center	955	929	929	991	930	687	2.8	39.0
Park/camp	5,357	4,928	4,708	4,820	4,662	4,281	8.7	25.1
Transportation	23,667	22,932	22,526	21,694	22,729	23,867	3.2	-0.8
Air	10,292	9,043	8,528	8,380	8,401	10,830	13.8	-5.0
Passenger terminal	5,382	4,629	4,375	4,705	4,785	6,095	16.3	-11.7
Runway	3,982	3,886	3,870	3,357	3,432	4,217	2.5	-5.6
Land	11,499	12,178	11,975	11,791	12,870	11,320	-5.6	1.6
Passenger terminal	2,965	2,833	2,783	3,075	3,155	3,359	4.7	-11.7
Mass transit	5,517	5,823	5,958	5,756	6,255	5,237	-5.3	5.3
Water	1,876	1,711	2,023	1,524	1,458	1,717	9.6	9.3
Dock/marina	1,470	1,326	1,430	1,202	917	1,271	10.9	15.7
Power	7,934	8,153	7,774	7,606	8,264	9,790	-2.7	-19.0
Highway and street	79,805	78,558	78,817	76,843	76,701	76,511	1.6	4.3
Pavement	46,370	46,463	45,143	43,507	44,603	46,691	-0.2	-0.7
Lighting	1,779	1,741	2,284	1,855	2,097	1,554	2.2	14.5
Bridge	28,850	27,517	28,809	28,299	26,760	25,144	4.8	14.7
Rest facility	696	470	443	741	713	701	48.1	-0.7
Sewage and waste disposal	21,228	20,974	21,040	21,238	22,051	21,568	1.2	-1.6
Sewage/dry waste	12,135	12,517	12,152	12,392	12,944	12,014	-3.1	1.0
Plant	2,963	3,004	3,068	3,390	3,446	3,704	-1.4	-20.0
Line/pump station	9,096	9,317	9,004	8,985	9,395	8,253	-2.4	10.2
Waste water	9,093	8,457	8,889	8,846	9,108	9,554	7.5	-4.8
Plant	7,713	6,720	7,257	7,614	7,660	8,305	14.8	-7.1
Line/drain	1,380	1,737	1,632	1,231	1,447	1,249	-20.6	10.5
Water supply	12,364	12,879	12,972	12,941	13,075	12,690	-4.0	-2.6
Plant	5,274	5,316	5,176	5,247	5,197	5,427	-0.8	-2.8
Line	4,900	5,072	5,633	5,743	5,544	5,360	-3.4	-8.6
Pump station	556	520	398	456	491	490	6.9	13.5
Conservation and development	2,293	2,385	2,254	2,187	2,093	2,389	-3.9	-4.0
Dam/levee	810	856	898	811	858	944	-5.4	-14.2
Breakwater/jetty	728	630	619	722	638	607	15.6	19.9

Table 2-60. Value of State and Local Construction Put in Place, 2011 (Year to Date) and 2012

[Dollars in millions, percent.]

Characteristics	Not seasonally adjusted								
	June 2012[1]	May 2012[2]	April 2012[2]	March 2012	February 2012	June 2011	Percent change, June 2012 from:		
							May 2012	June2011	Percent change
Total state and local construction	23,334	20,964	18,962	16,938	15,981	24,035	112,141	113,949	-1.6
Residential	409	390	398	371	392	594	2,390	3,130	-23.6
Multi-family	349	329	348	322	342	508	2,054	2,756	-25.5
Nonresidential	22,925	20,573	18,564	16,567	15,589	23,442	109,751	110,819	-1.0
Office	559	555	547	486	459	695	3,125	3,786	-17.5
Commercial	128	136	118	108	119	174	725	863	-16.0
Automotive	97	87	87	72	77	85	493	440	12.0
Parking	78	68	70	54	60	67	385	365	5.5
Health care	595	591	573	544	543	615	3,388	3,435	-1.4
Hospital	463	458	433	401	412	461	2,573	2,632	-2.2
Medical building	93	93	96	85	79	80	527	433	21.7
Special care	39	40	43	58	52	75	288	370	-22.2
Educational	6,142	5,342	5,025	4,786	4,537	6,525	30,454	30,946	-1.6
Primary/secondary	3,751	3,014	2,844	2,646	2,510	4,076	17,285	17,877	-3.3
Elementary	1,090	858	838	763	656	1,059	4,884	4,714	3.6
Middle/junior high	718	559	530	487	475	840	3,274	3,417	-4.2
Secondary	1,918	1,566	1,419	1,368	1,348	2,150	8,925	9,510	-6.2
Higher Education	2,124	2,071	1,944	1,844	1,760	2,195	11,560	11,567	-0.1
Instructional	1,113	1,111	1,068	1,044	982	1,166	6,310	6,617	-4.6
Dormitory	410	350	328	315	307	406	2,000	1,885	6.1
Sports/recreation	196	193	193	178	163	240	1,093	1,075	1.7
Infrastructure	171	177	131	97	87	102	765	502	52.4
Other educational	194	204	169	219	186	157	1,173	962	21.9
Library/archive	118	134	115	137	116	99	730	669	9.1
Public safety	689	660	631	623	600	661	3,824	3,463	10.4
Correctional	477	446	423	409	399	450	2,557	2,329	9.8
Detention	314	295	281	272	240	298	1,665	1,480	12.5
Police/sheriff	163	152	142	136	159	152	891	848	5.1
Other public safety	212	214	208	215	201	211	1,267	1,134	11.7
Fire/rescue	149	142	131	139	134	137	839	665	26.2
Amusement and recreation	799	770	711	668	618	751	4,200	4,146	1.3
Sports	74	73	83	76	84	106	474	598	-20.7
Performance/meeting center	152	169	150	154	151	165	928	851	9.0
Convention center	113	118	115	109	107	89	672	488	37.7
Social center	90	86	84	90	79	80	511	498	2.6
Neighborhood center	81	73	71	78	65	60	436	413	5.6
Park/camp	476	434	390	344	301	390	2,259	2,039	10.8
Transportation	2,092	1,907	1,809	1,630	1,597	2,113	10,628	11,295	-5.9
Air	949	740	646	564	543	988	4,021	4,913	-18.2
Passenger terminal	469	381	368	377	380	522	2,341	3,078	-23.9
Runway	400	316	254	165	152	418	1,475	1,628	-9.4
Land	987	1,024	994	938	933	982	5,772	5,682	1.6
Passenger terminal	256	237	224	236	222	289	1,413	1,637	-13.7
Mass transit	467	500	512	488	480	453	2,873	2,757	4.2
Water	156	143	169	127	122	143	835	700	19.3
Dock/marina	123	111	119	100	76	106	605	503	20.3
Power	716	722	730	574	584	877	3,918	4,511	-13.1
Highway and street	7,959	6,785	5,457	4,281	3,813	7,700	31,888	30,937	3.1
Pavement	4,797	4,009	2,903	2,195	2,014	4,827	17,730	18,264	-2.9
Lighting	170	139	196	142	117	153	884	824	7.3
Bridge	2,742	2,392	2,152	1,719	1,460	2,444	11,908	10,399	14.5
Rest facility	63	40	34	44	44	63	260	382	-31.9
Sewage and waste disposal	1,890	1,765	1,652	1,612	1,543	1,916	9,997	9,903	0.9
Sewage/dry waste	1,092	1,035	929	911	886	1,088	5,731	5,362	6.9
Plant	262	256	229	251	240	332	1,467	1,461	0.4
Line/pump station	824	763	693	659	638	751	4,219	3,837	10.0
Waste water	798	730	723	700	657	828	4,266	4,541	-6.1
Plant	678	584	588	608	567	718	3,581	3,912	-8.5
Line/drain	121	146	135	92	91	110	686	629	9.1
Water supply	1,093	1,092	1,070	1,003	955	1,143	6,168	6,309	-2.2
Plant	458	435	436	431	392	470	2,545	2,736	-7.0
Line	445	445	459	417	373	510	2,555	2,666	-4.2
Pump station	46	43	33	38	41	41	242	360	-32.8
Conservation and development	195	188	166	157	149	206	1,002	938	6.8
Dam/levee	69	63	61	54	54	80	355	341	4.1
Breakwater/jetty	61	53	52	60	53	51	335	266	25.9

Note: Total state and local construction includes the following categories of construction not shown separately: lodging, religious, communication, and manufacturing.

[1] = Preliminary.

[2] = Revised.

Source: U.S. Census Bureau, Value of Construction Put in Place

Table 2-61. Value of Federal Construction Put in Place, 2011 (Year to Date) and 2012

[Dollars in millions, percent.]

Characteristics	Seasonally adjusted							
	June 2012[1]	May 2012[2]	April 2012[2]	March 2012	February 2012	June 2011	Percent change, June 2012 from:	
							May 2012	June 2011
Total federal construction	26,406	26,845	25,486	27,126	26,709	30,819	-1.6	-14.3
Residential	1,911	1,840	1,697	1,792	1,753	2,557	3.9	-25.3
Nonresidential	24,495	25,005	23,788	25,334	24,957	28,262	-2.0	-13.3
Office	4,358	4,445	4,756	4,903	4,593	4,395	-2.0	-0.8
Commercial	1,678	1,804	1,792	1,750	1,558	1,819	-7.0	-7.8
Health care	4,035	4,131	3,744	3,770	3,663	4,524	-2.3	-10.8
Educational	2,351	2,279	2,131	2,200	2,238	2,906	3.2	-19.1
Public safety	2,368	2,541	2,486	2,562	2,801	2,655	-6.8	-10.8
Amusement and recreation	325	375	287	427	492	717	-13.3	-54.7
Transportation	2,015	1,837	1,745	1,753	1,713	1,771	9.7	13.8
Power	731	798	798	811	1,146	1,428	-8.4	-48.8
Highway and street	625	703	581	844	783	808	-11.1	-22.6
Conservation and development	3,824	3,992	3,774	4,050	3,872	5,144	-4.2	-25.7

Characteristics	Not seasonally adjusted								
	June 2012[1]	May 2012[2]	April 2012[2]	March 2012	February 2012	June 2011	Percent change, June 2012 from:		
							May 2012	June 2011	Percent change
Total federal construction	2,220	2,216	2,044	2,214	2,038	2,640	12,625	14,790	-14.6
Residential	165	152	133	139	140	225	845	1,319	-35.9
Nonresidential	2,055	2,063	1,912	2,075	1,898	2,414	11,780	13,471	-12.6
Office	358	360	399	410	350	368	2,214	2,122	4.3
Commercial	142	144	136	145	120	154	812	799	1.6
Health care	337	349	315	331	296	375	1,925	2,136	-9.9
Educational	202	194	167	172	169	252	1,052	1,465	-28.2
Public safety	198	218	192	205	212	227	1,205	1,247	-3.4
Amusement and recreation	29	29	25	32	34	67	182	339	-46.3
Transportation	171	155	135	138	134	153	848	792	7.1
Power	66	64	61	67	82	130	421	677	-37.8
Highway and street	54	60	32	44	36	74	262	305	-14.1
Conservation and development	316	319	320	334	296	443	1,869	2,684	-30.4

[1] = Preliminary.
[2] = Revised.

Source: U.S. Census Bureau, Value of Construction Put in Place

Table 2-62. Value of Nonfinancial Assets of All Families, by Type of Asset, 1989–2010

[Percent.]

Type of nonfinancial asset	From internal Federal Reserve Board data							
	1989	1992	1995	1998	2001	2004	2007	2010
Total	100.0	100.0	100.0	100.0	100.0	100.0	100.0	100.0
Vehicles	5.6	5.7	7.1	6.5	5.9	5.1	4.4	5.2
Primary residence	46.0	47.0	47.5	47.0	46.9	50.3	48.0	47.4
Other residential property	8.2	8.5	8.0	8.5	8.1	9.9	10.7	11.2
Equity in nonresidential property	11.1	11.0	7.9	7.7	8.2	7.3	5.8	6.7
Business equity	26.7	26.3	27.2	28.5	29.3	25.9	29.7	28.2
Other	2.5	1.6	2.3	1.7	1.6	1.5	1.3	1.3
Nonfinancial assets as a share of total assets	69.5	68.4	63.2	59.3	57.8	64.2	66.0	62.1

Type of nonfinancial asset	From public data							
	1989	1992	1995	1998	2001	2004	2007	2010
Total	100.0	100.0	100.0	100.0	100.0	100.0	100.0	100.0
Vehicles	5.6	5.7	7.1	6.5	6.0	5.1	4.5	5.2
Primary residence	45.7	47.0	47.3	47.0	47.3	50.3	48.3	47.6
Other residential property	8.1	8.5	8.2	8.7	8.2	10.2	11.2	11.3
Equity in nonresidential property	11.3	10.9	7.6	7.6	8.2	7.1	5.4	6.7
Business equity	27.1	26.4	27.7	28.6	28.8	25.8	29.6	28.1
Other	2.2	1.5	2.2	1.6	1.5	1.5	1.0	1.1
Nonfinancial assets as a share of total assets	68.9	68.3	63.1	59.1	57.4	64.2	65.7	62.2

Note: For questions on income, respondents were asked to base their answers on the calendar year preceding the interview.

Source: Federal Reserve Board, Survey of Consumer Finances

Table 2-63. Type of Home-Secured Debt Held by Homeowners Carrying Home-Secured Debt, 1989–2010

[Percent.]

Characteristics	From Federal Reserve internal data							
	1989	1992	1995	1998	2001	2004	2007	2010
First-lien mortgage	58.5	60.0	61.0	62.2	62.5	65.2	66.1	66.4
Purchase loan	NC	NC	37.8	36.8	35.8	28.2	30.4	30.5
Refinanced								
Extracted equity	NC	NC	6.4	9.8	9.7	12.9	14.3	11.4
No extracted equity	NC	NC	16.7	15.6	17.1	24.0	21.5	24.5
Junior-lien mortgage	9.0	7.7	7.8	9.4	8.5	6.1	8.5	5.8
For home purchase	1.6	1.5	1.2	1.0	1.3	1.5	2.1	1.7
Other purpose	7.4	6.2	6.6	8.5	7.2	4.7	6.4	4.0
Home equity line of credit	7.1	9.9	7.9	10.6	11.2	17.8	18.4	15.3
Currently borrowing	4.9	6.7	4.4	6.7	7.1	12.4	12.4	10.7

Characteristics	From public data							
	1989	1992	1995	1998	2001	2004	2007	2010
First-lien mortgage	58.5	60.1	61.0	62.2	62.5	65.2	66.1	66.4
Purchase loan	NC	NC	37.8	36.8	35.8	28.2	30.4	30.5
Refinanced								
Extracted equity	NC	NC	6.4	9.8	9.7	12.9	14.3	11.4
No extracted equity	NC	NC	16.7	15.6	17.1	24.0	21.5	24.5
Junior-lien mortgage	9.0	7.7	7.8	9.4	8.5	6.1	8.5	5.8
For home purchase	1.7	1.5	1.2	1.0	1.5	1.7	2.2	1.8
Other purpose	7.4	6.2	6.6	8.4	7.0	4.5	6.3	4.0
Home equity line of credit	7.1	9.9	7.9	10.6	11.2	17.8	18.4	15.3
Currently borrowing	4.9	6.7	4.4	6.7	7.1	12.4	12.4	10.7

NC = Relevant data not collected.

Source: Federal Reserve Board, Survey of Consumer Finances

Table 2-64. Amount of Debt of All Families, by Purpose of Debt, 1989–2010

[Percent.]

Purpose of debt	From Federal Reserve internal data							
	1989	1992	1995	1998	2001	2004	2007	2010
Total debt	100.0	100.0	100.0	100.0	100.0	100.0	100.0	100.0
Primary residence								
Purchase	64.0	67.2	70.3	67.9	70.9	70.2	69.5	69.5
Improvement	2.5	2.5	2.0	2.1	2.0	1.9	2.3	1.9
Other residential property	8.8	10.8	8.2	7.8	6.5	9.5	10.8	10.5
Investments excluding real estate	3.9	1.8	1.0	3.3	2.8	2.2	1.6	2.0
Vehicles	10.6	7.0	7.6	7.6	7.8	6.7	5.5	4.7
Goods and services	6.1	5.6	5.7	6.3	5.8	6.0	6.2	5.7
Education	2.4	2.8	2.7	3.5	3.1	3.0	3.6	5.2
Other	1.7	2.3	2.4	1.5	1.1	0.6	0.5	0.4

Purpose of debt	From public data							
	1989	1992	1995	1998	2001	2004	2007	2010
Total debt	100.0	100.0	100.0	100.0	100.0	100.0	100.0	100.0
Primary residence								
Purchase	71.3	77.2	78.0	75.4	77.2	79.3	79.8	79.5
Improvement	2.4	2.5	2.0	2.1	2.0	1.9	2.3	1.9
Other residential property	2.3	2.4	2.4	1.5	1.1	.5	.5	.4
Investments excluding real estate	5.1	2.6	1.6	3.6	3.1	2.6	2.2	2.5
Vehicles	10.5	7.0	7.5	7.6	7.7	6.6	5.5	4.7
Goods and services	5.2	5.1	5.4	6.0	5.5	5.5	5.8	5.2
Education	3.1	3.4	3.1	3.7	3.5	3.5	4.0	5.8
Other	*	*	*	*	*	*	*	*

* = Ten or fewer observations.

Source: Federal Reserve Board, Survey of Consumer Finances

Table 2-65. Average Length of Time from Authorization to Start of New Privately Owned Residential Buildings, 1976–2011

[Months, average from authorization to start of buildings started in permit-issuing places.]

Region and year	Buildings with 1 unit				Buildings with 2 units or more				
	Total[1]	Purpose of construction			Total[2]	Number of units in building			
		Built for sale	Contractor built	Owner built		2 to 4	5 to 9	10 to 19	20 or more
United States									
RSE[3]	10.0	10.0	10.0	12.0	9.0	29.0	17.0	17.0	7.0
2011	0.9	0.8	0.8	1.1	2.5	2.5	2.0	3.0	2.2
2010	1.0	0.9	0.9	1.3	2.7	2.2	3.2	2.9	3.0
2009	1.0	1.1	0.8	1.0	2.0	1.8	2.2	1.8	2.2
2008	1.1	1.2	0.7	1.1	2.1	2.1	2.0	2.1	2.1
2007	1.1	1.1	0.9	1.0	2.2	2.1	2.5	2.3	2.2
2006	1.0	1.0	0.9	1.2	2.0	2.0	2.3	1.8	2.1
2005	0.9	0.9	0.8	1.0	1.7	1.6	1.6	1.7	1.9
2004	0.8	0.8	0.8	1.0	1.7	1.4	2.1	2.0	1.7
2003	0.8	0.7	0.7	1.0	1.7	1.6	1.6	1.6	2.0
2002	0.7	0.7	0.6	0.9	1.4	1.4	1.5	1.2	1.2
2001	0.7	0.7	0.6	0.8	1.6	1.3	2.0	1.8	1.4
2000	0.7	0.7	0.6	0.9	1.6	1.4	1.5	1.7	1.9
1999	0.7	0.7	0.6	0.8	1.5	1.1	1.5	1.9	2.0
1998	0.6	NA	NA	NA	1.5	1.0	NA	NA	NA
1997	0.7	NA	NA	NA	1.9	0.8	NA	NA	NA
1996	0.7	NA	NA	NA	1.8	1.3	NA	NA	NA
1995	0.7	NA	NA	NA	1.6	1.1	NA	NA	NA
1994	0.7	NA	NA	NA	1.8	1.1	NA	NA	NA
1993	0.8	NA	NA	NA	1.6	1.2	NA	NA	NA
1992	0.8	NA	NA	NA	2.0	0.9	NA	NA	NA
1991	0.8	NA	NA	NA	1.8	1.5	NA	NA	NA
1990	0.8	NA	NA	NA	2.2	1.5	NA	NA	NA
1989	0.8	NA	NA	NA	2.0	1.5	NA	NA	NA
1988	0.8	NA	NA	NA	1.6	1.3	NA	NA	NA
1987	0.8	NA	NA	NA	1.9	1.2	NA	NA	NA
1986	0.8	NA	NA	NA	1.7	1.1	NA	NA	NA
1985	0.7	NA	NA	NA	1.6	1.0	NA	NA	NA
1984	0.8	NA	NA	NA	1.6	1.1	NA	NA	NA
1983	0.7	NA	NA	NA	1.7	1.2	NA	NA	NA
1982	0.8	NA	NA	NA	1.9	0.9	NA	NA	NA
1981	0.8	NA	NA	NA	2.0	1.2	NA	NA	NA
1980	0.9	NA	NA	NA	2.1	1.1	NA	NA	NA
1979	0.9	NA	NA	NA	2.2	1.3	NA	NA	NA
1978	0.9	NA	NA	NA	2.2	1.2	NA	NA	NA
1977	0.7	NA	NA	NA	1.7	1.1	NA	NA	NA
1976	0.6	NA	NA	NA	1.8	0.8	NA	NA	NA
Northeast									
RSE[3]	48.0	55.0	28.0	32.0	33.0	41.0	45.0	40.0	33.0
2011	1.5	1.2	1.0	0.9	2.4	2.7	1.1	1.8	1.2
2010	1.5	1.5	1.1	1.1	2.2	2.4	1.0	1.6	1.4
2009	0.8	0.8	0.7	0.8	2.1	2.3	1.9	0.9	1.7
2008	1.0	1.2	0.7	1.2	1.3	1.5	1.3	0.7	1.3
2007	1.1	1.0	0.8	0.9	1.5	1.4	2.2	2.1	1.5
2006	0.9	0.8	0.9	1.4	2.5	2.6	2.4	0.9	2.9
2005	0.9	0.9	1.0	1.0	2.1	2.4	1.3	1.6	1.3
2004	1.0	0.9	1.1	1.4	1.3	1.3	1.5	2.0	0.6
2003	1.0	1.1	0.9	1.2	1.8	2.0	1.2	1.1	0.9
2002	0.9	0.9	0.7	1.1	1.5	1.6	1.4	0.9	1.1
2001	0.8	0.8	0.6	1.0	1.9	1.9	2.0	1.9	1.1
2000	1.1	0.7	0.8	1.0	1.8	1.9	1.3	1.6	1.3
1999	0.8	0.7	0.6	1.1	1.4	1.5	1.1	1.0	1.4
1998	0.7	NA	NA	NA	1.0	1.0	NA	NA	NA
1997	0.9	NA	NA	NA	2.2	1.2	NA	NA	NA
1996	1.0	NA	NA	NA	1.2	1.8	NA	NA	NA
1995	1.0	NA	NA	NA	2.2	2.2	NA	NA	NA
1994	1.2	NA	NA	NA	2.4	1.7	NA	NA	NA
1993	1.3	NA	NA	NA	1.9	2.6	NA	NA	NA
1992	1.3	NA	NA	NA	2.4	1.5	NA	NA	NA
1991	1.3	NA	NA	NA	3.2	2.1	NA	NA	NA
1990	1.4	NA	NA	NA	3.7	2.7	NA	NA	NA
1989	1.2	NA	NA	NA	2.2	2.7	NA	NA	NA
1988	1.1	NA	NA	NA	1.3	2.2	NA	NA	NA
1987	1.1	NA	NA	NA	1.6	1.8	NA	NA	NA

Table 2-65. Average Length of Time from Authorization to Start of New Privately Owned Residential Buildings, 1976–2011—*Continued*

[Months, average from authorization to start of buildings started in permit-issuing places.]

Region and year	Buildings with 1 unit				Buildings with 2 units or more				
	Total[1]	Purpose of construction			Total[2]	Number of units in building			
		Built for sale	Contractor built	Owner built		2 to 4	5 to 9	10 to 19	20 or more
1986	1.0	NA	NA	NA	2.4	1.5	NA	NA	NA
1985	1.0	NA	NA	NA	2.0	1.0	NA	NA	NA
1984	1.0	NA	NA	NA	2.1	1.7	NA	NA	NA
1983	1.1	NA	NA	NA	1.9	1.9	NA	NA	NA
1982	1.3	NA	NA	NA	2.9	1.2	NA	NA	NA
1981	1.1	NA	NA	NA	4.2	1.3	NA	NA	NA
1980	1.1	NA	NA	NA	3.3	1.2	NA	NA	NA
1979	1.0	NA	NA	NA	5.2	2.2	NA	NA	NA
1978	1.2	NA	NA	NA	4.0	2.0	NA	NA	NA
1977	1.1	NA	NA	NA	3.5	2.8	NA	NA	NA
1976	1.0	NA	NA	NA	3.9	2.0	NA	NA	NA
Midwest									
RSE[3]	15.0	22.0	23.0	26.0	28.0	22.0	11.0	93.0	103.0
2011	0.7	0.7	0.5	0.8	0.7	0.7	1.4	0.2	0.5
2010	0.6	0.6	0.5	0.8	2.0	1.3	2.2	2.9	2.1
2009	0.7	0.7	0.6	0.7	1.4	1.4	1.9	1.7	0.7
2008	0.8	0.8	0.5	0.8	3.1	4.7	1.4	3.2	3.0
2007	0.8	0.8	0.7	0.7	3.1	4.2	2.2	2.2	1.2
2006	0.8	0.8	0.7	1.0	2.0	2.2	2.3	1.6	1.1
2005	0.7	0.7	0.6	0.9	1.4	1.7	1.6	1.0	0.6
2004	0.6	0.6	0.6	0.9	1.7	1.6	2.4	1.5	0.8
2003	0.6	0.6	0.5	0.8	1.3	2.0	1.0	1.1	0.8
2002	0.6	0.6	0.4	0.8	0.8	0.8	1.1	1.1	-0.2
2001	0.6	0.5	0.5	0.7	1.0	0.9	1.3	1.2	0.3
2000	0.5	0.5	0.5	0.7	0.7	0.7	0.8	0.9	0.2
1999	0.5	0.5	0.5	0.6	1.0	0.6	1.1	1.2	2.2
1998	0.5	NA	NA	NA	0.8	0.6	NA	NA	NA
1997	0.5	NA	NA	NA	0.7	0.6	NA	NA	NA
1996	0.6	NA	NA	NA	1.3	0.5	NA	NA	NA
1995	0.5	NA	NA	NA	0.4	0.7	NA	NA	NA
1994	0.4	NA	NA	NA	1.1	0.7	NA	NA	NA
1993	0.5	NA	NA	NA	0.8	0.7	NA	NA	NA
1992	0.4	NA	NA	NA	1.6	0.5	NA	NA	NA
1991	0.4	NA	NA	NA	1.0	0.9	NA	NA	NA
1990	0.4	NA	NA	NA	1.1	0.5	NA	NA	NA
1989	0.4	NA	NA	NA	1.0	0.6	NA	NA	NA
1988	0.4	NA	NA	NA	0.6	0.4	NA	NA	NA
1987	0.4	NA	NA	NA	0.9	0.5	NA	NA	NA
1986	0.5	NA	NA	NA	1.3	0.7	NA	NA	NA
1985	0.4	NA	NA	NA	1.2	0.6	NA	NA	NA
1984	0.4	NA	NA	NA	0.8	0.6	NA	NA	NA
1983	0.3	NA	NA	NA	0.8	0.7	NA	NA	NA
1982	0.4	NA	NA	NA	0.9	0.6	NA	NA	NA
1981	0.4	NA	NA	NA	1.4	0.6	NA	NA	NA
1980	0.5	NA	NA	NA	1.3	0.8	NA	NA	NA
1979	0.6	NA	NA	NA	1.5	0.8	NA	NA	NA
1978	0.6	NA	NA	NA	1.4	0.8	NA	NA	NA
1977	0.5	NA	NA	NA	1.1	0.7	NA	NA	NA
1976	0.4	NA	NA	NA	1.1	0.5	NA	NA	NA
South									
RSE[3]	7.0	9.0	9.0	19.0	14.0	38.0	21.0	27.0	7.0
2011	0.8	0.8	0.7	1.2	2.6	1.1	3.0	3.3	2.9
2010	1.1	1.0	1.0	1.6	2.9	1.3	2.7	2.9	4.0
2009	1.0	1.1	0.8	1.0	1.7	0.5	1.8	2.0	2.4
2008	1.1	1.2	0.7	1.1	2.1	1.6	1.9	2.3	2.2
2007	1.1	1.1	0.9	1.1	2.4	2.1	2.5	2.4	2.7
2006	1.1	1.1	1.0	1.2	1.7	1.0	2.4	2.1	2.3
2005	1.0	1.0	0.8	1.0	1.9	1.6	1.9	2.0	2.2
2004	0.9	0.9	0.8	1.3	2.1	1.5	3.2	2.2	2.0
2003	0.9	0.8	0.8	1.2	1.8	0.7	2.2	1.8	2.4
2002	0.8	0.7	0.7	0.9	1.7	1.9	1.9	1.3	1.5
2001	0.8	0.7	0.7	0.8	1.6	0.7	2.2	2.2	1.8
2000	0.8	0.8	0.7	1.2	2.3	1.8	2.2	2.4	2.7
1999	0.8	0.8	0.7	0.9	2.0	0.9	2.0	2.5	2.2
1998	0.8	NA	NA	NA	2.0	1.3	NA	NA	NA
1997	0.8	NA	NA	NA	2.7	0.8	NA	NA	NA

Table 2-65. Average Length of Time from Authorization to Start of New Privately Owned Residential Buildings, 1976–2011—*Continued*

[Months, average from authorization to start of buildings started in permit-issuing places.]

Region and year	Buildings with 1 unit				Buildings with 2 units or more				
	Total[1]	Purpose of construction			Total[2]	Number of units in building			
		Built for sale	Contractor built	Owner built		2 to 4	5 to 9	10 to 19	20 or more
1996	0.9	NA	NA	NA	2.3	1.0	NA	NA	NA
1995	0.8	NA	NA	NA	2.0	0.7	NA	NA	NA
1994	0.9	NA	NA	NA	2.2	0.8	NA	NA	NA
1993	0.9	NA	NA	NA	1.9	0.9	NA	NA	NA
1992	0.8	NA	NA	NA	2.1	1.0	NA	NA	NA
1991	0.9	NA	NA	NA	2.2	0.8	NA	NA	NA
1990	0.9	NA	NA	NA	2.7	2.0	NA	NA	NA
1989	0.8	NA	NA	NA	2.6	0.8	NA	NA	NA
1988	0.8	NA	NA	NA	2.2	1.2	NA	NA	NA
1987	0.9	NA	NA	NA	2.7	1.2	NA	NA	NA
1986	0.9	NA	NA	NA	2.3	1.1	NA	NA	NA
1985	0.7	NA	NA	NA	2.0	1.4	NA	NA	NA
1984	0.8	NA	NA	NA	2.1	0.9	NA	NA	NA
1983	0.8	NA	NA	NA	1.9	1.2	NA	NA	NA
1982	0.8	NA	NA	NA	2.2	0.8	NA	NA	NA
1981	0.8	NA	NA	NA	2.1	1.3	NA	NA	NA
1980	0.9	NA	NA	NA	2.5	1.1	NA	NA	NA
1979	1.0	NA	NA	NA	2.6	1.5	NA	NA	NA
1978	0.9	NA	NA	NA	2.8	1.1	NA	NA	NA
1977	0.8	NA	NA	NA	2.1	1.0	NA	NA	NA
1976	0.7	NA	NA	NA	2.4	0.9	NA	NA	NA
West									
RSE[3]	14.0	16.0	16.0	17.0	22.0	57.0	15.0	14.0	21.0
2011	0.9	0.7	1.2	1.8	3.5	6.1	1.3	4.3	2.2
2010	0.8	0.6	0.8	1.6	3.3	2.9	4.9	3.3	1.8
2009	1.4	1.3	1.2	1.4	2.8	2.7	2.9	2.1	3.4
2008	1.5	1.6	1.0	1.6	2.3	2.3	2.7	2.1	1.9
2007	1.2	1.2	0.9	1.0	2.3	2.0	2.9	2.3	1.8
2006	1.1	1.0	1.2	1.4	2.0	2.0	2.3	2.0	1.6
2005	0.8	0.8	0.9	1.1	0.9	0.2	1.2	1.4	1.9
2004	0.7	0.7	0.8	0.8	1.5	1.4	1.1	2.0	1.9
2003	0.6	0.6	0.9	0.8	1.7	1.5	1.5	1.8	2.2
2002	0.7	0.6	0.7	0.9	1.2	1.0	1.2	1.0	1.5
2001	0.7	0.7	0.6	0.9	1.7	1.5	2.3	1.6	1.2
2000	0.6	0.6	0.6	0.7	1.2	1.3	1.1	1.2	1.2
1999	0.5	0.5	0.6	0.8	1.2	1.0	1.0	1.5	1.4
1998	0.5	NA	NA	NA	1.2	0.8	NA	NA	NA
1997	0.5	NA	NA	NA	0.9	0.9	NA	NA	NA
1996	0.6	NA	NA	NA	1.4	1.2	NA	NA	NA
1995	0.5	NA	NA	NA	1.8	1.0	NA	NA	NA
1994	0.6	NA	NA	NA	1.5	1.0	NA	NA	NA
1993	0.7	NA	NA	NA	1.5	1.1	NA	NA	NA
1992	0.9	NA	NA	NA	2.2	0.8	NA	NA	NA
1991	0.9	NA	NA	NA	2.0	1.9	NA	NA	NA
1990	0.9	NA	NA	NA	2.0	1.6	NA	NA	NA
1989	0.8	NA	NA	NA	1.8	1.8	NA	NA	NA
1988	0.7	NA	NA	NA	1.5	1.4	NA	NA	NA
1987	0.8	NA	NA	NA	1.8	1.4	NA	NA	NA
1986	0.6	NA	NA	NA	1.2	1.0	NA	NA	NA
1985	0.7	NA	NA	NA	1.1	0.7	NA	NA	NA
1984	0.7	NA	NA	NA	1.1	1.5	NA	NA	NA
1983	0.7	NA	NA	NA	1.5	1.1	NA	NA	NA
1982	0.8	NA	NA	NA	1.4	0.8	NA	NA	NA
1981	0.8	NA	NA	NA	1.7	1.5	NA	NA	NA
1980	1.0	NA	NA	NA	1.8	1.3	NA	NA	NA
1979	1.0	NA	NA	NA	1.5	1.4	NA	NA	NA
1978	0.9	NA	NA	NA	1.7	1.3	NA	NA	NA
1977	0.7	NA	NA	NA	1.3	1.0	NA	NA	NA
1976	0.6	NA	NA	NA	1.1	0.6	NA	NA	NA

NA = Not available.
[1] = Includes units built for rent (not shown separately).
[2] = For years up through 1998, this only represents 5 units or more.
[3] = Relative standard error.

Source: U.S. Census Bureau, New Residential Construction

Table 2-66. Percent Distribution of New Privately Owned Residential Buildings Started in Permit-Issuing Places, by Number of Months from Authorization, 2011

[Percent.]

Region and characteristic	Buildings with 1 unit				Buildings with 2 units or more				
	Total[1]	Purpose of construction			Total	Number of units in building			
		Built for sale	Contractor built	Owner built		2 to 4	5 to 9	10 to 19	20 or more
Percent distribution									
United States									
Prior to or same month as authorization	56.0	58.0	54.0	51.0	37.0	41.0	28.0	35.0	38.0
1 month	31.0	31.0	33.0	31.0	25.0	33.0	23.0	21.0	17.0
2 months	6.0	6.0	6.0	7.0	10.0	5.0	16.0	10.0	14.0
3 months	2.0	2.0	3.0	4.0	13.0	10.0	22.0	11.0	13.0
4 months or more	5.0	4.0	4.0	7.0	15.0	10.0	12.0	23.0	18.0
Northeast									
Prior to or same month as authorization	60.0	63.0	55.0	63.0	42.0	42.0	54.0	36.0	40.0
1 month	23.0	23.0	25.0	23.0	29.0	28.0	24.0	38.0	32.0
2 months	6.0	6.0	6.0	5.0	4.0	3.0	4.0	2.0	13.0
3 months	3.0	2.0	5.0	2.0	12.0	15.0	7.0	1.0	2.0
4 months or more	8.0	6.0	10.0	7.0	13.0	12.0	11.0	24.0	13.0
Midwest									
Prior to or same month as authorization	59.0	63.0	56.0	52.0	57.0	35.0	32.0	81.0	77.0
1 month	30.0	29.0	36.0	31.0	24.0	55.0	30.0	10.0	4.0
2 months	5.0	4.0	4.0	8.0	9.0	10.0	22.0	4.0	3.0
3 months	3.0	2.0	2.0	3.0	3.0	W	8.0	1.0	4.0
4 months or more	3.0	2.0	2.0	6.0	6.0	W	7.0	4.0	12.0
South									
Prior to or same month as authorization	53.0	54.0	52.0	50.0	30.0	47.0	14.0	25.0	28.0
1 month	34.0	34.0	38.0	34.0	23.0	44.0	9.0	18.0	18.0
2 months	6.0	7.0	6.0	6.0	12.0	1.0	14.0	12.0	17.0
3 months	2.0	2.0	2.0	4.0	18.0	4.0	46.0	14.0	18.0
4 months or more	4.0	4.0	2.0	7.0	18.0	4.0	17.0	30.0	18.0
West									
Prior to or same month as authorization	58.0	60.0	55.0	42.0	31.0	28.0	36.0	27.0	34.0
1 month	28.0	29.0	22.0	26.0	23.0	21.0	36.0	23.0	17.0
2 months	6.0	5.0	10.0	12.0	17.0	24.0	19.0	14.0	12.0
3 months	3.0	2.0	6.0	8.0	10.0	5.0	2.0	16.0	13.0
4 months or more	5.0	4.0	7.0	12.0	19.0	23.0	8.0	19.0	24.0
RSE[2]									
United States									
Prior to or same month as authorization	3.0	3.0	6.0	8.0	8.0	16.0	19.0	19.0	7.0
1 month	4.0	4.0	10.0	14.0	13.0	18.0	19.0	25.0	15.0
2 months	7.0	8.0	15.0	15.0	15.0	36.0	34.0	23.0	11.0
3 months	12.0	13.0	19.0	20.0	24.0	62.0	40.0	32.0	17.0
4 months or more	9.0	10.0	24.0	22.0	15.0	25.0	33.0	39.0	14.0
Northeast									
Prior to or same month as authorization	8.0	8.0	13.0	10.0	18.0	25.0	35.0	47.0	16.0
1 month	11.0	12.0	16.0	22.0	22.0	27.0	44.0	52.0	31.0
2 months	17.0	29.0	25.0	32.0	42.0	64.0	82.0	85.0	45.0
3 months	28.0	40.0	31.0	67.0	64.0	69.0	80.0	97.0	66.0
4 months or more	29.0	32.0	40.0	42.0	31.0	34.0	72.0	70.0	69.0
Midwest									
Prior to or same month as authorization	6.0	4.0	16.0	18.0	12.0	44.0	22.0	12.0	13.0
1 month	11.0	7.0	26.0	18.0	22.0	34.0	28.0	57.0	58.0
2 months	17.0	18.0	27.0	38.0	55.0	67.0	51.0	69.0	52.0
3 months	25.0	21.0	54.0	50.0	44.0	W	26.0	56.0	63.0
4 months or more	20.0	26.0	41.0	32.0	47.0	W	39.0	43.0	66.0
South									
Prior to or same month as authorization	4.0	4.0	7.0	12.0	16.0	28.0	45.0	34.0	12.0
1 month	5.0	5.0	8.0	21.0	26.0	32.0	77.0	38.0	17.0
2 months	9.0	10.0	22.0	20.0	22.0	117.0	68.0	36.0	13.0
3 months	15.0	17.0	33.0	28.0	25.0	80.0	38.0	35.0	18.0
4 months or more	11.0	12.0	34.0	37.0	31.0	62.0	50.0	54.0	13.0
West									
Prior to or same month as authorization	7.0	8.0	7.0	16.0	19.0	31.0	20.0	31.0	23.0
1 month	8.0	10.0	11.0	14.0	21.0	45.0	24.0	47.0	31.0
2 months	17.0	21.0	34.0	21.0	21.0	40.0	50.0	28.0	21.0
3 months	21.0	24.0	24.0	37.0	38.0	77.0	64.0	57.0	42.0
4 months or more	18.0	19.0	23.0	29.0	20.0	54.0	32.0	17.0	26.0

W = Less than 0.5 percent.
[1] = Includes units built for rent (not shown separately).
[2] = Relative standard error.

Source: U.S. Census Bureau, New Residential Construction

Table 2-67. Conventional, Conforming 30-Year Fixed-Rate Mortgage Series, 1971–2012

[Percent.]

Month and year	Rate	Points
2012		
January	3.92	0.8
February	3.89	0.8
March	3.95	0.8
April	3.91	0.7
May	3.80	0.8
June	3.68	0.7
July	3.55	0.7
August	NA	NA
September	NA	NA
October	NA	NA
November	NA	NA
December	NA	NA
Annual average	NA	NA
2011		
January	4.76	0.8
February	4.95	0.7
March	4.84	0.7
April	4.84	0.7
May	4.64	0.7
June	4.51	0.7
July	4.55	0.7
August	4.27	0.7
September	4.11	0.7
October	4.07	0.8
November	3.99	0.7
December	3.96	0.7
Annual average	4.45	0.7
2010		
January	5.03	0.7
February	4.99	0.7
March	4.97	0.7
April	5.10	0.7
May	4.89	0.7
June	4.74	0.7
July	4.56	0.7
August	4.43	0.7
September	4.35	0.7
October	4.23	0.8
November	4.30	0.8
December	4.71	0.7
Annual average	4.69	0.7
2009		
January	5.05	0.7
February	5.13	0.7
March	5.00	0.7
April	4.81	0.7
May	4.86	0.7
June	5.42	0.7
July	5.22	0.7
August	5.19	0.7
September	5.06	0.7
October	4.95	0.7
November	4.88	0.7
December	4.93	0.7
Annual average	5.04	0.7
2008		
January	5.76	0.4
February	5.92	0.5
March	5.97	0.5
April	5.92	0.4
May	6.04	0.5
June	6.32	0.7
July	6.43	0.6
August	6.48	0.7
September	6.04	0.7
October	6.20	0.6
November	6.09	0.7
December	5.29	0.7
Annual average	6.03	0.6
2007		
January	6.22	0.4
February	6.29	0.4
March	6.16	0.4
April	6.18	0.5
May	6.26	0.4
June	6.66	0.4
July	6.70	0.4
August	6.57	0.4
September	6.38	0.5
October	6.38	0.5
November	6.21	0.4
December	6.10	0.5
Annual average	6.24	0.4
2006		
January	6.15	0.5
February	6.25	0.6
March	6.32	0.6
April	6.51	0.6
May	6.60	0.5
June	6.68	0.5
July	6.76	0.5
August	6.52	0.4
September	6.40	0.5
October	6.36	0.4
November	6.24	0.5
December	6.14	0.4
Annual average	6.41	0.5
2005		
January	5.71	0.7
February	5.63	0.7
March	5.93	0.7
April	5.86	0.6
May	5.72	0.6
June	5.58	0.6
July	5.70	0.5
August	5.82	0.5
September	5.77	0.6
October	6.07	0.5
November	6.33	0.6
December	6.27	0.5
Annual average	5.87	0.6
2004		
January	5.71	0.7
February	5.64	0.7
March	5.45	0.7
April	5.83	0.7
May	6.27	0.7
June	6.29	0.6
July	6.06	0.6
August	5.87	0.7
September	5.75	0.7
October	5.72	0.7
November	5.73	0.6
December	5.75	0.6
Annual average	5.84	0.7
2003		
January	5.92	0.6
February	5.84	0.6
March	5.75	0.6
April	5.81	0.6
May	5.48	0.6
June	5.23	0.6
July	5.63	0.5
August	6.26	0.7
September	6.15	0.6
October	5.95	0.6
November	5.93	0.6
December	5.83	0.7
Annual average	5.83	0.6
2002		
January	7.00	0.8
February	6.89	0.7
March	7.01	0.7
April	6.99	0.7
May	6.81	0.7
June	6.65	0.6
July	6.49	0.6
August	6.29	0.6
September	6.09	0.6
October	6.11	0.6
November	6.07	0.6
December	6.05	0.6
Annual average	6.54	0.6

Table 2-67. Conventional, Conforming 30-Year Fixed-Rate Mortgage Series, 1971–2012—*Continued*

[Percent.]

Month and year	Rate	Points
2001		
January	7.03	0.9
February	7.05	1.0
March	6.95	0.9
April	7.08	0.9
May	7.15	1.0
June	7.16	1.0
July	7.13	0.9
August	6.95	0.9
September	6.82	0.9
October	6.62	0.9
November	6.66	0.8
December	7.07	0.8
Annual average	6.97	0.9
2000		
January	8.21	1.0
February	8.33	1.0
March	8.24	1.0
April	8.15	1.0
May	8.52	1.0
June	8.29	0.9
July	8.15	0.9
August	8.03	1.0
September	7.91	1.0
October	7.80	1.0
November	7.75	0.9
December	7.38	1.0
Annual average	8.05	1.0
1999		
January	6.79	0.9
February	6.81	1.0
March	7.04	0.9
April	6.92	1.0
May	7.15	1.0
June	7.55	1.0
July	7.63	1.0
August	7.94	1.0
September	7.82	1.0
October	7.85	1.0
November	7.74	1.0
December	7.91	1.0
Annual average	7.44	1.0
1998		
January	6.99	1.4
February	7.04	1.2
March	7.13	1.2
April	7.14	1.0
May	7.14	1.1
June	7.00	1.0
July	6.95	1.1
August	6.92	1.1
September	6.72	1.0
October	6.71	0.9
November	6.87	0.9
December	6.74	1.0
Annual average	6.94	1.1
1997		
January	7.82	1.8
February	7.65	1.7
March	7.90	1.8
April	8.14	1.7
May	7.94	1.7
June	7.69	1.7
July	7.50	1.8
August	7.48	1.7
September	7.43	1.7
October	7.29	1.7
November	7.21	1.7
December	7.10	1.8
Annual average	7.60	1.7
1996		
January	7.03	1.8
February	7.08	1.7
March	7.62	1.8
April	7.93	1.8
May	8.07	1.7
June	8.32	1.7
July	8.25	1.8
August	8.00	1.7
September	8.23	1.7
October	7.92	1.7
November	7.62	1.8
December	7.60	1.7
Annual average	7.81	1.7
1995		
January	9.15	1.8
February	8.83	1.9
March	8.46	1.8
April	8.32	1.9
May	7.96	1.8
June	7.57	1.8
July	7.61	1.8
August	7.86	1.8
September	7.64	1.8
October	7.48	1.9
November	7.38	1.8
December	7.20	1.8
Annual average	7.93	1.8
1994		
January	7.07	1.7
February	7.15	1.8
March	7.68	1.7
April	8.32	1.8
May	8.60	1.8
June	8.40	1.8
July	8.61	1.8
August	8.51	1.8
September	8.64	1.8
October	8.93	1.8
November	9.17	1.8
December	9.20	1.8
Annual average	8.38	1.8
1993		
January	7.99	1.6
February	7.68	1.5
March	7.50	1.6
April	7.46	1.7
May	7.47	1.8
June	7.42	1.6
July	7.21	1.6
August	7.11	1.5
September	6.91	1.5
October	6.83	1.5
November	7.16	1.6
December	7.17	1.7
Annual average	7.31	1.6
1992		
January	8.43	1.8
February	8.76	1.8
March	8.94	1.9
April	8.85	1.7
May	8.67	1.7
June	8.51	1.7
July	8.13	1.6
August	7.98	1.7
September	7.92	1.7
October	8.09	1.8
November	8.31	1.9
December	8.21	1.6
Annual average	8.39	1.7
1991		
January	9.64	2.1
February	9.37	2.0
March	9.50	2.1
April	9.50	2.0
May	9.47	2.0
June	9.62	2.1
July	9.58	2.0
August	9.24	1.9
September	9.01	1.9
October	8.86	1.9
November	8.71	1.8
December	8.50	1.8
Annual average	9.25	2.0

Table 2-67. Conventional, Conforming 30-Year Fixed-Rate Mortgage Series, 1971–2012—*Continued*

[Percent.]

Month and year	Rate	Points
1990		
January	9.90	2.1
February	10.20	2.1
March	10.27	2.1
April	10.37	2.1
May	10.48	2.0
June	10.16	2.0
July	10.04	2.0
August	10.10	2.0
September	10.18	2.1
October	10.17	2.2
November	10.01	2.1
December	9.67	1.9
Annual average	10.13	2.1
1989		
January	10.73	2.1
February	10.65	2.2
March	11.03	2.2
April	11.05	2.2
May	10.77	2.1
June	10.20	2.1
July	9.88	2.1
August	9.99	2.1
September	10.13	2.0
October	9.95	2.0
November	9.77	2.0
December	9.74	2.0
Annual average	10.32	2.1
1988		
January	10.38	2.0
February	9.89	2.1
March	9.93	2.0
April	10.20	2.1
May	10.46	2.1
June	10.46	2.0
July	10.43	2.0
August	10.60	2.2
September	10.48	2.1
October	10.30	1.9
November	10.27	2.1
December	10.61	2.1
Annual average	10.34	2.1
1987		
January	9.20	2.2
February	9.08	2.1
March	9.04	2.1
April	9.83	2.3
May	10.60	2.3
June	10.54	2.2
July	10.28	2.2
August	10.33	2.1
September	10.89	2.2
October	11.26	2.2
November	10.65	2.1
December	10.64	2.1
Annual average	10.21	2.2
1986		
January	10.89	2.3
February	10.71	2.3
March	10.08	2.3
April	9.94	2.2
May	10.15	2.3
June	10.69	2.3
July	10.51	2.2
August	10.20	2.1
September	10.01	2.2
October	9.98	2.1
November	9.70	2.0
December	9.32	2.1
Annual average	10.19	2.2
1985		
January	13.08	2.5
February	12.92	2.4
March	13.17	2.6
April	13.20	2.6
May	12.91	2.5
June	12.22	2.5
July	12.03	2.5
August	12.19	2.6
September	12.19	2.6
October	12.14	2.5
November	11.78	2.4
December	11.26	2.3
Annual average	12.43	2.5
1984		
January	13.37	2.3
February	13.23	2.4
March	13.39	2.4
April	13.65	2.4
May	13.94	2.5
June	14.42	2.5
July	14.67	2.6
August	14.47	2.6
September	14.35	2.6
October	14.13	2.6
November	13.64	2.5
December	13.18	2.5
Annual average	13.88	2.5
1983		
January	13.25	2.2
February	13.04	2.0
March	12.80	2.2
April	12.78	2.1
May	12.63	2.1
June	12.87	2.1
July	13.43	2.2
August	13.81	2.2
September	13.73	2.2
October	13.54	2.1
November	13.44	2.1
December	13.42	2.2
Annual average	13.24	2.1
1982		
January	17.48	2.2
February	17.60	2.2
March	17.16	2.2
April	16.89	2.3
May	16.68	2.3
June	16.70	2.2
July	16.82	2.2
August	16.27	2.3
September	15.43	2.3
October	14.61	2.2
November	13.82	2.2
December	13.62	2.2
Annual average	16.04	2.2
1981		
January	14.90	2.0
February	15.13	2.0
March	15.40	2.0
April	15.58	2.0
May	16.40	2.1
June	16.70	2.1
July	16.83	2.1
August	17.28	2.1
September	18.16	2.1
October	18.45	2.3
November	17.82	2.1
December	16.95	2.1
Annual average	16.63	2.1
1980		
January	12.88	1.6
February	13.04	1.6
March	15.28	2.0
April	16.32	1.9
May	14.26	1.9
June	12.71	1.8
July	12.19	1.8
August	12.56	1.7
September	13.20	1.7
October	13.79	1.7
November	14.21	1.7
December	14.79	1.7
Annual average	13.74	1.8

Table 2-67. Conventional, Conforming 30-Year Fixed-Rate Mortgage Series, 1971–2012—*Continued*

[Percent.]

Month and year	Rate	Points
1979		
January	10.39	1.5
February	10.41	1.5
March	10.43	1.5
April	10.50	1.5
May	10.69	1.6
June	11.04	1.6
July	11.09	1.7
August	11.09	1.7
September	11.30	1.6
October	11.64	1.7
November	12.83	1.7
December	12.90	1.6
Annual average	11.20	1.2
1978		
January	9.01	1.3
February	9.14	1.3
March	9.20	1.3
April	9.35	1.3
May	9.57	1.3
June	9.71	1.4
July	9.74	1.4
August	9.78	1.3
September	9.76	1.3
October	9.86	1.2
November	10.11	1.2
December	10.35	1.4
Annual average	9.64	1.3
1977		
January	8.72	1.1
February	8.67	1.1
March	8.69	1.2
April	8.75	1.1
May	8.83	1.1
June	8.86	1.1
July	8.94	1.1
August	8.94	1.1
September	8.90	1.1
October	8.92	1.2
November	8.92	1.1
December	8.96	1.2
Annual average	8.85	1.1
1976		
January	9.02	1.1
February	8.81	1.0
March	8.76	1.3
April	8.73	1.3
May	8.76	1.3
June	8.85	1.3
July	8.93	1.2
August	9.00	1.2
September	8.98	1.2
October	8.92	1.2
November	8.81	1.3
December	8.79	1.2
Annual average	8.87	1.2
1975		
January	9.43	1.2
February	9.10	1.2
March	8.89	1.1
April	8.82	1.0
May	8.91	1.1
June	8.89	1.0

Month and year	Rate	Points
July	8.89	1.1
August	8.94	1.1
September	9.12	1.1
October	9.22	1.1
November	9.15	1.1
December	9.10	1.1
Annual average	9.05	1.1
1974		
January	8.54	1.0
February	8.46	1.0
March	8.41	1.0
April	8.58	1.0
May	8.97	1.1
June	9.09	1.2
July	9.28	1.3
August	9.59	1.3
September	9.96	1.4
October	9.98	1.5
November	9.79	1.4
December	9.62	1.3
Annual average	9.19	1.2
1973		
January	7.44	0.9
February	7.44	1.0
March	7.46	0.9
April	7.54	0.9
May	7.65	0.9
June	7.73	0.9
July	8.05	1.0
August	8.50	1.0
September	8.82	1.1
October	8.77	1.1
November	8.58	1.0
December	8.54	1.0
Annual average	8.04	1.0
1972		
January	7.44	1.0
February	7.32	0.9
March	7.29	0.9
April	7.29	0.9
May	7.37	0.9
June	7.37	0.9
July	7.40	0.9
August	7.40	0.9
September	7.42	1.0
October	7.42	1.0
November	7.43	1.0
December	7.44	1.0
Annual average	7.38	0.9
1971		
January	NA	NA
February	NA	NA
March	NA	NA
April	7.31	NA
May	7.43	NA
June	7.53	NA
July	7.60	NA
August	7.70	NA
September	7.69	NA
October	7.63	NA
November	7.55	NA
December	7.48	NA
Annual average	NA	NA

NA = Not available.

Source: Freddie Mac, Primary Mortgage Market Survey

Table 2-68. Conventional, Conforming 15-Year Fixed-Rate Mortgage Series, 1991–2012

[Percent, number.]

Month and year	Rate	Points
2012		
January	3.92	0.8
February	3.89	0.8
March	3.95	0.8
April	3.91	0.7
May	3.80	0.8
June	3.68	0.7
July	3.55	0.7
August	NA	NA
September	NA	NA
October	NA	NA
November	NA	NA
December	NA	NA
Annual average	NA	NA
2011		
January	4.76	0.8
February	4.95	0.7
March	4.84	0.7
April	4.84	0.7
May	4.64	0.7
June	4.51	0.7
July	4.55	0.7
August	4.27	0.7
September	4.11	0.7
October	4.07	0.8
November	3.99	0.7
December	3.96	0.7
Annual average	4.45	0.7
2010		
January	4.44	0.6
February	4.37	0.7
March	4.33	0.7
April	4.42	0.6
May	4.28	0.7
June	4.18	0.7
July	4.04	0.7
August	3.91	0.6
September	3.81	0.6
October	3.66	0.7
November	3.68	0.7
December	4.06	0.7
Annual average	4.10	0.7
2009		
January	4.72	0.7
February	4.77	0.7
March	4.64	0.7
April	4.50	0.7
May	4.52	0.7
June	4.90	0.7
July	4.69	0.7
August	4.61	0.7
September	4.49	0.6
October	4.39	0.6
November	4.34	0.6
December	4.39	0.6
Annual average	4.57	0.7
2008		
January	5.29	0.4
February	5.44	0.5
March	5.42	0.5
April	5.47	0.4
May	5.60	0.5
June	5.91	0.6
July	5.97	0.6
August	6.03	0.7
September	5.64	0.6
October	5.89	0.6
November	5.79	0.7
December	5.04	0.7
Annual average	5.62	0.6
2007		
January	5.97	0.4
February	6.02	0.4
March	5.88	0.4
April	5.88	0.5
May	5.97	0.4
June	6.34	0.4
July	6.36	0.4
August	6.23	0.4
September	6.05	0.5
October	6.04	0.6
November	5.85	0.5
December	5.75	0.5
Annual average	6.03	0.4
2006		
January	5.71	0.5
February	5.86	0.6
March	5.97	0.6
April	6.16	0.5
May	6.21	0.5
June	6.31	0.5
July	6.39	0.4
August	6.20	0.4
September	6.08	0.4
October	6.05	0.5
November	5.96	0.5
December	5.88	0.5
Annual average	6.07	0.5
2005		
January	5.17	0.6
February	5.15	0.7
March	5.46	0.7
April	5.41	0.6
May	5.28	0.6
June	5.17	0.6
July	5.28	0.6
August	5.40	0.6
September	5.36	0.6
October	5.63	0.6
November	5.86	0.6
December	5.82	0.6
Annual average	5.42	0.6
2004		
January	5.02	0.7
February	4.94	0.7
March	4.74	0.7
April	5.16	0.6
May	5.64	0.7
June	5.66	0.6
July	5.46	0.6
August	5.26	0.6
September	5.14	0.7
October	5.12	0.6
November	5.14	0.6
December	5.18	0.6
Annual average	5.21	0.6
2003		
January	5.30	0.6
February	5.22	0.6
March	5.07	0.6
April	5.12	0.6
May	4.86	0.7
June	4.63	0.6
July	4.97	0.5
August	5.59	0.7
September	5.46	0.6
October	5.27	0.6
November	5.27	0.7
December	5.20	0.6
Annual average	5.17	0.6
2002		
January	6.48	0.7
February	6.38	0.7
March	6.52	0.7
April	6.48	0.7
May	6.28	0.7
June	6.11	0.6
July	5.93	0.5
August	5.70	0.6
September	5.51	0.6
October	5.50	0.6
November	5.46	0.6
December	5.45	0.6
Annual average	5.98	0.6

Table 2-68. Conventional, Conforming 15-Year Fixed-Rate Mortgage Series, 1991–2012—*Continued*

[Percent, number.]

Month and year	Rate	Points
2001		
January	6.64	0.9
February	6.64	0.9
March	6.51	1.0
April	6.60	1.0
May	6.68	1.0
June	6.70	1.0
July	6.68	0.9
August	6.50	0.9
September	6.34	0.9
October	6.10	0.9
November	6.15	0.8
December	6.54	0.8
Annual average	6.50	0.9
2000		
January	7.80	1.0
February	7.93	1.0
March	7.83	0.9
April	7.80	1.0
May	8.18	1.0
June	7.99	0.9
July	7.87	0.9
August	7.76	1.0
September	7.60	1.0
October	7.47	1.0
November	7.42	0.9
December	7.06	0.9
Annual average	7.72	1.0
1999		
January	6.43	1.0
February	6.44	1.0
March	6.68	0.9
April	6.53	0.9
May	6.75	1.0
June	7.18	1.0
July	7.26	1.0
August	7.53	1.0
September	7.44	1.0
October	7.47	1.0
November	7.36	1.0
December	7.52	1.0
Annual average	7.06	1.0
1998		
January	6.58	1.4
February	6.64	1.2
March	6.74	1.2
April	6.78	1.0
May	6.78	1.0
June	6.67	1.0
July	6.62	1.1
August	6.61	1.1
September	6.40	1.0
October	6.36	0.9
November	6.51	0.9
December	6.39	0.9
Annual average	6.59	1.1
1997		
January	7.33	1.7
February	7.15	1.7
March	7.41	1.7
April	7.68	1.7
May	7.47	1.6
June	7.24	1.7
July	7.04	1.8
August	7.02	1.7
September	6.99	1.7
October	6.85	1.7
November	6.76	1.7
December	6.66	1.8
Annual average	7.13	1.7
1996		
January	6.55	1.7
February	6.56	1.7
March	7.11	1.8
April	7.44	1.7
May	7.58	1.7
June	7.83	1.7
July	7.77	1.7
August	7.52	1.7
September	7.75	1.7
October	7.43	1.7
November	7.14	1.7
December	7.10	1.7
Annual average	7.32	1.7
1995		
January	8.80	1.8
February	8.46	1.8
March	8.06	1.8
April	7.88	1.8
May	7.51	1.7
June	7.06	1.7
July	7.09	1.7
August	7.36	1.8
September	7.16	1.8
October	7.01	1.8
November	6.89	1.8
December	6.74	1.7
Annual average	7.48	1.8
1994		
January	6.57	1.7
February	6.66	1.7
March	7.18	1.7
April	7.80	1.7
May	8.08	1.7
June	7.91	1.8
July	8.11	1.7
August	8.02	1.8
September	8.13	1.8
October	8.39	1.8
November	8.67	1.8
December	8.80	1.8
Annual average	7.86	1.8
1993		
January	7.51	1.7
February	7.17	1.5
March	7.00	1.6
April	6.94	1.6
May	6.93	1.8
June	6.92	1.6
July	6.72	1.6
August	6.63	1.5
September	6.43	1.5
October	6.37	1.5
November	6.69	1.5
December	6.68	1.5
Annual average	6.83	1.6
1992		
January	8.01	1.7
February	8.38	1.8
March	8.58	1.9
April	8.47	1.7
May	8.29	1.7
June	8.08	1.7
July	7.67	1.6
August	7.49	1.6
September	7.41	1.6
October	7.55	1.7
November	7.80	1.8
December	7.74	1.6
Annual average	7.96	1.7
1991		
January	NA	NA
February	NA	NA
March	NA	NA
April	NA	NA
May	NA	NA
June	NA	NA
July	NA	NA
August	NA	NA
September	8.69	1.8
October	8.49	1.8
November	8.33	1.7
December	8.07	1.7
Annual average	NA	NA

NA = Not available.

Source: Freddie Mac, Primary Mortgage Market Survey

Table 2-69. Conventional, Conforming, Treasury-Indexed 5/1 Hybrid Adjustable Rate Mortgage Series, 2005–2012

[Percent, number.]

Month and year	Rate	Points	Margin
2012			
January	2.84	0.7	2.74
February	2.81	0.7	2.74
March	2.87	0.7	2.74
April	2.84	0.7	2.74
May	2.83	0.6	2.74
June	2.80	0.6	2.74
July	2.74	0.6	2.74
August	NA	NA	NA
September	NA	NA	NA
October	NA	NA	NA
November	NA	NA	NA
December	NA	NA	NA
Annual average	NA	NA	NA
2011			
January	3.72	0.7	2.75
February	3.82	0.6	2.75
March	3.67	0.6	2.74
April	3.66	0.6	2.74
May	3.44	0.6	2.74
June	3.29	0.6	2.74
July	3.28	0.6	2.74
August	3.12	0.5	2.73
September	2.99	0.6	2.74
October	3.03	0.6	2.74
November	2.96	0.6	2.74
December	2.88	0.6	2.74
Annual average	3.31	0.6	2.74
2010			2.74
January	4.32	0.6	2.74
February	4.19	0.6	2.74
March	4.10	0.6	2.75
April	4.09	0.6	2.74
May	3.95	0.7	2.75
June	3.90	0.7	
			2.74
July	3.79	0.7	2.74
August	3.58	0.6	2.75
September	3.54	0.6	2.75
October	3.45	0.6	2.75
November	3.37	0.7	2.75
December	3.68	0.6	2.74
Annual average	3.82	0.6	
2009			
January	5.31	0.6	2.74
February	5.15	0.6	2.73
March	5.00	0.7	2.71
April	4.88	0.6	2.74
May	4.83	0.6	2.74
June	5.00	0.6	2.75
July	4.80	0.7	2.74
August	4.68	0.6	2.74
September	4.53	0.5	2.74
October	4.39	0.6	2.74
November	4.27	0.6	2.74
December	4.33	0.6	2.74
Annual average	4.75	0.6	2.74

Month and year	Rate	Points	Margin
2008			
January	5.45	0.5	2.75
February	5.30	0.4	2.75
March	5.54	0.7	2.75
April	5.58	0.6	2.76
May	5.64	0.5	2.76
June	5.77	0.6	2.76
July	5.93	0.6	2.74
August	6.02	0.6	2.73
September	5.88	0.6	2.74
October	6.09	0.6	2.74
November	5.98	0.6	2.74
December	5.65	0.6	2.74
Annual average	5.74	0.5	2.75
2007			
January	6.02	0.5	2.76
February	6.00	0.5	2.76
March	5.90	0.6	2.76
April	5.91	0.6	2.77
May	5.98	0.5	2.77
June	6.31	0.6	2.76
July	6.32	0.5	2.76
August	6.33	0.5	2.76
September	6.21	0.6	2.76
October	6.09	0.5	2.76
November	5.91	0.5	2.75
December	5.86	0.5	2.76
Annual average	6.07	0.5	2.76
2006			
January	5.76	0.6	2.78
February	5.92	0.6	2.78
March	5.98	0.7	2.78
April	6.15	0.7	2.78
May	6.22	0.6	2.78
June	6.28	0.5	2.77
July	6.36	0.5	2.75
August	6.18	0.4	2.76
September	6.08	0.5	2.76
October	6.09	0.6	2.76
November	6.02	0.6	2.76
December	5.95	0.5	2.76
Annual average	6.08	0.6	2.77
2005			
January	5.04	0.6	2.79
February	5.02	0.7	2.79
March	5.30	0.7	2.78
April	5.27	0.6	2.77
May	5.13	0.7	2.79
June	5.06	0.5	2.79
July	5.22	0.6	2.78
August	5.34	0.6	2.79
September	5.31	0.6	2.78
October	5.57	0.7	2.78
November	5.80	0.6	2.78
December	5.78	0.6	2.77
Annual average	5.32	0.6	2.78

NA = Not available.

Source: Freddie Mac, Primary Mortgage Market Survey

Table 2-70. Terms on Conventional Home Mortgages: National Averages for All Major Lenders, Loans Closed, by Property Type, June 2011–June 2012

[Percent, years, dollars in thousands.]

Characteristics	Contract interest rates	Initial fees and charges	Effective rate	Term to maturity	Loan amount	Purchase price	Loan-to-price ratio	Percent of loans by loan-to-price ratio class, loan-to-price ratio			
								70.0-less	70.1-80.0	80.1-90.0	90.1-over
All loans											
2011											
June^	4.61	0.94	4.74	28.2	219.1	301.3	76.3	23	50	15	13
July^	4.55	0.85	4.67	28.3	213.8	296.9	76.0	21	55	13	11
August^	4.52	0.90	4.65	27.6	214.3	293.3	77.2	20	52	14	13
September^	4.36	0.94	4.49	29.0	220.7	298.3	78.3	23	45	10	21
October^	4.17	0.83	4.29	28.7	218.5	298.0	78.4	21	44	13	22
November^	4.20	0.78	4.31	28.5	220.5	299.8	77.1	22	50	11	17
December^	4.13	0.83	4.24	28.8	221.7	297.7	78.7	18	51	10	21
2012											
January^	4.19	0.82	4.31	28.3	223.0	311.1	75.5	25	49	11	15
February	4.05	0.93	4.17	28.8	244.3	347.2	75.3	26	48	9	17
March	3.89	0.93	3.93	27.3	247.1	346.5	74.8	29	47	10	15
April	3.93	0.90	4.03	27.3	256.2	354.0	75.3	26	49	10	15
May	3.78	1.03	3.91	27.7	263.2	357.5	76.4	25	49	10	17
June	3.67	1.07	3.81	27.5	263.2	363.3	75.6	26	47	11	15
Purchase of newly built houses											
2011											
June^	4.45	1.13	4.61	28.0	255.8	359.6	73.7	27	54	10	8
July^	4.48	0.52	4.55	28.1	224.8	300.8	77.0	19	43	28	10
August^	4.19	0.72	4.29	25.3	223.6	314.5	75.5	21	58	13	8
September^	4.24	0.85	4.36	29.1	225.5	289.0	83.0	15	40	9	36
October^	4.11	0.58	4.19	29.4	241.6	311.9	80.8	17	42	15	27
November^	4.16	0.73	4.26	29.3	261.6	345.5	76.9	19	49	17	15
December^	4.08	0.68	4.18	28.7	258.9	338.3	79.0	20	43	12	25
2012											
January^	4.06	0.68	4.15	29.3	254.5	332.6	77.9	18	48	17	17
February	3.89	0.92	4.01	29.5	275.9	370.1	76.2	23	49	10	18
March	3.84	1.03	3.72	28.3	270.5	365.8	76.2	25	46	13	17
April	3.84	1.05	3.93	28.3	279.5	379.5	75.7	21	53	12	14
May	3.75	1.22	3.88	28.2	271.8	357.7	77.1	22	49	12	18
June	3.68	1.21	3.80	28.6	274.7	374.6	75.3	26	43	15	16
Purchase of previously occupied homes											
2011											
June^	4.62	0.92	4.75	28.2	216.4	297.0	76.5	22	50	15	13
July^	4.57	0.94	4.70	28.4	211.0	295.9	75.7	21	58	9	12
August^	4.56	0.92	4.69	27.9	213.2	290.8	77.4	20	52	14	14
September^	4.38	0.95	4.51	29.0	219.9	299.8	77.6	24	46	11	19
October^	4.19	0.93	4.32	28.5	209.9	292.7	77.5	23	44	13	20
November^	4.22	0.80	4.33	28.2	205.3	282.9	77.2	23	50	9	18
December^	4.15	0.90	4.27	28.9	205.3	279.8	78.5	17	54	10	19
2012											
January^	4.25	0.88	4.37	27.9	210.8	302.7	74.6	27	50	9	14
February	4.08	0.93	4.21	28.7	236.9	341.8	75.1	27	48	8	17
March	3.90	0.92	3.96	27.1	243.8	343.8	74.6	29	47	9	14
April	3.93	0.89	4.04	27.2	253.8	351.3	75.3	27	49	9	15
May	3.78	1.01	3.92	27.6	262.1	357.4	76.3	25	49	10	17
June	3.67	1.06	3.81	27.4	261.5	361.6	75.6	26	48	10	15

^ = Data are weighted.

Source: Federal Housing Finance Agency, Monthly Interest Rate Survey

Table 2-71. Terms on Conventional Home Mortgages: National Averages for All Major Lenders, Loans Closed, by Loan Type, June 2011–June 2012

[Percent, years, dollars in thousands.]

Characteristics	Fixed-rate loans closed							Adjustable-rate loans closed						
	Contract interest rate	Initial fees and charges	Effective rate	Term to maturity	Loan amount	Purchase price	Loan-to-price ratio	Contract interest rate	Initial fees and charges	Effective rate	Term to maturity	Loan amount	Purchase price	Loan-to-price ratio
All loans														
2011														
June^	4.72	0.95	4.85	28.0	207.9	282.1	76.7	NA	NA	NA	NA	NA	NA	NA
July^	4.63	0.87	4.75	28.1	200.5	273.8	76.7	NA	NA	NA	NA	NA	NA	NA
August^	4.57	0.95	4.71	27.3	204.9	277.7	77.3	NA	NA	NA	NA	NA	NA	NA
September^	4.52	0.96	4.66	29.0	208.3	275.3	79.3	NA	NA	NA	NA	NA	NA	NA
October^	4.31	0.85	4.43	28.7	204.6	271.2	79.7	NA	NA	NA	NA	NA	NA	NA
November^	4.35	0.81	4.46	28.3	206.4	275.3	77.9	NA	NA	NA	NA	NA	NA	NA
December^	4.29	0.89	4.41	28.6	207.8	273.4	79.6	NA	NA	NA	NA	NA	NA	NA
2012														
January^	4.32	0.87	4.45	28.2	210.0	284.0	77.0	NA	NA	NA	NA	NA	NA	NA
February	4.31	0.98	4.45	28.5	218.8	296.1	77.6	NA	NA	NA	NA	NA	NA	NA
March	4.00	1.04	4.05	26.8	230.0	319.7	75.3	NA	NA	NA	NA	NA	NA	NA
April	4.06	0.92	4.17	26.8	237.6	324.5	75.8	NA	NA	NA	NA	NA	NA	NA
May	3.92	1.07	4.07	27.3	243.8	327.5	76.7	NA	NA	NA	NA	NA	NA	NA
June	3.76	1.13	3.91	27.2	245.2	335.9	76.0	NA	NA	NA	NA	NA	NA	NA
Purchase of newly built houses														
2011														
June^	4.58	1.15	4.74	27.7	245.8	344.6	73.7	NA	NA	NA	NA	NA	NA	NA
July^	4.53	0.50	4.60	28.0	220.2	291.6	77.5	NA	NA	NA	NA	NA	NA	NA
August^	4.30	0.68	4.40	24.7	210.9	295.6	75.7	NA	NA	NA	NA	NA	NA	NA
September^	4.41	0.82	4.53	28.9	214.1	270.2	84.0	NA	NA	NA	NA	NA	NA	NA
October^	4.18	0.56	4.26	29.3	233.6	298.7	81.3	NA	NA	NA	NA	NA	NA	NA
November^	4.20	0.71	4.30	29.3	259.4	340.6	77.2	NA	NA	NA	NA	NA	NA	NA
December^	4.14	0.70	4.24	28.6	256.3	334.8	79.1	NA	NA	NA	NA	NA	NA	NA
2012														
January^	4.11	0.68	4.21	29.3	250.9	325.9	78.2	NA	NA	NA	NA	NA	NA	NA
February	4.05	0.89	4.17	29.4	261.6	346.0	76.9	NA	NA	NA	NA	NA	NA	NA
March	3.92	1.04	3.78	28.2	262.6	355.1	76.3	NA	NA	NA	NA	NA	NA	NA
April	3.98	1.05	4.07	28.1	265.1	353.1	76.6	NA	NA	NA	NA	NA	NA	NA
May	3.87	1.26	4.00	27.9	259.2	339.5	77.3	NA	NA	NA	NA	NA	NA	NA
June	3.76	1.24	3.88	28.5	265.2	359.4	75.8	NA	NA	NA	NA	NA	NA	NA
Purchase of previously occupied homes														
2011														
June^	4.73	0.94	4.86	28.0	205.1	277.6	76.9	NA	NA	NA	NA	NA	NA	NA
July^	4.65	0.97	4.79	28.1	195.1	268.8	76.4	NA	NA	NA	NA	NA	NA	NA
August^	4.61	0.98	4.75	27.6	204.1	275.6	77.5	NA	NA	NA	NA	NA	NA	NA
September^	4.54	0.98	4.68	29.0	207.4	276.1	78.6	NA	NA	NA	NA	NA	NA	NA
October^	4.37	0.97	4.50	28.5	192.2	259.5	79.1	NA	NA	NA	NA	NA	NA	NA
November^	4.41	0.86	4.53	27.9	183.8	247.4	78.3	NA	NA	NA	NA	NA	NA	NA
December^	4.36	0.99	4.50	28.6	183.4	242.5	79.9	NA	NA	NA	NA	NA	NA	NA
2012														
January^	4.42	0.96	4.56	27.8	191.4	265.0	76.5	NA	NA	NA	NA	NA	NA	NA
February	4.38	1.00	4.52	28.3	207.9	283.3	77.8	NA	NA	NA	NA	NA	NA	NA
March	4.01	1.04	4.09	26.6	224.8	314.1	75.1	NA	NA	NA	NA	NA	NA	NA
April	4.07	0.91	4.18	26.7	234.7	321.5	75.8	NA	NA	NA	NA	NA	NA	NA
May	3.93	1.05	4.08	27.2	241.8	325.9	76.7	NA	NA	NA	NA	NA	NA	NA
June	3.76	1.12	3.92	27.1	242.0	332.3	76.0	NA	NA	NA	NA	NA	NA	NA

NA = Not available.
^ = Data are weighted.

Source: Federal Housing Finance Agency, Monthly Interest Rate Survey

Table 2-72. Terms on Conventional Home Mortgages: National Averages for All Major Lenders, Loans Closed, 15- and 30-Year Fixed-Rate Loans, June 2011–June 2012

[Percent, dollars in thousands.]

Characteristics	Fixed-rate 30-year $417k or less loans							Fixed-rate 15-year $417k or less loans						
	Contract interest rate	Initial fees and charges	Effective rate	Loan amount	Purchase price	Loan-to-price ratio	Share of total market	Contract interest rate	Initial fees and charges	Effective rate	Loan amount	Purchase price	Loan-to-price ratio	Share of total market
All loans														
2011														
June^	4.79	0.97	4.92	175.8	230.5	78.6	69.9	4.30	0.75	4.43	151.9	232.3	69.0	7.1
July^	4.69	0.88	4.81	176.0	230.3	78.5	70.2	4.39	1.15	4.58	100.8	160.2	71.5	4.9
August^	4.63	1.02	4.77	176.4	234.5	78.7	64.1	4.49	0.88	4.64	164.0	211.7	77.9	7.9
September^	4.56	0.98	4.69	181.1	232.5	80.8	75.1	4.32	1.40	4.56	98.2	144.0	72.6	1.3
October^	4.36	0.89	4.48	179.0	226.5	82.1	72.4	4.03	0.66	4.14	151.6	235.5	70.7	2.0
November^	4.40	0.87	4.52	182.0	236.7	79.6	70.3	4.21	0.63	4.32	88.2	124.0	73.9	4.7
December^	4.32	0.94	4.45	180.7	230.4	81.2	70.0	4.31	0.52	4.40	111.0	160.0	78.5	3.3
2012														
January^	4.33	0.84	4.44	182.2	235.2	80.2	63.0	5.45	1.18	5.65	60.3	142.5	42.3	5.6
February	4.36	1.06	4.51	180.8	238.1	79.3	64.3	4.29	1.28	4.50	100.3	149.4	72.1	2.2
March	4.12	1.16	4.16	200.2	261.3	78.6	56.2	3.47	0.84	3.58	169.9	283.2	65.6	12.7
April	4.21	1.05	4.32	192.8	251.6	78.8	57.7	3.48	0.76	3.60	162.9	259.7	67.5	13.8
May	4.04	1.17	4.19	202.9	262.3	79.0	60.0	3.34	1.03	3.50	158.7	248.0	68.7	11.2
June	3.88	1.26	4.04	209.9	274.8	78.7	62.7	3.16	0.91	3.30	177.2	277.9	67.9	11.6

^ = Data are weighted.

Source: Federal Housing Finance Agency, Monthly Interest Rate Survey

Table 2-73. Terms on Conventional Single-Family Mortgages, All Homes, Annual National Averages, 1963–2010

[Percent, years, dollars in thousands.]

Year	Contract interest rate	Initial fees and charges	Effective interest rate	Term to maturity	Mortgage loan amount	Purchase price	Loan-to-price ratio	Percentage distribution of estimated number of loans by loan-to-price ratio				Percent of estimated number of loans with adjustable rates
								70.0-less	70.1-80.0	80.1-90.0	90.1-more	
2010	4.81	0.73	4.91	27.7	215.8	304.9	74.0	27	55	10	9	5
2009	5.05	0.61	5.14	28.2	217.8	307.3	74.5	26	52	13	8	NA
2008	6.06	0.53	6.14	28.4	219.8	306.1	76.9	24	40	17	20	7
2007	6.42	0.48	6.49	29.3	224.7	300.5	79.4	19	43	9	29	11
2006	6.54	0.41	6.60	29.0	222.9	307.1	76.6	22	52	7	19	22
2005	5.85	0.38	5.90	28.5	211.9	299.8	74.7	25	51	8	15	30
2004	5.68	0.40	5.74	27.9	185.5	262.0	74.9	25	48	9	18	35
2003	5.67	0.37	5.73	26.8	167.9	243.4	73.5	29	42	9	20	18
2002	6.44	0.46	6.51	27.3	163.4	231.2	75.1	27	42	10	21	17
2001	6.94	0.53	7.03	27.6	155.7	215.5	76.2	25	42	12	21	12
2000	7.86	0.67	7.96	28.7	148.3	198.9	77.8	21	43	14	22	24
1999	7.14	0.74	7.25	28.2	139.3	184.2	78.5	21	41	15	23	21
1998	6.97	0.85	7.10	27.8	131.8	173.4	78.9	21	39	15	25	12
1997	7.52	0.98	7.68	27.5	126.6	164.5	79.4	20	38	17	25	22
1996	7.58	0.97	7.74	26.9	118.7	155.1	79.0	21	36	17	25	27
1995	7.69	0.97	7.85	27.4	110.4	142.8	79.9	20	34	18	27	32
1994	7.31	1.10	7.49	27.1	109.9	142.0	79.9	20	34	21	25	39
1993	6.93	1.20	7.13	25.5	107.0	143.1	77.2	25	37	20	17	20
1992	7.83	1.58	8.11	25.4	108.7	146.4	76.6	26	38	21	14	20
1991	9.07	1.58	9.34	26.5	106.3	146.7	74.4	32	41	18	9	23
1990	9.74	1.79	10.05	27.0	104.0	142.6	74.7	29	45	18	8	28
1989	9.81	1.87	10.13	27.7	104.5	142.8	74.8	28	46	20	7	38
1988	8.98	1.96	9.30	27.7	97.4	131.6	76.0	25	44	23	8	58
1987	8.95	2.08	9.30	26.8	89.1	121.8	75.2	28	42	23	8	43
1986	9.79	2.21	10.18	25.6	79.3	110.6	74.1	28	41	20	11	30
1985	11.17	2.51	11.64	25.9	70.2	96.1	75.8	26	34	19	21	51
1984	11.99	2.57	12.48	26.8	64.5	86.6	77.0	24	30	20	27	62
1983	12.26	2.39	12.73	26.0	59.9	83.1	74.5	26	34	19	21	40
1982	14.73	2.65	15.31	25.6	55.0	78.4	72.9	29	31	20	21	41
1981	14.39	2.39	14.91	26.4	53.7	76.3	73.1	32	37	17	15	NA
1980	12.46	1.97	12.84	27.2	51.7	73.4	72.9	34	41	16	10	NA
1979	10.59	1.50	10.85	27.4	48.2	67.7	73.5	33	43	17	9	NA
1978	9.37	1.30	9.59	26.7	41.4	57.1	74.6	29	42	19	11	NA
1977	8.82	1.22	9.02	26.3	36.3	49.6	75.0	26	43	21	11	NA
1976	8.87	1.22	9.07	25.2	31.9	44.3	73.9	28	41	21	11	NA
1975	8.92	1.28	9.13	24.9	29.7	41.2	73.7	27	42	19	14	NA
1974	8.76	1.18	8.96	24.1	26.8	37.6	72.9	27	42	20	12	NA
1973	7.80	1.01	7.97	24.0	24.6	33.7	74.8	24	40	23	14	NA
1972	7.40	0.83	7.53	26.1	26.1	34.3	76.2	NA	NA	NA	NA	NA
1971	7.56	0.80	7.69	24.7	24.2	32.8	74.0	NA	NA	NA	NA	NA
1970	8.22	0.95	8.38	23.5	22.5	31.5	71.3	NA	NA	NA	NA	NA
1969	7.67	0.89	7.82	23.5	21.5	29.9	71.9	NA	NA	NA	NA	NA
1968	6.88	0.84	7.02	23.4	19.7	26.9	73.2	NA	NA	NA	NA	NA
1967	6.38	0.77	6.50	23.1	18.3	25.1	72.9	NA	NA	NA	NA	NA
1966	6.26	0.71	6.37	22.5	16.9	23.3	72.3	NA	NA	NA	NA	NA
1965	5.83	0.53	5.92	22.6	16.4	22.5	73.0	NA	NA	NA	NA	NA
1964	5.85	0.57	5.95	22.1	15.7	21.8	72.1	NA	NA	NA	NA	NA
1963	5.90	0.62	6.00	21.3	14.8	20.6	71.7	NA	NA	NA	NA	NA

NA = Not available.

Source: Federal Housing Finance Agency, Monthly Interest Rate Survey

Table 2-74. Terms on Conventional Single-Family Mortgages, Newly Built Homes, Annual National Averages, 1963–2010

[Percent, years, dollars in thousands.]

Year	Contract interest rate	Initial fees and charges	Effective interest rate	Term to maturity	Mortgage loan amount	Purchase price	Loan-to-price ratio	Percentage distribution of estimated number of loans by loan-to-price ratio				Percent of estimated number of loans with adjustable rates
								70.0-less	70.1-80.0	80.1-90.0	90.1-more	
2010	4.69	0.82	4.80	28.5	241.7	335.3	73.4	27	55	11	7	3
2009	5.00	1.00	5.14	28.8	239.7	332.3	73.9	26	51	14	8	NA
2008	5.93	0.84	6.05	29.1	257.3	350.6	76.2	26	39	17	18	4
2007	6.29	0.81	6.41	29.4	269.8	360.4	77.1	22	47	11	20	11
2006	6.53	0.67	6.63	29.5	254.1	346.4	75.4	23	54	10	13	21
2005	5.86	0.54	5.94	29.2	239.6	328.5	75.2	24	52	11	13	29
2004	5.70	0.50	5.77	28.8	216.3	293.6	76.0	22	52	11	16	42
2003	5.70	0.63	5.80	28.7	208.0	275.3	77.9	20	45	12	23	21
2002	6.34	0.61	6.43	28.9	197.4	261.7	77.7	21	46	13	21	27
2001	6.90	0.67	7.00	28.8	184.0	244.8	77.3	21	45	14	19	18
2000	7.42	0.69	7.52	29.2	177.2	234.9	77.4	22	45	16	18	40
1999	6.93	0.76	7.04	28.8	161.8	210.7	78.8	20	41	17	22	35
1998	6.94	0.88	7.07	28.4	151.2	195.0	80.1	19	38	14	29	17
1997	7.55	1.01	7.71	28.2	141.2	181.4	80.4	19	36	15	30	21
1996	7.60	1.21	7.80	27.1	139.1	182.6	78.1	22	35	17	25	26
1995	7.67	1.20	7.87	27.7	134.3	175.4	78.6	22	34	18	26	37
1994	7.28	1.29	7.49	27.5	130.9	170.7	78.7	23	32	20	25	41
1993	7.00	1.29	7.20	26.1	123.2	163.7	78.0	23	34	21	22	18
1992	7.97	1.59	8.24	25.6	118.1	158.1	76.6	26	35	20	19	17
1991	9.03	1.72	9.32	26.8	114.2	155.2	75.0	30	40	18	12	25
1990	9.71	1.98	10.05	27.3	113.2	154.1	74.9	29	44	17	10	31
1989	9.77	2.08	10.13	28.1	117.4	160.1	74.6	29	45	20	7	35
1988	8.83	2.19	9.19	28.0	110.9	150.5	75.6	27	42	23	8	19
1987	8.94	2.26	9.31	27.8	100.6	137.2	75.2	28	42	23	8	41
1986	9.74	2.48	10.17	26.8	87.6	119.8	75.3	28	41	20	11	27
1985	11.09	2.52	11.55	27.0	78.2	105.0	77.1	26	34	19	21	51
1984	11.88	2.66	12.38	27.8	73.7	96.8	78.6	24	30	20	27	59
1983	12.11	2.39	12.57	26.7	70.6	93.9	77.3	26	34	19	21	37
1982	14.49	2.96	15.14	27.5	69.5	94.1	76.6	29	31	20	21	41
1981	14.13	2.66	14.70	27.7	65.2	90.3	74.8	32	37	17	15	NA
1980	12.26	2.09	12.66	28.1	59.1	83.2	73.2	34	41	16	10	NA
1979	10.49	1.66	10.78	28.5	53.3	74.4	73.8	33	43	17	9	NA
1978	9.33	1.39	9.56	28.0	46.0	62.8	75.2	29	42	19	11	NA
1977	8.80	1.32	9.02	27.9	40.5	54.4	76.3	26	43	21	11	NA
1976	8.77	1.42	9.00	27.3	36.4	49.1	75.7	28	41	21	11	NA
1975	8.75	1.53	9.00	27.0	33.4	44.7	76.2	26	42	19	14	NA
1974	8.71	1.33	8.92	26.4	29.9	40.1	75.9	27	42	20	12	NA
1973	7.78	1.12	7.96	26.2	27.9	37.0	76.9	24	40	23	14	NA
1972	7.45	0.88	7.60	27.2	28.6	37.3	76.8	NA	NA	NA	NA	NA
1971	7.59	0.87	7.74	26.2	27.0	36.3	74.3	NA	NA	NA	NA	NA
1970	8.27	1.03	8.45	25.1	25.5	35.5	71.7	NA	NA	NA	NA	NA
1969	7.66	0.91	7.81	25.5	24.9	34.1	72.8	NA	NA	NA	NA	NA
1968	6.83	0.89	6.97	25.5	22.6	30.7	73.9	NA	NA	NA	NA	NA
1967	6.33	0.81	6.46	25.2	20.6	28.0	73.6	NA	NA	NA	NA	NA
1966	6.14	0.71	6.25	24.7	19.4	26.6	73.0	NA	NA	NA	NA	NA
1965	5.74	0.49	5.81	25.0	18.5	25.1	73.9	NA	NA	NA	NA	NA
1964	5.75	0.51	5.83	24.7	17.8	24.3	73.3	NA	NA	NA	NA	NA
1963	5.80	0.58	5.89	24.1	16.9	23.1	72.9	NA	NA	NA	NA	NA

NA = Not available.

Source: Federal Housing Finance Agency, Monthly Interest Rate Survey

Table 2-75. Terms on Conventional Single-Family Mortgages, Previously Occupied Homes, Annual National Averages, 1963–2010

[Percent, years, dollars in thousands.]

Year	Contract interest rate	Initial fees and charges	Effective interest rate	Term to maturity	Mortgage loan amount	Purchase price	Loan-to-price ratio	Percentage distribution of estimated number of loans by loan-to-price ratio				Percent of estimated number of loans with adjustable rates
								70.0-less	70.1-80.0	80.1-90.0	90.1-more	
2010	4.83	0.71	4.94	27.5	209.7	297.7	74.2	27	55	9	9	5
2009	5.06	0.55	5.14	28.1	239.7	303.6	74.6	26	53	13	8	NA
2008	6.09	0.46	6.16	28.3	211.7	296.4	77.0	23	40	17	20	8
2007	6.46	0.40	6.51	29.3	213.9	286.2	79.9	18	42	8	31	11
2006	6.54	0.33	6.59	28.9	214.0	295.9	76.9	22	51	7	21	22
2005	5.84	0.33	5.89	28.3	203.6	291.3	74.6	26	51	7	16	30
2004	5.68	0.37	5.73	27.7	177.0	253.2	74.6	26	47	8	19	33
2003	5.67	0.32	5.72	26.5	159.9	237.0	72.6	31	41	8	19	17
2002	6.46	0.44	6.52	27.1	159.2	227.5	74.8	28	42	10	21	16
2001	6.95	0.51	7.03	27.5	151.8	211.5	76.0	25	42	11	21	11
2000	7.94	0.66	8.05	28.6	142.6	191.8	77.9	21	43	13	22	21
1999	7.18	0.73	7.29	28.1	135.1	179.3	78.4	21	41	15	23	18
1998	6.97	0.84	7.10	27.7	128.4	169.5	78.7	22	39	16	24	12
1997	7.51	0.97	7.67	27.3	123.5	161.0	79.2	21	39	17	24	22
1996	7.57	0.93	7.73	26.8	115.1	150.2	79.1	21	36	17	25	27
1995	7.69	0.93	7.84	27.4	106.4	137.3	80.1	20	34	19	28	31
1994	7.31	1.07	7.49	27.1	105.9	136.4	80.1	20	34	21	25	39
1993	6.92	1.19	7.12	25.4	104.2	139.6	77.1	25	38	20	17	20
1992	7.81	1.58	8.08	25.4	106.9	144.1	76.5	26	39	22	13	21
1991	9.07	1.54	9.33	26.5	105.2	145.8	74.4	32	41	19	9	22
1990	9.75	1.74	10.05	27.0	102.5	140.3	74.9	29	45	18	8	27
1989	9.81	1.79	10.12	27.7	101.6	138.4	75.2	27	47	20	6	37
1988	9.01	1.88	9.32	27.7	94.3	126.6	76.4	25	44	24	8	24
1987	8.94	2.02	9.28	26.6	86.4	117.7	75.4	27	45	22	8	44
1986	9.80	2.13	10.18	25.4	77.4	108.5	73.9	30	43	19	8	31
1985	11.18	2.50	11.64	25.5	67.5	92.7	75.7	28	38	19	16	50
1984	12.00	2.54	12.49	26.5	60.9	82.2	76.8	27	35	19	20	64
1983	12.29	2.40	12.75	25.9	56.8	79.3	74.3	33	36	17	15	41
1982	14.78	2.55	15.33	24.9	48.7	70.7	71.9	37	36	16	11	39
1981	14.51	2.27	15.00	25.9	47.7	68.5	72.9	36	38	16	10	NA
1980	12.53	1.91	12.90	26.9	48.4	68.3	73.5	34	41	17	9	NA
1979	10.63	1.44	10.89	27.1	46.4	64.8	74.0	31	43	19	6	NA
1978	9.40	1.26	9.61	26.4	39.6	54.5	75.0	28	45	21	7	NA
1977	8.83	1.17	9.02	25.8	34.8	47.6	75.1	27	48	20	6	NA
1976	8.90	1.14	9.10	24.6	30.2	42.0	73.8	30	47	18	5	NA
1975	8.97	1.16	9.17	24.2	28.2	39.2	73.5	31	47	17	5	NA
1974	8.78	1.10	8.97	23.3	25.0	35.5	72.4	35	45	16	4	NA
1973	7.82	0.95	7.98	23.3	23.1	31.5	75.0	28	44	20	8	NA
1972	7.38	0.81	7.51	25.7	25.4	33.4	76.0	NA	NA	NA	NA	NA
1971	7.54	0.77	7.67	24.2	23.4	31.7	73.9	NA	NA	NA	NA	NA
1970	8.20	0.92	8.36	22.8	21.3	30.0	71.1	NA	NA	NA	NA	NA
1969	7.68	0.88	7.82	22.7	20.2	28.3	71.5	NA	NA	NA	NA	NA
1968	6.90	0.83	7.03	22.7	18.7	25.6	73.0	NA	NA	NA	NA	NA
1967	6.40	0.76	6.52	22.4	17.5	24.1	72.7	NA	NA	NA	NA	NA
1966	6.30	0.72	6.41	21.7	16.0	22.2	72.0	NA	NA	NA	NA	NA
1965	5.87	0.55	5.95	21.8	15.7	21.6	72.7	NA	NA	NA	NA	NA
1964	5.89	0.59	5.99	21.3	15.0	20.9	71.7	NA	NA	NA	NA	NA
1963	5.94	0.63	6.04	20.4	14.0	19.7	71.2	NA	NA	NA	NA	NA

NA = Not available.

Source: Federal Housing Finance Agency, Monthly Interest Rate Survey

Table 2-76. Terms on Conventional Single-Family Mortgages, Fixed-Rate Mortgages, Annual National Averages, 1985–2010

[Percent, years, dollars in thousands.]

Characteristics	Contract interest rate	Initial fees and charges	Effective interest rate	Term to maturity	Mortgage loan amount	Purchase price	Loan-to-price ratio
All property types							
2010	4.84	0.73	4.94	27.6	212.6	300.0	74.0
2009	5.06	0.61	5.15	28.1	215.8	304.4	74.4
2008	6.09	0.54	6.17	28.3	213.1	296.9	76.8
2007	6.44	0.48	6.51	29.2	210.7	283.1	79.4
2006	6.60	0.44	6.66	28.7	200.3	279.4	76.4
2005	6.00	0.42	6.07	27.9	183.0	266.3	73.9
2004	5.95	0.43	6.02	26.9	158.2	234.5	73.0
2003	5.83	0.37	5.88	26.2	155.4	230.7	72.5
2002	6.62	0.48	6.69	26.8	148.9	214.0	74.6
2001	7.03	0.56	7.11	27.3	143.9	200.4	76.1
2000	8.14	0.75	8.25	28.3	129.2	174.0	77.9
1999	7.32	0.78	7.44	27.8	126.4	167.4	78.6
1998	7.05	0.86	7.19	27.5	124.9	164.3	79.0
1997	7.73	1.01	7.89	26.9	118.7	155.0	79.3
1996	7.81	1.03	7.98	26.1	107.2	141.6	78.6
1995	8.01	1.01	8.18	26.5	99.4	129.9	79.5
1994	7.98	1.14	8.17	25.8	96.1	125.3	79.7
1993	7.27	1.21	7.48	24.7	101.9	136.7	77.3
1992	8.21	1.61	8.50	24.4	104.4	141.4	76.5
1991	9.38	1.63	9.66	25.8	101.0	141.7	73.8
1990	10.06	1.87	10.39	26.1	97.4	136.1	73.9
1989	10.21	1.92	10.54	27.0	96.7	135.2	73.7
1988	10.04	2.07	10.41	26.0	82.8	117.3	73.7
1987	9.52	2.18	9.90	25.5	81.9	114.8	73.9
1986	10.09	2.31	10.50	24.9	75.5	107.7	73.2
1985	11.93	2.56	12.43	24.1	65.3	93.3	73.5
New homes							
2010	4.70	0.82	4.82	28.4	240.7	33.9	73.3
2009	5.01	1.00	5.15	28.7	239.2	331.5	73.8
2008	5.94	0.85	6.07	29.0	253.3	344.6	76.2
2007	6.30	0.83	6.42	29.4	258.6	346.6	77.1
2006	6.63	0.74	6.74	29.3	240.0	329.6	75.2
2005	6.10	0.61	6.19	28.8	222.6	310.7	74.3
2004	5.95	0.60	6.04	28.0	199.1	279.6	73.9
2003	5.87	0.68	5.97	28.4	200.4	267.2	77.6
2002	6.63	0.70	6.73	28.6	183.0	243.8	77.6
2001	7.02	0.73	7.14	28.6	171.7	229.0	77.4
2000	8.04	0.85	8.17	28.6	152.3	204.6	76.9
1999	7.29	0.87	7.42	28.2	144.5	189.2	78.8
1998	7.29	0.87	7.42	28.2	144.5	189.2	78.8
1997	7.73	1.02	7.90	27.8	132.8	170.9	80.4
1996	7.80	1.29	8.02	26.4	129.0	170.3	77.9
1995	7.95	1.28	8.17	26.7	120.8	159.7	78.0
1994	7.85	1.38	8.08	26.4	118.2	155.1	78.4
1993	7.27	1.32	7.49	25.8	120.0	158.4	78.4
1992	8.25	1.61	8.53	25.1	115.8	154.6	77.0
1991	9.32	1.79	9.63	26.1	107.3	147.8	74.4
1990	10.06	2.09	10.43	26.4	104.0	144.3	74.2
1989	10.17	2.22	10.56	27.5	110.8	153.9	73.4
1988	9.98	2.43	10.40	26.1	97.2	140.7	71.9
1987	9.48	2.41	9.89	26.8	93.2	129.9	74.0
1986	10.03	2.62	10.49	26.4	85.0	118.0	74.7
1985	11.86	2.55	12.35	25.4	74.3	103.2	75.4

Table 2-76. Terms on Conventional Single-Family Mortgages, Fixed-Rate Mortgages, Annual National Averages, 1985–2010—*Continued*

[Percent, years, dollars in thousands.]

Characteristics	Contract interest rate	Initial fees and charges	Effective interest rate	Term to maturity	Mortgage loan amount	Purchase price	Loan-to-price ratio
Previously occupied homes							
2010	4.87	0.71	4.97	27.4	205.8	291.9	74.2
2009	5.07	0.56	5.15	28.0	212.2	300.2	74.5
2008	6.12	0.47	6.19	28.1	204.1	286.2	77.0
2007	6.48	0.40	6.53	29.2	199.2	267.8	80.0
2006	6.59	0.35	6.64	28.6	188.8	264.8	76.8
2005	5.97	0.37	6.03	27.6	171.0	252.8	73.8
2004	5.95	0.38	6.01	26.6	148.4	223.8	72.7
2003	5.82	0.31	5.86	25.8	146.8	223.8	71.6
2002	6.62	0.46	6.69	26.6	145.2	210.8	74.3
2001	7.03	0.54	7.11	27.2	140.4	196.8	75.9
2000	8.15	0.73	8.27	28.2	125.8	169.4	78.1
1999	7.32	0.77	7.44	27.7	123.7	164.2	78.6
1998	7.05	0.86	7.18	27.4	121.9	161.1	78.8
1997	7.72	1.01	7.89	26.7	115.7	151.7	79.0
1996	7.81	0.98	7.97	26.1	103.3	136.4	78.8
1995	8.02	0.97	8.18	26.5	96.2	125.4	79.8
1994	8.00	1.09	8.19	25.7	92.0	119.9	80.0
1993	7.27	1.19	7.47	24.5	98.7	132.8	77.1
1992	8.20	1.61	8.49	24.3	102.1	138.7	76.4
1991	9.39	1.58	9.66	25.8	100.3	141.0	73.8
1990	10.06	1.81	10.38	26.1	96.1	134.2	74.0
1989	10.21	1.82	10.53	26.9	93.1	129.9	74.1
1988	10.05	1.97	10.40	26.1	79.3	111.3	74.4
1987	9.51	2.11	9.88	25.2	78.8	110.4	74.1
1986	10.10	2.22	10.50	24.5	73.0	104.8	72.9
1985	11.92	2.56	12.42	23.6	62.0	89.3	73.3

Source: Federal Housing Finance Agency, Monthly Interest Rate Survey

Table 2-77. Terms on Conventional Single-Family Mortgages, by State, 1978–2010

[Percent, years, dollars in thousands.]

Characteristics	Contract interest rate	Initial fees and charges	Effective interest rate	Term to maturity	Purchase price	Loan-to-price ratio	Adjustable-rate loans
Alabama							
2010	4.78	1.07	4.93	28.1	236.8	77.3	4.78
2009	4.93	0.98	5.07	27.8	239.8	76.8	3.18
2008	6.02	0.64	6.12	28.9	234.3	80.7	NA
2007	6.54	0.71	6.65	29.0	205.8	83.0	6.10
2006	6.73	0.52	6.81	28.4	199.8	80.7	15.32
2005	0.56	6.06	28.0	197.8	79.8	26	
2004	5.89	0.68	5.99	28.0	165.4	80.7	31.00
2003	5.75	0.51	5.82	27.2	154.0	81.6	13.00
2002	6.54	0.74	6.65	27.2	147.0	80.8	10.00
2001	6.93	0.68	7.04	26.8	142.9	79.6	5.00
2000	8.08	0.69	8.19	28.4	140.8	82.3	7.00
1999	7.32	0.75	7.43	27.6	148.8	81.9	5.00
1998	0.91	7.13	27.5	146.8	82.8	5	8.00
1997	7.62	1.23	7.83	26.4	131.2	83.4	8.00
1996	7.81	0.92	7.97	23.5	126.5	82.0	8.00
1995	8.23	0.93	8.38	24.5	122.3	79.4	14.00
1994	7.82	0.94	7.99	21.7	103.5	82.3	23.00
1993	7.18	0.66	7.30	20.5	95.5	76.0	13.00
1992	7.83	1.05	8.03	21.3	124.0	73.9	15.00
1991	9.13	1.62	9.40	25.2	121.7	77.8	11.00
1990	9.80	1.99	10.14	25.4	131.6	75.8	16.00
1989	9.88	2.34	10.28	26.8	121.4	77.6	23.00
1988	8.77	2.34	9.15	27.8	109.2	80.0	62.00
1987	9.03	2.34	9.42	26.5	104.7	78.7	34.00
1986	9.76	2.37	10.16	25.6	90.4	78.4	16.00
1985	10.54	3.00	11.07	27.5	80.5	83.0	NA
1984	11.33	2.86	11.85	28.4	70.7	86.4	NA
1983	11.87	3.00	12.44	24.5	61.5	81.1	NA
1982	14.21	2.10	14.64	28.9	53.0	86.2	NA
1981	13.21	2.82	13.77	28.9	59.6	82.5	NA
1980	11.94	2.26	12.36	28.5	69.7	75.7	NA
1979	10.53	2.04	10.89	27.5	60.7	77.0	NA
1978	9.40	2.26	9.78	27.5	53.4	79.1	NA
Alaska							
2010	4.65	0.90	4.77	25.7	317.0	74.5	4.03
2009	4.96	0.85	5.08	28.9	316.3	76.5	1.27
2008	6.01	1.06	6.17	27.5	280.7	77.3	NA
2007	6.29	1.04	6.44	29.3	267.8	80.6	2.61
2006	6.39	0.97	6.54	29.2	249.7	78.7	3.33
2005	5.86	1.11	6.02	28.4	239.9	78.3	7.28
2004	5.59	1.30	5.78	28.4	203.2	77.1	8.00
2003	5.55	1.33	5.75	26.8	191.1	81.3	2.00
2002	6.31	1.14	6.49	27.7	208.0	77.1	10.00
2001	6.88	1.12	7.05	28.5	189.3	80.8	6.00
2000	8.20	1.03	8.37	27.9	188.1	79.2	6.00
1999	7.55	1.13	7.73	27.1	182.3	79.7	5.00
1998	7.01	1.00	7.17	27.4	192.3	81.4	2.00
1997	7.89	1.53	8.15	25.8	175.0	80.7	2.00
1996	7.62	1.54	7.88	24.1	167.1	75.7	21.00
1995	7.66	1.10	7.84	23.7	168.5	82.1	14.00
1994	7.60	1.00	7.78	26.2	180.5	78.4	32.00
1993	6.79	0.72	6.92	19.4	168.9	72.1	12.00
1992	7.32	1.77	7.62	23.1	146.3	73.8	16.00
1991	9.41	1.57	9.67	27.8	147.2	80.6	8.00
1990	9.16	1.73	9.42	58.9	133.8	86.7	11.00
1989	8.97	1.82	9.26	29.3	104.4	88.1	21.00
1988	9.77	1.53	10.02	29.7	99.5	79.9	5.00
1987	9.03	0.96	8.81	23.2	147.9	79.4	6.00
1986	9.76	1.31	9.79	19.5	158.9	81.8	5.00
1985	10.54	1.19	10.86	18.5	134.5	85.7	NA
1984	11.02	1.29	11.27	17.9	131.3	85.2	NA
1983	10.59	1.20	10.82	18.3	120.0	86.7	NA
1982	11.92	1.67	12.24	25.3	105.3	86.0	NA
1981	10.71	1.65	10.99	29.7	104.1	87.3	NA
1980	9.70	1.49	9.95	29.8	95.3	88.1	NA
1979	9.78	2.00	10.13	29.2	89.4	83.7	NA
1978	9.72	1.58	9.99	29.3	89.7	84.2	NA

Table 2-77. Terms on Conventional Single-Family Mortgages, by State, 1978–2010—*Continued*

[Percent, years, dollars in thousands.]

Characteristics	Contract interest rate	Initial fees and charges	Effective interest rate	Term to maturity	Purchase price	Loan-to-price ratio	Adjustable-rate loans
Arizona							
2010	4.81	1.19	4.98	27.3	237.1	74.1	4.76
2009	5.15	0.92	5.28	28.6	252.1	73.7	3.03
2008	6.12	0.78	6.23	28.7	299.4	75.1	NA
2007	6.46	0.65	6.56	29.9	302.8	77.6	15.39
2006	6.57	0.46	6.63	29.4	313.4	74.3	31.84
2005	5.86	0.39	5.92	28.6	280.5	72.9	39.29
2004	5.73	0.58	5.81	27.8	207.2	75.3	35.00
2003	5.72	0.52	5.80	27.1	193.6	74.8	19.00
2002	6.51	0.68	6.62	27.8	180.8	77.7	18.00
2001	7.00	0.68	7.10	28.2	175.8	80.1	12.00
2000	7.99	0.83	8.12	28.9	169.0	78.9	19.00
1999	7.24	0.94	7.38	28.7	167.8	79.3	17.00
1998	7.05	0.97	7.19	28.4	163.1	78.8	9.00
1997	7.56	1.09	7.74	27.1	158.7	78.5	16.00
1996	7.54	0.89	7.68	28.1	145.4	77.5	27.00
1995	7.29	0.87	7.42	28.6	128.6	79.0	46.00
1994	7.04	1.71	7.31	28.1	126.7	77.6	39.00
1993	6.98	1.63	7.23	27.3	119.4	74.4	11.00
1992	7.83	1.91	8.15	27.3	121.2	77.4	18.00
1991	9.18	1.56	9.44	27.9	118.4	75.8	15.00
1990	9.95	2.11	10.31	28.1	111.8	74.9	9.00
1989	9.82	2.32	10.21	28.5	123.5	73.9	25.00
1988	8.92	2.10	9.27	28.9	117.2	76.4	52.00
1987	8.85	2.25	9.22	28.9	126.1	75.8	46.00
1986	9.69	2.33	10.08	28.7	121.7	73.9	32.00
1985	10.98	2.70	11.47	28.5	109.3	77.1	NA
1984	12.04	2.59	12.53	29.6	98.0	80.2	NA
1983	12.08	2.90	12.62	29.6	95.9	79.6	NA
1982	14.34	3.59	15.08	28.9	83.8	80.2	NA
1981	13.64	3.00	14.28	28.0	82.1	78.4	NA
1980	12.26	2.13	12.65	29.6	83.4	75.1	NA
1979	10.71	1.99	11.06	29.4	66.9	76.4	NA
1978	1978	9.40	2.03	9.74	29.3	57.3	77.8
Arkansas							
2010	4.70	0.49	4.78	25.5	216.0	74.8	1.1
2009	4.93	0.39	4.99	27.0	212.7	78.9	3.7
2008	6.15	0.34	6.20	28.9	183.3	84.2	NA
2007	6.47	0.24	6.50	30.0	143.0	88.7	2
2006	6.52	0.34	6.57	29.1	156.2	84.9	9
2005	5.94	0.51	6.02	28.0	161.0	81.2	23
2004	6.00	0.44	6.07	27.4	144.4	80.7	24
2003	5.84	0.31	5.89	26.6	139.5	78.2	12
2002	6.55	0.41	6.61	27.4	131.3	82.6	12
2001	6.82	0.61	6.91	28.1	115.5	87.6	9
2000	7.98	0.78	8.10	28.5	113.7	87.0	11
1999	7.29	0.85	7.42	27.8	122.7	82.9	14
1998	6.88	0.92	7.02	25.5	115.6	79.0	18
1997	7.40	0.94	7.56	23.1	109.0	74.4	38
1996	7.35	0.88	7.51	21.7	113.3	71.0	50
1995	7.32	0.98	7.49	20.5	106.9	73.7	52
1994	6.90	0.97	7.07	20.2	86.4	68.2	57
1993	7.00	1.38	7.25	24.0	103.4	80.7	14
1992	7.99	1.88	8.31	25.8	100.4	81.7	16
1991	9.29	1.88	8.31	25.8	100.4	81.7	7
1990	9.75	1.93	9.61	28.1	111.3	78.2	19
1989	9.54	2.62	10.20	25.7	97.9	80.5	36
1988	8.20	2.30	9.93	27.0	85.6	77.4	71
1987	8.88	2.81	8.64	28.1	104.4	78.3	47
1986	9.86	3.04	9.38	27.2	88.7	76.4	21
1985	10.22	2.67	10.33	25.3	78.0	75.0	NA
1984	11.48	3.25	12.08	27.8	60.2	83.0	NA
1983	12.08	2.47	12.55	26.5	61.8	79.9	NA
1982	13.85	2.73	14.41	27.2	64.9	76.9	NA
1981	12.67	2.46	13.17	27.6	67.6	75.8	NA
1980	10.56	1.98	10.91	28.7	62.0	79.6	NA
1979	9.21	1.34	9.43	28.1	53.2	78.9	NA
1978	9.31	1.03	9.49	25.0	38.6	74.7	NA

Table 2-77. Terms on Conventional Single-Family Mortgages, by State, 1978–2010—*Continued*

[Percent, years, dollars in thousands.]

Characteristics	Contract interest rate	Initial fees and charges	Effective interest rate	Term to maturity	Purchase price	Loan-to-price ratio	Adjustable-rate loans
California							
2010	4.83	0.86	4.95	28.9	488.3	71.6	6.8
2009	5.08	0.47	5.15	29.2	463.0	72.0	3.4
2008	6.13	0.39	6.19	28.4	461.9	71.2	NA
2007	6.38	0.38	6.43	30.5	513.0	75.9	25
2006	6.49	0.23	6.53	29.9	545.1	71.7	46
2005	5.65	0.18	5.67	28.8	516.7	67.0	59
2004	5.48	0.20	5.51	28.0	434.5	68.6	58
2003	5.54	0.19	5.57	26.4	378.6	65.2	29
2002	6.20	0.36	6.25	27.1	350.0	68.6	30
2001	6.78	0.42	6.84	27.9	328.3	70.4	26
2000	7.18	0.49	7.26	29.4	300.2	74.9	52
1999	6.65	0.69	6.75	29.0	277.1	74.8	47
1998	6.78	0.87	6.91	28.8	265.8	74.0	30
1997	7.26	1.07	7.42	29.0	242.0	76.8	32
1996	7.35	1.04	7.51	29.0	231.6	78.1	38
1995	7.10	1.13	7.27	30.1	220.9	79.4	50
1994	6.27	1.12	6.43	30.6	220.8	79.8	63
1993	6.37	1.18	6.55	29.3	216.1	76.5	46
1992	7.37	1.44	7.61	28.3	225.4	76.0	41
1991	8.87	1.27	9.07	28.3	215.9	73.5	33
1990	9.52	1.47	9.76	29.0	204.3	75.1	42
1989	9.65	1.55	9.90	29.8	199.6	75.6	46
1988	8.67	1.46	8.90	29.7	182.7	77.0	70
1987	8.64	1.75	8.92	29.4	164.3	77.6	58
1986	9.61	1.87	9.92	28.9	154.8	76.8	47
1985	11.23	1.86	11.56	29.0	143.1	77.2	NA
1984	11.81	1.89	12.15	30.0	130.2	79.3	NA
1983	11.87	1.90	12.22	29.5	129.4	77.5	NA
1982	14.63	1.92	15.04	29.0	121.5	75.3	NA
1981	14.57	1.93	15.04	27.6	113.9	75.9	NA
1980	12.86	1.56	13.16	29.7	110.4	75.5	NA
1979	10.94	1.42	11.19	29.8	91.2	74.7	NA
1978	9.76	1.40	9.99	29.6	80.6	75.3	NA
Colorado							
2010	4.88	0.96	5.02	28.3	309.3	75.1	4.0
2009	5.06	0.94	5.19	28.3	276.7	75.9	2.2
2008	6.00	0.93	6.13	28.5	296.7	77.5	NA
2007	6.40	0.81	6.51	29.3	297.6	75.6	12
2006	6.52	0.58	6.60	28.7	297.5	74.9	28
2005	5.74	0.54	5.82	28.8	310.2	73.1	39
2004	5.56	0.55	5.64	29.0	280.8	74.7	53
2003	5.54	0.45	5.61	28.2	258.0	73.7	30
2002	6.28	0.58	6.37	28.4	265.6	73.0	32
2001	6.91	0.53	6.99	28.5	254.9	73.6	17
2000	7.81	0.63	7.91	29.0	235.2	74.6	26
1999	7.20	0.68	7.30	28.7	210.3	75.9	20
1998	6.96	0.73	7.07	28.4	194.5	76.5	10
1997	7.58	0.79	7.70	27.6	181.0	76.8	25
1996	7.59	0.76	7.72	27.3	176.7	73.8	39
1995	7.64	0.84	7.78	28.2	172.5	76.6	47
1994	6.84	0.98	6.99	27.5	165.5	76.2	55
1993	6.66	0.99	6.83	25.2	149.2	74.7	30
1992	7.80	1.36	8.04	24.4	130.4	75.6	18
1991	9.14	1.57	9.40	26.6	125.1	73.5	17
1990	9.81	1.26	10.02	25.7	129.9	73.9	23
1989	9.62	1.47	9.86	27.3	129.7	74.3	37
1988	9.10	1.68	9.38	27.7	118.6	76.4	49
1987	8.88	1.79	9.17	28.2	123.8	78.1	45
1986	9.83	1.74	10.13	26.8	127.6	73.4	34
1985	11.08	2.12	11.46	28.1	112.2	78.6	NA
1984	12.09	2.48	12.56	28.4	103.1	80.3	NA
1983	12.32	2.52	12.80	27.7	103.5	79.6	NA
1982	13.92	2.73	14.51	27.6	80.3	80.1	NA
1981	12.93	2.00	13.33	29.4	79.1	80.1	NA
1980	11.66	1.73	11.97	29.6	77.0	78.1	NA
1979	10.72	1.44	10.98	29.5	71.9	77.2	NA
1978	9.65	1.37	9.23	29.1	53.1	77.1	NA

Table 2-77. Terms on Conventional Single-Family Mortgages, by State, 1978–2010—*Continued*

[Percent, years, dollars in thousands.]

Characteristics	Contract interest rate	Initial fees and charges	Effective interest rate	Term to maturity	Purchase price	Loan-to-price ratio	Adjustable-rate loans
Connecticut							
2010	4.86	0.46	4.92	28.5	416.7	70.9	3.2
2009	4.93	0.36	4.99	28.7	397.4	71.9	3.3
2008	6.05	0.32	6.09	28.9	374.2	76.1	NA
2007	6.39	0.22	6.42	29.4	372.9	77.4	8
2006	6.40	0.25	6.44	29.4	395.2	75.0	19
2005	5.73	0.27	5.77	28.6	382.5	72.2	29
2004	5.63	0.30	5.67	28.1	344.8	71.7	34
2003	5.68	0.26	5.72	26.8	299.0	69.9	17
2002	6.44	0.41	6.51	27.5	303.4	73.6	19
2001	6.96	0.66	7.06	27.7	259.0	73.2	14
2000	7.84	0.74	7.96	28.7	249.3	73.6	26
1999	7.04	0.80	7.16	28.5	227.8	76.4	22
1998	6.89	0.91	7.02	28.7	210.4	78.4	15
1997	7.28	0.91	7.42	28.6	196.4	79.1	27
1996	7.35	1.18	7.53	28.1	180.4	77.9	31
1995	7.25	1.11	7.42	28.8	166.0	78.8	34
1994	6.59	1.25	6.78	28.4	189.7	75.1	52
1993	6.60	1.38	6.83	26.3	197.2	71.7	27
1992	7.53	1.81	7.84	26.4	201.0	71.0	26
1991	8.50	1.44	8.74	28.7	169.6	74.9	40
1990	9.48	1.72	9.77	28.0	177.2	71.2	30
1989	9.43	1.75	9.71	29.4	190.2	72.7	48
1988	8.32	1.79	8.60	29.3	182.4	71.5	78
1987	8.40	2.00	8.72	29.0	176.6	69.8	64
1986	9.50	2.04	9.84	27.9	151.7	68.2	45
1985	10.87	2.31	11.28	28.2	122.6	72.4	NA
1984	11.96	2.14	12.36	28.1	110.1	70.3	NA
1983	12.31	2.22	12.73	28.2	104.0	68.2	NA
1982	15.09	2.49	15.62	28.6	102.9	66.5	NA
1981	14.90	2.33	15.39	28.8	92.5	66.7	NA
1980	12.68	2.10	13.08	28.6	85.8	68.8	NA
1979	10.61	1.33	10.85	28.8	80.1	69.0	NA
1978	9.00	0.78	9.13	28.4	70.5	70.6	NA
Delaware							
2010	4.74	0.73	4.84	28.8	325.1	70.5	1.1
2009	4.97	0.95	5.10	29.2	328.9	70.1	0.5
2008	5.97	0.53	6.04	29.4	352.4	73.3	NA
2007	6.33	0.69	6.43	29.5	364.3	74.1	4
2006	6.59	0.65	6.69	29.7	368.5	74.6	7
2005	6.13	0.33	6.18	29.2	326.2	74.3	9
2004	5.78	0.40	5.84	28.7	273.9	75.1	20
2003	5.87	0.48	5.94	28.3	256.0	74.8	7
2002	6.53	0.60	6.62	28.5	222.1	76.9	9
2001	6.92	0.74	7.03	28.1	207.7	77.5	5
2000	8.01	0.97	8.16	28.9	180.2	77.8	12
1999	7.21	1.05	7.37	28.5	177.3	78.5	9
1998	6.97	1.27	7.16	28.9	168.8	80.1	4
1997	7.54	1.48	7.78	28.5	155.8	82.2	10
1996	7.45	1.87	7.75	28.0	149.4	81.9	15
1995	7.54	1.85	7.84	28.2	142.1	83.0	24
1994	7.32	1.92	7.63	27.4	142.0	77.6	29
1993	6.84	1.75	7.11	26.0	164.3	77.1	11
1992	7.85	2.70	8.33	25.5	148.3	79.4	7
1991	9.21	2.34	9.60	28.7	125.2	78.7	17
1990	9.59	2.82	10.08	26.7	125.4	76.4	18
1989	9.87	3.01	10.42	22.3	113.7	73.0	29
1988	9.67	2.82	10.20	20.4	122.7	70.7	22
1987	9.66	2.63	10.15	19.0	116.2	66.7	6
1986	10.16	3.00	10.71	20.8	115.2	67.0	15
1985	12.59	2.31	13.03	21.9	101.9	61.4	NA
1984	13.59	1.77	13.95	19.6	97.4	68.2	NA
1983	13.50	1.19	13.74	19.3	83.0	60.3	NA
1982	14.23	2.31	14.72	27.2	69.3	76.4	NA
1981	15.07	1.39	15.39	22.0	59.8	67.9	NA
1980	12.65	0.37	12.72	18.5	55.5	60.8	NA
1979	10.62	0.30	10.67	21.5	45.9	69.5	NA
1978	9.13	0.13	9.15	19.9	50.8	74.8	NA

Table 2-77. Terms on Conventional Single-Family Mortgages, by State, 1978–2010—*Continued*

[Percent, years, dollars in thousands.]

Characteristics	Contract interest rate	Initial fees and charges	Effective interest rate	Term to maturity	Purchase price	Loan-to-price ratio	Adjustable-rate loans
District of Columbia							
2010	4.84	0.63	4.93	29.6	607.0	74.1	5.7
2009	4.96	0.40	5.02	29.5	600.0	74.3	4.6
2008	6.08	0.39	6.14	28.2	563.7	70.7	NA
2007	6.50	0.28	6.54	29.7	525.9	75.3	18
2006	6.51	0.15	6.53	30.1	513.7	75.8	31
2005	5.64	0.23	5.67	29.0	504.6	73.8	55
2004	5.50	0.22	5.53	27.6	418.7	70.3	52
2003	5.69	0.27	5.73	27.2	363.2	69.7	25
2002	6.56	0.36	6.62	27.4	329.4	73.0	15
2001	7.02	0.34	7.07	27.7	326.8	72.5	19
2000	7.82	0.48	7.90	29.5	288.3	78.1	33
1999	7.13	0.64	7.22	29.5	271.2	80.2	33
1998	6.96	0.65	7.05	29.3	248.9	82.5	21
1997	7.47	0.88	7.61	29.0	220.6	82.4	28
1996	7.30	1.37	7.52	28.4	278.4	79.8	51
1995	7.43	1.24	7.62	29.2	266.5	80.9	56
1994	7.29	1.17	7.47	29.3	218.0	83.0	46
1993	6.63	1.19	6.81	28.6	209.0	80.4	34
1992	7.88	1.41	8.14	24.9	201.8	74.6	17
1991	8.15	2.21	8.52	27.9	214.2	78.7	52
1990	9.44	2.50	9.86	27.8	190.4	79.1	40
1989	9.43	2.64	9.87	29.4	224.7	78.1	61
1988	8.60	2.53	9.01	29.4	191.8	77.5	68
1987	8.99	2.41	9.40	26.7	140.8	77.7	26
1986	9.61	2.37	10.03	26.0	152.5	78.3	36
1985	10.65	2.60	11.12	27.0	194.3	75.2	NA
1984	11.62	2.72	12.15	27.4	143.3	79.9	NA
1983	12.50	2.26	12.95	28.0	121.7	80.5	NA
1982	15.19	2.81	15.79	28.7	127.1	76.3	NA
1981	14.47	2.03	14.88	29.6	118.3	73.6	NA
1980	13.04	1.78	13.38	29.4	97.4	75.7	NA
1979	10.81	1.61	11.10	29.5	97.0	76.1	NA
1978	9.62	1.01	9.79	29.5	90.1	77.3	NA
Florida							
2010	4.87	0.96	5.00	27.9	246.2	72.9	5.6
2009	5.11	0.62	5.20	28.6	252.0	73.3	2.8
2008	6.17	0.50	6.25	28.9	293.3	75.6	NA
2007	6.55	0.35	6.60	29.8	295.4	79.8	13
2006	6.70	0.37	6.75	29.3	298.7	75.8	30
2005	5.94	0.33	5.99	28.7	279.9	75.1	37
2004	5.75	0.34	5.80	28.1	230.3	75.5	37
2003	5.78	0.17	5.80	26.9	196.7	73.5	15
2002	6.53	0.21	6.56	27.2	182.5	75.5	12
2001	7.03	0.28	7.08	27.4	173.6	76.8	8
2000	7.96	0.40	8.02	28.5	161.8	78.3	21
1999	7.19	0.64	7.29	28.0	148.8	78.9	21
1998	6.97	0.73	7.09	27.6	138.9	77.9	14
1997	7.52	0.85	7.66	27.8	134.5	78.3	22
1996	7.66	0.85	7.80	27.3	126.4	79.1	22
1995	7.74	0.80	7.87	27.9	127.3	78.7	35
1994	7.29	0.95	7.45	28.0	121.2	79.5	43
1993	6.78	1.06	6.95	27.1	117.5	78.0	25
1992	7.35	1.47	7.59	26.3	112.4	73.3	41
1991	8.93	1.41	9.16	27.6	114.6	74.3	29
1990	9.67	1.67	9.95	28.0	119.9	74.3	36
1989	9.69	1.83	9.99	28.1	106.4	74.5	46
1988	8.65	1.89	8.96	28.7	101.2	76.0	67
1987	8.64	2.07	8.98	27.4	100.4	75.0	49
1986	9.52	2.49	9.96	27.1	93.3	75.4	39
1985	10.68	2.85	11.19	28.0	84.6	77.9	NA
1984	11.68	2.82	12.21	28.6	80.2	80.1	NA
1983	12.29	2.98	12.86	27.9	78.1	76.6	NA
1982	15.20	2.81	15.83	26.7	85.0	73.9	NA
1981	14.84	2.99	15.48	28.2	78.1	72.6	NA
1980	12.86	3.00	13.45	27.4	66.8	71.5	NA
1979	10.61	2.70	11.10	28.1	55.8	75.1	NA
1978	9.10	2.31	9.48	26.6	48.0	75.4	NA

Table 2-77. Terms on Conventional Single-Family Mortgages, by State, 1978–2010—*Continued*

[Percent, years, dollars in thousands.]

Characteristics	Contract interest rate	Initial fees and charges	Effective interest rate	Term to maturity	Purchase price	Loan-to-price ratio	Adjustable-rate loans
Georgia							
2010	4.75	1.04	4.90	28.2	279.1	76.2	7.7
2009	4.95	0.87	5.07	28.5	278.5	76.6	4.4
2008	6.05	0.76	6.16	28.9	262.9	81.6	NA
2007	6.37	0.54	6.45	29.8	235.4	84.3	11
2006	6.56	0.45	6.62	29.3	231.1	80.5	23
2005	5.87	0.42	5.93	28.6	230.9	78.0	35
2004	5.69	0.39	5.75	27.6	215.5	75.6	39
2003	5.72	0.34	5.77	26.5	201.1	74.3	16
2002	6.45	0.48	6.52	27.4	195.3	78.2	14
2001	6.90	0.53	6.98	27.8	195.8	78.5	10
2000	7.96	0.67	8.06	28.8	191.3	81.1	19
1999	7.23	0.80	7.35	28.5	187.8	82.3	15
1998	6.95	0.89	7.08	28.1	169.3	82.2	9
1997	7.50	0.98	7.65	27.8	155.1	83.0	21
1996	7.57	1.08	7.76	25.8	125.1	81.2	22
1995	7.84	1.15	8.05	26.1	129.5	83.3	34
1994	7.57	1.36	7.79	27.5	118.4	82.2	34
1993	7.00	1.23	7.19	25.8	121.1	81.4	21
1992	7.90	1.69	8.18	25.0	106.2	80.9	17
1991	9.21	1.80	9.50	27.4	112.5	81.4	19
1990	9.33	2.10	9.69	26.8	125.3	79.4	30
1989	9.76	2.24	10.15	27.7	129.2	77.3	31
1988	8.85	2.40	9.24	28.2	123.1	79.4	60
1987	8.78	2.38	9.17	27.4	115.1	78.2	41
1986	9.64	2.49	10.07	26.6	104.9	79.6	22
1985	10.60	3.29	11.19	27.2	92.8	81.6	NA
1984	11.90	2.87	12.45	27.3	83.0	81.9	NA
1983	12.48	2.85	13.03	26.9	81.6	79.2	NA
1982	14.76	3.91	15.74	24.6	78.7	76.3	NA
1981	14.11	3.17	14.78	27.9	73.4	76.6	NA
1980	12.31	2.79	12.84	28.0	72.9	76.4	NA
1979	10.49	2.69	10.97	28.0	61.1	77.7	NA
1978	9.30	2.48	9.72	27.7	52.3	78.9	NA
Hawaii							
2010	4.83	1.29	5.01	29.2	552.9	68.4	10.1
2009	4.79	1.66	5.03	29.0	503.0	71.6	1.3
2008	5.73	1.31	5.92	28.9	481.9	77.8	NA
2007	6.01	1.19	6.18	29.6	485.5	72.8	4
2006	6.15	0.97	6.30	29.3	516.7	73.6	15
2005	5.73	0.70	5.83	28.7	454.2	71.8	31
2004	5.40	0.78	5.51	28.8	386.6	73.4	34
2003	5.43	0.81	5.55	28.6	335.9	74.9	23
2002	6.44	1.27	6.62	29.0	284.6	78.0	14
2001	6.81	1.48	7.03	28.7	259.6	81.2	6
2000	7.59	1.42	7.81	29.2	264.4	80.2	41
1999	7.04	1.49	7.27	29.0	263.3	80.9	21
1998	6.76	1.59	7.00	29.1	264.7	79.2	7
1997	7.32	1.83	7.61	29.0	260.2	79.3	25
1996	6.96	1.52	7.20	29.4	271.2	80.1	39
1995	7.28	1.62	7.55	29.1	275.0	79.6	41
1994	6.37	1.40	6.57	29.7	284.1	76.3	76
1993	5.78	1.84	6.05	29.2	300.8	72.9	73
1992	6.32	1.99	6.63	28.3	281.9	68.1	72
1991	8.42	1.87	8.72	28.6	271.1	67.7	44
1990	9.47	1.81	9.77	27.9	241.4	67.0	48
1989	9.50	1.87	9.82	28.4	202.7	71.4	50
1988	8.82	1.90	9.12	28.5	170.0	71.4	62
1987	9.16	2.01	9.49	27.5	168.1	74.9	37
1986	9.52	2.13	9.88	26.6	161.2	71.9	37
1985	11.55	2.17	11.96	27.1	141.1	70.5	NA
1984	12.20	2.22	12.66	26.7	134.5	70.6	NA
1983	12.33	1.92	12.71	27.7	131.8	75.0	NA
1982	13.31	2.04	13.75	26.6	137.9	73.7	NA
1981	13.81	1.99	14.25	27.6	126.9	70.7	NA
1980	12.04	2.08	12.44	28.9	126.4	72.8	NA
1979	11.05	1.87	11.39	28.9	97.7	73.2	NA
1978	9.43	1.65	9.70	28.9	80.9	75.2	NA

Table 2-77. Terms on Conventional Single-Family Mortgages, by State, 1978–2010—*Continued*

[Percent, years, dollars in thousands.]

Characteristics	Contract interest rate	Initial fees and charges	Effective interest rate	Term to maturity	Purchase price	Loan-to-price ratio	Adjustable-rate loans
Idaho							
2010	4.79	1.02	4.94	27.5	247.8	74.1	5.2
2009	5.00	0.74	5.11	29.1	244.2	75.8	3.2
2008	5.99	0.85	6.11	28.9	280.8	77.3	NA
2007	6.43	0.71	6.53	29.5	262.3	77.8	7
2006	6.49	0.59	6.58	29.1	232.1	77.4	18
2005	5.86	0.67	5.95	28.8	198.9	76.9	19
2004	5.63	0.76	5.74	28.2	183.4	76.0	31
2003	5.66	0.52	5.74	26.3	164.6	75.0	14
2002	6.53	0.53	6.61	26.1	161.1	74.5	11
2001	6.93	0.53	7.01	27.2	162.0	76.1	5
2000	7.77	0.70	7.88	28.5	160.0	76.1	15
1999	7.15	0.81	7.27	27.5	147.3	76.3	12
1998	7.04	0.81	7.16	27.0	143.8	76.0	5
1997	7.69	1.03	7.86	27.1	143.4	75.2	9
1996	7.72	0.84	7.86	27.4	140.8	72.9	17
1995	7.67	0.75	7.79	27.2	135.1	75.6	32
1994	7.29	0.88	7.43	27.8	112.2	76.4	37
1993	7.08	0.96	7.24	25.4	95.8	71.0	6
1992	8.00	2.38	8.39	26.5	103.1	76.3	20
1991	9.26	2.48	9.68	26.8	100.0	76.3	3
1990	10.09	1.37	10.32	28.0	133.8	72.8	0
1989	9.87	1.78	10.17	29.6	140.4	70.1	31
1988	8.42	1.83	8.73	25.8	100.1	75.1	57
1987	9.22	1.61	9.49	26.6	106.3	77.3	17
1986	10.02	2.08	10.39	24.3	89.6	75.7	8
1985	10.39	2.57	10.84	29.5	76.8	82.8	NA
1984	11.20	2.47	11.64	29.3	73.3	83.2	NA
1983	12.92	2.06	13.37	21.6	76.9	60.4	NA
1982	14.72	3.70	15.53	26.3	90.6	73.7	NA
1981	13.38	1.74	14.18	26.7	81.1	68.5	NA
1980	12.27	2.12	12.66	29.6	66.9	80.4	NA
1979	10.84	1.80	11.16	28.7	64.6	76.3	NA
1978	9.55	1.76	9.84	28.3	57.5	75.9	NA
Illinois							
2010	4.97	0.53	5.05	26.6	228.7	77.1	11.2
2009	5.20	0.44	5.27	26.9	238.6	74.4	9.3
2008	6.09	0.40	6.15	27.2	263.4	74.6	NA
2007	6.56	0.24	6.60	28.7	254.9	78.5	16
2006	6.54	0.21	6.57	28.5	259.9	77.1	34
2005	5.78	0.21	5.81	28.8	275.9	76.2	45
2004	5.56	0.24	5.59	28.5	259.4	76.1	49
2003	5.54	0.20	5.57	26.6	250.0	73.5	27
2002	6.36	0.26	6.40	27.5	243.2	74.3	28
2001	6.97	0.29	7.01	27.4	222.2	75.2	19
2000	7.79	0.37	7.85	28.9	201.3	77.1	37
1999	7.15	0.35	7.20	27.8	182.4	77.3	28
1998	6.97	0.47	7.04	28.0	174.7	78.6	19
1997	7.50	0.58	7.60	27.3	162.0	78.6	27
1996	7.67	0.43	7.74	26.6	161.5	75.0	23
1995	7.96	0.54	8.04	27.9	157.5	77.3	33
1994	7.67	0.61	7.77	27.3	159.6	78.8	39
1993	7.14	0.83	7.28	25.1	151.3	76.3	20
1992	8.08	1.46	8.33	25.7	150.5	76.1	19
1991	9.09	1.52	9.35	24.1	126.3	73.0	23
1990	9.82	1.70	10.12	23.7	118.6	73.8	24
1989	9.89	1.93	10.23	25.3	117.0	73.2	36
1988	9.34	1.91	9.66	25.9	107.7	73.3	53
1987	9.18	2.09	9.54	24.5	101.5	71.3	29
1986	9.94	2.28	10.35	23.8	95.1	71.9	24
1985	11.56	2.66	12.07	23.8	82.6	71.8	NA
1984	11.97	2.85	12.52	25.6	78.8	72.3	NA
1983	12.26	2.85	12.81	26.3	84.3	70.4	NA
1982	14.10	2.69	14.70	24.2	72.5	69.7	NA
1981	13.94	2.64	14.50	25.7	74.3	70.3	NA
1980	12.06	2.41	12.52	26.8	71.7	70.2	NA
1979	10.20	2.04	10.56	26.6	62.8	72.1	NA
1978	9.22	1.63	9.50	25.7	60.2	70.4	NA

Table 2-77. Terms on Conventional Single-Family Mortgages, by State, 1978–2010—*Continued*

[Percent, years, dollars in thousands.]

Characteristics	Contract interest rate	Initial fees and charges	Effective interest rate	Term to maturity	Purchase price	Loan-to-price ratio	Adjustable-rate loans
Indiana							
2010	5.01	0.81	5.13	25.6	169.9	72.2	5.0
2009	5.39	0.90	5.53	27.0	200.6	76.4	7.3
2008	6.14	0.47	6.21	26.8	187.0	80.3	NA
2007	6.55	0.42	6.62	28.0	160.7	82.6	23
2006	6.67	0.33	6.72	27.9	167.5	81.3	26
2005	5.97	0.29	6.01	28.3	163.6	79.7	22
2004	5.89	0.26	5.93	27.7	140.4	80.3	27
2003	5.97	0.29	6.02	27.0	135.8	80.2	18
2002	6.67	0.53	6.75	27.0	145.1	80.1	15
2001	7.08	0.51	7.16	27.0	139.4	78.7	13
2000	8.13	0.67	8.23	28.4	136.6	79.5	26
1999	7.38	0.51	7.46	27.7	127.3	80.3	15
1998	7.12	0.67	7.22	27.1	125.1	79.5	12
1997	7.69	0.79	7.82	26.9	117.5	80.5	22
1996	7.76	0.73	7.89	25.3	108.0	80.5	25
1995	8.01	0.95	8.17	26.3	106.3	80.9	22
1994	7.66	1.10	7.85	23.8	109.5	78.6	34
1993	7.08	0.92	7.24	21.9	106.9	75.6	27
1992	8.09	1.02	8.27	21.7	100.3	75.5	12
1991	9.34	1.47	9.59	21.3	82.7	73.0	24
1990	9.91	1.85	10.25	21.7	83.0	73.1	29
1989	10.02	1.95	10.38	22.7	76.4	72.4	42
1988	8.90	2.08	9.25	23.5	74.0	75.1	68
1987	9.07	2.07	9.44	22.2	67.2	72.6	47
1986	9.88	2.28	10.30	21.6	64.4	74.3	27
1985	11.28	2.63	11.78	23.2	55.1	75.2	NA
1984	12.12	2.41	12.60	23.4	53.4	76.3	NA
1983	12.45	2.06	12.87	22.8	51.2	74.3	NA
1982	14.97	2.46	15.53	21.7	47.3	73.1	NA
1981	14.53	2.49	15.07	23.6	54.9	70.3	NA
1980	12.68	2.04	13.09	23.2	49.3	69.9	NA
1979	10.86	1.61	11.15	24.4	52.7	71.7	NA
1978	9.40	1.27	9.62	23.4	46.7	71.2	NA
Iowa							
2010	4.80	0.88	4.92	28.6	135.9	81.2	1.9
2009	5.02	0.92	5.15	28.2	182.5	78.6	2.7
2008	6.04	0.99	6.19	28.1	166.0	82.1	NA
2007	6.39	0.87	6.52	28.2	162.0	83.1	6
2006	6.47	0.63	6.57	27.9	166.5	79.6	16
2005	5.80	0.70	5.91	28.2	147.6	82.0	18
2004	5.70	0.97	5.85	27.9	133.0	81.9	21
2003	5.66	0.97	5.80	26.7	126.5	80.9	15
2002	6.53	0.85	6.65	27.2	121.2	83.5	14
2001	6.92	0.74	7.03	27.6	132.6	82.4	9
2000	8.06	0.84	8.20	27.5	127.4	80.1	20
1999	7.32	0.72	7.43	27.0	111.8	82.0	12
1998	7.05	0.86	7.18	26.5	117.8	79.9	9
1997	7.73	0.96	7.89	26.3	112.9	80.0	13
1996	7.78	0.43	7.86	21.3	87.6	77.4	35
1995	8.02	0.53	8.11	21.0	91.6	77.0	25
1994	7.33	0.89	7.50	20.3	84.9	78.1	36
1993	7.06	0.72	7.18	16.6	98.9	70.0	10
1992	8.17	1.12	8.39	16.0	84.4	71.7	8
1991	9.46	1.09	9.64	25.4	101.0	72.4	9
1990	9.88	1.64	10.17	25.2	86.5	76.9	21
1989	9.69	1.16	9.89	25.7	72.0	77.3	37
1988	8.97	1.43	9.21	25.4	58.5	75.1	62
1987	8.85	1.69	9.15	24.9	72.2	77.8	54
1986	9.89	2.02	10.29	20.7	64.8	73.6	45
1985	10.84	2.05	11.24	23.6	76.1	72.6	NA
1984	12.12	2.19	12.54	25.0	56.9	77.6	NA
1983	12.33	1.83	12.69	23.4	52.2	76.7	NA
1982	13.81	1.62	14.14	24.0	57.4	75.0	NA
1981	14.00	1.94	14.42	25.6	60.0	73.6	NA
1980	12.45	2.12	12.86	25.2	58.3	72.1	NA
1979	10.62	0.48	10.71	25.4	58.9	71.7	NA
1978	9.29	1.24	9.50	24.8	50.6	73.6	NA

Table 2-77. Terms on Conventional Single-Family Mortgages, by State, 1978–2010—*Continued*

[Percent, years, dollars in thousands.]

Characteristics	Contract interest rate	Initial fees and charges	Effective interest rate	Term to maturity	Purchase price	Loan-to-price ratio	Adjustable-rate loans
Kansas							
2010	4.77	0.18	4.80	27.8	226.5	77.3	8.0
2009	5.03	0.16	5.06	28.1	231.8	77.7	
2008	5.83	0.17	5.85	27.5	232.5	79.6	NA
2007	6.14	0.15	6.16	28.1	206.9	81.0	10
2006	6.27	0.17	6.30	28.4	188.1	80.6	15
2005	5.78	0.19	5.81	27.9	173.2	80.0	19
2004	5.72	0.34	5.77	27.3	170.3	79.9	30
2003	5.69	0.32	5.73	27.6	164.4	80.6	18
2002	6.54	0.25	6.58	27.3	143.6	82.3	14
2001	6.94	0.21	6.97	27.8	150.1	83.5	13
2000	7.90	0.37	7.96	28.7	137.6	83.2	29
1999	7.03	0.34	7.08	28.0	145.3	81.2	27
1998	6.95	0.42	7.01	27.9	134.8	81.8	16
1997	7.52	0.66	7.63	28.0	127.8	82.2	35
1996	7.63	0.85	7.76	26.9	113.7	82.5	33
1995	7.77	0.92	7.91	27.4	114.6	82.1	37
1994	7.28	0.79	7.40	27.1	113.8	82.8	58
1993	6.69	1.30	6.91	25.8	109.6	80.8	28
1992	7.88	1.69	8.17	26.0	103.6	79.7	18
1991	9.28	1.78	9.57	26.5	95.4	80.1	10
1990	9.93	1.76	10.23	26.1	99.7	77.3	16
1989	9.76	2.07	10.12	26.8	98.5	77.5	35
1988	9.08	1.95	9.40	27.1	92.2	78.6	54
1987	8.99	1.99	9.31	27.4	91.4	79.3	46
1986	9.79	2.03	10.14	25.5	83.6	77.4	35
1985	10.83	2.31	11.24	26.2	77.2	77.4	NA
1984	12.06	2.29	12.49	28.1	73.3	79.9	NA
1983	12.17	2.35	12.61	28.4	69.1	80.2	NA
1982	13.94	2.63	14.49	26.0	59.4	78.5	NA
1981	13.29	2.23	13.74	27.6	65.8	77.4	NA
1980	12.10	2.07	12.49	27.8	54.7	77.9	NA
1979	10.53	1.39	10.77	27.7	50.7	78.6	NA
1978	9.57	1.32	9.80	27.4	46.1	77.9	NA
Kentucky							
2010	4.84	0.71	4.94	26.6	206.6	74.7	1.8
2009	5.09	0.78	5.20	27.7	217.3	75.6	1.6
2008	6.12	0.71	6.23	28.6	202.7	79.6	NA
2007	6.48	0.66	6.58	29.0	201.5	80.3	5
2006	6.62	0.50	6.70	28.7	196.4	78.1	12
2005	5.94	0.47	6.02	27.7	193.0	78.5	23
2004	5.71	0.54	5.79	28.5	168.0	79.1	36
2003	5.68	0.55	5.76	26.9	168.2	76.8	15
2002	6.49	0.59	6.58	26.9	164.1	78.1	13
2001	7.00	0.57	7.08	27.1	153.7	77.2	8
2000	8.09	0.90	8.24	28.5	150.7	77.4	12
1999	7.28	0.79	7.40	27.9	142.5	79.2	10
1998	6.91	1.09	7.08	27.9	138.4	79.5	14
1997	7.39	1.20	7.58	28.5	138.7	78.4	34
1996	7.52	1.17	7.71	27.7	123.3	80.6	19
1995	7.76	1.04	7.93	27.5	112.9	80.6	20
1994	7.59	1.12	7.77	26.7	106.0	80.1	32
1993	7.03	1.02	7.20	24.2	103.6	78.2	24
1992	7.86	1.58	8.14	24.0	110.5	75.6	18
1991	9.35	1.11	9.55	23.8	85.5	76.0	45
1990	10.03	1.53	10.29	24.5	81.5	79.4	40
1989	10.22	1.32	10.45	24.6	75.1	75.9	44
1988	9.35	1.49	9.60	24.6	73.4	77.7	57
1987	9.04	1.40	9.28	23.2	72.0	76.7	56
1986	10.05	1.64	10.35	22.1	62.3	75.2	45
1985	11.53	1.85	11.89	22.3	57.6	75.6	NA
1984	12.25	2.14	12.67	23.5	52.9	73.2	NA
1983	12.59	1.68	12.91	20.5	48.2	71.7	NA
1982	14.49	2.03	14.91	23.6	48.3	76.7	NA
1981	14.34	2.64	14.88	25.3	53.3	74.6	NA
1980	12.42	2.06	12.81	24.6	51.0	73.1	NA
1979	10.42	1.29	10.66	21.8	53.1	70.7	NA
1978	9.18	1.06	9.36	24.8	45.2	74.7	NA

Table 2-77. Terms on Conventional Single-Family Mortgages, by State, 1978–2010—*Continued*

[Percent, years, dollars in thousands.]

Characteristics	Contract interest rate	Initial fees and charges	Effective interest rate	Term to maturity	Purchase price	Loan-to-price ratio	Adjustable-rate loans
Louisiana							
2010	4.81	0.57	4.90	26.9	241.1	70.2	1.9
2009	4.99	0.75	5.09	26.8	246.6	75.8	3.8
2008	6.10	0.45	6.17	28.9	211.2	81.5	NA
2007	6.51	1.00	6.66	29.2	220.2	79.4	2
2006	6.54	0.60	6.62	28.6	216.2	79.5	9
2005	5.91	0.59	6.00	28.4	187.0	81.5	17
2004	5.75	0.54	5.83	28.1	169.2	82.4	20
2003	5.65	0.59	5.74	27.7	163.0	81.5	11
2002	6.43	0.68	6.53	27.9	161.5	81.3	9
2001	6.86	0.74	6.98	27.8	157.8	80.3	7
2000	7.89	0.73	8.01	28.0	161.9	80.2	26
1999	7.13	0.75	7.25	27.9	153.3	80.5	30
1998	6.97	0.90	7.11	27.4	137.1	80.2	4
1997	7.65	1.15	7.84	26.9	126.9	82.6	9
1996	7.78	1.00	7.95	24.2	115.4	83.8	7
1995	7.99	1.07	8.17	25.9	113.0	81.1	18
1994	7.91	1.21	8.12	25.0	121.6	80.8	25
1993	7.08	1.26	7.30	23.5	118.0	78.9	8
1992	7.85	1.79	8.20	23.1	120.3	77.1	13
1991	9.37	2.43	9.79	26.6	96.7	79.3	4
1990	9.97	2.41	10.40	27.3	85.9	81.6	5
1989	9.78	2.67	10.24	27.6	81.5	82.3	10
1988	9.16	2.77	9.62	28.1	86.4	83.1	33
1987	9.51	2.78	9.98	27.6	96.5	79.1	14
1986	10.01	2.95	10.52	27.5	93.1	80.0	5
1985	11.41	3.53	12.07	27.0	89.0	81.4	NA
1984	11.86	3.27	12.47	28.3	77.7	83.2	NA
1983	12.51	2.47	12.98	27.2	88.4	78.8	NA
1982	14.36	2.77	14.95	27.4	83.7	76.2	NA
1981	13.87	2.85	14.51	26.4	75.9	70.9	NA
1980	11.93	2.29	12.37	27.8	75.7	73.2	NA
1979	10.07	2.84	10.57	27.8	67.4	75.2	NA
1978	9.41	1.68	9.70	28.0	57.2	77.4	NA
Maine							
2010	4.80	0.44	4.87	26.7	230.6	75.5	3.5
2009	5.00	0.45	5.06	26.8	222.6	77.3	0.9
2008	5.95	0.47	6.02	28.0	205.4	75.9	NA
2007	6.38	0.39	6.44	28.3	217.5	77.0	4
2006	6.53	0.41	6.60	27.9	219.9	76.1	8
2005	5.95	0.34	6.00	27.4	241.0	73.7	19
2004	5.80	0.47	5.86	27.1	221.1	72.9	21
2003	5.72	0.30	5.76	25.4	232.4	71.0	14
2002	6.58	0.59	6.68	26.2	159.8	74.0	7
2001	7.01	0.77	7.13	26.9	154.0	78.2	6
2000	8.23	0.74	8.35	27.6	150.1	78.5	7
1999	7.30	0.75	7.42	23.7	131.6	73.3	5
1998	7.11	0.72	7.22	24.4	140.0	74.3	4
1997	7.71	1.01	7.87	27.0	131.1	78.1	12
1996	7.67	0.74	7.79	26.1	129.6	75.0	21
1995	7.87	1.62	8.13	26.9	123.6	76.8	24
1994	7.43	1.74	7.71	27.2	118.4	75.3	43
1993	7.07	1.49	7.31	26.0	131.5	71.8	24
1992	7.79	1.92	8.10	26.8	127.3	75.0	30
1991	9.21	1.81	9.51	28.4	105.5	75.7	52
1990	9.93	1.33	10.17	27.0	127.3	68.1	36
1989	10.71	1.71	11.02	27.5	120.9	65.3	28
1988	9.83	1.78	10.13	25.5	101.0	66.8	32
1987	9.71	1.59	9.97	28.0	92.0	68.3	55
1986	9.72	2.13	10.09	27.7	94.4	72.3	46
1985	11.27	2.31	11.70	26.3	73.6	79.6	NA
1984	12.15	2.56	12.63	27.2	65.7	75.8	NA
1983	12.17	2.95	12.74	25.5	63.9	73.2	NA
1982	15.17	2.73	15.77	23.3	64.1	74.8	NA
1981	14.80	2.13	15.25	28.0	53.1	72.8	NA
1980	12.39	2.12	12.80	26.8	51.8	73.8	NA
1979	10.81	1.16	11.02	28.1	51.2	74.6	NA
1978	9.33	1.05	9.50	26.9	44.9	74.8	NA

Table 2-77. Terms on Conventional Single-Family Mortgages, by State, 1978–2010—*Continued*

[Percent, years, dollars in thousands.]

Characteristics	Contract interest rate	Initial fees and charges	Effective interest rate	Term to maturity	Purchase price	Loan-to-price ratio	Adjustable-rate loans
Maryland							
2010	4.72	0.75	4.82	28.7	424.1	71.9	1.6
2009	5.03	0.81	5.14	29.1	425.0	71.2	1.3
2008	6.12	0.57	6.20	29.2	455.3	72.6	NA
2007	6.49	0.63	6.58	30.2	449.9	76.1	5
2006	6.67	0.66	6.77	29.9	446.0	73.2	12
2005	6.05	0.67	6.15	29.0	400.9	72.4	22
2004	5.81	0.63	5.90	28.1	327.5	72.5	28
2003	5.91	0.64	6.00	27.6	299.9	73.4	11
2002	6.58	0.56	6.66	27.7	267.6	74.3	10
2001	7.05	0.62	7.14	28.0	251.3	74.8	7
2000	8.00	0.73	8.12	29.0	235.6	76.4	16
1999	7.21	0.76	7.32	28.5	223.9	77.6	14
1998	7.01	0.82	7.13	28.4	213.5	78.3	13
1997	7.53	1.08	7.70	28.2	200.0	79.4	22
1996	7.52	1.33	7.74	27.3	199.9	78.2	23
1995	7.57	1.36	7.79	28.3	192.8	82.0	25
1994	7.27	1.39	7.50	28.3	183.5	83.3	32
1993	6.90	1.27	7.10	27.0	181.8	80.0	13
1992	7.84	1.85	8.16	26.3	179.3	80.2	10
1991	9.18	2.12	9.55	24.5	150.8	74.6	26
1990	9.80	2.56	10.24	27.4	153.5	73.7	20
1989	9.76	2.56	10.20	26.7	151.9	75.9	35
1988	9.15	2.48	9.57	27.2	144.2	76.5	48
1987	9.23	2.41	9.64	24.9	119.6	75.3	27
1986	9.77	2.48	10.22	24.1	112.9	74.1	29
1985	11.18	2.70	11.68	24.7	104.8	77.0	NA
1984	11.99	2.32	12.43	26.7	93.0	78.3	NA
1983	12.24	1.21	12.47	23.6	82.8	72.5	NA
1982	15.07	1.74	15.44	25.2	82.9	67.6	NA
1981	14.66	1.09	14.88	23.6	81.3	69.5	NA
1980	12.57	1.09	12.77	26.1	72.5	71.3	NA
1979	10.55	0.27	10.61	25.1	71.6	69.7	NA
1978	9.48	0.19	9.52	26.3	60.1	73.5	NA
Massachusetts							
2010	4.76	0.21	4.79	28.0	368.8	64.8	9.8
2009	4.86	0.20	4.89	28.6	380.0	65.3	7.2
2008	5.96	0.21	5.99	29.1	366.0	72.5	NA
2007	6.30	0.23	6.33	29.8	354.1	78.9	13
2006	6.32	0.25	6.36	29.6	363.7	76.4	21
2005	5.62	0.22	5.66	28.9	388.5	72.8	39
2004	5.38	0.27	5.42	28.5	375.9	69.9	45
2003	5.55	0.22	5.58	27.4	328.6	69.1	32
2002	6.38	0.33	6.43	28.3	307.0	73.7	27
2001	6.93	0.52	7.01	28.3	281.3	73.4	22
2000	7.88	0.55	7.97	29.0	256.4	74.6	38
1999	7.16	0.67	7.26	28.6	223.1	77.3	25
1998	7.04	0.80	7.17	28.7	220.4	78.7	13
1997	7.56	0.82	7.72	27.7	208.5	78.2	23
1996	7.53	0.80	7.66	27.9	177.6	78.9	36
1995	7.74	0.87	7.88	28.2	177.5	78.9	34
1994	7.47	1.04	7.64	28.0	182.8	79.3	40
1993	7.06	1.24	7.27	26.7	169.5	77.6	13
1992	8.11	1.77	8.41	27.6	167.6	78.3	14
1991	9.10	1.66	9.38	28.6	150.9	77.4	22
1990	9.73	1.51	9.98	29.0	157.7	75.0	28
1989	10.07	1.65	10.34	29.3	163.9	73.9	31
1988	9.18	1.59	9.44	29.3	175.4	72.8	68
1987	9.00	1.50	9.24	28.4	167.9	68.7	56
1986	10.07	1.65	10.35	27.1	146.9	65.6	38
1985	11.82	1.59	12.11	26.3	116.8	69.2	NA
1984	12.78	1.67	13.10	26.9	94.4	72.6	NA
1983	12.82	1.90	13.19	26.7	82.6	71.2	NA
1982	15.75	1.94	16.17	26.3	72.2	69.3	NA
1981	15.68	1.65	16.03	27.5	71.9	71.4	NA
1980	12.96	2.05	13.36	27.0	67.0	72.0	NA
1979	10.78	1.42	11.05	25.6	59.3	72.4	NA
1978	8.98	0.41	9.05	24.7	51.7	72.3	NA

Table 2-77. Terms on Conventional Single-Family Mortgages, by State, 1978–2010—*Continued*

[Percent, years, dollars in thousands.]

Characteristics	Contract interest rate	Initial fees and charges	Effective interest rate	Term to maturity	Purchase price	Loan-to-price ratio	Adjustable-rate loans
Michigan							
2010	5.05	0.34	5.11	26.7	185.9	79.1	1.2
2009	5.19	0.15	5.21	27.5	180.8	79.6	4.2
2008	6.21	0.11	6.22	28.6	172.8	84.5	NA
2007	6.66	0.16	6.68	29.0	176.4	83.0	12
2006	6.67	0.15	6.69	28.9	179.9	82.5	19
2005	5.84	0.27	5.88	28.5	196.5	77.6	31
2004	5.63	0.25	5.67	28.4	183.4	77.7	33
2003	5.54	0.25	5.58	27.9	173.2	79.6	30
2002	6.41	0.58	6.50	27.6	188.1	77.1	22
2001	6.99	0.59	7.08	27.9	186.5	76.8	12
2000	8.04	0.84	8.17	28.7	169.1	77.8	21
1999	7.33	0.74	7.44	28.3	156.0	78.3	17
1998	7.07	0.73	7.18	28.0	165.2	77.8	13
1997	7.67	0.72	7.79	25.6	152.5	77.0	21
1996	7.87	0.83	8.01	25.8	116.7	78.8	30
1995	7.89	1.27	8.12	25.9	120.3	78.4	23
1994	7.58	1.40	7.82	24.5	125.4	76.8	30
1993	6.99	1.96	7.33	23.0	112.3	75.1	20
1992	7.92	1.92	8.28	20.9	119.9	71.6	15
1991	9.01	1.89	9.33	24.7	112.2	71.8	13
1990	9.92	2.05	10.28	25.6	106.3	72.3	14
1989	9.89	2.30	10.30	25.4	103.4	71.7	23
1988	9.19	2.58	9.64	25.0	93.9	73.0	42
1987	9.38	2.68	9.86	23.0	88.0	73.0	20
1986	10.08	2.36	10.51	21.8	77.8	72.8	8
1985	11.41	2.50	11.89	22.6	72.0	74.5	NA
1984	11.50	2.48	11.97	27.0	68.3	77.2	NA
1983	11.81	2.15	12.22	28.3	68.2	75.6	NA
1982	14.22	2.07	14.66	27.2	73.0	72.7	NA
1981	14.33	1.74	14.70	27.6	71.8	72.4	NA
1980	12.68	1.35	12.98	27.6	62.7	73.4	NA
1979	10.97	0.97	11.15	27.4	55.3	74.9	NA
1978	9.41	0.87	9.56	27.8	51.0	74.9	NA
Minnesota							
2010	4.72	1.09	4.88	27.6	256.9	75.0	7.3
2009	4.95	1.09	5.11	28.2	262.0	74.9	4.0
2008	5.94	0.93	6.08	28.7	266.4	80.0	NA
2007	6.29	0.93	6.43	29.2	266.3	79.7	6
2006	6.37	0.80	6.48	29.2	274.7	77.1	19
2005	5.62	0.81	5.74	29.0	272.6	76.4	31
2004	5.44	1.03	5.58	28.9	250.0	77.5	41
2003	5.46	1.06	5.62	28.0	232.8	77.2	25
2002	6.37	1.16	6.54	28.0	205.1	78.4	15
2001	6.88	1.03	7.04	28.0	199.4	78.2	7
2000	7.96	1.15	8.14	28.8	179.6	79.9	12
1999	7.26	1.10	7.43	28.3	155.6	82.2	10
1998	6.96	1.19	7.14	27.8	153.5	81.6	4
1997	7.53	1.27	7.74	26.8	147.7	81.1	11
1996	7.69	1.10	7.90	24.2	128.4	77.6	11
1995	7.84	1.17	8.03	26.7	119.7	81.2	13
1994	7.71	1.18	7.91	25.7	125.2	79.6	26
1993	7.00	1.33	7.22	24.9	123.8	77.5	9
1992	7.99	1.90	8.33	25.4	117.5	81.0	10
1991	9.13	1.78	9.42	28.5	110.2	76.2	23
1990	9.53	2.27	9.91	28.6	131.3	73.7	45
1989	9.73	1.79	10.03	29.6	129.9	77.9	26
1988	8.82	1.83	9.11	29.7	133.7	73.8	59
1987	8.63	1.80	8.91	29.3	133.2	76.9	48
1986	9.75	2.06	10.10	27.3	125.6	76.6	19
1985	10.80	3.17	11.37	28.2	84.1	85.0	NA
1984	11.45	3.66	12.13	28.9	89.4	82.8	NA
1983	11.87	2.85	12.40	27.9	75.8	78.1	NA
1982	13.91	2.68	14.46	27.1	86.4	73.8	NA
1981	13.65	2.25	14.12	28.2	80.3	74.9	NA
1980	12.18	1.31	12.41	28.4	76.6	70.8	NA
1979	10.43	0.92	10.59	28.0	70.5	70.5	NA
1978	9.41	0.84	9.55	27.1	60.4	71.2	NA

Table 2-77. Terms on Conventional Single-Family Mortgages, by State, 1978–2010—*Continued*

[Percent, years, dollars in thousands.]

Characteristics	Contract interest rate	Initial fees and charges	Effective interest rate	Term to maturity	Purchase price	Loan-to-price ratio	Adjustable-rate loans
Mississippi							
2010	4.73	0.97	4.87	24.6	172.2	74.3	2.3
2009	5.15	0.82	5.27	28.0	206.3	73.3	0.5
2008	6.29	0.72	6.40	28.3	186.1	83.7	NA
2007	6.62	0.60	6.71	29.0	171.5	84.9	6
2006	6.66	0.49	6.73	27.7	176.1	80.4	11
2005	5.89	0.46	5.96	27.8	163.6	80.1	17
2004	5.85	0.57	5.94	27.2	142.0	80.4	16
2003	5.66	0.68	5.77	26.9	147.8	81.5	16
2002	6.52	0.93	6.67	26.2	135.4	80.7	8
2001	6.89	0.82	7.02	26.3	129.4	81.5	7
2000	8.04	0.81	8.17	27.3	134.3	81.9	10
1999	7.22	0.78	7.34	27.6	142.3	81.8	23
1998	7.03	1.00	7.18	26.7	116.9	83.5	10
1997	7.88	1.03	8.06	25.6	107.3	82.9	10
1996	7.92	0.82	8.06	25.6	106.1	83.7	6
1995	8.23	1.09	8.42	22.1	88.5	81.0	11
1994	7.95	1.31	8.17	23.5	106.9	77.1	17
1993	7.27	1.11	7.45	22.6	83.4	84.4	9
1992	8.22	1.52	8.48	22.5	95.9	84.0	16
1991	9.35	1.95	9.70	21.8	80.6	79.1	28
1990	9.72	2.31	10.13	23.3	79.9	82.1	31
1989	9.80	2.43	10.23	23.4	75.4	80.6	45
1988	9.18	2.71	9.65	24.0	65.2	83.1	55
1987	9.26	2.91	9.77	25.7	91.5	81.0	39
1986	9.78	2.02	10.13	25.6	70.2	79.6	28
1985	10.82	2.92	11.35	26.0	67.1	81.0	NA
1984	11.76	3.04	12.38	24.5	70.4	80.7	NA
1983	12.84	1.91	13.23	20.3	58.2	70.9	NA
1982	13.85	1.59	14.19	22.0	65.5	79.5	NA
1981	13.99	1.80	14.37	21.1	57.8	69.3	NA
1980	12.54	1.61	12.85	23.5	63.3	68.3	NA
1979	10.08	1.73	10.39	25.5	51.4	72.7	NA
1978	9.41	1.46	9.66	24.2	39.2	75.6	NA
Missouri							
2010	5.02	0.66	5.11	26.4	195.5	77.4	3.0
2009	5.09	0.46	5.16	27.5	214.1	76.1	2.3
2008	6.14	0.28	6.18	28.7	211.4	81.7	NA
2007	6.48	0.20	6.51	29.4	179.6	85.4	4
2006	6.47	0.16	6.49	29.2	170.7	83.6	11
2005	5.90	0.19	5.93	28.2	180.2	80.7	19
2004	5.93	0.32	5.98	27.1	165.5	79.0	26
2003	5.84	0.35	5.89	26.6	156.6	78.7	15
2002	6.62	0.32	6.67	26.7	144.8	80.9	18
2001	7.03	0.29	7.08	27.5	142.8	82.0	14
2000	7.99	0.43	8.06	28.6	135.2	82.7	25
1999	7.23	0.30	7.28	26.0	137.0	77.3	19
1998	7.00	0.46	7.07	26.5	143.9	77.5	15
1997	7.54	0.58	7.64	27.0	136.8	79.4	35
1996	7.64	0.60	7.77	27.1	126.3	78.5	39
1995	7.95	0.63	8.05	26.6	116.1	78.3	36
1994	7.35	0.81	7.49	27.4	117.3	79.6	46
1993	7.09	0.85	7.23	25.0	111.6	77.3	15
1992	7.91	1.30	8.22	23.0	116.2	76.4	15
1991	9.09	1.33	9.31	26.0	103.1	77.4	28
1990	9.83	1.59	10.10	25.8	93.6	74.6	36
1989	10.00	1.70	10.29	27.1	98.7	72.6	36
1988	8.83	1.77	9.12	26.5	94.3	76.3	70
1987	8.85	1.88	9.16	26.0	88.8	75.1	55
1986	9.68	1.85	10.00	24.7	79.0	75.8	44
1985	11.00	2.00	11.37	25.4	70.5	77.6	NA
1984	11.99	2.28	12.42	26.4	67.2	76.9	NA
1983	12.22	2.22	12.65	25.7	63.4	76.7	NA
1982	14.41	2.60	14.96	24.0	59.6	71.2	NA
1981	14.47	2.12	14.98	23.8	68.5	71.2	NA
1980	12.51	1.73	12.85	25.1	56.1	75.6	NA
1979	10.29	1.09	10.49	25.7	55.6	73.2	NA
1978	9.37	1.10	9.56	24.7	44.6	76.5	NA

Table 2-77. Terms on Conventional Single-Family Mortgages, by State, 1978–2010—*Continued*

[Percent, years, dollars in thousands.]

Characteristics	Contract interest rate	Initial fees and charges	Effective interest rate	Term to maturity	Purchase price	Loan-to-price ratio	Adjustable-rate loans
Montana							
2010	4.79	0.99	4.93	27.7	264.0	73.8	2.6
2009	4.97	0.90	5.10	28.4	268.4	73.3	1.6
2008	6.01	0.85	6.14	28.7	241.0	77.5	NA
2007	6.40	0.84	6.52	29.0	233.0	77.8	9
2006	6.50	0.70	6.61	28.4	266.4	73.9	20
2005	5.76	0.74	5.87	28.8	226.8	75.7	24
2004	5.64	0.89	5.77	27.3	193.3	75.6	32
2003	5.74	0.90	5.88	25.3	180.7	73.7	14
2002	6.59	1.03	6.75	26.3	156.9	78.3	14
2001	6.92	0.89	7.06	27.0	155.4	77.0	4
2000	8.10	1.07	8.27	28.3	144.9	77.2	10
1999	7.40	1.14	7.58	27.5	133.4	77.6	6
1998	7.10	1.09	7.27	26.7	135.2	76.8	3
1997	7.84	1.20	8.04	26.2	129.0	77.0	8
1996	7.93	0.99	8.10	24.6	134.0	70.5	12
1995	7.89	0.82	8.02	25.0	140.0	72.2	8
1994	7.91	1.62	8.19	27.5	130.1	72.2	21
1993	7.29	1.04	7.47	25.1	123.6	72.2	5
1992	8.19	1.77	8.48	27.2	109.3	75.4	12
1991	9.40	1.44	9.64	24.0	134.5	73.6	0
1990	9.90	2.38	10.31	25.1	115.2	63.4	0
1989	10.42	1.97	10.78	21.9	93.0	71.8	0
1988	9.59	1.13	9.78	25.9	112.8	69.7	28
1987	9.60	1.89	9.92	25.8	72.4	81.2	30
1986	9.60	2.07	9.94	28.0	88.1	78.4	25
1985	9.49	4.07	10.17	26.5	78.4	77.4	NA
1984	13.39	1.79	13.77	19.8	48.5	74.6	NA
1983	13.01	1.36	13.28	25.1	71.4	65.8	NA
1982	15.87	2.85	16.48	28.5	98.6	65.6	NA
1981	15.05	2.31	15.54	26.3	87.1	65.6	NA
1980	13.02	0.43	13.15	28.5	85.7	70.2	NA
1979	10.63	0.95	10.80	29.8	73.3	70.2	NA
1978	9.47	1.30	9.69	29.6	67.1	68.8	NA
Nebraska							
2010	4.95	0.89	5.08	26.7	183.8	74.6	1.7
2009	5.14	0.88	5.27	28.0	171.7	78.3	0.3
2008	6.08	0.71	6.19	28.3	160.7	81.1	NA
2007	6.35	0.50	6.42	28.9	147.9	85.5	2
2006	6.47	0.51	6.55	28.7	155.2	82.5	6
2005	5.91	0.53	5.99	28.8	161.1	79.2	15
2004	5.82	0.76	5.93	28.5	159.3	79.9	30
2003	5.79	0.75	5.90	28.1	158.0	80.2	15
2002	6.57	0.73	6.68	28.5	156.5	81.4	18
2001	6.96	0.62	7.05	27.4	156.9	79.1	10
2000	8.07	0.64	8.17	28.5	144.8	79.0	15
1999	7.30	0.69	7.41	27.7	138.8	79.2	11
1998	7.19	0.60	7.29	24.6	82.6	96.7	6
1997	7.87	0.67	7.98	23.0	84.7	95.8	10
1996	7.74	0.57	7.83	25.0	97.2	84.5	20
1995	7.87	0.78	8.00	26.5	104.9	79.1	21
1994	7.49	0.84	7.63	26.8	102.5	79.3	39
1993	7.08	0.77	7.21	23.4	89.5	77.4	15
1992	7.82	1.25	8.04	26.6	93.3	78.1	17
1991	9.22	1.89	9.53	28.1	104.0	77.6	11
1990	9.49	2.54	9.91	27.7	77.5	81.5	19
1989	9.61	2.59	10.04	28.3	91.1	79.2	26
1988	9.17	2.45	9.58	27.6	91.9	77.0	46
1987	8.98	2.50	9.40	27.3	81.5	79.2	22
1986	9.66	3.02	10.18	26.4	77.3	75.8	12
1985	10.81	3.74	11.50	25.9	67.0	78.4	NA
1984	11.45	3.19	12.05	27.2	69.3	80.2	NA
1983	11.67	3.66	12.38	23.0	70.8	77.2	NA
1982	14.79	3.29	15.51	25.0	67.2	74.2	NA
1981	12.07	2.47	12.54	29.3	46.4	85.0	NA
1980	11.41	2.39	11.84	29.1	49.0	82.0	NA
1979	10.59	1.84	10.92	28.3	49.2	78.9	NA
1978	9.49	1.77	9.79	28.0	46.7	78.7	NA

Table 2-77. Terms on Conventional Single-Family Mortgages, by State, 1978–2010—*Continued*

[Percent, years, dollars in thousands.]

Characteristics	Contract interest rate	Initial fees and charges	Effective interest rate	Term to maturity	Purchase price	Loan-to-price ratio	Adjustable-rate loans
Nevada							
2010	4.93	1.34	5.12	28.7	212.8	74.6	3.0
2009	5.19	0.87	5.31	28.9	242.5	75.5	2.1
2008	6.09	0.65	6.18	28.9	313.3	76.5	NA
2007	6.51	0.53	6.59	29.9	358.6	77.5	25
2006	6.56	0.41	6.62	28.7	398.4	70.5	42
2005	5.82	0.39	5.88	28.4	347.6	70.3	47
2004	5.66	0.40	5.72	27.9	287.1	71.5	46
2003	5.74	0.37	5.79	26.4	226.4	71.4	18
2002	6.44	0.60	6.53	27.5	216.5	76.3	16
2001	6.98	0.65	7.08	27.9	196.3	78.9	10
2000	7.99	0.90	8.13	28.9	187.6	79.2	15
1999	7.25	0.92	7.40	28.6	178.4	79.7	15
1998	7.04	0.90	7.18	28.4	174.2	79.9	9
1997	7.60	0.98	7.76	27.7	171.4	78.9	15
1996	7.52	0.76	7.64	28.3	164.5	78.8	22
1995	7.28	0.56	7.37	28.9	149.4	80.2	37
1994	7.14	1.12	7.31	28.4	148.2	78.6	32
1993	7.10	1.27	7.30	28.4	142.9	78.2	8
1992	8.10	1.63	8.37	27.2	145.9	76.1	8
1991	9.22	1.61	9.49	27.7	147.1	71.6	10
1990	9.93	1.72	10.23	28.0	146.3	73.1	11
1989	9.83	1.88	10.15	28.2	141.6	70.9	23
1988	8.88	2.01	9.20	28.9	138.1	74.7	56
1987	9.16	1.54	9.41	29.1	139.5	78.8	38
1986	9.96	1.93	10.30	26.8	129.4	76.0	24
1985	11.23	2.75	11.74	27.2	121.0	80.2	NA
1984	12.34	3.19	12.96	28.6	91.0	83.7	NA
1983	12.29	2.86	12.83	29.3	100.3	79.6	NA
1982	14.61	4.35	15.59	28.2	91.3	79.3	NA
1981	14.98	2.58	15.52	28.8	97.7	74.4	NA
1980	12.45	2.28	12.87	29.5	105.9	73.5	NA
1979	10.78	1.94	11.12	29.3	91.5	75.0	NA
1978	9.70	2.09	10.05	29.0	73.6	75.6	NA
New Hampshire							
2010	4.65	0.11	4.66	27.8	237.8	75.6	26.7
2009	4.87	0.16	4.90	27.3	290.2	72.1	19.6
2008	6.05	0.35	6.10	28.1	283.6	76.1	NA
2007	6.44	0.28	6.48	28.1	255.6	77.4	13
2006	6.39	0.30	6.44	28.0	292.1	77.2	25
2005	5.75	0.34	5.80	27.7	310.9	73.6	22
2004	5.55	0.36	5.60	28.2	287.9	73.6	38
2003	5.74	0.30	5.78	26.9	235.7	71.8	15
2002	6.60	0.40	6.66	27.4	221.3	74.3	11
2001	7.07	0.58	7.16	27.4	207.0	75.3	8
2000	8.17	0.76	8.29	29.0	183.4	78.6	14
1999	7.38	0.89	7.52	28.3	173.4	79.0	10
1998	7.10	1.09	7.27	28.1	161.6	79.9	5
1997	7.64	1.00	7.80	28.0	157.4	79.9	15
1996	7.72	0.85	7.86	26.5	135.3	78.0	22
1995	7.91	0.97	8.07	27.1	136.0	78.7	16
1994	7.85	1.23	8.05	26.8	136.7	77.7	26
1993	6.97	1.24	7.17	25.6	139.4	74.5	18
1992	7.94	1.76	8.23	26.2	143.9	75.8	22
1991	9.16	1.98	9.51	25.7	120.1	78.1	15
1990	9.78	1.91	10.11	28.2	124.9	72.0	27
1989	10.14	1.73	10.43	28.8	148.9	76.2	28
1988	9.29	1.56	9.54	29.4	159.5	74.0	66
1987	8.75	1.83	9.04	28.3	139.7	73.8	68
1986	9.82	2.01	10.16	26.5	118.8	66.6	49
1985	11.39	1.99	11.75	26.4	99.4	71.0	NA
1984	12.61	2.15	13.02	26.8	85.9	71.7	NA
1983	12.80	2.24	13.24	23.7	75.8	71.4	NA
1982	15.92	2.19	16.40	25.9	64.8	70.5	NA
1981	15.75	2.56	16.30	28.5	61.0	71.9	NA
1980	12.81	2.01	13.20	27.5	61.2	73.6	NA
1979	10.83	1.09	11.02	26.9	57.0	70.1	NA
1978	9.21	1.17	9.41	27.2	52.2	74.1	NA

Table 2-77. Terms on Conventional Single-Family Mortgages, by State, 1978–2010—*Continued*

[Percent, years, dollars in thousands.]

Characteristics	Contract interest rate	Initial fees and charges	Effective interest rate	Term to maturity	Purchase price	Loan-to-price ratio	Adjustable-rate loans
New Jersey							
2010	4.79	0.49	4.86	28.7	408.1	72.2	2.3
2009	5.01	0.49	5.08	28.6	408.3	71.1	1.9
2008	6.01	0.31	6.05	28.9	396.3	71.1	NA
2007	6.38	0.26	6.41	29.6	396.5	74.5	8
2006	6.61	0.25	6.65	29.5	417.4	72.0	20
2005	5.88	0.24	5.91	28.9	407.6	71.6	28
2004	5.66	0.27	5.70	28.4	351.5	71.4	31
2003	5.67	0.25	5.71	26.7	326.9	68.4	12
2002	6.43	0.37	6.49	27.6	301.1	71.8	14
2001	6.95	0.52	7.03	27.6	264.0	72.9	10
2000	7.84	0.60	7.94	28.9	241.1	75.7	28
1999	7.18	0.61	7.28	28.5	224.0	76.8	13
1998	7.01	0.72	7.12	28.2	212.8	76.8	7
1997	7.49	0.84	7.62	28.4	208.3	77.2	25
1996	7.53	1.01	7.69	27.8	208.3	75.8	33
1995	7.78	1.22	7.98	27.7	191.7	75.6	30
1994	7.61	1.31	7.83	27.6	193.6	76.1	31
1993	7.11	1.51	7.36	25.9	186.7	73.9	9
1992	7.97	2.15	8.33	26.0	178.4	73.8	9
1991	8.89	1.96	9.22	27.1	176.2	70.8	20
1990	9.54	2.10	9.89	27.9	174.8	72.2	31
1989	9.69	1.88	10.01	28.8	175.8	71.1	36
1988	8.90	1.88	9.21	28.8	168.8	70.6	61
1987	9.00	2.30	9.39	27.8	159.6	69.9	44
1986	9.76	2.64	10.22	25.7	138.9	67.1	24
1985	11.44	2.76	11.97	25.2	118.5	69.1	NA
1984	12.45	2.93	13.03	25.1	108.6	69.1	NA
1983	12.59	2.94	13.17	25.5	104.8	65.5	NA
1982	15.26	3.19	15.95	28.1	98.5	65.5	NA
1981	14.88	2.59	15.44	28.3	92.3	65.6	NA
1980	12.29	1.43	12.58	27.2	87.4	62.5	NA
1979	10.02	0.45	10.09	26.6	70.6	64.7	NA
1978	8.93	0.39	8.99	26.7	61.3	67.2	NA
New Mexico							
2010	4.77	0.81	4.88	26.4	230.8	72.1	0.4
2009	5.19	0.85	5.31	27.1	233.8	71.1	1.3
2008	6.08	0.64	6.18	26.3	227.6	80.0	NA
2007	6.48	0.57	6.57	28.8	203.5	83.9	3
2006	6.45	0.78	6.57	29.0	216.3	79.4	6
2005	5.94	0.73	6.04	29.1	206.3	80.4	9
2004	5.82	0.47	5.89	28.1	163.3	84.1	15
2003	5.83	0.52	5.91	28.1	149.1	86.0	9
2002	6.49	0.57	6.58	27.5	160.2	82.2	8
2001	6.88	0.60	6.97	27.6	150.3	81.6	5
2000	8.06	0.73	8.18	27.6	159.6	79.3	12
1999	7.33	0.91	7.47	27.4	153.5	79.1	9
1998	6.99	1.01	7.15	27.7	158.4	80.0	6
1997	7.58	1.09	7.76	26.6	146.2	79.4	14
1996	7.09	0.74	7.21	27.9	139.9	79.4	40
1995	7.02	0.65	7.12	28.7	132.7	80.1	54
1994	7.01	1.00	7.17	27.4	121.9	80.3	40
1993	7.12	1.53	7.37	25.5	116.1	78.6	6
1992	7.95	2.01	8.28	26.9	123.3	79.6	11
1991	9.27	1.97	9.61	25.6	95.5	76.9	15
1990	9.90	1.86	10.22	27.1	95.8	80.8	5
1989	9.93	2.07	10.29	27.6	87.6	81.5	18
1988	9.54	2.17	9.91	27.0	85.1	78.0	26
1987	9.22	2.66	9.66	27.3	94.5	76.1	31
1986	9.73	2.22	10.11	27.4	78.2	77.8	35
1985	11.21	2.63	11.69	26.0	66.8	81.5	NA
1984	12.29	2.58	12.78	27.2	70.9	82.0	NA
1983	12.43	2.79	12.96	27.5	75.9	77.6	NA
1982	14.56	2.33	15.04	27.5	69.9	81.3	NA
1981	14.22	1.81	14.58	28.6	72.3	74.1	NA
1980	11.27	2.20	11.68	28.5	55.6	77.7	NA
1979	9.18	2.11	9.52	28.9	50.0	83.8	NA
1978	9.44	1.90	9.76	27.4	47.0	82.7	NA

Table 2-77. Terms on Conventional Single-Family Mortgages, by State, 1978–2010—*Continued*

[Percent, years, dollars in thousands.]

Characteristics	Contract interest rate	Initial fees and charges	Effective interest rate	Term to maturity	Purchase price	Loan-to-price ratio	Adjustable-rate loans
New York							
2010	4.80	0.50	4.87	28.1	336.1	73.8	1.5
2009	5.06	0.59	5.15	28.6	374.2	73.7	1.5
2008	6.03	0.39	6.09	28.9	360.3	76.4	NA
2007	6.40	0.31	6.45	29.1	337.7	77.6	11
2006	6.44	0.25	6.47	28.6	327.7	75.1	16
2005	5.78	0.29	5.82	28.1	331.9	73.0	20
2004	5.70	0.28	5.75	27.3	298.1	73.1	23
2003	5.63	0.21	5.66	26.1	300.4	70.8	12
2002	6.47	0.20	6.50	27.5	325.8	73.4	18
2001	7.02	0.27	7.06	27.6	269.9	74.5	12
2000	8.10	0.47	8.17	27.8	237.0	74.8	19
1999	7.32	0.49	7.40	27.4	215.8	75.5	13
1998	7.03	0.81	7.16	27.7	195.5	77.8	9
1997	7.60	0.87	7.74	27.0	177.9	77.2	16
1996	7.73	0.55	7.81	26.0	163.0	75.9	17
1995	7.84	0.83	7.97	26.7	156.4	76.3	23
1994	7.47	1.02	7.64	25.5	158.9	74.7	35
1993	7.19	0.90	7.34	23.7	154.5	71.6	20
1992	8.26	1.29	8.49	24.9	150.4	72.4	14
1991	9.40	1.21	9.60	25.9	147.1	70.6	18
1990	9.94	1.40	10.18	27.0	151.0	70.5	25
1989	9.84	1.62	10.11	28.1	154.6	72.0	42
1988	8.87	1.84	9.17	27.8	155.2	72.4	65
1987	8.58	2.01	8.91	27.1	142.7	72.4	60
1986	9.79	2.21	10.18	24.9	126.3	70.0	34
1985	11.15	2.72	11.65	25.6	109.5	71.2	NA
1984	11.84	3.35	12.48	26.2	91.6	71.4	NA
1983	12.31	3.07	12.90	25.2	86.4	67.3	NA
1982	15.42	2.82	16.04	24.4	76.7	65.1	NA
1981	14.85	2.57	15.40	25.1	68.9	65.9	NA
1980	12.09	1.23	12.33	25.4	63.0	67.4	NA
1979	9.56	0.49	9.65	25.0	59.9	66.0	NA
1978	8.51	0.46	8.58	24.7	51.0	69.0	NA
North Carolina							
2010	4.74	0.78	4.85	28.6	274.6	76.3	5.0
2009	4.96	0.72	5.06	28.6	262.5	76.5	3.8
2008	5.99	0.65	6.09	28.7	258.8	78.6	NA
2007	6.32	0.55	6.40	28.9	252.0	79.6	5
2006	6.49	0.49	6.57	28.6	236.5	76.7	12
2005	5.93	0.44	5.99	28.2	228.9	74.8	21
2004	5.76	0.44	5.83	27.3	210.3	74.0	28
2003	5.72	0.45	5.79	26.5	194.7	74.2	13
2002	6.43	0.58	6.52	27.6	186.6	78.0	15
2001	6.87	0.61	6.96	28.4	179.3	81.1	9
2000	7.88	0.67	7.99	28.9	175.1	81.0	17
1999	7.11	0.81	7.24	28.5	175.4	81.0	21
1998	6.87	0.91	7.00	28.3	166.0	82.0	13
1997	7.42	1.01	7.58	28.2	162.3	81.3	27
1996	7.44	1.28	7.66	26.2	152.7	81.5	21
1995	7.67	1.15	7.85	28.1	145.4	82.0	44
1994	7.67	0.94	7.83	27.7	118.8	85.0	36
1993	6.98	1.30	7.20	25.6	124.5	81.6	11
1992	7.85	1.58	8.13	25.4	122.5	79.7	15
1991	9.11	1.14	9.30	25.0	124.7	74.4	19
1990	9.75	1.41	10.01	24.2	112.2	74.1	20
1989	9.98	1.77	10.29	24.8	106.6	76.0	27
1988	9.33	1.62	9.60	25.7	101.9	75.6	46
1987	9.20	1.74	9.51	25.1	99.6	74.7	27
1986	9.97	1.63	10.25	24.7	91.8	74.4	17
1985	11.09	2.33	11.52	25.5	77.5	77.7	NA
1984	12.34	2.16	12.76	26.1	70.9	78.2	NA
1983	12.61	1.88	12.98	25.9	74.6	76.0	NA
1982	15.01	2.16	15.50	25.4	66.2	75.0	NA
1981	14.80	1.67	15.16	24.9	60.1	73.6	NA
1980	12.68	1.43	12.96	25.7	56.4	73.7	NA
1979	10.87	1.23	11.09	26.0	52.8	76.2	NA
1978	9.43	1.30	9.65	25.3	45.8	77.7	NA

Table 2-77. Terms on Conventional Single-Family Mortgages, by State, 1978–2010—*Continued*

[Percent, years, dollars in thousands.]

Characteristics	Contract interest rate	Initial fees and charges	Effective interest rate	Term to maturity	Purchase price	Loan-to-price ratio	Adjustable-rate loans
North Dakota							
2010	4.58	0.98	4.73	23.9	203.9	70.8	5.3
2009	4.79	1.08	4.95	24.8	213.2	70.3	4.1
2008	5.63	0.98	5.78	26.6	207.3	73.3	NA
2007	5.97	1.00	6.11	29.4	190.5	76.2	8
2006	6.12	0.77	6.24	28.3	188.6	76.6	14
2005	5.55	0.68	5.65	28.3	174.3	79.0	20
2004	5.58	0.97	5.72	27.8	152.2	79.2	26
2003	5.58	0.99	5.72	27.2	142.2	80.4	17
2002	6.44	0.85	6.57	27.1	130.8	80.4	8
2001	6.88	0.87	7.02	27.3	128.4	78.1	4
2000	8.04	0.88	8.18	27.8	121.5	79.2	8
1999	7.25	1.02	7.41	26.8	119.8	78.3	6
1998	6.92	1.27	7.12	27.1	123.4	80.6	4
1997	7.46	1.17	7.66	27.0	117.0	80.2	9
1996	7.62	1.09	7.80	25.9	103.4	78.9	22
1995	7.52	0.55	7.61	25.4	93.6	82.7	27
1994	7.52	0.68	7.63	25.9	93.7	80.6	54
1993	6.82	1.23	7.02	23.3	86.4	79.5	16
1992	7.95	1.53	8.22	21.6	88.5	76.5	2
1991	9.31	2.23	9.69	26.3	84.0	71.7	3
1990	9.92	2.61	10.37	28.6	104.3	76.1	8
1989	9.81	2.96	10.32	28.0	85.3	73.4	22
1988	9.20	3.22	9.76	27.5	77.1	75.0	56
1987	9.02	3.27	9.56	27.5	72.0	76.5	42
1986	10.03	1.87	10.35	27.2	71.1	82.8	17
1985	10.67	3.01	11.20	28.3	66.8	80.2	NA
1984	11.42	3.44	12.05	28.3	58.9	84.7	NA
1983	12.90	2.19	13.34	24.2	73.7	63.8	NA
1982	14.26	1.20	14.54	21.0	51.0	68.2	NA
1981	13.62	2.13	14.25	16.5	58.0	66.9	NA
1980	13.25	1.94	13.89	17.6	49.8	74.5	NA
1979	10.43	0.97	10.61	23.5	55.5	65.5	NA
1978	9.35	1.15	9.55	22.4	55.7	75.0	NA
Ohio							
2010	4.77	0.97	4.91	27.7	210.5	75.7	0.8
2009	5.07	1.20	5.24	28.3	212.7	76.8	1.0
2008	5.97	1.16	6.14	28.8	208.0	81.2	NA
2007	6.37	0.90	6.50	29.3	221.5	81.8	3
2006	6.48	0.82	6.60	29.5	243.3	79.1	5
2005	5.90	0.60	5.98	29.1	238.3	79.0	11
2004	5.67	0.56	5.75	28.8	200.6	80.5	30
2003	5.66	0.59	5.74	28.2	200.9	80.9	14
2002	6.53	0.57	6.61	27.4	173.5	78.8	13
2001	7.03	0.56	7.11	27.7	166.0	78.6	6
2000	8.02	0.76	8.14	28.6	163.2	77.9	17
1999	7.21	0.72	7.32	28.3	155.5	79.2	14
1998	6.98	1.03	7.14	27.5	149.4	78.3	8
1997	7.54	1.08	7.72	27.6	139.8	78.0	29
1996	7.73	1.05	7.90	26.4	122.5	78.8	23
1995	8.00	0.86	8.14	27.1	108.3	80.0	17
1994	7.65	0.89	7.80	26.4	112.8	78.7	23
1993	7.14	1.48	7.40	23.5	116.3	72.4	13
1992	7.97	1.80	8.29	23.1	114.0	73.5	15
1991	9.01	1.96	9.34	25.2	103.8	74.1	22
1990	9.75	2.21	10.15	24.9	98.5	73.8	25
1989	9.86	2.35	10.28	26.3	96.2	74.7	29
1988	9.33	2.33	9.73	26.4	89.0	75.6	41
1987	9.25	2.54	9.69	25.5	84.9	75.5	31
1986	9.88	2.73	10.38	23.6	79.5	73.9	20
1985	11.36	3.05	11.94	23.9	71.6	74.1	NA
1984	12.24	3.06	12.83	25.8	67.4	76.2	NA
1983	12.19	2.95	12.76	26.6	68.0	74.5	NA
1982	14.34	3.11	15.01	25.7	65.9	72.0	NA
1981	14.17	2.76	14.75	26.9	68.3	72.6	NA
1980	12.55	2.36	13.01	26.6	58.1	72.8	NA
1979	10.70	1.70	11.01	26.3	57.3	72.6	NA
1978	9.34	1.46	9.59	25.8	50.9	73.1	NA

Table 2-77. Terms on Conventional Single-Family Mortgages, by State, 1978–2010—*Continued*

[Percent, years, dollars in thousands.]

Characteristics	Contract interest rate	Initial fees and charges	Effective interest rate	Term to maturity	Purchase price	Loan-to-price ratio	Adjustable-rate loans
Oklahoma							
2010	4.79	0.12	4.81	25.9	173.0	76.3	0.1
2009	5.21	0.26	5.24	26.4	184.1	75.4	0.4
2008	6.28	0.28	6.32	27.5	173.0	82.8	NA
2007	6.57	0.25	6.60	28.3	149.6	85.8	2
2006	6.65	0.23	6.68	27.1	144.3	82.1	5
2005	6.04	0.31	6.09	26.9	154.9	78.9	10
2004	6.00	0.39	6.06	27.2	141.7	79.7	22
2003	5.94	0.25	5.98	25.7	137.3	76.3	8
2002	6.59	0.32	6.64	26.9	134.2	82.4	8
2001	7.01	0.42	7.08	27.4	129.1	84.0	6
2000	8.19	0.76	8.31	27.9	126.3	81.2	9
1999	7.39	0.82	7.52	27.2	125.9	80.5	8
1998	7.05	0.83	7.18	27.1	117.9	81.9	4
1997	7.99	1.00	8.16	25.8	106.5	80.7	11
1996	7.83	1.10	8.01	25.1	102.3	82.3	15
1995	8.15	1.15	8.35	24.7	93.6	83.4	16
1994	8.00	1.93	8.34	25.2	101.3	82.7	25
1993	7.66	1.08	7.86	21.2	91.3	80.0	4
1992	8.31	1.86	8.66	23.2	96.6	82.5	5
1991	9.40	1.65	9.68	25.6	87.0	75.9	30
1990	9.78	1.64	10.06	26.9	109.2	74.1	22
1989	9.50	2.30	9.90	25.6	110.6	76.5	46
1988	9.20	2.61	9.64	28.1	104.4	77.1	52
1987	8.75	2.03	9.09	27.4	86.0	79.2	54
1986	9.99	1.97	10.33	26.8	86.3	78.6	32
1985	10.49	2.97	11.01	27.8	90.0	81.8	NA
1984	11.48	2.90	12.02	27.8	73.4	84.3	NA
1983	12.66	2.42	13.14	26.0	71.4	80.0	NA
1982	14.85	2.84	15.47	27.0	79.3	79.6	NA
1981	14.58	2.14	15.04	27.6	74.8	77.9	NA
1980	12.29	1.96	12.66	28.7	67.9	78.7	NA
1979	10.92	1.88	11.26	28.5	57.3	79.0	NA
1978	9.64	1.87	9.95	28.2	51.9	79.7	NA
Oregon							
2010	4.73	0.75	4.83	28.2	320.0	69.6	6.9
2009	4.96	0.66	5.05	28.5	363.4	71.2	4.6
2008	6.00	0.56	6.08	29.0	358.5	74.6	NA
2007	6.41	0.42	6.47	29.9	335.9	77.7	11
2006	6.48	0.37	6.53	29.7	323.8	74.5	28
2005	5.78	0.34	5.82	28.4	277.9	72.3	29
2004	5.68	0.33	5.72	27.7	141.7	79.7	38
2003	5.55	0.22	5.58	25.8	220.0	68.9	17
2002	6.38	0.43	6.44	26.1	214.7	69.7	16
2001	6.86	0.64	6.96	27.0	200.7	71.7	9
2000	7.59	0.72	7.70	28.8	191.2	75.4	28
1999	6.86	0.83	6.99	28.0	182.0	74.5	26
1998	6.96	0.87	7.10	27.3	179.8	73.6	9
1997	7.58	0.87	7.72	26.9	175.2	75.8	16
1996	7.48	0.93	7.63	27.6	167.6	77.9	40
1995	7.36	0.72	7.47	28.6	139.8	80.2	45
1994	6.63	0.83	6.76	28.9	131.2	80.5	60
1993	6.93	1.25	7.13	27.1	128.2	75.0	15
1992	7.84	1.46	8.08	25.9	124.0	73.3	18
1991	9.29	1.94	9.63	27.1	116.3	73.0	16
1990	9.97	1.91	10.30	27.9	106.2	74.6	24
1989	9.85	2.09	10.21	27.5	93.6	72.9	28
1988	9.16	2.16	9.53	26.9	86.3	78.3	48
1987	9.20	2.00	9.53	27.3	96.5	75.1	40
1986	9.90	2.02	10.25	27.1	96.9	75.2	27
1985	11.11	2.25	11.52	27.8	79.8	77.0	NA
1984	12.15	2.27	12.58	28.0	75.9	79.2	NA
1983	12.17	2.45	12.65	28.5	73.6	79.0	NA
1982	14.55	2.25	15.01	28.5	88.7	75.9	NA
1981	13.81	2.03	14.21	29.1	76.7	76.3	NA
1980	12.00	1.85	12.34	29.0	68.3	76.7	NA
1979	10.60	1.57	10.88	28.8	62.7	76.5	NA
1978	9.64	1.56	9.90	28.1	54.3	77.2	NA

Table 2-77. Terms on Conventional Single-Family Mortgages, by State, 1978–2010—*Continued*

[Percent, years, dollars in thousands.]

Characteristics	Contract interest rate	Initial fees and charges	Effective interest rate	Term to maturity	Purchase price	Loan-to-price ratio	Adjustable-rate loans
Pennsylvania							
2010	4.85	0.69	4.96	27.8	251.0	74.4	2.4
2009	5.16	0.60	5.25	28.1	246.7	77.7	1.4
2008	6.04	0.51	6.11	28.7	259.4	78.6	NA
2007	6.31	0.53	6.39	28.9	252.3	80.5	4
2006	6.49	0.50	6.56	28.9	280.8	76.8	8
2005	6.02	0.40	6.08	28.8	270.2	76.7	12
2004	5.85	0.38	5.91	28.0	217.6	77.8	15
2003	5.78	0.43	5.84	26.8	202.5	76.9	9
2002	6.53	0.49	6.61	26.8	182.1	76.8	9
2001	7.00	0.66	7.10	27.2	169.4	77.6	7
2000	7.97	0.92	8.11	28.3	158.2	78.8	14
1999	7.16	0.98	7.32	27.6	150.9	78.8	10
1998	6.91	1.06	7.07	27.7	150.1	79.9	6
1997	7.49	1.31	7.69	27.6	143.8	80.4	13
1996	7.43	1.51	7.67	26.7	122.2	81.0	11
1995	7.75	1.46	7.98	26.6	115.6	81.3	13
1994	7.46	1.68	7.73	26.4	121.8	80.8	23
1993	6.95	1.62	7.22	24.3	127.0	77.0	15
1992	7.95	2.31	8.34	25.4	127.8	76.3	14
1991	9.16	2.23	9.54	25.1	113.5	71.2	14
1990	9.79	2.41	10.22	24.8	111.8	72.8	18
1989	10.01	2.42	10.44	24.2	100.3	74.5	44
1988	9.53	2.40	9.95	23.8	97.7	75.1	58
1987	9.36	2.22	9.75	23.8	87.9	74.7	37
1986	9.93	2.65	10.41	23.3	79.4	73.4	23
1985	11.59	2.79	12.13	22.9	70.2	73.0	NA
1984	12.52	2.72	13.06	23.4	62.9	72.9	NA
1983	12.50	2.62	13.02	23.1	60.9	71.7	NA
1982	15.50	2.66	16.09	22.2	56.1	68.8	NA
1981	14.85	2.09	15.31	23.2	55.0	70.0	NA
1980	12.47	1.61	12.78	24.4	56.8	69.6	NA
1979	10.43	0.98	10.60	24.0	48.9	72.2	NA
1978	9.13	0.92	9.28	23.4	45.4	72.9	NA
Rhode Island							
2010	4.62	0.41	4.67	27.1	361.1	71.0	15.8
2009	4.94	0.19	4.97	28.7	324.9	74.5	0.2
2008	6.06	0.32	6.11	28.7	331.1	75.7	NA
2007	6.33	0.08	6.35	31.5	311.9	83.8	5
2006	6.31	0.19	6.34	31.0	329.5	80.9	18
2005	5.70	0.25	5.74	28.1	397.0	72.1	29
2004	5.56	0.27	5.60	28.4	315.1	71.4	39
2003	5.81	0.26	5.85	27.1	280.1	72.0	15
2002	6.49	0.44	6.56	28.5	273.9	73.3	17
2001	6.91	0.54	6.99	27.9	225.9	75.5	12
2000	8.08	0.65	8.18	28.9	199.9	77.3	17
1999	7.22	0.69	7.32	28.5	173.8	79.6	19
1998	6.96	0.83	7.09	28.5	171.1	78.8	5
1997	7.50	0.83	7.63	28.2	153.7	81.0	10
1996	7.67	0.85	7.81	26.5	150.3	76.6	16
1995	7.93	0.76	8.06	26.5	137.6	76.8	17
1994	7.62	1.20	7.82	28.3	150.1	78.0	29
1993	7.11	1.03	7.28	26.1	138.6	79.0	6
1992	8.04	1.85	8.34	27.5	130.3	81.1	8
1991	8.70	1.54	8.95	29.8	113.5	83.6	36
1990	9.58	1.33	9.81	28.8	131.4	75.5	24
1989	10.17	1.33	10.40	29.3	152.2	71.9	29
1988	9.11	1.49	9.35	28.8	140.7	74.7	67
1987	8.93	1.84	9.23	28.1	119.0	71.3	47
1986	9.92	1.90	10.25	25.6	92.0	70.7	16
1985	11.35	2.26	11.76	24.4	75.1	74.0	NA
1984	12.06	2.72	12.58	25.0	70.3	75.9	NA
1983	11.51	2.68	12.02	25.6	62.2	76.4	NA
1982	14.37	2.73	14.95	23.3	53.9	74.1	NA
1981	13.73	2.12	14.16	25.6	57.4	75.1	NA
1980	11.22	1.84	11.56	27.4	58.5	72.1	NA
1979	9.41	1.30	9.63	27.0	53.8	73.9	NA
1978	8.92	0.73	9.04	24.7	47.9	72.3	NA

Table 2-77. Terms on Conventional Single-Family Mortgages, by State, 1978–2010—*Continued*

[Percent, years, dollars in thousands.]

Characteristics	Contract interest rate	Initial fees and charges	Effective interest rate	Term to maturity	Purchase price	Loan-to-price ratio	Adjustable-rate loans
South Carolina							
2010	4.68	0.62	4.77	28.4	258.7	74.8	11.9
2009	4.93	0.53	5.00	28.5	267.1	76.4	6.2
2008	6.06	0.44	6.12	28.8	253.3	78.3	NA
2007	6.42	0.46	6.48	29.0	235.4	79.7	5
2006	6.59	0.42	6.65	28.5	220.9	76.7	13
2005	5.95	0.39	6.01	27.9	217.5	74.7	20
2004	5.71	0.39	5.77	27.6	194.7	77.4	26
2003	5.67	0.30	5.71	27.2	176.5	78.4	13
2002	6.43	0.34	6.48	27.9	163.3	81.2	11
2001	6.84	0.43	6.90	28.3	158.3	83.1	8
2000	7.98	0.60	8.07	28.8	154.1	82.9	17
1999	7.09	0.77	7.21	28.6	152.1	83.6	20
1998	6.86	0.94	7.00	28.4	142.1	83.6	15
1997	7.45	1.00	7.61	28.2	136.1	83.2	28
1996	7.48	1.06	7.66	27.1	130.5	83.0	21
1995	7.79	0.98	7.94	28.0	127.2	83.4	38
1994	7.68	0.96	7.84	27.9	111.1	85.6	38
1993	7.07	1.02	7.23	25.9	114.3	82.5	9
1992	8.10	1.54	8.37	24.8	110.7	80.0	10
1991	9.19	1.42	9.43	26.8	111.1	77.2	16
1990	9.91	1.78	10.22	26.5	108.5	77.4	16
1989	10.00	2.02	10.36	25.8	97.9	76.7	31
1988	9.01	2.06	9.35	27.7	99.6	78.7	64
1987	9.05	2.25	9.44	25.8	95.7	76.9	54
1986	9.68	2.77	10.16	25.3	88.1	78.1	42
1985	10.90	3.34	11.52	26.6	78.1	79.3	NA
1984	12.04	3.14	12.64	27.3	72.5	80.1	NA
1983	12.17	3.13	12.77	27.3	70.5	78.5	NA
1982	14.70	2.70	15.29	24.8	65.0	73.8	NA
1981	14.32	1.99	14.73	26.2	67.1	73.2	NA
1980	12.25	1.62	12.56	26.6	61.8	74.4	NA
1979	10.74	1.42	11.00	26.9	54.8	77.9	NA
1978	9.18	1.37	9.41	25.8	47.0	78.4	NA
South Dakota							
2010	4.68	1.36	4.88	27.4	210.5	76.5	4.1
2009	4.94	0.97	5.08	28.4	203.3	78.6	0.5
2008	5.91	0.87	6.04	28.0	206.0	80.3	NA
2007	6.30	0.76	6.41	28.7	189.4	80.1	4
2006	6.40	0.76	6.51	28.5	173.8	78.1	10
2005	5.72	0.71	5.83	28.6	183.3	78.4	17
2004	5.66	1.18	5.84	28.0	165.3	78.7	22
2003	5.56	1.32	5.76	27.6	167.2	78.0	16
2002	6.51	1.35	6.71	26.9	148.7	79.4	21
2001	6.91	0.97	7.06	27.1	159.2	77.7	2
2000	8.11	0.99	8.27	27.7	156.7	77.7	7
1999	7.40	0.84	7.54	26.5	139.4	79.4	8
1998	7.02	1.06	7.19	27.1	143.1	79.3	5
1997	7.72	1.13	7.92	26.6	128.4	77.7	11
1996	8.07	0.96	8.27	22.7	101.1	72.5	30
1995	8.21	0.85	8.36	24.8	97.4	77.4	36
1994	7.69	1.11	7.87	23.5	101.9	77.3	22
1993	7.07	1.03	7.25	20.6	91.3	76.9	8
1992	8.06	0.97	8.23	19.3	84.7	73.3	25
1991	9.11	0.77	9.24	19.2	83.2	74.8	34
1990	9.93	1.39	10.17	22.5	71.6	74.0	66
1989	9.69	1.09	9.88	22.1	101.3	76.4	56
1988	9.33	1.29	9.53	19.3	87.4	81.0	57
1987	8.71	2.23	9.08	21.7	52.9	75.0	62
1986	10.57	1.60	10.83	29.8	66.0	81.9	12
1985	11.96	2.44	12.58	18.1	37.4	70.5	NA
1984	12.01	4.26	12.81	29.4	56.3	85.4	NA
1983	12.97	1.00	13.16	24.9	57.2	78.5	NA
1982	NA	NA	NA	NA	NA	NA	NA
1981	13.65	2.47	14.16	27.2	48.1	69.8	NA
1980	12.43	1.96	12.81	24.9	38.1	72.4	NA
1979	9.93	1.58	10.21	25.2	54.0	65.7	NA
1978	9.27	1.19	9.47	26.0	43.4	70.7	NA

Table 2-77. Terms on Conventional Single-Family Mortgages, by State, 1978–2010—*Continued*

[Percent, years, dollars in thousands.]

Characteristics	Contract interest rate	Initial fees and charges	Effective interest rate	Term to maturity	Purchase price	Loan-to-price ratio	Adjustable-rate loans
Tennessee							
2010	4.70	0.83	4.82	25.8	231.3	73.1	5.6
2009	4.95	0.78	5.06	26.4	239.6	73.4	4.3
2008	6.03	0.63	6.12	27.5	235.1	79.1	NA
2007	6.34	0.63	6.44	28.2	203.0	81.5	6
2006	6.58	0.54	6.67	28.1	205.6	78.8	12
2005	5.96	0.43	6.02	27.6	193.4	76.3	17
2004	5.85	0.44	5.92	26.9	177.7	77.0	22
2003	5.80	0.44	5.87	26.2	173.2	76.2	10
2002	6.55	0.64	6.64	26.9	166.8	79.9	11
2001	6.95	0.72	7.06	26.9	167.3	78.6	7
2000	7.99	0.74	8.11	28.0	151.2	81.4	12
1999	7.22	0.84	7.35	27.9	157.0	81.7	13
1998	6.88	1.01	7.03	27.1	150.3	80.8	12
1997	7.47	1.13	7.65	27.6	144.3	81.0	27
1996	7.77	1.23	8.03	23.3	127.2	80.6	28
1995	8.02	1.13	8.25	23.3	133.6	79.6	35
1994	7.58	1.20	7.83	25.3	124.7	81.8	38
1993	7.34	0.87	7.52	21.2	110.4	81.5	11
1992	8.18	1.12	8.42	20.4	109.4	79.5	6
1991	9.91	1.03	10.08	22.2	98.2	77.6	14
1990	10.04	1.50	10.31	23.5	100.9	78.7	16
1989	10.53	1.90	10.87	26.2	102.7	77.5	22
1988	8.82	2.52	9.23	27.5	113.9	78.7	59
1987	8.99	2.49	9.41	26.3	101.8	77.2	42
1986	9.75	1.94	10.11	23.7	88.0	77.2	36
1985	10.71	2.49	11.16	25.0	81.2	76.8	NA
1984	11.30	2.58	11.76	27.1	71.7	82.2	NA
1983	12.40	1.98	12.78	25.1	73.1	74.2	NA
1982	14.34	1.77	14.72	20.0	66.9	66.5	NA
1981	14.98	2.14	15.43	25.5	65.8	77.0	NA
1980	12.36	2.05	12.74	26.2	62.4	75.3	NA
1979	10.76	1.87	11.09	23.7	52.0	71.8	NA
1978	9.36	1.80	9.66	25.6	47.9	76.3	NA
Texas							
2010	4.76	0.88	4.88	26.3	258.3	74.5	3.1
2009	5.04	0.56	5.12	27.3	249.5	77.9	1.5
2008	6.15	0.49	6.22	27.4	226.6	81.1	NA
2007	6.54	0.44	6.60	28.5	189.4	84.3	3
2006	6.71	0.41	6.77	28.2	188.2	81.1	8
2005	5.98	0.41	6.04	27.7	184.6	80.4	15
2004	5.94	0.37	5.99	26.3	173.5	75.7	19
2003	5.81	0.30	5.85	25.4	171.5	73.7	8
2002	6.61	0.46	6.68	25.8	170.8	74.9	8
2001	7.01	0.54	7.10	26.5	168.0	77.4	7
2000	8.03	0.77	8.16	27.7	159.7	79.5	13
1999	7.23	0.81	7.35	27.6	155.2	80.9	13
1998	6.99	0.88	7.13	26.9	144.5	80.9	8
1997	7.57	0.93	7.72	26.6	144.2	81.3	12
1996	7.66	0.82	7.79	27.0	147.0	83.4	24
1995	7.64	0.72	7.76	27.5	112.9	84.4	28
1994	7.55	0.81	7.68	27.0	105.2	84.4	26
1993	7.05	0.93	7.21	25.9	112.2	83.4	10
1992	8.02	1.30	8.24	25.9	120.4	82.1	10
1991	9.17	1.80	9.48	26.6	114.4	80.4	9
1990	9.89	2.43	10.31	26.7	119.5	78.4	7
1989	9.92	2.33	10.32	27.5	117.6	79.3	15
1988	9.48	2.73	9.95	27.4	107.3	81.8	24
1987	9.20	2.34	9.59	27.7	111.2	81.4	21
1986	9.83	2.12	10.19	26.3	110.2	79.8	20
1985	11.20	2.69	11.70	26.2	94.5	81.3	NA
1984	11.98	3.04	12.55	27.5	89.8	82.6	NA
1983	12.41	2.95	13.01	26.7	89.1	81.6	NA
1982	14.48	4.38	15.47	26.8	83.6	82.9	NA
1981	13.62	3.80	14.42	27.9	84.5	79.1	NA
1980	11.84	2.83	12.37	28.1	76.8	79.6	NA
1979	10.01	2.65	10.48	28.2	65.6	79.2	NA
1978	9.46	1.57	9.72	27.9	54.9	81.4	NA

Table 2-77. Terms on Conventional Single-Family Mortgages, by State, 1978–2010—*Continued*

[Percent, years, dollars in thousands.]

Characteristics	Contract interest rate	Initial fees and charges	Effective interest rate	Term to maturity	Purchase price	Loan-to-price ratio	Adjustable-rate loans
Utah							
2010	4.82	0.74	4.93	27.8	296.6	74.6	2.3
2009	4.99	0.80	5.10	28.2	307.9	74.9	4.0
2008	6.01	1.04	6.16	28.8	312.4	77.0	NA
2007	6.51	0.80	6.63	28.8	311.6	76.1	13
2006	6.60	0.55	6.68	29.3	290.0	75.7	30
2005	5.78	0.47	5.85	28.0	247.0	74.0	31
2004	5.59	0.53	5.67	27.6	217.5	75.3	43
2003	5.44	0.45	5.50	25.9	199.8	73.9	23
2002	6.29	0.61	6.39	25.8	206.2	72.8	20
2001	6.77	0.72	6.88	27.0	199.5	76.1	11
2000	7.27	0.80	7.39	29.1	192.6	77.9	38
1999	6.95	0.91	7.09	28.5	187.2	78.3	26
1998	6.92	1.02	7.07	27.4	181.6	76.5	8
1997	7.58	1.15	7.76	28.0	161.3	78.2	13
1996	7.68	0.86	7.83	26.9	164.3	75.6	21
1995	7.74	0.92	7.89	27.5	153.0	76.7	24
1994	7.18	1.47	7.41	27.4	158.2	77.7	34
1993	7.21	1.24	7.41	24.2	138.5	73.5	9
1992	8.09	1.41	8.33	23.2	126.1	73.9	4
1991	9.15	1.11	9.33	26.8	129.4	76.6	13
1990	9.79	1.40	10.03	28.2	133.3	75.1	17
1989	9.87	1.55	10.13	28.7	115.8	75.9	6
1988	9.24	1.50	9.48	27.9	105.3	78.6	39
1987	9.00	1.81	9.30	27.8	120.4	77.5	37
1986	10.01	2.01	10.36	25.6	105.6	72.9	4
1985	10.97	3.25	11.55	29.1	92.0	82.8	NA
1984	11.96	2.60	12.45	28.3	86.7	81.8	NA
1983	12.47	2.44	12.95	27.3	79.5	76.3	NA
1982	13.36	2.37	13.85	27.7	85.2	78.5	NA
1981	13.97	1.96	14.37	28.7	90.8	78.0	NA
1980	11.90	2.36	12.34	29.5	73.6	78.4	NA
1979	10.87	1.59	11.14	29.6	69.0	76.5	NA
1978	9.71	1.67	9.99	28.7	61.0	75.2	NA
Vermont							
2010	4.67	0.03	4.68	27.8	159.7	79.1	6.2
2009	5.13	0.17	5.15	28.0	200.7	79.8	8.6
2008	6.15	0.07	6.16	28.8	191.4	82.1	NA
2007	6.38	0.09	6.39	27.4	253.8	76.3	17
2006	6.44	0.13	6.46	28.8	221.0	77.4	18
2005	5.84	0.16	5.86	28.5	235.9	75.8	19
2004	5.66	0.07	5.67	28.2	144.4	83.8	17
2003	5.66	0.38	5.72	27.9	196.9	77.6	20
2002	6.54	0.30	6.59	27.7	175.2	76.7	16
2001	7.07	0.41	7.13	27.0	164.1	76.1	8
2000	8.03	0.50	8.11	28.6	140.4	81.1	17
1999	7.29	0.30	7.34	28.1	136.6	79.0	10
1998	7.05	0.51	7.13	28.3	137.2	80.4	3
1997	7.60	0.82	7.73	28.2	120.0	81.9	9
1996	7.80	1.06	7.96	27.8	112.8	83.8	11
1995	8.00	1.04	8.19	27.7	116.0	82.3	9
1994	7.70	1.06	7.87	27.5	121.9	77.7	25
1993	6.96	1.12	7.15	27.0	123.3	75.5	28
1992	7.72	1.53	7.97	27.7	111.3	70.9	23
1991	9.04	1.59	9.30	27.9	136.1	72.7	24
1990	9.63	1.47	9.87	28.1	121.9	69.2	29
1989	9.97	1.61	10.25	27.4	120.7	72.2	28
1988	9.36	1.94	9.68	28.1	111.2	75.3	60
1987	9.20	2.09	9.54	28.3	98.9	75.3	44
1986	9.78	1.99	10.12	27.3	86.2	71.9	18
1985	11.52	2.26	11.94	26.1	73.3	75.9	NA
1984	12.28	2.19	12.70	26.9	75.8	77.7	NA
1983	12.71	2.08	13.11	27.0	64.3	69.4	NA
1982	15.06	2.41	15.57	24.8	72.6	68.9	NA
1981	15.92	1.54	16.25	24.9	56.3	71.8	NA
1980	12.36	1.28	12.60	25.8	53.1	69.2	NA
1979	10.11	0.24	10.15	24.6	51.3	72.1	NA
1978	9.38	0.16	9.41	25.5	51.0	67.9	NA

Table 2-77. Terms on Conventional Single-Family Mortgages, by State, 1978–2010—*Continued*

[Percent, years, dollars in thousands.]

Characteristics	Contract interest rate	Initial fees and charges	Effective interest rate	Term to maturity	Purchase price	Loan-to-price ratio	Adjustable-rate loans
Virginia							
2010	4.71	0.74	4.82	28.7	417.6	73.4	3.5
2009	4.97	0.77	5.07	29.0	391.2	74.5	2.2
2008	6.02	0.73	6.13	29.1	395.0	74.8	NA
2007	6.41	0.87	6.54	29.8	397.7	77.7	7
2006	6.54	0.80	6.66	29.3	416.2	73.5	19
2005	5.93	0.58	6.01	28.6	388.9	72.4	33
2004	5.70	0.53	5.78	27.9	323.5	71.3	37
2003	5.82	0.62	5.91	27.3	294.8	71.6	13
2002	6.54	0.62	6.64	27.6	256.6	73.2	12
2001	7.02	0.76	7.13	27.9	246.0	74.2	9
2000	8.03	0.94	8.18	28.8	225.3	75.8	18
1999	7.17	1.12	7.34	28.5	211.3	77.7	17
1998	6.91	1.14	7.09	28.5	191.0	81.0	10
1997	7.45	1.36	7.66	28.3	181.4	80.9	22
1996	7.46	1.74	7.74	27.1	184.1	78.7	23
1995	7.61	1.58	7.86	27.8	180.9	79.6	32
1994	7.36	1.60	7.62	27.5	179.0	81.2	37
1993	6.90	1.34	7.11	26.7	173.4	80.2	16
1992	7.83	1.60	8.11	26.6	165.5	79.3	12
1991	8.75	2.15	9.11	27.5	169.3	76.7	20
1990	9.63	2.63	10.08	27.4	160.5	74.8	22
1989	9.52	2.40	9.92	28.3	157.7	76.4	43
1988	8.85	2.43	9.24	28.9	153.1	77.9	57
1987	9.04	2.49	9.46	28.0	142.6	77.3	28
1986	9.66	2.49	10.09	27.3	125.9	76.8	25
1985	10.59	2.84	11.10	27.4	113.4	80.1	NA
1984	11.66	2.66	12.15	28.0	101.6	81.5	NA
1983	12.11	1.72	12.44	27.1	88.5	78.5	NA
1982	14.28	2.04	14.70	28.3	91.0	77.0	NA
1981	13.85	2.27	14.32	28.6	80.0	78.4	NA
1980	12.34	1.90	12.70	28.8	82.3	74.8	NA
1979	10.54	1.68	10.84	28.5	70.2	76.0	NA
1978	9.28	1.64	9.56	27.8	60.9	76.7	NA
Washington							
2010	4.77	0.96	4.91	28.2	370.3	72.6	6.0
2009	5.00	0.69	5.10	28.7	390.3	72.5	4.5
2008	5.97	0.58	6.05	28.6	381.7	74.3	NA
2007	6.40	0.52	6.48	29.3	365.5	75.4	16
2006	6.46	0.38	6.52	29.0	357.1	72.2	29
2005	5.71	0.28	5.75	28.1	321.2	70.8	32
2004	5.55	0.39	5.60	27.6	269.5	72.9	40
2003	5.50	0.26	5.54	26.0	252.6	69.8	19
2002	6.31	0.44	6.37	26.6	245.9	71.1	20
2001	6.85	0.57	6.94	27.4	234.8	72.8	12
2000	7.59	0.66	7.69	29.1	223.0	75.8	30
1999	6.95	0.82	7.08	28.3	209.1	75.9	26
1998	6.93	0.98	7.08	27.5	194.6	75.4	9
1997	7.52	1.10	7.69	27.1	190.6	76.7	17
1996	7.47	1.07	7.64	27.9	186.3	77.8	34
1995	7.50	1.07	7.66	28.2	162.0	78.7	29
1994	6.82	1.03	6.98	28.5	150.8	79.2	55
1993	6.84	1.29	7.05	25.7	148.6	72.5	18
1992	7.92	1.69	8.22	24.9	147.1	75.1	17
1991	9.20	1.61	9.47	27.3	160.7	72.3	19
1990	10.06	1.80	10.37	28.4	144.5	73.6	23
1989	9.93	1.71	10.22	28.6	134.7	74.4	36
1988	8.88	1.80	9.17	28.6	119.0	76.1	59
1987	8.85	1.92	9.17	28.4	116.8	77.7	51
1986	9.87	2.22	10.24	28.3	109.8	77.2	22
1985	10.75	2.34	11.16	29.3	90.4	80.7	NA
1984	11.71	2.59	12.18	29.5	89.7	79.6	NA
1983	12.52	2.57	13.01	27.9	86.4	77.5	NA
1982	14.17	3.35	14.89	26.6	83.1	74.5	NA
1981	14.08	3.12	14.73	28.8	77.8	77.9	NA
1980	12.41	2.30	12.85	28.9	78.1	75.1	NA
1979	10.75	1.88	11.09	28.5	68.6	74.8	NA
1978	9.67	1.80	9.97	28.1	55.4	77.3	NA

Table 2-77. Terms on Conventional Single-Family Mortgages, by State, 1978–2010—*Continued*

[Percent, years, dollars in thousands.]

Characteristics	Contract interest rate	Initial fees and charges	Effective interest rate	Term to maturity	Purchase price	Loan-to-price ratio	Adjustable-rate loans
West Virginia							
2010	4.86	0.38	4.92	24.9	153.3	74.7	0.4
2009	5.17	0.46	5.23	25.8	160.4	78.2	0.3
2008	6.02	0.51	6.10	26.6	176.8	81.1	NA
2007	6.46	0.51	6.53	26.3	190.5	82.7	2
2006	6.53	0.58	6.62	25.5	221.8	75.1	7
2005	6.01	0.71	6.11	28.1	232.3	76.2	17
2004	5.84	0.80	5.95	27.6	187.9	78.8	25
2003	5.87	0.80	5.99	27.6	196.3	78.6	12
2002	6.65	0.68	6.76	27.4	155.1	80.8	7
2001	7.08	0.81	7.21	25.6	138.6	80.5	7
2000	8.31	0.92	8.46	25.8	109.4	78.1	14
1999	7.71	0.63	7.81	23.9	106.3	79.6	25
1998	7.04	0.49	7.11	25.7	115.7	79.5	11
1997	7.48	0.55	7.57	23.4	129.9	76.7	27
1996	7.64	0.63	7.74	25.5	128.2	82.8	30
1995	7.91	0.72	8.03	24.6	106.0	79.5	16
1994	7.79	0.56	7.89	21.7	92.0	84.5	48
1993	7.44	0.85	7.58	20.8	94.8	74.8	39
1992	7.83	1.23	8.04	23.2	121.0	79.3	75
1991	9.19	1.79	9.51	19.7	75.8	75.4	38
1990	10.42	1.77	10.75	19.9	56.5	82.0	27
1989	10.14	2.32	10.56	24.0	80.9	76.4	19
1988	9.68	2.08	10.04	25.5	83.9	78.4	28
1987	9.57	2.06	9.93	23.9	74.5	74.0	16
1986	9.97	2.20	10.39	19.3	59.1	67.4	20
1985	11.65	1.96	12.10	19.1	45.4	72.0	NA
1984	12.12	1.91	12.50	23.5	60.6	66.8	NA
1983	12.79	1.99	13.19	21.4	59.2	70.7	NA
1982	15.68	1.94	16.23	14.1	58.2	62.7	NA
1981	14.46	2.35	14.97	23.1	60.7	69.1	NA
1980	11.93	1.51	12.22	24.2	54.1	72.7	NA
1979	10.12	0.88	10.28	20.5	54.1	63.8	NA
1978	9.58	0.67	9.70	20.8	50.1	70.2	NA
Wisconsin							
2010	4.74	0.76	4.85	27.3	237.2	75.1	3.8
2009	5.06	0.51	5.14	27.9	241.6	75.2	1.7
2008	6.13	0.51	6.20	28.6	225.5	80.1	NA
2007	6.49	0.42	6.56	29.0	220.2	78.9	6
2006	6.56	0.27	6.60	28.9	228.1	76.5	15
2005	5.91	0.29	5.95	28.3	214.4	77.1	20
2004	5.75	0.39	5.81	28.7	190.0	79.1	26
2003	5.69	0.42	5.75	27.9	181.2	78.8	12
2002	6.47	0.58	6.55	27.8	172.2	79.2	13
2001	7.03	0.46	7.10	28.1	161.0	80.2	11
2000	8.06	0.56	8.15	28.7	147.3	79.7	24
1999	7.25	0.52	7.33	28.2	136.0	80.8	24
1998	7.09	0.42	7.15	26.6	143.0	78.0	12
1997	7.73	0.49	7.81	26.6	133.0	77.9	26
1996	7.77	0.59	7.87	26.6	112.5	77.8	40
1995	7.99	0.48	8.07	27.1	102.9	81.4	25
1994	7.50	0.56	7.59	22.3	111.3	80.0	53
1993	7.30	0.55	7.39	19.7	92.1	79.9	30
1992	8.18	0.90	8.38	21.6	81.8	77.1	40
1991	9.26	1.11	9.46	25.7	92.0	74.2	28
1990	9.88	1.12	10.08	25.2	94.9	75.4	43
1989	10.09	1.22	10.33	25.4	84.4	76.4	39
1988	9.42	1.27	9.64	26.4	85.7	76.7	51
1987	9.09	1.51	9.35	24.1	80.9	73.7	30
1986	9.83	1.67	10.13	23.4	72.2	75.7	17
1985	11.19	2.40	11.64	24.0	70.7	75.0	NA
1984	11.94	2.66	12.44	26.2	67.0	74.1	NA
1983	11.97	2.27	12.40	26.1	67.7	71.2	NA
1982	13.79	2.64	14.37	26.3	66.3	70.6	NA
1981	14.70	2.35	15.26	26.2	58.0	71.6	NA
1980	12.21	1.67	12.53	26.9	61.3	70.8	NA
1979	10.58	1.51	10.86	25.9	58.6	71.2	NA
1978	9.40	1.35	9.63	25.6	50.4	73.0	NA

Table 2-77. Terms on Conventional Single-Family Mortgages, by State, 1978–2010—*Continued*

[Percent, years, dollars in thousands.]

Characteristics	Contract interest rate	Initial fees and charges	Effective interest rate	Term to maturity	Purchase price	Loan-to-price ratio	Adjustable-rate loans
Wyoming							
2010	4.76	1.27	4.93	28.7	284.5	73.9	8.0
2009	4.97	1.03	5.12	28.7	275.4	75.8	3.0
2008	6.11	1.00	6.26	28.4	242.8	79.8	NA
2007	6.40	0.94	6.54	29.4	235.4	81.8	4
2006	6.55	0.84	6.67	28.2	218.3	75.9	7
2005	5.88	0.94	6.03	27.2	179.8	79.1	14
2004	5.74	1.17	5.91	28.3	167.4	80.9	29
2003	5.67	1.26	5.86	27.2	171.7	78.4	16
2002	6.56	1.21	6.74	27.7	161.9	80.1	8
2001	6.98	1.11	7.15	27.2	143.0	79.1	4
2000	8.19	1.19	8.38	28.5	151.2	78.6	9
1999	7.44	1.24	7.63	27.6	126.1	79.8	3
1998	7.07	1.20	7.26	27.0	122.9	79.5	2
1997	7.74	1.31	7.95	26.9	124.6	77.8	3
1996	7.85	0.89	7.99	25.1	130.7	74.7	3
1995	8.09	1.18	8.28	27.4	115.9	72.0	23
1994	7.35	1.81	7.65	25.6	106.4	78.1	19
1993	7.18	1.13	7.39	17.7	95.6	67.6	2
1992	7.51	2.09	7.88	22.4	88.8	76.1	16
1991	9.52	1.32	9.78	22.5	67.4	68.8	5
1990	10.52	2.00	10.88	25.3	62.4	79.7	0
1989	10.55	0.64	10.66	26.7	88.7	81.5	0
1988	10.60	1.18	10.81	20.5	48.4	65.6	0
1987	9.83	1.71	10.12	23.7	124.8	72.8	0
1986	10.05	2.26	10.45	26.1	98.8	75.7	0
1985	12.15	2.00	12.56	15.3	44.8	61.4	NA
1984	13.36	1.84	13.88	17.4	105.6	50.6	NA
1983	14.73	2.00	15.18	15.6	44.0	79.3	NA
1982	16.32	1.58	16.78	11.5	73.2	25.7	NA
1981	17.11	1.46	17.91	8.9	53.2	79.2	NA
1980	14.78	1.50	15.16	20.6	74.0	65.1	NA
1979	11.65	1.19	11.90	15.8	67.4	69.6	NA
1978	9.78	1.09	9.96	28.0	53.9	77.3	NA

NA = Not available.

Source: Federal Housing Finance Agency, Monthly Interest Rate Survey

Table 2-78. Terms on Conventional Single-Family Mortgages, All Homes, Monthly National Averages, 1973–2010

[Percent, years, dollars in thousands.]

Year and month	Contract interest rate	Initial fees and charges	Effective interest rate	Term to maturity	Mortgage loan amount	Purchase price	Loan-to-price ratio	Adjustable-rate loans
2010								
January	4.99	0.54	5.07	27.8	218.0	314.7	72.7	NA
February	5.03	0.63	5.12	27.5	208.6	292.4	74.8	NA
March	4.99	0.61	5.08	27.6	212.6	298.3	74.2	NA
April	5.02	0.63	5.12	27.6	218.8	307.4	74.3	NA
May	4.99	0.72	5.10	27.5	218.6	305.1	74.1	NA
June	4.90	0.80	5.02	27.7	219.9	309.6	74.3	NA
July	4.77	0.87	4.90	27.6	223.4	315.3	74.4	NA
August	4.63	0.81	4.74	27.5	216.7	309.6	73.3	NA
September	4.52	0.82	4.64	27.6	210.9	299.6	73.3	NA
October	4.44	0.87	4.57	28.0	215.0	310.7	72.2	NA
November	4.35	0.80	4.46	28.1	214.8	303.4	74.8	NA
December	4.52	0.80	4.63	28.4	209.5	291.0	75.6	NA
2009								
January	5.11	0.64	5.20	28.4	211.5	297.5	75.2	NA
February	5.03	0.57	5.12	28.1	208.9	296.8	74.4	NA
March	5.05	0.60	5.14	28.1	209.9	298.5	74.7	NA
April	4.88	0.57	4.96	28.3	217.0	304.0	75.1	NA
May	4.87	0.58	4.95	28.3	221.2	315.7	74.2	NA
June	5.08	0.58	5.16	28.5	233.0	330.0	74.4	NA
July	5.25	0.67	5.35	28.4	227.3	317.3	74.9	NA
August	5.23	0.67	5.33	28.1	221.8	311.6	74.6	NA
September	5.15	0.62	5.24	28.0	212.4	298.4	74.5	NA
October	5.02	0.63	5.11	28.1	211.2	297.0	74.0	NA
November	5.00	0.61	5.09	28.0	211.2	299.0	73.9	NA
December	4.92	0.62	5.01	27.4	217.8	306.4	73.9	NA
2008								
January	5.96	0.56	6.04	28.6	222.6	306.2	78.4	7
February	5.87	0.46	5.94	28.0	218.0	310.4	76.3	8
March	6.00	0.52	6.08	28.1	212.7	297.3	77.6	10
April	5.96	0.46	6.02	28.1	221.7	310.7	77.2	6
May	6.02	0.45	6.09	28.5	220.0	305.2	77.5	8
June	6.19	0.47	6.26	28.4	228.0	317.7	77.0	10
July	6.37	0.55	6.45	28.5	219.7	309.1	76.2	9
August	6.42	0.56	6.50	28.4	221.2	307.3	76.3	9
September	6.13	0.63	6.22	28.5	221.1	306.1	76.3	6
October	6.12	0.58	6.21	28.7	214.7	293.7	76.1	4
November	6.15	0.60	6.24	28.7	211.2	289.7	76.6	NA
December	5.52	0.64	5.61	28.7	218.0	302.2	75.1	NA
2007								
January	6.35	0.43	6.41	29.3	219.5	296.9	78.3	11
February	6.36	0.46	6.43	29.4	223.4	304.8	77.9	11
March	6.29	0.45	6.35	29.4	225.5	305.3	78.6	12
April	6.25	0.44	6.31	29.4	222.0	299.1	79.1	11
May	6.33	0.48	6.40	29.4	226.6	297.0	80.4	10
June	6.55	0.47	6.61	29.6	234.2	309.7	79.7	11
July	6.71	0.48	6.78	29.4	226.3	299.6	79.8	14
August	6.70	0.50	6.78	29.3	228.1	301.3	80.0	13
September	6.56	0.51	6.64	29.3	215.8	291.0	79.5	8
October	6.48	0.50	6.56	29.0	221.8	295.6	79.7	9
November	6.34	0.49	6.41	29.0	228.2	307.5	78.9	8
December	6.20	0.55	6.28	28.9	222.7	297.1	80.3	7
2006								
January	6.26	0.36	6.32	28.7	209.9	295.7	75.3	31
February	6.31	0.36	6.37	28.7	221.6	309.5	75.2	28
March	6.44	0.36	6.49	29.0	224.0	309.5	75.9	25
April	6.51	0.37	6.57	29.0	222.0	306.3	76.5	24
May	6.61	0.37	6.66	28.9	224.3	309.6	76.4	25
June	6.66	0.39	6.72	29.0	229.8	317.9	76.1	27
July	6.76	0.39	6.82	28.9	219.8	302.4	76.9	24
August	6.75	0.44	6.82	29.1	221.6	306.1	76.6	20
September	6.59	0.47	6.66	29.1	218.2	297.2	77.3	14
October	6.55	0.47	6.62	29.2	223.2	306.3	76.9	15
November	6.45	0.47	6.52	29.4	227.0	310.8	77.2	14
December	6.36	0.43	6.43	29.2	225.8	305.2	78.0	13
2005								
January	5.78	0.41	5.84	28.3	197.8	275.7	76.1	37
February	5.68	0.28	5.72	28.3	200.4	287.3	74.8	30
March	5.76	0.37	5.81	28.5	204.9	285.5	75.9	30
April	5.84	0.41	5.90	28.5	202.3	283.8	75.1	33
May	5.79	0.40	5.85	28.5	207.9	290.1	75.6	34
June	5.66	0.39	5.72	28.5	215.9	308.8	73.7	32

Table 2-78. Terms on Conventional Single-Family Mortgages, All Homes, Monthly National Averages, 1973–2010—*Continued*

[Percent, years, dollars in thousands.]

Year and month	Contract interest rate	Initial fees and charges	Effective interest rate	Term to maturity	Mortgage loan amount	Purchase price	Loan-to-price ratio	Adjustable-rate loans
July	5.68	0.36	5.73	28.5	213.1	305.1	74.4	29
August	5.81	0.35	5.86	28.5	214.4	301.9	74.8	29
September	5.86	0.39	5.92	28.6	216.4	307.1	74.4	27
October	5.98	0.35	6.03	28.6	215.5	306.8	74.1	27
November	6.19	0.40	6.25	28.7	219.6	314.4	74.1	30
December	6.29	0.41	6.35	28.8	221.3	311.1	74.8	29
2004								
January	5.58	0.49	5.66	27.4	171.8	241.8	75.3	30
February	5.67	0.39	5.73	27.1	168.5	248.0	72.4	21
March	5.42	0.37	5.47	27.1	170.4	250.6	72.3	31
April	5.38	0.35	5.43	27.5	182.3	262.1	73.7	32
May	5.72	0.35	5.77	27.6	183.2	261.0	74.1	36
June	5.91	0.38	5.97	27.8	188.8	267.6	74.1	40
July	5.88	0.37	5.94	28.3	191.0	263.8	76.1	39
August	5.78	0.44	5.84	28.3	188.6	261.6	76.4	38
September	5.63	0.49	5.70	28.4	191.0	264.9	76.1	36
October	5.66	0.43	5.73	28.3	188.9	264.5	75.9	37
November	5.70	0.40	5.75	28.4	194.2	271.9	75.7	37
December	5.78	0.39	5.83	28.4	196.5	272.2	76.4	35
2003								
January	5.93	0.37	5.98	26.7	167.5	243.6	73.2	15
February	5.87	0.31	5.92	26.8	160.2	233.5	73.4	17
March	5.75	0.28	5.79	26.6	159.9	234.6	72.9	15
April	5.70	0.32	5.75	26.7	169.0	244.1	73.8	16
May	5.59	0.35	5.64	26.7	166.2	244.3	72.7	15
June	5.37	0.33	5.42	26.7	169.4	247.8	72.6	13
July	5.36	0.37	5.41	26.6	170.8	247.4	73.9	13
August	5.62	0.40	5.68	26.9	174.6	253.9	73.3	20
September	5.88	0.43	5.95	26.9	163.8	237.9	73.6	22
October	5.79	0.39	5.85	27.3	169.9	243.8	73.8	25
November	5.80	0.47	5.87	27.5	174.5	246.7	74.6	26
December	5.70	0.52	5.77	27.5	167.5	233.9	75.7	29
2002								
January	6.81	0.52	6.89	26.9	155.7	220.2	75.3	15
February	6.77	0.50	6.84	27.2	159.2	222.0	75.9	17
March	6.76	0.45	6.83	27.4	161.5	226.1	75.8	18
April	6.85	0.49	6.92	27.7	163.1	224.1	76.8	19
May	6.71	0.51	6.79	27.9	165.8	226.3	77.0	21
June	6.59	0.52	6.67	27.9	169.1	236.9	75.7	21
July	6.46	0.50	6.53	27.7	166.5	231.5	76.1	20
August	6.30	0.47	6.37	27.5	166.0	236.2	74.7	20
September	6.22	0.45	6.28	27.3	164.5	237.6	73.9	15
October	6.08	0.40	6.14	26.7	161.0	235.7	73.3	13
November	6.02	0.37	6.08	26.5	163.5	238.5	73.3	14
December	6.03	0.39	6.09	26.6	162.4	233.0	74.0	13
2001								
January	7.23	0.58	7.32	28.5	152.5	207.8	77.0	14
February	7.08	0.57	7.17	27.9	152.5	210.0	76.5	10
March	7.01	0.58	7.10	27.8	153.7	210.9	76.7	10
April	7.00	0.53	7.09	27.5	152.3	210.0	76.4	10
May	7.08	0.58	7.17	27.6	155.1	214.6	76.1	12
June	7.09	0.54	7.17	27.7	157.6	216.6	76.6	12
July	7.09	0.54	7.18	27.8	156.5	215.3	76.5	14
August	6.99	0.52	7.07	27.9	157.9	216.5	76.7	15
September	6.86	0.48	6.93	27.8	158.7	219.9	76.0	15
October	6.66	0.46	6.73	27.5	157.5	219.6	75.8	12
November	6.56	0.45	6.62	27.0	157.6	222.7	75.1	11
December	6.69	0.52	6.77	26.6	155.7	221.7	74.6	13
2000								
January	7.70	0.71	7.82	28.7	145.4	192.0	78.9	30
February	7.86	0.69	7.97	28.6	143.9	189.8	78.9	32
March	7.92	0.68	8.02	28.7	146.9	195.2	78.4	32
April	7.92	0.66	8.03	28.7	144.2	192.0	78.3	29
May	7.99	0.68	8.10	28.8	147.5	196.0	78.4	30
June	8.05	0.68	8.16	28.8	150.9	202.5	77.6	30
July	7.98	0.66	8.09	28.8	150.1	201.7	77.6	24
August	7.91	0.66	8.01	28.7	149.2	201.2	77.3	21
September	7.81	0.69	7.92	28.6	148.8	199.9	77.6	19
October	7.75	0.64	7.85	28.5	148.0	200.8	77.2	17
November	7.67	0.63	7.77	28.6	150.9	204.8	77.1	16
December	7.54	0.63	7.64	28.5	151.7	206.1	76.8	15

Table 2-78. Terms on Conventional Single-Family Mortgages, All Homes, Monthly National Averages, 1973–2010—*Continued*

[Percent, years, dollars in thousands.]

Year and month	Contract interest rate	Initial fees and charges	Effective interest rate	Term to maturity	Mortgage loan amount	Purchase price	Loan-to-price ratio	Adjustable-rate loans
1999								
January	6.78	0.82	6.90	27.7	133.3	177.9	77.8	11
February	6.82	0.75	6.93	27.8	137.6	183.0	78.0	11
March	6.88	0.76	7.00	28.0	138.6	183.2	78.5	13
April	6.91	0.75	7.02	28.0	136.5	181.2	78.2	14
May	6.93	0.71	7.04	27.9	138.6	184.3	78.2	16
June	7.11	0.76	7.22	28.2	143.4	189.3	78.4	22
July	7.33	0.80	7.46	28.2	137.7	181.1	78.7	25
August	7.40	0.72	7.51	28.3	141.2	186.3	78.5	30
September	7.47	0.69	7.58	28.5	141.4	185.8	79.0	29
October	7.46	0.70	7.57	28.6	140.2	184.5	79.0	30
November	7.48	0.68	7.59	28.6	141.8	187.3	78.6	29
December	7.48	0.65	7.58	28.5	143.3	187.7	79.3	30
1998								
January	7.12	0.89	7.26	27.4	127.3	168.7	78.2	13
February	7.07	0.89	7.20	27.1	127.3	170.2	78.0	12
March	7.07	0.85	7.20	27.5	128.4	167.8	79.3	13
April	7.09	0.82	7.21	27.8	130.2	170.2	79.4	13
May	7.08	0.89	7.21	27.9	133.1	174.7	78.8	14
June	7.05	0.87	7.19	28.0	134.1	175.3	79.5	14
July	7.01	0.84	7.14	28.0	134.7	177.1	78.8	13
August	6.97	0.89	7.11	28.1	133.1	172.6	80.1	13
September	6.87	0.83	7.00	28.1	131.2	171.9	79.3	11
October	6.74	0.75	6.86	27.7	131.7	175.2	78.3	8
November	6.75	0.77	6.87	27.4	131.2	174.9	77.9	11
December	6.76	0.95	6.91	28.0	136.4	179.6	78.7	10
1997								
January	7.58	0.97	7.73	27.0	121.2	160.0	78.3	26
February	7.55	0.95	7.71	27.2	121.8	157.9	79.4	26
March	7.63	0.95	7.78	27.1	120.3	156.1	79.5	24
April	7.75	1.02	7.92	26.9	124.3	159.9	79.9	26
May	7.77	0.98	7.93	27.3	125.0	161.0	79.8	25
June	7.69	1.07	7.87	27.4	129.6	168.4	79.4	25
July	7.54	0.96	7.69	27.8	128.1	166.0	79.5	21
August	7.46	1.02	7.63	27.7	127.9	167.1	78.9	20
September	7.45	0.99	7.61	27.6	127.2	166.0	78.9	20
October	7.37	0.98	7.53	27.6	126.8	166.0	79.0	18
November	7.33	0.92	7.47	27.8	128.1	166.3	79.6	18
December	7.26	0.93	7.41	27.6	130.2	169.0	79.9	16
1996								
January	7.17	0.87	7.31	26.6	111.7	148.4	77.8	16
February	7.12	0.90	7.26	26.3	111.5	146.8	78.7	14
March	7.29	1.02	7.46	26.5	115.4	150.3	79.3	18
April	7.55	0.99	7.72	26.5	114.6	148.8	79.7	23
May	7.71	0.97	7.87	27.2	122.5	158.1	79.9	31
June	7.77	0.99	7.94	26.6	121.1	157.5	79.4	29
July	7.86	1.01	8.03	27.0	123.7	161.4	78.8	36
August	7.78	1.00	7.94	27.3	122.1	158.8	79.2	31
September	7.78	0.99	7.94	26.9	121.1	159.4	78.3	33
October	7.70	0.95	7.85	27.2	120.4	156.8	78.7	33
November	7.56	0.96	7.72	27.4	120.7	158.0	78.5	29
December	7.49	0.88	7.63	27.2	118.3	155.7	78.8	26
1995								
January	7.80	1.10	7.98	28.1	110.8	141.7	80.5	59
February	8.01	1.14	8.20	28.0	109.6	139.4	80.7	53
March	8.08	0.96	8.23	28.1	109.0	140.2	80.2	44
April	7.99	0.96	8.14	27.8	107.9	138.1	80.5	41
May	7.86	1.06	8.03	27.6	109.2	141.2	79.9	38
June	7.61	0.96	7.77	27.2	110.6	143.2	80.2	25
July	7.56	0.97	7.72	27.1	111.3	143.4	80.1	23
August	7.60	0.96	7.75	27.1	111.0	143.9	79.6	23
September	7.59	0.91	7.74	27.2	110.5	144.7	79.2	23
October	7.51	0.94	7.67	27.0	111.0	144.6	79.2	22
November	7.45	0.86	7.59	27.1	112.6	147.6	78.8	19
December	7.21	0.77	7.34	26.9	111.8	146.2	79.1	26
1994								
January	6.74	1.07	6.91	26.2	105.4	141.4	76.7	24
February	6.68	0.99	6.84	26.0	108.4	144.6	77.8	21
March	6.84	1.05	7.00	26.6	108.6	140.9	79.4	23
April	7.05	1.06	7.23	26.8	110.8	143.7	79.3	31
May	7.31	1.19	7.51	26.7	109.3	140.2	80.0	36
June	7.37	1.11	7.55	27.3	112.0	144.2	80.3	43

Table 2-78. Terms on Conventional Single-Family Mortgages, All Homes, Monthly National Averages, 1973–2010—*Continued*

[Percent, years, dollars in thousands.]

Year and month	Contract interest rate	Initial fees and charges	Effective interest rate	Term to maturity	Mortgage loan amount	Purchase price	Loan-to-price ratio	Adjustable-rate loans
July	7.49	1.15	7.68	27.3	110.7	141.5	80.6	42
August	7.57	1.06	7.74	27.7	109.3	140.2	80.7	43
September	7.56	1.09	7.74	27.5	109.8	140.4	80.5	46
October	7.59	1.04	7.76	27.7	110.5	141.9	80.3	49
November	7.56	1.05	7.74	27.8	110.9	141.4	80.8	55
December	7.72	1.35	7.94	27.8	111.4	143.3	80.8	55
1993								
January	7.51	1.50	7.77	25.1	107.4	143.8	77.2	25
February	7.32	1.35	7.55	25.3	110.8	151.0	76.2	22
March	7.17	1.35	7.40	25.5	106.1	142.1	76.9	19
April	7.09	1.20	7.29	24.7	105.5	142.7	76.3	23
May	7.09	1.28	7.31	24.9	102.2	133.6	78.1	20
June	7.02	1.32	7.23	25.3	108.0	146.0	77.5	23
July	6.95	1.19	7.15	25.9	108.6	143.7	77.9	18
August	6.87	1.08	7.05	25.4	106.8	143.0	76.9	16
September	6.75	1.10	6.93	25.6	106.3	140.6	77.8	17
October	6.59	1.03	6.76	25.6	107.0	144.0	76.5	18
November	1.12	6.78	26.2	108.0	145.9	77.0	19	
December	1.17	6.85	26.6	109.3	143.9	78.3	24	
1992								
January	8.05	1.32	8.28	25.7	114.3	159.7	74.0	16
February	8.18	1.61	8.48	24.9	101.1	140.7	74.5	15
March	8.15	1.64	8.44	25.3	107.6	143.9	76.6	22
April	8.26	1.72	8.55	26.1	106.4	140.9	77.6	20
May	8.22	1.64	8.50	26.5	113.1	148.9	78.1	20
June	8.06	1.67	8.35	25.7	111.9	148.2	77.6	23
July	7.78	1.46	8.04	25.5	112.5	151.4	76.6	20
August	7.60	1.77	7.91	25.0	111.2	147.9	77.3	20
September	7.48	1.54	7.74	25.3	104.4	141.4	76.2	20
October	7.44	1.40	7.68	24.9	108.0	148.4	75.4	21
November	7.54	1.57	7.82	24.9	105.1	144.3	75.7	22
December	7.55	1.50	7.81	25.0	109.1	145.1	77.8	25
1991								
January	9.53	1.54	9.80	26.3	103.0	142.1	74.4	24
February	9.46	1.58	9.73	26.1	105.5	148.4	73.8	21
March	9.25	1.45	9.50	25.6	101.2	143.1	73.6	18
April	9.24	1.71	9.53	26.4	107.3	149.0	73.7	18
May	9.23	1.66	9.52	26.8	106.2	146.1	74.3	20
June	9.13	1.57	9.39	27.2	109.1	150.0	74.6	23
July	9.12	1.72	9.41	26.5	109.4	150.2	75.1	23
August	9.11	1.59	9.38	26.7	103.9	143.2	74.5	27
September	8.93	1.52	9.19	26.6	104.8	145.5	74.4	23
October	8.79	1.46	9.03	26.2	105.8	147.7	73.8	23
November	8.42	1.55	8.68	26.2	104.7	143.9	75.4	27
December	8.26	1.52	8.51	26.2	107.5	147.0	75.4	25
1990								
January	9.66	1.84	9.97	27.6	104.6	145.5	73.9	19
February	9.73	1.83	10.04	27.1	105.0	144.1	74.6	25
March	9.73	1.95	10.07	27.3	103.8	141.3	75.2	27
April	9.82	1.89	10.15	26.9	106.8	145.3	75.3	27
May	9.84	1.90	10.17	27.0	104.4	142.8	74.8	30
June	9.85	1.85	10.16	27.3	103.5	141.5	75.0	33
July	9.83	1.79	10.14	27.2	107.1	146.2	74.7	30
August	9.71	1.72	10.01	26.7	102.8	140.6	74.6	28
September	9.69	1.71	9.98	26.3	99.7	137.7	73.9	28
October	9.67	1.71	9.96	26.5	101.0	139.6	74.2	30
November	9.69	1.62	9.97	26.6	103.2	141.1	74.9	32
December	9.56	1.58	9.83	27.5	105.6	145.7	74.3	29
1989								
January	9.30	1.83	9.61	28.2	108.4	147.1	75.2	55
February	9.46	2.07	9.81	28.0	102.3	138.6	75.2	57
March	9.63	1.92	9.95	27.9	103.8	140.2	75.6	55
April	9.78	1.82	10.09	28.3	111.0	149.5	75.8	55
May	10.06	1.97	10.40	27.6	104.8	142.2	75.5	53
June	10.23	1.89	10.56	27.8	98.9	134.5	75.2	47
July	10.09	1.88	10.41	27.9	107.5	148.3	74.5	31
August	9.82	1.83	10.13	28.1	107.8	146.2	75.2	24
September	9.85	1.88	10.17	27.2	100.6	138.1	74.5	25
October	9.85	1.80	10.16	27.0	98.7	136.8	73.8	25
November	9.81	1.84	10.13	27.3	103.3	142.6	73.9	24
December	9.70	1.77	10.00	27.5	107.4	148.7	74.1	21

Table 2-78. Terms on Conventional Single-Family Mortgages, All Homes, Monthly National Averages, 1973–2010—*Continued*

[Percent, years, dollars in thousands.]

Year and month	Contract interest rate	Initial fees and charges	Effective interest rate	Term to maturity	Mortgage loan amount	Purchase price	Loan-to-price ratio	Adjustable-rate loans
1988								
January	8.90	2.02	9.24	27.4	93.7	128.3	75.1	64
February	8.83	2.03	9.16	28.0	93.3	126.2	76.2	64
March	8.82	1.94	9.14	27.7	93.7	127.9	75.8	54
April	8.91	1.86	9.21	27.5	95.8	129.5	76.0	49
May	8.86	1.97	9.19	27.0	94.4	126.8	73.3	53
June	8.96	1.94	9.28	27.6	96.2	129.1	76.4	54
July	8.95	2.06	9.29	27.7	95.7	129.6	76.1	59
August	8.94	2.01	9.28	27.8	97.7	131.2	76.5	61
September	8.97	2.00	9.30	27.8	98.9	133.0	76.0	63
October	9.05	1.88	9.36	27.8	100.8	136.9	75.5	63
November	9.14	1.98	9.47	27.9	102.1	137.8	76.0	60
December	9.27	1.78	9.56	28.1	102.6	137.8	76.0	55
1987								
January	9.18	2.09	9.53	26.3	83.2	114.0	74.9	28
February	8.90	1.98	9.23	26.8	87.5	120.0	75.0	29
March	8.80	1.87	9.11	26.7	89.0	121.3	74.9	24
April	8.80	1.91	9.11	26.5	91.3	124.7	74.8	22
May	8.95	2.08	9.30	26.0	88.3	122.3	74.3	27
June	9.03	2.18	9.39	26.6	88.7	121.2	75.3	37
July	9.05	2.19	9.42	26.7	87.6	120.2	74.9	49
August	9.05	2.08	9.40	26.5	87.6	120.0	75.2	50
September	8.95	2.04	9.29	26.8	89.6	122.7	74.9	54
October	8.89	2.19	9.25	27.4	90.8	123.1	76.0	60
November	8.95	2.18	9.31	27.3	90.5	123.1	75.6	64
December	8.86	2.11	9.21	28.0	93.0	125.4	76.3	69
1986								
January	10.41	2.34	10.84	25.6	74.7	102.6	75.1	46
February	10.41	2.21	10.80	25.2	74.1	103.9	74.1	40
March	10.19	2.27	10.60	25.3	76.2	106.6	74.3	31
April	9.98	2.15	10.36	24.7	75.7	105.9	74.1	29
May	9.81	2.07	10.18	24.6	76.5	107.6	73.4	27
June	9.81	2.18	10.19	25.0	78.0	110.4	73.3	21
July	9.89	2.20	10.27	25.3	77.9	110.2	73.2	23
August	9.87	2.19	10.26	25.7	78.2	109.7	73.9	28
September	9.71	2.20	10.09	26.0	81.5	114.1	73.6	31
October	9.59	2.30	9.99	25.9	80.9	111.7	74.7	30
November	9.47	2.23	9.86	26.2	82.3	113.9	74.6	30
December	9.29	2.20	9.67	26.8	86.0	118.4	74.9	35
1985								
January	12.07	2.69	12.58	27.1	67.8	92.0	76.7	50
February	11.88	2.53	12.36	26.3	67.6	91.9	76.4	46
March	11.67	2.47	12.13	26.3	68.5	92.3	76.8	49
April	11.60	2.61	12.09	26.2	67.0	89.7	77.2	50
May	11.60	2.56	12.09	26.0	67.7	92.4	75.9	52
June	11.31	2.50	11.77	26.3	70.6	95.2	76.3	56
July	11.00	2.42	11.45	26.1	75.2	101.9	76.2	53
August	10.86	2.51	11.32	25.1	69.6	96.3	75.3	52
September	10.74	2.50	11.19	25.8	69.7	96.2	75.2	49
October	10.82	2.47	11.28	25.0	69.4	97.2	74.6	50
November	10.74	2.51	11.20	25.4	71.1	98.9	74.5	49
December	10.64	2.40	11.08	25.8	74.4	103.5	74.7	48
1984								
January	11.76	2.46	12.23	27.1	63.9	85.8	77.3	NA
February	11.77	2.40	12.23	26.5	65.9	88.7	77.0	NA
March	11.70	2.49	12.17	26.7	64.2	85.5	77.5	NA
April	11.59	2.53	12.07	27.1	62.7	83.1	78.0	NA
May	11.67	2.54	12.15	27.1	66.5	87.6	78.5	NA
June	11.77	2.52	12.24	27.0	65.0	86.4	77.4	NA
July	12.00	2.72	12.52	26.9	64.9	87.2	77.0	NA
August	12.17	2.69	12.69	26.8	63.5	85.5	76.6	NA
September	12.34	2.53	12.83	26.3	64.2	88.3	75.6	NA
October	12.45	2.62	12.96	26.6	62.2	84.1	76.7	NA
November	12.38	2.59	12.88	26.3	62.9	86.3	75.8	NA
December	12.23	2.65	12.75	26.4	67.4	91.5	76.2	NA
1983								
January	13.03	2.49	13.53	25.7	58.5	83.4	73.2	NA
February	12.82	2.67	13.34	26.2	59.1	82.7	73.9	NA
March	12.73	2.24	13.17	24.6	54.6	78.1	72.4	NA
April	12.34	2.29	12.78	25.7	58.4	82.3	72.8	NA
May	12.33	2.36	12.79	26.2	59.0	82.1	74.4	NA
June	12.17	2.38	12.63	26.0	57.7	80.8	73.9	NA

Table 2-78. Terms on Conventional Single-Family Mortgages, All Homes, Monthly National Averages, 1973–2010—*Continued*

[Percent, years, dollars in thousands.]

Year and month	Contract interest rate	Initial fees and charges	Effective interest rate	Term to maturity	Mortgage loan amount	Purchase price	Loan-to-price ratio	Adjustable-rate loans
July	12.15	2.39	12.61	26.5	60.7	84.7	74.1	NA
August	12.20	2.32	12.66	25.9	60.3	86.0	72.9	NA
September	12.33	2.45	12.81	26.1	61.6	84.3	75.5	NA
October	12.15	2.36	12.60	25.9	60.2	83.1	75.2	NA
November	12.07	2.46	12.55	25.9	61.3	83.0	76.2	NA
December	11.96	2.45	12.42	26.5	62.4	83.6	76.6	NA
1982								
January	15.13	2.46	15.69	26.1	57.5	83.5	71.7	NA
February	15.03	2.52	15.60	26.3	57.7	82.0	73.8	NA
March	15.03	2.78	15.67	26.3	56.1	78.8	73.9	NA
April	15.35	2.90	16.00	26.3	55.3	78.1	73.9	NA
May	15.50	2.56	16.11	23.1	49.2	74.4	68.6	NA
June	14.97	2.62	15.55	26.0	54.9	77.9	73.2	NA
July	15.00	2.73	15.60	26.1	55.2	78.6	72.6	NA
August	15.07	2.63	15.65	25.3	52.8	75.6	72.7	NA
September	14.63	2.73	15.21	26.1	56.2	78.9	74.0	NA
October	14.26	2.72	14.83	26.1	56.4	78.9	74.3	NA
November	13.62	2.66	14.17	25.8	57.3	79.3	74.9	NA
December	13.42	2.50	13.93	24.7	53.9	77.9	71.2	NA
1981								
January	13.12	2.23	13.57	27.5	53.1	73.6	75.4	NA
February	13.49	2.23	13.94	27.2	54.4	76.8	73.7	NA
March	13.76	2.41	14.25	27.4	54.3	77.3	73.6	NA
April	13.86	2.36	14.36	26.8	52.1	72.2	74.4	NA
May	14.01	2.29	14.49	26.2	51.3	71.6	73.9	NA
June	14.32	2.32	14.82	26.0	54.5	78.0	72.7	NA
July	14.57	2.47	15.10	26.9	55.8	79.6	73.1	NA
August	14.88	2.53	15.45	26.2	55.1	79.4	71.9	NA
September	15.14	2.48	15.70	25.6	53.4	76.8	72.0	NA
October	15.35	2.44	15.89	25.9	52.7	77.9	70.1	NA
November	15.75	2.52	16.37	24.6	53.1	76.6	73.2	NA
December	15.41	2.55	15.98	26.2	54.6	78.0	72.0	NA
1980								
January	11.68	1.82	12.02	27.1	48.1	69.2	71.9	NA
February	12.02	1.70	12.35	27.5	51.8	73.4	72.4	NA
March	12.42	1.75	12.75	26.9	51.5	73.1	72.3	NA
April	13.09	1.86	13.46	27.5	53.5	75.5	73.0	NA
May	13.59	2.06	14.01	27.2	51.8	75.2	71.8	NA
June	12.73	2.07	13.14	26.7	48.8	71.3	71.5	NA
July	12.21	2.00	12.59	27.6	53.2	75.9	73.0	NA
August	11.89	2.00	12.27	27.2	53.5	75.6	72.8	NA
September	11.99	2.03	12.37	27.4	54.0	76.9	72.8	NA
October	12.29	2.02	12.67	27.1	51.4	71.7	74.1	NA
November	12.77	2.07	13.18	26.7	49.7	69.8	73.9	NA
December	13.06	2.12	13.48	27.0	51.9	73.5	73.2	NA
1979								
January	10.02	1.48	10.28	27.9	49.5	68.4	74.6	NA
February	10.07	1.45	10.32	27.4	46.4	64.9	73.9	NA
March	10.16	1.50	10.43	27.1	45.4	63.8	73.9	NA
April	10.23	1.50	10.49	27.7	50.1	69.6	74.3	NA
May	10.31	1.45	10.56	27.0	45.4	63.8	73.4	NA
June	10.45	1.44	10.70	27.2	46.4	64.9	73.5	NA
July	10.63	1.44	10.89	26.7	47.8	68.2	72.6	NA
August	10.83	1.50	11.10	27.7	50.7	72.0	72.7	NA
September	10.89	1.45	11.15	27.4	50.4	71.8	73.1	NA
October	10.98	1.54	11.25	27.2	48.4	68.2	73.3	NA
November	11.17	1.65	11.47	27.6	49.9	69.5	74.1	NA
December	11.49	1.71	11.80	27.3	49.4	70.3	72.5	NA
1978								
January	8.94	1.28	9.15	26.6	38.7	53.0	74.9	NA
February	8.97	1.27	9.19	26.2	38.7	52.8	75.3	NA
March	9.03	1.27	9.24	26.5	39.3	53.7	75.2	NA
April	9.11	1.31	9.32	26.9	40.5	55.1	75.6	NA
May	9.15	1.27	9.36	26.5	39.9	54.4	75.5	NA
June	9.25	1.26	9.46	26.8	40.9	56.4	74.6	NA
July	9.38	1.31	9.60	26.8	40.7	55.9	74.7	NA
August	9.51	1.32	9.73	26.7	41.5	57.3	74.7	NA
September	9.57	1.29	9.79	26.8	42.5	59.5	73.7	NA
October	9.64	1.29	9.86	26.8	42.2	58.7	74.1	NA
November	9.70	1.35	9.94	26.9	44.1	61.3	74.4	NA
December	9.81	1.37	10.05	27.2	45.2	63.4	73.6	NA

Table 2-78. Terms on Conventional Single-Family Mortgages, All Homes, Monthly National Averages, 1973–2010—*Continued*

[Percent, years, dollars in thousands.]

Year and month	Contract interest rate	Initial fees and charges	Effective interest rate	Term to maturity	Mortgage loan amount	Purchase price	Loan-to-price ratio	Adjustable-rate loans
1977								
January	8.84	1.21	9.04	25.9	34.9	47.8	74.8	NA
February	8.79	1.27	9.00	26.1	34.9	48.0	74.6	NA
March	8.76	1.22	8.95	26.0	35.9	48.4	75.7	NA
April	8.73	1.25	8.94	26.1	35.4	47.8	75.6	NA
May	8.75	1.22	8.95	26.2	35.9	48.6	75.8	NA
June	8.78	1.21	8.98	26.2	36.0	49.2	75.1	NA
July	8.81	1.19	9.01	26.3	35.9	49.1	75.0	NA
August	8.84	1.21	9.04	26.5	36.7	50.4	74.9	NA
September	8.84	1.20	9.04	26.3	37.2	51.4	74.5	NA
October	8.87	1.22	9.07	26.1	35.7	49.0	74.6	NA
November	8.87	1.25	9.08	26.5	37.9	52.3	74.7	NA
December	8.91	1.23	9.11	26.6	37.9	52.0	74.7	NA
1976								
January	8.97	1.36	9.20	25.2	30.8	43.0	73.8	NA
February	8.95	1.31	9.17	24.6	29.5	40.6	74.2	NA
March	8.85	1.32	9.07	25.1	30.6	42.3	74.0	NA
April	8.82	1.26	9.03	25.2	30.9	42.7	73.7	NA
May	8.82	1.24	9.03	25.2	30.9	42.4	74.7	NA
June	8.79	1.17	8.99	25.1	32.4	45.0	73.5	NA
July	8.83	1.15	9.02	25.3	33.0	46.0	73.9	NA
August	8.87	1.21	9.07	25.5	32.4	44.9	74.1	NA
September	8.91	1.21	9.11	25.0	32.2	44.9	73.7	NA
October	8.90	1.19	9.10	25.3	32.4	45.0	73.6	NA
November	8.90	1.19	9.10	24.9	32.2	44.8	73.8	NA
December	8.89	1.18	9.09	25.3	33.0	45.9	73.3	NA
1975								
January	9.26	1.35	9.49	23.7	26.5	38.6	69.6	NA
February	9.12	1.34	9.35	24.5	29.0	40.4	73.2	NA
March	9.02	1.39	9.25	24.3	27.8	38.8	72.9	NA
April	8.88	1.30	9.09	25.0	30.2	41.6	73.7	NA
May	8.81	1.26	9.02	24.8	28.9	39.9	74.1	NA
June	8.85	1.21	9.05	25.0	30.2	41.8	73.9	NA
July	8.84	1.20	9.04	25.0	30.9	42.8	73.6	NA
August	8.86	1.25	9.06	25.0	30.3	41.9	74.3	NA
September	8.86	1.23	9.06	24.9	30.2	41.7	73.8	NA
October	8.91	1.29	9.13	25.1	29.9	40.8	74.8	NA
November	8.98	1.37	9.21	25.2	30.0	41.3	74.3	NA
December	8.98	1.29	9.20	24.7	29.8	41.3	73.5	NA
1974								
January	8.44	1.11	8.63	23.7	25.9	37.0	72.5	NA
February	8.45	1.16	8.64	24.1	28.2	38.7	74.0	NA
March	8.44	1.13	8.63	24.2	26.2	35.8	74.6	NA
April	8.45	1.10	8.63	23.8	25.3	35.1	73.9	NA
May	8.52	1.15	8.71	24.4	27.0	37.0	74.5	NA
June	8.67	1.20	8.87	24.3	26.8	37.1	73.6	NA
July	8.79	1.14	8.99	24.2	27.4	39.3	72.1	NA
August	8.94	1.19	9.14	24.0	26.6	38.0	72.0	NA
September	9.09	1.21	9.29	24.0	27.1	38.8	71.7	NA
October	9.24	1.33	9.47	24.2	27.1	38.9	71.7	NA
November	9.23	1.35	9.47	24.0	27.0	38.6	71.4	NA
December	9.32	1.25	9.54	23.9	26.9	38.8	71.1	NA
1973								
January	7.51	1.04	7.68	24.1	24.3	32.8	75.4	NA
February	7.54	1.06	7.71	24.5	23.6	31.1	77.8	NA
March	7.53	1.01	7.70	23.9	24.1	32.2	76.3	NA
April	7.54	1.03	7.71	24.3	24.4	32.8	75.9	NA
May	7.59	1.00	7.76	24.1	23.9	32.2	76.4	NA
June	7.62	1.00	7.78	24.2	24.8	33.6	75.6	NA
July	7.69	0.99	7.85	24.6	25.6	35.0	74.8	NA
August	7.85	0.99	8.01	24.1	25.1	34.3	75.0	NA
September	8.08	1.05	8.25	24.0	25.2	34.9	74.3	NA
October	8.26	1.03	8.44	23.3	24.3	34.2	72.6	NA
November	8.35	1.00	8.52	23.0	24.6	34.9	71.3	NA
December	8.37	0.99	8.53	22.8	24.0	33.7	72.2	NA

NA = Not available.

Source: Federal Housing Finance Agency, Monthly Interest Rate Survey

Table 2-79. Terms on Conventional Single-Family Mortgages, Newly Built Homes, Monthly National Averages, 1973–2010

[Percent, years, dollars in thousands.]

Year and month	Contract interest rate	Initial fees and charges	Effective interest rate	Term to maturity	Mortgage loan amount	Purchase price	Loan-to-price ratio	Adjustable-rate loans
2010								
January	4.91	0.92	5.04	28.5	252.5	346.4	74.2	NA
February	4.95	0.92	5.08	28.2	227.9	314.9	74.0	NA
March	4.96	0.93	5.09	28.5	228.8	317.6	72.9	NA
April	5.08	0.94	5.21	27.9	234.1	320.2	74.1	NA
May	4.99	0.91	5.12	28.6	237.5	328.1	74.3	NA
June	4.88	0.85	5.00	28.2	224.4	316.1	73.1	NA
July	4.75	0.87	4.87	28.8	266.0	374.7	73.2	NA
August	4.56	0.75	4.67	28.4	253.6	348.6	73.2	NA
September	4.42	0.73	4.52	28.7	251.0	349.7	73.1	NA
October	4.31	0.63	4.40	29.1	256.3	361.7	71.4	NA
November	4.16	0.72	4.26	28.2	237.7	328.9	73.2	NA
December	4.33	0.77	4.44	28.7	252.8	343.7	74.5	NA
2009								
January	4.98	0.92	5.11	29.0	255.1	356.6	74.7	NA
February	4.97	0.86	5.09	28.9	245.4	340.1	74.2	NA
March	4.98	0.86	5.10	29.0	244.2	336.5	75.2	NA
April	4.83	0.93	4.96	29.0	234.3	319.4	75.6	NA
May	4.78	1.00	4.92	29.0	248.7	342.7	74.1	NA
June	5.01	1.11	5.17	29.0	244.7	344.0	72.9	NA
July	5.25	1.08	5.40	29.0	240.6	328.1	75.0	NA
August	5.16	1.15	5.32	28.4	238.1	330.1	73.5	NA
September	5.11	1.06	5.26	28.5	238.2	329.6	73.8	NA
October	5.01	0.94	5.14	28.7	232.7	325.0	74.0	NA
November	4.95	0.93	5.08	28.5	225.6	312.9	73.0	NA
December	4.89	0.84	5.01	28.4	245.9	347.9	72.1	NA
2008								
January	5.90	0.78	6.02	29.0	269.5	360.2	78.6	5
February	5.87	0.66	5.96	29.2	275.9	373.1	78.1	6
March	5.80	0.80	5.92	28.8	248.6	329.8	77.9	13
April	5.89	0.64	5.98	28.9	252.4	346.3	76.4	4
May	5.92	0.67	6.01	29.2	254.2	339.4	77.3	3
June	5.99	0.91	6.13	29.1	258.3	352.7	75.6	5
July	6.15	0.94	6.29	29.3	254.8	349.1	75.5	5
August	6.18	1.03	6.33	29.1	261.2	358.1	75.2	5
September	5.93	1.07	6.09	28.6	253.4	353.5	73.9	4
October	5.97	0.91	6.10	29.3	244.4	333.7	75.2	1
November	6.03	0.82	6.16	28.7	247.7	346.4	74.0	NA
December	5.53	0.94	5.67	29.1	256.1	351.6	74.9	NA
2007								
January	6.24	0.80	6.35	29.5	267.3	368.2	75.4	9
February	6.20	0.74	6.31	29.5	270.3	361.9	76.3	16
March	6.10	0.79	6.22	29.3	270.5	369.0	75.3	10
April	6.09	0.82	6.21	29.5	268.8	368.4	76.3	10
May	6.11	0.76	6.22	29.4	265.8	355.0	77.0	10
June	6.41	0.88	6.54	29.5	267.2	357.9	76.7	10
July	6.58	0.85	6.70	29.4	270.1	356.1	77.6	15
August	6.60	0.88	6.73	29.6	282.9	368.9	78.6	15
September	6.45	0.87	6.58	29.6	266.5	358.3	76.9	8
October	6.43	0.81	6.55	29.4	266.3	350.7	78.6	9
November	6.30	0.80	6.42	29.2	273.7	366.8	77.1	6
December	6.10	0.74	6.21	29.2	268.8	347.7	79.4	8
2006								
January	6.06	0.43	6.12	28.9	243.4	337.7	74.4	48
February	6.32	0.52	6.40	29.3	248.2	338.1	75.4	27
March	6.45	0.59	6.53	29.7	254.8	341.8	76.4	25
April	6.55	0.63	6.64	29.5	248.2	335.0	76.5	20
May	6.60	0.65	6.69	29.5	255.4	350.0	75.2	22
June	6.69	0.70	6.79	29.4	258.5	355.5	75.0	22
July	6.71	0.67	6.81	29.2	253.2	346.0	75.5	23
August	6.77	0.69	6.87	29.5	248.9	343.1	74.8	20
September	6.61	0.76	6.72	29.7	255.8	347.6	75.3	14
October	6.57	0.81	6.69	29.7	257.7	349.7	75.7	15
November	6.44	0.75	6.55	29.7	260.6	354.8	75.7	13
December	6.26	0.73	6.37	29.3	255.8	348.6	74.9	11

Table 2-79. Terms on Conventional Single-Family Mortgages, Newly Built Homes, Monthly National Averages, 1973–2010—*Continued*

[Percent, years, dollars in thousands.]

Year and month	Contract interest rate	Initial fees and charges	Effective interest rate	Term to maturity	Mortgage loan amount	Purchase price	Loan-to-price ratio	Adjustable-rate loans
2005								
January	5.95	0.48	6.01	29.2	223.1	303.0	76.3	44
February	5.68	0.48	5.75	28.9	232.2	317.1	75.5	23
March	5.75	0.47	5.82	28.9	231.1	315.2	75.6	23
April	5.77	0.50	5.84	29.1	223.8	307.0	75.3	32
May	5.75	0.51	5.82	29.1	235.6	320.8	75.5	34
June	5.69	0.52	5.76	29.2	238.6	329.9	74.4	30
July	5.69	0.48	5.76	29.2	240.4	330.7	75.1	31
August	5.75	0.52	5.83	29.1	237.7	323.1	75.9	30
September	5.91	0.58	5.99	29.2	243.3	332.3	75.5	26
October	5.95	0.58	6.03	29.4	246.3	338.6	75.1	27
November	6.11	0.66	6.20	29.5	249.6	345.6	74.4	27
December	6.30	0.65	6.39	29.5	260.4	358.5	74.4	25
2004								
January	5.40	0.54	5.48	29.2	199.0	263.2	78.1	47
February	5.63	0.59	5.72	28.6	211.0	288.0	75.6	28
March	5.36	0.45	5.42	28.0	198.7	283.9	72.9	42
April	5.42	0.50	5.49	28.6	213.6	292.9	75.5	38
May	5.70	0.49	5.77	28.7	213.2	291.6	75.3	39
June	5.73	0.50	5.81	28.6	213.2	288.1	75.8	44
July	5.89	0.48	5.96	28.9	214.1	289.2	76.2	45
August	5.81	0.48	5.88	29.1	221.8	297.5	76.9	47
September	5.63	0.57	5.72	29.2	225.1	301.5	77.0	45
October	5.75	0.47	5.82	29.0	218.7	297.6	76.0	49
November	5.84	0.49	5.91	29.2	224.3	304.8	75.7	41
December	5.94	0.50	6.02	28.8	227.0	305.5	76.6	39
2003								
January	6.00	0.79	6.12	28.9	214.0	278.9	79.3	13
February	5.76	0.37	5.82	28.3	179.3	235.1	78.0	27
March	5.69	0.40	5.75	28.2	184.2	252.9	76.2	26
April	5.83	0.62	5.92	29.0	205.0	266.0	78.8	14
May	5.66	0.61	5.75	28.8	210.7	275.3	78.7	16
June	5.42	0.64	5.51	28.8	213.7	283.3	78.0	17
July	5.44	0.62	5.53	28.7	214.4	283.4	78.2	15
August	5.68	0.66	5.77	28.5	212.1	280.1	78.0	22
September	5.87	0.68	5.97	28.8	208.1	275.6	77.8	25
October	5.83	0.62	5.92	28.5	200.8	273.7	75.8	27
November	5.82	0.69	5.92	29.0	214.5	284.6	78.0	22
December	5.49	0.66	5.59	28.9	206.3	275.9	77.6	41
2002								
January	6.77	0.66	6.87	28.8	186.7	245.8	78.1	21
February	6.72	0.62	6.82	28.8	190.1	250.6	78.2	25
March	6.66	0.62	6.76	29.1	193.3	255.6	78.2	26
April	6.65	0.64	6.74	28.8	198.9	262.9	77.7	29
May	6.51	0.59	6.59	29.0	199.1	265.0	77.2	31
June	6.38	0.56	6.47	29.0	201.1	268.2	77.1	32
July	6.28	0.62	6.37	29.1	201.6	268.2	77.5	30
August	6.17	0.59	6.26	29.0	199.1	267.5	77.3	29
September	6.09	0.60	6.17	29.1	201.1	266.7	77.6	27
October	6.00	0.63	6.09	28.8	195.0	258.7	77.7	22
November	5.99	0.61	6.08	28.4	193.3	256.7	77.4	23
December	5.95	0.64	6.04	28.7	205.1	266.9	79.0	20
2001								
January	7.09	0.71	7.20	29.4	181.6	238.7	78.2	24
February	6.99	0.70	7.10	29.0	185.4	245.0	77.9	17
March	6.94	0.66	7.04	28.8	182.9	244.5	77.2	16
April	6.96	0.71	7.07	28.5	181.5	240.8	77.6	16
May	7.02	0.69	7.12	28.6	181.4	241.4	77.6	16
June	7.02	0.66	7.12	28.7	188.7	250.6	77.3	15
July	7.01	0.66	7.11	28.8	182.7	242.9	77.3	20
August	7.06	0.61	7.15	28.7	181.3	241.5	76.6	22
September	6.80	0.61	6.89	29.0	184.3	246.6	77.1	21
October	6.63	0.67	6.73	28.5	181.2	242.9	76.9	16
November	6.54	0.63	6.63	28.6	189.1	252.2	77.2	16
December	6.68	0.69	6.79	28.9	190.0	253.0	77.2	20

Table 2-79. Terms on Conventional Single-Family Mortgages, Newly Built Homes, Monthly National Averages, 1973–2010—*Continued*

[Percent, years, dollars in thousands.]

Year and month	Contract interest rate	Initial fees and charges	Effective interest rate	Term to maturity	Mortgage loan amount	Purchase price	Loan-to-price ratio	Adjustable-rate loans
2000								
January	7.34	0.75	7.45	29.1	169.9	223.7	77.9	43
February	7.43	0.71	7.54	29.1	165.6	216.9	78.4	46
March	7.49	0.68	7.60	29.0	170.7	226.0	77.7	46
April	7.52	0.68	7.63	29.1	170.2	224.2	77.9	43
May	7.44	0.71	7.55	29.2	176.3	232.2	78.0	45
June	7.40	0.69	7.50	29.2	178.3	238.6	76.9	46
July	7.41	0.66	7.51	29.3	178.3	235.8	77.7	42
August	7.44	0.68	7.54	29.3	179.7	237.0	77.7	40
September	7.41	0.70	7.52	29.2	182.5	241.9	77.1	36
October	7.43	0.69	7.53	29.2	180.4	240.2	77.2	31
November	7.36	0.69	7.47	29.2	184.2	247.2	76.2	30
December	7.29	0.73	7.40	29.1	187.3	250.0	76.5	27
1999								
January	6.81	1.01	6.96	28.4	153.3	202.3	78.0	18
February	6.78	0.92	6.92	28.7	155.4	204.1	78.2	20
March	6.74	0.82	6.86	28.8	162.9	211.0	79.4	26
April	6.74	0.77	6.85	28.9	162.4	209.4	79.5	27
May	6.78	0.69	6.89	28.7	161.6	207.5	79.8	30
June	6.92	0.72	7.03	28.6	162.0	211.0	79.0	38
July	7.16	0.83	7.29	28.5	158.2	207.6	78.6	29
August	6.99	0.68	7.09	28.5	163.1	213.8	78.3	50
September	6.99	0.64	7.09	29.1	161.8	210.3	78.8	50
October	7.06	0.71	7.17	29.1	165.1	214.4	79.0	44
November	7.13	0.73	7.24	29.0	167.0	220.8	77.4	43
December	7.18	0.71	7.28	29.0	167.2	216.3	78.6	41
1998								
January	7.13	0.91	7.27	28.5	142.3	184.1	80.5	15
February	7.09	0.99	7.24	28.0	148.5	195.3	78.6	15
March	7.03	0.95	7.17	28.3	149.5	191.7	81.0	19
April	7.05	0.87	7.19	28.4	147.1	189.5	80.4	16
May	7.05	0.85	7.18	28.3	150.2	195.6	79.1	19
June	7.03	0.85	7.16	28.3	151.0	193.7	81.0	17
July	6.99	0.90	7.13	28.5	160.1	208.7	78.7	19
August	6.95	0.87	7.09	28.6	150.4	191.5	81.3	18
September	6.85	0.85	6.98	28.7	150.8	192.7	80.9	16
October	6.72	0.86	6.85	28.6	155.8	201.4	79.8	14
November	6.68	0.76	6.80	28.3	148.1	192.1	79.5	18
December	6.80	0.98	6.94	28.7	159.0	206.0	79.4	15
1997								
January	7.65	1.02	7.81	27.9	133.6	172.4	79.7	21
February	7.61	1.03	7.78	28.2	130.9	166.6	80.9	24
March	7.72	0.99	7.88	28.0	132.1	169.2	80.8	19
April	7.86	1.04	8.03	27.8	134.8	172.5	81.1	22
May	7.85	1.00	8.01	28.2	137.7	177.6	80.0	23
June	7.79	1.04	7.95	28.0	140.6	181.4	79.9	21
July	7.62	1.05	7.78	28.7	142.7	181.4	81.2	19
August	7.42	1.06	7.59	28.2	148.2	191.2	79.8	23
September	7.43	1.12	7.61	28.3	147.0	190.6	79.3	25
October	7.39	0.94	7.54	28.1	142.4	183.4	80.1	19
November	7.26	0.95	7.40	28.6	143.5	184.0	80.8	22
December	7.25	0.96	7.40	28.2	149.8	190.7	81.0	18
1996								
January	7.15	1.07	7.32	27.7	135.8	179.2	77.3	22
February	7.00	1.24	7.20	27.8	143.2	181.7	80.3	20
March	7.25	1.30	7.49	26.4	141.5	184.5	77.8	20
April	7.57	1.17	7.76	27.1	133.2	175.2	78.4	20
May	7.61	1.16	7.80	27.2	137.6	179.5	79.3	25
June	7.75	1.31	8.05	25.8	139.4	180.1	78.7	23
July	7.80	1.25	8.01	26.7	144.2	194.0	76.2	33
August	7.85	1.38	8.08	27.2	141.1	184.8	77.7	26
September	7.77	1.28	7.98	27.7	141.7	187.1	77.2	32
October	7.76	1.11	7.95	27.4	139.0	183.9	77.7	32
November	7.60	1.19	7.80	27.4	143.3	188.1	78.0	27
December	7.63	1.01	7.79	27.5	129.9	170.8	79.3	22

Table 2-79. Terms on Conventional Single-Family Mortgages, Newly Built Homes, Monthly National Averages, 1973–2010—*Continued*

[Percent, years, dollars in thousands.]

Year and month	Contract interest rate	Initial fees and charges	Effective interest rate	Term to maturity	Mortgage loan amount	Purchase price	Loan-to-price ratio	Adjustable-rate loans
1995								
January	7.96	1.31	8.18	28.0	134.2	176.5	78.0	59
February	8.07	1.32	8.28	28.3	135.6	175.6	79.3	56
March	8.02	1.18	8.21	28.6	132.6	173.3	78.2	53
April	7.96	1.14	8.15	28.1	134.6	174.7	79.2	45
May	7.79	1.30	7.99	28.4	136.3	178.1	78.7	40
June	7.54	1.18	7.73	27.2	137.7	181.7	78.2	36
July	7.58	1.18	7.78	26.6	130.4	169.4	78.9	29
August	7.56	1.12	7.75	27.3	130.6	170.4	78.9	28
September	7.50	1.20	7.69	28.0	131.8	174.8	78.1	21
October	7.39	1.11	7.58	26.6	133.0	174.3	77.8	28
November	7.27	1.22	7.46	27.7	136.4	178.6	78.9	25
December	7.20	1.21	7.40	27.6	140.9	181.7	79.1	21
1994								
January	6.77	1.18	6.95	27.2	127.9	168.1	78.0	25
February	6.67	1.16	6.85	27.0	124.1	157.9	80.2	23
March	6.81	1.20	6.99	27.6	131.0	167.8	80.2	21
April	7.13	1.16	7.31	26.7	127.6	166.1	79.3	31
May	7.20	1.45	7.43	27.6	132.2	171.6	78.5	35
June	7.41	1.30	7.62	26.5	130.0	172.6	78.0	42
July	7.50	1.35	7.71	27.5	129.0	166.0	79.4	37
August	7.45	1.38	7.67	28.0	129.3	167.6	79.0	46
September	7.48	1.36	7.70	27.9	133.7	170.6	79.4	49
October	7.55	1.22	7.76	27.6	131.9	173.4	78.3	55
November	7.59	1.30	7.81	27.9	136.2	178.2	78.0	58
December	7.61	1.38	7.83	28.0	136.2	184.9	76.9	63
1993								
January	7.57	1.49	7.82	25.7	119.5	158.6	76.8	23
February	7.52	1.43	7.77	23.8	114.5	159.7	75.4	12
March	7.22	1.50	7.46	26.9	121.5	156.2	79.3	19
April	7.26	1.23	7.46	24.9	115.0	150.9	78.5	28
May	7.14	1.43	7.37	26.9	118.8	153.1	79.5	12
June	7.02	1.32	7.23	25.4	125.3	185.6	75.3	23
July	6.99	1.28	7.20	26.2	127.4	168.7	77.8	14
August	6.86	1.21	7.05	26.4	122.2	158.1	78.4	15
September	6.76	1.13	6.95	26.5	120.8	155.3	78.5	16
October	6.61	1.23	6.80	26.7	128.4	169.2	78.0	19
November	6.61	1.23	6.80	26.9	134.0	174.4	79.1	18
December	6.74	1.10	6.92	26.8	128.7	167.9	79.2	19
1992								
January	8.17	1.85	8.49	26.2	114.9	153.9	75.2	13
February	8.29	1.84	8.65	24.5	110.2	154.7	72.9	12
March	8.21	1.75	8.51	25.2	123.2	167.0	76.1	17
April	8.26	1.88	8.58	26.6	122.7	162.5	76.9	19
May	8.30	1.69	8.59	26.4	119.7	158.7	77.3	16
June	8.15	1.57	8.43	25.0	116.1	154.4	77.3	18
July	7.81	1.19	8.00	26.4	132.6	173.5	77.5	18
August	7.72	1.62	8.00	24.8	113.6	148.4	78.7	18
September	7.68	1.52	7.93	25.7	109.3	146.0	77.0	12
October	7.65	1.42	7.90	25.2	119.7	159.2	77.3	23
November	7.81	1.54	8.07	24.9	117.3	165.4	75.3	22
December	7.65	1.31	7.88	26.1	117.7	154.0	77.7	21
1991								
January	9.36	1.75	9.65	28.1	112.3	148.3	77.2	28
February	9.28	1.73	9.57	28.3	113.8	153.2	76.3	30
March	9.16	1.59	9.43	25.7	100.4	136.7	74.6	23
April	9.24	2.12	9.60	26.8	114.5	151.4	76.4	19
May	9.26	1.54	9.52	26.1	109.2	146.8	75.2	26
June	9.18	1.69	9.46	26.8	121.9	166.7	74.2	26
July	9.12	1.85	9.43	27.0	121.6	165.1	75.0	26
August	9.19	1.74	9.48	27.1	115.7	159.0	74.6	24
September	9.00	1.86	9.30	25.9	114.3	157.8	73.3	23
October	8.78	1.61	9.04	27.5	115.0	153.4	76.5	23
November	8.38	1.53	8.64	26.4	116.0	162.6	73.5	29
December	8.28	1.50	8.53	26.4	113.8	159.1	73.1	24

Table 2-79. Terms on Conventional Single-Family Mortgages, Newly Built Homes, Monthly National Averages, 1973–2010—*Continued*

[Percent, years, dollars in thousands.]

Year and month	Contract interest rate	Initial fees and charges	Effective interest rate	Term to maturity	Mortgage loan amount	Purchase price	Loan-to-price ratio	Adjustable-rate loans
1990								
January	9.59	1.86	9.91	27.1	107.1	148.5	73.4	24
February	9.56	1.87	9.88	27.4	109.1	148.9	74.6	29
March	9.70	1.96	10.03	26.6	100.9	138.2	74.7	25
April	9.83	2.01	10.17	26.5	114.6	155.5	75.4	27
May	9.87	2.41	10.28	28.1	119.7	162.0	75.0	27
June	9.79	1.96	10.13	26.9	111.8	149.7	76.3	42
July	9.75	1.93	10.08	28.0	120.9	163.5	75.2	33
August	9.75	2.07	10.11	27.2	118.3	161.5	74.5	25
September	9.60	1.82	9.90	27.2	114.8	156.6	74.7	32
October	9.68	1.80	9.98	26.9	105.1	146.1	73.4	37
November	9.61	1.70	9.90	27.1	111.2	151.5	74.9	38
December	9.45	1.88	9.76	28.6	115.4	156.3	74.9	37
1989								
January	9.20	1.90	9.52	28.8	121.3	165.2	75.2	57
February	9.46	2.14	9.82	28.3	111.8	153.7	73.5	58
March	9.63	2.11	9.99	27.7	117.7	159.7	74.4	50
April	9.88	1.70	10.17	28.4	124.5	169.2	75.0	47
May	9.82	2.12	10.18	28.3	112.3	151.8	75.3	57
June	10.09	1.91	10.42	27.8	111.0	150.5	75.2	53
July	10.06	2.42	10.48	28.6	125.3	174.5	73.8	22
August	9.83	2.31	10.22	28.3	119.4	160.8	75.6	19
September	9.87	2.14	10.24	28.4	118.6	160.6	75.3	15
October	9.77	1.95	10.11	27.3	111.3	153.1	73.2	29
November	9.78	1.81	10.09	27.1	110.4	152.8	73.0	26
December	9.70	2.18	10.07	27.9	119.9	162.7	74.4	18
1988								
January	8.75	2.17	9.10	28.2	108.4	150.1	74.0	68
February	8.76	2.23	9.12	28.1	104.3	139.4	76.4	69
March	8.77	2.28	9.15	27.3	106.3	147.2	75.0	55
April	8.76	2.20	9.13	27.7	112.1	151.4	76.2	52
May	8.59	2.15	8.95	28.1	108.0	145.3	76.4	59
June	8.90	2.16	9.26	27.5	110.2	152.0	73.8	57
July	8.80	2.24	9.17	28.4	111.9	152.9	75.2	63
August	8.68	2.35	9.06	28.5	114.9	154.2	76.7	66
September	8.90	2.14	9.26	27.6	109.8	148.3	75.4	63
October	8.77	1.98	9.10	28.4	114.0	153.8	75.8	72
November	9.05	2.28	9.43	28.4	115.6	155.3	76.1	60
December	9.04	2.08	9.39	28.3	110.8	150.0	75.6	63
1987								
January	9.14	2.23	9.51	27.7	97.3	132.6	75.5	25
February	8.87	2.21	9.23	27.6	99.1	135.6	75.3	22
March	8.77	2.20	9.14	27.1	95.0	130.2	74.3	22
April	8.84	2.23	9.21	27.1	100.9	136.9	75.2	19
May	8.99	2.26	9.37	28.0	99.0	132.9	76.1	25
June	9.05	2.40	9.45	28.0	97.5	131.8	75.9	34
July	9.01	2.42	9.41	27.9	99.4	134.6	75.4	45
August	9.01	2.19	9.38	27.8	102.6	141.2	75.0	47
September	9.03	2.08	9.37	27.3	100.8	140.2	74.6	49
October	8.87	2.34	9.25	28.3	106.1	145.3	75.0	60
November	8.92	2.33	9.30	28.3	100.1	135.9	75.4	65
December	8.78	2.22	9.15	28.2	107.7	147.3	74.9	73
1986								
January	10.40	2.55	10.89	25.4	77.6	108.4	74.4	43
February	10.21	2.64	10.68	26.8	84.3	115.1	75.6	45
March	10.04	2.60	10.50	26.9	79.6	108.2	75.4	34
April	9.87	2.34	10.27	25.9	83.9	114.2	75.9	29
May	9.84	2.19	10.22	25.8	82.9	114.7	74.7	27
June	9.74	2.40	10.15	26.6	88.0	122.1	74.9	21
July	9.89	2.35	10.30	26.2	83.4	115.7	73.9	23
August	9.84	2.40	10.26	26.5	84.8	117.9	74.5	26
September	9.74	2.49	10.17	27.1	90.4	124.0	75.2	21
October	9.57	2.66	10.02	27.9	93.9	127.5	75.6	24
November	9.45	2.64	9.91	27.3	92.5	124.2	76.2	24
December	9.28	2.46	9.69	27.4	93.2	124.8	76.4	31

Table 2-79. Terms on Conventional Single-Family Mortgages, Newly Built Homes, Monthly National Averages, 1973–2010—*Continued*

[Percent, years, dollars in thousands.]

Year and month	Contract interest rate	Initial fees and charges	Effective interest rate	Term to maturity	Mortgage loan amount	Purchase price	Loan-to-price ratio	Adjustable-rate loans
1985								
January	11.77	2.65	12.27	27.7	71.4	94.8	77.9	55
February	11.74	2.58	12.21	28.1	76.5	101.8	77.6	42
March	11.42	2.65	11.92	27.2	69.9	91.3	79.8	53
April	11.55	2.65	12.05	27.4	76.9	101.4	78.9	50
May	11.55	2.49	12.01	26.8	78.4	106.4	76.1	50
June	11.31	2.40	11.75	27.7	79.7	102.4	79.9	51
July	10.94	2.24	11.34	27.5	89.4	119.4	77.5	47
August	10.78	2.46	11.24	24.5	74.4	104.4	74.6	58
September	10.69	2.62	11.17	26.7	76.7	104.6	76.0	46
October	10.64	2.49	11.09	26.7	77.1	104.1	76.0	54
November	10.55	2.57	11.01	26.4	78.5	107.5	75.5	52
December	10.47	2.59	10.94	26.7	80.3	111.5	75.0	52
1984								
January	11.80	2.61	12.29	27.8	71.7	92.9	79.2	NA
February	11.78	2.41	12.23	27.3	77.8	104.1	77.8	NA
March	11.56	2.52	12.02	27.9	73.4	94.0	80.4	NA
April	11.55	2.63	12.04	28.0	71.1	92.4	79.2	NA
May	11.68	2.63	12.18	27.6	72.8	93.9	79.8	NA
June	11.61	2.58	12.10	28.1	72.5	93.4	79.9	NA
July	11.91	3.07	12.50	28.2	74.6	98.3	78.4	NA
August	11.89	2.82	12.43	28.0	71.8	94.3	78.1	NA
September	12.03	2.63	12.53	27.6	72.5	97.4	77.3	NA
October	12.27	2.58	12.77	27.6	74.0	98.4	78.2	NA
November	12.27	2.54	12.75	27.5	75.2	99.5	77.9	NA
December	12.05	2.65	12.55	28.0	76.9	102.6	77.9	NA
1983								
January	13.00	2.46	13.49	26.5	65.4	88.9	75.2	NA
February	12.62	2.78	13.16	27.2	66.6	88.4	77.9	NA
March	12.97	2.21	13.41	24.2	60.5	80.1	76.8	NA
April	12.02	2.09	12.42	26.9	66.5	89.5	74.2	NA
May	12.21	2.44	12.67	26.8	67.8	92.1	77.5	NA
June	11.90	2.43	12.36	27.3	69.2	93.0	76.9	NA
July	12.02	2.54	12.50	28.1	72.3	97.3	76.5	NA
August	12.01	1.96	12.38	25.7	67.3	94.4	73.3	NA
September	12.08	2.45	12.54	27.2	76.5	100.7	78.4	NA
October	11.80	2.33	12.25	26.9	72.5	95.8	78.4	NA
November	11.82	2.54	12.34	26.5	76.7	98.0	80.5	NA
December	11.94	2.56	12.42	27.3	73.3	94.8	79.1	NA
1982								
January	14.67	2.55	15.25	27.4	71.3	102.0	73.5	NA
February	14.44	3.01	15.12	28.1	71.1	97.3	76.5	NA
March	14.93	2.90	15.67	27.4	65.4	90.0	75.7	NA
April	15.13	3.28	15.84	28.6	70.4	95.7	77.2	NA
May	15.11	3.16	15.89	25.9	64.8	86.4	77.4	NA
June	14.74	3.00	15.40	27.4	66.2	89.4	77.0	NA
July	15.01	3.15	15.70	28.4	73.1	98.4	77.3	NA
August	15.05	2.87	15.68	26.4	66.5	91.4	74.1	NA
September	14.34	3.04	14.98	28.1	71.6	95.0	78.7	NA
October	13.86	2.74	14.41	28.4	74.4	99.1	77.9	NA
November	13.26	2.76	13.81	27.9	75.6	97.9	79.0	NA
December	13.09	2.98	13.69	26.9	67.6	91.8	75.2	NA
1981								
January	12.80	2.40	13.26	29.1	63.0	87.0	75.6	NA
February	13.02	2.59	13.54	29.0	65.6	90.3	75.6	NA
March	13.48	2.64	14.02	28.7	64.5	10.0	73.9	NA
April	13.62	2.61	14.15	28.6	64.1	88.5	74.7	NA
May	13.56	2.60	14.10	28.5	65.5	88.9	76.7	NA
June	14.12	2.50	14.67	27.5	66.8	94.1	72.6	NA
July	14.14	2.73	14.72	28.3	67.9	95.2	73.9	NA
August	14.60	2.98	15.27	27.2	70.3	98.1	74.7	NA
September	14.69	2.75	15.29	26.6	64.8	89.1	74.4	NA
October	15.04	2.86	15.65	27.4	63.5	89.2	73.0	NA
November	15.68	2.52	16.38	23.4	62.7	84.5	77.3	NA
December	15.23	2.87	15.87	27.7	64.4	88.7	75.3	NA

Table 2-79. Terms on Conventional Single-Family Mortgages, Newly Built Homes, Monthly National Averages, 1973–2010—*Continued*

[Percent, years, dollars in thousands.]

Year and month	Contract interest rate	Initial fees and charges	Effective interest rate	Term to maturity	Mortgage loan amount	Purchase price	Loan-to-price ratio	Adjustable-rate loans
1980								
January	11.48	2.11	11.87	28.1	54.4	76.9	73.0	NA
February	11.60	1.79	11.93	28.8	56.6	79.8	72.5	NA
March	12.25	1.98	12.62	27.4	55.1	77.7	72.0	NA
April	12.64	2.04	13.03	28.3	59.4	83.1	73.6	NA
May	13.26	2.17	13.68	28.8	61.3	88.0	72.4	NA
June	12.24	2.21	12.66	28.4	58.0	81.3	74.1	NA
July	12.08	2.12	12.48	28.9	64.2	90.1	73.9	NA
August	11.84	2.12	12.25	27.7	61.5	88.6	71.2	NA
September	11.95	2.10	12.35	27.6	58.7	83.7	72.2	NA
October	12.20	2.16	12.61	28.2	61.3	84.0	75.0	NA
November	12.62	2.15	13.04	27.6	56.1	77.1	75.2	NA
December	12.86	2.15	13.28	28.2	63.9	90.1	72.9	NA
1979								
January	9.92	1.56	10.18	28.6	52.0	71.9	74.7	NA
February	9.94	1.56	10.20	28.6	49.5	68.3	74.5	NA
March	10.02	1.65	10.30	28.5	49.9	68.1	75.4	NA
April	10.06	1.75	10.36	29.0	54.9	75.4	75.1	NA
May	10.20	1.59	10.47	28.2	51.4	72.3	73.2	NA
June	10.39	1.53	10.66	28.4	52.5	73.7	73.5	NA
July	10.49	1.63	10.78	28.1	52.7	74.3	73.0	NA
August	10.73	1.60	11.01	28.1	56.9	80.0	73.1	NA
September	10.72	1.67	11.02	28.6	53.9	75.5	73.4	NA
October	10.91	1.70	11.21	28.5	54.9	76.4	73.7	NA
November	11.04	1.82	11.37	28.5	55.4	77.1	73.8	NA
December	11.30	1.85	11.64	28.8	56.0	79.4	72.9	NA
1978								
January	8.93	1.41	9.15	28.3	43.3	58.0	76.4	NA
February	8.96	1.32	9.18	27.3	44.0	59.9	75.3	NA
March	9.03	1.37	9.26	27.4	43.5	58.8	75.5	NA
April	9.07	1.44	9.30	28.4	45.7	61.6	76.1	NA
May	9.14	1.34	9.37	27.7	44.2	59.8	75.5	NA
June	7.61	1.14	7.79	26.4	27.7	62.6	77.9	NA
July	7.68	1.08	7.85	26.2	27.9	61.9	77.2	NA
August	7.76	1.09	7.93	26.8	29.1	63.6	76.6	NA
September	7.99	1.18	8.17	26.6	28.3	64.6	76.9	NA
October	8.14	1.23	8.34	26.1	28.2	66.8	76.5	NA
November	8.21	1.13	8.40	25.8	28.9	65.1	75.4	NA
December	8.28	1.13	8.47	25.8	28.0	68.1	75.8	NA
1977								
January	8.82	1.38	9.05	28.2	39.0	52.5	76.3	NA
February	8.78	1.31	8.99	27.8	39.3	53.1	75.8	NA
March	8.74	1.34	8.95	28.0	40.9	53.8	77.5	NA
April	8.73	1.30	8.94	27.3	39.6	53.4	75.5	NA
May	8.74	1.34	8.96	27.9	39.9	52.8	77.4	NA
June	8.78	1.25	8.98	27.2	39.5	53.1	76.0	NA
July	8.79	1.31	9.00	27.9	40.0	53.7	76.2	NA
August	8.81	1.30	9.02	28.2	40.8	54.9	76.5	NA
September	8.82	1.34	9.04	28.2	41.7	56.0	76.3	NA
October	8.84	1.35	9.07	27.6	40.2	54.0	76.1	NA
November	8.85	1.38	9.07	28.2	42.0	56.4	76.5	NA
December	8.87	1.32	9.09	28.0	42.6	57.7	75.5	NA
1976								
January	8.72	1.80	9.01	27.7	35.9	47.8	76.9	NA
February	8.69	1.62	8.95	26.4	34.2	46.1	75.7	NA
March	8.66	1.62	8.92	27.3	35.3	47.2	76.7	NA
April	8.67	1.50	8.92	27.1	35.3	48.0	75.0	NA
May	8.74	1.39	8.97	26.9	35.9	47.2	77.4	NA
June	8.71	1.30	8.92	26.9	36.7	49.9	74.6	NA
July	8.76	1.32	8.97	27.3	37.2	50.2	75.6	NA
August	8.79	1.39	9.01	27.8	37.1	50.4	75.7	NA
September	8.85	1.40	9.07	27.6	37.4	50.7	75.3	NA
October	8.83	1.38	9.06	27.8	36.3	49.2	75.0	NA
November	8.83	1.31	9.05	26.8	36.1	48.6	75.8	NA
December	8.87	1.38	9.10	27.8	37.7	51.1	75.6	NA

Table 2-79. Terms on Conventional Single-Family Mortgages, Newly Built Homes, Monthly National Averages, 1973–2010—*Continued*

[Percent, years, dollars in thousands.]

Year and month	Contract interest rate	Initial fees and charges	Effective interest rate	Term to maturity	Mortgage loan amount	Purchase price	Loan-to-price ratio	Adjustable-rate loans
1975								
January	9.08	1.54	9.34	26.6	31.5	43.0	73.9	NA
February	8.92	1.48	9.16	26.8	33.0	44.5	76.4	NA
March	8.82	1.58	9.07	26.1	33.3	46.1	74.0	NA
April	8.69	1.57	8.94	26.8	34.2	45.7	76.2	NA
May	8.65	1.63	8.91	27.1	32.3	43.7	75.7	NA
June	8.74	1.36	8.96	26.6	32.1	42.7	76.3	NA
July	8.68	1.39	8.90	26.2	33.0	44.1	75.9	NA
August	8.64	1.58	8.90	26.9	34.1	45.3	76.9	NA
September	8.71	1.46	8.94	26.9	34.2	45.7	76.2	NA
October	8.82	1.56	9.07	27.5	32.9	43.3	77.6	NA
November	8.73	1.65	9.00	27.6	35.0	46.9	76.4	NA
December	8.75	1.66	9.02	27.9	34.7	46.1	76.6	NA
1974								
January	8.34	1.25	8.54	26.4	29.1	38.7	76.9	NA
February	8.39	1.38	8.61	26.2	28.6	38.1	76.5	NA
March	8.42	1.35	8.64	26.3	29.3	38.9	77.2	NA
April	8.45	1.25	8.65	26.3	29.2	38.5	77.3	NA
May	8.55	1.24	8.75	25.9	29.0	38.2	76.9	NA
June	8.66	1.28	8.87	26.3	29.7	39.3	76.4	NA
July	8.72	1.26	8.93	26.4	29.8	40.8	74.3	NA
August	8.88	1.32	9.10	26.2	29.4	40.2	75.0	NA
September	8.96	1.42	9.20	26.1	31.4	43.1	74.6	NA
October	8.96	1.46	9.20	26.8	31.1	42.8	74.8	NA
November	9.06	1.47	9.31	26.7	30.8	41.7	74.6	NA
December	9.18	1.39	9.41	27.7	31.6	42.5	76.2	NA
1973								
January	7.53	1.01	7.69	25.3	26.2	35.1	75.9	NA
February	7.52	1.15	7.70	26.8	27.6	35.9	78.6	NA
March	7.51	1.11	7.69	26.7	27.8	36.3	78.1	NA
April	7.55	1.09	7.72	25.8	26.9	35.2	77.8	NA
May	7.55	1.09	7.72	25.8	26.9	35.2	77.8	NA
June	7.61	1.14	7.79	26.4	27.7	36.4	77.9	NA
July	7.68	1.08	7.85	26.2	27.9	36.8	77.2	NA
August	7.76	1.09	7.93	26.8	29.1	38.8	76.6	NA
September	7.99	1.18	8.17	26.6	28.3	37.8	76.9	NA
October	8.14	1.23	8.34	26.1	28.2	37.7	76.5	NA
November	8.21	1.13	8.40	25.8	28.9	39.1	75.4	NA
December	8.28	1.13	8.47	25.8	28.0	37.7	75.8	NA

NA = Not available.

Source: Federal Housing Finance Agency, Monthly Interest Rate Survey

Table 2-80. Terms on Conventional Single-Family Mortgages, Previously Occupied Homes, Monthly National Averages, 1973–2010

[Percent, years, dollars in thousands.]

Year and month	Contract interest rate	Initial fees and charges	Effective interest rate	Term to maturity	Mortgage loan amount	Purchase price	Loan-to-price ratio	Adjustable-rate loans
2010								
January	5.01	0.47	5.08	27.6	211.4	308.7	72.4	NA
February	5.05	0.58	5.13	27.4	205.1	288.3	74.9	NA
March	4.99	0.54	5.07	27.4	209.4	294.6	74.4	NA
April	5.02	0.58	5.10	27.6	216.4	305.5	74.3	NA
May	4.99	0.69	5.09	27.3	215.5	301.4	74.1	NA
June	4.91	0.79	5.02	27.5	218.6	307.5	74.7	NA
July	4.78	0.87	4.90	27.4	214.8	303.4	74.6	NA
August	4.65	0.83	4.76	27.2	207.5	299.9	73.3	NA
September	4.55	0.86	4.68	27.3	198.5	284.2	73.4	NA
October	4.49	0.95	4.62	27.6	202.0	294.6	72.5	NA
November	4.42	0.83	4.54	28.0	205.7	293.3	75.4	NA
December	4.58	0.81	4.69	28.4	196.0	274.6	76.0	NA
2009								
January	5.12	0.61	5.21	28.3	207.9	292.6	75.2	NA
February	5.04	0.53	5.12	28.0	203.4	290.3	74.4	NA
March	5.06	0.58	5.14	28.1	208.0	296.4	74.7	NA
April	4.88	0.53	4.96	28.2	214.8	302.0	75.0	NA
May	4.88	0.53	4.95	28.2	217.7	312.2	74.2	NA
June	5.09	0.50	5.16	28.4	231.3	328.0	74.6	NA
July	5.26	0.60	5.34	28.3	225.2	315.5	74.9	NA
August	5.25	0.58	5.33	28.0	218.9	308.3	74.8	NA
September	5.16	0.55	5.24	27.9	208.1	293.1	74.6	NA
October	5.02	0.57	5.10	27.9	206.9	291.5	74.0	NA
November	5.01	0.55	5.09	27.9	208.2	296.0	74.1	NA
December	4.92	0.57	5.00	27.2	212.0	297.8	74.3	NA
2008								
January	5.97	0.50	6.04	28.5	210.3	292.1	78.3	8
February	5.87	0.43	5.94	27.8	206.7	298.1	76.0	8
March	6.03	0.49	6.10	28.0	208.9	293.8	77.5	10
April	5.97	0.42	6.03	27.9	215.5	303.5	77.4	7
May	6.04	0.41	6.10	28.3	213.1	298.3	77.6	9
June	6.23	0.38	6.28	28.3	221.6	310.3	77.3	11
July	6.41	0.47	6.48	28.3	212.4	300.9	76.4	10
August	6.46	0.46	6.53	28.3	212.8	296.7	76.6	9
September	6.17	0.52	6.25	28.5	213.5	294.8	76.9	7
October	6.16	0.50	6.23	28.6	207.4	283.9	76.4	5
November	6.18	0.53	6.26	28.7	199.6	271.6	77.4	NA
December	5.51	0.54	5.59	28.5	204.6	284.9	75.1	NA
2007								
January	6.37	0.35	6.42	29.2	208.8	281.1	79.0	12
February	6.40	0.40	6.46	29.4	212.1	291.0	78.3	10
March	6.33	0.37	6.38	29.5	214.9	290.3	79.4	12
April	6.28	0.36	6.34	29.4	212.8	285.6	79.7	11
May	6.37	0.43	6.43	29.4	219.1	286.0	81.1	10
June	6.58	0.37	6.63	29.7	226.1	297.9	80.4	11
July	6.74	0.40	6.80	29.4	217.3	287.9	80.2	14
August	6.73	0.41	6.79	29.3	214.2	284.2	80.4	13
September	6.59	0.43	6.66	29.2	203.2	274.2	80.2	9
October	6.50	0.41	6.56	28.9	209.2	280.0	80.0	9
November	6.35	0.40	6.41	28.9	215.5	291.0	79.4	9
December	6.23	0.49	6.31	28.9	207.1	280.0	80.6	7
2006								
January	6.30	0.35	6.35	28.6	204.0	288.2	75.5	28
February	6.31	0.31	6.36	28.5	213.2	300.4	75.2	28
March	6.43	0.29	6.47	28.8	213.7	298.7	75.8	26
April	6.50	0.30	6.55	28.8	214.6	298.3	76.4	25
May	6.61	0.30	6.65	28.8	215.8	298.6	76.7	26
June	6.65	0.30	6.69	28.8	221.4	306.9	76.5	28
July	6.77	0.33	6.82	28.9	212.3	292.6	77.2	24
August	6.75	0.37	6.81	29.0	214.0	295.8	77.1	20
September	6.59	0.38	6.64	29.0	207.9	283.5	77.9	14
October	6.54	0.37	6.60	29.0	213.1	293.5	77.3	16
November	6.45	0.37	6.51	29.3	215.4	295.4	77.7	15
December	6.40	0.34	6.45	29.1	216.8	292.1	78.9	13

Table 2-80. Terms on Conventional Single-Family Mortgages, Previously Occupied Homes, Monthly National Averages, 1973–2010—*Continued*

[Percent, years, dollars in thousands.]

Year and month	Contract interest rate	Initial fees and charges	Effective interest rate	Term to maturity	Mortgage loan amount	Purchase price	Loan-to-price ratio	Adjustable-rate loans
2005								
January	5.72	0.39	5.78	28.1	189.0	266.2	76.0	35
February	5.68	0.23	5.71	28.1	191.3	278.7	74.6	32
March	5.76	0.34	5.81	28.5	197.7	277.3	76.0	32
April	5.86	0.39	5.92	28.4	196.1	277.0	75.1	33
May	5.80	0.37	5.85	28.3	200.8	282.2	75.6	34
June	5.65	0.35	5.71	28.3	209.6	302.9	73.4	32
July	5.68	0.33	5.73	28.3	206.7	299.0	74.2	29
August	5.83	0.30	5.87	28.2	206.9	295.1	74.5	28
September	5.85	0.33	5.90	28.4	208.2	299.4	74.1	27
October	5.98	0.28	6.03	28.3	206.8	297.8	73.9	27
November	6.22	0.30	6.26	28.4	208.5	302.9	74.0	31
December	6.29	0.30	6.33	28.5	203.7	289.6	75.0	31
2004								
January	5.63	0.47	5.70	26.9	164.5	236.0	74.6	26
February	5.69	0.33	5.74	26.7	156.0	236.3	71.5	18
March	5.43	0.35	5.48	26.8	164.6	243.7	72.2	29
April	5.37	0.31	5.42	27.2	175.6	255.5	73.3	31
May	5.73	0.31	5.77	27.3	175.9	253.4	73.8	35
June	5.96	0.35	6.01	27.6	181.9	261.7	73.7	38
July	5.88	0.34	5.93	28.1	184.2	256.4	76.1	37
August	5.77	0.43	5.83	28.1	179.6	251.8	76.2	35
September	5.63	0.47	5.70	28.2	181.2	254.3	75.8	34
October	5.64	0.42	5.70	28.2	180.2	254.9	75.8	34
November	5.65	0.37	5.70	28.1	183.7	260.5	75.6	35
December	5.71	0.34	5.76	28.3	185.0	259.6	76.3	33
2003								
January	5.91	0.29	5.96	26.3	159.1	237.2	72.1	16
February	5.88	0.30	5.93	26.7	158.3	233.3	72.9	16
March	5.76	0.26	5.80	26.4	157.6	232.9	72.6	14
April	5.68	0.27	5.72	26.2	162.7	240.3	72.9	16
May	5.58	0.30	5.62	26.3	157.7	238.4	71.6	15
June	5.36	0.27	5.40	26.3	161.4	241.4	71.7	12
July	5.34	0.31	5.39	26.1	161.1	239.4	72.9	13
August	5.61	0.35	5.66	26.6	166.6	248.3	72.3	20
September	5.89	0.37	5.94	26.4	153.4	229.0	72.6	21
October	5.78	0.33	5.83	26.9	161.8	236.0	73.3	25
November	5.79	0.38	5.85	27.0	158.0	230.9	73.2	27
December	5.74	0.49	5.82	27.2	158.3	223.9	75.2	26
2002								
January	6.81	0.50	6.89	26.7	152.0	217.2	74.9	15
February	6.77	0.49	6.85	27.0	155.3	218.3	75.7	16
March	6.77	0.43	6.84	27.2	157.3	222.3	75.4	17
April	6.88	0.48	6.95	27.5	158.1	218.6	76.7	18
May	6.74	0.50	6.82	27.8	161.2	220.9	77.0	19
June	6.62	0.52	6.70	27.8	164.4	232.3	75.5	20
July	6.48	0.48	6.55	27.5	161.7	226.5	75.9	19
August	6.32	0.45	6.38	27.3	161.8	232.2	74.4	19
September	6.23	0.43	6.29	27.1	160.2	234.2	73.5	13
October	6.09	0.38	6.14	26.4	157.5	233.3	72.8	13
November	6.03	0.35	6.08	26.3	160.5	236.7	72.9	14
December	6.04	0.37	6.10	26.4	157.7	229.3	73.5	12
2001								
January	7.25	0.56	7.34	28.3	147.4	202.3	76.8	12
February	7.10	0.55	7.18	27.7	147.7	204.9	76.3	9
March	7.02	0.57	7.11	27.7	149.9	206.5	76.7	9
April	7.01	0.51	7.09	27.3	148.6	206.0	76.3	9
May	7.08	0.56	7.17	27.4	151.5	211.0	75.9	12
June	7.10	0.53	7.18	27.5	153.4	211.9	76.5	11
July	7.10	0.53	7.19	27.7	152.8	211.4	76.4	13
August	6.99	0.50	7.06	27.7	154.7	213.0	76.7	14
September	6.86	0.46	6.93	27.7	155.0	216.0	75.9	14
October	6.66	0.43	6.73	27.4	154.1	216.3	75.6	12
November	6.56	0.43	6.62	26.8	153.8	219.1	74.9	10
December	6.69	0.50	6.77	26.3	152.0	218.3	74.3	12

Table 2-80. Terms on Conventional Single-Family Mortgages, Previously Occupied Homes, Monthly National Averages, 1973–2010—*Continued*

[Percent, years, dollars in thousands.]

Year and month	Contract interest rate	Initial fees and charges	Effective interest rate	Term to maturity	Mortgage loan amount	Purchase price	Loan-to-price ratio	Adjustable-rate loans
2000								
January	7.79	0.71	7.90	28.5	139.8	184.8	79.1	27
February	7.95	0.69	8.06	28.5	139.1	183.8	79.0	29
March	8.01	0.67	8.11	28.6	141.8	188.6	78.6	29
April	8.00	0.66	8.10	28.6	139.5	186.1	78.4	26
May	8.08	0.67	8.19	28.7	142.5	189.7	78.4	27
June	8.17	0.68	8.27	28.7	146.1	196.1	77.8	26
July	8.09	0.66	8.20	28.7	144.7	195.2	77.6	21
August	8.00	0.66	8.10	28.5	143.2	194.3	77.3	18
September	7.89	0.69	8.00	28.5	141.8	191.2	77.7	15
October	7.81	0.63	7.91	28.4	141.3	192.6	77.2	14
November	7.73	0.61	7.83	28.4	144.2	196.2	77.2	13
December	7.59	0.62	7.68	28.3	145.3	198.2	76.9	13
1999								
January	6.77	0.79	6.89	27.5	129.9	173.7	77.7	10
February	6.82	0.73	6.93	27.7	134.6	179.5	78.0	9
March	6.91	0.75	7.02	27.9	134.7	178.7	78.4	11
April	6.94	0.75	7.05	27.8	132.0	176.4	78.0	11
May	6.96	0.72	7.07	27.8	134.1	179.7	77.8	14
June	7.14	0.77	7.26	28.1	139.7	185.0	78.3	18
July	7.35	0.80	7.48	28.2	135.1	177.8	78.8	25
August	7.48	0.72	7.59	28.3	136.8	180.8	78.5	26
September	7.57	0.70	7.68	28.4	137.5	181.0	79.0	25
October	7.56	0.70	7.67	28.5	134.3	177.5	79.0	26
November	7.56	0.67	7.66	28.5	136.5	180.3	78.9	26
December	7.55	0.63	7.65	28.4	137.1	180.3	79.5	28
1998								
January	7.26	0.93	7.41	27.5	126.4	164.8	79.7	15
February	7.12	0.88	7.26	27.2	124.5	165.8	77.8	12
March	7.06	0.88	7.20	27.0	124.1	166.5	77.9	12
April	7.07	0.83	7.20	27.4	124.8	163.7	79.0	12
May	7.09	0.81	7.21	27.7	127.4	167.0	79.2	12
June	7.08	0.89	7.22	27.8	130.4	171.4	78.8	14
July	7.06	0.88	7.19	27.9	130.8	171.8	79.3	14
August	7.01	0.83	7.14	27.9	131.2	172.7	78.8	12
September	6.98	0.90	7.11	28.0	129.2	168.4	79.8	12
October	6.88	0.82	7.00	27.9	127.4	167.9	79.0	11
November	6.77	0.77	6.89	27.3	127.9	171.7	77.6	9
December	6.76	0.95	6.90	27.9	132.6	175.1	78.6	10
1997								
January	7.55	0.95	7.71	26.6	117.3	156.1	77.8	28
February	7.53	0.93	7.69	26.9	119.3	155.5	79.0	27
March	7.61	0.95	7.76	26.9	117.7	153.3	79.2	25
April	7.73	1.01	7.90	26.7	122.2	157.3	79.7	27
May	7.75	0.97	7.91	27.2	122.6	157.8	79.7	26
June	7.67	1.07	7.85	27.3	127.5	165.8	79.3	25
July	7.52	0.95	7.68	27.7	125.2	162.9	79.1	22
August	7.47	1.01	7.63	27.6	123.9	162.4	78.7	20
September	7.46	0.97	7.61	27.4	123.3	161.2	78.8	20
October	7.37	0.98	7.53	27.4	123.6	162.5	78.8	18
November	7.34	0.91	7.48	27.6	124.8	162.4	79.4	17
December	7.26	0.93	7.41	27.5	126.4	164.8	79.7	15
1996								
January	7.18	0.84	7.31	26.5	108.4	144.2	77.9	15
February	7.13	0.86	7.27	26.2	107.4	142.3	78.4	14
March	7.29	0.99	7.45	26.6	112.0	145.7	79.5	18
April	7.55	0.97	7.71	26.4	111.9	144.8	79.9	23
May	7.72	0.94	7.88	27.2	120.1	154.7	80.0	32
June	7.77	0.94	7.93	26.7	118.4	154.2	79.4	30
July	7.87	0.97	8.03	27.0	120.6	156.6	79.2	37
August	7.76	0.93	7.92	27.4	118.8	154.2	79.5	32
September	7.78	0.93	7.94	26.8	116.9	153.7	78.5	33
October	7.68	0.91	7.83	27.2	115.8	150.2	79.0	33
November	7.55	0.89	7.70	27.4	114.4	149.6	78.7	29
December	7.45	0.85	7.59	27.2	114.8	151.2	78.7	27

Table 2-80. Terms on Conventional Single-Family Mortgages, Previously Occupied Homes, Monthly National Averages, 1973–2010—*Continued*

[Percent, years, dollars in thousands.]

Year and month	Contract interest rate	Initial fees and charges	Effective interest rate	Term to maturity	Mortgage loan amount	Purchase price	Loan-to-price ratio	Adjustable-rate loans
1995								
January	7.77	1.05	7.94	28.1	105.7	134.2	81.0	59
February	8.00	1.11	8.19	27.9	104.0	131.7	81.1	52
March	8.09	0.91	8.24	28.0	103.7	132.7	80.6	42
April	7.99	0.93	8.14	27.8	103.7	132.3	80.7	40
May	7.87	1.02	8.04	27.5	104.6	135.0	80.1	37
June	7.62	0.93	7.77	27.2	107.1	138.3	80.4	24
July	7.56	0.94	7.71	27.2	108.6	139.7	80.3	22
August	7.60	0.94	7.75	27.1	108.0	139.8	79.7	22
September	7.61	0.87	7.75	27.1	107.2	140.0	79.4	23
October	7.53	0.92	7.68	27.1	107.4	139.8	79.4	21
November	7.48	0.79	7.61	26.9	108.5	142.4	78.8	17
December	7.22	0.68	7.33	26.8	106.4	139.5	79.1	27
1994								
January	6.73	1.04	6.89	25.9	100.2	135.2	76.4	23
February	6.68	0.96	6.83	25.8	105.6	142.2	77.4	21
March	6.84	1.02	7.01	26.4	104.0	135.4	79.3	23
April	7.04	1.05	7.21	26.8	108.2	140.1	79.3	31
May	7.33	1.14	7.52	26.5	105.0	134.2	80.2	36
June	7.36	1.07	7.54	27.5	108.7	139.0	80.8	43
July	7.49	1.12	7.68	27.3	107.4	137.1	80.8	42
August	7.59	1.00	7.76	27.7	105.7	135.2	81.1	42
September	7.57	1.04	7.74	27.5	105.7	135.2	80.7	45
October	7.60	1.01	7.76	27.7	106.1	135.4	80.7	48
November	7.56	1.00	7.72	27.8	106.1	134.5	81.3	55
December	7.75	1.34	7.97	27.7	105.4	133.3	81.8	53
1993								
January	7.49	1.50	7.75	25.0	105.1	141.0	77.2	26
February	7.28	1.34	7.51	25.6	110.0	149.1	76.3	24
March	7.17	1.33	7.39	25.3	103.7	140.0	76.5	19
April	7.06	1.20	7.26	24.6	103.7	141.3	75.9	22
May	7.08	1.25	7.30	24.5	98.9	129.8	77.8	21
June	7.02	1.32	7.23	25.2	104.6	138.4	77.9	23
July	6.95	1.18	7.14	25.8	105.6	139.8	77.9	19
August	6.87	1.06	7.05	25.3	104.4	140.7	76.7	16
September	6.75	1.10	6.93	25.4	103.9	138.2	77.7	17
October	6.59	1.00	6.75	25.5	103.4	139.8	76.2	18
November	6.60	1.11	6.77	26.1	104.0	141.5	76.7	45
December	6.65	1.18	6.84	26.5	106.0	139.8	78.1	48
1992								
January	8.02	1.18	8.23	25.6	114.2	161.2	73.7	17
February	8.15	1.55	8.43	24.9	98.5	136.9	74.9	15
March	8.14	1.62	8.42	25.3	104.6	139.3	76.7	23
April	8.26	1.70	8.55	26.0	103.8	137.5	77.7	20
May	8.20	1.63	8.48	26.5	111.9	147.1	78.2	21
June	8.04	1.69	8.34	25.9	111.1	146.9	77.6	24
July	7.78	1.52	8.05	25.3	107.8	146.3	76.4	20
August	7.58	1.79	7.90	25.0	110.8	147.8	77.0	20
September	7.44	1.54	7.70	25.2	103.5	140.5	76.0	22
October	7.40	1.40	7.64	24.9	106.0	146.5	75.0	20
November	7.49	1.58	7.77	24.9	102.7	140.2	75.7	22
December	7.53	1.53	7.80	24.9	107.7	143.6	77.8	25
1991								
January	9.54	1.50	9.80	26.1	102.2	141.7	74.1	23
February	9.49	1.53	9.75	25.9	104.1	147.1	73.7	20
March	9.26	1.40	9.50	25.7	101.7	144.7	73.4	17
April	9.24	1.60	9.51	26.4	106.9	149.5	73.4	18
May	9.23	1.65	9.51	27.0	106.3	146.3	74.3	20
June	9.12	1.52	9.37	27.3	108.3	148.7	74.8	23
July	9.12	1.69	9.41	26.4	108.7	149.1	75.3	22
August	9.10	1.54	9.36	26.7	102.6	141.1	74.7	27
September	8.93	1.47	9.17	26.7	104.0	144.1	74.7	23
October	8.78	1.42	9.02	26.1	105.1	147.2	73.7	23
November	8.43	1.55	8.69	26.1	101.9	139.3	75.8	27
December	8.25	1.53	8.51	26.2	106.2	144.5	75.9	26

Table 2-80. Terms on Conventional Single-Family Mortgages, Previously Occupied Homes, Monthly National Averages, 1973–2010—*Continued*

[Percent, years, dollars in thousands.]

Year and month	Contract interest rate	Initial fees and charges	Effective interest rate	Term to maturity	Mortgage loan amount	Purchase price	Loan-to-price ratio	Adjustable-rate loans
1990								
January	9.68	1.82	9.99	27.7	104.6	145.5	74.1	17
February	9.75	1.83	10.06	27.1	104.4	143.3	74.6	23
March	9.74	1.94	10.07	27.6	103.8	140.8	75.5	27
April	9.82	1.86	10.15	27.0	106.1	144.0	75.6	27
May	9.83	1.75	10.14	26.7	101.1	138.0	75.1	30
June	9.85	1.82	10.16	27.4	102.4	140.1	75.0	31
July	9.85	1.72	10.15	27.0	104.2	142.2	74.9	28
August	9.70	1.61	9.98	26.6	98.8	134.9	74.7	27
September	9.70	1.69	10.00	26.2	98.0	135.2	74.0	25
October	9.67	1.66	9.96	26.5	100.9	138.7	74.7	29
November	9.69	1.60	9.97	26.6	101.5	138.5	75.2	30
December	9.58	1.50	9.84	27.4	104.2	144.0	74.4	27
1989								
January	9.31	1.79	9.61	28.2	106.5	143.7	75.6	55
February	9.44	1.99	9.78	27.9	100.4	134.4	76.3	58
March	9.62	1.85	9.93	28.1	99.7	133.6	76.2	56
April	9.76	1.84	10.08	28.3	107.4	144.0	76.3	57
May	10.13	1.93	10.46	27.5	103.3	139.9	75.8	51
June	10.27	1.86	10.59	27.9	96.7	131.2	75.4	45
July	10.10	1.69	10.39	27.8	103.0	140.9	75.1	32
August	9.81	1.67	10.10	28.1	104.7	142.0	75.4	24
September	9.82	1.74	10.13	26.7	93.1	128.1	74.5	27
October	9.86	1.76	10.16	27.1	97.6	134.6	74.3	22
November	9.80	1.85	10.12	27.4	102.1	140.6	74.4	22
December	9.69	1.62	9.96	27.5	104.3	145.2	74.3	21
1988								
January	8.92	1.97	9.24	27.4	90.3	122.1	75.9	65
February	8.84	1.96	9.16	28.0	90.4	122.3	76.5	63
March	8.84	1.81	9.14	27.9	90.5	122.5	76.4	53
April	8.93	1.76	9.21	27.5	91.6	123.1	76.3	48
May	8.90	1.91	9.22	26.9	90.9	121.8	76.5	51
June	8.98	1.86	9.28	27.7	93.1	123.7	77.2	54
July	8.98	2.00	9.32	27.6	92.2	124.1	76.6	58
August	9.00	1.92	9.32	27.7	94.3	126.2	76.7	60
September	8.98	1.95	9.30	27.9	96.1	128.8	76.3	63
October	9.11	1.81	9.41	27.7	98.1	132.6	75.8	61
November	9.16	1.87	9.48	27.7	98.3	132.4	76.2	60
December	9.31	1.69	9.59	28.2	101.0	134.8	76.3	54
1987								
January	9.19	2.05	9.53	26.1	79.3	108.4	75.1	28
February	8.89	1.89	9.21	26.6	84.5	115.7	75.3	30
March	8.80	1.76	9.09	26.8	87.6	118.4	75.3	24
April	8.79	1.81	9.09	26.3	89.1	121.7	74.9	22
May	8.93	2.02	9.27	25.6	86.2	120.0	74.1	27
June	9.03	2.13	9.38	26.3	86.7	118.7	75.3	38
July	9.05	2.12	9.41	26.5	85.2	117.2	74.9	50
August	9.05	2.03	9.40	26.3	84.6	115.3	75.5	51
September	8.91	2.02	9.25	26.6	86.8	118.1	75.1	56
October	8.86	2.13	9.22	27.3	87.0	117.1	76.6	61
November	8.89	2.12	9.25	27.3	88.5	119.5	76.3	65
December	8.86	2.05	9.20	28.0	88.3	118.2	76.9	69
1986								
January	10.40	2.26	10.81	25.8	74.5	101.5	75.6	47
February	10.46	2.08	10.83	24.9	71.4	100.7	74.0	38
March	10.24	2.17	10.62	25.0	75.3	105.6	74.4	30
April	10.00	2.09	10.37	24.5	74.1	104.2	73.8	29
May	9.80	2.01	10.15	24.3	75.0	106.0	73.1	36
June	9.83	2.13	10.20	24.7	76.1	108.5	72.8	20
July	9.89	2.16	10.26	25.2	76.6	108.9	73.1	22
August	9.88	2.14	10.26	25.5	77.3	108.5	73.8	28
September	9.71	2.11	10.08	25.7	78.9	111.1	73.3	34
October	9.59	2.20	9.97	25.5	78.5	108.6	74.7	32
November	9.48	2.11	9.84	25.9	79.5	110.7	74.3	32
December	9.29	2.11	9.65	26.7	83.7	116.1	74.7	36

Table 2-80. Terms on Conventional Single-Family Mortgages, Previously Occupied Homes, Monthly National Averages, 1973–2010—*Continued*

[Percent, years, dollars in thousands.]

Year and month	Contract interest rate	Initial fees and charges	Effective interest rate	Term to maturity	Mortgage loan amount	Purchase price	Loan-to-price ratio	Adjustable-rate loans
1985								
January	12.09	2.70	12.61	26.6	64.4	87.5	77.0	52
February	11.90	2.51	12.39	25.6	64.5	88.1	76.4	46
March	11.72	2.43	12.19	25.6	65.2	88.5	76.1	50
April	11.62	2.55	12.11	25.8	63.6	85.2	77.0	50
May	11.62	2.58	12.11	25.8	64.1	87.0	76.5	52
June	11.29	2.52	11.76	25.9	67.9	93.0	75.7	59
July	11.02	2.46	11.47	25.6	70.4	95.7	76.0	55
August	10.87	2.50	11.33	25.2	68.3	93.7	75.7	49
September	10.76	2.47	11.20	25.6	68.4	94.5	75.3	49
October	10.86	2.47	11.32	24.6	67.4	95.1	74.6	48
November	10.80	2.49	11.26	25.2	68.7	95.8	74.3	47
December	10.70	2.34	11.12	25.5	72.6	100.8	74.8	47
1984								
January	11.70	2.44	12.16	27.0	61.2	82.7	77.1	NA
February	11.73	2.40	12.19	26.2	60.9	81.8	77.1	NA
March	11.69	2.50	12.17	26.4	59.9	80.1	77.1	NA
April	11.61	2.47	12.07	26.8	60.1	80.0	77.9	NA
May	11.63	2.50	12.10	27.1	63.7	84.4	78.4	NA
June	11.79	2.51	12.26	26.8	63.3	84.1	77.3	NA
July	12.03	2.58	12.53	26.4	61.0	82.8	76.5	NA
August	12.24	2.65	12.75	26.5	60.8	82.4	76.3	NA
September	12.43	2.48	12.91	26.1	61.1	84.5	75.4	NA
October	12.52	2.62	13.04	26.3	57.0	77.3	76.5	NA
November	12.38	2.62	12.89	26.0	58.0	79.7	75.7	NA
December	12.26	2.62	12.77	26.1	62.2	84.3	76.1	NA
1983								
January	13.04	2.48	13.54	25.4	55.3	80.5	72.6	NA
February	12.88	2.65	13.40	25.8	55.7	79.3	72.9	NA
March	12.61	2.27	13.05	25.2	52.6	74.7	72.4	NA
April	12.42	2.34	12.88	25.4	55.6	78.9	72.8	NA
May	12.36	2.32	12.82	26.2	56.5	79.0	73.9	NA
June	12.21	2.36	12.67	25.8	55.5	77.9	74.0	NA
July	12.18	2.35	12.63	26.2	58.2	81.6	73.8	NA
August	12.25	2.42	12.72	26.1	58.5	83.2	73.4	NA
September	12.38	2.45	12.85	25.8	57.1	78.6	75.1	NA
October	12.19	2.39	12.65	25.9	56.7	78.8	75.2	NA
November	12.11	2.45	12.58	25.8	56.9	77.7	75.9	NA
December	11.94	2.41	12.39	26.4	58.6	79.2	76.2	NA
1982								
January	15.37	2.44	15.92	25.3	47.6	70.0	70.6	NA
February	15.22	2.31	15.73	25.5	50.3	72.7	72.7	NA
March	15.07	2.71	15.65	25.8	50.5	71.1	73.4	NA
April	15.39	2.73	16.00	25.3	47.8	69.1	72.5	NA
May	15.57	2.33	16.11	22.3	42.9	69.3	65.1	NA
June	15.01	2.47	15.56	25.4	49.5	71.2	72.2	NA
July	14.96	2.60	15.52	25.2	49.2	71.1	71.6	NA
August	15.03	2.56	15.59	24.9	47.7	69.2	72.5	NA
September	14.71	2.64	15.27	25.4	49.7	71.4	72.6	NA
October	14.37	2.73	14.95	25.2	49.4	70.5	73.4	NA
November	13.74	2.61	14.29	25.0	49.7	70.8	73.6	NA
December	13.44	2.47	13.95	24.8	50.0	71.6	72.3	NA
1981								
January	13.24	2.16	13.67	27.1	48.6	66.7	76.1	NA
February	13.73	2.06	14.16	26.3	48.9	69.6	73.3	NA
March	13.91	2.25	14.38	26.7	47.1	66.5	74.2	NA
April	13.99	2.25	14.47	26.0	45.1	62.2	74.8	NA
May	14.19	2.17	14.66	25.4	44.8	63.5	73.0	NA
June	14.40	2.22	14.88	25.3	49.3	70.8	73.1	NA
July	14.77	2.36	15.28	26.3	50.2	72.4	72.9	NA
August	15.03	2.31	15.54	25.7	48.1	70.3	70.9	NA
September	15.38	2.40	15.93	25.2	47.2	69.4	71.2	NA
October	15.47	2.42	16.01	25.7	48.1	71.9	70.9	NA
November	15.80	2.52	16.38	25.4	46.0	70.1	70.8	NA
December	15.53	2.30	16.04	25.3	48.1	70.0	70.6	NA

Table 2-80. Terms on Conventional Single-Family Mortgages, Previously Occupied Homes, Monthly National Averages, 1973–2010—*Continued*

[Percent, years, dollars in thousands.]

Year and month	Contract interest rate	Initial fees and charges	Effective interest rate	Term to maturity	Mortgage loan amount	Purchase price	Loan-to-price ratio	Adjustable-rate loans
1980								
January	11.78	1.68	12.10	26.8	44.8	63.7	72.6	NA
February	12.30	1.67	12.62	26.9	48.9	69.3	72.7	NA
March	12.56	1.61	12.87	26.9	49.1	69.1	73.3	NA
April	13.21	1.77	13.57	27.0	50.3	71.0	73.2	NA
May	13.74	2.00	14.15	26.4	46.2	66.6	72.3	NA
June	12.88	2.05	13.30	26.5	43.7	64.2	71.8	NA
July	12.23	1.96	12.61	27.2	48.5	68.8	73.7	NA
August	11.89	1.94	12.26	27.0	50.9	71.3	73.6	NA
September	12.00	1.98	12.37	27.4	51.9	73.6	73.4	NA
October	12.31	1.95	12.68	26.8	48.1	67.1	74.2	NA
November	12.85	2.03	13.26	26.5	47.5	66.3	74.5	NA
December	13.15	2.12	13.58	26.5	46.3	65.3	73.7	NA
1979								
January	10.08	1.43	10.33	27.7	48.7	66.7	75.3	NA
February	10.14	1.40	10.39	26.9	44.4	61.9	74.0	NA
March	10.22	1.43	10.47	26.8	44.1	62.2	73.8	NA
April	10.29	1.41	10.54	27.4	48.8	67.6	74.6	NA
May	10.35	1.41	10.60	26.8	43.3	59.8	74.5	NA
June	10.46	1.41	10.71	27.0	44.7	61.9	74.3	NA
July	10.67	1.43	10.93	26.9	44.7	64.0	73.2	NA
August	10.88	1.46	11.14	27.6	48.6	68.6	73.2	NA
September	10.94	1.34	11.20	27.0	48.5	67.9	73.5	NA
October	11.01	1.46	11.28	26.9	46.2	64.7	73.8	NA
November	11.23	1.56	11.52	27.3	47.2	65.4	74.6	NA
December	11.59	1.64	11.89	26.9	46.2	64.7	73.6	NA
1978								
January	8.95	1.22	9.15	26.1	36.9	50.6	74.8	NA
February	8.99	1.23	9.20	25.8	36.4	49.4	75.9	NA
March	9.04	1.22	9.24	26.2	37.6	51.0	75.6	NA
April	9.14	1.26	9.35	26.6	38.6	52.1	76.1	NA
May	9.17	1.22	9.37	26.2	38.2	51.7	76.0	NA
June	9.27	1.21	9.48	26.5	39.2	53.9	74.8	NA
July	9.41	1.27	9.63	26.5	39.2	53.7	75.1	NA
August	9.55	1.27	9.77	26.4	39.7	54.7	74.9	NA
September	9.62	1.26	9.84	26.6	41.3	57.5	74.4	NA
October	9.68	1.28	9.90	26.6	39.9	55.0	74.9	NA
November	9.74	1.30	9.97	26.6	42.6	59.4	74.8	NA
December	9.85	1.32	10.08	27.0	43.7	61.5	73.7	NA
1977								
January	8.84	1.15	9.03	25.4	33.6	45.9	75.2	NA
February	8.80	1.23	9.00	25.6	33.2	45.9	74.5	NA
March	8.76	1.17	8.95	25.4	33.9	46.1	75.4	NA
April	8.74	1.23	8.94	25.8	34.1	45.7	76.1	NA
May	8.75	1.17	8.95	25.9	34.8	46.9	76.2	NA
June	8.78	1.17	8.98	26.0	34.8	47.4	75.3	NA
July	8.83	1.13	9.02	25.9	34.6	47.4	75.1	NA
August	8.86	1.16	9.05	26.1	35.3	48.5	74.9	NA
September	8.86	1.14	9.05	25.9	35.8	49.5	74.5	NA
October	8.88	1.16	9.08	25.6	34.1	46.6	74.8	NA
November	8.89	1.18	9.08	26.0	36.2	50.2	74.5	NA
December	8.93	1.17	9.12	26.1	36.0	49.4	74.8	NA
1976								
January	9.06	1.20	9.26	24.6	28.8	40.4	73.5	NA
February	9.05	1.20	9.25	24.0	27.4	37.7	74.2	NA
March	8.91	1.19	9.11	24.3	28.7	40.0	73.5	NA
April	8.86	1.18	9.06	24.7	29.3	40.5	73.6	NA
May	8.84	1.16	9.04	24.7	29.0	40.1	74.3	NA
June	8.81	1.11	9.00	24.6	30.7	42.8	73.5	NA
July	8.85	1.09	9.03	24.7	31.5	43.7	73.9	NA
August	8.90	1.13	9.09	24.8	31.0	43.1	73.9	NA
September	8.93	1.14	9.13	24.3	30.7	43.2	73.5	NA
October	8.93	1.12	9.12	24.6	30.7	42.7	73.8	NA
November	8.93	1.16	9.13	24.5	30.3	41.9	74.3	NA
December	8.91	1.11	9.09	24.6	31.3	43.8	73.1	NA

Table 2-80. Terms on Conventional Single-Family Mortgages, Previously Occupied Homes, Monthly National Averages, 1973–2010—*Continued*

[Percent, years, dollars in thousands.]

Year and month	Contract interest rate	Initial fees and charges	Effective interest rate	Term to maturity	Mortgage loan amount	Purchase price	Loan-to-price ratio	Adjustable-rate loans
1975								
January	9.33	1.22	9.55	22.4	23.8	35.5	68.1	NA
February	9.20	1.30	9.43	23.4	26.5	37.2	72.5	NA
March	9.10	1.23	9.31	23.9	25.9	35.6	73.8	NA
April	8.94	1.15	9.13	24.4	28.4	39.3	73.5	NA
May	8.86	1.11	9.04	24.0	27.3	37.9	73.8	NA
June	8.87	1.13	9.06	24.8	29.3	40.5	74.0	NA
July	8.89	1.12	9.08	24.6	30.1	41.9	73.5	NA
August	8.92	1.12	9.11	24.4	28.8	39.8	74.3	NA
September	8.92	1.15	9.11	24.6	29.2	40.6	73.8	NA
October	8.96	1.18	9.16	24.4	28.6	39.3	74.2	NA
November	9.09	1.24	9.30	24.4	27.7	38.3	74.0	NA
December	9.07	1.15	9.27	23.6	27.8	38.8	72.9	NA
1974								
January	8.51	1.07	8.69	22.6	23.5	34.3	71.6	NA
February	8.48	1.05	8.66	23.4	28.0	38.4	73.7	NA
March	8.46	1.07	8.64	23.6	24.3	33.4	74.2	NA
April	8.44	1.04	8.62	23.0	23.7	33.4	73.0	NA
May	8.50	1.09	8.68	23.9	25.8	35.4	74.5	NA
June	8.65	1.12	8.84	23.7	25.3	35.1	73.5	NA
July	8.82	1.08	9.01	23.7	26.0	37.1	72.2	NA
August	8.97	1.13	9.17	23.3	25.2	36.3	71.4	NA
September	9.17	1.10	9.36	23.0	24.9	35.9	71.1	NA
October	9.37	1.20	9.58	23.1	25.0	36.7	70.6	NA
November	9.35	1.20	9.57	22.2	24.2	35.9	69.5	NA
December	9.43	1.20	9.65	21.8	23.2	34.2	69.1	NA
1973								
January	7.51	0.99	7.67	23.6	23.1	31.1	75.6	NA
February	7.55	1.03	7.72	23.6	22.0	29.2	77.5	NA
March	7.54	0.96	7.70	23.1	22.1	29.5	76.3	NA
April	7.55	0.97	7.71	23.8	23.0	30.6	76.6	NA
May	7.61	0.95	7.76	23.5	22.6	30.4	77.0	NA
June	7.62	0.93	7.78	23.5	23.4	31.8	75.5	NA
July	7.69	0.93	7.85	24.1	24.5	33.6	74.5	NA
August	7.89	0.93	8.04	23.4	23.7	32.1	75.4	NA
September	8.13	0.99	8.29	23.1	23.7	32.8	74.3	NA
October	8.36	0.95	8.52	22.1	22.1	31.5	71.8	NA
November	8.43	0.97	8.59	22.1	22.3	31.7	71.6	NA
December	8.45	0.92	8.61	21.6	21.8	30.6	72.1	NA

NA = Not available.

Source: Federal Housing Finance Agency, Monthly Interest Rate Survey

Table 2-81. Terms on Conventional Single-Family Mortgages, Fixed-Rate Mortgages, All Homes, Monthly National Averages, 1986–2010

[Percent, years, dollars in thousands.]

Year and month	Contract interest rate	Initial fees and charges	Effective interest rate	Term to maturity	Mortgage loan amount	Purchase price	Loan-to-price ratio
2010							
January	5.01	0.55	5.09	27.7	214.5	309.9	72.8
February	5.07	0.63	5.16	27.4	206.1	288.4	74.7
March	5.02	0.61	5.11	27.5	209.4	293.0	74.3
April	5.06	0.63	5.15	27.5	216.1	302.9	74.4
May	5.04	0.70	5.15	27.3	214.8	298.9	74.1
June	4.92	0.81	5.04	27.5	214.6	302.4	74.1
July	4.80	0.87	4.92	27.5	220.3	310.6	74.3
August	4.66	0.81	4.78	27.4	212.4	303.5	73.2
September	4.55	0.82	4.67	27.6	208.3	295.8	73.3
October	4.45	0.88	4.58	28.0	215.8	311.7	72.2
November	4.39	0.80	4.50	27.9	212.7	301.0	74.6
December	4.57	0.79	4.68	28.4	204.4	283.2	75.8
2009							
January	5.09	0.64	5.18	28.4	207.3	294.8	74.9
February	5.03	0.57	5.11	28.1	209.9	298.4	74.3
March	5.03	0.58	5.12	28.1	211.0	300.2	74.6
April	4.87	0.58	4.95	28.3	215.6	302.0	75.0
May	4.87	0.58	4.95	28.3	220.2	314.7	74.0
June	5.10	0.59	5.18	28.4	228.7	324.2	74.3
July	5.28	0.67	5.37	28.3	224.5	312.6	75.0
August	5.26	0.67	5.36	28.0	218.3	306.0	74.6
September	5.18	0.63	5.27	27.9	211.1	296.3	74.4
October	5.04	0.64	5.14	28.0	207.8	291.4	74.2
November	5.04	0.61	5.13	27.9	208.3	293.6	74.0
December	4.96	0.62	5.05	27.3	216.7	303.9	73.9
2008							
January	5.97	0.58	6.05	28.5	213.6	294.1	78.4
February	5.90	0.48	5.97	27.8	205.9	294.4	76.3
March	6.06	0.54	6.14	27.9	199.8	280.2	77.6
April	5.98	0.47	6.05	27.9	215.9	302.3	77.1
May	6.06	0.46	6.12	28.4	216.2	300.4	77.4
June	6.23	0.49	6.31	28.3	218.3	303.7	77.0
July	6.41	0.57	6.50	28.3	211.9	298.8	76.1
August	6.46	0.58	6.55	28.3	215.7	298.8	76.5
September	6.15	0.65	6.24	28.4	216.2	297.9	76.7
October	6.12	0.59	6.21	28.7	212.3	291.4	75.9
November	6.15	0.62	6.25	28.7	214.1	294.1	76.3
December	5.52	0.65	5.61	28.7	218.2	302.7	75.1
2007							
January	6.36	0.44	6.42	29.2	207.0	281.4	78.4
February	6.37	0.45	6.44	29.4	208.7	287.1	77.8
March	6.30	0.45	6.37	29.4	213.8	290.8	78.7
April	6.27	0.44	6.33	29.3	208.2	282.4	79.1
May	6.35	0.48	6.42	29.4	213.0	280.4	80.4
June	6.57	0.47	6.64	29.6	221.1	292.6	79.9
July	6.76	0.47	6.83	29.3	206.2	274.0	79.9
August	6.73	0.51	6.81	29.2	206.9	275.3	80.1
September	6.57	0.52	6.65	29.2	203.9	275.9	79.6
October	6.49	0.51	6.57	28.9	208.3	278.2	79.8
November	6.36	0.50	6.43	28.9	215.0	291.3	78.7
December	6.22	0.58	6.30	28.8	214.1	286.8	80.1
2006							
January	6.40	0.40	6.46	28.1	173.8	249.6	75.1
February	6.43	0.41	6.49	28.2	191.1	270.6	75.2
March	6.51	0.40	6.57	28.7	197.6	277.4	75.7
April	6.57	0.41	6.63	28.6	197.0	275.4	76.3
May	6.67	0.41	6.73	28.5	199.7	280.3	76.0
June	6.72	0.45	6.79	28.6	203.6	287.1	75.8
July	6.83	0.42	6.90	28.6	195.1	271.0	77.0
August	6.78	0.47	6.85	28.9	196.7	275.5	76.5
September	6.64	0.47	6.71	28.9	203.8	280.5	77.1
October	6.59	0.47	6.67	29.0	207.2	287.2	76.6
November	6.47	0.47	6.54	29.3	212.1	292.8	77.0
December	6.38	0.43	6.44	29.0	210.8	287.0	78.0

Table 2-81. Terms on Conventional Single-Family Mortgages, Fixed-Rate Mortgages, All Homes, Monthly National Averages, 1986–2010—*Continued*

[Percent, years, dollars in thousands.]

Year and month	Contract interest rate	Initial fees and charges	Effective interest rate	Term to maturity	Mortgage loan amount	Purchase price	Loan-to-price ratio
2005							
January	5.87	0.48	5.94	27.4	171.4	249.7	74.7
February	5.87	0.32	5.91	27.6	172.6	256.5	73.8
March	5.95	0.41	6.00	28.0	180.1	255.9	75.4
April	6.06	0.45	6.13	27.8	172.7	251.0	73.9
May	5.98	0.44	6.05	27.7	177.6	257.6	74.1
June	5.82	0.42	5.88	27.8	184.7	273.8	72.4
July	5.80	0.40	5.86	27.8	183.5	270.4	73.5
August	5.95	0.40	6.01	27.8	188.6	273.0	73.9
September	5.99	0.43	6.05	28.0	187.7	271.5	74.0
October	6.10	0.40	6.16	28.0	185.7	269.3	73.8
November	6.33	0.47	6.40	28.1	187.8	273.8	74.0
December	6.46	0.47	6.53	28.3	191.0	273.6	74.5
2004							
January	5.88	0.49	5.95	26.3	149.0	219.0	73.8
February	5.86	0.37	5.92	26.4	152.4	233.1	70.9
March	5.76	0.37	5.82	25.8	142.8	223.9	69.7
April	5.72	0.36	5.77	26.4	155.8	235.2	71.6
May	6.10	0.36	6.16	26.4	157.2	238.6	71.1
June	6.28	0.40	6.34	26.5	157.6	239.3	70.9
July	6.22	0.40	6.28	27.4	161.6	233.5	74.5
August	6.07	0.48	6.14	27.4	160.7	231.6	75.2
September	5.86	0.54	5.94	27.5	160.1	229.4	75.1
October	5.86	0.47	5.93	27.4	157.5	229.0	74.9
November	5.87	0.45	5.93	27.5	166.4	244.7	74.0
December	5.88	0.45	5.94	27.7	177.8	254.7	75.1
2003							
January	6.05	0.38	6.11	26.1	156.4	231.4	72.5
February	6.02	0.31	6.06	26.2	147.7	220.5	72.4
March	5.89	0.27	5.93	26.0	148.4	222.5	72.1
April	5.84	0.33	5.89	26.1	158.0	234.1	72.6
May	5.70	0.33	5.75	26.1	159.8	238.3	72.2
June	5.47	0.32	5.52	26.2	162.4	241.0	72.0
July	5.46	0.36	5.51	26.2	161.2	237.2	73.2
August	5.82	0.40	5.88	26.2	157.6	236.7	72.0
September	6.10	0.42	6.17	26.1	148.5	221.7	72.6
October	6.03	0.41	6.09	26.5	149.7	222.4	72.6
November	6.03	0.50	6.11	26.7	159.1	232.4	73.3
December	5.98	0.52	6.06	26.6	143.6	208.2	74.3
2002							
January	6.95	0.54	7.04	26.4	143.2	204.7	75.0
February	6.94	0.53	7.02	26.6	144.7	204.1	75.7
March	6.95	0.48	7.02	26.9	145.9	206.8	75.4
April	7.07	0.54	7.15	27.2	146.5	203.5	76.5
May	6.97	0.55	7.06	27.4	150.0	207.7	76.5
June	6.85	0.56	6.93	27.4	151.0	215.4	75.2
July	6.72	0.52	6.80	27.1	149.8	211.1	75.6
August	6.53	0.48	6.60	26.9	149.0	215.7	74.2
September	6.36	0.45	6.43	26.9	152.5	223.2	73.4
October	6.20	0.40	6.26	26.2	150.1	223.1	72.8
November	6.14	0.37	6.19	26.0	151.4	224.3	72.7
December	6.14	0.39	6.20	26.1	150.3	219.2	73.6
2001							
January	7.34	0.62	7.44	28.3	137.4	187.5	77.2
February	7.13	0.60	7.23	27.7	139.5	192.5	76.6
March	7.06	0.61	7.16	27.6	141.4	194.9	76.7
April	7.07	0.56	7.15	27.2	142.0	197.0	76.3
May	7.16	0.61	7.25	27.3	144.1	201.4	75.7
June	7.19	0.57	7.28	27.4	147.5	204.4	76.3
July	7.19	0.57	7.28	27.5	143.9	199.5	76.4
August	7.11	0.55	7.19	27.5	143.8	198.2	76.6
September	6.96	0.50	7.03	27.5	145.7	202.9	75.9
October	6.74	0.49	6.82	27.2	147.0	206.0	75.7
November	6.62	0.47	6.69	26.7	147.5	210.1	74.9
December	6.79	0.54	6.88	26.1	145.4	209.0	74.3

Table 2-81. Terms on Conventional Single-Family Mortgages, Fixed-Rate Mortgages, All Homes, Monthly National Averages, 1986–2010—*Continued*

[Percent, years, dollars in thousands.]

Year and month	Contract interest rate	Initial fees and charges	Effective interest rate	Term to maturity	Mortgage loan amount	Purchase price	Loan-to-price ratio
2000							
January	8.05	0.82	8.18	28.2	126.0	166.6	79.1
February	8.24	0.80	8.37	28.1	124.0	164.1	78.9
March	8.28	0.78	8.40	28.1	125.4	166.9	78.6
April	8.26	0.76	8.38	28.2	122.7	163.7	78.6
May	8.34	0.78	8.47	28.3	125.0	166.5	78.5
June	8.42	0.80	8.55	28.3	126.3	170.2	77.7
July	8.29	0.75	8.41	28.4	129.0	174.0	77.7
August	8.17	0.73	8.29	28.4	130.6	176.9	77.6
September	8.04	0.75	8.16	28.4	132.4	178.7	77.7
October	7.96	0.70	8.07	28.3	131.6	179.1	77.4
November	7.87	0.67	7.97	28.3	136.2	185.4	77.2
December	7.70	0.68	7.81	28.2	137.2	187.2	77.0
1999							
January	6.86	0.82	6.98	27.4	125.3	167.4	77.9
February	6.89	0.76	7.01	27.6	129.6	172.2	78.2
March	6.99	0.76	7.11	27.7	129.7	171.4	78.7
April	7.03	0.75	7.15	27.7	127.8	170.0	78.3
May	7.07	0.71	7.18	27.6	128.6	171.4	78.1
June	7.31	0.77	7.43	27.8	130.5	172.8	78.4
July	7.56	0.82	7.69	27.8	127.0	167.8	78.8
August	7.75	0.81	7.88	27.7	122.1	161.2	78.6
September	7.84	0.80	7.97	28.0	121.3	159.4	79.3
October	7.85	0.82	7.97	28.1	119.7	157.2	79.5
November	7.84	0.82	7.97	28.1	123.2	162.6	79.0
December	7.87	0.78	7.99	28.1	123.7	162.1	79.8
1998							
January	7.21	0.89	7.35	27.2	122.2	162.7	78.0
February	7.15	0.90	7.29	26.8	121.9	163.4	77.9
March	7.16	0.86	7.29	27.2	122.1	159.4	79.4
April	7.18	0.83	7.31	27.5	123.1	160.6	79.6
May	7.18	0.90	7.32	27.6	126.3	166.2	78.8
June	7.17	0.88	7.31	27.6	126.0	164.7	79.7
July	7.12	0.86	7.25	27.7	126.6	165.9	79.1
August	7.06	0.90	7.20	27.9	126.0	163.0	80.3
September	6.96	0.84	7.09	27.9	125.2	164.1	79.5
October	6.80	0.77	6.92	27.5	126.0	167.8	78.3
November	6.82	0.79	6.94	27.2	122.7	163.8	77.9
December	6.84	0.99	7.00	27.8	129.5	170.1	78.9
1997							
January	7.84	1.00	8.01	26.1	111.5	149.2	77.8
February	7.82	1.00	7.99	26.3	110.4	145.3	78.7
March	7.86	0.98	8.03	26.5	112.0	146.6	79.3
April	8.02	1.08	8.21	26.0	113.7	147.1	79.9
May	8.08	1.03	8.25	26.6	116.2	150.6	79.6
June	7.95	1.11	8.13	26.7	120.1	156.8	79.2
July	7.77	0.99	7.93	27.4	120.9	157.1	79.4
August	7.66	1.05	7.83	27.2	120.2	157.5	79.0
September	7.66	1.02	7.82	27.1	119.6	157.3	78.6
October	7.54	1.01	7.70	27.1	119.5	157.1	79.0
November	7.48	0.91	7.63	27.4	122.1	158.9	79.6
December	7.40	0.94	7.55	27.3	124.7	161.7	80.1
1996							
January	7.23	0.89	7.38	26.4	108.2	144.6	77.7
February	7.19	0.92	7.33	26.1	106.3	140.6	78.6
March	7.40	1.07	7.58	26.0	105.6	138.6	79.0
April	7.76	1.06	7.93	25.9	105.6	138.2	79.6
May	7.99	1.07	8.18	26.4	107.0	139.7	79.6
June	8.10	1.09	8.30	25.4	106.8	140.6	79.1
July	8.24	1.13	8.43	26.1	106.8	141.0	78.5
August	8.13	1.09	8.32	26.4	107.9	141.9	79.1
September	8.15	1.06	8.33	25.7	106.5	142.3	77.6
October	8.09	0.99	8.25	26.2	109.1	144.7	77.9
November	7.88	0.99	8.05	26.6	109.1	145.5	77.7
December	7.75	0.87	7.89	26.7	109.7	145.8	78.5

Table 2-81. Terms on Conventional Single-Family Mortgages, Fixed-Rate Mortgages, All Homes, Monthly National Averages, 1986–2010—*Continued*

[Percent, years, dollars in thousands.]

Year and month	Contract interest rate	Initial fees and charges	Effective interest rate	Term to maturity	Mortgage loan amount	Purchase price	Loan-to-price ratio
1995							
January	9.02	1.33	9.25	25.9	88.3	116.5	79.4
February	8.96	1.34	9.19	26.5	92.9	119.8	80.3
March	8.79	1.03	8.96	27.0	91.6	118.1	80.5
April	8.57	1.05	8.75	26.8	95.0	121.3	80.8
May	8.28	1.15	8.47	26.5	95.0	123.7	79.8
June	7.85	0.96	8.02	26.4	99.7	130.9	79.7
July	7.72	0.98	7.88	26.5	102.1	132.4	80.0
August	7.84	0.98	8.00	26.3	100.5	131.5	79.2
September	7.78	0.95	7.93	26.7	101.5	134.1	78.9
October	7.70	0.98	7.86	26.5	103.4	135.9	78.9
November	7.60	0.88	7.74	26.5	104.6	137.8	78.7
December	7.48	0.83	7.62	26.3	106.3	140.1	78.5
1994							
January	7.13	1.12	7.32	25.7	99.0	133.1	77.1
February	7.06	0.97	7.22	25.3	101.9	136.9	77.8
March	7.26	1.08	7.43	26.0	100.8	131.1	79.8
April	7.61	1.08	7.80	25.7	102.1	132.2	79.5
May	8.06	1.28	8.28	25.2	94.6	122.1	80.2
June	8.24	1.14	8.43	25.9	96.4	125.2	80.3
July	8.31	1.24	8.53	25.8	95.0	122.5	80.4
August	8.41	1.07	8.60	26.5	92.7	120.0	81.2
September	8.44	1.14	8.64	25.9	92.9	120.6	80.1
October	8.57	1.09	8.76	26.1	91.9	119.2	80.1
November	8.74	1.15	8.94	26.0	94.3	123.1	80.1
December	8.82	1.36	9.06	25.6	82.6	107.6	80.9
1993							
January	7.97	1.55	8.26	23.8	97.0	129.9	77.6
February	7.77	1.38	8.01	24.0	103.3	143.3	75.7
March	7.56	1.37	7.80	24.5	100.6	135.1	77.0
April	7.48	1.23	7.69	23.9	102.2	139.0	76.4
May	7.42	1.30	7.64	24.2	98.5	129.0	78.2
June	7.43	1.32	7.65	24.1	101.8	136.7	77.9
July	7.25	1.17	7.45	25.2	104.3	138.4	78.0
August	7.12	1.07	7.30	24.9	103.2	139.0	76.9
September	7.01	1.08	7.19	24.9	101.1	134.7	77.7
October	6.87	1.02	7.04	25.0	104.1	140.1	76.7
November	6.91	1.11	7.10	25.4	102.5	139.0	76.9
December	7.12	1.19	7.31	25.7	101.6	134.3	78.5
1992							
January	8.30	1.34	8.59	25.1	112.3	158.0	73.7
February	8.40	1.63	8.71	24.4	101.1	142.2	74.1
March	8.57	1.73	8.88	24.3	103.9	140.1	76.3
April	8.64	1.77	8.95	25.1	103.1	136.3	78.2
May	8.60	1.66	8.89	25.7	107.2	141.7	78.3
June	8.46	1.71	8.77	24.7	105.7	139.9	77.7
July	8.16	1.47	8.43	24.4	104.5	141.7	76.5
August	7.96	1.84	8.29	24.0	105.9	141.7	77.2
September	7.83	1.57	8.10	24.3	101.5	138.3	76.3
October	7.82	1.41	8.07	23.9	107.1	147.9	75.2
November	7.96	1.62	8.25	23.7	100.4	138.1	75.6
December	8.06	1.52	8.34	23.8	101.3	135.1	77.9
1991							
January	9.77	1.54	10.04	25.6	98.5	138.1	73.8
February	9.70	1.57	9.97	25.3	101.3	145.0	73.1
March	9.41	1.44	9.66	25.1	98.3	140.8	73.2
April	9.43	1.75	9.73	25.8	103.1	145.5	72.9
May	9.50	1.71	9.80	26.3	101.3	140.7	73.9
June	9.49	1.63	9.76	26.5	102.9	143.7	74.0
July	9.48	1.81	9.80	25.8	103.9	144.8	74.4
August	9.50	1.67	9.78	26.3	98.6	137.8	73.9
September	9.32	1.56	9.58	26.1	100.7	141.4	73.9
October	9.15	1.50	9.40	25.4	102.1	144.4	73.2
November	8.77	1.60	9.05	25.2	95.7	133.1	75.2
December	8.53	1.56	8.80	25.4	100.1	136.7	75.5

Table 2-81. Terms on Conventional Single-Family Mortgages, Fixed-Rate Mortgages, All Homes, Monthly National Averages, 1986–2010—*Continued*

[Percent, years, dollars in thousands.]

Year and month	Contract interest rate	Initial fees and charges	Effective interest rate	Term to maturity	Mortgage loan amount	Purchase price	Loan-to-price ratio
1990							
January	9.80	1.91	10.13	26.3	100.7	142.5	72.4
February	9.87	1.95	10.21	26.5	105.0	144.8	74.7
March	9.98	1.98	10.33	25.7	92.7	129.5	74.0
April	10.16	2.14	10.54	25.5	102.4	142.4	74.6
May	10.24	2.50	10.68	27.4	111.0	153.5	73.9
June	10.21	2.19	10.60	25.9	102.0	138.9	75.5
July	10.15	2.05	10.51	27.1	109.5	149.9	74.9
August	10.01	2.17	10.38	26.8	113.8	156.6	74.4
September	10.04	1.89	10.35	25.6	101.9	143.2	73.3
October	10.04	1.98	10.38	25.9	95.1	136.0	72.6
November	10.09	1.81	10.41	25.7	98.5	135.8	74.6
December	9.95	2.03	10.30	27.7	97.9	136.8	73.8
1989							
January	10.25	1.99	10.60	26.4	92.0	131.0	72.9
February	10.38	2.37	10.80	26.0	82.4	116.6	73.1
March	10.48	1.98	10.83	26.7	88.9	124.6	73.8
April	10.60	1.85	10.93	26.9	93.2	130.9	73.9
May	10.78	2.01	11.14	25.7	89.1	125.4	74.9
June	10.69	1.92	11.03	27.0	90.2	124.6	74.2
July	10.33	1.88	10.66	27.6	104.3	146.7	73.6
August	9.99	1.84	10.30	28.0	104.8	142.9	75.0
September	10.00	2.01	10.35	26.8	96.1	133.4	74.0
October	10.05	1.85	10.37	26.7	95.0	133.2	73.2
November	10.03	1.90	10.36	27.0	99.2	139.3	73.1
December	9.88	1.81	10.20	27.2	102.9	144.5	73.5
1988							
January	10.06	2.08	10.43	24.7	78.1	111.2	73.0
February	9.88	2.04	10.24	26.6	81.0	114.3	74.6
March	9.70	1.91	10.03	26.4	86.9	124.1	73.4
April	9.79	1.88	10.12	26.2	86.2	121.6	73.9
May	9.79	2.10	10.17	25.4	82.3	114.4	74.6
June	9.99	2.04	10.35	26.0	84.5	118.2	74.5
July	10.11	2.21	10.50	25.8	79.4	113.5	73.5
August	10.17	2.15	10.56	26.0	82.4	117.6	73.4
September	10.23	2.30	10.64	25.7	78.0	111.2	73.2
October	10.33	1.99	10.69	25.9	80.6	115.5	73.0
November	10.16	2.13	10.54	26.5	86.4	124.3	73.1
December	10.19	1.91	10.53	26.6	85.1	119.1	74.2
1987							
January	9.44	2.14	9.81	25.9	79.3	110.7	74.2
February	9.17	1.99	9.50	26.3	83.6	116.1	74.6
March	9.03	1.88	9.35	26.3	86.3	118.6	74.5
April	9.00	1.94	9.32	26.0	88.3	121.8	74.3
May	9.25	2.15	9.61	25.2	84.1	118.6	73.6
June	9.60	2.32	10.00	25.4	83.3	116.6	74.1
July	9.86	2.41	10.29	25.0	77.9	110.7	73.1
August	9.89	2.26	10.30	24.5	77.8	110.5	73.4
September	9.87	2.18	10.26	24.8	78.5	112.0	72.9
October	10.01	2.43	10.45	25.3	77.2	109.3	74.0
November	10.12	2.49	10.57	24.8	77.9	111.0	73.0
December	10.01	2.38	10.43	25.7	77.2	108.6	74.4
1986							
January	10.93	2.48	11.41	23.6	66.3	94.5	73.2
February	10.82	2.29	11.24	23.6	67.0	96.0	73.2
March	10.46	2.30	10.87	24.3	74.2	105.7	73.7
April	10.16	2.22	10.56	24.0	73.1	104.4	73.2
May	9.94	2.16	10.33	23.8	74.4	106.7	72.4
June	9.98	2.25	10.38	24.5	75.1	108.1	72.6
July	10.10	2.32	10.51	25.0	75.3	108.4	72.7
August	10.17	2.31	10.58	25.0	73.8	106.0	72.7
September	10.05	2.35	10.47	25.4	77.9	111.3	73.2
October	9.96	2.42	10.39	25.4	77.6	109.1	73.8
November	9.87	2.33	10.28	25.6	78.7	110.8	73.9
December	9.72	2.31	10.13	25.9	80.2	113.4	73.9

Source: Federal Housing Finance Agency, Monthly Interest Rate Survey

Table 2-82. Terms on Conventional Single-Family Mortgages, Fixed-Rate Mortgages, Newly Built Homes, Monthly National Averages, 1986–2010

[Percent, years, dollars in thousands.]

Year and month	Contract interest rate	Initial fees and charges	Effective interest rate	Term to maturity	Mortgage loan amount	Purchase price	Loan-to-price ratio
2010							
January	4.93	0.95	5.07	28.5	249.1	342.7	74.1
February	4.98	0.89	5.10	28.3	227.8	313.5	73.9
March	4.97	0.93	5.10	28.5	228.0	316.0	73.0
April	5.10	0.94	5.23	27.9	234.1	319.0	74.2
May	5.01	0.88	5.14	28.5	235.0	325.7	73.7
June	4.89	0.86	5.01	28.1	223.4	315.8	72.7
July	4.77	0.87	4.89	28.8	264.2	370.6	73.4
August	4.59	0.74	4.69	28.4	253.7	347.4	73.4
September	4.42	0.75	4.53	28.6	250.1	348.9	72.9
October	4.31	0.63	4.40	29.1	256.5	361.9	71.3
November	4.17	0.72	4.27	28.1	237.6	328.9	73.0
December	4.35	0.76	4.45	28.6	249.4	339.5	74.5
2009							
January	4.98	0.92	5.11	29.0	255.1	356.6	74.7
February	4.97	0.86	5.09	28.9	244.9	339.6	74.2
March	4.98	0.86	5.10	29.0	244.2	336.5	75.2
April	4.84	0.95	4.97	29.0	238.8	325.1	75.4
May	4.78	1.00	4.92	29.0	248.7	342.2	74.1
June	5.02	1.17	5.18	28.9	244.8	345.6	72.4
July	5.26	1.08	5.41	29.0	240.2	326.9	75.1
August	5.17	1.15	5.33	28.4	237.2	329.2	73.3
September	5.13	1.06	5.28	28.5	236.4	327.2	73.8
October	5.02	0.94	5.15	28.7	230.7	321.0	74.1
November	4.97	0.92	5.10	28.4	223.7	309.6	72.9
December	4.91	0.84	5.02	28.4	244.6	345.5	72.2
2008							
January	5.91	0.79	6.02	29.0	262.7	349.3	78.5
February	5.86	0.67	5.96	29.2	267.7	362.3	78.1
March	5.88	0.82	6.00	28.6	235.1	310.4	78.6
April	5.90	0.65	5.99	28.9	246.5	336.2	76.6
May	5.93	0.68	6.03	29.2	253.2	337.4	77.2
June	6.01	0.93	6.15	29.1	255.6	347.0	75.6
July	6.17	0.96	6.31	29.3	250.9	344.5	75.2
August	6.20	1.05	6.36	29.0	259.7	355.1	75.4
September	5.94	1.10	6.10	28.6	248.9	347.2	74.0
October	5.97	0.92	6.11	29.3	242.8	331.3	75.2
November	6.04	0.83	6.16	28.7	247.5	346.4	73.9
December	5.53	0.94	5.67	29.1	256.4	352.0	75.0
2007							
January	6.26	0.81	6.38	29.5	258.8	357.3	75.3
February	6.18	0.77	6.30	29.4	257.3	346.6	76.0
March	6.10	0.79	6.22	29.2	264.9	362.2	75.1
April	6.09	0.82	6.21	29.4	258.0	356.2	75.9
May	6.12	0.76	6.23	29.3	253.5	339.6	77.0
June	6.43	0.89	6.56	29.4	259.6	348.8	76.6
July	6.61	0.89	6.74	29.3	253.3	335.5	77.5
August	6.61	0.94	6.75	29.5	254.4	335.1	78.3
September	6.46	0.89	6.59	29.5	257.9	346.7	77.2
October	6.43	0.84	6.55	29.4	257.5	339.1	78.7
November	6.32	0.80	6.44	29.2	262.2	350.7	77.1
December	6.11	0.77	6.22	29.2	263.4	341.3	79.4
2006							
January	6.48	0.49	6.55	27.9	190.7	270.4	73.6
February	6.54	0.59	6.63	28.9	228.5	313.5	75.1
March	6.62	0.68	6.72	29.6	240.9	325.2	76.2
April	6.67	0.69	6.77	29.4	234.7	317.5	76.7
May	6.70	0.74	6.81	29.4	234.9	324.4	75.1
June	6.76	0.80	6.88	29.2	246.2	341.1	74.8
July	6.83	0.76	6.95	29.0	233.8	322.7	75.2
August	6.81	0.77	6.93	29.4	238.5	331.4	74.5
September	6.69	0.77	6.80	29.6	247.4	338.0	75.1
October	6.61	0.85	6.74	29.7	245.4	334.5	75.4
November	6.46	0.77	6.57	29.6	251.5	345.1	75.4
December	6.27	0.74	6.38	29.2	246.0	338.0	74.5

Table 2-82. Terms on Conventional Single-Family Mortgages, Fixed-Rate Mortgages, Newly Built Homes, Monthly National Averages, 1986–2010—*Continued*

[Percent, years, dollars in thousands.]

Year and month	Contract interest rate	Initial fees and charges	Effective interest rate	Term to maturity	Mortgage loan amount	Purchase price	Loan-to-price ratio
2005							
January	5.93	0.64	6.03	28.5	214.5	304.2	73.9
February	5.94	0.55	6.02	28.5	213.0	295.9	74.5
March	6.00	0.50	6.07	28.5	217.3	301.2	74.6
April	6.11	0.54	6.19	28.7	199.9	282.5	73.9
May	6.08	0.55	6.16	28.5	214.2	297.8	74.2
June	5.93	0.56	6.01	28.9	219.3	308.0	73.9
July	5.92	0.53	6.00	28.8	218.3	306.4	74.1
August	6.03	0.59	6.12	28.7	225.6	312.9	74.6
September	6.10	0.63	6.19	28.9	225.8	311.9	75.0
October	6.14	0.67	6.23	29.1	226.6	314.9	74.7
November	6.33	0.76	6.44	29.2	233.5	328.0	73.8
December	6.54	0.74	6.65	29.2	247.8	345.6	73.8
2004							
January	5.86	0.58	5.95	28.5	180.6	244.6	77.2
February	5.90	0.63	6.00	28.0	200.6	281.0	74.0
March	5.80	0.49	5.88	26.6	166.4	255.5	69.2
April	5.77	0.57	5.85	27.8	197.5	279.6	73.8
May	6.05	0.58	6.14	27.8	193.9	274.5	73.2
June	6.02	0.60	6.11	27.5	192.6	271.2	73.1
July	6.24	0.57	6.32	28.0	194.6	273.1	73.8
August	6.11	0.58	6.19	28.2	204.6	282.7	75.1
September	5.77	0.70	5.87	28.5	204.5	279.1	75.9
October	5.90	0.59	5.99	28.1	198.4	279.7	74.0
November	5.92	0.59	6.01	28.7	212.7	298.7	73.4
December	6.00	0.64	6.09	28.1	223.7	309.9	75.0
2003							
January	6.10	0.86	6.22	28.8	213.0	278.0	79.4
February	5.94	0.41	6.00	27.7	165.4	220.3	76.6
March	5.89	0.44	5.95	27.5	166.0	235.2	75.0
April	5.92	0.67	6.02	28.9	199.9	260.4	78.6
May	5.78	0.66	5.87	28.7	205.6	269.7	78.6
June	5.54	0.69	5.64	28.5	209.1	279.2	77.6
July	5.54	0.65	5.63	28.5	210.9	280.4	77.7
August	5.86	0.70	5.96	28.1	201.4	268.1	77.6
September	6.13	0.72	6.24	28.4	197.8	263.3	77.6
October	6.06	0.67	6.16	28.1	186.1	258.9	74.6
November	6.02	0.75	6.13	28.7	211.1	281.8	77.8
December	5.85	0.66	5.95	28.3	180.2	244.9	77.0
2002							
January	6.97	0.73	7.08	28.5	174.8	231.1	78.0
February	6.95	0.72	7.06	28.5	176.7	233.7	78.0
March	6.91	0.72	7.02	28.7	176.8	235.1	78.0
April	7.00	0.75	7.12	28.5	183.3	243.6	77.3
May	6.93	0.70	7.04	28.5	180.2	241.3	77.0
June	6.80	0.66	6.90	28.6	179.4	242.2	76.8
July	6.68	0.71	6.79	28.8	183.4	245.4	77.4
August	6.50	0.68	6.60	28.6	182.5	245.3	77.6
September	6.33	0.69	6.43	28.9	187.3	249.8	77.4
October	6.20	0.69	6.30	28.5	184.0	245.0	77.7
November	6.16	0.67	6.26	28.0	183.2	245.6	76.9
December	6.12	0.69	6.22	28.4	204.4	266.0	79.2
2001							
January	7.28	0.81	7.40	29.2	163.0	213.9	78.5
February	7.09	0.77	7.20	28.8	168.2	222.1	78.2
March	7.03	0.71	7.14	28.6	169.0	226.6	77.2
April	7.04	0.77	7.16	28.3	170.9	227.0	77.8
May	7.12	0.74	7.23	28.4	171.7	229.3	77.5
June	7.17	0.71	7.27	28.5	178.3	237.6	77.2
July	7.16	0.71	7.27	28.5	168.5	225.5	77.1
August	7.24	0.67	7.34	28.4	166.1	222.5	76.7
September	6.95	0.67	7.05	28.7	171.0	229.8	77.0
October	6.74	0.73	6.86	28.3	172.5	230.3	77.3
November	6.62	0.70	6.72	28.5	180.8	242.0	77.2
December	6.82	0.79	6.94	28.8	181.5	244.1	77.1

Table 2-82. Terms on Conventional Single-Family Mortgages, Fixed-Rate Mortgages, Newly Built Homes, Monthly National Averages, 1986–2010—*Continued*

[Percent, years, dollars in thousands.]

Year and month	Contract interest rate	Initial fees and charges	Effective interest rate	Term to maturity	Mortgage loan amount	Purchase price	Loan-to-price ratio
2000							
January	7.96	0.95	8.11	28.4	149.9	200.7	77.4
February	8.17	0.89	8.31	28.3	142.9	189.6	77.6
March	8.18	0.85	8.31	28.1	145.6	196.1	77.0
April	8.17	0.85	8.31	28.4	142.0	189.6	77.3
May	8.22	0.91	8.37	28.6	150.8	201.5	77.5
June	8.30	0.88	8.44	28.6	145.3	198.8	76.1
July	8.21	0.82	8.34	28.7	148.5	199.0	77.2
August	8.09	0.83	8.22	28.8	153.4	204.6	77.3
September	8.00	0.86	8.13	28.7	158.5	213.0	76.5
October	7.88	0.80	8.01	28.9	156.2	209.8	76.9
November	7.78	0.80	7.91	28.8	160.3	218.1	75.7
December	7.57	0.81	7.70	28.9	167.1	224.3	76.8
1999							
January	6.94	1.06	7.10	28.1	145.5	192.2	78.2
February	6.96	0.99	7.11	28.3	146.3	192.3	78.3
March	6.94	0.87	7.07	28.4	152.1	196.6	79.9
April	6.96	0.83	7.09	28.5	149.1	192.8	79.6
May	7.04	0.74	7.15	28.3	146.8	188.8	80.0
June	7.26	0.77	7.38	27.8	138.4	183.0	78.6
July	7.39	0.87	7.53	28.2	143.6	189.9	78.5
August	7.66	0.81	7.78	27.3	135.4	178.7	78.2
September	7.79	0.82	7.92	28.2	135.5	177.6	78.5
October	7.79	0.92	7.93	28.5	143.7	186.6	79.4
November	7.78	0.96	7.93	28.3	146.0	196.0	76.8
December	7.81	0.90	7.95	28.2	145.2	190.0	78.3
1998							
January	7.23	0.90	7.37	28.3	136.7	176.9	80.7
February	7.21	1.00	7.37	27.7	142.5	188.0	78.6
March	7.15	0.96	7.30	27.9	139.5	177.7	81.6
April	7.18	0.89	7.32	28.1	138.0	177.6	80.6
May	7.19	0.88	7.32	27.9	140.1	183.0	79.1
June	7.15	0.87	7.29	28.0	141.6	180.8	81.4
July	7.13	0.95	7.28	28.1	150.4	196.2	78.8
August	7.08	0.91	7.22	28.2	142.2	180.2	81.8
September	6.95	0.88	7.08	28.5	143.8	183.1	81.4
October	6.83	0.91	6.97	28.4	148.7	192.5	80.0
November	6.79	0.80	6.91	28.0	138.2	179.3	79.8
December	6.89	1.01	7.05	28.5	152.4	197.7	79.5
1997							
January	7.83	1.04	8.00	27.6	124.9	161.8	79.8
February	7.83	1.04	8.00	27.8	121.8	155.3	80.7
March	7.88	0.99	8.04	27.6	123.9	159.3	80.9
April	8.03	1.06	8.21	27.5	127.8	163.1	81.6
May	8.06	1.02	8.22	27.7	128.1	165.7	80.0
June	7.95	1.05	8.12	27.6	134.4	173.6	79.9
July	7.76	1.07	7.93	28.5	135.4	173.1	80.9
August	7.68	1.06	7.85	27.7	138.8	179.6	80.0
September	7.68	1.15	7.86	27.8	137.8	180.0	78.9
October	7.57	0.96	7.72	27.7	133.8	172.9	80.1
November	7.44	0.93	7.58	28.3	135.3	173.6	80.7
December	7.39	0.97	7.54	27.8	140.4	178.0	81.5
1996							
January	7.23	1.16	7.41	27.4	130.6	173.4	77.5
February	7.10	1.28	7.31	27.6	135.9	172.5	80.4
March	7.42	1.37	7.69	25.8	134.0	175.3	77.8
April	7.75	1.28	7.96	26.6	127.7	169.8	78.2
May	7.81	1.26	8.03	26.4	122.7	160.5	78.8
June	7.94	1.41	8.28	24.6	127.8	166.2	78.4
July	8.06	1.39	8.30	25.6	128.3	171.4	76.5
August	8.09	1.48	8.34	26.6	132.0	172.6	78.4
September	8.08	1.41	8.32	26.6	128.0	171.5	76.6
October	8.08	1.14	8.27	26.3	130.1	176.4	76.1
November	7.85	1.27	8.06	26.5	131.6	175.1	77.3
December	7.78	1.03	7.95	27.4	121.9	160.8	78.6

Table 2-82. Terms on Conventional Single-Family Mortgages, Fixed-Rate Mortgages, Newly Built Homes, Monthly National Averages, 1986–2010—*Continued*

[Percent, years, dollars in thousands.]

Year and month	Contract interest rate	Initial fees and charges	Effective interest rate	Term to maturity	Mortgage loan amount	Purchase price	Loan-to-price ratio
1995							
January	9.01	1.42	9.26	25.2	115.3	157.7	75.6
February	8.82	1.38	9.06	26.9	122.8	162.2	78.2
March	8.59	1.38	8.82	27.8	108.7	148.0	75.6
April	8.45	1.29	8.66	26.9	118.3	152.8	79.4
May	8.16	1.44	8.40	27.6	116.5	153.4	78.3
June	7.85	1.22	8.06	26.2	123.7	165.1	77.4
July	7.79	1.26	8.01	25.8	122.2	159.2	78.9
August	7.81	1.17	8.01	26.3	119.3	158.7	77.9
September	7.64	1.27	7.84	27.9	122.7	165.3	77.7
October	7.59	1.16	7.80	25.9	122.0	159.1	78.3
November	7.42	1.34	7.64	27.4	127.5	168.2	78.5
December	7.31	1.27	7.52	26.9	126.9	164.8	78.8
1994							
January	7.07	1.31	7.28	27.2	118.0	153.8	78.5
February	7.03	1.16	7.22	26.6	117.3	149.7	80.4
March	7.22	1.27	7.42	27.2	124.8	161.5	79.8
April	7.57	1.27	7.78	26.2	123.0	159.1	78.7
May	7.87	1.61	8.14	26.6	119.8	156.6	78.1
June	8.13	1.42	8.37	24.9	122.0	166.5	76.6
July	8.15	1.43	8.39	26.8	116.3	150.9	79.2
August	8.20	1.47	8.45	26.8	111.1	145.5	78.7
September	8.31	1.49	8.57	26.0	115.4	148.6	79.1
October	8.43	1.38	8.66	26.8	120.1	158.5	78.0
November	8.55	1.46	8.81	25.6	118.2	159.6	76.3
December	8.82	1.40	9.08	25.3	104.5	145.5	75.3
1993							
January	7.99	1.53	8.26	24.6	107.3	143.8	76.6
February	7.74	1.42	7.99	23.1	108.7	154.3	74.9
March	7.54	1.47	7.79	26.2	118.2	150.4	80.0
April	7.51	1.41	7.74	26.0	123.0	161.6	78.5
May	7.36	1.45	7.59	26.7	115.0	147.2	80.0
June	7.40	1.36	7.62	25.0	125.1	173.8	77.8
July	7.21	1.30	7.42	25.6	123.9	164.6	77.6
August	7.09	1.22	7.29	25.9	118.3	153.1	78.5
September	6.97	1.14	7.16	26.1	116.9	150.8	78.6
October	6.91	1.27	7.12	26.3	123.4	160.7	78.8
November	6.89	1.27	7.09	26.5	132.0	173.0	79.0
December	7.06	1.11	7.24	26.4	121.8	159.7	79.3
1992							
January	8.31	1.91	8.65	26.1	113.9	152.4	75.3
February	8.43	1.85	8.80	24.6	111.2	155.7	73.5
March	8.54	1.78	8.85	24.6	122.7	167.2	76.0
April	8.63	1.94	8.96	26.1	125.6	161.6	79.7
May	8.60	1.69	8.90	26.1	118.5	156.3	78.0
June	8.40	1.59	8.69	24.4	115.6	153.6	77.9
July	8.12	1.17	8.31	25.7	117.5	155.8	77.1
August	8.00	1.66	8.29	24.5	112.9	147.8	79.1
September	7.92	1.54	8.18	25.2	105.9	142.0	77.0
October	7.93	1.43	8.18	24.8	126.1	165.5	78.0
November	8.13	1.59	8.41	24.4	111.0	153.8	75.4
December	8.11	1.28	8.34	25.1	110.5	145.7	77.3
1991							
January	9.75	1.81	10.06	27.5	101.5	135.0	77.2
February	9.58	1.85	9.89	27.3	103.3	141.2	75.9
March	9.39	1.71	9.68	25.0	92.9	128.1	73.9
April	9.47	2.14	9.84	26.2	110.9	148.1	75.8
May	9.53	1.68	9.81	26.0	108.8	148.4	74.4
June	9.47	1.72	9.76	26.0	113.3	158.2	73.2
July	9.46	1.91	9.80	26.1	113.0	154.0	75.1
August	9.50	1.79	9.81	26.5	106.1	148.5	73.9
September	9.31	1.75	9.60	24.9	104.6	148.0	72.1
October	9.02	1.63	9.29	27.0	110.5	149.3	76.0
November	8.69	1.72	8.99	25.6	109.2	155.6	73.1
December	8.57	1.55	8.83	25.9	108.3	152.1	73.2

Table 2-82. Terms on Conventional Single-Family Mortgages, Fixed-Rate Mortgages, Newly Built Homes, Monthly National Averages, 1986–2010—*Continued*

[Percent, years, dollars in thousands.]

Year and month	Contract interest rate	Initial fees and charges	Effective interest rate	Term to maturity	Mortgage loan amount	Purchase price	Loan-to-price ratio
1990							
January	9.80	1.91	10.13	26.3	100.7	142.5	72.4
February	9.87	1.95	10.21	26.5	105.0	144.8	74.7
March	9.98	1.98	10.33	25.7	92.7	129.5	74.0
April	10.16	2.14	10.54	25.5	102.4	142.4	74.6
May	10.24	2.50	10.68	27.4	111.0	153.5	73.9
June	10.21	2.19	10.60	25.9	102.0	138.9	75.5
July	10.15	2.05	10.51	27.1	109.5	149.9	74.9
August	10.01	2.17	10.38	26.8	113.8	156.6	74.4
September	10.04	1.89	10.35	25.6	101.9	143.2	73.3
October	10.04	1.98	10.38	25.9	95.1	136.0	72.6
November	10.09	1.81	10.41	25.7	98.5	135.8	74.6
December	9.95	2.03	10.30	27.7	97.9	136.8	73.8
1989							
January	10.17	2.02	10.53	27.6	107.4	152.9	72.6
February	10.33	2.49	10.77	26.8	95.2	136.3	70.6
March	10.48	2.27	10.89	25.8	100.2	141.3	71.4
April	10.65	1.53	10.93	26.9	110.0	154.5	73.3
May	10.60	2.34	11.02	26.4	94.2	133.6	72.6
June	10.70	2.04	11.07	26.5	99.8	137.2	74.5
July	10.23	2.57	10.68	28.4	122.9	173.6	72.9
August	9.89	2.38	10.39	28.3	118.8	160.6	75.5
September	10.01	2.26	10.40	28.3	116.6	157.9	75.4
October	10.07	2.07	10.43	26.8	105.6	150.2	71.1
November	10.03	1.91	10.36	27.1	105.9	149.8	71.9
December	9.87	2.29	10.26	27.6	114.6	157.1	73.8
1988							
January	10.01	2.23	10.42	25.8	91.4	129.3	75.3
February	9.77	2.46	10.20	26.8	94.8	128.2	76.0
March	9.64	2.28	10.03	26.0	104.7	154.6	70.9
April	9.73	2.29	10.13	26.1	106.5	149.1	74.4
May	9.75	2.39	10.17	26.5	93.9	132.0	73.9
June	9.95	2.46	10.39	25.7	102.0	149.6	70.2
July	10.04	2.51	10.47	26.4	95.8	140.4	71.3
August	10.07	2.73	10.54	26.6	97.0	141.7	71.9
September	10.14	2.43	10.57	24.7	90.8	134.1	70.1
October	10.25	2.35	10.67	26.1	88.9	134.4	70.3
November	10.12	2.53	10.56	26.8	101.6	147.4	71.0
December	10.18	2.32	10.59	26.4	91.1	130.5	73.0
1987							
January	9.35	2.36	9.75	27.3	95.3	132.1	74.8
February	9.07	2.26	9.45	27.0	95.8	132.6	74.8
March	9.00	2.28	9.38	26.8	94.5	131.2	73.5
April	9.01	2.31	9.39	27.1	100.9	137.3	75.3
May	9.39	2.34	9.78	27.5	94.4	128.5	75.3
June	9.58	2.54	10.01	27.4	92.1	126.3	75.4
July	9.67	2.73	10.14	26.6	88.8	123.1	73.9
August	9.86	2.31	10.26	26.4	90.4	128.3	73.9
September	9.86	2.20	10.24	25.7	89.4	131.4	71.7
October	9.99	2.57	10.44	26.2	93.1	131.4	72.6
November	10.17	2.69	10.65	26.2	85.2	122.4	72.1
December	10.08	2.61	10.54	25.0	87.2	127.6	70.1
1986							
January	10.93	2.72	11.45	24.1	72.1	106.2	71.7
February	10.68	2.95	11.22	24.9	75.0	105.7	74.0
March	10.36	2.76	10.85	25.9	78.6	109.0	74.5
April	10.03	2.46	10.47	25.2	81.0	112.2	75.2
May	9.96	2.29	10.37	24.8	80.8	114.4	73.3
June	9.94	2.50	10.37	26.1	84.6	119.2	74.2
July	10.14	2.49	10.58	26.0	79.3	111.5	73.7
August	10.07	2.58	10.53	26.1	82.9	117.6	73.3
September	10.01	2.63	10.47	27.1	89.5	122.8	75.5
October	9.89	2.81	10.37	27.7	91.6	126.6	74.7
November	9.82	2.76	10.31	26.9	88.8	120.2	75.8
December	9.69	2.61	10.13	27.3	90.8	122.8	76.4

Source: Federal Housing Finance Agency, Monthly Interest Rate Survey

Table 2-83. Terms on Conventional Single-Family Mortgages, Adjustable-Rate Mortgages, All Homes, Monthly National Averages, 1986–2010

[Percent, years, dollars in thousands.]

Year and month	Contract interest rate	Initial fees and charges	Effective interest rate	Term to maturity	Mortgage loan amount	Purchase price	Loan-to-price ratio
2010							
January	NA	NA	NA	NA	NA	NA	NA
February	NA	NA	NA	NA	NA	NA	NA
March	NA	NA	NA	NA	NA	NA	NA
April	NA	NA	NA	NA	NA	NA	NA
May	NA	NA	NA	NA	NA	NA	NA
June	NA	NA	NA	NA	NA	NA	NA
July	NA	NA	NA	NA	NA	NA	NA
August	NA	NA	NA	NA	NA	NA	NA
September	NA	NA	NA	NA	NA	NA	NA
October	NA	NA	NA	NA	NA	NA	NA
November	NA	NA	NA	NA	NA	NA	NA
December	NA	NA	NA	NA	NA	NA	NA
2009							
January	NA	NA	NA	NA	NA	NA	NA
February	NA	NA	NA	NA	NA	NA	NA
March	NA	NA	NA	NA	NA	NA	NA
April	NA	NA	NA	NA	NA	NA	NA
May	NA	NA	NA	NA	NA	NA	NA
June	NA	NA	NA	NA	NA	NA	NA
July	NA	NA	NA	NA	NA	NA	NA
August	NA	NA	NA	NA	NA	NA	NA
September	NA	NA	NA	NA	NA	NA	NA
October	NA	NA	NA	NA	NA	NA	NA
November	NA	NA	NA	NA	NA	NA	NA
December	NA	NA	NA	NA	NA	NA	NA
2008							
January	5.80	0.27	5.84	30.3	339.3	462.5	78.8
February	5.51	0.30	5.55	30.2	364.0	503.2	76.6
March	5.54	0.36	5.59	30.1	324.8	444.4	77.3
April	5.60	0.25	5.63	30.0	305.6	432.6	79.1
May	5.59	0.34	5.64	29.5	264.2	361.1	79.6
June	5.74	0.32	5.79	29.8	317.9	447.2	77.5
July	5.91	0.36	5.96	29.9	299.1	414.5	77.8
August	5.89	0.32	5.94	29.8	280.0	398.0	74.4
September	5.81	0.27	5.84	29.9	295.0	429.0	71.0
October	6.10	0.31	6.14	30.0	266.6	344.9	80.5
November	NA	NA	NA	NA	NA	NA	NA
December	NA	NA	NA	NA	NA	NA	NA
2007							
January	6.25	0.39	6.31	30.1	316.2	417.2	77.6
February	6.27	0.55	6.35	29.9	337.5	441.7	78.8
March	6.15	0.45	6.22	29.9	313.6	415.2	77.5
April	6.10	0.46	6.16	30.3	338.6	440.2	79.2
May	6.17	0.48	6.24	30.1	343.4	439.8	80.4
June	6.35	0.50	6.42	30.1	337.5	445.6	78.0
July	6.39	0.54	6.46	30.1	346.3	452.0	79.1
August	6.52	0.46	6.58	30.1	365.1	469.4	79.6
September	6.52	0.45	6.58	30.2	346.6	456.3	78.7
October	6.38	0.39	6.44	29.6	352.1	463.3	78.1
November	6.12	0.41	6.18	30.4	378.1	493.0	80.3
December	6.01	0.25	6.05	30.0	329.0	424.6	82.5
2006							
January	5.97	0.27	6.01	30.0	289.6	397.3	75.8
February	6.01	0.24	6.04	30.1	300.8	410.0	75.4
March	6.23	0.26	6.26	30.1	301.4	403.6	76.5
April	6.34	0.26	6.37	30.0	301.9	405.3	76.9
May	6.42	0.26	6.46	30.1	298.6	398.1	77.5
June	6.48	0.24	6.52	30.0	301.9	402.9	77.0
July	6.53	0.31	6.58	30.1	297.9	401.5	76.6
August	6.66	0.32	6.70	30.0	320.0	426.7	76.9
September	6.30	0.47	6.37	30.2	303.6	396.6	78.6
October	6.30	0.45	6.36	29.8	311.7	411.7	78.5
November	6.31	0.46	6.37	29.9	315.5	417.4	78.2
December	6.29	0.44	6.35	30.1	330.2	431.5	78.2

Table 2-83. Terms on Conventional Single-Family Mortgages, Adjustable-Rate Mortgages, All Homes, Monthly National Averages, 1986–2010—*Continued*

[Percent, years, dollars in thousands.]

Year and month	Contract interest rate	Initial fees and charges	Effective interest rate	Term to maturity	Mortgage loan amount	Purchase price	Loan-to-price ratio
2005							
January	5.62	0.29	5.66	29.9	242.3	319.7	78.4
February	5.24	0.19	5.26	29.9	265.7	359.5	77.3
March	5.32	0.29	5.36	29.9	263.4	355.2	77.0
April	5.40	0.33	5.44	29.9	263.4	351.4	77.5
May	5.41	0.32	5.45	30.0	266.9	353.3	78.4
June	5.33	0.30	5.37	30.0	283.4	384.5	76.3
July	5.39	0.26	5.42	30.0	284.1	388.1	76.3
August	5.46	0.24	5.49	30.0	279.0	374.2	77.2
September	5.53	0.28	5.57	30.0	294.0	403.3	75.5
October	5.63	0.22	5.66	30.0	297.3	409.6	75.2
November	5.84	0.24	5.88	30.0	293.9	409.4	74.6
December	5.86	0.27	5.90	30.1	295.7	403.0	75.6
2004							
January	4.91	0.46	4.98	29.9	224.2	294.3	78.9
February	4.94	0.46	5.01	30.0	230.4	305.4	78.2
March	4.66	0.35	4.71	29.8	231.1	309.2	78.0
April	4.66	0.32	4.70	29.8	239.2	319.8	78.2
May	5.04	0.32	5.09	29.8	229.6	301.0	79.3
June	5.34	0.36	5.39	29.8	236.4	310.6	79.1
July	5.36	0.34	5.41	29.7	236.9	310.9	78.5
August	5.31	0.37	5.36	29.7	234.5	310.8	78.3
September	5.24	0.41	5.29	29.9	245.2	327.1	77.8
October	5.33	0.36	5.38	29.9	242.0	324.8	77.6
November	5.40	0.31	5.45	29.9	242.0	318.6	78.5
December	5.58	0.26	5.62	29.8	232.0	305.3	78.8
2003							
January	5.22	0.32	5.26	29.9	229.9	311.8	77.2
February	5.15	0.34	5.19	29.9	222.5	298.2	78.2
March	5.00	0.32	5.04	29.8	224.9	302.8	77.7
April	4.98	0.32	5.02	29.7	227.4	297.9	79.9
May	4.93	0.45	4.99	29.7	202.7	278.7	75.9
June	4.65	0.36	4.70	29.9	217.6	294.6	76.9
July	4.67	0.43	4.73	29.3	234.5	314.7	78.2
August	4.85	0.39	4.91	29.8	241.7	321.8	78.4
September	5.09	0.48	5.16	29.8	219.3	296.3	77.4
October	5.08	0.32	5.13	29.6	229.9	307.2	77.6
November	5.13	0.40	5.18	29.9	218.8	287.7	78.3
December	5.00	0.52	5.07	29.8	226.4	297.3	79.0
2002							
January	6.01	0.38	6.07	29.7	224.8	306.0	76.6
February	5.95	0.35	6.00	29.8	229.0	307.5	77.3
March	5.92	0.33	5.97	29.6	231.7	313.2	77.6
April	5.91	0.32	5.96	29.8	232.6	310.2	78.4
May	5.72	0.37	5.78	29.8	226.7	297.7	79.0
June	5.64	0.40	5.70	29.9	236.0	316.3	77.5
July	5.44	0.44	5.50	29.8	231.7	311.0	78.2
August	5.38	0.40	5.43	29.6	234.4	318.4	77.1
September	5.39	0.41	5.45	29.9	232.5	319.2	76.6
October	5.31	0.43	5.37	29.5	231.2	316.8	76.5
November	5.34	0.40	5.40	29.7	235.4	322.2	76.9
December	5.26	0.41	5.32	29.7	243.6	326.2	77.4
2001							
January	6.51	0.32	6.56	29.7	248.9	337.4	76.1
February	6.65	0.27	6.69	29.7	268.6	366.5	75.9
March	6.53	0.29	6.57	29.7	270.5	363.2	76.7
April	6.46	0.32	6.51	29.8	244.1	326.1	77.5
May	6.48	0.33	6.53	29.9	235.2	310.9	78.7
June	6.37	0.36	6.42	29.8	232.3	307.0	78.2
July	6.47	0.38	6.53	29.9	235.3	314.2	77.4
August	6.36	0.35	6.41	29.7	235.4	316.7	76.7
September	6.27	0.37	6.32	29.9	234.1	318.0	76.6
October	6.05	0.31	6.10	29.5	231.5	315.2	76.5
November	6.02	0.25	6.06	29.6	241.1	327.5	76.8
December	6.02	0.35	6.08	29.8	225.2	307.4	76.3

Table 2-83. Terms on Conventional Single-Family Mortgages, Adjustable-Rate Mortgages, All Homes, Monthly National Averages, 1986–2010—*Continued*

[Percent, years, dollars in thousands.]

Year and month	Contract interest rate	Initial fees and charges	Effective interest rate	Term to maturity	Mortgage loan amount	Purchase price	Loan-to-price ratio
2000							
January	6.88	0.46	6.95	29.8	191.4	252.2	78.2
February	7.06	0.46	7.13	29.9	186.3	244.2	78.8
March	7.14	0.46	7.21	29.8	192.8	255.4	77.9
April	7.09	0.41	7.16	29.8	197.6	262.4	77.8
May	7.16	0.44	7.23	29.8	200.1	264.6	78.1
June	7.16	0.41	7.22	29.9	209.8	279.8	77.5
July	7.01	0.39	7.07	29.9	216.6	289.3	77.1
August	6.92	0.40	6.98	29.8	217.9	291.3	76.5
September	6.83	0.41	6.89	29.8	218.7	290.7	77.0
October	6.73	0.38	6.78	29.9	226.8	305.0	76.3
November	6.63	0.38	6.69	29.9	227.8	306.0	76.3
December	6.66	0.36	6.72	29.8	231.6	310.7	75.8
1999							
January	6.16	0.79	6.27	29.8	195.6	259.2	76.8
February	6.17	0.73	6.28	29.9	203.3	271.4	76.8
March	6.20	0.75	6.31	29.9	196.7	260.0	77.4
April	6.13	0.73	6.23	29.8	190.8	251.5	77.8
May	6.21	0.71	6.32	29.6	189.4	250.0	78.4
June	6.39	0.71	6.49	29.7	189.6	248.7	78.2
July	6.65	0.75	6.76	29.3	169.6	220.9	78.4
August	6.58	0.50	6.66	29.8	185.1	244.0	78.2
September	6.60	0.43	6.66	29.8	189.7	249.1	78.3
October	6.55	0.41	6.61	29.9	189.1	249.6	77.9
November	6.59	0.32	6.64	29.8	187.2	247.7	77.7
December	6.57	0.36	6.62	29.6	188.5	246.5	78.2
1998							
January	6.55	0.86	6.68	29.2	162.3	209.6	79.5
February	6.48	0.84	6.60	29.2	166.7	219.5	78.3
March	6.48	0.80	6.59	29.5	169.6	222.3	78.5
April	6.45	0.72	6.55	29.3	178.5	235.0	78.1
May	6.44	0.81	6.56	29.8	173.5	225.0	79.1
June	6.36	0.85	6.49	29.9	182.3	238.5	78.6
July	6.30	0.73	6.40	29.6	188.5	250.7	77.2
August	6.37	0.83	6.49	29.6	180.3	236.2	78.4
September	6.21	0.70	6.31	29.7	177.6	232.4	77.9
October	6.13	0.54	6.21	29.4	193.7	254.9	77.7
November	6.18	0.54	6.26	29.7	202.5	269.0	77.4
December	6.09	0.64	6.18	29.6	195.8	261.4	77.0
1997							
January	6.83	0.86	6.96	29.3	148.7	190.9	79.7
February	6.81	0.82	6.93	29.7	153.5	192.9	81.2
March	6.89	0.86	7.02	28.9	146.1	186.0	80.0
April	7.00	0.84	7.13	29.2	153.8	195.4	80.1
May	6.86	0.82	6.99	29.6	150.7	191.3	80.3
June	6.91	0.93	7.06	29.5	158.9	204.1	79.7
July	6.70	0.85	6.83	29.5	155.0	199.0	79.6
August	6.68	0.91	6.82	29.6	158.2	205.0	78.7
September	6.67	0.88	6.80	29.5	156.7	199.8	80.1
October	6.59	0.84	6.72	29.4	160.3	207.4	79.2
November	6.60	0.94	6.74	29.4	156.1	200.5	79.9
December	6.53	0.90	6.67	29.6	160.0	208.1	78.8
1996							
January	6.86	0.77	6.98	27.5	130.2	168.2	78.4
February	6.72	0.83	6.85	27.7	142.3	183.6	79.1
March	6.75	0.83	6.88	29.2	160.6	203.5	80.7
April	6.85	0.76	6.97	28.5	145.1	184.8	80.0
May	7.07	0.75	7.19	29.2	157.0	199.0	80.6
June	6.96	0.72	7.07	29.6	156.1	199.1	80.0
July	7.20	0.79	7.32	28.5	153.7	197.6	79.4
August	6.99	0.80	7.11	29.5	153.6	196.4	79.4
September	7.02	0.84	7.15	29.5	151.2	194.5	79.6
October	6.89	0.87	7.02	29.2	143.7	181.9	80.6
November	6.77	0.88	6.90	29.3	149.6	189.2	80.7
December	6.76	0.93	6.90	28.9	142.8	184.0	79.6

Table 2-83. Terms on Conventional Single-Family Mortgages, Adjustable-Rate Mortgages, All Homes, Monthly National Averages, 1986–2010—*Continued*

[Percent, years, dollars in thousands.]

Year and month	Contract interest rate	Initial fees and charges	Effective interest rate	Term to maturity	Mortgage loan amount	Purchase price	Loan-to-price ratio
1995							
January	6.95	0.94	7.09	29.6	126.6	159.4	81.3
February	7.18	0.97	7.33	29.3	124.3	156.8	81.2
March	7.18	0.88	7.32	29.4	131.0	168.0	79.9
April	7.14	0.82	7.26	29.4	126.8	162.5	80.1
May	7.16	0.92	7.30	29.4	132.8	170.3	80.1
June	6.89	0.96	7.03	29.4	143.0	179.8	81.5
July	7.00	0.95	7.15	29.2	142.8	181.3	80.5
August	6.80	0.92	6.94	29.8	146.2	185.0	81.0
September	6.97	0.78	7.09	29.0	140.6	180.3	80.1
October	6.87	0.80	6.99	28.8	137.2	175.0	80.1
November	6.80	0.75	6.91	29.4	147.8	190.7	79.3
December	6.45	0.58	6.54	28.7	127.9	163.7	80.6
1994							
January	5.46	0.90	5.59	27.8	125.9	168.4	75.5
February	5.26	1.07	5.42	28.8	132.3	173.0	77.8
March	5.42	0.97	5.56	28.8	135.2	174.4	78.4
April	5.79	1.04	5.95	29.2	130.2	169.2	78.8
May	5.95	1.03	6.10	29.2	136.0	172.9	79.5
June	6.22	1.06	6.38	29.2	132.7	169.4	80.3
July	6.33	1.03	6.49	29.5	132.8	168.3	80.8
August	6.44	1.04	6.59	29.3	131.6	167.3	80.2
September	6.51	1.02	6.66	29.5	129.8	163.9	81.1
October	6.58	1.00	6.73	29.3	129.7	165.1	80.5
November	6.61	0.97	6.76	29.3	124.4	156.3	81.3
December	6.83	1.33	7.03	29.6	134.8	172.4	80.8
1993							
January	6.12	1.35	6.31	28.9	138.0	184.9	76.1
February	5.76	1.25	5.95	29.7	136.7	177.6	77.8
March	5.49	1.26	5.67	29.9	129.5	172.3	76.5
April	5.75	1.11	5.91	27.1	116.7	155.7	75.8
May	5.75	1.21	5.93	27.7	117.3	152.8	77.5
June	5.63	1.32	5.82	29.0	128.6	176.8	76.0
July	5.61	1.26	5.80	28.8	128.0	168.0	77.7
August	5.53	1.16	5.70	28.4	125.7	164.1	77.1
September	5.48	1.21	5.66	28.8	131.8	170.0	78.3
October	5.35	1.07	5.51	28.4	120.1	161.4	75.4
November	5.23	1.18	5.40	29.9	131.6	175.6	77.6
December	5.21	1.10	5.36	29.5	134.1	175.0	77.5
1992							
January	6.78	1.23	6.97	28.9	124.5	168.6	75.8
February	6.91	1.47	7.14	27.3	100.7	132.3	77.0
March	6.64	1.32	6.84	29.0	121.0	157.2	77.6
April	6.73	1.54	6.96	30.0	119.4	159.3	75.4
May	6.71	1.54	6.94	29.7	136.2	177.3	77.5
June	6.73	1.53	6.95	29.0	133.2	176.2	77.2
July	6.27	1.39	6.48	29.8	144.4	190.4	77.0
August	6.19	1.48	6.40	28.9	132.6	172.4	77.6
September	6.10	1.42	6.31	29.2	115.8	153.9	75.9
October	5.95	1.37	6.16	28.8	111.4	150.6	76.0
November	6.06	1.41	6.27	29.0	121.8	166.3	76.0
December	5.99	1.42	6.20	28.9	132.9	175.4	77.7
1991							
January	8.79	1.52	9.03	28.5	117.1	154.5	76.4
February	8.62	1.64	8.89	29.1	120.1	160.1	76.3
March	8.56	1.47	8.80	28.0	113.3	153.1	75.5
April	8.39	1.57	8.64	29.2	125.9	164.2	77.1
May	8.21	1.46	8.45	28.8	125.2	166.4	75.7
June	7.94	1.35	8.15	29.5	129.7	170.8	76.5
July	7.91	1.40	8.14	28.7	127.6	168.0	77.5
August	8.03	1.36	8.24	27.9	118.6	158.1	76.3
September	7.71	1.42	7.93	28.5	117.6	158.2	76.1
October	7.55	1.33	7.76	28.6	118.2	158.8	75.9
November	7.50	1.39	7.72	28.8	128.9	172.7	75.9
December	7.43	1.41	7.65	28.7	129.1	177.5	75.2

Table 2-83. Terms on Conventional Single-Family Mortgages, Adjustable-Rate Mortgages, All Homes, Monthly National Averages, 1986–2010—*Continued*

[Percent, years, dollars in thousands.]

Year and month	Contract interest rate	Initial fees and charges	Effective interest rate	Term to maturity	Mortgage loan amount	Purchase price	Loan-to-price ratio
1990							
January	9.06	1.73	9.34	29.6	120.8	158.6	76.2
February	9.02	1.51	9.26	29.2	116.4	154.6	74.9
March	8.95	1.68	9.22	29.5	121.5	157.7	78.1
April	8.94	1.66	9.21	29.3	127.0	166.3	77.0
May	9.00	1.73	9.28	29.4	119.0	155.9	77.1
June	9.07	1.59	9.33	29.1	118.7	156.6	77.0
July	8.98	1.65	9.25	29.0	124.0	165.6	75.6
August	8.93	1.51	9.12	28.8	116.4	153.1	76.7
September	8.83	1.47	9.06	29.0	119.6	156.9	76.7
October	8.79	1.48	9.03	28.8	121.2	161.3	76.3
November	8.84	1.41	9.07	29.3	121.9	161.2	77.0
December	8.70	1.51	8.94	29.2	122.0	159.9	77.1
1989							
January	8.54	1.69	8.80	29.6	121.7	160.3	77.2
February	8.78	1.85	9.07	29.4	117.2	155.1	76.8
March	8.93	1.88	9.24	28.8	116.0	153.0	77.0
April	9.11	1.80	9.41	29.4	125.6	164.8	77.4
May	9.42	1.94	9.74	29.2	118.8	157.3	76.9
June	9.72	1.85	10.03	28.7	108.9	145.8	76.4
July	9.52	1.89	9.84	28.5	114.8	152.1	76.7
August	9.26	1.82	9.56	28.5	117.4	157.2	75.8
September	9.37	1.49	9.62	28.3	114.2	152.3	76.1
October	9.25	1.64	9.52	28.1	109.9	147.4	75.4
November	9.12	1.67	9.39	28.3	116.2	153.0	76.4
December	8.99	1.64	9.25	29.1	127.7	164.4	76.2
1988							
January	8.27	1.98	8.58	28.9	102.2	137.7	76.2
February	8.23	2.02	8.55	28.8	100.4	133.0	77.1
March	8.07	1.96	8.38	28.8	99.5	131.2	71.9
April	7.98	1.84	8.27	28.8	105.7	137.7	78.3
May	8.02	1.86	8.31	28.4	105.3	138.1	77.9
June	8.10	1.86	8.39	28.9	106.0	138.3	78.0
July	8.13	1.95	8.44	29.0	107.1	140.9	77.9
August	8.17	1.92	8.47	28.9	107.4	139.8	78.4
September	8.22	1.83	8.51	29.1	111.2	145.9	77.6
October	8.30	1.81	8.58	28.9	112.7	149.4	76.9
November	8.46	1.88	8.76	28.8	112.5	146.8	77.9
December	8.52	1.67	8.78	29.4	116.6	152.8	77.4
1987							
January	8.51	1.97	8.83	27.6	93.5	122.5	76.8
February	8.23	1.93	8.54	28.2	97.5	129.6	76.2
March	8.07	1.84	8.36	28.2	97.7	129.9	76.1
April	8.08	1.79	8.36	28.2	102.0	135.3	76.4
May	8.13	1.89	8.43	28.1	99.8	132.6	76.3
June	8.06	1.94	8.37	28.6	97.7	129.0	77.3
July	8.20	1.97	8.51	28.6	97.7	130.1	76.8
August	8.21	1.91	8.51	28.5	97.3	129.5	76.9
September	8.15	1.92	8.45	28.5	99.2	132.0	76.6
October	8.14	2.03	8.46	28.7	99.8	132.2	77.3
November	8.28	2.00	8.59	28.8	97.8	130.1	77.1
December	8.35	1.99	8.67	29.0	99.9	132.7	77.1
1986							
January	9.80	2.16	10.17	28.1	84.7	112.2	77.3
February	9.78	2.08	10.14	27.7	85.0	116.0	75.4
March	9.60	2.21	9.97	27.4	80.5	108.8	75.6
April	9.53	1.99	9.87	26.6	82.1	109.5	76.2
May	9.45	1.83	9.76	26.6	82.1	110.0	75.8
June	9.17	1.91	9.48	27.0	88.9	119.1	75.9
July	9.17	1.80	9.47	26.4	86.3	116.5	75.0
August	9.09	1.85	9.40	27.5	89.9	119.5	77.1
September	8.94	1.88	9.25	27.1	89.5	120.4	74.5
October	8.74	2.02	9.07	27.0	88.6	117.6	76.6
November	8.54	2.01	8.87	27.7	90.8	121.2	76.2
December	8.49	2.00	8.81	28.4	96.8	127.7	76.6

NA = Not available.

Source: Federal Housing Finance Agency, Monthly Interest Rate Survey

Table 2-84. Terms on Conventional Single-Family Mortgages, Fixed-Rate Mortgages, Previously Occupied Homes, Monthly National Averages, 1986–2010

[Percent, years, dollars in thousands.]

Year and month	Contract interest rate	Initial fees and charges	Effective interest rate	Term to maturity	Mortgage loan amount	Purchase price	Loan-to-price ratio
2010							
January	5.03	0.47	5.10	27.5	207.9	303.5	72.6
February	5.08	0.58	5.17	27.2	202.0	283.7	74.9
March	5.03	0.55	5.11	27.3	205.7	288.4	74.5
April	5.05	0.58	5.13	27.5	213.2	300.4	74.4
May	5.05	0.67	5.15	27.1	211.4	294.4	74.1
June	4.93	0.80	5.04	27.4	211.8	298.1	74.6
July	4.80	0.88	4.93	27.3	211.3	298.2	74.5
August	4.68	0.83	4.80	27.1	201.9	292.4	73.2
September	4.59	0.85	4.71	27.3	195.4	279.4	73.4
October	4.50	0.96	4.63	27.6	202.8	295.6	72.5
November	4.47	0.83	4.59	27.9	202.7	289.9	75.2
December	4.64	0.80	4.75	28.3	190.1	265.3	76.2
2009							
January	5.10	0.61	5.19	28.4	203.3	289.6	75.0
February	5.04	0.53	5.11	28.0	204.6	292.1	74.3
March	5.04	0.57	5.12	28.1	209.1	298.2	74.6
April	4.87	0.53	4.95	28.2	212.7	299.1	74.9
May	4.88	0.53	4.96	28.2	216.4	311.0	74.0
June	5.11	0.51	5.18	28.4	226.4	321.2	74.6
July	5.28	0.60	5.37	28.2	221.8	310.2	74.9
August	5.28	0.59	5.36	27.9	214.9	301.7	74.9
September	5.19	0.56	5.27	27.8	206.7	291.0	74.6
October	5.05	0.58	5.13	27.8	203.2	285.3	74.2
November	5.05	0.54	5.13	27.8	205.0	290.1	74.2
December	4.97	0.57	5.06	27.1	210.7	294.8	74.3
2008							
January	5.98	0.52	6.06	28.3	200.3	279.2	78.3
February	5.91	0.44	5.98	27.6	193.5	280.8	76.0
March	6.08	0.51	6.15	27.8	196.1	277.1	77.5
April	6.00	0.43	6.06	27.7	209.5	295.2	77.2
May	6.08	0.42	6.14	28.2	208.3	292.5	77.4
June	6.28	0.39	6.34	28.1	209.9	294.0	77.2
July	6.46	0.49	6.54	28.1	203.5	289.0	76.3
August	6.52	0.47	6.59	28.1	206.1	286.5	76.7
September	6.20	0.54	6.28	28.4	208.1	285.7	77.4
October	6.16	0.51	6.23	28.5	204.5	281.1	76.1
November	6.19	0.55	6.27	28.7	203.1	276.9	77.0
December	5.51	0.55	5.59	28.5	204.6	285.2	75.1
2007							
January	6.38	0.35	6.43	29.1	195.1	264.0	79.1
February	6.41	0.38	6.47	29.3	197.7	273.7	78.2
March	6.35	0.37	6.41	29.4	201.5	273.6	79.6
April	6.30	0.36	6.36	29.3	198.4	267.9	79.7
May	6.39	0.42	6.45	29.4	205.3	269.1	81.1
June	6.61	0.36	6.66	29.6	211.6	278.6	80.7
July	6.79	0.38	6.85	29.3	196.6	261.5	80.4
August	6.76	0.41	6.82	29.2	195.1	260.5	80.6
September	6.59	0.43	6.66	29.2	190.3	258.1	80.2
October	6.51	0.42	6.57	28.8	194.3	250.9	80.2
November	6.37	0.41	6.43	28.8	201.5	274.3	79.2
December	6.25	0.51	6.33	28.7	197.5	268.5	80.4
2006							
January	6.39	0.39	6.44	28.1	171.6	247.0	75.3
February	6.40	0.35	6.45	27.9	178.9	256.7	75.2
March	6.47	0.31	6.51	28.4	183.0	261.4	75.6
April	6.54	0.33	6.59	28.4	185.8	262.9	76.2
May	6.66	0.31	6.70	28.3	189.7	267.8	76.3
June	6.71	0.34	6.76	28.4	190.2	270.0	76.1
July	6.83	0.34	6.88	28.5	186.2	259.2	77.4
August	6.77	0.39	6.83	28.7	185.0	259.9	77.1
September	6.63	0.38	6.68	28.8	191.9	264.8	77.6
October	6.59	0.36	6.64	28.8	195.8	273.1	77.0
November	6.48	0.36	6.53	29.2	198.0	274.0	77.6
December	6.41	0.33	6.46	29.0	199.9	271.3	79.0

Table 2-84. Terms on Conventional Single-Family Mortgages, Fixed-Rate Mortgages, Previously Occupied Homes, Monthly National Averages, 1986–2010—*Continued*

[Percent, years, dollars in thousands.]

Year and month	Contract interest rate	Initial fees and charges	Effective interest rate	Term to maturity	Mortgage loan amount	Purchase price	Loan-to-price ratio
2005							
January	5.85	0.43	5.92	27.1	158.6	233.5	74.9
February	5.84	0.25	5.88	27.2	159.7	243.9	73.5
March	5.93	0.38	5.98	27.8	168.7	241.9	75.7
April	6.05	0.43	6.11	27.6	164.7	241.7	74.0
May	5.96	0.41	6.02	27.5	168.2	247.3	74.1
June	5.78	0.38	5.84	27.5	174.8	264.0	72.0
July	5.77	0.37	5.83	27.6	175.5	262.1	73.4
August	5.93	0.34	5.98	27.6	177.0	260.5	73.6
September	5.95	0.37	6.00	27.8	175.9	258.9	73.7
October	6.09	0.32	6.14	27.7	174.2	256.5	73.5
November	6.34	0.35	6.39	27.7	169.8	252.4	74.0
December	6.43	0.34	6.48	27.8	163.4	238.5	74.9
2004							
January	5.88	0.48	5.95	25.9	142.9	214.0	73.1
February	5.85	0.30	5.90	25.9	140.0	220.8	70.1
March	5.76	0.35	5.81	25.6	138.9	218.7	69.8
April	5.71	0.32	5.75	26.1	147.8	226.7	71.2
May	6.11	0.31	6.16	26.0	148.7	230.2	70.7
June	6.35	0.35	6.40	26.2	148.5	231.1	70.3
July	6.22	0.35	6.27	27.2	153.1	223.4	74.7
August	6.06	0.46	6.13	27.2	151.0	220.3	75.2
September	5.88	0.50	5.95	27.3	149.6	217.6	74.9
October	5.85	0.45	5.92	27.3	148.4	217.8	75.0
November	5.85	0.40	5.91	27.2	151.9	227.8	74.2
December	5.84	0.38	5.89	27.6	161.8	235.5	75.1
2003							
January	6.05	0.29	6.09	25.6	145.8	222.8	71.2
February	6.02	0.30	6.07	26.1	146.2	220.5	72.1
March	5.89	0.25	5.92	25.9	146.9	221.5	71.8
April	5.82	0.27	5.86	25.6	150.6	229.4	71.6
May	5.69	0.27	5.73	25.7	151.2	232.4	71.0
June	5.46	0.26	5.50	25.8	154.5	234.5	71.1
July	5.45	0.30	5.49	25.7	150.3	227.8	72.3
August	5.81	0.34	5.86	25.8	148.5	230.2	70.8
September	6.10	0.35	6.15	25.6	137.5	212.5	71.5
October	6.02	0.34	6.07	26.1	140.5	213.2	72.0
November	6.04	0.38	6.10	25.9	136.0	210.3	71.3
December	6.01	0.49	6.08	26.2	136.6	201.2	73.8
2002							
January	6.95	0.52	7.03	26.2	139.7	201.8	74.7
February	6.94	0.51	7.01	26.4	141.0	200.7	75.4
March	6.95	0.45	7.02	26.7	142.3	203.5	75.1
April	7.08	0.51	7.16	27.0	142.1	198.7	76.4
May	6.98	0.53	7.06	27.3	146.4	203.7	76.4
June	6.85	0.54	6.94	27.3	147.5	212.1	75.0
July	6.72	0.49	6.80	27.0	145.8	207.1	75.4
August	6.53	0.46	6.60	26.7	145.3	212.5	73.8
September	6.36	0.43	6.43	26.7	149.1	220.6	73.0
October	6.20	0.37	6.25	26.0	146.9	221.1	72.3
November	6.14	0.34	6.19	25.8	148.5	222.4	72.3
December	6.15	0.36	6.20	25.9	144.9	214.5	73.0
2001							
January	7.35	0.60	7.44	28.2	133.5	183.4	77.0
February	7.14	0.58	7.23	27.5	135.7	188.5	76.4
March	7.07	0.60	7.16	27.5	138.1	191.0	76.7
April	7.07	0.53	7.15	27.1	138.6	193.4	76.2
May	7.16	0.59	7.26	27.1	140.6	197.8	75.5
June	7.19	0.55	7.28	27.2	143.5	200.0	76.2
July	7.20	0.55	7.28	27.4	140.7	196.1	76.3
August	7.09	0.53	7.18	27.4	141.0	195.2	76.6
September	6.96	0.47	7.03	27.3	142.2	199.2	75.8
October	6.74	0.45	6.81	27.1	143.5	202.7	75.4
November	6.62	0.45	6.69	26.5	143.8	206.5	74.7
December	6.79	0.52	6.87	25.8	141.8	205.5	74.0

Table 2-84. Terms on Conventional Single-Family Mortgages, Fixed-Rate Mortgages, Previously Occupied Homes, Monthly National Averages, 1986–2010—*Continued*

[Percent, years, dollars in thousands.]

Year and month	Contract interest rate	Initial fees and charges	Effective interest rate	Term to maturity	Mortgage loan amount	Purchase price	Loan-to-price ratio
2000							
January	8.06	0.80	8.19	28.1	121.8	160.6	79.4
February	8.25	0.79	8.37	28.0	120.8	159.9	79.1
March	8.29	0.77	8.42	28.1	122.1	162.2	78.9
April	8.27	0.75	8.39	28.2	120.0	160.0	78.7
May	8.36	0.76	8.48	28.3	121.6	162.0	78.6
June	8.44	0.79	8.56	28.3	123.8	166.4	77.9
July	8.30	0.74	8.42	28.4	126.3	170.5	77.8
August	8.19	0.71	8.30	28.3	127.4	173.0	77.6
September	8.04	0.74	8.16	28.3	128.3	173.3	77.9
October	7.97	0.68	8.08	28.2	127.6	174.0	77.5
November	7.88	0.65	7.98	28.2	132.3	180.1	77.5
December	7.72	0.67	7.82	28.1	132.7	181.6	77.1
1999							
January	6.84	0.79	6.96	27.3	122.1	163.5	77.8
February	6.89	0.72	7.00	27.5	127.1	169.2	78.2
March	7.00	0.75	7.11	27.6	126.7	168.1	78.5
April	7.04	0.74	7.16	27.5	124.8	166.8	78.1
May	7.07	0.71	7.18	27.5	125.7	168.6	77.8
June	7.31	0.78	7.43	27.8	129.4	171.3	78.4
July	7.58	0.82	7.71	27.8	125.1	165.3	78.9
August	7.76	0.81	7.89	27.8	120.3	158.8	78.6
September	7.85	0.80	7.97	28.0	119.5	157.1	79.4
October	7.85	0.81	7.98	28.1	115.4	152.0	79.5
November	7.86	0.80	7.98	28.1	119.5	157.2	79.3
December	7.88	0.75	8.00	28.0	119.2	156.2	80.1
1998							
January	7.20	0.89	7.34	27.0	119.5	160.1	77.6
February	7.14	0.89	7.28	26.7	118.9	159.8	77.8
March	7.16	0.84	7.29	27.1	119.3	156.5	79.1
April	7.18	0.82	7.31	27.5	120.7	157.9	79.4
May	7.18	0.90	7.32	27.5	124.2	163.8	78.8
June	7.17	0.88	7.31	27.6	123.1	161.8	79.4
July	7.11	0.84	7.24	27.7	123.5	162.0	79.1
August	7.06	0.90	7.20	27.8	122.6	159.5	80.0
September	6.96	0.84	7.09	27.7	121.8	160.6	79.1
October	6.79	0.75	6.91	27.3	122.1	163.6	78.1
November	6.83	0.79	6.95	27.0	120.0	161.1	77.6
December	6.84	0.98	6.99	27.7	125.9	165.7	78.8
1997							
January	7.84	0.99	8.01	25.7	106.9	144.8	77.1
February	7.81	0.99	7.98	25.9	107.2	142.5	78.2
March	7.86	0.98	8.02	26.3	109.2	143.6	78.9
April	8.02	1.08	8.21	25.7	110.6	143.6	79.5
May	8.08	1.03	8.25	26.3	113.9	147.6	79.5
June	7.95	1.12	8.13	26.5	117.1	153.3	79.1
July	7.77	0.98	7.93	27.2	117.9	153.8	79.1
August	7.66	1.04	7.83	27.1	116.8	153.4	78.8
September	7.65	1.00	7.81	27.0	116.3	153.2	78.6
October	7.54	1.02	7.70	27.0	116.7	153.9	78.8
November	7.49	0.91	7.63	27.2	119.3	155.8	79.3
December	7.40	0.94	7.55	27.1	121.7	158.6	79.9
1996							
January	7.23	0.85	7.37	26.3	105.3	141.0	77.8
February	7.20	0.87	7.34	25.9	102.8	136.8	78.4
March	7.40	1.03	7.57	26.0	101.9	133.9	79.1
April	7.76	1.03	7.93	25.8	102.2	133.3	79.8
May	8.02	1.04	8.21	26.4	104.3	136.1	79.7
June	8.13	1.04	8.30	25.5	103.5	136.5	79.2
July	8.26	1.09	8.45	26.1	103.4	136.2	78.8
August	8.14	1.01	8.32	26.3	103.3	136.0	79.3
September	8.17	0.99	8.34	25.4	102.0	136.2	77.8
October	8.09	0.95	8.25	26.2	103.9	136.9	78.3
November	7.89	0.91	8.05	26.6	102.6	137.0	77.8
December	7.74	0.82	7.87	26.4	105.9	141.1	78.5

Table 2-84. Terms on Conventional Single-Family Mortgages, Fixed-Rate Mortgages, Previously Occupied Homes, Monthly National Averages, 1986–2010—*Continued*

[Percent, years, dollars in thousands.]

Year and month	Contract interest rate	Initial fees and charges	Effective interest rate	Term to maturity	Mortgage loan amount	Purchase price	Loan-to-price ratio
1995							
January	9.02	1.30	9.25	26.1	82.5	107.6	80.2
February	8.99	1.34	9.22	26.4	87.1	111.4	80.7
March	8.82	0.96	8.99	26.9	88.5	112.7	81.3
April	8.59	1.02	8.76	26.8	91.6	116.8	80.9
May	8.30	1.10	8.48	26.4	91.6	119.0	80.0
June	7.85	0.93	8.01	26.5	97.2	127.2	80.0
July	7.71	0.94	7.87	26.6	99.5	128.9	80.1
August	7.84	0.95	8.00	26.3	97.7	127.6	79.4
September	7.80	0.91	7.95	26.5	98.1	129.1	79.2
October	7.71	0.96	7.87	26.6	100.7	132.4	79.0
November	7.63	0.81	7.76	26.4	101.0	133.1	78.7
December	7.51	0.74	7.64	26.1	102.1	135.2	78.5
1994							
January	7.15	1.07	7.32	25.3	94.7	128.3	76.8
February	7.07	0.94	7.22	25.0	99.2	134.6	77.4
March	7.26	1.04	7.43	25.7	95.7	124.6	79.7
April	7.62	1.05	7.80	25.6	98.9	128.0	79.6
May	8.09	1.22	8.31	25.0	89.7	115.5	80.6
June	8.26	1.09	8.45	26.1	91.7	117.5	81.0
July	8.35	1.20	8.56	25.6	90.8	116.9	80.6
August	8.45	1.01	8.62	26.5	89.5	115.6	81.6
September	8.46	1.09	8.65	25.8	89.3	116.1	80.2
October	8.60	1.04	8.78	26.0	86.9	112.3	80.4
November	8.77	1.09	8.96	26.1	90.2	116.8	80.8
December	8.82	1.36	9.06	25.6	78.5	100.4	82.0
1993							
January	7.97	1.55	8.26	23.7	95.0	127.1	77.8
February	7.78	1.37	8.02	24.3	102.0	140.6	75.9
March	7.57	1.36	7.80	24.3	98.0	132.8	76.5
April	7.47	1.20	7.68	23.6	98.7	135.2	76.1
May	7.44	1.26	7.66	23.7	95.0	125.0	77.9
June	7.44	1.31	7.66	24.0	97.3	129.6	77.9
July	7.26	1.15	7.45	25.1	101.0	134.0	78.0
August	7.13	1.04	7.30	24.7	100.8	136.7	76.7
September	7.02	1.07	7.20	24.7	98.5	132.0	77.6
October	6.86	0.98	7.02	24.8	100.8	136.7	76.4
November	6.92	1.08	7.10	25.2	97.9	133.8	76.5
December	7.13	1.20	7.33	25.5	97.9	129.6	78.4
1992							
January	8.30	1.18	8.52	24.8	111.9	159.5	73.2
February	8.39	1.57	8.69	24.4	98.3	138.3	74.2
March	8.57	1.72	8.89	24.2	99.0	134.4	76.4
April	8.64	1.74	8.95	25.0	99.6	132.2	78.0
May	8.60	1.65	8.89	25.6	105.0	138.9	78.3
June	8.47	1.73	8.78	24.8	103.4	136.8	77.6
July	8.17	1.55	8.46	24.2	101.4	138.3	76.4
August	7.95	1.87	8.29	23.9	104.7	140.7	76.8
September	7.81	1.57	8.08	24.1	100.6	137.5	76.1
October	7.81	1.41	8.05	23.8	104.0	144.9	74.7
November	7.93	1.63	8.22	23.6	98.4	135.1	75.6
December	8.05	1.56	8.34	23.5	99.6	133.2	78.0
1991							
January	9.75	1.51	10.02	25.3	98.8	139.4	73.4
February	9.71	1.51	9.97	25.1	100.4	144.2	73.0
March	9.41	1.39	9.65	25.1	99.1	142.4	73.2
April	9.42	1.63	9.71	25.7	102.7	146.3	72.6
May	9.50	1.69	9.79	26.4	100.4	139.7	73.9
June	9.48	1.59	9.75	26.6	102.3	142.6	74.3
July	9.48	1.79	9.79	25.7	103.4	144.3	74.4
August	9.50	1.63	9.78	26.3	97.6	136.2	74.0
September	9.32	1.51	9.57	26.2	100.3	140.5	74.2
October	9.16	1.45	9.41	25.3	101.5	143.9	73.2
November	8.79	1.57	9.06	25.1	92.4	127.8	75.7
December	8.53	1.56	8.80	25.3	98.4	133.4	76.0

Table 2-84. Terms on Conventional Single-Family Mortgages, Fixed-Rate Mortgages, Previously Occupied Homes, Monthly National Averages, 1986–2010—*Continued*

[Percent, years, dollars in thousands.]

Year and month	Contract interest rate	Initial fees and charges	Effective interest rate	Term to maturity	Mortgage loan amount	Purchase price	Loan-to-price ratio
1990							
January	9.81	1.84	10.12	27.3	101.0	142.6	73.6
February	9.97	1.94	10.30	26.5	100.5	140.0	74.4
March	10.03	2.05	10.39	26.8	97.4	135.0	74.3
April	10.15	1.94	10.49	26.1	98.9	136.6	75.0
May	10.18	1.81	10.50	25.6	95.2	132.8	74.2
June	10.22	1.93	10.56	26.6	95.1	133.1	74.1
July	10.19	1.77	10.51	26.2	97.5	134.7	74.5
August	10.00	1.67	10.30	25.7	92.7	129.3	73.6
September	10.01	1.79	10.33	25.3	91.1	128.6	72.9
October	10.06	1.76	10.37	25.5	92.2	129.1	73.7
November	10.09	1.68	10.39	25.4	93.6	130.5	74.1
December	9.91	1.53	10.18	26.7	98.7	139.8	73.2
1989							
January	10.25	1.98	10.60	26.4	89.8	126.8	73.4
February	10.39	2.23	10.79	25.6	77.6	107.9	74.7
March	10.48	1.85	10.81	27.1	84.4	117.4	74.8
April	10.58	1.94	10.92	27.0	87.7	123.0	74.3
May	10.82	1.95	11.17	25.7	88.0	123.4	74.3
June	10.68	1.87	11.01	27.2	89.1	123.0	74.3
July	10.37	1.61	10.65	27.5	98.2	137.1	74.2
August	9.99	1.65	10.27	28.0	100.6	137.2	75.1
September	10.00	1.87	10.33	26.1	85.5	120.1	73.5
October	10.05	1.79	10.36	26.7	93.6	130.8	73.7
November	10.01	1.90	10.34	27.0	98.1	137.3	73.5
December	9.87	1.64	10.15	27.1	99.8	141.0	73.9
1988							
January	10.06	2.03	10.43	24.5	75.6	106.6	73.5
February	9.90	1.95	10.25	26.5	77.1	109.2	74.9
March	9.71	1.77	10.02	26.6	82.4	115.7	74.5
April	9.80	1.75	10.10	26.4	80.5	113.3	74.1
May	9.79	2.01	10.15	25.4	78.6	109.0	74.8
June	10.00	1.91	10.33	26.2	80.7	111.1	75.7
July	10.13	2.14	10.51	25.8	76.1	107.6	74.2
August	10.20	2.04	10.56	26.0	80.2	113.1	74.2
September	10.25	2.25	10.65	26.1	73.9	103.7	74.4
October	10.34	1.87	10.68	25.9	78.3	110.6	73.7
November	10.17	2.00	10.52	26.4	81.6	116.7	73.7
December	10.18	1.82	10.50	26.7	84.1	116.7	74.7
1987							
January	9.47	2.08	9.82	25.6	74.2	103.4	74.3
February	9.18	1.88	9.50	26.1	79.9	111.0	74.8
March	9.03	1.75	9.32	26.3	84.1	114.5	75.0
April	8.99	1.83	9.29	25.7	85.0	117.5	74.3
May	9.21	2.08	9.56	24.8	81.9	116.1	73.4
June	9.60	2.26	10.00	25.0	80.9	113.6	73.9
July	9.92	2.31	10.33	24.6	74.9	107.6	72.8
August	9.91	2.21	10.31	24.2	74.7	105.5	73.7
September	9.87	2.16	10.26	24.5	75.1	106.1	73.3
October	9.99	2.39	10.42	25.3	72.3	102.3	74.6
November	10.06	2.42	10.49	24.7	75.8	106.2	74.3
December	9.98	2.29	10.39	25.8	73.1	101.6	75.7
1986							
January	10.93	2.40	11.38	23.6	65.2	91.7	74.2
February	10.84	2.14	11.24	23.4	65.1	93.6	73.3
March	10.49	2.17	10.88	24.1	72.9	103.7	73.9
April	10.18	2.15	10.57	23.7	71.6	102.8	73.0
May	9.93	2.10	10.30	23.7	72.6	104.4	72.3
June	9.98	2.19	10.37	24.1	73.1	106.0	72.1
July	10.09	2.28	10.49	24.8	74.5	107.8	72.4
August	10.20	2.25	10.60	24.7	71.8	103.4	72.6
September	10.07	2.24	10.47	24.9	73.6	106.7	72.6
October	9.98	2.31	10.39	24.9	73.8	104.5	73.6
November	9.89	2.19	10.28	25.2	75.4	107.3	73.5
December	9.73	2.20	10.12	25.6	76.2	109.4	73.4

Source: Federal Housing Finance Agency, Monthly Interest Rate Survey

Table 2-85. Terms on Conventional Single-Family Mortgages, Adjustable-Rate Mortgages, Newly Built Homes, Monthly National Averages, 1986–2010

[Percent, years, dollars in thousands.]

Year and month	Contract interest rate	Initial fees and charges	Effective interest rate	Term to maturity	Mortgage loan amount	Purchase price	Loan-to-price ratio
2010							
January	NA	NA	NA	NA	NA	NA	NA
February	NA	NA	NA	NA	NA	NA	NA
March	NA	NA	NA	NA	NA	NA	NA
April	NA	NA	NA	NA	NA	NA	NA
May	NA	NA	NA	NA	NA	NA	NA
June	NA	NA	NA	NA	NA	NA	NA
July	NA	NA	NA	NA	NA	NA	NA
August	NA	NA	NA	NA	NA	NA	NA
September	NA	NA	NA	NA	NA	NA	NA
October	NA	NA	NA	NA	NA	NA	NA
November	NA	NA	NA	NA	NA	NA	NA
December	NA	NA	NA	NA	NA	NA	NA
2009							
January	NA	NA	NA	NA	NA	NA	NA
February	NA	NA	NA	NA	NA	NA	NA
March	NA	NA	NA	NA	NA	NA	NA
April	NA	NA	NA	NA	NA	NA	NA
May	NA	NA	NA	NA	NA	NA	NA
June	NA	NA	NA	NA	NA	NA	NA
July	NA	NA	NA	NA	NA	NA	NA
August	NA	NA	NA	NA	NA	NA	NA
September	NA	NA	NA	NA	NA	NA	NA
October	NA	NA	NA	NA	NA	NA	NA
November	NA	NA	NA	NA	NA	NA	NA
December	NA	NA	NA	NA	NA	NA	NA
2008							
January	5.78	0.56	5.86	30.0	394.7	561.3	80.9
February	5.88	0.44	5.94	30.0	410.6	549.1	78.3
March	5.30	0.64	5.39	30.0	336.8	456.5	73.5
April	5.60	0.37	5.65	29.5	393.8	588.7	73.3
May	5.50	0.41	5.56	30.0	284.4	398.0	77.6
June	5.66	0.42	5.72	30.1	310.9	465.2	74.4
July	5.88	0.65	5.97	30.0	324.2	432.0	80.9
August	5.87	0.57	5.95	30.0	288.0	413.2	70.7
September	5.76	0.38	5.82	29.6	366.7	511.8	73.6
October	5.71	0.66	5.80	30.0	371.6	516.7	77.1
November	NA	NA	NA	NA	NA	NA	NA
December	NA	NA	NA	NA	NA	NA	NA
2007							
January	6.05	0.68	6.14	30.0	348.8	473.0	76.4
February	6.28	0.61	6.36	30.0	337.7	441.0	78.0
March	6.11	0.78	6.22	30.0	319.3	427.5	76.6
April	6.08	0.78	6.19	30.2	367.3	479.1	79.4
May	5.99	0.74	6.10	30.0	377.1	494.2	76.8
June	6.24	0.77	6.35	30.0	331.8	435.7	77.3
July	6.36	0.65	6.46	29.8	365.4	472.9	78.6
August	6.52	0.51	6.59	30.1	447.8	564.6	80.2
September	6.28	0.59	6.36	30.3	371.6	498.9	72.9
October	6.42	0.44	6.48	29.2	354.8	467.9	77.2
November	6.08	0.80	6.19	30.0	447.2	609.9	76.7
December	6.08	0.31	6.13	28.3	333.2	424.2	79.9
2006							
January	5.61	0.37	5.66	30.0	299.6	409.5	75.3
February	5.74	0.33	5.79	30.2	302.0	404.8	76.1
March	5.93	0.35	5.98	30.0	296.3	391.1	76.9
April	6.10	0.38	6.15	30.0	301.7	404.2	76.1
May	6.24	0.32	6.29	29.7	326.0	438.5	75.6
June	6.44	0.34	6.49	30.0	302.8	407.0	75.6
July	6.31	0.37	6.36	30.1	316.8	422.7	76.4
August	6.58	0.36	6.63	30.0	290.0	388.7	76.1
September	6.13	0.73	6.23	29.9	307.0	406.1	76.5
October	6.33	0.55	6.41	29.9	330.1	438.3	77.1
November	6.34	0.59	6.43	30.0	323.0	421.8	77.6
December	6.21	0.65	6.31	30.1	332.9	431.8	78.6

Table 2-85. Terms on Conventional Single-Family Mortgages, Adjustable-Rate Mortgages, Newly Built Homes, Monthly National Averages, 1986–2010—*Continued*

[Percent, years, dollars in thousands.]

Year and month	Contract interest rate	Initial fees and charges	Effective interest rate	Term to maturity	Mortgage loan amount	Purchase price	Loan-to-price ratio
2005							
January	5.96	0.28	6.00	30.0	233.8	301.4	79.4
February	4.83	0.22	4.86	30.0	295.4	386.8	78.7
March	4.93	0.37	4.99	30.0	276.2	360.9	78.9
April	5.05	0.42	5.11	29.9	274.4	358.6	78.3
May	5.09	0.44	5.15	30.1	277.9	366.2	77.9
June	5.12	0.45	5.19	30.1	283.5	380.8	75.7
July	5.18	0.38	5.23	30.1	288.9	384.2	77.3
August	5.11	0.35	5.16	30.0	265.6	346.7	78.8
September	5.36	0.42	5.42	30.1	293.7	390.9	76.8
October	5.43	0.33	5.48	30.0	300.1	403.2	76.0
November	5.50	0.38	5.55	30.1	293.9	394.0	76.2
December	5.59	0.40	5.64	30.2	297.5	396.2	76.1
2004							
January	4.89	0.50	4.95	30.0	219.9	284.2	79.1
February	4.93	0.48	5.00	30.1	237.7	305.9	79.4
March	4.76	0.40	4.81	30.0	242.5	322.5	77.8
April	4.85	0.39	4.90	29.9	240.2	315.0	78.3
May	5.14	0.35	5.19	30.0	243.2	318.4	78.6
June	5.36	0.38	5.42	30.0	239.5	309.7	79.3
July	5.47	0.38	5.52	29.9	237.8	308.6	79.0
August	5.49	0.36	5.54	30.0	241.1	314.1	78.9
September	5.48	0.40	5.53	29.9	249.8	328.4	78.2
October	5.60	0.34	5.65	30.0	239.6	316.1	78.1
November	5.72	0.34	5.76	30.0	240.9	313.5	78.8
December	5.86	0.29	5.90	29.8	232.3	298.6	79.3
2003							
January	5.39	0.36	5.44	29.5	220.9	285.2	78.6
February	5.29	0.28	5.33	29.9	215.8	274.3	81.7
March	5.12	0.30	5.16	30.0	235.7	303.0	79.6
April	5.28	0.32	5.32	30.0	236.3	300.1	80.4
May	5.02	0.35	5.07	29.7	237.3	304.8	79.3
June	4.83	0.39	4.89	29.9	236.0	302.9	79.8
July	4.90	0.42	4.95	29.8	235.0	300.6	80.5
August	5.00	0.49	5.07	30.0	251.0	323.5	79.3
September	5.11	0.55	5.18	30.0	238.9	312.1	78.6
October	5.20	0.47	5.27	29.8	241.2	314.4	79.0
November	5.14	0.47	5.21	30.0	226.5	294.8	78.4
December	4.97	0.66	5.06	29.8	244.3	321.0	78.5
2002							
January	6.04	0.42	6.11	30.0	231.4	301.3	78.5
February	6.05	0.33	6.10	29.6	230.2	300.7	78.8
March	5.95	0.34	6.00	29.9	240.6	314.2	79.0
April	5.77	0.35	5.82	29.5	237.2	310.3	78.7
May	5.57	0.34	5.62	30.0	241.0	317.4	77.5
June	5.47	0.35	5.52	29.9	248.0	324.2	77.7
July	5.32	0.41	5.37	29.9	244.9	322.4	77.8
August	5.35	0.38	5.40	29.9	240.8	323.3	76.3
September	5.44	0.38	5.49	29.8	237.5	311.0	78.2
October	5.31	0.42	5.37	29.8	233.0	306.4	78.0
November	5.41	0.43	5.47	29.7	227.1	293.8	79.1
December	5.27	0.47	5.33	30.0	208.1	270.3	78.4
2001							
January	6.47	0.40	6.53	30.0	241.4	318.5	77.2
February	6.53	0.37	6.59	29.9	271.1	359.2	76.3
March	6.47	0.40	6.53	29.9	256.0	338.6	77.0
April	6.57	0.40	6.63	29.8	236.8	312.3	76.8
May	6.49	0.39	6.55	29.5	232.8	305.6	77.9
June	6.18	0.41	6.24	29.8	248.5	325.6	78.2
July	6.41	0.44	6.48	29.9	239.2	312.3	78.3
August	6.42	0.39	6.47	29.6	233.8	307.5	76.4
September	6.26	0.40	6.32	29.9	233.5	309.2	77.3
October	6.01	0.35	6.07	29.1	226.8	308.6	74.8
November	6.12	0.27	6.16	29.4	231.5	304.2	77.6
December	6.11	0.29	6.15	29.4	224.9	289.5	77.5

Table 2-85. Terms on Conventional Single-Family Mortgages, Adjustable-Rate Mortgages, Newly Built Homes, Monthly National Averages, 1986–2010—*Continued*

[Percent, years, dollars in thousands.]

Year and month	Contract interest rate	Initial fees and charges	Effective interest rate	Term to maturity	Mortgage loan amount	Purchase price	Loan-to-price ratio
2000							
January	6.51	0.48	6.58	30.1	196.2	254.0	78.7
February	6.56	0.49	6.64	30.0	192.2	248.8	79.3
March	6.70	0.49	6.77	30.0	199.9	260.8	78.4
April	6.65	0.44	6.72	30.0	208.0	270.6	78.7
May	6.49	0.47	6.56	29.9	206.9	269.0	78.6
June	6.35	0.46	6.42	30.1	216.3	284.4	77.9
July	6.30	0.43	6.37	30.0	219.2	286.4	78.3
August	6.44	0.44	6.50	30.0	219.9	286.6	78.4
September	6.38	0.42	6.44	30.0	224.3	292.3	78.1
October	6.42	0.44	6.48	30.1	233.9	307.1	77.9
November	6.39	0.43	6.45	30.0	239.1	314.3	77.5
December	6.55	0.51	6.63	29.7	241.0	318.2	75.8
1999							
January	6.17	0.76	6.28	29.9	189.5	249.5	76.9
February	6.08	0.67	6.17	30.1	192.3	251.6	77.9
March	6.17	0.68	6.27	29.8	194.2	252.7	77.9
April	6.12	0.61	6.21	29.9	198.6	254.3	79.2
May	6.19	0.60	6.28	29.8	195.8	250.9	79.3
June	6.39	0.64	6.48	30.0	199.9	256.1	79.6
July	6.60	0.72	6.71	29.2	193.9	250.5	78.7
August	6.33	0.56	6.42	29.6	190.2	248.2	78.3
September	6.21	0.46	6.28	30.0	187.6	242.4	79.2
October	6.13	0.45	6.20	29.9	192.4	249.6	78.5
November	6.26	0.41	6.32	29.9	194.9	254.0	78.2
December	6.26	0.44	6.33	30.0	198.8	254.0	79.2
1998							
January	6.53	0.99	6.68	29.8	173.3	224.1	79.7
February	6.41	0.90	6.54	30.1	182.4	237.0	78.1
March	6.48	0.89	6.61	29.9	193.4	253.4	78.6
April	6.39	0.77	6.51	29.8	193.3	250.2	78.9
May	6.43	0.75	6.54	29.8	193.6	249.7	78.9
June	6.39	0.75	6.50	30.0	198.5	258.4	79.0
July	6.39	0.69	6.49	30.0	201.3	261.7	78.1
August	6.38	0.71	6.49	30.0	188.3	243.4	78.7
September	6.33	0.69	6.43	29.6	188.8	244.6	78.2
October	6.05	0.57	6.13	29.7	199.0	255.9	79.1
November	6.20	0.59	6.29	29.6	192.6	249.5	78.0
December	6.24	0.76	6.35	29.8	198.1	254.6	78.8
1997							
January	6.96	0.93	7.10	29.4	165.7	211.8	79.1
February	6.89	1.02	7.04	29.6	160.1	203.0	81.6
March	7.07	1.01	7.22	29.7	166.6	210.7	80.3
April	7.24	1.00	7.39	28.9	159.6	205.7	79.4
May	7.16	0.96	7.31	29.5	169.8	217.2	80.2
June	7.18	1.02	7.33	29.5	163.4	210.5	79.7
July	7.03	0.96	7.17	29.9	172.7	215.8	82.1
August	6.56	1.05	6.72	29.9	179.3	230.0	79.3
September	6.69	1.01	6.84	29.8	174.9	222.6	80.6
October	6.63	0.88	6.75	29.9	179.4	228.5	79.9
November	6.61	1.01	6.76	29.5	172.3	220.5	81.0
December	6.62	0.91	6.76	29.7	192.9	248.9	78.6
1996							
January	6.88	0.76	6.99	28.5	153.9	199.5	76.4
February	6.61	1.07	6.76	28.6	173.2	219.1	80.1
March	6.54	0.99	6.69	28.7	172.3	222.0	77.6
April	6.83	0.73	6.94	29.2	155.8	197.7	79.3
May	7.03	0.88	7.16	29.5	181.1	235.3	80.6
June	7.13	0.97	7.27	29.9	179.1	227.3	80.1
July	7.26	0.96	7.41	29.0	177.0	240.9	75.7
August	7.20	1.09	7.37	28.7	166.6	219.1	75.8
September	7.12	1.02	7.27	29.8	170.6	220.0	78.4
October	7.10	1.06	7.26	29.6	157.8	199.8	80.8
November	6.96	0.99	7.11	29.6	174.0	222.3	79.8
December	7.09	0.97	7.23	27.9	157.7	205.2	81.8

Table 2-85. Terms on Conventional Single-Family Mortgages, Adjustable-Rate Mortgages, Newly Built Homes, Monthly National Averages, 1986–2010—*Continued*

[Percent, years, dollars in thousands.]

Year and month	Contract interest rate	Initial fees and charges	Effective interest rate	Term to maturity	Mortgage loan amount	Purchase price	Loan-to-price ratio
1995							
January	7.24	1.23	7.42	29.9	147.5	189.6	79.7
February	7.48	1.27	7.68	29.4	145.5	186.0	80.2
March	7.53	1.00	7.68	29.4	153.5	195.3	80.5
April	7.38	0.96	7.53	29.5	154.3	201.0	79.1
May	7.23	1.08	7.39	29.8	166.1	215.2	79.2
June	6.99	1.11	7.16	29.1	162.7	211.1	79.5
July	7.06	0.98	7.21	28.5	150.5	194.5	78.9
August	6.92	0.97	7.06	29.8	160.4	201.0	81.5
September	6.98	0.97	7.12	28.4	165.4	209.7	79.7
October	6.86	0.98	7.01	28.6	161.5	213.8	76.6
November	6.80	0.86	6.93	28.6	163.1	209.7	80.0
December	6.76	1.01	6.91	29.9	193.5	245.6	79.9
1994							
January	5.87	0.81	5.99	27.1	157.0	210.4	76.7
February	5.43	1.15	5.60	28.4	147.4	185.7	79.4
March	5.25	0.94	5.38	28.9	154.5	191.8	81.5
April	6.13	0.93	6.27	27.8	137.9	181.7	80.8
May	5.95	1.16	6.12	29.6	155.0	199.5	79.1
June	6.43	1.13	6.59	28.7	141.2	181.1	79.9
July	6.38	1.21	6.56	28.9	150.7	191.8	79.7
August	6.55	1.28	6.74	29.4	150.7	193.7	79.3
September	6.62	1.22	6.80	29.8	152.8	193.7	79.7
October	6.84	1.08	7.03	28.2	141.4	185.4	78.5
November	6.92	1.18	7.09	29.5	149.0	191.4	79.2
December	6.90	1.38	7.11	29.5	154.5	207.7	77.9
1993							
January	6.12	1.39	6.32	29.4	161.6	209.7	77.7
February	5.95	1.53	6.17	29.1	156.0	198.1	79.6
March	5.81	1.62	6.04	29.8	136.1	181.7	75.9
April	6.64	0.75	6.75	22.3	94.3	123.1	78.6
May	5.63	1.25	5.81	28.6	146.2	194.9	76.3
June	5.72	1.20	5.90	26.8	126.0	226.1	67.0
July	5.65	1.13	5.81	29.5	149.7	194.6	78.9
August	5.49	1.12	5.65	28.9	145.0	187.1	78.1
September	5.67	1.07	5.82	28.5	141.4	179.4	78.2
October	5.31	1.05	5.45	28.4	149.4	205.1	74.5
November	5.30	1.04	5.45	28.9	143.0	181.0	79.4
December	5.39	1.06	5.54	28.5	158.1	202.7	78.9
1992							
January	7.29	1.48	7.52	27.0	121.2	164.0	74.4
February	7.31	1.78	7.62	24.0	103.2	147.1	68.8
March	6.62	1.59	6.86	28.2	125.5	166.3	76.2
April	6.74	1.60	6.98	28.9	110.5	166.4	65.1
May	6.69	1.63	6.93	28.4	126.5	171.9	73.6
June	7.02	1.45	7.24	27.9	118.4	157.9	74.7
July	6.38	1.27	6.57	29.7	202.5	255.2	79.2
August	6.44	1.45	6.66	26.4	117.0	151.2	76.7
September	5.99	1.41	6.20	28.9	133.0	173.5	76.8
October	6.71	1.40	6.93	26.6	98.0	137.6	74.7
November	6.65	1.36	6.86	26.5	139.7	206.4	75.1
December	5.94	1.45	6.14	29.9	144.7	184.8	79.3
1991							
January	8.37	1.59	8.62	29.4	139.8	181.9	77.1
February	8.58	1.47	8.81	30.5	138.6	181.1	77.3
March	8.43	1.18	8.61	28.1	124.7	165.1	77.0
April	8.24	2.04	8.56	29.1	129.8	165.1	79.0
May	8.50	1.12	8.68	26.3	110.3	142.0	77.2
June	8.34	1.60	8.58	29.0	146.3	190.8	77.2
July	8.14	1.67	8.40	29.6	146.0	196.8	74.7
August	8.15	1.57	8.39	29.0	147.4	193.4	76.7
September	7.96	1.98	8.27	29.5	147.1	191.0	77.8
October	7.96	1.55	8.20	29.1	130.3	167.5	78.4
November	7.62	1.06	7.78	28.2	132.5	179.3	74.5
December	7.33	1.36	7.54	28.2	131.4	181.8	72.8

Table 2-85. Terms on Conventional Single-Family Mortgages, Adjustable-Rate Mortgages, Newly Built Homes, Monthly National Averages, 1986–2010—*Continued*

[Percent, years, dollars in thousands.]

Year and month	Contract interest rate	Initial fees and charges	Effective interest rate	Term to maturity	Mortgage loan amount	Purchase price	Loan-to-price ratio
1990							
January	8.93	1.71	9.21	29.7	127.8	167.3	76.4
February	8.82	1.68	9.09	29.7	119.2	159.0	74.3
March	8.83	1.89	9.13	29.5	125.3	164.2	76.9
April	8.92	1.64	9.18	29.3	147.6	191.0	77.6
May	8.87	2.17	9.22	30.0	143.1	185.1	77.8
June	9.20	1.64	9.47	28.3	125.6	165.0	77.5
July	8.92	1.68	9.19	29.9	144.3	191.6	75.9
August	8.99	1.78	9.27	28.3	132.0	176.4	74.5
September	8.69	1.69	8.95	30.3	141.6	184.4	77.6
October	9.05	1.50	9.29	28.6	122.5	163.3	75.0
November	8.83	1.51	9.06	29.5	132.1	177.5	75.5
December	8.60	1.62	8.86	30.2	145.1	189.7	76.8
1989							
January	8.47	1.81	8.76	29.6	131.8	174.4	77.2
February	8.81	1.97	9.11	29.5	124.0	166.5	75.7
March	8.79	1.95	9.11	29.6	134.5	177.8	77.3
April	8.99	1.91	9.30	30.0	141.0	186.0	76.8
May	9.24	1.95	9.55	29.6	125.7	165.4	77.3
June	9.56	1.80	9.85	28.8	120.8	162.2	75.9
July	9.44	1.88	9.75	29.1	133.4	177.7	76.9
August	9.18	2.03	9.52	28.3	122.1	161.5	76.1
September	9.09	1.50	9.34	29.5	129.7	175.6	75.3
October	9.05	1.67	9.32	28.4	125.1	160.3	78.5
November	9.08	1.52	9.33	27.2	123.4	161.5	76.3
December	8.91	1.70	9.19	29.4	144.7	189.1	77.1
1988							
January	8.15	2.14	8.48	29.3	116.4	159.9	74.4
February	8.30	2.13	8.64	28.7	108.6	144.4	76.6
March	8.06	2.27	8.42	28.4	107.1	141.1	78.3
April	7.86	2.12	8.19	29.2	117.4	153.7	77.9
May	7.80	1.99	8.11	29.3	117.7	154.3	78.1
June	8.09	1.94	8.39	28.9	116.4	153.8	76.6
July	8.08	2.09	8.41	29.5	121.3	160.2	77.6
August	7.98	2.16	8.31	29.5	123.9	160.5	79.0
September	8.16	1.97	8.47	29.4	121.2	156.8	78.7
October	8.21	1.84	8.50	29.3	23.6	161.3	77.9
November	8.32	2.11	8.65	29.6	125.5	160.7	79.6
December	8.38	1.93	8.68	29.4	122.4	161.5	77.1
1987							
January		1.85	8.80	29.0	103.3	134.2	77.7
February	8.18	2.02	8.50	29.7	110.4	145.7	77.2
March	7.97	1.93	8.28	28.4	96.4	126.8	77.3
April	8.10	1.86	8.40	26.9	100.8	135.1	75.0
May	7.79	2.05	8.10	29.6	113.0	146.2	78.5
June	8.02	2.11	8.34	29.2	107.9	142.7	77.0
July	8.21	2.05	8.53	29.5	112.2	148.5	77.1
August	8.06	2.05	8.38	29.3	116.4	155.6	76.2
September	8.17	1.96	8.48	29.0	112.5	149.3	77.6
October	8.10	2.18	8.44	29.7	114.9	154.8	76.6
November	8.24	2.13	8.57	29.4	108.3	143.2	77.1
December	8.30	2.07	8.62	29.4	115.4	154.7	76.7
1986							
January	9.71	2.34	10.15	27.1	84.7	111.3	77.9
February	9.62	2.26	10.00	29.2	95.8	126.6	77.4
March	9.44	2.31	9.82	28.8	81.3	106.6	77.0
April	9.47	2.06	9.81	27.8	90.8	118.8	77.6
May	9.50	1.91	9.82	28.3	88.9	115.4	78.9
June	8.96	2.02	9.28	28.4	101.4	133.2	77.6
July	9.07	1.86	9.38	26.8	97.1	129.8	74.7
August	9.21	1.90	9.52	27.8	89.9	118.7	78.0
September	8.70	1.93	9.01	27.3	93.6	128.6	73.9
October	8.57	2.19	8.92	28.4	101.0	130.3	78.6
November	8.30	2.24	8.66	28.8	104.0	136.6	77.3
December	8.38	2.12	8.73	27.7	98.4	129.3	76.2

NA = Not available.

Source: Federal Housing Finance Agency, Monthly Interest Rate Survey

Table 2-86. Terms on Conventional Single-Family Mortgages, Adjustable-Rate Mortgages, Previously Occupied Homes, Monthly National Averages, 1986–2010

[Percent, years, dollars in thousands.]

Year and month	Contract interest rate	Initial fees and charges	Effective interest rate	Term to maturity	Mortgage loan amount	Purchase price	Loan-to-price ratio
2010							
January	NA	NA	NA	NA	NA	NA	NA
February	NA	NA	NA	NA	NA	NA	NA
March	NA	NA	NA	NA	NA	NA	NA
April	NA	NA	NA	NA	NA	NA	NA
May	NA	NA	NA	NA	NA	NA	NA
June	NA	NA	NA	NA	NA	NA	NA
July	NA	NA	NA	NA	NA	NA	NA
August	NA	NA	NA	NA	NA	NA	NA
September	NA	NA	NA	NA	NA	NA	NA
October	NA	NA	NA	NA	NA	NA	NA
November	NA	NA	NA	NA	NA	NA	NA
December	NA	NA	NA	NA	NA	NA	NA
2009							
January	NA	NA	NA	NA	NA	NA	NA
February	NA	NA	NA	NA	NA	NA	NA
March	NA	NA	NA	NA	NA	NA	NA
April	NA	NA	NA	NA	NA	NA	NA
May	NA	NA	NA	NA	NA	NA	NA
June	NA	NA	NA	NA	NA	NA	NA
July	NA	NA	NA	NA	NA	NA	NA
August	NA	NA	NA	NA	NA	NA	NA
September	NA	NA	NA	NA	NA	NA	NA
October	NA	NA	NA	NA	NA	NA	NA
November	NA	NA	NA	NA	NA	NA	NA
December	NA	NA	NA	NA	NA	NA	NA
2008							
January	5.81	0.22	5.84	30.4	329.7	445.3	78.4
February	5.45	0.28	5.49	30.3	357.4	496.7	76.4
March	5.57	0.32	5.61	30.1	323.1	442.8	77.9
April	5.60	0.24	5.63	30.0	295.3	414.3	79.8
May	5.60	0.33	5.65	29.4	262.7	358.4	79.7
June	5.75	0.31	5.79	29.8	318.6	445.5	77.8
July	5.92	0.32	5.96	29.9	296.2	412.5	77.4
August	5.89	0.29	5.93	29.8	279.0	396.1	74.9
September	5.81	0.26	5.85	30.0	285.5	418.1	70.7
October	6.12	0.29	6.16	30.0	260.1	334.3	80.7
November	NA	NA	NA	NA	NA	NA	NA
December	NA	NA	NA	NA	NA	NA	NA
2007							
January	6.29	0.34	6.34	30.1	310.4	407.3	77.8
February	6.27	0.53	6.34	29.9	337.4	442.0	79.1
March	6.16	0.38	6.21	29.9	312.4	412.7	77.7
April	6.10	0.40	6.16	30.4	333.5	433.2	79.2
May	6.21	0.43	6.27	30.1	337.3	430.1	81.0
June	6.37	0.43	6.43	30.1	338.8	447.8	78.2
July	6.39	0.52	6.47	30.1	342.1	447.4	79.2
August	6.52	0.44	6.58	30.1	341.6	442.3	79.4
September	6.57	0.41	6.63	30.2	341.0	446.8	80.0
October	6.37	0.38	6.43	29.7	351.4	462.1	78.4
November	6.13	0.33	6.17	30.5	364.2	469.4	81.1
December	5.99	0.23	6.02	30.7	327.5	424.8	83.5
2006							
January	6.08	0.24	6.11	30.0	286.6	393.6	76.0
February	6.09	0.21	6.12	30.0	300.5	411.6	75.2
March	6.32	0.23	6.36	30.1	303.0	407.7	76.3
April	6.39	0.23	6.42	30.0	301.9	405.5	77.1
May	6.46	0.25	6.50	30.2	292.0	388.4	78.0
June	6.49	0.22	6.52	30.0	301.7	401.9	77.3
July	6.58	0.30	6.63	30.1	293.8	396.9	76.7
August	6.68	0.31	6.72	30.0	328.5	437.3	77.1
September	6.34	0.40	6.40	30.3	302.7	394.1	79.1
October	6.29	0.42	6.35	29.8	306.7	404.3	78.9
November	6.30	0.42	6.36	29.9	313.3	416.1	78.3
December	6.30	0.39	6.36	30.1	329.5	431.4	78.1

Table 2-86. Terms on Conventional Single-Family Mortgages, Adjustable-Rate Mortgages, Previously Occupied Homes, Monthly National Averages, 1986–2010—*Continued*

[Percent, years, dollars in thousands.]

Year and month	Contract interest rate	Initial fees and charges	Effective interest rate	Term to maturity	Mortgage loan amount	Purchase price	Loan-to-price ratio
2005							
January	5.47	0.30	5.51	29.9	246.1	327.8	77.9
February	5.32	0.19	5.35	29.9	259.4	353.8	77.0
March	5.39	0.27	5.43	29.9	260.8	354.0	76.6
April	5.49	0.30	5.54	30.0	260.3	349.4	77.3
May	5.49	0.29	5.53	29.9	264.2	350.0	78.6
June	5.38	0.27	5.42	30.0	283.4	385.4	76.4
July	5.44	0.23	5.47	30.0	282.9	389.0	76.0
August	5.58	0.20	5.61	30.0	283.6	383.7	76.7
September	5.58	0.23	5.62	30.0	294.1	406.8	75.1
October	5.68	0.19	5.71	30.0	296.5	411.4	75.0
November	5.95	0.20	5.98	30.0	293.9	414.2	74.0
December	5.97	0.22	6.00	30.1	295.0	405.6	75.4
2004							
January	4.92	0.45	4.99	29.9	226.4	299.2	78.8
February	4.95	0.44	5.01	30.0	227.2	305.1	77.7
March	4.63	0.34	4.68	29.8	227.6	305.1	78.1
April	4.61	0.31	4.65	29.8	238.9	321.1	78.1
May	5.01	0.31	5.06	29.8	225.8	296.2	79.5
June	5.34	0.35	5.39	29.8	235.5	310.9	79.0
July	5.32	0.32	5.37	29.7	236.5	311.8	78.3
August	5.24	0.38	5.29	29.6	232.1	309.6	78.1
September	5.14	0.41	5.20	29.9	243.4	326.7	77.6
October	5.21	0.37	5.26	29.8	243.0	328.4	77.4
November	5.28	0.30	5.32	29.9	242.5	320.7	78.3
December	5.46	0.25	5.49	29.8	231.9	308.3	78.6
2003							
January	5.19	0.32	5.23	29.9	231.2	315.9	77.0
February	5.12	0.35	5.17	29.8	223.6	302.4	77.6
March	4.98	0.32	5.02	29.8	223.0	302.8	77.4
April	4.93	0.31	4.97	29.7	226.1	297.5	79.8
May	4.91	0.48	4.98	29.7	195.5	273.2	75.1
June	4.60	0.36	4.65	29.9	212.8	292.4	76.1
July	4.61	0.43	4.67	29.2	234.4	318.3	77.6
August	4.82	0.37	4.87	29.8	239.5	321.4	78.1
September	5.09	0.46	5.15	29.7	213.8	291.8	77.0
October	5.05	0.28	5.09	29.5	226.7	305.2	77.2
November	5.12	0.37	5.18	29.8	216.2	285.4	78.2
December	5.00	0.47	5.07	29.8	219.7	288.4	79.1
2002							
January	6.01	0.38	6.06	29.7	223.6	306.8	76.3
February	5.93	0.35	5.98	29.8	228.8	308.8	77.1
March	5.92	0.33	5.96	29.5	229.9	313.0	77.3
April	5.95	0.31	5.99	29.8	231.5	310.2	78.4
May	5.76	0.38	5.81	29.8	223.5	293.2	79.4
June	5.68	0.41	5.74	29.9	233.1	314.5	77.4
July	5.47	0.44	5.53	29.7	228.9	308.6	78.2
August	5.38	0.40	5.44	29.6	233.2	317.4	77.2
September	5.38	0.42	5.44	29.9	231.3	321.1	76.2
October	5.31	0.43	5.37	29.5	230.9	318.7	76.2
November	5.33	0.40	5.39	29.7	236.8	327.1	76.6
December	5.26	0.40	5.32	29.7	250.0	336.1	77.2
2001							
January	6.53	0.29	6.57	29.7	251.6	344.1	75.8
February	6.68	0.25	6.71	29.7	268.0	368.4	75.8
March	6.54	0.26	6.58	29.7	274.0	369.2	76.7
April	6.44	0.30	6.48	29.8	245.7	329.2	77.7
May	6.47	0.32	6.52	29.9	235.6	311.9	78.8
June	6.40	0.35	6.45	29.8	229.4	303.7	78.3
July	6.49	0.37	6.54	29.9	234.5	314.6	77.2
August	6.34	0.34	6.39	29.7	235.7	318.7	76.8
September	6.27	0.36	6.32	29.9	234.2	320.0	76.5
October	6.06	0.30	6.10	29.6	232.4	316.5	76.8
November	6.00	0.25	6.04	29.6	243.0	332.1	76.6
December	6.01	0.36	6.06	29.8	225.2	310.5	76.1

Table 2-86. Terms on Conventional Single-Family Mortgages, Adjustable-Rate Mortgages, Previously Occupied Homes, Monthly National Averages, 1986–2010—*Continued*

[Percent, years, dollars in thousands.]

Year and month	Contract interest rate	Initial fees and charges	Effective interest rate	Term to maturity	Mortgage loan amount	Purchase price	Loan-to-price ratio
2000							
January	7.02	0.45	7.09	29.7	189.6	251.5	78.1
February	7.23	0.45	7.30	29.8	184.2	242.6	78.6
March	7.30	0.45	7.36	29.8	190.4	253.6	77.7
April	7.22	0.40	7.29	29.7	194.5	260.0	77.5
May	7.36	0.42	7.42	29.8	198.1	263.4	78.0
June	7.41	0.40	7.48	29.9	207.7	278.4	77.3
July	7.29	0.37	7.34	29.8	215.5	290.5	76.6
August	7.14	0.38	7.19	29.7	216.9	293.4	75.7
September	7.05	0.40	7.11	29.7	216.0	289.9	76.5
October	6.86	0.35	6.92	29.8	223.6	304.1	75.6
November	6.74	0.35	6.80	29.8	222.5	302.2	75.8
December	6.71	0.30	6.75	29.8	228.0	307.8	75.8
1999							
January	6.16	0.80	6.27	29.7	197.3	262.0	76.7
February	6.20	0.76	6.31	29.9	207.2	278.4	76.4
March	6.21	0.78	6.32	29.9	197.7	262.6	77.2
April	6.13	0.78	6.24	29.8	187.7	250.4	77.3
May	6.22	0.77	6.33	29.5	186.7	249.7	78.1
June	6.39	0.74	6.50	29.6	185.3	245.6	77.6
July	6.65	0.75	6.76	29.3	166.0	216.5	78.3
August	6.68	0.47	6.75	29.8	183.1	242.3	78.1
September	6.75	0.42	6.81	29.7	190.5	251.7	78.0
October	6.71	0.40	6.77	29.8	187.8	249.5	77.6
November	6.71	0.29	6.75	29.8	184.6	245.5	77.6
December							
1998							
January	6.56	0.83	6.68	29.1	159.8	206.2	79.4
February	6.49	0.83	6.62	29.0	163.8	216.2	78.3
March	6.48	0.77	6.59	29.4	163.5	214.3	78.5
April	6.46	0.71	6.56	29.2	175.2	231.7	77.9
May	6.45	0.83	6.57	29.8	169.2	219.7	79.1
June	6.35	0.87	6.48	29.9	178.6	233.9	78.5
July	6.28	0.74	6.38	29.5	185.8	248.3	76.9
August	6.36	0.86	6.49	29.5	177.7	233.9	78.3
September	6.18	0.70	6.28	29.7	174.5	228.9	77.8
October	6.16	0.53	6.24	29.3	191.8	254.5	77.3
November	6.18	0.52	6.25	29.8	206.3	276.4	77.1
December	6.05	0.61	6.14	29.6	195.2	263.2	76.5
1997							
January	6.80	0.84	6.93	29.2	144.5	185.8	79.8
February	6.79	0.77	6.91	29.7	151.9	190.5	81.1
March	6.86	0.84	6.99	28.7	142.7	181.9	80.0
April	6.96	0.82	7.09	29.3	152.8	193.7	80.2
May	6.81	0.80	6.94	29.6	147.6	187.0	80.3
June	6.87	0.92	7.01	29.5	158.2	203.0	79.7
July	6.64	0.83	6.76	29.4	151.9	195.9	79.2
August	6.71	0.87	6.84	29.5	153.3	199.3	78.6
September	6.66	0.84	6.79	29.5	152.2	194.2	80.0
October	6.58	0.83	6.71	29.3	156.2	202.8	79.1
November	6.60	0.92	6.74	29.4	151.4	194.7	79.6
December	6.51	0.90	6.64	29.6	152.4	198.8	78.9
1996							
January	6.86	0.77	6.98	27.3	125.4	161.8	78.8
February	6.74	0.79	6.86	27.5	136.6	177.1	78.9
March	6.78	0.81	6.90	29.2	158.8	200.8	81.1
April	6.86	0.76	6.98	28.4	143.7	183.2	80.1
May	7.08	0.73	7.19	29.1	153.9	194.4	80.6
June	6.94	0.70	7.04	29.6	153.6	196.0	80.0
July	7.20	0.77	7.31	28.5	150.6	191.9	79.9
August	6.96	0.76	7.07	29.6	151.8	193.1	79.9
September	7.00	0.81	7.12	29.5	147.3	189.4	79.9
October	6.83	0.83	6.96	29.1	140.3	177.6	80.5
November	6.72	0.85	6.85	29.3	143.1	180.4	81.0
December	6.68	0.92	6.82	29.1	139.2	178.7	79.1

Table 2-86. Terms on Conventional Single-Family Mortgages, Adjustable-Rate Mortgages, Previously Occupied Homes, Monthly National Averages, 1986–2010—*Continued*

[Percent, years, dollars in thousands.]

Year and month	Contract interest rate	Initial fees and charges	Effective interest rate	Term to maturity	Mortgage loan amount	Purchase price	Loan-to-price ratio
1995							
January	6.89	0.87	7.02	29.5	122.1	152.9	81.7
February	7.11	0.90	7.25	29.3	119.4	150.1	81.4
March	7.08	0.84	7.21	29.4	124.7	160.2	79.7
April	7.09	0.80	7.21	29.4	121.9	155.6	80.2
May	7.15	0.89	7.28	29.3	126.8	162.2	80.3
June	6.87	0.93	7.01	29.5	139.2	173.7	81.9
July	6.99	0.95	7.14	29.3	141.4	178.8	80.8
August	6.78	0.91	6.92	29.8	143.5	182.0	80.9
September	6.97	0.75	7.08	29.1	137.0	176.1	80.2
October	6.87	0.76	6.99	28.8	132.1	166.9	80.8
November	6.79	0.73	6.90	29.5	144.1	186.1	79.1
December	6.41	0.52	6.49	28.5	118.2	151.6	80.7
1994							
January	5.36	0.93	5.49	28.0	118.0	157.8	75.2
February	5.23	1.05	5.38	28.8	129.4	170.5	77.5
March	5.45	0.98	5.59	28.7	131.7	171.2	77.8
April	5.74	1.06	5.90	29.4	129.0	167.2	78.5
May	5.95	1.01	6.10	29.2	132.5	168.0	79.6
June	6.19	1.05	6.34	29.3	131.2	167.3	80.4
July	6.32	1.00	6.47	29.6	130.0	164.6	81.0
August	6.41	0.99	6.56	29.3	127.8	162.0	80.4
September	6.49	0.99	6.64	29.4	125.5	158.3	81.3
October	6.52	0.98	6.66	29.6	126.9	160.4	81.0
November	6.55	0.93	6.69	29.3	119.4	149.2	81.8
December	6.81	1.32	7.00	29.6	129.1	162.2	81.6
1993							
January	6.12	1.34	6.31	28.9	134.1	180.8	75.8
February	5.74	1.23	5.92	29.8	134.6	175.4	77.7
March	5.44	1.20	5.61	30.0	128.5	170.8	76.6
April	5.54	1.19	5.71	28.2	121.9	163.3	75.2
May	5.76	1.21	5.94	27.6	113.9	147.9	77.6
June	5.62	1.34	5.81	29.4	129.0	167.6	77.7
July	5.61	1.27	5.80	28.8	125.5	164.9	77.6
August	5.54	1.16	5.71	28.3	123.0	160.9	76.9
September	5.45	1.23	5.63	28.8	130.4	168.5	78.3
October	5.36	1.08	5.51	28.4	114.9	153.8	75.6
November	5.22	1.20	5.39	30.0	130.0	174.9	77.3
December	5.18	1.10	5.34	29.6	130.9	171.3	77.3
1992							
January	6.68	1.17	6.85	29.3	125.2	169.6	76.1
February	6.82	1.40	7.03	28.0	100.1	129.0	78.9
March	6.64	1.28	6.84	29.1	120.3	155.9	77.8
April	6.73	1.53	6.96	30.2	120.7	158.3	76.9
May	6.71	1.53	6.94	29.9	137.5	178.0	78.0
June	6.68	1.54	6.91	29.2	135.6	179.2	77.6
July	6.25	1.42	6.46	29.8	132.7	177.2	76.6
August	6.15	1.49	6.36	29.3	134.9	175.6	77.7
September	6.11	1.42	6.32	29.2	114.0	151.7	75.8
October	5.81	1.36	6.01	29.2	114.0	153.1	76.2
November	5.95	1.41	6.15	29.5	118.3	158.4	76.2
December	5.99	1.42	6.20	28.8	131.2	174.0	77.5
1991							
January	8.83	1.49	9.07	28.4	113.5	149.3	76.7
February	8.63	1.62	8.89	29.0	118.7	158.2	76.7
March	8.50	1.48	8.74	28.5	114.9	156.4	74.7
April	8.41	1.48	8.64	29.3	125.7	164.2	77.1
May	8.14	1.49	8.37	29.4	130.3	173.3	75.9
June	7.87	1.28	8.07	29.6	128.9	169.2	76.6
July	7.85	1.33	8.06	28.8	127.3	166.2	78.3
August	7.99	1.31	8.19	27.8	116.4	154.6	76.7
September	7.66	1.33	7.87	28.4	116.2	156.0	76.6
October	7.48	1.29	7.68	28.6	117.3	158.3	75.7
November	7.47	1.48	7.70	29.0	127.9	171.0	76.3
December	7.45	1.42	7.67	28.8	128.6	176.7	75.7

Table 2-86. Terms on Conventional Single-Family Mortgages, Adjustable-Rate Mortgages, Previously Occupied Homes, Monthly National Averages, 1986–2010—*Continued*

[Percent, years, dollars in thousands.]

Year and month	Contract interest rate	Initial fees and charges	Effective interest rate	Term to maturity	Mortgage loan amount	Purchase price	Loan-to-price ratio
1990							
January	9.06	1.71	9.34	29.8	121.8	159.2	76.6
February	9.00	1.64	9.22	29.1	117.4	154.7	75.6
March	8.95	1.64	9.22	29.6	121.5	156.6	78.7
April	8.92	1.65	9.19	29.3	125.8	164.3	77.2
May	9.00	1.60	9.26	29.3	115.2	150.6	77.4
June	9.02	1.55	9.27	29.3	118.8	156.1	77.3
July	8.98	1.59	9.24	28.9	121.2	161.1	76.0
August	8.89	1.44	9.12	29.1	115.2	150.1	77.6
September	8.80	1.40	9.02	29.0	118.5	154.4	77.2
October	8.70	1.43	8.93	28.9	122.8	162.6	77.1
November	8.76	1.41	8.98	29.4	120.2	157.4	77.8
December	8.68	1.44	8.91	29.1	119.1	155.2	77.5
1989							
January	8.54	1.64	8.80	29.7	120.2	157.7	77.4
February	8.75	1.82	9.04	29.6	117.1	153.7	77.4
March	8.94	1.85	9.24	28.8	111.8	146.4	77.4
April	9.15	1.76	9.43	29.3	122.4	159.9	77.8
May	9.47	1.92	9.79	29.1	117.9	155.5	77.2
June	9.76	1.84	10.07	28.7	106.1	141.4	76.7
July	9.53	1.88	9.84	28.5	113.1	149.0	77.1
August	9.26	1.73	9.54	28.7	118.1	157.4	76.3
September	9.35	1.42	9.58	28.4	113.7	149.6	77.2
October	9.20	1.66	9.48	28.5	112.1	148.1	76.5
November	9.05	1.67	9.32	28.6	116.7	152.5	77.3
December	8.97	1.58	9.22	29.1	122.9	161.1	76.5
1988							
January	8.29	1.93	8.59	28.9	98.4	130.5	77.2
February	8.20	1.96	8.51	28.9	98.4	130.1	77.4
March	8.07	1.85	8.36	29.0	97.7	128.5	78.1
April	7.99	1.76	8.26	28.8	103.4	133.7	78.7
May	8.06	1.82	8.35	28.3	102.6	133.9	78.1
June	8.10	1.81	8.39	29.0	103.7	134.4	78.5
July	8.14	1.91	8.44	28.9	104.1	136.2	78.3
August	8.20	1.84	8.49	28.8	103.8	135.1	78.4
September	8.23	1.77	8.51	29.0	109.2	143.5	77.5
October	8.31	1.77	8.59	28.9	110.8	146.8	77.1
November	8.49	1.78	8.78	28.7	109.5	142.9	77.9
December	8.55	1.57	8.80	29.5	115.5	150.4	77.8
1987							
January	8.48	1.98	8.80	27.5	92.2	121.0	76.9
February	8.24	1.90	8.54	28.0	95.3	126.4	76.4
March	8.09	1.80	8.38	28.3	98.4	130.6	76.1
April	8.07	1.76	8.35	28.6	103.7	136.5	77.1
May	8.19	1.84	8.48	27.8	98.0	130.7	76.0
June	8.07	1.90	8.36	28.5	96.4	127.1	77.5
July	8.19	1.94	8.50	28.4	95.3	126.7	77.1
August	8.24	1.86	8.53	28.4	94.0	124.6	77.3
September	8.14	1.90	8.44	28.4	96.3	127.8	76.6
October	8.14	1.97	8.45	28.6	96.3	126.5	77.8
November	8.28	1.96	8.59	28.6	95.2	126.5	77.4
December	8.36	1.95	8.67	28.9	95.2	125.6	77.4
1986							
January	9.81	2.09	10.17	28.3	84.9	112.6	77.3
February	9.84	1.99	10.18	27.2	81.5	112.2	75.0
March	9.65	2.15	10.02	27.0	80.9	110.0	75.5
April	9.55	1.94	9.88	26.4	80.4	107.7	75.9
May	9.43	1.77	9.73	26.1	81.6	110.3	75.1
June	9.22	1.88	9.53	26.8	88.3	118.5	75.6
July	9.17	1.75	9.46	26.4	84.0	113.1	75.4
August	9.05	1.85	9.36	27.7	91.6	121.8	76.9
September	8.99	1.86	9.30	27.1	89.4	119.9	74.6
October	8.76	1.99	9.08	27.0	88.4	117.4	77.0
November	8.59	1.95	8.91	27.5	88.3	118.2	76.1
December	8.52	1.94	8.83	28.7	96.9	127.8	77.0

NA = Not available.

Source: Federal Housing Finance Agency, Monthly Interest Rate Survey

Table 2-87. Terms on Conventional Single-Family Mortgages, Fixed-Rate 30-Year and 15-Year Nonjumbo Loans, 1990–2010

[Percent, years, dollars in thousands.]

Year and month	Contract interest rate	Initial fees and charges	Effective interest rate	Term to maturity	Mortgage loan amount	Purchase price	Loan-to-price ratio	Share of total market
30-year								
2010								
January	5.10	0.58	5.18	30	190.0	265.2	74.8	72.4
February	5.13	0.67	5.23	30	180.5	244.6	76.9	70.0
March	5.09	0.65	5.18	30	187.4	253.5	76.1	71.7
April	5.12	0.68	5.22	30	187.2	256.8	76.1	70.0
May	5.12	0.75	5.23	30	186.0	251.1	76.4	67.2
June	5.00	0.88	5.12	30	185.4	251.9	76.3	69.4
July	4.84	0.91	4.96	30	188.4	255.0	76.7	69.7
August	4.70	0.91	4.82	30	184.6	256.0	75.8	68.4
September	4.58	0.88	4.70	30	186.8	256.0	75.2	70.6
October	4.46	0.96	4.59	30	183.9	259.2	73.9	73.8
November	4.38	0.84	4.50	30	185.5	253.9	76.6	71.1
December	4.61	0.86	4.73	30	180.9	241.8	77.5	77.1
2009								
January	5.09	0.66	5.18	30	189.4	260.1	76.6	79.3
February	5.03	0.59	5.11	30	193.9	266.1	76.2	78.4
March	5.05	0.62	5.13	30	186.3	254.3	76.9	77.5
April	4.87	0.60	4.95	30	195.3	262.8	77.4	78.2
May	4.88	0.62	4.96	30	195.4	266.8	76.5	76.4
June	5.12	0.63	5.21	30	193.4	264.8	76.3	74.3
July	5.31	0.72	5.41	30	193.9	261.3	76.9	75.2
August	5.30	0.70	5.40	30	189.3	258.0	76.1	73.4
September	5.23	0.68	5.33	30	183.7	249.8	75.9	73.5
October	5.10	0.68	5.19	30	182.1	245.5	76.3	74.7
November	5.09	0.65	5.19	30	182.0	247.3	76.0	73.7
December	5.05	0.69	5.14	30	188.2	254.7	76.3	69.2
2008								
January	5.98	0.62	6.07	30	197.2	246.1	83.0	73.7
February	5.93	0.49	6.00	30	194.2	247.5	81.8	71.5
March	6.10	0.57	6.18	30	187.4	236.6	82.3	70.2
April	5.98	0.50	6.06	30	201.9	258.7	81.1	73.3
May	6.07	0.49	6.14	30	196.6	253.1	80.8	74.9
June	6.24	0.51	6.31	30	195.8	254.9	80.1	72.2
July	6.42	0.59	6.51	30	193.5	258.7	78.6	74.2
August	6.49	0.60	6.58	30	196.2	262.0	78.2	73.1
September	6.16	0.67	6.26	30	195.2	257.5	78.7	76.5
October	6.12	0.62	6.21	30	192.4	255.2	77.9	78.9
November	6.17	0.64	6.26	30	190.4	251.9	78.0	80.7
December	5.51	0.68	5.61	30	200.8	268.6	77.1	82.9
2007								
January	6.36	0.47	6.43	30	182.2	243.2	80.1	69.4
February	6.37	0.49	6.44	30	181.0	243.7	79.5	70.0
March	6.31	0.47	6.38	30	183.8	244.9	80.4	69.6
April	6.26	0.48	6.33	30	180.6	240.0	80.5	70.2
May	6.36	0.52	6.44	30	185.6	236.7	82.3	70.7
June	6.59	0.49	6.66	30	191.8	248.6	81.2	70.3
July	6.77	0.50	6.84	30	184.0	239.5	81.4	69.0
August	6.73	0.54	6.81	30	188.1	240.1	82.2	70.5
September	6.56	0.53	6.64	30	186.8	241.4	81.8	75.8
October	6.50	0.53	6.57	30	190.5	240.3	82.7	72.7
November	6.36	0.52	6.44	30	194.6	249.5	81.7	74.5
December	6.20	0.61	6.29	30	196.6	243.8	83.5	75.0
2006								
January	6.40	0.42	6.46	30	163.4	222.9	78.3	56.7
February	6.42	0.42	6.48	30	175.5	237.4	78.3	58.4
March	6.47	0.42	6.53	30	180.7	242.5	78.8	60.6
April	6.55	0.44	6.61	30	179.1	239.6	79.4	61.2
May	6.65	0.44	6.71	30	181.9	244.6	78.8	60.5
June	6.71	0.47	6.78	30	183.0	246.5	78.7	59.2
July	6.83	0.45	6.90	30	176.9	233.9	80.0	60.9
August	6.78	0.50	6.85	30	177.3	240.3	78.8	64.8
September	6.63	0.48	6.70	30	184.9	247.5	79.3	68.4
October	6.60	0.51	6.68	30	181.6	244.8	78.8	66.4
November	6.48	0.50	6.55	30	184.1	249.9	78.5	68.2
December	6.38	0.45	6.45	30	187.3	248.4	79.7	67.3

Table 2-87. Terms on Conventional Single-Family Mortgages, Fixed-Rate 30-Year and 15-Year Nonjumbo Loans, 1990–2010—*Continued*

[Percent, years, dollars in thousands.]

Year and month	Contract interest rate	Initial fees and charges	Effective interest rate	Term to maturity	Mortgage loan amount	Purchase price	Loan-to-price ratio	Share of total market
2005								
January	5.90	0.50	5.97	30	180.7	247.6	78.4	51.9
February	5.91	0.35	5.96	30	162.4	230.8	77.0	55.4
March	5.99	0.43	6.06	30	165.6	225.3	78.6	56.3
April	6.09	0.48	6.16	30	163.3	224.6	77.4	53.9
May	5.99	0.47	6.06	30	167.3	228.4	77.9	52.2
June	5.81	0.45	5.88	30	172.4	241.4	76.3	53.8
July	5.78	0.42	5.84	30	168.7	233.0	77.7	55.9
August	5.94	0.41	6.00	30	172.6	236.6	77.6	56.4
September	5.97	0.45	6.04	30	170.9	234.3	77.6	58.0
October	6.08	0.41	6.14	30	168.9	232.3	77.4	58.1
November	6.32	0.48	6.39	30	170.9	236.0	77.7	55.8
December	6.44	0.47	6.50	30	169.6	232.3	77.7	56.0
2004								
January	5.92	0.55	6.00	30	160.8	213.4	80.0	52.4
February	5.85	0.41	5.90	30	169.5	227.3	79.0	59.8
March	5.71	0.44	5.77	30	160.2	213.3	79.8	49.1
April	5.72	0.39	5.78	30	169.4	227.0	79.2	51.4
May	6.07	0.39	6.13	30	174.2	233.2	79.1	48.5
June	6.25	0.44	6.32	30	173.4	234.8	78.4	46.3
July	6.26	0.41	6.32	30	169.5	229.6	78.6	50.3
August	6.10	0.50	6.17	30	168.8	226.1	79.5	51.3
September	5.90	0.57	5.98	30	167.3	223.9	78.9	53.0
October	5.91	0.49	5.98	30	166.5	227.2	78.4	51.6
November	5.89	0.48	5.96	30	175.1	241.4	77.8	52.7
December	5.90	0.47	5.97	30	186.1	253.9	78.2	55.5
2003								
January	6.09	0.44	6.16	30	171.4	229.9	78.8	62.0
February	6.02	0.34	6.07	30	161.0	216.2	79.1	61.2
March	5.90	0.30	5.94	30	162.5	217.3	79.3	61.4
April	5.90	0.38	5.96	30	171.2	226.4	79.8	61.2
May	5.74	0.38	5.80	30	174.9	233.0	79.4	62.4
June	5.50	0.36	5.55	30	177.8	238.3	78.9	64.3
July	5.53	0.41	5.59	30	176.2	234.5	79.6	64.0
August	5.88	0.46	5.94	30	171.7	230.4	78.9	58.7
September	6.19	0.47	6.25	30	163.2	216.1	80.1	57.8
October	6.05	0.46	6.12	30	164.0	217.1	79.9	56.9
November	6.06	0.55	6.14	30	174.0	228.7	80.1	58.0
December	6.00	0.57	6.09	30	155.5	204.1	80.8	54.3
2002								
January	7.02	0.56	7.10	30	151.9	200.1	80.2	63.0
February	6.98	0.57	7.07	30	153.6	200.1	80.7	62.8
March	6.98	0.51	7.06	30	155.0	203.2	80.1	63.5
April	7.11	0.56	7.20	30	154.7	201.3	80.8	64.3
May	6.99	0.58	7.08	30	158.0	205.2	80.7	64.4
June	6.87	0.59	6.96	30	158.7	213.0	79.2	64.0
July	6.72	0.56	6.81	30	159.9	209.2	80.6	62.9
August	6.53	0.54	6.61	30	159.6	213.2	79.6	62.1
September	6.36	0.50	6.44	30	163.2	220.0	78.9	66.0
October	6.23	0.44	6.29	30	162.2	218.3	79.0	63.2
November	6.20	0.41	6.26	30	162.6	218.5	78.9	61.4
December	6.21	0.43	6.28	30	161.2	215.1	79.4	63.8
2001								
January	7.31	0.63	7.40	30	143.4	188.5	79.8	76.1
February	7.13	0.61	7.22	30	146.4	192.1	79.9	75.5
March	7.06	0.62	7.15	30	148.5	194.4	80.1	75.3
April	7.09	0.56	7.17	30	149.7	197.0	80.0	72.4
May	7.18	0.61	7.27	30	152.4	201.5	79.5	71.2
June	7.21	0.57	7.30	30	154.7	203.6	79.8	72.1
July	7.21	0.57	7.29	30	150.9	198.2	80.0	71.1
August	7.13	0.56	7.21	30	149.9	196.4	80.0	69.9
September	6.97	0.51	7.04	30	153.1	201.9	79.5	70.0
October	6.76	0.50	6.83	30	155.4	205.1	79.6	70.3
November	6.67	0.49	6.74	30	156.5	208.0	79.4	68.1
December	6.89	0.56	6.97	30	155.0	204.8	79.7	62.6

Table 2-87. Terms on Conventional Single-Family Mortgages, Fixed-Rate 30-Year and 15-Year Nonjumbo Loans, 1990–2010—*Continued*

[Percent, years, dollars in thousands.]

Year and month	Contract interest rate	Initial fees and charges	Effective interest rate	Term to maturity	Mortgage loan amount	Purchase price	Loan-to-price ratio	Share of total market
2000								
January	8.08	0.81	8.20	30	129.9	166.8	81.1	61.1
February	8.27	0.78	8.39	30	127.8	163.7	81.2	58.6
March	8.31	0.76	8.43	30	129.2	166.2	80.9	59.0
April	8.27	0.76	8.39	30	126.6	162.9	80.9	62.2
May	8.35	0.77	8.47	30	128.6	165.6	80.8	61.7
June	8.43	0.79	8.55	30	130.2	169.5	80.1	62.1
July	8.29	0.75	8.41	30	133.0	173.5	80.0	67.3
August	8.16	0.73	8.27	30	135.4	176.5	79.9	69.7
September	8.03	0.75	8.15	30	137.2	178.4	80.0	71.8
October	7.95	0.70	8.05	30	137.2	179.3	79.9	72.6
November	7.85	0.68	7.96	30	141.4	185.4	79.7	74.1
December	7.68	0.69	7.78	30	143.1	187.4	79.6	74.1
1999								
January	6.89	0.82	7.01	30	131.7	168.9	80.8	72.0
February	6.92	0.76	7.04	30	134.8	173.0	80.7	73.5
March	7.01	0.76	7.12	30	135.0	171.7	81.6	72.6
April	7.05	0.76	7.17	30	133.0	170.4	81.0	71.7
May	7.09	0.72	7.20	30	134.8	172.8	80.8	69.4
June	7.34	0.77	7.46	30	135.9	173.9	80.9	66.1
July	7.59	0.82	7.72	30	132.0	168.7	81.1	63.4
August	7.79	0.81	7.91	30	126.8	161.6	81.0	58.9
September	7.87	0.79	7.99	30	124.7	158.4	81.6	60.7
October	7.87	0.82	7.99	30	123.2	156.9	81.6	61.2
November	7.87	0.81	7.99	30	126.5	161.6	81.2	61.5
December	7.90	0.77	8.02	30	127.4	161.7	82.0	60.1
1998								
January	7.24	0.90	7.38	30	128.5	164.6	80.8	70.0
February	7.19	0.91	7.33	30	127.4	164.1	80.8	68.4
March	7.19	0.88	7.32	30	128.0	161.8	81.9	70.0
April	7.21	0.84	7.33	30	127.8	161.2	82.0	72.0
May	7.21	0.90	7.34	30	130.1	165.1	81.4	70.9
June	7.20	0.88	7.33	30	131.5	166.3	82.0	71.2
July	7.13	0.87	7.26	30	131.8	167.0	81.4	72.6
August	7.09	0.90	7.22	30	130.9	164.7	82.3	74.1
September	6.97	0.85	7.09	30	130.7	165.9	81.7	75.0
October	6.82	0.79	6.94	30	131.1	168.0	81.2	75.0
November	6.85	0.80	6.97	30	128.8	164.3	81.2	71.4
December	6.88	0.98	7.03	30	133.9	169.9	81.5	75.7
1997								
January	7.87	1.03	8.03	30	117.3	149.4	81.0	55.9
February	7.87	0.99	8.03	30	114.7	144.2	82.0	56.7
March	7.91	1.02	8.07	30	115.7	145.3	82.0	59.1
April	8.10	1.06	8.27	30	116.6	145.8	82.3	55.8
May	8.14	1.04	8.30	30	118.7	149.0	81.8	58.9
June	8.00	1.12	8.17	30	123.4	155.8	81.6	60.3
July	7.79	0.99	7.95	30	124.8	156.7	81.8	65.4
August	7.69	1.07	7.85	30	124.7	158.2	81.2	65.0
September	7.69	1.04	7.85	30	123.5	156.6	81.2	64.8
October	7.57	1.02	7.72	30	124.0	157.5	81.4	67.2
November	7.50	0.92	7.64	30	127.4	161.1	81.6	68.0
December	7.41	0.95	7.56	30	130.1	163.5	82.4	69.2
1996								
January	7.28	0.90	7.41	30	112.8	144.0	81.0	64.4
February	7.24	0.95	7.38	30	112.8	142.9	81.8	64.5
March	7.47	1.11	7.64	30	110.4	138.8	82.1	61.0
April	7.82	1.08	7.98	30	110.9	139.1	82.6	57.3
May	8.05	1.05	8.22	30	110.2	138.0	82.2	53.9
June	8.17	1.13	8.35	30	113.0	142.6	82.0	52.1
July	8.27	1.14	8.45	30	111.7	141.8	81.3	48.3
August	8.19	1.11	8.36	30	111.1	141.3	81.5	53.6
September	8.20	1.12	8.37	30	112.9	144.8	80.7	49.5
October	8.12	1.02	8.28	30	114.5	145.7	81.1	51.6
November	7.92	1.02	8.07	30	115.1	147.1	80.7	56.2
December	7.77	0.91	7.91	30	114.7	146.2	81.3	57.9

Table 2-87. Terms on Conventional Single-Family Mortgages, Fixed-Rate 30-Year and 15-Year Nonjumbo Loans, 1990–2010—*Continued*

[Percent, years, dollars in thousands.]

Year and month	Contract interest rate	Initial fees and charges	Effective interest rate	Term to maturity	Mortgage loan amount	Purchase price	Loan-to-price ratio	Share of total market
1995								
January	9.06	1.34	9.27	30	93.5	116.2	83.5	31.1
February	8.96	1.37	9.18	30	94.9	118.1	82.8	36.4
March	8.82	1.02	8.98	30	95.8	120.1	82.5	45.0
April	8.60	1.06	8.77	30	98.7	122.0	83.2	46.7
May	8.30	1.14	8.47	30	100.0	125.7	82.4	48.6
June	7.88	0.97	8.03	30	105.5	132.3	82.9	57.8
July	7.76	0.98	7.91	30	105.9	132.5	82.4	60.3
August	7.88	0.99	8.03	30	104.9	131.8	82.3	58.5
September	7.82	0.95	7.96	30	106.1	135.0	81.8	60.1
October	7.71	1.00	7.87	30	108.6	137.3	81.8	60.5
November	7.63	0.89	7.77	30	110.8	141.2	81.2	62.4
December	7.51	0.83	7.64	30	112.8	143.1	81.3	56.5
1994								
January	7.19	1.18	7.37	30	105.8	135.5	80.5	53.9
February	7.14	0.98	7.29	30	108.4	138.3	81.5	55.1
March	7.32	1.09	7.48	30	108.1	135.3	82.4	57.1
April	7.68	1.03	7.84	30	108.2	135.2	82.2	50.8
May	8.15	1.29	8.35	30	99.7	122.5	84.1	46.3
June	8.33	1.12	8.50	30	97.4	120.5	83.6	41.7
July	8.36	1.26	8.55	30	99.6	123.4	83.1	43.8
August	8.50	1.04	8.66	30	94.6	117.6	83.9	44.0
September	8.50	1.12	8.67	30	98.2	122.6	82.8	40.7
October	8.64	1.07	8.80	30	97.1	120.7	83.3	37.5
November	8.79	1.11	8.97	30	98.0	123.1	83.0	33.9
December	8.90	1.38	9.11	30	87.1	108.4	84.0	32.4
1993								
January	8.08	1.58	8.32	30	104.9	134.7	80.3	47.2
February	7.86	1.41	8.08	30	112.8	145.4	80.1	50.2
March	7.67	1.41	7.88	30	108.3	138.8	80.2	54.3
April	7.56	1.27	7.75	30	112.6	145.6	80.3	48.2
May	7.48	1.38	7.69	30	107.8	134.9	82.1	53.3
June	7.48	1.36	7.69	30	111.6	141.3	81.4	48.9
July	7.34	1.17	7.51	30	109.9	139.2	81.4	57.6
August	7.24	1.07	7.40	30	110.0	140.4	81.0	56.2
September	7.08	1.08	7.24	30	108.8	138.0	81.2	56.8
October	6.93	1.06	7.08	30	112.1	143.5	80.5	56.3
November	6.99	1.12	7.15	30	108.6	140.4	80.3	56.9
December	7.20	1.16	7.37	30	108.3	136.7	81.7	55.3
1992								
January	8.35	1.39	8.57	30	121.0	164.1	76.7	56.2
February	8.46	1.72	8.73	30	111.0	147.2	78.4	55.9
March	8.65	1.82	8.94	30	111.0	141.7	80.8	50.6
April	8.71	1.81	9.00	30	105.7	134.4	80.7	56.6
May	8.68	1.68	8.94	30	112.8	144.1	80.6	58.3
June	8.52	1.79	8.80	30	114.2	146.3	80.3	51.9
July	8.28	1.55	8.52	30	111.0	145.2	78.8	53.8
August	8.09	1.86	8.37	30	113.0	145.6	80.3	51.4
September	7.92	1.66	8.18	30	109.0	140.9	80.1	51.8
October	7.92	1.47	8.15	30	116.2	152.0	79.3	49.9
November	8.06	1.64	8.32	30	109.8	142.7	79.5	47.6
December	8.18	1.53	8.41	30	108.4	137.7	81.3	47.9
1991								
January	9.75	1.58	10.01	30	105.6	143.8	75.8	53.7
February	9.62	1.59	9.88	30	107.4	150.0	74.4	53.6
March	9.45	1.46	9.69	30	104.5	146.4	74.8	54.9
April	9.47	1.69	9.75	30	111.9	153.7	75.0	58.2
May	9.52	1.65	9.79	30	108.6	146.7	76.2	58.1
June	9.49	1.58	9.75	30	109.9	149.2	76.0	59.2
July	9.49	1.85	9.80	30	111.4	150.5	76.7	54.4
August	9.52	1.64	9.79	30	105.2	144.0	76.0	54.0
September	9.33	1.55	9.58	30	108.5	147.3	76.5	55.7
October	9.10	1.50	9.33	30	114.1	156.0	75.7	53.9
November	8.77	1.66	9.03	30	105.6	141.7	77.6	49.0
December	8.58	1.60	8.84	30	109.4	142.2	79.0	50.4

Table 2-87. Terms on Conventional Single-Family Mortgages, Fixed-Rate 30-Year and 15-Year Nonjumbo Loans, 1990–2010—*Continued*

[Percent, years, dollars in thousands.]

Year and month	Contract interest rate	Initial fees and charges	Effective interest rate	Term to maturity	Mortgage loan amount	Purchase price	Loan-to-price ratio	Share of total market
1990								
January	9.81	1.87	10.12	30	106.1	148.0	74.5	63.1
February	9.97	2.04	10.31	30	108.4	148.0	76.0	53.4
March	10.03	2.07	10.38	30	105.4	143.6	75.7	54.5
April	10.14	2.07	10.49	30	107.5	146.5	75.8	51.1
May	10.22	2.00	10.56	30	103.2	140.8	75.6	49.5
June	10.21	2.01	10.55	30	101.2	138.7	75.7	49.2
July	10.20	1.89	10.52	30	105.2	142.9	75.6	51.1
August	9.99	1.80	10.29	30	103.4	141.8	75.5	51.3
September	9.99	1.81	10.29	30	99.3	136.9	75.0	47.5
October	10.06	1.86	10.38	30	96.0	131.3	75.7	47.4
November	10.11	1.75	10.40	30	99.0	135.1	75.4	45.1
December	9.87	1.57	10.13	30	104.8	144.1	75.1	51.1
15-year								
2010								
January	4.54	0.55	4.63	15	141.6	240.4	65.3	11.6
February	4.65	0.52	4.74	15	140.7	226.4	67.2	12.5
March	4.57	0.59	4.66	15	146.6	235.4	67.9	11.2
April	4.52	0.56	4.62	15	142.2	229.3	66.1	12.0
May	4.58	0.56	4.67	15	137.9	225.0	67.0	12.6
June	4.47	0.64	4.58	15	140.1	240.7	65.8	12.2
July	4.66	0.92	4.81	15	126.2	226.4	64.6	10.0
August	4.46	0.55	4.56	15	140.4	230.7	66.7	9.4
September	4.57	0.64	4.68	15	129.0	226.1	65.5	9.1
October	4.24	0.60	4.34	15	142.5	260.1	62.1	6.1
November	4.62	0.65	4.73	15	94.0	167.5	68.2	7.3
December	4.18	0.50	4.26	15	136.5	224.3	64.7	6.0
2009								
January	5.11	0.70	5.23	15	139.3	241.4	66.2	7.1
February	4.92	0.64	5.03	15	139.4	251.7	63.2	8.7
March	4.78	0.57	4.87	15	167.0	294.7	63.6	8.6
April	4.75	0.53	4.84	15	144.8	249.2	65.2	7.8
May	4.71	0.56	4.80	15	136.6	249.5	60.6	8.7
June	4.80	0.63	4.91	15	148.0	257.0	63.7	7.5
July	4.89	0.48	4.97	15	143.6	236.2	65.5	8.5
August	4.92	0.70	5.04	15	143.4	227.4	67.9	10.6
September	4.77	0.49	4.85	15	157.2	254.4	68.3	10.2
October	4.62	0.54	4.71	15	146.2	255.3	62.5	10.4
November	4.63	0.55	4.72	15	148.1	252.0	63.9	10.5
December	4.54	0.48	4.62	15	155.9	255.5	64.7	13.8
2008								
January	5.58	0.41	5.65	15	141.3	347.3	49.5	6.5
February	5.52	0.44	5.59	15	145.0	325.8	54.9	8.8
March	5.66	0.56	5.75	15	159.0	316.7	61.6	8.0
April	5.65	0.44	5.72	15	165.4	304.0	64.2	7.7
May	5.75	0.44	5.82	15	152.0	290.0	61.0	6.6
June	5.92	0.52	6.01	15	158.1	288.0	63.1	6.3
July	6.15	0.60	6.25	15	150.9	268.4	65.6	6.9
August	6.10	0.61	6.21	15	150.4	246.6	69.7	7.3
September	5.96	0.67	6.07	15	138.5	244.0	65.7	7.8
October	5.96	0.57	6.06	15	139.2	244.4	62.5	6.3
November	5.87	0.69	5.99	15	166.1	297.6	62.4	6.5
December	5.43	0.64	5.54	15	144.7	247.4	64.5	5.3
2007								
January	6.16	0.41	6.24	15	132.2	225.9	65.5	4.6
February	6.20	0.58	6.31	15	140.7	255.5	60.6	3.9
March	5.99	0.66	6.10	15	143.5	264.0	62.7	3.7
April	6.02	0.45	6.10	15	149.9	255.5	65.3	4.0
May	6.04	0.56	6.13	15	144.6	250.1	64.0	4.0
June	6.25	0.52	6.34	15	158.2	279.7	62.3	3.8
July	6.46	0.47	6.55	15	149.1	253.1	65.1	3.7
August	6.34	0.52	6.43	15	149.2	269.1	62.6	3.9
September	6.16	0.56	6.26	15	121.6	232.1	61.6	4.0
October	6.17	0.58	6.27	15	135.2	262.5	60.7	5.0
November	6.07	0.50	6.15	15	139.3	289.6	55.4	5.1
December	5.85	0.72	5.97	15	148.0	280.1	63.0	4.6

Table 2-87. Terms on Conventional Single-Family Mortgages, Fixed-Rate 30-Year and 15-Year Nonjumbo Loans, 1990–2010—*Continued*

[Percent, years, dollars in thousands.]

Year and month	Contract interest rate	Initial fees and charges	Effective interest rate	Term to maturity	Mortgage loan amount	Purchase price	Loan-to-price ratio	Share of total market
2006								
January	5.97	0.42	6.05	15	138.6	262.5	61.4	5.3
February	6.00	0.43	6.07	15	133.3	236.6	63.0	5.5
March	6.06	0.45	6.14	15	138.4	251.5	60.6	3.8
April	6.16	0.38	6.23	15	135.0	246.1	61.3	4.1
May	6.27	0.47	6.36	15	147.7	252.2	65.1	4.7
June	6.33	0.42	6.40	15	156.7	275.6	62.9	4.0
July	6.50	0.41	6.57	15	141.6	261.8	61.0	4.5
August	6.32	0.50	6.41	15	141.8	254.2	62.2	4.1
September	6.18	0.51	6.27	15	137.6	246.2	62.2	4.3
October	6.08	0.49	6.17	15	144.7	267.8	61.7	4.2
November	6.03	0.47	6.11	15	149.4	268.4	63.1	3.8
December	6.11	0.50	6.19	15	138.3	240.0	66.3	4.7
2005								
January	5.35	0.47	5.44	15	157.4	282.1	61.1	6.5
February	5.33	0.21	5.37	15	133.3	250.5	61.8	7.2
March	5.41	0.31	5.47	15	138.5	255.2	60.8	6.5
April	5.58	0.40	5.65	15	137.5	264.6	58.3	5.9
May	5.55	0.41	5.62	15	137.1	256.9	61.0	6.1
June	5.45	0.33	5.51	15	132.6	265.2	57.0	6.0
July	5.43	0.40	5.49	15	138.5	273.2	58.2	5.8
August	5.52	0.32	5.57	15	138.2	258.5	59.7	6.1
September	5.56	0.44	5.63	15	138.9	261.8	59.9	5.2
October	5.67	0.38	5.73	15	129.6	250.3	60.9	5.2
November	5.84	0.44	5.92	15	132.8	253.3	59.1	5.0
December	6.10	0.43	6.17	15	129.3	247.6	60.8	5.1
2004								
January	5.62	0.35	5.68	15	119.3	233.5	56.9	13.3
February	5.84	0.25	5.88	15	104.0	247.5	47.1	15.1
March	5.88	0.21	5.91	15	99.4	249.5	44.0	15.1
April	5.63	0.24	5.67	15	119.1	265.2	47.9	13.4
May	6.14	0.26	6.19	15	108.1	262.8	45.3	12.1
June	6.25	0.28	6.30	15	113.0	253.7	48.2	10.6
July	5.71	0.40	5.78	15	144.4	251.8	63.3	7.0
August	5.58	0.45	5.66	15	140.4	254.7	61.4	7.0
September	5.38	0.44	5.45	15	141.2	263.4	60.5	7.3
October	5.34	0.43	5.42	15	128.8	247.0	59.7	7.4
November	5.34	0.39	5.40	15	146.8	266.2	60.1	6.5
December	5.52	0.40	5.59	15	147.2	261.3	62.2	7.1
2003								
January	5.88	0.21	5.92	15	118.9	243.7	55.2	17.8
February	5.96	0.19	6.00	15	111.4	238.8	52.2	17.2
March	5.81	0.18	5.84	15	110.8	236.3	52.2	18.5
April	5.56	0.18	5.60	15	127.0	261.6	53.1	18.1
May	5.52	0.19	5.55	15	121.4	257.4	52.1	17.6
June	5.31	0.20	5.35	15	120.7	249.6	52.7	17.9
July	5.19	0.23	5.23	15	125.4	256.1	54.6	17.1
August	5.54	0.27	5.58	15	120.4	255.4	52.3	16.1
September	5.79	0.28	5.84	15	111.0	235.8	52.7	16.4
October	5.88	0.26	5.93	15	107.4	240.2	49.4	14.7
November	5.82	0.33	5.87	15	112.0	240.0	51.7	12.2
December	5.79	0.36	5.85	15	109.8	224.7	53.9	12.5
2002								
January	6.73	0.49	6.81	15	116.4	217.4	59.3	16.6
February	6.73	0.42	6.80	15	115.4	215.0	59.0	14.5
March	6.77	0.37	6.84	15	112.6	221.1	57.3	12.9
April	6.85	0.47	6.93	15	112.9	210.1	58.8	11.5
May	6.82	0.41	6.89	15	114.8	218.7	57.2	10.1
June	6.67	0.41	6.75	15	119.9	230.0	58.2	10.1
July	6.63	0.36	6.69	15	108.7	222.4	53.8	11.4
August	6.44	0.29	6.49	15	111.9	235.0	52.3	12.1
September	6.30	0.28	6.35	15	114.8	240.0	52.3	13.0
October	6.05	0.25	6.09	15	118.5	242.6	54.7	16.5
November	5.93	0.26	5.97	15	123.6	240.2	56.2	18.6
December	5.88	0.28	5.93	15	125.4	237.7	57.3	17.8

Table 2-87. Terms on Conventional Single-Family Mortgages, Fixed-Rate 30-Year and 15-Year Nonjumbo Loans, 1990–2010—*Continued*

[Percent, years, dollars in thousands.]

Year and month	Contract interest rate	Initial fees and charges	Effective interest rate	Term to maturity	Mortgage loan amount	Purchase price	Loan-to-price ratio	Share of total market
2001								
January	7.59	0.57	7.69	15	94.1	188.5	55.9	7.7
February	7.14	0.53	7.23	15	105.0	198.7	58.4	11.8
March	7.07	0.54	7.17	15	109.5	207.0	58.4	12.1
April	6.94	0.53	7.03	15	110.7	200.8	60.0	14.4
May	7.06	0.59	7.17	15	109.5	204.8	58.4	13.6
June	7.05	0.54	7.14	15	116.0	212.5	59.5	13.1
July	7.09	0.51	7.18	15	110.8	208.9	58.2	12.1
August	6.99	0.48	7.07	15	116.7	213.4	59.4	11.6
September	6.89	0.39	6.96	15	112.6	214.6	57.7	11.4
October	6.62	0.38	6.68	15	113.0	215.6	57.9	12.5
November	6.39	0.43	6.47	15	118.4	221.9	59.0	15.5
December	6.47	0.53	6.56	15	118.8	219.6	59.5	18.0
2000								
January	7.84	0.93	8.01	15	103.0	173.6	64.7	7.0
February	8.01	0.91	8.18	15	100.5	172.8	63.1	7.2
March	8.08	0.87	8.24	15	101.2	176.9	62.7	7.2
April	8.19	0.73	8.33	15	95.8	175.8	60.1	6.9
May	8.33	0.81	8.48	15	96.2	178.6	58.4	6.4
June	8.40	0.82	8.55	15	97.3	181.6	58.2	6.4
July	8.32	0.76	8.46	15	97.9	182.5	58.6	6.6
August	8.28	0.71	8.41	15	94.4	185.4	57.3	6.9
September	8.09	0.78	8.23	15	96.2	187.0	58.4	7.4
October	8.06	0.71	8.19	15	92.0	184.9	56.6	7.8
November	7.96	0.66	8.08	15	98.2	190.7	57.0	7.9
December	7.84	0.65	7.95	15	96.1	189.8	57.3	8.3
1999								
January	6.69	0.90	6.85	15	96.2	165.0	63.1	12.4
February	6.71	0.83	6.86	15	105.6	176.4	63.9	11.0
March	6.88	0.81	7.03	15	102.5	176.6	62.0	10.6
April	6.92	0.75	7.05	15	103.5	176.2	62.4	10.9
May	6.94	0.71	7.06	15	101.1	173.5	63.5	10.7
June	7.11	0.91	7.27	15	102.4	175.6	62.6	8.5
July	7.35	0.84	7.50	15	102.3	172.7	64.5	8.8
August	7.55	0.89	7.71	15	98.9	168.0	63.9	7.8
September	7.63	0.88	7.79	15	100.6	170.7	63.3	7.7
October	7.64	0.88	7.80	15	96.1	164.4	63.6	7.3
November	7.65	0.90	7.81	15	103.5	174.5	63.6	7.0
December	7.68	0.81	7.83	15	103.0	172.7	65.1	7.4
1998								
January	7.04	0.92	7.20	15	96.8	157.6	65.9	13.5
February	6.93	0.92	7.10	15	104.4	166.7	66.8	14.7
March	6.97	0.83	7.11	15	96.6	152.9	67.5	12.9
April	6.99	0.83	7.14	15	103.2	163.9	67.1	11.9
May	7.01	0.90	7.17	15	111.7	180.3	65.4	11.6
June	6.98	0.89	7.14	15	99.6	161.2	67.0	11.1
July	6.99	0.82	7.14	15	100.6	166.7	64.9	10.5
August	6.86	0.94	7.02	15	98.9	158.2	68.5	9.8
September	6.88	0.85	7.03	15	95.4	159.8	65.2	10.1
October	6.64	0.72	6.77	15	101.7	171.1	63.5	12.0
November	6.67	0.79	6.80	15	98.4	167.6	62.8	13.4
December	6.60	1.07	6.79	15	106.4	176.4	64.1	10.9
1997								
January	7.70	0.99	7.88	15	93.9	154.4	65.5	11.7
February	7.63	0.95	7.80	15	94.8	156.1	64.5	11.3
March	7.69	0.82	7.84	15	94.0	151.1	66.6	11.0
April	7.79	1.18	8.01	15	96.7	149.8	68.9	10.8
May	7.84	1.02	8.02	15	100.8	156.8	67.8	9.1
June	7.72	1.13	7.92	15	104.5	166.2	66.2	9.6
July	7.61	1.00	7.79	15	98.2	160.7	64.6	9.1
August	7.56	0.94	7.73	15	98.7	157.9	66.5	10.6
September	7.48	1.01	7.67	15	102.3	166.6	65.0	10.4
October	7.38	0.98	7.56	15	99.8	162.0	65.4	10.6
November	7.38	0.94	7.55	15	96.0	152.8	67.7	10.2
December	7.22	0.98	7.40	15	101.2	160.4	67.5	11.1

Table 2-87. Terms on Conventional Single-Family Mortgages, Fixed-Rate 30-Year and 15-Year Nonjumbo Loans, 1990–2010—*Continued*

[Percent, years, dollars in thousands.]

Year and month	Contract interest rate	Initial fees and charges	Effective interest rate	Term to maturity	Mortgage loan amount	Purchase price	Loan-to-price ratio	Share of total market
1996								
January	6.92	0.85	7.07	15	97.5	156.0	66.3	14.7
February	6.85	0.88	7.00	15	89.6	142.9	66.5	15.1
March	7.13	0.92	7.30	15	87.6	139.4	66.5	15.2
April	7.54	1.09	7.74	15	88.3	137.8	68.2	13.5
May	7.77	1.14	7.98	15	93.9	148.0	67.0	10.0
June	7.94	1.10	8.15	15	89.5	145.8	66.7	10.5
July	8.16	1.19	8.38	15	85.5	138.2	66.1	10.1
August	7.97	1.00	8.15	15	88.3	139.7	68.2	9.7
September	8.05	0.97	8.23	15	80.5	135.8	64.7	10.2
October	8.00	0.90	8.16	15	86.6	145.0	63.0	10.7
November	7.77	0.80	7.92	15	85.4	145.5	63.7	9.7
December	7.61	0.73	7.75	15	92.8	153.7	65.6	11.3
1995								
January	8.89	1.23	9.12	15	76.7	119.1	67.9	6.4
February	8.93	1.22	9.16	15	81.1	125.3	69.6	7.0
March	8.60	1.03	8.79	15	78.8	121.9	68.8	7.3
April	8.39	1.08	8.59	15	78.6	124.4	68.1	7.6
May	8.12	1.24	8.35	15	81.1	124.5	69.6	9.5
June	7.60	0.90	7.76	15	82.4	132.2	67.3	12.8
July	7.37	1.04	7.55	15	90.0	138.3	68.6	12.5
August	7.54	0.97	7.71	15	89.3	139.7	67.4	13.2
September	7.57	0.99	7.75	15	84.5	132.3	67.7	13.1
October	7.55	0.88	7.71	15	82.5	130.5	67.5	12.7
November	7.32	0.94	7.49	15	90.0	143.2	66.2	11.9
December	7.26	0.83	7.41	15	87.5	137.5	67.3	12.3
1994								
January	6.85	1.05	7.04	15	79.2	125.0	67.8	13.2
February	6.88	0.91	7.04	15	84.4	134.8	67.7	15.9
March	7.03	1.09	7.22	15	75.9	116.8	70.6	13.8
April	7.43	1.23	7.66	15	80.9	124.4	69.4	12.0
May	7.87	1.31	8.11	15	77.0	122.0	66.8	9.9
June	8.08	1.20	8.30	15	89.9	136.8	70.0	9.2
July	8.19	1.18	8.41	15	79.1	123.9	69.4	8.9
August	8.18	1.21	8.40	15	78.8	124.5	68.2	8.1
September	8.25	1.25	8.48	15	74.9	116.4	70.3	8.0
October	8.46	1.04	8.65	15	69.4	110.7	68.9	8.2
November	8.59	1.19	8.81	15	79.6	123.2	68.6	6.9
December	8.55	1.32	8.80	15	67.2	103.8	71.0	8.8
1993								
January	7.85	1.60	8.14	15	79.8	123.6	68.3	16.5
February	7.64	1.33	7.88	15	82.2	136.3	68.1	18.6
March	7.43	1.30	7.67	15	82.9	131.5	67.2	18.2
April	7.39	1.18	7.60	15	81.0	126.3	68.3	20.1
May	7.27	1.24	7.50	15	80.5	122.3	68.4	17.0
June	7.40	1.27	7.63	15	81.4	129.0	70.2	18.2
July	7.04	1.19	7.25	15	84.1	131.8	68.2	16.4
August	6.92	0.99	7.09	15	85.3	135.6	66.9	20.2
September	6.81	1.05	7.00	15	84.7	132.1	67.7	18.0
October	6.71	0.99	6.88	15	82.9	132.2	67.1	16.8
November	6.72	1.07	6.91	15	87.5	138.3	67.9	18.2
December	6.98	1.31	7.21	15	76.8	122.1	69.2	14.9
1992								
January	8.17	0.98	8.35	15	97.2	155.1	65.4	18.2
February	8.24	1.48	8.52	15	82.8	139.0	63.7	20.7
March	8.49	1.63	8.80	15	79.3	127.8	65.1	16.2
April	8.53	1.74	8.86	15	80.7	127.7	67.8	13.8
May	8.43	1.64	8.73	15	83.2	129.2	68.6	13.4
June	8.38	1.50	8.66	15	77.8	117.2	71.0	14.5
July	7.91	1.24	8.14	15	82.3	130.8	68.1	16.3
August	7.84	1.78	8.16	15	81.0	124.9	68.3	18.0
September	7.64	1.45	7.90	15	83.7	134.7	66.3	18.9
October	7.65	1.31	7.89	15	86.7	138.0	66.5	20.6
November	7.77	1.67	8.07	15	79.5	129.0	66.2	20.9
December	7.92	1.60	8.21	15	80.6	124.9	68.4	16.3

Table 2-87. Terms on Conventional Single-Family Mortgages, Fixed-Rate 30-Year and 15-Year Nonjumbo Loans, 1990–2010—*Continued*

[Percent, years, dollars in thousands.]

Year and month	Contract interest rate	Initial fees and charges	Effective interest rate	Term to maturity	Mortgage loan amount	Purchase price	Loan-to-price ratio	Share of total market
1991								
January	9.76	1.50	10.04	15	77.7	121.8	67.5	14.7
February	9.74	1.56	10.04	15	80.7	126.2	69.3	14.6
March	9.29	1.42	9.56	15	81.6	127.8	67.7	20.9
April	9.31	1.95	9.68	15	79.2	128.0	65.6	15.6
May	9.45	1.77	9.78	15	76.2	121.3	65.9	14.5
June	9.40	1.70	9.72	15	82.2	133.3	66.0	13.0
July	9.44	1.78	9.77	15	85.6	134.4	67.3	16.7
August	9.42	1.82	9.75	15	75.0	115.2	67.7	12.8
September	9.14	1.52	9.42	15	81.6	130.6	65.8	15.6
October	8.99	1.55	9.28	15	80.0	127.3	67.4	16.9
November	8.75	1.58	9.04	15	67.3	111.3	66.5	15.9
December	8.46	1.47	8.73	15	73.1	117.0	67.3	17.4
1990								
January	9.73	1.86	10.07	15	78.1	122.1	66.5	11.8
February	9.78	1.94	10.14	15	83.3	128.7	66.5	10.8
March	9.91	2.03	10.30	15	72.3	111.1	69.0	12.4
April	10.06	2.00	10.44	15	74.9	115.8	68.4	10.7
May	10.06	1.96	10.43	15	83.4	129.3	68.0	11.7
June	10.14	1.98	10.52	15	84.1	127.8	67.4	11.1
July	10.13	1.88	10.49	15	77.3	119.0	68.0	10.6
August	10.05	2.01	10.43	15	76.6	114.9	68.8	12.1
September	9.99	1.79	10.33	15	71.7	115.4	65.8	15.3
October	9.98	1.83	10.33	15	74.3	118.8	65.3	13.3
November	9.98	1.81	10.32	15	82.0	124.2	68.8	13.1
December	9.83	1.73	10.15	15	82.3	133.8	64.4	11.1

Source: Federal Housing Finance Agency, Monthly Interest Rate Survey

Table 2-88. Placements of New Manufactured Homes, by Region and Size of Home, 2000–2012

[Units in thousands.]

Characteristics	United States			Northeast			Midwest			South			West		
	Total[1]	Single	Double	Total[1]	Single	Double	Total[1]	Single	Double	Total[1]	Single	Double	Total[1]	Single	Double
Annual data															
2011 [2]	47.0	20.8	25.5	3.3	1.4	1.8	6.3	3.3	3.0	31.1	13.9	16.8	6.3	2.2	3.9
2010 [2]	50.7	19.3	30.4	3.7	1.5	2.3	5.7	2.6	3.1	34.7	13.8	20.4	6.6	1.4	4.6
2009	54.5	20.2	33.1	3.6	1.2	2.3	5.5	1.9	3.6	38.0	15.7	21.9	7.5	1.5	5.3
2008	80.5	27.8	50.8	5.0	1.6	3.3	8.2	2.7	5.4	54.0	21.0	32.4	13.3	2.4	9.7
2007	94.8	28.6	63.1	7.0	2.4	4.5	10.8	3.4	7.3	59.4	20.6	38.1	17.7	2.3	13.3
2006	112.4	28.9	79.2	7.9	1.9	6.0	14.5	4.0	10.4	66.1	21.0	43.9	23.9	2.0	18.9
2005	122.9	28.7	89.4	9.2	2.4	6.8	17.1	3.8	13.2	68.1	20.4	46.5	28.5	2.2	22.9
2004	124.4	28.2	91.7	11.0	3.1	7.8	20.6	3.7	16.6	67.4	19.4	46.8	25.5	2.0	20.5
2003	139.8	29.4	106.0	11.2	3.4	7.8	25.2	4.9	20.0	77.2	19.1	57.0	26.1	1.9	21.3
2002	174.3	41.1	128.7	11.8	3.1	8.7	34.2	8.1	25.7	101.0	27.6	72.0	27.2	2.4	22.2
2001	196.2	53.3	139.3	12.2	3.9	8.3	37.6	10.4	27.0	116.4	35.2	80.0	30.0	3.8	24.0
2000	280.9	88.3	190.3	14.9	4.2	10.6	48.7	14.2	34.4	178.7	64.3	113.4	38.6	5.6	31.9
Monthly data: not seasonally adjusted															
2012															
January	2.9	1.3	1.6	0.2	0.1	0.1	0.4	0.2	0.2	2.0	0.9	1.1	0.3	0.1	0.2
February	3.2	1.2	2.0	0.2	0.1	0.1	0.4	0.2	0.2	2.2	0.7	1.5	0.4	0.2	0.3
March [2]	4.4	2.2	2.1	0.2	0.1	0.1	0.6	0.3	0.3	3.2	1.7	1.5	0.4	0.2	0.2
April [2]	4.3	1.9	2.3	0.3	0.1	0.2	0.6	0.3	0.2	2.8	1.2	1.6	0.7	0.3	0.4
May [3]	4.4	2.1	2.3	0.3	0.2	0.1	0.7	0.4	0.3	2.7	1.2	1.5	0.6	0.3	0.3
June	NA	NA	NA	NA	NA	NA	NA	NA	NA	NA	NA	NA	NA	NA	NA
July	NA	NA	NA	NA	NA	NA	NA	NA	NA	NA	NA	NA	NA	NA	NA
August	NA	NA	NA	NA	NA	NA	NA	NA	NA	NA	NA	NA	NA	NA	NA
September	NA	NA	NA	NA	NA	NA	NA	NA	NA	NA	NA	NA	NA	NA	NA
October	NA	NA	NA	NA	NA	NA	NA	NA	NA	NA	NA	NA	NA	NA	NA
November	NA	NA	NA	NA	NA	NA	NA	NA	NA	NA	NA	NA	NA	NA	NA
December	NA	NA	NA	NA	NA	NA	NA	NA	NA	NA	NA	NA	NA	NA	NA
2011 [2]															
January	2.3	1.0	1.3	0.1	0.1	0.1	0.2	0.1	0.1	1.5	0.7	0.8	0.4	0.1	0.3
February	2.7	1.2	1.4	0.1	S	0.1	0.2	0.1	0.1	2.0	1.0	1.0	0.4	0.1	0.3
March	3.5	1.4	2.0	0.2	0.1	0.1	0.4	0.2	0.1	2.6	1.0	1.6	0.4	0.1	0.3
April	4.0	2.1	1.9	0.2	0.1	0.1	0.3	0.2	0.1	2.9	1.5	1.4	0.6	0.3	0.3
May	3.9	1.6	2.2	0.3	0.1	0.2	0.5	0.3	0.2	2.5	1.0	1.4	0.6	0.2	0.4
June	4.9	2.4	2.5	0.4	0.2	0.2	0.7	0.4	0.3	3.4	1.7	1.6	0.5	0.1	0.4
July	4.1	1.7	2.4	0.2	0.1	0.1	0.6	0.3	0.4	2.7	1.1	1.6	0.6	0.2	0.3
August	4.6	1.8	2.8	0.4	0.2	0.2	0.7	0.3	0.4	3.0	1.2	1.8	0.6	0.2	0.4
September	4.0	1.7	2.2	0.3	0.1	0.2	0.6	0.3	0.3	2.6	1.2	1.4	0.4	0.1	0.3
October	4.4	2.1	2.2	0.3	0.1	0.2	0.7	0.4	0.3	2.8	1.3	1.4	0.5	0.2	0.3
November	4.9	2.3	2.5	0.5	0.2	0.2	0.8	0.5	0.4	2.9	1.3	1.5	0.7	0.3	0.4
December	3.7	1.5	2.0	0.3	0.1	0.1	0.5	0.3	0.3	2.3	0.9	1.3	0.5	0.2	0.3
2010 [2]															
January	2.8	0.9	1.9	0.2	S	0.1	0.2	S	0.1	2.1	0.7	1.4	0.4	0.1	0.2
February	2.8	1.1	1.7	0.1	S	0.1	0.2	0.1	0.1	2.1	0.8	1.3	0.4	0.1	0.2
March	4.0	1.4	2.6	0.2	0.1	0.1	0.2	0.1	0.1	3.1	1.1	2.0	0.5	0.1	0.3
April	5.0	2.0	2.8	0.2	0.1	0.1	0.6	0.4	0.2	3.6	1.5	2.0	0.7	0.2	0.5
May	5.4	2.1	3.2	0.4	0.2	0.2	0.5	0.2	0.3	3.9	1.6	2.2	0.7	0.1	0.5
June	5.9	2.1	3.7	0.5	0.2	0.3	0.6	0.2	0.4	4.0	1.5	2.5	0.8	0.2	0.6
July	4.7	1.6	3.0	0.4	0.2	0.3	0.6	0.2	0.3	3.2	1.1	2.1	0.5	0.1	0.4
August	4.8	2.2	2.6	0.4	0.2	0.2	0.7	0.3	0.4	3.1	1.5	1.6	0.6	0.1	0.4
September	3.8	1.6	2.2	0.4	0.2	0.2	0.5	0.2	0.3	2.3	1.1	1.3	0.6	0.1	0.4
October	4.4	1.6	2.6	0.3	0.1	0.3	0.7	0.3	0.4	2.8	1.1	1.6	0.5	0.1	0.4
November	3.4	1.3	2.1	0.4	0.1	0.3	0.5	0.3	0.2	2.1	0.8	1.2	0.5	0.1	0.3
December	3.6	1.5	2.0	0.3	0.1	0.2	0.5	0.3	0.2	2.3	1.0	1.3	0.5	0.1	0.4
2009															
January	4.0	1.4	2.5	0.2	0.1	0.1	0.4	0.1	0.2	3.0	1.1	1.8	0.5	0.1	0.3
February	3.2	1.3	1.9	S	S	S	0.2	S	0.1	2.7	1.1	1.5	0.4	0.1	0.2
March	4.7	1.8	2.8	0.1	S	0.1	0.5	0.2	0.3	3.3	1.5	1.8	0.8	0.1	0.6
April	4.8	2.0	2.8	0.2	0.1	0.1	0.4	0.2	0.2	3.5	1.5	2.0	0.7	0.2	0.5
May	4.7	2.0	2.6	0.2	0.1	0.1	0.5	0.1	0.3	3.3	1.6	1.7	0.7	0.1	0.5
June	4.7	1.8	2.8	0.4	0.1	0.3	0.3	S	0.3	3.4	1.5	1.8	0.6	0.2	0.4
July	4.6	1.5	3.0	0.6	0.2	0.4	0.4	0.2	0.2	3.0	1.0	1.9	0.6	S	0.5
August	4.2	1.2	3.0	0.2	0.1	0.1	0.5	0.1	0.4	2.8	1.0	1.8	0.7	S	0.6
September	4.9	1.8	3.0	0.5	0.2	0.3	0.7	0.2	0.5	3.1	1.2	1.9	0.6	0.2	0.4
October	5.2	1.7	3.3	0.4	0.2	0.3	0.7	0.2	0.6	3.3	1.2	2.1	0.8	0.2	0.4
November	5.4	2.0	3.3	0.4	0.1	0.3	0.5	0.2	0.3	3.8	1.5	2.2	0.8	0.2	0.5
December	4.0	1.7	2.2	0.2	S	0.1	0.4	0.2	0.2	2.9	1.4	1.5	0.4	S	0.3

Table 2-88. Placements of New Manufactured Homes, by Region and Size of Home, 2000–2012—*Continued*

[Units in thousands.]

Characteristics	United States			Northeast			Midwest			South			West		
	Total[1]	Single	Double	Total[1]	Single	Double	Total[1]	Single	Double	Total[1]	Single	Double	Total[1]	Single	Double
Monthly data: seasonally adjusted annual rate															
2012															
January	52.0	X	X	4.0	X	X	8.0	X	X	34.0	X	X	5.0	X	X
February	56.0	X	X	6.0	X	X	11.0	X	X	33.0	X	X	6.0	X	X
March [2]	55.0	X	X	3.0	X	X	10.0	X	X	37.0	X	X	6.0	X	X
April [2]	51.0	X	X	4.0	X	X	9.0	X	X	31.0	X	X	7.0	X	X
May [3]	47.0	X	X	3.0	X	X	8.0	X	X	29.0	X	X	6.0	X	X
June	NA	NA	NA	NA	NA	NA	NA	NA	NA	NA	NA	NA	NA	NA	NA
July	NA	NA	NA	NA	NA	NA	NA	NA	NA	NA	NA	NA	NA	NA	NA
August	NA	NA	NA	NA	NA	NA	NA	NA	NA	NA	NA	NA	NA	NA	NA
September	NA	NA	NA	NA	NA	NA	NA	NA	NA	NA	NA	NA	NA	NA	NA
October	NA	NA	NA	NA	NA	NA	NA	NA	NA	NA	NA	NA	NA	NA	NA
November	NA	NA	NA	NA	NA	NA	NA	NA	NA	NA	NA	NA	NA	NA	NA
December	NA	NA	NA	NA	NA	NA	NA	NA	NA	NA	NA	NA	NA	NA	NA
2011 [2]															
January	38.0	X	X	2.0	X	X	4.0	X	X	26.0	X	X	7.0	X	X
February	46.0	X	X	3.0	X	X	6.0	X	X	30.0	X	X	7.0	X	X
March	47.0	X	X	4.0	X	X	7.0	X	X	31.0	X	X	5.0	X	X
April	46.0	X	X	3.0	X	X	4.0	X	X	32.0	X	X	7.0	X	X
May	42.0	X	X	3.0	X	X	6.0	X	X	26.0	X	X	6.0	X	X
June	49.0	X	X	4.0	X	X	6.0	X	X	34.0	X	X	5.0	X	X
July	47.0	X	X	2.0	X	X	6.0	X	X	31.0	X	X	7.0	X	X
August	50.0	X	X	4.0	X	X	7.0	X	X	34.0	X	X	6.0	X	X
September	45.0	X	X	3.0	X	X	6.0	X	X	31.0	X	X	4.0	X	X
October	46.0	X	X	3.0	X	X	6.0	X	X	32.0	X	X	5.0	X	X
November	56.0	X	X	5.0	X	X	8.0	X	X	36.0	X	X	8.0	X	X
December	48.0	X	X	4.0	X	X	7.0	X	X	30.0	X	X	6.0	X	X
2010 [2]															
January	50.0	X	X	4.0	X	X	4.0	X	X	35.0	X	X	7.0	X	X
February	48.0	X	X	3.0	X	X	6.0	X	X	32.0	X	X	7.0	X	X
March	51.0	X	X	4.0	X	X	4.0	X	X	37.0	X	X	7.0	X	X
April	59.0	X	X	3.0	X	X	9.0	X	X	39.0	X	X	8.0	X	X
May	58.0	X	X	5.0	X	X	6.0	X	X	41.0	X	X	7.0	X	X
June	59.0	X	X	5.0	X	X	5.0	X	X	40.0	X	X	9.0	X	X
July	53.0	X	X	4.0	X	X	6.0	X	X	37.0	X	X	6.0	X	X
August	52.0	X	X	4.0	X	X	7.0	X	X	35.0	X	X	6.0	X	X
September	43.0	X	X	4.0	X	X	5.0	X	X	27.0	X	X	7.0	X	X
October	46.0	X	X	3.0	X	X	6.0	X	X	32.0	X	X	6.0	X	X
November	41.0	X	X	4.0	X	X	5.0	X	X	26.0	X	X	6.0	X	X
December	48.0	X	X	4.0	X	X	7.0	X	X	30.0	X	X	6.0	X	X
2009															
January	68.0	X	X	4.0	X	X	8.0	X	X	47.0	X	X	8.0	X	X
February	55.0	X	X	S	X	X	6.0	X	X	42.0	X	X	8.0	X	X
March	62.0	X	X	2.0	X	X	9.0	X	X	39.0	X	X	11.0	X	X
April	56.0	X	X	3.0	X	X	6.0	X	X	39.0	X	X	8.0	X	X
May	50.0	X	X	2.0	X	X	6.0	X	X	35.0	X	X	7.0	X	X
June	48.0	X	X	4.0	X	X	3.0	X	X	35.0	X	X	7.0	X	X
July	50.0	X	X	6.0	X	X	4.0	X	X	34.0	X	X	6.0	X	X
August	46.0	X	X	2.0	X	X	5.0	X	X	32.0	X	X	7.0	X	X
September	55.0	X	X	5.0	X	X	6.0	X	X	37.0	X	X	7.0	X	X
October	56.0	X	X	3.0	X	X	6.0	X	X	37.0	X	X	9.0	X	X
November	68.0	X	X	4.0	X	X	5.0	X	X	48.0	X	X	11.0	X	X
December	52.0	X	X	3.0	X	X	6.0	X	X	39.0	X	X	4.0	X	X

NA = Not available.
S = Suppressed to avoid disclosing data for individual dealers; data are included in higher-level estimates.
X = Not applicable.
[1] = Includes manufactured homes with more than two sections.
[2] = Revised.
[3] = Preliminary.

Source: Census Bureau via survey sponsored by the Department of Housing and Urban Development

Table 2-89. Dealers' Inventory of New Manufactured Homes, by Region and Size of Home, 2000–2012

[Units in thousands.]

Characteristics	United States			Northeast			Midwest			South			West		
	Total[1]	Single	Double	Total[1]	Single	Double	Total[1]	Single	Double	Total[1]	Single	Double	Total[1]	Single	Double
Annual data															
2011[2]	20.1	7.6	12.1	1.2	0.5	0.8	2.3	1.0	1.3	14.6	5.8	8.6	2.0	0.4	1.4
2010[2]	20.4	7.0	13.0	1.1	0.4	0.7	2.6	1.0	1.5	14.3	5.1	9.0	2.4	0.5	1.7
2009	23.2	6.8	15.7	1.7	0.6	1.1	2.9	1.0	1.8	15.7	4.8	10.6	2.9	0.4	2.2
2008	30.6	8.9	21.0	2.1	0.6	1.5	3.5	0.9	2.6	20.8	6.7	13.9	4.2	0.7	3.0
2007	34.4	9.8	23.6	2.5	0.6	1.9	4.4	1.2	3.2	22.4	7.4	14.7	5.1	0.5	3.8
2006	36.8	10.0	25.6	2.4	0.8	1.6	4.9	1.2	3.6	23.6	7.6	15.7	6.0	0.3	4.7
2005	35.3	9.0	25.3	2.1	0.4	1.7	6.2	1.4	4.7	21.4	6.7	14.4	5.6	0.4	4.5
2004	35.3	8.0	26.1	1.7	0.4	1.3	5.7	0.9	4.6	22.3	6.4	15.6	5.5	0.2	4.5
2003	36.4	7.1	28.1	2.6	0.9	1.7	7.0	1.0	5.9	22.0	4.8	16.8	4.8	0.4	3.7
2002	47.2	10.2	36.0	2.7	0.8	1.9	8.7	1.5	7.2	29.9	7.6	22.0	5.9	0.4	4.8
2001	55.3	15.3	39.3	3.1	1.0	2.1	11.0	2.8	8.0	35.1	10.8	24.0	6.3	0.6	5.2
2000	59.3	19.6	39.3	2.9	0.8	2.1	11.3	4.0	7.3	38.5	14.1	24.2	6.7	0.7	5.7
Monthly data: not seasonally adjusted															
2012															
January	20.8	7.9	12.5	1.3	0.4	0.8	2.4	1.0	1.3	15.2	6.0	9.0	2.0	0.4	1.3
February	21.3	8.2	12.8	1.2	0.3	0.8	2.4	1.1	1.3	15.6	6.3	9.1	2.1	0.5	1.5
March[2]	21.2	8.3	12.5	1.4	0.5	0.9	2.7	1.3	1.4	14.9	6.1	8.7	2.2	0.5	1.5
April[2]	21.4	8.5	12.4	1.5	0.6	0.9	2.8	1.4	1.4	15.0	6.1	8.6	2.1	0.5	1.5
May[3]	22.0	8.7	12.9	1.6	0.6	1.0	2.9	1.4	1.4	15.3	6.1	8.9	2.3	0.6	1.5
June	NA	NA	NA	NA	NA	NA	NA	NA	NA	NA	NA	NA	NA	NA	NA
July	NA	NA	NA	NA	NA	NA	NA	NA	NA	NA	NA	NA	NA	NA	NA
August	NA	NA	NA	NA	NA	NA	NA	NA	NA	NA	NA	NA	NA	NA	NA
September	NA	NA	NA	NA	NA	NA	NA	NA	NA	NA	NA	NA	NA	NA	NA
October	NA	NA	NA	NA	NA	NA	NA	NA	NA	NA	NA	NA	NA	NA	NA
November	NA	NA	NA	NA	NA	NA	NA	NA	NA	NA	NA	NA	NA	NA	NA
December	NA	NA	NA	NA	NA	NA	NA	NA	NA	NA	NA	NA	NA	NA	NA
2011[2]															
January	20.3	7.0	12.8	1.1	0.4	0.7	2.5	1.0	1.5	14.5	5.2	9.1	2.1	0.4	1.6
February	20.2	6.9	12.8	1.2	0.5	0.7	2.6	1.0	1.5	14.4	5.1	9.1	2.1	0.4	1.5
March	20.7	7.5	12.8	1.2	0.4	0.7	2.7	1.0	1.6	14.6	5.5	8.9	2.3	0.5	1.6
April	20.6	7.2	12.9	1.2	0.4	0.8	2.9	1.1	1.7	14.3	5.3	8.8	2.2	0.4	1.5
May	20.9	7.6	12.9	1.2	0.4	0.8	3.0	1.2	1.8	14.6	5.5	8.9	2.1	0.4	1.5
June	21.0	7.6	12.9	1.2	0.4	0.8	3.0	1.2	1.8	14.6	5.5	8.9	2.1	0.4	1.5
July	20.4	7.4	12.6	1.4	0.5	0.8	2.7	1.0	1.7	14.3	5.5	8.6	2.0	0.4	1.5
August	20.4	7.6	12.4	1.3	0.5	0.9	2.7	1.0	1.6	14.4	5.7	8.5	2.1	0.4	1.5
September	20.9	7.9	12.6	1.4	0.5	0.9	2.7	1.1	1.5	14.6	5.8	8.7	2.2	0.4	1.5
October	20.9	7.8	12.7	1.4	0.6	0.9	2.8	1.2	1.6	14.6	5.6	8.8	2.1	0.4	1.5
November	20.4	7.7	12.3	1.2	0.5	0.8	2.5	1.1	1.4	14.5	5.7	8.6	2.1	0.4	1.5
December	20.1	7.6	12.1	1.2	0.5	0.8	2.3	1.0	1.3	14.6	5.8	8.6	2.0	0.4	1.4
2010[2]															
January	23.3	7.2	15.5	1.3	0.5	0.8	2.7	0.9	1.7	16.3	5.3	10.7	3.0	0.4	2.3
February	23.6	7.3	15.7	1.4	0.6	0.8	2.7	0.9	1.8	16.5	5.5	10.8	2.9	0.4	2.2
March	23.9	7.9	15.4	1.5	0.6	0.9	3.0	1.1	1.9	16.5	5.8	10.4	3.0	0.4	2.3
April	23.7	7.9	15.2	1.6	0.7	0.9	2.9	1.0	1.9	16.4	5.9	10.2	2.9	0.4	2.2
May	23.0	7.5	15.0	1.6	0.6	1.0	3.0	1.1	1.9	15.8	5.5	10.0	2.7	0.4	2.1
June	22.4	7.5	14.4	1.5	0.6	0.9	3.0	1.2	1.9	15.3	5.4	9.6	2.6	0.4	2.0
July	21.8	7.5	13.8	1.5	0.6	0.9	2.9	1.1	1.8	14.7	5.3	9.2	2.6	0.4	2.0
August	21.5	7.2	13.8	1.5	0.5	1.0	2.9	1.1	1.7	14.6	5.1	9.2	2.6	0.4	1.9
September	22.0	7.4	14.1	1.5	0.5	1.0	2.9	1.1	1.7	15.0	5.3	9.4	2.6	0.5	1.9
October	21.3	7.2	13.6	1.4	0.5	0.9	2.7	1.1	1.6	14.6	5.2	9.1	2.6	0.5	1.9
November	21.3	7.5	13.4	1.2	0.4	0.8	2.7	1.1	1.6	14.8	5.4	9.1	2.6	0.5	1.9
December	20.4	7.0	13.0	1.1	0.4	0.7	2.6	1.0	1.5	14.3	5.1	9.0	2.4	0.5	1.7
2009															
January	29.3	8.6	20.0	2.0	0.5	1.5	3.2	0.8	2.4	19.9	6.5	13.2	4.2	0.8	2.9
February	29.5	8.8	20.0	2.0	0.5	1.5	3.4	1.0	2.4	19.8	6.6	13.1	4.2	0.7	3.0
March	28.4	8.4	19.4	2.0	0.6	1.4	3.1	0.8	2.3	19.5	6.4	12.9	3.8	0.6	2.8
April	27.9	8.0	19.1	2.0	0.6	1.4	3.3	1.0	2.3	18.9	6.0	12.7	3.7	0.5	2.7
May	27.5	7.8	19.0	2.2	0.7	1.5	3.3	1.0	2.2	18.3	5.6	12.5	3.6	0.5	2.7
June	27.0	7.5	18.9	2.1	0.7	1.5	3.5	1.3	2.1	17.9	5.1	12.5	3.5	0.4	2.7
July	26.7	7.5	18.6	1.9	0.6	1.3	3.4	1.2	2.2	17.9	5.3	12.4	3.5	0.4	2.7
August	26.7	7.8	18.3	2.1	0.7	1.4	3.4	1.2	2.1	17.9	5.3	12.4	3.3	0.5	2.5
September	26.5	8.0	17.8	1.9	0.6	1.3	3.3	1.2	2.0	17.9	5.6	12.1	3.4	0.6	2.4
October	25.6	7.7	17.2	1.9	0.6	1.3	3.0	1.1	1.9	17.5	5.6	11.7	3.3	0.4	2.4
November	23.9	7.2	16.1	1.8	0.6	1.2	2.9	1.1	1.8	16.2	5.1	10.9	3.0	0.4	2.2
December	23.2	6.8	15.7	1.7	0.6	1.1	2.9	1.0	1.8	15.7	4.8	10.6	2.9	0.4	2.2

Table 2-89. Dealers' Inventory of New Manufactured Homes, by Region and Size of Home, 2000–2012—*Continued*

[Units in thousands.]

Characteristics	United States			Northeast			Midwest			South			West		
	Total[1]	Single	Double	Total[1]	Single	Double	Total[1]	Single	Double	Total[1]	Single	Double	Total[1]	Single	Double
Monthly data: seasonally adjusted annual rate															
2012															
January	21.0	X	X	1.0	X	X	3.0	X	X	15.0	X	X	2.0	X	X
February	21.0	X	X	1.0	X	X	2.0	X	X	15.0	X	X	2.0	X	X
March [2]	21.0	X	X	1.0	X	X	3.0	X	X	15.0	X	X	2.0	X	X
April [2]	21.0	X	X	1.0	X	X	3.0	X	X	15.0	X	X	2.0	X	X
May [3]	21.0	X	X	1.0	X	X	3.0	X	X	15.0	X	X	2.0	X	X
June	NA	NA	NA	NA	NA	NA	NA	NA	NA	NA	NA	NA	NA	NA	NA
July	NA	NA	NA	NA	NA	NA	NA	NA	NA	NA	NA	NA	NA	NA	NA
August	NA	NA	NA	NA	NA	NA	NA	NA	NA	NA	NA	NA	NA	NA	NA
September	NA	NA	NA	NA	NA	NA	NA	NA	NA	NA	NA	NA	NA	NA	NA
October	NA	NA	NA	NA	NA	NA	NA	NA	NA	NA	NA	NA	NA	NA	NA
November	NA	NA	NA	NA	NA	NA	NA	NA	NA	NA	NA	NA	NA	NA	NA
December	NA	NA	NA	NA	NA	NA	NA	NA	NA	NA	NA	NA	NA	NA	NA
2011 [2]															
January	21.0	X	X	1.0	X	X	3.0	X	X	15.0	X	X	2.0	X	X
February	20.0	X	X	1.0	X	X	3.0	X	X	14.0	X	X	2.0	X	X
March	20.0	X	X	1.0	X	X	3.0	X	X	14.0	X	X	2.0	X	X
April	20.0	X	X	1.0	X	X	3.0	X	X	14.0	X	X	2.0	X	X
May	20.0	X	X	1.0	X	X	3.0	X	X	14.0	X	X	2.0	X	X
June	21.0	X	X	1.0	X	X	3.0	X	X	15.0	X	X	2.0	X	X
July	21.0	X	X	1.0	X	X	3.0	X	X	15.0	X	X	2.0	X	X
August	20.0	X	X	1.0	X	X	3.0	X	X	14.0	X	X	2.0	X	X
September	21.0	X	X	1.0	X	X	3.0	X	X	14.0	X	X	2.0	X	X
October	21.0	X	X	1.0	X	X	3.0	X	X	15.0	X	X	2.0	X	X
November	21.0	X	X	1.0	X	X	3.0	X	X	15.0	X	X	2.0	X	X
December	21.0	X	X	1.0	X	X	2.0	X	X	15.0	X	X	2.0	X	X
2010 [2]															
January	24.0	X	X	1.0	X	X	3.0	X	X	16.0	X	X	3.0	X	X
February	24.0	X	X	2.0	X	X	3.0	X	X	16.0	X	X	3.0	X	X
March	24.0	X	X	2.0	X	X	3.0	X	X	16.0	X	X	3.0	X	X
April	23.0	X	X	2.0	X	X	3.0	X	X	16.0	X	X	3.0	X	X
May	23.0	X	X	1.0	X	X	3.0	X	X	16.0	X	X	3.0	X	X
June	22.0	X	X	1.0	X	X	3.0	X	X	15.0	X	X	3.0	X	X
July	22.0	X	X	1.0	X	X	3.0	X	X	15.0	X	X	3.0	X	X
August	21.0	X	X	1.0	X	X	3.0	X	X	15.0	X	X	3.0	X	X
September	22.0	X	X	1.0	X	X	3.0	X	X	15.0	X	X	3.0	X	X
October	22.0	X	X	1.0	X	X	3.0	X	X	15.0	X	X	3.0	X	X
November	22.0	X	X	1.0	X	X	3.0	X	X	15.0	X	X	3.0	X	X
December	21.0	X	X	1.0	X	X	3.0	X	X	15.0	X	X	3.0	X	X
2009															
January	30.0	X	X	2.0	X	X	3.0	X	X	20.0	X	X	4.0	X	X
February	29.0	X	X	2.0	X	X	3.0	X	X	20.0	X	X	4.0	X	X
March	28.0	X	X	2.0	X	X	3.0	X	X	19.0	X	X	4.0	X	X
April	27.0	X	X	2.0	X	X	3.0	X	X	19.0	X	X	4.0	X	X
May	27.0	X	X	2.0	X	X	3.0	X	X	18.0	X	X	4.0	X	X
June	27.0	X	X	2.0	X	X	3.0	X	X	18.0	X	X	3.0	X	X
July	27.0	X	X	2.0	X	X	3.0	X	X	18.0	X	X	4.0	X	X
August	27.0	X	X	2.0	X	X	3.0	X	X	18.0	X	X	3.0	X	X
September	26.0	X	X	2.0	X	X	3.0	X	X	18.0	X	X	3.0	X	X
October	26.0	X	X	2.0	X	X	3.0	X	X	18.0	X	X	3.0	X	X
November	24.0	X	X	2.0	X	X	3.0	X	X	16.0	X	X	3.0	X	X
December	24.0	X	X	2.0	X	X	3.0	X	X	16.0	X	X	3.0	X	X

NA = Not available.
X = Not applicable.
[1] = Includes manufactured homes with more than two sections.
[2] = Revised.
[3] = Preliminary.

Source: Census Bureau via survey sponsored by the Department of Housing and Urban Development

Table 2-90. Average Sales Price of New Manufactured Homes, by Region and Size of Home, 2000–2012

[Dollars.]

Characteristics	United States			Northeast			Midwest			South			West		
	Total[1]	Single	Double	Total[1]	Single	Double	Total[1]	Single	Double	Total[1]	Single	Double	Total[1]	Single	Double
Annual data															
2011 [2]	60,600	40,600	74,200	63,100	42,000	76,300	60,400	43,000	76,900	58,700	40,000	72,400	70,500	41,200	79,900
2010 [2]	62,800	39,500	74,500	65,700	44,000	76,900	60,600	41,400	74,500	60,100	38,600	72,700	78,600	42,100	82,000
2009	63,100	39,600	74,500	61,400	44,200	69,300	66,200	41,100	75,700	59,400	38,700	72,800	82,100	44,500	83,300
2008	64,700	38,000	75,800	68,400	46,100	77,700	65,700	39,400	74,500	59,600	36,900	72,700	84,900	42,700	87,100
2007	65,400	37,300	74,200	66,100	43,300	75,200	64,900	39,200	72,700	59,900	36,100	71,100	85,500	41,300	84,800
2006	64,300	36,100	71,300	65,300	40,500	73,100	59,100	35,900	67,400	58,900	35,400	68,700	83,400	41,200	79,600
2005	62,600	34,100	68,700	67,000	40,400	75,700	60,600	35,800	66,500	55,700	32,700	64,700	79,900	38,900	76,400
2004	58,200	32,900	63,400	60,200	38,100	67,600	58,800	34,500	63,100	52,300	31,200	59,600	73,200	38,600	71,100
2003	54,900	31,900	59,700	57,300	36,800	66,000	55,100	32,800	59,400	50,500	30,400	56,700	67,700	37,000	65,900
2002	51,300	30,900	56,100	53,200	33,800	59,100	51,700	32,300	56,500	48,000	29,900	54,100	62,600	35,800	61,200
2001	48,900	30,400	55,200	50,000	34,500	57,400	49,100	32,300	55,200	46,500	29,400	53,800	58,000	32,000	59,500
2000	46,400	30,200	53,600	47,000	31,200	53,000	47,900	31,600	54,400	44,300	29,700	52,500	54,100	32,100	56,900
Monthly data															
2012															
January	61,100	40,200	76,400	55,400	41,700	67,000	55,700	41,500	69,200	60,700	40,100	77,700	76,400	33,700	79,700
February	63,500	40,300	75,600	63,500	44,200	75,000	55,900	39,900	75,900	63,400	40,900	74,500	68,000	35,900	81,700
March	57,700	39,600	73,300	63,400	36,200	79,700	57,300	39,800	75,100	55,900	39,600	71,400	76,000	41,300	85,600
April	62,500	41,300	76,000	64,200	40,100	82,100	59,500	44,300	74,900	61,400	41,000	74,800	68,900	40,100	80,000
May	59,900	40,300	74,600	59,400	43,400	72,400	56,500	41,600	70,500	59,200	39,500	74,700	67,500	43,300	78,000
June	NA	NA	NA	NA	NA	NA	NA	NA	NA	NA	NA	NA	NA	NA	NA
July	NA	NA	NA	NA	NA	NA	NA	NA	NA	NA	NA	NA	NA	NA	NA
August	NA	NA	NA	NA	NA	NA	NA	NA	NA	NA	NA	NA	NA	NA	NA
September	NA	NA	NA	NA	NA	NA	NA	NA	NA	NA	NA	NA	NA	NA	NA
October	NA	NA	NA	NA	NA	NA	NA	NA	NA	NA	NA	NA	NA	NA	NA
November	NA	NA	NA	NA	NA	NA	NA	NA	NA	NA	NA	NA	NA	NA	NA
December	NA	NA	NA	NA	NA	NA	NA	NA	NA	NA	NA	NA	NA	NA	NA
2011 [2]															
January	59,800	37,700	72,700	53,700	36,300	67,600	57,100	42,200	68,800	57,900	37,700	71,700	72,300	34,100	79,600
February	60,400	40,100	74,800	81,700	S	88,700	68,000	43,700	86,000	57,300	40,300	71,500	71,100	33,200	80,000
March	59,300	41,000	70,500	48,700	36,500	78,100	54,200	44,600	75,900	58,600	40,300	68,700	73,600	44,800	79,000
April	57,100	39,500	74,300	68,700	37,800	88,100	53,500	42,400	72,200	56,000	39,200	73,600	61,700	39,900	74,700
May	64,700	39,900	79,500	64,100	42,600	73,800	59,700	41,800	78,400	62,600	38,900	78,000	79,100	42,400	88,800
June	59,300	39,900	74,300	68,200	43,800	84,200	59,800	42,100	77,300	56,100	39,100	71,200	75,800	44,200	81,600
July	61,800	41,500	74,200	57,200	41,000	70,900	60,800	43,400	71,100	61,000	40,600	73,600	68,900	44,900	81,300
August	60,500	39,900	72,800	65,900	42,600	80,100	62,800	41,700	73,800	59,200	39,900	71,600	62,200	36,700	74,000
September	61,300	40,200	74,200	63,800	36,800	71,400	62,800	41,500	79,600	58,700	40,100	73,000	76,000	40,000	76,400
October	60,400	41,500	75,100	64,300	38,800	77,800	61,700	42,400	86,600	58,100	41,000	72,000	70,100	45,100	78,500
November	60,200	42,300	73,400	61,600	49,200	71,900	60,200	46,300	76,200	58,100	40,400	71,100	71,000	42,000	83,400
December	62,500	42,200	74,300	61,200	41,100	71,500	60,200	41,900	76,700	61,700	42,200	73,300	69,100	42,500	79,100
2010 [2]															
January	64,900	37,900	74,600	62,500	S	75,100	86,200	S	88,400	61,900	37,700	72,500	74,300	40,700	79,400
February	66,000	40,400	80,200	91,300	S	92,500	62,100	44,200	78,100	62,700	39,800	76,900	80,700	41,300	95,100
March	61,900	38,100	71,500	64,700	40,500	79,500	56,400	40,900	68,600	60,100	37,000	70,000	76,500	44,600	81,200
April	61,300	38,500	74,000	79,600	55,900	85,400	53,700	39,500	78,200	59,800	37,600	72,300	72,000	40,900	76,700
May	62,600	39,600	73,400	57,200	40,700	68,100	59,300	39,700	69,500	59,900	39,500	73,000	85,300	40,500	80,200
June	63,000	38,800	73,300	68,600	44,300	83,600	64,000	43,800	72,000	60,200	38,000	71,700	73,700	35,700	77,300
July	63,700	40,200	72,300	68,400	46,600	77,100	63,300	41,900	74,500	60,500	39,100	70,200	85,100	42,300	79,900
August	60,600	39,900	75,600	60,600	45,200	73,000	58,500	41,100	74,900	56,900	39,000	72,900	83,800	41,700	88,900
September	62,100	39,600	75,900	61,300	48,000	69,300	58,600	38,500	73,000	58,500	38,600	74,600	81,400	39,600	85,500
October	64,700	40,800	76,700	80,400	51,000	87,900	64,000	46,800	74,000	61,700	38,200	75,100	73,900	47,400	80,200
November	62,200	39,900	73,900	60,500	37,900	72,400	60,200	42,900	76,100	59,900	38,800	72,500	78,400	48,800	79,400
December	62,900	40,100	76,800	59,000	42,700	68,800	57,000	38,500	77,100	60,600	39,500	75,200	80,400	46,500	86,200
2009															
January	64,000	41,600	73,400	65,400	58,100	68,300	66,900	40,400	76,500	60,100	38,100	72,700	85,700	69,000	77,100
February	59,400	38,600	70,400	S	S	S	73,800	S	73,800	57,500	38,900	70,400	76,600	29,500	71,800
March	62,200	41,300	71,900	71,600	S	71,600	64,300	45,000	67,900	57,000	40,800	70,200	82,900	43,300	79,700
April	61,700	38,000	76,800	62,800	41,300	75,200	53,400	42,500	69,100	59,700	36,400	75,300	76,700	45,300	86,300
May	62,400	40,600	76,000	60,100	53,300	68,400	69,800	43,500	76,800	58,200	39,100	75,400	78,900	44,600	79,300
June	63,100	38,800	75,000	58,200	34,100	65,700	85,300	S	82,700	59,500	39,000	74,100	77,100	40,000	80,800
July	63,600	38,600	73,000	60,200	47,300	66,200	60,600	38,800	78,000	60,800	37,000	71,800	81,800	S	79,900
August	65,500	39,600	76,100	57,600	34,700	72,800	68,100	41,600	74,700	62,000	40,200	73,900	81,900	S	84,700
September	65,700	41,700	78,100	66,400	46,200	76,300	65,200	41,500	76,000	62,400	39,900	75,600	85,400	52,200	95,300
October	64,600	38,600	74,800	60,700	40,300	71,800	70,500	41,700	76,600	60,400	37,600	73,700	80,100	42,300	79,200
November	64,500	38,100	75,500	57,300	42,900	63,500	62,200	33,000	73,900	60,600	38,500	72,300	90,100	32,800	95,900
December	58,500	39,400	70,000	64,300	S	70,900	61,200	42,700	77,500	53,700	39,000	67,300	86,900	S	78,900

NA = Not available.
S = Suppressed to avoid disclosing data for individual dealers; data are included in higher-level estimates.
[1] = Includes manufactured homes with more than two sections.
[2] = Revised.
[3] = Preliminary.
Source: Census Bureau via survey sponsored by the Department of Housing and Urban Development.

Table 2-91. Shipments of New Manufactured Homes, 2009–2012

[Thousands of units.]

Year and month	Not seasonally adjusted	Seasonal index	Seasonally adjusted annual rate
2012			
Total	27.7	X	X
January	4.0	80.1	60
February	4.1	85.1	58
March	4.7	98.8	57
April	4.6	99.0	56
May	5.2	115.7	54
June	5.1	111.9	54
July	NA	NA	NA
August	NA	NA	NA
September	NA	NA	NA
October	NA	NA	NA
November	NA	NA	NA
December	NA	NA	NA
2011			
Total	51.6	X	X
January	2.8	76.0	44
February	2.9	79.0	44
March	4.0	103.1	47
April	3.9	100.8	47
May	4.5	110.2	49
June	5.0	119.3	50
July	3.7	92.4	48
August	5.2	123.1	51
September	5.1	110.6	55
October	5.4	106.5	61
November	5.3	100.0	64
December	3.8	77.6	59
2010			
Total	50	X	X
January	3.2	76.1	51
February	3.5	78.8	53
March	4.5	101.2	54
April	4.8	105.5	55
May	5.0	105.8	57
June	5.4	119.0	55
July	4.3	97.7	52
August	4.9	117.1	50
September	4.4	112.5	47
October	3.8	106.7	43
November	3.5	96.5	43
December	2.7	82.5	40
2009			
Total	49.8	X	X
January	3.8	79.9	57
February	3.6	79.2	54
March	4.0	94.6	50
April	4.3	107.2	48
May	4.3	106.4	48
June	4.5	115.4	46
July	4.4	105.1	50
August	4.5	113.0	48
September	4.5	112.9	48
October	4.6	111.0	49
November	3.8	90.7	51
December	3.5	82.5	51

NA = Not available.
X = Not applicable.
[1] = Revised.
[2] = Preliminary.

Source: Not seasonally adjusted statistics on shipments compiled from manufacturer's reports to the Institute for Building Technology and Safety (IBTS).

Table 2-92. Existing Home Sales, by Year and Region, 2009–2012

[Numbers in thousands, months, percent.]

Characteristics	Seasonally adjusted annual rate					Not seasonally adjusted					Inventory	Supply (months)
	United States	Northeast	Midwest	South	West	United States	Northeast	Midwest	South	West		
2011	4,340	590	980	1,640	1,130	X	X	X	X	X	2,740	8.8
2010	4,190	570	910	1,630	1,080	X	X	X	X	X	3,020	9.4
2009	4,260	540	910	1,680	1,130	X	X	X	X	X	2,320	8.2
2012												
January	4,630	600	1,010	1,760	1,260	260	30	53	101	76	2,330	6.0
February	4,600	590	1,020	1,77-	1,220	287	38	64	112	73	2,400	6.3
March	4,470	590	1,020	1,730	1,130	360	43	82	140	95	2,320	6.2
April	4,620	620	1,030	1,790	1,080	400	52	89	155	104	2,500	6.5
May	4,620	610	1,040	1,810	1,160	448	57	108	169	114	2,470	6.4
June [1]	4,370	540	1,020	1,730	1,080	463	58	111	180	114	2,370	6.5
July [2]	4,470	580	1,040	1,770	1,080	429	64	106	166	93	2,400	6.4
2011												
July	4,050	510	890	1,630	1,020	385	57	88	151	89	3,150	9.3
August	4,410	580	950	1,710	1,170	429	57	92	170	110	3,020	8.2
September	4,280	550	920	1,690	1,120	369	47	83	149	91	2,900	8.1
October	4,320	510	940	1,730	1,140	343	43	71	140	89	2,740	7.6
November	4,400	540	980	1,740	1,140	335	40	68	132	95	2,620	7.1
December	4,380	580	970	1,700	1,130	349	44	76	136	93	2,320	6.4
Vs last month (percent)	2.3	7.4	2.0	2.3	0.0	7.3	10.3	-4.5	-7.8	-18.4	1.3	-1.5
Vs last year (percent)	10.4	13.7	16.9	8.6	5.9	11.4	12.3	20.5	9.9	4.5	-23.8	-31.2
Year to date	X	X	X	X	X	2.647	0.342	0.613	1.023	0.669	X	X

Note: Annual inventory figures are from December of each year.
X = Not applicable.
[1] = Revised.
[2] = Preliminary.

Source: National Association of Realtors, Existing Home Sales Survey

Table 2-93. Sales Prices of Existing Homes, by Year and Region, 2009–2012

[Dollars, percent.]

Characteristics	Median price					Mean price				
	United States	Northeast	Midwest	South	West	United States	Northeast	Midwest	South	West
2011	166,100	237,500	135,400	144,200	201,300	214,000	276,900	166,900	188,100	252,300
2010	172,900	243,500	141,600	150,100	214,800	220,000	281,500	172,500	193,000	264,100
2009	172,500	240,500	144,100	153,000	211,100	216,900	276,300	171,100	192,700	256,700
2012										
January	154,600	225,200	121,400	134,000	189,300	200,900	266,600	150,600	175,700	240,400
February	155,600	222,000	119,800	137,500	193,500	201,600	263,300	147,900	178,100	245,200
March	164,800	230,200	131,600	146,500	204,600	212,100	269,000	160,200	189,300	256,000
April	173,700	233,100	139,900	152,500	224,000	221,700	273,800	168,900	198,000	272,000
May	180,300	239,900	147,700	159,400	230,700	229,600	280,200	178,100	206,400	278,500
June [1]	188,800	253,200	156,200	164,100	235,100	238,200	294,600	190,000	212,300	283,400
July [2]	187,300	254,200	154,100	162,600	238,600	236,000	291,700	186,400	207,100	287,900
2011										
July	171,200	245,600	145,700	152,600	191,600	220,400	287,000	178,700	198,700	246,100
August	171,200	243,700	141,400	150,300	208,100	219,500	283,300	174,400	193,400	258,900
September	165,300	229,400	135,700	144,600	208,100	212,800	271,100	165,800	186,000	259,500
October	160,800	222,300	131,700	140,700	199,700	205,900	259,300	160,400	181,300	250,300
November	164,000	237,600	132,300	142,500	200,400	210,400	274,700	162,000	184,500	250,600
December	162,200	220,000	128,900	145,100	204,500	209,500	262,000	158,700	188,600	252,600
Vs last year (percent)	9.4	3.5	5.8	6.6	24.5	7.1	1.6	4.3	4.2	17.0

Note: Monthly data are not seasonally adjusted.
[1] = Revised.
[2] = Preliminary.

Source: National Association of Realtors, Existing Home Sales Survey

Table 2-94. National Existing Home Sales, by Type of Dwelling, 2009–2012

[Numbers in thousands, months, percent.]

Characteristics	Seasonally adjusted annual rate			Not seasonally adjusted			National supply (months)	Single family supply (months	Condo/ co-op supply (months
	Existing home price	Single family price	Condo/co-op price	Existing home price	Single family price	Condo/co-op price			
2011	4,260	3,787	477	X	X	X	8.2	8.1	9.7
2010	4,190	3,708	474	X	X	X	9.4	9.0	12.0
2009	4,340	3,870	464	X	X	X	8.8	8.3	12.7
2012									
January	4,630	4,100	530	260	234	26	6.0	6.1	5.7
February	4,600	4,070	530	287	252	35	6.3	6.1	7.2
March	4,470	3,970	500	360	316	44	6.2	6.1	7.1
April	4,620	4,090	530	400	355	45	6.5	6.4	7.2
May	4,620	4,110	510	448	399	49	6.4	6.4	6.8
June [1]	4,370	3,900	470	463	416	47	6.5	6.5	6.8
July [2]	4,470	3,980	490	429	378	51	6.4	6.3	7.4
2011									
July	4,050	3,620	430	385	340	45	9.3	8.9	13.4
August	4,410	3,910	500	429	383	46	8.2	8.1	9.2
September	4,280	3,800	480	369	327	42	8.1	7.9	10.3
October	4,320	3,850	470	343	305	38	7.6	7.4	8.8
November	4,400	3,950	450	335	304	31	7.1	7.1	7.8
December	4,380	3,900	480	349	310	39	6.4	6.2	7.3
Vs last month (percent)	2.3	2.1	4.3	-7.3	-9.1	8.5	-1.5	-3.1	8.8
Vs last year (percent)	10.4	9.9	14.0	11.4	11.2	13.3	-31.2	-29.2	-44.8
Year to date	X	X	X	2.647	2.350	0.297	X	X	X

X = Not applicable.
[1] = Revised.
[2] = Preliminary.

Source: National Association of Realtors, Existing Home Sales Survey

Table 2-95. National Sales Prices of Existing Single Family Homes and Condos/Co-ops, by Type of Dwelling, 2009–2012

[Dollars, percent.]

Characteristics	Median price			Mean price		
	Existing home price	Single family price	Condo/co-op price	Existing home price	Single family price	Condo/co-op price
2011	166,100	166,200	165,100	214,000	214,300	211,300
2010	172,900	173,100	171,700	220,000	220,600	215,700
2009	172,500	172,100	175,600	216,900	217,000	216,300
2012						
January	154,600	154,600	155,000	200,900	201,000	200,300
February	155,600	156,100	151,500	201,600	202,100	198,000
March	164,800	165,100	162,000	212,100	212,500	208,500
April	173,700	174,100	170,200	221,700	222,200	218,100
May	180,300	180,200	180,700	229,600	229,500	230,500
June [1]	188,800	189,600	182,200	238,200	238,900	232,100
July [2]	187,300	188,100	180,700	236,000	237,000	228,300
2011						
July	171,200	171,700	167,800	220,400	221,200	214,400
August	171,200	171,200	171,100	219,500	219,800	217,400
September	165,300	165,400	164,500	212,800	212,900	212,200
October	160,800	161,100	158,900	205,900	206,400	201,900
November	164,000	164,000	163,600	210,400	210,700	208,100
December	162,200	162,600	158,700	209,500	209,800	206,800
Vs last year (percent)	9.4	9.6	7.7	7.1	7.1	6.5

Note: Monthly data are not seasonally adjusted.
[1] = Revised.
[2] = Preliminary.

Source: National Association of Realtors, Existing Home Sales Survey

Table 2-96. Existing Single Family Home Sales, by Year and Region, 2009–2012

[Numbers in thousands, months, percent.]

Characteristics	Seasonally adjusted annual rate					Not seasonally adjusted					Inventory	Supply (months)
	United States	Northeast	Midwest	South	West	United States	Northeast	Midwest	South	West		
2011	3,787	449	863	1,471	1,004	X	X	X	X	X	2,330	8.3
2010	3,708	465	859	1,426	958	X	X	X	X	X	2,590	9.0
2009	3,870	480	918	1,460	1,012	X	X	X	X	X	2,030	8.1
2012												
January	4,100	500	950	1,540	1,110	234	26	50	90	68	2,080	6.1
February	4,070	490	960	1,540	1,080	252	33	61	95	63	2,080	6.1
March	3,970	490	960	1,520	1,000	316	37	78	119	82	2,020	6.1
April	4,090	510	970	1,570	1,040	355	43	84	136	92	2,180	6.4
May	4,110	510	980	1,590	1,030	399	46	102	149	102	2,180	6.4
June [1]	3,900	450	960	1,520	970	416	49	104	159	104	2,100	6.5
July [2]	3,980	480	980	1,560	960	378	51	98	146	83	2,100	6.3
2011												
July	3,620	440	840	1,430	910	340	46	82	132	80	2,670	8.9
August	3,910	460	900	1,510	1,040	383	47	87	152	96	2,640	8.1
September	3,800	450	870	1,480	1,000	327	39	77	130	81	2,490	7.9
October	3,850	430	890	1,520	1,010	305	36	67	123	79	2,390	7.4
November	3,950	470	920	1,530	1,030	304	34	64	118	88	2,330	7.1
December	3,900	480	920	1,500	1,000	319	36	72	120	82	2,030	6.2
Vs last month (percent)	2.1	6.7	2.1	2.6	-1.0	-9.1	4.1	-5.8	-8.2	-20.2	0.0	-3.1
Vs last year (percent)	9.9	9.1	16.7	9.1	5.5	11.2	10.9	19.5	10.6	3.8	-21.3	-29.2
Year to date	X	X	X	X	X	2.350	0.285	0.577	0.894	0.594	X	X

Note: Annual inventory figures are from December of each year.
X = Not applicable.
[1] = Revised.
[2] = Preliminary.

Source: National Association of Realtors, Existing Home Sales Survey

Table 2-97. Sales Prices of Existing Single Family Homes, by Year and Region, 2009–2012

[Dollars, percent.]

Characteristics	Median price					Mean price				
	United States	Northeast	Midwest	South	West	United States	Northeast	Midwest	South	West
2011	166,200	237,500	135,800	149,300	204,500	214,300	277,000	166,900	192,800	256,500
2010	173,100	243,900	140,800	153,700	220,700	220,600	282,200	170,700	196,500	270,200
2009	172,100	243,200	142,900	155,000	215,400	217,000	279,300	168,700	194,700	261,100
2012										
January	154,600	226,800	121,900	137,800	192,300	201,000	268,100	150,500	178,600	245,000
February	156,100	223,800	120,500	141,700	197,500	202,100	264,900	148,100	181,200	250,300
March	165,100	231,800	132,200	150,700	207,800	212,500	271,000	160,100	192,600	260,000
April	174,100	233,900	140,600	156,800	228,400	222,200	273,800	169,100	201,200	277,400
May	180,200	238,300	148,700	163,100	234,500	229,500	278,200	178,400	209,200	282,900
June [1]	189,600	251,800	157,500	168,600	241,100	238,900	293,200	190,700	216,200	289,600
July [2]	188,100	254,600	155,400	167,500	241,900	237,000	291,800	187,000	212,100	292,400
2011										
July	171,700	244,600	146,700	157,000	195,500	221,200	286,900	179,000	203,000	250,600
August	171,200	239,300	142,100	154,100	211,300	219,800	280,100	174,500	197,500	262,800
September	165,400	226,300	136,400	148,900	211,100	212,900	268,500	165,400	189,700	263,000
October	161,100	222,700	132,800	144,200	201,700	206,400	260,700	160,900	184,100	253,400
November	164,000	238,700	133,000	146,500	202,800	210,700	275,200	162,300	188,000	254,300
December	162,600	218,900	129,400	149,600	207,800	209,800	261,500	158,800	192,200	257,100
Vs last year (percent)	9.6	4.1	5.9	6.7	23.7	7.1	1.7	4.5	4.5	16.7

Note: Monthly data are not seasonally adjusted.
[1] = Revised.
[2] = Preliminary.

Source: National Association of Realtors, Existing Home Sales Survey

Table 2-98. Existing Condo/Co-op Sales, by Year and Region, 2009–2012

[Numbers in thousands, months, percent.]

Characteristics	Seasonally adjusted annual rate					Not seasonally adjusted					Inventory	Supply (months)
	United States	Northeast	Midwest	South	West	United States	Northeast	Midwest	South	West		
2011	477	89	52	210	126	X	X	X	X	X	291	9.7
2010	474	95	53	202	124	X	X	X	X	X	429	12
2009	464	105	58	180	121	X	X	X	X	X	411	12.7
2012												
January	530	100	60	220	150	26	4	3	11	8	253	5.7
February	530	100	60	230	140	35	5	3	17	10	316	7.2
March	500	100	60	210	130	44	6	4	21	13	295	7.1
April	530	110	60	220	140	45	9	5	19	12	318	7.2
May	510	100	60	220	130	49	11	6	20	12	289	6.8
June [1]	470	90	60	210	110	47	9	7	21	10	268	6.8
July [2]	490	100	60	210	120	51	13	8	20	10	303	7.4
2011												
July	430	70	50	200	110	45	11	6	19	9	480	13.4
August	500	120	50	200	130	46	10	5	17	14	383	9.2
September	480	100	50	210	120	42	8	5	19	10	410	10.3
October	470	80	50	210	130	38	7	4	17	10	346	8.8
November	450	70	60	210	110	31	6	4	14	7	294	7.8
December	480	100	50	200	130	39	8	4	16	11	291	7.3
Vs last month (percent)	4.3	11.1	0.0	0.0	9.1	8.5	44.4	14.3	-4.8	0.0	13.1	8.8
Vs last year (percent)	14.0	42.9	20.0	5.0	9.1	13.3	18.2	33.3	5.3	11.1	-36.9	-44.8
Year to date	X	X	X	X	X	0.297	0.057	0.036	0.129	0.075	X	X

Note: Annual inventory figures are from December of each year.
X = Not applicable.
[1] = Revised.
[2] = Preliminary.
Source: National Association of Realtors, Existing Home Sales Survey

Table 2-99. Sales Prices of Existing Condos/Co-ops, by Year and Region, 2009–2012

[Dollars, percent.]

Characteristics	Median price					Mean price				
	United States	Northeast	Midwest	South	West	United States	Northeast	Midwest	South	West
2011	165,100	237,700	129,000	107,800	176,000	211,300	276,300	167,500	155,200	218,900
2010	171,700	242,200	150,500	118,500	154,700	215,700	279,500	192,100	162,200	202,000
2009	175,600	232,800	157,100	132,700	162,100	216,300	267,800	197,200	172,500	206,200
2012										
January	155,000	217,300	113,800	107,600	167,400	200,300	258,900	153,000	155,300	206,300
February	151,500	213,400	108,800	109,700	162,900	198,000	255,600	145,000	157,000	206,300
March	162,000	222,500	122,600	116,200	179,600	208,500	259,100	161,800	165,700	225,400
April	170,200	229,600	128,500	121,700	191,800	218,100	273,600	165,700	174,900	232,000
May	180,700	248,300	131,700	133,100	200,300	230,500	290,300	173,600	186,000	243,500
June [1]	182,200	260,200	135,200	131,500	182,300	232,100	301,700	178,100	184,100	229,300
July [2]	180,700	252,400	132,800	126,000	212,600	228,300	291,300	176,000	169,700	251,900
2011										
July	167,800	248,700	135,600	114,000	150,200	214,400	287,300	175,000	160,800	199,400
August	171,100	257,200	134,000	112,700	175,200	217,400	292,900	173,300	152,900	218,100
September	164,500	238,000	128,400	108,200	172,700	212,200	278,200	169,800	154,200	218,900
October	158,900	221,300	120,400	110,000	177,500	201,900	255,300	155,000	157,300	216,800
November	163,600	230,300	120,700	113,500	177,300	208,100	271,000	157,800	159,300	215,700
December	158,700	225,300	119,100	111,600	178,800	206,800	264,600	156,400	161,500	218,000
Vs last year (percent)	7.7	1.5	-2.1	10.5	41.5	6.5	1.4	0.6	5.5	26.3

Note: Monthly data are not seasonally adjusted.
[1] = Revised.
[2] = Preliminary.

Source: National Association of Realtors, Existing Home Sales Survey

PART III
PHYSICAL CHARACTERISTICS

PART III: PHYSICAL CHARACTERISTICS

Figure 3-1. House Heating Fuel Used in the United States, American Housing Survey, 2009

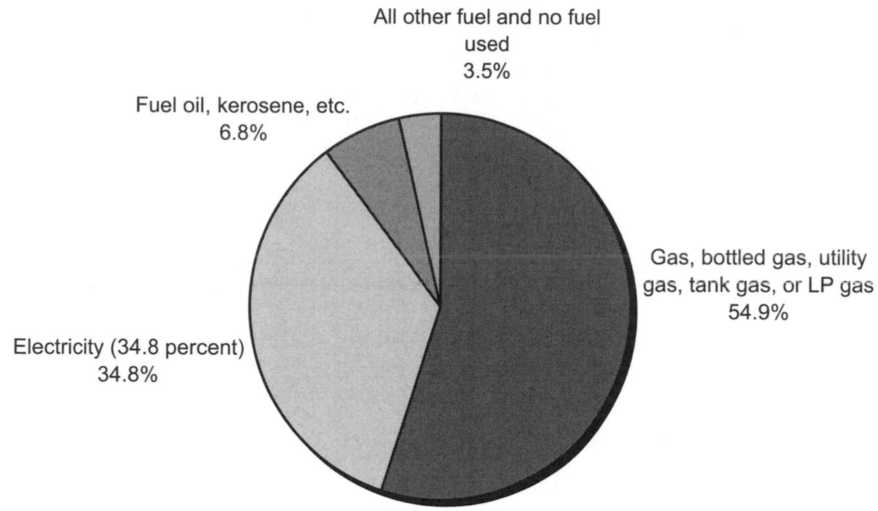

- In 2009, piped gas was the most frequently used house heating fuel, followed by electricity, fuel oil, bottled gas, and wood. Approximately 98,000 occupied units used coal or coke as fuel. (Table 3-15)
- Electrical fuses, circuit breakers, heating, sewage systems, and flush toilets represented the most fallible household equipment in 2009. (Table 3-18)
- Approximately 4 and a half million renters had utilities included in their rents, while 33 to 35 million others paid for at least a single utility. (Table 3-26, 1-, 3-, and 5-year estimates)
- Nearly half of all occupied units had between 5 and 6 rooms. (Table 3-9)

Table 3-1. Height and Condition of Building, All Housing Units, 2009

[Numbers in thousands.]

Characteristics	Total housing units	Seasonal	Year-round											New construction 4 years	Manufactured/ mobile homes
			Total	Occupied			Vacant								
				Total	Owner	Renter	Total	For rent	Rental vacancy rate	For sale only	Rented or sold	Occasional use/URE	Other vacant		
Total	130,112	4,618	125,494	111,806	76,428	35,378	13,688	4,018	10.1	2,108	879	3,314	3,368	5,955	8,769
Stories in structure[1]															
1	41,537	1,880	39,657	35,364	26,216	9,148	4,292	815	8.1	745	266	1,031	1,435	1,554	X
2	43,447	1,145	42,302	37,867	25,210	12,657	4,435	1,536	10.7	727	288	939	945	2,392	X
3	27,574	542	27,031	24,508	16,721	7,787	2,524	988	11.2	373	162	494	506	1,205	X
4 to 6	6,051	160	5,891	5,134	2,349	2,785	757	320	10.2	77	69	185	106	288	X
7 or more	2,734	160	2,573	2,094	515	1,580	479	182	10.3	42	29	178	48	192	X
Stories between main and apartment entrances															
Multiunits, 2 or more floors	28,329	775	27,553	22,962	3,458	19,503	4,592	2,572	11.5	284	272	822	641	1,054	X
None (on same floor)	9,076	159	8,916	7,616	1,187	6,429	1,300	718	10.0	76	76	197	233	249	X
1 (up or down)	7,916	189	7,727	6,447	911	5,536	1,280	743	11.7	88	86	188	175	251	X
2 or more (up or down)	11,337	427	10,910	8,899	1,361	7,538	2,012	1,111	12.7	120	110	437	233	553	X
Elevator on floor															
Multiunits, 2 or more floors	28,329	775	27,553	22,962	3,458	19,503	4,592	2,572	11.5	284	272	822	641	1,054	X
With 1 or more elevators working	5,585	311	5,274	4,348	1,045	3,303	926	426	11.3	80	41	276	103	400	X
With elevator, none in working condition	58	–	58	46	11	35	12	8	19.2	–	–	–	4	2	X
No elevator	22,686	464	22,222	18,568	2,403	16,165	3,654	2,138	11.6	204	231	546	535	652	X
Units, 3 or more floors from main entrance	1,805	43	1,763	1,436	133	1,302	327	184	12.2	17	22	66	37	72	X
Foundation															
1-unit building, excluding manufactured/mobile homes	89,525	3,047	86,478	79,052	67,276	11,776	7,427	1,018	7.9	1,652	519	1,926	2,312	4,518	X
With basement under all of building	29,104	490	28,614	26,713	23,821	2,892	1,902	214	6.8	480	139	479	590	1,237	X
With basement under part of building	8,991	170	8,821	8,208	7,350	858	613	82	8.6	135	64	157	176	156	X
With crawl space	20,955	965	19,991	18,022	14,783	3,240	1,968	280	7.9	360	92	538	698	727	X
On concrete slab	28,693	1,011	27,682	24,917	20,431	4,486	2,765	405	8.2	655	217	717	771	2,327	X
Other	1,782	411	1,371	1,192	892	300	179	37	11.0	22	7	35	77	71	X
External building conditions[2]															
Sagging roof	2,765	249	2,516	1,888	1,370	517	628	82	13.4	83	50	76	338	3	491
Missing roofing material	5,805	252	5,553	4,640	3,682	958	914	110	10.3	146	85	143	429	82	496
Hole in roof	2,020	139	1,881	1,458	1,029	429	424	37	7.9	52	33	40	262	6	423
Missing bricks, siding, or other outside wall material	3,175	211	2,964	2,323	1,661	661	641	80	10.7	68	47	86	359	22	374
Sloping outside walls	1,687	164	1,523	1,167	781	386	356	42	9.9	40	26	55	193	10	317
Boarded up windows	1,511	180	1,331	821	558	262	510	58	18.1	42	44	65	301	13	273
Broken windows	3,850	201	3,649	2,984	2,112	872	666	91	9.4	65	48	97	364	37	703
Bars on windows	3,552	32	3,520	3,318	2,616	702	202	47	6.3	26	20	44	65	22	65
Foundation crumbling or has open crack or hole	2,822	160	2,662	2,227	1,687	540	435	53	8.9	53	21	65	243	17	152
None of the above	78,826	3,031	75,795	69,766	60,037	9,730	6,029	860	8.1	1,419	401	1,890	1,458	4,555	6,807
Not reported	2,591	102	2,489	2,173	1,832	341	315	29	7.8	48	7	78	153	115	189
Site placement															
Manufactured/mobile homes	8,769	730	8,040	6,839	5,418	1,421	1,201	176	11.0	143	65	487	329	324	8,769
First site	5,912	509	5,403	4,600	4,002	598	803	85	12.3	98	52	353	215	272	5,912
Moved from another site	1,726	174	1,552	1,301	1,047	254	251	51	16.6	23	8	83	87	38	1,726
Don't know	553	46	506	362	97	265	144	41	13.3	22	5	48	28	9	553
Not reported	579	–	579	576	272	304	2	–	–	–	–	2	–	4	579

– = Zero or rounds to zero.
X = Not applicable.
[1] = Figures exclude manufactured/mobile homes.
[2] = Figures may not add to total because more than one category may apply to a unit. Figures do not include multiunit structures.

Source: U.S. Census Bureau, American Housing Survey

Table 3-2. Size of Unit and Lot, All Housing Units, 2009

[Numbers in thousands, except as noted.]

Characteristics	Total housing units	Seasonal	Year-round											New construction 4 years	Manufactured/ mobile homes
			Total	Occupied			Vacant								
				Total	Owner	Renter	Total	For rent	Rental vacancy rate	For sale only	Rented or sold	Occasional use/URE	Other vacant		
Total	130,112	4,618	125,494	111,806	76,428	35,378	13,688	4,018	10.1	2,108	879	3,314	3,368	5,955	8,769
Rooms															
1 room	579	104	475	352	26	326	123	57	14.6	–	9	27	30	12	7
2 rooms	1,423	194	1,229	946	68	879	283	128	12.6	9	8	68	70	22	39
3 rooms	11,290	697	10,593	8,711	1,036	7,675	1,882	949	10.9	100	92	385	356	295	420
4 rooms	23,036	1,374	21,662	17,828	6,475	11,354	3,834	1,442	11.2	323	182	998	890	606	2,753
5 rooms	29,888	1,108	28,779	25,444	17,232	8,212	3,336	822	9.0	534	209	838	933	1,367	3,082
6 rooms	27,480	632	26,848	24,596	20,364	4,232	2,252	408	8.7	463	207	547	627	1,240	1,573
7 rooms	17,877	315	17,562	16,489	14,754	1,735	1,073	126	6.8	358	82	241	266	954	689
8 rooms	10,623	89	10,533	10,033	9,410	622	501	46	6.9	171	49	98	136	710	150
9 rooms	4,629	68	4,561	4,344	4,130	214	217	30	12.3	69	26	52	40	403	36
10 rooms or more	3,286	36	3,250	3,063	2,933	130	187	8	5.9	81	16	60	21	344	19
Bedrooms															
None	1,265	187	1,077	789	45	744	288	129	14.7	7	11	69	72	29	32
1	14,690	806	13,884	11,434	1,714	9,720	2,450	1,262	11.4	128	133	500	427	358	508
2	34,514	1,834	32,680	27,671	13,471	14,200	5,008	1,717	10.7	502	254	1,321	1,215	1,015	3,533
3	53,734	1,317	52,417	48,082	39,723	8,359	4,335	704	7.7	973	335	1,057	1,267	2,548	4,076
4 or more	25,909	473	25,437	23,830	21,475	2,354	1,607	206	8.0	498	147	368	388	2,005	620
Complete bathrooms															
None	1,678	557	1,121	403	175	229	717	88	27.3	60	42	99	429	21	185
1	46,977	1,899	45,078	38,662	15,767	22,894	6,416	2,617	10.2	524	386	1,344	1,545	582	2,861
1 1/2	17,233	363	16,870	15,656	12,081	3,575	1,214	335	8.5	228	77	260	314	213	796
2 or more	64,223	1,798	62,425	57,085	48,405	8,680	5,340	978	10.0	1,296	375	1,611	1,080	5,138	4,927
Square footage of unit															
Single detached and manufactured/ mobile homes	91,241	3,524	87,717	79,918	68,742	11,176	7,799	996	8.1	1,620	536	2,200	2,447	4,291	8,769
Less than 500	988	225	764	603	383	220	161	21	8.7	25	7	65	43	10	331
500 to 749	2,765	462	2,303	1,771	1,085	686	532	62	8.2	46	13	245	166	19	1,020
750 to 999	6,440	593	5,847	5,014	3,519	1,495	833	179	10.6	100	31	238	285	68	1,935
1,000 to 1,499	21,224	814	20,410	18,419	14,978	3,441	1,991	297	7.9	416	127	527	624	557	2,779
1,500 to 1,999	20,636	521	20,115	18,519	16,284	2,235	1,596	165	6.8	391	143	435	461	827	1,309
2,000 to 2,499	14,361	284	14,077	13,190	12,057	1,134	886	103	8.2	199	88	236	260	813	334
2,500 to 2,999	7,589	141	7,448	7,050	6,622	429	398	35	7.5	128	15	111	109	535	126
3,000 to 3,999	7,252	137	7,115	6,692	6,391	301	424	39	11.3	102	35	101	146	751	54
4,000 or more	4,456	113	4,343	4,030	3,787	243	313	25	9.2	103	39	85	62	469	146
Not reported (includes don't know)	5,529	234	5,295	4,630	3,638	992	666	70	6.6	110	38	156	291	241	735
Median (square feet)	1,700	1,150	1,736	1,800	1,800	1,300	1,500	1,250	X	1,658	1,680	1,400	1,400	2,300	1,092
Lot size															
1-unit structures[1]	95,216	3,512	91,704	83,466	70,643	12,823	8,239	1,157	8.2	1,680	556	2,274	2,571	4,550	8,628
Less than 1/8 acre	13,931	515	13,416	11,824	9,107	2,717	1,593	295	9.7	309	106	447	435	698	1,891
1/8 up to 1/4 acre	25,008	880	24,129	21,793	17,771	4,022	2,336	367	8.3	490	182	585	712	1,110	1,424
1/4 up to 1/2 acre	17,825	518	17,307	15,921	13,837	2,084	1,386	188	8.2	359	87	349	402	931	732
1/2 up to 1 acre	11,292	372	10,920	10,036	8,874	1,162	884	112	8.8	190	33	274	275	447	808
1 up to 5 acres	19,172	754	18,418	17,014	14,895	2,120	1,404	157	6.9	247	106	411	483	922	2,700
5 up to 10 acres	3,104	120	2,984	2,750	2,545	205	234	20	8.7	44	14	70	86	205	509
10 acres or more	4,885	354	4,530	4,127	3,614	513	403	19	3.5	41	28	138	177	235	564
Median (acres)	0.26	0.32	0.26	0.27	0.32	0.22	0.25	0.18	X	0.25	0.23	0.25	0.25	0.27	0.50

– = Zero or rounds to zero.
X = Not applicable.
[1] = Does not include cooperatives or condominiums.

Source: U.S. Census Bureau, American Housing Survey

Table 3-3. Selected Equipment and Plumbing, All Housing Units, 2009

[Numbers in thousands.]

Characteristics	Total housing units	Seasonal	Year-round: Total	Year-round: Occupied: Total	Year-round: Occupied: Owner	Year-round: Occupied: Renter	Year-round: Vacant: Total	Year-round: Vacant: For rent	Year-round: Vacant: Rental vacancy rate	Year-round: Vacant: For sale only	Year-round: Vacant: Rented or sold	Year-round: Vacant: Occasional use/URE	Year-round: Vacant: Other vacant	New construction 4 years	Manufactured/ mobile homes
Total	130,112	4,618	125,494	111,806	76,428	35,378	13,688	4,018	10.1	2,108	879	3,314	3,368	5,955	8,769
Equipment[1]															
Lacking complete kitchen facilities	5,586	667	4,919	1,751	378	1,374	3,168	677	32.2	678	243	298	1,272	299	367
With complete kitchen (sink, refrigerator, and oven or burners)	124,526	3,951	120,575	110,054	76,050	34,004	10,520	3,342	8.9	1,430	636	3,017	2,096	5,656	8,402
Kitchen sink	128,769	4,291	124,478	111,510	76,329	35,180	12,968	3,914	9.9	2,044	821	3,215	2,974	5,914	8,613
Refrigerator	126,534	4,056	122,478	111,530	76,336	35,193	10,948	3,527	9.0	1,462	669	3,104	2,185	5,726	8,429
Cooking stove or range	126,744	4,127	122,617	111,038	76,153	34,886	11,579	3,650	9.4	1,744	726	3,114	2,344	5,858	8,448
Burners, no stove or range	258	22	237	208	109	99	29	17	14.5	–	–	2	11	5	17
Microwave oven only	496	14	481	378	127	251	103	29	10.4	18	3	37	16	10	30
Dishwasher	82,397	2,111	80,286	73,584	57,191	16,393	6,702	1,919	10.4	1,305	489	1,820	1,168	5,533	3,831
Washing machine	101,387	2,482	98,905	93,372	73,826	19,545	5,534	963	4.7	849	333	2,132	1,257	5,279	7,324
Clothes dryer	98,657	2,360	96,297	90,905	72,562	18,343	5,392	949	4.9	824	328	2,085	1,205	5,236	7,017
Disposal in kitchen sink	63,776	1,505	62,271	56,531	40,597	15,933	5,740	1,890	10.5	1,063	441	1,438	908	4,414	1,286
Trash compactor	4,511	146	4,365	3,896	3,166	730	469	105	12.5	98	38	158	69	415	62
Air conditioning[2]															
Central	82,475	2,077	80,398	72,808	54,647	18,161	7,590	2,211	10.8	1,456	534	1,888	1,501	5,279	5,469
Additional central	6,193	120	6,073	5,629	4,709	920	444	106	10.2	101	45	107	85	672	319
1 room unit	13,020	383	12,637	11,532	5,303	6,229	1,105	435	6.5	91	54	239	285	86	988
2 room units	8,670	144	8,527	8,132	4,800	3,332	395	129	3.7	32	20	110	104	88	790
3 room units or more	5,160	54	5,105	4,918	3,604	1,314	187	41	3.0	17	14	84	31	32	301
Safety equipment[1]															
Working smoke detector															
Yes	116,141	2,989	113,152	104,362	71,797	32,565	8,789	3,253	9.0	1,396	610	2,293	1,237	5,595	7,338
Powered by:															
Electricity	9,217	267	8,949	8,149	5,620	2,528	801	278	9.8	139	56	208	120	524	854
Batteries	72,868	1,547	71,321	66,536	43,210	23,326	4,785	1,785	7.1	701	303	1,252	744	1,832	4,263
Both	32,128	983	31,145	28,421	22,461	5,960	2,724	1,083	15.1	471	204	698	269	3,098	2,134
Not reported	1,928	191	1,736	1,257	506	751	480	108	12.4	85	47	136	104	142	87
No	9,101	824	8,276	6,157	3,686	2,472	2,119	356	12.5	280	126	284	1,073	142	911
Not reported	4,870	804	4,066	1,286	945	341	2,780	409	53.2	433	143	737	1,059	217	520
Batteries replaced in last 6 months[3]															
Yes	77,933	1,626	76,308	71,505	50,073	21,432	4,803	2,146	9.0	606	361	1,236	453	3,371	4,506
No	23,706	579	23,127	21,466	14,678	6,788	1,661	367	5.1	362	103	455	374	1,415	1,632
Not reported	3,357	326	3,031	1,986	920	1,066	1,045	354	24.5	204	43	259	186	144	259
Fire extinguisher purchased or recharged in the last 2 years	49,902	X	49,902	49,902	37,922	11,980	X	X	X	X	X	X	X	2,298	2,983
Sprinkler system inside home	6,401	246	6,155	5,167	2,086	3,081	988	488	13.5	119	85	221	76	1,099	95
Working carbon monoxide detector	43,494	673	42,822	40,698	31,691	9,007	2,123	762	7.7	294	164	647	255	2,107	1,676
Main heating equipment															
Warm-air furnace	81,629	2,034	79,595	71,141	51,691	19,450	8,454	2,442	11.1	1,523	588	1,941	1,961	4,037	6,306
Steam or hot water system	13,969	259	13,710	12,506	7,494	5,012	1,204	507	9.1	121	73	291	213	139	33
Electric heat pump	16,059	868	15,191	13,264	9,764	3,500	1,927	531	13.1	315	107	578	395	1,466	1,327
Built-in electric units	5,730	320	5,410	4,761	2,120	2,641	649	230	7.9	33	44	192	149	104	111
Floor, wall, or other built-in hot-air units without ducts	5,525	202	5,322	4,802	2,043	2,760	520	167	5.7	46	31	105	170	79	220
Room heaters with flue	1,173	73	1,100	950	580	370	150	23	5.6	15	15	37	61	23	68
Room heaters without flue	1,365	99	1,266	1,109	694	414	157	25	5.6	9	1	45	77	13	148
Portable electric heaters	1,405	107	1,298	1,167	535	632	131	44	6.4	12	3	24	48	6	234
Stoves	1,364	203	1,160	1,035	845	190	125	4	2.0	13	8	59	41	28	98
Fireplaces with inserts	192	10	182	172	155	18	10	–	–	2	–	4	5	–	4
Fireplaces without inserts	98	32	66	43	35	7	24	1	16.4	–	–	2	20	–	8
Other	570	69	501	386	232	154	115	22	12.2	6	4	16	67	22	79
Cooking stove	103	11	92	84	34	49	8	3	6.3	3	–	2	–	–	10
None	930	330	600	386	206	180	215	20	10.0	11	4	18	161	38	123

Table 3-3. Selected Equipment and Plumbing, All Housing Units, 2009—*Continued*

[Numbers in thousands.]

Characteristics	Total housing units	Seasonal	Year-round											New construction 4 years	Manufactured/ mobile homes
			Total	Occupied			Vacant								
				Total	Owner	Renter	Total	For rent	Rental vacancy rate	For sale only	Rented or sold	Occasional use/URE	Other vacant		
Other heating equipment[1]															
Warm-air furnace	258	–	258	251	225	26	7	–	–	–	1	6	–	15	19
Steam or hot water system	62	2	59	56	51	5	3	3	42.8	–	–	–	–	3	–
Electric heat pump	102	1	102	97	91	6	5	–	–	–	–	3	2	9	16
Built-in electric units	2,116	54	2,062	1,882	1,428	454	180	41	8.2	40	4	68	28	74	93
Floor, wall, or other built-in hot-air units without ducts	78	–	78	75	63	12	3	3	18.3	–	–	–	–	14	3
Room heaters with flue	879	21	858	822	716	106	36	9	7.4	6	2	18	–	23	65
Room heaters without flue	1,540	15	1,525	1,471	1,207	264	54	8	2.9	1	7	17	20	20	260
Portable electric heaters	14,290	174	14,116	13,719	9,886	3,832	397	135	3.4	61	25	119	58	365	922
Stoves	4,661	205	4,456	4,165	3,740	425	291	27	6.0	55	14	118	77	133	339
Fireplaces with inserts	5,532	104	5,428	5,205	4,742	464	223	17	3.5	77	15	76	38	404	326
Fireplaces without inserts	6,313	155	6,158	5,765	4,869	896	392	86	8.7	108	31	93	74	460	176
Other	832	11	820	790	707	83	30	3	2.8	–	9	15	3	53	56
Cooking stove	74	4	70	66	50	17	4	–	–	–	–	–	4	2	3
None	93,453	3,142	90,311	80,034	51,171	28,863	10,277	3,438	10.5	1,546	684	2,370	2,240	4,403	6,305
Plumbing															
With all plumbing facilities	127,290	4,006	123,284	110,574	75,852	34,722	12,710	3,872	9.9	2,036	825	3,195	2,783	5,928	8,452
Lacking some or all plumbing facilities[1]	2,822	611	2,210	1,232	576	656	978	146	17.8	72	55	119	586	27	317
No hot piped water	1,395	516	879	113	54	58	766	76	52.9	52	39	75	524	12	244
No bathtub and no shower	846	397	449	113	37	75	336	35	29.8	15	15	47	226	9	99
No flush toilet	817	369	448	102	37	64	346	36	33.8	16	15	41	238	13	104
No exclusive use	1,257	32	1,225	1,065	507	558	160	61	9.7	20	13	36	31	12	70
Primary source of water															
Public system or private company	113,489	3,238	110,251	98,027	64,372	33,655	12,224	3,898	10.3	1,909	798	2,734	2,884	5,157	6,283
Well serving 1 to 5 units	15,846	1,070	14,776	13,430	11,769	1,660	1,346	113	6.3	192	77	538	426	774	2,318
Drilled	14,141	892	13,249	12,175	10,772	1,404	1,074	90	6.0	150	68	442	324	673	2,048
Dug	999	106	892	822	700	122	70	6	4.6	8	–	26	30	38	163
Not reported	706	72	634	432	298	135	202	17	11.0	34	9	70	72	63	107
Other	777	309	467	349	287	63	118	7	9.6	7	4	42	58	23	169
Safety of primary source of water															
Selected primary water sources[4]	130,054	4,594	125,460	111,772	76,406	35,366	13,688	4,018	10.1	2,108	879	3,314	3,368	5,951	8,765
Safe to drink	118,091	3,885	114,206	102,247	71,152	31,095	11,959	3,737	10.6	1,881	778	2,819	2,745	5,436	7,656
Not safe to drink	9,236	325	8,911	8,412	4,530	3,882	500	105	2.6	46	44	162	143	371	831
Safety not reported	2,727	384	2,343	1,113	724	389	1,230	177	30.7	181	58	333	480	144	277
Means of sewage disposal															
Public sewer	103,155	2,596	100,559	89,467	56,736	32,732	11,092	3,764	10.2	1,752	725	2,393	2,458	4,546	4,170
Septic tank, cesspool, or chemical toilet	26,662	1,800	24,862	22,307	19,667	2,640	2,555	253	8.6	351	153	921	877	1,402	4,576
Other	295	222	73	31	25	6	41	1	16.1	5	1	–	34	6	23

– = Zero or rounds to zero.
X = Not applicable.
[1] = Figures may not add to total because more than one category may apply to a unit.
[2] = Includes only those who responded they had some type of air conditioning.
[3] = Restricted to units with smoke detector powered by both electricity and batteries, or batteries only.
[4] = Excludes unit where primary source of drinking water is commercial bottled water.

Source: U.S. Census Bureau, American Housing Survey

Table 3-4. Fuels, All Housing Units, 2009

[Numbers in thousands.]

Characteristics	Total housing units	Seasonal	Year-round											New construction 4 years	Manufactured/ mobile homes
			Total	Occupied			Vacant								
				Total	Owner	Renter	Total	For rent	Rental vacancy rate	For sale only	Rented or sold	Occasional use/URE	Other vacant		
Total	130,112	4,618	125,494	111,806	76,428	35,378	13,688	4,018	10.1	2,108	879	3,314	3,368	5,955	8,769
Main house heating fuel															
Housing units with heating fuel	129,181	4,288	124,894	111,420	76,222	35,198	13,473	3,998	10.1	2,097	875	3,296	3,207	5,916	8,646
Electricity	45,939	2,165	43,774	37,851	22,219	15,632	5,923	2,008	11.3	795	349	1,521	1,250	3,058	4,548
Piped gas	63,361	837	62,525	56,806	41,233	15,573	5,719	1,719	9.8	1,052	420	1,095	1,433	2,371	1,884
Bottled gas	7,366	694	6,673	5,817	4,889	929	855	75	7.3	129	46	358	248	327	1,444
Fuel oil	9,065	212	8,852	8,214	5,693	2,521	639	162	6.0	84	45	212	136	66	208
Kerosene or other liquid fuel	732	56	675	599	444	154	76	9	5.7	16	3	22	26	24	335
Coal or coke	126	5	122	98	91	7	24	2	24.4	2	–	8	11	3	–
Wood	2,215	284	1,931	1,780	1,503	277	150	4	1.4	16	8	65	57	57	199
Solar energy	18	7	11	11	8	3	–	–	–	–	–	–	–	3	–
Other	359	28	330	243	142	101	87	20	16.2	3	5	15	44	9	29
Cooking fuel															
With cooking fuel	127,453	4,129	123,323	111,623	76,388	35,235	11,700	3,694	9.4	1,761	729	3,149	2,367	5,868	8,485
Electricity	77,848	2,795	75,053	67,078	45,512	21,567	7,975	2,622	10.7	1,183	507	2,124	1,539	3,745	5,372
Gas	49,486	1,306	48,179	44,477	30,827	13,650	3,703	1,069	7.2	577	222	1,019	816	2,114	3,106
Kerosene or other liquid fuel	27	5	22	14	7	7	8	1	8.6	–	–	3	5	–	2
Coal or coke	–	–	–	–	–	–	–	–	–	–	–	–	–	–	–
Wood	53	17	35	29	17	12	6	1	6.9	–	–	–	5	2	4
Other	39	6	33	25	25	–	8	1	100.0	1	–	4	2	7	1
Water heating fuel															
With hot piped water	128,676	4,100	124,575	111,691	76,371	35,319	12,885	3,939	9.9	2,048	838	3,233	2,826	5,942	8,522
Electricity	54,871	2,706	52,164	45,435	29,341	16,095	6,729	2,054	11.2	981	376	1,929	1,389	3,034	6,416
Gas	68,198	1,252	66,946	61,202	43,645	17,556	5,745	1,773	9.1	1,027	435	1,158	1,351	2,828	2,049
Fuel oil	5,126	97	5,029	4,692	3,087	1,604	337	98	5.7	38	23	124	55	52	37
Kerosene or other liquid fuel	25	–	25	21	18	3	4	–	–	–	–	–	4	4	7
Coal or coke	31	3	28	23	23	–	5	2	100.0	2	–	1	–	–	–
Wood	134	23	112	104	96	9	7	1	14.6	–	–	1	5	10	10
Solar energy	159	12	147	135	121	14	11	–	–	–	–	11	–	5	–
Other	132	8	124	78	40	39	46	10	20.5	1	4	9	23	8	2
Central air conditioning fuel															
With central air conditioning	82,475	2,077	80,398	72,808	54,647	18,161	7,590	2,211	10.8	1,456	534	1,888	1,501	5,279	5,469
Electricity	80,201	2,029	78,172	70,863	53,098	17,765	7,309	2,154	10.7	1,363	497	1,826	1,469	5,120	5,396
Gas	2,175	40	2,135	1,891	1,502	389	244	52	11.5	88	28	50	26	146	73
Other	98	8	91	54	48	6	37	5	45.2	5	10	11	5	13	–
Clothes dryer fuel															
With clothes dryer	98,657	2,360	96,297	90,905	72,562	18,343	5,392	949	4.9	824	328	2,085	1,205	5,236	7,017
Electricity	76,936	2,036	74,900	70,497	55,059	15,438	4,403	815	5.0	605	263	1,740	980	4,289	6,450
Gas	21,667	318	21,348	20,364	17,478	2,886	984	134	4.4	219	65	343	223	947	564
Other	55	6	49	45	26	19	4	–	–	–	–	1	3	–	3
Units using each fuel[1]															
Electricity	127,483	3,743	123,740	111,746	76,378	35,368	11,994	4,014	10	1,811	786	2,945	2,438	5,886	8,460
Gas	88,285	2,114	86,171	77,702	55,091	22,611	8,469	2,718	11	1,363	581	1,849	1,959	3,575	4,253
Fuel oil	11,206	228	10,978	9,208	6,409	2,800	1,770	1,046	27	143	139	304	138	150	361
Kerosene or other liquid fuel	761	61	700	616	451	164	84	10	6	16	3	25	31	24	337
Coal or coke	132	5	128	104	97	7	24	2	24	2	–	8	11	3	–
Wood	2,226	287	1,940	1,787	1,510	278	153	5	2	16	8	65	59	57	203
Solar energy	177	19	158	147	130	17	11	–	–	–	–	11	–	8	–
Other	605	54	552	405	254	151	147	32	17	7	10	28	70	30	33
All electric units	37,198	1,978	35,220	30,166	17,951	12,216	5,053	1,701	12.1	690	283	1,309	1,070	2,460	4,101

– = Zero or rounds to zero.
[1] = Figures may not add to total because more than one category may apply to a unit.

Source: U.S. Census Bureau, American Housing Survey

Table 3-5. Housing and Neighborhood Quality, All Housing Units, 2009

[Numbers in thousands.]

Characteristics	Total housing units	Seasonal	Year-round												New construction 4 years	Manufactured/ mobile homes
			Total	Occupied			Vacant									
				Total	Owner	Renter	Total	For rent	Rental vacancy rate	For sale only	Rented or sold	Occasional use/URE	Other vacant			
Total	130,112	4,618	125,494	111,806	76,428	35,378	13,688	4,018	10.1	2,108	879	3,314	3,368	5,955	8,769
Selected amenities[1]															
Porch, deck, balcony, or patio	109,246	3,706	105,540	95,406	70,421	24,984	10,135	2,608	9.4	1,723	679	2,670	2,455	5,266	7,314
Usable fireplace	42,829	985	41,844	38,998	34,458	4,540	2,846	385	7.8	720	202	869	669	2,680	1,269
Separate dining room	59,738	1,220	58,518	53,676	43,717	9,959	4,842	1,158	10.3	1,081	385	1,018	1,200	2,979	2,482
With 2 or more living rooms or recreation rooms, etc.	36,333	469	35,864	33,912	30,978	2,934	1,952	219	6.9	604	186	538	405	2,213	1,023
Garage or carport included with home	82,484	1,931	80,553	74,236	60,979	13,258	6,317	1,131	7.8	1,455	458	1,685	1,588	4,757	3,130
Not included	47,421	2,668	44,753	37,525	15,420	22,105	7,227	2,862	11.3	641	413	1,597	1,716	1,188	5,636
Off-street parking included	39,020	2,218	36,802	30,963	13,287	17,676	5,839	2,349	11.6	532	342	1,304	1,312	1,041	5,083
Off-street parking not reported	17	2	15	3	2	2	11	1	41.4	3	–	–	7	1	–
Garage or carport not reported	206	18	188	44	29	15	144	26	58.2	12	9	32	64	10	4
Owner or manager on property															
Rental, multiunit[2]	25,502	X	25,502	22,181	X	22,181	3,321	2,824	11.2	X	245	252	X	778	X
Owner or manager lives on property	8,252	X	8,252	7,461	X	7,461	790	665	8.1	X	64	61	X	262	X
Neither owner nor manager lives on property	17,251	X	17,251	14,720	X	14,720	2,531	2,159	12.7	X	181	191	X	516	X
Selected deficiencies[1]															
Holes in floors	1,923	170	1,753	1,141	581	560	612	73	11.4	72	28	84	354	29	322
Open cracks or holes (interior)	7,011	313	6,698	5,517	3,101	2,416	1,180	172	6.6	158	72	141	637	111	643
Broken plaster or peeling paint (interior)	3,339	220	3,118	2,378	1,246	1,132	741	76	6.2	85	51	94	435	42	267
No electrical wiring	320	135	185	84	57	26	101	12	28.7	8	4	14	64	19	35
Exposed wiring	617	81	536	355	221	134	182	17	10.7	11	25	23	105	28	73
Rooms without electric outlets	1,926	223	1,703	1,274	650	624	430	58	8.4	25	47	60	241	65	174
Description of area within 300 feet[1]															
Single-family detached houses	109,633	3,324	106,309	95,916	68,909	27,007	10,393	2,760	9.2	1,783	667	2,441	2,742	4,725	6,282
Single-family attached	24,742	581	24,161	21,832	10,973	10,860	2,328	1,000	8.4	338	147	485	359	1,064	365
Multiunit residential buildings[3]	39,210	797	38,413	33,635	11,514	22,121	4,778	2,486	10.0	397	298	860	737	1,296	658
1- to 3-story multiunit is tallest	28,805	410	28,395	25,143	9,014	16,130	3,252	1,773	9.8	262	197	467	552	841	591
4- to 6-story multiunit is tallest	5,969	205	5,764	4,937	1,464	3,473	827	404	10.3	77	59	188	99	246	46
7-or-more-story multiunit is tallest	3,997	180	3,817	3,172	929	2,243	645	282	11.1	45	34	204	80	206	10
Manufactured/mobile homes	16,360	1,081	15,280	13,388	10,276	3,112	1,892	308	8.9	256	99	625	603	656	7,003
Commercial or institutional	40,535	732	39,803	35,649	16,992	18,657	4,154	1,886	9.1	441	285	709	832	1,151	1,580
Industrial or factories	5,888	53	5,834	5,376	2,520	2,856	458	203	6.6	47	19	55	134	149	369
Open space, park, woods, farm, or ranch	53,290	2,482	50,808	45,816	33,110	12,706	4,992	1,215	8.7	725	323	1,444	1,285	3,140	5,155
4-or-more-lane highway, railroad, or airport	22,064	415	21,649	19,612	10,380	9,232	2,037	899	8.8	232	119	326	461	754	1,324
Not reported	2,828	15	2,813	2,624	1,836	788	189	33	4.0	17	7	47	85	121	143
Bodies of water within 300 feet															
Water in area	23,326	2,053	21,273	18,656	13,824	4,832	2,617	630	11.4	315	134	1,067	472	1,367	2,105
With waterfront property	5,483	1,217	4,266	3,331	2,653	678	934	129	15.7	89	39	545	133	300	371
Waterfront property not reported	403	11	392	360	266	94	32	2	2.5	2	–	13	14	15	28
With flood plain	3,971	674	3,297	2,622	1,929	692	675	106	13.1	74	12	348	135	194	416
Flood plain not reported	166	11	155	116	41	74	39	8	9.4	7	6	12	7	28	14
Water not reported	753	7	746	676	521	156	70	10	5.9	12	–	18	29	73	35
No water in area	106,033	2,558	103,475	92,474	62,083	30,390	11,001	3,379	9.9	1,781	746	2,229	2,867	4,515	6,629
Age of other residential buildings within 300 feet															
Older	14,973	783	14,190	12,638	7,710	4,928	1,552	424	7.9	143	90	371	523	99	1,527
About the same	86,813	2,340	84,473	75,613	52,299	23,313	8,860	2,765	10.5	1,451	565	2,073	2,006	3,123	3,780
Newer	11,371	409	10,962	9,774	7,126	2,648	1,188	341	11.3	261	98	314	175	2,181	1,615
Very mixed	8,264	514	7,750	6,701	4,582	2,120	1,049	250	10.4	116	66	293	323	110	1,150
No other residential buildings	4,412	498	3,914	3,316	2,425	891	598	136	13.0	78	45	178	160	309	481
Not reported	4,279	73	4,205	3,764	2,286	1,478	441	102	6.4	59	14	84	183	133	216
Manufactured/mobile homes in group															
Manufactured/mobile homes	8,769	730	8,040	6,839	5,418	1,421	1,201	176	11.0	143	65	487	329	324	8,769
1 to 6	6,084	425	5,658	4,918	3,952	966	740	119	10.9	64	50	244	262	270	6,084
7 to 20	463	43	420	370	217	153	50	29	15.8	7	–	7	7	23	463
21 or more	2,222	261	1,961	1,550	1,249	301	411	28	8.5	72	15	236	60	30	2,222

Table 3-5. Housing and Neighborhood Quality, All Housing Units, 2009—*Continued*

[Numbers in thousands.]

Characteristics	Total housing units	Seasonal	Year-round											New construction 4 years	Manufactured/ mobile homes
			Total	Occupied			Vacant								
				Total	Owner	Renter	Total	For rent	Rental vacancy rate	For sale only	Rented or sold	Occasional use/URE	Other vacant		
None	113,769	3,956	109,813	98,452	67,919	30,533	11,361	3,444	10.0	1,782	760	2,882	2,492	5,296	7,419
1 building	3,759	79	3,680	3,246	2,034	1,211	435	119	8.9	56	19	65	175	96	336
More than 1 building	4,847	67	4,780	3,856	2,031	1,825	924	270	12.8	113	50	105	386	118	355
No buildings	3,832	467	3,364	2,871	2,245	626	493	87	11.9	71	37	161	138	272	476
Not reported	3,905	48	3,857	3,381	2,198	1,182	476	98	7.6	86	13	101	178	173	184
Bars on windows of buildings within 300 feet															
No bars on windows	108,704	3,991	104,713	93,406	66,383	27,024	11,307	3,269	10.7	1,806	729	2,827	2,677	5,308	7,816
1 building with bars	2,286	15	2,271	2,108	1,256	851	163	59	6.5	19	4	24	57	41	119
2 or more buildings with bars	10,230	60	10,170	9,101	3,927	5,174	1,069	439	7.8	116	85	155	274	144	147
No buildings	3,832	467	3,364	2,871	2,245	626	493	87	11.9	71	37	161	138	272	476
Not reported	5,061	85	4,975	4,320	2,617	1,703	656	165	8.8	96	25	147	223	190	211
Condition of streets within 300 feet															
No repairs needed	73,426	2,523	70,903	63,186	44,404	18,782	7,717	2,184	10.3	1,345	484	2,060	1,643	4,048	3,955
Minor repairs needed	43,170	1,521	41,649	36,976	24,133	12,843	4,674	1,512	10.4	582	318	979	1,282	1,215	3,375
Major repairs needed	7,523	268	7,255	6,604	4,375	2,228	651	183	7.6	82	42	118	227	381	1,029
No streets	2,158	241	1,916	1,678	1,259	419	238	56	11.8	34	15	79	53	140	205
Not reported	3,835	64	3,771	3,362	2,257	1,106	408	82	6.9	65	20	78	163	170	205
Trash, litter, or junk on streets or any properties within 300 feet															
None	115,242	4,346	110,896	99,010	69,415	29,595	11,886	3,459	10.4	1,918	755	3,049	2,706	5,458	7,675
Minor accumulation	8,439	137	8,302	7,250	3,491	3,759	1,052	388	9.3	110	83	155	316	247	590
Major accumulation	3,007	85	2,921	2,519	1,426	1,093	403	112	9.3	31	26	45	189	86	324
Not reported	3,424	49	3,374	3,027	2,096	931	348	59	5.9	49	16	66	157	164	181

– = Zero or rounds to zero.
X = Not applicable.
[1] = Figures may not add to total because more than one category may apply to a unit.
[2] = Two or more units of any tenure in the structure.
[3] = Figures do not add up because of nonrespondents.

Source: U.S. Census Bureau, American Housing Survey

Table 3-6. Height and Condition of Building, Occupied Units, 2009

[Numbers in thousands.]

Characteristics	Total occupied units	Tenure		Housing unit characteristics		Household characteristics				Regions			
		Owner	Renter	New construction 4 years	Manufactured/ mobile homes	Black alone	Hispanic	Elderly (65 years or over)	Below poverty level	Northeast	Midwest	South	West
Total	111,806	76,428	35,378	4,771	6,839	13,993	12,739	23,095	15,739	20,451	25,368	41,586	24,401
Stories in structure[1]													
1	35,364	26,216	9,148	1,240	X	4,512	5,359	8,757	5,340	1,109	4,072	19,803	10,381
2	37,867	25,210	12,657	2,004	X	4,388	3,960	6,886	4,677	6,291	10,192	12,065	9,320
3	24,508	16,721	7,787	954	X	3,172	1,731	4,023	2,824	8,689	8,530	4,611	2,678
4 to 6	5,134	2,349	2,785	179	X	777	712	1,152	868	2,813	1,045	721	554
7 or more	2,094	515	1,580	93	X	501	255	740	538	1,009	385	469	231
Stories between main and apartment entrances													
Multiunits, 2 or more floors	22,962	3,458	19,503	692	X	4,780	4,034	3,764	5,458	6,514	4,638	6,382	5,428
None (on same floor)	7,616	1,187	6,429	184	X	1,505	1,320	1,290	1,842	1,921	1,476	2,255	1,964
1 (up or down)	6,447	911	5,536	168	X	1,341	1,207	754	1,486	1,616	1,426	1,807	1,598
2 or more (up or down)	8,899	1,361	7,538	339	X	1,934	1,507	1,720	2,129	2,976	1,735	2,320	1,867
Elevator on floor													
Multiunits, 2 or more floors	22,962	3,458	19,503	692	X	4,780	4,034	3,764	5,458	6,514	4,638	6,382	5,428
With 1 or more elevators working	4,348	1,045	3,303	219	X	834	594	1,647	996	1,744	825	891	888
With elevator, none in working condition	46	11	35	–	X	7	16	9	15	11	4	10	20
No elevator	18,568	2,403	16,165	472	X	3,939	3,425	2,108	4,447	4,760	3,808	5,480	4,519
Units, 3 or more floors from main entrance	1,436	133	1,302	55	X	326	243	135	319	650	305	306	174
Foundation													
1-unit building, excluding manufactured/mobile homes	79,052	67,276	11,776	3,727	X	7,944	7,404	17,102	7,790	13,240	18,999	29,999	16,814
With basement under all of building	26,713	23,821	2,892	1,038	X	2,473	1,176	5,624	2,067	9,022	11,276	4,269	2,145
With basement under part of building	8,208	7,350	858	119	X	438	326	1,937	645	2,226	3,280	1,565	1,137
With crawl space	18,022	14,783	3,240	602	X	1,961	1,692	4,229	2,029	740	2,523	9,517	5,242
On concrete slab	24,917	20,431	4,486	1,946	X	2,946	4,034	4,995	2,823	1,146	1,758	13,941	8,071
Other	1,192	892	300	23	X	125	176	318	225	105	162	707	218
External building conditions[2]													
Sagging roof	1,888	1,370	517	3	292	292	171	275	461	314	500	776	299
Missing roofing material	4,640	3,682	958	71	342	573	506	836	752	673	1,312	1,761	893
Hole in roof	1,458	1,029	429	6	307	296	186	232	370	202	356	639	260
Missing bricks, siding, or other outside wall material	2,323	1,661	661	21	252	363	240	329	545	401	678	806	437
Sloping outside walls	1,167	781	386	10	183	241	113	230	279	168	305	515	179
Boarded up windows	821	558	262	11	142	168	132	149	235	101	214	374	131
Broken windows	2,984	2,112	872	33	518	371	408	349	636	353	829	1,171	631
Bars on windows	3,318	2,616	702	17	60	954	1,018	896	600	362	425	1,422	1,110
Foundation crumbling or has open crack or hole	2,227	1,687	540	17	71	306	165	354	373	382	820	650	375
None of the above	69,766	60,037	9,730	3,794	5,416	6,128	5,901	15,628	6,456	11,449	16,245	27,575	14,497
Not reported	2,173	1,832	341	98	143	278	161	431	371	376	403	954	441
Previous occupancy													
Unit built 1990 or later	27,805	21,908	5,897	4,771	3,416	2,818	2,612	4,034	2,579	2,550	5,569	13,016	6,671
Not previously occupied	11,223	10,515	708	3,295	1,581	1,045	909	1,941	732	1,142	2,460	5,464	2,157
Not reported	297	242	55	43	8	35	20	36	46	49	46	147	55
Site placement													
Manufactured/mobile homes	6,839	5,418	1,421	301	6,839	643	722	1,537	1,492	540	1,145	3,918	1,236
First site	4,600	4,002	598	259	4,600	463	467	1,228	894	390	705	2,630	874
Moved from another site	1,301	1,047	254	34	1,301	123	85	247	318	107	252	785	157
Don't know	362	97	265	3	362	28	37	29	98	25	73	188	75
Not reported	576	272	304	4	576	29	134	32	182	18	115	314	130
Manufactured/mobile home size													
Manufactured/mobile homes	6,839	5,418	1,421	301	6,839	643	722	1,537	1,492	540	1,145	3,918	1,236
Single-wide	3,923	2,867	1,056	133	3,923	363	475	779	1,029	366	766	2,319	472
Double-wide	2,803	2,444	358	165	2,803	267	233	704	454	174	370	1,544	715
Triple-wide or larger	106	103	3	3	106	13	14	53	8	–	2	55	49
Size not reported	8	4	4	–	8	–	–	–	1	1	7	–	–
Manufactured/mobile home tiedowns													
Manufactured/mobile homes	6,839	5,418	1,421	301	6,839	643	722	1,537	1,492	540	1,145	3,918	1,236
Anchored by tiedowns, bolts, or other means	6,136	4,914	1,222	273	6,136	611	639	1,377	1,299	417	1,034	3,668	1,017
Not anchored	545	426	119	19	545	27	66	141	139	91	88	204	161
Anchoring not reported	158	78	79	8	158	4	17	19	55	32	22	46	57
Manufactured/mobile home setup													
Manufactured/mobile homes	6,839	5,418	1,421	301	6,839	643	722	1,537	1,492	540	1,145	3,918	1,236
Set on permanent masonry foundation	1,367	1,158	209	50	1,367	101	85	364	171	119	303	659	285
Resting on concrete pad	1,076	870	206	72	1,076	27	127	253	236	141	346	326	263
Up on blocks, but not on concrete pad	4,194	3,251	943	166	4,194	499	477	886	1,048	260	455	2,851	628
Setup in some other way	113	99	14	4	113	8	18	26	23	14	24	42	33
Setup not reported	90	40	50	8	90	7	15	9	15	6	17	40	27

– = Zero or rounds to zero.
X = Not applicable.
[1] = Figures exclude manufactured/mobile homes.
[2] = Figures may not add to total because more than one category may apply to a unit. Figures do not include multiunit structures.

Source: U.S. Census Bureau, American Housing Survey

Table 3-7. Height and Condition of Building, Owner-Occupied Units, 2009

[Numbers in thousands.]

Characteristics	Total occupied units	Housing unit characteristics		Household characteristics				Regions			
		New construction 4 years	Manufactured/ mobile homes	Black alone	Hispanic	Elderly (65 years and over)	Below poverty level	Northeast	Midwest	South	West
Total	76,428	3,830	5,418	6,547	6,439	18,472	6,405	13,378	18,249	29,193	15,607
Stories in structure[1]											
1	26,216	1,053	X	2,684	3,531	7,499	2,740	807	2,882	15,155	7,372
2	25,210	1,709	X	1,611	1,552	5,717	1,555	4,404	7,633	7,671	5,502
3	16,721	702	X	1,482	698	3,102	925	6,333	6,072	2,846	1,469
4 to 6	2,349	68	X	225	128	589	134	1,193	630	324	202
7 or more	515	25	X	43	39	186	43	205	88	124	97
Stories between main and apartment entrances											
Multiunits, 2 or more floors	3,458	160	X	329	340	1,019	276	1,181	628	815	835
None (on same floor)	1,187	29	X	97	106	322	83	399	187	270	330
1 (up or down)	911	53	X	102	103	268	64	306	165	200	239
2 or more (up or down)	1,361	78	X	130	132	429	128	476	275	344	265
Elevator on floor											
Multiunits, 2 or more floors	3,458	160	X	329	340	1,019	276	1,181	628	815	835
With 1 or more elevators working	1,045	63	X	79	86	427	80	356	180	284	225
With elevator, none in working condition	11	–	X	–	3	2	–	–	2	5	4
No elevator	2,403	97	X	250	252	590	196	825	446	525	607
Units, 3 or more floors from main entrance	133	5	X	19	11	19	13	52	52	12	18
Foundation											
1-unit building, excluding manufactured/mobile homes	67,276	3,391	X	5,694	5,547	15,951	5,075	11,732	16,645	25,189	13,709
With basement under all of building	23,821	986	X	1,897	901	5,350	1,447	8,056	10,066	3,805	1,893
With basement under part of building	7,350	113	X	363	254	1,824	463	2,017	2,941	1,398	993
With crawl space	14,783	554	X	1,348	1,167	3,914	1,259	655	2,123	7,715	4,290
On concrete slab	20,431	1,717	X	2,026	3,113	4,568	1,764	927	1,371	11,758	6,374
Other	892	20	X	59	113	295	143	77	145	512	159
External building conditions[2]											
Sagging roof	1,370	–	199	196	115	252	270	252	350	561	207
Missing roofing material	3,682	52	254	415	338	747	493	564	1,073	1,401	644
Hole in roof	1,029	3	220	194	118	210	210	141	258	465	165
Missing bricks, siding, or other outside wall material	1,661	17	193	225	128	289	309	315	486	569	291
Sloping outside walls	781	7	146	172	63	207	144	116	204	354	107
Boarded up windows	558	8	96	112	84	131	119	62	136	268	93
Broken windows	2,112	30	377	236	242	304	346	274	591	809	438
Bars on windows	2,616	14	54	739	743	835	363	281	353	1,188	794
Foundation crumbling or has open crack or hole	1,687	15	48	191	111	319	209	316	631	468	272
None of the above	60,037	3,456	4,357	4,468	4,469	14,563	4,292	10,243	14,471	23,268	12,055
Not reported	1,832	92	101	174	129	407	279	327	340	792	374
Previous occupancy											
Unit built 1990 or later	21,908	3,830	2,829	1,728	1,876	3,215	1,349	2,042	4,480	10,403	4,982
Not previously occupied	10,515	2,953	1,506	897	795	1,737	545	1,053	2,326	5,158	1,978
Not reported	242	36	–	18	17	27	16	45	39	104	53
Site placement											
Manufactured/mobile homes	5,418	272	5,418	503	490	1,379	1,009	436	943	3,072	966
First site	4,002	242	4,002	405	368	1,135	716	348	620	2,280	755
Moved from another site	1,047	30	1,047	88	71	207	226	71	223	630	123
Don't know	97	–	97	–	5	17	16	6	31	35	25
Not reported	272	–	272	9	45	19	50	11	69	128	64
Manufactured/mobile home size											
Manufactured/mobile homes	5,418	272	5,418	503	490	1,379	1,009	436	943	3,072	966
Single-wide	2,867	122	2,867	242	313	652	634	277	599	1,643	347
Double-wide	2,444	148	2,444	249	167	673	367	159	338	1,375	572
Triple-wide or larger	103	3	103	13	11	53	8	–	2	55	47
Size not reported	4	–	4	–	–	–	–	–	4	–	–
Manufactured/mobile home tiedowns											
Manufactured/mobile homes	5,418	272	5,418	503	490	1,379	1,009	436	943	3,072	966
Anchored by tiedowns, bolts, or other means	4,914	253	4,914	476	442	1,240	886	344	874	2,900	796
Not anchored	426	19	426	23	43	127	87	80	65	143	137
Anchoring not reported	78	–	78	4	5	12	36	12	4	29	32
Manufactured/mobile home setup											
Manufactured/mobile homes	5,418	272	5,418	503	490	1,379	1,009	436	943	3,072	966
Set on permanent masonry foundation	1,158	33	1,158	93	56	341	135	104	260	575	219
Resting on concrete pad	870	68	870	21	90	235	153	116	283	249	223
Up on blocks, but not on concrete pad	3,251	163	3,251	377	326	774	695	207	369	2,195	480
Setup in some other way	99	4	99	8	16	24	18	8	24	34	33
Setup not reported	40	4	40	3	3	5	7	1	8	19	11

– = Zero or rounds to zero.
X = Not applicable.
[1] = Figures exclude manufactured/mobile homes.
[2] = Figures may not add to total because more than one category may apply to a unit. Figures do not include multiunit structures.

Source: U.S. Census Bureau, American Housing Survey

Table 3-8. Height and Condition of Buildings, Renter-Occupied Units, 2009

[Numbers in thousands.]

Characteristics	Total occupied units	Housing unit characteristics: New construction 4 years	Housing unit characteristics: Manufactured/ mobile homes	Household characteristics: Black alone	Household characteristics: Hispanic	Household characteristics: Elderly (65 years and over)	Household characteristics: Below poverty level	Regions: Northeast	Regions: Midwest	Regions: South	Regions: West
Total	35,378	941	1,421	7,446	6,300	4,623	9,334	7,073	7,119	12,392	8,794
Stories in structure[1]											
1	9,148	186	X	1,828	1,828	1,258	2,600	302	1,189	4,648	3,010
2	12,657	295	X	2,777	2,408	1,169	3,122	1,887	2,559	4,393	3,818
3	7,787	251	X	1,691	1,033	921	1,899	2,356	2,458	1,765	1,209
4 to 6	2,785	111	X	553	584	563	734	1,621	415	397	353
7 or more	1,580	68	X	458	216	554	495	804	297	345	134
Stories between main and apartment entrances											
Multiunits, 2 or more floors	19,503	532	X	4,451	3,694	2,745	5,182	5,333	4,010	5,567	4,593
None (on same floor)	6,429	155	X	1,408	1,214	968	1,759	1,522	1,289	1,985	1,633
1 (up or down)	5,536	116	X	1,239	1,105	486	1,422	1,310	1,261	1,607	1,358
2 or more (up or down)	7,538	261	X	1,804	1,376	1,290	2,000	2,500	1,460	1,976	1,602
Elevator on floor											
Multiunits, 2 or more floors	19,503	532	X	4,451	3,694	2,745	5,182	5,333	4,010	5,567	4,593
With 1 or more elevators working	3,303	156	X	755	508	1,220	916	1,387	645	607	664
With elevator, none in working condition	35	–	X	7	14	7	15	11	2	5	17
No elevator	16,165	375	X	3,689	3,173	1,518	4,251	3,935	3,363	4,955	3,912
Units, 3 or more floors from main entrance	1,302	49	X	307	232	116	305	598	253	295	156
Foundation											
1-unit building, excluding manufactured/mobile homes	11,776	337	X	2,251	1,857	1,151	2,715	1,508	2,353	4,810	3,105
With basement under all of building	2,892	51	X	576	275	273	620	966	1,210	464	252
With basement under part of building	858	5	X	75	72	113	183	209	339	166	144
With crawl space	3,240	48	X	614	525	315	771	85	400	1,801	952
On concrete slab	4,486	229	X	920	921	427	1,059	219	387	2,183	1,697
Other	300	3	X	66	64	24	83	28	17	195	60
External building conditions[2]											
Sagging roof	517	3	93	96	56	23	192	62	149	214	91
Missing roofing material	958	19	89	158	168	89	259	110	239	360	249
Hole in roof	429	3	87	102	68	23	160	61	99	175	95
Missing bricks, siding, or other outside wall material	661	5	59	138	112	40	235	87	192	237	146
Sloping outside walls	386	3	37	69	50	22	135	52	101	161	72
Boarded up windows	262	3	46	56	48	18	116	39	79	107	38
Broken windows	872	3	141	135	166	45	290	79	238	362	193
Bars on windows	702	3	6	215	276	60	237	81	72	234	316
Foundation crumbling or has open crack or hole	540	2	23	115	54	36	164	66	189	182	102
None of the above	9,730	338	1,059	1,660	1,432	1,065	2,164	1,207	1,774	4,307	2,442
Not reported	341	6	42	104	32	24	92	50	63	161	67
Previous occupancy											
Unit built 1990 or later	5,897	941	587	1,090	736	819	1,230	507	1,089	2,613	1,688
Not previously occupied	708	342	75	148	115	204	187	89	134	306	179
Not reported	55	7	8	17	3	10	30	5	7	42	1
Site placement											
Manufactured/mobile homes	1,421	28	1,421	140	232	158	483	104	201	845	270
First site	598	17	598	58	99	93	178	43	85	350	120
Moved from another site	254	4	254	35	14	40	92	36	29	155	34
Don't know	265	3	265	28	31	12	81	19	42	154	51
Not reported	304	4	304	19	88	13	132	6	46	186	66
Manufactured/mobile home size											
Manufactured/mobile homes	1,421	28	1,421	140	232	158	483	104	201	845	270
Single-wide	1,056	11	1,056	121	162	127	395	88	167	676	125
Double-wide	358	17	358	19	67	31	87	15	31	169	143
Triple-wide or larger	3	–	3	–	3	–	–	–	–	–	3
Size not reported	4	–	4	–	–	–	1	1	3	–	–
Manufactured/mobile home tiedowns											
Manufactured/mobile homes	1,421	28	1,421	140	232	158	483	104	201	845	270
Anchored by tiedowns, bolts, or other means	1,222	20	1,222	135	197	137	412	73	160	768	221
Not anchored	119	–	119	5	23	14	52	11	23	61	24
Anchoring not reported	79	8	79	–	12	6	19	20	18	16	25
Manufactured/mobile home setup											
Manufactured/mobile homes	1,421	28	1,421	140	232	158	483	104	201	845	270
Set on permanent masonry foundation	209	17	209	8	29	23	35	16	43	84	65
Resting on concrete pad	206	4	206	6	37	18	83	25	63	77	40
Up on blocks, but not on concrete pad	943	4	943	122	151	111	352	52	87	656	149
Setup in some other way	14	–	14	–	2	2	5	6	–	8	–
Setup not reported	50	4	50	4	12	4	8	5	9	20	16

– = Zero or rounds to zero.
X = Not applicable.
[1] = Figures exclude manufactured/mobile homes.
[2] = Figures may not add to total because more than one category may apply to a unit. Figures do not include multiunit structures.

Source: U.S. Census Bureau, American Housing Survey

Table 3-9. Size of Unit and Lot, Occupied Units, 2009

[Numbers in thousands.]

Characteristics	Total occupied units	Tenure		Housing unit characteristics		Household characteristics				Regions			
		Owner	Renter	New construction 4 years	Manufactured/ mobile homes	Black alone	Hispanic	Elderly (65 years or over)	Below poverty level	Northeast	Midwest	South	West
Total	111,806	76,428	35,378	4,771	6,839	13,993	12,739	23,095	15,739	20,451	25,368	41,586	24,401
Rooms													
1 room	352	26	326	7	3	45	56	82	141	111	60	33	149
2 rooms	946	68	879	13	7	153	134	176	324	269	130	209	337
3 rooms	8,711	1,036	7,675	201	155	1,569	1,364	2,121	2,562	2,235	1,891	2,461	2,124
4 rooms	17,828	6,475	11,354	384	1,888	2,764	2,953	3,376	4,035	3,277	3,889	6,376	4,287
5 rooms	25,444	17,232	8,212	1,084	2,578	3,620	3,282	5,477	4,009	3,854	5,758	10,355	5,476
6 rooms	24,596	20,364	4,232	983	1,383	2,958	2,532	5,440	2,622	4,435	5,400	9,918	4,842
7 rooms	16,489	14,754	1,735	813	627	1,548	1,339	3,428	1,231	3,080	3,904	6,110	3,394
8 rooms	10,033	9,410	622	646	143	811	624	1,802	483	1,898	2,465	3,533	2,136
9 rooms	4,344	4,130	214	334	36	336	259	677	225	751	1,124	1,468	1,000
10 rooms or more	3,063	2,933	130	306	19	191	196	515	105	540	747	1,121	655
Rooms used for business													
Business only													
1 or more rooms with direct access	8,518	6,120	2,398	420	701	1,076	901	1,914	1,394	1,363	1,764	3,654	1,737
1 or more rooms, no direct access	6,718	5,359	1,359	460	187	726	573	872	505	1,063	1,439	2,389	1,828
Not reported	688	536	152	39	25	65	18	130	127	153	117	302	115
Business and other use													
1 or more rooms	18,912	14,629	4,283	1,041	797	1,830	1,577	2,721	1,672	2,796	4,329	6,833	4,954
Not reported	760	580	181	47	27	72	30	131	135	187	150	308	115
Bedrooms													
None	789	45	744	17	8	100	118	156	282	225	142	97	324
1	11,434	1,714	9,720	229	202	2,067	1,749	2,726	3,183	2,973	2,391	3,292	2,777
2	27,671	13,471	14,200	714	2,495	3,891	3,959	6,116	5,245	5,279	6,499	9,480	6,413
3	48,082	39,723	8,359	2,088	3,571	5,715	4,820	10,223	5,228	7,784	10,885	20,062	9,352
4 or more	23,830	21,475	2,354	1,724	563	2,220	2,093	3,874	1,801	4,190	5,451	8,655	5,534
Complete bathrooms													
None	403	175	229	3	16	58	51	75	141	98	93	115	97
1	38,662	15,767	22,894	389	1,897	6,665	5,895	8,183	9,168	9,418	9,760	11,847	7,636
1 1/2	15,656	12,081	3,575	149	671	2,130	1,330	3,929	1,934	4,066	4,770	4,217	2,603
2 or more	57,085	48,405	8,680	4,231	4,254	5,140	5,462	10,908	4,496	6,869	10,746	25,406	14,064
Square footage of unit													
Single detached and manufactured/ mobile homes	79,918	68,742	11,176	3,611	6,839	7,492	7,529	17,449	8,441	11,971	19,088	31,981	16,878
Less than 500	603	383	220	6	161	63	122	139	150	86	104	247	166
500 to 749	1,771	1,085	686	14	638	198	337	440	466	249	415	810	298
750 to 999	5,014	3,519	1,495	67	1,500	614	720	1,088	1,096	614	1,340	2,086	973
1,000 to 1,499	18,419	14,978	3,441	478	2,315	2,044	2,079	4,180	2,521	2,047	4,331	7,834	4,207
1,500 to 1,999	18,519	16,284	2,235	667	1,082	1,605	1,733	4,162	1,708	2,458	4,039	7,564	4,457
2,000 to 2,499	13,190	12,057	1,134	697	307	908	936	2,888	830	2,000	3,282	5,165	2,743
2,500 to 2,999	7,050	6,622	429	455	112	501	363	1,365	308	1,211	1,594	2,819	1,426
3,000 to 3,999	6,692	6,391	301	643	54	422	390	1,237	308	1,119	1,700	2,488	1,385
4,000 or more	4,030	3,787	243	399	120	314	225	813	231	805	994	1,519	712
Not reported	4,630	3,638	992	186	550	823	625	1,138	823	1,382	1,288	1,449	510
Median	1,800	1,800	1,300	2,300	1,120	1,500	1,500	1,700	1,350	1,900	1,800	1,700	1,700
Lot size													
1-unit structures[1]	83,466	70,643	12,823	3,814	6,800	8,433	7,914	18,024	9,052	13,297	19,555	33,222	17,392
Less than 1/8 acre	11,824	9,107	2,717	552	1,346	1,654	1,849	2,478	1,603	2,146	2,577	3,439	3,661
1/8 up to 1/4 acre	21,793	17,771	4,022	907	975	2,598	3,051	4,496	2,588	2,625	5,235	7,241	6,692
1/4 up to 1/2 acre	15,921	13,837	2,084	805	529	1,645	1,351	3,296	1,450	2,383	4,044	6,523	2,970
1/2 up to 1 acre	10,036	8,874	1,162	388	690	962	558	2,135	810	1,974	1,964	4,945	1,153
1 up to 5 acres	17,014	14,895	2,120	806	2,335	1,319	842	3,767	1,854	3,072	3,669	8,310	1,963
5 up to 10 acres	2,750	2,545	205	183	433	97	104	595	250	464	737	1,106	443
10 acres or more	4,127	3,614	513	173	492	157	158	1,258	497	633	1,329	1,656	509
Median	0.27	0.32	0.22	0.30	0.75	0.24	0.16	0.32	0.25	0.34	0.28	0.36	0.18

Table 3-9. Size of Unit and Lot, Occupied Units, 2009—*Continued*

[Numbers in thousands.]

Characteristics	Total occupied units	Tenure		Housing unit characteristics		Household characteristics				Regions			
		Owner	Renter	New construction 4 years	Manufactured/ mobile homes	Black alone	Hispanic	Elderly (65 years or over)	Below poverty level	Northeast	Midwest	South	West
Persons per room													
0.50 or less	79,735	57,341	22,394	3,453	4,601	9,342	5,917	21,553	10,184	14,509	18,703	30,136	16,388
0.51 to 1.00	29,566	18,082	11,484	1,267	1,998	4,292	5,521	1,496	4,587	5,548	6,343	10,600	7,075
1.01 to 1.50	2,142	922	1,220	48	224	319	1,075	38	796	328	285	768	761
1.51 or more	362	83	279	3	17	40	226	7	172	67	38	81	177
Persons per bedroom													
0.50 or less	28,101	22,004	6,097	1,242	1,936	3,366	1,675	9,987	4,450	4,774	6,609	11,111	5,607
0.51 to 1.00	55,124	38,173	16,951	2,447	3,024	6,552	4,761	11,654	6,265	10,044	12,702	20,773	11,605
1.01 to 1.50	15,596	10,733	4,863	735	1,061	2,133	2,326	614	1,817	2,921	3,603	5,687	3,385
1.51 or more	12,197	5,475	6,722	329	809	1,843	3,860	684	2,924	2,487	2,313	3,918	3,479
No bedrooms	789	45	744	17	8	100	118	156	282	225	142	97	324
Square feet per person													
Single detached and manufactured/ mobile homes	79,918	68,742	11,176	3,611	6,839	7,492	7,529	17,449	8,441	11,971	19,088	31,981	16,878
Less than 200	1,502	955	548	52	394	241	585	93	489	184	255	687	376
200 to 299	4,230	2,899	1,331	65	773	550	1,114	224	855	454	864	1,751	1,162
300 to 399	6,326	4,932	1,394	191	887	677	945	463	779	816	1,444	2,577	1,489
400 to 499	7,205	5,933	1,272	289	719	656	846	756	615	964	1,743	2,758	1,740
500 to 599	7,115	6,018	1,097	255	584	682	641	936	587	1,021	1,768	2,764	1,561
600 to 699	7,227	6,333	894	313	529	576	505	1,194	487	1,036	1,748	2,936	1,506
700 to 799	5,848	5,257	591	362	468	502	427	1,273	438	759	1,423	2,406	1,261
800 to 899	4,764	4,255	509	249	372	390	319	1,065	346	710	1,082	1,893	1,079
900 to 999	4,538	4,181	357	195	358	316	247	1,238	366	608	1,145	1,796	990
1,000 to 1,499	14,582	13,289	1,293	790	781	1,083	769	4,540	1,300	2,090	3,513	6,053	2,927
1,500 or more	11,950	11,052	899	665	424	997	506	4,530	1,356	1,948	2,815	4,911	2,276
Not reported	4,630	3,638	992	186	550	823	625	1,138	823	1,382	1,288	1,449	510
Median	750	800	520	850	550	675	490	1,035	690	800	750	750	717

[1] = Does not include cooperatives or condominiums.

Source: U.S. Census Bureau, American Housing Survey

Table 3-10. Size of Unit and Lot, Owner-Occupied Units, 2009

[Numbers in thousands.]

Characteristics	Total occupied units	Housing unit characteristics		Household characteristics				Regions			
		New construction 4 years	Manufactured/ mobile homes	Black alone	Hispanic	Elderly (65 years and over)	Below poverty level	Northeast	Midwest	South	West
Total	76,428	3,830	5,418	6,547	6,439	18,472	6,405	13,378	18,249	29,193	15,607
Rooms											
1 room	26	5	3	–	3	3	7	5	7	3	11
2 rooms	68	3	5	6	9	16	28	21	3	24	21
3 rooms	1,036	41	100	90	82	358	184	303	220	230	283
4 rooms	6,475	147	1,349	401	691	2,037	1,067	1,147	1,576	2,379	1,372
5 rooms	17,232	825	2,028	1,635	1,731	4,698	1,968	2,431	4,151	7,052	3,598
6 rooms	20,364	821	1,213	2,004	1,841	5,128	1,616	3,645	4,582	8,234	3,903
7 rooms	14,754	739	531	1,263	1,092	3,312	875	2,815	3,552	5,498	2,890
8 rooms	9,410	628	139	682	559	1,746	394	1,789	2,344	3,304	1,973
9 rooms	4,130	323	32	295	242	670	174	714	1,086	1,404	926
10 rooms or more	2,933	298	19	172	190	503	91	509	728	1,067	629
Rooms used for business											
Business only											
1 or more rooms with direct access	6,120	342	601	523	433	1,596	676	944	1,347	2,658	1,171
1 or more rooms, no direct access	5,359	409	154	454	395	723	284	801	1,180	1,929	1,449
Not reported	536	39	23	25	8	102	83	94	95	257	90
Business and other use											
1 or more rooms	14,629	925	677	1,059	962	2,362	889	2,148	3,493	5,331	3,657
Not reported	580	43	23	28	11	106	81	113	116	261	90
Bedrooms											
None	45	5	5	–	5	7	10	16	10	5	14
1	1,714	43	142	140	124	602	282	526	366	409	413
2	13,471	400	1,854	902	1,197	4,530	1,795	2,595	3,444	4,487	2,945
3	39,723	1,746	2,938	3,752	3,360	9,626	3,147	6,457	9,413	16,501	7,353
4 or more	21,475	1,636	479	1,753	1,754	3,707	1,171	3,785	5,017	7,791	4,883
Complete bathrooms											
None	175	3	13	17	10	53	51	25	51	72	27
1	15,767	106	1,286	1,681	1,607	4,714	2,374	3,705	4,668	4,955	2,440
1 1/2	12,081	112	535	1,277	821	3,547	1,061	3,411	3,875	2,957	1,838
2 or more	48,405	3,610	3,584	3,573	4,002	10,159	2,919	6,237	9,656	21,211	11,302
Square footage of unit											
Single detached and manufactured/mobile homes	68,742	3,339	5,418	5,603	5,739	16,368	5,741	10,875	16,907	26,996	13,964
Less than 500	383	6	114	42	52	112	66	58	86	146	93
500 to 749	1,085	10	452	83	173	338	257	182	264	493	146
750 to 999	3,519	67	1,052	316	469	943	632	493	986	1,391	650
1,000 to 1,499	14,978	434	1,956	1,507	1,504	3,857	1,670	1,828	3,684	6,193	3,273
1,500 to 1,999	16,284	593	916	1,252	1,453	3,959	1,224	2,248	3,672	6,585	3,778
2,000 to 2,499	12,057	618	288	759	818	2,801	666	1,896	3,054	4,677	2,429
2,500 to 2,999	6,622	430	108	398	329	1,320	252	1,162	1,529	2,623	1,308
3,000 to 3,999	6,391	634	51	384	349	1,196	256	1,069	1,617	2,400	1,304
4,000 or more	3,787	391	103	295	185	790	195	751	951	1,442	644
Not reported	3,638	157	379	566	408	1,051	521	1,189	1,063	1,047	339
Median	1,800	2,400	1,200	1,656	1,600	1,764	1,470	2,000	1,800	1,800	1,800
Lot size											
1-unit structures[1]	70,643	3,472	5,380	6,095	5,874	16,769	5,917	11,742	17,073	27,712	14,116
Less than 1/8 acre	9,107	474	1,059	1,077	1,250	2,209	896	1,710	2,075	2,581	2,742
1/8 up to 1/4 acre	17,771	795	657	1,802	2,284	4,128	1,521	2,305	4,371	5,693	5,401
1/4 up to 1/2 acre	13,837	730	375	1,208	1,035	3,099	979	2,176	3,655	5,493	2,513
1/2 up to 1 acre	8,874	366	534	769	466	2,035	587	1,803	1,818	4,262	991
1 up to 5 acres	14,895	780	1,936	1,028	640	3,525	1,351	2,771	3,281	7,204	1,638
5 up to 10 acres	2,545	176	390	88	87	565	208	424	693	1,012	416
10 acres or more	3,614	152	428	122	112	1,208	375	551	1,181	1,466	416
Median	0.32	0.32	1.00	0.25	0.17	0.32	0.29	0.39	0.32	0.50	0.19

Table 3-10. Size of Unit and Lot, Owner-Occupied Units, 2009—*Continued*

[Numbers in thousands.]

Characteristics	Total occupied units	Housing unit characteristics		Household characteristics				Regions			
		New construction 4 years	Manufactured/ mobile homes	Black alone	Hispanic	Elderly (65 years and over)	Below poverty level	Northeast	Midwest	South	West
Persons per room											
0.50 or less	57,341	2,823	3,833	4,747	3,462	17,430	4,809	9,972	13,780	22,278	11,312
0.51 to 1.00	18,082	971	1,422	1,697	2,539	1,011	1,327	3,284	4,296	6,496	4,006
1.01 to 1.50	922	34	153	94	391	31	244	117	161	381	264
1.51 or more	83	3	10	9	48	–	26	6	13	39	26
Persons per bedroom											
0.50 or less	22,004	1,058	1,595	2,116	1,177	8,694	2,962	3,722	5,204	8,719	4,359
0.51 to 1.00	38,173	1,988	2,470	2,952	2,692	8,874	2,100	6,520	9,069	14,905	7,679
1.01 to 1.50	10,733	573	778	977	1,255	503	559	2,056	2,685	3,834	2,159
1.51 or more	5,475	206	570	502	1,310	394	774	1,064	1,282	1,731	1,397
No bedrooms	45	5	5	–	5	7	10	16	10	5	14
Square feet per person											
Single detached and manufactured/mobile homes	68,742	3,339	5,418	5,603	5,739	16,368	5,741	10,875	16,907	26,996	13,964
Less than 200	955	49	292	124	335	77	233	128	190	409	227
200 to 299	2,899	55	498	288	714	189	429	371	680	1,093	756
300 to 399	4,932	166	681	446	701	417	446	706	1,163	1,943	1,120
400 to 499	5,933	257	527	464	653	672	341	876	1,497	2,227	1,333
500 to 599	6,018	216	491	512	507	830	367	955	1,554	2,240	1,269
600 to 699	6,333	297	470	443	443	1,130	312	953	1,528	2,558	1,294
700 to 799	5,257	337	391	412	370	1,194	330	710	1,290	2,157	1,099
800 to 899	4,255	218	302	272	276	1,005	239	648	995	1,665	948
900 to 999	4,181	191	298	277	225	1,203	293	570	1,043	1,625	943
1,000 to 1,499	13,289	756	703	918	659	4,290	1,073	1,963	3,285	5,459	2,583
1,500 or more	11,052	641	385	883	448	4,310	1,155	1,806	2,619	4,576	2,052
Not reported	3,638	157	379	566	408	1,051	521	1,189	1,063	1,047	339
Median	800	894	600	750	533	1,050	840	800	800	800	750

– = Zero or rounds to zero.
[1] = Does not include cooperatives or condominiums.

Source: U.S. Census Bureau, American Housing Survey

Table 3-11. Size of Unit and Lot, Renter-Occupied Units, 2009

[Numbers in thousands.]

Characteristics	Total occupied units	Housing unit characteristics		Household characteristics				Regions			
		New construction 4 years	Manufactured/ mobile homes	Black alone	Hispanic	Elderly (65 years and over)	Below poverty level	Northeast	Midwest	South	West
Total	35,378	941	1,421	7,446	6,300	4,623	9,334	7,073	7,119	12,392	8,794
Rooms											
1 room	326	2	–	45	54	79	134	106	53	30	137
2 rooms	879	10	2	147	125	160	297	248	128	186	317
3 rooms	7,675	160	55	1,479	1,282	1,763	2,378	1,932	1,670	2,231	1,841
4 rooms	11,354	237	539	2,363	2,262	1,340	2,968	2,130	2,312	3,997	2,915
5 rooms	8,212	260	550	1,984	1,551	779	2,041	1,423	1,608	3,303	1,878
6 rooms	4,232	161	170	954	691	312	1,007	791	817	1,685	939
7 rooms	1,735	75	96	285	247	116	355	265	352	613	505
8 rooms	622	18	4	129	65	55	89	110	121	229	162
9 rooms	214	10	5	41	18	7	51	37	38	64	74
10 rooms or more	130	8	–	18	6	12	14	31	19	55	25
Rooms used for business											
Business only											
1 or more rooms with direct access	2,398	78	100	553	468	318	718	419	417	996	565
1 or more rooms, no direct access	1,359	52	33	272	177	148	221	261	258	461	379
Not reported	152	–	2	40	10	27	44	59	22	45	26
Business and other use											
1 or more rooms	4,283	116	119	771	615	359	783	649	836	1,501	1,297
Not reported	181	4	3	44	19	25	54	74	34	47	26
Bedrooms											
None	744	12	2	100	113	149	273	209	132	92	311
1	9,720	185	60	1,927	1,626	2,123	2,900	2,447	2,026	2,883	2,364
2	14,200	314	642	2,989	2,762	1,586	3,450	2,684	3,055	4,993	3,468
3	8,359	341	634	1,963	1,460	598	2,081	1,327	1,472	3,561	1,999
4 or more	2,354	88	83	467	339	167	630	406	434	863	652
Complete bathrooms											
None	229	–	3	42	42	22	90	73	42	43	70
1	22,894	284	612	4,984	4,288	3,469	6,794	5,713	5,093	6,893	5,196
1 1/2	3,575	36	136	853	509	383	872	654	895	1,261	765
2 or more	8,680	621	670	1,567	1,461	749	1,577	632	1,090	4,196	2,762
Square footage of unit											
Single detached and manufactured/mobile homes	11,176	272	1,421	1,890	1,790	1,081	2,700	1,096	2,181	4,985	2,914
Less than 500	220	–	47	21	70	27	84	28	18	101	73
500 to 749	686	4	186	115	164	101	209	67	150	318	151
750 to 999	1,495	–	449	298	251	145	464	122	354	695	324
1,000 to 1,499	3,441	44	359	537	575	323	850	219	647	1,641	934
1,500 to 1,999	2,235	74	166	353	279	203	484	211	367	979	679
2,000 to 2,499	1,134	79	19	149	118	87	164	104	228	487	314
2,500 to 2,999	429	25	4	102	34	45	55	49	65	196	118
3,000 to 3,999	301	9	3	38	41	41	52	49	83	88	81
4,000 or more	243	8	17	19	40	23	36	54	43	77	68
Not reported	992	29	171	257	218	86	302	193	225	403	171
Median	1300	1904	980	1280	1200	1205	1200	1500	1248	1280	1400
Lot size											
1-unit structures[1]	12,823	342	1,421	2,338	2,040	1,255	3,135	1,554	2,482	5,510	3,276
Less than 1/8 acre	2,717	78	287	577	600	269	707	435	503	859	920
1/8 up to 1/4 acre	4,022	112	318	796	766	368	1,067	320	863	1,548	1,291
1/4 up to 1/2 acre	2,084	75	154	437	317	198	471	207	390	1,030	457
1/2 up to 1 acre	1,162	23	156	194	92	100	223	171	146	683	162
1 up to 5 acres	2,120	26	399	291	202	241	503	301	388	1,106	325
5 up to 10 acres	205	7	43	9	18	29	43	39	44	94	28
10 acres or more	513	21	64	34	46	50	122	82	149	190	93
Median	0.22	0.21	0.32	0.14	0.13	0.23	0.15	0.25	0.20	0.25	0.13

Table 3-11. Size of Unit and Lot, Renter-Occupied Units, 2009—*Continued*

[Numbers in thousands.]

Characteristics	Total occupied units	Housing unit characteristics		Household characteristics				Regions			
		New construction 4 years	Manufactured/ mobile homes	Black alone	Hispanic	Elderly (65 years and over)	Below poverty level	Northeast	Midwest	South	West
Persons per room											
0.50 or less	22,394	631	768	4,595	2,455	4,123	5,375	4,537	4,923	7,858	5,076
0.51 to 1.00	11,484	296	576	2,595	2,982	486	3,260	2,264	2,047	4,104	3,069
1.01 to 1.50	1,220	14	71	225	684	7	553	211	125	387	498
1.51 or more	279	–	6	31	179	7	146	60	25	43	151
Persons per bedroom											
0.50 or less	6,097	184	341	1,251	497	1,293	1,488	1,052	1,405	2,392	1,248
0.51 to 1.00	16,951	459	555	3,600	2,069	2,780	4,165	3,524	3,633	5,868	3,926
1.01 to 1.50	4,863	162	284	1,155	1,071	112	1,258	865	918	1,853	1,227
1.51 or more	6,722	123	239	1,341	2,550	290	2,150	1,423	1,031	2,187	2,082
No bedrooms	744	12	2	100	113	149	273	209	132	92	311
Square feet per person											
Single detached and manufactured/mobile homes	11,176	272	1,421	1,890	1,790	1,081	2,700	1,096	2,181	4,985	2,914
Less than 200	548	3	102	117	251	16	256	56	64	278	149
200 to 299	1,331	10	275	262	401	34	426	83	185	658	405
300 to 399	1,394	25	206	231	244	46	333	110	281	634	369
400 to 499	1,272	32	191	192	193	84	274	88	245	531	407
500 to 599	1,097	39	92	170	133	107	220	66	215	525	292
600 to 699	894	16	59	133	62	63	174	83	219	378	213
700 to 799	591	25	77	90	56	79	107	48	133	249	162
800 to 899	509	30	70	119	43	60	107	62	88	228	131
900 to 999	357	4	60	39	23	35	73	38	102	171	47
1,000 to 1,499	1,293	34	79	165	110	250	227	127	228	594	344
1,500 or more	899	25	39	114	58	220	201	143	196	336	224
Not reported	992	29	171	257	218	86	302	193	225	403	171
Median	520	625	400	500	340	900	450	625	567	500	500

– = Zero or rounds to zero.
[1] = Does not include cooperatives or condominiums.

Source: U.S. Census Bureau, American Housing Survey

Table 3-12. Selected Equipment and Plumbing, Occupied Units, 2009

[Numbers in thousands.]

Characteristics	Total occupied units	Tenure		Housing unit characteristics		Household characteristics				Regions			
		Owner	Renter	New construction 4 years	Manufactured/ mobile homes	Black alone	Hispanic	Elderly (65 years or over)	Below poverty level	Northeast	Midwest	South	West
Total	111,806	76,428	35,378	4,771	6,839	13,993	12,739	23,095	15,739	20,451	25,368	41,586	24,401
Equipment[1]													
Lacking complete kitchen facilities	1,751	378	1,374	39	28	315	329	243	461	487	385	406	474
With complete kitchen (sink, refrigerator, and oven or burners)	110,054	76,050	34,004	4,732	6,811	13,679	12,410	22,852	15,277	19,964	24,984	41,180	23,927
Kitchen sink	111,510	76,329	35,180	4,766	6,830	13,953	12,695	23,019	15,638	20,344	25,308	41,532	24,326
Refrigerator	111,530	76,336	35,193	4,762	6,824	13,941	12,702	23,049	15,639	20,372	25,328	41,502	24,328
Cooking stove or range	111,038	76,153	34,886	4,761	6,790	13,878	12,622	22,906	15,451	20,329	25,207	41,347	24,155
Burners, no stove or range	208	109	99	3	15	28	30	37	52	29	32	79	69
Microwave oven only	378	127	251	3	26	60	64	102	159	40	103	108	127
Dishwasher	73,584	57,191	16,393	4,526	3,324	6,430	6,062	13,973	6,250	11,900	15,487	28,691	17,505
Washing machine	93,372	73,826	19,545	4,599	6,395	9,883	8,943	19,751	10,370	15,327	21,537	36,611	19,896
Clothes dryer	90,905	72,562	18,343	4,561	6,210	9,104	8,208	18,982	9,454	14,512	21,327	35,578	19,489
Disposal in kitchen sink	56,531	40,597	15,933	3,525	1,058	5,604	6,332	10,495	5,435	5,332	13,048	20,217	17,934
Trash compactor	3,896	3,166	730	302	55	460	378	885	294	512	610	1,569	1,206
Air conditioning:[2]													
Central	72,808	54,647	18,161	4,240	4,406	8,668	7,312	14,807	8,237	6,600	17,684	35,825	12,699
Additional central	5,629	4,709	920	576	269	607	576	986	541	331	656	3,676	966
1 room unit	11,532	5,303	6,229	71	793	1,727	1,515	2,707	2,696	3,895	3,186	1,765	2,686
2 room units	8,132	4,800	3,332	85	713	1,261	1,117	1,672	1,426	3,846	1,717	1,891	677
3 room units or more	4,918	3,604	1,314	30	281	718	685	884	561	2,758	575	1,323	263
Safety equipment[1]													
Working smoke detector													
Yes	104,362	71,797	32,565	4,656	6,263	13,034	11,216	21,165	13,929	19,479	24,153	37,942	22,788
Powered by:													
Electricity	8,149	5,620	2,528	434	772	951	789	2,128	1,186	1,680	1,534	3,238	1,696
Batteries	66,536	43,210	23,326	1,626	3,547	9,365	8,243	13,996	10,050	12,985	16,379	22,831	14,341
Both	28,421	22,461	5,960	2,496	1,909	2,531	2,084	4,684	2,418	4,654	5,971	11,370	6,426
Not reported	1,257	506	751	100	35	187	100	356	276	160	269	503	325
No	6,157	3,686	2,472	77	504	839	1,447	1,599	1,586	739	974	3,045	1,399
Not reported	1,286	945	341	38	72	121	76	331	224	233	241	598	214
Batteries replaced in last 6 months[3]													
Yes	71,505	50,073	21,432	2,808	4,022	8,871	7,869	14,146	9,341	14,175	17,336	25,312	14,682
No	21,466	14,678	6,788	1,257	1,328	2,809	2,253	4,218	2,718	3,133	4,557	8,179	5,597
Not reported	1,986	920	1,066	57	106	217	205	317	410	331	457	710	488
Fire extinguisher purchased or recharged in the last 2 years	49,902	37,922	11,980	2,298	2,983	5,518	4,304	9,625	5,422	9,405	11,183	19,118	10,196
Sprinkler system inside home	5,167	2,086	3,081	773	69	830	533	1,313	877	938	877	1,845	1,507
Working carbon monoxide detector	40,698	31,691	9,007	1,833	1,506	4,395	3,121	8,250	4,055	12,483	12,688	9,927	5,600
Main heating equipment													
Warm-air furnace	71,141	51,691	19,450	3,340	5,040	8,625	7,125	14,124	8,970	8,925	20,671	25,268	16,277
Steam or hot water system	12,506	7,494	5,012	109	20	1,778	1,381	2,910	1,789	9,088	2,015	592	811
Electric heat pump	13,264	9,764	3,500	1,095	1,009	1,734	1,403	2,670	1,511	336	706	10,785	1,436
Built-in electric units	4,761	2,120	2,641	77	83	453	444	1,115	890	1,159	1,134	827	1,641
Floor, wall, or other built-in hot-air units without ducts	4,802	2,043	2,760	68	152	593	1,438	951	1,140	435	388	1,154	2,825
Room heaters with flue	950	580	370	16	58	147	84	316	253	124	103	478	244
Room heaters without flue	1,109	694	414	8	125	360	219	340	345	24	52	992	41
Portable electric heaters	1,167	535	632	6	175	172	394	224	418	29	65	769	304
Stoves	1,035	845	190	14	92	29	61	233	200	226	158	341	310
Fireplaces with inserts	172	155	18	–	2	8	11	56	4	24	34	38	76
Fireplaces without inserts	43	35	7	–	5	2	3	16	5	3	6	16	18
Other	386	232	154	22	55	58	59	63	111	57	35	212	82
Cooking stove	84	34	49	–	10	12	37	23	26	18	–	53	13
None	386	206	180	17	12	21	82	56	76	3	3	58	321
Other heating equipment[1]													
Warm-air furnace	251	225	26	14	16	5	4	53	21	50	62	65	74
Steam or hot water system	56	51	5	3	–	2	3	12	7	27	18	7	4
Electric heat pump	97	91	6	9	16	2	11	26	–	9	31	36	20
Built-in electric units	1,882	1,428	454	54	75	166	135	464	244	316	398	640	528
Floor, wall, or other built-in hot-air units without ducts	75	63	12	14	–	3	7	21	15	12	16	28	20
Room heaters with flue	822	716	106	19	57	58	43	240	86	200	131	310	182
Room heaters without flue	1,471	1,207	264	20	236	156	70	381	226	218	370	745	138
Portable electric heaters	13,719	9,886	3,832	335	854	1,712	1,318	3,028	1,773	2,188	4,082	4,406	3,043
Stoves	4,165	3,740	425	99	306	160	197	976	371	1,231	863	1,010	1,061
Fireplaces with inserts	5,205	4,742	464	356	314	330	220	1,036	265	692	1,106	1,942	1,466
Fireplaces without inserts	5,765	4,869	896	370	169	563	547	941	449	555	903	2,542	1,766
Other	790	707	83	52	56	29	22	178	32	197	192	225	176
Cooking stove	66	50	17	2	3	4	7	18	12	9	14	29	14
None	80,034	51,171	28,863	3,521	4,886	10,982	10,246	16,321	12,297	15,135	17,772	30,637	16,490

Table 3-12. Selected Equipment and Plumbing, Occupied Units, 2009—*Continued*

[Numbers in thousands.]

Characteristics	Total occupied units	Tenure		Housing unit characteristics		Household characteristics				Regions			
		Owner	Renter	New construction 4 years	Manufactured/ mobile homes	Black alone	Hispanic	Elderly (65 years or over)	Below poverty level	Northeast	Midwest	South	West
Plumbing													
With all plumbing facilities	110,574	75,852	34,722	4,768	6,782	13,768	12,555	22,815	15,446	20,040	25,128	41,249	24,158
Lacking some or all plumbing facilities[1]	1,232	576	656	3	57	226	184	280	292	411	241	337	243
No hot piped water	113	54	58	–	7	33	10	27	54	39	25	43	6
No bathtub and no shower	113	37	75	–	–	22	24	25	52	33	21	33	26
No flush toilet	102	37	64	–	–	16	21	18	42	29	20	23	29
No exclusive use	1,065	507	558	3	50	188	157	248	216	364	206	282	213
Primary source of water													
Public system or private company	98,027	64,372	33,655	4,117	4,839	13,435	12,224	19,774	14,345	17,101	21,435	36,594	22,897
Well serving 1 to 5 units	13,430	11,769	1,660	642	1,941	543	495	3,221	1,315	3,275	3,878	4,821	1,455
Drilled	12,175	10,772	1,404	553	1,726	476	451	2,962	1,167	2,940	3,566	4,321	1,348
Dug	822	700	122	35	146	52	26	220	116	244	192	316	70
Not reported	432	298	135	54	69	14	18	38	32	92	120	183	38
Other	349	287	63	12	59	15	20	101	78	75	55	171	48
Safety of primary source of water													
Selected primary water sources[4]	111,772	76,406	35,366	4,768	6,839	13,983	12,726	23,091	15,731	20,448	25,368	41,569	24,385
Safe to drink	102,247	71,152	31,095	4,362	6,114	12,518	10,261	21,669	13,718	18,913	23,950	38,041	21,344
Not safe to drink	8,412	4,530	3,882	344	646	1,362	2,378	1,203	1,764	1,304	1,243	3,074	2,790
Safety not reported	1,113	724	389	61	79	102	87	220	249	231	176	455	251
Source of drinking water													
Primary source not safe to drink	8,412	4,530	3,882	344	646	1,362	2,378	1,203	1,764	1,304	1,243	3,074	2,790
Drinking and primary water source the same	1,486	976	509	64	109	224	309	249	292	272	307	578	329
Public or private system	1,445	941	505	60	103	224	304	241	292	261	294	562	329
Individual well	40	35	5	4	6	–	5	8	1	11	13	16	–
Spring	–	–	–	–	–	–	–	–	–	–	–	–	–
Cistern	–	–	–	–	–	–	–	–	–	–	–	–	–
Stream or lake	–	–	–	–	–	–	–	–	–	–	–	–	–
Other	–	–	–	–	–	–	–	–	–	–	–	–	–
Drinking and primary water source different	6,926	3,554	3,372	280	537	1,138	2,069	954	1,471	1,032	936	2,497	2,462
Public or private system	10	8	2	–	–	–	–	–	2	5	2	3	–
Individual well	40	25	15	–	11	8	10	14	7	6	4	24	7
Spring	129	69	61	3	10	24	20	25	34	71	9	37	13
Cistern	25	16	9	–	3	–	12	6	5	2	2	3	18
Stream or lake	10	4	6	3	–	–	–	–	1	–	1	6	3
Commercial bottled water	5,421	2,620	2,801	217	458	956	1,733	738	1,237	731	718	1,977	1,995
Other	1,291	812	479	57	55	151	294	171	186	217	200	448	426
Source of drinking water not reported	–	–	–	–	–	–	–	–	–	–	–	–	–
Means of sewage disposal													
Public sewer	89,467	56,736	32,732	3,558	3,153	12,961	11,791	17,583	13,435	16,263	20,432	31,288	21,484
Septic tank, cesspool, or chemical toilet	22,307	19,667	2,640	1,213	3,686	1,025	945	5,506	2,289	4,185	4,930	10,279	2,913
Other	31	25	6	–	–	7	3	6	15	3	6	18	3

– = Zero or rounds to zero.
[1] = Figures may not add to total because more than one category may apply to a unit.
[2] = Includes only those who responded they had some type of air conditioning.
[3] = Restricted to units with smoke detector powered by both electricity and batteries, or batteries only.
[4] = Excludes units where primary source of drinking water is commercial bottled water.

Source: U.S. Census Bureau, American Housing Survey

Table 3-13. Selected Equipment and Plumbing, Owner-Occupied Units, 2009

[Numbers in thousands.]

Characteristics	Total occupied units	Housing unit characteristics		Household characteristics				Regions			
		New construction 4 years	Manufactured/ mobile homes	Black alone	Hispanic	Elderly (65 years and over)	Below poverty level	Northeast	Midwest	South	West
Total	76,428	3,830	5,418	6,547	6,439	18,472	6,405	13,378	18,249	29,193	15,607
Equipment[1]											
Lacking complete kitchen facilities	378	13	22	29	53	99	65	106	83	120	69
With complete kitchen (sink, refrigerator, and oven or burners)	76,050	3,817	5,396	6,518	6,386	18,373	6,340	13,272	18,167	29,074	15,538
Kitchen sink	76,329	3,827	5,409	6,537	6,423	18,437	6,386	13,350	18,221	29,158	15,601
Refrigerator	76,336	3,821	5,409	6,540	6,435	18,451	6,384	13,364	18,232	29,151	15,589
Cooking stove or range	76,153	3,824	5,382	6,522	6,408	18,402	6,331	13,344	18,194	29,084	15,530
Burners, no stove or range	109	–	12	2	13	26	11	14	11	50	34
Microwave oven only	127	2	20	18	14	28	47	16	30	45	36
Dishwasher	57,191	3,651	2,912	3,579	3,722	12,351	3,298	9,885	12,704	21,879	12,723
Washing machine	73,826	3,780	5,169	6,142	6,081	17,696	5,963	12,576	17,763	28,400	15,088
Clothes dryer	72,562	3,771	5,056	5,806	5,783	17,191	5,599	12,221	17,620	27,858	14,864
Disposal in kitchen sink	40,597	2,786	903	2,570	3,485	8,512	2,159	4,110	9,911	14,506	12,071
Trash compactor	3,166	249	39	261	254	799	150	375	500	1,265	1,026
Air conditioning[2]											
Central	54,647	3,442	3,589	4,482	4,500	12,505	3,860	5,371	14,165	25,902	9,209
Additional central	4,709	516	221	358	414	884	307	298	572	3,018	821
1 room unit	5,303	49	591	537	342	1,670	760	1,820	1,324	819	1,340
2 room units	4,800	59	541	542	410	1,310	598	2,250	1,071	1,121	358
3 room units or more	3,604	24	208	481	362	791	275	2,109	422	902	171
Safety equipment[1]											
Working smoke detector											
Yes	71,797	3,730	5,032	6,092	5,749	16,858	5,531	12,821	17,411	26,833	14,733
Powered by:											
Electricity	5,620	337	683	492	399	1,505	516	1,103	1,081	2,317	1,119
Batteries	43,210	1,186	2,666	4,099	3,967	11,264	3,809	8,094	11,393	15,160	8,564
Both	22,461	2,143	1,652	1,458	1,361	3,900	1,146	3,547	4,852	9,127	4,935
Not reported	506	64	31	43	23	190	60	77	85	230	115
No	3,686	67	336	413	647	1,343	744	389	660	1,908	729
Not reported	945	33	50	43	42	271	130	169	179	452	145
Batteries replaced in last 6 months[3]											
Yes	50,073	2,298	3,215	4,094	4,107	11,405	3,737	9,533	12,680	18,220	9,641
No	14,678	1,008	1,027	1,404	1,162	3,513	1,150	1,962	3,322	5,737	3,657
Not reported	920	23	75	59	59	245	69	147	243	330	200
Fire extinguisher purchased or recharged in the last 2 years	37,922	1,914	2,469	3,095	2,567	8,329	2,702	7,146	8,860	14,434	7,481
Sprinkler system inside home	2,086	358	46	220	180	456	150	295	308	766	717
Working carbon monoxide detector	31,691	1,579	1,264	2,453	1,727	7,020	1,971	8,757	10,421	8,130	4,383
Main heating equipment											
Warm-air furnace	51,691	2,701	3,986	4,336	4,196	11,881	3,987	6,459	15,653	17,862	11,717
Steam or hot water system	7,494	80	20	649	344	2,083	524	5,541	1,072	388	494
Electric heat pump	9,764	877	832	844	843	2,222	716	260	547	7,995	962
Built-in electric units	2,120	44	62	118	106	627	165	545	460	502	612
Floor, wall, or other built-in hot-air units without ducts	2,043	54	112	174	486	602	302	200	177	678	987
Room heaters with flue	580	13	48	78	33	253	120	71	69	303	138
Room heaters without flue	694	8	94	218	132	286	188	13	29	633	19
Portable electric heaters	535	6	119	71	152	143	152	8	43	364	120
Stoves	845	14	80	27	44	197	143	213	132	266	234
Fireplaces with inserts	155	–	2	8	9	55	4	21	34	32	68
Fireplaces without inserts	35	–	5	2	3	16	5	3	6	16	11
Other	232	20	42	13	30	49	55	41	28	106	57
Cooking stove	34	–	7	4	26	17	15	–	–	29	5
None	206	14	8	7	35	42	29	3	–	19	183
Other heating equipment[1]											
Warm-air furnace	225	12	16	5	4	49	16	47	55	53	70
Steam or hot water system	51	3	–	2	–	12	5	27	18	4	3
Electric heat pump	91	9	13	2	8	26	–	9	31	31	20
Built-in electric units	1,428	46	61	95	76	381	125	256	331	492	348
Floor, wall, or other built-in hot-air units without ducts	63	14	–	–	4	18	7	9	13	28	13
Room heaters with flue	716	19	51	47	24	220	56	186	122	273	136
Room heaters without flue	1,207	20	207	114	46	335	154	184	315	611	98
Portable electric heaters	9,886	292	675	966	759	2,570	891	1,533	3,130	3,240	1,983
Stoves	3,740	85	238	126	154	942	270	1,142	806	890	901
Fireplaces with inserts	4,742	316	260	263	175	1,002	182	660	1,035	1,751	1,297
Fireplaces without inserts	4,869	345	154	455	427	909	328	499	803	2,213	1,354
Other	707	48	52	18	16	163	15	177	170	205	155
Cooking stove	50	2	3	–	3	18	3	7	9	26	7
None	51,171	2,708	3,814	4,653	4,877	12,422	4,454	9,041	11,972	20,356	9,802

Table 3-13. Selected Equipment and Plumbing, Owner-Occupied Units, 2009—*Continued*

[Numbers in thousands.]

Characteristics	Total occupied units	Housing unit characteristics		Household characteristics				Regions			
		New construction 4 years	Manufactured/ mobile homes	Black alone	Hispanic	Elderly (65 years and over)	Below poverty level	Northeast	Midwest	South	West
Plumbing											
With all plumbing facilities	75,852	3,830	5,381	6,466	6,396	18,285	6,311	13,225	18,122	28,994	15,510
Lacking some or all plumbing facilities[1]	576	–	37	81	43	187	94	153	127	199	97
No hot piped water	54	–	3	14	3	20	22	5	14	30	6
No bathtub and no shower	37	–	–	3	1	14	20	3	11	24	–
No flush toilet	37	–	–	3	–	11	19	2	13	19	3
No exclusive use	507	–	33	67	38	165	64	147	111	162	87
Primary source of water											
Public system or private company	64,372	3,238	3,733	6,117	6,050	15,385	5,356	10,416	14,720	24,892	14,345
Well serving 1 to 5 units	11,769	580	1,635	422	373	2,991	998	2,904	3,479	4,164	1,222
Drilled	10,772	495	1,447	372	352	2,753	902	2,615	3,234	3,781	1,142
Dug	700	34	131	44	18	202	86	219	162	257	62
Not reported	298	51	57	7	3	36	9	70	84	126	17
Other	287	12	50	8	16	95	52	58	50	138	41
Safety of primary source of water											
Selected primary water sources[4]	76,406	3,827	5,418	6,541	6,426	18,468	6,402	13,378	18,249	29,184	15,594
Safe to drink	71,152	3,507	4,865	5,942	5,334	17,478	5,689	12,571	17,368	27,081	14,132
Not safe to drink	4,530	267	490	568	1,058	816	591	661	773	1,798	1,299
Safety not reported	724	53	63	31	34	174	121	146	109	305	164
Source of drinking water											
Primary source not safe to drink	4,530	267	490	568	1,058	816	591	661	773	1,798	1,299
Drinking and primary water source the same	976	62	91	124	161	200	131	177	207	392	200
Public or private system	941	58	85	124	156	192	131	168	194	379	200
Individual well	35	4	6	–	5	8	1	9	13	13	–
Spring	–	–	–	–	–	–	–	–	–	–	–
Cistern	–	–	–	–	–	–	–	–	–	–	–
Stream or lake	–	–	–	–	–	–	–	–	–	–	–
Other	–	–	–	–	–	–	–	–	–	–	–
Drinking and primary water source different	3,554	205	398	444	897	616	460	484	566	1,406	1,098
Public or private system	8	–	–	–	–	–	–	5	–	3	–
Individual well	25	–	7	2	4	11	1	4	4	10	7
Spring	69	3	6	11	6	14	16	30	6	26	6
Cistern	16	–	3	–	6	4	5	2	2	3	10
Stream or lake	4	3	–	–	–	–	1	–	1	3	–
Commercial bottled water	2,620	148	336	364	717	462	387	333	416	1,070	800
Other	812	51	46	67	163	126	49	109	137	291	275
Source of drinking water not reported	–	–	–	–	–	–	–	–	–	–	–
Means of sewage disposal											
Public sewer	56,736	2,700	2,363	5,702	5,697	13,296	4,670	9,662	13,797	20,173	13,103
Septic tank, cesspool, or chemical toilet	19,667	1,130	3,055	842	742	5,170	1,724	3,716	4,447	9,004	2,500
Other	25	–	–	3	–	6	12	–	5	16	3

– = Zero or rounds to zero.
[1] = Figures may not add to total because more than one category may apply to a unit.
[2] = Includes only those who responded they had some type of air conditioning.
[3] = Restricted to units with smoke detector powered by both electricity and batteries, or batteries only.
[4] = Excludes units where primary source of drinking water is commercial bottled water.

Source: U.S. Census Bureau, American Housing Survey

Table 3-14. Selected Equipment and Plumbing, Renter-Occupied Units, 2009

[Numbers in thousands.]

Characteristics	Total occupied units	Housing unit characteristics		Household characteristics				Regions			
		New construction 4 years	Manufactured / mobile homes	Black alone	Hispanic	Elderly (65 years and over)	Below poverty level	Northeast	Midwest	South	West
Total	35,378	941	1,421	7,446	6,300	4,623	9,334	7,073	7,119	12,392	8,794
Equipment[1]											
Lacking complete kitchen facilities	1,374	26	6	286	276	144	396	381	302	286	404
With complete kitchen (sink, refrigerator, and oven or burners)	34,004	915	1,415	7,161	6,024	4,479	8,937	6,692	6,817	12,106	8,389
Kitchen sink	35,180	939	1,421	7,417	6,273	4,582	9,251	6,994	7,087	12,374	8,725
Refrigerator	35,193	941	1,415	7,401	6,267	4,598	9,255	7,007	7,097	12,351	8,738
Cooking stove or range	34,886	937	1,409	7,357	6,213	4,504	9,121	6,985	7,013	12,263	8,625
Burners, no stove or range	99	3	3	26	18	12	41	14	21	29	34
Microwave oven only	251	1	6	42	50	74	112	24	73	64	91
Dishwasher	16,393	874	413	2,851	2,340	1,621	2,953	2,016	2,783	6,813	4,782
Washing machine	19,545	819	1,225	3,741	2,862	2,056	4,407	2,751	3,775	8,211	4,808
Clothes dryer	18,343	791	1,153	3,297	2,425	1,791	3,855	2,291	3,707	7,720	4,625
Disposal in kitchen sink	15,933	739	155	3,034	2,847	1,983	3,276	1,222	3,137	5,711	5,863
Trash compactor	730	54	15	199	124	86	145	137	110	304	180
Air conditioning[2]											
Central	18,161	797	817	4,186	2,812	2,302	4,377	1,229	3,519	9,923	3,490
Additional central	920	60	48	249	162	102	235	33	84	658	145
1 room unit	6,229	22	202	1,190	1,173	1,036	1,936	2,075	1,862	946	1,346
2 room units	3,332	26	172	719	707	362	828	1,596	647	770	319
3 room units or more	1,314	6	73	237	323	93	286	649	153	421	92
Safety equipment[1]											
Working smoke detector											
Yes	32,565	926	1,231	6,942	5,467	4,307	8,398	6,659	6,742	11,109	8,055
Powered by:											
Electricity	2,528	97	89	459	390	623	670	577	453	921	577
Batteries	23,326	440	881	5,266	4,276	2,733	6,241	4,892	4,986	7,671	5,777
Both	5,960	353	257	1,073	723	785	1,272	1,107	1,119	2,244	1,491
Not reported	751	36	4	145	78	166	216	83	184	273	210
No	2,472	10	168	426	799	256	842	350	314	1,137	669
Not reported	341	5	21	78	34	59	93	64	62	146	69
Batteries replaced in last 6 months[3]											
Yes	21,432	510	807	4,777	3,761	2,741	5,603	4,643	4,656	7,093	5,040
No	6,788	250	301	1,405	1,091	705	1,568	1,171	1,235	2,442	1,940
Not reported	1,066	34	31	158	146	72	341	184	214	380	288
Fire extinguisher purchased or recharged in the last 2 years	11,980	385	513	2,423	1,738	1,296	2,719	2,259	2,323	4,684	2,715
Sprinkler system inside home	3,081	415	23	611	353	857	726	643	570	1,078	790
Working carbon monoxide detector	9,007	254	242	1,943	1,393	1,230	2,084	3,726	2,268	1,797	1,216
Main heating equipment											
Warm-air furnace	19,450	639	1,054	4,289	2,930	2,243	4,983	2,466	5,017	7,406	4,560
Steam or hot water system	5,012	29	–	1,129	1,036	827	1,264	3,547	943	204	318
Electric heat pump	3,500	218	178	890	561	447	795	75	160	2,790	474
Built-in electric units	2,641	33	21	336	338	488	725	614	674	325	1,029
Floor, wall, or other built-in hot-air units without ducts	2,760	15	39	420	952	349	838	235	211	476	1,838
Room heaters with flue	370	3	11	69	51	63	133	54	34	176	107
Room heaters without flue	414	–	31	142	87	53	157	11	23	358	22
Portable electric heaters	632	–	55	102	241	81	266	22	22	405	184
Stoves	190	–	12	2	16	36	57	14	25	76	76
Fireplaces with inserts	18	–	–	–	2	1	–	3	–	6	9
Fireplaces without inserts	7	–	–	–	–	–	–	–	–	–	7
Other	154	2	12	45	29	14	57	16	8	106	24
Cooking stove	49	–	3	9	11	5	11	18	–	24	8
None	180	3	5	14	47	14	47	–	3	39	138
Other heating equipment[1]											
Warm-air furnace	26	2	–	–	–	4	5	3	7	11	4
Steam or hot water system	5	–	–	–	3	–	2	–	–	3	2
Electric heat pump	6	–	3	–	3	–	–	–	–	6	–
Built-in electric units	454	8	15	71	60	83	119	60	66	148	180
Floor, wall, or other built-in hot-air units without ducts	12	–	–	3	3	3	7	3	3	–	7
Room heaters with flue	106	–	6	11	19	20	30	15	9	37	46
Room heaters without flue	264	–	29	43	24	46	71	34	55	134	41
Portable electric heaters	3,832	42	179	747	559	458	882	655	952	1,166	1,059
Stoves	425	13	69	34	43	33	102	89	57	119	160
Fireplaces with inserts	464	41	54	68	44	35	83	32	72	191	169
Fireplaces without inserts	896	25	15	109	121	32	121	56	99	329	412
Other	83	4	4	11	7	15	18	20	22	20	21
Cooking stove	17	–	–	4	4	–	9	2	4	3	6
None	28,863	813	1,072	6,329	5,369	3,899	7,843	6,094	5,800	10,281	6,688

Table 3-14. Selected Equipment and Plumbing, Renter-Occupied Units, 2009—*Continued*

[Numbers in thousands.]

Characteristics	Total occupied units	Housing unit characteristics		Household characteristics				Regions			
		New construction 4 years	Manufactured/ mobile homes	Black alone	Hispanic	Elderly (65 years and over)	Below poverty level	Northeast	Midwest	South	West
Plumbing											
With all plumbing facilities	34,722	938	1,400	7,302	6,160	4,530	9,135	6,814	7,005	12,254	8,648
Lacking some or all plumbing facilities[1]	656	3	21	145	140	93	198	259	114	138	146
No hot piped water	58	–	3	19	7	8	32	35	11	13	–
No bathtub and no shower	75	–	–	19	22	12	32	30	10	9	26
No flush toilet	64	–	–	13	21	7	24	27	7	4	26
No exclusive use	558	3	17	121	119	83	153	217	95	120	125
Primary source of water											
Public system or private company	33,655	879	1,106	7,318	6,174	4,388	8,990	6,685	6,715	11,702	8,552
Well serving 1 to 5 units	1,660	62	306	121	123	229	318	371	399	657	234
Drilled	1,404	58	279	105	99	209	265	324	332	541	206
Dug	122	2	15	8	8	18	30	25	30	59	8
Not reported	135	3	12	8	16	2	23	22	36	56	20
Other	63	–	9	7	4	5	26	17	5	34	8
Safety of primary source of water											
Selected primary water sources[4]	35,366	941	1,421	7,442	6,300	4,623	9,329	7,070	7,119	12,386	8,791
Safe to drink	31,095	855	1,249	6,576	4,927	4,191	8,029	6,342	6,582	10,959	7,212
Not safe to drink	3,882	77	156	795	1,320	387	1,173	643	470	1,276	1,492
Safety not reported	389	8	16	71	53	46	128	85	67	150	87
Source of drinking water											
Primary source not safe to drink	3,882	77	156	795	1,320	387	1,173	643	470	1,276	1,492
Drinking and primary water source the same	509	3	17	100	148	49	161	95	100	186	128
Public or private system	505	3	17	100	148	49	161	93	100	183	128
Individual well	5	–	–	–	–	–	–	2	–	3	–
Spring	–	–	–	–	–	–	–	–	–	–	–
Cistern	–	–	–	–	–	–	–	–	–	–	–
Stream or lake	–	–	–	–	–	–	–	–	–	–	–
Other	–	–	–	–	–	–	–	–	–	–	–
Drinking and primary water source different	3,372	75	139	695	1,172	338	1,012	548	370	1,091	1,364
Public or private system	2	–	–	–	–	–	2	–	2	–	–
Individual well	15	–	4	6	6	3	6	2	–	13	–
Spring	61	–	4	13	13	11	18	40	3	11	6
Cistern	9	–	–	–	6	2	–	–	–	–	9
Stream or lake	6	–	–	–	–	–	–	–	–	3	3
Commercial bottled water	2,801	69	122	591	1,016	276	849	397	302	907	1,195
Other	479	6	9	84	132	45	137	108	62	157	151
Source of drinking water not reported	–	–	–	–	–	–	–	–	–	–	–
Means of sewage disposal											
Public sewer	32,732	858	790	7,259	6,094	4,287	8,765	6,602	6,635	11,114	8,381
Septic tank, cesspool, or chemical toilet	2,640	83	631	184	203	336	566	468	483	1,276	413
Other	6	–	–	3	3	–	3	3	1	2	–

– = Zero or rounds to zero.
[1] = Figures may not add to total because more than one category may apply to a unit.
[2] = Includes only those who responded they had some type of air conditioning.
[3] = Restricted to units with smoke detector powered by both electricity and batteries, or batteries only.
[4] = Excludes units where primary source of drinking water is commercial bottled water.

Source: U.S. Census Bureau, American Housing Survey

Table 3-15. Fuels, Occupied Units, 2009

[Numbers in thousands.]

Characteristics	Total occupied units	Tenure		Housing unit characteristics		Household characteristics				Regions			
		Owner	Renter	New construction 4 years	Manufactured/ mobile homes	Black alone	Hispanic	Elderly (65 years or over)	Below poverty level	Northeast	Midwest	South	West
Total	111,806	76,428	35,378	4,771	6,839	13,993	12,739	23,095	15,739	20,451	25,368	41,586	24,401
Main house heating fuel													
Housing units with heating fuel	111,420	76,222	35,198	4,755	6,826	13,973	12,657	23,039	15,662	20,448	25,366	41,527	24,079
Electricity	37,851	22,219	15,632	2,370	3,559	5,652	4,951	7,173	6,522	2,448	4,362	24,280	6,761
Piped gas	56,806	41,233	15,573	1,991	1,508	6,925	6,558	11,596	6,925	9,941	17,720	13,355	15,791
Bottled gas	5,817	4,889	929	259	1,107	435	267	1,521	758	691	2,163	2,179	784
Fuel oil	8,214	5,693	2,521	57	155	812	731	2,118	986	6,613	564	844	192
Kerosene or other liquid fuel	599	444	154	21	299	97	57	141	161	236	12	322	29
Coal or coke	98	91	7	3	–	–	–	11	10	80	8	5	6
Wood	1,780	1,503	277	42	192	43	78	416	266	412	418	501	449
Solar energy	11	8	3	3	–	3	–	5	–	3	2	–	6
Other	243	142	101	9	6	6	14	58	35	24	116	41	62
Cooking fuel													
With cooking fuel	111,623	76,388	35,235	4,767	6,831	13,967	12,716	23,045	15,661	20,398	25,341	41,534	24,351
Electricity	67,078	45,512	21,567	2,933	4,305	7,645	5,830	14,528	9,229	8,915	14,930	30,821	12,412
Piped gas	39,476	26,553	12,923	1,562	1,364	5,906	6,532	7,222	5,694	10,015	9,194	8,937	11,330
Bottled gas	5,001	4,274	726	268	1,158	413	349	1,278	716	1,451	1,193	1,758	599
Kerosene or other liquid fuel	14	7	7	–	–	3	–	3	1	6	4	4	–
Coal or coke	–	–	–	–	–	–	–	–	–	–	–	–	–
Wood	29	17	12	–	4	–	4	10	20	4	8	12	4
Other	25	25	–	4	–	1	1	4	–	6	11	3	6
Water heating fuel													
With hot piped water	111,691	76,371	35,319	4,771	6,832	13,960	12,729	23,066	15,684	20,410	25,343	41,543	24,395
Electricity	45,435	29,341	16,095	2,316	5,135	6,051	4,464	9,723	7,432	4,558	7,532	26,921	6,424
Piped gas	57,145	40,280	16,865	2,119	1,149	7,194	7,445	11,216	7,162	10,476	16,391	13,222	17,056
Bottled gas	4,057	3,365	692	270	519	251	255	886	497	745	1,326	1,210	776
Fuel oil	4,692	3,087	1,604	43	10	450	546	1,138	572	4,529	27	132	4
Kerosene or other liquid fuel	21	18	3	4	7	4	–	8	1	11	–	8	2
Coal or coke	23	23	–	–	–	–	–	3	3	17	3	3	–
Wood	104	96	9	10	9	–	–	22	5	43	43	10	9
Solar energy	135	121	14	5	–	9	10	48	6	14	5	23	93
Other	78	40	39	4	2	1	8	22	6	16	17	15	31
Central air conditioning fuel													
With central air conditioning	72,808	54,647	18,161	4,240	4,406	8,668	7,312	14,807	8,237	6,600	17,684	35,825	12,699
Electricity	70,863	53,098	17,765	4,121	4,346	8,430	7,167	14,322	8,040	6,182	17,083	35,413	12,185
Piped gas	1,722	1,353	369	101	24	220	140	424	162	381	535	341	465
Other	223	196	27	17	35	19	5	61	35	37	66	70	49
Other central air fuel													
With other central air	5,629	4,709	920	576	269	607	576	986	541	331	656	3,676	966
Electricity	5,466	4,563	903	561	267	589	566	948	523	305	627	3,598	936
Gas	148	134	14	15	3	18	10	39	18	25	26	76	21
Other	15	12	3	–	–	–	–	–	–	1	3	3	8
Clothes dryer fuel													
With clothes dryer	90,905	72,562	18,343	4,561	6,210	9,104	8,208	18,982	9,454	14,512	21,327	35,578	19,489
Electricity	70,497	55,059	15,438	3,713	5,689	7,327	5,770	14,749	7,807	9,878	14,843	32,930	12,846
Piped gas	19,111	16,326	2,785	787	368	1,733	2,387	3,878	1,548	4,203	6,086	2,391	6,431
Other	1,298	1,178	120	62	152	44	51	354	100	431	399	256	212
Units using each fuel[1]													
Electricity	111,746	76,378	35,368	4,763	6,839	13,993	12,739	23,093	15,727	20,431	25,342	41,572	24,401
Piped gas	67,886	46,700	21,186	2,507	1,723	8,838	8,701	13,548	8,940	13,048	19,005	17,083	18,750
Bottled gas	9,816	8,391	1,425	473	1,647	663	504	2,492	1,245	2,042	2,705	3,927	1,141
Fuel oil	9,208	6,409	2,800	74	249	912	818	2,369	1,172	7,274	694	1,019	222
Kerosene or other liquid fuel	616	451	164	21	299	99	57	146	162	242	16	328	29
Coal or coke	104	97	7	3	–	–	–	11	10	82	8	8	6
Wood	1,787	1,510	278	42	197	43	78	417	270	413	418	507	449
Solar energy	147	130	17	8	–	12	10	54	6	17	8	23	99
Other	405	254	151	19	9	13	40	98	50	61	148	85	111
All electric units	30,166	17,951	12,216	1,862	3,177	4,455	3,457	5,894	5,166	1,677	3,351	20,653	4,486

– = Zero or rounds to zero.
[1] = Figures may not add to total because more than one category may apply to a unit.

Source: U.S. Census Bureau, American Housing Survey

Table 3-16. Fuels, Owner-Occupied Units, 2009

[Numbers in thousands.]

Characteristics	Total occupied units	Housing unit characteristics		Household characteristics				Regions			
		New construction 4 years	Manufactured/mobile homes	Black alone	Hispanic	Elderly (65 years and over)	Below poverty level	Northeast	Midwest	South	West
Total	76,428	3,830	5,418	6,547	6,439	18,472	6,405	13,378	18,249	29,193	15,607
Main house heating fuel											
Housing units with heating fuel	76,222	3,816	5,410	6,540	6,404	18,430	6,376	13,375	18,249	29,174	15,424
Electricity	22,219	1,750	2,847	2,175	2,203	5,045	2,211	1,140	2,112	15,644	3,323
Piped gas	41,233	1,726	1,147	3,632	3,724	9,750	2,903	6,596	13,353	10,386	10,897
Bottled gas	4,889	231	881	296	183	1,400	511	554	1,881	1,788	665
Fuel oil	5,693	47	124	338	206	1,675	430	4,416	438	696	143
Kerosene or other liquid fuel	444	18	249	57	27	131	105	200	8	218	18
Coal or coke	91	3	–	–	–	11	5	75	8	3	6
Wood	1,503	28	157	41	59	377	199	375	385	406	338
Solar energy	8	3	–	–	–	2	–	3	2	–	3
Other	142	9	6	1	3	40	11	16	62	33	31
Cooking fuel											
With cooking fuel	76,388	3,826	5,413	6,541	6,435	18,456	6,388	13,374	18,234	29,179	15,601
Electricity	45,512	2,227	3,452	3,442	2,806	11,552	3,640	6,291	10,351	21,255	7,614
Piped gas	26,553	1,348	1,016	2,804	3,372	5,742	2,218	5,853	6,810	6,427	7,463
Bottled gas	4,274	247	942	295	255	1,153	522	1,220	1,056	1,482	516
Kerosene or other liquid fuel	7	–	–	–	–	3	–	3	4	–	–
Coal or coke	–	–	–	–	–	–	–	–	–	–	–
Wood	17	–	4	–	2	2	8	1	2	12	2
Other	25	4	–	1	1	4	–	6	11	3	6
Water heating fuel											
With hot piped water	76,371	3,830	5,415	6,533	6,436	18,450	6,383	13,371	18,235	29,164	15,601
Electricity	29,341	1,710	4,076	2,651	2,082	7,500	3,031	3,000	4,772	18,029	3,539
Piped gas	40,280	1,814	886	3,574	4,058	9,226	2,808	6,744	12,240	9,975	11,322
Bottled gas	3,365	251	424	162	164	805	334	577	1,140	1,006	642
Fuel oil	3,087	32	10	136	122	835	198	2,956	27	104	–
Kerosene or other liquid fuel	18	4	7	4	–	5	1	11	–	5	2
Coal or coke	23	–	–	–	–	3	3	17	3	3	–
Wood	96	10	9	–	–	19	5	38	43	10	6
Solar energy	121	5	–	6	7	46	3	14	5	21	81
Other	40	4	2	–	3	10	–	13	6	11	9
Central air conditioning fuel											
With central air conditioning	54,647	3,442	3,589	4,482	4,500	12,505	3,860	5,371	14,165	25,902	9,209
Electricity	53,098	3,343	3,536	4,337	4,404	12,085	3,728	5,039	13,676	25,594	8,789
Piped gas	1,353	82	20	136	93	367	105	296	430	252	375
Other	196	17	32	10	2	53	27	37	58	56	44
Other central air fuel											
With other central air	4,709	516	221	358	414	884	307	298	572	3,018	821
Electricity	4,563	501	218	341	406	846	289	276	547	2,947	794
Gas	134	15	3	17	8	38	18	21	25	68	19
Other	12	–	–	–	–	–	–	1	–	3	8
Clothes dryer fuel											
With clothes dryer	72,562	3,771	5,056	5,806	5,783	17,191	5,599	12,221	17,620	27,858	14,864
Electricity	55,059	3,031	4,615	4,547	3,916	13,177	4,479	8,179	11,887	25,526	9,467
Piped gas	16,326	680	316	1,230	1,827	3,677	1,042	3,635	5,370	2,108	5,212
Other	1,178	60	124	29	40	337	78	407	362	224	184
Units using each fuel[1]											
Electricity	76,378	3,822	5,418	6,547	6,439	18,470	6,397	13,364	18,223	29,183	15,607
Piped gas	46,700	2,125	1,306	4,263	4,486	10,939	3,443	7,819	13,959	12,638	12,284
Bottled gas	8,391	441	1,343	463	337	2,302	864	1,724	2,370	3,332	966
Fuel oil	6,409	55	212	373	229	1,887	513	4,846	550	845	167
Kerosene or other liquid fuel	451	18	249	57	27	133	105	203	12	218	18
Coal or coke	97	3	–	–	–	11	5	78	8	6	6
Wood	1,510	28	161	41	59	377	203	375	385	412	338
Solar energy	130	8	–	6	7	48	3	17	8	21	84
Other	254	19	6	6	17	71	12	49	83	63	59
All electric units	17,951	1,331	2,541	1,744	1,506	4,200	1,772	840	1,611	13,268	2,232

– = Zero or rounds to zero.
[1] = Figures may not add to total because more than one category may apply to a unit.

Source: U.S. Census Bureau, American Housing Survey

Table 3-17. Fuels, Renter-Occupied Units, 2009

[Numbers in thousands.]

Characteristics	Total occupied units	Housing unit characteristics		Household characteristics				Regions			
		New construction 4 years	Manufactured/mobile homes	Black alone	Hispanic	Elderly (65 years and over)	Below poverty level	Northeast	Midwest	South	West
Total	35,378	941	1,421	7,446	6,300	4,623	9,334	7,073	7,119	12,392	8,794
Main house heating fuel											
Housing units with heating fuel	35,198	938	1,416	7,432	6,253	4,609	9,286	7,073	7,116	12,353	8,655
Electricity	15,632	619	712	3,477	2,749	2,129	4,311	1,307	2,250	8,637	3,438
Piped gas	15,573	265	362	3,293	2,834	1,845	4,022	3,344	4,367	2,969	4,893
Bottled gas	929	28	226	139	84	122	247	138	282	390	119
Fuel oil	2,521	9	31	474	525	444	556	2,197	126	148	50
Kerosene or other liquid fuel	154	3	50	39	30	10	56	36	3	103	11
Coal or coke	7	–	–	–	–	–	4	5	–	2	–
Wood	277	13	35	2	19	39	67	38	33	96	110
Solar energy	3	–	–	3	–	3	–	–	–	–	3
Other	101	–	–	5	11	18	24	8	54	8	31
Cooking fuel											
With cooking fuel	35,235	941	1,417	7,425	6,281	4,589	9,273	7,024	7,107	12,355	8,750
Electricity	21,567	706	853	4,203	3,025	2,976	5,589	2,624	4,579	9,566	4,798
Piped gas	12,923	214	348	3,102	3,160	1,480	3,476	4,162	2,384	2,510	3,867
Bottled gas	726	21	217	117	94	124	194	230	138	275	83
Kerosene or other liquid fuel	7	–	–	3	–	–	1	4	–	4	–
Coal or coke	–	–	–	–	–	–	–	–	–	–	–
Wood	12	–	–	–	3	9	12	4	6	–	3
Other	–	–	–	–	–	–	–	–	–	–	–
Water heating fuel											
With hot piped water	35,319	941	1,417	7,427	6,293	4,616	9,301	7,038	7,108	12,379	8,794
Electricity	16,095	605	1,059	3,400	2,383	2,223	4,401	1,558	2,760	8,892	2,885
Piped gas	16,865	305	263	3,620	3,387	1,989	4,354	3,732	4,151	3,247	5,734
Bottled gas	692	19	95	88	91	81	164	167	186	204	134
Fuel oil	1,604	11	–	314	424	302	374	1,573	–	28	4
Kerosene or other liquid fuel	3	–	–	–	–	3	–	–	–	3	–
Coal or coke	–	–	–	–	–	–	–	–	–	–	–
Wood	9	–	–	–	–	3	–	6	–	–	3
Solar energy	14	–	–	3	3	2	3	–	–	2	12
Other	39	–	–	1	6	12	6	2	11	4	22
Central air conditioning fuel											
With central air conditioning	18,161	797	817	4,186	2,812	2,302	4,377	1,229	3,519	9,923	3,490
Electricity	17,765	778	811	4,093	2,762	2,238	4,313	1,143	3,407	9,819	3,396
Piped gas	369	19	4	85	47	57	57	86	105	89	89
Other	27	–	3	8	2	8	7	–	8	14	5
Other central air fuel											
With other central air	920	60	48	249	162	102	235	33	84	658	145
Electricity	903	60	48	248	160	102	235	29	80	651	143
Gas	14	–	–	1	2	1	–	4	1	7	2
Other	3	–	–	–	–	–	–	–	3	–	–
Clothes dryer fuel											
With clothes dryer	18,343	791	1,153	3,297	2,425	1,791	3,855	2,291	3,707	7,720	4,625
Electricity	15,438	682	1,074	2,780	1,854	1,572	3,328	1,699	2,956	7,405	3,378
Piped gas	2,785	107	51	502	560	202	505	568	715	283	1,219
Other	120	2	28	15	11	17	22	24	36	32	28
Units using each fuel[1]											
Electricity	35,368	941	1,421	7,446	6,300	4,623	9,330	7,067	7,119	12,389	8,794
Piped gas	21,186	381	417	4,575	4,215	2,610	5,497	5,230	5,046	4,444	6,466
Bottled gas	1,425	32	304	200	167	189	382	318	336	595	175
Fuel oil	2,800	19	37	539	589	482	659	2,428	144	174	55
Kerosene or other liquid fuel	164	3	50	42	30	13	57	40	3	110	11
Coal or coke	7	–	–	–	–	–	4	5	–	2	–
Wood	278	13	35	2	19	40	67	38	33	96	110
Solar energy	17	–	–	6	3	5	3	–	–	2	15
Other	151	–	3	8	23	27	38	11	65	22	52
All electric units	12,216	531	637	2,711	1,952	1,694	3,394	836	1,740	7,385	2,254

– = Zero or rounds to zero.
[1] = Figures may not add to total because more than one category may apply to a unit.

Source: U.S. Census Bureau, American Housing Survey

Table 3-18. Failures in Equipment, Occupied Units, 2009

[Numbers in thousands.]

Characteristics	Total occupied units	Tenure		Housing unit characteristics		Household characteristics				Regions			
		Owner	Renter	New construction 4 years	Manufactured/ mobile homes	Black alone	Hispanic	Elderly (65 years or over)	Below poverty level	Northeast	Midwest	South	West
Total	111,806	76,428	35,378	4,771	6,839	13,993	12,739	23,095	15,739	20,451	25,368	41,586	24,401
Water supply stoppage													
With hot and cold piped water	111,691	76,371	35,319	4,771	6,832	13,960	12,729	23,066	15,684	20,410	25,343	41,543	24,395
No stoppage in last 3 months	106,864	73,494	33,370	4,595	6,249	13,469	12,269	22,217	14,824	19,582	24,333	39,755	23,194
With stoppage in last 3 months	3,632	2,031	1,601	111	517	352	387	609	607	612	826	1,188	1,006
No stoppage lasting 6 hours or more	833	439	394	13	130	64	89	165	118	142	172	269	250
1 time lasting 6 hours or more	1,861	1,100	760	49	249	161	171	297	281	284	510	612	455
2 times	470	249	221	18	37	59	75	78	76	97	72	154	147
3 times	190	98	92	27	31	26	20	20	25	28	33	61	68
4 times or more	231	120	111	3	62	32	29	43	83	56	25	78	73
Number of times not reported	46	25	22	–	8	10	3	5	24	6	14	14	13
Stoppage not reported	1,194	846	348	65	65	139	73	239	253	216	184	599	194
Flush toilet breakdowns													
With one or more flush toilets	111,704	76,391	35,313	4,771	6,839	13,977	12,718	23,077	15,696	20,422	25,348	41,563	24,371
With at least one working toilet at all times in last 3 months	108,440	74,674	33,766	4,694	6,631	13,382	12,303	22,528	14,879	19,833	24,724	40,200	23,683
None working some time in last 3 months	2,094	884	1,210	16	144	459	352	308	565	374	451	778	491
No breakdowns lasting 6 hours or more	568	197	371	10	16	117	99	110	143	107	151	178	133
1 time lasting 6 hours or more	1,061	512	549	3	90	229	157	163	265	198	224	407	231
2 times	261	95	167	3	10	59	38	28	78	36	33	103	89
3 times	42	12	30	–	8	7	14	–	17	4	4	25	9
4 times or more	139	55	83	–	18	43	37	5	58	21	30	65	23
Number of times not reported	23	13	9	–	3	4	6	2	4	8	9	–	6
Breakdowns not reported	1,170	833	337	62	63	137	63	241	253	214	174	585	197
Sewage disposal breakdowns													
With public sewer	89,467	56,736	32,732	3,558	3,153	12,961	11,791	17,583	13,435	16,263	20,432	31,288	21,484
No breakdowns in last 3 months	88,307	56,096	32,211	3,538	3,095	12,703	11,572	17,394	13,157	16,093	20,118	30,893	21,203
With breakdowns in last 3 months	1,160	640	521	20	58	258	220	189	278	171	314	395	281
No breakdowns lasting 6 hours or more	224	130	94	3	2	22	45	31	47	40	67	54	62
1 time lasting 6 hours or more	699	415	283	10	43	168	128	128	164	110	173	256	160
2 times	127	50	77	3	–	43	20	17	26	10	47	40	30
3 times	50	17	33	3	6	11	8	–	19	5	10	26	10
4 times or more	60	27	33	–	6	15	18	13	22	5	17	18	19
With septic tank or cesspool	22,307	19,667	2,640	1,213	3,686	1,025	945	5,506	2,289	4,185	4,930	10,279	2,913
No breakdowns in last 3 months	22,053	19,462	2,591	1,208	3,646	1,016	934	5,461	2,263	4,145	4,879	10,151	2,878
With breakdowns in last 3 months	252	204	48	5	40	10	10	45	25	38	51	128	36
No breakdowns lasting 6 hours or more	35	31	3	–	3	–	–	17	3	3	5	19	9
1 time lasting 6 hours or more	180	140	40	3	28	3	10	26	16	31	38	84	27
2 times	21	21	–	–	7	7	–	–	6	4	3	15	–
3 times	6	2	3	–	2	–	–	–	–	–	–	6	–
4 times or more	10	8	2	2	–	–	–	2	–	–	5	5	–
Heating problems													
With heating equipment and occupied last winter	106,459	75,215	31,244	4,375	6,590	13,135	11,786	22,827	14,437	19,761	24,385	39,640	22,673
Not uncomfortably cold for 24 hours or more last winter	94,725	67,769	26,957	4,080	5,654	11,375	10,666	20,906	12,149	17,018	21,528	35,788	20,391
Uncomfortably cold for 24 hours or more last winter[1]	9,677	6,055	3,622	232	799	1,485	986	1,441	1,856	2,245	2,522	2,959	1,951
Equipment breakdowns	2,738	1,594	1,144	47	214	573	366	366	572	701	786	773	478
No breakdowns lasting 6 hours or more	27	14	12	–	–	1	6	1	4	7	10	7	2
1 time lasting 6 hours or more	1,719	1,119	600	39	117	319	190	245	308	405	516	482	315
2 times	399	208	191	9	34	91	53	57	71	115	124	100	60
3 times	206	120	86	–	23	44	20	26	53	64	58	71	13
4 times or more	339	125	214	–	38	95	84	35	113	101	70	95	73
Number of times not reported	49	8	41	–	2	22	13	3	23	10	7	18	14
Other causes	7,152	4,571	2,581	185	598	964	646	1,086	1,343	1,626	1,792	2,234	1,501
Utility interruption	2,635	2,139	496	106	251	201	121	493	295	619	692	993	332
Inadequate heating capacity	1,025	350	675	13	55	235	174	128	348	215	234	281	295
Inadequate insulation	917	394	523	13	92	214	105	96	246	184	236	247	249
Cost of heating	1,200	778	421	32	99	159	103	167	242	258	304	295	343
Other	1,699	1,022	677	33	128	226	186	248	304	398	430	486	384
Not reported	10	3	7	3	–	2	–	–	2	3	2	3	3
Reason for discomfort not reported	26	2	24	–	–	8	7	8	4	17	3	3	3
Discomfort not reported	2,057	1,391	666	63	137	275	134	480	432	498	335	893	330
Electric fuses and circuit breakers													
With electrical wiring	111,722	76,371	35,351	4,760	6,837	13,991	12,722	23,091	15,724	20,428	25,348	41,556	24,391
No fuses or breakers blown in last 3 months	100,576	68,697	31,879	4,297	6,223	12,673	11,814	21,504	14,229	18,514	22,493	37,564	22,004
With fuses or breakers blown in last 3 months	9,767	6,685	3,082	400	549	1,166	817	1,285	1,233	1,710	2,641	3,273	2,143
1 time	5,334	3,795	1,540	228	318	567	443	850	559	875	1,478	1,836	1,146
2 times	2,297	1,596	701	87	119	305	184	284	305	464	595	742	496
3 times	873	571	303	38	32	122	68	77	129	169	234	273	197
4 times or more	1,193	686	507	43	77	142	113	67	213	180	310	405	298
Number of times not reported	70	37	33	3	3	30	10	6	27	22	25	18	5
Problem not reported or don't know	1,380	989	391	63	65	153	91	303	262	204	214	718	244

– = Zero or rounds to zero.
[1] = Other causes and equipment breakdowns may not add to the total as both may be reported.

Source: U.S. Census Bureau, American Housing Survey

Table 3-19. Failures in Equipment, Owner-Occupied Units, 2009

[Numbers in thousands.]

Characteristics	Total occupied units	Housing unit characteristics		Household characteristics				Regions			
		New construction 4 years	Manufactured/mobile homes	Black alone	Hispanic	Elderly (65 years and over)	Below poverty level	Northeast	Midwest	South	West
Total	76,428	3,830	5,418	6,547	6,439	18,472	6,405	13,378	18,249	29,193	15,607
Water supply stoppage											
With hot and cold piped water	76,371	3,830	5,415	6,533	6,436	18,450	6,383	13,371	18,235	29,164	15,601
No stoppage in last 3 months	73,494	3,687	4,956	6,381	6,280	17,819	6,061	12,888	17,566	28,034	15,007
With stoppage in last 3 months	2,031	93	414	102	123	427	189	337	519	713	461
No stoppage lasting 6 hours or more	439	8	87	13	26	104	38	71	95	161	112
1 time lasting 6 hours or more	1,100	40	213	52	60	219	92	160	337	381	223
2 times	249	18	25	21	23	57	8	66	44	92	48
3 times	98	27	28	3	5	12	7	8	19	36	35
4 times or more	120	–	52	10	7	32	34	29	16	37	38
Number of times not reported	25	–	8	4	3	4	9	4	8	7	6
Stoppage not reported	846	50	45	50	33	204	133	147	150	417	133
Flush toilet breakdowns											
With one or more flush toilets	76,391	3,830	5,418	6,544	6,439	18,461	6,387	13,376	18,236	29,175	15,604
With at least one working toilet at all times in last 3 months	74,674	3,771	5,265	6,373	6,311	18,083	6,137	13,092	17,901	28,412	15,269
None working some time in last 3 months	884	12	110	123	103	174	113	138	192	351	203
No breakdowns lasting 6 hours or more	197	6	5	27	25	53	25	35	49	78	35
1 time lasting 6 hours or more	512	3	74	62	56	105	57	77	107	210	118
2 times	95	3	9	11	6	12	11	9	12	34	40
3 times	12	–	5	5	2	–	5	–	3	10	–
4 times or more	55	–	14	13	12	3	13	11	17	20	8
Number of times not reported	13	–	3	4	3	–	3	5	5	–	3
Breakdowns not reported	833	47	43	48	25	204	136	146	143	412	132
Sewage disposal breakdowns											
With public sewer	56,736	2,700	2,363	5,702	5,697	13,296	4,670	9,662	13,797	20,173	13,103
No breakdowns in last 3 months	56,096	2,687	2,312	5,596	5,621	13,163	4,584	9,572	13,604	19,953	12,967
With breakdowns in last 3 months	640	13	51	106	77	133	86	89	194	221	136
No breakdowns lasting 6 hours or more	130	3	2	2	11	26	13	25	45	36	24
1 time lasting 6 hours or more	415	7	36	95	62	89	62	61	108	158	88
2 times	50	3	–	7	–	9	3	3	28	11	8
3 times	17	–	6	–	1	–	–	1	4	6	6
4 times or more	27	–	6	2	2	9	8	–	9	9	9
With septic tank or cesspool	19,667	1,130	3,055	842	742	5,170	1,724	3,716	4,447	9,004	2,500
No breakdowns in last 3 months	19,462	1,127	3,020	832	742	5,125	1,710	3,682	4,398	8,903	2,479
With breakdowns in last 3 months	204	3	35	10	–	45	12	32	49	101	21
No breakdowns lasting 6 hours or more	31	–	3	–	–	17	–	3	5	15	9
1 time lasting 6 hours or more	140	3	23	3	–	26	6	26	36	65	13
2 times	21	–	7	7	–	–	6	4	3	15	–
3 times	2	–	2	–	–	–	–	–	–	2	–
4 times or more	8	–	–	–	–	2	–	–	5	3	–
Heating problems											
With heating equipment and occupied last winter	75,215	3,626	5,329	6,465	6,319	18,370	6,260	13,220	18,033	28,839	15,123
Not uncomfortably cold for 24 hours or more last winter	67,769	3,390	4,638	5,763	5,838	16,815	5,348	11,565	16,140	26,272	13,791
Uncomfortably cold for 24 hours or more last winter[1]	6,055	190	586	602	413	1,181	677	1,364	1,649	1,945	1,098
Equipment breakdowns	1,594	39	168	224	158	304	157	363	494	460	277
No breakdowns lasting 6 hours or more	14	–	–	1	1	–	–	3	6	5	–
1 time lasting 6 hours or more	1,119	30	103	158	112	222	108	245	362	305	207
2 times	208	9	30	32	11	40	12	47	66	62	33
3 times	120	–	14	15	8	22	14	35	28	51	7
4 times or more	125	–	19	18	22	16	21	30	33	35	27
Number of times not reported	8	–	2	–	3	3	2	3	–	2	3
Other causes	4,571	151	429	390	258	891	528	1,034	1,190	1,504	843
Utility interruption	2,139	88	171	124	75	444	168	495	579	793	272
Inadequate heating capacity	350	8	47	39	52	69	68	62	93	106	89
Inadequate insulation	394	7	55	80	39	53	56	88	94	106	105
Cost of heating	778	32	79	92	39	139	131	173	202	203	200
Other	1,022	30	90	74	64	203	122	235	258	313	215
Not reported	3	–	–	–	–	–	–	–	–	3	–
Reason for discomfort not reported	2	–	–	–	–	2	–	2	–	–	–
Discomfort not reported	1,391	46	105	100	68	375	235	291	244	621	234
Electric fuses and circuit breakers											
With electrical wiring	76,371	3,822	5,416	6,547	6,429	18,470	6,394	13,363	18,229	29,175	15,604
No fuses or breakers blown in last 3 months	68,697	3,431	4,953	5,911	5,938	17,113	5,808	12,059	16,144	26,408	14,085
With fuses or breakers blown in last 3 months	6,685	339	425	560	449	1,094	437	1,158	1,922	2,254	1,351
1 time	3,795	206	255	289	281	715	204	626	1,114	1,298	757
2 times	1,596	71	93	165	100	255	136	325	416	544	311
3 times	571	19	23	51	28	69	35	102	175	175	118
4 times or more	686	40	50	45	39	50	57	94	198	232	162
Number of times not reported	37	3	3	10	1	5	5	10	19	6	2
Problem not reported or don't know	989	52	39	77	42	263	150	146	163	512	168

– = Zero or rounds to zero.

[1] = Other causes and equipment breakdowns may not add to the total as both may be reported.

Source: U.S. Census Bureau, American Housing Survey

Table 3-20. Failures in Equipment, Renter-Occupied Units, 2009

[Numbers in thousands.]

Characteristics	Total occupied units	Housing unit characteristics: New construction 4 years	Housing unit characteristics: Manufactured/ mobile homes	Household characteristics: Black alone	Household characteristics: Hispanic	Household characteristics: Elderly (65 years and over)	Household characteristics: Below poverty level	Regions: Northeast	Regions: Midwest	Regions: South	Regions: West
Total	35,378	941	1,421	7,446	6,300	4,623	9,334	7,073	7,119	12,392	8,794
Water supply stoppage											
With hot and cold piped water	35,319	941	1,417	7,427	6,293	4,616	9,301	7,038	7,108	12,379	8,794
No stoppage in last 3 months	33,370	908	1,294	7,088	5,989	4,397	8,763	6,694	6,768	11,722	8,187
With stoppage in last 3 months	1,601	18	103	251	264	182	418	275	306	475	545
No stoppage lasting 6 hours or more	394	5	43	51	63	61	80	71	77	108	139
1 time lasting 6 hours or more	760	10	36	109	111	79	190	124	173	231	232
2 times	221	–	12	39	53	22	69	31	28	63	99
3 times	92	–	3	24	15	8	17	20	14	24	34
4 times or more	111	3	10	22	23	12	48	27	9	41	35
Number of times not reported	22	–	–	6	–	1	15	2	6	8	6
Stoppage not reported	348	15	20	89	40	36	120	69	34	183	62
Flush toilet breakdowns											
With one or more flush toilets	35,313	941	1,421	7,434	6,279	4,616	9,310	7,046	7,112	12,388	8,768
With at least one working toilet at all times in last 3 months	33,766	923	1,366	7,008	5,992	4,445	8,742	6,741	6,823	11,788	8,415
None working some time in last 3 months	1,210	3	34	336	249	134	452	237	258	427	288
No breakdowns lasting 6 hours or more	371	3	11	90	74	57	118	71	102	100	98
1 time lasting 6 hours or more	549	–	16	167	101	57	208	122	117	198	113
2 times	167	–	1	47	33	16	67	26	22	69	50
3 times	30	–	3	2	12	–	12	4	2	15	9
4 times or more	83	–	4	30	25	2	44	10	13	45	16
Number of times not reported	9	–	–	–	4	2	1	3	4	–	3
Breakdowns not reported	337	15	20	89	38	37	116	68	31	173	65
Sewage disposal breakdowns											
With public sewer	32,732	858	790	7,259	6,094	4,287	8,765	6,602	6,635	11,114	8,381
No breakdowns in last 3 months	32,211	851	783	7,108	5,951	4,231	8,573	6,520	6,515	10,941	8,236
With breakdowns in last 3 months	521	7	6	151	143	55	192	81	120	174	145
No breakdowns lasting 6 hours or more	94	–	–	20	34	5	34	15	22	18	38
1 time lasting 6 hours or more	283	3	6	72	66	39	102	49	65	98	71
2 times	77	–	–	35	20	8	23	8	19	29	22
3 times	33	3	–	11	6	–	19	4	6	20	3
4 times or more	33	–	–	13	16	4	14	5	8	10	10
With septic tank or cesspool	2,640	83	631	184	203	336	566	468	483	1,276	413
No breakdowns in last 3 months	2,591	81	626	184	193	336	552	463	481	1,249	399
With breakdowns in last 3 months	48	2	5	–	10	–	13	6	2	27	14
No breakdowns lasting 6 hours or more	3	–	–	–	–	–	3	–	–	3	–
1 time lasting 6 hours or more	40	–	5	–	10	–	10	6	2	18	14
2 times	–	–	–	–	–	–	–	–	–	–	–
3 times	3	–	–	–	–	–	–	–	–	3	–
4 times or more	2	2	–	–	–	–	–	–	–	2	–
Heating problems											
With heating equipment and occupied last winter	31,244	749	1,261	6,670	5,467	4,457	8,177	6,541	6,352	10,802	7,550
Not uncomfortably cold for 24 hours or more last winter	26,957	689	1,016	5,612	4,828	4,091	6,801	5,452	5,388	9,516	6,601
Uncomfortably cold for 24 hours or more last winter[1]	3,622	43	212	883	573	260	1,179	881	873	1,014	853
Equipment breakdowns	1,144	9	46	349	208	62	415	338	292	313	201
No breakdowns lasting 6 hours or more	12	–	–	–	5	1	4	3	4	2	2
1 time lasting 6 hours or more	600	9	14	161	78	23	200	160	154	177	108
2 times	191	–	4	59	42	17	59	68	58	38	27
3 times	86	–	9	28	12	3	38	29	31	20	6
4 times or more	214	–	19	77	61	18	92	71	37	60	46
Number of times not reported	41	–	–	22	10	–	21	7	7	16	11
Other causes	2,581	34	169	574	388	196	815	592	602	730	657
Utility interruption	496	18	81	78	46	49	126	123	113	200	60
Inadequate heating capacity	675	5	8	196	121	59	280	153	141	176	205
Inadequate insulation	523	6	37	134	65	43	189	96	142	141	144
Cost of heating	421	–	19	68	63	28	111	85	102	92	142
Other	677	3	38	153	122	45	183	163	172	173	169
Not reported	7	3	–	2	–	–	2	3	2	–	3
Reason for discomfort not reported	24	–	–	8	7	6	4	15	3	3	3
Discomfort not reported	666	17	33	175	66	105	198	207	91	272	96
Electric fuses and circuit breakers											
With electrical wiring	35,351	938	1,421	7,444	6,293	4,621	9,330	7,065	7,119	12,381	8,787
No fuses or breakers blown in last 3 months	31,879	867	1,271	6,762	5,876	4,391	8,422	6,455	6,349	11,156	7,919
With fuses or breakers blown in last 3 months	3,082	61	124	606	368	191	796	552	719	1,019	792
1 time	1,540	23	62	278	162	135	356	249	364	538	388
2 times	701	17	26	141	84	29	169	139	179	198	185
3 times	303	19	9	71	40	8	94	67	59	98	79
4 times or more	507	3	27	97	74	17	155	86	112	172	137
Number of times not reported	33	–	–	19	8	1	23	11	6	12	3
Problem not reported or don't know	391	11	26	76	49	39	112	58	51	206	77

– = Zero or rounds to zero.
[1] = Other causes and equipment breakdowns may not add to the total as both may be reported.

Source: U.S. Census Bureau, American Housing Survey

Table 3-21. Additional Indicators of Housing Quality, Occupied Units, 2009

[Numbers in thousands.]

Characteristics	Total occupied units	Tenure		Housing unit characteristics		Household characteristics				Regions			
		Owner	Renter	New construction 4 years	Manufactured/ mobile homes	Black alone	Hispanic	Elderly (65 years or over)	Below poverty level	Northeast	Midwest	South	West
Total	111,806	76,428	35,378	4,771	6,839	13,993	12,739	23,095	15,739	20,451	25,368	41,586	24,401
Selected amenities[1]													
Porch, deck, balcony, or patio	95,406	70,421	24,984	4,246	5,955	10,717	9,798	19,712	11,854	15,067	21,854	37,281	21,204
Telephone available	109,325	75,129	34,196	4,462	6,647	13,502	12,452	22,783	15,178	19,740	24,781	40,796	24,009
Usable fireplace	38,998	34,458	4,540	2,236	1,195	2,866	2,846	7,876	2,424	5,431	8,127	14,517	10,923
Separate dining room	53,676	43,717	9,959	2,481	2,106	6,273	5,152	11,183	5,145	11,008	11,774	20,400	10,493
With 2 or more living rooms or recreation rooms, etc.	33,912	30,978	2,934	1,879	918	2,578	2,071	7,092	1,794	5,852	8,705	11,923	7,431
Garage or carport included with home	74,236	60,979	13,258	3,926	2,639	6,194	7,412	16,551	6,867	10,731	18,726	25,052	19,727
Not included	37,525	15,420	22,105	843	4,200	7,792	5,327	6,525	8,868	9,701	6,629	16,528	4,667
Off-street parking included	30,963	13,287	17,676	732	3,891	6,150	4,018	5,380	7,070	6,271	5,624	15,119	3,950
Off-street parking not reported	3	2	2	–	–	1	1	–	2	1	2	–	–
Garage or carport not reported	44	29	15	3	–	7	–	19	4	18	13	5	7
Cars and trucks available[1]													
No cars, trucks, or vans	8,738	2,069	6,669	116	308	2,541	1,398	3,084	3,946	3,232	1,658	2,450	1,398
Other households without cars	13,421	9,006	4,415	569	1,372	1,284	1,908	2,128	2,081	1,562	3,354	5,902	2,603
1 car with or without trucks or vans	52,458	35,040	17,418	2,232	3,602	6,634	5,487	12,711	7,473	8,846	12,275	20,023	11,314
2 cars	28,103	22,384	5,719	1,438	1,160	2,793	2,871	4,255	1,872	5,180	6,178	10,195	6,550
3 or more cars	9,085	7,929	1,157	416	396	741	1,075	916	367	1,632	1,903	3,015	2,535
With cars, no trucks or vans	51,465	33,456	18,009	2,171	2,390	6,996	5,421	11,541	6,917	10,489	11,193	18,063	11,721
1 truck or van with or without cars	35,951	28,026	7,925	1,724	2,693	3,279	3,969	6,244	3,593	4,802	8,800	14,305	8,044
2 or more trucks or vans	15,652	12,876	2,775	760	1,449	1,177	1,952	2,226	1,283	1,928	3,717	6,767	3,239
Selected deficiencies[1]													
Signs of rats in last 3 months	613	354	258	7	63	124	139	111	148	85	56	295	177
Signs of mice in last 3 months	6,122	3,984	2,138	90	690	905	703	1,140	1,134	1,709	1,465	2,117	831
Signs of rodents, not sure which kind in last 3 months	353	164	189	9	11	102	37	42	98	83	60	164	46
Holes in floors	1,141	581	560	14	190	255	177	157	343	231	208	478	225
Open cracks or holes (interior)	5,517	3,101	2,416	75	472	999	690	646	1,295	1,081	1,338	2,049	1,049
Broken plaster or peeling paint (interior)	2,378	1,246	1,132	27	158	495	311	343	606	531	642	819	386
No electrical wiring	84	57	26	11	2	2	17	4	14	23	21	30	10
Exposed wiring	355	221	134	13	33	68	50	79	81	63	85	155	52
Rooms without electric outlets	1,274	650	624	45	86	275	179	207	318	215	371	501	187
Special living[2]													
Services available to residents[1]	1,077	101	976	27	X	168	80	878	342	246	328	310	193
Meals	656	45	611	18	X	63	38	577	187	116	236	177	127
Transportation	762	76	686	18	X	119	55	652	226	162	243	229	127
Housekeeping	548	44	504	11	X	60	19	503	144	78	208	145	117
Financial management	273	26	247	6	X	35	9	219	94	74	79	75	45
Aid with telephone	267	16	251	12	X	23	15	225	76	48	84	83	53
Shopping	446	35	411	10	X	47	17	403	114	81	158	136	70
Services and assistance available to residents[1, 3]	325	18	308	8	X	25	8	299	86	54	124	93	54
Bathing	275	15	261	5	X	17	7	259	74	43	112	75	45
Eating	247	13	234	4	X	20	4	231	61	36	102	66	42
Moving about	274	15	259	2	X	24	6	251	70	46	111	70	47
Dressing	255	11	244	5	X	19	5	239	64	36	103	67	49
Toilet use	234	11	223	2	X	18	5	218	59	36	96	59	43
Access to structure													
Entering building from outside[4]	25,915	3,734	22,181	743	–	5,407	4,613	4,456	6,457	6,671	5,225	7,669	6,350
Use of steps not required	9,771	1,532	8,239	382	–	2,005	1,705	2,345	2,535	2,039	1,663	3,436	2,633
Use of steps required	16,136	2,201	13,935	362	–	3,401	2,906	2,106	3,922	4,628	3,557	4,233	3,718
Use of steps not reported	8	2	6	–	–	–	2	5	–	4	5	–	–
Entering home from outside[5]	85,891	72,694	13,197	4,028	6,839	8,587	8,126	18,639	9,282	13,781	20,144	33,916	18,050
Use of steps not required	38,011	32,654	5,357	2,151	1,135	3,657	4,304	8,805	3,900	4,860	6,641	16,898	9,611
Use of steps required	47,752	39,928	7,824	1,877	5,704	4,926	3,820	9,799	5,362	8,891	13,477	16,973	8,411
Use of steps not reported	128	112	16	–	–	4	2	35	20	30	25	45	28

Table 3-21. Additional Indicators of Housing Quality, Occupied Units, 2009—*Continued*

[Numbers in thousands.]

Characteristics	Total occupied units	Tenure		Housing unit characteristics		Household characteristics				Regions			
		Owner	Renter	New construction 4 years	Manufactured/ mobile homes	Black alone	Hispanic	Elderly (65 years or over)	Below poverty level	Northeast	Midwest	South	West
Selected physical problems													
Severe physical problems[1]	1,864	870	994	11	128	392	294	346	490	596	398	533	337
Plumbing	1,232	576	656	3	57	226	184	280	292	411	241	337	243
Heating	545	245	300	–	61	139	104	60	166	165	128	166	86
Electric	71	58	13	8	6	7	4	2	19	21	30	20	–
Upkeep	74	30	44	–	12	24	7	11	29	14	20	29	10
Moderate physical problems[1]	3,893	1,625	2,269	52	285	896	697	642	1,064	723	695	1,800	676
Plumbing	164	62	101	–	23	44	46	–	58	26	24	82	32
Heating	1,073	669	404	8	125	345	214	325	331	20	52	965	36
Upkeep	1,177	616	560	11	145	267	154	125	345	267	277	459	174
Kitchen	1,629	335	1,293	37	19	291	314	218	409	443	357	374	455
Overall opinion of structure													
1 (worst)	530	203	327	–	44	154	114	84	240	114	94	222	100
2	331	122	209	9	49	93	56	30	99	33	79	123	96
3	611	175	436	6	50	151	74	42	230	129	110	194	179
4	1,153	444	708	14	147	229	111	115	309	209	261	431	251
5	5,275	2,365	2,910	77	595	969	733	825	1,365	864	1,204	2,071	1,137
6	5,208	2,655	2,553	75	436	889	608	706	963	966	1,237	1,820	1,185
7	15,045	8,899	6,146	377	898	2,037	1,653	1,835	2,074	2,724	3,461	5,391	3,468
8	30,667	21,042	9,625	1,006	1,640	3,582	3,426	5,459	3,654	5,599	7,212	10,987	6,870
9	17,844	13,627	4,217	880	739	1,568	1,978	3,936	1,716	3,323	3,989	6,434	4,099
10 (best)	30,909	23,967	6,941	2,148	2,023	3,660	3,634	9,226	4,263	5,601	6,990	12,077	6,241
Not reported	4,233	2,926	1,306	179	218	662	354	836	826	889	731	1,837	775
Water leakage during the last 12 months													
No leakage from inside structure	101,540	70,356	31,184	4,479	6,133	12,417	11,606	21,687	13,999	18,549	22,981	37,787	22,223
With leakage from inside structure[1]	9,007	5,170	3,836	227	635	1,439	1,063	1,123	1,483	1,679	2,199	3,179	1,951
Fixtures backed up or overflowed	2,141	1,188	952	37	95	388	248	221	362	333	572	704	533
Pipes leaked	3,809	2,145	1,664	100	328	617	466	465	639	838	830	1,349	791
Broken water heater	1,041	714	327	31	144	132	123	177	140	154	219	436	233
Other or unknown (includes not reported)	2,351	1,263	1,088	59	85	364	268	294	412	405	644	813	488
Interior leakage not reported	1,260	902	357	65	71	138	70	285	256	224	188	620	227
No leakage from outside structure	99,592	67,686	31,906	4,484	5,943	12,382	11,678	21,049	13,860	17,947	21,473	37,587	22,586
With leakage from outside structure[1]	10,963	7,842	3,121	222	825	1,474	997	1,778	1,620	2,285	3,694	3,383	1,600
Roof	5,747	4,168	1,579	75	620	847	646	965	891	1,147	1,426	2,313	860
Basement	2,847	2,309	538	46	20	292	97	467	288	812	1,643	228	164
Walls, closed windows, or doors	1,960	1,165	795	78	134	292	174	255	369	317	632	625	386
Other or unknown (includes not reported)	1,101	691	410	29	81	145	121	171	181	199	299	373	230
Exterior leakage not reported	1,250	900	350	65	71	137	65	268	259	219	201	615	215

– = Zero or rounds to zero.
X = Not applicable.
[1] = Figures may not add to total because more than one category may apply to a unit.
[2] = Restricted to multiunits with five or more apartments with a resident 55 years of age or older.
[3] = Limited to units that reported meals, transportation, housekeeping, financial management, aid with telephone, or shopping.
[4] = Restricted to multiunits.
[5] = Restricted to single units.

Source: U.S. Census Bureau, American Housing Survey

Table 3-22. Additional Indicators of Housing Quality, Owner-Occupied Units, 2009

[Numbers in thousands.]

Characteristics	Total occupied units	Housing unit characteristics		Household characteristics				Regions			
		New construction 4 years	Manufactured/ mobile homes	Black alone	Hispanic	Elderly (65 years and over)	Below poverty level	Northeast	Midwest	South	West
Total	76,428	3,830	5,418	6,547	6,439	18,472	6,405	13,378	18,249	29,193	15,607
Selected amenities[1]											
Porch, deck, balcony, or patio	70,421	3,506	4,774	5,668	5,732	16,876	5,690	11,742	16,799	27,257	14,623
Telephone available	75,129	3,601	5,277	6,388	6,329	18,286	6,245	13,054	17,904	28,752	15,419
Usable fireplace	34,458	2,085	1,072	2,207	2,222	7,563	1,799	5,096	7,578	12,728	9,056
Separate dining room	43,717	2,208	1,820	3,975	3,372	10,171	2,982	8,906	9,812	16,781	8,219
With 2 or more living rooms or recreation rooms, etc.	30,978	1,736	829	2,156	1,773	6,842	1,444	5,462	8,088	10,863	6,565
Garage or carport included with home	60,979	3,429	2,357	4,257	5,030	14,988	4,275	9,346	15,978	21,441	14,214
Not included	15,420	398	3,061	2,287	1,409	3,472	2,129	4,017	2,262	7,750	1,391
Off-street parking included	13,287	352	2,843	1,824	1,227	2,942	1,783	3,083	1,907	7,089	1,209
Off-street parking not reported	2	–	–	–	–	–	2	–	2	–	–
Garage or carport not reported	29	3	–	3	–	12	1	15	9	3	2
Cars and trucks available[1]											
No cars, trucks, or vans	2,069	22	177	400	159	1,251	743	701	391	716	261
Other households without cars	9,006	471	1,024	609	934	1,789	999	998	2,375	4,098	1,535
1 car with or without trucks or vans	35,040	1,704	2,891	3,111	2,663	10,616	3,352	5,868	8,687	13,576	6,909
2 cars	22,384	1,252	1,005	1,842	1,843	3,935	1,081	4,317	5,087	8,148	4,832
3 or more cars	7,929	381	321	584	839	882	231	1,494	1,710	2,655	2,070
With cars, no trucks or vans	33,456	1,602	1,840	3,223	2,541	9,536	2,947	7,276	7,547	11,680	6,952
1 truck or van with or without cars	28,026	1,519	2,212	2,066	2,388	5,683	1,974	3,834	7,106	11,197	5,889
2 or more trucks or vans	12,876	688	1,188	858	1,351	2,003	741	1,566	3,206	5,600	2,504
Selected deficiencies[1]											
Signs of rats in last 3 months	354	7	45	36	58	96	59	29	29	182	114
Signs of mice in last 3 months	3,984	78	500	356	239	915	445	1,002	1,050	1,443	489
Signs of rodents, not sure which kind in last 3 months	164	9	5	27	13	34	18	27	29	79	30
Holes in floors	581	14	151	78	61	115	119	96	129	234	122
Open cracks or holes (interior)	3,101	57	350	383	288	496	433	536	814	1,188	562
Broken plaster or peeling paint (interior)	1,246	24	110	189	101	269	183	263	373	444	166
No electrical wiring	57	8	2	–	10	2	11	15	21	18	3
Exposed wiring	221	10	28	37	23	52	34	24	61	112	24
Rooms without electric outlets	650	33	58	88	58	151	86	116	227	228	78
Special living[2]											
Services available to residents[1]	101	1	X	3	4	76	11	17	21	39	25
Meals	45	1	X	–	–	40	9	6	15	11	13
Transportation	76	1	X	3	4	65	11	14	16	29	17
Housekeeping	44	1	X	–	–	37	9	7	13	13	12
Financial management	26	–	X	–	–	21	4	8	8	6	4
Aid with telephone	16	1	X	–	–	14	6	3	8	3	2
Shopping	35	1	X	–	4	35	8	6	14	12	2
Services and assistance available to residents[1, 3]	18	–	X	–	–	15	5	2	7	9	–
Bathing	15	–	X	–	–	12	5	2	7	5	–
Eating	13	–	X	–	–	13	5	2	7	3	–
Moving about	15	–	X	–	–	15	5	2	7	6	–
Dressing	11	–	X	–	–	11	5	2	7	3	–
Toilet use	11	–	X	–	–	11	5	2	7	3	–
Access to structure											
Entering building from outside[4]	3,734	167	–	351	401	1,142	321	1,210	661	932	932
Use of steps not required	1,532	90	–	91	186	565	149	388	225	465	453
Use of steps required	2,201	78	–	260	216	577	172	819	435	467	479
Use of steps not reported	2	–	–	–	–	–	–	2	–	–	–
Entering home from outside[5]	72,694	3,663	5,418	6,196	6,038	17,330	6,084	12,169	17,589	28,261	14,675
Use of steps not required	32,654	1,921	939	2,706	3,354	8,253	2,668	4,369	5,888	14,518	7,879
Use of steps required	39,928	1,742	4,479	3,487	2,681	9,048	3,406	7,770	11,679	13,711	6,768
Use of steps not reported	112	–	–	4	2	28	10	30	22	32	28

Table 3-22. Additional Indicators of Housing Quality, Owner-Occupied Units, 2009—*Continued*

[Numbers in thousands.]

Characteristics	Total occupied units	Housing unit characteristics		Household characteristics				Regions			
		New construction 4 years	Manufactured/ mobile homes	Black alone	Hispanic	Elderly (65 years and over)	Below poverty level	Northeast	Midwest	South	West
Selected physical problems											
Severe physical problems[1]	870	8	77	125	78	228	142	234	210	296	130
Plumbing	576	–	37	81	43	187	94	153	127	199	97
Heating	245	–	33	34	31	39	36	65	60	86	33
Electric	58	8	4	4	4	2	12	14	30	14	–
Upkeep	30	–	9	7	–	8	8	4	12	14	–
Moderate physical problems[1]	1,625	26	221	345	254	436	333	258	259	943	164
Plumbing	62	–	16	19	14	–	13	11	14	30	8
Heating	669	8	94	203	132	271	179	12	29	609	19
Upkeep	616	11	117	112	64	99	123	136	155	253	73
Kitchen	335	11	17	26	53	83	51	104	66	96	69
Overall opinion of structure											
1 (worst)	203	–	23	38	15	55	62	28	43	95	38
2	122	4	32	20	26	14	25	2	25	45	50
3	175	4	40	21	15	16	27	29	41	56	49
4	444	9	105	48	29	88	71	71	110	192	70
5	2,365	57	399	271	209	568	396	381	601	946	436
6	2,655	49	279	290	162	472	268	482	686	967	520
7	8,899	261	715	791	672	1,344	674	1,584	2,225	3,247	1,843
8	21,042	794	1,311	1,660	1,732	4,368	1,437	3,666	5,255	7,690	4,431
9	13,627	684	609	923	1,183	3,248	872	2,424	3,184	5,062	2,957
10 (best)	23,967	1,821	1,742	2,206	2,211	7,598	2,143	4,169	5,547	9,606	4,646
Not reported	2,926	149	162	279	184	700	430	542	531	1,286	568
Water leakage during last 12 months											
No leakage from inside structure	70,356	3,595	4,898	6,013	5,964	17,375	5,833	12,345	16,695	26,922	14,394
With leakage from inside structure[1]	5,170	185	467	480	443	861	424	893	1,406	1,825	1,047
Fixtures backed up or overflowed	1,188	33	68	137	104	177	90	168	349	369	302
Pipes leaked	2,145	78	228	187	185	341	179	443	526	797	379
Broken water heater	714	29	122	60	86	148	47	94	169	283	169
Other or unknown (includes not reported)	1,263	45	65	108	87	224	120	212	401	418	232
Interior leakage not reported	902	50	53	53	32	236	148	141	149	446	167
No leakage from outside structure	67,686	3,593	4,748	5,686	5,848	16,698	5,508	11,578	15,346	26,381	14,381
With leakage from outside structure[1]	7,842	187	617	808	562	1,548	746	1,660	2,750	2,365	1,067
Roof	4,168	65	480	487	387	856	473	841	1,040	1,683	603
Basement	2,309	38	18	200	65	426	159	655	1,329	190	135
Walls, closed windows, or doors	1,165	71	79	129	85	201	107	189	385	367	225
Other or unknown (includes not reported)	691	18	60	59	49	139	63	119	219	230	123
Exterior leakage not reported	900	50	53	53	29	227	151	140	153	447	159

– = Zero or rounds to zero.
X = Not applicable.
[1] = Figures may not add to total because more than one category may apply to a unit.
[2] = Restricted to multiunits with five or more apartments with a resident 55 years of age or older.
[3] = Limited to units that reported meals, transportation, housekeeping, financial management, aid with telephone, or shopping.
[4] = Restricted to multiunits.
[5] = Restricted to single units.

Source: U.S. Census Bureau, American Housing Survey

Table 3-23. Additional Indicators of Housing Quality, Renter-Occupied Units, 2009

[Numbers in thousands.]

Characteristics	Total occupied units	Housing unit characteristics		Household characteristics				Regions			
		New construction 4 years	Manufactured/ mobile homes	Black alone	Hispanic	Elderly (65 years and over)	Below poverty level	Northeast	Midwest	South	West
Total	35,378	941	1,421	7,446	6,300	4,623	9,334	7,073	7,119	12,392	8,794
Selected amenities[1]											
Porch, deck, balcony, or patio	24,984	740	1,181	5,049	4,066	2,836	6,164	3,325	5,055	10,024	6,580
Telephone available	34,196	861	1,369	7,114	6,123	4,498	8,933	6,685	6,877	12,044	8,590
Usable fireplace	4,540	151	123	659	625	314	626	335	550	1,789	1,866
Separate dining room	9,959	273	287	2,298	1,780	1,012	2,163	2,103	1,963	3,620	2,274
With 2 or more living rooms or recreation rooms, etc.	2,934	143	89	421	298	250	350	390	618	1,060	866
Garage or carport included with home	13,258	497	281	1,937	2,382	1,563	2,592	1,385	2,748	3,612	5,513
Not included	22,105	444	1,139	5,505	3,918	3,053	6,739	5,685	4,367	8,778	3,276
Off-street parking included	17,676	380	1,048	4,326	2,790	2,439	5,287	3,188	3,717	8,030	2,742
Off-street parking not reported	2	–	–	1	1	–	1	1	1	–	–
Garage or carport not reported	15	–	–	4	–	7	2	3	5	3	5
Cars and trucks available[1]											
No cars, trucks, or vans	6,669	94	130	2,141	1,238	1,834	3,203	2,531	1,267	1,734	1,136
Other households without cars	4,415	98	348	674	974	340	1,082	564	979	1,804	1,068
1 car with or without trucks or vans	17,418	528	712	3,523	2,824	2,095	4,121	2,978	3,588	6,447	4,405
2 cars	5,719	186	155	951	1,027	320	791	862	1,091	2,047	1,718
3 or more cars	1,157	35	75	156	236	35	136	138	194	360	465
With cars, no trucks or vans	18,009	569	550	3,772	2,880	2,005	3,970	3,213	3,645	6,383	4,768
1 truck or van with or without cars	7,925	206	480	1,214	1,581	561	1,619	968	1,695	3,107	2,155
2 or more trucks or vans	2,775	72	260	319	601	223	541	362	512	1,168	734
Owner or Manager on Property											
Rental, multiunit[2]	22,181	576	X	5,056	4,212	3,314	6,136	5,461	4,564	6,737	5,419
Owner or manager lives on property	7,461	198	X	1,419	1,568	1,182	1,838	1,615	1,176	1,966	2,704
Neither owner nor manager lives on property	14,720	378	X	3,636	2,644	2,132	4,298	3,846	3,388	4,771	2,715
Selected deficiencies[1]											
Signs of rats in last 3 months	258	–	18	87	82	15	90	55	26	114	63
Signs of mice in last 3 months	2,138	13	190	549	464	225	689	707	415	674	342
Signs of rodents, not sure which kind in last 3 months	189	–	6	75	24	8	81	57	31	85	16
Holes in floors	560	–	38	177	116	42	223	134	80	244	103
Open cracks or holes (interior)	2,416	18	123	617	402	149	862	545	524	861	487
Broken plaster or peeling paint (interior)	1,132	3	48	306	210	74	423	269	270	375	219
No electrical wiring	26	3	–	2	7	2	4	8	–	12	6
Exposed wiring	134	4	5	31	27	27	46	40	23	43	28
Rooms without electric outlets	624	11	28	187	121	56	232	99	144	272	109
Special living[3]											
Services available to residents[1]	976	26	X	165	76	802	331	229	307	271	168
Meals	611	17	X	63	38	537	178	110	221	166	114
Transportation	686	17	X	115	51	587	215	148	227	200	110
Housekeeping	504	10	X	60	19	466	135	71	195	132	105
Financial management	247	6	X	35	9	198	91	66	71	69	41
Aid with telephone	251	11	X	23	15	211	71	45	76	79	51
Shopping	411	9	X	47	13	369	106	75	144	124	68
Services and assistance available to resdents[1, 4]	308	8	X	25	8	284	81	51	118	85	54
Bathing	261	5	X	17	7	247	69	41	105	70	45
Eating	234	4	X	20	4	218	56	34	95	63	42
Moving about	259	2	X	24	6	236	65	44	104	64	47
Dressing	244	5	X	19	5	227	59	34	97	65	49
Toilet use	223	2	X	18	5	206	53	34	89	57	43
Access to structure											
Entering building from outside[5]	22,181	576	–	5,056	4,212	3,314	6,136	5,461	4,564	6,737	5,419
Use of steps not required	8,239	292	–	1,915	1,519	1,780	2,386	1,650	1,438	2,972	2,180
Use of steps required	13,935	284	–	3,141	2,690	1,529	3,750	3,809	3,122	3,766	3,239
Use of steps not reported	6	–	–	–	2	5	–	2	5	–	–
Entering home from outside[6]	13,197	365	1,421	2,391	2,089	1,309	3,198	1,612	2,555	5,655	3,375
Use of steps not required	5,357	230	196	951	950	551	1,231	491	754	2,380	1,732
Use of steps required	7,824	135	1,225	1,439	1,139	751	1,956	1,121	1,798	3,262	1,643
Use of steps not reported	16	–	–	–	–	7	11	–	4	13	–

Table 3-23. Additional Indicators of Housing Quality, Renter-Occupied Units, 2009—*Continued*

[Numbers in thousands.]

Characteristics	Total occupied units	Housing unit characteristics		Household characteristics				Regions			
		New construction 4 years	Manufactured/ mobile homes	Black alone	Hispanic	Elderly (65 years and over)	Below poverty level	Northeast	Midwest	South	West
Selected physical problems											
Severe physical problems[1]	994	3	51	267	216	118	348	363	188	236	207
Plumbing	656	3	21	145	140	93	198	259	114	138	146
Heating	300	–	28	105	73	22	130	100	68	79	53
Electric	13	–	3	3	1	–	6	7	–	7	–
Upkeep	44	–	3	17	7	2	21	10	9	15	10
Moderate physical problems[1]	2,269	26	64	551	443	206	731	466	435	856	511
Plumbing	101	–	7	26	33	–	45	14	10	53	24
Heating	404	–	31	142	82	53	152	7	23	356	18
Upkeep	560	–	28	155	90	27	222	131	122	206	101
Kitchen	1,293	26	3	265	261	135	358	339	291	278	386
Overall opinion of structure											
1 (worst)	327	–	21	117	98	29	178	86	51	127	62
2	209	5	16	73	29	16	74	31	54	78	45
3	436	2	9	129	59	26	203	100	69	138	129
4	708	5	42	181	81	27	238	138	151	239	180
5	2,910	20	196	698	524	257	969	482	603	1,124	701
6	2,553	27	156	598	446	235	695	484	551	852	665
7	6,146	116	183	1,246	981	490	1,400	1,140	1,236	2,144	1,625
8	9,625	212	330	1,922	1,695	1,091	2,217	1,933	1,956	3,296	2,439
9	4,217	196	130	645	794	688	844	899	805	1,371	1,143
10 (best)	6,941	328	282	1,454	1,424	1,628	2,120	1,432	1,443	2,471	1,596
Not Reported	1,306	30	56	383	170	136	396	348	200	551	208
Water leakage during last 12 months											
No leakage from inside structure	31,184	884	1,234	6,404	5,643	4,312	8,166	6,204	6,287	10,864	7,829
With leakage from inside structure[1]	3,836	42	168	958	620	262	1,059	786	792	1,354	904
Fixtures backed up or overflowed	952	4	28	251	143	44	271	164	223	335	231
Pipes leaked	1,664	22	100	430	282	124	460	395	304	552	413
Broken water heater	327	2	22	72	37	29	93	60	50	153	64
Other or unknown (includes not reported)	1,088	14	20	256	181	70	291	193	243	395	256
Interior leakage not reported	357	15	18	84	38	49	108	83	40	174	60
No leakage from outside structure	31,906	891	1,195	6,696	5,830	4,352	8,352	6,369	6,126	11,206	8,205
With leakage from outside structure[1]	3,121	35	208	667	434	230	874	625	945	1,019	533
Roof	1,579	10	140	360	259	109	418	306	386	631	257
Basement	538	8	2	92	32	41	129	157	314	38	29
Walls, closed windows, or doors	795	6	56	163	89	54	262	128	247	258	162
Other or unknown (includes not reported)	410	11	20	86	72	32	117	80	80	142	108
Exterior leakage not reported	350	15	18	84	36	41	107	79	48	168	56
Renter maintenance quality											
Major repairs needed[7]	25,554	514	938	5,512	4,577	3,664	6,744	5,225	5,281	8,814	6,234
Work usually started quickly	22,183	455	837	4,495	3,831	3,412	5,634	4,544	4,692	7,548	5,398
Management solved problem quickly	23,246	484	865	4,849	4,078	3,484	5,976	4,750	4,865	7,929	5,702
Management polite and considerate	24,967	505	926	5,338	4,473	3,596	6,568	5,107	5,168	8,613	6,079
Minor repairs needed[7]	27,123	590	956	5,761	4,839	3,897	7,084	5,565	5,605	9,261	6,693
Started quickly enough usually	23,940	541	868	4,897	4,214	3,649	6,078	4,829	5,008	8,209	5,894
Solved the problem quickly	25,190	563	907	5,268	4,410	3,731	6,437	5,084	5,310	8,596	6,200
Polite	26,624	586	935	5,611	4,731	3,854	6,922	5,482	5,495	9,081	6,566
Building and ground maintenance											
Building maintenance quality											
Completely satisfied	25,026	781	956	4,791	4,411	3,822	6,163	4,839	5,054	8,799	6,334
Partly satisfied	6,809	105	212	1,795	1,266	504	2,003	1,485	1,445	2,200	1,679
Dissatisfied	1,939	11	63	580	392	119	735	475	381	628	455
Landlord not responsible	967	28	161	107	157	98	226	101	170	464	233
Not reported	637	16	29	173	74	79	207	173	69	302	92
Ground maintenance quality											
Completely satisfied	23,997	695	884	4,612	4,252	3,695	6,111	4,931	4,829	8,192	6,044
Partly satisfied	5,392	100	129	1,424	1,055	445	1,529	1,226	1,130	1,625	1,412
Dissatisfied	1,813	16	77	607	395	137	657	427	339	618	429
Landlord not responsible	3,564	113	301	646	531	268	830	313	772	1,659	819
Not reported	612	16	29	158	67	78	205	176	48	298	90
Building and ground maintenance quality											
Completely satisfied with both	21,201	648	790	3,951	3,789	3,463	5,294	4,379	4,232	7,236	5,354
Completely dissatisfied with both	994	5	38	350	247	67	419	284	168	295	247

– = Zero or rounds to zero.
X = Not applicable.
[1] = Figures may not add to total because more than one category may apply to a unit.
[2] = Two or more units of any tenure in structure.
[3] = Restricted to multiunits with five or more apartments with a resident 55 years of age or older.
[4] = Limited to units that reported meals, transportation, housekeeping, financial management, aid with telephone, or shopping.
[5] = Restricted to multiunits.
[6] = Restricted to single units.
[7] = When landlord responsible for repairs and when at least 1 condition answered.

Source: U.S. Census Bureau, American Housing Survey

Table 3-24. New Privately Owned Housing Units, Authorized, Physical Features, Unadjusted Data for the United States, 2011

[Numbers in thousands.]

Characteristics	Total housing units	Seasonal	Year-round											New construction 4 years	Manufactured/ mobile homes
				Occupied			Vacant								
			Total	Total	Owner	Renter	Total	For rent	Rental vacancy rate	For sale only	Rented or sold	Occasional use/URE	Other vacant		
Total	130,112	4,618	125,494	111,806	76,428	35,378	13,688	4,018	10.1	2,108	879	3,314	3,368	5,955	8,769
Stories in structure[1]															
1	41,537	1,880	39,657	35,364	26,216	9,148	4,292	815	8.1	745	266	1,031	1,435	1,554	X
2	43,447	1,145	42,302	37,867	25,210	12,657	4,435	1,536	10.7	727	288	939	945	2,392	X
3	27,574	542	27,031	24,508	16,721	7,787	2,524	988	11.2	373	162	494	506	1,205	X
4 to 6	6,051	160	5,891	5,134	2,349	2,785	757	320	10.2	77	69	185	106	288	X
7 or more	2,734	160	2,573	2,094	515	1,580	479	182	10.3	42	29	178	48	192	X
Stories between main and apartment entrances															
Multiunits, 2 or more floors	28,329	775	27,553	22,962	3,458	19,503	4,592	2,572	11.5	284	272	822	641	1,054	X
None (on same floor)	9,076	159	8,916	7,616	1,187	6,429	1,300	718	10.0	76	76	197	233	249	X
1 (up or down)	7,916	189	7,727	6,447	911	5,536	1,280	743	11.7	88	86	188	175	251	X
2 or more (up or down)	11,337	427	10,910	8,899	1,361	7,538	2,012	1,111	12.7	120	110	437	233	553	X
Elevator on floor															
Multiunits, 2 or more floors	28,329	775	27,553	22,962	3,458	19,503	4,592	2,572	11.5	284	272	822	641	1,054	X
With 1 or more elevators working	5,585	311	5,274	4,348	1,045	3,303	926	426	11.3	80	41	276	103	400	X
With elevator, none in working condition	58	–	58	46	11	35	12	8	19.2	–	–	–	4	2	X
No elevator	22,686	464	22,222	18,568	2,403	16,165	3,654	2,138	11.6	204	231	546	535	652	X
Units, 3 or more floors from main entrance	1,805	43	1,763	1,436	133	1,302	327	184	12.2	17	22	66	37	72	X
Foundation															
1-unit building, excluding manufactured/mobile homes	89,525	3,047	86,478	79,052	67,276	11,776	7,427	1,018	7.9	1,652	519	1,926	2,312	4,518	X
With basement under all of building	29,104	490	28,614	26,713	23,821	2,892	1,902	214	6.8	480	139	479	590	1,237	X
With basement under part of building	8,991	170	8,821	8,208	7,350	858	613	82	8.6	135	64	157	176	156	X
With crawl space	20,955	965	19,991	18,022	14,783	3,240	1,968	280	7.9	360	92	538	698	727	X
On concrete slab	28,693	1,011	27,682	24,917	20,431	4,486	2,765	405	8.2	655	217	717	771	2,327	X
Other	1,782	411	1,371	1,192	892	300	179	37	11.0	22	7	35	77	71	X
External building conditions[2]															
Sagging roof	2,765	249	2,516	1,888	1,370	517	628	82	13.4	83	50	76	338	3	491
Missing roofing material	5,805	252	5,553	4,640	3,682	958	914	110	10.3	146	85	143	429	82	496
Hole in roof	2,020	139	1,881	1,458	1,029	429	424	37	7.9	52	33	40	262	6	423
Missing bricks, siding, or other outside wall material	3,175	211	2,964	2,323	1,661	661	641	80	10.7	68	47	86	359	22	374
Sloping outside walls	1,687	164	1,523	1,167	781	386	356	42	9.9	40	26	55	193	10	317
Boarded up windows	1,511	180	1,331	821	558	262	510	58	18.1	42	44	65	301	13	273
Broken windows	3,850	201	3,649	2,984	2,112	872	666	91	9.4	65	48	97	364	37	703
Bars on windows	3,552	32	3,520	3,318	2,616	702	202	47	6.3	26	20	44	65	22	65
Foundation crumbling or has open crack or hole	2,822	160	2,662	2,227	1,687	540	435	53	8.9	53	21	65	243	17	152
None of the above	78,826	3,031	75,795	69,766	60,037	9,730	6,029	860	8.1	1,419	401	1,890	1,458	4,555	6,807
Not reported	2,591	102	2,489	2,173	1,832	341	315	29	7.8	48	7	78	153	115	189
Site placement															
Manufactured/mobile homes	8,769	730	8,040	6,839	5,418	1,421	1,201	176	11.0	143	65	487	329	324	8,769
First site	5,912	509	5,403	4,600	4,002	598	803	85	12.3	98	52	353	215	272	5,912
Moved from another site	1,726	174	1,552	1,301	1,047	254	251	51	16.6	23	8	83	87	38	1,726
Don't know	553	46	506	362	97	265	144	41	13.3	22	5	48	28	9	553
Not reported	579	–	579	576	272	304	2	–	–	–	–	2	–	4	579

– = Zero or rounds to zero.
X = Not applicable.
[1]Figures exclude manufactured/mobile homes.
[2]Figures may not add to total because more than one category may apply to a unit. Figures do not include multiunit structures.

Source: U.S. Census Bureau, Building Permits Survey

Table 3-25. Selected Housing Characteristics, 2010 American Community Survey, 1-, 3-, and 5-Year Estimates

[Numbers in thousands, rate, percent.]

Characteristics	United States											
	1-year estimates				3-year estimates				5-year estimates			
	Estimate	Estimate margin of error (+/-)	Percent	Percent margin of error (+/-)	Estimate	Estimate margin of error (+/-)	Percent	Percent margin of error (+/-)	Estimate	Estimate margin of error (+/-)	Percent	Percent margin of error (+/-)
Housing occupancy												
Total housing units	131,791.0	5.74	100.0	X	131,210.6	6.08	100.0	X	130,038.1	11.17	100.0	X
Occupied housing units	114,567.0	163.25	86.9	0.1	114,596.9	112.09	87.3	0.1	114,236.0	248.11	87.8	0.2
Vacant housing units	17,223.0	167.25	13.1	0.1	16,613.7	107.44	12.7	0.1	15,802.1	237.53	12.2	0.2
Homeowner vacancy rate	2.5	0.10	X	X	2.5	0.10	X	X	2.4	0.10	X	X
Rental vacancy rate	8.2	0.10	X	X	8.1	0.10	X	X	7.8	0.10	X	X
Units in structure												
Total housing units	131,791.0	5.74	100.0	X	131,210.6	6.08	100.0	X	130,038.1	11.17	100.0	X
1-unit, detached	80,965.0	113.53	61.4	0.1	80,772.1	78.48	61.6	0.1	80,135.9	124.02	61.6	0.1
1-unit, attached	7,661.0	35.44	5.8	0.1	7,551.8	21.71	5.8	0.1	7,461.7	25.50	5.7	0.1
2 units	5,049.0	40.36	3.8	0.1	5,080.4	27.59	3.9	0.1	5,043.9	31.91	3.9	0.1
3 or 4 units	5,847.0	40.62	4.4	0.1	5,868.6	25.19	4.5	0.1	5,817.3	25.84	4.5	0.1
5 to 9 units	6,338.0	40.17	4.8	0.1	6,363.8	30.33	4.9	0.1	6,293.0	31.66	4.8	0.1
10 to 19 units	5,930.0	42.34	4.5	0.1	5,959.6	26.80	4.5	0.1	5,876.2	33.35	4.5	0.1
20 or more units	11,250.0	49.31	8.5	0.1	10,868.3	24.50	8.3	0.1	10,618.2	21.30	8.2	0.1
Mobile home	8,636.0	48.98	6.6	0.1	8,636.7	30.88	6.6	0.1	8,684.4	39.32	6.7	0.1
Boat, RV, van, etc.	110.0	4.87	0.1	0.1	109.2	3.11	0.1	0.1	107.5	2.45	0.1	0.1
Year structure built												
Total housing units	131,791.0	5.74	100.0	X	131,210.6	6.08	100.0	X	130,038.1	11.17	100.0	X
2005 or later	8,007.0	43.95	6.1	0.1	6,509.2	27.59	5.0	0.1	5,273.9	27.24	4.1	0.1
2000 to 2004	11,549.0	52.99	8.8	0.1	11,346.0	29.44	8.6	0.1	11,282.6	28.20	8.7	0.1
1990 to 1999	18,302.0	63.35	13.9	0.1	18,378.3	36.82	14.0	0.1	18,316.3	24.29	14.1	0.1
1980 to 1989	18,408.0	73.24	14.0	0.1	18,471.0	30.79	14.1	0.1	18,473.0	26.54	14.2	0.1
1970 to 1979	21,105.0	64.30	16.0	0.1	21,340.4	31.01	16.3	0.1	21,353.3	27.34	16.4	0.1
1960 to 1969	14,692.0	54.44	11.1	0.1	14,791.8	29.99	11.3	0.1	14,808.7	24.61	11.4	0.1
1950 to 1959	14,428.0	58.39	10.9	0.1	14,640.2	28.54	11.2	0.1	14,654.7	23.15	11.3	0.1
1940 to 1949	7,304.0	40.39	5.5	0.1	7,503.5	22.85	5.7	0.1	7,526.5	16.66	5.8	0.1
1939 or earlier	17,992.0	52.99	13.7	0.1	18,230.2	32.76	13.9	0.1	18,349.0	34.73	14.1	0.1
Rooms												
Total housing units	131,791.0	5.74	100.0	X	131,210.6	6.08	100.0	X	130,038.1	11.17	100.0	X
1 room	2,594.0	34.12	2.0	0.1	2,589.1	19.88	2.0	0.1	2,061.7	18.68	1.6	0.1
2 rooms	3,145.0	25.39	2.4	0.1	2,990.0	15.31	2.3	0.1	3,406.0	17.59	2.6	0.1
3 rooms	12,001.0	57.92	9.1	0.1	11,682.0	35.82	8.9	0.1	11,732.8	30.01	9.0	0.1
4 rooms	22,075.0	76.80	16.8	0.1	21,753.9	56.63	16.6	0.1	21,915.4	71.77	16.9	0.1
5 rooms	26,947.0	81.75	20.4	0.1	26,767.4	50.13	20.4	0.1	27,215.1	63.02	20.9	0.1
6 rooms	24,047.0	71.72	18.2	0.1	24,035.7	41.04	18.3	0.1	24,138.9	27.53	18.6	0.1
7 rooms	16,203.0	66.46	12.3	0.1	16,272.7	34.93	12.4	0.1	16,103.5	43.44	12.4	0.1
8 rooms	11,212.0	53.28	8.5	0.1	11,300.0	36.88	8.6	0.1	10,913.8	47.29	8.4	0.1
9 rooms or more	13,563.0	68.32	10.3	0.1	13,820.0	50.90	10.5	0.1	12,550.9	70.45	9.7	0.1
Median rooms	5.5	0.1	X	X	5.5	0.10	X	X	5.5	0.10	X	X
Bedrooms												
Total housing units	131,791.0	5.74	100.0	X	131,210.6	6.08	100.0	X	130,038.1	11.17	X	X
No bedroom	2,875.0	32.78	2.2	0.1	2,873.7	19.48	2.2	0.1	2,393.3	17.25	1.8	0.1
1 bedroom	14,828.0	55.90	11.3	0.1	14,597.3	31.62	11.1	0.1	14,724.1	27.13	11.3	0.1
2 bedrooms	35,514.0	83.60	26.9	0.1	35,398.4	58.33	27.0	0.1	35,368.6	73.99	27.2	0.1
3 bedrooms	52,286.0	94.14	39.7	0.1	52,060.5	52.34	39.7	0.1	51,750.6	60.69	39.8	0.1
4 bedrooms	20,826.0	61.15	15.8	0.1	20,833.9	40.71	15.9	0.1	20,550.3	57.80	15.8	0.1
5 or more bedrooms	5,458.0	31.68	4.1	0.1	5,446.8	17.72	4.2	0.1	5,251.2	13.90	4.0	0.1
Housing tenure												
Occupied housing units	114,567.0	163.25	X	X	114,596.9	112.09	X	X	114,236.0	248.11	X	X
Owner-occupied	74,873.0	216.09	65.4	0.1	75,557.7	165.35	65.9	0.1	76,089.7	362.76	66.6	0.2
Renter-occupied	39,694.0	91.88	34.6	0.1	39,039.3	74.53	34.1	0.1	38,146.3	120.18	33.4	0.2
Average household size of owner-occupied unit	2.7	0.01	X	X	2.7	0.01	X	X	2.7	0.01	X	X
Average household size of renter-occupied unit	2.5	0.01	X	X	2.5	0.01	X	X	2.4	0.01	X	X
Year householder moved into unit												
Occupied housing units	114,567.0	163.25	X	X	114,596.9	112.09	X	X	114,236.0	248.11	X	X
2005 or later	51,277.0	86.70	44.8	0.1	46,731.4	55.63	40.8	0.1	39,766.0	70.05	34.8	0.1
2000 to 2004	20,276.0	72.89	17.7	0.1	22,789.6	56.45	19.9	0.1	26,516.8	95.00	23.2	0.1
1990 to 1999	21,140.0	84.50	18.5	0.1	22,225.8	54.77	19.4	0.1	23,883.4	107.43	20.9	0.1
1980 to 1989	9,903.0	45.53	8.6	0.1	10,304.7	33.31	9.0	0.1	10,803.7	60.38	9.5	0.1
1970 to 1979	6,564.0	39.67	5.7	0.1	6,817.0	20.23	5.9	0.1	7,146.5	31.23	6.3	0.1
1969 or earlier	5,404.0	32.18	4.7	0.1	5,728.4	16.28	5.0	0.1	6,119.6	29.40	5.4	0.1

Table 3-25. Selected Housing Characteristics, 2010 American Community Survey, 1-, 3-, and 5-Year Estimates—*Continued*

[Numbers in thousands, rate, percent.]

Characteristics	United States											
	1-year estimates				3-year estimates				5-year estimates			
	Estimate	Estimate margin of error (+/-)	Percent	Percent margin of error (+/-)	Estimate	Estimate margin of error (+/-)	Percent	Percent margin of error (+/-)	Estimate	Estimate margin of error (+/-)	Percent	Percent margin of error (+/-)
Vehicles available												
Occupied housing units	114,567.0	163.25	X	X	114,596.9	112.09	X	X	114,236.0	248.11	X	X
No vehicles	10,397.0	50.79	9.1	0.1	10,256.0	28.14	8.9	0.1	10,113.3	26.00	8.9	0.1
1 vehicle	38,742.0	74.04	33.8	0.1	38,440.5	48.66	33.5	0.1	38,014.2	36.17	33.3	0.1
2 vehicles	43,057.0	120.25	37.6	0.1	43,144.2	70.54	37.6	0.1	43,265.0	142.05	37.9	0.1
3 or more vehicles	22,370.0	75.37	19.5	0.1	22,756.2	51.40	19.9	0.1	22,843.6	94.28	20.0	0.1
House heating fuel												
Occupied housing units	114,567.0	163.25	X	X	114,596.9	112.09	X	X	114,236.0	248.11	X	X
Utility gas	56,691.0	106.55	49.5	0.1	56,983.8	77.31	49.7	0.1	57,018.5	162.99	49.9	0.1
Bottled, tank, or LP gas	5,779.0	37.11	5.0	0.1	5,907.5	24.48	5.2	0.1	6,146.4	24.18	5.4	0.1
Electricity	40,579.0	72.64	35.4	0.1	39,909.3	48.32	34.8	0.1	39,066.3	63.60	34.2	0.1
Fuel oil, kerosene, etc.	7,389.0	34.00	6.5	0.1	7,739.1	19.10	6.8	0.1	8,073.2	15.68	7.1	0.1
Coal or coke	134.0	5.44	0.1	0.1	133.5	2.71	0.1	0.1	135.3	2.19	0.1	0.1
Wood	2,382.0	24.48	2.1	0.1	2,346.2	12.21	2.0	0.1	2,249.6	9.27	2.0	0.1
Solar energy	41.0	3.07	0.0	0.1	38.0	1.37	0.0	0.1	38.0	1.27	0.0	0.1
Other fuel	511.0	10.19	0.4	0.1	491.1	6.78	0.4	0.1	483.5	4.05	0.4	0.1
No fuel used	1,058.0	14.96	0.9	0.1	1,048.6	8.64	0.9	0.1	1,025.3	7.75	0.9	0.1
Selected characteristics												
Occupied housing units	114,567.0	163.25	X	X	114,596.9	112.09	X	X	114,236.0	248.11	X	X
Lacking complete plumbing facilities	652.0	15.84	0.6	0.1	696.0	8.87	0.6	0.1	602.3	9.02	0.5	0.1
Lacking complete kitchen facilities	1,101.0	21.05	1.0	0.1	1,079.1	11.01	0.9	0.1	899.2	9.34	0.8	0.1
No telephone service available	2,862.0	22.25	2.5	0.1	2,803.2	16.16	2.4	0.1	4,209.5	21.58	3.7	0.1
Occupants per room												
Occupied housing units	114,567.0	163.25	X	X	114,596.9	112.09	X	X	114,236.0	248.11	X	X
1.00 or less	110,685.0	177.58	96.6	0.1	110,915.9	121.90	96.8	0.1	110,699.8	262.34	96.9	0.1
1.01 to 1.50	2,709.0	28.74	2.4	0.1	2,535.8	18.44	2.2	0.1	2,546.2	15.71	2.2	0.1
1.51 or more	1,172.0	19.59	1.0	0.1	1,145.2	11.72	1.0	0.1	990.0	7.10	0.9	0.1
Value												
Owner-occupied units	74,873.0	216.09	X	X	75,557.7	165.35	X	X	76,089.7	362.76	X	X
Less than $50,000	6,439.0	41.24	8.6	0.1	6,361.8	23.49	8.4	0.1	6,203.3	26.93	8.2	0.1
$50,000 to $99,999	11,369.0	66.66	15.2	0.1	10,991.0	40.43	14.5	0.1	11,301.6	61.90	14.9	0.1
$100,000 to $149,999	11,993.0	59.27	16.0	0.1	11,562.8	35.27	15.3	0.1	11,794.5	61.12	15.5	0.1
$150,000 to $199,999	11,374.0	60.16	15.2	0.1	11,177.2	36.67	14.8	0.1	10,874.9	56.38	14.3	0.1
$200,000 to $299,999	13,950.0	64.35	18.6	0.1	14,124.3	44.01	18.7	0.1	13,534.2	66.85	17.8	0.1
$300,000 to $499,999	11,920.0	48.78	15.9	0.1	12,603.3	32.57	16.7	0.1	12,883.8	69.78	16.9	0.1
$500,000 to $999,999	6,268.0	30.36	8.4	0.1	6,984.9	20.90	9.2	0.1	7,679.5	35.62	10.1	0.1
$1,000,000 or more	1,558.0	16.25	2.1	0.1	1,752.4	9.39	2.3	0.1	1,817.8	8.14	2.4	0.1
Median (dollars)	179,900.0	292.00	X	X	187,500.00	198.00	X	X	188,400.00	184.00	X	X
Mortgage status												
Owner-occupied units	74,873.0	216.09	X	X	75,557.7	165.35	X	X	76,089.7	362.76	X	X
Housing units with a mortgage	50,339.0	146.04	67.2	0.1	51,197.5	120.72	67.8	0.1	51,696.8	255.19	67.9	0.1
Housing units without a mortgage	24,533.0	94.65	32.8	0.1	24,360.2	56.27	32.2	0.1	24,392.8	111.57	32.1	0.1
Selected monthly owner costs (SMOC)												
Housing units with a mortgage	50,339.0	146.04	X	X	51,197.5	120.72	X	X	51,696.8	255.19	X	X
Less than $300	102.0	4.60	0.2	0.1	111.5	3.05	0.2	0.1	112.6	1.92	0.2	0.1
$300 to $499	931.0	14.03	1.8	0.1	950.8	8.87	1.9	0.1	955.0	7.33	1.8	0.1
$500 to $699	2,755.0	24.64	5.5	0.1	2,781.9	15.51	5.4	0.1	2,785.4	14.59	5.4	0.1
$700 to $999	7,503.0	41.80	14.9	0.1	7,402.9	28.01	14.5	0.1	7,450.3	36.12	14.4	0.1
$1,000 to $1,499	13,995.0	67.14	27.8	0.1	13,863.7	42.91	27.1	0.1	13,998.2	71.67	27.1	0.1
$1,500 to $1,999	10,062.0	54.18	20.0	0.1	10,191.0	34.19	19.9	0.1	10,309.6	58.92	19.9	0.1
$2,000 or more	14,987.0	51.91	29.8	0.1	15,895.8	41.42	31.0	0.1	16,085.7	86.60	31.1	0.1
Median (dollars)	1,496.0	3.00	X	X	1,521.00	2.00	X	X	1,524.00	1.00	X	X
Housing units without a mortgage	24,533.0	94.65	X	X	24,360.2	56.27	X	X	24,392.8	111.57	X	X
Less than $100	312.0	8.39	1.3	0.1	323.1	5.10	1.3	0.1	322.1	3.63	1.3	0.1
$100 to $199	1,825.0	19.78	7.4	0.1	1,871.7	11.08	7.7	0.1	1,853.9	11.53	7.6	0.1
$200 to $299	4,054.0	30.02	16.5	0.1	4,060.9	20.12	16.7	0.1	4,069.2	21.34	16.7	0.1
$300 to $399	4,829.0	34.62	19.7	0.1	4,721.6	21.62	19.4	0.1	4,733.5	24.40	19.4	0.1
$400 or more	13,511.0	55.63	55.1	0.1	13,383.0	34.98	54.9	0.1	13,414.1	63.09	55.0	0.1
Median (dollars)	431.0	1.00	X	X	431.00	1.00	X	X	431.00	1.00	X	X

Table 3-25. Selected Housing Characteristics, 2010 American Community Survey, 1-, 3-, and 5-Year Estimates—*Continued*

[Numbers in thousands, rate, percent.]

Characteristics	United States											
	1-year estimates				3-year estimates				5-year estimates			
	Estimate	Estimate margin of error (+/-)	Percent	Percent margin of error (+/-)	Estimate	Estimate margin of error (+/-)	Percent	Percent margin of error (+/-)	Estimate	Estimate margin of error (+/-)	Percent	Percent margin of error (+/-)
Selected monthly owner costs as a percentage of household income (SMOCAPI)												
Housing units with a mortgage (excluding units where SMOCAPI cannot be computed)	50,082.0	145.24	X	X	50,970.8	120.73	X	X	51,483.0	256.08	X	X
Less than 20.0 percent	16,883.0	73.19	33.7	0.1	17,220.3	57.63	33.8	0.1	17,447.8	113.62	33.9	0.1
20.0 to 24.9 percent	7,982.0	46.44	15.9	0.1	8,136.3	34.03	16.0	0.1	8,257.5	56.76	16.0	0.1
25.0 to 29.9 percent	6,176.0	37.77	12.3	0.1	6,328.8	24.27	12.4	0.1	6,433.4	40.42	12.5	0.1
30.0 to 34.9 percent	4,458.0	33.22	8.9	0.1	4,559.2	21.33	8.9	0.1	4,636.2	24.48	9.0	0.1
35.0 percent or more	14,581.0	53.41	29.1	0.1	14,726.2	32.34	28.9	0.1	14,708.2	35.68	28.6	0.1
Not computed	256.0	9.72	X	X	226.7	5.01	X	X	213.8	3.54	X	X
Housing units without a mortgage (excluding units where SMOCAPI cannot be computed)	24,236.0	95.19	X	X	24,090.0	56.47	X	X	24,142.9	111.61	X	X
Less than 10.0 percent	9,396.0	54.82	38.8	0.1	9,513.9	29.90	39.5	0.1	9,493.0	44.58	39.3	0.1
10.0 to 14.9 percent	4,910.0	32.25	20.3	0.1	4,840.2	19.29	20.1	0.1	4,841.0	23.66	20.1	0.1
15.0 to 19.9 percent	3,026.0	23.68	12.5	0.1	2,945.3	13.09	12.2	0.1	2,960.5	15.58	12.3	0.1
20.0 to 24.9 percent	1,884.0	20.65	7.8	0.1	1,840.2	11.74	7.6	0.1	1,854.6	12.51	7.7	0.1
25.0 to 29.9 percent	1,248.0	14.33	5.2	0.1	1,222.1	8.69	5.1	0.1	1,234.8	9.34	5.1	0.1
30.0 to 34.9 percent	853.0	14.23	3.5	0.1	835.6	7.40	3.5	0.1	839.7	7.82	3.5	0.1
35.0 percent or more	2,915.0	25.77	12.0	0.1	2,892.7	16.11	12.0	0.1	2,919.3	18.00	12.1	0.1
Not computed	297.0	8.65	X	X	270.2	4.57	X	X	249.9	3.43	X	X
Gross rent												
Occupied units paying rent	37,521.0	92.18	X	X	36,882.3	74.13	X	X	35,969.3	119.81	X	X
Less than $200	741.0	11.73	2.0	0.1	785.8	8.42	2.1	0.1	811.0	5.67	2.3	0.1
$200 to $299	1,241.0	15.87	3.3	0.1	1,241.5	10.57	3.4	0.1	1,227.4	8.00	3.4	0.1
$300 to $499	3,405.0	28.50	9.1	0.1	3,488.6	18.08	9.5	0.1	3,526.6	13.53	9.8	0.1
$500 to $749	9,208.0	41.99	24.5	0.1	9,078.6	32.81	24.6	0.1	8,956.5	30.28	24.9	0.1
$750 to $999	9,171.0	54.51	24.4	0.1	8,943.4	31.35	24.2	0.1	8,772.9	32.04	24.4	0.1
$1,000 to $1,499	9,072.0	47.63	24.2	0.1	8,818.2	35.94	23.9	0.1	8,457.8	44.44	23.5	0.1
$1,500 or more	4,679.0	36.37	12.5	0.1	4,526.2	20.63	12.3	0.1	4,217.1	29.70	11.7	0.1
Median (dollars)	855.0	0.00	X	X	850.00	1.00	X	X	841.00	1.00	X	X
No rent paid	2,172.0	25.27	X	X	2,156.9	14.25	X	X	2,177.0	8.64	X	X
Gross rent as a percentage of household income (GRAPI)												
Occupied units paying rent (excluding units where GRAPI cannot be computed)	36,656.0	91.11	X	X	36,118.4	71.94	X	X	35,274.2	115.47	X	X
Less than 15.0 percent	4,119.0	36.08	11.2	0.1	4,285.6	25.00	11.9	0.1	4,324.8	26.42	12.3	0.1
15.0 to 19.9 percent	4,333.0	35.33	11.8	0.1	4,412.1	21.36	12.2	0.1	4,383.5	20.50	12.4	0.1
20.0 to 24.9 percent	4,537.0	33.57	12.4	0.1	4,573.3	20.88	12.7	0.1	4,511.1	22.51	12.8	0.1
25.0 to 29.9 percent	4,244.0	33.59	11.6	0.1	4,199.4	19.61	11.6	0.1	4,117.0	19.76	11.7	0.1
30.0 to 34.9 percent	3,373.0	33.87	9.2	0.1	3,307.8	18.84	9.2	0.1	3,215.0	16.05	9.1	0.1
35.0 percent or more	16,047.0	61.86	43.8	0.1	15,340.2	43.34	42.5	0.1	14,722.9	46.74	41.7	0.1
Not computed	3,037.0	31.64	X	X	2,920.8	15.42	X	X	2,872.1	11.66	X	X

X = Not applicable.

Source: U.S. Census Bureau, 2008--2010 American Community Survey

Table 3-26. Inclusion of Utilities in Rent, Renter-Occupied Housing Units in the United States, 2010 American Community Survey, 1-, 3-, and 5-Year Estimates

[Numbers in thousands.]

Characteristics	United States					
	1-year estimates		3-year estimates		5-year estimates	
	Estimate	Margin of error (+/-)	Estimate	Margin of error (+/-)	Estimate	Margin of error (+/-)
Total	39,694.0	91.9	39,039.3	74.5	38,146.3	120.2
Pay extra for one or more utilities	35,202.9	91.9	34,675.3	70.6	33,829.4	119.1
No extra payment for any utilities	4,491.6	35.0	4,364.0	18.7	4,316.9	13.2

Source: U.S. Census Bureau, American Community Survey

Table 3-27. Year Structure Built, 2010 American Community Survey, 1-, 3-, and 5-Year Estimates

[Numbers in thousands, except as noted.]

Characteristics	United States					
	1-year estimates		3-year estimates		5-year estimates	
	Estimate	Margin of error (+/-)	Estimate	Margin of error (+/-)	Estimate	Margin of error (+/-)
Total units	131,791.1	5.7	131,210.6	6.1	130,038.1	11.2
Built 2005 or later	8,007.6	44.0	6,509.2	27.6	5,273.9	27.2
Built 2000 to 2004	11,549.6	53.0	11,346.0	29.4	11,282.60	28.2
Built 1990 to 1999	18,302.1	63.3	18,378.3	36.8	18,316.3	24.3
Built 1980 to 1989	18,408.4	73.2	18,471.0	30.8	18,473.0	26.5
Built 1970 to 1979	21,105.7	64.3	21,340.4	31.0	21,353.3	27.3
Built 1960 to 1969	14,692.1	54.4	14,791.8	30.0	14,808.7	24.6
Built 1950 to 1959	14,428.8	58.4	14,640.2	28.5	14,654.7	23.1
Built 1940 to 1949	7,304.4	40.4	7,503.5	22.9	7,526.5	16.7
Built 1939 or earlier	17,992.3	53.0	18,230.2	32.8	18,349.0	34.7
Median year structure built (years)	1975	1	1975	1	1975	1

Source: U.S. Census Bureau, 2010 American Community Survey

Table 3-28. Percent of Housing Units That Were Built in 2005 or Later, United States and Puerto Rico, by State and Urban Designation, 2010 American Community Survey, 1-, 3-, and 5-Year Estimates

[Percent.]

Characteristics	United States					
	1-year estimates		3-year estimates		5-year estimates	
	Estimate	Margin of error (+/-)	Estimate	Margin of error (+/-)	Estimate	Margin of error (+/-)
United States	6.1	0.1	5.0	0.1	4.1	0.1
Urban and rural						
Urban	4.4	0.1	3.6	0.1	3.0	0.1
Rural	10.9	0.1	9.0	0.1	7.4	0.1
Inside and outside metropolitan statistical area						
In metropolitan or micropolitan statistical area	6.2	0.1	5.1	0.1	4.2	0.1
In metropolitan statistical area	6.3	0.1	5.2	0.1	4.3	0.1
In principal city	5.3	0.1	4.3	0.1	3.5	0.1
Not in principal city	7.0	0.1	5.8	0.1	4.8	0.1
In micropolitan statistical area	5.6	0.1	4.4	0.1	3.5	0.1
In principal city	5.1	0.2	4.0	0.1	3.1	0.1
Not in principal city	5.8	0.1	4.6	0.1	3.6	0.1
Not in metropolitan or micropolitan statistical area	4.3	0.1	3.1	0.1	2.4	0.1
Alabama	7.2	0.3	5.8	0.1	4.6	0.1
Alaska	6.6	0.7	4.5	0.3	3.3	0.2
Arizona	10.5	0.3	8.7	0.2	7.6	0.1
Arkansas	7.5	0.4	6.1	0.2	4.8	0.2
California	4.9	0.1	4.0	0.1	3.3	0.1
Colorado	6.6	0.2	5.5	0.1	4.6	0.1
Connecticut	3.0	0.2	2.4	0.1	1.9	0.1
Delaware	7.8	0.7	6.6	0.3	5.6	0.2
District of Columbia	4.7	0.6	3.5	0.3	2.8	0.2
Florida	7.2	0.2	6.2	0.1	5.5	0.1
Georgia	9.4	0.3	7.7	0.1	6.3	0.1
Hawaii	5.8	0.4	4.4	0.2	3.6	0.2
Idaho	9.8	0.5	8.4	0.2	6.8	0.2
Illinois	4.7	0.2	3.9	0.1	3.3	0.1
Indiana	4.9	0.2	4.2	0.1	3.4	0.1
Iowa	5.3	0.2	4.3	0.1	3.4	0.1
Kansas	5.0	0.3	4.0	0.1	3.2	0.1
Kentucky	5.9	0.2	4.6	0.1	3.8	0.1
Louisiana	8.2	0.3	6.2	0.1	5.0	0.1
Maine	4.3	0.4	3.2	0.2	2.6	0.1
Maryland	4.8	0.2	4.0	0.1	3.3	0.1
Massachusetts	3.2	0.2	2.5	0.1	2.0	0.1
Michigan	3.1	0.1	2.6	0.1	2.2	0.1
Minnesota	5.2	0.2	4.3	0.1	3.6	0.1
Mississippi	8.1	0.4	6.5	0.2	5.2	0.2
Missouri	6.1	0.2	4.8	0.1	3.9	0.1
Montana	6.7	0.5	5.1	0.3	4.0	0.2
Nebraska	5.2	0.3	4.2	0.2	3.3	0.1
Nevada	11.8	0.5	10.2	0.2	8.9	0.2
New Hampshire	4.1	0.4	3.3	0.2	2.7	0.1
New Jersey	3.7	0.1	3.0	0.1	2.5	0.1
New Mexico	6.4	0.4	5.3	0.2	4.3	0.1
New York	2.8	0.1	2.1	0.1	1.6	0.1
North Carolina	8.8	0.2	7.3	0.1	5.7	0.1
North Dakota	6.4	0.5	4.9	0.3	3.8	0.2
Ohio	3.4	0.1	2.9	0.1	2.4	0.1
Oklahoma	6.3	0.3	5.1	0.1	4.0	0.1
Oregon	6.6	0.3	5.4	0.2	4.4	0.1
Pennsylvania	3.4	0.1	2.7	0.1	2.2	0.1
Rhode Island	2.4	0.4	2.0	0.2	1.6	0.1
South Carolina	9.5	0.3	7.6	0.2	6.0	0.1
South Dakota	6.9	0.6	5.3	0.3	4.1	0.2
Tennessee	7.3	0.2	6.2	0.1	5.0	0.1
Texas	10.2	0.1	8.3	0.1	6.7	0.1
Utah	10.4	0.5	8.2	0.3	6.5	0.1
Vermont	3.3	0.4	2.5	0.2	2.0	0.1
Virginia	6.5	0.2	5.3	0.1	4.2	0.1
Washington	7.6	0.3	6.0	0.1	4.8	0.1
West Virginia	4.1	0.3	3.2	0.1	2.4	0.1
Wisconsin	4.9	0.1	3.9	0.1	3.2	0.1
Wyoming	7.7	0.8	5.8	0.4	4.3	0.3
Puerto Rico	2.7	0.2	1.2	0.1	0.9	0.1

Source: U.S. Census Bureau, 2010 American Community Survey

Table 3-29. Tenure, by Age of Householder, Occupants Per Room, Telephone Service Available, and Vehicles Available, 2010 American Community Survey, 1-, 3-, and 5-Year Estimates

[Numbers in thousands.]

Characteristics	United States					
	1-year estimates		3-year estimates		5-year estimates	
	Estimate	Margin of error (+/-)	Estimate	Margin of error (+/-)	Estimate	Margin of error (+/-)
Total units, occupants per room	114,567.4	163.2	114,596.9	112.1	114,236.0	248.1
Owner-occupied units	74,873.4	216.1	75,557.7	165.3	76,089.7	362.8
Householder 15 to 34 years	8,061.9	66.3	8,446.3	48.1	8,874.5	89.5
1.00 or less occupants per room	7,803.8	65.8	8,190.4	47.3	8,608.9	89.1
1.01 to 1.50 occupants per room	207.1	8.0	206.2	4.1	217.7	3.4
1.51 or more occupants per room	51.1	3.2	49.7	2.2	48.0	1.4
Householder 35 to 64 years	47,265.3	125.1	47,816.9	89.2	48,242.6	189.8
1.00 or less occupants per room	46,299.3	125.8	46,913.2	88.5	47,336.5	189.0
1.01 to 1.50 occupants per room	750.0	14.4	705.1	7.3	725.0	6.0
1.51 or more occupants per room	216.0	7.3	198.7	3.9	181.2	3.0
Householder 65 years and over	19,546.2	60.0	19,294.4	40.6	18,972.5	86.7
1.00 or less occupants per room	19,452.2	60.0	19,208.3	40.9	18,891.8	86.8
1.01 to 1.50 occupants per room	64.9	3.5	59.9	2.0	59.0	1.5
1.51 or more occupants per room	29.1	2.8	26.3	1.3	21.8	0.9
Renter-occupied units	39,694.0	91.9	39,039.3	74.5	38,146.3	120.2
Householder 15 to 34 years	14,633.3	48.7	14,779.6	33.6	14,670.5	22.3
1.00 or less occupants per room	13,503.8	45.6	13,685.4	32.8	13,629.2	23.4
1.01 to 1.50 occupants per room	744.8	16.7	704.8	8.9	710.1	7.8
1.51 or more occupants per room	384.6	12.2	389.4	7.1	331.2	4.6
Householder 35 to 64 years	19,732.8	75.7	19,079.0	62.5	18,409.0	136.7
1.00 or less occupants per room	18,371.8	70.8	17,804.7	58.5	17,225.7	127.9
1.01 to 1.50 occupants per room	911.3	14.8	832.5	9.7	806.6	9.1
1.51 or more occupants per room	449.8	12.4	441.8	7.4	376.6	5.0
Householder 65 years and over	5,327.9	31.5	5,180.7	16.6	5,066.9	23.7
1.00 or less occupants per room	5,254.3	31.5	5,114.0	16.3	5,007.8	23.9
1.01 to 1.50 occupants per room	31.8	3.2	27.4	1.5	27.8	1.1
1.51 or more occupants per room	41.9	3.6	39.3	1.8	31.2	1.3
Total units, telephone service available	114,567.4	163.2	114,596.9	112.1	114,236.0	248.1
Owner-occupied units	74,873.4	216.1	75,557.7	165.3	76,089.7	362.8
With telephone service available	73,795.8	210.7	74,595.1	165.5	74,639.1	365.0
Householder 15 to 34 years	7,844.9	63.4	8,243.2	46.9	8,445.6	86.2
Householder 35 to 64 years	46,564.7	122.5	47,200.4	90.5	47,379.4	195.1
Householder 65 years and over	19,386.3	59.9	19,151.5	40.7	18,814.1	86.9
No telephone service available	1,077.6	14.8	962.5	8.7	1,450.6	7.5
Householder 15 to 34 years	217.1	6.9	203.1	4.6	428.9	5.5
Householder 35 to 64 years	700.6	12.0	616.5	6.2	863.3	7.8
Householder 65 years and over	159.9	5.5	142.9	3.5	158.4	2.4
Renter-occupied units	39,694.0	91.9	39,039.3	74.5	38,146.3	120.2
With telephone service available	37,909.1	92.1	37,198.6	70.8	35,387.4	105.8
Householder 15 to 34 years	13,932.3	46.4	14,008.0	33.9	13,282.6	20.7
Householder 35 to 64 years	18,825.8	74.4	18,168.6	58.3	17,200.8	121.9
Householder 65 years and over	5,151.0	31.2	5,021.9	16.6	4,904.0	24.5
No telephone service available	1,785.0	21.4	1,840.7	13.7	2,759.0	19.4
Householder 15 to 34 years	701.0	14.4	771.5	9.2	1,387.9	10.7
Householder 35 to 64 years	907.1	15.4	910.4	9.5	1,208.2	17.3
Householder 65 years and over	176.9	7.5	158.8	4.8	162.9	3.3
Total units, vehicles available	114,567.4	163.2	114,596.9	112.1	114,236.0	248.1
Owner-occupied units	74,873.4	216.1	75,557.7	165.3	76,089.7	362.8
No vehicle available	2,512.0	23.5	2,522.0	15.1	2,533.9	21.2
Householder 15 to 34 years	176.0	6.9	181.1	4.1	189.9	4.4
Householder 35 to 64 years	1,010.6	15.3	986.3	9.1	972.5	8.6
Householder 65 years and over	1,325.4	16.1	1,354.6	8.8	1,371.5	12.5
1 or more vehicles available	72,361.4	206.4	73,035.7	157.7	73,555.7	344.6
Householder 15 to 34 years	7,885.9	63.9	8,265.2	46.9	8,684.6	86.6
Householder 35 to 64 years	46,254.7	119.2	46,830.7	86.8	47,270.2	185.1
Householder 65 years and over	18,220.8	57.1	17,939.8	36.7	17,601.0	76.5
Renter-occupied units	39,694.0	91.9	39,039.3	74.5	38,146.3	120.2
No vehicle available	7,885.0	48.1	7,734.0	24.5	7,579.3	18.9
Householder 15 to 34 years	2,101.0	27.7	2,115.9	13.5	2,088.4	11.0
Householder 35 to 64 years	3,641.1	33.9	3,542.2	16.2	3,447.1	21.1
Householder 65 years and over	2,143.0	24.3	2,076.0	10.4	2,043.8	12.2
1 or more vehicles available	31,809.0	83.0	31,305.2	71.1	30,567.0	116.7
Householder 15 to 34 years	12,532.3	41.4	12,663.7	33.4	12,582.1	22.5
Householder 35 to 64 years	16,091.8	69.4	15,536.8	59.7	14,961.9	121.4
Householder 65 years and over	3,185.0	23.7	3,104.7	14.4	3,023.0	15.6

Source: U.S. Census Bureau, 2010 American Community Survey

Table 3-30. Physical Characteristics of Occupied Housing Units, 2010 American Community Survey, 1-, 3-, and 5-Year Estimates

[Number, percent, except where noted.]

Characteristics	1-year estimates						3-year estimates					
	Occupied housing units		Owner-occupied housing units		Renter-occupied housing units		Occupied housing units		Owner-occupied housing units		Renter-occupied housing units	
	Estimate	Margin of error (+/-)	Estimate	Margin of error (+/-)	Estimate	Margin of error (+/-)	Estimate	Margin of error (+/-)	Estimate	Margin of error (+/-)	Estimate	Margin of error (+/-)
Total occupied housing units (numbers in thousands)	114,567.4	163.2	74,873.4	216.1	39,694.0	91.9	114,596.9	112.1	75,557.7	165.3	39,039.3	74.5
Units in structure												
1, detached	63.1	0.1	82	0.1	27.4	0.1	63.2	0.1	81.9	0.1	27	0.1
1, attached	5.9	0.1	5.9	0.1	6.1	0.1	5.9	0.1	5.8	0.1	6	0.1
2 apartments	3.6	0.1	1.3	0.1	8.1	0.1	3.7	0.1	1.3	0.1	8.3	0.1
3 or 4 apartments	4.2	0.1	0.9	0.1	10.6	0.1	4.3	0.1	0.9	0.1	10.8	0.1
5 to 9 apartments	4.6	0.1	0.8	0.1	11.8	0.1	4.6	0.1	0.8	0.1	12	0.1
10 apartments or more	12.4	0.1	2.4	0.1	31.2	0.1	12.2	0.1	2.5	0.1	31.2	0.1
Mobile home or other type of housing	6.1	0.1	6.8	0.1	4.7	0.1	6.1	0.1	6.9	0.1	4.7	0.1
Year structure built												
2000 or later	14.8	0.1	15.9	0.1	12.7	0.1	13.6	0.1	14.7	0.1	11.4	0.1
1990 to 1999	14.1	0.1	15.4	0.1	11.8	0.1	14.3	0.1	15.6	0.1	11.7	0.1
1980 to 1989	13.9	0.1	13.7	0.1	14.3	0.1	14	0.1	13.8	0.1	14.3	0.1
1960 to 1979	27.2	0.1	25.9	0.1	29.7	0.1	27.6	0.1	26.3	0.1	30.1	0.1
1940 to 1959	16.7	0.1	17	0.1	16.2	0.1	17.1	0.1	17.3	0.1	16.7	0.1
1939 or earlier	13.2	0.1	12.1	0.1	15.3	0.1	13.5	0.1	12.3	0.1	15.7	0.1
Rooms												
1 room	1.6	0.1	0.2	0.1	4	0.1	1.6	0.1	0.2	0.1	4.2	0.1
2 or 3 rooms	10.6	0.1	2.7	0.1	25.6	0.1	10.4	0.1	2.7	0.1	25.4	0.1
4 or 5 rooms	35.7	0.1	28.8	0.1	48.8	0.1	35.5	0.1	28.6	0.1	48.9	0.1
6 or 7 rooms	31.8	0.1	39.7	0.1	16.8	0.1	31.9	0.1	39.7	0.1	16.7	0.1
8 or more rooms	20.3	0.1	28.5	0.1	4.9	0.1	20.6	0.1	28.8	0.1	4.8	0.1
Bedrooms												
No bedroom	1.8	0.1	0.3	0.1	4.5	0.1	1.8	0.1	0.3	0.1	4.7	0.1
1 bedroom	10.6	0.1	2.5	0.1	26	0.1	10.5	0.1	2.5	0.1	26.1	0.1
2 or 3 bedrooms	66.4	0.1	68.4	0.1	62.5	0.1	66.4	0.1	68.5	0.1	62.4	0.1
4 or more bedrooms	21.2	0.1	28.8	0.1	7	0.1	21.3	0.1	28.7	0.1	6.8	0.1
Complete facilities												
With complete plumbing facilities	99.4	0.1	99.6	0.1	99.2	0.1	99.4	0.1	99.6	0.1	99.1	0.1
With complete kitchen facilities	99	0.1	99.5	0.1	98.1	0.1	99.1	0.1	99.5	0.1	98.2	0.1
Vehicles available												
No vehicles	9.1	0.1	3.4	0.1	19.9	0.1	8.9	0.1	3.3	0.1	19.8	0.1
1 vehicle	33.8	0.1	26.7	0.1	47.1	0.1	33.5	0.1	26.5	0.1	47.2	0.1
2 vehicles	37.6	0.1	44	0.1	25.5	0.1	37.6	0.1	44	0.1	25.4	0.1
3 or more vehicles	19.5	0.1	25.9	0.1	7.5	0.1	19.9	0.1	26.2	0.1	7.5	0.1
Telephone service available												
With telephone service available	97.5	0.1	98.6	0.1	95.5	0.1	97.6	0.1	98.7	0.1	95.3	0.1
House heating fuel												
Utility gas	49.5	0.1	53	0.1	42.9	0.1	49.7	0.1	53.1	0.1	43.1	0.1
Bottled, tank, or LP gas	5	0.1	6.2	0.1	2.9	0.1	5.2	0.1	6.3	0.1	2.9	0.1
Electricity	35.4	0.1	29.8	0.1	46.1	0.1	34.8	0.1	29.3	0.1	45.4	0.1
Fuel oil, kerosene, etc.	6.5	0.1	7.1	0.1	5.2	0.1	6.8	0.1	7.4	0.1	5.5	0.1
Coal or coke	0.1	0.1	0.2	0.1	0.1	0.1	0.1	0.1	0.1	0.1	0.1	0.1
All other fuels	2.6	0.1	3.2	0.1	1.4	0.1	2.5	0.1	3.1	0.1	1.4	0.1
No fuel used	0.9	0.1	0.6	0.1	1.6	0.1	0.9	0.1	0.6	0.1	1.6	0.1
Percent imputed												
Units in structure	1.7	X	X	X	X	X	1.5	X	X	X	X	X
Year structure built	18.7	X	X	X	X	X	18.1	X	X	X	X	X
Rooms	6	X	X	X	X	X	5.5	X	X	X	X	X
Bedrooms	5	X	X	X	X	X	4.6	X	X	X	X	X
Plumbing facilities	2.6	X	X	X	X	X	2.3	X	X	X	X	X
Kitchen facilities	3.3	X	X	X	X	X	3	X	X	X	X	X
Vehicles available	1.3	X	X	X	X	X	1	X	X	X	X	X
Telephone service available	1.1	X	X	X	X	X	0.9	X	X	X	X	X
House heating fuel	3.3	X	X	X	X	X	3.1	X	X	X	X	X

Table 3-30. Physical Characteristics of Occupied Housing Units, 2010 American Community Survey, 1-, 3-, and 5-Year Estimates—*Continued*

[Number, percent, except where noted.]

Characteristics	5-year estimates					
	Occupied housing units		Owner-occupied housing units		Renter-occupied housing units	
	Estimate	Margin of error (+/-)	Estimate	Margin of error (+/-)	Estimate	Margin of error (+/-)
Total occupied housing units (numbers in thousands)	114,236.0	248.1	76,089.7	362.8	38,146,3	120.2
Units in structure						
1, detached	63.2	0.1	81.7	0.1	26.2	0.1
1, attached	5.9	0.1	5.8	0.1	5.9	0.1
2 apartments	3.7	0.1	1.3	0.1	8.4	0.1
3 or 4 apartments	4.3	0.1	0.9	0.1	11	0.1
5 to 9 apartments	4.6	0.1	0.8	0.1	12.3	0.1
10 apartments or more	12.1	0.1	2.5	0.1	31.5	0.1
Mobile home or other type of housing	6.2	0.1	6.9	0.1	4.8	0.1
Year structure built						
2000 or later	12.7	0.1	13.8	0.1	10.7	0.1
1990 to 1999	14.4	0.1	15.7	0.1	11.6	0.1
1980 to 1989	14.1	0.1	14	0.1	14.5	0.1
1960 to 1979	27.9	0.1	26.6	0.1	30.5	0.1
1940 to 1959	17.3	0.1	17.5	0.1	16.8	0.1
1939 or earlier	13.7	0.1	12.5	0.1	15.9	0.1
Rooms						
1 room	1.3	0.1	0.2	0.1	3.5	0.1
2 or 3 rooms	10.9	0.1	2.8	0.1	27	0.1
4 or 5 rooms	36.4	0.1	29.7	0.1	49.6	0.1
6 or 7 rooms	32.1	0.1	40.3	0.1	15.8	0.1
8 or more rooms	19.4	0.1	27	0.1	4.2	0.1
Bedrooms						
No bedroom	1.5	0.1	0.3	0.1	4.1	0.1
1 bedroom	10.7	0.1	2.5	0.1	27	0.1
2 or 3 bedrooms	66.8	0.1	68.9	0.1	62.5	0.1
4 or more bedrooms	21	0.1	28.4	0.1	6.4	0.1
Complete facilities						
With complete plumbing facilities	99.5	0.1	99.6	0.1	99.2	0.1
With complete kitchen facilities	99.2	0.1	99.6	0.1	98.5	0.1
Vehicles available						
No vehicles	8.9	0.1	3.3	0.1	19.9	0.1
1 vehicle	33.3	0.1	26.3	0.1	47.3	0.1
2 vehicles	37.9	0.1	44.1	0.1	25.4	0.1
3 or more vehicles	20	0.1	26.3	0.1	7.4	0.1
Telephone service available						
With telephone service available	96.3	0.1	98.1	0.1	92.8	0.1
House heating fuel						
Utility gas	49.9	0.1	53.3	0.1	43.2	0.1
Bottled, tank, or LP gas	5.4	0.1	6.5	0.1	3	0.1
Electricity	34.2	0.1	28.8	0.1	44.9	0.1
Fuel oil, kerosene, etc.	7.1	0.1	7.7	0.1	5.8	0.1
Coal or coke	0.1	0.1	0.1	0.1	0.1	0.1
All other fuels	2.4	0.1	3	0.1	1.4	0.1
No fuel used	0.9	0.1	0.6	0.1	1.6	0.1
Percent imputed						
Units in structure	X	X	X	X	X	X
Year structure built	X	X	X	X	X	X
Rooms	X	X	X	X	X	X
Bedrooms	X	X	X	X	X	X
Plumbing facilities	X	X	X	X	X	X
Kitchen facilities	X	X	X	X	X	X
Vehicles available	0.9	X	X	X	X	X
Telephone service available	0.7	X	X	X	X	X
House heating fuel	2.6	X	X	X	X	X

X = Not applicable.

Source: U.S. Census Bureau, 2010 American Community Survey

Table 3-31. Tenure, by Bedrooms, 2010 American Community Survey, 1-, 3-, and 5-Year Estimates

[Numbers in thousands.]

Characteristics	United States					
	1-year estimates		3-year estimates		5-year estimates	
	Estimate	Margin of error (+/-)	Estimate	Margin of error (+/-)	Estimate	Margin of error (+/-)
Total units	114,567.4	163.2	114,596.9	112.1	114,236.0	248.1
Owner-occupied units	74,873.4	216.1	75,557.7	165.3	76,089.7	362.8
No bedroom	235.6	7.0	240.0	4.3	204.3	3.3
1 bedroom	1,861.1	18.7	1,874.2	12.0	1,906.5	11.0
2 bedrooms	13,861.5	60.9	14,095.9	40.1	14,341.3	55.4
3 bedrooms	37,383.5	132.4	37,640.7	96.0	38,065.7	198.9
4 bedrooms	17,054.6	67.1	17,199.5	51.6	17,199.8	98.6
5 or more bedrooms	4,477.0	30.4	4,507.4	16.1	4,372.0	16.0
Renter-occupied units	39,694.0	91.9	39,039.3	74.5	38,146.3	120.2
No bedroom	1,799.7	27.3	1,851.4	16.1	1,545.5	12.3
1 bedroom	10,315.1	46.7	10,191.0	27.8	10,312.5	25.5
2 bedrooms	15,412.0	65.6	15,250.9	40.5	15,170.6	43.8
3 bedrooms	9,377.4	56.1	9,093.9	39.1	8,682.4	63.4
4 bedrooms	2,238.9	27.3	2,127.2	16.3	1,949.2	20.8
5 or more bedrooms	551.0	11.7	524.9	8.6	486.1	6.5

Source: U.S. Census Bureau, 2010 American Community Survey

Table 3-32. Bedrooms, by Gross Rent, 2010 American Community Survey, 1-, 3-, and 5-Year Estimates

[Numbers in thousands.]

Characteristics	United States					
	1-year estimates		3-year estimates		5-year estimates	
	Estimate	Margin of error (+/-)	Estimate	Margin of error (+/-)	Estimate	Margin of error (+/-)
Total units	39,694.0	91.9	39,039.3	74.5	38,146.3	120.2
No bedroom	1,799.7	27.3	1,851.4	16.1	1,545.5	12.3
With cash rent	1,761.7	27.2	1,813.4	16.0	1,510.9	12.1
Less than $200	65.4	3.7	78.0	3.0	64.9	1.9
$200 to $299	119.3	6.5	124.5	3.5	104.1	2.1
$300 to $399	318.7	10.9	333.9	6.0	287.1	4.1
$500 to $749	501.3	11.6	507.4	7.6	424.6	5.7
$750 to $999	342.1	12.5	349.1	5.9	286.9	4.5
$1,000 or more	414.9	11.4	420.6	6.2	343.3	5.3
No cash rent	38.0	3.3	37.9	2.0	34.6	1.4
1 bedroom	10,315.1	46.7	10,191.0	27.8	10,312.5	25.5
With cash rent	10,113.3	46.3	9,992.7	26.5	10,094.8	25.5
Less than $200	359.2	8.1	377.5	5.4	402.5	3.8
$200 to $299	672.0	12.4	659.2	7.2	667.5	6.1
$300 to $399	1,397.8	18.9	1,400.0	9.7	1,452.2	9.6
$500 to $749	3,066.6	28.9	3,009.2	15.6	3,036.2	13.9
$750 to $999	2,291.0	25.2	2,257.6	15.3	2,294.5	12.0
$1,000 or more	2,326.8	26.6	2,289.1	13.8	2,241.9	9.9
No cash rent	201.7	8.2	198.3	4.4	217.7	3.5
2 bedrooms	15,412.0	65.6	15,250.9	40.5	15,170.6	43.8
With cash rent	14,711.0	66.6	14,543.0	40.4	14,439.8	44.2
Less than $200	218.1	8.3	226.1	4.5	235.5	3.7
$200 to $299	299.7	7.6	304.9	5.5	305.9	4.2
$300 to $399	1,106.9	18.5	1,156.5	10.7	1,188.4	7.8
$500 to $749	3,934.2	29.9	3,881.7	22.0	3,872.0	15.2
$750 to $999	4,198.4	41.7	4,079.7	20.6	4,043.4	19.9
$1,000 or more	4,953.7	38.7	4,894.1	19.5	4,794.7	21.4
No cash rent	701.0	13.9	707.9	7.8	730.8	5.6
3 or more bedrooms	12,167.3	67.6	11,746.0	48.9	11,117.7	85.7
With cash rent	10,935.1	67.3	10,533.2	48.7	9,923.8	84.7
Less than $200	98.5	4.6	104.2	3.1	108.2	2.3
$200 to $299	151.0	7.6	152.9	3.8	149.8	2.6
$300 to $399	581.8	11.7	598.3	8.5	599.0	6.0
$500 to $749	1,706.8	21.3	1,680.3	14.5	1,623.7	14.1
$750 to $999	2,340.4	27.6	2,257.0	17.1	2,148.0	19.7
$1,000 or more	6,056.7	44.5	5,740.6	31.5	5,295.1	53.6
No cash rent	1,232.2	19.1	1,212.8	8.6	1,194.0	6.3

Source: U.S. Census Bureau, 2010 American Community Survey

Table 3-33. House Heating Fuel, 2010 American Community Survey, 1-, 3-, and 5-Year Estimates

[Numbers in thousands.]

Characteristics	United States					
	1-year estimates		3-year estimates		5-year estimates	
	Estimate	Margin of error (+/-)	Estimate	Margin of error (+/-)	Estimate	Margin of error (+/-)
Total units	114,567.4	163.2	114,596.9	112.1	114,236.0	248.1
Utility gas	56,691.1	106.6	56,983.8	77.3	57,018.5	163.0
Bottled, tank, or LP gas	5,779.1	37.1	5,907.5	24.5	6,146.4	24.2
Electricity	40,579.1	72.6	39,909.3	48.3	39,066.3	63.6
Fuel oil, kerosene, etc.	7,389.6	34.0	7,739.1	19.1	8,073.2	15.7
Coal or coke	134.0	5.4	133.5	2.7	135.3	2.2
Wood	2,382.7	24.5	2,346.2	12.2	2,249.6	9.3
Solar energy	41.5	3.1	38.0	1.4	38.0	1.3
Other fuel	511.4	10.2	491.1	6.8	483.5	4.1
No fuel used	1,058.9	15.0	1,048.6	8.6	1,025.3	7.8

Source: U.S. Census Bureau, 2010 American Community Survey

Table 3-34. Tenure, House Heating Fuel, 2010 American Community Survey, 1-, 3-, and 5-Year Estimates

[Numbers in thousands.]

Characteristics	United States					
	1-year estimates		3-year estimates		5-year estimates	
	Estimate	Margin of error (+/-)	Estimate	Margin of error (+/-)	Estimate	Margin of error (+/-)
Total units	114,567.4	163.2	114,596.9	112.1	114,236.0	248.1
Owner-occupied units	74,873.4	216.1	75,557.7	165.3	76,089.7	362.8
Utility gas	39,665.7	121.5	40,143.7	98.7	40,537.7	227.2
Bottled, tank, or LP gas	4,643.1	33.2	4,771.9	22.3	4,983.5	20.8
Electricity	22,294.1	77.9	22,173.1	51.3	21,928.2	96.6
Fuel oil, kerosene, etc.	5,339.6	31.2	5,591.5	16.8	5,852.6	22.7
Coal or coke	113.1	5.0	111.1	2.4	112.7	1.9
Wood	2,050.8	21.4	2,017.3	10.6	1,935.7	9.4
Solar energy	32.0	2.5	28.9	1.2	28.7	1.1
Other fuel	312.9	8.7	297.5	5.1	290.0	3.2
No fuel used	422.1	9.7	422.7	5.1	420.6	4.6
Renter-occupied units	39,694.0	91.9	39,039.3	74.5	38,146.3	120.2
Utility gas	17,025.4	66.8	16,840.1	45.8	16,480.8	69.4
Bottled, tank, or LP gas	1,136.0	16.3	1,135.5	10.0	1,162.9	7.5
Electricity	18,285.0	67.8	17,736.2	47.2	17,138.2	49.9
Fuel oil, kerosene, etc.	2,050.0	19.5	2,147.6	13.9	2,220.5	14.9
Coal or coke	21.0	1.9	22.4	1.3	22.5	1.0
Wood	331.9	9.4	328.8	5.2	314.0	4.3
Solar energy	9.5	1.3	9.1	0.8	9.4	0.7
Other fuel	198.5	6.9	193.6	3.9	193.4	3.0
No fuel used	636.7	12.9	625.9	7.4	604.7	6.4

Source: U.S. Census Bureau, 2010 American Community Survey

Table 3-35. Percent of Occupied Housing Units with Gas as the Principal Heating Fuel, by State and Urban Designation, 2010 American Community Survey, 1-, 3-, and 5-Year Estimates

[Percent.]

Characteristics	1-year estimates		3-year estimates		5-year estimates	
	Percent	Margin of error (+/-)	Percent	Margin of error (+/-)	Percent	Margin of error (+/-)
United States	54.5	0.1	54.9	0.1	55.3	0.1
Urban and rural						
Urban	58.2	0.1	58.5	0.1	58.8	0.1
Rural	42.8	0.2	43.3	0.1	43.8	0.1
Inside and outside metropolitan areas						
In metropolitan or micropolitan statistical area	55.1	0.1	55.4	0.1	55.8	0.1
In metropolitan statistical area	56.2	0.1	56.5	0.1	56.8	0.1
In principal city	58.2	0.1	58.4	0.1	58.8	0.1
Not in principal city	54.9	0.1	55.1	0.1	55.4	0.1
In micropolitan statistical area	46.3	0.2	47.1	0.1	47.9	0.1
In principal city	57.5	0.4	58.5	0.2	59.2	0.2
Not in principal city	40.7	0.3	41.4	0.1	42.2	0.1
Not in metropolitan or micropolitan statistical area	46.5	0.2	47.3	0.1	48.2	0.1
Alabama	38.7	0.6	40.1	0.3	41.8	0.2
Alaska	49.5	1.2	50.7	0.7	50.7	0.5
Arizona	38.4	0.6	38.9	0.3	39.6	0.2
Arkansas	49.6	0.7	50.7	0.4	52.3	0.4
California	70.0	0.2	70.2	0.1	70.8	0.1
Colorado	79.0	0.4	80.1	0.3	80.4	0.2
Connecticut	34.4	0.5	34.1	0.3	33.8	0.3
Delaware	50.8	1	50.8	0.6	50.5	0.5
District of Columbia	65.4	1.4	64.5	0.9	64.8	0.6
Florida	5.9	0.1	5.9	0.1	6.3	0.1
Georgia	47.3	0.4	48.9	0.2	50.4	0.2
Hawaii	3.0	0.3	3.2	0.2	3.7	0.2
Idaho	57.7	0.8	56.6	0.6	56.5	0.4
Illinois	84.5	0.2	84.9	0.1	85.1	0.1
Indiana	69.1	0.4	70.2	0.2	70.9	0.2
Iowa	78.0	0.5	78.8	0.3	79.6	0.2
Kansas	77.4	0.6	78.0	0.4	78.6	0.2
Kentucky	45.5	0.5	47.1	0.3	48.4	0.2
Louisiana	39.9	0.6	41.0	0.4	42.2	0.3
Maine	11.0	0.7	10.7	0.3	10.3	0.2
Maryland	47.5	0.6	48.1	0.3	48.4	0.2
Massachusetts	51.8	0.5	50.6	0.3	50.0	0.2
Michigan	86.4	0.2	86.7	0.1	87.1	0.1
Minnesota	77.4	0.3	77.8	0.2	78.0	0.2
Mississippi	45.7	0.8	46.7	0.4	48.7	0.4
Missouri	62.6	0.4	64.0	0.3	65.0	0.2
Montana	68.6	1	68.8	0.5	69.4	0.5
Nebraska	71.1	0.7	72.1	0.4	73.1	0.3
Nevada	67.7	0.8	66.8	0.5	67.0	0.3
New Hampshire	33.3	1	32.9	0.4	32.6	0.4
New Jersey	75.9	0.3	75.4	0.2	74.6	0.2
New Mexico	77.8	0.8	78.1	0.4	78.3	0.3
New York	58.2	0.2	57.4	0.1	56.5	0.1
North Carolina	33.9	0.4	34.5	0.2	35.3	0.2
North Dakota	55.0	1.3	55.8	0.7	55.7	0.4
Ohio	73.5	0.3	73.6	0.2	73.8	0.1
Oklahoma	63.5	0.6	64.5	0.3	65.3	0.2
Oregon	39.8	0.5	40.0	0.4	39.9	0.2
Pennsylvania	54.9	0.3	54.9	0.2	54.9	0.1
Rhode Island	51.1	1.1	51.5	0.7	50.9	0.5
South Carolina	28.3	0.5	29.7	0.3	30.5	0.2
South Dakota	65.5	1	66.8	0.6	67.7	0.4
Tennessee	38.5	0.5	39.4	0.2	40.7	0.2
Texas	41.7	0.3	42.4	0.1	43.2	0.2
Utah	87.8	0.5	88.2	0.3	88.1	0.2
Vermont	29.9	0.9	29.6	0.6	29.3	0.5
Virginia	39.0	0.4	39.0	0.2	39.6	0.2
Washington	38.7	0.4	38.8	0.3	38.8	0.2
West Virginia	47.6	0.8	47.8	0.4	48.8	0.4
Wisconsin	76.3	0.4	76.8	0.2	77.1	0.1
Wyoming	73.9	1.4	72.8	0.8	72.8	0.6
Puerto Rico	1.2	0.1	1.2	0.1	1.5	0.1

Source: U.S. Census Bureau, 2010 American Community Survey

Table 3-36. Percent of Occupied Housing Units with Electricity as the Principal Heating Fuel, by State and Urban Designation, 2010 American Community Survey, 1-, 3-, and 5-Year Estimates

[Percent.]

Characteristics	1-year estimates		3-year estimates		5-year estimates	
	Percent	Margin of error (+/-)	Percent	Margin of error (+/-)	Percent	Margin of error (+/-)
United States	35.4	0.1	34.8	0.1	34.2	0.1
Urban and rural						
Urban	34.0	0.1	33.5	0.1	33.0	0.1
Rural	39.9	0.2	39.1	0.1	38.2	0.1
Inside and outside metropolitan areas						
In metropolitan or micropolitan statistical area	35.4	0.1	34.8	0.1	34.2	0.1
In metropolitan statistical area	34.9	0.1	34.3	0.1	33.8	0.1
In principal city	35.5	0.1	35.0	0.1	34.4	0.1
Not in principal city	34.4	0.1	33.9	0.1	33.4	0.1
In micropolitan statistical area	39.2	0.2	38.3	0.1	37.4	0.1
In principal city	37.0	0.4	35.8	0.2	34.9	0.2
Not in principal city	40.3	0.3	39.6	0.1	38.6	0.1
Not in metropolitan or micropolitan statistical area	36.2	0.3	35.4	0.1	34.3	0.1
Alabama	59.6	0.6	58.2	0.3	56.5	0.2
Alaska	10.4	0.9	9.5	0.4	9.5	0.4
Arizona	58.2	0.6	57.7	0.3	57.0	0.2
Arkansas	45.3	0.7	44.1	0.5	42.5	0.4
California	24.5	0.2	24.3	0.1	23.8	0.1
Colorado	17.9	0.4	16.8	0.2	16.4	0.2
Connecticut	15.0	0.5	14.9	0.3	14.9	0.2
Delaware	30.3	1.1	29.3	0.6	29.2	0.6
District of Columbia	29.8	1.4	30.9	0.8	30.3	0.6
Florida	92.3	0.1	92.0	0.1	91.5	0.1
Georgia	51.1	0.4	49.5	0.2	48.0	0.2
Hawaii	31.5	1.1	32.9	0.6	34.5	0.6
Idaho	31.8	0.9	32.4	0.6	32.0	0.4
Illinois	14.0	0.2	13.6	0.1	13.3	0.1
Indiana	26.7	0.4	25.6	0.2	24.9	0.2
Iowa	18.0	0.5	17.1	0.3	16.2	0.2
Kansas	20.2	0.5	19.5	0.3	19.0	0.2
Kentucky	49.6	0.6	48.1	0.3	46.6	0.3
Louisiana	59.1	0.6	57.8	0.4	56.5	0.3
Maine	5.1	0.4	4.9	0.2	4.7	0.1
Maryland	39.1	0.5	38.2	0.3	37.6	0.2
Massachusetts	13.6	0.4	13.4	0.2	13.3	0.2
Michigan	7.5	0.2	7.3	0.1	7.0	0.1
Minnesota	14.9	0.3	14.4	0.2	14.0	0.1
Mississippi	52.2	0.8	51.1	0.4	49.0	0.4
Missouri	32.6	0.4	31.3	0.3	30.4	0.2
Montana	19.8	0.9	19.5	0.5	18.8	0.4
Nebraska	25.2	0.6	24.4	0.4	23.4	0.3
Nevada	29.1	0.7	30.3	0.4	30.2	0.3
New Hampshire	8.1	0.6	7.7	0.4	7.7	0.2
New Jersey	10.8	0.3	10.6	0.2	10.6	0.1
New Mexico	14.5	0.6	14.2	0.3	14.0	0.2
New York	9.4	0.2	8.9	0.1	8.9	0.1
North Carolina	58.1	0.5	57.1	0.2	55.7	0.2
North Dakota	37.4	1.4	36.1	0.6	35.7	0.5
Ohio	20.5	0.3	20.4	0.1	20.1	0.1
Oklahoma	33.3	0.6	32.2	0.3	31.5	0.2
Oregon	48.8	0.5	48.4	0.3	48.1	0.2
Pennsylvania	20.2	0.3	19.6	0.2	19.0	0.1
Rhode Island	8.9	0.7	8.4	0.4	8.1	0.2
South Carolina	68.6	0.5	66.8	0.3	65.8	0.2
South Dakota	26.8	1	25.6	0.6	24.4	0.4
Tennessee	58.5	0.5	57.6	0.3	56.1	0.2
Texas	57.1	0.3	56.4	0.1	55.6	0.1
Utah	10.2	0.5	9.8	0.3	9.8	0.2
Vermont	5.3	0.7	4.6	0.4	4.4	0.3
Virginia	50.6	0.4	50.1	0.2	48.9	0.2
Washington	53.1	0.5	52.7	0.2	52.4	0.2
West Virginia	40.8	0.9	40.4	0.5	38.8	0.3
Wisconsin	14.1	0.3	13.3	0.2	13.0	0.1
Wyoming	19.1	1.2	19.5	0.7	19.9	0.6
Puerto Rico	14.6	0.4	15.6	0.2	15.5	0.2

Source: U.S. Census Bureau, 2010 American Community Survey

Table 3-37. Percent of Occupied Housing Units with Fuel Oil/Kerosene/Etc. as the Principal Heating Fuel, by State and Urban Designation, 2010 American Community Survey, 1-, 3-, and 5-Year Estimates

[Percent.]

Characteristics	1-year estimates		3-year estimates		5-year estimates	
	Percent	Margin of error (+/-)	Percent	Margin of error (+/-)	Percent	Margin of error (+/-)
United States	6.5	0.1	6.8	0.1	7.1	0.1
Urban and rural						
Urban	5.7	0.1	6.0	0.1	6.2	0.1
Rural	8.8	0.1	9.2	0.1	9.8	0.1
Inside and outside metropolitan areas						
In metropolitan or micropolitan statistical area	6.4	0.1	6.7	0.1	7.0	0.1
In metropolitan statistical area	6.3	0.1	6.6	0.1	6.9	0.1
In principal city	4.4	0.1	4.7	0.1	4.9	0.1
Not in principal city	7.6	0.1	7.9	0.1	8.2	0.1
In micropolitan statistical area	7.1	0.1	7.4	0.1	7.8	0.1
In principal city	3.1	0.1	3.3	0.1	3.5	0.1
Not in principal city	9.2	0.1	9.5	0.1	10.0	0.1
Not in metropolitan or micropolitan statistical area	7.3	0.1	7.6	0.1	8.1	0.1
Alabama	0.2	0.1	0.3	0.1	0.3	0.1
Alaska	33.4	1.2	32.8	0.6	33.4	0.5
Arizona	0.1	0.1	0.1	0.1	0.1	0.1
Arkansas	0.1	0.1	0.2	0.1	0.2	0.1
California	0.3	0.1	0.3	0.1	0.3	0.1
Colorado	0.1	0.1	0.1	0.1	0.1	0.1
Connecticut	47.9	0.6	48.4	0.3	48.9	0.3
Delaware	17.4	1.0	18.1	0.5	18.6	0.4
District of Columbia	3.3	0.5	3.3	0.3	3.7	0.2
Florida	0.3	0.1	0.3	0.1	0.3	0.1
Georgia	0.3	0.1	0.3	0.1	0.3	0.1
Hawaii	0.0	0.1	0.0	0.1	0.0	0.1
Idaho	2.3	0.3	2.6	0.2	2.9	0.1
Illinois	0.2	0.1	0.3	0.1	0.3	0.1
Indiana	1.2	0.1	1.2	0.1	1.4	0.1
Iowa	0.8	0.1	1.0	0.1	1.1	0.1
Kansas	0.1	0.1	0.1	0.1	0.1	0.1
Kentucky	1.2	0.1	1.3	0.1	1.4	0.1
Louisiana	0.1	0.1	0.1	0.1	0.1	0.1
Maine	70.4	0.9	72.1	0.5	74.1	0.4
Maryland	11.3	0.3	11.7	0.2	12.1	0.1
Massachusetts	32.1	0.4	33.7	0.2	34.6	0.2
Michigan	1.6	0.1	1.9	0.1	2.0	0.1
Minnesota	3.1	0.1	3.4	0.1	3.8	0.1
Mississippi	0.2	0.1	0.1	0.1	0.2	0.1
Missouri	0.3	0.1	0.3	0.1	0.3	0.1
Montana	1.7	0.2	1.8	0.2	1.9	0.1
Nebraska	0.8	0.1	0.8	0.1	0.8	0.1
Nevada	0.9	0.1	0.9	0.1	0.9	0.1
New Hampshire	49.2	1.0	50.8	0.6	52.3	0.4
New Jersey	12.4	0.3	13.1	0.2	14.0	0.1
New Mexico	0.1	0.1	0.2	0.1	0.1	0.1
New York	28.7	0.2	30.2	0.1	31.3	0.1
North Carolina	5.4	0.2	5.8	0.1	6.4	0.1
North Dakota	4.5	0.4	5.0	0.2	5.5	0.2
Ohio	2.9	0.1	3.0	0.1	3.3	0.1
Oklahoma	0.1	0.1	0.1	0.1	0.1	0.1
Oregon	3.3	0.2	3.5	0.1	3.9	0.1
Pennsylvania	20.1	0.2	20.8	0.1	21.5	0.1
Rhode Island	37.7	1.1	38.1	0.7	39.2	0.5
South Carolina	1.8	0.2	2.0	0.1	2.3	0.1
South Dakota	2.9	0.3	3.5	0.2	3.7	0.2
Tennessee	0.6	0.1	0.7	0.1	0.8	0.1
Texas	0.1	0.1	0.1	0.1	0.1	0.1
Utah	0.2	0.1	0.2	0.1	0.3	0.1
Vermont	47.8	1.1	49.9	0.7	51.7	0.5
Virginia	7.0	0.2	7.6	0.1	8.2	0.1
Washington	2.8	0.1	3.1	0.1	3.4	0.1
West Virginia	3.8	0.4	3.9	0.2	4.5	0.2
Wisconsin	3.6	0.1	4.0	0.1	4.4	0.1
Wyoming	0.4	0.2	0.4	0.1	0.4	0.1
Puerto Rico	0.0	0.1	0.0	0.1	0.0	0.1

Source: U.S. Census Bureau, 2010 American Community Survey

Table 3-38. Kitchen Facilities for All Housing Units, 2010 American Community Survey, 1-, 3-, and 5-Year Estimates

[Numbers in thousands.]

Characteristics	United States					
	1-year estimates		3-year estimates		5-year estimates	
	Estimate	Margin of error (+/-)	Estimate	Margin of error (+/-)	Estimate	Margin of error (+/-)
Total units	131,791.1	5.7	131,210.6	6.1	130,038.1	11.2
With complete kitchen facilities	127,533.2	48.5	127,166.5	34.2	126,566.6	55.8
Lacking complete kitchen facilities	4,257.9	51.4	4,044.1	30.4	3,471.5	45.6

Source: U.S. Census Bureau, 2010 American Community Survey

Table 3-39. Tenure, Kitchen Facilities for All Housing Units, 2010 American Community Survey, 1-, 3-, and 5-Year Estimates

[Numbers in thousands.]

Characteristics	United States					
	1-year estimates		3-year estimates		5-year estimates	
	Estimate	Margin of error (+/-)	Estimate	Margin of error (+/-)	Estimate	Margin of error (+/-)
Total units	114,567.4	163.2	114,596.9	112.1	114,236.0	248.1
Owner-occupied units	74,873.4	216.1	75,557.7	165.3	76,089.7	362.8
With complete kitchen facilities	74,513.3	217.0	75,188.3	167.0	75,776.2	365.8
Lacking complete kitchen facilities	360.0	11.6	369.4	5.9	313.5	4.7
Renter-occupied units	39,694.0	91.9	39,039.3	74.5	38,146.3	120.2
With complete kitchen facilities	38,952.1	87.1	38,329.6	71.2	37,560.7	117.8
Lacking complete kitchen facilities	741.9	17.4	709.7	9.0	585.7	6.3

Source: U.S. Census Bureau, 2010 American Community Survey

Table 3-40. Plumbing Facilities for All Housing Units, 2010 American Community Survey, 1-, 3-, and 5-Year Estimates

[Numbers in thousands.]

Characteristics	United States					
	1-year estimates		3-year estimates		5-year estimates	
	Estimate	Margin of error (+/-)	Estimate	Margin of error (+/-)	Estimate	Margin of error (+/-)
Total units	131,791.1	5.7	131,210.6	6.1	130,080.1	11.2
Complete plumbing facilities	128,938.5	37.6	128,463.1	25.4	127,652.3	39.1
Lacking complete plumbing facilities	2,852.6	40.3	2,747.5	21.0	2,385.8	28.7

Source: U.S. Census Bureau, 2010 American Community Survey

Table 3-41. Tenure, Plumbing Facilities for All Housing Units, by Occupants Per Room, 2010 American Community Survey, 1-, 3-, and 5-Year Estimates

[Numbers in thousands.]

Characteristics	United States					
	1-year estimates		3-year estimates		5-year estimates	
	Estimate	Margin of error (+/-)	Estimate	Margin of error (+/-)	Estimate	Margin of error (+/-)
Total units	114,567.4	163.2	114,596.9	112.1	114,236.0	248.1
Owner-occupied units	74,873.4	216.1	75,557.7	165.3	76,089.7	362.8
With complete plumbing facilities	74,554.3	217.5	75,222.9	167.0	75,778.2	365.5
1.00 or less occupants per room	73,258.0	218.1	73,998.6	166.0	74,545.5	364.1
1.01 to 1.50 occupants per room	1,011.4	18.6	959.6	8.9	991.2	7.1
1.51 or more occupants per room	285.0	7.9	264.8	4.6	241.5	3.5
Lacking complete plumbing facilities	319.0	10.7	334.7	6.7	311.5	4.9
1.00 or less occupants per room	297.3	10.7	313.3	6.5	291.6	4.5
1.01 to 1.50 occupants per room	10.6	1.4	11.6	1.0	10.4	0.7
1.51 or more occupants per room	11.1	1.9	9.9	0.8	9.5	0.7
Renter-occupied units	39,694.0	91.9	39,039.3	74.5	38,146.3	120.2
With complete plumbing facilities	39,360.6	91.3	38,678.0	71.7	37,855.5	116.6
1.00 or less occupants per room	36,829.8	85.5	36,278.6	66.6	35,599.7	102.9
1.01 to 1.50 occupants per room	1,671.1	21.4	1,547.8	15.1	1,531.4	14.2
1.51 or more occupants per room	859.7	17.7	851.6	10.5	724.4	7.4
Lacking complete plumbing facilities	333.4	11.3	361.2	6.5	290.9	6.2
1.00 or less occupants per room	300.1	11.2	325.5	6.4	263.0	5.8
1.01 to 1.50 occupants per room	16.7	2.3	16.8	1.4	13.2	0.9
1.51 or more occupants per room	16.6	2.4	18.9	1.4	14.6	0.9

Source: U.S. Census Bureau, 2010 American Community Survey

Table 3-42. Total Rooms, Median Number of Rooms, and Aggregate Number of Rooms in Housing Units, 2010 American Community Survey, 1-, 3-, and 5-Year Estimates

[Numbers in thousands, except as noted.]

Characteristics	United States					
	1-year estimates		3-year estimates		5-year estimates	
	Estimate	Margin of error (+/-)	Estimate	Margin of error (+/-)	Estimate	Margin of error (+/-)
Total units	131,791.1	5.7	131,210.6	6.1	130,038.1	11.2
1 room	2,594.2	34.1	2,589.1	19.9	2,061.7	18.7
2 rooms	3,145.2	25.4	2,990.0	15.3	3,406.0	17.6
3 rooms	12,001.4	57.9	11,682.0	35.8	11,732.8	30.0
4 rooms	22,075.5	76.8	21,753.9	56.6	21,915.4	71.8
5 rooms	26,947.3	81.7	26,767.4	50.1	27,215.1	63.0
6 rooms	24,047.0	72.7	24,035.7	41.0	24,138.90	27.5
7 rooms	16,203.9	66.5	16,272.7	34.9	16,103.5	43.4
8 rooms	11,212.7	53.3	11,300.0	36.9	10,913.8	47.3
9 or more rooms	13,563.8	68.3	13,820.0	50.9	12,550.9	70.5
Median number of rooms (number)	5.5	0.1	5.5	0.1	5.5	0.1
Aggregate number of rooms	755,972.8	714.5	756,107.8	524.1	725,635.5	678.2

Source: U.S. Census Bureau, 2010 American Community Survey

Table 3-43. Tenure, Total Rooms, Median Number of Rooms, and Aggregate Number of Rooms in Housing Units, 2010 American Community Survey, 1-, 3-, and 5-Year Estimates

[Numbers in thousands, except as noted.]

Characteristics	United States					
	1-year estimates		3-year estimates		5-year estimates	
	Estimate	Margin of error (+/-)	Estimate	Margin of error (+/-)	Estimate	Margin of error (+/-)
Total units	114,567.4	163.2	114,596.9	112.1	114,236.0	248.1
Owner-occupied units	74,873.4	216.1	75,557.7	165.3	76,089.7	362.8
1 room	180.5	6.2	185.1	3.9	145.1	2.6
2 rooms	347.9	7.8	333.6	4.3	363.5	4.8
3 rooms	1,686.8	18.6	1,674.6	11.9	1,733.7	11.5
4 rooms	6,661.9	35.8	6,654.9	22.7	6,924.6	29.2
5 rooms	14,881.2	64.7	14,927.4	36.1	15,699.5	56.2
6 rooms	16,894.0	68.0	16,997.7	43.6	17,538.6	74.5
7 rooms	12,847.7	68.0	12,993.8	37.0	13,127.5	69.5
8 rooms	9,430.8	52.7	9,566.7	37.6	9,398.4	61.2
9 or more rooms	11,942.4	68.3	12,223.9	53.1	11,158.8	80.5
Renter-occupied units	39,694.0	91.9	39,039.3	74.5	38,146.3	120.2
1 room	1,601.5	27.4	1,647.3	16.0	1,317.5	13.1
2 rooms	2,181.1	20.3	2,095.8	13.7	2,437.8	18.1
3 rooms	7,974.3	43.1	7,813.8	28.2	7,880.6	20.3
4 rooms	11,176.9	62.1	11,039.1	39.7	11,033.8	42.1
5 rooms	8,177.9	51.9	8,059.8	34.9	7,875.9	47.4
6 rooms	4,603.1	31.7	4,520.2	21.7	4,225.2	29.8
7 rooms	2,049.6	25.9	1,998.0	12.4	1,791.2	13.1
8 rooms	1,027.8	16.5	994.7	9.1	849.8	7.7
9 or more rooms	901.7	15.4	870.6	8.6	734.5	6.4
Median number of rooms (number)						
Total units	5.6	0.1	5.6	0.1	5.6	0.1
Owner-occupied units	6.3	0.1	6.3	0.1	6.3	0.1
Renter-occupied units	4.2	0.1	4.2	0.1	4.2	0.1
Aggregate number of rooms						
Total units	672,678.7	1,450.9	675,100.3	1,026.9	649,657.6	1,872.5
Owner-occupied units	495,692.1	1,600.8	501,411.6	1,243.7	485,009.2	2,462.2
Renter-occupied units	176,966.6	460.1	173,688.7	349.5	164,648.4	614.2

Source: U.S. Census Bureau, 2010 American Community Survey

Table 3-44. Aggregate Number of Rooms in Housing Units, by Vacancy, 2010 American Community Survey, 1-, 3-, and 5-Year Estimates

[Numbers in thousands.]

Characteristics	United States					
	1-year estimates		3-year estimates		5-year estimates	
	Estimate	Margin of error (+/-)	Estimate	Margin of error (+/-)	Estimate	Margin of error (+/-)
Total aggregate number of rooms	83,324.1	834.7	81,007.5	554.8	75,977.9	1,207.6
For rent	14,219.5	202.3	14,094.9	128.0	13,234.2	263.7
Rented, not occupied	2,469.1	78.5	2,480.1	43.6	2,434.5	61.6
For sale only	11,196.3	212.4	11,621.1	131.6	10,802.3	251.5
Sold, not occupied	3,481.0	90.2	2,481.2	63.1	3,592.8	88.6
For seasonal, recreational, or occasional use	25,018.6	293.4	23,926.1	136.7	22,523.6	180.0
For migrant workers	131.0	17.7	143.2	8.2	142.6	7.4
Other vacant	26,808.6	356.0	25,260.9	229.8	23,247.8	404.3

Source: U.S. Census Bureau, American Community Survey

Table 3-45. Tenure, by Units in Structure, 2010 American Community Survey, 1-, 3-, and 5-Year Estimates

[Numbers in thousands.]

Characteristics	United States					
	1-year estimates		3-year estimates		5-year estimates	
	Estimate	Margin of error (+/-)	Estimate	Margin of error (+/-)	Estimate	Margin of error (+/-)
Total units	114,567.4	163.2	114,596.9	112.1	114,236.0	248.1
Owner-occupied units	74,873.4	216.1	75,557.7	165.3	76,089.7	362.8
1, detached	61,374.9	197.4	61,844.4	153.7	62,190.1	318.6
1, attached	4,404.8	27.2	4,411.2	19.4	4,445.9	34.0
2	946.8	15.9	993.8	7.7	1,022.8	7.0
3 or 4	643.3	13.3	668.7	5.9	681.6	5.0
5 to 9	577.5	10.1	602.6	6.2	605.4	4.5
10 to 19	455.6	10.1	469.5	5.9	475.2	4.4
20 to 49	492.3	9.6	500.3	5.9	503.3	5.0
50 or more	869.0	13.8	884.8	7.9	888.5	8.3
Mobile home	5,033.8	29.5	5,109.2	16.1	5,204.5	11.5
Boat, RV, van, etc.	75.2	3.9	73.3	2.3	72.4	2.0
Renter-occupied units	39,694.0	91.9	39,039.3	74.5	38,146.3	120.2
1, detached	10,890.5	60.1	10,526.4	41.5	10,003.8	74.9
1, attached	2,410.6	23.6	2,328.3	13.3	2,245.1	9.7
2	3,230.5	26.9	3,224.7	21.4	3,186.1	19.9
3 or 4	4,212.1	31.4	4,233.3	21.0	4,207.8	15.4
5 to 9	4,674.8	31.9	4,701.2	22.3	4,679.6	19.7
10 to 19	4,385.2	37.1	4,420.5	20.8	4,383.9	22.1
20 to 49	3,413.0	31.5	3,315.8	16.7	3,271.8	10.8
50 or more	4,605.6	34.8	4,440.7	17.9	4,342.9	26.9
Mobile home	1,836.7	23.2	1,812.5	15.3	1,790.2	18.1
Boat, RV, van, etc.	35.0	3.4	35.9	2.0	35.1	1.5

Source: U.S. Census Bureau, 2010 American Community Survey

Table 3-46. Tenure, Total Population in Housing Units, by Units in Structure, 2010 American Community Survey, 1-, 3-, and 5-Year Estimates

[Numbers in thousands.]

Characteristics	United States					
	1-year estimates		3-year estimates		5-year estimates	
	Estimate	Margin of error (+/-)	Estimate	Margin of error (+/-)	Estimate	Margin of error (+/-)
Total units	301,362.4	*****	298,732.7	*****	295,968.3	*****
Owner-occupied units	201,961.0	474.6	202,674.1	375.2	203,526.1	694.3
1, detached or attached	180,962.7	489.0	181,500.0	395.9	182,118.7	718.0
2 to 4	3,888.3	63.6	4,030.0	30.6	4,117.0	25.0
5 or more	4,197.4	49.3	4,256.6	28.3	4,263.7	22.2
Mobile home	12,786.6	86.9	12,764.3	51.9	12,904.3	45.2
Boat, RV, van, etc.	126.0	8.0	123.2	5.3	122.3	3.8
Renter-occupied units	99,401.4	474.6	96,058.7	375.2	92,442.1	694.3
1, detached or attached	41,196.1	271.3	39,257.4	201.3	36,698.8	380.7
2 to 4	18,057.7	134.3	17,765.6	101.1	17,405.4	132.5
5 or more	34,884.5	169.6	34,062.1	109.1	33,402.1	138.4
Mobile home	5,196.2	86.1	5,006.2	63.9	4,869.8	72.0
Boat, RV, van, etc.	66.9	8.8	67.4	3.8	65.9	3.1

***** = Estimate is controlled. A statistical test for sampling variability is not appropriate.

Source: U.S. Census Bureau, 2010 American Community Survey

Table 3-47. Percent of Housing Units That Are Mobile Homes, United States and Puerto Rico, by State and Urban Designation, 2010 American Community Survey, 1-, 3-, and 5-Year Estimates

[Percent.]

State and territory	United States					
	1-year estimates		3-year estimates		5-year estimates	
	Percent	Margin of error (+/-)	Percent	Margin of error (+/-)	Percent	Margin of error (+/-)
United States	6.6	0.1	6.6	0.1	6.7	0.1
Urban and rural						
Urban	3.5	0.1	3.6	0.1	3.7	0.1
Rural	15.3	0.1	15.5	0.1	15.8	0.1
Inside and outside metropolitan areas						
In metropolitan or micropolitan statistical area	5.7	0.1	5.8	0.1	5.9	0.1
In metropolitan statistical area	4.7	0.1	4.8	0.1	4.9	0.1
In principal city	1.9	0.1	1.9	0.1	2.0	0.1
Not in principal city	6.6	0.1	6.7	0.1	6.8	0.1
In micropolitan statistical area	13.5	0.1	13.5	0.1	13.6	0.1
In principal city	5.0	0.2	5.1	0.1	5.2	0.1
Not in principal city	17.4	0.2	17.5	0.1	17.5	0.1
Not in metropolitan or micropolitan statistical area	16.4	0.2	16.1	0.1	16.3	0.1
Alabama	13.8	0.4	14.2	0.2	14.5	0.2
Alaska	5.1	0.6	5.3	0.3	5.4	0.2
Arizona	10.8	0.3	10.8	0.2	11.0	0.1
Arkansas	13.1	0.4	12.9	0.3	13.0	0.2
California	3.8	0.1	3.9	0.1	3.9	0.1
Colorado	4.3	0.3	4.5	0.1	4.6	0.1
Connecticut	0.8	0.1	0.8	0.1	0.9	0.1
Delaware	9.3	0.7	9.6	0.3	9.9	0.2
District of Columbia	0.1	0.1	0.0	0.1	0.0	0.1
Florida	9.3	0.2	9.6	0.1	9.8	0.1
Georgia	9.3	0.2	9.5	0.1	9.9	0.1
Hawaii	0.2	0.1	0.1	0.1	0.2	0.1
Idaho	9.6	0.6	9.7	0.3	9.8	0.2
Illinois	2.7	0.1	2.7	0.1	2.7	0.1
Indiana	5.2	0.2	5.3	0.1	5.4	0.1
Iowa	4.2	0.3	4.2	0.1	4.2	0.1
Kansas	5.2	0.3	5.1	0.2	5.2	0.1
Kentucky	12.6	0.3	12.4	0.2	12.4	0.2
Louisiana	13.2	0.4	13.1	0.2	13.4	0.2
Maine	8.9	0.4	8.8	0.3	9.0	0.2
Maryland	1.7	0.2	1.7	0.1	1.7	0.1
Massachusetts	0.8	0.1	0.8	0.1	0.8	0.1
Michigan	5.5	0.1	5.5	0.1	5.6	0.1
Minnesota	3.7	0.2	3.7	0.1	3.7	0.1
Mississippi	15.6	0.6	15.2	0.3	15.3	0.2
Missouri	6.9	0.2	6.8	0.1	6.9	0.1
Montana	11.1	0.5	11.5	0.4	11.7	0.3
Nebraska	3.8	0.3	3.8	0.2	4.0	0.1
Nevada	6.3	0.3	6.2	0.2	6.3	0.1
New Hampshire	6.0	0.5	6.1	0.2	6.0	0.2
New Jersey	0.9	0.1	1.0	0.1	1.0	0.1
New Mexico	16.5	0.6	16.3	0.4	16.7	0.3
New York	2.4	0.1	2.5	0.1	2.5	0.1
North Carolina	14.0	0.3	14.1	0.2	14.3	0.1
North Dakota	7.9	0.7	7.4	0.3	7.6	0.2
Ohio	4.0	0.1	3.9	0.1	4.0	0.1
Oklahoma	9.5	0.3	9.3	0.2	9.4	0.1
Oregon	8.3	0.3	8.4	0.2	8.6	0.1
Pennsylvania	4.2	0.1	4.3	0.1	4.3	0.1
Rhode Island	0.8	0.2	0.9	0.1	1.0	0.1
South Carolina	17.6	0.4	17.7	0.2	17.9	0.2
South Dakota	9.0	0.6	9.1	0.4	9.3	0.3
Tennessee	9.9	0.3	10.1	0.2	10.2	0.1
Texas	7.6	0.2	7.5	0.1	7.7	0.1
Utah	3.8	0.3	4.1	0.1	4.1	0.1
Vermont	6.9	0.6	7.1	0.3	7.0	0.2
Virginia	5.6	0.2	5.7	0.1	5.7	0.1
Washington	7.1	0.2	7.2	0.1	7.3	0.1
West Virginia	16.1	0.6	14.8	0.3	14.9	0.3
Wisconsin	3.7	0.1	3.8	0.1	3.9	0.1
Wyoming	13.4	1.1	14.2	0.6	14.6	0.3
Puerto Rico	0.2	0.1	0.2	0.1	0.2	0.1

Source: U.S. Census Bureau, 2010 American Community Survey

Table 3-48. Tenure, by Year Structure Built, 2010 American Community Survey, 1-, 3-, and 5-Year Estimates

[Numbers in thousands, except as noted.]

Characteristics	United States					
	1-year estimates		3-year estimates		5-year estimates	
	Estimate	Margin of error (+/-)	Estimate	Margin of error (+/-)	Estimate	Margin of error (+/-)
Total units	114,567.4	163.2	114,596.9	112.1	114,236.0	248.1
Owner-occupied units	74,873.4	216.1	75,557.7	165.3	76,089.7	362.8
Built 2005 or later	5,214.9	40.4	4,384.9	27.1	3,488.3	30.2
Built 2000 to 2004	6,680.3	40.7	6,753.6	30.3	6,984.2	50.5
Built 1990 to 1999	11,520.4	54.9	11,765.3	33.5	11,969.6	49.9
Built 1980 to 1989	10,241.1	46.1	10,428.3	28.8	10,615.7	45.8
Built 1970 to 1979	11,246.9	55.1	11,543.9	31.6	11,768.5	48.5
Built 1960 to 1969	8,168.6	42.7	8,315.1	27.9	8,445.3	40.4
Built 1950 to 1959	8,810.0	47.5	8,999.5	26.4	9,145.9	48.6
Built 1940 to 1949	3,909.4	28.9	4,053.0	17.5	4,143.2	25.0
Built 1939 or earlier	9,081.8	48.6	9,314.0	29.8	9,528.9	47.0
Renter-occupied units	39,694.0	91.9	39,039.3	74.5	38,146.3	120.2
Built 2005 or later	2,520.0	25.7	1,913.5	12.2	1,434.1	8.0
Built 2000 to 2004	2,540.8	25.4	2,524.5	17.3	2,635.3	13.3
Built 1990 to 1999	4,676.9	35.5	4,576.8	21.5	4,426.6	18.3
Built 1980 to 1989	5,664.5	45.6	5,594.9	23.7	5,521.7	21.8
Built 1970 to 1979	7,054.8	39.2	7,064.4	28.6	6,965.2	25.1
Built 1960 to 1969	4,725.6	38.6	4,702.9	22.5	4,659.6	20.9
Built 1950 to 1959	4,029.9	33.1	4,071.3	20.1	4,002.8	19.7
Built 1940 to 1949	2,399.8	26.9	2,455.9	14.3	2,417.5	13.1
Built 1939 or earlier	6,081.8	38.9				
Median year structure built (years)						
Total	1976	2	1975	1	1975	1
Owner-occupied units	1977	1	1976	1	1976	1
Renter-occupied units	1974	1	1973	1	1973	1

Source: U.S. Census Bureau, 2010 American Community Survey

APPENDIXES

APPENDIX A: SOURCE OVERVIEW

American Community Survey (ACS)

Web site: http://www.census.gov/acs/www/

The American Community Survey is an ongoing survey that provides data every year, giving communities the information they need to plan investments and services. Information from the survey generates data that help determine how more than $400 billion in federal and state funds are distributed each year. Questions are asked regarding age, sex, race, disability, work and commute, living expenses, income and benefits, health insurance, education, veteran status, and family.

Data from the ACS can be used to obtain demographic, social, economic, and housing information and characteristics. All ACS data are survey estimates. To help users interpret the reliability of the estimates, the Census Bureau publishes a margin of error for every ACS estimate. The value shown here is the 90 percent margin of error. The margin of error can be interpreted roughly as providing a 90 percent probability that the interval defined by the estimate minus the margin of error and the estimate plus the margin of error (the lower and upper confidence bounds) contains the true value. In addition to sampling variability, the ACS estimates are subject to nonsampling error (for a discussion of nonsampling variability, see the Accuracy of the Data section on the website). The effect of nonsampling error is not represented in these tables.

ACS data comprise 1-, 3-, and 5-year estimates. In the 2010 survey, 1-year estimates, which are best for populations of 65,000+, cover the time period between January 1, 2010, and December 31, 2010. The 3-year estimates, best for populations of 20,000+, cover the time period between January 1, 2008, and December 31, 2010. The 5-year estimates, ideal for populations of almost any size, cover the time period between January 1, 2006, and December 31, 2010.

The methodology for calculating median income and median earnings changed between 2008 and 2009. Medians over $75,000 were most likely affected. The underlying income and earning distribution now uses $2,500 increments up to $250,000 for households, nonfamily households, families, and individuals. It employs a linear interpolation method for median calculations. Before 2009, the highest income category was $200,000 for households, families and nonfamily households ($100,000 for individuals), and portions of the income and earnings distribution contained intervals wider than $2,500. Those cases used a Pareto Interpolation Method.

Supporting documentation on code lists, subject definitions, data accuracy, and statistical testing can be found on the ACS website in the Data and Documentation section.

Sample size and data quality measures (including coverage rates, allocation rates, and response rates) can be found on the ACS website in the Methodology section.

While the ACS data generally reflect the December 2009 Office of Management and Budget (OMB) definitions of metropolitan and micropolitan statistical areas, in certain instances the names, codes, and boundaries of the principal cities shown in ACS tables may differ from the OMB definitions due to differences in the effective dates of the geographic entities.

Estimates of urban and rural population, housing units, and characteristics reflect boundaries of urban areas defined based on Census 2000 data. Boundaries for urban areas have not been updated since Census 2000. As a result, data for urban and rural areas from the ACS do not necessarily reflect the results of ongoing urbanization.

For more information, please consult:
http://www.census.gov/acs/www/guidance_for_data_users/estimates/.

American Housing Survey (AHS)

Web site: http://www.census.gov/housing/ahs/

The American Housing Survey is sponsored by the Department of Housing and Urban Development (HUD) and conducted by the U.S. Census Bureau. It represents the most comprehensive national housing survey in the United States. It provides current information on a wide range of housing subjects, including size and composition of the nation's housing inventory, vacancies, physical condition of housing units, characteristics of occupants, indicators of housing and neighborhood quality, mortgages and other housing costs, persons eligible for and beneficiaries of assisted housing, home values, and characteristics of those who have recently moved.

The AHS is a longitudinal housing unit survey that asks questions about the quality of housing in the United States. By returning to the same housing units every other year to gather data, users are afforded the unique opportunity of analyzing housing and household changes over long periods of time. When gathering information, Census Bureau interviewers visit or telephone the household occupying each housing unit in the sample. For unoccupied units, they obtain information from landlords, rental agents, or neighbors. The survey is redesigned from time to time to make sure it meets current needs, and new topics are introduced for specific survey years.

Data release for the 2011 AHS was delayed three months due to budgetary issues. The data are subject to error from sampling and other causes, such as incomplete data and wrong answers.

Each housing unit in the AHS national sample is weighted and represents about 2,000 housing units in the United States. The weighting is designed to minimize sampling error and utilize independent estimates of occupied and vacant housing units.

Housing units participating in the AHS have been scientifically selected to represent a cross section of all housing units in the nation. The same basic sample of housing units is interviewed every two years until a new sample is selected. The U.S. Census Bureau updates the sample by adding newly constructed housing units and units discovered through coverage improvement efforts.

Respondents include:

- Occupied Housing Units – A household respondent, who must be a knowledgeable household member 16 years of age or over, provides information on the unit, the household composition, and income. Census prefers to select the reference person or spouse as the household respondent.

- Vacant Housing Units – A landlord, owner, real estate agent, or knowledgeable neighbor can provide data on the unit.

The survey is generally conducted biennially between May and September in odd-numbered years.

The first AHS was conducted in 1973, under the name the Annual Housing Survey, with a sample size of 60,000 housing units. The survey was conducted on an annual basis from 1973 to 1981. Due to budget constraints, it became biennial, and its name was changed to the American Housing Survey. The national sample underwent a redesign in 1985 based on data from the 1980 decennial census, with a base sample size of approximately 47,000 housing units. In 2005, the national sample was improved in two ways. Mobile home coverage was adjusted by replacing the units currently in the sample with mobile homes selected from Census 2000, and assisted living housing units selected from Census 2000 were introduced into the sample, thereby improving coverage of the elderly population.

The paper questionnaire was eliminated in 1997. All interviews from that point on were conducted by computer-assisted personal interviewing (CAPI). The 1997 AHS national-level data were also the first AHS data processed under a redesigned system using SAS software. In 2007, the newly converted Blaise CAPI survey instrument was adopted. A Spanish version of the instrument was first implemented in 2009.

Current plans call for a complete AHS sample redesign, beginning with the 2015 survey. Should this occur, data from the new sample will not be comparable with those from the previous sample.

Building Permits Survey

Web site: http://www.census.gov/construction/bps/

The purpose of the Building Permits Survey is to provide national, state, and local statistics on new, privately owned residential construction. The United States Code, Title 13, authorizes this survey, provides for voluntary responses, and provides an exception to confidentiality for public records. Data collected include number of buildings, number of housing units, and permit valuation by size of structure.

The monthly sample of 9,000 permit-issuing places was selected using a stratified systematic sample procedure. All permit places located in selected large metropolitan areas were selected with certainty. The remaining places were stratified by state. Places that exceed a cutoff value, which varies by state, were selected with certainty. Remaining places were sampled at a rate of 1 in 10. Monthly estimates represent all permit-issuing places nationwide. If a survey report is not received, missing data on permits for new construction are imputed, except for places that are also selected for the Survey of Construction (SOC). For these places, SOC permit data are used.

Existing Home Sales (EHS)

Web site: http://www.realtor.org/topics/existing-home-sales/expansion-and-survey

The National Association of Realtors® (NAR) issues Existing Home Sales data on a monthly basis to provide accurate and timely information about the U.S. housing market.

The research division receives data every month on existing home sales (single family, condos, and co-ops) from local associations/boards and multiple listing services (MLS) nationwide. NAR captures between 30 and 40 percent of all existing homes sales transactions with its monthly survey. The data provide the total number of closed existing home sales in each association/board/MLS and also total sales within price categories ranging from less than $30,000 to more than $600,000. Participants of the survey are located in every region of the country and provide wide geographic coverage of the existing home market. The statistics are published for the United States and for the four census regions of the country. State volume is based on the entire survey of nearly 700 associations/boards/MLSs and is reported quarterly to ensure each state receives optimal representation.

The monthly Existing Home Sales economic indicator is based on a representative sample of 160 Boards/MLSs. The home sales data (raw data) is divided into the four census regions: Northeast, South, Midwest, and West. NAR economists carefully evaluate the raw sales volume from the participating Boards/MLSs for accuracy. Once the "problematic data" have been extricated from the sample, the aggregated raw volume figures are weighted to accurately represent sales activity for each region of the country. This is also called the non-seasonally-adjusted volume. The weights are benchmarked every 10 years to reflect shifts in regional demand. The non-seasonally adjusted volume is then converted into seasonally adjusted annualized rates.

Median and mean (average) prices are computed for the nation and four census regions on a monthly basis. Median prices are also calculated for selected metropolitan areas and are reported quarterly. Due to the nature of the distribution of home sales prices, the mean sales price is usually higher than the median price.

There is a slight degree of seasonal variation in reporting selling prices. Sales prices generally experience the largest gains in the summer months, as favorable weather conditions create an ideal atmosphere for buying and selling a home. Demand for homes usually hits its seasonal peak in the third quarter, and strong price appreciation generally follows suit and then declines moderately over the next three months. Despite the slight seasonal variances that exist in the price series, sales prices are not seasonally adjusted. The reason for this is that seasonal variances are extremely fickle and difficult to gauge. Furthermore, changes in the characteristics and size of a home have a more pronounced effect on home prices.

Housing Vacancies and Homeownership (CPS/HVS)

Web site: http://www.census.gov/hhes/www/housing/hvs/hvs.html

The Housing Vacancies and Homeownership Survey provides current information on the rental and homeowner vacancy rates and characteristics of vacant units available for occupancy. These data are used extensively by public and private sector organizations to evaluate the need for new housing programs and initiatives. In addition, the rental vacancy rate is a component of the index of leading economic indicators and is thereby used by the federal government and economic forecasters to gauge the current economic climate.

Rental and homeowner vacancy rates and homeownership rates are available for the United States, regions, states, and for the 75 largest Metropolitan Statistical Areas (MSAs). These data are available both quarterly and annually. Homeownership rates are also tabulated by age of householder, by family status for the United States and regions, by race/ethnicity of householder, and by median family income for the United States. In addition, estimates of the total housing inventory and percent distributions of vacant for-rent and for-sale-only units are available for the United States and regions.

Computer-assisted telephone and personal visit interviews. All units in sample are visited if a telephone interview is not obtained. The CPS/HVS is a voluntary survey.

There are about 72,000 housing units both occupied and vacant contained in the Current Population Survey (CPS) sample. Of these units, about 61,200 are occupied and are eligible for interview each month. In addition to the 61,200, about 10,800 are visited but found to be vacant or otherwise not interviewed each month. About half of the 10,800 units are vacant and interviewed for the HVS. The HVS is a supplement of the CPS.

Multifamily vacancy rates are only available nationally from the HVS. Overall vacancy rates (which include single and multifamily units) are available by region and state and for the 75 largest MAs. Multifamily vacancy rates, by region, are available every two years from the American Housing Survey (AHS - national). MA data are also available for the 44 largest MAs from the AHS, each completed every four years on a rotating basis.

Housing unit estimates are available for the United States and regions by type of vacant unit and tenure. Estimates are also available for the United States and regions by age of householder. However, estimates by state or by MA are not provided. Some MA housing unit estimates are available from the AHS. County level data or smaller are only available from the decennial censuses.

The four quarterly press releases are issued during the last week of the month following the previous quarter. The detailed tables previously shown in quarterly reports will normally be available on the day of the press release. The annual data will be available after the fourth quarter press release is issued each year and as soon as it can be compiled.

Foreclosures may be in any of the housing stock categories in the estimates of the total housing inventory for the United States contained in the press release. They could still be occupied by the owner or still be occupied by the renter, making them "owner occupied" or "renter occupied," respectively.

They could also be vacant and available for sale or for rent. If the unit is classified as "vacant for sale only," it will be included in the "vacant for sale" category. If the unit is for rent or "for sale OR rent," it will be included in the "vacant for rent" category.

Many foreclosures will be in the "vacant other" category, because they are neither for sale or for rent; instead, they are still in the foreclosure process and tied up in legal proceedings, or being held off the market until the legal owner of the property decides what to do. In addition, it is possible the unit could be undergoing repair for future use. Also included in the "vacant other" category are units "for occasional use" and units "temporarily occupied by persons with usual residence elsewhere," both of which may contain foreclosures. Foreclosures could also be included in the seasonal category, depending on the specific situation.

Thus, foreclosed properties may appear in all of the housing unit categories, not just the "vacant for sale" category. However, please note that the formulas for calculating the rental and homeowner vacancy rates do not include "vacant other" or "seasonal" units in the calculation of the vacancy rates.

Changes in 2012

In the second quarter 2012, historical housing inventory estimates were revised based on the latest series of independent housing controls, the vintage 2011 independent housing estimates issued by Population Division. This includes the housing inventory time-series data from 2010 through the first quarter 2012. The vintage 2011 estimates are benchmarked to the 2010 Census. The same general procedure will be followed each year in revising housing inventory estimates with the most up-to-date independent housing estimates available.

For an explanation of the methodology used in producing the housing inventory independent estimates, please see: http://www.census.gov/popest/methodology/.

Note: This time series is by the latest "vintage year." For example, vintage 2011 means that all of the estimates in this time series are identified as belonging to "vintage 2011." The 2010 data are from the 2011 vintage, the 2011 data are from the 2011 vintage, and so on.

Beginning in the first quarter 2012, the population controls reflect the results of the 2010 decennial census. This change has virtually no effect on vacancy and homeownership rates, as described below.

Research has shown that the new 2010-based controls increased the rental vacancy rate in April 2010 from 10.43 percent to 10.45 percent—a difference of less than 1/10 of 1 percent. The homeowner vacancy rate remained the same at 2.63 percent, while the homeownership rate was up from 66.67 percent to 66.74 percent.

Changes in 2011

In the third quarter 2011, historical housing inventory estimates were revised based on the latest series of independent housing controls, the vintage 2010 independent housing estimates issued by Population Division. This includes the housing inventory time-series data from 2000 through the second quarter 2011. The vintage 2010 estimates are benchmarked to the 2000 and 2010 Census.

Note: This time series is by the latest "vintage year." For example, vintage 2010 means that all of the estimates in this time series are identified as belonging to "vintage 2010." The 2000 data are from the 2010 vintage, the 2001 data are from the 2010 vintage, and so on.

Changes in 2010

In the third quarter 2010, historical housing inventory estimates were revised based on the latest series of independent housing controls, the vintage 2009 independent housing estimates issued by Population Division. The vintage 2010 estimates are benchmarked to the 2000 Census.

In the first quarter 2010, Census began imputing missing values for the family income question, which is used in the homeownership table 8 of the press release. Previously, householders not responding to this question were excluded from the homeownership calculations for those below/above the median family income level. When compared to previous procedures, this change resulted in an increase in the homeownership rate of 2.2 percentage points for those at or below the median family income and an increase of 0.5 percentage points for those above the median family income level for the second quarter 2012. Data users should keep this in mind when comparing data from 2010 and later to earlier data.

Manufactured Homes Survey

Web site: http://www.census.gov/construction/mhs/mhsindex.html

The Manufactured Homes Survey is conducted by the U.S. Census Bureau and sponsored by the Department of Housing and Urban Development (HUD). MHS produces monthly regional estimates of new manufactured home placements, average sales prices, and dealers' inventories and more detailed annual estimates including selected characteristics of new manufactured homes. The statistics on shipments of new manufactured homes are produced by the Institute for Building Technology and Safety (IBTS) and published by the Manufactured Housing Institute (MHI).

The purpose of the survey is to provide current monthly estimates of new manufactured (mobile) homes placed for residential use and dealer inventories. The United States Code, Title 13, authorizes this survey and provides for voluntary responses. The Department of Housing and Urban Development funds this survey.

Coverage includes all new manufactured homes that have received a Federal inspection (i.e., HUD-code homes). Data collected include manufacturer's date of shipment, sales price, date of placement for residential use, placement location (state, county, and community), how titled, and home physical characteristics such as foundation, number of bedrooms, floor area, and air conditioning. Data collection begins about 40 days after each reference month, and continues for about 9 days. Reported data are for activities taking place two months earlier. The sample is updated each month. The survey is conducted monthly and has been since 1974.

A mail-out and telephone interview survey of about 1,000 dealers covering an inventory of some 1,200 selected new manufactured homes is conducted each month. In addition, a sample of newly manufactured homes is selected from lists obtained from the Institute for Building Technology and Safety. Dealers that take shipment of the selected homes are mailed a survey form for recording the status of the manufactured home. Each successive month, the dealer is contacted by telephone and provides updated status information about the home. Contact continues until the selected home is placed. From the sample data, monthly placements in the United States are estimated and seasonally adjusted.

Monthly survey results are placed on the Census Web site and include preliminary estimates and the two prior month figures for units placed, average sales price, and dealers' inventories by geographical region. This data is available about 8 weeks after each reference month.

Annual data for units placed, average sales price, and dealers' inventories are available by state. Annual manufactured homes data on selected characteristics by location and type of home placed, and detailed price data on units sold are also available. The annual data is available about five months after each calendar year and placed on the Census Web site.

Methodology

The methodology for collecting information on new manufactured homes for 1974 through 1979 involved contacting a sample of manufactured home dealers each month within 137 geographic areas or primary sampling units. The dealers were requested to provide data on the number of manufactured homes received from manufacturers, the number placed on a site for residential use, and the number held in inventory.

The methodology used after 1979 involves a monthly sample of new manufactured homes shipped by manufacturers. The dealer to whom the sampled unit was shipped is contacted by telephone and asked about the status of the unit. This is done each month until that unit is reported as placed.

Reliability of Estimates

The various estimates shown in the tables are based on sample surveys and may differ from statistics that would have been obtained from a complete census using the same schedules and procedures. For a particular estimate, statisticians define this difference as the total error of the estimate. When describing the reliability of survey results, total error is defined as the sum of sampling error and nonsampling error. Sampling error is the error arising from the use of a sample, rather than a census, to estimate population values. Nonsampling error encompasses all other factors that contribute to the total error of a sample survey estimate. The sampling error of an estimate can usually be estimated from the sample, whereas the nonsampling error of an estimate is difficult to measure and can rarely be estimated. Consequently, the actual error in an estimate exceeds the error that can be estimated. Further descriptions of sampling error and nonsampling error are provided in the following sections. Data users should take into account the estimates of sampling error and the potential effects of nonsampling error when using the published estimates.

Sampling Error

Sampling error reflects the fact that only a particular sample was surveyed rather than the entire population. Each sample selected for the MHS is one of a large number of similar probability samples that, by chance, might have been selected under the same specifications. Estimates derived from the different samples would differ from each other. The standard error (SE), or sampling error, of a survey estimate is a measure of the variation among the estimates from all possible sample. It is thus a measure of the precision with which an estimate from a particular sample approximates the average from all possible samples.

Estimates of the standard errors have been computed from the sample data for selected statistics. They are presented in the form of relative standard errors. The relative standard error equals the standard error divided by the estimated value to which it refers.

The sample estimate and an estimate of its standard error allow us to construct interval estimates with prescribed confidence that the interval includes the average result of all possible samples with the same size and design. To illustrate, if all possible samples were surveyed under essentially the same conditions, and estimates calculated from each sample, then:

1. Approximately 68 percent of the intervals from one standard error below the estimate to one standard error above the estimate would include the average value of all possible samples.

2. Approximately 90 percent of the intervals from 1.6 standard errors below the estimate to 1.6 standard errors above the estimate would include the average value of all possible samples.

Thus, for a particular sample, one can say with specified confidence that the average of all possible samples is included in the constructed interval.

For example, suppose that an estimated 30,000 manufactured homes were placed in a particular month and that the average relative standard error of this estimate is 4 percent. Multiplying 30,000 by .04, 1,200 is obtained as the standard error. This means that Census is confident, with 68 percent chance of being correct, that the average estimate from all possible samples of manufactured homes placed during the particular month is between 28,800 and 31,200 homes. To increase the probability to a 90 percent chance that the interval contains the average value over all possible samples (this is called a 90-percent confidence interval), multiply 1,200 by 1.6, yielding limits of 28,080 and 31,920 (30,000 units plus or minus 1,920 units). The average estimate of manufactured homes placed during the specified month may or may not be contained in any one of these computed intervals; but for a particular sample, one can say that the average estimate from all possible samples is included in the constructed interval with a specified confidence of 90 percent. It is important to note that the standard error and the relative standard error only measure sampling variability. They do not measure any systematic nonsampling errors in the estimates.

Nonsampling Errors

Nonsampling error encompasses all other factors, other than sampling error, that contribute to the total error of a sample survey estimate and may also occur in censuses. It is often helpful to think of nonsampling error as arising from deficiencies or mistakes in the survey process. Nonsampling errors are usually attributed to many possible sources: (1) coverage error—failure to accurately represent all population units in the sample, (2) inability to obtain information about all sample cases, (3) response errors, possibly due to definitional difficulties or misreporting, (4) mistakes in recording or coding the data obtained, and (5) other errors of coverage, collection and nonresponse, response, processing, or imputing for missing or inconsistent data. Although nonsampling error is not measured directly, the Census Bureau employs quality control procedures throughout the process to minimize this type of error.

A potential source of nonsampling error in the estimates is nonresponse. Nonresponse is the inability to obtain all the intended measurements or responses about all selected units. Unit nonresponse is used to describe the inability to obtain any of the substantive measurements about a sampled unit. For the 2011 survey, the average unit nonresponse rate was 14 percent.

Seasonal Adjustment

For analyzing general trends in the economy, seasonally adjusted data are usually preferred since seasonal adjustment eliminates the effect of changes that normally occur at about the same time and in about the same magnitude every year. For example, suppose that the normal month-to-month change in an unadjusted series between February and March was an increase of 20 percent. Then, an increase in the unadjusted series of less than 20 percent would be viewed as a decrease in the seasonally adjusted series; an increase of exactly 20 percent would be viewed as no change in the adjusted series; and an increase of more than 20 percent would be viewed as an increase in the adjusted series.

The recurring changes in a series that are removed by seasonal adjustment result from such factors as normal changes in weather and differing lengths of months. It should be emphasized that seasonal adjustment does not account for abnormal weather conditions or for year-to-year changes in weather.

Most of the seasonally adjusted series are shown as seasonally adjusted annual rates (SAAR). A SAAR is the seasonally adjusted monthly rate multiplied by 12.

The seasonal adjustment indexes were developed using X-13ARIMA-SEATS software. X-13ARIMA-SEATS software improves upon the X-12-ARIMA seasonal adjustment software by providing enhanced diagnostics as well as incorporating an enhanced version of the Bank of Spain's SEATS (Signal Extraction in ARIMA Time Series) software, which uses an ARIMA model-based procedure instead of the X-11 filter-based approach to estimate seasonal factors. The X-13ARIMA-SEATS and X-12-ARIMA software produce identical results when using the X-11 filter-based adjustment methodology. The X-13ARIMA-SEATS software will be available from the Census Bureau's Internet site in the coming months. Note that MHS estimates continue to be adjusted using the X-11 filter-based adjustment procedure.

The X-13ARIMA-SEATS program provides summary statistics to indicate the overall effect of the seasonal adjustment. A description of X-13ARIMA-SEATS appears in The X-13A-S Seasonal Adjustment Program and Update on the Development of X-13ARIMA-SEATS by Brian C. Monsell, U.S. Census Bureau. For more information on X-12-ARIMA see the reference manuals posted on the Census Bureau's Web site.

An assumption underlying the seasonal adjustment process is that the original series can be separated into a seasonal component, a trading-day component, a trend-cycle component, and an irregular component. The seasonally adjusted series consists of the trend-cycle and irregular components taken together. The trend-cycle component includes the long-term trend and the business cycle. The irregular component is made up of residual variations, such as the sudden impact of political events and the effects of strikes, unusual weather conditions, reporting and sampling errors, etc.

Seasonal indexes are developed concurrently for each month for shipments, regional estimates of manufactured homes placements and manufactured homes on dealer lots. The seasonally adjusted U.S. total is the sum of the four regional components.

Monthly Interest Rate Survey

Web site: http://www.fhfa.gov/Default.aspx?Page=250

The survey provides monthly information on interest rates, loan terms, and house prices by property type (all, new, previously occupied), by loan type (fixed or adjustable rate), and by lender type (savings associations, mortgage companies, commercial banks, and savings banks), as well as information on 15-year and 30-year fixed-rate loans. In addition, the survey provides quarterly information on conventional loans by major metropolitan area and by FHLBank district.

To conduct this survey, the Finance Board asks a sample of mortgage lenders to report the terms and conditions on all single-family, fully amortized, purchase-money, nonfarm loans that they close during the last five business days of the month. The survey excludes FHA-insured and VA-guaranteed loans, multifamily loans, mobile home loans, and loans created by refinancing another mortgage.

The final July value of the National Average Contract Mortgage Rate for the Purchase of Previously Occupied Homes by Combined Lenders is 3.66 percent. This is a decrease of 0.01 percent from the previous month. Many lenders use this rate in adjusting some adjustable-rate mortgages. This index was the only index rate that federally chartered savings and loan associations could use as an adjustable-rate mortgage index in the early 1980s.

Interested parties can receive up-to-date information on this index value by calling (202) 649-3206. The release date for the August index, as of August 2012, was scheduled for September 27, 2012.

New Residential Construction

Web site: http://www.census.gov/construction/nrc/

This page provides national and regional data on the number of new housing units authorized by building permits; authorized, but not started; started; under construction; and completed. The data are for new, privately owned housing units, excluding "HUD-code" manufactured (mobile) homes. The data are from the Building Permits Survey and from the Survey of Construction (SOC), which is partially funded by the Department of Housing and Urban Development (HUD). Local building permit data may be found on the Building Permits Survey Web site.

Residential construction data is comprised of 2 surveys, the Survey of Construction (SOC) and the Building Permits Survey (BPS). The following links provide additional information about each of the surveys.

The Survey of Construction estimates the amount of new, privately owned construction in areas that require a building permit and in areas that do not require a building permit. Areas that do not require a building permit are referred to as non-permit (NP) areas. Less than 2 percent of all new construction takes place in NP areas. Census Field Representatives collect data for both of these areas. For areas requiring a permit, they visit a sample of permit offices and select a sample of permits authorizing private new residential construction. These permits are then followed through to see when they are started and completed, and when they are sold for single-family units that are built to be sold. Information on physical and financial characteristics are also collected. For NP areas, roads in sampled NP areas are driven as least once every 3 months to see if there is any new construction.

Each month, the Census Bureau publishes preliminary estimates of building permits, housing starts, and housing completions. The Census Bureau releases these estimates to provide government and private data users with early measures of new privately owned residential construction and new residential sales activity. A necessary part of the process of issuing these early data involves the issuance of subsequent revisions. The revisions are primarily the result of the replacement of imputed data with data reported in subsequent months.

Certain apartments are included in the data. A housing unit, as defined for purposes of these data, is a house, an apartment, a group of rooms, or a single room intended for occupancy as separate living quarters. Each apartment unit in an apartment building is counted as one housing unit. Housing units, as distinguished from "HUD-code" manufactured (mobile) homes, include conventional "site-built" units, prefabricated, panelized, sectional, and modular units.

Most of the seasonally adjusted series are shown as seasonally adjusted annual rates (SAAR). The seasonally adjusted annual rate is the seasonally adjusted monthly value multiplied by 12. The benefit of the annual rate is that not only can one monthly estimate be compared with another; monthly data can also be compared with an annual total. The seasonally adjusted annual rate is neither a forecast nor a projection; rather it is a description of the rate of building permits, housing starts, housing completions, or new home sales in the particular month for which they are calculated.

Seasonal movements are often large enough that they mask other characteristics of the data that are of interest to analysts of current economic trends. For example, if each month has a different seasonal tendency toward high or low values it can be difficult to detect the general direction of a time series' recent monthly movement (increase, decrease, turning point, no change, consistency with another economic indicator, etc.). Seasonal adjustment produces data in which the values of neighboring months are usually easier to compare. Many data users prefer seasonally adjusted data because they want to see those characteristics that seasonal movements tend to mask, especially changes in the direction of the series.

The estimated standard error expressed as a percent of the estimated total or proportion, that is, the estimated standard error times 100 divided by the estimate. This is also called coefficient of variation (CV). It is a measure of sampling error.

The sample estimate and an estimate of its standard error allow us to construct interval estimates with prescribed confidence that the interval includes the average result of all possible samples with the same size and design.

The only series on new residential construction that is available at a smaller geographic area is the housing units authorized by building permits. Building permits data are collected from individual permit offices, most of which are municipalities; the remainder are counties, townships, or New England and Middle Atlantic-type towns. Because building permits are public records, local area data can be published without any confidentiality concerns. From local area data, estimates are tabulated for counties, states, metropolitan areas, census divisions, census regions, and the United States.

A (Z) is not necessarily a true zero. It represents a relative standard error less than 0.5 percent.

Primary Mortgage Market Survey (PMMS)

Web site: http://www.freddiemac.com/pmms/

Freddie Mac's Primary Mortgage Market Survey (PMMS) surveys lenders each week on the rates and points for their most popular 30-year fixed-rate, 15-year fixed-rate, 5/1 hybrid amortizing adjustable-rate, and 1-year amortizing adjustable-rate mortgage products. The survey is based on first-lien prime conventional conforming mortgages with a loan-to-value of 80 percent. In addition, the adjustable-rate mortgage (ARM) products are indexed to U.S. Treasury yields and lenders are asked for both the initial coupon rate and points as well as the margin on the ARM products.

Since April 1971, Freddie Mac has surveyed lenders across the nation weekly to determine the average 30-year fixed-rate mortgage rate; in 1984, the 1-year ARM was added to the survey and the 15-year fixed-rate mortgage rate was included beginning in 1991. In January 2005, Freddie Mac added a 5/1 hybrid ARM series to the survey. Currently, about 125 lenders are surveyed each week and the mix of lender types (thrifts, credit unions, commercial banks, and mortgage lending companies) is roughly proportional to the level of mortgage business that each type commands nationwide.

The survey is collected from Monday through Wednesday and the results are posted on Thursdays. Average rates and points (and margin for ARMs) for each product are reported for the nation and the five Freddie Mac regions. The PMMS results are published extensively in the media, used in several government agency reports, and many other industry-related publications. For example, the Federal Reserve Board includes the average 30-year rate on its list of Selected Interest Rates (Statistical Release H.15) as the measure of conventional mortgage rates.

The PMMS has evolved into the foremost reliable, representative source of regional and national mortgage rate trends and is relied upon by the mortgage industry and the public in gauging market conditions and evaluating mortgage loan options.

The PMMS rate is based on current lender quotes. These rates and points are indicative of what a consumer could expect to be offered if they were to request a loan on that day.

A "point" equals one percent of the loan amount. Discount points are used by consumers to buy down their mortgage interest rate. Therefore, an inverse relationship exists between the number of points paid and the given mortgage rate. Origination points are points paid by consumers but are used to cover the costs of originating the mortgage, such as compensation for the loan officer, application processing costs, etc. The way "points" are measured for PMMS is by total points, which includes both discount and origination fees that have historically averaged around one point. The points quoted in the PMMS represent the average points charged for mortgages offered at the PMMS rate during the survey week.

In some areas it is common for home sellers to pay points on a home-buyer's loan. This results in loans from areas with seller-paid points displaying lower rates and higher points relative to loans from areas without seller-paid points. Historically, originators have attributed one point for origination costs, and charged for it either explicitly (paid at origination) or implicitly with a higher mortgage rate. Automated underwriting systems, such as Loan Prospector®, and shifts in the mortgage origination channels (e.g., emergence of Internet commerce) have increased loan processing efficiencies. However, it is not clear if these cost-savings are passed on to consumers through lower interest rates, lower points, or a combination of the two. Many lenders offer their customers a menu of rate-point combinations and are asked to provide their most popular combination for the survey.

Currently, about 25 lenders from each of Freddie Mac's five regions are surveyed each week. The mix of lenders surveyed approximates the volume of mortgage loans that each lender type originates nationwide.

The survey results each week are weighted based on the most recently released dollar volume of conventional, single-family originations within the Freddie Mac one-unit loan limit reported under the Home Mortgage Disclosure Act (HMDA) data—prior survey averages are not adjusted. The HMDA data are typically published in September of each year for the immediately prior year. To do the weighting, the HMDA state origination volumes are taken and aggregated to the five regions to establish regional weightings. A national average is then calculated as the weighted average of the five regional averages. In addition, when calculating the regional averages, any rate/point combination outlier that is more than one standard deviation from the region's mean is discarded.

Survey of Consumer Finances (SCF)

Web site: http://www.federalreserve.gov/econresdata/scf/scfindex.htm

The Survey of Consumer Finances (SCF) is normally a triennial cross-sectional survey of U.S. families, but over the 1983–1989 and 2007–2009 periods, the survey collected panel data. The survey data include information on families' balance sheets, pensions, income, and demographic characteristics. Information is also included from related surveys of pension providers and the earlier such surveys conducted by the Federal Reserve Board. By selecting a given survey in the drop-down box below, users may obtain summary results, codebooks, and other documentation, and the publicly available data for that survey. Additional information about the survey, recent changes, answers to frequently asked questions and working papers on the surveys are available through the link above.

The regular SCF cross-sectional surveys are conducted every three years to provide detailed information on the finances of U.S. families. No other study for the country collects comparable information. Data from the SCF are widely used, from analysis at the Federal Reserve and other branches of government to scholarly work at the major economic research centers.

The survey has contained a panel element over two periods. Respondents to the 1983 survey were re-interviewed in 1986 and 1989. Respondents to the 2007 survey were re-interviewed in 2009.

The study is sponsored by the Federal Reserve Board in cooperation with the Department of the Treasury. Since

1992, data have been collected by the NORC at the University of Chicago.

To ensure the representativeness of the study, respondents are selected randomly using procedures described in the technical working papers on the Web site. A strong attempt is made to select families from all economic strata.

Participation in the study is strictly voluntary. However, because only about 6,500 families were interviewed in the most recent study, every family selected is very important to the results. To maintain the scientific validity of the study, interviewers are not allowed to substitute respondents for families that do not participate. Thus, if a family declines to participate, it means that families like theirs may not be represented clearly in national discussions.

The confidentiality of the information provided in the study is of the highest importance to NORC and the Federal Reserve. Strenuous efforts are made to protect the privacy of participants, and in the history of the survey, there has never been a leak. The names of the participants in the survey are known only to NORC, which has more than 50 years of successful experience in collecting confidential information.

For the 1983 and 1989 surveys, a separate Survey of Pension Providers (SPP) was conducted to obtain detailed technical information on the pensions of SCF participants; data and documentation for the SPP appear under a separate link.

A link is also given for data and documentation from the 1962 Survey of Financial Characteristics of Consumers (SFCC) and the 1963 Survey of Changes in Family Finances (SCFF); these surveys are the most direct precursors of the SCF.

For information about recent changes, please see:
http://www.federalreserve.gov/econresdata/scf/scf_recent changes.htm.

Survey of Market Absorption (SOMA)

Web site: http://www.census.gov/hhes/www/housing/soma/soma.html

The Survey of Market Absorption (SOMA), sponsored by the Department of Housing and Urban Development (HUD), uses the Census Bureau's Survey of Construction (SOC) as its sampling base. Each month, a sample of residential buildings containing five or more units is selected for SOMA. The initial 3-month interview collects information on amenities, rent or sales price levels, number of units, type of building, and the number of units taken off the market (absorbed). Field representatives conduct subsequent interviews, if necessary, at 6, 9, and 12 months after completion. Beginning in 2002, the survey started collecting information on "Senior Housing."

Data are tabulated quarterly and annually and are released on the Internet along with selected metro area quarterly absorption rates. Additionally, an annual report on the "Characteristics of Apartments Completed" is produced. Quarterly reports, including basic tabulations, are published and released on the Internet. These quarterly reports are generally available the first week of March, June, September, and December. Additionally, data on absorption rates for selected metropolitan areas are also released on the Internet at the same time. Pre-publication data, detailing information for regular rental units and condominiums is published approximately one month earlier. There are also two annual publications released on the Internet, the H-130 Annual, which provides 12-month absorption data for the previous year and is released the first week in April, and the H-131, Characteristics of Apartments Report, which provides annual 3-month absorption rates and is released the first week of July.

Preferred interviewees are the building manager or rental/sales agent for the unit. The owner or builder may also respond.Buildings selected for the SOMA come from the Bureau's Survey of Construction (SOC). New buildings are brought into sample each month. The actual number will vary based on construction activity.

Value of Construction Put in Place

Web site: http://www.census.gov/econ/overview/co0300.html

The purpose of this information is to provide monthly estimates of the total dollar value of construction work done in the United States. The United States Code, Title 13, authorizes this program and provides for voluntary responses. Coverage includes construction work done each month on new structures or improvements to existing structures for private and public sectors.Data estimates include the cost of labor and materials, architectural and engineering work, overhead, interest and taxes paid during construction, and contractor's profits.

Data collection and estimation activities begin on the first day after the reference month and continue for about three weeks. Reported data and estimates are for activity taking place during the previous calendar month. The survey has been conducted monthly since 1960.

Composite estimates are based on mail-out/mail-back and interview surveys of selected construction projects and building owners, and estimates developed or compiled from other Census Bureau, federal agency, and private data sources. Directly measured (survey) estimates account for 65 percent of total monthly Value of Construction Put in Place; other estimates cover the remaining 35 percent of work done.

The *Construction Progress Reporting Surveys* are mail-out/mail-back surveys of owners of sampled construction projects that collect data on expenditures for 4 types of construction: privately owned nonresidential construction, state and local construction, privately owned multifamily, and federal construction projects.

Projects are selected using stratified systematic sample procedures. Privately owned nonresidential, state and local, and federal projects are selected from lists compiled by the McGraw-Hill Construction Company (and supplemented with a small sample of projects in non-permit issuing areas), with strata based on type of construction and estimated project value. Multifamily projects are a subsample of multi-unit projects identified in the Survey of Construction, with strata based on building location and number of housing units.

Owners of selected projects report on the value of work done each month from project start through completion. These four surveys currently cover about 6,500 private nonresidential; 10,500 state and local; 1,500 multifamily; and 700 federal projects each month.

The *Consumer Expenditure Survey (CE)* is a personal interview survey of 7,500 owner-occupied housing units. Monthly Value Put in Place data for residential improvements to owner-occupied housing units are derived from CE.

Other estimates are developed or compiled for the Value of Construction Put in Place through various sources and surveys. Examples include estimates of new home construction activity for houses identified in the Survey of Construction; expenditures for railroad construction obtained from the Surface Transportation Board; and data on cable television construction obtained from industry trade association statistics.

Value of Construction Put in Place press releases are issued on the first working day of each month, 2 months after the reference month. Data are shown by type of construction in seasonally adjusted and unadjusted dollars. Statistics are available at the U.S. level monthly, and by division, region, and state annually for selected categories.

The Bureau of Economic Analysis uses these data directly in producing GDP statistics. Other government agencies and construction-related businesses use the data for economic forecasts, market research, and financial decision making.

The data also provide a designated principal economic indicator and a major source of data for monthly estimates of fixed capital investment.

Supplemental Table Notes

This part of Appendix A contains additional information about specific tables included in Part I, Part II, and Part III of this publication. These tables have information beyond the footnotes that is important to understanding and analyzing the data. Please note that not all tables have supplementary notes. Definitions, organized by source, can be found in Appendix B. Each table contains a note regarding its source material.

Table 1-22

For more information on understanding race and Hispanic origin data, please see the Census 2010 Brief entitled "Overview of Race and Hispanic Origin: 2010," issued March 2011. The ACS questions on Hispanic origin and race were revised in 2008 to make them consistent with the Census 2010 question wording. Any changes in estimates for 2008 and beyond may be due to demographic changes, as well as factors including questionnaire changes, differences in ACS population controls, and methodological differences in the population estimates, and therefore should be used with caution.

For a summary of questionnaire changes, see http://www.census.gov/acs/www/methodology/questionnaire_changes/. For more information about changes in the estimates, see http://www.census.gov/population/www/socdemo/hispanic/reports.html.

Tables 1-28 through 1-30

The Census Bureau introduced a new set of disability questions in the 2008 ACS questionnaire. Accordingly, comparisons of disability data from 2008 or later with data from prior years are not recommended. For more information on these questions and their evaluation in the 2006 ACS Content Test, see the Evaluation Report Covering Disability.

Occupation codes are 4-digit codes and are based on Standard Occupational Classification 2010.

Note that the data do not meet all of the criteria outlined in the Census Bureau Standard *Quality Requirements for Releasing Data Products* and they should be used with caution. In particular, the item response rates for certain key characteristics and the coverage rates for certain segments of the group quarters population do not meet the criteria outlined in the standard. See the ACS User Notes on the Web site for a detailed description of the specific quality issues and information about the impact on the data.

Table 1-31

See the definitions in Appendix B and/or the ACS Web site for more information on the definitions of the following population groups: Arab, Arab/Arabic, European, Subsaharan African, African, American, and All Other Hispanic or Latino.

Data for the households, families, occupied housing units, owner-occupied housing units, and renter-occupied housing units lines refer to the specified race, Hispanic or Latino, American Indian or Alaska Native, or ancestry of the householder shown in the table. Data in the "Total population" column are shown regardless of the race, Hispanic or Latino, American Indian or Alaska Native, or ancestry of the person.

The Census Bureau introduced a new set of disability questions in the 2008 ACS questionnaire. Accordingly, comparisons of disability data from 2008 or later with data from prior years are not recommended. For more information on these questions and their evaluation in the 2006 ACS Content Test, see the Evaluation Report Covering Disability.

There were changes in the edit between 2009 and 2010 regarding Supplemental Security Income (SSI) and Social Security. The changes in the edit loosened restrictions on disability requirements for receipt of SSI resulting in an increase in the total number of SSI recipients in the American Community Survey. The changes also loosened restrictions on possible reported monthly amounts in Social Security income resulting in higher Social Security aggregate amounts. These results more closely match administrative counts compiled by the Social Security Administration.

The Census Bureau introduced an improved sequence of labor force questions in the 2008 ACS questionnaire. Accordingly, caution is recommended when making labor force data comparisons from 2008 or later with data from prior years. For more information on these questions and their evaluation in the 2006 ACS Content Test, see the "Evaluation Report Covering Employment Status" at http://www.census.gov/acs/www/Downloads/methodology/content_test/P6a_Employment_Status.pdf, and the "Evaluation Report Covering Weeks Worked" at http://www.census.gov/acs/www/Downloads/methodology/content_test/P6b_Weeks_Worked_Final_Report.pdf. Additional information can also be found at http://www.census.gov/hhes/www/laborfor/laborforce.html.

Industry codes are 4-digit codes and are based on the North American Industry Classification System 2007. The Industry categories adhere to the guidelines issued in Clarification Memorandum No. 2, "NAICS Alternate Aggregation Structure for Use by U.S. Statistical Agencies," issued by the Office of Management and Budget.

Occupation codes are 4-digit codes and are based on Standard Occupational Classification 2010.

The health insurance coverage category names were modified in 2010. See ACS Health Insurance Definitions for a list of the insurance type definitions.

Table 2-22

This table was included in the 2000 SF3 file.

Table 2-23

To increase the size of the distribution for real estate taxes.

Table 2-29

Median calculations for base table sourcing VAL, MHC, SMOC, and TAX should exclude zero values.

Tables 2-34 and 2-35 (CPS/HVS)

Vacancy rates are based in part on forecasts of occupied housing units. These forecasts are periodically revised to incorporate more recent data and improved forecasting procedures.

Beginning in the first quarter 2003, these data are based on data from the 2001 AHS. Beginning in 2005, first quarter 2005 data are based on data from the 2003 AHS. Beginning in 2007, first quarter 2007 data are based on data from the 2005 AHS. Beginning in 2009, first quarter 2009 data are based on data from the 2007 AHS. Beginning in 2011, first quarter 2011 data are based on data from the 2009 AHS.

For the occupied unit forecasts for the monthly rent categories, the AHS data are updated quarterly to reflect the rise in the cost of renting through the use of the residential rent index, and the latest available asking rent data for newly constructed rental units.

Table 3-25

The median gross rent excludes no cash renters.

In prior years, the universe included all owner-occupied units with a mortgage. It is now restricted to include only those units where SMOCAPI is computed, that is, SMOC and household income are valid values.

In prior years, the universe included all owner-occupied units without a mortgage. It is now restricted to include only those units where SMOCAPI is computed, that is, SMOC and household income are valid values.

In prior years, the universe included all renter-occupied units. It is now restricted to include only those units where GRAPI is computed, that is, gross rent and household Income are valid values.

The 2009 and 2010 plumbing data for Puerto Rico will not be shown. Research indicates that the questions on plumbing facilities that were introduced in 2008 in the stateside American Community Survey and the 2008 Puerto Rico Community Survey may not have been appropriate for Puerto Rico.

Table 3-30

The percent imputed for units in structure, year structure built, rooms, bedrooms, plumbing facilities, and kitchen facilities is based on all housing units (both occupied and vacant housing units) instead of occupied housing units only.

The 2009 and 2010 plumbing data for Puerto Rico will not be shown. Research indicates that the questions on plumbing facilities that were introduced in 2008 in the stateside American Community Survey and the 2008 Puerto Rico Community Survey may not have been appropriate for Puerto Rico.

The imputation rates for some items—Units in Structure, Year Structure Built, Rooms, Bedrooms, Plumbing Facilities, and Kitchen Facilities—are calculated using the number of imputations in total housing units in the numerator but using total occupied housing units in the denominator. This results in artificially inflated imputation rates for all areas, but particularly in areas where there are unusually high percentages of vacant housing units.

APPENDIX B: DEFINITIONS

Absorption. When a unit in a building with five or more units has been initially rented or sold after construction and is no longer available on the market.

Aggregate contract rent. This is calculated by adding all of the contract rents for occupied housing units in an area. Aggregate contract rent is subject to rounding, which means that all cells in a matrix are rounded to the nearest hundred dollars.

Aggregate earnings. This refers to the sum of wage/salary and net self-employment income for a particular universe of people 16 years old and over. Aggregate earnings are rounded to the nearest hundred dollars.

Aggregate income. This is the sum of all incomes for a particular universe.

Aggregate rent asked. This is calculated by adding all of the rents for vacant-for-rent housing units in an area. Aggregate rent asked is subject to rounding, which means that all cells in a matrix are rounded to the nearest hundred dollars.

Aggregate rooms. This is calculated by adding all of the rooms for housing units in an area.

Aggregate value. This is calculated by adding all of the value estimates for owner occupied housing units in an area. Aggregate value is rounded to the nearest hundred dollars.

Authorization. The act of a local jurisdiction approving construction projects by issuing building or zoning permits.

Available housing vacancy rate. The proportion of the housing inventory that is vacant-for-sale only and vacant-for-rent. It is computed by dividing the sum of vacant-for-sale only housing units and vacant-for-rent housing units, by the sum of occupied units, vacant-for-sale only housing units, vacant-sold-not occupied housing units, vacant-for-rent housing units, and vacant-rented-not-occupied housing units, and then multiplying by 100.

Average. The arithmetic mean, which is calculated by adding a set of numbers and dividing the resulting sum by the quantity of numbers summed.

Average family size. A measure obtained by dividing the number of people in families by the total number of families (or family householders). In cases where the measures, "people in family" or "people per family" are cross-tabulated by race or Hispanic origin, the race or Hispanic origin refers to the householder rather than the race or Hispanic origin of each individual.

Average household size. A measure obtained by dividing the number of people in households by the number of households. In cases where people in households are cross-classified by race or Hispanic origin, people in the household are classified by the race or Hispanic origin of the householder rather than the race or Hispanic origin of each individual.

Average household size of occupied unit. A measure obtained by dividing the number of people living in occupied housing units by the total number of occupied housing units. This measure is rounded to the nearest hundredth.

Average household size of owner-occupied unit. A measure obtained by dividing the number of people living in owner-occupied housing units by the total number of owner-occupied housing units.

Average household size of renter-occupied unit. A measure obtained by dividing the number of people living in renter-occupied housing units by the total number of renter-occupied housing units.

Bedrooms. Those rooms used mainly for sleeping or designed to be a bedroom, even if used for other purposes. A housing unit consisting of only one room, such as a one–room efficiency apartment, is classified by definition as having no bedroom.

Building or zoning permit. The approval given by a local jurisdiction to proceed on a construction project. Note that not all areas of the country require a permit for construction.

Built for rent. This category includes all houses built on builder's land with the intention of renting the housing unit. A lease-purchase, rent-purchase, or other option to eventually buy the house may exist. This also would include retirement community units, occupied under a "life-lease"/"continuing-care" arrangement (occupants pay an up front fee or small monthly fees for lifelong use).

Built for sale. This category includes all houses built on builder's land with the intention of selling the house and land in one transaction. Such a sale is called "fee simple." These units are often called "speculatively-built" houses.

Citizenship. Place of birth was asked for each householder and every household member. There are five categories of citizenship status: (1) born in the United States, (2) born in Puerto Rico or another U.S. outlying area, (3) born abroad of U.S. citizen parents, (4) naturalized citizens, or (5) non-citizens. People born in the United States are citizens at birth.

Commercial purpose. The use of property by persons for any fare, fee, rate, charge or other consideration, or directly or indirectly in connection with any business, or other undertaking intended for profit.

Commitment rate. The interest rate a lender would charge to lend mortgage money to a qualified borrower exclusive of the fees and points required by the lender. This commitment rate applies only to conventional financing on conforming mortgages with loan-to-value rates of 80 percent or less.

Complete bathrooms. A housing unit is classified as having a complete bathroom if it has a room or adjoining areas with a flush toilet, bathtub or shower, sink, and hot and cold-piped water. A half bathroom has hot and cold piped water and either a flush toilet or a bathtub or shower, but does not have all the facilities for a complete bathroom.

Completed housing. A house is defined as completed when all finished flooring has been installed (or carpeting if used in place of finished flooring). If the building is occupied before all construction is finished, it is classified as completed at the time of occupancy. In privately owned buildings with two or more housing units, all of the units in the buildings are counted as completed when 50 percent or more of the units are occupied or available for occupancy.

Condominium and cooperative fee. A condominium fee is charged to the owners of the individual condominium unit on a regular basis. The fee covers operating and maintenance costs of the common property; for example: halls, lobby, parking areas, laundry room, swimming pool; as well as related administrative costs, such as utilities billed communally and management fees. A cooperative maintenance fee (also called carrying charge) is a fee charged to the owners of the cooperative on a regular basis.

Condominium status. Condominium is a type of ownership that enables a person to own an apartment or house in a development of similarly owned units and to hold a common or joint ownership in some or all of the common areas and facilities such as land, roof, hallways, entrances, elevators, swimming pool, etc. Condominiums may be single-family houses as well as units in apartment buildings.

Consolidated metropolitan statistical areas. A consolidated metropolitan statistical area (CMSA) is made up of at least two primary metropolitan statistical areas. The microdata identify specific CMSAs.

Contract rent. For renter-occupied units, the contract rent is the monthly rent agreed upon regardless of any furnishings, utilities, or services that may be included. For vacant units, rent is the amount asked for the unit at the time of interview; the amount may differ from the rent contracted for when the unit is occupied.

Contractor-built houses. This category includes all houses built for owner occupancy on the owner's land with construction under the supervision of a single general contractor. Also includes houses built for rent-free use such as a church that builds a house for its clergy (built by a builder or general contractor who does not own the land).

Cooperatives. A type of ownership whereby a group of housing units is owned by a corporation of member–owners. Each individual member is entitled to occupy or rent out an individual housing unit and is a shareholder in the corporation that owns the property, but does not own the unit directly. The corporation may have a mortgage on the whole group of units. The member may have a loan or mortgage to buy his or her shares in the corporation.

Core based statistical area (CBSA). CBSAs include an urban center of at least 10,000 people and adjacent areas that are socioeconomically tied to the urban center by commuting. The term "CBSA" refers collectively to both metropolitan statistical areas and micropolitan areas. Micropolitan areas are based around Census Bureau-defined urban clusters of at least 10,000 and fewer than 50,000 people.

Cost and ownership sharing. This item is restricted to owner-occupied housing units. Shared ownership is two or more names on a deed or title. Shared costs include only payments designated for mortgage or utility costs (not taxes or insurance), whether paid directly to a mortgage or utility company, or to household members. Not living here means that one of the people sharing the ownership or costs is not a household member.

Current income. This is defined as the total income of the family and any primary individuals in the past year.

Current interest rate. This item refers to the annual percentage rate of the mortgage in effect as of the date of the interview, not the rate when the mortgage was made, nor any future changes of variable rates of which the respondent may be aware. In this publication, medians for current interest rate are rounded to the nearest tenth of a percent.

Current line-of-credit interest rate. This item refers to the annual percentage rate in effect on current line-of-credit outstanding balances.

Down payment. This item refers to the total amount of money used for the down payment or outright purchase of the home. Respondents were allowed to answer by giving a total dollar amount or by giving a percent of the purchase price.

Duration of vacancy. The length of time a housing unit was vacant was computed from the day the unit became vacant until the day of the interview. The data, therefore, do not provide a direct measure of the total length of time units remain vacant. For newly constructed units, the duration of vacancy represents the time period since the date when the unit was considered a vacant housing unit; that is, when construction had reached the point that all exterior windows and doors were installed and final usable floors were in place. For recently converted or merged units, the length of time is reported from the date the conversion or merger was completed.

Earnings. Earnings are defined as the sum of wage or salary income and net income from self-employment. "Earnings" represent the amount of income received regularly for people 16 years old and over before deductions for personal income taxes, Social Security, bond purchases, union dues, Medicare deductions, etc. An individual with earnings is one who has either wage/salary income or self-employment income, or both.

Educational attainment. Data on educational attainment are derived from a question that asks, "What is the highest level of school . . . completed or the highest degree . . . has received?" The question on educational attainment applies only to progress in "regular" schools. Regular schools include public, private, and parochial elementary and high schools (both junior and senior), colleges and universities, professional, vocational, trade, and business schools.

Employed. This category includes all civilians 16 years old and over who either (1) were "at work," that is, those who did any work at all during the reference week as paid employees, worked in their own business or profession, worked on their own farm, or worked 15 hours or more as unpaid workers on a family farm or in a family business; or (2) were "with a job but not at work," that is, those who did not work during the reference week but had jobs or businesses from which they were temporarily absent due to illness, bad weather, industrial dispute, vacation, or other personal reasons. Excluded from the employed are people whose only activity consisted of work around the house or unpaid volunteer work for religious, charitable, and similar organizations; also excluded are all institutionalized people and people on active duty in the United States Armed Forces.

Family households. A family consists of a householder and one or more other people living in the same household who are related to the householder by birth, marriage, or adoption. All people in a household who are related to the householder are regarded as members of his or her family. A family household may contain people not related to the householder, but those people are not included as part of the householder's family in tabulations.

FIPS state and county codes. Federal Information Processing Standard (FIPS) codes uniquely identify states, counties, and other related location entities. These are now more properly named the ANSI codes for the American National Standards Institute. For details, see the ANSI Web site: <http://www.census.gov/geo/www/ansi/ansi.html>.

First-time owners. If neither the owner nor any co-owner has ever owned or co-owned another home as a usual residence, then the housing unit is reported as the first home ever owned. Previous homes purchased solely as vacation homes or homes purchased for commercial rental purposes are not considered usual residences. However, if a previously owned home was originally purchased as a usual residence and later used as a vacation home or for commercial or rental purposes, the owner is not a first time owner.

Food stamps. These data are restricted to families and primary individuals with total incomes of $25,000 per year or less. Housing units are counted in these data if the householder or any relative currently living in the unit received food stamps in the past year, even at another address. Throughout most of the United States, stamps have been replaced by the electronic benefit transfer (EBT), which is a system allowing transfer via debit card of government benefits from a federal account to a retail outlet's account.

For seasonal, recreational, or occasional use. These are vacant units used or intended for use only in certain seasons or for weekends or other occasional use throughout the year. Seasonal units include those used for summer or winter sports or recreation, such as beach cottages and hunting cabins. Seasonal units also may include quarters for such workers as herders and loggers.

Foreign born. The foreign-born population includes anyone who was not a U.S. citizen or a U.S. national at birth. This includes respondents who indicated they were a U.S. citizen by naturalization or not a U.S. citizen.

Gini Index. The Gini is a measure of how much a distribution varies from a proportionate distribution. A purely proportionate distribution would have every value in the distribution being equal (that is 20% of the values would equal 20 percent of the aggregate total of all the values). This is also known as "perfect equality." All households have an equal share of income.

Government workers. Includes people who were employees of any local, state, or federal governmental unit, regardless of the activity of the particular agency.

Government subsidy for repairs. "Government subsidy for repairs" refers to an assistance program provided by the federal, state, or local government for the purpose of obtaining or installing energy conservation products for low-income households. The money must be spent that way. The type of products include insulation, storm doors, storm windows, weather stripping, caulking, furnace tune ups, or for repair of broken doors and windows.

Group quarters. A place where people live or stay, in a group living arrangement that is owned or managed by an entity or organization providing housing and/or services for the residents. These services may include custodial or medical care, as well as other types of assistance, and residency is commonly restricted to those receiving these services.

Hispanic. "Hispanic" refers to the origin of the householder, and was determined by asking respondents to identify people living in the unit who were Hispanic or Spanish-American. There is no intent to include people of Brazilian or Portuguese ancestry. Hispanics may be of any race.

Home-equity line-of-credit. This revolving home-equity loan allows the property owner to borrow against the equity up to a fixed limit set by the lender without reapplying for a loan.

Home-equity lump-sum loan. This home-equity loan is paid out in a one-time lump-sum amount and must be repaid over a set period.

Homeowner vacancy rate. The homeowner vacancy rate is the proportion of the homeowner inventory, which is vacant for sale.

Homeownership by age of householder. This homeownership rate is calculated by dividing the number of owner households in a particular age group by the total number of occupied households in that age group.

Homeownership rates. The proportion of households that are owners is termed the homeownership rate. It is computed by dividing the number of households that are owners by the total number of occupied households.

Homes currently for sale or rent. The data are presented in the publication for owner-occupied units, year round units temporarily occupied by people who have a usual residence elsewhere, and vacant units. The owner may offer the unit up for rent only, up for rent or for sale, or for sale only. In addition, the owner may have contracted to rent or sell the unit, but the transfer has not yet taken place. Finally, the housing unit may not be on the market at all.

Household. A household consists of all people who occupy a particular housing unit as their usual residence, or who live there at the time of the interview and have no usual residence elsewhere. The usual residence is the place where the person lives and sleeps most of the time. This place is not necessarily the same as a legal residence, voting residence, or domicile.

Householder. The householder is the first household member listed on the questionnaire who is an owner or renter of the sample unit and is 18 years or older. An owner is a person whose name is on the deed, mortgage, or contract to purchase. A renter is a person whose name is on the lease.

Housing units. A housing unit is a house, apartment, group of rooms, or single room occupied or intended for occupancy as separate living quarters.

"HUD-code" manufactured (mobile) home. A manufactured home is defined as a movable dwelling, 8 feet or more wide and 40 feet or more long, designed to be towed on its own chassis, with transportation gear integral to the unit when it leaves the factory, and without need of a permanent foundation. These homes are built in accordance with the U.S. Department of Housing and Urban Development (HUD) building code.

Labor force. All people classified in the civilian labor force plus members of the U.S. Armed Forces (people on active duty with the United States Army, Air Force, Navy, Marine Corps, or Coast Guard).

Labor force participation rate. The labor force participation rate represents the proportion of the population that is in the labor force.

Land contract. A land contract is an arrangement for the sale of real estate whereby the buyer may use, occupy, and enjoy land, but no deed is given by the seller (and no title passes) until all of the sale price has been paid.

Land rent. In some parts of the country people own their homes, but rent the land on which their homes sit. Mobile homes, cooperatives, and condominiums are not asked if land rent is paid.

Lenders of primary and secondary mortgages. This item is presented for units with two or more mortgages. The data are classified by whether the money was borrowed from a firm (bank or other organization), the seller of the property, or from another individual. Other organizations consist of mortgage corporations, pension plans, credit unions, and savings and loan associations.

Line-of-credit amount used for home additions, improvements, or repairs. This is the percentage of the dollar amount of home-equity loans used for home additions, improvements, or repairs.

Line-of-credit monthly payment. This is the monthly payment on the line-of-credit paid to the bank at the present interest rate.

Living quarters. These are classified as either housing units or group quarters. Living quarters are usually found in structures intended for residential use, but also may be found in structures intended for nonresidential use as well as in places such as tents, vans, and emergency and transitional shelters.

Lot size. Lot size includes all connecting land that is owned or rented with the home. Excluded are two-or more-unit buildings and two-or-more-unit mobile homes. In the publication, median lot size is shown to hundredths of an acre.

Loan-to-value ratio (LTV). The ratio of the loan amount of a mortgage loan to the lower of the appraisal value or purchase price of the property securing the loan.

Maintenance in last year. Routine maintenance consists of regular maintenance activities necessary for the preventive care of the structure, property, and fixed equipment items. Included are such things as painting; papering; floor sanding; restoring of shingles; fixing water pipes; replacing parts of large equipment, such as a furnace; repairing fences, gutters, sidewalks, decks or patios; removing dangerous trees; or termite inspection.

Major source of down payment. This item refers to the source of the cash used for down payment or outright purchase of the property (house or lot). If more than one source applied, the one providing the largest amount was recorded.

Manufactured/mobile home. A manufactured/mobile home is defined as a housing unit that was originally constructed to be towed on its own chassis (also called HUD Code homes). It may be built in one or more sections. Since the sections are attached side-by-side at the home site, the final home comprises the number of sections referring to as house "wide." A unit composed of two sections is a double-wide; three sections is a triple-wide, etc. Single-wide units come from the factory as one section. It also may have permanent rooms attached at its present site or other structural modifications. The term does not include prefabricated buildings, modular homes, travel campers, boats, or self-propelled vehicles like motor homes.

Manufactured/mobile home setup. Manufactured/mobile homes that are placed on a permanent masonry foundation; rest on concrete pads; or are up on blocks, but not on concrete pads.

Manufactured/mobile home tiedowns. Manufactured/mobile home or trailer tiedowns that are ground-anchor foundation systems and give physical stability to manufactured/mobile homes.

Manufactured/mobile homes in group. Manufactured/mobile homes or mobile home sites that are gathered close together are considered to be in a "group." This may be a mobile home park or it may be a number grouped together on adjacent individually owned lots not in a mobile home park.

Margin. A fixed amount added to the underlying index to establish the fully indexed rate for an ARM.

Marital history. Beginning in 2008, people 15 years and over who were ever married (married, widowed, separated, or divorced) were asked if they had been married, widowed, or divorced in the past 12 months. They were asked how many times (once, two times, three or more times) they have been married, and the year of their last marriage.

Mean. This measure represents an arithmetic average of a set of values. It is derived by dividing the sum (or aggregate) of a group of numerical questions by the total number of questions in that group.

Mean earnings. Mean earnings are calculated by dividing aggregate earnings by the population 16 years old and over with earnings. Mean earnings are rounded to the nearest whole dollar.

Mean income. Mean income is the amount obtained by dividing the aggregate income of a particular statistical universe by the number of units in that universe.

Mean of household income by quintiles. Means of household income by quintiles are calculated by dividing aggregate household income in each quintile by the number of households in each quintile (one-fifth of the total number of households).

Mean travel time to work (in minutes). Mean travel time to work (in minutes) is the average travel time that workers usually took to get from home to work (one way) during the reference week.

Median. Median is the 50th percentile and is often the better measure of "typical" than is the mean or average. It is found by ordering all values in a data set from lowest to highest and then finding the value that lies in the exact middle.

Median age at first marriage. The median age at first marriage is calculated indirectly by estimating the proportion of young people who will marry during their lifetime, calculating one-half of this proportion, and determining the age (at the time of the survey) of people at this half-way mark by osculatory interpolation. It does not represent the actual median age of the population who married during the calendar year.

Median and quartile contract rent. The median divides the rent distribution into two equal parts: one-half of the cases falling below the median contract rent and one-half above the median. Quartiles divide the rent distribution into four equal parts.

Median and quartile value. The median divides the value distribution into two equal parts: one-half of the cases falling below the median value of the property (house and lot, mobile home and lot, or condominium unit) and one-half above the median. Quartiles divide the value distribution into four equal parts.

Median earnings. The median divides the earnings distribution into two equal parts: one-half of the cases falling below the median and one-half above the median. Median earnings is restricted to individuals 16 years old and over with earnings and is computed on the basis of a standard distribution.

Median gross rent. Median gross rent divides the gross rent distribution into two equal parts: one-half of the cases falling below the median gross rent and one-half above the median. Median gross rent is computed on the basis of a standard distribution. Median gross rent is rounded to the nearest whole dollar.

Median income. The median divides the income distribution into two equal parts: one-half of the cases falling below the median income and one-half above the median. For households and families, the median income is based on the distribution of the total number of households and families including those with no income. The median income for individuals is based on individuals 15 years old and over with income.

Median monthly housing costs. This measure divides the monthly housing costs distribution into two equal parts: one-half of the cases falling below the median monthly housing costs and one-half above the median. Medians are shown separately for units "with a mortgage" and for units "not mortgaged." Median monthly housing costs are computed on the basis of a standard distribution. Median monthly housing costs are rounded to the nearest whole dollar.

Median rooms. This measure divides the room distribution into two equal parts: one-half of the cases falling below the median number of rooms and one-half above the median. In computing median rooms, the whole number is used as the midpoint of the interval; thus, the category "3 rooms" is treated as an interval ranging from 2.5 to 3.5 rooms. Median rooms is rounded to the nearest tenth.

Median selected monthly owner costs. This measure divides the selected monthly owner costs distribution into two equal parts; one-half of the cases falling below the median selected monthly owner costs and one-half above the median. Medians are shown separately for units "with a mortgage" and for units "not mortgaged."

Median selected monthly owner costs as a percentage of household income. This measure divides the selected monthly owner costs as a percentage of household income distribution into two equal parts: one-half of the cases falling below the median selected monthly owner costs as a percentage of household income and one-half above the median. Median selected monthly owner costs as a percentage of household income is computed on the basis of a standard distribution.

Median year householder moved into unit. Median year householder moved into unit divides the distribution into two equal parts: one-half of the cases falling below the median year householder moved into unit and one-half above the median. Median year householder moved into unit is rounded to the nearest calendar year.

Metropolitan areas. Metropolitan areas are composed of whole counties (towns in New England) that have significant levels of commuting and contiguous urban areas in common. They may cross state lines, and usually include large amounts of rural land and farmland, provided the county or town as a whole qualifies.

Multifamily housing. Residential buildings containing units built one on top of another and those built side-by-side which do not have a ground-to-roof wall and/or have common facilities (i.e., attic, basement, heating plant, plumbing, etc.).

Native population The native population includes anyone who was a U.S. citizen or a U.S. national at birth. This includes respondents who indicated they were born in the United States, Puerto Rico, a U.S. Island Area (such as Guam), or abroad of American (U.S. citizen) parent or parents.

New England city and town areas. The New England city and town areas (NECTAs) are defined using the same criteria as metropolitan and micropolitan statistical areas and are identified as either metropolitan or micropolitan, based, respectively, on the presence of either an urbanized area of 50,000 or more population or an urban cluster of at least 10,000 but less than 50,000 population.

New houses for sale. A house is considered to be for sale when it is being built to be sold and a permit to build has been issued (in permit-issuing places) or work has begun on the footings or foundation (in nonpermit areas) and a sales contract has not been signed nor a deposit accepted.

New residential construction. The category of statistics called "New Residential Construction" consists of data on the five phases of a residential construction project: (1) housing units authorized to be built by a building or zoning permit; (2) housing units authorized to be built, but not yet started; (3) housing units started; (4) housing units under construction; and (5) housing units completed.

Nonfamily household. A householder living alone or with nonrelatives only. Same-sex couple households with no relatives of the householder present are tabulated in nonfamily households.

Not in labor force. All people 16 years old and over who are not classified as members of the labor force. This category consists mainly of students, homemakers, retired workers, seasonal workers interviewed in an off season who were not looking for work, institutionalized people, and people doing only incidental unpaid family work (less than 15 hours during the reference week).

Number of rooms. Included in the count of rooms were whole rooms such as living rooms, dining rooms, bedrooms, kitchens, finished basements or attics, recreation rooms, permanently enclosed sun porches, which are suitable for year-round use, and lodger's rooms.

Occupants per room. This is obtained by dividing the number of people in each occupied housing unit by the number of rooms in the unit. The figures show the number of occupied housing units having the specified ratio of people per room.

Occupied housing unit. A housing unit is classified as occupied if it is the current place of residence of the person or group of people living in it at the time of interview, or if the occupants are only temporarily absent from the residence for two months or less, that is, away on vacation or a business trip. If all the people staying in the unit at the time of the interview are staying there for two months or less, the unit is considered to be temporarily occupied and classified as "vacant."

Origination fees and discount points. The total charged by the lender at settlement. One point equals one percent of the loan amount.

Other housing costs per month. A homeowner's association fee (excludes condominium and cooperative fees) is a fee charged for services such as upkeep of common property, including painting hallways, cleaning lobbies, mowing lawns, repairing laundry facilities, paving parking areas, and repairing street lights. The fee may include the use and maintenance of either indoor or outdoor swimming facilities or other recreational facilities (party rooms, tennis courts, basketball courts, exercise rooms, and playground areas). In addition, the homeowner association fee can include payments for security personnel such as security guards or services such as telephone answering service, maid service, or other domestic help.

Other occupancy and vacancy rates. The percent distributions of vacant and occupied housing units are shown as a percent of all housing units.

Owner occupied. A housing unit is owner occupied if the owner or co-owner lives in the unit even if it is mortgaged or not fully paid for. The owner or co-owner must live in the unit and usually is Person 1 on the questionnaire. The unit is "Owned by you or someone in this household with a mortgage or loan" if it is being purchased with a mortgage or some other debt arrangement such as a deed of trust, trust deed, contract to purchase, land contract, or purchase agreement.

Per capita income. Per capita income is the mean income computed for every man, woman, and child in a particular group including those living in group quarters. It is derived by dividing the aggregate income of a particular group by the total population in that group.

Permit-issuing place. A geographic area that issues building or zoning permits for the construction of residential structures. The area may be a single municipality or county or a combination of multiple municipalities.

Placement and average sales price data. The placement and average sales price figures are based on the initial sale to private individuals for residential use. The MHS does not collect data for resales, repossessions, or placements for nonresidential use. Purchases by state, local, and federal government agencies (i.e., FEMA) are not included in the survey.

Previous occupancy. The statistics presented are restricted to housing units built in 1990 or later. "Previously occupied" indicates that someone, or people not now in the household, occupied the housing unit prior to the householder or other related household members' occupancy. "Not previously occupied" indicates that either the householder or some other current household member was the first occupant of the housing unit.

Primary metropolitan statistical area (PMSA). A PMSA is one subcomponent of a CMSA. For example, Washington is one PMSA of the Washington-Baltimore CMSA.

Primary mortgage. Detailed information on regular and lump-sum home-equity mortgages was collected in the AHS on the first three mortgages reported, even if the unit had four or more mortgages. If the owner(s) had both a regular and a lump-sum home-equity mortgage, priority was given to the regular mortgage(s) for collecting detailed information. On the basis of this information, one of the mortgages was considered to be primary.

Principal. Principal is the amount of money raised by a mortgage or other loan, as distinct from the interest paid for its use. It is the amount of debt excluding interest.

Principal cities and metropolitan and micropolitan statistical area. The largest city in each metropolitan or micropolitan statistical area is designated a "principal city." Additional cities qualify if specified requirements are met concerning population size and employment.

Private mortgage insurance. Private mortgage insurance is insurance that a lender generally requires a homebuyer to obtain if the down payment made by the home buyer is below a certain percentage (often 20 percent down payment for conventional loans).

Privately owned. Structures not owned by any federal, state, or local government. Units in structures built by private developers with partial public subsidies or which are for sale upon completion to local public housing authorities under the HUD "Turnkey" program are all classified as private housing.

Property insurance. This item refers to insurancc on the structure and/or its contents (such as furniture, appliances, or clothing) and usually contains some liability insurance. Renters usually do not have property insurance, (renter's property insurance) but, if they do have it, its cost is counted. The total cost is the most recent yearly cost for which the occupants have actually been billed.

Public housing. Public housing is a residential building owned by a federal, state or local agency. Units in structures built by private developers with partial public subsidies or which are for sale upon completion to local public housing authorities under the HUD "Turnkey" program are all classified as private housing.

Purchase price. The purchase price refers to the price of the house or apartment and lot at the time the property was purchased. Closing costs are excluded from the purchase price, and for mobile homes the value of the land is excluded. In the publications, the median purchase price is rounded to the nearest dollar.

Rate. This is a measure of occurrences in a given period of time divided by the possible number of occurrences during that period. For example, the homeowner vacancy rate is calculated by dividing the number of vacant units "for sale only" by the sum of owner-occupied units and vacant units that are "for sale only," and then multiplying by 100. Rates are sometimes presented as percentages.

Ratio. This is a measure of the relative size of one number to a second number expressed as the quotient of the first number divided by the second. For example, the sex ratio is calculated by dividing the total number of males by the total number of females, and then multiplying by 100.

Real estate taxes. This item includes special assessments, school taxes, county taxes, and any other real estate taxes. Excluded are payments on delinquent taxes due from prior years. Rebates are subtracted from the total. When the real estate taxes are included with the mortgage, a separate amount for the taxes is obtained. To determine average monthly cost, yearly cost was divided by 12.

Reason primary mortgage refinanced. If the current primary mortgage was a regular mortgage (not a lump sum home-equity loan) and was not an assumed or wraparound mortgage, the respondent was asked if it was a refinancing of a previous mortgage and the reason for the refinancing.

Reference week. The data on employment status and journey to work relate to the reference week, that is, the calendar week preceding the date on which the respondents completed their questionnaires or were interviewed. This week is not the same for all respondents since the interviewing was conducted over a 12-month period. The occurrence of holidays during the relative reference week could affect the data on actual hours worked during the reference week, but probably had no effect on overall measurement of employment status.

Regions. States and the District of Columbia contained in each region are as follows:

Northeast. Maine, New Hampshire, Vermont, Massachusetts, Rhode Island, Connecticut, New York, Pennsylvania, and New Jersey.

Midwest. Ohio, Indiana, Illinois, Michigan, Wisconsin, Minnesota, Iowa, Missouri, Kansas, Nebraska, North Dakota, and South Dakota.

South. Delaware, Maryland, District of Columbia, Virginia, West Virginia, North Carolina, South Carolina, Georgia, Florida, Alabama, Mississippi, Tennessee, Kentucky, Arkansas, Louisiana, Oklahoma, and Texas.

West. Montana, Wyoming, Colorado, New Mexico, Arizona, Utah, Idaho, Alaska, Washington, Oregon, Nevada, California, and Hawaii.

Remaining years mortgaged. The owner or owner's spouse was asked the length of time it would take to pay off the loan at the current payments. The response reflects the amortization schedule. For example, in many balloon mortgages the initial monthly payments are calculated to pay off the loan in 30 years, though the mortgage is due in 5 years, and the 60th payment is very large. Such a mortgage would count here as 30 years, not 5 years, minus whatever number of years have passed.

Rent. A set amount of money, billed or charged, which is paid at regular intervals (weekly, bi-weekly or monthly) to a property owner in exchange for right of occupancy.

Rent control. This refers to cases in which increases in rent are limited by state or local law. The jurisdiction, state, or local agency, mandates that rent increases may not exceed some level, or must be approved by the government. This category does not include limits that HUD puts on all rental projects insured by the Federal Housing Administration.

Rent paid by lodgers. This item refers to regular, fixed rent: a set amount of money, billed or charged, which is paid at regular intervals by a lodger (usually weekly or monthly) to a member of the household. This category is restricted to lodgers who are 16 years and older, nonrelatives of the householder, and people who are not spouses of a co-owner or co-renter, not children of a co-owner or co-renter, and not co-owners or co-renters themselves.

Rental vacancy rate. The proportion of the rental inventory that is vacant for rent.

Renter occupied. All occupied housing units which are not owner occupied, whether they are rented or occupied without payment of rent, are classified as renter occupied. "No rent paid" units are separately identified in the rent tabulations. Such units are generally provided free by friends or relatives or in exchange for services such as resident manager, caretaker, minister, or tenant farmer.

Renter's property insurance. Renter's property insurance or renter's coverage policy covers those aspects of the apartment and its contents not specifically covered in the blanket policy written for the complex. This policy can also cover liabilities arising from accidents and intentional injuries for guests as well as passers-by. Common coverage areas are events such as lightning, riot, aircraft, explosion, vandalism, smoke, theft, windstorm or hail, falling objects, volcanic eruption, snow, sleet, and weight of ice.

Residential building. A residential building is a building consisting primarily of housing units. In a new building combining residential and nonresidential floor areas, every effort is made to include the residential units in these statistics, even if the primary function of the entire building is for nonresidential purposes.

Respondent. Any knowledgeable adult household member 16 years of age or older is technically eligible to act as the respondent. That is, the one who is the most knowledgeable household member who appears to know—or might reasonably be expected to know—the answers to all or the majority of thc questions.

Reverse annuity mortgages. These were defined to the respondent as "reverse annuity mortgage or home-equity conversion mortgage." These mortgages involve borrowing against home equity for retirement or income and sometimes do not need to be repaid until after the owner's death.

Rooms. Rooms counted include whole rooms used for living purposes, such as bedrooms, living rooms, dining rooms, kitchens, recreation rooms, permanently enclosed porches that are suitable for year-round use, lodger's rooms, and other finished rooms. Also included are rooms used for offices by a person living in the unit.

Seasonally adjusted annual rate. Seasonal adjustment is the process of estimating and removing seasonal effects from a time series to better reveal certain non-seasonal features such as underlying trends and business cycles. Seasonal adjustment procedures estimate effects that occur in the same calendar month with similar magnitude and direction from year to year. In series whose seasonal effects come primarily from weather, the seasonal factors are estimates of average weather effects for each month.

Self-employed in own not incorporated business workers. Includes people who worked for profit or fees in their own unincorporated business, profession, or trade, or who operated a farm.

Secured communities. These types of communities are typically residential communities in which public access by nonresidents is restricted, usually by physical boundaries, such as gates, walls, and fences, or through private security. These communities sometimes require a special entry system, such as entry codes, key cards, or security guard approval. A public access restriction refers to the community, not a building or units.

Secured multiunits. Secured multiunits refer to one or more multiunit buildings that require some sort of special entry procedure, such as entry codes, key cards, or security guard approval for access. This also includes intercom systems where the occupants can identify and buzz-in visitors.

Sex ratio. The sex ratio represents the balance between the male and female populations. Ratios above 100 indicate a larger male population, and ratios below 100 indicate a larger female population. This measure is derived by dividing the total number of males by the total number of females and then multiplying by 100. It is rounded to the nearest tenth.

Shares of household income by quintiles. Negative incomes are converted to zero for these measures. These measures are the aggregate household income in each quintile as a percentage of the total aggregate household income.

Shipments data. The shipments figures are based on reports submitted by manufacturers on the number of manufactured homes actually shipped during the survey month. Shipments to dealers may not necessarily be placed for residential use in the same month as they are shipped. The number of manufactured "homes" used for nonresidential purposes is not known.

Single-family house. The single-family statistics include fully detached, semidetached (semiattached, side-by-side), row houses, and townhouses. In the case of attached units, each must be separated from the adjacent unit by a ground-to-roof wall in order to be classified as a single-family structure. Also, these units must not share heating/air-conditioning systems or utilities, such as water supply, power supply, or sewage disposal lines.

Standard error. Measure of the variation among the estimates from all possible samples; measure of the precision with which an estimate from a particular sample approximates the average results of all possible samples; square root of the sampling variance.

Start. Start of construction occurs when excavation begins for the footings or foundation of a building. All housing units in a multifamily building are defined as being started when this excavation begins. Beginning with data for September 1992, estimates of housing starts include units in structures being totally rebuilt on an existing foundation.

Structure, type of. The statistics, by type of structure, refer to the structural characteristics of the building. The one-unit structure category is a single-family home. It includes fully detached, semidetached (semiattached, side-by-side), row houses, and townhouses. Multifamily structures are classified by the number of housing units in the structure. Data are tabulated for 2 units, 3 and 4 units combined, and 5 or more unit structures.

Special or assisted living. Special living refers to services that management of multiunit complexes with 5 or more units in a building provides for residents where at least one household member is age 55 or older. The questions determine whether the management offers the following services to residents: meals, transportation, housekeeping, managing finances, phone use, and shopping. If the resident said yes to any of the above services, then questions are asked if the management offers assistance with personal care, such as bathing, eating, moving about, dressing, and toilet use.

Subfamily. A subfamily is a married couple (husband and wife interviewed as members of the same household) with or without never-married children under 18 years old, or one parent with one or more never-married children under 18 years old. A subfamily does not maintain its own household, but lives in a household where the householder or householder's spouse is a relative.

Subsidized units. Households paying a lower rent because a federal, state, or local government program pays part of the cost of construction, mortgage, or operating expenses. These programs include rental assistance programs where part of the rent for low-income families is paid by HUD, and direct loan programs of HUD and the Department of Agriculture for reduced cost housing. Units requiring income verification are usually subsidized.

Suburbs. The portion of each metropolitan area that is not in any central city.

Term of primary mortgage at origination or assumption. The term is the number of years from the date the present owner-occupants first obtained the present mortgage to the date the last payment is due according to the terms of the contract. On a balloon mortgage this term may be short and the last payment very large. In this publication, medians for term of primary mortgage are rounded to the nearest year.

Timeshare. A timeshare is a form of ownership or right to the use of a property. These can be either single-family or multifamily structures.

Total home-equity line-of-credit limit. Total home equity line-of-credit limit is a mortgage loan that is usually in a subordinate position and allows the property owner to obtain multiple advances of the loan proceeds at the borrower's discretion, up to an amount that represents a specified percentage of the borrower's equity in a property. This line-of-credit allows the property owner to borrow against the equity in the home from time to time without reapplying for a loan.

Total outstanding line-of-credit loans. The total outstanding line-of-credit loan is the current balance on the home-equity line-of-credit. The current balance is usually reported on the monthly or quarterly statement.

Transient Use. Units not used as a regular or permanent residence (i.e., motel/hotel).

Turnkey Housing. Units in structures built by private developers with partial public subsidies or that are for sale upon completion to local public housing authorities.

Under construction. Estimates of housing units started, but not yet completed, are shown in the "under construction" data series. Housing units under construction are estimated for all areas of the United States, regardless of whether permits are required.

Units. The number of housing units in a structure, all units, occupied and vacant. The statistics are presented for the number of housing units, not the number of residential structures.

Units in structure. In determining the number of housing units in a structure, all units, occupied and vacant, are counted. The statistics are presented for the number of housing units, not the number of residential structures. A structure either has open space on all sides or is separated from other structures by dividing walls that extend from ground to roof.

Unemployed. All civilians 16 years old and over are classified as unemployed if they (1) were neither "at work" nor "with a job but not at work" during the reference week, and (2) were actively looking for work during the last 4 weeks, and (3) were available to start a job. Also included as unemployed are civilians who did not work at all during the reference week, were waiting to be called back to a job from which they had been laid off, and were available for work except for temporary illness.

Unemployment rate. The unemployment rate represents the number of unemployed people as a percentage of the civilian labor force. For example, if the civilian labor force equals 100 people and 7 people are unemployed, then the unemployment rate would be 7 percent.

Unpaid family workers. Includes people who worked without pay in a business or on a farm operated by a relative.

Unrelated individual. An unrelated individual is: (1) a householder living alone or with nonrelatives only, (2) a household member who is not related to the householder, or (3) a person living in group quarters who is not an inmate of an institution.

U.S. citizen. Respondents who indicated that they were born in the United States, Puerto Rico, a U.S. Island Area (such as Guam), or abroad of American (U.S. citizen) parent or parents are considered U.S. citizens at birth. Foreign-born people who indicated that they were U.S. citizens through naturalization also are considered U.S. citizens.

Vacancy, seasonality. A housing unit is vacant if no one is living in it at the time of the interview, unless its occupants are only temporarily absent. In addition, housing units where all the occupants have a usual residence elsewhere are grouped with vacant units.

Vacant housing units. A housing unit is vacant if no one is living in it at the time of the interview, unless its occupants are only temporarily absent. In addition, a vacant unit may be one which is entirely occupied by persons who have a usual residence elsewhere. New units not yet occupied are classified as vacant housing units if construction has reached a point where all exterior windows and doors are installed and final usable floors are in place.

Valuation. The valuation is the estimated value of the residential structure as shown on the building permit. If no value is listed on the permit, we accept estimates from the permit official.

Value. Value is the respondent's estimate of how much the property would sell for on the current market. For vacant units, value is the sales price asked for the property at the time of the interview and may differ from the price at which the property is sold. The "sales price asked" includes the price of a one-housing-unit structure and the land on which it is located. The "sales price asked" may also include additional structures such as garages, sheds, barns, etc.

Veteran status. Veterans are men and women who have served (even for a short time), but are not currently serving, on active duty in the U.S. Army, Navy, Air Force, Marine Corps, or the Coast Guard, or who served in the U.S. Merchant Marine during World War II. People who served in the National Guard or Reserves are classified as veterans only if they were ever called or ordered to active duty, not counting the 4-6 months for initial training or yearly summer camps. All other civilians are classified as nonveterans.

Women's earnings as a percentage of men's earnings. This is defined as median earnings for females who worked full-time, year-round divided by median earnings for males who worked full-time, year-round, multiplied by 100.

Worker. This term appears in connection with several subjects: employment status, journey-to-work questions, class of worker, weeks worked in the past 12 months, and number of workers in family in the past 12 months. The meaning varies and, therefore, should be determined in each case by referring to the definition of the subject in which it appears.

Year-round vacant units. Beginning in 1990, year-round vacant mobile homes were included as part of the year-round vacant count of housing units. Year-round units are those intended for occupancy at any time of the year, even though they may not be in use the year round. In resort areas, a housing unit that is usually occupied on a year-round basis is considered a year-round unit.

Year structure built. "Year structure built" refers to the date the original construction of the structure was completed, and not to any later remodeling, addition, or conversion. The figures on the number of units built during a given period relate to the number of units in existence at the time of interview. For both occupied and vacant mobile homes, "model year" is the year built.

INDEX